MW01028970

PSALTER
HYMNAL
Handbook

PSALTER HYMNAL

Emily R. Brink and Bert Polman, Editors

CRC Publications
Grand Rapids, Michigan

Unless otherwise indicated, the Scripture quotations in this publication are from the HOLY BIBLE, NEW INTERNATIONAL VERSION © 1973, 1978, 1984, International Bible Society. Used by permission of Zondervan Bible Publishers.

© 1998 by CRC Publications, 2850 Kalamazoo Ave. SE, Grand Rapids, MI 49560. All rights reserved. With the exception of brief excerpts for review purposes, no part of this book may be reproduced in any manner whatsoever without written permission from the publisher. Printed in the United States of America on recycled paper. ♻
1-800-333-8300

"The *Revised Common Lectionary* with Related Songs" is adapted from *The Revised Common Lectionary,* © 1992 by the Consultation on Common Texts (CCT). Used with permission. Attn: Daniel T. Benedict, Jr.; P.O. Box 840 (Rm. 381); Nashville, TN 37202.

Library of Congress Cataloging-in-Publication Data
Psalter hymnal handbook / Emily R. Brink and Bert Polman, editors.
    p.   cm.
Based on the 1987 ed. of the Psalter hymnbook.
Includes indexes.
ISBN 1-56212-269-X
1. Christian Reformed Church—Hymns—History and criticism. 2. Hymns, English—History and criticism. I. Brink, Emily Ruth, 1940 - . II. Polman, Bertus Frederick, 1945 - . III. Psalter hymnal.
ML3164.P73 1998
264'.05731023—dc21   97-39977
                                                                            CIP
                                                                            MN

10 9 8 7 6 5 4 3 2 1

CONTENTS

Part 1
Historical Essays

Part 2
Commentary on the Psalms, Bible Songs, and Hymns

Part 3
Commentary on the Ecumenical Creeds, Confessions, and Liturgical Forms

CONTRIBUTORS

Henry Admiraal prepared the scripture references for all the hymn entries. He is pastor of Westend Christian Reformed Church, Grand Rapids, Michigan.

Harry Boonstra contributed several of the biographies and wrote the commentary on the ecumenical creeds. He serves as theological librarian for Calvin Theological Seminary, Grand Rapids, Michigan.

Emily R. Brink wrote the essays on the Genevan Psalter and English metrical psalmody and served as general editor of the *Handbook*. She is music and liturgy editor for CRC Publications, Grand Rapids, Michigan.

David J. Diephouse coauthored the commentary on the liturgical forms (along with Carl G. Kromminga and Bert Polman). He is an academic dean at Calvin College.

Morris N. Greidanus contributed the commentary on the contemporary testimony *Our World Belongs to God*. He is pastor of First Christian Reformed Church, Grand Rapids, Michigan.

Roy Hopp wrote early research drafts of the hymnody essays, provided many of the biographies, and prepared the index of songs keyed to the *Revised Common Lectionary*. He is director of music at Woodlawn Christian Reformed Church, Grand Rapids, Michigan.

Fred H. Klooster contributed the commentary on the Heidelberg Catechism. He is professor of systematic theology emeritus, Calvin Theological Seminary.

Carl G. Kromminga coauthored the commentary on the liturgical forms (together with David J. Diephouse and Bert Polman). He is professor of practical theology emeritus, Calvin Theological Seminary.

Bert Polman wrote and coauthored several of the essays, was the primary author of the song entries, edited all the biographical entries, and prepared the index of songs keyed to the Heidelberg Catechism (along with Joan Ringerwole). He is professor of music at Redeemer College, Ancaster, Ontario.

Jack Reiffer coauthored the article on Christian Reformed psalters and hymnals (together with Bert Polman). He is pastor of the Washington, D.C., Christian Reformed Church.

Joan Ringerwole, together with several of her students, contributed to the index of songs keyed to the Heidelberg Catechism (along with Bert Polman). She is professor of music at Dordt College, Sioux Center, Iowa.

Pam Ruiter Feenstra initiated correspondence with living authors and composers and wrote the music sections of the psalm entries. She is professor of music at Eastern Michigan University, Ypsilanti, Michigan.

Donald Sinnema contributed the commentary on the Canons of Dort. He is professor of theology at Trinity Christian College, Palos Heights, Illinois.

Calvin R. Stapert wrote the essay on early psalmody and coauthored the article on Greek and Latin hymnody (with Roy Hopp and Bert Polman). He is professor of music at Calvin College.

John H. Stek wrote the text sections of the psalm entries. He is professor of Old Testament emeritus, Calvin Theological Seminary.

Henry Zwaanstra contributed the commentary on the Belgic Confession. He is professor of historical theology at Calvin Theological Seminary.

PREFACE

When the 1987 *Psalter Hymnal* was finally completed after ten years of effort, the *Psalter Hymnal* Revision Committee posed for a group photograph. Everyone was given a framed copy with the inscription "Ten Years of Labor, a Lifetime of Praise." Another ten years later, the same inscription could appropriately be applied to the many different people who contributed to this handbook for the *Psalter Hymnal* (see list of contributors on pp. 7-8).

It is appropriate that as co-editors of this *Psalter Hymnal Handbook* we say a brief word about each other.

Bert Polman was not only a member of the revision committee, he is also the primary contributor to this volume. For twenty years (most of his professional life to date), Bert devoted the better parts of his summers and weekends, and many more days and nights, initially to the *Psalter Hymnal* and then to this *Psalter Hymnal Handbook*. His contribution is a labor of love—love for the songs that nurture the faith of God's people, and love for the saints who wrote and still write songs for God's people to sing. A church organist, Bert's deep commitment to helping those who sing from the *Psalter Hymnal* do so with greater devotion and understanding was one of his responses to his own inability to sing (due to vocal paralysis). He is probably the only member of the Christian Reformed Church who has a doctorate in musicology with hymnology as his area of specialization. He took on the research, writing, and editing of the *Psalter Hymnal Handbook* with selfless dedication and good cheer.

Emily Brink was also a member of the revision committee initially, until it was decided that the new hymnal should be published by CRC Publications. In 1983 she was appointed full-time music editor for CRC Publications. As editor, she was responsible for shepherding the new hymnal through the entire publishing process—from working with the committee to guiding the project through synodical approval to getting the hymnal into the hands of the churches. Blessed with both vision and great energy, Emily is a church organist, choir director, and composer (with a doctorate in music theory). She quickly demonstrated her superlative skills as a project administrator, editor, and promoter of the *Psalter Hymnal* and, more recently, of this *Handbook*. As her responsibilities at CRC Publications increased to include the whole domain of worship, the editing of the journal *Reformed Worship* and other hymnic ventures such as *Songs for LiFE,* Emily earned the confidence of the entire Christian Reformed denomination and respect in ecumenical circles for her leadership in liturgy and hymnody.

We would be the first to admit that the research that led to this *Psalter Hymnal Handbook* depended on countless others who have written and preserved records over the centuries. We were indebted to many hymnal companions, particularly the *Hymnal Companion to the Lutheran Book of Worship* by Marilyn Kay Stulken (Fortress, 1981), the *Companion to the United Methodist Hymnal* by Carlton R. Young (Abingdon, 1993), and *The Hymnal 1982 Companion* (The Church Hymnal Corporation, 1990-1994), a massive four-volume work edited by Raymond F. Glover for the Episcopal Church. However, much of what appears in the *Psalter Hymnal Handbook* is new, particularly the material on the psalms and on many of the Bible songs. We were able to uncover some new information on older hymns and some first-time information on new hymns that we trust will serve succeeding generations of companion and handbook writers and readers.

From the start, CRC Publications knew that producing a handbook to the *Psalter Hymnal* would not be a self-supporting venture and that some outside funding would be necessary. An appeal for funds resulted in a generous response on the part of many. With gratitude for all those gifts, we mention two in particular: a matching grant of $7,500 from the Holland American Wafer Company, in tribute to Anne Vander Heide (1907-1997), a longtime church musician and cultural leader in Grand Rapids; and a $5,000 grant from the Rainbow Foundation, a private foundation dedicated to supporting Christian educational efforts in western Michigan.

We chose to call this book a "handbook" rather than a "companion." Though these terms are often used interchangeably, a companion generally provides historical and biographical information; whereas a handbook may also include instructional material. The *Psalter Hymnal Handbook* includes both: in addition to historical and biographical information, the song entries include Scripture references and exegetical commentary on the texts, metronome markings and performance suggestions for the music, and suggestions for liturgical use. Confessional and liturgical resources are also included in this volume, since they are part of the *Psalter Hymnal*'s Worship Edition, the edition used in most Christian Reformed congregations. The indexes keying songs to the Heidelberg Catechism and the *Revised Common Lectionary* will be helpful in choosing songs for worship. Our intent is that this volume not be merely informative but also useful as a resource for worship planning.

May this *Psalter Hymnal Handbook* add to the understanding of the Reformed tradition in the context of the broader Christian heritage of songs included in the *Psalter Hymnal*. Even more, may all those who find a song to sing in that collection learn to sing with greater gratitude to God for the great cloud of witnesses represented in that book who even now sing before the throne.

—Emily R. Brink and Bert Polman, Editors

PART 1
HISTORICAL ESSAYS

Singing Psalms from Bible Times to the Protestant Reformation

by Calvin R. Stapert

In Christian worship, psalmody holds the first place. . . . Psalms and biblical canticles rank before all lyrical compositions of merely ecclesiastical origin, since they are the inspired word of God. This is why they have always been given a special preference, as is shown by the dominant place they hold in all the offices of the Church.

—*Joseph Gelineau, S.J.;* Voices and Instruments in Christian Worship *(Collegeville, Minn.: Liturgical Press, 1964), p. 67.*

This observation by the twentieth-century Catholic composer and liturgy scholar Joseph Gelineau sounds remarkably like what John Calvin said four centuries earlier: "Wherefore, although we look far and wide and search on every hand, we shall not find better songs nor songs better suited to [worship] than the Psalms of David which the Holy Spirit made and uttered through him" (Foreword to the *Geneva Psalter* of 1543, tr. Oliver Strunk, *Source Readings in Music History;* New York: W. W. Norton and Co., 1950; p. 348.)

Calvin was not saying something new either. He, like Gelineau, was echoing early Christian enthusiasm for the psalms, an enthusiasm that reached an unprecedented and unsurpassed peak in the fourth century when church fathers such as Basil, John Chrysostom, and Ambrose gave voice to unstinting praise of the psalms. They mustered all of their considerable eloquence to urge the faithful to sing the psalms daily. For example, Basil said,

All Scripture is given by inspiration of God and is profitable. . . . But the book of the Psalms embraces whatever in all the others is helpful. It prophesies things to come, it recalls histories to the mind, it gives laws for living, it counsels what is to be done. And altogether it is a storehouse of good instructions, diligently providing for each what is useful to him. For it heals the ancient wounds of souls and to the newly wounded brings prompt relief; it ministers to what is sick and preserves what is in health; and it wholly removes the ills, howsoever great and of whatsoever kind, that attack souls in our human life; and this by means of a certain well-timed persuasion which inspires wholesome reflection. . . .

A psalm is the tranquillity of souls, the arbitrator of peace, restraining the disorder and turbulence of thoughts, for it softens the passion of the soul and moderates its unruliness. A psalm forms friendships, unites the divided, mediates between enemies. For who can still consider him an enemy with whom he has sent forth one voice to God? So that the singing of psalms brings love, the greatest of good things, contriving harmony like some bond of union and uniting the people in a symphony of a single choir.

A psalm drives away demons, summons the help of angels, furnishes arms against nightly terrors, and gives respite from daily toil; to little children it is safety, to men in their prime an adornment, to the old a solace, to women their most fitting ornament. It peoples solitudes, it chastens market places. To beginners it is a beginning; to those who are advancing, an increase; to those who are concluding, a support. A psalm is the voice of the church. It gladdens feast days; it creates grief which is in accord with God's will, for a psalm brings a tear even from a heart of stone.

—Homily on the First Psalm, tr. *Oliver Strunk*, Source Readings, *pp. 64-65.*

While it is obvious that Basil is not afraid to use hyperbole to make a point, it is equally obvious to those who have looked into the history of music in the Christian church that the psalms have held a special place—and not without reason: Undergirding all of Basil's specific reasons for valuing the psalms stands a feature that makes them unique: they can function simultaneously as God's Word to us and our words to God. As Gelineau put it, "psalmody never loses its double character of word of God and prayer of the community" (p. 68).

A close look at the history of the church's music will show that Gelineau was exaggerating only a bit when he said that the psalms "have always been given special preference." For although that claim cannot hold up in every instance, still there can be no doubt that the psalms have been the most widely used and universally loved texts that Christians have sung. If the psalms have not been at every moment in every place the preferred texts to sing, they have rarely been neglected. Usually they have been prominent; often they have been dominant. And at some times among some Christians they have been the only texts sung in public worship.

Psalms in Temple Worship

The psalms, of course, came to the church from the Jews. But beyond that there is little that we can say with certainty about their origin and early history. Tradition long ascribed all the psalms to David. But although it is likely that some go back to him, it is impossible to determine with certainty which he wrote and which others wrote in his style. During the centuries after David—and probably under the influence of this "sweet psalmist of Israel" (2 Sam. 23:1, RSV)—psalms continued to be composed, edited, and compiled until, by the third century before Christ, the 150 psalms stood together as a canonical Jewish hymnbook of unrivaled value.

If the early history of the psalms is obscure to our view, so is their function. Were they composed originally for liturgical purposes? Some scholars think so; others disagree. Most agree, however, that whatever their original functions might have been, the psalms, in the process of being collected and compiled, were adapted for liturgical purposes—in particular, for singing at the sacrificial rites carried out in the temple.

There is scanty information about how the psalms were used in temple worship. The few references in the Old Testament historical and prophetic books do not go very far toward giving us ideas about what music in temple worship was like. And since none of the music was written down, we will never know much about it—beyond the facts that it was in the hands of the Levites and that it included instrumental accompaniment as well as singing. We can surmise that in the worship in at least the first and second temples the singing of psalms at the times of sacrifice was quite an elaborate affair, performed by highly trained singers and instrumentalists who used melodic formulas or recitation patterns.

We have a somewhat clearer picture of temple worship around the time of Jesus, thanks to some fairly detailed description found in the *Mishnah,* a redaction of the *Talmud* from about A.D. 200. Every day of the year there were two solemn sacrifices, one in the morning and one in the afternoon. On sabbaths and feast days there were additional sacrifices. Services began with the priests blowing three blasts on their silver trumpets. Then

> the great gate of the sanctuary was opened, the lamb was slaughtered and its limbs made ready for the sacrifice. At this point the participants retired for prayer to the Chamber of Hewn Stone. . . . They recited three items: (1) the Ten Commandments; (2) the *Shema,* "Hear, O Israel" [Deut. 6:4-9]; and (3) a number of benedictions which constituted the nucleus of what would become the eighteen benedictions of the *Tefillah* [prayers]. . . .
>
> The service continued as two priests chosen by lot went to the Sanctuary for the solemn incense offering before the Holy of Holies. As they moved across the court towards the Sanctuary, an officer threw down a large rake, the *magrefah,* with a legendary loud clatter. This was the signal for the participants to prepare for the final acts of the service, and accordingly the Levite musicians assembled on the *duchan,* a platform adjoining the people's portion of the inner court towards the east. While the incense was being offered the people both within and without the temple court prayed. After performing the offering, the chosen priests withdrew from the Sanctuary and together with the other priests blessed the people from the Sanctuary steps. The limbs of the lamb were then carried up the altar ramp and cast upon the fire. Two priests gave three blasts on their trumpets, the *segan* waved a cloth, the temple officer who was "over the cymbals" clashed them together, and as the libation of wine was poured on to the fire, the Levites sang a psalm accompanied by the string instruments *nevel* and *kinnor.* The morning service—and the afternoon service as well—ended with the conclusion of the psalm.
>
> —*James McKinnon, "The Question of Psalmody in the Ancient Synagogue," Early Music History 6, pp. 162-63.*

This description of the temple liturgy confirms the impression we have about temple psalmody from Old Testament sources:

- It was part of a highly formalized liturgy.
- It was closely associated with the sacrifice.
- It was performed by the Levites {that is, by highly trained, "professional" musicians).

- It was accompanied by stringed instruments (that is, by the softer instruments that could support the singing but would not drown out or obscure the words).

This last feature points to the word-oriented nature of Jewish psalmody, a characteristic that set it apart from the music of the sacrificial rites of Israel's pagan neighbors. Pagan sacrificial music typically featured the frenzy-inducing sound of loud, double-reed instruments and the rhythms of dancing in which words were superfluous. In contrast, in Jewish temple music words were primary and governed the rhythms. The stringed instruments that accompanied the singing supported the monophonic vocal line, perhaps with some heterophonic embellishments, but never overpowering the words. Trumpets and cymbals were used independently only to signal the beginning of the psalm and the places at the ends of sections where the worshipers were to prostrate themselves.

Psalmody in the Synagogue

Psalmody in Jewish synagogues was very different from that in the temple. The gatherings in the synagogues did not focus on sacrifice and therefore did not require the priestly and Levitical classes—or their specially trained musicians. Synagogue psalmody, therefore, was undoubtedly simple—probably little more than a slightly embellished recitation—and did not make use of instruments.

When did chanting the psalms become a regular feature at synagogue gatherings? For a long time most scholars agreed that psalmody played an important role in Jewish synagogues during pre-Christian times and that the chanting of psalms in early Christian worship was a carryover from synagogue practice. It was thought that synagogue worship before the Christian era consisted of four main ingredients—Scripture reading, discourse upon the reading, prayer, and psalm chanting.

The hypothesis that early Christian psalmody was an inheritance from synagogue practice, however, rested more on reasonable assumption and conjecture than on concrete evidence. A careful search of surviving evidence reveals that Scripture reading and discourse were regular occurrences at synagogue gatherings. For example, note the familiar accounts of Jesus and of Paul in the synagogue, recorded in Luke 4:14-27 and Acts 13:14-43, respectively. Jesus read from and commented upon a passage in Isaiah, and Paul, after hearing the readings from the Law and the Prophets, spoke to the assembly in response to the invitation from the synagogue rulers to anyone who had "a word of exhortation for the people" (Acts 13:15, RSV).

But evidence is lacking for prayer and psalmody as regular, fixed activities. There's no doubt that praying took place, but nowhere is the synagogue, like the temple, referred to as a "house of prayer." And nowhere in the New Testament are we told that anyone went to the synagogue to pray. When we are told that people went to pray, it is invariably to the temple or to a house. When we are told that people went to the synagogue, it was to speak or debate. The picture of the synagogue that emerges from pre-Christian and early Christian times, then, is that of a public forum for reading, studying, and discussing the law and the prophets, and of a place to settle disputes in what we would think of as secular matters.

When the temple was destroyed in A.D. 70, changes took place in the synagogue. With the temple no longer in existence, the synagogue began to take over some of the elements of formal worship, excluding, of course, the sacrifices. It seems, for example, that after the destruction of the temple, the *Shema*—"Hear, O Israel: the LORD our God, the LORD is one" (Deut. 6:4)—and the *Tefillah*—a series of eighteen prayers beginning "Blessed art thou, O Lord"—moved into the synagogue and eventually became regular features of synagogue liturgy.

Regular chanting of the psalms is as noticeably absent as formal prayer is from the sources of information about the synagogue in pre-Christian and early Christian times. It seems likely that psalms were sometimes among the Scripture readings (although technically they were not among the law and prophets that are explicitly mentioned in our sources, but part of the *Hagiographa* ["Writings"], the third part of the Jewish Scriptures). As Scripture readings they would have been intoned in a simple recitation formula like the other readings. Owing to their poetic qualities, the recitation of the psalms may have tended toward a more melodious and lyrical rendition. But as a regular, fixed, distinctively musical part of the activities in the synagogues, psalmody seems to have been a latecomer. In fact, the earliest concrete evidence for psalmody as a distinct musical ingredient in synagogue liturgy comes from the eighth century A.D. The eighth-century treatise *Sopherim* lists the daily psalms used in the synagogue. They were to be chanted at the end of the synagogue service, preceded by a clear reference to temple psalmody: "This is the first [or second, etc.] day of the week, on which the Levites used to say . . ." Particularly interesting, as James McKinnon has pointed out, is that even at this late date, it was "found necessary . . . to contrive some justification for [the psalms'] use in the absence of sacrifice" (p. 183)—another indication that it took a considerable amount of time after the destruction of the temple for psalmody as a specific musical-liturgical activity to find its way into synagogue worship.

Psalms in Early Christian Worship

Early Christian psalmody was probably more similar in style, method of performance, and character to the psalmody eventually found in the synagogue than to the psalmody of the temple. It was simple, performed by "amateurs," and devoid of instrumental accompaniment. Given temple psalmody's close association with sacrifice and early Christianity's lack of opportunity for the institutional development of trained choirs and instrumental ensembles like those of the Levites, it is not surprising that early Christianity did not follow the lead of the temple in its psalmody. But if it did not come from the temple, and if synagogue psalmody was such a late development, where did early Christian psalmody come from?

That question betrays a hidden assumption that lurked in scholars' minds for a long time. The assumption was that the psalms were exclusively, or at least primarily, temple or synagogue music. The fact is, as careful reading of the sources will show, the psalms were as much "house music" as they were "church music." Both for the Jews and for the early Christians, the psalms were an important part of daily life.

Jewish households provided many occasions, both formal and informal, for singing.

The pertinent informal religious assemblies of the family are those intimate occasions when parents discharge their duties as religious instructors of their children. The context of 4 Maccabees xviii. 15 suggests that it was not unusual in a devout household for the father to sing psalms to his children on such occasions. Psalm singing may therefore be considered to have been a normal concomitant of the religious life of the family in the home.

—*J. A. Smith, "The Ancient Synagogue, the Early Church and Singing," Music and Letters 65, 1984, p. 10.*

Formal occasions that included psalm singing were weddings, funerals, and, most important, the Passover.

The Passover ritual had two consecutive parts. The first was public and took place in the temple. . . . The second part was private and took place in rooms within the city. This consisted of the Passover meal at which each household, each in its respective room, ate the roasted meat of the lambs that had earlier been sacrificed. During the meal . . . blessings and prayers were offered by the head of the household, and explanations of the meaning of the occasion and the symbolism of the foods were given. Also included was the obligatory singing of the *Hallel* [Ps. 113-118]. . . . After the destruction of the temple the domestic part of the ritual was retained.

—*Smith, pp. 9-10.*

It is most likely that the "hymn" that Jesus and his disciples sang at the Last Supper was this group of *Hallel* psalms (see Matt. 26:30).

It seems from the surviving evidence, then, that the source of early Christian psalmody was more likely the Jewish household than the Jewish synagogue. Further, although evidence is sparse, it appears that early Christian psalmody was more a regular feature in Christian households than it was in formal worship.

The clearest and most complete surviving description of an early Christian Sunday Eucharist comes from Justin Martyr (d. c. 165). In it there is not a word about singing:

And on the day named for the sun there is an assembly in one place for all who live in the towns and in the country; and the memoirs of the Apostles and the writings of the Prophets are read as long as time permits. Then, when the reader has finished, he who presides speaks, giving admonishment and exhortation to imitate those noble deeds. Then we all stand together and offer prayers. And when, as we said above, we are finished with the prayers, bread is brought, and wine and water, and he who presides likewise offers prayers and thanksgiving, according to his ability, and the people give their assent by exclaiming Amen. And there takes place the distribution to each and the partaking of that over which thanksgiving has been said, and it is brought to those not present by the deacon.

—*Apology I, 67, trans. James McKinnon, Music in Early Christian Literature (Cambridge: Cambridge University Press, 1987), p. 20.*

Of course, it is dangerous to argue from silence. But Justin's silence is compelling because his description is so clear, straightforward, and sequential. Again, as with the synagogue, it would be putting too much weight on skimpy evidence and flying in the face of common sense to claim that the Psalms were totally absent from early Christian worship. They could very well have been among "the writings of the Prophets" that were read or (more likely) intoned. And given the positive attitude toward singing that the apostles Paul and James displayed in their letters, it would stretch credulity to maintain that singing was totally absent from early Christian worship. But the evidence does not permit us to maintain a picture of early Christian worship in which psalm singing was a fixed and regular liturgical feature.

It is particularly interesting to note that the surviving evidence gives us a much clearer picture of early Christian psalmody in homes, especially at communal meals among which the *agape* (love-feast) is best known. This parallels the Jewish situation and adds support to the theory that it was Jewish daily life more than the synagogue that was the source of early Christian psalmody. The following passage by Cyprian (d. 258) is an example of the descriptions of psalmody at meals that we find in early Christian literature:

> Now as the sun is sinking towards evening, let us spend what remains of the day in gladness and not let the hour of repast go untouched by heavenly grace. Let a psalm be heard at the sober banquet, and since your memory is sure and your voice pleasant, undertake this task as is your custom. You will better nurture your friends, if you provide a spiritual recital for us and beguile our ears with sweet religious strains.
>
> —Ad Donatum *xvi, trans. McKinnon,* Music, *p. 49.*

Here a point needs to be made about terminology. Cyprian, in the above passage, used the word "psalm." He was not necessarily referring to one of the canonical psalms. He could just as easily have been referring to a newly composed Christian "hymn." The early Christian writers, including the New Testament authors, hardly distinguished between what we would now call "psalms" and "hymns"—that is, between songs with texts taken from the 150 psalms and songs with newly composed texts. Either term could be used for either category. Prior to the fourth century, newly composed texts were as common as, or perhaps even more common than, the psalms in worship.

So the surviving evidence suggests that early Christian psalmody came out of Jewish daily life and grew into Christian daily life. It is difficult to deny that psalmody occurred in formal worship, but it is impossible to prove that it did. In any case, it is clear that the psalms were not only (probably not even primarily) for formal, public worship among the early Christians any more than they were among the Jews. Wherever Christians sang—and particularly in the home—the psalms were included.

Psalmody in Monastic Life

Compared to the scarcity of information about psalmody in the church during the second and third centuries, the amount of evidence coming from the fourth century is abundant. We have already heard one example of the exuberant praise the fourth-century church fathers heaped upon the singing of the psalms. The unprecedented enthusiasm for the psalms found in fourth-century Christian writings has rarely been matched in the subsequent history of the church. But it certainly has helped to establish the psalms as the primary texts used in the singing of the church.

During the earlier centuries newly composed hymns were at least as prominent among the church's songs as were the psalms. But during the fourth century psalmody became overwhelmingly more prominent than hymnody. Undoubtedly one of the reasons for the waning of hymn singing in favor of psalm singing was the threat of heresy. The success with which heretical sects spread their ideas through hymns made the church wary of noncanonical texts.

Another feature of the fourth century that contributed to the enthusiasm for psalmody was the growth of monasticism. In monastic communities the singing of the psalms became the backbone of the liturgical day. Although initially varying from time to time and place to place, a schedule of periods of worship throughout each day was an important feature of monastic life. By the sixth century, owing to the influence of the order founded by Benedict of Nursia, the monastic liturgical day typically consisted of eight periods of worship (not including Mass). These periods of worship—collectively referred to as the Divine Office or the Hours—were short and consisted of prayers, Scripture reading, and the chanting of psalms and canticles.

Though there were variants throughout the Middle Ages, the usual pattern of daily worship for many inhabitants of a monastery or nunnery began with Vigils (often called Matins) during the night. This period was followed by Lauds ("praise," before dawn), Prime (the first hour of the day, about 6 A.M.), and then at three-hour intervals by Terce, Sext, and None during the working day. Vespers was sung in the evening, followed by Compline. All these Offices involved the singing of psalms in sequence—for example, Lauds included seven psalms, Vespers had five psalms, Compline involved four, and so on. In many monastic institutions, the 150 psalms were chanted *in toto* each week, a well-known practice from the Rule of Benedict.

Obviously the general populace did not participate in this rigorous schedule of worship in its entirety, though evidence suggests that at least some of these Offices in the early Middle Ages and in the Eastern church were intended for nonmonastic Christians as well. In addition, the hospitality that many monastic institutions provided to pilgrims and other travelers in later medieval times suggests that guests would be present at some of these Offices and that especially Vespers would be attended by the laity as well as by monks or nuns. It is also worth noting in this context that the popularity of Matins and Vespers has survived to this day in services of Morning and Evening Prayer, particularly among Anglicans and Lutherans. The practice of daily services of prayer has also been introduced recently among some Presbyterians.

It would be difficult to exaggerate the importance of the psalms in monastic life throughout the Middle Ages and beyond. It was not unusual (in fact, it was often required) for a monk to know the entire Psalter by memory. In the monasteries the psalms were predominant, or as one anonymous early Christian put it, "David is first and middle and last." Sung in unison, with responsorial and/or antiphonal performance, the psalms were a monk's daily bread, the foundation of his prayer life; they were a nun's daily food for meditation.

The Psalms Among the Laity

While the psalms became and remained the cornerstone of monastic prayer and meditation, what happened to them in the daily life and communal worship of Christians outside the monastic communities?

In daily life outside the monasteries there seems to have been a short period—the fourth century and perhaps a little beyond—when the singing of psalms played a role analogous to, if not as extensive as, the role it had in the monasteries. At least that was the ideal held out by fourth-century church fathers like Ambrose, who urged believers,

> At least divide your time between God and the world. When the darkness of night prevents you from performing in public the deeds of this world, then, as you have leisure time for God, give yourself to prayer, and, lest you sleep, sing psalms, thus cheating your sleep by means of a beneficent fraud. In the morning hasten to church and offer the first fruits of your pious devotion, and afterwards, if worldly necessity calls, you are not excluded from saying: "My eyes have anticipated the morning that I might meditate upon thy words" (Ps. 119:148). You may now with peace of mind proceed to your duties.
>
> —Expositio psalmi cxviii, *xix, 32, trans. McKinnon,* Music, *p. 128.*

It cannot be maintained that most Christians lived up to this ideal, but neither can it be denied that some tried and that in some Christian households the singing of psalms was regularly and frequently heard.

After the fourth century there is little evidence to suggest that Christians outside monastic communities maintained anything approaching the ideal advanced in the fourth century. Sad to say, it seems all too likely that while the psalms were nourishing the monastic communities, they were falling into disuse among other Christians, as far as daily life was concerned.

The psalms did become prominent, however, in the Mass of the Western church, the main occasion for public communal worship. Again the fourth century was pivotal in this development. Before that time we can find little evidence of regular, fixed singing of psalms in the Mass. The fourth century marked the birth of psalmody as a regular feature at two points in the Mass—at the reading of the Scripture lessons and at the communion. Later, during the early Middle Ages, psalmody became a regular feature at the beginning of the Mass as well—the introit—and at the offertory. So in the full-fledged medieval Mass, the chants sung at the introit, offertory, and communion, as well as the chants sung between the Scripture lessons—the graduals, alleluias, and tracts—overwhelmingly drew from the psalms. In other words, the singing of psalm texts in Latin was a big part in the medieval Mass, and all who attended regularly received a generous exposure to them.

But that exposure had two serious defects. First, for many people it involved hearing but not understanding, because Latin remained the liturgical language long after it ceased to be the daily language of the uneducated majority. And, second, the exposure involved hearing but not singing, because the Mass was performed by the clergy and choir, giving the congregation little opportunity for direct participation.

The music that carried the psalm texts (and all other liturgical texts to be sung) of both Mass and Office throughout the Middle Ages is known as plainchant, or Gregorian chant, in honor of Pope Gregory I (sixth century). It is music that consists of melody only and is sung in unison without the use of instruments. Its rhythm is flexible and prose-like rather than rigidly metered, and its melodic curves are gentle, graceful, and a bit elusive as to destination, at least for ears used more to tonal than to modal structures.

Though singing the psalms is an ancient tradition, it is only from the late ninth century on (when early music notations developed) that we can decipher the chants used for the psalms. The pitches were structured according to the medieval scale patterns of the modal system, which were more varied than the major/minor constructs of the later tonal system. Usually each melody or psalm tone was a recitation formula, composed in one of the eight musical modes: Dorian (I), Hypodorian (II), Phrygian (III), Hypophrygian (IV), Lydian (V), Hypolydian (VI), Mixolydian (VII), and Hypomixolydian (VIII). (Many manuscripts simply indicated one of these Roman numerals with each psalm.) Later other chant melodies were devised in the more recent Aeolian and Ionian modes. Though it was possible to sing any psalm to various chants, it was customary to associate a specific psalm to a specific psalm tone in a specific mode, as an aid to memorization and group performance.

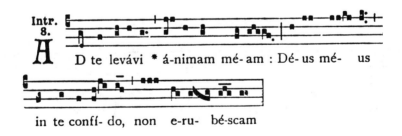

Example 1: Gregorian Chant Setting of Psalm 25:1-2

Without denying the positive characteristics of plainchant—its austere beauty, liturgical appropriateness, and spiritual depth—it's important to recognize that by the late Middle Ages reform was long overdue. The chant and liturgy of the church had become an elaborate affair, rivaling and perhaps "surpassing in splendor the psalmody of the temple" (James McKinnon, *Antiquity and the Middle Ages;* Prentice-Hall, 1990;

p. 12). But the people were spectators, not participants. What is more, they were spectators who at best had only a hazy idea of what was happening and what was being sung.

Much earlier, the elaborate Jewish temple psalmody had come under severe prophetic attack, for example, by Amos, who said, on the Lord's behalf,

> "I hate, I despise your religious feasts;
> I cannot stand your assemblies. . . .
> Away with the noise of your songs!
> I will not listen to the music of your harps."
>
> —*Amos 5:21-23*

Chanted Psalmody in the Reformation

In some ways there is a parallel between the worship of Amos's day and the late Middle Ages and Renaissance, when the elaborate music and ritual of the church became "the object of prophetic scorn on the part of the more radical Protestant reformers" (McKinnon, *Antiquity*, p. 12).

John Calvin was one of those more radical Reformers, advocating the exclusive use of the psalms and returning them to the whole body of Christians, in worship and in everyday life, in the form of vernacular, metrical versifications sung in unison and unaccompanied. Arranging the psalms in poetic meters (hence, the term *metrical psalmody*) meant an abandonment of the chant tradition (see the following article on Calvin's role in the development of the Genevan Psalter).

Martin Luther was not as radical. He was reluctant to abandon the musical treasures of the medieval church, including the use of choirs and instruments. He retained the practice of chanting parts of the service—for example, the following intonation of a psalm for the beginning of his *Deutsche Messe* (German Mass of 1526), translated here into English:

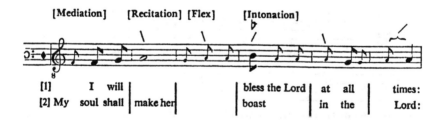

Example 2: Introit from Luther's German Mass (Psalm 34:1-2)

Although some of his chorales were psalm versifications (for example, "A Mighty Fortress Is Our God," 468/469, based on Ps. 46) to be sung by the congregation in unison and unaccompanied, he also translated older Latin hymns and encouraged new hymn texts. "Savior of the Nations, Come" (336), for example, is a chorale adapted from an early Latin hymn text and a chant melody.

Luther was even reluctant to let go of the Latin language, for that would mean losing musical treasures that he wanted to retain, especially for the youth:

> For in no wise would I want to discontinue the service in the Latin language, because the young are my chief concern. And if I could bring it to pass, and Greek and Hebrew were as familiar to us as the Latin and had as many fine melodies and songs, we would hold mass, sing, and read on successive Sundays in all four languages, German, Latin, Greek, and Hebrew.
>
> *—Preface to* The German Mass and Order of Service, *trans. A. Steimle, rev. Ulrich S. Leupold;*
> Luther's Works *vol. 53, ed. U. S. Leupold (Philadelphia: Fortress Press, 1965), p. 63.*

The Anglican Church developed the chanting of psalms and canticles in a style called Anglican chant. Anglican chants are sung not in unison but in four parts. These chants generally consist of two phrases, one for each half of a psalm verse (some "double chants" consist of four phrases). Most of the text syllables are chanted on the first chord of the phrase, and the last syllables are reserved for the cadential chords. The following example of Psalm 51:17 is set to the psalm tone TONUS REGIUS.

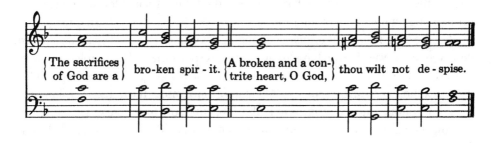

Example 3: Psalm 51:17 (KJV), set to Tonus Regius *(Royal Tone),*
possibly a French adaptation of a Gregorian chant used in the French Royal Chapel

Although it's called Anglican chant, the use of this chant style has not been exclusively Anglican; some other Protestant churches have used it as well.

Vestiges of Pre-Reformation Psalmody in the *Psalter Hymnal*

What vestiges of the long and rich pre-Reformation tradition of chanting the psalms are retained in the *Psalter Hymnal,* the songbook of a denomination that descends from one of the more radical Reformers? Most conspicuous, and most important in this regard, is the prominence of the psalm texts. The *Psalter Hymnal* opens with a selection of 150 psalm settings, one for each psalm in Scripture, and provides alternate versifications and musical settings for some psalms among the Bible songs and hymns that follow in subsequent sections of the songbook. (References to these alternates are listed at each of the corresponding psalms in the first 150.)

Because the Calvinist Reformation turned so exclusively to metrical psalmody, and because the modern convention of harmonized accompaniments is so firmly entrenched, the heritage of medieval musical styles and methods of performance is not prominent in the *Psalter Hymnal*, but it is not entirely missing.

Chant style is nearly nonexistent in the *Psalter Hymnal*. The melody of the great early Christian hymn "Of the Father's Love Begotten" (342) is the closest that the melodies in the *Psalter Hymnal* come to plainchant. "O Come, O Come, Immanuel" (328) and "Savior of the Nations, Come" (336) still have a few earmarks of their chant origins (see also 398 and 407, both of which derive from the same chant). Some scholars also detect plainchant influences in some Genevan tunes. In his classic study, *Le Psautier Huguenot* (1962), Pierre Pidoux points to chant fragments in the Genevan tunes for Psalms 17, 20, 31, 32, 55, 80, 124, and 129. Of these, the tune for Psalm 124 is represented in the *Psalter Hymnal*. The *Psalter Hymnal* does contain one Anglican chant: a setting of the Lord's Prayer (207).

A slightly stronger vestige of ancient and medieval musical practice retained in the *Psalter Hymnal* are those songs that lend themselves to the responsorial method of singing. Responsorial singing is a prominent feature of the song of oral cultures. Without access to written music, the only way to involve a large group of people in song is to have them participate through responses and refrains. Ancient Jewish and early Christian singing relied heavily on responsorial methods, and that pattern is maintained in the New Testament principle of singing "as with one voice" (*una voces dicentes*). There were many ways in which psalms were sung responsorially. The simplest way was to have a soloist sing most of the verses and to have the congregation respond periodically with a short acclamation such as "Alleluia" or "Hosanna." It was also very simple to turn a short phrase into a refrain, as in Psalm 136. Often the first verse was turned into a refrain, and occasionally more elaborate refrains were used, as in Psalm 42-43. A more difficult method, requiring that everyone know the psalm, is to have the leader and the congregation sing alternate verses or half-verses.

The *Psalter Hymnal* includes many psalms that lend themselves to responsorial singing—for example, see Psalms 8, 16, 23 (162), 24(163), 100 (176), and 148 (188). Some of these, like the setting of Psalm 100 by Lucien Deiss at 176, are modern pieces inspired by ancient and medieval sources. More of them, such as the setting of Psalm 46 at 610, come out of oral musical traditions that, like ancient and early medieval traditions, needed to make use of responsorial methods to involve everyone in the singing. What developed out of a musical need in those traditions can be an enriching musical alternative for us today.

In addition to responsorial singing involving a solo cantor with congregational refrains, there is some evidence that antiphonal singing was known in the Jewish temple. Presumably the large Levite choirs sang some of the longer psalms by assigning stanzas to smaller groups within the choir. Such *alternatim praxis* was also known in the Greek-speaking Eastern church, and Ambrose is usually credited for encouraging antiphonal singing in the Latin-speaking Western church. Some of the liturgical manuscripts from various monasteries in both the early and late Middle Ages show symbols that indicate antiphonal singing of the psalms. The custom developed of having two groups sing a psalm, with each group singing one biblical verse at a time in order and then concluding with the "Gloria Patri." The very architecture of most medieval churches and cathedrals, with their divided chancels and choir seats, is lasting evidence of this antiphonal practice.

Though antiphonal singing of the psalms is not specifically indicated in the *Psalter Hymnal,* this traditional practice is useful for singing the longer psalms (such as 9, 18, 22, 68, 89, 104, 119, and 145, and so on). To reflect the nuances within some psalms, antiphony may also be combined with the responsorial style—that is, using solo voices, two or more groups, and the entire congregation for singing a psalm (such as 10, 50, and 132).

* * * * * * *

The psalms have been the heart of the church's singing throughout its history. Christians throughout the ages, whenever they have made the psalms central in their singing, have learned what Calvin and Basil knew: "Although we look far and wide . . . we shall not find better songs . . . than the Psalms of David," for the Psalter in Scripture "embraces whatever . . . is helpful." As vehicles of prayer and as sources of spiritual nourishment, the psalms remain unparalleled. The church ignores them to its harm but sings them to its health. For, as Ambrose said,

> A psalm is the blessing of the people, the praise of God, the commendation of the multitude, the applause of all, the speech of every man, the voice of the Church, the sonorous profession of faith, devotion full of authority, the joy of liberty, the noise of good cheer, and the echo of gladness. It softens anger, it gives release to anxiety, it alleviates sorrow; it is protection at night, instruction by day, a shield in time of fear, a feast of holiness, the image of tranquility, a pledge of peace and harmony. . . . A psalm joins those with differences, unites those at odds and reconciles those who have been offended, for who will not concede to him with whom one sings to God in one voice? It is after all a great bond of unity for the full number of people to join in one chorus.

—Explanatio psalmi i, *9, trans. McKinnon,* Music, *pp. 126-27.*

The Genevan Psalter

by Emily R. Brink

The psalms have always had a central place in both Jewish and Christian prayer. But after centuries of chanting the psalms, a new approach was introduced in the sixteenth century: metrical psalmody. In chant, the psalm texts remained intact; they were set to melodic patterns that could be adapted to the varied lines of text. In metrical psalmody, the psalm texts themselves were adapted into poetic meters for singing to tunes that remained intact. The Reformed branch of the Reformation that spoke of *sola scriptura* was willing to adapt Scripture in order to allow people to sing the psalms to tunes that were closer to their cultural song traditions. That decision was based on a firm commitment to congregational song and the conviction that metrical structure was the most accessible form for the people of that day. Metrical psalmody became the hallmark of the Reformed tradition.

The Lutheran branch of the sixteenth century Reformation was also committed to congregational song, but as an addition to the church's rich heritage of chant and choral and instrumental music. Martin Luther (1483-1546), a former monk who had chanted the psalms daily and probably knew them by heart, preferred to sing the Scriptures directly even while introducing hymns and a few metrical psalms. Lutherans chant the psalms to this day. But under the leadership of John Calvin (1509-1564), metrical psalmody was to become the virtually exclusive form of congregational song for the Reformed tradition. The Reformed branch of the Reformation (in distinction from Lutherans) restricted church music to unison (no harmony) congregational singing (no choirs) of the psalms (no hymns) in meter (no chant), sung unaccompanied (no instruments).

That simplistic comparison doesn't begin to tell the story of the power of the metrical psalm tradition. The city of Geneva became the focal point for the creation of a metrical psalter that was to have a profound impact on the spiritual lives of countless people and was an important factor in the spread of Calvinism throughout Europe. The development and spread of that psalter happened very quickly in an intense period of Reformation history. The various names by which this psalter came to be known gives testimony to its widespread and continuing use. Probably the most common name is the Genevan Psalter, after the city at the center of the development of Calvinism; but it is also known as the Dutch Psalter, from its adoption in the Low Countries; the Huguenot Psalter among French-speaking Calvinists; and the Hungarian Psalter in Hungary. In fact, it is the only psalter from Reformation times still published in its entirety and used in several countries.

The Development of the Genevan Psalter

The story of the Calvinist psalter begins in Strasbourg. In April 1538 John Calvin was expelled from Geneva, where he had served as pastor for less than two years. When passing through Geneva in 1536, just after his *Institutes of the Christian Religion* were written, Calvin was persuaded to stay and help the French evangelical preacher Guillaume Farel to pastor the Protestant church there. The city council had officially voted to become Protestant that same year. So Calvin, the quiet scholar, reluctantly became a pastor in Geneva. The city had just suffered an iconoclastic riot, and the next two years were anything but peaceful. Under the influence of Ulrich Zwingli (PHH 261), the church in Geneva had banned all music from worship; there was no singing at all. Calvin's attempts to introduce singing were rejected; in his *Articles* of 1537 he lamented, "We are not able to estimate the benefit and edification which will derive from this [congregational singing] until after having experienced it. Certainly at present the prayers of the faithful are so cold that we should be greatly ashamed and confused." After two difficult years, Calvin was expelled from Geneva and went to Strasbourg, the city he had been traveling to while first passing through Geneva.

Calvin's next three years in Strasbourg were much more peaceful: he married Idelette van Buren, pastored a congregation of French refugees, and gave lectures in theology. And there he experienced the power of congregational singing. Charles Garside, in *The Origins of Calvin's Theology of Music: 1536-1543* (1979), provides this description:

> Calvin had his own congregation there, and from his own parishioners he had quickly learned at first hand the depth of their appreciation for the singing of the psalms in their own language. How much, in fact, it meant to them is revealed in a letter by a young man from Antwerp who had sought refuge in Strasbourg. . . . He wrote to his cousins at Lille as follows: "On Sundays . . . we sing a psalm of David or some other prayer taken from the New Testament. The psalm or prayer is sung by everyone together, men as well as women, with a beautiful unanimity, which is something beautiful to behold. For you must understand that each one has a music book in his hand; that is why they cannot lose touch with one another. Never did I think that it could be as pleasing and delightful as it is. For five or six days at first, as I looked upon this little company, exiled from countries everywhere for having upheld the honor of God and his Gospel, I would begin to weep, not at all from sadness, but from joy at hearing them sing so heartily, and, as they sang, giving thanks to the Lord that he had led them to a place where his name is honored and glorified. No one could believe the joy which one experiences when one is singing the praises and wonders of the Lord in the mother tongue as one sings them here.
>
> —*Alfred Erichson*, L 'Église française de Strasbourg au seizième siècle d'après des documents inédits *(Strasbourg, Librairie C. F. Schmidt, 1886), pp. 21-22.*

Calvin's own reactions must have been similar, since he quickly decided to begin versifying the psalms for congregational singing. During the next several years, Calvin was involved in the development of several collections, which were published in installments until the entire psalter was completed in 1562. He contributed several of his own versifications in the early development, but he withdrew them later when other, more skilled poets became involved.

The 1539 Collection

Calvin's first little psalter, *Certain Psalms and Canticles with Melodies* (*Aulcuns pseaulmes et cantiques mys en chant*, Strasbourg, 1539), included six psalm texts by Calvin and thirteen (greatly altered texts) by Clément Marot, the most famous poet in France. Also included were the Ten Commandments, the Song of Simeon, and a prose (chant) setting of the Apostles' Creed. Marot was not aware of the (corrupted) use of his texts until later.

In 1537 Marot, a valet to King François I, had prepared rhymed translations of thirty psalms; he had earlier translated Greek and Latin poetry into French, and now he was interested in doing the same for Hebrew poetry. Chroniclers reported that the monarch, courtiers, and courtesans sang his psalm texts to popular tunes. In 1540 Marot gave a manuscript of his psalms to Charles V, who urged the poet to continue his work. Evidently some of Marot's early popular settings resulted in pirated and altered copies that found their way into Calvin's first collection.

The psalm texts were set to melodies borrowed from earlier Strasbourg songbooks; some were probably composed by Matthäus Greiter (PHH 68), a cantor in a German-speaking congregation in Strasbourg. Melodies from the 1539 collection included in the *Psalter Hymnal* are found at 68, 103, 130, and 143 (see those entries for more information).

The 1542 Collection

When Calvin returned to Geneva in 1541, he immediately sought and this time gained approval from the city council to introduce congregational singing. In the *Ecclesiastical Ordinances* he presented for approval just two months after he returned, two little sentences are inserted in a section dealing with marriage:

> It will be good to introduce ecclesiastical songs, the better to incite the people to pray to and praise God. For a beginning the little children are to be taught; then with time all the church will be able to follow.

One year later Calvin brought out his second psalter, *The Liturgy of Prayers and Ecclesiastical Songs* (*La forme des prieres et chantz ecclesiastiques*, Geneva, 1542). This book contains thirty psalms and two canticles by Marot, five psalms and two canticles by Calvin, a catechism, and directions for baptism, communion, and marriage. Some tunes from 1539 were retained, some were adapted, and others were new. Melodies from the 1542 edition included in the *Psalter Hymnal* are found at 6, 19, and 173 (Ps. 95).

The first collection had no preface, but for this second collection Calvin prepared an "Epistle to the Reader," a preface that reveals his theological and liturgical thinking on the sacraments and psalm singing. The edition concluded with liturgical texts (prayers and forms for the sacraments). In his "Epistle" (expanded in subsequent printings)

Calvin calls congregational singing a "public prayer with song" that "has existed since the first origin of the Church." Calvin believed congregational singing "has great force and vigor to move and inflame the hearts of men to invoke and praise God with a more vehement and ardent zeal." For this reason, the melody must not be "light and frivolous, but have weight and majesty" appropriate to the text. Though "we look far and wide and search on every hand," Calvins says that the best texts for religious use are the psalms of David. "We shall not find better songs nor songs better suited" to praise God than those that the Holy Spirit made and uttered through David. "When we sing them, we may be certain that God puts the words in our mouths as if he himself sang in us to exalt his glory" (*Source Readings in Music History,* Strunck, p. 346).

The 1543 Collection

In 1542 Marot fled to Geneva to escape religious persecution. There he discovered his altered texts in use, and Calvin enlisted him in making corrections and additions to the next edition, *Fifty Psalms of David* (*Cinquante Pseaumes de David*), published in Geneva in 1543. No copy of this edition survives. Calvin urged Marot to continue his work of providing more psalm versifications, but Marot left Geneva and died suddenly in 1544. His prominence as a poet combined with his work on the psalms during those tense days may have made him a target of those opposed to the Reformation. It is not known who served as composer or music editor of the 1542 or 1543 editions. Melodies from the 1543 edition included in the *Psalter Hymnal* are found at 65 and 128.

The 1551 Collection

The next person to take up the textual work was Théodore de Bèze, who came to Geneva in 1548 and eventually succeeded Calvin as ecclesiastical leader in Geneva. De Bèze prepared thirty-four more texts, which were published in the *Eighty-Three Psalms of David* (*Pseaumes octantetrois de David Geneva,*1551).

Louis Bourgeois (PHH 3), who had been active as a music teacher in Geneva since 1545, was responsible for the melodies in this collection. Bourgeois explained his work on the melodies in a preface, claiming that he wrote new melodies for the de Bèze psalms, rewrote or revised some of the old melodies, and left others untouched. Although Bourgeois is often credited for work on other Genevan psalters, his role, though substantial, was confined to this publication. Fourteen tunes in the *Psalter Hymnal* come from the 1551 psalter: 3, 12, 25, 27, 42, 47, 51, 100, 101, 119, 124, 133, 134, and 180 (Ps. 121).

The Complete Psalter of 1562

Calvin's goal of a complete psalter was finally realized in 1562 with the publication of *The Psalms Rhymed in French by Clement Marot and Théodore de Bèze* (*Les pseaumes mis en rime françoise, par Clement Marot et Théodore de Bèze*). The complete psalter was included along with only two other texts: the Ten Commandments and the Song of Simeon. Eighty-five melodies are repeated from the 1551 edition; forty are new. The creator of the new melodies was a certain "Maitre Pierre." The identity of "Maitre Pierre" remains a mystery because a number of Pierres—Dagues, Vallette, Davantes, and du Buisson—were all active as musicians in Geneva at this time. Ten melodies first appearing in the 1562 psalter are included in the *Psalter Hymnal* at 81, 84, 87, 89, 97, 105, 116, 136, 150, and 172 (Ps. 93).

As previous installments of the psalter grew in popularity, the completion of the psalter was eagerly awaited. Antoine Vincent was the publisher in charge of producing the tens of thousands of copies that poured from printing presses in Geneva, Paris, Lyons, Caen, St. Lo, and elsewhere, each copy duly marked "pour Antoine Vincent." This extensive printing venture, involving twenty-four printers in Paris alone, shows the immense popularity of the Calvinist psalms. As hostile a commentator as Florimond de Raemond wrote in his *Story of the Birth of Heresy* (*L'histoire de la naissance de l'heresie*, Paris, 1610) that the psalms of Marot and de Bèze "were received and welcomed by everyone with as much favor as ever any book was, not only by those with Protestant sympathies, but also by Catholics; everyone enjoyed singing them." French scholar Édith Weber states, "Printing launched it practically into orbit, for in 1562 alone more than 30,000 copies were sold—and more would have been, had not the civil and religious situation in France been so explosive" (as translated in *Hymnology Annual* 1992, from her 1983 article first published in France).

The Texts of the Genevan Psalter

The texts of Marot and de Bèze are no longer in use—singing in the vernacular brought about translations of their original work as well as eventual updates in the French language. Further, the intense persecution of the French Huguenots resulted in increased use of the psalter in other places and in other languages. But since the basic structure of the original French texts determined the structure of the melodies, it's clear that the translations and updates, when sung to the Genevan tunes, still reflect the influence of Marot.

Marot's texts reveal a stunning variety in metrical structure and rhyme scheme. A sophisticated poet, Marot gave full play to his skills in casting the psalms into meter. There were no fewer than 110 varieties of stanza structure (line length and number of lines per stanza) and 33 different rhyme schemes.

An interesting study could be made of the relationship between the original Hebrew poetry and Marot's metrical settings of the psalms. It is impossible to cast psalm texts into metrical form without some interpretation and "padding" to fill out lines and allow for rhyme. Subsequent translations sung to the same tunes usually tried to keep the same rhyme schemes, but the number of stanzas varied greatly. The melodies in a sense were "rhymed" as well to match the texts; many of the repetitions of musical phrases grew out of the textual rhymes and rhythms.

Most of the versifications to the Genevan tunes in the 1987 *Psalter Hymnal* are new, and many follow the same rhyme schemes as the original French. In a few cases, a prose versification was prepared; Psalm 119 in one Dutch translation took eighty-eight stanzas, compared to the tight (and unrhymed) virtual prose setting of twenty-two stanzas in the *Psalter Hymnal*. The intent was to stay as close to Scripture as possible, with a minimum of padding.

The Tunes of the Genevan Psalter

Calvin's goal was to provide a distinct tune for every psalm, so that each psalm would have its own identity. Every tune would then bring to mind a particular psalm. The psalter didn't quite reach this goal: it contains 125 different melodies for 152 texts (the 150 psalms and two canticles). Fifteen tunes were used twice, four tunes were used three times each, and one tune is used four times (see chart below).

Most of the Genevan melodies were newly composed, but some were adapted from various sources. Although there are reliable reports that Marot's first psalms were sung to popular tunes, there are only a few Genevan tunes that contain melodic segments borrowed from French chansons. Similarly, there are a few Genevan tunes that were adapted from Latin chants. Indeed, the Genevan tunes are actually much closer in form and contour to Latin chants than to the French chanson. Calvin insisted that melodies should not be light or flighty, but should "have weight and majesty." Therefore whatever was used was adapted to Calvin's principles for congregational singing.

Like Latin chants, the Genevan psalms are modal. The scales upon which the various melodies are based are not limited to the major and minor modes we use today. Instead, the composers used all of the medieval church modes (see p. 23). The Dorian, Phrygian, Lydian, and Mixolydian modes may sound slightly strange to modern ears, but their use increases the emotional range of the entire Genevan repertoire.

Calvin's interest in melodies that exhibit "weight and majesty" resulted in a rhythmic structure much simpler than in surrounding secular music, or even in many German chorales (for example, "A Mighty Fortress"; see 468 for the original rhythm). In the Genevan tunes there are only two note values: long and short. In the *Psalter Hymnal* only quarter and half notes are used; the whole notes at the ends of some phrases are used instead of rests. Usually the quarter notes come in pairs, but occasionally in groups of three, which creates a syncopation that enlivens the rhythm (47).

Also unlike Latin chants or chansons and madrigals of the time, the Genevan psalms are almost exclusively syllabic (see 6 for one exception). The melodic motion is primarily stepwise, with a range limited to an octave. This is music designed to be sung not by professional musicians or the clergy but by the congregation, and the tunes are designed so that the text clearly comes through and is not obscured by the music.

Tune Repetitions in the Genevan Psalter

5 = 64
14 = 53
17 = 63 = 70
18 = 144
24 = 62 = 95 = 111
28 = 109
30 = 76 = 139
31 = 71
33 = 67
36 = 68
46 = 82
51 = 69
60 = 108
65 = 72
66 = 98 = 118
74 = 116
77 = 86
78 = 90
100 = 131 = 142
117 = 127

The Calvinist (and Lutheran) congregations of the sixteenth century sang unaccompanied. Each congregation used a precentor (cantor) with a strong voice to lead the singing. This person would teach the melodies to the children and lead the people during worship. The precentor may even have directed the congregation by raising and lowering his hand. In 1556 Pierre Vallette (perhaps the "Maitre Pierre" credited with writing the psalm melodies after Bourgeois left Geneva) wrote a preface to one edition of the Genevan psalters in which he gave instructions for singing the psalms. He specifies that the semibreve (half note in the *Psalter Hymnal*) should have the value of one beat, shown by the raising and lowering of the hand. Vallete's instruction that the long note get the beat implies that the tempo for psalm singing was brisk. The tempo indications for Renaissance music state that the beat should equal the pulse rate of a quietly breathing adult.

The Spread of the Genevan Psalter

Though the Genevan Psalter was created for communal worship, the people soon began singing psalms at home, at work, and on the streets. People found great encouragement in singing the psalms, especially in the difficult days when taking a stand for the Reformed faith could mean imprisonment and even death. When armed resistance came, Psalm 68 became the "Huguenot Marseillaise" (see PHH 68). Laws in France became increasingly restrictive, banning psalm singing from streets and shops (1623), at executions (1657), outdoors at all (1659), and anywhere in French territory worldwide (1661). James Hastings Nichols writes: "The courage and joy of these martyrs who, like the ancient Christians, could have had release for a word, won converts among the onlookers. The authorities tried gags, but the cord would burn and from out of the smoke the psalm would begin again" (*Corporate Worship in the Reformed Tradition*, p. 39). The popularity of the Genevan Psalter continued to grow.

Composers also were attracted to the melodies of the Genevan Psalter, and thousands of choral settings were published beginning already in the first decade after its publication in 1562; organ compositions on the Genevan tunes began in the next century. The following information is based in part on research by Howard Slenk, retired professor of music at Calvin College, published in his article on metrical psalmody in *The New Groves Dictionary of Music and Musicians* (1980).

France and Switzerland

The immense popularity of the Calvinist psalms inspired composers to use the texts for polyphonic choral compositions. The first settings came soon after Calvin's first psalter of 1539 and are scattered singly in various chanson collections. These compositions make use of the texts, not the psalter melodies. But with the growing popularity of the subsequent collections, French printers soon began issuing publications devoted exclusively to polyphonic settings of the fifty Marot psalms with the Genevan tunes. Bourgeois, who had himself written some of the melodies, made two different polyphonic settings of the fifty psalms in 1547. One of the publications was in a simple chordal style, with the unchanged psalm melody in the tenor, which was the contemporary place for the main tune in many Renaissance choral works. The other collection of psalm settings by Bourgeois featured more elaborate motets, which also used the Genevan tunes.

Soon after the publication of the complete Genevan Psalter in 1562, composers began to write polyphonic settings of all 150 psalms. In their prefaces the composers of this Calvinist choral repertory stated that they had retained "the usual melody which is sung in church," because so many people enjoyed singing the psalms outside of the church, "in a more melodious setting, from the art of music." The most well-known composers involved were Claude Goudimel and Claude le Jeune. They and their colleagues either used the simple chordal style or wrote elaborate psalm motets. Goudimel set the whole psalter three times, once in simple chordal style, once in simple motet style, and once again in multi-movement elaborate settings. The given melody was clearly present in the simple harmonizations but was treated with more freedom in the more elaborate motets. Goudimel also usually placed the melody in the tenor voice in his simple harmonizations; in his more elaborate psalm motets the Genevan melodies appear in all voice parts. The very practice of women singing in the congregation was influential in eventually moving the melody line to the soprano voice. The *Psalter Hymnal* includes several of Goudimel's four-part settings with the melody in the tenor (6, 33, 68, 100, 138).

These compositions were to be sung in homes and in places where amateurs gathered to make music, not in church, since Calvin was concerned that polyphony could obscure the text. The goal was to keep the text clear and to have the entire congregation joined in singing the same text at the same time. Goudimel prefaced his chordal settings, published in Geneva in 1565, with the instruction that these settings were not be to sung in church but in the home. As for the more difficult motet-like settings, they were frequently dedicated to *colleges musicaux*, which were groups of accomplished amateurs. However, Robin A. Leaver recently uncovered one reference to part singing in church by English exiles living in Wesel, a German town on the Rhein. They had produced for their use a small English psalter, *Psalmes of David in Metre* (c. 1556), which included the following statement: "Item. that some psalm or invocation may at sometyme be sung ether in one tune, or in severall parts, at the discreation of all thelders provided alwayes that the verse wich shalbe so sung be befoer playnly & disctinctly read of the minister" (quoted in Leaver's *'Goostly Psalmes and Spirituall Songes': English and Dutch Metrical Psalms from Coverdale to Uitenhove—1535-1566*, Oxford, 1991, p. 214). That "item" indicates that at least one congregation was singing at times in harmony during the sixteenth century.

In France and Switzerland, there was little instrumental music to match the vast amount of choral music based on the Genevan Psalter. Perhaps that lack is due to the extreme persecution that so weakened the Huguenot churches in the following centuries. Not until the twentieth century do we find any significant French or Swiss instrumental compositions based on the Genevan Psalter. The most prominent of these are by Henri Gagnebin, a Swiss composer, teacher, and musicologist who wrote several orchestral suites and many organ pieces based on the Genevan psalm tunes.

Through the leadership of French scholars like Édith Weber, the Genevan Psalter has received much renewed attention in the last quarter of the twentieth century. Weber was involved in preparing a new French edition of the Genevan Psalter, *Le Psautier française* (1995). She also wrote a *Historie de la musique française de 1500-1650* (1996), which includes a substantial treatment of the Genevan Psalter.

The Low Countries

The teachings of John Calvin found their most receptive audience in the Low Countries. In Antwerp and Ghent, printers issued psalters in both French and Dutch, and psalm singing became very popular. The public singing of psalms was forbidden by Spanish royal decree, and if the Inquisition found psalters in homes, the owners were imprisoned. But beginning in April 1566 there was a period of relative religious freedom. The Protestants held their first open-air services, usually in the fields just outside the city walls. Thousands of people in Flanders, Holland, and Zeeland forsook the Catholic mass to hear the preachers of the new religion. Several chroniclers have described the singing of psalms at these gatherings, and pictures of the famous *hagepreeken* (hedge-sermons) show people carrying small psalmbooks in their hands. Psalm singing accompanied the frenzied outburst of image breaking in August 1566, which in turn led to strong repressive measures from ruling Spain. The singing of psalms became a heretical activity, punishable by death.

The French-speaking Low Countries and the Dutch-speaking provinces that lay below the Rhine delta were unable to throw off the Spanish yoke; they remained Catholic, controlled by a foreign power. The northern provinces, however, gained independence, and Calvinism flourished. The churches there used the Dutch Psalter translated from the Genevan Psalter in 1566 by Peter Datheen, a Flemish monk turned Protestant preacher. He translated the texts of Marot and de Bèze, often quite literally, and fitted his translations to the Genevan melodies. His psalter was accepted by the Synod of Wesel in 1568 and remained the official songbook of the Dutch-speaking Calvinist church for more than two centuries. The Datheen texts were finally replaced by a more modern version in 1773. Although for this and subsequent revisions the French texts no longer served as models, the Genevan melodies were retained.

Today these congregations sing the psalms in the lively "long-and-short-note style" in which they were written. But it was not always that way. Quite soon after the Calvinist Reformation had gained a solid hold in the Netherlands, the psalm melodies began to lose their lively tempo and rhythmic variety. Eventually congregations sang them slowly and in isorhythm, that is, with all equal notes. Exactly why, when, and how this happened to Dutch psalmody we do not know (the same phenomenon was true of Lutheran chorale singing). One can only speculate that the subtle rhythms of the Genevan melodies were too difficult for the precentors and the people, most of whom could not read, let alone read music. Or perhaps the influence of pietism was partly responsible for the change. It is certainly true that the Baroque musical style of the seventeenth century had made significant alterations to Renaissance ideals of tempo and rhythm.

To help the people sing, organists began accompanying congregational singing in the late seventeenth century. But if the organists supplied one chord per note of the psalm tune, as was the custom, they probably stemmed the flow of the melody even more. Slow, even-note congregational singing became the norm throughout Protestant Europe, not just in the Netherlands. Even though the Calvinist psalms and the Lutheran chorales were often still printed with long and short notes, they were not sung that way. Many harmonizations for organists, like the popular settings by Johannes Worp of the nineteenth century, used even notes.

In the nineteenth century, Abraham Kuyper and other religious leaders in the Netherlands made urgent calls for reform in liturgy and church music. These were finally answered, at least in part, by the creation of a new psalter and hymnal issued in 1938 for the Nederlandse Hervormde Kerk. Although the psalm melodies were restored to their original form, the text was still the old translation from 1773! In 1949 the Gereformeerde Kerken in Nederland approved a new rhymed translation of the psalms by Hendrik Hasper, a minister in that church who later left to join the Hervormde Kerk. The latter, ironically, did not accept Hasper's translation, and his work was not used.

The 1773 texts remained in use until 1968, when the interdenominational committee "Interkerkelijke Stichting" released a newly revised metrical psalter using the Genevan tunes. The texts were prepared by an interdenominational team of the best poets in the Netherlands. The new texts were included in the 1973 *Liedboek voor de kerken,* an ecumenical psalter hymnal now used in several different denominations in the Netherlands. If history repeats itself, this translation will serve the Reformed churches in the Netherlands for the next two hundred years! The Genevan tunes in the *Liedboek voor de kerken* (1973) have all been restored to their original rhythms.

During the first century of the Genevan Psalter in the Low Countries, composers wrote and published polyphonic choral settings of the Genevan psalms. Although the activity was not as prolific as in France and Switzerland, it included important composers like Lassus, Clemens non Papa, de Monte, Pevernage, and Sweelinck. Sweelinck was the only composer anywhere ever to accomplish the task of setting all of the Genevan psalms in a florid motet style. He brought out his 153 compositions in four books published in Amsterdam between 1604 and 1621. Into a rich fabric of late Renaissance polyphony, ranging from two to eight voices, Sweelinck wove the Genevan melodies in an imaginative variety of ways, using chromaticism, word-painting, echo effects, and double-chorus writing to great effect in these contrapuntal masterpieces. His work is the climax and crown of the Calvinist repertory.

Since Sweelinck there has been no great composer of Genevan-based choral music in the Low Countries. This is primarily due to the absence of choirs in Calvinist churches there, though there are many community choirs in the Netherlands. The organ, however, has become the dominant instrument in Dutch churches, and there is a fair amount of Dutch organ music based on the Genevan psalms. The repertory begins with Sweelinck, who wrote several sets of organ variations on Genevan psalm tunes. Other composers include Hendrik Spuy in the seventeenth century, and Jan Zwart, Cor Kee, and Jaap Dragt in the twentieth century. Many Dutch organists are brilliant improvisers and have given the Genevan psalms skilled settings in services and in concerts.

Germany

The Netherlands was not the only country that welcomed the Genevan Psalter. Metrical translations of psalms had been prominent in the very earliest Lutheran songbooks, before the advent of Calvinism, some of them versified by Luther himself. The metrical psalms of Lutheran poets, however, did not gain the popularity in Germany that the Marot-de Bèze psalter did in France, Switzerland, the Low Countries, and eventually in Germany itself.

A translation of the Marot-de Bèze psalms became by far the best-known psalter in Germany. In 1565 Ambrosius Lobwasser finished his translation of the entire French psalter into German. *The Psalter of the Royal Prophet David, Translated into Clear and Understandable German Verse* (*Der Psalter dess koeniglichen Propheten Davids, in deutsche Reymen verstendiglich und deutlich gebracht*) was published in Leipzig in 1573. The Lobwasser translation enjoyed immediate popularity and was used by Lutheran congregations as well as Calvinist. As a result, several Genevan tunes found a permanent place in the repertory of Lutheran chorales. One of the best known is the tune for Psalm 42, which was set in German to the chorale text *Freu dich sehr, o meine Seele*.

Lobwasser's work was popular partly because his texts were accompanied in print by the chordal settings of Goudimel with the melody in the tenor. (Part-singing of the psalms was introduced into German Calvinist services long before it was permitted in Geneva or the Low Countries.) Goudimel's chordal psalm settings influenced the texture of the later Lutheran *cantional* style, in which the melody was placed in the soprano. The approach was first used in a Lutheran hymnal by Osiander in 1586. The chordal style with the melody in the soprano is a style familiar to all who have sung a Protestant hymn.

Hungary and the Balkans

Calvinism also spread to southeastern Europe, especially to Hungary. The Reformed faith nurtured Hungary for many centuries and remains an important component in the spiritual and political makeup of that country. With the demise of communism in eastern Europe, Reformed churches around the world are once more becoming aware of the renewed energy among churches not only in Hungary but also in Hungarian-speaking congregations in present-day Romania and parts of former Yugoslavia.

Their history also includes periods of decline. Evidently hymns were part of the Hungarian tradition from early on. The 1948 preface printed in their most recent psalter hymnal (1988) refers to an earlier time:

> The contents of the Debrecen-type psalter hymnals were expanded around 1730, comprising all that had been borrowed from times before the Reformation and also what has been accepted from the contemporary Hungarian and foreign singing traditions under first German, then Swiss and Dutch influence. But already a year before the most complete "old Debrecen" psalter hymnals were published (1778), the elimination of the old songs had started . . . replaced by the products of late Pietism and early rationalism.

—translated by Dóra Sallay, student at Calvin College

In 1921 the Hungarian Reformed church issued a new psalter hymnal that restored many older songs and introduced new material. A Yugoslavian psalter hymnal of 1939 led the way to more thorough reforms, and in 1948 the Hungarian church published a complete Genevan Psalter in Hungarian. The goal of the revision committee with regard to the psalms, as stated in the preface to their 1988 psalter hymnal, was "to find a way to reinstall gradually the Genevan psalms—which had a deep and blessed effect on our Reformed church and nation—in a fresh, complete, and suitable form."

The most recent psalter hymnal of the Hungarian Reformed churches, *Énekeskönyv—Magyar Reformátusok Hasznnálatára* (Budapest, 1988), is organized like the *Liedboek voor de kerken*; the first 150 songs include the entire psalter set to the Genevan tunes, restored to their original rhythms.

The great Hungarian composer and music educator Zoltan Kodaly took a keen interest in this project and selected several Genevan psalm tunes as bases for choral compositions. Many of his composition students also prepared settings; a collection of choral settings of seventy Genevan psalms, all by twentieth-century Hungarian composers, is available in *Magyar Zsoltárok* (Budapest, 1979).

Other Communities

Other Reformed communities around the world, particularly in places of Dutch influence, also use the Genevan Psalter today, at least in part. These communities can be found in Australia, Indonesia, South Africa, Canada, and the United States. Of these, the Canadian Reformed churches have published the only available complete Genevan Psalter in the English language: *The Book of Praise: Anglo-Genevan Psalter* (1984; available from Premier Printing, 1249 Plessis Road, Winnipeg, Manitoba, Canada R2C 3L9).

England and Scotland have also been influenced by the Genevan Psalter. The more diverse story of metrical psalmody in the English and Scottish tradition is told briefly in the next essay. The role of the Genevan Psalter in the Christian Reformed Church is described in the essay beginning on page 97.

English Metrical Psalmody

by Emily R. Brink

When the Christian Reformed Church (CRC) made the decision in 1914 to adopt an English-language psalter, more than a change of language was involved. The CRC left behind one psalm-singing tradition and adopted another. For more than three hundred years, the members and forebears of the CRC had sung only psalms, in Dutch, to tunes from the Genevan Psalter. The history of that tradition is told in the previous essay, "The Genevan Psalter" (see p. 28).

This essay offers an overview of another tradition, just as old, that developed in parallel but distinct ways across the English Channel from the Netherlands. The CRC entered the English and Scottish psalm-singing tradition when it adopted the 1912 United Presbyterian *Psalter* in 1914. Since then, the Genevan and the English/Scottish traditions have existed side by side in the life of the CRC and in various editions of the *Psalter Hymnal.*

Those two traditions share a similar beginning: both the Genevan Psalter and the first English metrical psalter for public worship began in royal courts; both came out in installments; both were conceived and begun by authors who did not live to see the completed project; both were completed and released in the same year (1562); both became extremely popular for centuries thereafter, going through countless editions; and both served as the main, even exclusive, songbook for generations of Christians in their respective traditions. In spite of so many similarities, however, the two traditions developed in distinct ways.

Beginnings in England

Thomas Sternhold prepared the first installment of the English psalter that eventually bore his name. He was a groomsman in the court of Henry VIII, whose break with the Roman Catholic Church brought about the birth of the Church of England. In 1547 Sternhold prepared a small collection of nineteen psalms in ballad meter and dedicated them to the young son and successor of Henry VIII, Edward VI, who ascended the throne that year at age ten. Sternhold's psalms were intended not for public worship but for private devotional use by the young king and the court. They were probably sung to popular tunes. Two years later, Sternhold died, and his friend John Hopkins published a collection of the thirty-seven psalm texts Sternhold had completed, adding seven of his own. Several other writers became involved in many ways before the project was completed, but the completed psalter, published in 1562, became popularly known as the "Sternhold and Hopkins Psalter."

One distinction between the English and the Genevan metrical psalm traditions was the English origin in devotional use rather than liturgical use. In writing psalms in meter, Sternhold was following an old practice; many English writers developed both their poetic writing skills and devotional life by recasting into meter the great works of the past, works from Greek and Latin classics as well as the Psalms, which were now available in English translation. The art of "imitation," in which the writer would seek to capture in verse form the essence of an earlier text, was part of a classical education.

One example of that continuing practice can be found John Milton's versification of Psalm 136 (136), written many years after the publication of the Sternhold and Hopkins Psalter. In 1623, when he was only fifteen years old, John Milton set Psalm 136 in 24 stanzas; his original text is included in the *The Hymnal 1982 Companion* (Vol. 3B, 389) along with this comment: "The youthful poet's stanzas have required some tidying in order to make them regular enough for singing." Here is an example of Milton's original text for Psalm 136:7-9:

And caus'd the Golden-tressed Sun,
All the day long his course to run.
For his mercies aye endure,
Ever faithful, ever sure.

The horned Moon to shine by night,
Amongst her spangled sisters bright,
For his mercies aye endure,
Ever faithful, ever sure.

The *Psalter Hymnal* recasts those lines as follows in 136, stanza 4:

sun to stride across the day,
moon and stars in vast array:
for his mercies shall endure,
ever faithful, ever sure.

Interaction with Europe: The Anglo-Genevan Psalters

In contrast to the devotional origins of English metrical psalmody, Martin Luther and John Calvin had developed a liturgical approach to psalmody. Miles Coverdale had traveled in Germany and knew of Luther's 1532 translation of the Bible into German, which influenced his own translation of the entire Bible into English in 1539. Coverdale had also experienced congregational singing of the psalms, and he translated and published fifteen psalm texts in his collection of forty-one texts and tunes, *Goostley Psalmes and Spirituall Songes* (London, 1535). Coverdale, like Luther, had included hymns as well as psalms, and tunes as well as texts. But Henry VIII banned them, and the Lutheran approach to congregational song did not take hold in England.

Protestant traffic across the English Channel increased, however. During the early development of the Church of England, Britain became a safe place for Protestant leaders. Entire congregations from Europe, especially from the Low Countries, fled to England to escape the persecution of the Spanish Inquisition. But when young Edward VI died of tuberculosis in 1553 after only six years on the throne, his half-sister Queen Mary, an ardent Roman Catholic, restored the Roman Mass and began a period of intense persecution of all Protestants. Now traffic flowed in the other direction. "Bloody Mary" reigned only until 1558, but during those five years European exiles returned home, and entire English and Scottish congregations fled across the channel, settling as refugees in a number of European cities, including Geneva. The complex story of that ebb and flow of refugees and their developing psalters is told in *'Goostly Psalmes and Spirituall Songes': English and Dutch Metrical Psalms from Coverdale to Uitenhove, 1535-1566* by Robin A. Leaver (Oxford, 1991).

The "Marian Exiles" took their incomplete Sternhold and Hopkins psalters with them, evidence of the growing popularity of psalm singing, though the collections included only texts, not tunes. The refugees added to these collections in various cities. Several editions of English psalters printed in Geneva during the Marian Exile became known as the Anglo-Genevan psalters. Several new texts were added, and some earlier ones were revised to be more literally faithful to Scripture. Tunes were added to their collections of texts, showing an important influence from Calvin's approach in the developing Genevan Psalter.

The earliest English metrical psalm text in the *Psalter Hymnal* dates from the 1561 Anglo-Genevan Psalter: William Kethe's versification of Psalm 100, "All People That on Earth Do Dwell" (100). In that psalter Kethe's text was set to the Genevan tune for Psalm 134, a relationship found ever since in most English psalters. In fact, the tune became known as OLD HUNDREDTH because of its relationship to Kethe's text. However, the *Psalter Hymnal* retains the original Genevan tune for Kethe's Psalm 100, which happens to be in the same meter as the Genevan tune for Psalm 134. That choice by the *Psalter Hymnal* Revision Committee provides a glimpse into another distinction between the Genevan and English psalm-singing traditions. Whereas the Genevan Psalter closely identified tunes with texts from the beginning, the English metrical psalm tradition was essentially a poetic tradition for which a variety of tunes could be sung to a given text. The revision committee maintained the original Genevan relationship between the psalm text with the tune that was composed for it, in spite of the more widely known tune associated with it in the English tradition.

The First Completed English Metrical Psalter

After Queen Mary died and Queen Elizabeth began her long and more peaceful rule, it was safe for the Protestant exiles to return home. The English Protestants returned with their expanded psalter collections developed in the various places they had found refuge. John Day (1522-1584) obtained a monopoly from the British crown for printing *The Whole Booke of Psalmes, collected into Englysh metre by T. Starnhold, I. Hopkins, & others . . . , with apt Notes to singe them withal* (London, 1562). Day eventually published thirty-six separate editions of this enormously popular psalter.

When Sternhold began writing his texts for the young King Edward VI, he chose the common ballad meters, which were to become the dominant metrical structure of English psalmody and, later, of English hymnody. Those meters consisted of four-line stanzas, with each line including six or, more often, eight syllables. One meter, known as common meter, became so popular for psalm texts that it became known as "psalm meter." The completed Sternhold and Hopkins Psalter contained 131 texts in common meter (86 86), six in short meter (66 86), three in long meter (88 88), and fourteen in other meters. Thirty-seven texts were by Sternhold, sixty by Hopkins, and the rest by a variety of writers working in exile in Frankfort, Geneva, Strasbourg, and Wesel.

The primary legacy of the Sternhold and Hopkins Psalter is more musical than textual. The only text that the *Psalter Hymnal* includes from that psalter is William Kethe's setting of Psalm 100, which actually dates back to the 1561 Anglo-Genevan Psalter. Yet the texts are responsible for the structure of the tunes. Just as the complex metrical variety in the Genevan Psalter by the French poet Marot necessitated distinct tunes for most psalms in the Genevan Psalter, so the repetition of a few meters in the English psalter created the possibility for easy exchanges of texts and tunes. Not only were texts and tunes interchangeable, the English attitude toward the relationship of texts and tunes was much looser than in the Genevan tradition. To this day, some English hymnals include only the texts, assuming that tunes will be supplied from another source.

The first edition of the English metrical psalter in 1562 included fifty tunes; the next year another edition provided harmony for the tunes. Almost half have Genevan origins, dating first from the days of European exile in London, and later from the Anglo-Genevan Psalter dating from the days of English exile in Geneva. The English refugees freely "bent" many of the Genevan tunes into a shape they were used to, usually into common meter double. Many of those tunes are still found in English and North American hymnals with the word "old" in front of them, indicating that the tune was set in the Sternhold and Hopkins Psalter to a particular psalm text. For example, OLD HUNDRETH indicated that the melody was set to Psalm 100 in that psalter. Another example in the *Psalter Hymnal* is the tune TOULON (521), a squared-off four-line version of GENEVAN 124 (124), originally in five lines and with more energetic rhythms. The *Psalter Hymnal* includes no other examples of such "old" tunes, largely because it goes back to the original Genevan tunes rather than to the English adaptations of them. OLD 107TH and OLD 124TH are other examples of "old" tunes adapted from various editions of the Genevan Psalter and present in many modern North American hymnals.

Several of the English tunes composed for texts in the Sternhold and Hopkins Psalter are still found in contemporary hymnals. The *Psalter Hymnal* includes one attributed to John Day from his 1562 edition—the tune ST. FLAVIAN (69). Other English tunes followed in various editions, including SOUTHWELL (380), and WINCHESTER OLD (215). Only one of those tunes (ST. FLAVIAN) is still set to a psalm, though not to the psalm for which it was originally composed. The freedom with which English psalm tunes have since been set to various psalm and hymn texts is typical of the English metrical psalm tradition.

In subsequent publications of the Sternhold and Hopkins Psalter throughout the seventeenth century, other tunes were composed for the existing psalm texts, including John Dowland's elaborated harmonization of OLD HUNDREDTH (134), the Irish tune

COLERAINE (31), and BRISTOL (53). But the texts remained unchanged, in spite of efforts to replace them with better poetry. One of those efforts was a complete psalter published in 1569 by Matthew Parker, the Archbishop of Canterbury, known today mainly because of the nine tunes written for it by the great English composer Thomas Tallis. Of those tunes, three are found in the *Psalter Hymnal:* THIRD MODE MELODY (62), TALLIS CANON (441), and TALLIS' ORDINAL (583).

The Sternhold and Hopkins Psalter became the most popular psalter in English history and remained the official psalter and the basic congregational repertoire of the Church of England for more than 250 years.

Scottish Psalters

Just when the Reformation was making headway in England, pressed not so much by religious turmoil as political necessity, the persecution under Queen Mary scattered the leadership, including John Knox (c. 1505-1572), who became the leader of the Scottish Protestants. He had worked earlier with Thomas Cranmer, the first Protestant archbishop of Canterbury, who was executed in 1556. That same year, Knox, already in Frankfort as an exile, moved to Geneva to be closer to Calvin. One reason for his move was related to a rift over the use of the Prayer Book in worship, and another to the Genevan approach in versifying the psalms. Robin A. Leaver describes the tensions:

> A division developed within the Frankfort exiles with one party favoring Prayer Book worship and the other demanding a form more akin to the French liturgy of Calvin in Geneva. The division of opinion became a physical split. The Prayer Book party remained in Frankfort, and the others, including Whittingham and eventually, Knox, migrated to Geneva.
>
> —*"English Metrical Psalmody,"* in The Hymnal 1982 Companion, *Vol. 1, p. 327.*

In Geneva, Knox was undoubtedly involved at some level in the development of the Anglo-Genevan psalters, which reworked some earlier Sternhold and Hopkins texts. Many of those texts were "corrected" according to the approach taken by the Genevan psalters, which involved a more strict and literal approach to versifying the psalms. The Anglo-Genevan Psalter of 1556 included this note on its title page: "One and fiftie Psalmes of David in English meter . . . . , in certeyn places corrected as the sens of the Prophete required."

When Knox returned home to Scotland from Geneva, he took with him the Anglo-Genevan liturgy of 1556 and the Anglo-Genevan Psalter of 1560, both clearly influenced by Calvin's reforms. The Scottish Reformers continued work on completing the Scottish Psalter, retaining and revising some of the earlier work of Sternhold and Hopkins, some of the work of other writers working in exile, and some new Scottish texts and tunes.

In 1564 both the complete psalter and liturgy were published in Edinburgh. *The CL psalmes of David in English metre* was published as part of *The Forme of Prayers and Ministrations of the Sacraments,* the Anglo-Genevan liturgy of 1556 with only minor revisions. About a third of the metrical psalm texts were of Scottish origin. In contrast to the fifty tunes of the English psalter, the Scottish Psalter of 1564 included 105 tunes, many more from the Genevan Psalter, and with more metrical variety than found in the completed English psalter of Sternhold and Hopkins.

Subsequent editions of the Scottish Psalter reworked the texts and added tunes. Two tunes from the 1615 edition are included in the *Psalter Hymnal:* DUNFERMLINE (266) and DUNDEE (434), both common-meter tunes now set to hymn texts. Two texts from the 1650 Scottish Psalter are also included in the *Psalter Hymnal:* the famous setting of Psalm 23, "The Lord's My Shepherd" (161); and "Now Blessed Be the Lord Our God" (630).

The 1650 edition, however, which has remained the official psalter of the Church of Scotland, included no tunes. By then a decline in the practice of psalm singing was evident, and the repertoire of known psalm tunes was small. Efforts to improve congregational singing included a restoration of music in subsequent editions. The current *Scottish Psalter* (1929) was printed in a "Dutch door" format, with each page cut in half. The lower halves of the pages contain the texts of the 150 psalms, seven doxologies, sixty-seven scriptural paraphrases, and five hymns. The upper halves contain 188 harmonized tunes in only three meters, permitting the mixing and matching of texts and tunes.

A New Version

Back in the Church of England, the first serious contender to the Sternhold and Hopkins Psalter was a complete psalter released in 1696 by the Irishmen William Tate and Nicholas Brady, who published *A New Version of the Psalms of David, fitted to the tunes used in Churches.* The very title indicates the intent to replace Sternhold and Hopkins, which thereafter became known as the "Old Version." Both Tate and Brady had connections to royalty; Tate was named poet laureate by King William III, and Brady was a royal chaplain. The King approved their new version for use in the Church of England.

Though the texts in the *New Version* were poetically superior, the beloved "Old Version" was entrenched, particularly in rural communities, and the *New Version* never became as popular. One old man is said to have objected, "David speaks so plain that we cannot mistake his meaning, but as for Mr. Tate and Mr. Brady, they have taken away my Lord, and I know not where they have laid him."

Like the early editions of the "Old Version," the *New Version* was published with texts only. Because of changes in the English language throughout the centuries, however, few of the early texts have been retained in current hymnals, and no text examples from this *New Version* are included in the 1987 *Psalter Hymnal.* Composers, however, continued to write new tunes for many of the texts. Three well-known tunes by the composer and editor William Croft, for example, published in his 1708 *Supplement to the New Version,* are included in the *Psalter Hymnal* and in most English and North American hymnals to this day: HANOVER (149, 477), ST. ANNE (170), and ST. MATTHEW

(21). Another tune found in most subsequent English and North American hymnals is DARWALL'S 148TH (408), one of a complete set of tunes and basses composed by the minister John Darwall for all 150 psalm texts in Tate and Brady's *New Version*.

The Influence of Isaac Watts

By the beginning of the eighteenth century, the metrical psalm tradition still dominated congregational song in England and Scotland. But under the influence of Isaac Watts (1674-1748; see biographical notes at PHH 155) the English hymn began to flourish, and the metrical psalm tradition began to decline significantly.

Already as a teenager, Watts expressed frustration with the quality of poetry found in the English psalm texts, and his father challenged him to provide better texts. He took up the challenge, writing many new psalm versifications and hymn texts even before he was twenty. The quality of his poetry ensured a place for hymnody in England, and Watts later became known as the father of English hymnody.

But Watts's approach to setting psalm texts caused great controversy. He was a pivotal figure in freeing psalmody from a rigid traditionalism. Until this time, the English metrical psalms were versifications of Scripture, more or less faithful to the actual psalm texts. The Scottish Psalters were concerned with an almost literal faithfulness to the biblical texts. Watts introduced much greater freedom, moving from versification to paraphrase.

In 1719 Watts published *The Psalms of David Imitated in the Language of the New Testament and Applied to the Christian State and Worship*. In his preface, titled "An Inquiry into the Right Way of Fitting the Book of Psalms for Christian Worship," Watts maintained that the psalms are inappropriate for New Testament Christians unless recast in "the language of the New Testament." His reasoning for singing in New Testament language helped on the one hand to create an acceptance for hymnody. On the other hand, his theology of the psalms created a gulf between the Old and New Testaments, and his approach contributed to the decline and even disappearance of metrical psalmody in some traditions that had once practiced exclusive psalm singing.

> Though the Psalms of David are a work of admirable and divine composure, though they contain the noblest sentiments of piety, and breathe a most exalted spirit of devotion, yet when the best of Christians attempt to sing many of them in our common translation, that spirit of devotion vanishes, and is lost, the psalm dies away upon their lips, and they feel scarcely any thing of the holy pleasure.
>
> If I were to render the reasons of it, I would give this as one of the chief; namely, that the Royal Psalmist here expresses his own concerns . . . in the language of his own religion. . . . But when we who are Christians sing the same lines, we express nothing but the character, the concerns, and the religion of the Jewish king, while our own circumstances, and our own religion (which are so widely different from his) have little to do in the sacred song. . . .
>
> [Therefore, I propose to] accommodate the book of Psalms to Christian

worship. And in order to do this, it is necessary to divest David and Asaph, &c. of every other character but that of a psalmist and a saint, and to make them always speak the common sense of a Christian.

. . . Attempting the work with this view, I have entirely omitted some whole psalms, and large pieces of many others, and have chosen out of all of them such parts only as might easily and naturally be accommodated to the various occasions of the Christian life. . . .

Where the psalmist uses sharp invectives against his personal enemies, I have endeavored to turn the edge of them against our spiritual adversaries, sin, Satan, and temptation. . . .

Where the original runs in the form of prophecy concerning Christ and his salvation, I have given an historical turn to the sense. There is no necessity that we should always sing in the obscure and doubtful style of prediction, when the things foretold are brought into open light by a full accomplishment. Where the writers of the New Testament have cited or alluded to any part of the psalms, I have often indulged the liberty of paraphrase, according to the words of Christ, or his apostles.

Watts's approach blurred the distinction between metrical psalms and hymns—and indeed, several of his psalm paraphrases from that collection are popularly identified as hymns. Examples in the *Psalter Hymnal* include "O God, Our Help in Ages Past" (170, from Ps. 90), "Joy to the World! The Lord Is Come" (337, from Ps. 98), "Jesus Shall Reign" (412, from Ps. 72), "My Shepherd Will Supply My Need" (550, from Ps. 23), and "Let Children Hear the Mighty Deeds" (585, from Ps. 78).

The influence of Watts's approach was great not only in Great Britain but also in North America. With the movement from versification to paraphrase, the division of psalms into hymn-like units, the disappearance of some sections and even of entire psalms, the metrical psalm tradition in England gradually became absorbed into a growing body of hymnody—although in Scotland exclusive psalmody continued.

Only two psalm texts from England written after Watts's 1719 collection and before the last part of the twentieth century are included in the 1987 *Psalter Hymnal:* Psalm 148 from the Foundling Hospital Collection (148), and Psalm 72 by James Montgomery (72).

Metrical Psalmody in North America

During the seventeenth century many groups left the British Isles and Europe for North America. Since most of the early settlers in the New World were Calvinists, they were also metrical psalm singers. Many different psalters were in use simultaneously.

The Eclipse of the Genevan Tradition

French Huguenots had taken the Genevan Psalter with them to Florida (near present-day Jacksonville) and had taught their songs to Native Americans. Historian Robert Stevenson wrote that "after the Spaniards massacred the encroaching French colonists, the Indians for many years continued to sing snatches of these vigorous Huguenot tunes as 'code words' to determine whether any stragglers along the seacoast were friendly French or sullen Spanish" (in *Protestant Church Music: A History*, by Friedrich Blume, W. W. Norton, 1975, p. 639).

Dutch Reformed settlers began arriving with their Dutch Genevan psalters in 1628. They may even have worshiped at times with French and German settlers in New York, who were singing the psalms in their own languages but to the same Genevan tunes. Though the Dutch prospered and sang the Genevan psalm tunes to Peter Datheen's translation for the next 150 years (see the previous essay, "The Genevan Psalter," p. 28), they gradually adapted to using the English language in business, in education, and, finally, in the church.

Francis Hopkinson (1737-1791) was hired by the Reformed Protestant Church of the City of New York (the present-day Middle Collegiate Church) to prepare a translation of the Dutch Psalter when the church began worshiping in English in 1764. Hopkinson was an American organist/composer trained in England and is remembered today chiefly as one of the signers of the Declaration of Independence. But he probably didn't even know the Dutch language. He actually took many Tate and Brady texts and added some words here and there to make them fit about a dozen mangled Genevan tunes, used repeatedly. In a letter to Benjamin Franklin in 1765 he wrote, "I have finished the Translation of the Psalms of David, to the great Satisfaction of the Dutch Congregation at New York." But that assessment was hardly accurate, for the project, completed in 1767, was a dismal failure. James Brumm relates the sad story, commenting that it was reasonable to assume that "his primary motivation for taking on the job was to make some quick money" (in *Singing the Lord's Song: A History of the English Language Hymnals of the Reformed Church in America*, published by the Historical Society of the Reformed Church in America, New Brunswick, New Jersey, 1990). As a result of that debacle, the Genevan tradition virtually disappeared from the Reformed Church in North America. In the Reformed Protestant Church's English-language collection *Psalms and Hymns* (1789), only twenty-two of the psalm settings chosen by Hopkinson had survived; none were retained in the second edition of 1812. The tunes of the Genevan Psalter were not to reappear in North America until Dutch immigrants who formed the Christian Reformed Church brought them in the mid-nineteenth century. English texts for some of their Genevan tunes were not provided until the publication of their first *Psalter Hymnal* (1934).

English and Scottish Psalters in the USA

English Pilgrims, separatists who sailed for the New World after a lengthy exile in the Netherlands, took the Ainsworth Psalter of 1612 with them to the Massachusetts Bay area in 1620, where they later founded Plymouth. Their psalter had been developed by the separatist minister and Hebrew scholar Henry Ainsworth. Ten years later the Puritans came with their copies of Sternhold and Hopkins, but soon they developed their own Bay Psalm Book, printed in Cambridge, Massachusetts in 1640, the first book published in British North America. The Bay Psalm book included no music, but the texts were referenced to tunes from the Ravenscroft Psalter, a collection published in

England by Thomas Ravenscroft in 1621. The *Psalter Hymnal* includes two tunes that were published in that collection: MANCHESTER (59) and DUNDEE (434). Only six different meters were included in the Bay Psalm Book, as compared to fifteen in the Ainsworth Psalter, which were more difficult to sing. The Presbyterians revered the Scottish Psalter of 1650, while the Protestant Episcopalians, being associated with the Church of England, preferred the *New Version* of Tate and Brady (1696). Therefore, many psalters were in use.

During the eighteenth century two psalters were eventually to dominate the North American scene: the Scottish Psalter of 1650 and the *Psalms of David Imitated* by Isaac Watts. Watts had as much influence in North America as in England. Only ten years after his 1719 *Psalms of David Imitated* was released in England, Benjamin Franklin published a reprint in Philadelphia, the first of many American editions of Watts's texts.

Many tensions developed over the merits and shortcomings of those psalters, especially among Presbyterians, where churches split and new denominations were formed, in part over whether to sing hymns and what psalm settings to use. The 1788 Synod of New York and Philadelphia approved a new *Directory for the Worship of God* which stated, "It is the duty of Christians to praise God by singing psalms, or hymns, publicly in the church, as also privately in the family." The addition was hymns, changing the longstanding history of exclusive psalmody established in the 1646 Westminster Confession, which had limited public worship to the "singing of psalms with grace in the heart." Most of the more Americanized Presbyterian groups moved to psalter hymnals, and eventually to hymnals in which psalms and hymns were integrated. A history of the psalters among the many different Presbyterian groups that went their separate ways on the issue of psalmody and hymnody has yet to be written.

There were many denominations without a tradition of metrical psalmody, and among them were growing numbers of Lutherans and Roman Catholics. Groups of Methodists came singing the hymns of Charles Wesley. And the Baptists never developed a psalter tradition. The denominational scene in the eighteenth century reflects far more communions which sang hymns than psalms. So profound was the shift to hymnody throughout North America that psalm singers were in the minority by 1800.

Early North American Contributions

For a number of reasons, the state of singing in the New World declined. One reason was certainly that many of the English psalters did not include tunes. Another was the general lack of musical education in the colonies. The number of tunes that people used shrank, until by 1700 only about a dozen tunes were in general use.

The custom of "lining-out" the psalms and then embellishing them created a rather chaotic sound in many congregations. The Presbyterian tradition had been one of singing under the leadership of a precentor, who had his own pulpit below that of the minister. Rather than following an organ, the congregation depended on the precentor to "line out" the psalm, reading or singing line by line, with the congregation following.

Thomas Symmes (1678-1725), both a preacher and precentor, took the lead in introducing new tunes and abolishing the custom of "lining-out" the psalms. His advocacy of singing-schools was influential in providing basic music education for many church members. The movement paved the way for many new psalm tunes and other church music, including music by William Billings (1746-1800), the most famous early American composer. Singing schools became very popular, also in the Christian Reformed Church. For example, before he became a pastor, John R. Brink (1860-1972) led singing schools, which became important for social interaction in the lives of CRC young people of the early twentieth century and were influential in the eventual acceptance of church choirs and of hymn singing.

Some of the tunes that found their way into various shape-note collections were set to psalm texts, especially the popular texts of Isaac Watts, though the distinction between psalms and hymns had become very blurred, and the terms *hymn* and *psalm* were even used interchangeably. With the free movement of tunes to various texts in the English tradition, many of the tunes originally set to psalms were matched with hymn texts and still are associated with those texts today. The reverse is also true. For example, some early American hymn tunes have been set to psalm texts in the *Psalter Hymnal* (see the essay titled "North American Hymnody: 1800-1950," p. 99).

By the middle of the nineteenth century, most metrical psalters were abandoned or absorbed into growing collections of hymns. *Psalms and Hymns adapted to public worship, and approved by the General Assembly of the Presbyterian Church in the United States of America* (Philadelphia, 1831) was the only hymnbook of the undivided Presbyterian Church, which split in 1837. This hymnbook included the entire Watts psalter followed by doxologies and then by 531 hymns. Several other collections of both psalms and hymns were published until *The Hymnal of the Presbyterian Church* (1866) deleted the word *psalm* from the title, representing a break with metrical psalmody as a distinct body of congregational song.

Pockets of Exclusive Metrical Psalmody

But not all churches abandoned exclusive psalmody. A group of conservative Presbyterians joined in 1858 to form the United Presbyterian Church. One of their first actions was to revise the two-hundred-year-old texts of the Scottish Psalter. And, more significant, they began work on preparing "a new and improved version of the Psalms." Their 1871 *Book of Psalms* (texts only, no tunes) included updated Scottish Psalter texts along with a second section of 140 new texts. Here, finally, was a break from the past and the first truly American collection of metrical psalm texts. That collection was published with tunes in the 1887 *Psalter.* Several psalm texts from that collection are included in the *Psalter Hymnal:* texts for Psalms 27 (at 164), 46, 48, 67, 112, 117, 135 (at 181), and 146.

Actually, the presence of those texts in the *Psalter Hymnal* is due to their retention in the 1912 *Psalter,* also published by the United Presbyterian Church. The 1912 *Psalter,* adopted as the first English-language song collection of the Christian Reformed

Church in 1914, was the first ecumenical psalter published in the United States, involving nine denominations. Sixty-five psalm texts from the 1912 *Psalter* have been retained in the 1987 *Psalter Hymnal,* though in most cases the texts have been altered for reasons of faithfulness to Scripture, completeness, and inclusivity, and many have been updated for intelligibility.

Although the nine denominations that contributed to the 1912 *Psalter* represent a small slice of conservative Presbyterian and Reformed Christianity in North America, that collection became the most widely used metrical psalter of the twentieth century. It is still in print (Grand Rapids, Mich.: Eerdmans, 1927) and used by two small denominations of Dutch Reformed heritage that have retained exclusive psalmody, the Protestant Reformed Church and the Netherlands Reformed Church. More information on the 1912 *Psalter* is available on page 98.

The Reformed Presbyterian Church in North America is another small denomination still practicing exclusive metrical psalmody. Often called "Covenanters," their practice is rooted in the Scottish Psalter tradition. Their latest psalter, *The Book of Psalms for Singing* (1973), represents several generations of textual revision but is still clearly rooted in the old Scottish texts. The concern for biblical accuracy and completeness is shown by indicating directly on each line the exact verse of the biblical text. The psalms are also numbered according to their biblical numbers, with number-letter combinations distinguishing alternate or additional texts (for example, Psalm 1A, 1B, and so on). The 1987 *Psalter Hymnal* includes four versifications from *The Book of Psalms for Singing:* Psalms 9, 10, 54, and 64.

The Canadian Reformed Churches form another small denomination that has prepared English translations of all the psalms for use with the Genevan psalm tunes (see page 39).

Late Twentieth Century Revival of Metrical Psalmody

After years of decline in psalmody, even in communions that once sang only the psalms, a remarkable resurgence of psalm singing began in the second half of the twentieth century. Virtually every denomination has produced a new hymnal in the last quarter of the century, and virtually every hymnal committee has greatly increased the presence of psalms in its denominational worship book. A few of the older classics have been retained. But an enormous number of new psalm settings have been written in the past generation. A number of factors have contributed to a revival of psalmody as a regular part of Christian worship:

- New translations of the Bible have made the psalms come alive again. The texts of the 1912 *Psalter* no longer sound fresh; in fact, with the many changes in English usage since 1912, some older psalm settings look as archaic to late-twentieth-century Christians as the older English texts had appeared to Isaac Watts two centuries earlier. Many writers have returned to the psalms for inspiration, writing either new versifications, looser paraphrases, or hymns closely based on Scripture.

- The Scripture-song movement has provided additional resources for singing the psalms, though usually not in metrical form (see the following essay, "Canticles and Other Bible Songs," especially page 55).
- The liturgical renewal movement, especially after Vatican II, has stimulated interest in preparing an ecumenical lectionary. Many congregations, including those with roots in the Reformed/Presbyterian tradition, have begun using the *Common Lectionary* (1983) and the *Revised Common Lectionary* (1992). The lectionary always appoints a psalm to be sung after the Old Testament lesson. But hymnals of most denominations were sorely lacking in psalm resources. As a result, along with the "hymn explosion" of the past generation has come an enormous increase in the writing of new psalm settings and in the regular singing of psalms. Many of the newer settings are not metrical but have returned to the even older responsorial style (see the essay "Singing Psalms from Bible Times to the Protestant Reformation," especially the final section, p. 25).

While many new settings go back to traditions that came before metrical psalmody, many other new settings are metrical. After all, the metrical structure has sustained not only a four-hundred-year tradition of psalm singing but also the entire English hymn tradition. One of the first publications to introduce a wide range of new psalm texts was *Psalm Praise,* published in England in 1973 by the Jubilate Group of clergy and musicians in the Church of England. That collection, immediately made available in the United States by G.I.A. Publications, reveals the diversity that has marked congregational song collections ever since: contemporary texts, revision of older texts, and many different styles, ranging from chant to folk. The different textual styles are part and parcel of different musical styles, and once again some settings of the psalms are integral units of text and tune rather than the easily separable approach of English metrical psalmody. Four metrical psalm settings—text and music— from *Psalm Praise* are included in the 1987 *Psalter Hymnal:* Psalms 15, 16, 20, and 30. In addition, the *Psalter Hymnal* includes from that collection a tune at Psalm 61 (LISTENING) that was specifically composed for that biblical psalm.

Faced with the task of preparing a new edition of the *Psalter Hymnal,* the *Psalter Hymnal* Revision Committee took courage from the work of the Jubilate Group and eventually decided to prepare an essentially new metrical psalter. As mentioned earlier, sixty-five texts from the 1912 *Psalter* have been retained, though altered and updated, in order to preserve the communal memory of those settings that had served the denomination for most of this century. Also for the sake of memory, and to preserve the Genevan heritage, many new psalm texts have been prepared for singing to original Genevan tunes. All together, some 102 new psalm versifications have been prepared for the 1987 *Psalter Hymnal.*

Some new tunes were also commissioned by the revision committee for these new texts, including PHILIP (4) and ELEANOR (66) by Dale Grotenhuis, MAPLE AVENUE (14) by Richard L. Van Oss, GREELEY by Roy Hopp (41; originally composed for Psalm 14), ROSALIE MCMILLAN by James Ward (56, originally composed for Psalm 17), and ST.

JAMES THE APOSTLE by F. William Voetberg (78). However, when those tunes are added to the forty Genevan tunes and tunes associated with particular psalms from the 1912 *Psalter,* only a little more than a third of the psalms are set in the tradition of a unified text and tune. Almost two thirds of the psalms in the *Psalter Hymnal* are set to tunes originally composed for other texts, following the admittedly easier pattern of the English tradition.

Summary Comparison of the English and Genevan Metrical Psalm Traditions

Whereas Lutherans sang both hymns and psalms from the earliest days of the Protestant Reformation, congregational song in the British Isles followed the Calvinist approach of exclusive psalmody. The English metrical psalm tradition began as private devotional texts sung to tunes not necessarily composed for those texts. That practice contrasts with the Genevan tradition, which had a liturgical beginning, with composers as well as text writers involved from the start. English psalters, as a result, were often printed with texts only, whereas the continental Genevan Psalters in various languages, including Dutch, always included melodies.

The English metrical psalm texts were composed by many different writers, but all wrote in relatively few distinct meters, permitting the easy exchange of texts and tunes. As a result, many composers followed with tune books that continued to offer new ways of singing increasingly older texts. Even those Genevan tunes that were adopted in England were also adapted to fit the few meters that dominated English metrical poetry. English tunes subsequently were set to a variety of psalm and also hymn texts. Therefore the study of English metrical psalmody is essentially a study of the texts.

In contrast, the Genevan Psalter texts were written by only two writers who used a great number of meters, requiring melodies that were closely linked to the texts. Those tunes were developed with the character of the psalm in mind. Therefore, even when psalm texts were translated into different languages, the tunes were retained, with one tune provided for a given psalm text. What remains of the continental Calvinist tradition is a body of tunes to which successive generations of psalm texts in various languages have been written.

When Isaac Watts moved in the eighteenth century from versification to paraphrase that included New Testament language, the English metrical psalm tradition moved in the direction of hymnody; metrical psalmody began to decline even as a very strong hymn tradition began to develop. Watts also dropped some psalms and psalm sections. Subsequent English-language psalters often included more than one versification of a given psalm, and the numbering system in many hymnals eventually lost the direct relationship between versifications and the biblical psalms. The possibilities of more than one versification, sung to any possible number of tunes, created a body of songs that at first were given separate treatment in psalters, then were placed in separate sections in psalm and hymn collections, and finally were integrated into hymn sections, becoming indistinguishable from hymns. This pattern occurred in one denomination after another that left exclusive psalmody and began to sing hymns. Only a few small pockets of exclusive psalmody remain, found in churches of Scottish or Dutch origin.

Again, in contrast, the Genevan Psalter tradition was one of keeping the complete psalm (text and tune)—and, indeed, the complete psalter—intact. Even though not all the psalms were sung, they were all available, and they were separated from the hymns that eventually were added in many psalter hymnals.

When the *Psalter Hymnal* Revision Committee developed an essentially new psalter section in the 1987 *Psalter Hymnal*, it retained the metrical heritage but left behind part of the English heritage reflected in earlier editions. The committee also left behind multiple and divided psalm settings with sequential numbers that were not related to the biblical psalm numbers. Instead, the committee returned to the continental European practice of a one-on-one presentation of complete psalms, each with its own tune, numbered in biblical order, with extra settings and non-metrical settings placed either in the Bible Song or Hymn sections, and with a distinct tune for almost every psalm.

Though this essentially new metrical psalter in the *Psalter Hymnal* has been lauded for this approach as well as for the excellent new body of texts in it, the sheer amount of new texts and especially new melodies is proving daunting to the churches. Further, the broad and growing interest in Scripture choruses and responsorial psalmody throughout the world suggests that metrical psalmody will no longer be the dominant form of psalmody. Since the metrical structure has so long been associated with hymnody, perhaps a distinct style for psalmody, especially the responsorial, is to be welcomed. At the same time, the concept of what constitutes a hymn is also broadening, so much so that the term *metrical hymnody* may become helpful to describe what was once the exclusive structure for English psalmody.

Canticles and Other Bible Songs

by Bert Polman

Early Christian and Medieval Traditions

In addition to the Book of Psalms, the Bible contains a number of other songs, prayers, and confessions that have gained prominence as liturgical texts. The tradition of singing such biblical songs from outside the psalter is reflected in the Bible Songs portion of the *Psalter Hymnal* (151-236). Perhaps the best known of these songs, or canticles, from Scripture are the three found in the gospel of Luke and sometimes referred to as the Lukan canticles: the Song of Mary (Luke 1:46-55), the Song of Zechariah (Luke 1:68-79), and the Song of Simeon (Luke 2:29-32). However, several Old Testament texts such as the Song of Moses (Exodus 15:1-18) and the Song of the Three Young Men (also known as the Song of the Three Children, an apocryphal writing found in the Greek version of Daniel between 3:23 and 3:24) already enjoyed special status in Jewish worship at the temple and later in the synagogue.

Many biblical scholars think that poetic texts in the New Testament such as Philippians 2:6-11 or the choruses in Revelation 4-5 may be early Christian hymns that the biblical authors incorporated into their writings. However, we have little, if any, evidence as to which songs were sung by the Christians of the first few centuries. From the fourth century (when Christianity became an official religion and when monasticism began to develop), however, we have much reliable evidence of the use of biblical canticles and similar songs in Christian worship. The Song of Moses was incorporated into the Easter Vigil from the early fourth century. In the *Codex Alexandrinus*, a Greek text of the Bible produced in the first half of fifth century, some fourteen canticles were placed after the Psalms. Of these, ten were from the Old Testament, and four were from the New Testament; the last one was the *Gloria in excelsis Deo* (whose initial line is taken from Luke 2:14—the Song of the Angels).

In the Eastern Church, the Byzantine practice of nine canticles or odes developed for use during the morning Office, or *Orthos*, on Sundays and feast days:

1. Exodus 15:1-18 (Moses' Song of Thanksgiving)
2. Deuteronomy 32:1-43 (Moses' Final Admonition)
3. 1 Samuel 2:1-10 (Prayer of Hannah)
4. Habakkuk 3:2-19 (Prayer of Habakkuk)
5. Isaiah 26:1-21 (Prayer of Isaiah)
6. Jonah 2:2-9 (Prayer of Jonah)
7. Apocryphal Daniel 3:26-45, 52-56 (Prayer of Azariah, First Song of the Three Children)
8. Apocryphal Daniel 3:57-88 (Song of the Three Children)
9. Luke 1:46-55, 68-79 (Song of Mary, Song of Zechariah)

In time this Byzantine order of canticles became known as the *kanon* (meaning "rule"). During the seventh century the practice of paraphrasing these canticles arose, and that led to the poetic form of the *kanon* from which several well-known Easter hymns derive (for example, 389, 390). In modern practice, the Eastern Church emphasizes the Song of Mary and often omits the other traditional canticles.

In the Western Church the Rule of Benedict (c. 540) prescribed the use of canticles (and psalms) in the Office without naming individual canticles (see p. 21 for an explanation of the various Office Hours). But soon various patterns arose for each of the daily Hours. Though some regional variants are common throughout the Middle Ages, those canticles in customary use for Lauds were as follows:

Sunday: Apocryphal Daniel 3:57-88 (Song of the Three Children)
Monday: Isaiah 12:1-6 (Song of Isaiah)
Tuesday: Isaiah 38:10-20 (Prayer of Hezekiah)
Wednesday: 1 Samuel 2:1-10 (Prayer of Hannah)
Thursday: Exodus 15:1-18 (Song of Moses)
Friday: Habakkuk 3:2-19 (Prayer of Habakkuk)
Saturday: Deuteronomy 32:1-43 (Prayer of Moses)

Other canticles were customary for Matins. For example, a thirteenth-century manuscript prescribes the following three canticles for Matins on Christmas Day: Isaiah 9:2-7, 26:1-12, and 66:10-16. The three well-known Lukan canticles have honored places in the Roman Catholic Church and are sung daily at the climax of specific Offices: the Song of Zechariah (*Benedictus*) in Lauds, the Song of Mary (*Magnificat*) in Vespers, and the Song of Simeon (*Nunc Dimittis*) in Compline. The *Nunc Dimittis* was usually chanted to a psalm tone, but the *Benedictus* and *Magnificat* each had special canticle tones, somewhat more elaborate than ordinary psalm tones.

Based on this heritage, modern usage in the Roman Catholic Church's Liturgy of the Hours prescribes the use of the *major* canticles in Luke's gospel and of some 35 *minor* canticles from elsewhere in Scripture. Included with the Old Testament songs are those mentioned above as well as Isaiah 40:10-17; 61:10-62:5; Jeremiah 31:10-14; Ezekiel 36:24-28; and several selections from the Apocrypha. The *minor* canticles from the New Testament come from the Epistles and Revelation—for example, Philippians 2:6-11; Ephesians 1:3-10; Colossians 1:12-20; Revelation 5:9-12; 19:1-7.

The Scripture texts of the *classic* canticles and Bible songs from the Orthodox and Roman traditions (though not in their original musical settings) are represented in the *Psalter Hymnal* as follows:

- 152   Song of Moses and Miriam (Exodus 15)
- 157   Song of Moses (Deuteronomy 32, 33)
- 158   Song of Hannah (1 Samuel 2)
- 193   Song of Isaiah (Isaiah 12)
- 202   Song of Jonah (Jonah 2)
- 212, 478   Song of Mary (Luke 1)
- 213   Song of Zechariah (Luke 1)

- 214   Song of the Angels (Luke 2)
- 216   Song of Simeon (Luke 2)

Reformation and Later Protestant Traditions

The Protestant Reformers had various reactions to the Roman Catholic liturgy and its use of the Lukan canticles and other Bible songs. In adapting plainsong (or plain-chant) and various medieval texts and in composing new songs for worship, Luther promoted the singing of the Ten Commandments, the Lord's Prayer, the Nicene Creed, and the Song of Mary for every Sunday. He also composed a canticle-like hymn, "From Heaven Above to Earth I Come" (339), based on the Christmas gospel in Luke 2. Though the Lutheran tradition is primarily known for its thousands of chorales or hymns, various Lutheran hymnists paraphrased certain Bible texts into hymns (for example, "Comfort, Comfort Now My People" [194], from Isaiah 40).

In urging the singing of psalms as the voice of God's people in worship, Calvin established what would become a long tradition of metrical psalmody for the Reformed and Presbyterian communities. However, the reign of psalmody was not an exclusive one, not even in Calvin's Geneva. Following the medieval practice, various editions of the Genevan Psalter included metrical settings of such canticles as the Songs of Zechariah, Mary, and Simeon and of other texts such as the Song of Moses, the Ten Command-ments, and the *Te Deum* (504). Other Calvinist publications also encouraged the singing of various portions of the Bible. Though not sanctioned for use in church, these Bible songs were certainly used in many Calvinist homes. For example, in 1556 Théodore de Bèze had cast Proverbs 31 (titled "Les Vertus de la Femme Fidele") into meter for singing to the Genevan tune for Psalm 15. That same year Accace d'Albiac du Plessis versified portions of Proverbs and Ecclesiastes as *Les Proverbes de Salomon* to tunes by Gindron. And in 1595 de Bèze's *Les Saincts Cantiques* was published; this collection consisted of fourteen metrical settings of the time-honored Old Testament canticles and two New Testament canticles: the Songs of Mary and Zechariah. This Genevan heritage of Bible songs is represented in the *Psalter Hymnal* with the Calvinist setting of the Ten Commandments (153) and with Calvin Seerveld's recent paraphrase of themes from Ecclesiastes (190).

The Anglican *Book of Common Prayer* used the term *canticle* to refer only to the Song of the Three Children, but in colloquial use it has become a general term for the psalms, hymns, and Bible songs that are prescribed for daily use in Morning Prayer and Evening Prayer. Given with their customary Latin titles (each one the incipit of the Latin text) and their alternates or occasional substitutions, these canticles are

Morning Prayer
- *Venite* (Psalm 95)
- *Te Deum,* or *Benedicite* (Song of the Three Children)
- *Benedictus* (Song of Zechariah), or *Jubilate* (Psalm 100)

Evening Prayer
- *Magnificat* (Song of Mary), or *Cantate Domino* (Psalm 98)
- *Nunc Dimittis* (Song of Simeon), or *Deus misereatur* (Psalm 67)

The Anglican liturgical tradition also makes use of the Beatitudes (Matt. 5:3-10), other portions of Scripture such as 1 Chronicles 29:10-13, excerpts from Isaiah 60, and special biblical canticles for Christmas, Good Friday, Easter, and Whitsunday (Pentecost). In Anglican parish churches these "canticles" are either spoken responsively or chanted, while in the cathedrals and colleges they are sung in Anglican chant or (more usually) elaborated in choral settings. One setting of the Lord's Prayer in the *Psalter Hymnal* (207) comes from this Anglican heritage.

The medieval tradition of singing canticles and other songs from Scripture, affirmed in various ways by the churches of the Reformation and continued in such phenomena as the famous singing of Scripture texts by the Moravians in Herrnhut (see PHH 513), was further boosted in the English-speaking world of the eighteenth century by the publication of several collections of those biblical songs. Britain had long made use of the Sternhold and Hopkins Psalter (1562) with its metrical psalms and Lukan canticles in meter, but that "Old Version" was gradually replaced by the *New Version of the Psalms . . .* published by William Tate and Nicholas Brady (1696). The *Supplement* to this latter volume (1702) contained paraphrases of various well-known canticles but also included new ones such as "While Shepherds Watched Their Flocks" (215). Shortly afterward the work of Isaac Watts began to appear. Though he is best known for his many "Christianized" paraphrases of psalms (see 337, 412) and for numerous hymns (for example, 384, 430), Watts also wrote a number of paraphrases of other portions of Scripture, such as "Love God with All Your Soul and Strength" (155), based on Deuteronomy 6:5.

Scottish Presbyterians had periodically included some Bible songs in their various psalters; the 1634 edition contained fourteen such "spiritual songs," though none were retained in the important 1650 edition. But after various collections of Scripture songs were provided (and frequently debated and "corrected") in the first half of the eighteenth century, the Scottish *Translations and Paraphrases* were finally published in 1781 (but still not officially sanctioned). The thirty-two Old Testament and thirty-five New Testament Bible songs in this significant collection were drawn from paraphrases by well-known hymn writers such as Isaac Watts and Philip Doddridge and from Scottish ministers such as John Morison and William Cameron. Some examples from the *Paraphrases* (with their original 1781 numbering) are

- 2   O God of Bethel, by Whose Hand (Gen. 28:20-22)
- 18   Behold! the Mountain of the Lord (Isa. 2:2-6)
- 19   The People Who in Darkness Walked (Isa. 9:2-3, 6-7)
- 30   Come, Let Us to the Lord our God (Hosea 6:1-4)
- 58   Where High the Heavenly Temple Stands (Heb. 4:14-16)
- 63   Behold, th'Amazing Gift of Love (1 John 3:1-4)

Used in the wider community of English-speaking churches during the nineteenth century, some of these Scottish paraphrases still appear in modern hymnals and are often still identified with their original numbering, by which they became popularly known. Thus "The People Who in Darkness Walked" (192), the *Psalter Hymnal*'s only entry from the Scottish *Paraphrases* of 1781, was originally called "Paraphrase Nineteen."

The Modern Reemergence

In the footsteps of the Scottish *Paraphrases* the nineteenth century witnessed the publication of the Irish *Paraphrases* (1880), along with various other canticles in hymn form and small collections of Bible songs. This proliferation occurred on both sides of the Atlantic. Narrative African American spirituals such as "When Israel Was in Egypt's Land" (476) could be placed in this genre as well. But generally the nineteenth century saw a decline in the singing of psalms and traditional canticles by common people and instead witnessed a great prominence of hymns, gospel songs, and Sunday school songs.

In the second half of the twentieth century, however, various phenomena coincided to produce a significant revival in the singing of Scripture texts. The first of these phenomena was the rise of the "Jesus people," especially in California. This "Jesus movement" grew out of Christian ministries among disenchanted young people of the 1950s and '60s. Adherents of this movement liked folk music and strummed guitars; they developed a fervor for Bible study (often from the King James Version) and began to set excerpts from Scripture to simple melodies. In this they followed the pattern of the staff members of various evangelical organizations, who themselves sang short biblical texts to older chorus-type tunes such as "I Will Sing of the Mercies of the LORD" (169). The parachurch organization Maranatha! Music, with its numerous *Praise* publications and recordings, is a typical representative of this movement, as are Bible songs such as "Seek Ye First the Kingdom" (209), "Rejoice in the Lord Always" (228), and "You Are Worthy" (232).

A second influence on the revival of Bible songs was the rise of the charismatic movement. Birthed by Pentecostalism, this movement, which has significantly influenced many other Protestant denominations and the Roman Catholic Church, emphasized renewal in worship, the use of all believers' gifts, and the appropriateness of expressing Christian joy through lively music and dance. Provided by both amateur and professional musicians (such as Betty Pulkingham) and widely published in numerous booklets (such as *Scripture in Song* by David and Dale Garratt), the charismatic repertoire includes many Scripture songs and other praise choruses. Some of these Bible songs have gained wide acceptance in the official hymnbooks of various churches. Three examples in the *Psalter Hymnal* are "Our God Reigns" (195), "Fear Not, Rejoice and Be Glad" (201), and "This Is the Day" (241); the latter is an example of how a single psalm verse became expanded by oral tradition into a composite Bible song.

A third factor is the evangelical revival in the parish churches of British Anglicanism. Initially focused on youth ministries, this revival movement found its musical expression in the Jubilate Group, a collective body of hymn authors and composers who specialized in paraphrasing psalms and other Scripture passages and who gained exposure in *Psalm Praise* (1973). Leaders such as Timothy Dudley-Smith, Christopher

M. Idle, Michael A. Perry, and Norman L. Warren have contributed their biblical paraphrases and metered précis to Jubilate Group publications such as *Hymns for Today's Church* (1982) and *Psalms for Today* (1990). These texts are set to music whose styles range from hymn to pop to folk tunes. Representative examples of such Bible songs in the *Psalter Hymnal* are "Since Our Great High Priest, Christ Jesus" (230), "Heavenly Hosts in Ceaseless Worship" (233), and "Then I Saw a New Heaven and Earth" (236).

The renewal in Roman Catholic worship after Vatican II is a fourth influence on the re-emergence of Scripture singing in the late twentieth century. In the wake of the official decision to worship in the vernacular, many English-speaking priests and nuns such as James Quinn, Willard F. Jabusch, and Miriam Therese Winter began to write hymns, biblical paraphrases, and other liturgical texts to folk and folk-like music. Roman Catholic publications in the United States such as *Glory & Praise: Comprehensive Edition* (1987, 1997) and *Gather* (1988, 1994) include a number of psalms and other Scripture songs, many of which require responsorial performance between cantor and congregation. Examples of Bible versifications in the *Psalter Hymnal* that come from Roman Catholic sources are "See, Christ Was Wounded for Our Sake" (196), "Whatsoever You Do to the Least" (210), and "Give Thanks to God, the Father" (225).

In addition to these major phenomena are smaller ventures that have also brought renewed interest to the singing of canticles and other Scripture texts. The influence of Jewish music and of songs by Jews for Jesus music teams can be seen in such *Psalter Hymnal* selections as "I Will Sing unto the LORD" (152), "The Trees of the Field" (197), "Arise, Shine, for Your Light Is Come" (198), and the Jewish tune LINDESFARNE (218). The Taizé Community, an ecumenical movement in France that cultivates the singing of Scripture texts to memorable music, often in simple patterns, has given us "Jesus, Remember Me" (217), "Eat This Bread" (312), and "Magnify the Lord" (622), to name just a few. Various ethnic traditions have also contributed Bible songs to the *Psalter Hymnal*. For example, see "In the Beginning" (151) and "The Lord Is Risen, Yes, Indeed" (211), both originally from the Dutch, and "Alabaré" (234) and "Santo, Santo, Santo" (626), both of which are Spanish *canticos*.

Consciously affected by the several historic traditions of singing canticles and other portions of Scripture, influenced by the various contemporary renewal movements that promote Scripture singing, and encouraged by the model of a sizable group of Bible songs in the Dutch ecumenical *Liedboek* (1973), the *Psalter Hymnal* Revision Committee determined to include many of these historic and contemporary Scripture songs in the *Psalter Hymnal*. In addition, new paraphrases were commissioned from or submitted by committee members such as Bert Polman (213, 222, 229), Marie Post (200, 219, 223), Calvin Seerveld (157, 191, 221); by the *Psalter Hymnal* editor, Emily Brink (158); and by several other members of the Christian Reformed Church (199, 208, 226, 227, 231). Committee members Calvin Seerveld and Dale Grotenhuis also composed several new tunes for *Psalter Hymnal* Bible songs (154, 205, 221, 224), and other Christian Reformed composers provided the music for additional Scripture texts (196, 200, 226).

Always noted for its Calvinist heritage and historic commitment to the singing of psalms, the Christian Reformed Church offers in the 1987 *Psalter Hymnal* settings of many other passages of Scripture in unity with Christians throughout history and the contemporary world. It is a time-honored tradition in Christianity that Bible songs (as well as psalms) are "useful for worship, teaching, and testifying"—the more so as they become memorized and integrated into full-orbed Christian lives and communities.

Greek and Latin Hymnody

by Roy Hopp, Bert Polman, and Calvin R. Stapert

The dispersion of the early Christian Jews and the missionary enterprises of the young church produced two bodies of early Christian hymnody: hymns in Greek, associated with the Eastern segment of the church in Palestine, Asia Minor, and North Africa; and hymns in Latin, associated with the Western church in Europe.

Greek Hymnody

Greek was the language of the earliest Christian hymns. Although Greece, at the time the church was born, was just a province of the ruling Roman Empire, the Greek language and Hellenistic culture were dominant throughout most of the empire. It is not surprising, therefore, that the hymns sung by the first Christians were in the Greek language, just as were the inspired writings of the apostles that became the New Testament. The New Testament, in fact, is the source of what are probably the oldest extant fragments of Christian hymns (see the essay "Canticles and Other Bible Songs," p. 55).

What is generally regarded as the oldest surviving complete Greek hymn text is one that Clement of Alexandria (see PHH 590) appended to his book *Paedagogus* (c. 200). The first stanza, literally translated from the Greek, reads as follows:

> Bridle of colts untamed, wing of unwandering birds,
> sure helm of ships, shepherd of royal lambs,
> assemble your simple children to praise holily,
> to hymn guilessly with innocent mouths,
> Christ, the guide of children.

Modern English paraphrases of this hymn include "Jesus, Our Mighty Lord" (590) and "Shepherd of Tender Youth" (414 in the 1959 *Psalter Hymnal*).

A few other examples of Greek hymns from the early church still appear quite regularly in modern hymnbooks. "Father, We Give You Thanks, Who Planted" (314) is based on a eucharistic prayer from the *Didache*, the "Teachings of the Apostles" (early third century). The anonymous *Phos hilaron*, or "Lamplighting Hymn," was a prayer sung as Christians gathered for evening devotions from as early as the third century; in many hymnals this hymn is translated as "O Gladsome Light, O Grace." Another hymn also derived from a eucharistic prayer is "Let All Mortal Flesh Keep Silence" (341); it comes from the Jerusalem Liturgy of St. James (fifth century).

There is, however, a scarcity of early Greek hymns, a situation resulting from more than just the normal attrition that takes place over a long period of time. Because of the impact of heretical hymns by people like Bardaisan (154-222) and Paul of Samosta (third century), orthodox church leaders discouraged the use of nonbiblical hymns. So during the early centuries of Christianity, "free" hymn writing sometimes languished in favor of hymns more strictly modeled on biblical texts.

In the fifth century, short musical prayers called *troparia* were developed in the Byzantine Church. These were extended into longer, more elaborate hymns, called *kontakion* from the sixth century on. *Kontakion* were essentially metrical sermons paraphrasing a biblical narrative and consisting of multiple stanzas. Almost none of this material has survived into modern Protestant hymnody. In the eighth century the *kontakion* was superseded by the acrostic *kanon*, which was a cycle of eight or nine hymnic odes modeled on the biblical canticles sung during the monastic daily Office, or prayer services (see p. 56). The developments of the *kanon* occurred initially at the monastery of Mar Saba, between Jerusalem and the Dead Sea, and later at the Studium monastery in Constantinople. Two important names in the history of the *kanon* are Andrew of Crete (660-732), whose style seems to have inspired "Christian, Do You Struggle" (575), and John of Damascus (d. c. 780), from whose Easter *kanon* are derived "Come, You Faithful, Raise the Strain" (389) and "The Day of Resurrection" (390).

Although the vestiges of the rich heritage of Greek hymnody are small in modern Protestant hymnody, the little that survives enriches our modern worship of God greatly. The chief characteristics of Greek hymn texts are their strong emphasis on objective and cosmic praise of God, their consistent use of biblical images, their exploration of mystery and awe, and their orthodox confessional language. Music notation, however, was not yet developed during the era in which Greek hymnody flourished, so we have no knowledge of melodies associated with these texts and we know little about any related performance practices.

Early Latin Hymnody

Beginning in the third century, Latin began to replace Greek in the Western churches, and during the fourth century Latin hymnody was born. Hilary, a fourth-century bishop of Poiters, was the first-known Latin hymn writer. Using as his models the Greek hymns that he knew, he wrote trinitarian hymns in Latin designed to combat the then current Arian heresy, which denied the deity of Christ. Unfortunately his *Liber Hymnorum* is lost.

Ambrose, a fourth-century bishop of Milan, followed in Hilary's footsteps by writing hymns and leading the fight against Arianism. The story of his introduction of hymn singing into the church at Milan is told by Augustine in Book IX of his *Confessions:*

It was not long before [my baptism] that the church at Milan had begun to seek comfort and spiritual strength in the practice of singing hymns, in which the faithful fervently united with heart and voice. . . . In those days your faithful people used to keep watch in the church, ready to die with their bishop, your servant. It was then that the practice of singing hymns and psalms was introduced, in keeping with the usage of the Eastern churches, to revive the flagging spirits of the people during their long and cheerless watch. Ever since then the custom has been retained, and the example of Milan has been followed in many other places, in fact in almost every church throughout the world.

—*trans. R. S. Pine-Coffin (Harmondsworth: Penguin Classics, 1961), p. 191.*

Ambrose, who is sometimes called the "father of Latin hymnody," made popular the syllabic metrical hymn and the antiphonal singing of hymns. Though almost a hundred hymn texts are attributed to him, only four can be definitely ascribed to him. His best-known hymn, *Veni, Redemptor Gentium,* was translated by Martin Luther as "Nun komm, der Heiden Heiland" in the early sixteenth century; for the *Psalter Hymnal* Calvin Seerveld prepared "Savior of the Nations, Come" (336), a translation based on both the original Ambrose text and Luther's German text.

Marcus Aurelius C. Prudentius (348-413), a contemporary of Ambrose living in Spain, has been called the "first Christian poet." He converted to Christianity at age fifty-seven, entered a monastery, and then wrote long, didactic, and apologetic poetry for devotional use, not for congregational singing. Nevertheless, an extract from one of his poems in his *Liber Cathemerinon* provides us with the beautiful Christmas hymn "Of the Father's Love Begotten" (342).

The best known of all early Latin hymns, *Te Deum laudamus,* also comes from this early period. A story that circulated during the Middle Ages claimed that this hymn was improvised by Ambrose and Augustine as Ambrose baptized Augustine. Though appealing, that story is no doubt apocryphal, for the more likely author of the initial part of this hymn is an obscure church father named Niceta of Remesiana, a fourth-century missionary and bishop to what more recently was called Yugoslavia. Appearing in most modern hymnals as "Holy God, We Praise Your Name" (504), the *Te Deum* remains one of the church's richest expressions of praise.

After the fall of the Roman Empire in 476, the development of Latin hymnody is mostly associated with the monastic movement. The key figure in establishing hymns as a regular feature of the daily monastic prayer services was Benedict. In the influential Rule of Benedict (c. 530) and in later monastic orders, hymns were assigned specific places in the daily Offices (see p. 21).

In the latter part of the sixth century Fortunatus (c. 530-609) wrote a cycle of "Hymns for All the Festivals of the Christian Year" (now lost). Among his hymns that continue to be published in modern hymnals are "The Royal Banners Forward Go," "Hail Thee, Festival Day," and "Praise the Savior Now and Ever" (400). Theodulph of Orleans's popular hymn for Palm Sunday, "All Glory, Laud, and Honor" (375, 376), dates from the time of the Carolingian Renaissance (ninth century). From the same era comes *Veni, Creator Spiritus,* usually attributed to Rabanus Maurus (776-856) and variously translated as "Creator Spirit, by Whose Aid" (425) and "O Holy Spirit, by Whose Breath" (426).

Medieval Latin Hymnody

During the high Middle Ages, the monks and other clergy, Europe's most literate class of people, continued to provide large numbers of hymns for the monastic Offices, as well as *sequences*, which were hymn-like texts used during the Mass. The twelfth century marks the beginning of what some have called the "Golden Age of Latin Hymnody." Some of the church's most-loved devotional hymns come from this time. "O Sacred Head, Now Wounded" (383), often ascribed to Bernard of Clairvaux (1091-1153), epitomizes the mystic contemplation of Christ's suffering that was so characteristic of medieval piety. Also ascribed by some to Bernard and by others to an anonymous Benedictine abbess is the long Latin poem *Jesu dulcis memoria*, from which came "O Jesus, Joy of Loving Hearts" (307) and "Jesus, the Very Thought of You" (480).

A well-known Latin hymn from the same era is *Veni Immanuel*. Translated as "O Come, O Come, Immanuel" (328), it contains many Old Testament names for the Messiah. "All Creatures of Our God and King" (431) comes from Francis of Assisi's famous *lauda* (or devotional song), "Canticle to the Sun" (c. 1225); while "Jerusalem the Golden" (618) derives from Bernard of Cluny's satirical poem *De Contemptu Mundi* about the glories of the new Jerusalem. "O Love, How Deep, How Broad, How High" (364) and "O Sons and Daughters" (393) are versions of Latin hymns that come from the fifteenth and early sixteenth centuries.

As with the Greek hymns, a number of earlier Latin hymns come to us without tunes. After the development of musical notation in the ninth century, however, the chant music of the medieval Mass and of the Office hymns becomes discernible. Originally sung in unison, medieval chant tunes such as VENI IMMANUEL (328) and DIVINUM MYSTERIUM (342) are now commonly sung also in harmony. The large repertoire of medieval chant tunes was also used by some Lutheran musicians to compose chorale tunes, and later composers used medieval chants to fashion modern hymn tunes— PENTECOST (212) and HAMBURG (384) are two obvious examples in the *Psalter Hymnal*.

While the Latin hymns of the early church were written for all members of the congregation to sing, by medieval times the state of congregational singing had gradually deteriorated to the point at which only clergy and trained choirs were singing these hymns in a language (Latin) that most laypeople could not understand. Some folk hymns were sung in local languages, however, and there are some bilingual (*macaronic*) carols such as "In dulci jubilo/Nun singet und seyt fro," which we know as "Good Christian Friends, Rejoice" (355).

A constant factor in the performance of Latin hymns in traditional Roman Catholic liturgies has been *alternatum praxis:* alternate phrases of each hymn sung by different parts of the choir. Today this is commonly done by singing alternate hymn stanzas between choir and congregation, or between worshipers on the left of the center aisle and those on the right, or between men and women.

Modern Latin Hymnody

Following the Protestant Reformation, the Roman Catholic authorities revised and then fixed (some say "froze"!) the Latin rite in the *Missale Romanum* (1570) issued after the Council of Trent (1545-1563). Most of the *sequences* were banned by that council, and many of the Office hymns were more uniformly assigned to specific occasions in the liturgy. As a result, there was less impetus to produce new Latin hymnody during the next three centuries. However, some notable Latin hymns were written during these post-Tridentine years. Significant among these later Latin hymns are "The Strife Is O'er, the Battle Done" (391), "On Jordan's Bank the Baptist's Cry" (327), and what may be the most widely used and best loved of all Christmas hymns, *Adeste Fideles*, written in the eighteenth century by John Francis Wade and known to Christians throughout the English-speaking world as "O Come, All Ye Faithful" (340).

Following the Council of Trent various persons and bodies in the Roman Catholic Church also produced tunebooks from time to time, in part to foster renewal in the congregational singing of Latin hymns. Some of the melodies from these hymnals have enriched ecumenical Christian hymnody. Examples include LASST UNS ERFREUEN (431) from a Jesuit hymnal in Cologne, O QUANTA QUALIA (235) from a diocesan hymnal in Paris, and MELCOMBE (112, 274) from a British Roman Catholic source. (For more recent hymnic developments in the Roman Catholic Church following the Second Vatican Council and its revised *Missale Romanum* [1969], see p. 55 in the essay "Canticles and Other Bible Songs" and p. 84 in the essay "North American Hymnody: 1800-1950.")

The treasures of Greek and Latin hymnody could not be sung by the English-speaking world without the skill and artistry of translators. Many have contributed hymnic translations, but none stands so dominant in the field as does John Mason Neale (1818-1866), an Anglican clergyman who knew about twenty languages (see PHH 342). His publication *Hymns of the Eastern Church* (1862) brought the treasures of the ancient Greek hymns to the English-speaking world for the first time. He also published three major collections of hymns from the Latin: *Medieval Hymns and Sequences* (1851), *The Hymnal Noted* (1854), and *Hymns, Chiefly Medieval, on the Joys and Glories of Paradise* (1865). The *Psalter Hymnal* includes seven of his translations (342, 355, 375/376, 389, 390, 393, 618) and one of his (apparently) original hymn texts (575).

Continental European Hymnody: 1500-1900

by Roy Hopp and Bert Polman

Lutheran Hymnody

Though there were earlier revival leaders such as John Wycliffe and John Hus in the Roman Catholic Church, the Protestant Reformation sprang to life when Martin Luther (1483-1546) nailed his "ninety-five theses" to the door of the Wittenberg castle church on October 31, 1517. In addition to being a theologian and a primary architect of the Protestant movement, Luther was also a liturgist, a musician, and a hymn author. He wanted worship to occur in the vernacular, so he translated the Bible into German, revised the Roman Catholic liturgy for Protestant use, and wrote hymns to be sung by the entire congregation, not just by clergy choirs. Luther and his associates published their first hymnal, *Etlich Christliche Lieder,* in 1524. This was followed by several hundred Lutheran hymnals during the remainder of the sixteenth century. Collectively these hymnals constitute the first phase of Lutheran hymnody.

Phase One

Luther favored the continuity of song from the medieval era, and thus, in addition to writing new texts and tunes, he and the first several generations of Lutheran hymn authors and composers often simply adapted texts and tunes from the chants of medieval Roman Catholicism. The texts that made up the *Ordinary* of the Mass (that is, its unchanging texts)—the *Kyrie, Gloria, Credo, Sanctus,* and *Agnus Dei,* were each paraphrased into hymns. The *Psalter Hymnal* inherits "All Glory Be to God on High" (247) and "O Christ, the Lamb of God" (257) from this tradition. Some medieval hymn texts with *Kyrie eleison* phrases, known in Germany as *Leisen,* were also reshaped to become Lutheran chorales—see, for example, the tunes CHRIST IST ERSTANDEN (407) and CHRIST LAG IN TODESBANDEN (398), both of which are related to "Victimae paschali laudes," the Roman Catholic sequence for Easter. Luther himself is best known for his "battle hymn of the Reformation," which we sing as "A Mighty Fortress Is Our God" (469); for his rhythmic tune for this hymn, EIN FESTE BURG (468); and for his reworking of a folk song about garlands into the hymn "From Heaven Above to Earth I Come" (339).

These early Lutheran chorales often made use of the Ionian mode (later known as *major tonality*) and lively rhythms. The chorales were usually sung in unison by the assembled congregation, sometimes with polyphonic harmonizations sung by choirs. The published harmonizations in much of the sixteenth century routinely offered the melody in the tenor part. Lukas Osiander, however, published *Fünfzig geistliche Lieder und Psalmen* in 1586, which featured the melody in the soprano part, and that simple "cantional" approach became the common practice for congregational hymnals after that date.

The first phase of Lutheran hymnody came to a close by the turn of the seventeenth century. From the end of this first phase come two popular chorales by Philipp Nicolai (1536-1608): "Wake, Awake, for Night Is Flying" (613) and "How Bright Appears the Morning Star" (357). Also from this phase comes the tune for "O Sacred Head, Now Wounded," HERZLICH TUT MICH VERLANGEN (383) by Hans Leo Hassler (1564-1612), and several tunes from the 1609 *Gesangbuch* of Melchior Vulpius (1560-1615): GELOBT SEI GOTT (397), DAS NEUGEBORNE KINDELEIN (426), and CHRISTUS, DER IST MEIN LEBEN (565). The most significant Lutheran collection of hymns from this period is *Musae Sioniae* (1605-1610), compiled by Michael Praetorius (1571-1621). Aptly summarizing the sixteenth-century Lutheran repertoire, this multivolume anthology includes 1,244 settings of chorales, ranging from two-part harmonizations to settings for twelve or more parts. Praetorius's popular setting ES IST EIN ROS (351) is from this collection.

Phase Two

The second phase of Lutheran hymnody was dominated by the preacher-poet Paul Gerhardt (1607-1676), the church musician and publisher Johann Crüger (1598-1662), and the disastrous Thirty Years' War (1618-1648). What began as a local Catholic-Protestant conflict in Bohemia spread to a political and religious war waged throughout large parts of Europe. The earlier hymns of a more objective nature gave way to the more subjective hymns written during and after the Thirty Years' War, as hymn writers sought to express a more personal relationship with God. The devastations of the war led to a renewed hymnic focus on the cross and on comfort. Some of the most noble hymn texts written during this period are "Ah, Holy Jesus, How Have You Offended" (386) by Johann Heermann (1585-1647), "Now Thank We All Our God" (454) by Martin Rinkart (1587-1649), "If You But Trust in God to Guide You" (446) by Georg Neumark (1621-1681), and two by Johann Franck (1618-1677): "Clothe Yourself, My Soul, with Gladness" (305) and "Jesus, Priceless Treasure" (572).

But the greatest hymn author of this period was Paul Gerhardt, whose "O Lord, How Shall I Meet You" (331) is a splendid example of the fervently evangelical content of his original hymns. Associated with Gerhardt in Berlin for some years was Johann Crüger, the compiler of the most significant hymnal of this period: *Praxis Pietatis Melica* (first edition c. 1644). Crüger clearly inherited the rhythmic chorales from the first phase of Lutheran hymnody, but he contributed to the hymnody of this second phase through his original tunes and harmonizations and his editing of hymnals. His music often reveals the influence of Genevan psalm-tune rhythms. And it is striking that many of the texts of this time period that are still sung today feature tunes by Crüger. Some examples of his music included in the *Psalter Hymnal* are the tunes SCHMÜCKE DICH (305), WIE SOLL ICH DICH EMPFANGEN (331), HERZLIEBSTER JESU (386), JESUS, MEINE ZUVERZICHT (399), NUN DANKET (454), and JESU, MEINE FREUDE (572).

Phase Three

The third phase of the main body of Lutheran hymnody is marked by the influence of the Pietist movement. Begun by Jakob Spener and August Francke in the 1670s, this evangelical movement desired more piety in one's personal walk with the Lord, and it arose in opposition to the prevailing dead orthodoxy of the earlier seventeenth century. Pietism also expressed itself, however, in public acts of charity, especially in the running of orphanages. Among the first examples of Pietist hymnody in the *Psalter Hymnal* are "Sing Praise to God Who Reigns Above" (465) by Johann Schütz (1640-1690) and "Praise to the Lord, the Almighty" (253) by Joachim Neander (1650-1680).

The primary hymnbook of this phase is *Geistreiche Gesangbuch* (1704), compiled by the noted Pietist preacher and orphanage administrator Johann Freylinghausen (1670-1739). The 1741 edition of this hymnal contained some sixteen hundred texts and six hundred tunes. By this time, however, many of the settings were intended for solo voice with *basso continuo* (keyboard and cello) accompaniment, and many of the chorales had lost their initial rhythmic vitality, having been altered into even rhythm, or *isorhythm.* RATISBON (34), MONKLAND (223) and DIE TUGEND WIRD (439) are examples of Freylinghausen's isorhythmic tunes in the *Psalter Hymnal.*

The lamentable loss of the original lively rhythms of the Lutheran chorales during this time is counteracted, in part, by the high-quality harmonizations provided by the great baroque composer Johann Sebastian Bach (1685-1750) for many of these chorales. Bach used the melodies from the Freylinghausen *Gesangbuch* to fashion his chorale harmonizations for his church music. Many of these harmonizations still appear in modern hymnals and have come to be called "the Bach chorales," which erroneously implies that Bach composed the tunes. The *Psalter Hymnal* features a number of (sometimes simplified) harmonizations by Bach—for example, DARMSTADT (574), ERMUNTRE DICH (343), FAITHFUL (429), JESU JOY (122), LOBT GOTT, IHR CHRISTEN (192), ST. THEODULPH (376), WACHET AUF (613), and WIE SCHÖN LEUCHTET (357). The Bach settings VATER UNSER (208, 562) and HERZLICH TUT MICH VERLANGEN (383) come from his *St. John Passion* and *St. Matthew Passion,* respectively.

The 1741 edition of Freylinghausen's *Gesangbuch* and the chorale harmonizations by Bach mark the close of this third phase of Lutheran hymnody. Among the last hymn writers of this era who were influenced by Pietism were the Reformed preacher Gerhardt Tersteegen (1697-1769), who wrote "God Himself Is with Us" (244), and the Lutheran philosophy teacher Christian Gellert (1715-1759), whose Easter ode "Jesus Lives, and So Do We" (399) is still popular today.

Phase Four

A nineteenth-century stage in European Lutheran hymnody comes from Scandinavia. The Danish pastor and hymn author Nicolai Grundtvig (1783-1872) wrote the classic hymn texts "Bright and Glorious Is the Sky" (360) and "Built on the Rock" (503). For this latter text a Norwegian church musician, Ludwig Lindemann (1812-1887), composed the tune KIRKEN (503). The most prolific of the Scandinavian hymn writers was Caroline Sandell Berg (1832-1903), the Swedish poet whose work is represented in the *Psalter Hymnal* by her "Children of the Heavenly Father" (440), suitably set to a Swedish tune: TRYGGARE KAN INGEN VARA. Another anonymous Swedish tune, O STORE GUD, also dates to the nineteenth century; it regained popularity in the later twentieth century through its association with Stuart Hine's text "How Great Thou Art" (483).

Translations

Lutheran hymnody arose and initially remained in German-speaking lands, but eventually it spread also to English-speaking branches of Christianity. One of the most important translators of these German chorales into English was Catherine Winkworth (1827-1878), a pioneer in the higher education of women in England. She translated almost four hundred hymns from some 170 authors who represent the various phases of Lutheran hymnody, and she published them in collections such as her *Lyra Germanica* (vol. 1, 1855; vol. 2, 1858) and her *Chorale Book for England* (1863). The high quality of Winkworth's translations has rarely been surpassed, although modern hymnals usually incorporate some alterations in her work. "Blessed Jesus, at Your Word" (280), "Comfort, Comfort Now My People" (194), "Jesus, Priceless Treasure" (572), "Now Thank We All Our God" (454), and "Praise to the Lord, the Almighty" (253) are select examples of the thirteen Winkworth translations of Lutheran chorales included in the *Psalter Hymnal.*

Moravian Hymnody

The followers of John Hus (d. 1415), who were first known as Bohemian Brethren and later as Moravians, were the first Protestant group to reemphasize congregational singing in worship. They published eighty-nine Czech hymns in their first Protestant hymnbook in 1501—almost a full generation before Luther's first hymnal. Other hymnals followed in 1505 and 1519; these were followed by *Ein Neu Gesengbuchlen* (1531), a collection of 157 high-quality hymns, and by further hymnals in 1541 and 1561. The Moravians' *Kirchengesange* (1566) contained both Czech and German hymns and included MIT FREUDEN ZART (465). A Moravian hymnal of 1661 quaintly indicated that it included "Psalms of the Royal Prophet David, Songs by John Hus, and Songs by Doctor Martin Luther."

The Bohemian Brethren developed a communal life style and used antiphonal a cappella singing of complete hymns and select stanzas in their daily times of worship. Much persecuted by the Roman Catholic Church, they were often forced to move from one region to another.

In the eighteenth century the Moravians made their greatest contributions to hymnody and to the missionary enterprise of Christianity. After two centuries of persecution for their religious zeal, these followers of John Hus fled Moravia in 1722 and found refuge on the estate of Count Nicolaus von Zinzendorf (1700-1760) at Herrnhut, Saxony. There the enthusiastic singing of the Moravians inspired the prolific

Zinzendorf to write some two thousand hymns and to publish several hymnals. His "Christian Hearts in Love United" (513) was published in *Das Gesangbuch der Gemeine in Herrnhut* (1735), a text-only book with almost a thousand hymns. Corresponding tunes for this hymnal were issued only in manuscript form. Under Zinzendorf's leadership, the daily times of worship became more formalized, although the Moravians' traditional improvisation of prayer and hymn medleys continued, with antiphonal singing between "liturgist, chorus, brethren, sisters, and the [full] congregation." From Herrnhut and later also from London, the Moravians sent out missionaries to various parts of the world. (Their influence on the Wesleys is recounted in the essay titled "English Hymnody," p. 73.)

The Moravians' "London" hymnal (1753-54), compiled under Zinzendorf's direction, contained 3,627 hymns in chronological order(!) in two volumes, and their *Kleines Brudergesangbuch* (1754) contained some three thousand hymns and hymn excerpts. By that time the Moravians also used brass ensembles for their hymn accompaniment. Later in that century Christian Gregor (1723-1801) emerged as their most influential hymnodist. He was both an organist and a hymn writer; he compiled their 1778 text-only hymnal, and he edited its tunebook, *Choralbuch* (1784), which included among its excellent tunes GREGOR'S 112TH METRE (445).

In the next century the hymn texts of the Moravian poet and newspaper editor James Montgomery (1771-1854) made a significant impact on European hymnody. The *Psalter Hymnal* includes his "Hail to the LORD's Anointed" (72), "According to Thy Gracious Word" (298), "Angels from the Realms of Glory" (354), and "Go to Dark Gethsemane" (381).

Other European Hymnody

The *Psalter Hymnal* contains a number of texts and tunes from the Netherlands. "Come and Stand Amazed, You People" (338) is an anonymous Dutch medieval hymn; while IN BABILONE (117) is a Dutch folk tune. The *Evangelische Gezangen* (1806) included the original Dutch texts of "Hours and Days and Years and Ages" (443) and "We Come to Thank You, God, by Singing" (439). Later Dutch hymnals provide us with the source texts of "Awake, All Who Sleep" (537) by the preacher Petro Parson; the Easter hymn "A Shout Rings Out, a Joyful Voice (392) by Eduard Gerdes; the most famous Dutch Christmas carol, "Glory to God" (214); and "Our Faithful God" (445) by the missions-preaching Hendrik Pierson.

"I Greet My Sure Redeemer" (248) is a French hymn from the Reformation era. Originally a Marian prayer in Latin, the Protestant reworking of this text into French has sometimes been (erroneously) attributed to John Calvin. Another French hymn in the *Psalter Hymnal* is the noel "Angels We Have Heard on High" and its tune GLORIA (347).

One of the early Reformers in Switzerland was Ulrich Zwingli (1484-1531), who wrote the original version of "Lord, We Cry to You for Help" (261), even though he banned hymn singing and all other music from his church services in Zurich. Some of

Zwingli's followers disagreed with his convictions on infant baptism and fostered what soon became known as the Anabaptist movement. The early Anabaptists sang hymns in the vernacular, and their most significant hymnal, first published in the 1560s, was the *Ausbund.* Its 1583 edition contained some hymns written by early Anabaptists who were later martyred. Various versions of the *Ausbund* were used by Mennonite communities, and more recent editions are still used by the Old Order Amish in the United States. Because many of the early Anabaptists were viewed with suspicion and hatred by both Roman Catholics and Protestants, there was little Protestant acceptance of Anabaptist hymnody. The *Psalter Hymnal* is typical in this respect in that it contains no hymns from the *Ausbund* tradition.

English Hymnody

by Roy Hopp and Bert Polman

Early British Hymnody

While the Reformation in many European lands led to an outpouring of hymns, congregational singing in Britain took a much different course. Following the lead of John Calvin, who advocated the exclusive use of psalmody in congregational singing, the English-speaking churches became psalm singers for the first century and a half after the Reformation (see the essay "English Metrical Psalmody," p. 40). There were, nevertheless, a few attempts to introduce hymn singing to the British people. The first English hymnal was *Goostly Psalmes and Spirituall Songes drawen out of the Holy Scripture* (1535). Compiled by Miles Coverdale, it was a small collection of forty-one hymns, most of them translations of German hymns, including the first English version of Martin Luther's "Ein feste Burg" (see 468, 469). This attempt to introduce hymns to psalm-singing England was thwarted by King Henry VIII, who placed the hymnal on a list of banned books.

But even the early English psalters included a few hymns: for example, there were nineteen hymns in John Day's 1562 edition of the Sternhold and Hopkins Psalter, thirteen hymns in the Scottish Psalter of 1635, and sixteen hymns in the 1700 *Supplement* to *A New Version of the Psalms . . .* (1696). That supplement included "While Shepherds Watched Their Flocks" (215). Many of these early hymns were paraphrases of New Testament canticles or other biblical texts. Late in the sixteenth and early seventeenth centuries devotional poetry abounded from authors such as John Donne and George Wither, and some of Wither's texts were published in *Hymns and Songs of the Church* (1623) with tunes by Orlando Gibbons such as SONG 13 (423) and SONG 24 (167). Also in the late sixteenth century John Playford interspersed hymns among the psalms in his *Psalms and Hymns* (1671).

Hymnody began to take a more significant foothold in England late in the seventeenth century. The Baptist preacher Benjamin Keach began writing hymns for use at the Lord's Supper in 1673, and by the time he published his hymnal *Spiritual Melody* (1691), he was using hymns weekly. Another Baptist preacher, Joseph Stennett, published his *Hymns . . . for the Celebration of the Holy Supper* in 1697. By that time there were English Presbyterian hymnals: Richard Baxter's *Paraphrases on the Psalms of David with Other Hymns* (1692), Joseph Boyse's *Sacramental Hymns* (1693), and Matthew Henry's *Family Hymns* (1695).

Thus the English psalm-singing tradition was gradually enriched by the introduction of hymns. As the early literal (and often unpoetic) versifications of the psalms and canticles were eventually replaced by more poetically pleasing and freer paraphrases of those biblical texts, and as the domestic use of sung devotional poetry and the church's use of New Testament-inspired hymns written for the Lord's Supper increased, the way was prepared for a whole new repertoire of English-language hymns to follow in the eighteenth century.

Isaac Watts

Though he wasn't by any means the first English author to write hymns, Isaac Watts (1674-1748) has been called by some the "father of the English hymn" and by others the "liberator of English hymnody." He and Charles Wesley are certainly the most significant English hymn authors who wrote in the eighteenth century. By the beginning of that century congregational singing was, at best, lethargic, and the psalters in use contained versifications that Watts thought to be inferior. Thus he took on the challenge of improving psalm singing and of recasting what he saw as inappropriate psalm lyrics into "the language of the New Testament" for singing in Christian worship.

Watts's more than seven hundred hymns are, for the most part, either "hymns of human composure," as he called them, or new versifications of psalms. He tested the public's acceptance of his early texts in *Horae Lyricae* (1705), and then devoted the next dozen years to producing new psalms and hymns. His *Hymns and Spiritual Songs* (1707) included 78 texts based on Scripture, 110 on "divine subjects," and 23 for use with the Lord's Supper. A new edition in 1709 provided 135 additional texts. In 1715 he published a children's hymnal, *Divine Songs and Moral Songs,* which included "Love God with All Your Soul and Strength" (155). His *Psalms of David Imitated . . .* (1719) contained paraphrases of 138 psalms, since he deemed some psalms (those with imprecations) to be unworthy of Christian singing.

In paraphrasing the psalms somewhat loosely, Watts interpreted the Old Testament texts Christologically. Thus the Old Testament text of Psalm 72 became "Jesus Shall Reign" (412). Watts also inserted British references into his paraphrases. For example, his version of Psalm 100 included these lines:

Sing to the Lord with joyful voice;
let every land his name adore;
the British Isles shall send the noise
across the ocean to the shore.

Later editions of Watts's *Psalms* (and certainly those in the United States after 1776) have excised such British references. On the other hand, Watts's attempt to reflect the "common sense and language of a [modern] Christian" in his psalm paraphrases has been well received. Most modern hymnals still include his version of Psalm 23, "My Shepherd Will Supply My Need" (550); of Psalm 90, "O God, Our Help in Ages Past" (170); and of Psalm 98, "Joy to the World! The Lord Is Come" (337).

Watts wrote his "hymns of human composure" as contemporary expressions of devotion and praise to complement his paraphrases of the psalms and other portions of Scripture. From among these hymns come some of Watts's finest texts, retained in most modern hymnals. His "When I Survey the Wondrous Cross" (384) is surely one of the greatest hymns ever written, and it should convince anyone that Calvin's principle of exclusive psalm singing is too narrow in modern Christian worship. Other examples of Watts's hymns include "The Lord Our God in Mercy Spoke" (275), "Alas! And Did My Savior Bleed" (385), and "We Sing the Mighty Power of God" (430).

The poetry found in the hymns of Watts shares certain characteristics. Almost all have four lines to a stanza and use iambic meter (consisting of alternating unaccented and accented syllables). The second and fourth lines usually rhyme with each other in an ABCB pattern or sometimes in a cross-rhymed pattern, ABAB. His hymns usually appear in one of the three popular English ballad meters used for psalm-singing: common meter (8686), long meter (8888), or short meter (6686). Thus Watts's texts could be readily sung to the familiar psalm tunes of his day. The vocabulary he uses is simple, but he often captures the essence of a hymn in a memorable opening phrase. Note the epigrammatic opening lines from the following memorable hymns: "O God, Our Help in Ages Past," "Joy to the World! The Lord Is Come," and "Jesus Shall Reign."

The content of Watts's hymns also share certain characteristics. Many are Christocentric; as indicated above, even in his hymns inspired by the psalms, Christ is often the focus. Watts's hymns display the strong influence of John Calvin and other Reformed theologians. Many of Watts's hymns were written to be sung after a particular sermon was preached. His texts appealed to the subjective experience of Christians, but that subjectivity was held in check by his thorough study of Scripture and his emphasis on the corporate nature of Christian worship. Many allusions as well as entire themes in his hymns are derived from and reveal Watts's great knowledge of Scripture.

The Wesleys

In the same year that Isaac Watts published his first collection of hymns, a child was born who would become, along with Watts, one of the two most important figures in eighteenth-century English hymnody. Charles Wesley (1707-1788), who with his older brother John (1703-1791), became one of the cofounders of Methodism, wrote thousands of devotional poems, more than 6,500 of which can be considered hymns. They were published in more than sixty books and pamphlets of hymns during his lifetime. What is so remarkable about this immense output is that so many of Wesley's hymns are unsurpassed in their excellence and have become indispensable to the singing church ever since.

Ordained as Anglican clergymen, both John and Charles left England in 1735 to take up mission work in the English colony of Georgia. Sailing with the Wesleys on their journey to the New World were twenty-six German-speaking Moravian missionaries. The Wesleys were impressed by the Moravians' piety and especially by their hearty hymn singing. While still on board the ship John learned the German language and began to translate the hymns of the Moravians into English. They were eventually published along with hymns of Isaac Watts as a *Collection of Psalms and Hymns* (1737). This was the first of many hymnals published by the Wesleys.

By early 1738 John and Charles were back in England, both disappointed with failing in their mission in Georgia. They began associating with a Moravian colony that met in

Aldersgate, London. Later that year, first Charles, and then John, three days later, both experienced a dramatic conversion. From then on they were to dedicate their lives to a gospel ministry in England that sparked an evangelical revival. They ministered especially to the poor and the outcast in British society, and in their itinerant work they founded Methodist "societies" in which they taught a discipline, or "method," of daily prayer and Bible study. John was an able preacher and administrator, and the nature of his hymn translations resembled those of Paul Gerhardt and Nicolaus von Zinzendorf. Charles was most effective as a prolific author of hymns. Their Methodist societies eventually became the Methodist Church, though both John and Charles themselves remained Anglican throughout their lives.

Most of Charles Wesley's hymns appear in three wide-ranging categories: hymns of the church year, hymns expressing glory to Christ in response to a conversion experience, and hymns of Christian experience. In his personal devotions Charles read daily in his Anglican prayer book, which is organized around the liturgical year. This practice bore fruit in his hymn writing: he wrote many hymns for the various seasons of the church year. A quick glance at the hymns in the Advent, Christmas, or Easter sections of any modern hymnal will reveal that some of the most often sung seasonal hymns are by Charles Wesley. In the *Psalter Hymnal* we find such examples as "Come, Thou Long-Expected Jesus" (329), "Hark! The Herald Angels Sing" (345), "Christ the Lord Is Risen Today" (388), "Rejoice, the Lord Is King" (408), "Hail the Day That Sees Him Rise" (409), and "Lo! He Comes with Clouds Descending" (612).

Considering that he had a dramatic conversion experience and that he advocated a theology encouraging others to seek the same, it comes as no surprise that Charles Wesley's second major contribution to hymnody falls in the category of conversion hymns. His autobiographical "And Can It Be" (267) was written shortly after his own conversion experience, while "Oh, for a Thousand Tongues to Sing" (501) was a segment of a hymn he wrote to celebrate the first anniversary of his conversion.

Charles Wesley also contributed much to the broad category of hymns of Christian experience. Foremost among them are "Forth in Your Name, O Lord, I Go" (324), "You Servants of God, Your Master Proclaim" (477), "Christ, Whose Glory Fills the Skies" (481), "Love Divine, All Loves Excelling" (568), "Soldiers of Christ, Arise" (570) and "Jesus, Lover of My Soul" (578).

The poetry in Charles's hymns is rich and varied in many ways, and it certainly contributed to the literary improvement of hymn texts. He used the trochaic foot (an accented syllable followed by an unaccented one) as much as the iambic foot (an unaccented syllable followed by an accented one), and he incorporated more than thirty meters into his hymns, going well beyond the three meters commonly found in the English psalters and in the hymns of Isaac Watts. Rarely can one find a line in one of Charles Wesley's hymns that does not rhyme with another line. The cross-rhymed pattern, ABAB, is used as frequently as the rhymed couplet, AABB.

John Wesley described his brother's hymns as "a body of experiential and practical divinity." Charles emphasized the work of Christ in many of his texts; in others he stressed the ups and downs of everyday Christian experience. The theology expressed in his greatest hymns has found ecumenical acceptance, while some of his infrequently used hymns reflect Arminian teachings. Like the hymns of Isaac Watts, Charles Wesley's hymns are replete with scriptural quotations and allusions. Wesley intended his hymns to be useful in liturgical Christian worship and for the observance of the sacraments, but he also maintained a strong evangelical call to conversion in his texts, and he provided lyrics expressing many facets of Christian life and doctrine. Incidentally, most of the tunes that were originally associated with the Wesley hymn texts are no longer in use in modern hymnody, in part because a number of these tunes (some by Handel) are melismatic—that is, they often require the singing of several tones per syllable of text.

The Olney Hymns

The life story of John Newton (1725-1807) is a fascinating account about a sea captain and slave trader who became an Anglican clergyman in the small English village of Olney. It was there that he formed a friendship with the poet William Cowper (1731-1800). Together they compiled a hymnbook known as the *Olney Hymns* (1779), a collection that has profoundly influenced the later developments of English hymnody. While they faithfully sang psalms on Sundays, the Olney congregation held midweek devotional meetings at which they sang hymns. Newton and Cowper wrote their hymns for the villagers who attended these midweek meetings. The intent was to use the hymns to assist in the religious education of the congregation.

A well-known British poet, Cowper suffered periodically from depression, sometimes to the brink of suicide. But he managed to write sixty-eight of the hymns found in the Olney collection; of these "There Is a Fountain Filled with Blood," "Oh, for a Closer Walk with God" (551), and "God Moves in a Mysterious Way" (434) are exemplary of his profound faith even in the midst of severe trials. John Newton wrote the remaining 280 hymns in the Olney book; many of his hymns reflect a Calvinist theology in their emphasis on the love of Christ and the experiences of a redeemed sinner. This emphasis is clear in his most popular and autobiographical text, "Amazing Grace—How Sweet the Sound" (462). Other examples of Newton's hymns in the *Psalter Hymnal* are "How Sweet the Name of Jesus Sounds (487), "Glorious Things of Thee Are Spoken" (506), and "Day of Judgment! Day of Wonders!" (614).

Other Eighteenth-Century English Hymnody

The Evangelical Revival in the eighteenth century in England was spearheaded by noted preachers such as George Whitefield and the Wesleys. One group of these revival leaders followed the Arminian theology of the Wesleys, but another group followed the Calvinism of Whitefield. Hymn singing was an important part of this revival movement, and it affected not only the beginnings of the Methodist Church but also the other traditional English denominations: Anglicans, Baptists, Presbyterians, and Congregationalists.

William Williams (1717-1781) was a great Welsh revivalist preacher who first served in the Wesleyan tradition and later in the Calvinist Methodist church. He wrote some eight hundred Welsh hymns; of the few that have been translated into English, "Guide Me, O My Great Redeemer" (543) is still sung today. Edward Perronet (1726-1792), a Calvinist Methodist, wrote "All Hail the Power of Jesus' Name" (470, 471); while Thomas Olivers (1725-1799), another Welsh Methodist preacher and sometime assistant to John Wesley, provided the translation and reworking of a Jewish doxology into a familiar hymn, "The God of Abraham Praise" (621).

Augustus Toplady (1740-1778) was a militant Calvinist who wrote the serene "Rock of Ages" as well as the more doctrinally explicit "How Vast the Benefits Divine" (497); he also reworked some of the Wesley hymns to conform to his own Calvinism. Anne Steele (1716-1778) was a Baptist poet whose work is still evident in select modern hymnals. More ecumenically known are two parting hymns by the Baptist preacher John Fawcett (1740-1817): "Lord, Dismiss Us with Your Blessing" (320, 321) and "Blest Be the Tie That Binds" (315). During this same era Thomas Haweis (1734-1820), an Anglican preacher who turned Methodist, wrote hymn texts such as "Our Children, Lord, in Faith and Prayer" (270), but he is best known today for his tune RICHMOND (335).

Some fine psalm tunes that were composed early in the eighteenth century came to serve later as hymn tunes. These include HANOVER (149, 477) and WAREHAM (463). From the middle part of the eighteenth century come the hymn tunes YORKSHIRE (80, 350), ST. BRIDE (546), HALTON HOLGATE (553), and ITALIAN HYMN (246). Other notable tunes of the later eighteenth century are DARWALL'S 148TH (408), ROCKING-HAM (178), MORNING HYMN (592), DUKE STREET (412), and TRURO (413).

Early Nineteenth-Century British Hymnody

Under the influence of English Romantic poets such as Byron, Shelley, and Keats, a number of English hymn authors in the early nineteenth century wrote hymn texts that were respectable works of literature and not merely didactic or evangelistic texts. Many of these new hymns were also more closely tied to liturgical worship throughout the church year. Reginald Heber (1783-1826) wrote fifty-seven hymns in this new style; among them is his well-known text "From Greenland's Icy Mountains," which is still found in some modern hymnals. Heber's hymn texts were published posthumously in *Hymns Written & Adapted to the Weekly Church Services of the Year* (1827), and they included "Holy, Holy, Holy! Lord God Almighty" (249) and "Bread of the World, in Mercy Broken" (310). His hymns were instrumental in opening the way for hymn singing in the Church of England.

Other hymn texts of this period that demonstrate more careful attention to poetic expression include "In the Cross of Christ I Glory" (474) by John Bowring (1792-1872), "Ride On, Ride On in Majesty" (382) by Henry Milman (1791-1868), "O Worship the King" (428) by Robert Grant (1779-1838), "The Head That Once Was Crowned with

Thorns" (411) by Thomas Kelly (1769-1855), and "Abide with Me" (442) and "Praise, My Soul, the King of Heaven" (475)—both by Henry F. Lyte (1793-1847).

Early nineteenth-century British hymn tunes were often compiled into tunebooks, which were used in singing classes and in the many churches that used text-only hymnals. William Gardiner (1770-1853), for example, borrowed melodies from Haydn, Mozart, and Beethoven to fashion hymn tunes such as GERMANY (111, 602) and LYONS (428), and published them in the six volumes of his *Sacred Melodies* (1812-1815). The British music publisher Vincent Novello issued a similar set of four tunebooks called *The Psalmist* (1833-1843); the fourth volume of this set includes WESTMINSTER ABBEY (612) which was originally part of an anthem by Henry Purcell. From this same era come the tunes SAGINA (267) and ST. PETER (487).

Hymnody of the Oxford Movement

Sometimes known as the "Tractarian Movement" because of its publication of numerous tracts, the Oxford Movement began in 1833 under leaders such as John Keble, E. B. Pusey, and John Henry Newman. These men sought to recover theology and liturgy as practiced by the early Christian church, and they deplored the emotional individualism associated with evangelicalism. Influenced by a Romanticist veneration of the past, the Oxford Movement's greatest impact on hymnody was the recovery and translation of early Greek and Latin hymns and Lutheran chorales. John Chandler (1806-1876) initiated this development when he published his *Hymns of the Primitive Church* (1837, 1841), but he was soon followed by John Mason Neale, whose numerous translations from Greek and Latin are still found in many modern hymnals (see the end of the essay "Greek and Latin Hymnody," p. 62). Thomas Helmore (1811-1890) consolidated the revival of chant tunes in the two volumes of *The Hymnal Noted* (1852, 1858), while the primary translator of German chorales was Catherine Winkworth (see the subsection "Translations" in the essay "Continental European Hymnody: 1500-1900," p. 70).

Some of the early adherents to the Oxford Movement also produced original hymns. Once an Anglican, Frederick Faber (1814-1863) wrote "Faith of Our Fathers" and "My God, How Wonderful You Are" (499) after becoming a Roman Catholic, and Matthew Bridges (1800-1894) wrote "Crown Him with Many Crowns" (410) after a similar journey. Not a Tractarian but an evangelical, William Havergal (1793-1870) also displayed early-church interests in his *Old Church Psalmody* (1847), as did a Tractarian musician, Richard Redhead (1820-1901), whose REDHEAD 76 (255, 381) comes from one of his three volumes of hymn tunes.

Hymns Ancient and Modern

The history of English hymnody had long been characterized by a great assortment of psalters and hymnals (often with separate books for texts and tunes), many of which enjoyed only regional acceptance, and some of which competed with each other for popular use. By the mid-nineteenth century, work had begun on a new "concensus" hymnal, which was to incorporate the best of the old and the new. This hymnal was named *Hymns Ancient and Modern* (1860, 1861) which, in its numerous editions and with its various supplements (into the late twentieth century), constitutes the most enduring and influential hymnal tradition in England.

The Oxford emphasis on "high" liturgy and the order of the *Book of Common Prayer* are evident in the contents and structure of *Hymns Ancient and Modern*. Its first edition included 119 hymns from authors such as Isaac Watts, Charles Wesley, and John Newton; ten translations of German chorales, and only twelve new hymns. Its largest group of texts were its 132 translations of Latin hymns, many of which were set to chant tunes. The first edition also established the (now common) British practice of placing a hymn text adjacent to its tune (thereby avoiding the separation of songbook and tunebook) and of ending each hymn with an "Amen." Though the Church of England has never formally adopted *any* hymnal, the various editions of *Hymns Ancient and Modern* were gradually accepted in many Anglican congregations and have contributed significantly to the greater use of hymns in Anglican worship.

Much of the success of the first several editions of *Hymns Ancient and Modern* was due to the skill with which its editors were able to match texts and tunes into longlasting "marriages." Many of these classic combinations still appear in modern hymnals. Here are a few of the many "marriages" in the *Psalter Hymnal* that date back to *Hymns Ancient and Modern*:

- "Abide with Me" and EVENTIDE (442)
- "All Glory, Laud, and Honor" and ST. THEODULPH (375, 376)
- "Crown Him with Many Crowns" and DIADEMATA (410)
- "Holy, Holy, Holy! Lord God Almighty" and NICAEA (249)
- "How Sweet the Name of Jesus Sounds" and ST. PETER (487)
- "O God, Our Help in Ages Past" and ST. ANNE (170)
- "The Church's One Foundation" and AURELIA (502)
- "The Strife Is O'er, the Battle Done" and VICTORY (391)
- "When Morning Gilds the Sky" and LAUDES DOMINI (438)
- "While Shepherds Watched Their Flocks" and WINCHESTER OLD (215)

The primary text editor of the first several editions of *Hymns Ancient and Modern* was Henry Baker (1821-1877). He contributed thirty-three original texts and translations, including "Sing Praise to the Lord" (466), "O Perfect Life of Love" (380), and "O God of Love, O King of Peace" (608). William Monk (1823-1889) served as the music editor for those first editions, and he was most responsible for the hymnal's many successful "marriages" of text and tune. He also contributed fifty-six tunes, including EVENTIDE (442), MERTON (332), and CORONAE (464). Both of these editors ensured that the contents of *Hymns Ancient and Modern* was "restrained, serious, decorous, and demure," as the great British hymnologist Erik Routley has observed in his commentary *The Music of Christian Hymns* (1981).

Victorian Hymnody

It was during the reign of Queen Victoria in the latter half of the nineteenth century that Britain benefited most from the hymnodic effects of the Oxford Movement and the higher literary standards of nonconformist hymnody. This was the era that witnessed the passion of Christian socialists, the influence of higher criticism on biblical studies and theology, and the informal division of the Church of England into "high church" and "low church" groupings.

Among the most noted of Victorian hymn authors, listed here with the hymns representing them in the *Psalter Hymnal,* are

William Dix (1837-1898)	"As with Gladness Men of Old" (358) "Alleluia! Sing to Jesus" (406)
Christopher Wordsworth (1807-1885)	"Songs of Thankfulness and Praise" (361) "Alleluia! Alleluia!" (387) "See, the Conqueror Mounts in Triumph" (414)
Edward Plumptre (1821-1891)	"Your Hands, O Lord, in Days of Old" (363) "Your Hand, O God, Has Guided" (509) "Rejoice, O Pure in Heart" (561)
William How (1823-1897)	"O Word of God Incarnate" (279) "We Give You But Your Own" (296) "O Son of God the Father" (368) "For All the Saints" (505)
Cecil F. Alexander (1818-1895)	"Once in Royal David's City" (346) "All Things Bright and Beautiful" (435) "Jesus Calls Us; O'er the Tumult" (553)
John Ellerton (1826-1893)	"The Day You Gave Us, Lord, Is Ended" (318) "Savior, Again to Your Dear Name We Raise" (319)

Two other well-known hymn texts from this era are "Onward, Christian Soldiers" (522) and "The Church's One Foundation" (502)—both from the hands of "high churchmen": Sabine Baring-Gould and Samuel J. Stone, respectively.

Some evangelical women produced memorable Victorian hymns, of which the following are included in the *Psalter Hymnal:*

Frances R. Havergal (1836-1879)	"Take My Life and Let It Be" (288, 289) "Lord, Speak to Me That I May Speak" (528) "Like a River Glorious" (560)
Charlotte Elliott (1789-1871)	"Just as I Am, Without One Plea" (263)
Caroline Noel (1817-1877)	"At the Name of Jesus" (467)
A. Catherine Hankey (1834-1911)	"I Love to Tell the Story" (530)

The output of hymn tunes from Victorian composers is immense, though uneven in quality; fortunately some of those with weaker melodies have been complemented with rich harmonies! Associated with *Hymns Ancient and Modern,* John B. Dykes (1823-1876) composed tunes such as NICAEA (249) and MELITA (425). IRBY (346) by Henry Gauntlett (1805-1876), DIADEMATA (48, 410) by George Elvey (1816-1893), AURELIA (502) by Samuel S. Wesley (1810-1876), and LAUDA ANIMA (475) by John Goss (1800-1880) merit their continued popularity. Other important Victorian hymn composers are Henry Smart (1813-1879), who wrote such tunes as REGENT SQUARE (354) and LANCASHIRE (555); Joseph Barnby (1838-1896), from whose 246 tunes LAUDES DOMINI (438) and O PERFECT LOVE (580) are best known; and John Stainer (1840-1901), whose CREDO (127) and CROSS OF JESUS (581) exemplify the diverse characteristics of the hymn tunes of this era.

Finally, no survey of Victorian hymnody would be complete without reference to Arthur Sullivan (1841-1900), whose operettas have been judged more valuable than his work as editor of *The Hymnary* (1872) and *Church Hymns with Tunes* (1874), but whose tunes such as NOEL (46; also known as GERARD), ST. KEVIN (389), and ST. GERTRUDE (522) still appear in modern hymnals. Mention must also be made of the Scottish "Free Kirk" hymn writer Horatius Bonar (1808-1889), who produced such notable texts as "Not What My Hands Have Done" (260), "I Heard the Voice of Jesus Say" (488), and "Fill Thou My Life, O Lord, My God" (547).

The English Hymnal and Its Successors

By the turn of the twentieth century, *Hymns Ancient and Modern* had become a venerable, if somewhat stodgy, institution in English hymnody; its revision in 1904 was not widely accepted. It should not surprise that some reactions developed in opposition to its high church and Victorian tastes. Consequently the *English Hymnal* (1906) was a noticeably different volume, as was its successor, *Songs of Praise* (1925, 1931), which was deliberately designed to extend to all British parishes and schools. Both hymnals were joint efforts of literary editor Percy Dearmer (1867-1936) and music editor Ralph Vaughan Williams (1872-1958).

Dearmer and Vaughan Williams included hymns that were less universal and more English, textually less liturgical and more expressive of liberal theology and the social gospel—and to these texts they set a daring choice of tunes. "Christ Is the World's True Light" (600) by George Briggs (1875-1959) and "Lord of All Hopefulness" (558) by Jan Struther (1901-1953) are typical examples of Dearmer's editorial choices. But it is primarily the choice of tunes in the *English Hymnal* and its successors that make these hymnals so important. The refusal of the *Hymns Ancient and Modern* proprietors to let other groups use their copyrighted tunes contributed to Vaughan Williams's penchant for adapting English folk tunes into hymn tunes. Such arrangements as FOREST GREEN (422) and KINGSFOLD (430) first appeared in the *English Hymnal*, alongside Vaughan Williams's original tunes such as SINE NOMINE (505), RANDOLPH (316), and SALVE FESTA DIES (515). The several editions of *Songs of Praise* also featured Vaughan

Williams's KING'S WESTON (467), as well as original tunes by Martin Shaw (1875-1958): JULIUS (49), WESTRIDGE (204), and the wonderful canon PURPOSE (594).

Other important tunes from this era are those by C. Hubert Parry (1848-1918): JERUSALEM (145), LAUDATE DOMINUM (466), and RUSTINGTON (506, 532); as well as ENGELBERG (512) by Charles Stanford (1852-1924) and THORNBURY (368, 509) by Basil Harwood (1859-1949).

Although *Hymns Ancient and Modern* was losing ground by this time, it must be said that the 1916 supplement to this hymnal included the now well-known "Lift High the Cross" and its tune, CRUCIFER (373). The text of this hymn was collated from the writings of George Kitchin (1827-1912) and Michael Newbolt (1874-1956), and its uplifting tune was composed by the supplement's music editor, Sydney Nicholson (1875-1947).

Welsh Hymnody

Welsh music is rooted in a folk tradition of ballads and harpists. Early Welsh psalmody appeared in 1621, already using long meter, common meter, and variations of the 87 87 meter. The first Welsh hymnal dates from 1703. The appearance of the Methodist movement in Wales in the eighteenth century produced some great hymn texts, of which "Guide Me, O My Great Redeemer" (543) is one example of the eight hundred hymns written by William Williams (1717-1791). David Jones (1710-1777) translated the Isaac Watts hymns into Welsh, while Morgan Rhys (1716-1776) and Ann Griffiths (1776-1805) are other examples of hymn authors from this "golden age of Welsh hymnody."

More significant than Welsh hymn texts are the Welsh tunes that have become much loved among favorites—due, in part, to a number of them being included in the *English Hymnal*. These Welsh tunes are of two kinds: anonymous folk tunes and tunes by named composers. A number of the folk tunes were originally harp melodies, some of which were instrumental pieces, and some of which became ballads. This type of anonymous Welsh tune is represented in the *Psalter Hymnal* by melodies such as ASH GROVE (453), ST. DENIO (144, 460), and RHUDDLAN (591).

Among popular hymn tunes from the nineteenth century by known Welsh composers are LLANFAIR (409) by Robert Williams (1781-1821), HYFRYDOL (479, 568) by Rowland Prichard (1811-1887), ABERYSTWYTH (18, 578) by Joseph Parry (1841-1903), and EBENEZER (387) by Thomas Williams (1869-1944). Two other outstanding Welsh hymn tunes date from the early twentieth century: BLAENWERN (132, 416) by William Rowlands (1860-1937) and CWM RHONDDA (543) by John Hughes (1873-1932).

North American Hymnody: 1800-1950

by Roy Hopp and Bert Polman

The first European settlers of North America brought with them their European songbooks. The English-, Dutch-, and French-speaking colonists sang from their psalters, while the German- and Scandinavian-speaking settlers sang chorales from their hymnals. To improve congregational singing, various New England pastors and musicians in the early eighteenth century developed the "singing school," which used manuals such as John Tufts's *An Introduction to the Singing of Psalm Tunes* (1721). Such volumes included a section on the basics of music notation and an anthology of church songs. Later books in this tradition were known simply as "tunebooks" and usually included fuguing tunes and choral anthems as well as psalm and hymn tunes. By the end of the eighteenth century, hymn texts by Isaac Watts and Charles Wesley were included in these American tunebooks. Two period pieces from this era survive in most modern hymnals: the fuguing tune CORONATION (471), composed by Oliver Holden (1765-1844), who was a pastor, music teacher, and tunebook compiler; and the hymn text "I Love Your Church, O Lord" (510), written by Timothy Dwight (1752-1817), who is famous for his American revisions and editions of texts by Isaac Watts.

Southern Hymnody

One result of the singing-school tradition was the publication of tunebooks using the shape-note system. In an attempt to simplify sight-reading, tunebooks from 1802 began to use distinctive shapes such as a triangle, circle, square, or diamond to signify specific pitches; later tunebooks used seven shapes. As itinerant music teachers brought these shape-note tunebooks with them to the southern United States, they also notated the numerous folk songs of the South that earlier had thrived in oral transmission. Thus began the mixing of psalm and hymn texts with folk tunes—a practice that came to characterize the southern hymnodic repertoire. Pentatonic and modal scales are common characteristics of these tunes, many of which have been traced back to British roots, and some of which are early American originals. Some scholars refer to these southern hymns as "white spirituals."

A group of southern folk tunes including NETTLETON (486) and MORNING SONG (615) was first published in John Wyeth's *Repository of Sacred Music, Part Second,* (1813). The first truly southern shape-note hymnbook, *Kentucky Harmony*, compiled by Ananias Davisson (1816), featured SALVATION (120), and the 1820 *Supplement* to this hymnbook included DETROIT (83). HOLY MANNA (322) was published in William Moore's *The Columbian Harmony* (1825), and the famous tune NEW BRITAIN, now well associated with "Amazing Grace" (462), appeared first in another *Columbian Harmony* (1829), compiled by Benjamin Shaw and Charles Spillman. William Walker's *Southern Harmony* (1835) was one of the most successful shape-note hymnals of this era; its numerous editions included tunes such as DISTRESS (70), WONDROUS LOVE (379), and ARISE (534). BEACH

SPRING (579) was published in another popular volume, *The Sacred Harp* (1844), compiled by Benjamin White and Elisha King. Other typical tunes from this southern tradition are LAND OF REST (311) and FOUNDATION (500).

Facsimile of "Amazing Grace" (PHH 469) set for the first time to the tune NEW BRITAIN in William Walker's Southern Harmony *(1835). A facsimile edition of this "oblong" tune book was published in 1987 by the University of Kentucky Press, Louisville, Kentucky.*

Northern Hymnody

Lowell Mason (1792-1872) was the most important figure in the musical world of the northern states in the mid-nineteenth century. He is best known as the pioneer of music education in the Boston public schools, but his contribution to hymnody is also significant. Mason composed and arranged some sixteen hundred hymn tunes, compiled some eighty hymnbooks by himself or in association with others, and presided over the influential Handel & Haydn Society. He favored European models for his music, holding the opinion that most of the originally American music from singing-school tunebooks and revival hymnals was inferior. Among his popular hymn tunes are arrangements from previous sources: ANTIOCH (337), AZMON (501), and HAMBURG (384); among his enduring original tunes are OLIVET (262), RIPLEY (146), WESLEY (96) and BETHANY, associated in many hymnals with "Nearer My God to Thee."

Associated with Mason in his numerous musical activities were other musicians such as George Root, Thomas Hastings, and William Bradbury. Bradbury (1816-1868), who initially studied and sang under Mason, composed many hymn tunes for Sunday school use and published a number of Sunday school hymnals. Consequently he is sometimes called "the father of Sunday school hymnody." Currently popular examples of his work are tunes such as SOLID ROCK (183), WOODWORTH (263), AUGHTON (452), and JESUS LOVES ME (571). Bradbury's successors in producing Sunday school hymnody were Robert Lowry (1826-1899), who wrote the text and tune of "Low in the Grave Christ Lay" (396), and William Doane (1832-1915), who composed the tune TO GOD BE THE GLORY (473). A later associate of Mason was George Webb (1803-1887), whose tune WEBB became "married" to the text "Stand Up, Stand Up for Jesus" (559). One hymn text that became widely popular through use in Sunday school hymnals was "What a

Friend We Have in Jesus" (579), written by an Irish immigrant to Canada named Joseph Scriven (1819-1886).

Other important hymn texts from this era are "Holy Spirit, Truth Divine" (423) by a Unitarian hymnal editor, Samuel Longfellow (1819-1892); "O Christians, Haste" (525) by Mary Ann Thomson (1834-1923), an Episcopalian poet from Philadelphia; "God of All Ages, Whose Almighty Hand" (599) by another Episcopalian, Daniel Roberts (1841-1907); "O Master, Let Me Walk with Thee" (573) by a socially conscious Congregationalist minister, Washington Gladden (1836-1918); and "From Ocean unto Ocean" (596) by a Canadian Presbyterian editor, Robert Murray (1832-1910). Among the better-known American hymn tunes from this period are BEECHER (95) by a New York organist, John Zundel (1815-1882), and ALL SAINTS NEW (110) by another New York organist, Henry Cutler (1824-1902).

Gospel Hymns

The first American gospel hymns were created when the mid-eighteenth-century Evangelical Revival spread from England and western Europe to the United States, where it became known as the Great Awakening. In the States the revival ignited by means of numerous evangelistic camp meetings from about 1800 on. With hymn stanzas often sung by a soloist and their refrains sung by an entire assembly, these ballad-style texts focused on the call to conversion while emphasizing individualistic faith and eschatological imagery. While usually simple, the tunes often featured "catchy" refrains. One of the most popular of the early gospel hymnals was *The Christian Lyre* (1831), compiled by Joshua Leavitt, an associate of the famous evangelist Charles Finney. Leavitt stated his collection included "lighter and more songlike hymns with rippling rhythms and sometimes choruses." His volume contained the tunes ELLESDIE (171) and PLEADING SAVIOR (603) and was the first to publish James Alexander's translation "O Sacred Head, Now Wounded" (383).

The growing body of Sunday school hymnody, the hymns used at the large annual conventions of the Young Men's Christian Association and of the Sunday School Union, and the numerous hymns from "praise services" led by musicians such as Philip Phillips and Philip Bliss—all contributed to the rapid expansion of gospel hymns in the latter half of the nineteenth century. Bliss (1838-1876) was associated with music publishers in Chicago and Cincinnati and with evangelists such as Dwight Moody and Daniel Whittle. Bliss wrote texts such as "I Will Sing of My Redeemer" (479) and "Man of Sorrows—What A Name" (482), for which he also supplied the tune, HALLELUJAH! WHAT A SAVIOR. He also composed tunes for the texts of other authors—for example, VILLE DU HAVRE (489).

One of Bliss's many hymnals, *Gospel Songs* (1874), along with a hymnal he compiled with Ira Sankey, *Gospel Hymns and Sacred Solos* (1875), generated the collective term *gospel* for this style of evangelistic hymnody. The joint work of Bliss and Sankey (another musician associated with Moody) was followed by similarly titled later hymnals. These works also involved the work of James McGranaham (1840-1907), who composed EL

NATHAN (495), and the work of George Stebbins (1846-1945), who composed ADE-LAIDE (287). Ultimately this series culminated in two closely related works: *Gospel Hymns Nos. 1-6 Complete* (1894), a collection of 739 hymns that enjoyed immense popularity in the United States; and the equally successful British "Sankey" hymnal (1903), which contained some 1,200 gospel songs and solos! Daniel Towner (1850-1919), head of the music department at the Moody Bible Institute in Chicago, composed the popular tune TRUST AND OBEY (548) for the text "When We Walk with the Lord," written by John Sammis (1846-1919).

One of the best-known authors of gospel hymns during this era was Fanny Crosby (1820-1915), a Methodist teacher in New York who wrote well over eight thousand hymn texts. Crosby, who was blind, wrote under a variety of pseudonyms, including the name Martha J. Lankton ("Dwell in Me, O Blessed Spirit" [427]). Her typical style is represented in the *Psalter Hymnal* with "Blessed Assurance: Jesus Is Mine" (490), and more atypically with "To God Be the Glory" (473). Many of her texts were commissioned by Biglow and Main, a large church publishing company in New York, but she also supplied texts for composers such as William Bradbury, George Root, William Doane, Robert Lowry, Ira Sankey, and William Kirkpatrick. A Philadelphia Methodist, Kirkpatrick (1838-1921) was involved in compiling some one hundred gospel hymnals; his tunes range from the simple CRADLE SONG (349) to the more elaborate PRAISE JEHOVAH (188), which features the dotted rhythms characteristic of many gospel hymns.

The gospel-hymn tradition was continued in the first half of the twentieth century by musicians such as Charles Alexander and Homer Rodeheaver. Among its thousands of gospel hymns, the Rodeheaver Company published a favorite evangelical crucifix hymn: "The Old Rugged Cross." Rodeheaver employed such editors as Charles Gabriel (1856-1932), some of whose hymn tunes are paired with psalm texts in the *Psalter Hymnal* (24, 29, 94, 125, 242, 514), and Alfred Ackley (1887-1960), who wrote the text and tune of "I Serve a Risen Savior" (405). A favorite gospel hymn from this era is "Great Is Thy Faithfulness" (556), written by a Methodist pastor, Thomas Chisholm (1866-1960); the music for this text was composed by another Methodist, William Runyan (1870-1957), who was a music editor for the Hope Publishing Company. The leading southern publisher of shape-note gospel hymnody in this era was the Stamps-Baxter Music Company of Dallas. Gospel hymnody after World War II (1939-1945) became more the domain of professional singers and quartets and less a vibrant tradition for congregations.

African American Hymnody

The African slaves who were brought to the Americas since the early days of European colonization gradually became Christianized and eventually developed their own denominations and a repertoire of hymnody. Influenced textually by European hymnody and musically by some African performance traditions, African American spirituals developed in oral tradition for several centuries. The first hymnal in this tradition was *A Collection of Hymns and Spiritual Songs* (1801), compiled by Richard Allen for the African Methodist Episcopal Church.

After the American Civil War (1861-1865), African American spirituals developed in two traditions: the common style, as seen in *Slave Songs of the United States* (1867); and the concert style, as seen in concert arrangements featured by the Fisk Jubilee Singers of Nashville beginning in 1871. The concert settings became widely known by means of touring choirs, and in the twentieth century by soloists such as Marian Anderson and Paul Robeson. Vocal arrangements were composed by James and Rosamund Johnson, Clarence White, and Harry Burleigh (1866-1949), who harmonized MC KEE (540). Choral settings came from African American composers such as Robert Dett and William Dawson, as well as, later in the twentieth century, from white musicians such as Robert Shaw, Alice Parker, and Norman Luboff.

After World War II, African American spirituals were also published in mainline Protestant hymnals, often with typical hymnal-style harmonizations. The *Psalter Hymnal* includes African American spirituals such as "Lord, I Want to Be a Christian" (264), "Standing in the Need of Prayer" (265), "Let Us Break Bread Together" (304), "Go, Tell It on the Mountain" (356), "Amen" (365), "Oh, I Know the Lord Laid His Hands on Me" (367), "Were You There" (377), "He's Got the Whole World in His Hands" (457), "When Israel Was in Egypt's Land" (476), "There Is a Balm in Gilead" (494), and "Swing Low, Sweet Chariot" (617).

African American gospel hymnody, a later development emerging from the spirituals, was influenced by the blues tradition and by white gospel hymnody. The African American gospel style is both choral and congregational in local churches, and it usually incorporates keyboard and percussion instruments. Two early representatives of this style are the Philadelphia Methodist pastor Charles Tindley (1851-1933), who authored the text and tune of "Beams of Heaven" (577), and the Chicago blues and gospel composer Thomas Dorsey (1899-1993), who authored the text and arranged the music for "Precious Lord, Take My Hand" (493). "Lead Me, Guide Me" (544) by Doris Akers (b. 1922) is a more recent example of African American gospel hymnody. Through their concert tours and recordings, numerous African American gospel quartets and vocalists such as Mahalia Jackson have contributed as well to the wide appreciation of African American gospel style throughout North American.

American Hymnody into the Twentieth Century

Various American denominations issued important hymnals during the first half of the twentieth century. Several Methodist churches cooperated to publish the 1905 *Methodist Hymnal* and its 1935 successor with the same name. The Episcopal Church issued *The Hymnal* in 1916 and an authorized music edition named *The New Hymnal* in 1918; this was superseded by a distinguished volume, *The Hymnal 1940* (1943). The Presbyterian Church (USA) published its hymnbook, *The Hymnal*, in 1933. Many Southern Baptist congregations used McKinney's *Broadman Hymnal* (1940), and a variety of Lutherans used the *Common Service Book* (1917), the *American Lutheran Hymnal*

(1930), and *The Lutheran Hymnal* (1941). Some Mennonites sang from their *Church Hymnal* (1927) and *The Mennonite Hymnary* (1940), while the Christian Reformed denomination published its first *Psalter Hymnal*, the "red" book, in 1934; which first included the memorable "By the Sea of Crystal" and its tune CRYSTAL (620).

Among the beloved American hymn texts of the first half of the twentieth century are "This Is My Father's World" (436) by a Presbyterian pastor, Maltbie Babcock (1858-1901); "Where Cross the Crowded Ways of Life" (602) by Frank North (1850-1935), a Methodist minister and editor of *The Christian City*; "Let All Things Now Living" (453) by Katherine Davis (1892-1980), who is probably better known for "The Little Drummer Boy"; and "Father, We Give You Thanks, Who Planted" (314) by F. Bland Tucker (1895-1984), who contributed to *The Hymnal 1940*.

The Hymnal 1940 also reveals the work of hymnologist C. Winfred Douglas (1867-1944), some of whose harmonizations grace the *Psalter Hymnal* (342, 377, 596). Interesting in their diversity are some of the tunes from this era: HERMON (174) by Charles Pilcher (1879-1961), a Canadian; LIVING FOR JESUS (292) by C. Harold Lowden (1883-1963); IVERSON (424) by Daniel Iverson (1890-1977); and ORA LABORA (526) by T. Tertius Noble (1867-1953).

After World War II new developments such as the civil rights movement, the charismatic movement, ecological awareness, and the feminist movement stirred the North American churches' consciousness. New texts and tunes and important hymnals and supplements were issued by British and North American denominations and independent publishers. In fact, English-language hymnody throughout the entire world experienced an exciting period of rebirth and reformation after 1950 (see the next essay, "Hymnody After 1950").

Hymnody After 1950

by Bert Polman

One of the most exciting aspects of Christianity in the latter half of the twentieth century is the veritable outburst of modern Christian hymnody from all areas of the globe. The following survey introduces this new repertoire in seven categories, which, admittedly, overlap sometimes in content and may contain some terminology that will not be entirely satisfactory when more historical perspective is gained, *Deo volente*, by hymnologists in the twenty-first century who look back at this material. (For comments on contemporary psalmody and Scripture songs, see the essays "English Metrical Psalmody," p. 40; "Canticles and Other Bible Songs," p. 55; and "Christian Reformed Psalters and Hymnals," p. 97.)

1. Britain

Beginning with *Hymns Ancient and Modern Revised* (1950), Britain has witnessed a flurry of activity in producing new hymn texts and tunes and in publishing many new hymnal supplements and complete hymnals. A Congregationalist (now United Reformed) minister, Albert Bayly (1901-1984), signaled the new developments with socially conscious hymn texts such as "What Does the Lord Require" (293) and "Lord, Whose Love in Humble Service" (603). The musical editor of the *BBC Hymnal* (1951), Cyril Taylor (1907-1991), combined the musical traditions of the English cathedral, the parish church, and the public school in tunes such as ABBOT'S LEIGH (523) and MEAD HOUSE (533).

The great British hymnologist Erik Routley coined the term "English hymn renaissance" when he described the important work of three hymn authors from the 1960s onward: Fred Pratt Green (b. 1903), a Methodist minister who wrote "For the Fruits of His Creation" (455), "When in Our Music God Is Glorified" (512), and "God Is Here!" (516); Fred Kaan (b. 1926), a United Reformed Church minister who wrote "God Who Spoke in the Beginning" (277) and "Father, Help Your People" (607); and a United Reformed Church minister, Brian Wren (b. 1936), who wrote one of the finest modern "green" hymns, "Thank You, God, for Water, Soil, and Air" (437), as well as "Christ Is Alive! Let Christians Sing" (413). Routley himself (1917-1982) also belongs to this "renaissance" group: a United Reformed preacher and scholar (and one of my hymnology teachers), he has written texts such as "All Who Love and Serve Your City" and tunes such as CLIFF TOWN (129) and SHARPTHORNE (293). The numerous British hymnals and hymnal supplements of this era were the *Psalter Hymnal* sources for such texts as "'Forgive Our Sins as We Forgive'" (266) by Rosamond Herklots (1905-1987) and "We Know That Christ Is Raised" (271) by John Geyer (b. 1932), and for such tunes as LAUDS (278) by John W. Wilson (1905-1992) and EAST ACKLAM (455) by Francis Jackson (b. 1917).

A number of evangelical Anglican church leaders and musicians formed the Jubilate Group in the early 1960s to foster songs for church youth with the use of contemporary language and tunes in a popular style. Their work began with two volumes, *Youth Praise* (1966, 1969) and *Psalm Praise* (1973). More recently their efforts have included *Hymns for Today's Church* (1982), with its significant alterations in older hymn texts; *Carols for Today* (1986); and two volumes of psalmody: *Psalms for Today* (1990) and *Songs from the Psalms* (1990). The Jubilate presence in the *Psalter Hymnal* can be found in such texts as "No Weight of Gold or Silver" (374) and the much-loved "Tell Out, My Soul" (478) by Timothy Dudley-Smith (b. 1926); "How Shall They Hear the Word of God" (531) and "In Christ There Is No East or West" (540) by Michael Perry (1942-1996); and "Baptized in Water" (269) by Michael Saward (b. 1932). Various tunes by Norman Warren (b. 1934) in the *Psalter Hymnal* also represent the Jubilate repertoire: BISHOP TUCKER (30), NEW HEAVEN (236), BURNING HEART (299), and YVONNE (511).

After the wide acceptance of his *Twentieth-Century Folk Mass* (1958), Geoffrey Beaumont, an Anglican priest, joined with some friends to form the Twentieth-Century Church Light Music Group, which encouraged the use of popular-style tunes for hymnody. That style may be noted in the contemporary hymn tunes of composers such as Patrick Appleford, John Alldis, and Malcolm Williamson, and in hymn festivals broadcast by the BBC. Some of this material has been published in modern hymnals, but it is not represented in the *Psalter Hymnal*.

Hymnological study of the great range of traditional and modern British hymnody is promoted by the Hymn Society of Great Britain and Ireland through its conferences, hymn festivals, and a publication called *The Bulletin*.

2. Continental Europe

Until the time of World War II (1939-1945), Christian hymnody in continental Europe was largely dominated by romanticist traditions of singing psalms and chorales. In Germany the "standard" Lutheran hymnal, the *Evangelische Kirchengesangbuch* (1853, with numerous later revisions), witnessed the prominent return of the rhythmic chorale in mid-twentieth-century choir editions such as the *Spandauer Gesangbuch* (1963). A similar development occurred in the *Orgelbuch* (1953) of the German-speaking Swiss Reformed Church. Radical hymn texts with syncopated tunes, influenced by the songs of the postwar *Kirchentag* conventions, appear in various recent German hymnal supplements such as *Christen Lieder* (1971) and *Schalom* (1971). One of the prominent German church musicians, Heinz Werner Zimmermann (b. 1930), adopted certain jazz idioms in his church music; his hymn tunes include LAUDATE PUERI (177) and LITTLE FLOCK (366).

While metrical psalmody dominated the Netherlands since the time of the Reformation, hymns were introduced in 1806 with the *Evangelischen Gezangen* and were reaffirmed with its *Vervolgbundel* (1866). Since that time numerous Dutch hymnals have been published, often bound together with a psalter. "A Shout Rings Out, a Joyful Voice" (392), "We Come to Thank You, God, by Singing" (439), and "Hours and Days and Years and Ages" (443) are originally nineteenth-century Dutch hymns. The ecumenical *Liedboek voor de kerken* (1973) is an excellent example of a Dutch hymnal that includes not only old and new hymnody from the Netherlands along with a new psalter, but also a good selection of English hymnody translated into Dutch. Examples of modern Dutch hymnody in the *Psalter Hymnal* include "Our Faithful God" (445) by Hendrik Pierson, as well as the tunes VERGEEF, O HEER (88) by Gerben Baaij (b. 1929) and ANTHEA (301) and ROSE-MARIE (590) by Wim Mennes (1917-1996). "In the Beginning" (151) and "The Lord Is Risen Indeed" (211), with their respective tunes, IN HET BEGIN and OPGESTAAN, come from the volumes of the Dutch children's hymnal *Alles wordt nieuw* (1966, 1971).

Other important European hymnals and supplements from this era are the Hungarian Protestant *Hozsanna!* (1974) and the Swedish *Psalmer och Visor* (1975), with its fascinating biblically based hymnody. The ongoing study of European hymnody is promoted by a German-based organization called *International Arbeitsgemeinschaft für Hymnologie.*

3. United States of America

The latter half of the twentieth century also witnessed the publication of some significant hymnals in the United States. Outstanding examples from the past few decades are the *Lutheran Book of Worship* (1978), *The Hymnal 1982* (1985) of the Episcopal Church, the Christian Reformed *Psalter Hymnal* (1987), *The United Methodist Hymnal* (1989), Hope Publishing's *The Worshiping Church* (1990), *The Presbyterian Hymnal* (1990), the Southern *Baptist Hymnal* (1991), and the Brethren and Mennonite *Hymnal: A Worship Book* (1992). All of these hymnals, in greater or lesser measure, had editorial policies that favored inclusive language for human beings, and some (such as the United Methodist book) began to venture in new directions with language for God.

Some of the finest new hymn texts from the U.S. in the *Psalter Hymnal* are "Hope of the World" (524) by Georgia Harkness (1891-1974); "O God of Every Nation" (606) by William Reid, Jr. (b. 1923); and "Lord, You Give the Great Commission" (523) by Jeffrey Rowthorn (b. 1921). The important work of Carl Daw, Jr. (b. 1944), is represented in "Surely It Is God Who Saves Me" (193), while a typical text of Thomas Troeger (b. 1945) is "These Things Did Thomas Count as Real" (394), sung to the tune MERLE MARIE, composed by his publishing partner, Carol Doran (b. 1936).

Lutherans in the United States have produced outstanding texts and tunes during the past few decades. Jaroslav Vajda (b. 1919) has written hymn texts such as "Now the Silence, Now the Peace" in addition to translating texts such as "Greet Now the Swiftly Changing Year" (444). From this group of hymnodists the *Psalter Hymnal* also includes "Earth and All Stars" (433) by Herbert Brokering (b. 1926) along with its title tune by David Johnson (1922-1987); the tune FLENTGE (10), one of the many tunes composed by Carl Schalk (b. 1929); and Paul Bunjes's harmonizations of O MEIN JESU (79) and WORCESTER (168).

Two Episcopalian church musicians, Richard Dirksen (b. 1921) and David Hurd (b. 1950), produced VINEYARD HAVEN (163) and JULION (321), respectively. Various Christian Reformed authors and composers also contributed to the hymn section of the *Psalter Hymnal*: notable examples are the texts of Marie Post (1919-1990) and the tunes and musical settings of Dale Grotenhuis (b. 1931) and Roy Hopp (b. 1951).

The white gospel-song tradition in the U.S. has been carried forward by author/composers such as John W. Peterson, Ralph Carmichael, Kurt Kaiser, and William and Gloria Gaither, as is evident in evangelical hymnals such as *Hymns for the Family of God* (1976), *Praise! Our Songs and Hymns* (1979), and *Hymnal for Worship and Celebration* (1986). African American gospel style is evident in the *Psalter Hymnal* with "The Blood Will Never Lose Its Power" (552) and BLESS THE LORD (627) by Andraé Crouch (b. 1945). The wide range of modern African American hymnody may be noted in hymnal supplements such as the Episcopal *Lift Every Voice and Sing* (1981) and the United Methodists' *Songs of Zion* (1981), as well as in the full-size Roman Catholic hymnal, *Lead Me, Guide Me* (1987).

The Hymn Society in the United States and Canada has done much to promote new hymn texts and tunes in hymn contests, hymn-writing workshops, annual conventions, and its quarterly journal *The Hymn*. A selection of previously issued Hymn Society texts and tunes was republished as *Holding in Trust* (1992), while the society also initiated the publication of a text-only hymnal for devotional use called *Amazing Grace* (1994).

Three U.S. companies have encouraged new hymnody by their publishing ventures. Hope Publishing Company, under the leadership of George Shorney, issued numerous small volumes of new texts and tunes by single authors or composers and published small anthologies such as *Ecumenical Praise* (1977), *Hymnal Supplement* (1984), *Hymnal Supplement II* (1987), *100 Hymns of Hope* (1992), and *Supplement 96* (1996). G.I.A. Publications, under the leadership of Robert Batastini, is to be commended for its publication of significant Roman Catholic hymnals and collections of responsorial psalmody, and for making available the music of the ecumenical Taizé Community of France and the music of the Iona Community of Scotland, led by John Bell. Selah Publishing Company, under the direction of David Schaap, has published hymnic anthologies titled *Songs of Rejoicing* (1989) and *New Songs of Rejoicing* (1994) and has also issued single-author or -composer collections.

4. Canada and Australia

Modern Canadian hymnody is well represented in *The Hymn Book* (1971), a joint project of the Anglican and the United Church of Canada. One of Canada's finest hymn authors is Margaret Clarkson (b. 1915) who wrote "We Come, O Christ, to You" (238) and "For Your Gift of God the Spirit" (416). Frank De Vries (b. 1929), Bert Polman (b. 1945), Calvin Seerveld (b. 1930), and Bert Witvoet (b. 1934) are among Christian Reformed Canadians who contributed to the *Psalter Hymnal*. Other Canadian hymn authors whose works appear in various hymnals are Moir Waters, Herbert O'Driscoll, Walter Farquharson, and Sylvia Dunstan; a hymn tune by Graham George,

THE KING'S MAJESTY, has also been widely published. Several new Canadian hymnals are scheduled for release in the 1990's. The *Catholic Book of Worship III* (1994) and *Voices United* (1996) from the United Church of Canada will be followed by new Presbyterian and Anglican hymnals before the end of the decade.

Australian hymnody began with the import of a British Methodist hymnal in 1821. A century and a half later, the *Australian Hymn Book* (1977, also published as *With One Voice*), was a Protestant and Roman Catholic ecumenical venture that included some original Australian texts and tunes. Other Australian hymnals include *Rejoice! A Collection of Psalms, Hymns, and Spiritual Songs* (1987), the hymn book of the Presbyterian Churches of Australia, and *The Book of Worship* (1990), produced by the Reformed Churches of Australia. The modern hymn texts of the New Zealander Shirley Erena Murray are most noted for their Christian expressions of social and ecological issues.

5. Roman Catholic Hymnody

When the Second Vatican Council (1962-1965) permitted vernacular languages to be used in Roman Catholic worship and encouraged more active participation by the laity, a major shift of emphasis away from Latin led to a great outburst of new psalmody and hymnody in the Roman Catholic Church. This outburst is evident in the numerous small collections of new hymns and psalm settings that led eventually to the development of significant hymnals. Further evidence of the shift incited by Vatican II has been the eventual inclusion of Protestant hymnody into Catholic usage. (See the essay "Canticles and Other Bible Songs," p. 55, for more information on recent Roman Catholic developments.)

In Scotland, James Quinn wrote hymns such as "I Am the Holy Vine" (220) and "Forth in the Peace of Christ We Go" (323). The British *New Catholic Hymnal* (1971) featured texts such as Brian Foley's "See, Christ Was Wounded for Our Sake" (196). Another British Roman Catholic hymnal, *Praise the Lord* (1972), retained some traditional chants and responsorial psalms and canticles while encouraging the use of various Protestant hymns and new material.

Glory and Praise (latest edition 1997), the third edition of *Worship* (1985), and *Gather* (1988, 1994) are some of the best-known Roman Catholic hymnals in the United States, each one complementary in representing different musical traditions. Various publishers compete with each other in producing quarterly missals that contain the psalms and suggested hymns for each mass. One of the finest hymns from recent Roman Catholic vintage is "Gift of Finest Wheat" and its tune BICENTENNIAL (300), now published in many Protestant hymnals.

6. World Hymnody

Christianity is a worldwide religion, so its adherents sing their praise and prayer to God in numerous languages and in many different musical styles. While European and American missionary efforts initially produced Euro-American sounding hymnody from their Third World converts, indigenous church song has begun to flourish in the twentieth century. Begun in 1924 as an ecumenical hymnal for Christian students around the world, *Cantate Domino* has faithfully featured hymn texts in different languages and tunes from various countries. Its fourth edition (1974; with full music, 1980), produced by a committee that represented the Roman Catholic, Protestant, and Orthodox branches of Christianity, contained some two hundred international hymns with music.

Devoted to world peace and justice, the Iona Community (based on Iona, a small island off western Scotland) and its Wild Goose Worship Group, led by John Bell and Graham Maule, have published a series of songbooks that feature new hymn texts and often incorporate folk tunes from around the world: *Heaven Shall Not Wait* (1987), *Enemy of Apathy* (1988), *Love from Below* (1989), *Many and Great: Songs of the World Church*, Volume 1 (1990), and *Sent by the Lord: Songs of the World Church*, Volume 2 (1991).

Various recent U.S. hymnals have made a deliberate effort to include international Christian hymnody from Africa, Asia, Latin America, and Native America. Among the most successful in this endeavor are *The United Methodist Hymnal* (1989) and the Brethren and Mennonite *Hymnal: A Worship Book* (1992), though the international contents of the *Psalter Hymnal*, compiled a few years earlier, is also commendable. Three African hymns have received wide acceptance in modern hymnals: "Jesu, Jesu, Fill Us with Your Love" and its Ghanaian tune, CHEREPONI (601); "That Boy-Child of Mary" and its Malawian tune BLANTYRE (352); and "Jesus, We Love to Meet" associated with the Nigerian tune JESU A FE PADE (245). An important English source for African hymnody is *Africa Praise* (1969).

Asian hymnody is anthologized in collections such as the Chinese *Hymns of Universal Praise* (1936, 1948, 1977; English edition, 1981); the *East Asia Christian Council Hymn Book* (1962); the U.S. Methodists' *Hymns from the Four Winds* (1983); the Christian Conference of Asia's recent hymnal, *Sound the Bamboo* (1990); and the United Church of Christ in Japan hymnal, *The Hymnal 21* (1997). Chinese hymnody is evident in the *Psalter Hymnal* in the "underground church" text "Father, Long Before Creation" (464) and in the hymn "Fount of Love, Our Savior God," set to the ancient tune MAN-CHIANG-HUNG (564). The folk tune ARIRANG (229) comes from Korea, while "Here, O Lord, Your Servants Gather" (251) is an example of Japanese hymnody.

Hispanic hymnody from Spain, Latin America, and the United States is published in two United Methodist volumes called *Celebremos* (1979, 1983) and in the forthcoming Hispanic hymnals produced by the United Methodist, Episcopalian, United Church of Christ, and Presbyterian Church (USA) denominations. The Spanish "Alabaré" (234), the Ecuadorian "Te Exaltaré Mi Dios, Mi Rey" (186), the Mexican "Te Vengo a Decir" (250), and the Puerto Rican "Oh, Qué Bueno Es Jesús" (401) are select examples of Hispanic hymnody in the *Psalter Hymnal*.

The oldest Native American hymn to appear in modern hymn books is the Huron carol "'Twas in the Moon of Wintertime," while a mid-nineteenth century Dakota hymn, "Many and Great, O God," now also appears commonly in hymnals. Modern native hymnody is still scarce in mainline church hymnals, however, and was not included in the *Psalter Hymnal.* One hopes that this will change in the next generation of hymn books.

7. Praise and Worship Hymns

The "Jesus People," the charismatics, and various church renewal and growth movements have contributed to the development of a "praise and worship" tradition among modern Christians. This phenomenon spans across denominational lines and incorporates songs that are energetically performed with clapping and dancing, as well as songs that are more meditative in character. Numerous publishing companies issue this style of hymnody in songbooks and on recordings. One of the popular collections is Maranatha! Music's *Praise Chorus Book* (third edition, 1993). This music is typically sung from memory or from texts projected on a screen. In many congregations this reper-toire enriches the traditions of classic and twentieth-century hymnody; in some, however, this material has unfortunately replaced all previous traditions of congrega-tional song.

This category of hymnody includes short praise choruses and Scripture songs, many of which are "mini-hymns." Some of this repertoire features direct biblical quotations and paraphrases such as "Seek Ye First the Kingdom" (209) and "Rejoice in the Lord Always" (228). (See the essay "Canticles and Other Bible Songs" [p. 55] for more information on praise and Scripture songs.) "As the Deer" and many songs like it only allude briefly to a biblical text and should be considered praise hymns, not Scripture choruses.

"Alleluia, Alleluia! Give Thanks" (402) is one of the early charismatic hymns that has been widely published in modern hymnals. Written in a stream-of-consciousness style, "Majesty, Worship His Majesty" is another popular hymn of this genre that is finding acceptance in some mainline hymnbooks. Finally, the more recent "Jesus March" songs and hymns such as "Shine, Jesus, Shine" by Graham Kendrick are noteworthy for their orthodox evangelical texts and the enduring musical fervor of their tunes.

All through the ages the skilled writers and composers have sought not only to increase and develop the repertory of the singing congregation but to increase and develop that of the individual Christian. They have done this . . . sometimes by composing and writing new things, sometimes by reviving material long forgotten. So the Christian's faith is nourished by both new and old things. . . . [Hymnody] for people who are neither literary connoisscurs nor cultivated musicians, and what is designed to become part of their religious lives, must contain something which is already theirs, and something which is newly given.

—*Erik Routley in* The Music of Christian Hymns *(Chicago: G.I.A., 1981) p. 184.*

Christian Reformed Psalters and Hymnals

by Bert Polman and Jack Reiffer

The story of the worship-song collections of the Christian Reformed Church in North America (CRC) is one of movement from the Dutch language to English and from exclusive psalmody to both psalms and hymns. The story also moves from synodical control, which restricted worship songs to officially sanctioned psalters and hymnals to local congregational control with freedom to add to those collections. The essay on the Genevan Psalter (p. 28) covers the development of the Dutch Psalter in detail; this essay will briefly review that history and then focus on the psalters and hymnals that have been approved by Christian Reformed synods.

The Dutch Soil

The CRC was established in 1857 by Dutch immigrants who settled in Michigan and Iowa. These settlers were devout psalm singers who brought with them the 1773 version of the Dutch *Psalmen Davids,* a psalter that used all the tunes from the Calvinist Genevan Psalter (see "The Genevan Psalter," p. 28). For about two centuries after the Dutch Reformation, the forebears of these immigrants had used Peter Datheen's *Psalmboek* (1566), which was an earlier translation of the Genevan Psalter and which, for all its literary faults, had become hallowed by the memory of many Dutch martyrs who had sung from it.

John Calvin's practice of singing only the psalms was also the practice of the Dutch Reformed Churches, formalized in the church order accepted at the Synod of Dort in 1619. Those early Dutch Calvinists sang their psalms unaccompanied—and often with the help of a *voorzanger* (cantor).

Gradually, however, the modal and rhythmic characteristics of the sprightly Genevan tunes were altered into tonal patterns and into solemn *isorhythms* (in which all notes have the same time value—usually whole notes in slow tempo). One *voorzanger* reputedly took twelve minutes to sing one stanza of Psalm 68! As a means of strengthening congregational singing, by the end of the seventeenth century organ accompaniment had replaced the *voorzanger* in some Dutch churches. By the time the new translation of the psalms was introduced in the 1773 *Psalmen,* the use of organ was almost universal.

In the second half of the eighteenth century, a movement to sing hymns had arisen, and in 1805 the *Evangelischen Gezangen* were published. The enforced use of these hymns in the Dutch Reformed Church created much controversy and contributed to the Dutch Secession of 1834 (*De Afscheiding*), whereupon a number of exclusively psalm-singing seceders migrated to the American frontier and established the CRC in 1857.

The American Planting

These early immigrant congregations found strength in their isolation throughout much of the later nineteenth century. Still, they were subject to all the pressures of

Americanization—as were most other religious and ethnic minorities in the United States. Though these immigrants, as devout psalm singers, had left the Netherlands in part over the question of hymns, eventually hymns crept into the new Christian Reformed denomination as well.

In the mid-1880s a number of German-speaking Reformed congregations in Iowa and Illinois joined the denomination, and in 1888 the CRC synod approved the continued use of their liturgy and songbook, *Die Psalmen Davids zum gebrauch im den reformierten Gemeinde Ostfrieslands*. This book included not only the 150 psalms but also 355 *lieder*, or hymns.

In 1890 the True Reformed Protestant Dutch Church joined the CRC to become Classis Hackensack. This group of Reformed congregations had earlier adopted the United Presbyterian *Psalter* of 1887 and had also used 190 hymns grouped according to the fifty-two Lord's Days of the Heidelberg Catechism. These hymns came mostly from John Henry Livingstone's *Psalms and Hymns* (1789), used in the Reformed Church in America. This means that after 1890 two minority groups in the CRC were singing hymns in either German or English, while the majority of the denomination still sang only the Psalms in Dutch.

The 1912 Psalter

By the turn into the twentieth century, however, English was increasingly in use. LaGrave Avenue CRC in Grand Rapids, Michigan, was the first to organize as an English-speaking congregation in 1887, and others began to follow. Eventually the question of replacing the Dutch psalter had to be faced. The answer came in an invitation from the United Presbyterian Church, whose leaders wanted to revise their 1887 *Psalter*. (The texts actually dated back to the 1871 *Book of Psalms*; the 1887 edition had added music to the texts). They were interested in an ecumenical psalter, and they invited all other Reformed and Presbyterian denominations to join them in the effort of preparing new versifications of the psalms. The CRC, the Reformed Church in America, and six Presbyterian denominations joined in the effort. CRC ministers Johannes Groen and Henry Beets joined the committee in 1900 and in 1902, respectively. A group of versifiers met from 1897 to 1905; their work was again revised by 1909 and in 1912 it was published as the United Presbyterian *Psalter*.

The 1912 *Psalter* was to become the most widely used metrical psalter in North America during the twentieth century. It included all the psalms in 413 settings, eight doxologies, and the three Lukan canticles (Song of Mary, Song of Zechariah, Song of Simeon). Sixty-five text settings from the 1912 *Psalter* and eight versifications that were retained in 1912 from the 1887 *Psalter* have been published in the 1987 *Psalter Hymnal*, though many of the texts have been updated and revised.

Synod 1910 of the CRC permitted local use of the forthcoming *Psalter* (1912), and in 1914 synod adopted it as the first English-language songbook for the denomination. Classis Hackensack prepared its own edition, including the texts of the 190 hymns they had already been using. Presumably congregations beyond that classis also began to use those hymns, even though officially the denomination retained its tradition of singing only psalms.

The switch from the Dutch Genevan Psalter to the 1912 English *Psalter* was a dramatic change. The CRC gained a new language for worship and a whole new set of tunes for singing psalms, but it also lost a great deal. The people lost their psalm texts, well over a hundred years old, many of which were committed to memory and were important in shaping their piety. The people also lost their entire heritage of melodies, which had served them for more than 350 years and had connected them to their mother church in the Netherlands and to other immigrant Dutch communities around the world, such as Australia, Indonesia, and South Africa.

Henry Vander Werp, who had been appointed by synod as alternate to the committee, foresaw this loss and actually prepared and privately published in 1911 his own psalter, which retained many Genevan tunes as well as including some of the work of the 1912 committee. However, an overture by Classis Zeeland to approve his collection was rejected by Synod 1912, which judged that his volume was too much the work of one person.

The language change was the most basic and, in a way, the simplest change to take. However, the Presbyterian approach to metrical paraphrases of the psalms was very different from the Dutch approach. The Dutch pattern, following the French of the original Genevan Psalter, had been to keep the psalms intact, with 150 numbers for the 150 psalms. The Scottish heritage of the Presbyterians had a different practice, that of dividing the psalms into segments, and also using more than one versification of a given psalm. Following the pattern of English metrical psalmody, only a few meters, especially long meter and common meter, were employed in the various segments and duplications of the psalms in 413 song settings. In contrast, the 150 Dutch/Genevan psalm settings had a wealth of metrical stanza and rhyme structures chosen on the basis of the character of each psalm.

Probably the most profound change was melodic. Whereas the Genevan Psalter under Calvin's leadership involved not only text writers but also tune composers to form a complete psalter, the English tradition was primarily textual, without tunes "wedded" to texts. To this day, English psalters and hymnals are often printed without music, whereas Dutch (and French, German, and Hungarian) psalters and hymnals typically include the melodies. The Presbyterian committee preparing the 1912 *Psalter* was a text committee; little is known of how the tunes were chosen. Rather than being composed for the texts, the tunes were usually borrowed from typical British and American psalm and hymn tunes, many of them in long meter or common meter. Only two Genevan tunes were included in the 1912 *Psalter,* and neither was in its authentic form: GENEVAN 124 and GENEVAN 134, the famous "doxology" tune that had also become known as OLD HUNDREDTH.

The Ecumenical Flowering

By the end of World War I (1918) older members in the Christian Reformed Church had not forgotten that hymns were associated with liberalism and were, in part, responsible for the Dutch Secession of 1834. But peer pressure on the young people and the commercial promotion associated with Sunday school hymnody and gospel songs could not be ignored much longer. Further, synod had approved hymns for some segments of the church. Consequently a number of synodical committees struggled with the issues of liturgical uniformity. Finally, Synod 1928 appointed a specific committee to study the question of hymns; its members were William Heyns (chairman), Henry J. Kuiper, R. B. Kuiper, Seymour Swets, H. J. G. VanAndel, and J. M. VandeKieft. In 1930, amid strenuous debate, that committee reported in favor of hymns and submitted an initial draft of 197 hymn texts. By 1932 the church order was changed to permit the singing of "approved" hymns, and in 1934 the first Christian Reformed *Psalter Hymnal* was published.

The committee responsible for the final contents of the 1934 edition consisted of H. Denkema, J. B. Hulst, Henry J. Kuiper, Seymour Swets, H. J. G. VanAndel, and Daniel Zwier. They had surveyed some half dozen hymnals to recommend their choices of hymns, and they borrowed their title from the *Psalter Hymnal* published by the United Presbyterians in 1927.

The 1934 CRC *Psalter Hymnal*, later known as the "red" hymnal, introduced some 140 hymns of remarkably high quality to the denomination; most of these hymns were retained in the 1959 revision, and many are still found in the 1987 edition. Among them were many classics of Christian hymnody: medieval texts such as "All Glory, Laud, and Honor" (375, 376), Lutheran chorales such as "A Mighty Fortress Is Our God" (469), and Wesleyan hymns such as "Christ the Lord Is Risen Today" (388). In this first *Psalter Hymnal* the Christian Reformed denomination expressed its identity with the whole realm of Christian song and thus with ecumenical Christendom of all times and places.

The psalter section included 327 psalm versifications and settings. Most were retained from the 1912 *Psalter*, though many texts were significantly altered. In addition, thirty-five new English versifications of favorite psalms sung to Genevan tunes were prepared by Christian Reformed authors, thus restoring part of the denomination's musical heritage. Eighteen of these versifications were written by Dewey Westra, a school teacher in Detroit who keenly felt the loss of the "Dutch" psalms (that is, Genevan tunes) and who eventually cast all the psalms into English to fit the Genevan melodies. William Kuipers was responsible for another nine of these new versifications.

The restoration of those Genevan melodies, however, did not come easily. In the first printing of the "red" hymnal, these Genevan tunes were provided with rhythmic settings adapted from the original Genevan rhythms. Many older members who were pleased to have these "Dutch" psalm tunes back in the book were disappointed that they had not been set in isorhythm (all notes of equal rhythm), which is how they remembered them. Consequently Synod 1946 authorized the return of isorhythm for these tunes in future printings. Some of the harmonizations for these tunes had been "corrected" by Walter E. Buszin (a well-known Lutheran church musician who was hired for this task) in the 1939 printing, and again by Henry Bruinsma for the 1948 printing.

Thus the hymns in this "red" *Psalter Hymnal* brought an ecumenical breadth to the denomination and provided an opportunity to reintroduce the Genevan tunes. From many perspectives the book served the church well, though it is fair to point out that the overwhelming success of hymn singing contributed to the gradual erosion of psalm singing in the denomination.

After World War II (1939-1945), however, it became apparent that a revision of the *Psalter Hymnal* would be necessary. Synod 1951 appointed a revision committee, and its members were Henry Bruinsma (chairman), Marvin Baas, James DeJonge, Trena Haan, Adrian Hartog, Johanna Oranje, William Rutgers, Seymour Swets (who had served on the 1934 book), Dick VanHalsema, Dick Walters, and Henry Zylstra. After much work, including the processing of questionnaires to local churches, the committee proposed revisions to the Synod of 1956, which approved them. The new edition was to be known as the "centennial edition" to coincide with the 1957 celebration of the CRC's first hundred years. After further editorial work the new edition of the *Psalter Hymnal* was published in 1959, bound in a blue cover. That same year synod approved the preparation of a handbook to accompany this *Psalter Hymnal,* but without a staff or budget to work on it, a handbook never began.

This "blue" centennial edition contained 310 settings of the Psalms and 183 hymns. Some psalm versifications from the "red" edition (1934), which had originally been taken from the 1912 *Psalter,* were dropped or revised, and some were set to new tunes. Nine hymns were dropped from the "red" edition, and fifty more hymns were added from the rich history of Christian song. Many church members were delighted with "new" hymns such as "Praise to the Lord, the Almighty" (253), "Amazing Grace" (462), "For All the Saints" (505), and "Oh, for a Thousand Tongues to Sing" (501). The number of Genevan tunes decreased slightly, but some of them were again cast into their original rhythms.

The committee who prepared the revision spent part of their time at first on the formulation of a statement of principle for church music, adopted by Synod 1953:

Principle: The music of the church should be appropriate for worship.

1. *The music of the church should be liturgical*—In spirit, form, and content it must be a positive expression of Scripturally religious thought and feeling. It should serve the ministry of the Word.

2. *The music of the church should be beautiful*—Its religious thought or spirit should be embodied appropriately in the poetry as poetry, in the music as music, and in the blending of these in song. It should satisfy the aesthetic laws of balance, unity, variety, harmony, design, rhythm, restraint, and fitness which are the conditions of all art.

—*"Statement of Principle for Music in the Church,"* Psalter Hymnal *(Grand Rapids, Mich.: Board of Publications of the Christian Reformed Church, 1959), p. v.*

The committee elaborated on this statement of principle by articulating ten "Implications" that synod referred to the churches for study. The statement and implications provided guidance in matters of church music for the next generation.

Like its predecessor in 1934, the 1959 edition of the *Psalter Hymnal* was primarily a nineteenth-century book. The restoration of some Genevan tunes in original rhythm gave evidence of the vitality of the Genevan Psalter tradition, but the loss of those tunes for twenty years (from 1914-1934) and the multiple or partial settings of many psalms mainly to nineteenth-century tunes continued to contribute to a decline in psalm singing. Meanwhile, hymn singing was strong in a denomination that has always been known for excellent congregational singing. The greater number of hymns reflected the CRC's growing openness to the rich ecumenical heritage of Christianity.

The Multiethnic Grafting

Though initially quite comfortable in its isolation and Dutch characteristics, the Christian Reformed Church had a vision for mission beyond its own ethnic roots. By 1896 the denomination was working among the Navajo and Zuni peoples in the southwestern United States. Near the end of the twentieth century, the CRC was worshiping in eleven different languages; there are now congregations in which the membership is more African American, Asian, Hispanic, or Native American than Dutch. Thus other traditions have become grafted into the Dutch vine. That new diversity came to musical expression in the popularity of various other hymnals beyond the official *Psalter Hymnal*. As psalmody declined in all but the most recent Dutch-immigrant congregations (especially among the large number of congregations formed in Canada soon after World War II), the old issue of psalm singing versus hymn singing was replaced by the issue of the *Psalter Hymnal* versus other songbooks.

From 1970 onward, Christian Reformed leaders faced requests for more latitude and permission to sing songs beyond the "approved" repertoire found in the *Psalter Hymnal*. A change in the church order that permitted local consistorial discretion in the choice of songs beyond the *Psalter Hymnal* was finally ratified in 1975. By that time, a *Psalter Hymnal Supplement* (1974) was also available. That small collection of sixty-three songs was intended to be a guide and resource for new songs that were in common use throughout many Christian Reformed congregations. Typical of the more exploratory supplementary hymnals published during the 1960s and '70s, the *Psalter Hymnal Supplement* featured some traditional hymns as well as a number of folk settings, spirituals, and contemporary texts and tunes (some in a pop style and/or with guitar chords); also included were three psalm settings by Joseph Gelineau.

Approved by Synod 1974 for experimental use, this *Supplement* was prepared by a committee made up of Calvin Seerveld (chair), Arnold Brink, John Hamersma, Mike McGervey, Marie Post, Douglas Tjapkes, Nancy Van Halsema, Gary Warmink, and John Worst. Its first printing in 1974 merited some revisions after responses from some congregations; its second printing in 1976 contained sixty-four songs. In actuality, however, this *Supplement* received limited use, providing too little of what the churches wanted. Those who had been looking for a major increase in folk hymns found in it only a token collection; similar reactions came from those looking for hymns for urban African American congregations, for more classic Lutheran chorales and Anglican hymns, and for twentieth-century hymns and Scripture songs. The booklet could not compete with attractively marketed commercial songbooks that were flooding the market, nor with the practice of many congregations of producing their own songbooks (which were often copied illegally). In fact, one poll in 1980 showed that some 80 percent of Christian Reformed congregations were using other songbooks to comple-ment the *Psalter Hymnal,* and more than fifty different collections were in use.

In response to the growing cultural and ethnic diversity within the denomination, and acting upon a final recommendation from the Supplement Committee, Synod 1977 initiated another revision of the *Psalter Hymnal.* Chaired by Jack Van Laar, the *Psalter Hymnal* Revision Committee included Shirley Boomsma, Emily Brink, Dale Grotenhuis, John Hamersma, Anthony Hoekema, Bert Polman, Marie Post, Jack Reiffer, Verlyn Schultz, Calvin Seerveld, and Dale Topp. The *Psalter Hymnal* Revision Committee was initially responsible directly to synod, but before long it became clear that a functional relationship with the denominational publishing house was desirable. Synod approved this transition, and in 1983 Emily Brink was appointed as a full-time staff member of CRC Publications. As Music and Liturgy Editor, she served ably as the editor for the entire hymnal project, and with various members of the revision commit-tee she led a number of regional conferences to introduce proposed changes.

The contents of the new *Psalter Hymnal* were approved by Synods 1985 and 1986. After final editorial work, securing of copyrights, and tackling the challenges of producing a music book with the help of new computer technology, CRC Publications issued the current "gray" *Psalter Hymnal.* The publication date is cited as 1987, and the first copies reached the churches in spring 1988.

At the beginning of what became a ten-year project, the revision committee initiated various reviews of the "blue" book and its use, invited suggestions from the churches, and studied principles and guidelines—some of which were drawn from other denomi-nations' experiences of hymnal revision. Drawing on the 1968 Report of the Liturgical Committee with its four motifs of worship, the committee revised the Statement of Principle, which was adopted by the Synod of 1979:

> The music of the church should be appropriate for worship—that is, it should be liturgical and have aesthetic integrity. The music of worship should serve the dialogue between God and his people. It must be true to the full message of the Scriptures and reflective of biblical Christian experience. Along with the biblical motif, the music of worship should give expression to the other motifs of liturgy: the catholic, the confessional, and the pastoral. The music of worship should satisfy the aesthetic laws that are conditions of good art, such as imaginative craftsmanship and seriousness of expression. It should reflect the church at worship today and throughout the ages in ways that are relevant, enduring, festive, and dignified.

Various implications of this statement became guidelines for the committee's work; these are reflected in the "Introduction" to the *Psalter Hymnal* (pp. 11-15), which also gives an account of the criteria used to revise older psalm and hymn texts and determine the choice of new songs.

The revision committee proposed to synod that the entire psalter was essential for Reformed worship, that each psalm merited its own complete musical setting, and that the current psalm versifications (many of which dated from the 1912 United Presbyterian *Psalter*) needed thorough review and updating. Though there were some contrary opinions, synod approved the committee's recommendation. The review of psalm versifications resulted in the conviction that many psalms needed to be versified afresh. So a group of poets and several committee members formed a Poets' Workshop that included Helen Otte, Bert Polman, Marie Post, Calvin Seerveld, and Stanley Wiersma, among others, to take up the task of providing new versifications. Briefed by experts on meter, psalmody, and Hebrew imagery, these poets prepared a number of new psalm paraphrases for the new *Psalter Hymnal.* They used both the Revised Standard Version and New International Version of the Bible in their work, experimented sometimes with unrhymed verse, and received the benefit of extensive critique by members of the revision committee. The revision committee also decided that each of the 150 psalm texts should have its own tune as an aid to memorization, that these psalms should be numbered 1-150 in the new book, and that any duplicate psalm settings should be placed in a later section of the hymnal.

Influenced strongly by the various historic Christian traditions of singing canticles and other nonpsalm portions of Scripture, the revision committee resolved to include a sizable group of Bible songs in the new hymnal. An extensive search was made for paraphrases of biblical texts, and in a number of cases new versifications were prepared. Some of the duplicate psalm settings were also included in this "Bible Songs" section.

The revision of the "Hymns" section of the book proceeded along several lines. The revision committee conducted a survey of the denomination to determine current usage and solicit suggestions; a 157-page report on the survey was the subject of an editorial in *The Banner* (9/20/82). The committee reviewed the existing collection of hymns from 1957, compiled more than a thousand other hymns (both old and new) from other hymnals, and eventually grouped those deemed most desirable into topical categories. The revision committee then made final recommendations, considering such factors as usage by adults and children, duplications in theme, musical balance, and ethnic style. Task forces from Hispanic and African American Christian Reformed congregations contributed in significant ways to this process; unfortunately, attempts to get similar input from the Asian and Native American members were less successful.

The hymns were grouped into three large segments: hymns for the order of worship (following the pattern of the 1968 Liturgy Report), hymns for the seasons of the church year, and hymns on general themes (following the broad outline of the CRC's contemporary testimony, *Our World Belongs to God;* see p. 1019 of the Worship Edition). Each of these large segments had its own subcategories.

In its work the revision committee processed each of the songs through a text subcommittee and a music subcommittee. The recommendations about text revisions and number of stanzas, and the recommendations about tune and harmonization were then carefully reviewed by the committee as a whole. These "Samplers" of twenty-five songs each were tested in many congregations throughout the denomination; regional conferences worked their way through the proposed book in two large volumes; and informative articles about the new hymnal appeared in *The Banner*, the weekly magazine of the CRC. Final drafts were scrutinized by members of the board of CRC Publications, by various experts (such as John Stek and Henrietta Ten Harmsel in the case of psalm paraphrases), by the delegates to Synods 1986 and 1987, and then in the final editorial process by Emily Brink. During Synod 1988 the completion of the *Psalter Hymnal* was celebrated in a public service of dedication, and the revision committee met for the last time at a dinner given in their honor. The hymnal was also featured at the 1988 Conference on Liturgy and Music (COLAM), held at Calvin College that same summer. The many layers of review gave the denomination a large investment in the new hymnal project and helped to make approval and acceptance of the "gray" book a smooth process.

Even before the book was published, plans were being made to develop a handbook to this new *Psalter Hymnal*. Outlines and assignments were prepared, and during the next several years work began. The complexity and expense of the project, however, coupled with the press of other publishing work at hand, put the handbook project on the back burner several times throughout the following ten years.

Though other hymnals will continue to be used by segments of the Christian Reformed Church, the *Psalter Hymnal* is the main songbook of the denomination. The history of the *Psalter Hymnal* reveals the denomination's respect for its Dutch roots in American soil as well as its willingness to identify with the ecumenical church that transcends temporary divisions of race, culture, and era. As the preface to the "gray" *Psalter Hymnal* states,

> In this edition we present several new songs as our particular gift to the church. We see Christ's kingdom growing across the earth, and we join our voices in praise to God with those far away in place as well as in time.

Thus the *Psalter Hymnal* contributes to the song of the Christian church and reveals how other cultural and ethnic traditions are grafted into a musical repertoire of praise and prayer to God.

* * * * * * *

Postscript by 1987 *Psalter Hymnal* Editor Emily Brink

Several aspects of preparing the 1987 *Psalter Hymnal* were especially memorable. The revision committee grew to know and love each other well during ten years of long meetings. Every member gave readily of their time and energy throughout the process. They grew immensely in knowledge of the rich legacy of psalms and hymns, texts and tunes—gifts to the church from saints throughout the ages. Most of all, the committee members grew in discerning the high calling of their task and in understanding the importance of what and how Christians sing together in public worship. Calvin Seerveld has called his work on the revision committee the most important work of his life.

Here is an inside look at a few areas that were part of the process of preparing the 1987 *Psalter Hymnal:*

The Psalm Question

The issue that took the most energy was whether to retain the complete psalter, and if so, how to revise that large portion of the 1959 *Psalter Hymnal* (310 of 493 songs). One of the first decisions the committee made was to seek help from two theologians to make presentations on a wide range of issues regarding psalm singing as New Testament Christians in the late twentieth century: John Stek, professor of Old Testament at Calvin Theological Seminary and a member of the Committee on Bible Translation (New International Version); and Ford Lewis Battles, a Calvin scholar recently appointed to the Calvin Theological Seminary faculty and a member of the committee that produced *The Hymnal of the United Church of Christ* (1974). The committee reached agreement that "each psalm should normally have one complete musical setting—that is, a whole psalm set to a single tune. There should be an express reason for more than one musical setting of the same verses. Certainly, no more than two versifications of the same verses should be included" (Meeting 5, Art. 5; May 12-13, 1978).

However, following discussions at the July 1979 Conference on Liturgy and Music about the current practice of psalm singing in the Christian Reformed Church, the committee reopened the question of including all the psalms. On January 4, 1980, the committee hosted a public forum at Calvin Theological Seminary on the question "Should We Sing All the Psalms?" Howard Hageman of the Reformed Church in America's New Brunswick Theological Seminary, Andrew Kuyvenhoven, then editor of *The Banner,* and Marlin Van Elderen, then editor at Eerdmans Publishing Company, each presented position papers. A panel discussion followed. One hundred sixteen people were present. The following day the committee spent more time with Hageman, who was chair of the RCA Subcommittee on Hymnbooks. The committee, appointed in 1968, was then beginning work on the RCA hymnbook *Rejoice in the Lord,* released in 1985. Earlier correspondence had revealed that a joint hymnal project was unfeasible, partly over the issue of psalmody.

The committee maintained its commitment to retain the four-hundred-year-old Reformed tradition of a complete metrical psalter, but they were convinced that new versifications were needed. Although new Bible translations in contemporary English were becoming available, few complete contemporary metrical psalm texts were available. Synod approved the committee's request "to hold two workshops for the composition of new songs . . . [to] focus on the versification of certain psalms to be used with Genevan tunes" (*Acts of Synod 1978,* p. 473). That decision was significant, resulting in the formation of the Poets' Workshop and eventually an essentially new metrical psalter of remarkably high and even quality.

Ethnic Task Forces

The *Psalter Hymnal* was one of the first denominational hymnals to conscientiously include congregational songs from beyond the Anglo-European heritage of congregational song. Four consultants were appointed to gather task forces to prepare recommendations for songs from African American, Asian, Hispanic, and Native American sources. Millie Kurley was appointed for music from Native American traditions; Charles Park for Asian traditions; Donald Sherow for African American music; and Dante Venegas for music from Hispanic traditions.

Millie Kurley, writing on June 7, 1984, from the Christian Education Office of the Christian Reformed Indian Churches at Rehoboth, New Mexico, told of her disappointment in not submitting any songs; the response of the elders of her community was "overwhelmingly negative." The 1959 edition of the *Psalter Hymnal* had been translated into Navajo, which satisfied the needs of the Navajo Christian Reformed churches up until that point. Charles Park, a Korean from California, submitted a short list of possible songs, one of which was the suggestion that the committee provide new words for the Korean folk tune ARIRANG (229).

The African American task force prepared a substantial list of recommendations. Don Sherow, then pastor of Madison Avenue Christian Reformed Church in Paterson, New Jersey, invited Clinton Ingram and Ronald and Elesia Foster to work with him in proposing a priority list of spirituals, hymns, and gospel songs. He presented the recommendations to the entire revision committee in the context of an evening of presentations by Rodney Alexander, Anton Armstrong, Alice Finley, and James White. The presentation dealt with considerations of theology and liturgy, style and heritage, and distinctions among spirituals, hymns, and historic and modern African American gospel music.

Similarly, the Hispanic task force came with a prioritized list of "songs universally sung in Latin American countries." Members of the task force were Pedro Aviles, Raul Gilmenez, and Dante and Jackie Venegas. They also submitted a recording of several of the songs, since the rhythmic style and instrumentation would not be evident on paper and many of the submitted songs were not notated and were well known only in oral tradition. They also made a case for including both English and Spanish texts for the songs.

Sampler Test Program

During the committee selection process, three small samplers of twenty-five songs each were prepared for testing in a number of congregations. Rather than following the initial plan to select about thirty congregations to participate, the overwhelming response from the churches resulted in a much more extensive testing program. By the time the program got underway, 192 congregations had signed up. An article in *The Banner* of May 7, 1984, indicated just how eager the churches were to be part of the process. In a November 1984 letter to a congregation, however, the committee had to urge patience: "Your congregation is #208 on the list." Each congregation on the list was to use one of the samplers for four months, fill out response forms, and then send the samplers on to the next church on the list. By exception, Calvin Theological Seminary received all three samplers and kept them throughout the trial period. The sampler program was a great learning experience for the editor, for the committee, and for the churches.

Music Typesetting Process

The process for typesetting the songs in the *Psalter Hymnal* seems very primitive from the standpoint of ten years and great advances in computer technology. During the mid-1980s the vast majority of music was typeset manually, and music software was still in its infancy. The sampler program of trial booklets was a great learning experience for the editor as well as for the churches! The first booklet used a new computer program, but the results were less than satisfactory. So the process moved to the way the majority of music was set at that time. All the music in the entire *Psalter Hymnal* was set by hand by one person, Cliff Lehman, using a retooled manual Olympia typewriter on which the letters had been replaced by the symbols needed for setting music, including note heads, stems, flags, bar lines, sharps, flats, etc. He kept one hand on the scroll bar to position the bar precisely so that when his other hand hit the key for a quarter note head, for example, the note would be positioned exactly on a staff line or space, and not in between the line or space. His craftsmanship was impeccable.

However, all the song texts were entered on computer in order to generate the large print text-only edition of the *Psalter Hymnal,* from which the concordance could also be generated. The process was as follows: we sent Cliff "strips" of text lines that were to go between the music staves of each song. The syllables were separated with generic spacing and without hyphens. The longest syllables determined the proportional spacing that Cliff needed to set the music so that eventually each syllable would be centered under each note. After he submitted the finished music, we cut and pasted the syllables in place. The last step was adding the hyphens—one person actually pasted in every hyphen by hand! The final proofreading involved much "tweaking" of syllables that were slightly askew or of hyphens not centered precisely between the syllables. In fact, the word "skew" was used often enough in the proofing process that for our staff celebration when the *Psalter Hymnal* was finally completed, we were all given a T-shirt with the word "skew" splashed boldly askew in red ink across the front. I still have that T-shirt!

A History of Worship in the Christian Reformed Church

by Bert Polman

This article traces the development of worship practices in the Christian Reformed Church (CRC), beginning with a review of the Reformed liturgical tradition in the Netherlands and how this tradition was adapted by the early Christian Reformed immigrants in North America. This history concludes with an account of more recent worship developments in the denomination.

In the Footsteps of Datheen

The early development of the Dutch Reformed liturgy began with the work of Peter Datheen (1531-1588) one of the Dutch refugees who had settled in Frankenthal, Germany.

The early Dutch Protestants had fled persecution; the group in Frankenthal had first settled in England, and then after Queen Mary I ascended the throne in 1553, they moved again, this time to the German area along the middle Rhine region known as the Palatinate. In 1566 Datheen prepared Dutch paraphrases of the Genevan Psalter, which had been completed with French texts only four years earlier (see "The Genevan Psalter," p. 28). Datheen also translated into Dutch the church order used in the Palatinate. This church order contained not only the Heidelberg Catechism (which soon became one of the confessions of the Dutch Reformed Church) but also some liturgical materials that are known as the Palatinate Liturgy.

Like the Heidelberg Catechism, the Palatinate Liturgy was drawn up by Zacharius Ursinus and Caspar Olevianus in 1563 on the request of the Elector of the Palatinate, Frederick III, who wanted to unite the Lutherans, the Calvinists, and the Zwinglians in his domain. Consequently the Palatinate Liturgy represents a blending of various liturgical texts and traditions.

The compilers of the Palatinate Liturgy drew on the liturgy of the Dutch exile congregation in London, summarized in Marten Micron's *De Christelycke Ordinancien* (1554) and expanded in the *Forma ac Ratio* of Johannes à Lasco (1555). The Dutch liturgy from London represented Zwinglian teachings, since both Micron and à Lasco were Zwinglians who had been influenced by the teachings of continental Sacramentarians. The Calvinist strain in the Palatinate Liturgy can be traced to the *Liturgia Sacra* of Valerand Pullain (1551), used by the French Reformed refugees in London where the Dutch exiles had become familiar with it. Pullain had translated his liturgy from that of Calvin at Strasbourg, *La Forme de Prieres* (1545), which was itself based on Martin Bucer's *Grund und Ursach* (1524). The Lutheran influence on the Palatinate Liturgy came from the simple preaching service of the *Kirchenordnung* of Württemberg (1561).

The Palatinate Liturgy provided an outline for a Sunday-morning preaching service in which the sermon is preceded and followed by long prayers and one psalm is to be sung by the congregation. The second Sunday service was a teaching service that incorporated the Ten Commandments, the Apostles' Creed, and preaching on the Heidelberg Catechism. The Lord's Supper was to be administered once a month with the use of a largely didactic formulary.

Datheen translated this Palatinate Liturgy into Dutch, made some minor changes in it, and published his work in 1566 along with his Dutch Psalter. When the National Reformed Synod of Wesel adopted Datheen's *Psalmen* in 1568, the prayers and formularies from the Palatinate were also accepted for use in the Dutch Reformed congregations. The following years witnessed additional, if also minor, changes to the liturgy adapted by Datheen. The Provincial Synod of Dordrecht (1574) decreed that the Lord's Supper should be observed once every two months and that the Calvinist *votum* ("Our help . . ."—Ps. 124:8) be used at the beginning of the service. The lengthy confession of sin in the post-sermon prayer was replaced by a prayer of thanksgiving, and the sung Decalogue (Ten Commandments) shifted from the second service to the morning service. The great Synod of Dordrecht (Dort) brought an end to the formal revisions in 1619 and, in effect, "froze" any further developments to the Dutch Reformed liturgy until major revisions were undertaken in the twentieth century.

The Dutch Reformed liturgy is essentially a collection of prayers and liturgical formularies; it is not a complete order of worship, as were its Calvinian predecessors. It is thought that the skeleton nature of the early Dutch Reformed liturgy provided the minimum items of worship desired by the Zwinglians but allowed the interpolation of other acts of worship which the Calvinists may have wanted.

The following chart graphically summarizes the development of the early Dutch Reformed liturgy:

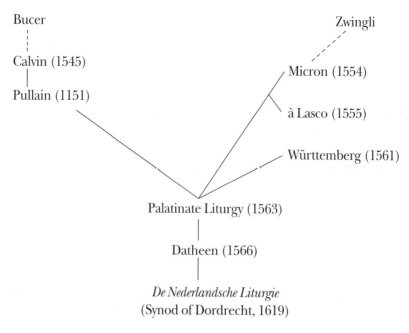

Bucer

Zwingli

Calvin (1545)

Micron (1554)

Pullain (1151)

à Lasco (1555)

Württemberg (1561)

Palatinate Liturgy (1563)

Datheen (1566)

De Nederlandsche Liturgie
(Synod of Dordrecht, 1619)

Howard Hageman aptly concludes his study of the early Dutch Reformed liturgy with these words:

> The liturgy of the Dutch church was German in origin, composed of elements drawn from the liturgies of the French church in Strasbourg, the Dutch church in London, the Lutheran church in Württemberg, woven together by a compiler whose theological cast was overwhelmingly Zwinglian.
>
> —from "The Liturgical Origins of the Reformed Churches" by Hageman in
> The Heritage of John Calvin, ed. John H. Bratt (Grand Rapids, 1973), p. 136.

And the Zwinglian pattern prevailed! The typical Dutch Reformed service of worship since the time of the Reformation is a Zwinglian preaching service from which the sacrament of the Lord's Supper and other traditional Christian rituals were largely absent. In addition, the formulary for the Lord's Supper leans strongly toward Zwingli's memorialist position. Though Calvinist in its creedal theology and its use of the psalms in worship, the Dutch Reformed Church became Zwinglian in its *orthodoxy* (that is, in its "proper manner of worship") and liturgical structures. The inherent tension between the Calvinist and Zwinglian practices of worship resulted in some struggles for the young Dutch Reformed Church. The same tension is still evident in the Christian Reformed Church today.

An Early Seventeenth-Century Service

To illustrate a local congregation's practice of psalmody and liturgy in the Dutch Reformed Church in the early seventeenth century (before the Synod of Dordrecht, 1618-1619), here follows a reconstruction of a typical Sunday-morning service (with some commentary).

As the people walk to the church, they bring their own Bible and *psalmboekje* (a small psalter, frequently bound into the same volume). As a preliminary exercise in the church sanctuary, the people join together in singing one or several psalms from the Datheen Psalter, using the corresponding Genevan melodies and rhythms. The singing is done in a strong unison, without the benefit of any organ accompaniment. A *voorzanger* (cantor or precentor—often the local school teacher) intones each of the psalms or uses a lining-out technique on the more difficult tunes. The *voorzanger* may also serve as *voorlezer* (lay-reader) by reading passages from the Bible. Some people perhaps lift their eyebrows or shake their heads as they stumble over the mismatched textual and musical accents in some of Datheen's psalm paraphrases. Neither the text nor the singing is polished, and the singing tends to slow down in places, but the people sing from the heart. At some point during the singing, the *dominee* (minister) and the elders enter the sanctuary, and at this time the service can begin properly.

That proper beginning involves the Calvinist *votum*, Psalm 124:8 ("Our help is in the name of the LORD, the Maker of heaven and earth"), and the apostolic greeting ("Grace and peace be unto you . . ."). Both are spoken by the minister. Then the minister uses Datheen's pre-sermon prayer to lead the congregation in a lengthy confession of sin. This prayer concludes with a petition for the right hearing of the preached Word and with the Lord's Prayer (possibly spoken in unison). Then follows the congregational singing of the Decalogue, after which the minister begins reading his Scripture text for the sermon and delivers his sermon. Reading and preaching constitute one single event. The minister chooses the Scripture according to the practice of *lectio continua*, preaching through a given book of the Bible.

After the sermon comes another lengthy prayer, again led by the *dominee*. This prayer consists of both thanksgiving and intercession for the needs of all Christendom. Like the first prayer, this one also concludes with the Lord's Prayer. Then the *voorzanger* takes up another psalm with the congregation, and the *dominee* concludes the service with the Aaronic benediction, Numbers 6:24-26. The people return to their homes perhaps two hours after beginning the first psalm.

Several things should be noted about this morning service. First, the liturgy consists primarily of form prayers and of preaching. The two long prayers are straight from Datheen's Dutch Reformed liturgy, while the singing of psalms by the congregation can also be understood as form prayers. Thus the prayers of this era are common prayers or corporate prayers—they are the prayers of the people, whether spoken or sung. (When the prescribed prayers are spoken only by the minister, they can still be followed by the people in their psalters.)

Second, the music of this morning service is music by all the people. There is no choir, and the organ is not used during the service. Though the singing is not without its difficulties—given the Datheen Psalter—and the singing tempo may be slower than that used originally in Calvin's Geneva, the people make a valiant attempt to sing the Genevan melodies and vibrant rhythms.

Finally, the order of the morning service is not yet totally fixed, as the preliminary singing of psalms and the initial Scripture readings are not yet integrated into the service proper. However, the order definitely indicates the preeminence of the sermon. The Lord's Supper is probably observed once every three months, appended to the typical morning service; baptism is administered as needed, and its formulary is probably used at some convenient point in the usual order of service.

From Passivity to Turmoil

Under the influence of the Pietist teachings of Jean de Labadie and his disciples, extemporaneous prayers gradually replaced the form prayers in the Dutch liturgy. By the mid-eighteenth century, free prayer had become commonplace and increasingly became the standard by which the piety of a minister was judged. Thus the spoken public prayers became entirely the domain of the clergy—they were no longer the corporate prayers of the congregation. Except for the singing of psalms, the people assumed a passive role in their worship of God. Always preaching-centered, the Dutch Reformed pattern of worship now also became preacher-centered as the *dominee* enacted most of the worship on behalf of the people—not unlike the role of the medieval Roman priest (a phenomenon to which all the Reformers had objected).

The psalm singing and Scripture readings that were part of the "preliminaries" in the early seventeenth-century service (see above) were gradually incorporated into the service proper during the next century—most often by placing the *votum* and greeting before these readings and psalms. The sermon retained its central and climactic role in the order of worship. But by the later eighteenth century the liturgical meaning of each part of the service in relation to the other parts and to the whole of the service was often spurious. For example, the Scripture reading(s) at the beginning of the service were not usually related to the sermon, and any observance of baptism or the Lord's Supper would simply be inserted into a service as a separate event. In summarizing the later eighteenth-century Dutch Reformed practices of worship, John Vriend suggests,

> The "law," for instance, appears as a floating element without any liturgical anchorage either in that which precedes or follows. Neither is there a clear logical progression, or movement, in this order. It is more a jumble of unconnected parts, held together loosely by a beginning *votum* or Salutation and a concluding Benediction.
>
> —*from "A History of Liturgy in the Christian Reformed Church" by Vriend in* Proceedings of a Conference on Liturgy and Music in Reformed Worship *(Grand Rapids, Mich.: 1979), pp. 9-10.*

A Late Eighteenth-Century Service

To illustrate a local congregation's practice of psalmody and liturgy in the Dutch Reformed Church in the late eighteenth century (after the French Revolution, 1789), here follows a reconstruction of a Sunday-morning service in which the Lord's Supper is observed (again with some commentary).

As in the previous century, the people walk to church carrying their Bibles and *psalmboekjes,* which contain the new psalm paraphrases published in 1773. An organ prelude is played, during which the people meditate or pray silently. When the *dominee* and elders enter, the service begins properly with the *votum* and the greeting, all spoken by the minister alone. Then all stand for the singing of an entire psalm. The singing is extremely slow; each stanza is begun with a "gathering note," and the organist plays *tussenspelen* (one-bar interludes) between the phrases of each stanza. After the psalm is sung—entirely in isorhythm (all tones in the same rhythm; for example, all half notes)—the *dominee* reads the Decalogue from Exodus 20 and follows this with another, though unrelated, Scripture reading. A penitential psalm is sung, and then the minister begins the "long prayer." It is a lengthy, extemporaneous prayer of confession of sin, filled with biblical quotations about human misery and humanity's hopeless condition; the prayer concludes with a petition for mercy and with brief intercessions for all humankind and for peace in the world.

After this prayer another psalm is sung, during which the deacons collect the offerings of the people. Then the *dominee* reads the Scripture text on which his sermon is based, and he delivers the sermon. As the sermon is also lengthy, he asks that the congregation sing another psalm midway. A shorter prayer of thanksgiving and another psalm bring this part of the service to a conclusion.

Then the formulary for the Lord's Supper is read by the minister from the pulpit, but he adds significantly to the "fencing of the table" by naming specific sins that prevail in the congregation. The Lord's Prayer and the Apostles' Creed, which are part of the formulary, are spoken only by the minister; the congregation is silent throughout. As most of the adult members of the congregation fear the Lord's Supper and are deeply aware of their own sin and lack of moral dignity, few actually come forward to sit down at the communion table to receive the elements. The service concludes with the reading (not singing) of Psalm 103, a prayer, and the benediction—all spoken by the minister. Then the people solemnly leave the church during an organ postlude.

A typical Dutch Reformed in the late eighteenth-century would include everything mentioned in the above description except for the observance of the Lord's Supper, which would probably occur every three months. The *dominee* established the entire liturgy by his own choice of Scripture readings, of the psalms to be sung, and by the wording of his prayers and sermon. Even the traditional formulary for the Lord's Supper might be altered at his discretion. The services were strongly didactic in tone, with much emphasis in the prayers and sermons on sin and moral righteousness.

Beyond the offering of alms, the primary liturgical act of the people was their singing of the psalms. And this they did with much fervor—even at a slow tempo. The psalms constituted their corporate worship, their ritual prayers, and no one would easily take these psalms away from them. When the nineteenth-century Dutch Reformed immigrants organized the Christian Reformed Church in North America, they sang these psalms with deep devotion and brought with them the liturgical practices described above.

Seeds of Transition

Noting the disarray of the Reformed churches after Napoleon's domination of the Netherlands, Dutch King William I reorganized the Reformed Church into a national church in 1816. The new changes in church governance, the imposed use of a collection of hymns in addition to the psalms (*Evangelische Gezangen*, 1806), and the theologically liberal trends in the Dutch church were opposed by a number of people who had been influenced by the *Reveille* or "Great Awakening" movement. The conflicts led to a formal Secession, the *Afscheiding*, in 1834, and after a disastrous potato-crop failure in 1846, a number of these Seceders left the Netherlands the following year and migrated to Michigan and Iowa in the United States. Initially these immigrants joined the Protestant Dutch Church of North America (now known as the Reformed Church in America), but in 1857 they separated again to establish what is now known as the Christian Reformed Church in North America.

Affirmation of the Dutch Tradition in North America

The new settlers and church planters found strength in their separation from the liberal church in the Netherlands but also in their isolation from American culture, for they safeguarded their ethnic heritage and language fiercely in their new homeland.

Up until World War I (1914-1918) these immigrants kept the Dutch liturgy and continued to sing the slow "Dutch" psalms.

The adoption of the English-language *Psalter* in 1914 was an important milestone in the Americanization of the Christian Reformed Church (see the essay "Christian Reformed Psalters and Hymnals," p. 97). The singing schools and church choirs in the denomination were similar products of the American environment. But it was not just the language of worship and the music that changed as the church became more American. The liturgical practices of the denomination were also influenced by the American culture and by American Christians from other denominations.

This influence was first noted officially at Synod 1916, where Classis Illinois wanted a "uniform order of service in our American-speaking churches in which the congrega-

Traditional Order (from *Acts of Synod 1928*, p. 287)	**Proposed Order** (adopted, *Acts of Synod 1928*, p. 55; rescinded in 1930)	**New Order** (permitted, *Acts of Synod 1930*, p. 187)
Votum	Votum	Psalm
Salutation	Salutation	Invocation
Psalm	Psalm	Salutation
The Law	Reading of the Law	Reading of the Law
Scripture Lesson	Confession of Sin or	Psalm of Consecration and
Psalm	Penitential Psalm (or both)	Devotion
	Absolution	
	Apostles' Creed	
	Psalm	
General Prayer	General Prayer	Prayer
Psalm with the	Offering and Psalm	Offering and Psalm
Offering	Offertory Prayer (optional)	Offertory Prayer (optional)
or following the Offering		
[Sermon Text]	Scripture Lesson	Scripture Lesson
Sermon	Sermon	Sermon
Closing Prayer	Prayer	Prayer
Psalm (and Doxology)	Psalm	Psalm
Benediction	Benediction	Benediction
	Doxology	Doxology

tion takes a more active part" (*Acts of Synod 1916*, p. 30). Synod appointed a study committee, which reported in 1918 that it recognized deficiencies in the denomination's worship life and yet affirmed a number of principles. An enlarged committee reported extensively in 1920 and proposed an order of worship for the morning service; this order of worship was clearly structured in a dialogic fashion, that is, "acts from God's side and acts from the side of God's people" were alternated in logical order. Much debate on the issue ensued during the next several years, but finally in 1928 synod adopted a revision of the "uniform order of worship" proposed in 1920. Severe protests led synod in 1930 to abolish the "absolution" section of the order and to rescind the obligation to use this new order. Instead, a modification of the traditional Dutch liturgical pattern was recommended, although its actual use was left to the discretion of local consistories. Thus ended a liturgical battle that lasted more than a decade. Synod never again adopted a compulsory order of worship.

Some crucial issues surfaced during this liturgical battle:

- It is clear that the denomination was gripped by a conservatism that declared essentially the eighteenth-century Dutch pattern of worship to be normative.
- Equally divisive was the question of whether synod had the right to establish an obligatory order of worship, and ultimately the denomination chose a congregationalist polity on liturgy and not a presbyterian one. This congregationalist trend has marked the worship life of the denomination ever since.
- The debates during the 1920s also affirmed the Zwinglian heritage of the denomination in favoring preaching as the central element of worship—there was virtually no concern for the celebration of the Lord's Supper.
- Though the various liturgy committees wanted to give a greater role to the people in worship, the dialogic structure of the liturgy was often interpreted to mean that the minister speaks for God but also speaks on behalf of the people.
- The need for liturgical education was evident not only among the common people but also among the ministers. However, the synodical debates did little to improve the understanding of liturgical principles and tended to generate more "heat" than "light."
- The various proposals and counterproposals on worship betray the catalytic influences of other American denominations but do not appear to be affected directly by the ecumenical liturgical movement of the late nineteenth and early twentieth centuries.

Toward Worship Renewal

When the Christian Reformed Church examined its liturgical practices in the 1920s, it did so under considerable pressure from its American environment, for there was a strong element in the denomination that had shed the initial desire for cultural isolation and now favored imitating the worship life of other Christian churches in North America. After the 1928 "uniform order of worship" was rejected in 1930 and the traditional Dutch liturgy prevailed, the Dutch-language prayers and liturgical formularies were translated into English and published in the first *Psalter Hymnal* (1934); later, formularies for marriage and public profession of faith were also introduced. Hymns were also included for the first time as officially accepted songs for worship in the 1934 *Psalter Hymnal.*

That first *Psalter Hymnal* introduced a large body of ecumenical hymnody into the denomination, and this phenomenon was even more prominent in the 1957 edition. It took almost another decade, however, for that ecumenical consciousness to be articulated in the general worship life of the denomination. Responding to various overtures, Synod 1964 appointed a group to serve as Liturgical Committee and gave them a wide-ranging mandate. The first members of the committee were John H. Stek (chair), Alvin L. Hoksbergen, Carl G. Kromminga, John F. Schuurmann, Calvin G. Seerveld, Lewis B. Smedes, John Vriend, and Nicholas P. Wolterstorff. In 1968, this committee presented to synod an extensive report that is now known as "the 1968 Liturgy Report"; its primary author was Lewis Smedes (the report is available in *Agenda for Synod 1968,* pp. 67-131 and in the 1974 *Psalter Hymnal Supplement*).

The report devotes many pages to a historical and principial discussion in which the dialogic structure of liturgy is reaffirmed but in which also the Lord's Supper has greater prominence as the desirable regular complement to preaching. The committee elaborated four criteria by which the church was to be guided in its worship life: the biblical motif, the catholic motif, the confessional motif, and the pastoral motif. The report also contains three "Models for the Morning Worship" and a model liturgy for the Lord's Supper. Prayers from various sources—from Chrysostom to Taizé—are included; the observance of the ecumenical church year receives a qualified commendation; and suggestions are given for singing canticles, hymns, and liturgical texts such as the *Kyrie* and the *Agnus Dei.*

In the footsteps of this significant report, the Liturgical Committee set out to revise traditional formularies and to prepare new ones for various worship acts and events. It also issued more model services with seasonal church-year emphases, and it provided a group of prayers and responsive readings of the Ten Commandments. Eventually most of these materials were published in the Christian Reformed *Service Book,* Parts 1-5 (1981), and some were incorporated into the 1987 *Psalter Hymnal.*

The position of Music and Liturgy Editor was created within CRC Publications in 1983. Emily R. Brink was appointed to that position to edit the 1987 *Psalter Hymnal.* After the completion of that project, the *Psalter Hymnal* Revision Committee was dismissed, the mandate of the Liturgical Committee was expanded to include church-music issues, and that committee was renamed. Now operating under the auspices of CRC Publications, the CRC Worship Committee has continued to prepare or revise formularies, and has begun to dialogue with other agencies of the Christian Reformed Church as well as to be consciously influenced by a liturgical consensus that is clearly ecumenical. The committee has also been instrumental in preparing several resources, including *In Life and in Death* (1992), written and compiled by Leonard Vander Zee, offering for the first time denominational materials for funerals; and *Lift Up Your Hearts:*

Resources for Planning Worship (1995) by Howard Vanderwell and Norma deWaal Malefyt, which was copublished with the Reformed Church in America.

Various studies of Christian Reformed worship from the 1970s to the early 1990s show clearly a number of diverse tendencies or patterns in the worship life of the denomination (see, for example, Chapter IV of *Church Music & Liturgy in the Christian Reformed Church of North America,* by Bert Polman, Univ. of Minnesota, 1981; and a survey of worship practices conducted by the denominational Worship Committee in 1990). Some of these developments are noted as follows:

- More congregational participation occurs in readings and prayers, but the centrality of the sermon is continued.
- Choirs, special music, and visual art such as banners are important components of worship in most congregations.
- There is a growing consciousness and celebration of the Christian year, especially in Advent and Lent, along with some interest in using the *Revised Common Lectionary.*
- Congregations are moving toward both a more joyful and more frequent celebration of the Lord's Supper.
- The second service is poorly attended, and various attempts are being made (often unsuccessfully) to alter its format to make it more attractive.
- There is greater concern for the role of children in worship, especially through the use of the Children and Worship program.
- The church-growth movement, "seeker" services, and the "praise and worship" style are making significant inroads into traditional Christian Reformed worship patterns.
- The denomination is beginning to address an educational role in worship through the journal *Reformed Worship* (beginning in 1986), through periodic regional and denomination-wide conferences on worship, and through new core courses as well as elective classes in worship at Calvin Theological Seminary.
- The diversity of worship practices is increasing not only with regard to differences in tradition between rural and urban churches or between established churches and new church plants, but also with regard to a variety of styles among congregations in the same community.
- Both the traditional and more recent liturgical forms are perceived to be "suggestions" only, for in actual practice many ministers, musicians, and local worship committees improvise their own worship materials.
- Psalmody continues to decline in the denomination.

The following assessment by John Vriend in 1979 with regard to the worship life in the Christian Reformed Church continues to be valid for a number of congregations:

New forms, revised forms, and new translations of old forms come down the conveyor belt year after year. The standing Committee on Liturgy provides us with materials and their rationale; it never imposes any action on a congregation, nor does synod. It leaves all the churches free to do as they wish. And the churches, by and large, continue to do what they have done before, though with increasing flexibility, increasing congregational participation, an increasing number of options, and ever growing diversity.

[The liturgical consciousness of the Christian Reformed Church] is of a people who were twice bitten in the Old World and somewhat unsure of themselves in the New. In the sixteenth century we were stung by the superstitions and corruptions of Rome, and in reply we exalted the gospel of justification as the thing that matters most. In the nineteenth century we were stung by the liberalism and laxity of the state-church under King William and, in reply, we exalted purity of doctrine as the thing that matters most.

The liturgical consequence of the first is that our services have one focus, the sermon; they tend to be catechetical rather than dialogic in structure, and often lack a clear climactic order. The liturgical consequence of the second is that, rather than leaving to the ministers the challenge of instruction in the sacraments and ceremonies of the church, we have insisted on the use of official forms that tend to be long, monologic, and "heavy," rather than worshipful in character.

—from "A History of Liturgy in the Christian Reformed Church" by Vriend in Proceedings of a
Conference on Liturgy and Music in Reformed Worship (Grand Rapids, 1979), pp. 13-14.

Given the declining influence of traditional Reformed worship materials, increasing ethnic and cultural diversity, and strong congregationalistic tendencies within the denomination as a whole, many Christian Reformed congregations today experience a worship life in which "everyone does what is right in their own eyes" without significant concern for denominational identification, ecumenical liturgical consensus, or application of Reformed principles to worship. Still other congregations are quite conscious of the 1968 Liturgy Report's four motives (biblical, catholic, confessional, and pastoral) as they modify the inherited Reformed patterns of worship to suit the needs of their particular ministries.

Building on the 1968 report, another major report titled "Authentic Worship in a Changing Culture" was prepared for Synod 1997 and then published separately. That report deals extensively with cultural analysis and theological reflection, and it offers pastoral guidance in the form of questions and answers on a number of issues that churches are struggling with. The leadership of the denomination will continue to be challenged by the various worship needs of the different segments of a church that is in transition from being a respected cultural institution to being a union of mission-oriented congregations. Admittedly, when worship practices venture into all different directions, some of the results are chaotic. But, equally important, the liberation from unthinking and unfeeling use of traditional, didactic liturgies presents new opportunities to achieve a worship life that honors God, employs diverse spiritual gifts, and meets the needs of people who live in a post-modern, relativistic society.

PART 2

THE PSALMS, BIBLE SONGS, AND HYMNS

PSALMS

1

How Blest Are They Who, Fearing God

A sharp contrast between the lot of the righteous and of the wicked.

Text

Psalm 1, the first of the "wisdom" psalms, directs all who enter the book of Psalms to the appropriate way to serve and worship God. In the tradition of the teachers of wisdom (also found in 34, 37, 49, 73, 112, and throughout Proverbs), this psalm sharply contrasts the results of righteousness with those of wickedness. Psalm 1 declares the blessedness of the righteous, who shun the counsel and company of the wicked (st. 1) and who meditatively review God's law (st. 2). While the righteous are blessedly secure, fruitful, and prosperous in all they do (st. 3), the wicked are as wind-blown chaff, excluded from the LORD's congregation and unable to stand in the place of judgment (st. 4). The LORD watches over the way chosen by the righteous, but the way of the wicked comes to nothing (st. 6). These two "ways" lead to such contrasting conditions not by chance or some natural law but because God is active in human affairs to protect and bless the one and denounce the other. The versification is from the 1912 *Psalter,* slightly altered and cast in plural rather than singular pronouns.

Scripture References
st. 1 = v. 1
st. 2 = v. 2
st. 3 = v. 3
st. 4 = vv. 4-5
st. 5 = v. 6

Tune

EPWORTH was composed by Charles Wesley, Jr. (b. Bristol, England, 1757; d. Marylebone, London, 1834), and was published posthumously under the tune name LOUGHTEN in the third part (1838) of Novello's *The Psalmist.* The heading there reads "Charles Wesley, arr. S. Wesley," which means that Charles's more musically accomplished brother Samuel prepared the harmonization. EPWORTH is named for Epworth in Lincolnshire, the birthplace of both John and Charles Wesley. Smooth movement in the second and third phrases complements the dramatic melodic leaps in the first and last phrases. The reflective text calls for a moderate tempo, played legato.

The Wesley brothers who composed this music were sons of the famous Methodist hymn writer Charles Wesley (PHH 267). The family was very musical, and young Charles and his brother Samuel gave private concerts at their home. Charles was a child prodigy who played the harpsichord at the age of three, although his father did not allow him to become a chorister at the Chapel Royal and discouraged him from becoming a professional musician. Charles did study organ, however, and became an accomplished organist, first at the Lock Hospital (1797-1802) and later at the Marylebone Parish Church (1817-1834). He composed some hymn tunes, anthems, voluntaries, concertos, and string quartets, and edited a new edition of his uncle John Wesley's *Sacred Harmony* in 1822.

Samuel Wesley (b. Bristol, 1766; d. London, 1837) began composing and taking organ lessons at the age of six. He was known as the finest organist of his time and composed much church music. He was also very involved in a revival in England of the music of J. S. Bach. His son Samuel Sebastian Wesley was even more influential; for more information on the Wesley family, see PHH 206 and 267.

Liturgical Use

Many occasions in Christian worship, especially with the liturgical reading of the law, and before or after sermons devoted to Christian wisdom themes.

2

MONSEY CHAPEL
♩ = 63

Wherefore Do the Nations Rage

A coronation song for God's anointed, proclaiming the new king's triumph over his enemies.

Text

This messianic psalm about Yahweh's anointed king from David's line applies both to earthly kings and to David's greatest Son, who now reigns on David's throne (Luke 1:32; Acts 13:33). In the ancient world the power of a newly crowned king was usually challenged by subject monarchs and peoples; here, too, those who would resist the reign of God's anointed conspire to throw off the

Scripture References
st. 1 = vv. 1-3
st. 2 = vv. 4-6
st. 3 = vv. 7-9
st. 4 = vv. 10-12

"chains" of God (v. 3) and of his appointed Son (vv. 7, 12). The versification is from the 1912 *Psalter,* with alterations mainly in stanzas 3 and 4. It follows the psalm's thematic structure closely: first comes the almost incredulous "Why?"—What folly funds their dreams!—(st. 1); then we hear God's laughter and rebuke (st. 2); next, the Messiah confidently announces God's imperial proclamation enthroning him (st. 3); and that calls forth a warning to the rebels to submit with joy or taste the wrath of God and his Son (st. 4). The phrase "You are my Son" (st. 3) is quoted several times in the New Testament.

Tune

Dick L.Van Halsema (b. Kentwood, MI, 1922) attended Calvin College and Seminary in Grand Rapids, Michigan; Princeton Theological Seminary in New Jersey; and Union Theological Seminary in New York City. Ordained in 1949, he served pastorates in Christian Reformed congregations in Monsey, New York; Miami, Florida; and Holland, Michigan. Home missionary-at-large and minister of evangelism for the Christian Reformed Church from 1957 to 1963, Van Halsema was president of Reformed Bible

College, Grand Rapids, from 1966 until his retirement in 1987. He was secretary of the committee that produced the 1959 *Psalter Hymnal,* and several of his hymn tunes and anthems have been published.

Van Halsema composed MONSEY CHAPEL in 1952 when he was a pastor in Monsey; the tune was first published in the 1959 *Psalter Hymnal.* When performed at a good tempo, this forceful tune corresponds well to the text. Organists should be sure to detach the many repeated tones in MONSEY CHAPEL to keep the brisk character this psalm needs.

Liturgical Use
Advent, Easter, Ascension, and other celebrations of the enthronement of the LORD's anointed.

3

O LORD, My Enemies

*A prayer for deliverance from enemies who attack in
brazen assurance that God will not lift a hand against them.*

Text

Even while threatened by many powerful enemies, the LORD's servant confesses so much confidence in the LORD's protection (st. 1) that peaceful rest and freedom from fear are possible (st. 2). The psalmist petitions God for deliverance and closes with a testimony to God's readiness and power to save, coupled with a prayer for God's blessing on the faithful (st. 3).

Scripture References
st. 1 = vv. 1-3
st. 2 = vv. 4-6
st. 3 = vv. 7-8

Paul Shuart (b. Grand Rapids, MI, 1957) versified the text in 1982 for the *Psalter Hymnal.* Educated at both Calvin College, Grand Rapids, Michigan, and Dordt College, Sioux Center, Iowa, Shuart is a composer and writer of hymns, including the fiftieth anniversary hymn text of the Reformed Bible College in Grand Rapids.

Tune

GENEVAN 3 is the first of some fourteen tunes in the *Psalter Hymnal* credited to Louis Bourgeois (b. Paris, France, c. 1510; d. Paris, 1561), who was the primary musical editor of the Genevan Psalter. In both his early and later years Bourgeois wrote French songs to entertain the rich, but in the history of church music he is known especially for his contribution to the Genevan Psalter. Apparently moving to Geneva in 1541, the same year John Calvin returned to Geneva from Strasbourg, Bourgeois served as cantor and master of the choristers at both St. Pierre and St. Gervais, which is to say he was music director there under the pastoral leadership of Calvin. Bourgeois used the choristers to teach the new psalm tunes to the congregation.

The extent of Bourgeois's involvement in the Genevan Psalter is a matter of scholarly debate. Calvin had published several partial psalters, including one in Strasbourg in 1539 and another in Geneva in 1542, with melodies by unknown composers. In 1551 another French psalter appeared in Geneva, *Eighty-three Psalms of David*, with texts by Marot and de Bèze, and with most of the melodies by Bourgeois, who supplied thirty-four original tunes and thirty-six revisions of older tunes. This edition was republished repeatedly, and later Bourgeois's tunes were incorporated into the complete Genevan Psalter (1562). However, his revision of some older tunes was not uniformly appreciated by those who were familiar with the original versions; he was actually imprisoned overnight for some of his musical arrangements but freed after Calvin's intervention. In addition to his contribution to the 1551 Psalter, Bourgeois produced a four-part harmonization of fifty psalms, published in Lyons (1547, enlarged 1554), and wrote a textbook on singing and sight-reading, *La Droit Chemin de Musique* (1550). He left Geneva in 1552 and lived in Lyons and Paris for the remainder of his life.

GENEVAN 3 was first published in the 1551 edition of the Genevan Psalter to Clement Marot's text for Psalm 3, "O Seigneur que de gens," which is sometimes used as a tune name. In the Anglo-Genevan Psalter of 1561 the tune became the setting for Psalm 122 as well and is therefore also known as OLD 122ND. In 1899 Robert Bridges chose this tune for his translation of "When Morning Gilds the Sky" (438); that combination is still found in some hymnals. In Ionian mode (major), this Genevan tune has no repetitions in its melodic structure. However, its regular rhythmic pattern helps to make it accessible; each group of three short phrases forms longer units, thereby making four long lines in the melody.

Howard J. Slenk (b. Holland, MI, 1931) provided the harmonization. Slenk received his undergraduate education from Calvin College and his Ph.D. from Ohio State University in Columbus; his dissertation was entitled *The Huguenot Psalter in the Low Countries*. He taught at Trinity Christian College in Palos Heights, Illinois, and at Calvin College from 1967 until retiring in 1995. From 1970 to 1993 Slenk served as organist and director of music at Woodlawn Christian Reformed Church in Grand Rapids. His published works include *A Well-Appointed Church Music* (1960) and various articles on Genevan psalmody, including the article on page 28.

Liturgical Use
Advent; Passion Week; whenever Christians experience or remember the hostile powers opposed to God's kingdom.

4

LORD, Hear Me When I Call to You

PHILIP
♩ = 100

An appeal to God to confirm the faith and loyalty of his servant in the face of others who are turning to false gods in a time of prolonged distress.

Text

Psalm 4 was liturgically assigned to the "director of music," probably for temple worship. It alludes to some prolonged national calamity, perhaps a drought (v. 7). The calamity has pushed the faith of many over the edge, and they are turning to whatever gods may possibly bring relief (v. 2). Such defection from the LORD also means that the divinely appointed king is rejected as having no authority. The psalmist appeals to God (st. 1), rebukes the faithless and calls them back to trust in the LORD (st. 2-4), asks God to show himself as the one from whom good comes (st. 5), and confesses joy and confidence in the LORD (st. 6-7).

Scripture References
st. 1 = v. 1
st. 2 = v. 2
st. 3 = v. 3
st. 4 = vv. 4-5
st. 5 = v. 6
st. 6 = v. 7
st. 7 = v. 8

Albertus (Bert) Witvoet (b. Joure, Friesland, the Netherlands, 1934) wrote the versification in 1983 for the *Psalter Hymnal*. Witvoet spent his childhood and youth in the Netherlands, where he developed a love for music and singing. Currently a Canadian citizen, he is a member of a Christian Reformed church in St. Catharines, Ontario. Educated at Calvin College, Grand Rapids, Michigan, and the University of Toronto, Witvoet taught English at Hamilton Christian High School, Toronto District Christian High School, and Harbord Collegiate Institute in Toronto. Since 1982 he has been editor of the weekly *Christian Courier* (previously known as *The Calvinist Contact*). He has written poetry and translated poems from Dutch into English.

Tune

Dale Grotenhuis (b. Cedar Grove, WI, 1931) composed PHILIP in 1985 for the *Psalter Hymnal*, naming it after his third son. The tune is well suited for part singing. The occasional stretching of the prevailing 2/2 meter into 3/2 supports the lament character of the tune.

Grotenhuis, a member of the *Psalter Hymnal* Revision Committee, was professor of music and director of choral music at Dordt College, Sioux Center, Iowa, from 1960 until he retired in 1994 to concentrate on composition. Educated at Calvin College; Michigan State University, Lansing; and Ohio State University, Columbus; he combined teaching with composition throughout his career and is a widely published composer of choral music. He also directed the Dordt choir in a large number of recordings, including many psalm arrangements found in the 1959 edition of the *Psalter Hymnal*.

Liturgical Use

Times when the church's faith is severely tried, when trust in the Lord is ridiculed, and when people turn from God to try to find relief elsewhere.

5

TEBBEN
♩ = 80

Hear, O LORD, My Urgent Prayer

A cry for help and comfort from God, asking that false accusers be brought to account.

Text

Offered in the morning at the temple, this prayer was probably uttered at the time of the regular morning sacrifice. Beset by false accusers who seek to destroy his standing in the community (vv. 6, 8-9), the psalmist prays to his heavenly King (st. 1) in the assurance that God abhors those who lie and do evil (st. 2). In singing this psalm, we join the psalmist in asking God to lead us in right ways (st. 3), to call accusers to account for their malicious attacks (st. 4),

Scripture References
st. 1 = vv. 1-3
st. 2 = vv. 4-6
st. 3 = vv. 7-8
st. 4 = vv. 9-10
st. 5 = vv. 11-12

and to protect all the godly who take refuge in the LORD—to their joy and God's praise (st. 5). Marie J. (Tuinstra) Post (b. Jenison, MI, 1919; d. Grand Rapids, MI, 1990) versified this psalm in 1983 for the *Psalter Hymnal.*

While attending Dutch church services as a child, Post was first introduced to the Genevan psalms, which influenced her later writings. She attended Calvin College, Grand Rapids, Michigan, where she studied with Henry Zylstra. From 1940 to 1942 she taught at the Muskegon Christian Junior High School. For over thirty years Post wrote poetry for the *Grand Rapids Press* and various church periodicals. She gave many readings of her poetry in churches and schools and has been published in a number of journals and poetry anthologies. Two important collections of her poems are *I Never Visited an Artist Before* (1977) and the posthumous *Sandals, Sails, and Saints* (1993). A member of the 1987 *Psalter Hymnal* Revision Committee, Post was a significant contributor to its array of original texts and paraphrases.

Tune

Timothy Hoekman composed TEBBEN in 1979 for the text "Take My Life and Let It Be" (288). See PHH 289 for more information on Hoekman and TEBBEN; the setting there is in a higher key.

Liturgical Use

For morning worship, for times of persecution or slander; also for commemoration of Christ's suffering at the hands of false accusers. Stanzas 1 and 5 are fitting as a choral introit or as a frame around a pastoral prayer.

6

LORD, Chasten Not in Anger

A prayer for physical healing and for deliverance from ill-wishing enemies.

Text

Psalm 6 is the first of seven psalms designated in early Christian liturgical use as penitential psalms (the others are 32, 38, 51, 102, 130, and 143). A severe illness subjects the psalmist to the unmasked glee of enemies who think to gain by his death. The psalmist prays urgently for God to lift this chastisement (st. 1), appealing for deliverance from death (st. 2), and expressing deep

Scripture References
st. 1 = vv. 1-3
st. 2 = vv. 4-5
st. 3 = vv. 6-7
st. 4 = vv. 8-10

emotional pain inflicted by the glee of his enemies (st. 3). Then follows a confession of joyful assurance that God hears and will foil the enemies' expectations (st. 4).

Clarence P. Walhout (b. Muskegon, MI, 1934) versified the text in 1982 for the *Psalter Hymnal;* he was a member of the Poets' Workshop, a group of several writers who worked on versifications for the 1987 *Psalter Hymnal.* Professor of English at his alma mater, Calvin College in Grand Rapids, Michigan, since 1969, Walhout also attended the University of Michigan in Ann Arbor and Northwestern University in Evanston, Illinois. He has been editor of the journal *Christianity and Literature* and is coauthor of *The Responsibility of Hermeneutics* (1985).

Tune

GENEVAN 6 was composed or adapted to be sung to Clement Marot's versification of Psalm 6 in the 1542 edition of the Genevan Psalter. This tune is one of the few in the Genevan Psalter to include a melisma, a syllable set to more than one note. Howard Slenk (PHH 3) harmonized the tune in 1985 for the *Psalter Hymnal.* The alternate harmonization with the melody in the tenor was composed by Claude Goudimel in 1564 as part of a collection of simple four-part settings of all the Genevan tunes. This setting is especially appropriate for choirs or for men's voices. A slow tempo is appropriate for this penitential psalm. The change in mood and address calls for a change in registration between stanzas 3 and 4.

The music of Claude Goudimel (b. Besançon, France, c. 1505; d. Lyons, France, 1572) was first published in Paris, and by 1551 he was composing harmonizations for some Genevan psalm tunes—initially for use by both Roman Catholics and Protestants. He became a Calvinist in 1557 while living in the Huguenot community in Metz. When the complete Genevan Psalter with its unison melodies was published in 1562, Goudimel began to compose various polyphonic settings of all the Genevan tunes. He actually composed three complete harmonizations of the Genevan Psalter, usually with the tune in the tenor part: simple hymn-style settings (1564), slightly more complicated harmonizations (1565), and quite elaborate, motet-like settings (1565-1566). The various Goudimel settings became popular throughout Calvinist Europe, both for domestic singing and later for use as organ harmonizations in church. Goudimel was one of the victims of the St. Bartholomew's Day massacre of Huguenots, which occurred throughout France.

Liturgical Use
Times of penitence and illness.

7

O LORD My God, from You Alone Comes Aid

The LORD's anointed asks God for deliverance from attacking enemies.

Text

Undefended by other helpers, the psalmist asks God to save him from pursuers who threaten his life (st. 1). He pleads his innocence of any wrongdoing that might warrant his violent death (st. 2) and appeals for a just judgment on his adversaries (st. 3). Confident of a righteous judgment, the psalmist describes God as a warrior and the wicked as those who give birth to evil (st. 4). The psalm concludes with a vow to thank and praise the LORD for his righteousness and deliverance (st. 5). Marie J. Post (PHH 5) wrote the versification in 1981 for the *Psalter Hymnal.*

Scripture References
st. 1 = vv. 1-2
st. 2 = vv. 3-5
st. 3 = vv. 6-9
st. 4 = vv. 10-16
st. 5 = v. 17

Tune

SO GEIBST DU (also called DRESDEN) was first published in the Dresden collection *Geist und Lehr-reiches Kirchen und Haus Buch* (1694). The complete translated title of this collection reads: "Spiritual and instructive church and house book, including familiar old Lutheran hymns (so lovely), new pure hymns—especially the Syrachis Catechism, Sunday hymns, feastday hymns, until now the formal edition of the Dresden court hymnal, for cantors and organists, with melody and figured bass. To make available for the first time for the Saxon nobility, relevant contributions of the past and with gladness to issue new hymns." The tune name SO GEIBST DU is the incipit of the 24-stanza German hymn text in that collection. Consisting of five long phrases, SO GIEBST DU is one of the more difficult melodies in the *Psalter Hymnal,* but it is surely worth the effort it may take to learn. A stately tempo works best. If the initial stanzas are performed in the manner of a prayer of petition, the vow of praise in stanza 5 merits full voice and full organ. Johann S. Bach composed the harmonization for the *Musicallisches Gesangbuch* of 1736, which he edited. He did not use this tune in any other extant works.

Johann Sebastian Bach (b. Eisenach, Germany, 1685; d. Leipzig, Germany, 1750) came from a family of musicians. He learned to play violin, organ, and harpsichord from his father and his older brother, Johann Christoph. Bach's early career developed in Arnstadt and Mühlhausen, particularly at the court of Duke Wilhelm Ernst in Weimar. During this period he composed cantatas and most of his large organ works. In 1717 Bach became director of music for Prince Leopold in Anhalt-Cöthen, for whom he composed much of his instrumental music—orchestral suites and concertos as well as *The Well-Tempered Clavier*. In 1723 he was appointed cantor of the Thomas Schule at Leipzig and director at St. Thomas and St. Nicholas churches and at the University of Leipzig. During that time he wrote his large choral works, 165 cantatas, and more compositions for organ and harpsichord. Although Bach's contribution to church music was immense and his stature as the finest composer of the Baroque era unparalleled, he composed no hymn tunes for congregational use. He did, however, harmonize many German chorales, which he used extensively in his cantatas, oratorios, and organ works. These harmonizations were published posthumously by his son Carl Phillip Emmanuel as *371 Vierstimmige Choralgesänge*.

Liturgical Use

Passion Week; occasions of persecution or personal distress when an appeal to God's righteous intervention is in order, especially when the powers of this age threaten to overwhelm God's children. Also for use in solidarity with Christians in other places who are persecuted.

8

EVENING PRAISE
♩ = 60

LORD, Our LORD, Your Glorious Name

Praise of the heavenly Creator's high majesty and of the dignity and authority God has bestowed on humanity.

Text

God's glory displayed in the heavens inspires the psalmist and us to proclaim the greatness of God's name (st. 1, refrain). So great is the LORD's name and glory "in all the earth" that praise from even the weakest members of society, infants and children, will silence God's enemies (st. 2). The starry heaven's majesty shows what puny creatures human beings are (st. 3), and yet the One who fashioned the moon and stars has also crowned humans with almost godlike glory and honor (st. 4),

Scripture References
st. 1 = v. 1
st. 2 = v. 2
st. 3 = vv. 3-4
st. 4 = vv. 4-5
st. 5 = vv. 6-8
ref. = vv. 1, 9

appointing them to authority over all creation (st. 5)—this thought evokes in the poet a wonder that refuses to be silent. New Testament writers see these divine appointments for humanity fully realized only in Jesus Christ (Heb. 2:5-9). The *Psalter Hymnal* versification is from the 1912 *Psalter.*

Tune

William Fiske Sherwin (b. Buckland, MA, 1826; d. Boston, MA, 1888) composed EVENING PRAISE (also called CHAUTAUQUA) in 1877 as the tune to Mary A. Lathbury's text "Day Is Dying in the West." The text and tune were included in the hymnal *The Calvary Selection of Spiritual Songs* (1878), and the song was sung at vespers at the Lake Chautauqua assembly in New York for more than one hundred years (see PHH 282 for information on the Chautauqua Institution).

Although he lacked much formal education, Sherwin's interest in music prompted him to attend singing schools and to study with Lowell Mason (PHH 96) and George Webb (PHH 559). He became the music director at Pearl Street Baptist Church in Albany and a teacher at the Albany Female Seminary. Later he taught voice at the New England Conservatory of Music in Boston. In 1874 Methodist Bishop John H. Vincent, founder of the Chautauqua Assembly in New York State, asked Sherwin to organize and direct the Assembly's choruses. Sherwin retained that position until his death. He wrote few hymn texts but many hymn tunes and contributed to song collections such as Robert Lowry's *Bright Jewels* (1869) and Silas Vail's *Songs of Grace and Glory* (1874).

EVENING PRAISE neatly reserves its melodic climax for the final phrase of the refrain. Perform this psalm at a good tempo, with two beats per measure. Try the following for a beautiful rendition of this song: sing stanza 1 together, gather the children to sing stanza 2 (memorized ahead of time), and sing stanzas 3 and 4 unaccompanied and stanza 5 with solid accompaniment. The refrain should always be accompanied. Emily R. Brink (PHH 158) composed the descant in 1987 for the *Psalter Hymnal.* The key lends itself well to voices as well as instruments such as recorders, flutes, or violins. Just before the refrain is an option of A-C-sharp-D or, if A is too high for comfortable performance, F-sharp-E-D.

Liturgical Use

Beginning of worship; anticipation of Christ's final victory and the reign of his people with him in the new heaven and earth.

9

Wholehearted Thanksgiving to You I Will Bring

WALTHER
♩ = 76

*Praise to God as the Defender and Deliverer of his anointed
and of his people in an often hostile world.*

Text

Psalm 9 contains hints that it was originally composed by or for a king in Israel who was under attack (vv. 3-6, 13-14). Praise predominates, but it is offered in the context of a prayer for deliverance. The psalmist begins with a vow to praise the LORD for his wonders (st. 1) and quickly moves to praise of God's past defense against enemies and for their defeat (st. 2-3). The security of God's throne and God's righteous rule over the world (st. 4) and the sure refuge the LORD provides under times of attack (st. 5) prompt additional praise and stir a call for the people to honor the LORD's unfailing attention to those who rely on him (st. 6). The psalmist voices our prayer for deliverance from the threat of enemies (st. 7) and our confession that they will suffer the very evil they perpetrate against

Scripture References

st. 1	=	vv. 1-2
st. 2	=	vv. 3-4
st. 3	=	vv. 5-6
st. 4	=	vv. 7-8
st. 5	=	vv. 9-10
st. 6	=	vv. 11-12
st. 7	=	vv. 13-14
st. 8	=	vv. 15-16
st. 9	=	vv. 17-18
st. 10	=	vv. 19-20

the LORD's anointed and his people (st. 8-9). The psalm ends in triumphant hope with a prayer asking God to show the enemies how powerless and vulnerable they are before him (st. 10).

The versification (altered) is from *The Book of Psalms for Singing* (1973) produced by the Reformed Presbyterian Church in North America, a denomination that limits its congregational song to unaccompanied psalm singing.

Tune

Charles Ferdinand Wilhelm Walther (b. Langenschursdorf, Saxony, 1811; d. St. Louis, MO, 1887) was an influential Lutheran theologian and leader. He studied theology at Leipzig, was ordained in 1837, and immigrated to the United States in 1839 with other orthodox Lutherans to escape from the rationalism of the state church in Saxony. He ministered to several congregations in the St. Louis region and assisted in building the log cabin college at Alternburg, which eventually became Concordia Seminary in St. Louis. Founder of the periodical *Der Lutheraner* in 1844, Walther also helped to establish the Evangelical Lutheran Synod in 1847 (of which he was elected president, 1847-1850, 1864-1878) and was professor of theology and president of Concordia Seminary. His publishing work eventually led to the establishment of Concordia Publishing House. He wrote numerous hymn tunes and texts and in 1847 compiled *Kirchengesangbuch* for the Saxon immigrants to Missouri and Ohio.

Walther composed the tune named after him for his text "He's Risen, He's Risen, Christ Jesus, the Lord" (originally *"Erstanden, erstanden"*) an Easter hymn of eleven stanzas. It may have been written in 1860, since it was included in his biography with the title "On the First Easter Day, April 8, 1860, on the Ocean," a reference to a trip Walther took that year. The tune begins like a fanfare, giving a dramatic flair to the melody. Sing it with enthusiasm, using antiphonal performance throughout.

Liturgical Use
Celebration of God's victory over enemies; as a prayer when the church reflects on or experiences the hostility of the present evil age.

10

FLENTGE
𝅗𝅥 = 56

Why Do You Stand So Far Away, O LORD?

A prayer for God's deliverance from those who scheme and terrorize in arrogant confidence that God will do nothing to stop them.

Text
Psalm 10 is thought to have been originally the conclusion to Psalm 9 (to which it is joined in the Septuagint); together the two form an acrostic poem in which the stanzas begin with successive letters of the Hebrew alphabet. Here we find a classic description of the arrogance (st. 1-3) and malice that spout from the tongue of the wicked (st. 4-5; in the Psalms the tongue is often the most destructive weapon). We join the psalmist, who cries plaintively for God to delay no longer in delivering the weak from the wicked (st. 1, 6)—in fact, as the eternal King, to break the power of the wicked and call their sin to account (st. 8). Yet the psalm conveys a confident note of assurance: because of God's sure defense of those who look to him, the wicked, for all their defiance, will be compelled to acknowlededge their mere humanity (st. 7, 9). The *Psalter Hymnal* versification is from *The Book of Psalms for Singing* (1973).

Scripture References
st. 1 = vv. 1-2
st. 2 = vv. 3-4
st. 3 = vv. 5-6
st. 4 = vv. 7-8
st. 5 = vv. 9-11
st. 6 = vv. 12-13
st. 7 = v. 14
st. 8 = vv. 15-16
st. 9 = vv. 17-18

Tune
FLENTGE was commissioned for *Songs of Thanks and Praise: A Hymnal Supplement* (1980), where it was set to "Eternal Spirit of the Living Christ." Composer Carl Schalk named the tune after his mother's family name, which is also his middle name. FLENTGE is music for unison singing, in four long phrases, with the organ providing additional rhythmic energy at the cadences. Because of the forceful nature of this lament text, sing the tune with intensity and at a tempo that moves it along.

Carl F. Schalk (b. Des Plaines, IL, 1929) is professor of music emeritus at Concordia University, River Forest, Illinois, where he has taught since 1965. He completed graduate work at the Eastman School of Music in Rochester, New York, and at Concordia Seminary, St. Louis, Missouri. From 1952 to 1956 he taught and directed music at Zion Lutheran Church in Wausau, Wisconsin, and from 1958 to 1965 served as director of music for the International Lutheran Hour. Honored as a fellow of the Hymn Society in the United States and Canada in 1992, Schalk was editor of the *Church Music* journal (1966-1980), a member of the committee that prepared the *Lutheran Book of Worship* (1978), and a widely published composer of church music. Included in his publications are *The Roots of Hymnody in The Lutheran Church-Missouri Synod* (1965), *Key Words in Church Music* (1978), and *Luther on Music: Paradigms of Praise* (1988). His numerous hymn tunes and carols are collected in the *Carl Schalk Hymnary* (1989) and its 1991 *Supplement.*

Liturgical Use
Times when the church, as either the victim or the guilty party, reflects on social injustice.

11

The LORD Is My Strength and My Refuge

HILLCREST
♩ = 116

A ringing confession of trust in God in the face of rampant evil so forceful that no human power can bring relief.

Text

The circumstances described in Psalm 11 occur frequently in human affairs (PHH 12). God's servant is threatened by a godless and arrogantly wicked alliance, and there seems to be no standing against its power. With the moral atmosphere so poisoned and wickedness in such complete control, the psalmist's friends counsel in despair: flee to some place of rescue in the creation.

Scripture References
st. 1 = vv. 1-2
st. 2 = vv. 3-4
st. 3 = vv. 5-6
st. 4 = v. 7

But the psalmist, and all who trust in the LORD, can stand firm, unshaken in our confidence that the LORD is all the refuge we need. Our trust in God rebukes those who urge us to flee (st. 1). We counter their despair by pointing to the all-seeing LORD on the throne (st. 2), assuring them that God's just wrath will not fail to be aroused against the violent acts of the wicked (st. 3). God's love for the upright, says the psalmist, will hold them secure (st. 4). Clarence P. Walhout (PHH 6) versified this psalm in 1983 for the *Psalter Hymnal.*

Tune

Roy Allen Hopp (b. Sheboygan, WI, 1951) composed HILLCREST for this text in 1984; it
was first sung in Denver, Colorado, by the choir and orchestra of Hillcrest Christian
Reformed Church on June 2, 1985. HILLCREST has the "stretched" cadence patterns
that are characteristic of Hopp's tunes; four-part singing or organ accompaniment
must keep the rhythmic energy moving through these cadences with their delightful
harmonies. Try to feel one broad beat per measure.

Hopp attended Calvin College, Grand Rapids, Michigan; Michigan State University;
and Concordia Teachers College, River Forest, Illinois. He has taught in the Christian
school systems in Grandville, Michigan, and Grand Rapids, and served as choir director
in Christian Reformed and Reformed congregations in Colorado and Michigan, most
recently at the Woodlawn Christian Reformed Church in Grand Rapids. Hopp also has
been involved in recording and music typesetting projects for CRC Publications.
Several of his anthems have been published, and his hymn tunes are collected in the
Roy Hopp Hymnary (1990). His oratorio "The House of the Lord" premiered in 1996,
sung by the Calvin College Oratorio Society.

Liturgical Use

Occasions when wickedness is especially rampant in the world or in a particular
community, and when human resources falter or fail, and only God can provide refuge.

12

GENEVAN 12
♩ = 66

Help, LORD, for Those Who Love Your Truth

*A prayer of the godly when oppressed by the arrogant wicked, who have
grown so powerful that they shape and control the social order.*

Text

The circumstances out of which Psalm 12 arises are not uncommon in human history. Whereas Psalm 11 features an individual
professing confidence in the LORD's protection against wicked,
formidable powers, Psalm 12 uses the voice of the oppressed (v.
7). We stand with the oppressed to ask God for help in a time
when the whole social order has become morally corrupt (st. 1),
to ask God to execute due penalties on the arrogant wicked (st. 2), to hear a reassuring
word from the divine Protector (st. 3), and to respond with confidence that God's
promised protection will not fail (st. 4). Marie J. Post (PHH 5) versified this psalm in
1983 for the *Psalter Hymnal*.

Scripture References
st. 1 = vv. 1-2
st. 2 = vv. 3-4
st. 3 = v. 5
st. 4 – vv. 6-8

Tune

GENEVAN 12 first appeared in the 1551 Genevan Psalter and has thus been attributed to Louis Bourgeois (PHH 3), music editor for the 1551 edition. It is also known as DONNE SECOURS, the first two words of the French text for Psalm 12. The tune is included in many English-language hymnals because of its frequent association with the well-known 1954 text "Hope of the World" (524). Composed in the Dorian mode, this Genevan tune has four phrases and two main rhythmic patterns: one for lines 1 and 3 and another for lines 2 and 4. Howard Slenk (PHH 3) harmonized GENEVAN 12 in 1985 for the *Psalter Hymnal.*

Liturgical Use

Any occasion of oppression in the world when God's people want to cry out to the Lord for justice.

13

How Long Will You Forget Me, LORD

THE CHURCH'S DESOLATION
♩ = 72

An anguished prayer asking God to restore the psalmist from a prolonged, serious illness that encourages enemies to gloat over the prospect of his death.

Text

This lament appears to rise from a time of serious illness that could lead to death (v. 3). In singing it, we take on our lips the prayer of an anguished, impatient psalmist who has waited long for God to restore health and vigor and thus deliver him from the gloating of his enemies (st. 1), and who prays for restoration lest death come and the enemies triumph (st. 2). In closing, we profess confidence in God's restoring power and vow to praise the LORD for his goodness (st. 3). Marie J. Post (PHH 5) versified Psalm 13 in 1982 for the *Psalter Hymnal.*

Scripture References
st. 1 = vv. 1-2
st. 2 = vv. 3-4
st. 3 = vv. 5-6

Tune

J. T. White composed THE CHURCH'S DESOLATION in 1844 for *The Sacred Harp* (1844), edited by B. F. White and E. J. King. There it became a setting for the text "Well May Thy Servants Mourn, My God, the Church's Desolation." Suitably plaintive for the text, this tune is reminiscent of other white spirituals from the southeastern United States. The melody was originally in the tenor and set to shape notes, an alternative style of tune writing used in several nineteenth-century tune books such as *The Sacred Harp.* THE CHURCH'S DESOLATION was originally in four lines; the *Psalter Hymnal* Revision

Committee omitted the repeat of the first line to fit the tune to the text for Psalm 13. Dale Grotenhuis (PHH 4) harmonized the tune in 1986 for the *Psalter Hymnal.*

Liturgical Use
Times when God's people are weakened by sickness or other distresses and opposing forces gloat over their vulnerability.

14

The Foolish in Their Hearts Deny

Denouncing the folly of those who deal with God's people as if there were no God.

Text

Psalm 14 (= Psalm 53) springs from a time when the many godless run roughshod over the few who walk humbly with God. The psalmist's lyrics refer to the godless as fools because they act as if there were no God to call them to account; yet God sees their folly (st. 1) and their God-defying oppression of his people (st. 2).

Scripture References
st. 1 = vv. 1-2
st. 2 = vv. 3-4
st. 3 = vv. 5-7

Confident that the LORD will expose such foolishness, the psalmist voices our prayer for the early deliverance of God's people and anticipates the time of their restoration and joy (st. 3). Marie J. Post (PHH 5) versified this psalm in 1983 for the *Psalter Hymnal.*

Tune

Richard L. Van Oss (b. Grand Rapids, MI, 1953) composed MAPLE AVENUE in 1984 for this text; it was first sung in 1985 by the senior choir of Maple Avenue Christian Reformed Church. Intended for unison singing, this tune consists of four phrases, the fourth being a repeat of the second. The repeated phrase has in its cadence an F-natural that singers and instrumentalists will want to observe carefully to preserve the tune's minor tonality. Keep the tempo somewhat stately.

Van Oss was educated at Grand Rapids Junior College and Hope College in Holland, Michigan. He served as music director at Maple Avenue CRC (1973-1985) and since 1985 at the First Reformed Church, Holland, Michigan. Since 1975 he has been a music and classroom teacher at the Ravenna (Michigan) Elementary School. Van Oss also served on the committee that compiled the children's hymnal *Songs for LiFE* (1994).

Liturgical Use
Occasions in which the church suffers from or laments the folly of unbelievers who act toward God's people as if God is dead.

15

LORD, Who Are They That May Dwell

STELLA CARMEL
$\downarrow$ = 92

A call to self-examination on the part of all who wish access to the presence of God.

Text

Though the details of temple worship are largely unknown, Psalm 15 may have served as part of an entrance liturgy. The song reminds all who would worship at the temple that entrance into God's presence requires self-examination (st. 1) and cannot be purchased with sacrifices; only those whose lives conform to God's moral law will be received by God (st. 2-4) and will be blessed with God's unfailing care (st. 5).

Scripture References
st. 1 = v. 1
st. 2 = vv. 2-3
st. 3 = vv. 3-4a
st. 4 = vv. 4b-5
st. 5 = vv. 1, 5

The unrhymed versification by James E. Seddon (b. Ormskirk, Lancashire, England, 1915; d. London, England, 1983) was first published in *Psalm Praise* (1973); in the *Psalter Hymnal* the singular "he" has been altered to "they." *Psalm Praise,* first published in England and subsequently in the United States, broke new ground in psalm singing by providing contemporary settings of the psalms and other portions of Scripture.

Seddon received his musical training at the London College of Music and Trinity College in London and his theological training at the Bible Churchmen's Theological College (now Trinity College) in Bristol. He served various Anglican parishes in England from 1939 to 1945 as well as from 1967 to 1980. Seddon was a missionary in Morocco from 1945 to 1955 and the home secretary for the Bible Churchmen's Missionary Society from 1955 to 1967. Many of his thirty hymns are based on missionary themes; he wrote some in Arabic while he lived in Morocco. Seddon joined other Jubilate Group participants to produce *Psalm Praise* (1973) and *Hymns for Today's Church* (1982).

Tune

Norman L. Warren (b. London, England, 1934) composed STELLA CARMEL in 1971 for Seddon's text; it was also first published in *Psalm Praise.* The tune consists of four phrases connected by cadential harmonies that help keep alive the song's rhythmic energy. To make clear the question-and-response structure of the text, a soloist or choir could sing stanza 1, and everyone could respond by singing stanzas 2 through 5.

Warren was educated at Dulwich College, Corpus Christi College, and Ridley Hall Theological College in Cambridge, and was ordained in the Church of England in 1961. He served as vicar of St. Paul's Church, Leamington Spa (1963-1977), rector of Morden (1977-1989), and since 1989 has been archdeacon of Rochester. His publications include *Journey into Life* (1964) and *What's the Point?* (1986). Warren was a member of the Jubilate Group committees that published *Psalm Praise* (1973) and *Hymns for Today's Church* (1982). He has composed over one hundred hymn tunes.

Liturgical Use
Beginning of worship; during service of confession and forgiveness; exposition on the lifestyle acceptable to God.

16

MEPHIBOSHETH
♩ = 88

Protect Me, God: I Trust in You

A prayer asking God to preserve the psalmist's life, coupled with a ringing confession of why he looks to the LORD.

Text

Like many psalm prayers, Psalm 16 includes a short petition to God, a lengthy declaration of trust and delight in the LORD, and gratitude for his many blessings. This psalm seems to arise out of some unspecified threat to the author's life—probably an illness, since no enemies are mentioned. Our voices join with the psalmist in a short prayer for protection and a confession of trust in the LORD (st. 1). Then we declare solidarity with God's people and repudiate all other gods and pagan ways (st. 2), acknowledging

Scripture References
st. 1 = vv. 1-2
st. 2 = vv. 3-4
st. 3 = vv. 5-6
st. 4 = vv. 7-8
st. 5 = vv. 9-10
st. 6 = v. 11

that the LORD has provided a secure and abundant source of all that blesses life (st. 3). The psalmist helps us gratefully rely only on the LORD as the One who assures life (st. 4)—even from the power of death (st. 5)—and who counsels in the way that leads to eternal joy in God's presence (st. 6). Michael John Saward (b. Blackheath, Kent, England, 1932) wrote this versification in 1970. It was commissioned for and first published in *Psalm Praise* (1973; see PHH 15).

Saward is residentiary Canon of St. Paul's Cathedral, London, and is a church commissioner and member of the general synod of the Church of England. Educated at Eltham College, Bristol University, and Tyndale Hall, he was ordained in the Church of England in 1956. Saward served in several congregations and was radio and television officer for the Church Information Office (1967-1972). His publications include *Leisure* (1963), *Couldn't Care Less* (1966), *Don't Miss the Party* (1974), and *All Change* (1983). Associated with the Jubilate Group for a number of years, he has written some sixty hymns and served as text editor for *Hymns for Today's Church* (1982).

Tune

Christian T. Strover (b. Colchester, Essex, England, 1932) wrote MEPHIBOSHETH for this text in 1973. He explains the naming of the tune as follows: "Mephibosheth, a son of Saul, was lame in both feet. He was welcomed by David and lived in his house and fed at his table. The prayer of the song is appropriately illustrated in David's care and provision." Filled with rhythmic interest and a tender character, MEPHIBOSHETH repeats the first part of the psalm's prayer (v. 1) in its refrain. The unison melody requires a strong solo stop on the organ, with lighter accompaniment. A solo voice or choir could sing the stanzas, and everyone could join in on the refrain. Guitar and string bass accompaniment is also very appropriate.

Strover received the B.Litt. and M.A. degrees from Hertford College in Oxford, England. He is director of music at Emmanuel School and organist and choirmaster at Christ Church in Beckenham, Kent, England. He has composed and arranged a number of hymn tunes, some of which appeared in *Psalm Praise* (1973).

Liturgical Use
When the Christian appeals to God for protection and expresses confidence in God's care; especially appropriate for Easter and for profession of faith.

17

LORD, Listen to My Righteous Plea

BERNARD
♩ = 96

An appeal for deliverance from ungodly foes.

Text

Psalm 17 asks God, the heavenly King and Judge, to protect his faithful servant from the unprovoked attacks of godless enemies. It appears that the enemies hope to profit from the psalmist's death or downfall, perhaps to fatten their purses with worldly wealth (v. 14), and they seem to have the power to bring him down (vv. 10-12). As in many psalms, it could be that the enemies attack the LORD's anointed with false accusations (v. 10), and the only

Scripture References
st. 1 = vv. 1-5
st. 2 = vv. 6-8
st. 3 = vv. 8-9
st. 4 = vv. 10-13
st. 5 = vv. 14-15

recourse is to call for God's righteous judgment. The psalmist appeals to God to hear his just cause (st. 1) and declares trust in God's safekeeping (st. 2). A prayer follows, in which the psalmist implores God for safe sanctuary and rescue from plotting and threatening enemies (st. 3-4) and expresses full confidence in God's provision and in the believer's ultimate joy in God's presence (st. 5).

Helen Ann (Brink) Otte (b. Grand Rapids, MI, 1931) versified this psalm in 1982 for the *Psalter Hymnal.* She received her education at Calvin College, Grand Rapids, Michigan, and has worked as a teacher, proofreader, and librarian. She was a member of the Poets' Workshop that worked with the revision committee to prepare psalm versifications for the 1987 *Psalter Hymnal.* Since 1986 Otte has resided in Downs, Kansas, where she is active as a freelance writer of children's stories and dramas, some of which have been published in *Reformed Worship* under the name Helen Walter.

Tune

Jack M. Grotenhuis (b. Bellingham, WA, 1956; d. Tempe, AZ, 1983) composed BERNARD for this text in November 1983, a few weeks before he died in a traffic accident. His wife, Kathy, first used BERNARD with her choir at Second Baptist Church in Phoenix, Arizona, in February 1984. Grotenhuis's parents named the tune in honor of Bernard Haan, a close boyhood friend of Jack's. The tune consists of two very long, almost identical lines; both resolve their quarter-note rhythms into stately half notes at the cadences. The harmony invites four-part singing at a moderate tempo.

Grotenhuis studied music at Dordt College, Sioux Center, Iowa, and the University of Iowa, and taught music at Lynden Christian High School, Lynden, Washington, from 1979 to 1981. Like his father, Dale (PHH 4), his main interest was in choral music, but he also loved jazz. He had almost completed his doctoral program in choral music at the University of Arizona when he died.

Liturgical Use

Situations of threat from the enemies of God's people; remembrance of the suffering of Christ at the hands of those who falsely accused him.

18

ABERYSTWYTH
♩ = 84

How I Love You, LORD, My God

The LORD's anointed praises God for delivering him,
causing him to triumph over all who opposed his reign.

Text

Psalm 18 is also found, with minor variants, in 2 Samuel 22. Faced with a mortal threat from Saul and others who opposed his divinely appointed rule over Israel, David had cried out to God from the depths, and he was marvelously delivered. With majestic imagery David praises God's deliverance from death in answer to prayer (st. 1), God's coming to deliver with creation-shaking power (st. 2), God's heaven-descending reach that lifted David from the overwhelming flood of enemies (st. 3), and God's just ways with humankind by which he saves (st. 4). The LORD has helped and enabled David to triumph over all his foes (st. 5-6) and has extended his reign over hostile nations (st. 7). David's victories in the strength of the

Scripture References
st. 1 = vv. 1-6
st. 2 = vv. 7-15
st. 3 = vv. 16-24
st. 4 = vv. 25-28
st. 5 = vv. 29-34
st. 6 = vv. 30-42
st. 7 = vv. 43-48
st. 8 = vv. 46-50

LORD have secured his throne for generations (st. 8). Psalm 138 is a similar song of thanksgiving for the LORD's saving acts.

Ada Roeper-Boulogne (b. Haarlem, the Netherlands, 1931) chose to versify this psalm because, she says, "It portrays so well my own struggle with depression and how the LORD lifted me out of the pit and made the whole world light up for me." She first wrote the versification in 1981 in a poem of fifteen stanzas. The *Psalter Hymnal* Revision Committee asked her to write the psalm in eight stanzas, which she did in 1985. This versification was first sung on March 16, 1986, in a psalm service at Eastern Avenue Christian Reformed Church, Grand Rapids, Michigan.

Roeper-Boulogne received her elementary education at the Dutch-Chinese Christian School in Central Java, Indonesia (then the Dutch East Indies), where her father, an organist and rebuilder of organs, served as a missionary and teacher. After Japan conquered Indonesia during World War II (1942), Roeper-Boulogne's family was placed in a concentration camp and remained there until 1945. Because a teacher organized a children's choir in the camp, even there Roeper-Boulogne was not totally devoid of music. In 1946 the family returned to the Netherlands and in 1951 immigrated to St. Catharines, Ontario, Canada. Roeper-Boulogne has translated several Dutch songs and is the author of "Little Children Be Happy," which was published in *Bible Steps* (1983).

Tune

Joseph Parry (b. Merthyr Tydfil, Glamorganshire, Wales, 1841; d. Penarth, Glamorganshire, 1903) was born into a poor but musical family. Although he showed musical gifts at an early age, he was sent to work in the puddling furnaces of a steel mill at the age of nine. His family immigrated to a Welsh settlement in Danville, Pennsylvania, in 1854, where Parry later started a music school. He traveled in the United States and in Wales, performing, studying, and composing music, and he won several *Eisteddfodau* (singing competition) prizes. Parry studied at the Royal Academy of Music and at Cambridge, where part of his tuition was paid by interested community people who were eager to encourage his talent. From 1873 to 1879 he was professor of music at the Welsh University College in Aberystwyth. After establishing private schools of music in Aberystwyth and in Swansea, he was lecturer and professor of music at the University College of South Wales in Cardiff (1888-1903). Parry composed oratorios, cantatas, an opera, orchestral and chamber music, as well as some four hundred hymn tunes.

ABERYSTWYTH, Parry's best known hymn tune, was composed in 1876 and named after the Welsh seaside resort where he was teaching. It was first published in Edward Stephen's *Ail Llyfr Tonau ac Emynau* (*The Second Book of Tunes and Hymns,* 1879) as a setting for the Welsh hymn "Beth sydd i mi yn byd." Parry later joined the tune to "Jesus, Lover of My Soul" (578), and that combination has remained in most hymnals. Like many Welsh tunes, it requires firm and majestic treatment. The vivid text invites sturdy and sometimes dramatic accompaniment, especially on stanza 2. Try singing stanza 3 or 4 in harmony. For one or two of the other inner stanzas, the congregation may sing in canon when using the alternative accompaniment by Donald Busarow (opposite 17 in the hymnal). The congregation may be divided into two sections, or treble voices could begin, followed by men's voices after one measure.

Donald Busarow (b. Racine, WI, 1934) graduated from Concordia University, River Forest, Illinois, and then studied at the University of Michigan, the Cleveland Institute, and Michigan State University, where he received a Ph.D. degree. Since 1975 he has been professor of music and chair of the department of sacred music at Wittenberg University, Springfield, Ohio. He has published many hymn concertatos, anthems, and organ compositions and is well-known for his hymn festivals.

Liturgical Use
Victory celebrations commemorating God's salvation in Christ or triumphs in the Christian life.

19

GENEVAN 19
♩ = 84

The Spacious Heavens Tell

Praise of God's glory as voiced by the heavens and discerned in God's life-enriching and sweet-tasting law.

Text

Psalm 19 appears to have been fashioned as a praise offering. The author has reflected long on the "voice" of God heard in the heavenly display of God's glory and in the covenant statutes given to Israel. These statutes are the good, righteous, and pure commandments that nourish life, gladden the heart, enlighten the eyes, and are sweet to the taste. Such reflection moves the psalmist and us to voice our appreciation of God's glory proclaimed in the heavens (st. 1) and of God's law, full of choice benefits (st. 2). We then pray that neither hidden nor willful sins may alienate us from God and that God will accept our sacrifice of praise (st. 3).

Scripture References
st. 1 = vv. 1-6
st. 2 = vv. 7-11
st. 3 = vv. 12-14

Helen Otte (PHH 17) versified this psalm in 1985 for the *Psalter Hymnal.* Another setting of Psalm 19 is found at 429.

Tune

GENEVAN 19 was first published in the 1542 Genevan Psalter and altered to its present shape in the 1549 edition. Dale Grotenhuis (PHH 4) wrote the harmonization in 1985. Composed in the Mixolydian mode, this tune consists of four long lines, each containing three short phrases. The repetition of the first line and the dependable rhythmic patterns make this tune quite accessible for congregational singing.

Liturgical Use
Beginning of worship; during service of confession and consecration; frequently sung for Epiphany and Easter.

20

In the Day of Need

SAMSON
♩ = 69

A prayer for the king (God's anointed—Messiah)
by those about to follow him into battle.

Text

The themes of Psalm 20 suggest that the people are assembled to follow the king into battle. They commend the king to God's protection and help (st. 1-2), confess their confident reliance on the LORD in the impending battle (st. 3), and close with an appeal to God for the king's safety and victory, professing trust in God rather than in human resources (st. 4).

Scripture References
st. 1 = vv. 1-3, 9
st. 2 = vv. 4-5
st. 3 = v. 6
st. 4 = vv. 7-9

Christopher Martin Idle (b. Bromley, Kent, England, 1938) wrote this versification in 1969; it was first published in *Psalm Praise* (1973). Idle suggests that "the fourth stanza seems to have a message peculiarly relevant to a world where many in east and west boast of their weapons of war and rely on them to preserve 'peace.'" Idle was educated at Elthan College, St. Peter's College, Oxford, and Clifton Theological College in Bristol, and was ordained in the Church of England. He served churches in Barrow-in-Furness, Cumbria; London; and Oakley, Suffolk; and recently returned to London, where he is involved in various hymnal projects. A prolific author of articles on the Christian's public responsibilities, Idle has also published *The Lion Book of Favorite Hymns* (1980) and at least one hundred of his own hymns and biblical paraphrases. Some of his texts first appeared in hymnals published by the Jubilate Group, with which he is associated. He was also editor of *Anglican Praise* (1987).

Tune

Norman L. Warren (PHH 15) composed SAMSON for this text in 1972 for publication in *Psalm Praise* (1973). The tune was named after Warren's "small, very friendly" dog, a Border terrier. This simple folklike tune requires strong unison for congregational singing, with two beats to the bar.

Liturgical Use

Occasions when the church contemplates following Christ into battle—thus fitting for adult baptism, profession of faith, or at the conclusion of worship, as God's people take up their service and spiritual warfare in the world.

21

The King Rejoices in Your Strength

A celebration of the prosperity and triumphs of God's anointed (Messiah).

Text

The people praise God for blessing the anointed king with wealth, long life, and victories (st. 1-2) and assure the king of future triumphs because he trusts in the faithful God of Israel (st. 3). Whereas Psalm 20 looks forward to an impending battle, this psalm celebrates blessings bestowed and victories won and what these promise for the future—a future Christians call the great Day of the Lord. Marie J. Post (PHH 5) versified this psalm in 1985 for the *Psalter Hymnal.*

Scripture References
st. 1 = vv. 1-3
st. 2 = vv. 4-7
st. 3 = vv. 8-13

Tune

ST. MATTHEW was published in the *Supplement to the New Version of Psalms by Dr. Brady and Mr. Tate* (1708), where it was set to Psalm 33 and noted as a new tune. The editor of the *Supplement,* William Croft (PHH 149), may be the composer of ST. MATTHEW. One of the longer British psalm tunes, it has a fine mix of larger and stepwise intervals. It bears forceful or even jubilant singing with one broad beat per measure. If taken at a brisk tempo (c. dotted half = 50), consider holding the last note of every long phrase an extra measure to provide a breathing space between sentences.

Liturgical Use

Celebrations of the triumphant march of Christ's kingdom; particularly appropriate for Easter and Ascension.

22

My God! O My God!

The anguished prayer of the godly when apparently abandoned by God to the fierce attacks of determined and powerful enemies.

Text

One of the two psalms most frequently evoked in the gospel accounts of Jesus' death (the other is Ps. 69), Psalm 22 is one of the most poignant prayers in the Psalms. Beset by a host of powerful enemies determined to bring him down to a disgraceful death (st. 3, 5-6), the psalmist feels abandoned by God (st. 1), the God on whom he has relied

Scripture References

st. 1 = vv. 1-2
st. 2 = vv. 3-5
st. 3 = vv. 6-8
st. 4 = vv. 9-11
st. 5 = vv. 12-15
st. 6 = vv. 16-18
st. 7 = vv. 19-21
st. 8 = vv. 22-24
st. 9 = vv. 26-29
st. 10 = vv. 25, 30-31

since birth (st. 4) and who never failed his ancestors whenever they cried to him (st. 2). Yet to God he lifts his anguished prayer, pleading his lifelong trust and desperate need (st. 1, 7). The prayer shifts suddenly to exuberant praise: God will save, and all generations will hear, and all humankind, the high and the humble, will take up the praise (st. 8-10).

The original occasion for this prayer is not known (yet see Ps. 18), but its circumstances foreshadow Christ's suffering at Calvary. Calvin George Seerveld (b. Bayshore, NY, 1930) wrote this paraphrase of Psalm 22 in 1985. Portions of the final verses of the psalm (vv. 22-31) are often sung (160, 239, 240, 542), but Seerveld versified the entire psalm in order to place those verses in context. He said, "I believe Christ quoted this psalm on the cross (Matt. 27:46; Mark 15:34) because Christ knew the last paragraph of the psalm was a triumphant section, and this Scripture . . . gave him courage to undergo the terrible ordeal."

Seerveld was professor of aesthetics at the Institute for Christian Studies in Toronto from 1972 until he retired in 1995. Educated at Calvin College, Grand Rapids, Michigan; the University of Michigan; and the Free University of Amsterdam (Ph.D.), he also studied at Basel University in Switzerland, the University of Rome, and the University of Heidelberg. Seerveld began his career by teaching at Bellhaven College in Jackson, Mississippi (1958-1959), and at Trinity Christian College in Palos Heights, Illinois (1959-1972). A fine Christian scholar, fluent in various biblical and modern languages, he is published widely in aesthetics, biblical studies, and philosophy. His books include *Take Hold of God and Pull* (1966), *The Greatest Song: In Critique of Solomon* (1967), *For God's Sake, Run with Joy* (1972), *Rainbows for the Fallen World: Aesthetic Life and Artistic Task* (1980), and *On Being Human* (1988). He credits the Dutch musician Ina Lohr for influencing his compositions of hymn tunes. Most of his Bible versifications and hymns were written for the *Psalter Hymnal* (1987), on whose revision committee he ably served.

Tune

MALDWYN, a personal name in Welsh, is a traditional Welsh tune thought to date from the seventeenth century. It was published in David Evan's (PHH 285) collection *Moliant Cenedl Dinbych* (1920). The tune consists of four long phrases, each of which has the same rhythmic scheme. In minor tonality, the melody is mostly stepwise; the strong music is a fitting vehicle for the powerful text. Seerveld chose this tune for this text. He writes, "MALDWYN has exactly the right tension to catch the complaint (st. 1-4), the expostulation (st. 5-7), and the exultation (st. 8-10) of the psalm." Antiphonal performance is suggested for the first seven stanzas, followed by strong unison singing on the final three; use a more majestic tempo for the final stanza.

Liturgical Use

Holy Week, especially Good Friday services. Stanzas 8 through 10, as the "vow to praise" part of this lament psalm, have many uses in Christian worship, especially at the beginning of services.

23

CRIMOND
♩ = 100

The LORD, My Shepherd, Rules My Life

A profession of joyful trust in the LORD as the good Shepherd-King.

Text

Psalm 23's tranquil confession of faith and hope builds on the common ancient Near East and Old Testament metaphor of the king as shepherd of his people. God is the true Shepherd-King, providing his people their every need (st. 1-2), protecting them against every danger (st. 3), and welcoming them to a banquet of bounty and fellowship at the LORD's royal table in the face of their enemies (st. 4). The people thus have the sure hope of God's unfailing care and of ready access to God's presence (st. 5). Jesus' use of the shepherd image (John 10) has further endeared this psalm to Christians everywhere.

Scripture References
st. 1 = vv. 1-2
st. 2 = v. 3
st. 3 = v. 4
st. 4 = v. 5
st. 5 = v. 6

The 1977 versification by Christopher M. Idle (PHH 20) was first published in *Jesus Praise* (1982). He wrote it, he said, "to provide a version of the twenty-third Psalm in familiar meter which would avoid the archaisms and inversions of the established sixteenth-century version from the Scottish Psalter" (161). Other settings of Psalm 23 include 161, 162, and 550.

Tune

CRIMOND was first published in *The Northern Psalter* (1872), where the tune was attributed to David Grant (b. Aberdeen, Scotland, 1833; d. Lewisham, London, England, 1893), who arranged many of the tunes in that collection. However, in 1911 Anna B. Irvine claimed that CRIMOND had been composed by her sister, Jessie Seymour Irvine (b. Dunnottar, Kincardineshire, Scotland, 1836; d. Aberdeen, Scotland, 1887), who had given it to Grant to be harmonized. Irvine's authorship is generally accepted today. Little is known of Irvine's life except that she was the daughter of an Anglican minister and lived in her parents' home for much of her life.

CRIMOND became very popular after it was used at the wedding of Queen Elizabeth II and Prince Philip in 1947. Named after the town of Crimond in Aberdeenshire, Scotland, the tune is considered by many to be among the finest of all Scottish psalm tunes.

David Grant composed the harmonization. A tobacco shop merchant by trade, Grant was an amateur musician. He composed music for bands, arranged tunes for *The Northern Psalter* (1872), and served as precentor of the Footdee Church in Aberdeen.

The descant composed by William Baird Ross (b. Montrose, Scotland, 1871; d. Edinburgh, Scotland, 1950) also gained popularity from royal use in 1947. Educated at Queen's College in Oxford, Ross became a Fellow of the Royal College of Organists. He was an educator and an organist in Montrose, Edinburgh, Glasgow, Aberdeen, and Stirling in Scotland.

Liturgical Use

As an expression of trust, Psalm 23 is appropriate for many liturgical uses, including baptism, the Lord's Supper, weddings, and funeral services.

24

The Earth and the Riches

LANSING
♩ = 132

A congregational celebration of the LORD's triumphal entry into Zion.

Text

Psalm 24 is a liturgy composed for use in one of Israel's annual religious festivals, perhaps the Feast of Tabernacles. In the postexilic liturgy of the temple, this psalm was sung at the time of the morning sacrifice on the first day of the week. The liturgy accompanied a procession that may have reenacted David's bringing of the ark (symbolic of God's throne) into Jerusalem and placing it there in its own tent sanctuary. In broader

Scripture References
st. 1 = vv. 1-2
st. 2 = vv. 3-4
st. 3 = vv. 5-6
st. 4 = vv. 7-8
st. 5 = vv. 9-10

perspective the liturgy no doubt celebrated the final triumphal march of the King of Glory from Mount Sinai (Ps. 68), or even from Egypt (Ex. 15:1-18), into his royal resting place (1 Chron. 28:2) in the royal city of his kingdom. While the focus is on this triumphal entry (st. 4-5), we also join in the people's confession that the whole world belongs to God (st. 1), and the priestly reminder that only those pure in hand and heart may have fellowship with the LORD (st. 2-3). Marie J. Post (PHH 5) versified this psalm in 1982 for the *Psalter Hymnal*. See 163 for another setting of the last part of this psalm.

Tune

LANSING is one of several tunes by Charles Hutchinson Gabriel (b. Wilton, IA, 1856; d. Los Angeles, CA, 1932) included in the 1912 *Psalter*, where it was set to the second part of Psalm 24, "Ye Gates Lift Your Heads." The tune title refers to the Illinois city just south of Chicago near which Gabriel settled in 1895. This tune is a fine accompaniment to the psalm text and should be sung with confidence and enthusiasm. To bring out the structure of the current versification, try singing stanzas 2 and 3 antiphonally, with one group asking the questions in the first two lines and the other responding. Then sing stanzas 4 and 5 with full voice and majestic accompaniment, though there also the questions in line 3 could be sung by select voices.

For the first seventeen years of his life Gabriel lived on an Iowa farm, where friends and neighbors often gathered to sing. Gabriel accompanied them on the family reed organ he had taught himself to play. At the age of sixteen he began teaching singing in schools (following in his father's footsteps) and soon was acclaimed as a fine teacher and composer. He moved to California in 1887 and served as Sunday school music director at the Grace Methodist Church in San Francisco. After moving to Chicago in 1892, Gabriel edited numerous collections of anthems, cantatas, and a large number of songbooks for the Homer Rodeheaver, Hope, and E. O. Excell publishing companies. He composed hundreds of tunes and texts, at times using pseudonyms such as Charlotte G. Homer. The total number of his compositions is estimated at about seven thousand. Gabriel's gospel songs became widely circulated through the Billy Sunday-Homer Rodeheaver urban crusades.

Liturgical Use
As an entrance psalm for Advent, Palm Sunday, and especially Ascension Day, but also to many other worship occasions.

25

GENEVAN 25
♩ = 72

LORD, to You My Soul Is Lifted

A prayer for God's mercies when suffering affliction for sins and when enemies seize the opportunity to attack.

Text
Enfeebled and distracted by illness or some other affliction (vv. 16-18), the psalmist in his distress recognizes the hand of God. But the affliction has also emboldened enemies to take advantage of the psalmist's weakened condition (v. 19), perhaps seeking to discredit him publicly through mischievous slander. In such straits, the psalmist encourages us also to humbly ask God for forgiveness and for instruction and guidance into right ways (st. 1), to appeal to God's covenant faithfulness toward those who are faithful (st. 2), and to plead for deliverance from affliction and for relief from the opportunistic attacks of enemies (st. 3). Stanley Marvin Wiersma

Scripture References
st. 1 = vv. 1-7
st. 2 = vv. 8-15
st. 3 = vv. 16-22

(b. Orange City, IA, 1930; d. Amsterdam, the Netherlands, 1986) versified Psalm 25 in 1980 for the *Psalter Hymnal.*

Wiersma was a poet and professor of English at Calvin College, Grand Rapids, Michigan, from 1959 until his sudden death in 1986. He attended Calvin as an undergraduate and received a Ph.D. from the University of Wisconsin in 1959. His love for the Genevan psalms is reflected in the two books of poetry for which he is most widely known: *Purpaleanie and Other Permutations* (1978) and *Style and Class* (1982), both written under the pseudonym Sietze Buning. He also wrote *More Than the Ear Discovers: God in the Plays of Christopher Fry* and translated many Dutch poems and hymn texts into English, including the children's hymns published in *All Will Be New* (1982).

Tune

Louis Bourgeois's (PHH 3) GENEVAN 25 was first published in the 1551 edition of the Genevan Psalter. Howard Slenk (PHH 3) harmonized the tune in 1985 for the *Psalter Hymnal.* One of the most beautifully constructed Genevan tunes, 25 is noted especially for its rhythmic interest and form (AABC). Like many melodies of its time, the rhythmic units move easily between groupings of two and three quarter-notes. For example, the first phrase is grouped 3+2+3+2+2; the first note of each group carries the stressed syllable of the text. Though set to a reflective text, the music should not be sung too slowly; feel the half note as the basic pulse.

Liturgical Use

When personal or communal distress forces the Christian to turn to a gracious Lord— especially when the distress appears to discredit the church.

26

LORD, Speak to Me, for I Am Yours

PERRY
♩ = 60

A prayer of the godly asking to be spared from the death God has appointed for the wicked.

Text

Psalm 26 appears to have been occasioned by a serious illness or some other mortal threat. In singing this lament, we share in the psalmist's appeal for God to examine the deepest commitments and moral integrity of the human heart (st. 1-2). Examples of that integrity follow: the psalmist is no partner with the morally corrupt (st. 3), worships with clean hands and a tongue that celebrates God's mighty deeds (st. 4), and loves the holy temple where God's glory dwells among the people in a marvelous display of grace (st. 5). Finally, the poet pleads with God for

Scripture References
st. 1 = vv. 1-2
st. 2 = vv. 2-3
st. 3 = vv. 4-5
st. 4 = vv. 6-7
st. 5 = v. 8
st. 6 = vv. 9-10
st. 7 = vv. 11-12

deliverance from the death designated for the wicked (st. 6) and confesses confidently that God will hear and give renewed occasion for praise (st. 7). Marie J. Post (PHH 5) versified this lament in 1983 for the *Psalter Hymnal.*

Tune
Leo Sowerby (b. Grand Rapids, MI, 1895; d. Port Clinton, OH, 1968) composed PERRY in 1962 at Put-in-Bay, Ohio, the site of an international peace monument and the place from which Commodore Oliver H. Perry (then a lieutenant) sailed to gain a naval victory during the War of 1812. The tune was originally composed for James A. Blaisdell's "Beneath the Form of Outward Rite" and was first published in *The Methodist Hymnal* (1964). PERRY is composed in the style of Scottish psalm tunes, but it has a delightful alternation of 2/2 and 3/2 time. The accompaniment should be firm but subdued, but play the last stanza brighter.

Sowerby moved to Chicago at the age of fourteen to study with Calvin Lampert. In 1913 the Chicago Symphony gave the first public performance of his violin concerto. At the age of fifteen Sowerby decided to become an organist. He took some lessons, but because he found practice time on the organ too expensive, he sketched the pedal keyboard on brown butcher paper and laid the paper beneath the piano, thus teaching himself to play the organ. From 1921 to 1924 Sowerby studied at the American Academy in Rome as the first recipient of the "Prix de Rome." After his return to the United States he taught music at the American Conservatory in Chicago (1925-1962), was organist and choirmaster at St. James Episcopal Church there, and earned a doctorate in music from the Eastman School of Music in Rochester, New York. In 1962 he moved to Washington, D.C., to organize the College for Church Musicians at National Cathedral. A respected composer of numerous instrumental works and some three hundred songs, Sowerby received many commissions and awards, including the Pulitzer Prize in 1946 for his oratorio *Canticle of the Sun,* which has lyrics taken from the famous text by Francis of Assisi. A member of the joint commission that revised the Episcopal *Hymnal 1940,* Sowerby is known for his prolific output of organ works, choir anthems, and service music.

Liturgical Use
Service of confession and forgiveness; Lent; occasions when an individual or the church is severely threatened.

27

The LORD God Is My Light and My Salvation

GENEVAN 27
♩ = 76

A prayer for deliverance from treacherous enemies who attack with the deadly weapons of slander and "false witness."

Text

The psalmist is surrounded by enemies who seek to destroy him. But their attacks are not brutal and open; their weapons are the poisoned arrows of slander and "false witness." Such weapons are no less deadly than missiles of bronze and iron and are more convenient for secret in-house treachery. Notice a hint that the attacks come from the psalmist's inner circle of associates—"though my father and mother forsake me" (v. 10). In the face of such circumstances, the psalmist offers a confession of trust in God that is unexcelled in the Psalms. In stanza 1, the psalmist's unwavering confidence in God's protective care removes all fear. Stanza 2 testifies that the LORD (and God's temple) is a sure stronghold for shelter and safety; stanza 3 is a prayer requesting God's help in this time of desperation and asking that God will not abandon us to false witnesses. That prayer moves to a confession that God will surely bring deliverance, followed by a self-exhortation that calls us to remain firm in that confession (st. 4). Marie J. Post (PHH 5) versified this psalm in 1980 for the *Psalter Hymnal*. See 164 for another setting of Psalm 27.

Scripture References
st. 1 = vv. 1-3
st. 2 = vv. 4-6
st. 3 = vv. 7-9
st. 4 = vv. 10-14

Tune

First published in the 1551 Genevan Psalter, GENEVAN 27 has been generally attributed to Louis Bourgeois (PHH 3), editor of that psalter. Dale Grotenhuis (PHH 4) composed the harmonization in 1986 for the *Psalter Hymnal*. Though one of the longer and more difficult Genevan tunes, 27 is accessible because of the repeat of the first two lines and the use of smaller intervals. The tune is mostly Mixolydian. Sing this music with a comfortable tempo that permits the long lines of text to be clearly expressed.

Liturgical Use

Times of persecution or other situations in which the Christian community wishes to express confidence in the Lord.

28

SPIRITUS VITAE
♩ = 63

O LORD My Rock, in Desperation

A prayer of the LORD's anointed for deliverance from unscrupulous and treacherous rebels.

Text

The psalmist's enemies appear to be rebels within the kingdom who plot against the LORD's anointed—they "speak cordially with their neighbors but harbor malice in their hearts" (v. 3). The psalm opens with a plea for God to defend his servant (st. 1). While praying to be spared from the fate of sinners (st. 2), the psalm singer calls upon God to deal with the rebels as they deserve (st. 3) and declares confidently that God "will cast them down" and "will never let them rise" (st. 4). A call to praise God for hearing this prayer (st. 5) accompanies a testimony to God's faithful defense of the anointed and a prayer to the Shepherd of Israel to save and bless the people (st. 5-6). Marie J. Post (PHH 5) prepared this versification in 1982 for the *Psalter Hymnal*.

Scripture References
st. 1 = v. 1
st. 2 = vv. 2-3
st. 3 = vv. 3-4
st. 4 = v. 5
st. 5 = vv. 6-7
st. 6 = vv. 8-9

Tune

The name SPIRITUS VITAE derives from the Latin translation of Bessie P. Head's text "O Breath of Life," for which Mary Jane Hammond (b. England, 1878; d. St. Albans, Hertfordshire, England, 1964) composed the tune around 1914. That text and SPIRITUS VITAE were first published in *Heavenly Places and Other Messages* (1920). Little is known about Hammond except that she lived in Harpenden, Hertfordshire, toward the end of her life and died at the Hillingdon Nursing Home in nearby St. Albans.

One of few tunes that begin on their highest tone, SPIRITUS VITAE virtually repeats lines 1 and 2 in lines 3 and 4, with only a cadential change. Antiphonal performance is appropriate if the entire psalm is sung. The setting with the melody in the tenor, composed by Emily R. Brink (PHH 158) in 1987, is well suited for a choral stanza or as an alternate organ setting.

Liturgical Use

Situations of personal or communal distress; occasions when the church recalls Christ's suffering; and times when Christians need to pray for other Christians who are being persecuted.

29

Give Glory to God, All You Heavenly Creatures

ARLES
♩ = 132

A call to praise the Creator, whose majesty and might as displayed in the thunderstorm is the source of the people's security and welfare.

Text

Psalm 29 attributes to the God of Israel what the Canaanites attributed to Baal—the divine majesty and power seen in the awesome sights and sounds and force of a thunderstorm. After the opening call to the great powers of creation to glorify the LORD (st. 1), the main body of the psalm (st. 2-4) evokes the experience of thunderstorms in northern Canaan as they form over the Mediterranean ("the waters"), sweep across the Lebanon ranges,

Scripture References
st. 1 = vv. 1-2
st. 2 = vv. 3-4
st. 3 = vv. 5-6
st. 4 = vv. 7-9
st. 5 = vv. 9-10

and spend themselves over the desert-like steppe to the east. Appropriately "the voice of the LORD," that is, thunder (in Baal mythology, the voice of Baal), sounds seven times in this psalm (vv. 3-9). Such displays of divine might may cause Baal worshipers to tremble, but true believers praise their God exuberantly, knowing that the LORD of the thunderstorm gives strength to his people and blesses them with peace (st. 5). Calvin Seerveld (PHH 22) versified this psalm in 1983 for the *Psalter Hymnal*.

Tune

ARLES was composed by Charles H. Gabriel (PHH 24), a prolific composer of gospel hymn tunes; it was associated with this psalm in the 1912 *Psalter.* Named after the French city, ARLES bears energetic, rhythmically precise accompaniment and four-part singing. For variety and contrast, sing the stanzas antiphonally, with men's voices on stanza 2 and treble voices on stanza 4.

Liturgical Use

Whenever the people of God want to express their praise to the Lord as the One who sits enthroned in the heavens, rules over all creation as King forever, and blesses and sustains his people.

BISHOP TUCKER
♩ = 96

I Worship You, O LORD

Praise for God's deliverance from death by healing his servant in answer to prayer.

Text

The superscript of this psalm states that it is "for the dedication of the temple." Most likely this superscript refers to the dedication of the second temple by the returned exiles (Ezra 6:16). In that case the "I" of the psalm came to refer to the repatriated community and the "healing" experienced in restoration from exile. Still later the Jews included this psalm in the liturgy for Hanukkah, the festival that celebrates the rededication of the temple in the days of Judas Maccabeus after its desecration by Antiochus IV Epiphanes.

Scripture References
st. 1 = vv. 1-3
st. 2 = vv. 4-5
st. 3 = vv. 6-8
st. 4 = vv. 9-10
st. 5 = vv. 11-12

In singing this thanksgiving psalm, we praise God for deliverance from the brink of death (st. 1) and call all "who know his name" to praise God for unfailing mercies (st. 2). Recalling the LORD's chastisement for proud self-reliance (st. 3), the psalmist reiterates a prayer offered while standing at death's door (st. 4) and closes in praise to God for turning sadness into gladness (st. 5). James Seddon (PHH 15) prepared this versification sometime before 1969; it was first published in *Psalm Praise* (1973). Calvin Seerveld (PHH 22) provided stanza 4 in 1982 to provide a complete versification of the psalm for the *Psalter Hymnal.*

Tune

Composed in 1969 by Norman L. Warren (PHH 15) for this text, BISHOP TUCKER was published in *Psalm Praise* (1973). The tune name is derived from Bishop Tucker Theological College in Uganda, where Warren and his wife led seminars on worship and counseling. Warren said the tune "is loosely based on a wisp of melody from Rochmaninov's D-flat Piano Concerto." BISHOP TUCKER is a tune of six very similar phrases, in which phrases 1 and 2 interchange to become phrases 5 and 6, and phrase 4 is a sequence of phrase 3. The testimony of God's healing and restoring power may be highlighted by having a soloist sing stanzas 3 and 4.

Liturgical Use

Easter; occasions for testimony upon restoration from serious illness or difficulty.

31

I Seek My Refuge in You, LORD

COLERAINE
♩ = *104*

A prayer for deliverance from enemies in a situation that appears so hopeless that even the psalmist's friends abandon him.

Text

In the face of heavy and sustained attack and the defection of close associates, there is only One who will not be false and who has the power to rescue. We join the psalmist in this urgent prayer that includes rousing confessions of trust. Calling upon the LORD to be our rock and our refuge from enemies (st. 1), we too commit our lives into God's saving hand (st. 2; Jesus used part of this passage on the cross). In other times of affliction God heard, answered, and delivered (st. 3), so the plea for God's mercy comes once again, expressing anguish

Scripture References
st. 1 = vv. 1-2
st. 2 = vv. 3-5
st. 3 = vv. 6-8
st. 4 = vv. 9-13
st. 5 = vv. 14-18
st. 6 = vv. 19-20
st. 7 = vv. 21-24

over being abandoned by all others (st. 4). The psalm singer declares trust in God and asks for God's judgment on those who slander the righteous (st. 5), for the LORD does not fail those who cling to him for aid (st. 6). In stanza 7, the psalmist further praises God's mercy and deliverance and calls all saints to trust the LORD. Marie J. Post (PHH 5) versified this lament in 1985 for the *Psalter Hymnal.*

Tune

COLERAINE (or VICENZA) was first published in *La Scala Santa* (1681) as a setting for Psalm 122 in long meter (88 88) without the repeat of the first two lines. The name COLERAINE derives from Lord Coleraine, the possible compiler of this Irish anthology. The tune entered English hymnody through publication in the 1904 edition of *Hymns Ancient and Modern.* This bar-form (AAB) melody finds its tonal and rhythmic climax in the last line. Have everyone sing stanzas 1, 4, and 7, and alternate the remaining stanzas between two parts of the congregation.

Erik Reginald Routley (b. Brighton, Sussex, England, 1917; d. Nashville, TN, 1982) composed the harmonization of COLERAINE for *Rejoice in the Lord* (1985). Routley is remembered as perhaps the most significant English hymnologist of the twentieth century. Educated at Magdalen and Mansfield Colleges, Oxford, and Oxford University, Routley was ordained to the ministry in the Congregational Church in 1943. He served Trinity Congregational Church in Wednesbury and the Dartford Congregational Church in Kent. In 1948 he became lecturer in church history as well as chaplain, librarian, and director of music at Mansfield College. He accepted a call to the Augustine Congregational Church in Edinburgh in 1959 and moved to Newscastle-upon-Tyne to minister to St. James Church in 1967. Coming to the United States in

1975, Routley took the position of visiting professor of music at Princeton Theological Seminary and professor of church music at Westminster Choir College, where he remained until his death. Routley wrote thirty-seven books on church music, church history, theology, and worship, including *Hymns and Human Life* (1959), *Words, Music, and the Church* (1968), *A Panorama of Christian Hymnody* (1979), and *The Music of Christian Hymns* (1981). Editor of the *Bulletin of the Hymn Society* in the British Isles from 1948 to 1974, he was also a member of the editorial committees of *Congregational Praise* (1951), *Cantate Domino* (1974), and *Ecumenical Praise* (1977). Routley wrote the musical notes for *Companion to Congregational Praise* (1953), compiled and edited *Rejoice in the Lord* (1985) for the Reformed Church in America, participated in issuing various hymnal supplements, and produced a number of recordings. A composer of numerous anthems as well as a frequent lecturer and outstanding teacher, he made invaluable contributions to church music and was especially appreciated for his critical opinions and wit, many examples of which occur in his *Organist's Companion to "The [1972 Presbyterian] Worshipbook"* (1975). His collected hymn texts, tunes, and carols were published as *Our Lives Be Praise* (1990). Routley was posthumously honored as a Fellow of the Hymn Society in the United States and Canada in 1985.

Liturgical Use
Good Friday; whenever believers are threatened by enemies of Christ.

32

RUTHERFORD
♩ = 60

How Blest Are They Whose Trespass

A testimony to the blessedness of the forgiven and an exhortation to the trust, obedience, and joyful worship that should mark their lives.

Text

Psalm 32 is traditionally considered a penitential psalm (along with 6, 38, 51, 102, 130, and 143). In the sequence of spiritual experience it follows the situation depicted in Psalm 51, the great plea for forgiveness. That psalm's traditional association with David's sin against Uriah, together with Psalm 32's reference to delayed confession, has suggested a historical link between the two. The psalm's thematic movement is noteworthy and is well represented in the versification, which is slightly altered from that of the 1912 *Psalter.*

Scripture References
st. 1 = vv. 1-2
st. 2 = vv. 3-5
st. 3 = vv. 6-7
st. 4 = vv. 8-9
st. 5 = vv. 10-11

The psalm begins with a testimony to the blessedness of those forgiven by God (st. 1). Retracing the spiritual movement from stubbornly denying sin to experiencing the joy of God's forgiveness (st. 2), the psalm exhorts all the godly to faithfully rely on

God and reaffirms the LORD as refuge and hiding place (st. 3). Next God speaks, instructing the saints in godly obedience (st. 4). The psalm then contrasts the lot of the wicked with that of those who trust in God, and it closes with a call to the righteous to rejoice in God for his unfailing mercies (st. 5).

Tune
RUTHERFORD was composed by Chrétien Urhan (b. Aix-la-Chappelle, France, 1790; d. Belleville, near Paris, France, 1845). Urhan was an accomplished violin and viola player at an early age. After hearing him play his instrument in 1805, the Empress Josephine took him to Paris to study composition and strings from the best teachers. Urhan revived the importance of the viola d'amore by giving virtuoso performances on this instrument with Pierre Baillot's quartet. A composer of chamber music and works for piano, he also served as organist of the Church of St. Vincent de Paul in Paris. In 1816 he joined the Paris Opera orchestra and became its leader in 1831. A mystic and devout Catholic, Urhan regarded his contribution to church music as the most important part of his career. Although he played in opera orchestras for some thirty years, he is reputed never to have looked at the opera itself from the orchestra pit because of his religious scruples.

RUTHERFORD originally was published in *Chants Chrétien* (1834). The tune became associated with Anne Ross Cousin's hymn text "The Sands of Time Are Sinking." Cousin based her hymn on writings from the *Last Words of Samuel Rutherford* (1857); Rutherford was a seventeenth-century Scottish Covenant preacher. The tune was later arranged by Edward Francis Rimbault (b. Soho, London, England, 1816; d. Soho, London, 1876) and published in its present form in *Psalms and Hymns for Divine Worship* (1867).

Rimbault first studied with his father, organist of St. Giles-in-the-Fields, London, and later was a student of both Samuel Wesley and William Crotch. Various London churches employed him as organist, including St. Peter's on Vere Street, St. John's Wood Presbyterian Church, the Swiss Church in Soho, and St. Giles-in-the-Fields. Active in the Motet Society and the Handel Society, Rimbault was also one of the founders of the Musical Antiquarian Society. He edited much music, including editions of Tallis's *Cathedral Service and Order of Daily Service,* Merbecke's *Book of Common Prayer Noted,* and Este's *The Whole Book of Psalms.*

RUTHERFORD consists of four long lines, each of which has its own melodic and rhythmic patterns. Sing this music with two beats per bar to get the sense of the longer textual and musical lines. Try singing in harmony, unaccompanied on one of the inner stanzas.

Liturgical Use
Though considered penitential, this psalm is properly used not so much in confession of sin as in thanksgiving for God's forgiveness of our sin. It is a joyful psalm! Within that context, the psalm could also serve as a call to confession (st. 1-3) and instruction for godly living following the assurance of pardon (st. 4-5).

33

Rejoice! Sing Praise to Your Creator

Praise for God's unfailing protection against all worldly powers.

Text

References in this psalm to "a new song" (v. 3) and to God's frustration of the plans of hostile nations may suggest a time when Israel experienced a remarkable deliverance from foreign enemies, as in the days of Jehoshaphat (2 Chron. 20) or Hezekiah (2 Kings 19). Relevant for any time the people of God reflect on their security in the face of hostile powers, the psalm calls on God's people to rejoice and sing because of God's faithful care (st. 1). As the almighty Creator, God has more than enough power to protect his people (st. 2). Possessing sovereign power over all the world, God can frustrate all plots against his people and effect his own plans for them (st. 3). God's all-seeing eye perceives the devices of worldly powers and watches protectively over his people (st. 4), so they wait in hope for the LORD, rejoicing and trusting in God's unfailing love and protection (st. 5). Marie J. Post (PHH 5) versified this psalm in 1980 for the *Psalter Hymnal*. See 449 for another (condensed) setting of Psalm 33.

Scripture References
st. 1 = vv. 1-5
st. 2 = vv. 6-9
st. 3 = vv. 10-12
st. 4 = vv. 13-19
st. 5 = vv. 20-22

Tune

Psalm 33 was first set to GENEVAN 33 in the 1551 edition of the Genevan Psalter. The tune is generally attributed to Louis Bourgeois (PHH 3), the composer who served as editor of that psalter. The *Psalter Hymnal* includes two versions of a harmonization by Claude Goudimel (PHH 6): an adapted one to place the melody in the soprano, and the original 1564 setting (opposite 32) with the melody in the tenor, which was customary for that time. GENEVAN 33 is in Dorian mode; the two long opening lines of this bar form (AABC) are contrasted by even longer lines of three phrases each. A majestic tempo is helpful in negotiating the rhythms and the bountiful text. Sing (and play) stanzas 1-4 antiphonally (with some use of the alternate harmonization), and have everyone join in unison on stanza 5.

Liturgical Use

Praise to God as Creator and Ruler of the universe; expressions of trust in God's saving power; reproach of the evil plans of human powers arrayed against the church and the kingdom of God; counsel against reliance on creaturely means; affirmation of the Lord as the believer's only hope for security.

34

LORD, I Bring My Songs to You

RATISBON
♩ = 52

Praise of God for deliverance in time of trouble; instruction in "the fear of the LORD."

Text

Psalm 34's thematic development is striking in that it moves from praise for God's deliverance to wisdom instruction in "the fear of the LORD" (a similar development is found in 92; see also 1, 37, 49, 73, and 112). The person who sings this psalm commits to praising the LORD and calls all people to do the same (st. 1), for God delivers and always protects those who fear the LORD (st. 2). "Taste and see," exhorts the psalmist; God shelters all who fear him (st. 3). Instruction in "the fear of the LORD" points to

Scripture References
st. 1 = vv. 1-3
st. 2 = vv. 4-7
st. 3 = vv. 8-10
st. 4 = vv. 11-14
st. 5 = vv. 15-18
st. 6 = vv. 19-22

seeking God's peace and keeping the tongue from evil (st. 4). God sees the needs and hears the cries of those who trust in him but turns away from the wicked (st. 5). Even though the troubles of the godly may multiply, God keeps safe those who fear him and condemns the wicked (st. 6). Marie J. Post (PHH 5) versified this psalm in 1985 for the *Psalter Hymnal.*

Tune

RATISBON was first published in Johann Freylinghausen's *Geistreiches Gesangbuch* (1704) as an adaptation of a Joachim Neander (PHH 244) tune. A subsequent adaptation appeared in Johann G. Werner's *Choralbuch* (1815) with the text "Jesu, meines Lebens Leben." There it appeared as an 87 87 88 77 tune with the third and fourth lines a repeat of the first two. In the 1861 *Hymns Ancient and Modern* the repeat was omitted and the tune further altered to its present predictable shape. A number of earlier tunes are similar to and also may have influenced the development of RATISBON; among them is JESUS, MEINE SUVERSICHT (399). The tune name probably derives from the ancient German city Ratisbon, now known as Regensburg. Sing with two beats to the bar and savor the harmony.

Johann Anastasius Freylinghausen (b. Gandersheim, Brunswick, Germany, 1670; d. Halle, Germany, 1739) attended the University of Jena in 1689 and came under the influence of August Francke and the Pietist movement. He followed Francke to Halle in 1692, became his live-in and unpaid assistant, and married his daughter in 1715. After Francke's death in 1727, Freylinghausen became pastor of St. Ulrich's Church and headed the school and orphanage that Francke had established. An effective Pietist preacher and hymnal publisher, Freylinghausen wrote about forty hymn texts and twenty-two hymn tunes. Besides *Geistreiches Gesangbuch,* he compiled another significant Lutheran hymnal, *Neues geistreiches Gesangbuch* (1714). Both volumes became very popular in Pietist and other congregations and went through numerous printings. They were combined in the editions of 1741 and 1772 to include almost fifteen hundred texts and three hundred tunes.

Liturgical Use
Thanksgiving to God for answered prayer; expressions of how Christian gratitude should result in godly living—trust in God and obedience to his will. Stanza 1 can be a choral call to worship; stanza 3 is appropriate in the liturgy of the Lord's Supper. In a communion service, the entire psalm could be framed by the refrain of 301, "Taste and see that God is good."

35

GOTTLOB
♩ = 108

O LORD, Arise, Come Help Me Now

*A king's prayer for deliverance from the plots of false friends,
who have turned against him in his time of trouble.*

Text

This psalm appears to be a prayer of the LORD's anointed ("his servant," v. 27) and evokes a situation similar to that in other psalm prayers (25, 41): when the psalmist is brought low through trouble ("when I stumbled," v. 15), those whom he has viewed as friends and associates plot to destroy him, using the weapons of slander and false accusation. Unable to defend himself against such treachery, and having no other court of appeal, the king presents his case to his heavenly King.

Scripture References
st. 1 = vv. 1-3
st. 2 = vv. 4-8
st. 3 = vv. 9-10
st. 4 = vv. 11-16
st. 5 = vv. 17-25
st. 6 = vv. 22-28

Appropriately in such an appeal, the anointed pleads that the LORD will both vindicate him (st. 1) and turn the plots of his enemies back upon them (st. 2). A vow to praise his heavenly Deliverer accompanies this appeal (st. 3). The treachery of the psalmist's enemies is such that they falsely accuse him even though he cared and prayed for them when they were ill (st. 4). The psalmist renews his appeal for God's judgment and again vows to praise the LORD, promising thankful rejoicing "amid the crowds of worshipers" (st. 5-6). Helen Otte (PHH 17) versified this psalm of lament in 1985 for the *Psalter Hymnal*.

Tune

Various forms of GOTTLOB are found in a number of collections of old German melodies. One form of the tune appeared in Johann G. Wagner's *Sammlung alter und neuer* (1742) with the burial hymn "Gottlob, es geht nunmehr zum Ende" ("Thanks Be to God; My End Is Near Me"). Although only the first line of this variant vaguely resembles the harmonization by Johann S. Bach (PHH 7) in the *Psalter Hymnal*, some scholars think it is the source for Bach's setting published posthumously in the second edition of his *Choralgesängbuch* (1769). Other scholars think Bach found another source, and still others think he composed the tune himself.

Like many German chorales, this tune is a bar form (AAB). Its superb melody is finely matched by Bach's harmonization, which invites four-part singing. A moderate tempo helps to underline the cheerful hope of this text.

Liturgical Use

Occasions of personal distress or times when the Christian church is under attack. Stanzas 1, 2, and 3 or stanzas 1, 5, and 6 work well as alternatives to the entire psalm in voicing an appeal for God's vindication against slander or false accusation.

36

My Heart Speaks Out on Those Who Sin

PALMARUM
$\quad$ = 96

A meditation on the godlessness of the wicked and on the great goodness of God.

Text

Psalm 36's reflections on the godless character of the wicked (st. 1) precede an especially rich observation of God's goodness: God's love, faithfulness, righteousness, and justice (st. 2) are manifest in God's preservation of all life, in his protection of all who take refuge in him, and in his bounteous provision for all their needs (st. 3). In rapid succession the psalm gives us three striking and fertile images: God's "river of delights" (v. 8), God's

Scripture References
st. 1 = vv. 1-4
st. 2 = vv. 5-6a
st. 3 = vv. 6b-8
st. 4 = vv. 9-10
st. 5 = vv. 11-12

"fountain of life," and God's "light" by which "we see light" (v. 9; st. 4). The psalmist asks God to continue loving and providing for the faithful (st. 4) and closes with a prayer for deliverance from the wicked (st. 5). Psalm 36 provides no clue to its original occasion, but its theme and tone suggest a time of quiet meditation at the temple (see 48:9; 63:2) or during a wakeful hour of the night (see 42:8; 77:6). Bert Witvoet (PHH 4) paraphrased this psalm in 1981 for the *Psalter Hymnal*.

Tune

John Frederick Wolle (b. Bethlehem, PA, 1863; d. Bethlehem, 1933) was a descendant of the Moravian missionaries who founded Bethlehem in 1741. Wolle taught mathematics at the parochial school in that city. From 1881 to 1884 he was also the organist of Trinity Episcopal Church in Bethlehem. After going to Munich, Germany, to study the organ with Joseph Rheinberger, Wolle returned to Bethlehem to become organist at the Moravian Church and Lehigh University (1887-1905). In 1898 he founded and conducted the Bethlehem Bach choir, which gave the American premiere of J. S. Bach's B Minor Mass in 1900. Wolle taught music at the University of California from 1905 to 1911 and then returned again to live and teach in Bethlehem. He conducted Bach festivals at Lehigh (1912-1932) and promoted interest in Bach's choral works throughout the United States. A founder of the American Guild of Organists, he wrote organ transcriptions of orchestral compositions by Bach and Richard Wagner.

Wolle wrote PALMARUM in 1888 for the Central Moravian Church of Bethlehem; the tune was first published in the *Moravian Offices of Worship and Hymns* (1891). It was first used as a setting for "Ride On, Ride On in Majesty" (382), which explains the tune's title. Later it became associated with the missionary hymn "Fling Out the Banner." PALMARUM's ascending melodic phrases give the tune a confident cast. Repeated melodic notes require clear articulation in accompaniment. The alternate setting by Roy Hopp (PHH 11) provides a helpful descant for stanzas 2 and 4.

Liturgical Use
Beginning of worship; occasions of wisdom teaching contrasting God's goodness with the godlessness of the wicked; praise of the Lord for providing in creation and for leading in our lives (st. 2-4). The middle portion of this psalm (st. 3-4) is also traditionally used in the Jewish morning prayer.

37

DINBYCH
♩ = 100

When Evil People Sin

A contrast of the way of the righteous and the way of the ungodly; the wages of the one and the hope of the other.

Text

In Old Testament wisdom style, Psalm 37 contrasts the way of the wicked and the way of the righteous (see also 1, 34, 49, 73, and 112). Even though the wicked, by their scheming and violence, appear to prosper, it is the righteous, those trusting in the LORD, who will possess the (promised) land. In a series of images, the psalm portrays the wicked in their apparent power and wealth and repeatedly overrides their folly with an image of the lasting salvation of the faithful. Do not envy the wicked; trust in God, says the psalmist (st. 1). Do not fret when wickedness succeeds; wait patiently for the LORD (st. 2). God frustrates the wicked but blesses the righteous (st. 3). The wicked are

Scripture References
st. 1 = vv. 1-6
st. 2 = vv. 7-11
st. 3 = vv. 12-20
st. 4 = vv. 21-26
st. 5 = vv. 27-33
st. 6 = vv. 34-40

miserly, but the righteous are generous; God will surely help the righteous (st. 4). The righteous live godly lives, and the LORD will always protect them (st. 5). God's blessing and salvation are reserved for those who trust and obey (st. 6). Reworking an earlier text of Christopher M. Idle (originally prepared for *Psalm Praise,* 1973), Bert Polman versified this psalm in 1985 for the *Psalter Hymnal.*

Bert Frederick Polman (b. Rozenburg, Zuid Holland, the Netherlands, 1945) immigrated to Canada in 1955. Trained in hymnology, he was a member of the revision committee that produced the 1987 *Psalter Hymnal* and is primary author of this companion volume. He was also a member of the editorial committees for *The Worshiping Church* (1990), *Songs for LiFE* (1994), and *Amazing Grace, Hymn Texts for Devotional Use* (1994). Educated at Dordt College, Sioux Center, Iowa, and the University of Minnesota (Ph.D. 1981; dissertation "Church Music and Liturgy in the Christian Reformed Church of North America"), he did postgraduate work at the Institute for Christian Studies in Toronto. Polman has served as organist and choirmaster at Oakland United Methodist Church, Minneapolis (1968-1972), and St. John's Anglican Church, Mississauga, Ontario (1972-1974). He was liturgist of the Campus Worship Community at the University of Toronto and organist at Fellowship Christian Reformed Church, Rexdale, Toronto (1977-1985) while teaching music at Ontario Bible College in Toronto (1975-1985). From 1985 to 1991 Polman was organist at Immanuel Christian Reformed Church in Hamilton, Ontario, and currently holds a similar position at Bethel Christian Reformed Church in nearby Waterdown. Since 1985 he has also taught music at Redeemer College in Ancaster, Ontario. He has served on the editorial council of *Reformed Worship,* the executive committee of the Hymn Society in the United States and Canada, and the denominational worship committee of the Christian Reformed Church. Despite partial vocal paralysis, Polman is a frequent conference speaker.

Tune

Joseph Parry (PHH 18) composed DINBYCH and named it after the city of Dinbych in northern Wales. The tune first appeared in *Llyfr Tonau Cynulleidfaol Cenedlaethol Cymru (The Welsh National Book of Congregational Tunes),* which was edited by Parry and published in several parts from 1887 to 1892. DINBYCH appears in the *Psalter Hymnal* in an abridged form, as found in other English hymnals. This anthem-like tune features a well designed mix of small and larger intervals and short and longer phrases and is supported by a colorful harmony. Part singing and optional antiphonal performance are appropriate.

Liturgical Use

Occasions of wisdom teaching contrasting the righteous with the wicked.

38

Rebuke Me Not in Anger, LORD

*A penitent prayer for restoration from severe illness and
for deliverance from the opportunistic attacks of enemies.*

Text

Psalm 38 is one of the traditional penitential psalms (along with 6,   *Scripture References*
32, 51, 102, 130, and 143). Though the occasion is unknown, the   st. 1 = vv. 1-4
author of Psalm 38 recognizes in a debilitating illness the chastis-   st. 2 = vv. 5-8
ing hand of God for some sin (st. 1). The prayer moves from   st. 3 = vv. 9-12
humble confessions of guilt (st. 1, 2, 5) to a lament over the illness   st. 4 = vv. 13-16
that repels friends and attracts enemies (st. 2-4). Utterly weak and   st. 5 = vv. 17-20
in pain, the psalmist waits on the LORD for help, renews the   st. 6 = vv. 21-22
lament and confession of sin (st. 5), and prays for God to "come
quickly" and "help" (st. 6). Helen Otte (PHH 17) wrote this versification in 1985 for the
Psalter Hymnal.

Tune

A pentatonic (five-pitch) folk tune from the southern United States, BOURBON fits well
with the penitential text of Psalm 38. The tune calls for unison singing, with accompaniment providing a firmly articulated rhythm. Like many pentatonic tunes, when unaccompanied it can be sung in canon after either one or two measures.

Included in *Columbian Harmony* (1825), BOURBON was credited there to Freeman
Lewis (1780-1859) and set to "'Twas on that Dark and Doleful Night," a text often
attributed to Isaac Watts. The tune appeared in several other nineteenth-century
songbooks, among them Hauser's *Hesperian Harp* (1848). The tune title presumably
refers to the aristocratic French family whose descendents included Henry IV, Phillip V,
and Charles III, and after which a Kentucky county is named.

The harmonization (1958) is by Louise McAllister (b. Louisville, KY, 1913; d.
Richmond, VA, 1960). She spent her childhood in Louisville, where her father was a
professor at Louisville Prebsyterian Theological Seminary. In 1925, when her father
began teaching at Union Theological Seminary, she moved to Richmond, Virginia, and
lived there the rest of her life. A pianist, composer, teacher, and writer, McAllister
attended the Collegiate School in Richmond, Virginia, and Mary Baldwin College,
Staunton, Virginia. She published many piano compositions and harmonizations of
folk-hymn melodies.

Liturgical Use

Serves well as a confession of sin, but may also be used in the context of sickness or other humbling circumstances—whenever God's people want to cry out, "Come quickly to help me, O Lord, my Savior."

39

Once I Said, "I Must Keep Quiet"

TYDDYN LLWYN
♩ = 88

Reflections on the fragility of life, and a prayer for God's gracious removal of disciplinary illness.

Text

The situation implied in this psalm is much like that suggested by Psalm 38: God is disciplining the psalmist because of some sin with an illness that invites "the scorn of fools" (v. 8). The psalmist tries to be silent in the presence of the wicked (st. 1) but cannot hold back. He speaks out on the fragility of life (st. 2) and then prays for deliverance from sin and its consequences (st. 3). In the same breath the psalmist prays to be saved from "the blow of [God's] hand" (v. 10), seeking removal of God's "discipline for sinning" (st. 4). The psalm closes with a plea for restoration to God's peace (st. 5), echoing the confession "My hope is in you" (v. 7). Calvin Seerveld (PHH 22) paraphrased this psalm of lament in 1983 for the *Psalter Hymnal.*

Scripture References
st. 1 = vv. 1-3
st. 2 = vv. 4-6
st. 3 = vv. 7-9
st. 4 = vv. 10-11
st. 5 = vv. 12-13

Tune

Evan Morgan (b. Tyn-dre, Morfa Bychan, Wales, 1846; d. Portmadoc, Wales, 1920) was a furniture maker by trade in Morfa Bychan in the Lleyn Peninsula. He took an interest in music at a young age, however, and became well-known in Wales as a singer and poet. He composed some hymn tunes and arranged folk tunes for the brass band in Portmadoc. His tune TYDDYN LLWYN was first published in the second appendix (1890) to Ieuan Gwyllt's *Llyfr Tonau Cynulleidfaol* (The Book of Congregational Tunes, 1859). The tune's phrases balance each other very well; the final phrase resolves the rhythmic energy and harmonic color of the initial lines. Part singing goes well with a moderate tempo.

Liturgical Use

Occasions when the church marks the brevity of life (perhaps New Year's Eve services or funerals); also appropriate in the service of confession and forgiveness of sin.

MERTHYR TYDFIL
♩ = 116

I Waited Patiently for God

*A penitent prayer for God's help when troubles abound and
enemies rejoice at the prospect of the psalmist's ruin.*

Text

Psalm 40 notes a time of "troubles without number"—troubles
the psalmist sees as brought on by sins outnumbering the hairs
of his head (v. 12). The occasion cannot be identified, but the
situation would fit the circumstances in David's life at the time
of Absalom's rebellion. The psalmist begins with an affirmation
of trust and a recollection of God's past mercies ("he lifted me

Scripture References
st. 1 = vv. 1-5
st. 2 = vv. 6-10
st. 3 = vv. 11-13
st. 4 = vv. 14-17

out of the slimy pit," st. 1), followed by a declaration of commitment to God's will and
to praising God (st. 2). Then comes an appeal that God not withhold mercy, but come
to the psalmist's aid—even though the troubles have come because of sin—for they are
overwhelming (st. 3). The psalmist also asks God not to delay in shaming enemies and
to let all who seek the LORD rejoice and magnify him (st. 4). Hebrews 10 applies vv. 6-8
(st. 2) of Psalm 40 to Christ as the One who has done God's will and has brought a
better sacrifice. Bert Polman (PHH 37) versified this psalm prayer in 1980 for morning
worship at a Christian Association for Psychological Studies convention for Christian
counselors. This unrhymed versification was published for the first time in the 1987
Psalter Hymnal.

Tune

Joseph Parry (PHH 18) composed MERTHYR TYDFIL (also called DIES IRAE), first
published in *Llyfr Tonau Cynulleidfaol Cenedlaethol Cymru (The Welsh National Book of
Congregational Tunes)*, a collection of hymn tunes Parry compiled and published in
several parts from 1887 to 1892. The tune is named after the town of Parry's birth and
means "the martyr Tydfil." The similarities of lines 1, 2, and 4 find a fitting contrast and
climax in line 3. The harmonization invites part singing, but the music must not be
taken too slowly.

Liturgical Use

Thanksgiving and dedication (st. 1-2); Advent or Lent (st. 2); pleas for God's help
(st. 3-4); times when the church reflects on the life-troubling consequences of sin.

41

How Blest Are Those Who Thoughtfully

GREELEY
♩ = 100

A prayer for mercy in time of illness, when friends betray and enemies attack.

Text

As in Psalms 38 and 39, the psalmist prays for God's mercy and restoration in a time of illness, which he views as discipline for his sins. The psalmist's enemies seize the occasion to publicly discredit him. Even his "close friend" (v. 9) turns against him. Apparently betrayal was not rare in ancient Israel. Jesus himself experienced profound betrayal by Judas at a time when Jesus seemed powerless before the growing opposition of Jewish religious leaders. This psalm expresses our confidence that the LORD delivers the godly from illness and from the attack of enemies (st. 1). In it we appeal for God's mercy in the face of our enemies' gloating and a friend's betrayal (st. 2) and pray that God will restore us and undo the slander of our enemies (st. 3). Bert Polman (PHH 37) versified this psalm in 1985 for the *Psalter Hymnal,* borrowing the opening lines from the paraphrase in the 1912 *Psalter.*

Scripture References
st. 1 = vv. 1-3
st. 2 = vv. 4-9
st. 3 = vv. 10-13

Tune

GREELEY, composed by Roy Hopp (PHH 11) in 1984 for the *Psalter Hymnal,* was first sung on tour by the Dordt College Concert Choir on March 31, 1985. Hopp named the tune after Greeley, Colorado, where his wife studied for a time. A classically designed tune (in which lines 1, 2, and 4 are similar and line 3 provides a suitable contrast), GREELEY is in the Aeolian mode and is well harmonized for part singing.

Liturgical Use

Suitable as a confession of sin, but also appropriate during illness or other distress occasioning slander or the alienation of friends. Because Jesus experienced a close parallel in the betrayal by Judas, this psalm is also fitting for Holy Week.

GENEVAN 42
♩ = 69

As a Deer in Want of Water

*The anguished yet hopeful prayer of a thirsty soul to be
restored to intimate fellowship with God at his temple.*

Text

Psalm 42 marks the beginning of Book II of the Psalms.
Exiled to the northern fringes of Israelite territory,
forced by taunting enemies to reside far from the house
of God (see also Ps. 63 and 84), the psalmist, who dearly
loves God, grieves over feeling forgotten and rejected
by God. Many throughout the ages have testified to that
same sense of abandonment, described here in terms
of a parching thirst for God (st. 1) and recalling past
seasons of worshiping God with multitudes in the
temple (st. 2). But faith revives hope in God's faithful-

Scripture References
st. 1 = vv. 42:1-2
st. 2 = vv. 42:3-4
st. 3 = vv. 42:5, 11; 43:5
(refrain)
st. 4 = vv. 42:6-8
st. 5 = vv. 42:9-10
st. 6 = vv. 43:1-2
st. 7 = vv. 43:3-4

ness (st. 3). Though overwhelmed by troubles, the exile still remembers God (st. 4) and
asks that God will remember him in the face of jeering unbelievers (st. 5). The psalmist
prays for vindication from enemies (st. 6) and for restoration to God's precious presence
(st. 7).

Psalms 42 and 43 were originally one psalm. To honor the structure of the original,
the *Psalter Hymnal* Revision Committee asked members Bert Polman (PHH 37) and
Jack Reiffer (b. Grand Rapids, MI, 1944) to versify both psalms so they could be sung
together to GENEVAN 42. As a result, Psalm 43 is the only psalm published in two
settings in the psalter section of the hymnal—first as stanzas 6 and 7 (and refrain)
under 42, and next as a separate entry under 43. The composite text includes several
lines from the 1931 versification by Dewey Westra (PHH 98) published in earlier
editions of the *Psalter Hymnal.*

Jack Reiffer was chair of the text subcommittee of the revision committee. A gradu-
ate of Calvin College and Seminary, he is currently pastor of the Washington, D.C.,
Christian Reformed Church; he has also served congregations in Chicago and
Champaign, Illinois.

Tune

Louis Bourgeois (PHH 3) composed or adapted GENEVAN 42 for the 1551 Genevan
Psalter. This tune, in bar form (AAB) with lilting rhythms fluctuating between groups of
three and two, is one of the best known and best loved in the Genevan Psalter. It is often
called FREU DICH SEHR after a German funeral hymn for which it became a setting in
Rhamba's *Harmoniae sacrae* (1613). Bach used the melody in seven different cantatas.

Adapted to long meter double, GENEVAN 42 was also published in English and Scottish psalters.

Johann Crüger (b. Grossbriesen, near Guben, Prussia, Germany, 1598; d. Berlin, Germany, 1662) published his harmonization of the tune in 1658 as part of his complete setting of the Genevan Psalter in simple four-part chorale style with instrumental accompaniment. The vocal parts are set with the text; the instrumental parts—two descants for melody instruments and a keyboard part—are found opposite 41 in the *Psalter Hymnal.*

Crüger attended the Jesuit College at Olmütz and the Poets' School in Regensburg, and later studied theology at the University of Wittenberg. He moved to Berlin in 1615, where he published music for the rest of his life. In 1622 he became the Lutheran cantor at the St. Nicholas Church and a teacher for the Gray Cloister. He wrote music instruction manuals, the best known of which is *Synopsis musica* (1630), and tirelessly promoted congregational singing. With his tunes he often included elaborate accompaniment for various instruments. Crüger's hymn collection, *Neues vollkömliches Gesangbuch* (1640), was one of the first hymnals to include figured bass accompaniment (musical shorthand) with the chorale melody rather than full harmonization written out. It included eighteen of Crüger's tunes. His next publication, *Praxis Pietatis Melica* (1644), is considered one of the most important collections of German hymnody in the seventeenth century. It was reprinted forty-four times in the following hundred years. Another of his publications, *Geistliche Kirchen Melodien* (1649), is a collection arranged for four voices, two descanting instruments, and keyboard and bass accompaniment. Crüger also published a complete psalter, *Psalmodia sacra* (1657), which included the Lobwasser translation set to all the Genevan tunes.

Psalm 42/43 invites division into two singing groups; have the congregation sing stanzas 1-2, 4-5, and 6-7 as units, punctuated by a soloist or the choir singing the refrain (st. 3), accompanied by the instrumental parts. Or, conversely, have a soloist or choir sing the lament accompanied by instruments, and have the whole congregation sing the refrain. See 194 for an alternate harmonization by Claude Goudimel (1564).

Liturgical Use
Psalm 42 (with 43) is fitting as a prayer for deliverance from distress or persecution or any forced separation from God. It also expresses the church's confidence in God in the face of present or potential threats—such as Revelation depicts—to its communion with God. Stanzas 1 and 3 serve well at the beginning of worship.

43

GENEVAN 43
♩ = 69

Defend Me, LORD, from Those Who Charge Me

A prayer for deliverance from jeering enemies and for return to God's precious presence.

Text

Marie J. Post (PHH 5) versified Psalm 43 in 1981 for the *Psalter Hymnal.* Other settings of Psalm 43 are at 42 and 165. For other commentary, see PHH 42.

Scripture References
st. 1 = vv. 1-2
st. 2 = vv. 3-4
st. 3 = v. 5

Tune

GENEVAN 43 was first published in the 1551 edition of the Genevan Psalter. Claude Goudimel (PHH 6) harmonized it in 1564. Though Goudimel usually placed the melody of his harmonizations in the tenor, which was typical of that time, he placed the melody of this one in the soprano, which was later to become the new style of writing for congregational singing. Each of the six phrases has its own delicate rhythm; the last two phrases should be sung as one long line. The mood should shift from a somber treatment in stanza 1 to increasingly joyful strains in stanzas 2 and 3.

Liturgical Use

See PHH 42. Stanza 2 serves as a call to worship; stanza 3 as a sung prayer of response to the sermon.

44

STAR IN THE EAST
♩ = 84

O God, We Have Heard

An anguished cry for God's renewed help after allowing his people to be crushingly defeated.

Text

Ascribed to (or assigned to) "the Sons of Korah," one of the Levitical choirs (1 Chron. 6:31-48), Psalm 44 is a communal prayer of ancient Israel. It reflects a cry of faith in the face of Judah's crushing defeat at the hands of Assyrian armies. That God had abandoned Judah to their enemies even though they had not turned their backs on him was a great enigma that tried their faith. Psalm 44 expresses that enigma in a prayer for God's renewed help. Impassioned as it is, this carefully designed prayer has its appropriate use in Christian

Scripture References
st. 1 = vv. 1-8
st. 2 = vv. 9-16
st. 3 = vv. 17-22
st. 4 = vv. 1-3, 23-26

worship. In singing it, we join the people who recall God's past victories on their behalf (st. 1), cite God's present abandonment of his people to their cruel enemies (st. 2), and wonder at the great enigma: "This happened though we have been faithful" (st. 3). Again recalling the LORD's past victories for them, the people cry for a renewal of God's help (st. 4). Bert Polman (PHH 37) prepared the versification of this psalm in 1985 for the *Psalter Hymnal*, adapting from the versifications in the 1912 *Psalter* and *The Book of Psalms for Singing* (1973).

Tune

STAR IN THE EAST was published with an Epiphany hymn in William Walker's *The Southern Harmony* (1835), a popular collection using shape notes. This modal tune is well matched to the lament character of Psalm 44. It is one of the longest in the *Psalter Hymnal*, yet is very accessible because of its repeated patterns and phrases (AABA). Sing with a solid and steady beat, feeling a slow two beats per measure. Two harmonizations are given—one for congregational singing by Dale Grotenhuis (PHH 4), and a three-part choral setting (opposite 43) by Roy Hopp (PHH 11). The Hopp setting can also accompany men's voices on stanza 3.

William Walker (b. Cross Keys, SC, 1809; d. Spartenburg, SC, 1875) was known as "Singin' Billy." A Southern Baptist singing school teacher, Walker composed his first hymn tune, SOLEMN CALL, at the age of eighteen. With his brother-in-law, Benjamin F. White, he compiled the famous hymnbook *The Southern Harmony and Musical Companion* (1835), which sold over six hundred thousand copies over the next thirty years. The first edition of *Southern Harmony* is considered to be primarily a borrowing from Ananias Davisson's *Kentucky Harmony* (1815), another four-shape-note tunebook. In his travels through Appalachia, Walker collected many folk tunes. His work represents one of the best collections of early American folk hymns, many of which were derived from traditional melodies of the British Isles.

Because White's work in compiling *The Southern Harmony* was uncredited by Walker in 1835, White and E. J. King published the equally important tunebook *The Sacred Harp* (1844), which led to rivalry between those who sang from the two books. In 1867 Walker expanded the four-shape notation in his book to seven shapes and published it as *Christian Harmony. The Southern Harmony* and *The Sacred Harp* are both still popular tunebooks today and are used in regular hymn-sings in various communities throughout the southeastern United States.

Liturgical Use

Because this communal lament wrestles with why God sometimes seems to forsake his faithful people, it is appropriate for occasions when the church is suffering at the hands of Christ's enemies or has been defeated (temporarily!) by the powers of this age.

45

O DASS ICH TAUSEND
♩ = 69

I Praise the King with All My Verses

A song exalting the LORD's anointed on his wedding day.

Text

Associated with "the Sons of Korah," this song in praise of the king
on his wedding day undoubtedly refers to the LORD's anointed
from the house of David. It may have been used at more than one
royal wedding. Since the bride is a foreign princess, the psalmist
highlights the king's standing as internationally significant. In
post-exilic times this psalm's importance as a description of the
Messiah came to the forefront, and the author of Hebrews applied

Scripture References
st. 1 = vv. 1-4
st. 2 = vv. 5-7
st. 3 = vv. 8-9
st. 4 = vv. 10-12
st. 5 = vv. 13-17

it directly to Christ (1:8-9). The main body of the song falls into two parts: words
addressed to the king (vv. 3-9) and words addressed to the bride (vv. 10-15). Each of the
two parts includes exhortations to and a description of the glory of the king or the
bride. The psalmist begins by announcing the praise of the king, the defender of truth
and right (st. 1). Hail to you, victorious and righteous king, blessed by God, says the
psalmist (st. 2); hail to you, glorious king, robed in splendor (st. 3). And to the bride:
Be loyal to your royal groom (st. 4). The psalmist then extols the bride's glory, the
certainty of the king's dynasty, and the king's international honor (st. 5). Marie J. Post
(PHH 5) versified this psalm in 1985 in four-line stanzas. Bert Polman (PHH 37), at the
request of the *Psalter Hymnal* Revision Committee, altered the versification to six-line
stanzas in 1986 to match the tune O DASS ICH TAUSEND.

Tune

Johann Balthaser König (b. Waltershausen, near Gotha, Germany, 1691; d. Frankfurt,
Germany, 1758) composed this tune, which later became associated with Johann
Mentzer's hymn "O dass ich tausend Zungen hätte" (Oh, That I Had a Thousand
Voices). The harmonization is from the *Württembergische Choralbuch* (1653). Music of
that time was not notated with bar lines every three or four beats; here a "quarter bar"
marks the division between the two sections of the first longer phrase, and a full bar line
delineates the other phrases. Like many of the German chorales, this tune is in bar
form (AAB) and may be sung in four-part harmony. The tune begins on an upbeat,
with the first accent on the second note.

A chorister in the Kapella of Frankfurt at a young age, König was a student of the
famous Georg Philipp Telemann, who later became godfather to König's son. He
succeeded Telemann as director of municipal music and became director of music at
the Barfüsserkirche and at St. Catherine's Church, all in Frankfurt. In 1727 he also
assumed the directorship of the Frankfurt Kapella. Mainly interested in congregational

singing, König presented a document to the Frankfurt city council in which he stated the problems of and solutions for the state of singing in the church. He edited the largest eighteenth-century German collection of hymns, *Harmonischer Lieder-Schatz* (1738), which also included O DASS ICH TAUSEND. This collection consisted of over nineteen hundred tunes with figured bass, including the 125 Genevan tunes set to Lobwasser's German translation of John Calvin's psalter. In accord with the style of his day, König "straightened out" (made all quarter notes) the originally lively rhythms of many tunes in this significant hymnal.

Liturgical Use
Any occasion on which the church celebrates the marriage of Christ and his bride—the church.

46

God Is Our Refuge and Our Strength

NOEL
♩ = 116

A celebration of the absolute security of the city of God.

Text

This song in celebration of Zion's security (see also 48 and 76) has heartened God's people throughout the ages. Luther echoed it in "A Mighty Fortress Is Our God" (469). Traditionally ascribed to (or assigned to) the "sons of Korah," the psalm was no doubt composed for liturgical use at the temple. As a song concerning the royal city of the kingdom of God on earth, it expresses Israel's hope in the certain triumph of God's kingdom. The psalm's

Scripture References
st. 1 = vv. 1-3
st. 2 = vv. 4-5
st. 3 = vv. 6-7
st. 4 = vv. 8-9
st. 5 = vv. 10-11

imagery of a river that "make[s] glad the city of God" (v. 4) serves as a metaphor for the unfailing flow of God's sustaining and refreshing blessings, which make the city of God like the Garden of Eden (Gen. 2:10). In this psalm we confess fearless trust in God, "our refuge" (st. 1), and extol God's refreshing river and protective presence (st. 2). God stills the rage of the nations, inspiring us with faith's strong confidence (st. 3). The LORD's mighty victories assure us of the people's peace (st. 4), and God's reassuring word "Be still, and know . . ." inspires us again with the confidence of faith (st. 5). The versification is based on the 1650 Scottish psalter version, which was altered in both the 1871 and 1912 American psalters and now again in the 1987 *Psalter Hymnal*. Hymns based on Psalm 46 are at 468, 469, and 610.

Tune

The tune NOEL (also used at 185) is also known as EARDISLEY or GERARD. Arthur Seymour Sullivan (b. Lambeth, London, England, 1842; d. Westminster, London,

1900) adapted this traditional English melody (probably one of the variants of the folk song "Dives and Lazarus"), added phrases of his own to recast the melody in common meter double, and published it first in his *Church Hymns with Tunes* (1874). In that collection Sullivan set this tune to the Christmas carol "It Came Upon a Midnight Clear," which explains one of the tune names. Though NOEL has frequent changes of harmony, do not sing it too slowly; keep the rhythmic energy moving. Antiphonal performance may highlight the refrain (second half of st. 3 and 5) in this psalm: all sing stanzas 1, 3, and 5; alternate groups sing stanzas 2 and 4. The folk origin of the tune suggests unison singing to most, but Sullivan's harmony will attract some choristers. Either way, this is lively music.

Sullivan was born of an Italian mother and an Irish father who was an army band-master and a professor of music. Sullivan entered the Chapel Royal as a chorister in 1854. He was elected as the first Mendelssohn scholar in 1856, when he began his studies at the Royal Academy of Music in London. He also studied at the Leipzig Conservatory (1858-1861) and in 1866 was appointed professor of composition at the Royal Academy of Music. Early in his career Sullivan composed oratorios and music for some Shakespeare plays. However, he is best known for writing the music for lyrics by William S. Gilbert, which produced popular operettas such as *H.M.S. Pinafore* (1878), *The Pirates of Penzance* (1879), *The Mikado* (1884), and *Yeomen of the Guard* (1888). These operettas satirized the court and everyday life in Victorian times. Although he com-posed some anthems, in the area of church music Sullivan is best remembered for his hymn tunes, written between 1867 and 1874 and published in *The Hymnary* (1872) and *Church Hymns* (1874), both of which he edited. He contributed hymns to *A Hymnal Chiefly from The Book of Praise* (1867) and to the Presbyterian collection *Psalms and Hymns for Divine Worship* (1867). A complete collection of his hymns and arrangements was published posthumously as *Hymn Tunes by Arthur Sullivan* (1902). Sullivan steadfastly refused to grant permission to those who wished to make hymn tunes from the popular melodies in his operettas.

Liturgical Use
Suitable for many occasions in Christian worship, especially for times of war or persecu-tion, confusion and loss, whenever the conflict between church and world sharpens. Also for Old or New Year services.

47

Nations, Clap Your Hands

A celebration of the LORD's universal reign and its recognition by the nations of the world.

Text

Ascribed to (or assigned to) "the Sons of Korah," this celebration of the universal reign of God serves as a powerful congregational testimony to the sure triumph of God's kingdom. The psalmist calls all nations to join in the praise of this "great King" (v. 2), whose victories make his people secure in their inheritance (st. 1).

Scripture References
st. 1 = vv. 1-4
st. 2 = vv. 5-7
st. 3 = vv. 8-9

God is "King of all the earth" (v. 7; st. 2), and God's universal reign draws the nobility of the nations to assemble around his throne (st. 3). In language and theme Psalm 47 shows much affinity with Psalms 93-99. It stands between two songs (46, 48) that celebrate the security of the city of God, thus reinforcing their theme. It's likely that this psalm played a role in the temple liturgy, but its place in that liturgy is uncertain. Cor Wm. Barendrecht (PHH 326) originally versified this psalm in an unrhymed text in 1980; the *Psalter Hymnal* Revision Committee added rhyme and recast a number of lines to arrive at the current versification. Another partial setting of Psalm 47 is at 166.

Tune

GENEVAN 47 was first published in the 1551 edition of the Genevan Psalter, which was supervised by Louis Bourgeois (PHH 3); Claude Goudimel (PHH 6) harmonized it in the tenor in 1564. Restored to its exciting original rhythms in this edition of the *Psalter Hymnal,* this tune could well serve as the model for what Shakespeare called "Genevan jigs." The rhythmic pattern is the same for each of the six long phrases of this major (Ionian) tune. Use a bright organ registration, and do not hesitate to try percussion; in fact, the biblical text calls for clapping.

Liturgical Use

Praise occasions; especially Ascension Day (st. 2).

48

Great Is the LORD Our God

A celebration of the absolute security of the city of God.

Text

Traditionally associated with the Levitical "Sons of Korah," this
celebration song matches the exuberant faith of Psalm 46 (see
also 76, 84, 87, 122, 125, and 137). In the post-exilic liturgy of
the temple, this psalm was sung at the time of the morning
sacrifice on the second day of the week. Because the LORD
Almighty is present in Zion, that hill's rather modest height is
likened to Mount Zaphon (North Mountain), the Mount

Scripture References
st. 1 = vv. 1-2
st. 2 = vv. 3-8
st. 3 = vv. 9-10
st. 4 = vv. 11-13a
st. 5 = vv. 13-14

Olympus where the Canaanite gods supposedly sat in counsel. Jerusalem, unlike the
imperial capitals of Egypt and Mesopotamia, was no grand city. But her walls and
citadels are impregnable because "the Great King" lives there. And in Jerusalem's
temple "we meditate on [God's] unfailing love" (v. 9). In this psalm we proclaim the
greatness of the LORD and the glory of his city (st. 1), extol God's triumphs over Zion's
enemies and his people's sense of security (st. 2), and praise the LORD's love, grace,
and righteousness (st. 3). Zion rejoices in its King and in the ramparts God maintains
(st. 4). The psalmist exhorts the people to let succeeding generations know Zion will
not fail—for God, the unfailing guide, is present there [by his Word and Spirit] (st. 5).
Emily R. Brink (PHH 158) versified stanza 1, and Bert Witvoet (PHH 4) versified stanza
2; stanzas 3 through 5 (with some alterations) are from *The Book of Psalms* (1871), a text-
only psalter that was later published with music in 1887.

Tune

George Job Elvey (b. Canterbury, England, 1816; d. Windlesham, Surrey, England,
1893) composed DIADEMATA (Greek for "crowns") for the Matthew Bridges text
"Crown Him with Many Crowns" (410). It was first published in the Appendix of *Hymns
Ancient and Modern* (1868). The tune is a splendid example of a nineteenth-century
English hymn tune and is equally appropriate for this joyful psalm of Zion. A stately
tempo is helpful, combined with a ritard on the final phrase of the fifth stanza. See 410
for a setting of DIADEMATA with the descant.

As a young boy, Elvey was a chorister in Canterbury Cathedral. Living and studying
with his brother Stephen, he was educated at Oxford and at the Royal Academy of
Music. At age nineteen Elvey became organist and master of the boys' choir at St.
George Chapel, Windsor, where he remained until his retirement in 1882. He was
frequently called upon to provide music for royal ceremonies such as Princess Louise's

wedding in 1871 (after which he was knighted). Elvey also composed hymn tunes, anthems, oratorios, and service music.

Liturgical Use

Beginning of worship; various points in festive services (including church anniversaries), since the New Testament temple is the whole people of God.

49

Listen, All People Who Live in This World

JULIUS
$\downarrow = 120$

Godly counsel against fear or awe of the godless wealthy.

Text

Traditionally ascribed to (or assigned to) "the Sons of Korah," Psalm 49, like Psalms 1, 34, 37, 73, and 112, gives instruction in godly wisdom. It calls God's people to hear wise counsel (st. 1) against fear or awe of the wealthy, especially those who trust in riches rather than in God. Death takes them too, and no ransom payment can ward it off (st. 2). They are fools whose final home is the grave (st. 3). While death is the shepherd of those who trust in themselves, God redeems the godly from the grave and takes them to himself (st. 4). "Do not be overawed," says the psalmist (v. 16), by the wealth and honor of the rich (st. 5); "one who has riches without understanding is like the beasts that perish" (v. 20). Helen Otte (PHH 17) paraphrased Psalm 49 in unrhymed dactylic meter in 1984 for the *Psalter Hymnal.*

Scripture References
st. 1 = vv. 1-4
st. 2 = vv. 5-9
st. 3 = vv. 10-11
st. 4 = vv. 12-15
st. 5 = vv. 16-20

Tune

Martin Edward Fallas Shaw (b. Kensington, London, England, 1875; d. Southwold, Suffolk, England, 1958) composed JULIUS for J. S. Arkwright's iambic text "O Valiant Hearts" and named the tune in memory of his brother, who was reported missing in World War I. JULIUS was first published in Sir Sydney Nicholson's *Gift Book* in 1935 for the School of English Church Music (which later became the Royal School of Church Music). Take this tune in two broad beats per bar; the resulting "triplets" lend a confident and sure spirit to the text.

Shaw was educated at the Royal College of Music in London and was organist and choirmaster at St. Mary's, Primrose Hill (1908-1920), St. Martin's in the Fields (1920-1924), and the Eccleston Guild House (1924-1935). From 1935 to 1945 he served as music director for the diocese of Chelmsford. He established the Purcell Operatic Society and was a founder of the Plainsong and Medieval Society and what later became the Royal Society of Church Music. Author of *The Principles of English Church Music*

Composition (1921), Shaw was a notable reformer of English church music. He worked with Percy Dearmer (his rector at St. Mary's in Primrose Hill; see PHH 595), Ralph Vaughan Williams (PHH 316), and his brother Geoffrey Shaw in publishing hymnals such as *Songs of Praise* (1925, 1931) and the *Oxford Book of Carols* (1928). A leader in the revival of English opera and folk music scholarship, Shaw composed some one hundred songs as well as anthems and service music; some of his best hymn tunes were published in his *Additional Tunes in Use at St. Mary's* (1915).

Liturgical Use
Occasions when the church speaks out against materialism and all forms of proud secularism.

50

ST. PETERSBURG
♩ = 132

The Mighty God and Sovereign LORD

The LORD calls the people to covenant account.

Text

Psalm 50 is the first of twelve psalms (the others are 73-83) ascribed by tradition to Asaph, head of one of the Levitical choirs (1 Chron. 6:31-48). It is unusual among the psalms in that, for the most part, it represents God's address to Israel rather than Israel's address to God. For Christians who sing this psalm, the LORD appears in Zion to confront the people (st. 1), to call them to covenant account. After summoning the covenant witnesses—the earth (v. 1) and the heavens (v. 4)—the LORD calls for an assembly of all "who made a covenant" with him (v. 5; st. 2). First God

Scripture References
st. 1 = vv. 1-3
st. 2 = vv. 4-6
st. 3 = vv. 7-8
st. 4 = vv. 9-11
st. 5 = vv. 12-15
st. 6 = vv. 16-17
st. 7 = vv. 18-21a
st. 8 = vv. 21b-23

instructs them with warnings against false notions about sacrifice, exhorting them, "Call upon me" (v. 15; st. 3-5). Then God turns to the wicked with indictments and rebukes, making clear that God desires people's complete trust and a wholehearted commitment to his moral will (st. 6-8). Marie J. Post (PHH 5) prepared this versification in 1985 for the *Psalter Hymnal* using the 1912 *Psalter* as her starting point.

Tune

Dmitri Stephanovich Bortnianski (b. Gloukoff, Ukraine, 1751; d. St. Petersburg, Russia, 1825) was a Russian composer of church music, operas, and instrumental music. His tune ST. PETERSBURG (also known as RUSSIAN HYMN) was first published in J. H. Tscherlitzky's *Choralbuch* (1825). The tune is supposedly from a Mass composed in 1822, though that work is not extant. Tchaikovsky included ST. PETERSBURG as the setting for a Russian hymn in his 1884 edition of Bortnianski's compositions for church use. The tune is named after the city where Bortnianski studied, worked, and died. Shaped into a strict bar form (AAB), this tune has a third line that brings a fine climax and resolution to the entire melody.

Bortnianski began his musical study as a chorister in the imperial chapel choir at the age of eight. With financial aid from Catherine the Great, he went to Venice in 1768 to study music; he also studied in Rome and Naples. After returning to Russia, he assumed the directorship of the imperial chapel choir in St. Petersburg. His choral music was published by Tchaikovsky (c. 1884) and continues to be used both in the Russian Orthodox Church and in western churches.

Liturgical Use
Times of self-examination; beginning of worship; service of confession of sin.

51

Be Merciful, Be Merciful, O God

GENEVAN 51
$\quad$ = 72

A fervent prayer for pardon, renewal, and reconciliation with God.

Text

Tradition ascribes this prayer to David on the occasion "when the prophet Nathan came to him after David had committed adultery with Bathsheba." No other psalm matches the frankness and fullness with which Psalm 51 faces the problem of human sinfulness. Sin is first of all sin against God, and no animal sacrifice can effect reconciliation. Only a heart "contrite and broken" can expect God's forgiveness. Moreover, sin springs

Scripture References
st. 1 = vv. 1-5
st. 2 = vv. 6-9
st. 3 = vv. 10-13
st. 4 = vv. 14-17
st. 5 = vv. 18-19

from a heart so defiled that it must be recreated, made new, to be clean. The psalm offers an unparalleled confession of sin and a fervent plea for pardon (st. 1); a prayer for forgiveness and restoration to joy (st. 2); a prayer for a new, undefiled heart and for reconciliation with God (st. 3); and a vow to praise when God grants pardon to a "contrite and broken" heart (st. 4). Added to this is a prayer that God's mercy will extend to the whole city of Zion (st. 5)—in Christian terms, to the whole church of Christ. Stanley Wiersma (PHH 25), who prepared this unrhymed versification in 1980 for the *Psalter Hymnal*, often spoke of this psalm sung to GENEVAN 51 as the "Calvinist *Kyrie*" (see PHH 258 for information on the *Kyrie*). Psalm 51 is also one of the traditional penitential psalms (along with 6, 32, 38, 102, 130, and 143). Other settings of Psalm 51 are at 167 and 255.

Tune

GENEVAN 51 first appeared in the 1551 edition of the Genevan Psalter and is attributed to Louis Bourgeois (PHH 3). Claude Goudimel (PHH 6) composed the harmonization in 1564; the melody was originally in the tenor. One of the longer and more difficult Genevan tunes in the *Psalter Hymnal*, this Phrygian melody is one of the most hauntingly suitable tunes for a penitential psalm. Though the initial stanzas of this psalm are subdued, it should not be sung too slowly, and the final stanzas have many phrases that abound in confidence and joy. Sing harmony on stanzas 3, 4, and/or 5.

Liturgical Use

Traditionally in the service of confession of sin; also appropriate for the liturgy of the Lord's Supper and during Lent.

52

MADILL
♩ = 69

Mighty Mortal, Boasting Evil

A godly man's denunciation of a rich and arrogant fool who has wronged him.

Text

Tradition ascribes this psalm to David on the occasion "when Doeg the Edomite had gone to Saul and told him: 'David has gone to the house of Ahimelech'" (1 Sam. 21). The psalmist has been attacked by one who has grown wealthy and powerful by taking advantage of others with the most vicious of weapons, an evil tongue. Here the psalmist addresses him with the bluntness his folly deserves (st. 1). The fool is evil and arrogant, and God will bring him "down to everlasting ruin" (v. 5); then the righteous ones he disdained will mock his folly (st. 2). We join the psalmist in a testimony that only those who trust in the LORD will flourish like the long-lived olive tree, enjoying a ready welcome in God's house (st. 3). This psalm has much in common with Psalm 49. Helen Otte (PHH 17) versified Psalm 52 in 1985 for the *Psalter Hymnal*.

Scripture References
st. 1 = vv. 1-4
st. 2 = vv. 5-7
st. 3 = vv. 8-9

Tune

Aubrey Lee Butler (b. Noble, OK, 1933) composed MADILL to accompany Milburn Price's text "Stir Thy Church, O God, Our Father." Butler named the tune after Madill, Oklahoma, where he served as a minister of music at the First Baptist Church. MADILL first appeared in a pamphlet, *New Hymns for This Day* (1971). This unison tune requires clear articulation of the repeated notes in the melody and a rather forceful (or even strident) performance of stanzas 1 and 2, with a more stately performance for stanza 3. The accompaniment establishes the half note as the primary beat.

Butler, known as "Pete" by his friends, began his music career as minister of music in several Baptist congregations in Madill and Ada, Oklahoma. He was educated at Oklahoma Baptist University and Southern Baptist Theological Seminary, Louisville, Kentucky. Since 1983 he has been a member of the faculty of Midwestern Baptist Theological Seminary, Kansas City, Missouri. He also established that school's church music program. Butler has composed hymn tunes, cantatas, and numerous anthems, and served on the editorial committee for *The Baptist Hymnal* (1991).

Liturgical Use
Whenever the church reflects on the folly of those who live by taking advantage of others. The confidence and hope of stanza 3 make the psalm useful for many occasions in Christian worship.

53

The Foolish in Their Hearts Exclaim

BRISTOL
♩ = 63

A denunciation of godless fools who oppress God's people.

Text
A slightly revised version of Psalm 14, this psalm is a denunciation of fools who devote themselves to evil and "devour" God's people as if there were no God to call them to account (v. 4). Although its original occasion is unknown, Psalm 53 appears to reflect a situation in which fools are crushed by the God they have disregarded. The psalmist describes their godlessness (st. 1) and how God examines the human race (st. 2) and finds "no one who does good," only "evildoers" who oppress God's people (vv. 3-4; st. 3). He proclaims that God will judge such fools (st. 4) and prays longingly for Zion's deliverance from them (st. 5). Marie J. Post (PHH 5) versified this psalm in 1982 for the *Psalter Hymnal.*

Scripture References
st. 1 = v. 1
st. 2 = v. 2
st. 3 = vv. 3-4
st. 4 = v. 5
st. 5 = v. 6

Tune
John Playford (b. Norwich, England, 1623; d. London, England, 1686) composed BRISTOL for his musical edition of *The Whole Book of Psalms* (1677). BRISTOL, named after the British city, was the only newly composed tune for that psalter. (Several other tunes use the same name.) BRISTOL was originally in three parts; the alto and tenor lines in the more typical four-part composition replaced the original middle part. The result is a rhythmically playful setting that moves into a triple meter on the last line. Emphasize the final stanza with a change in registration and a more stately tempo.

Playford was a bookseller, a clerk at the Temple Church, and choral vicar at St. Paul Cathedral. But he is primarily known for his music publishing. In order to publish in seventeenth-century England it was necessary to have the approval of the Stationers' Company, which Playford received. In 1603 King James I granted the Stationers' Company the privilege of being the sole printers of metrical psalters. Because Playford was the primary publisher of the time, he published nearly all the psalters. Through his publishing he also encouraged better congregational singing of the psalms, especially in three-part harmony. Playford's best-known collection is his 1677 psalter, *The Whole Book of Psalms; with the Usual Hymns and Spiritual Songs; together with all the Ancient and proper Tunes Sung in Churches, with some of Later Use. Composed in Three Parts, Cantus, Medius, and Bassus: In a More Plain and Useful Method than hath been formerly Published.*

Liturgical Use

Occasions in which the church suffers from or laments the folly of unbelievers who act toward God's people as if there is no God.

54

ENGADINE
♩ = 120

By Your Name, O God, Now Save Me

A prayer for rescue, with confidence that God will save.

Text

Though very short, this psalm is a classic example of a psalm prayer. It contains the most common elements of these prayers: an initial appeal for God to hear and save (vv. 1-2); an indication of distress and an indictment of the ruthless strangers who attack "without regard for God" (v. 3); a confession of confidence that God will help (v. 4); a call for God to deal as a judge with the attackers (v. 5); and a vow to praise God for his deliverance (vv. 6-7). The versification is a 1985 revision by Helen Otte (PHH 17) of the text published in *The Book of Psalms for Singing* (1973).

Scripture References
st. 1 = vv. 1-3
st. 2 = vv. 4-7

Tune

ENGADINE was included in Frizzoni's *Canzuns Spirituaelas* (1765); the tune is named after the valley of the Inn River in eastern Switzerland. Shaped in rounded bar form (AABA'), this Italian tune needs the sense of one broad beat per measure. The color of the four-part harmonization helps in congregational singing.

Liturgical Use

Reflection upon the church's or the individual's trust in God.

55

I Need Your Help, O LORD My God

RELEASE

♩ = 72

A prayer for God's help when threatened by a host of conspirators led by a former friend.

Text

Psalm 55 evokes a situation such as David experienced at the time of Absalom's revolt: the city is in turmoil, danger lurks everywhere, false reports circulate among the masses, and who can be trusted is uncertain. In the midst of this confusion and danger, the psalmist pleads for God's help (st. 1) and dreams of escape to some desert refuge "far from the tempest and

Scripture References
st. 1 = vv. 1-5
st. 2 = vv. 6-11
st. 3 = vv. 12-15, 20-21
st. 4 = vv. 16-19, 22-23

storm" (v. 8). He appeals to the LORD to frustrate the plans of the treacherous conspirators (st. 2). The chief adversary is a friend and close associate who shared fellowship with the psalmist at the house of God, and the psalmist must face the unbearable pain of this friend's betrayal (st. 3). (In David's case this could have been Ahithophel—2 Sam. 15:12. Christ experienced a similar betrayal by a close associate.) In singing this psalm we take refuge in God, who "will never let the righteous fall," and urge others to "cast [their] cares on the LORD" (v. 22; st. 4). Helen Otte (PHH 17) prepared this versification of Psalm 55 in 1984 for the *Psalter Hymnal.*

Tune

RELEASE is an anonymous Danish folk tune named by the publishers of the *Service Book and Hymnal* (1958), in which it was associated with the text "How Blessed from the Bonds of Sin." It is also known by its Danish name, JEG SER DIG. RELEASE is a simple tune with a simple harmony that invites part singing.

Liturgical Use

When the church is betrayed; when the church remembers Christ's betrayal by Judas.

56

O God, Be Merciful to Me

ROSALIE MCMILLAN

♩ = 60

A prayer for deliverance from enemies who conspire to destroy through slander and defamation.

Text

The psalmist is under such threats from enemies that he is in mortal danger. But because the enemies' weapons are defamation and slander, there is no human court of appeal to which he can plead his case. So the psalmist appeal to which he can plead his case. So the psalmist appeals to God for deliverance. The psalmist frames this prayer with an appeal to God (st. 1) and a confession of assurance (st. 5). An inner frame confesses confident trust that God will preserve the psalmist against the treachery of mortals (vv. 3-4, 10-11; st. 2, 4). And at the prayer's center the psalmist asks God to bring down the enemies and to respond to this lament (st. 3-4). Helen Otte (PHH 17) versified this psalm in 1986 for the *Psalter Hymnal*.

Scripture References
st. 1 = vv. 1-2
st. 2 = vv. 3-4
st. 3 = vv. 5-7
st. 4 = vv. 8-11
st. 5 = vv. 12-13

Tune

James Calvin Ward (b. Belleville, IL, 1950) composed ROSALIE MCMILLAN in 1984 for Psalm 17; the *Psalter Hymnal* Revision Committee, however, chose it as the setting for Psalm 56, which is versified in the same meter. Ward named the tune for his mother, whose Covenanter heritage in the Reformed Presbyterian Church in North America influenced his love for the psalms. This tune consists of two long lines with identical rhythmic patterns. The simple harmony invites four-part singing.

Ward received a B.A. in music from Covenant College, Lookout Mountain, Georgia, and a Masters in Jazz from the University of Tennessee at Knoxville. From 1973 to 1975 he worked as a campus intern and musician with InterVarsity Christian Fellowship, then codirected the progressive jazz group "Elan" in Pittsburgh until 1978. After working with Lamb and Lion Records (Pat Boone/Benson) and Greentree Records, Ward began working independently; he currently tours North America annually as a solo performer, recording artist, and songwriter. He also serves as director of music at New City Fellowship Presbyterian Church, Chattanooga, Tennessee. Among the recordings Ward has released are *Mourning to Dancing* (1980), *Faith Takes a Vision* (1983), *Good Advice* (1985), and *Over All the World* (1990). A number of his songs have been arranged as choral anthems.

Liturgical Use

When the church is under attack by worldly attempts to discredit its ministry.

57

Be Merciful to Me, O God

A prayer asking for God's deliverance from fierce and ruthless foes.

Text

Hounded by fierce foes (v. 4), the psalmist takes refuge in the protective "shadow of [God's] wings" (v. 1). The first half of the psalm is an appeal to God for mercy and refuge (st. 1) and a description of the ferocity of the psalmist's enemies (st. 2). The second half expresses both the psalmist's confidence that these enemies will fall into the trap they have set (st. 3) and praise for

Scripture References
st. 1 = vv. 1-3
st. 2 = vv. 4-5
st. 3 = vv. 6-8
st. 4 = vv. 9-11

God's saving help (st. 4). Both halves end with a refrain exalting God as the LORD over all creation (vv. 5, 11; st. 2, 4). Though originally a lament on being threatened by enemies, Psalm 57 expresses great confidence in God's help; the refrain in stanzas 2 and 4 highlights the tone of praise that often concludes such laments. Marie J. Post (PHH 5) versified this psalm in 1982 for the *Psalter Hymnal.*

Tune

Katherine Kennicott Davis (b. St. Joseph, MA, 1892; d. Concord, MA, 1980) composed MASSACHUSETTS in 1962 for *The Methodist Hymnal* (1964), in which it was set to Charles Kingsley's "From Thee All Skill and Science Flow." Davis named the tune after her home state. MASSACHUSSETTS exhibits the classic structure of a rounded bar form (AABA). The second half of stanzas 2 and 3 and all of stanza 4 bear an energetic and even jubilant performance; sing the entire psalm with two beats per measure.

Davis studied at Wellesley College, Wellesley, Massachusetts, where she was also a teaching assistant in music. From 1921 to 1929 she taught singing and piano in private schools in Concord, Massachusetts, and Philadelphia, Pennsylvania. After 1929 she devoted herself largely to music composition. She wrote some eight hundred pieces, most of which were choral (often writing under several pseudonyms). One of her most popular songs is "The Little Drummer Boy," originally called "Carol of the Drum" (1941). Her other publications include the folk operetta *Cinderella* (1933) and *Songs of Freedom* (1948).

Liturgical Use

The combined themes of distress, confidence in God, and praise to God suggest a number of uses in Christian worship.

58

O Mighty Rulers, Can You Claim

A denunciation of wicked rulers and an appeal to God to destroy their power to work harm.

Text

The psalmist's reproof of wicked rulers expresses a concern frequently addressed in the Old Testament. Nothing corrupts the social order more pervasively or causes more human pain than the perversion of justice by the powerful, especially those who are supposed to uphold it. The psalmist denounces wicked rulers for

Scripture References
st. 1 = vv. 1-2
st. 2 = vv. 3-9
st. 3 = vv. 10-11

corrupting justice (st. 1); appeals to God to destroy their power and bring their kind to an end (st. 2); and, in a final word, reassures the righteous that "there is a God who judges" (st. 3; see 82 for a similar theme). The early church applied Psalm 58 to Jesus' trial before the Sanhedrin (Matt. 26:57-68). Bert Polman (PHH 37) versified this psalm in 1983 for the *Psalter Hymnal.*

Tune

Annabeth McClelland Gay (b. Ottawa, IL, 1925) composed SHEPHERDS' PIPES in 1952, and her husband matched it with a hymn text to send as Christmas greetings. She wrote, "When I played it for him, he said, 'I wonder if Palestinian shepherds played on pipes, because that's what this tune reminds me of.' So his text followed ("The Shepherds' Pipes on Bethl'hem's Heights") and from the text, the tune name." The tune was first published in *Pilgrim Hymnal* (1958) with T. T. Lynch's text "The Lord Is Rich and Merciful." Gay was organist and choir director in churches in New York and Ohio, including the Hale United Church of Christ in Dayton, Ohio, where her husband served as pastor. She was educated at Knox College, Galesburg, Illinois, and received a masters degree in sacred music from Union Theological Seminary, New York City. Other of her hymn tunes were combined with texts by her husband and sent with Christmas greetings; "Carol of Hope" was included in *Worship II.*

Dale Grotenhuis (PHH 4) harmonized SHEPHERDS' PIPES in 1985. In a minor tonality, this tune offers melodic repetitions and dependable rhythms. To do justice to this text, use a *marcato* performance.

Liturgical Use

Many situations in which the Christian community needs to address government and the frequent miscarriages of justice perpetrated or condoned by government officials.

59

Protect and Save Me, O My God

MANCHESTER
♩ = 138

A prayer for deliverance from the fierce attacks of powerful and treacherous enemies.

Text

Like snarling dogs, the psalmist's enemies prowl the city at night and "spew out swords from their lips" (v. 7). Under such threat the psalmist turns to the LORD for protection (st. 1), declaring personal innocence, describing the unwarranted hatred of these enemies (st. 2), and pleading for God's help (st. 3). These enemies blindly disregard God, but the LORD "will turn them back" (st. 4). The psalmist professes reliance on God's sure help (st. 5) and asks God to confront the enemies' wickedness with his sovereign power (st. 6). Even though the enemies "slink back at night," the psalmist knows God will defeat them (st. 7) and

Scripture References
st. 1 = vv. 1-2
st. 2 = vv. 3-4a
st. 3 = vv. 4b-5
st. 4 = vv. 6-8
st. 5 = vv. 9-10
st. 6 = vv. 11-13
st. 7 = vv. 14-15, 16b
st. 8 = vv. 16-17

promises to praise the LORD "in the morning" (v. 16), confident that the night of woe will give way to the dawn of God's relief (st. 8). In the first part of this psalm (st. 1-5) we sing a prayer for deliverance, while in the second part (st. 6-8) we express assurance that the LORD will deliver. The versification (altered) is from the 1912 *Psalter.*

Tune

MANCHESTER (also known as ELY; both names refer to British cities) is from the musical edition of *The Whole Book of Psalms* (1621) by Thomas Ravenscroft (b. England, c. 1582; d. England, c. 1635). Ravenscroft was a chorister as well as a participant in a theater company of child actors at St. Paul's Cathedral in London (1598). He graduated from Cambridge University with a music degree in 1605 and served as music master at Christ's Hospital from 1618 to 1622. A composer of many songs for stage productions, Ravenscroft also published a number of works, of which the best known is *The Whole Book of Psalms, with the Hymnes Evangelical and Songs Spiritual, composed into four parts by sundry Authors, to such several Tunes as have been and are usually sung in England, Scotland, Wales, Germany, Italy, France, and the Netherlands, never as yet in one volume published* (1621). This psalter, with the tunes in the tenor, contains 105 settings (forty-eight by Ravenscroft) and was one of the earliest publications to list the composers' names as well as the tune names.

Emily R. Brink (PHH 158) harmonized the tune in 1985. MANCHESTER reveals the rhythmic vitality once present in British psalm tunes (partly as a result of Genevan influence). Think two beats per measure.

Liturgical Use

In situations of distress and persecution; or by Christians who sing this prayer on behalf of others in severe distress.

60

O God, You Have Rejected Us

A prayer for victory over Edom, the enemy of God's people.

Text

This lament, in contrast to the immediately preceding ones, takes on a national scope, focusing on Israel's defeat by a foreign nation. Though Israel has suffered God's rejection in battle, the psalmist appeals for help (st. 1) from God, who has declared that Israel is his kingdom ("Judah [is] my scepter"), and who will triumph over Edom and other enemies (st. 2). Relying on that declaration, the psalmist encourages us to pray with confidence that God will give victory to his people, his church (st. 3). Marie J. Post (PHH 5) versified this psalm in 1985 for the *Psalter Hymnal*.

Scripture References
st. 1 = vv. 1-5
st. 2 = vv. 6-8
st. 3 = vv. 9-12

Tune

Julius Robinson Tipton (b. Memphis, TN, 1942) composed XAVIER for the *Baptist Hymnal* (1975) as a setting for Harry Emerson Fosdick's text "O God, Who to a Loyal Home." The tune name derives from Xavier University in New Orleans, Louisiana, where Tipton was choral director and music department chair from 1969-1978. XAVIER is written in the style of *Southern Harmony* tunes from the southeastern United States (see PHH 44 for more information on *Southern Harmony*). Lines 1, 2, and 4 contrast with the climactic line 3. A moderate tempo and clear organ articulation help set the pace for this music.

Tipton graduated from Mississippi College, Louisiana State University, and New Orleans Baptist Theological Seminary, and served several churches as minister of music, including Woodland Presbyterian Church in New Orleans from 1969-1978. Tipton then received the M.Div. degree from Austin Presbyterian Seminary, was pastor of First Presbyterian Church of New Iberia, Louisiana (1980-1989), and is currently pastor at John Knox Presbyterian Church in Orlando, Florida. Tipton has composed vocal, choral, and instrumental works, including the opera *Judas*.

Liturgical Use

When the church has suffered defeat or is otherwise in need of encouragement in its spiritual warfare.

61

Listen to My Cry, LORD

A prayer that the LORD's anointed be restored to God's presence and be enthroned there forever.

Text

In this short prayer the psalmist seeks restoration to God's presence. Kept far from the temple by circumstances of which we cannot be certain (though there are hints about being driven away by enemies), the psalmist calls to God to hear him (st. 1) "from the ends of the earth" (v. 2) and pleads to be led back to the LORD's "rock" (st. 2) of refuge and protection from enemies (st. 3). Longing for the shelter of God's wings (st. 4), the psalmist recalls God's past mercies (st. 5) and prays for the security of the king's life and reign (st. 6-7), vowing to praise God for that protection (st. 7). The prayer that the king "be enthroned in God's presence forever" (v. 7) acknowledges that only under God's protection is the psalmist's life secure. Later, the Jews appropriately applied this psalm to the Messiah, and surely that is how Christians sing it today. (Some scholars propose that the enemy in view is death and that "from the ends of the earth" is a metaphor for the edge of the grave.)

Scripture References
st. 1 = v. 1
st. 2 = v. 2
st. 3 = v. 3
st. 4 = v. 4
st. 5 = v. 5
st. 6 = v. 6
st. 7 = vv. 7-8

Henrietta Ten Harmsel (b. Hull, IA, 1921) versified this psalm in 1985 for the *Psalter Hymnal.* Ten Harmsel attended Calvin College, Grand Rapids, Michigan, and the University of Michigan in Ann Arbor. From 1949 to 1957 she taught English at Western Christian High School in Hull, Iowa, and from 1960 until retirement in 1985 was a member of the English department at Calvin College. Many factors contributed to Ten Harmsel's interest in the psalms. As a child she learned Dutch from her parents, and they instilled in her a love for the Dutch Psalter. Later J. W. Schulte Nordholt, poet, hymnologist, and professor of American history at the University of Leiden, became a great promoter of her interest in Dutch language and literature and her translation work. Ten Harmsel's translations from Dutch include *Jacobus Revius: Dutch Metaphysical Poet* (1968) and two collections of children's poems: *Pink Lemonade* (1981) and *Good Friday* (1984). In 1984 Ten Harmsel was awarded the Martinus Nijhoff translation award.

Tune

Norman L. Warren (PHH 15) composed LISTENING in 1969 for another paraphrase of Psalm 61, a text, writes Warren, "which demanded a gentle tune." It was published in *Psalm Praise* (1973). Its two long lines flow together in apparent perpetual motion— they should be performed that way, too, with no significant breaks between stanzas. A final ritard is appropriate for the alternate ending on stanza 7.

Liturgical Use

Whenever the church reflects on past or present threats to Christ and his church and kingdom. Warren suggested using Psalm 61 as a solo before a time of quiet worship or prayer.

62

THIRD MODE MELODY
♩ = 56

My Soul Finds Rest in God Alone

A confession of trust in God by the LORD's anointed when
threatened by a powerfully backed internal conspiracy.

Text

Psalm 62 suggests that a strong conspiracy aims to topple the king from his throne. It even hints that the king is old and no longer vigorous (v. 3)—which may have occasioned the revolt. Such treachery and rebellion plagued King David in his old age (2 Sam. 15-20). Though threatened by a host of conspirators, including powerful elements in the land, the king "finds rest in God," his rock and refuge (st. 1-2), and exhorts the people to trust in the LORD, whose protection is sure (st. 2). These truths bring confidence when God's people are threatened: although our "mortal strength is vain," God is strong and loving and faithful (st. 3).

Scripture References
st. 1 = vv. 1-4
st. 2 = vv. 5-8
st. 3 = vv. 9-12

David James Diephouse (b. Grand Haven, MI, 1947) versified this psalm in 1986 for the *Psalter Hymnal.* Educated at Calvin College, Grand Rapids, Michigan, and Princeton University, Diephouse taught at Rutgers University, New Brunswick, New Jersey, from 1974 to 1976. Since 1976 he has been professor of history at Calvin College. In addition to a number of essays, Diephouse wrote *Pastors and Pluralism in Wurttemberg, 1918-1933.* A pianist and harpsichordist, Diephouse has served on the worship committee of the Church of the Servant, Grand Rapids, and on the Christian Reformed Church denominational worship committee.

Tune

THIRD MODE MELODY is the third of nine tunes Thomas Tallis composed for Matthew Parker's *The Whole Psalter* (c. 1561). This magnificent tune is worth the trouble it may take to learn. Diephouse set the text with this tune in mind, since it kept coming to him as he was working on the text. Many may know the tune from Ralph Vaughan Williams's orchestral work "Fantasia on a Theme of Thomas Tallis." The "third mode" is the Phrygian mode, and THIRD MODE MELODY is one of the few tunes in that mode included in the *Psalter Hymnal* (see also 51 and 100). This tune requires solid, yet rhythmically pliable organ support. The melody was originally in the tenor, and choirs

may switch parts between tenors and sopranos. Another suitable tune for Psalm 62 is
BETHLEHEM (497).

Thomas Tallis (b. Leicestershire [?], England, c. 1505; d. Greenwich, Kent, England,
1585) was one of the few Tudor musicians who served during the reigns of Henry VIII,
Edward VI, Mary, and Elizabeth I and managed to remain in the good favor of both
Catholic and Protestant monarchs. He was court organist and composer from 1543
until his death, composing music for Roman Catholic masses and Anglican liturgies
(depending on the monarch). With William Byrd, Tallis also enjoyed a long-term
monopoly on music printing. Prior to his court connections Tallis had served at
Waltham Abbey and Canterbury Cathedral. He composed mostly church music,
including Latin motets, English anthems, settings of the liturgy, magnificats, and two
sets of lamentations. His most extensive contrapuntal work was the choral composition,
"Spem in alium," a work in forty parts for eight five-voice choirs. He also provided nine
modal psalm tunes for Matthew Parker's *Psalter* (c. 1561).

Liturgical Use

Many occasions in which the church is under threat from human powers and wants to
express its confidence in the Lord.

63

O LORD, My God, Most Earnestly

THE GREEN HILL
♩ = 63

A profession of longing for God when hindered by enemies from communing with God at the temple.

Text

Like Psalm 42, Psalm 63 uses the metaphor of thirst to express the
longing for security in God's presence. Traditionally ascribed to
David "when he was in the Desert of Judah," this song expresses the
psalmist's yearning for God while forced to wander "in a desert
land" far from the LORD's sanctuary (st. 1; see also Ps. 84). There
the psalmist thinks of God's soul-satisfying love through "the watches of the night" (st.
2) and of the sense of security he enjoys from God's sheltering wings (st. 3). Though
explicit mention of the king (v. 11; st. 3) identifies the speaker as the LORD's anointed,
and references to enemies (vv. 9-10; st. 3) suggest that they are the ones who have
forced the king from the temple, Christians can sing this psalm today whenever we
yearn for the security that only God provides. The versification comes from the 1912
Psalter, with alterations mainly in stanza 3.

Scripture References
st. 1 = vv. 1-2
st. 2 = vv. 3-6
st. 3 = vv. 7-11

Tune

George Coles Stebbins (b. East Carlton, NY, 1846; d. Catskill, NY, 1945) composed THE GREEN HILL in 1877 to accompany Cecil F. Alexander's hymn "There Is a Green Hill Far Away." The tune was published in *Gospel Hymns No. 3* (1878). The slow harmonic rhythm and mostly stepwise melody build to a climax in the last line. This music bears an animated tempo, but organists must be sure to tie over many of the bass tones.

Stebbins grew up on a farm and attended a small country school. At the age of thirteen he enrolled in a singing school and became so enthralled with music that he decided to make it his career. In 1869 he moved to Chicago, where he worked at the Lyon and Healy Music Company and became music director at the First Baptist Church. There he also became acquainted with famous gospel musicians Root (PHH 93), Bliss (PHH 479), and Sankey (PHH 73). In 1874 he moved to Boston and became music director of the Clarendon Baptist Church and later of Tremont Temple Baptist Church. Associated with Dwight L. Moody and Ira D. Sankey from 1876 until 1899, Stebbins traveled on their evangelism campaigns throughout England and the United States as well as in India, Egypt, and Palestine. Along with Sankey and McGranahan, he edited and published three editions of *Gospel Hymns* (1878-1891). He also edited *The Northfield Hymnal* (1904) for Moody's Bible Conference in Massachusetts. Stebbins composed some fifteen hundred songs, many of them under the pseudonym "George Coles." His *Reminiscences and Gospel Hymn Stories* (1924) are a helpful account of gospel music in the urban revivals of the late nineteenth century.

Liturgical Use

Preserved in the early church for use in daily public prayers, this psalm fits well at the beginning of worship or whenever the church seeks to express its longing for God's presence and saving power.

64

WINDHAM
♩ = 63

Hear My Voice, O God, in My Complaint

A prayer for God's protection from a band of confident conspirators.

Text

As in many prayers of the psalms, the psalmist's enemies' chief weapon is an evil and vicious tongue. Curses, lies, threats, and plots in those days could dethrone kings more effectively than brandished spears and drawn swords. And only God could protect against the tongue's deadly arrows. So the psalmist turns to God for safety (st. 1), identifying the enemies' tongues as their weapons—like arrows shot from ambush (st. 2)—and marking

Scripture References
st. 1 = vv. 1-2
st. 2 = vv. 3-4
st. 3 = vv. 5-6
st. 4 = vv. 6-7
st. 5 = vv. 8-9
st. 6 = vv. 9-10

their plots and intrigue as their mode of operation (st. 3). Confident that God will shoot the conspirators with his own arrows (st. 4) and turn their tongues against them (st. 5), the psalmist proclaims that the saints (of all times) will praise and rejoice in the LORD "for his protecting care" (st. 6). Largely unrhymed, this versification was altered from *The Book of Psalms for Singing* (1973).

Tune

Daniel Read (b. Rehoboth [now Attleboro], MA, 1757; d. New Haven, CT, 1836) composed WINDHAM and published it in his collection *The American Singing Book* (1785). The tune, named after a village and a county in Connecticut, was also published in many shape-note books of the nineteenth century. Originally WINDHAM was in long meter with a half note beginning each phrase; the rhythmic pattern of its first three phrases is subtly altered in the final phrase. Erik Routley (PHH 31) composed the harmony in 1982. Sing this with three beats to the bar.

Although Read was one of the most significant American composers of psalmody of his time, he had a varied career. During the Revolutionary War he served in the Governor's Guards and after the war worked in engraving, publishing, and bookselling. He also manufactured ivory combs, taught singing schools, edited hymnals, and served as a stockbroker and librarian in New Haven. His publications include *The American Singing Book* (1785), which included forty-seven of his tunes, *The Columbian Harmonist* (1793), and *The New Haven Collection of Sacred Music* (1817). From 1786 to 1836 he published the *American Musical Magazine*, the earliest magazine of its kind.

Liturgical Use

Expressions of confidence in God's saving power in the face of persecution or slander; expressions of solidarity with those who are persecuted.

65

Praise Is Your Right, O God, in Zion

GENEVAN 65
♩ = 80

Praise for God's boundless goodness to his people.

Text

Psalm 65's praise of God's goodness ranges across the spectrum of his mercies: God forgives the people's sins so that they may enjoy sweet communion with him at the temple (st. 1); stills the turbulence of the nations so that his people are secure in their land (st. 2); blesses the promised land with a taste of Eden (st. 3). The range of these reflections and the power and beauty of their imagery make this psalm

Scripture References
st. 1 = vv. 1-4
st. 2 = vv. 5-8
st. 3 = vv. 9-13

one of the most beloved in the psalter. Stanley Wiersma (PHH 25) versified Psalm 65 in 1980 for the *Psalter Hymnal*. A hymn based on this psalm is found at 458.

Tune
GENEVAN 65 appears twice in the Genevan Psalter. It was originally composed to accompany Psalm 72 in the 1551 edition of that psalter and was later matched with Theodore de Bèze's versification of Psalm 65 in the 1554 edition. Composed in Aeolian (minor), this tune consists of four long phrases in bar form (AABC) unified by similar melodic and rhythmic patterns. Dale Grotenhuis (PHH 4) wrote the harmonization in 1985. Because 65 is a joyful psalm, it calls for jubilant singing, brisk accompaniment, and a moderate tempo.

Liturgical Use
Thanksgiving Day and other occasions of gratitude for God's blessings; whenever the church looks forward to redemption in the new creation.

66

ELEANOR
♩ = 58

Come, Everyone, and Join with Us

Praise of God for delivering his people from enemy oppression.

Text
The original occasion for Psalm 66 is unknown, but some scholars have proposed that it reflects Judah's remarkable deliverance from the Assyrians in the days of Hezekiah (2 Kings 18-19). After an initial call to praise (st. 1), the theme of this psalm develops in two movements. First, the psalmist exhorts the earth's peoples to join in praise to God for delivering his people from the heavy burdens they have suffered (st. 2-3). Then the psalmist offers personal praise to God, gratefully fulfilling vows made in troubled

Scripture References
st. 1 = vv. 1-4
st. 2 = vv. 5-7
st. 3 = vv. 8-12
st. 4 = vv. 13-15
st. 5 = vv. 16-19
st. 6 = vv. 20, 1-2

times (st. 4); giving testimony to God's grace, "Let me tell you what he has done for me" (v. 16; st. 5); and praising God for listening to the previous cries for help (st. 6). This thematic development suggests that the psalmist was a king whose distress and prayers, and now his praise, had national significance. These same themes are the testimony of Christians in every age. Marie J. Post (PHH 5) versified this psalm in 1985 for the *Psalter Hymnal*. Another setting of Psalm 66 is at 242.

Tune
Dale Grotenhuis (PHH 4) composed ELEANOR (named after his wife) in 1985. It is published for the first time in the 1987 *Psalter Hymnal*. The tune features melodic

197

devices such as repetition, sequence, and inversion; it is accompanied by part-writing that immediately suggests singing in harmony. ELEANOR requires crisp articulation of repeated tones and an energetic tempo.

Liturgical Use

Praise occasions, particularly at the beginning of worship, at the dedication of the offering, and at recognitions of answered prayer; anticipation of Christ's rule in the new heaven and new earth.

67

O God, to Us Show Mercy

OFFERTORIUM
$\quad$ ♩ = *100*

A communal prayer for God's promised blessing on his people;
a call to all nations to join in God's praise.

Text

This short communal prayer for God's blessing may have served as a liturgical prayer of the people at the close of worship. Its echoes of the priestly benediction (Num. 6:22-27) suggest that it may have been used just prior to that divinely authorized blessing. The prayer begins with an allusion to the priestly blessing and asks that

Scripture References
st. 1 = vv. 1-2
st. 2 = vv. 3-4
st. 3 = vv. 5-6

God will fulfill the purpose of that blessing—to bring "salvation among the nations" (v. 2; st. 1). In its request that all earth's people may join in praise to God, whose universal rule is just and good (st. 2), this prayer anticipates God's blessings upon the earth for such praise. And it anticipates as well the whole world's recognition that the LORD is the one true God (st. 3). The versification of this psalm was altered from *The Book of Psalms* (1871), a text-only psalter that was later published with music in 1887.

Tune

OFFERTORIUM is adapted from the offertorium of a choral Mass by Johann Michael Haydn (b. Rohrau, Austria, 1737; d. Salzburg, Austria, 1806). It first was treated as a hymn tune in the 1916 supplement to *Hymns Ancient and Modern* with William Cowper's "Sometimes a Light Surprises." This music suggests part singing and a stately tempo suitable for a solemn blessing.

Younger brother of the more famous Franz Joseph, J. Michael was a chorister, vocal soloist, and substitute organist at St. Stephen's Cathedral in Vienna. He served as music director to the bishop of Grosswarden, Hungary (1757-1762), and as concertmaster for the Archbishop of Salzburg (1762-1806). A devout Roman Catholic, Haydn composed both orchestral and church music, much of it still unpublished (and sometimes confused with his brother's music). He also edited *Der Heilige Gesang zum Gottesdienste in der Römisch-katholischen Kirche* (1790). Some of his music has been used as sources for hymn tunes.

Liturgical Use

The combination of blessing from God and praise to God in this psalm makes it most useful at the end of worship. It can also be used for Pentecost and whenever the church reflects on its evangelistic mission, since the psalmist calls all nations to acknowledge and praise God.

68

GENEVAN 68
♩ = 66

Let God Arise and by His Might

A celebration of God's triumphant march from Mount Sinai to Mount Zion—the establishment of his kingdom.

Text

At Sinai God established Israel as the people of his kingdom, organized them as his army, and set out as their head to conquer the promised land. When the conquest was at last completed through the wars fought by King David, God's royal temple (palace) was erected on Mount Zion, marking the full establishment of his kingdom among the kingdoms of the world. That triumph gave Israel hope that God's kingdom would never fail, that it would humble all the nations, and that ultimately it would engage all the kingdoms of the earth in God's praise. This psalm belonged to the liturgy of a religious festival celebrated at Jerusalem (perhaps the Feast of Tabernacles). It was probably accompanied by a liturgical procession that reenacted God's triumphant march from Sinai to the temple in Jerusalem (see also 24).

Scripture References
st. 1 = vv. 1-3
st. 2 = vv. 4-6
st. 3 = vv. 7-10
st. 4 = vv. 11-14
st. 5 = vv. 15-18
st. 6 = vv. 19-23
st. 7 = vv. 24-27
st. 8 = vv. 28-31
st. 9 = vv. 32-35

The striking thematic structure of the psalm is captured in the nine stanzas; the odd-numbered stanzas carry the action of the procession forward, and the even-numbered reflect on God's rule and power. Stanza 1 marks the beginning of God's march from Sinai (and of the liturgical procession; see Num. 10:35-36). Stanza 2 calls for praise of the LORD as "our salvation." Stanza 3 describes God's march through the desert to the promised land, and stanza 4 hails God's victories over the kings of Canaan. Stanza 5 reports the LORD's triumphant ascent of Mount Zion, and stanza 6 responds with praise of the LORD as the Savior from all that threatens his people. Stanza 7 celebrates the climactic entrance of the LORD (and the liturgical procession) into his holy temple on Zion. Stanza 8 offers a prayer that the LORD may continue to subdue the nations, and stanza 9 rouses all the nations to praise the almighty and triumphant King in his sanctuary.

The versification is mainly by Stanley Wiersma (PHH 25) and John H. Stek (b. Mahaska Co., IA, 1925), with some lines retained (in st. 1, 2, and 6) from the 1931 text by Benjamin Essenberg (1890-1976) included in previous editions of the *Psalter Hymnal* (1934, 1959). Essenberg was a Christian Reformed minister who served congregations in Michigan and Illinois; earlier editions of the *Psalter Hymnal* also included his versification of Psalm 81 to GENEVAN 81.

John Stek is professor of Old Testament, emeritus, at Calvin Seminary, Grand Rapids, Michigan, where he taught from 1961 until 1991. He is chair of the Committee on Bible Translation for the International Bible Society, to which he has belonged since 1965. He was translator and coeditor of the New International Version (NIV) of the Bible, of the New International Reader's Version (NIrV), and author and associate editor for the *NIV Study Bible*. Stek reviewed each of the psalm versifications of the PHH prior to publication for their faithfulness to the Hebrew, and he also prepared the textual commentary on the psalms for this handbook.

Tune
GENEVAN 68 is usually attributed to Matthäus Greiter (b. Aichach, Bavaria, 1490; d. Strasbourg, France, 1550). It was published as a setting for Psalm 119 in *Das dritt theil Strassburger Kirchenampt* (1525), which Greiter and his friend Wolfgang Dachstein edited. Greiter studied at Freiburg University and became a monk and musician at the Strassburg Cathedral. Influenced by Wolfgang Dachstein, Greiter joined the Lutheran Church in 1524 and served several Lutheran congregations in the Strassburg area. He also taught at the Gymnasium Argentinense (high school) and eventually directed a choir school. However, the year before his death Greiter returned to the Roman Catholic Church. He is thought to have been the music editor of John Calvin's first Strasbourg Psalter, *Aulcuns Pseaulmes et Cantiques* (1539).

Greiter's tune was later published with Psalm 36 in the 1539 Strasbourg Psalter approved by John Calvin for worship in Geneva, and still later with Psalm 68 in the 1562 edition of the Genevan Psalter. This sturdy tune is known among Lutherans as O MENSCH BEWEIN' and in the British tradition (with alterations) as OLD 113TH. Written in the Ionian (major) mode, GENEVAN 68 became the battle song of the Calvinist Reformation throughout Europe (analogous to Luther's "A Mighty Fortress Is Our God" in the Lutheran tradition). It has been called the "Huguenot Marseillaise," and stanzas 1 and 6 (1 and 10 in the old Dutch versification) are probably the best-known in the Dutch Reformed tradition.

The melody consists of four long phrases shaped into a bar form (AABC). Its first phrase is identical to the first phrase of LASST UNS ERFREUEN (431). Two harmonizations are given—one composed in 1985 by Howard Slenk (PHH 3), and the 1564 setting (opposite 67 in the hymnal) by Claude Goudimel (PHH 19) with the melody in the tenor, which was typical of that time. GENEVAN 68 is a fine processional tune requiring a stately tempo. Antiphonal singing is best for the entire psalm; try this pattern, alternating accompaniment as well:

Everyone: stanzas 1 and 9
Group A: stanzas 2, 4, 6, and 8
Group B: stanzas 3, 5, and 7

Liturgical Use
Many occasions in Christian worship, especially when the church reflects on the spiritual warfare and triumph of the kingdom of God. Psalm 68 has long been associated with observance of the Reformation.

69

ST. FLAVIAN
♩ = 88

Save Me, O God; I Sink in Floods

A plea for God to have mercy and to deliver from scornful enemies—to save from the miry depths.

Text
In this prayer a godly king pleads for God to save him from a host of enemies who conspire against him at a time when God has "wounded" him (v. 26) for some sin in his life (v. 5). The authors of the New Testament viewed this prayer as foreshadowing the sufferings of Christ. Only Psalm 22 is quoted or alluded to more often in the New Testament. The psalmist begins with a cry to God from the depths (st. 1); he is troubled by countless enemies and by personal sins (st. 2). He asks that God spare the saints from suffering shame on his account (st. 3); his zeal for God has brought only reproach from enemies (st. 4). In faith the psalmist turns to God for deliverance (st. 5), asking to be set free in God's mercy (st. 6). LORD, you know how I have been scorned, says the psalmist (st. 7); my enemies have fed me gall and curses (st. 8). Bring on them the judgment due them (st. 9), and grant my poor, troubled soul salvation (st. 10). This Messianic psalm closes with a vow to praise God, who "still hears the needy" (st. 11), and with a call to all creation to do the same, for God makes his people secure in Zion (st. 12). Marie J. Post (PHH 5) prepared this versification in 1985 for the *Psalter Hymnal*.

Scripture References
st. 1 = vv. 4-5
st. 2 = vv. 4-5
st. 3 = vv. 6-8
st. 4 = vv. 9-12
st. 5 = vv. 13-15
st. 6 = vv. 16-18
st. 7 = vv. 19-20
st. 8 = v. 21
st. 9 = vv. 22-28
st. 10 = v. 29
st. 11 = vv. 30-33
st. 12 = vv. 34-36

Tune
ST. FLAVIAN is found in John Day's *Whole Booke of Psalmes* (Day's *Psalter*, 1562) as an eight-line tune set to Psalm 132. The first four lines were published in the 1875 edition of

Hymns Ancient and Modern and given the name ST. FLAVIAN, after a fifth-century bishop of Constantinople. ST. FLAVIAN is notated in isorhythm, rather than in the more varied rhythms of the original tune in *Day's Psalter.* Though it has lost some of its rhythmic vitality, this music has a majestic character that suits the text.

An early English printer, John Day (b. Dunwich, Suffolk, England, 1522; d. Walden, Essex, England, 1584) is primarily known for his printing of the *Whole Booke of Psalmes* by Thomas Sternhold and John Hopkins (1562). In 1559 Day had already received a printing monopoly for this psalter from the crown; he printed thirty-six separate editions. Day further established his reputation by the excellence of his product, devising different printing types and illustrating his books with ornate woodcuts. His publications included Queen Elizabeth I's *Prayer Book*, Foxe's *Book of Martyrs*, and Archbishop Parker's *Psalmes* (for which Thomas Tallis provided some noteworthy tunes).

Organists will want to use the alternate harmonization by Alan Gray (b. York, England, 1855; d. Cambridge, England, 1935) for one or more stanzas. Gray composed the descant for Trinity College, Cambridge, where he studied law and music. A composer of church music and works for organ and chamber groups, Gray was music director at Wellington College (1883-1892) and Trinity College (1892-1930). He also conducted the Cambridge University Music Society. His *A Book of Descants* (1923) gained much popular use.

Liturgical Use

Good Friday (especially st. 7-8); stanza groups 5-6 and 10-12 may be used as prayers for deliverance.

70

Come Quickly, LORD, to Rescue Me

DISTRESS
$\quad \downarrow = 69$

A prayer asking God to deliver from mortal enemies and thus move all the saints to joyful praise.

Text

This short prayer for God's help from enemies who threaten the psalmist's life is a revision of Psalm 40:13-17. The prayer is framed by pleas to God to "come quickly" (vv. 1, 5; st. 1, 3). Between these urgent calls are prayers asking God to bring disgrace upon the psalmist's enemies (st. 1) and to bring joy to "all who seek" the LORD (st. 2). Bert Polman (PHH 37) versified this psalm in 1983 for the *Psalter Hymnal*.

Scripture References
st. 1 = vv. 1-3
st. 2 = v. 4
st. 3 = v. 5

Tune

DISTRESS was published in William Walker's (PHH 44) *Southern Harmony* (1835), set in shape notes to Anne Steele's "So Fades the Lovely Blooming Flow'r." The plaintive pentatonic (five-pitch) tune has a simple but effective design: the first phrase has an ascending melody that climaxes in phrases 2 and 3 and returns to the opening melody again in phrase 4. Sustain a leisurely tempo. Like many pentatonic folk tunes, DISTRESS may be sung in canon after two or three beats. Two harmonizations are given—one by Erik Routley (PHH 31) for *Rejoice in the Lord* (1985), and the original from *Southern Harmony* (opposite 69 in the hymnal). A concertato performance of this psalm could be planned as follows:

Choir: 639, singing "Maranatha" instead of "Alleluia"
Congregation: 70, stanza 1
Choir: 639, singing "Maranatha"
Choir: 70, stanza 2, in alternate choral harmonization
Choir: 639, singing "Alleluia"
Congregation: 70, stanza 3
Choir: 639, singing "Maranatha"

"Maranatha" was an Aramaic expression used in the early Christian church meaning "Lord, come!" (1 Cor. 16:22).

Liturgical Use

Before or after the congregational prayer, especially in time of threat to God's people; the more elaborate concertato version suggested is useful during Advent.

71

JUDSON
♩ = 56

In You, O LORD, I Put My Trust

A prayer for God's protection from treacherous enemies in old age "when strength has fled."

Text

The content of this prayer suggests that it was composed by a king, the LORD's anointed, in his old age. Seeing the king's vigor wane, his enemies suppose that "God has forsaken him" (v. 11), and they openly conspire against him. The king appeals for God's defense, recalling his lifelong trust in God (st. 1) and confessing that God has never failed to protect him (st. 2). Do not forsake me now, he prays, when my strength is gone and I am old and gray (st. 3). At the psalm's center the old king confesses with unfaltering faith, "But as for me, I will always have hope; I will praise you more and more" (v. 14; st. 4). Thereafter the psalm is a song of praise and thanks—for God's gracious display of power (st. 5); support of the king in his old age (st. 6); deliverance

Scripture References
st. 1 = vv. 1-4
st. 2 = vv. 5-8
st. 3 = vv. 9-11
st. 4 = vv. 12-14
st. 5 = vv. 15-16
st. 6 = vv. 17-18
st. 7 = vv. 19-21
st. 8 = vv. 22-24

from troubles (st. 7); rescue from harm, and provision of lasting hope (st. 8). Clarence P. Walhout (PHH 6) versified this psalm in 1985 for the *Psalter Hymnal.*

Tune

Roger Wayne Wischmeier (b. Sioux City, IA, 1935) composed JUDSON in 1974. It was first sung on October 31, 1975, with James D. Cramer's text "I Sing the Goodness of the Lord" at Judson College, Elgin, Illinois, in a drama about Adoniram Judson, the first American missionary to Burma. Wischmeier comments, "The original text by Cramer provides a vivid sense of God's providence in spite of affliction. The paraphrase of Psalm 71 for the *Psalter Hymnal* has much of this same flavor." The original version of the tune, which included a slightly different ending and an Amen, was included in a hymnal supplement prepared by Daniel Landes for a dissertation at Southern Baptist Seminary, Louisville, Kentucky.

An organist, music theorist, and church musician, Wischmeier teaches music at Sterling College, Kansas. He previously taught at Southern Baptist Seminary and Grace College of the Bible, Omaha, Nebraska. He attended the University of Nebraska, Lincoln, and received his D.M.A. from Southern Baptist Seminary. Wischmeier was a founding member of the Fellowship of American Baptist Musicians and served as editor of their *FABM Newsletter* (1973-1977).

Intended for unison singing, JUDSON consists of four phrases, of which the first and third are identical and the second and fourth are similar. The harmonization requires clear articulation on the organ and a moderate tempo. This psalm favors antiphonal performance: the outer stanzas (1, 8) and the theme stanza (4) may be sung by everyone; the other stanzas by alternating groups.

Liturgical Use

When Christians reflect on the frailty of life and sense the need for God's lifelong help.

72

Hail to the LORD's Anointed

ES FLOG EIN KLEINS WALDVOGELEIN
♩ = 60

A commemoration of Messiah's righteous and glorious reign.

Text

Psalm 72 is a prayer for blessing upon God's anointed king, probably intended for use in a liturgy for coronation. Later Jewish traditions and the early church saw in it a description of Messiah's righteous reign. The psalm expresses the people's desire that God so endow the king that righteousness and justice will characterize his reign (v. 1). This king will be worthy of high praise, for he will defend the poor and crush the oppressor (st. 1); his reign of

Scripture References
st. 1 = vv. 1-4
st. 2 = vv. 5-8
st. 3 = vv. 9-11
st. 4 = vv. 12-14
st. 5 = vv. 15-16
st. 6 = vv. 17-19

refreshing peace and blessing will extend "over every nation" (st. 2). All nations will submit to him and bring him tribute (st. 3). He will rescue the poor, oppressed, and needy, for they are "precious in his sight" (st. 4). Prayers for the longevity and prosperity of his kingdom and praise for him will never cease (st. 5). His name will endure forever, as will his blessings among all nations, invoking eternal praise of the God whose glory fills creation (st. 6; see also Ps. 101).

James Montgomery (b. Irvine, Ayrshire, Scotland, 1771; d. Sheffield, Yorkshire, England, 1854) wrote this text for Christmas 1821 as an ode based on Psalm 72. It was first published in its entirety (eight stanzas) in 1822 in Adam Clarke's *Commentary on the Bible,* and later that year Montgomery also published it in his *Songs of Zion.* Montgomery's original paraphrase contains explicit Christian messianic overtones; Bert Polman's (PHH 37) 1985 revision brings the versification closer to the biblical text. Other partial settings of Psalm 72 are at 359, 412, 541, and 630.

The son of Moravian parents who died on a West Indies mission field while he was in boarding school, Montgomery inherited a strong religious bent, a passion for missions, and an independent mind. He was editor of the *Sheffield Iris* (1796-1827), a newspaper that sometimes espoused radical causes. Montgomery was imprisoned briefly when he printed a song that celebrated the fall of the Bastille and again when he described a riot in Sheffield that reflected unfavorably on a military commander. He also protested against slavery, the lot of boy chimney sweeps, and lotteries. Associated with Christians of various persuasions, Montgomery supported missions and the British Bible Society. He published eleven volumes of poetry, mainly his own, and at least four hundred hymns. Some critics judge his hymn texts to be equal in quality to those of Isaac Watts (PHH 155) and Charles Wesley (PHH 267). Many were published in Thomas Cotterill's *Selection of Psalms and Hymns* (1819 edition) and in Montgomery's own *Songs of Zion* (1822), *Christian Psalmist* (1825), and *Original Hymns* (1853).

Tune
ES FLOG EIN KLEINS WALDVOGELEIN, a German folk tune, was first published in an early-seventeenth-century manuscript collection from Memmingen, Germany. It later became a setting for Christopher Wordsworth's (PHH 361) "O Day of Rest and Gladness" in George R. Woodward's *Songs of Syon* (1910 edition). The tune shares its opening motive and also its bar-form structure (AABA') with LOBE DEN HERREN (253). ES FLOG's combination of a sturdy tune and an able harmonization calls for energetic part singing that remains vibrant but not rushed. Psalm 72 also lends itself to antiphonal performance: the outer stanzas (1, 6) may be sung by everyone; the other stanzas by alternating groups.

Liturgical Use
Advent; Epiphany; Ascension celebrations; also suitable as a missionary song.

73

God Loves All the Righteous

HIDING IN THEE
♩ = 69

Godly wisdom concerning the destinies of the righteous and the wicked.

Text

Psalm 73, the first in Book III of the Psalms, addresses one of the most disturbing problems of the Old Testament saints: Why do the wicked often prosper while the righteous endure much suffering (see also 1, 34, 37, 49, and 112)? The psalmist confesses confidence in the LORD, but describes how his faith faltered when he considered this problem (st. 1). We too can see the wicked prosper and in good health (st. 2), even though they are proud and arrogant, "scoff at the helpless" (st. 3), and curse God Most High. Meanwhile our own troubles may increase (st. 4), and we may be tempted to become like the wicked and denounce

Scripture References
st. 1 = vv. 1-3
st. 2 = vv. 4-6
st. 3 = vv. 6-10
st. 4 = vv. 11-14
st. 5 = vv. 13-20
st. 6 = vv. 21-24
st. 7 = vv. 25-26
st. 8 = vv. 27-28

God. Resolution comes only when we stand in God's presence—then we can discern the final outcome of wicked living (st. 5). God will never fail to sustain us throughout our lives and afterward will take us to glory (st. 6). With that assurance, we confess our dependence on God alone and our conviction that God will sustain us forever (st. 7). The psalm concludes with renewed commitment to trust in God and a promise to make God's grace known to others (st. 8). The versification (somewhat altered) is from the 1912 *Psalter.* Another setting of Psalm 73 is at 554.

Tune

Ira David Sankey (b. Edinburgh, PA, 1840; d. Brooklyn, NY, 1908) composed HIDING IN THEE (also known as SANKEY) and first published it in *Welcome Tidings* (1887), compiled by Lowry, Doane (PHH 473), and Sankey. It was set to the text "O Safe to the Rock That Is Higher than I." The four lines of HIDING IN THEE are in ABAB' form and are accompanied by a simple harmonization that suggests part singing. Antiphonal singing is useful if the entire psalm is sung.

When Sankey's family moved to Newcastle, Pennsylvania, in 1857, he joined the local Methodist church and became its choir director and Sunday school superintendent. After the Civil War he worked for the Internal Revenue Service and became active in the YMCA. As a delegate to the YMCA convention in Indianapolis in 1870, he met evangelist Dwight L. Moody. After hearing Sankey sing, Moody asked Sankey to join him as music director in his Chicago church. Thus began their lengthy and famous association as an evangelism team, which ministered throughout the world for some thirty years. Although Sankey was an amateur musician, he became known worldwide for his gospel singing (accompanying himself on a reed organ), his songs (especially

"The Ninety and Nine"), and as a publisher of gospel music. With various collaborators he published the six volumes of *Gospel Hymns* (1875-1891; collected in one volume, 1894), a very successful venture. Sankey served as president of the Biglow and Main Publishing Company from 1895 until his death. Credited with composing some one hundred gospel hymn tunes, Sankey also published his autobiography, *My Life and the Story of the Gospel Hymns and of the Sacred Songs and Solos* in 1906.

Liturgical Use
Whenever "the fear of the LORD is the beginning of wisdom" is proclaimed; especially appropriate when Christians suffer and the wicked prosper and grow defiant in their prosperity.

74

LANGRAN
♩ = 66

O God, Why Have You Cast Us All Away?

A prayer asking God to remember his covenant, reassert his mighty power, and deliver his people from the enemies who have mocked God and destroyed his holy temple.

Text
Similar in theme to Psalms 79 and 137, this prayer most likely dates from the time when the kingdom of Judah was destroyed, the promised land devastated, and the temple reduced to ruins. The lament that "no prophets are left" (v. 9) suggests that the author was among the small remnant who remained in the land (Jer. 43:4-7). In these desperate circumstances the psalmist cries out to God to remember his people (st. 1) and to bring an end to the mockery of those who have destroyed the house of the LORD

Scripture References
st. 1 = vv. 1-2
st. 2 = vv. 3-11
st. 3 = vv. 12-14
st. 4 = vv. 15-17
st. 5 = vv. 18-19
st. 6 = vv. 20-23

(st. 2). Recalling the mighty displays of God's power in creation and in the Exodus (st. 3), the psalmist appeals to God as LORD over all creation (st. 4). Remember how these enemies have "reviled your name," says the psalmist; save us from these "wild, raging beasts" (st. 5). We pray with the psalmist, "Remember your covenant with us, O LORD; deliver your oppressed people and defend your cause against the rage of your foes" (st. 6). Marie J. Post (PHH 5) versified this psalm in 1985 for the *Psalter Hymnal*.

Tune
LANGRAN (also known as ST. AGNES) was composed by James Langran (b. London, England, 1835; d. London, 1909) and first published by Novello in a pamplet in 1861 as a setting for the hymn text "Abide with Me." Several other texts have also been set to the tune, which is one of Langran's best. Sing it in parts, perhaps unaccompanied on one or more stanzas.

Langran studied organ as a youth but did not receive his Bachelor of Music degree from Oxford until he was forty-nine years old. He had several organist positions—the longest was at St. Paul's Church, Tottenham, England, from 1870 to 1909. He also taught music at St. Katherine's Training College for Schoolmistresses (1878-1909). Music editor of the *New Mitre Hymnal* (1875), Langran composed around fifty hymn tunes and contributed several of them to early editions of *Hymns Ancient and Modern*.

Liturgical Use
Worship services focusing on the Israelites' exile; whenever Christians experience persecution; for services when we want to offer prayers on behalf of refugees who are exiled and displaced.

75

We Give Our Thanks to You, O God

WEYMOUTH
$\bullet = 112$

The reassurance of faith in the face of enemy threat.

Text
A song of assurance, Psalm 75 contains many thematic parallels to the Song of Hannah (1 Sam. 2:1-10; see PHH 158). Thanksgiving (v. 1) and praise (vv. 9-10) frame the song, while faith-reassuring words from heaven (vv. 2-5; st. 1) and a triumphant response from earth (vv. 6-8; st. 2) form the song's core. Helen Otte (PHH 17) versified this psalm in 1985 for the *Psalter Hymnal*.

Scripture References
st. 1 = vv. 1-5
st. 2 = vv. 6-10

Tune
Theodore Parker Ferris (b. Port Chester, NY, 1908; d. 1972) composed WEYMOUTH in 1941 for H. C. Robbins's text "And Have the Bright Immensities"; the tune was published in *The Hymnal 1940*. Ferris named the tune for his summer hometown, Weymouth, Nova Scotia. Well-crafted with an effective rhythmic climax in the final line, WEYMOUTH requires a brisk accompaniment at an energetic pace.

A graduate of Harvard University and General Theological Seminary (1934), Ferris was ordained a priest in the Episcopal church. He taught at General Theological Seminary and served Grace Church in New York City, Emmanuel Church in Baltimore, Maryland, and Trinity Church in Boston, Massachusetts. His publications include *This Created World* (1944) and *The Image of God* (1965).

Liturgical Use

Occasions of thanksgiving for and reassurance of God's faithful rescue of his people in the face of threats from enemies.

76

TEMPLE BORO
♩ = 76

God Is Known Among His People

Praise for God's mighty deliverance of Zion.

Text

Ancient tradition suggests that this psalm was composed after the destruction of Sennacherib's army outside Jerusalem (2 Kings 19:35). The psalm's main theme develops in the opening and closing stanzas (vv. 1-3, 11-12; st. 1, 4): God defends Zion and makes his name known; God requires commitment, worship, and praise, even from the kings of the earth. The seven Hebrew lines (vv. 4-10) that link the psalm's framing verses celebrate God's awesome act of judgment that brought relief to Zion: God's unequaled power overcomes human might (st. 2), and not even human hostility can frustrate the plans of the God who pronounces judgment from heaven (st. 3). The theme of God's protection of Zion links this psalm with 46 and 48 (see also 84, 87, 122, 125, and 137). The versification is significantly revised from that in the 1912 *Psalter.*

Scripture References
st. 1 = vv. 1-3
st. 2 = vv. 4-7
st. 3 = vv. 8-10
st. 4 = vv. 11-12

Tune

F. Pinder composed TEMPLE BORO, published as a setting for Psalm 76 in the 1912 *Psalter* and in every edition of the *Psalter Hymnal.* Nothing is known about the composer or the origin of the tune. TEMPLE BORO's three long lines have identical rhythms. Interesting facets of this music are its wide melodic range, its harmonization (undoubtedly intended for choral singing), and the climax in the final line. Strive for three long lines; avoid six choppy phrases.

Liturgical Use

Beginning of worship; celebrations of God's victories over the enemies of his kingdom.

77

I Cried to God to Help Me

GENEVAN 77
♩ = 60

Faith's bewilderment and recovery in the face of great distress.

Text

In this psalm, as in many others, remembrance of God's saving deeds in the Exodus restores peace to the troubled soul. Psalm 77 begins with a vivid description of the believer's struggle with unanswered prayer in a time of distress (st. 1). The psalmist is bewildered and his personal faith is shaken over God's seeming failure to respond (st. 2). But in reflecting on the mighty deeds

Scripture References
st. 1 = vv. 1-4
st. 2 = vv. 5-9
st. 3 = vv. 10-15
st. 4 = vv. 16-20

through which the LORD saved Israel from slavery in Egypt, the psalmist finds bewilderment put to rest (st. 3-4). Thus Christians find renewed hope in God's saving deeds in Christ. Helen Otte (PHH 17) versified this psalm in 1985 for the *Psalter Hymnal*.

Tune

GENEVAN 77 was first published in the 1551 edition of the Genevan Psalter as a setting for Psalm 86. It was set to Psalm 77 in the 1562 edition. Claude Goudimel (PHH 6) composed the harmonization in 1564. GENEVAN 77's many repeated phrases make it memorable; it is in Hypo-Dorian mode. The plaintive character of this music is well suited to the psalm text but must not become mournful. Sing stanzas 1 and 2 quietly and stanzas 3 and 4 with increasing strength and volume.

Liturgical Use

Evening worship; remembrance of the Exodus; situations in which this psalm of comfort may encourage people in distress.

78

The Mighty Deeds the LORD Has Done

ST. JAMES THE APOSTLE
♩ = 54

A warning to the worshipers in Zion not to sin against God as their ancestors did but to remember all of God's mercies.

Text

Like Psalms 105-106 and 135-136, Psalm 78 tells a story—it recounts part of the covenant history of God's Old Testament people. Since their freedom from captivity in Egypt, God's people Israel had repeatedly refused "to live by his law" (v. 10)—in spite of

God's unfailing mercies and occasional chastisement.

Psalm 78 teaches that people must remember God's mighty deeds through the generations to remain faithful (st. 1-2); they should learn from their history and not "put God to the test" (v. 41). God delivered Israel from Egypt, and Israel complained in the wilderness about the lack of food (st. 3); God provided food (manna and quail), and Israel was ungrateful (st. 4). "In spite of blessings they rebelled"; God became angry with Israel and punished an entire generation (st. 5). Yet God again showed mercy, and Israel showed fickleness of faith (st. 6). "How could they forget the plagues" God

Scripture References

st. 1	= vv. 1-4
st. 2	= vv. 5-8
st. 3	= vv. 12-14, 17-20
st. 4	= vv. 23-31
st. 5	= vv. 21-22, 31-33
st. 6	= vv. 34-41
st. 7	= vv. 42-51
st. 8	= vv. 15-16, 52-55
st. 9	= vv. 56-61
st. 10	= vv. 62-66
st. 11	= vv. 66-72, 9-11
st. 12	= Concluding exhortation from New Testament perspective

had used to free them from Egypt (st. 7)? How could they forget God's gift of water from the rock and God's gift of the promised land (st. 8)? Once established in Canaan, Israel rebelled against God again, and God withdrew from them completely (st. 9). But when they became desperate and desolate at the hands of their enemies, God awoke to their situation (st. 10). "The LORD beat back his enemies," reestablishing Israel in the promised land. Then the LORD, in a final great display of mercy, chose David of the tribe of Judah to shepherd the people with integrity and skill (st. 11). Mention of God's choice of Zion and Judah over Ephraim and Shiloh (vv. 9-11, 60, 67-68) was intended as a warning to worshipers at Jerusalem (Zion) not to fall away from God as their ancestors had done (Jer. 7:12-19; 26:5-6).

Calvin Seerveld (PHH 22) versified this psalm in 1985 for the *Psalter Hymnal.* His intent was "to condense this psalm of covenantal history so that it could be sung responsively in church and tell the 'history of salvation' for young and old to hear again." A setting of the first segment of Psalm 78 is at 585.

Tune

F. William Voetberg (b. Kalamazoo, MI, 1947) composed ST. JAMES THE APOSTLE in 1985 for a versification of Psalm 7—a psalm to be read for the feast of St. James the Apostle. The simple tune is well-suited to the telling of Israel's history. The condensed versification permits the singing of the entire psalm; try antiphonal singing of various stanzas in that case. Singing of select stanzas should always include the theme stanza (12).

A graduate of Calvin College, Grand Rapids, Michigan, Voetberg has served several congregations as choir director and organist; since 1993 he has been the director of music at St. Paul's on the Green Episcopal Church in Norwalk, Connecticut. He is also a technical consultant for AT&T. Among his published compositions are organ works in

Free Harmonizations of Hymn Tunes (1986) and music for instruments in *6 Christmas Trios* (1992).

Liturgical Use

As instruction on obedient living with God; as an exhortation to faithfulness in light of God's enthronement of Christ as the Shepherd-King of God's people.

79

In Your Heritage the Nations

O MEIN JESU
♩ = 76

A prayer for God's forgiveness and restoration and for his judgment on world powers that have defied and scorned him.

Text

Like Psalms 74 and 137, this song comes from the exile period. It is a community lament in which Israel pleads with God to turn his anger from Israel to the kingdoms that have treated her cruelly and shown utter contempt for the LORD (st. 1-2). Those nations have devastated God's kingdom ("heritage," st. 1), and God's people now beg for forgiveness and for deliverance that will return

Scripture References
st. 1 = vv. 1-4
st. 2 = vv. 5-7
st. 3 = vv. 8-9
st. 4 = vv. 10-13

glory to God's name (st. 3). In sympathy with the psalmist we sing, "Show the nations that you avenge the blood of your people, O God; save us, and we will praise you forever" (st. 4). The versification (altered) is from the 1912 *Psalter.* Another segment of Psalm 79 is at 254.

Tune

Set to a German chorale text, "O mein Jesu, ich muss sterben" (O my Jesus, I must die), O MEIN JESU was published in *Geistliche Volkslieder* (1850). Paul G. Bunjes (b. Frankenmuth, MI, 1914) composed the harmonization for *Lutheran Worship* (1982). O MEIN JESU is in rounded bar form (AABA') with identical rhythms in its four musical lines. The music is well suited to part singing and bears a stately tempo.

A graduate of Valparaiso (IN) University, Bunjes also earned a Ph.D. in music from the Eastman School of Music, Rochester, New York. He was an elementary school teacher and administrator for fifteen years and since 1951 has served on the faculty of Concordia Teachers College, River Forest, Illinois. Bunjes is noted as an organ-building consultant. He served as musical editor of *Lutheran Worship* (1982) and prepared many harmonizations for that hymnal, using his own name as well as two pseudonyms, Wilhelm Quampen and George Leonard.

Liturgical Use

Worship services focusing on the Jewish exile or on solidarity with Christians who suffer persecution or are refugees.

80

YORKSHIRE
♩ = 72

Hear Us, O Shepherd of Your Chosen Race

A prayer for God to restore his people after they have been ravaged by a foreign power.

Text

Psalm 80 was probably written upon the demise of the northern kingdom of Israel at the hands of the Assyrians (2 Kings 17:1-6), who made deep inroads into Judah as well (2 Kings 18:9-13). The psalmist prays, O Shepherd, show us your face and restore peace to your people (st. 1); turn away your anger, hear our prayer, and give us peace (st. 2). At the heart of this psalm is an image of Israel as a vine God brought from Egypt, planted in the "vineyard" of the promised land, and caused to flourish (st. 3). (Similar imagery occurs in Isa. 3:14-15; 5:1-7; Jer. 2:21; 12:10; Ezek. 17:6-10; 19:10-14; Hos. 10:1; 14:7; Mic. 7:1; Jesus used it in John 15.) The psalmist describes the devastation of this vine when no longer protected by the LORD, and asks that God return to restore his people (st. 4). We join the psalmist in praying, "Rest your hand once more upon us, LORD, that our moans may turn to praise" (st. 5). Borrowing a phrase here and there from the 1912 *Psalter,* Bert Polman (PHH 37) prepared this versification in 1985 for the *Psalter Hymnal.*

Scripture References
st. 1 = vv. 1-3
st. 2 = vv. 4-7
st. 3 = vv. 8-11
st. 4 = vv. 12-15
st. 5 = vv. 16-19

Tune

For information on YORKSHIRE and John Wainwright, see PHH 350, where the tune is in the key of C. Antiphonal part singing may be useful in this psalm, but the refrain lines in stanzas 1, 2, and 5 ("Restore us, LORD, your saving power release . . .") should always be sung by all or otherwise highlighted by a change in accompaniment registration.

Liturgical Use

Times of reflection on persecution, particularly in prayer services for God's restoring power.

81

Sing a Psalm of Joy

GENEVAN 81
♩ = 80

*An exhortation to Israel to renew their faithfulness to God as they
celebrate the LORD's deliverance out of Egypt.*

Text

The psalmist addresses the people of Israel at an annual festival celebrating their deliverance from slavery in Egypt. He begins with a call to joyful celebration (st. 1) and praise of the LORD (st. 2), remembering God's saving answer to the people's cry in bondage and God's test of their faith in the wilderness (st. 3). As God's spokesperson, the psalmist calls Israel once again to be faithful to the LORD and to reject all false gods (st. 4). In remembering the Exodus, Israel is reminded of its own unfaithfulness in the wilderness and how God dealt with them. The LORD, who

Scripture References
st. 1 = vv. 1-2
st. 2 = vv. 3-5
st. 3 = vv. 6-7
st. 4 = vv. 8-9
st. 5 = v. 10
st. 6 = vv. 11-15
st. 7 = vv. 8, 16

brought them out of Egypt and who has supplied all their needs, will surely bless the people if they wholly trust in him (st. 5). God's great desire is for the people to obey and trust him, so that they may enjoy his protection and abundant blessings (st. 6-7). In singing this psalm we too need to respond obediently to God's call. In the post-exilic temple liturgy this psalm was sung during the morning sacrifice on the fifth day of the week. Marie J. Post (PHH 5) versified Psalm 81 in 1984 for the *Psalter Hymnal.*

Tune

GENEVAN 81 was first published in the 1562 edition of the Genevan Psalter; Dale Grotenhuis (PHH 4) composed the harmonization in 1985. This bright tune in Ionian mode (major) has short phrases, two of which are repeated (AB, AC, CD), making it one of the simplest in the Genevan Psalter. For that reason, generations of Dutch children started their weekly school program of memorizing psalms with this one, beginning with the stanza that included "Open wide your mouth, surely I will fill it." The psalm should be sung with much energy, though the mood shifts between stanzas 5 and 6. The text suggests antiphonal performance: stanzas 1 and 2 to be sung by everyone, stanzas 3 through 7 by a solo voice or smaller group (possibly ending with a unison repeat of stanza 1 by all).

Liturgical Use

Call to commitment or rededication.

82

MEIRIONYDD
♩ = 104

There Where the Judges Gather

A prayer asking God, who calls all unjust rulers to account,
to establish his righteous reign on earth.

Text

Interpretations of Psalm 82 vary on many details, but one thing is clear: the psalmist has seen—and most likely experienced—that those who wield authority on earth are prone to promoting injustice rather than defending the powerless and oppressed (see also 58). Yet God sits in judgment as the great King over all

Scripture References
st. 1 = vv. 1-2
st. 2 = vv. 3-5
st. 3 = vv. 6-8

such rulers (st. 1), calling them sternly to account (st. 1-2). In spite of their arrogant confidence in their power (st. 2), the LORD will terminate their little season of authority with death. In faith the psalmist sees the supreme Judge presiding over the heavenly court and prays for God to establish his righteous rule over all the nations on earth (st. 3). In the post-exilic temple liturgy, this psalm was sung at the time of the morning sacrifice on the third day of the week. Henry Zylstra (b. Platte, SD, 1909; d. Amsterdam, the Netherlands, 1956) prepared the versification in 1953 for the 1959 *Psalter Hymnal;* it was slightly altered for the 1987 edition.

Zylstra earned an undergraduate degree at Calvin College, Grand Rapids, Michigan; studied German literature at Iowa State University; and received his Ph.D. in comparative literature from Harvard University. From 1943 to 1956 he taught in the English department at Calvin College. His tenure there was interrupted by service in the United States Navy (1943-1945), during which he received the Bronze Star for "unusually meritorious service." He was studying under a Fulbright professorship at the Free University of Amsterdam when he died of a heart attack in 1956. A founder of *Reformed Journal,* Zylstra was a greatly esteemed teacher and leader at Calvin College and in the Christian Reformed Church. His writings on education and on the relationship between culture and the Christian faith were especially valued; many of his essays were collected posthumously in *Testament of Vision* (1958). His translations of theological works from Dutch into English were also of a high calibre. From 1951 until his death Zylstra served on the committee that prepared the 1959 *Psalter Hymnal.*

Tune

William Lloyd (b. Rhos Goch, Llaniestyn, Caernarvonshire, Wales, 1786; d. Caernarvonshire, 1852) composed MEIRIONYDD, which was first published in manuscript form with the name BERTH in *Caniadau Seion* (*Songs of Zion*, 1840, ed. R. Mills). The tune is named after the Welsh county Meirionydd in which Lloyd lived; that county is also the site of the Harlech Castle made famous in story and song. A cattle farmer and dealer, Lloyd was also a self-taught musician. He had a fine voice and conducted various singing societies in his hometown as well as in other cities.

Although generally attributed to Lloyd, MEIRIONYDD could be a traditional Welsh melody that he arranged. Shaped in bar form (AABC), the tune is set in sturdy rhythms and harmonies for choral singing. Compared to the typical triadic outlines in Welsh melodies, this tune is more stepwise. Sing it rather boldly, in balance with the tone of the text. A higher setting is found at 472.

Liturgical Use

When the church needs to speak against unjust use of power—especially by government.

83

O God, Do Not in Silence Stand

DETROIT
♩ = 92

A communal prayer asking God for protection against a great conspiracy of nations in order to show all the world that the LORD is God.

Text

Psalm 83 dates from a time when Assyria was extending the tentacles of its power into Palestine. A great array of nations (all of Israel's near neighbors) jointly plotted—with Assyrian support—against the kingdom of the LORD. The psalmist appeals to God to rise in the face of these enemies (st. 1) who are plotting arrogantly (st. 2) and to destroy them as he did past enemies (st. 3). Blow these enemies away like chaff, O LORD, he prays (st. 4). Humble them so that they recognize their wickedness (st. 5). Show the world that you alone are "Most High over all the earth" (v. 18; st. 6). Clarence P. Walhout (PHH 6) versified this psalm in 1982 for the *Psalter Hymnal.*

Scripture References
st. 1 = vv. 1-3
st. 2 = vv. 4-8
st. 3 = vv. 9-12
st. 4 = vv. 13-15
st. 5 = vv. 15-17
st. 6 = v. 18

Tune

Presumably named after the Michigan city and river, DETROIT was published anonymously in Ananias Davisson's shape-note tune book *Supplement to Kentucky Harmony* (1820). The tune is credited to "Bradshaw" in *Virginia Harmony* (1831) and *Southern Harmony* (1835). Emily R. Brink (PHH 158) harmonized the tune in 1986. Thought to be an Appalachian adaptation of an old English folk song, DETROIT has a fine melodic curve over its two long lines, ascending and then descending. Feel two beats per measure.

Liturgical Use
When the church is under attack; when the church offers intercessory prayer for those suffering persecution.

84

GENEVAN 84
𝅝 = 66

How Lovely Is Your House, O LORD

The prayer of a yearning heart asking to be restored to the house of God.

Text
Psalm 84 expresses the longing of an outcast believer or a pilgrim for sweet communion with God at the temple (see also 42 and 63). Faint with longing, the psalmist yearns "for the courts of the LORD" (v. 2), where faithful worshipers of all times and places are blessed and even birds find safe haven (st. 1). Just the thought of being in God's presence invigorates those who are on pilgrimage to God's holy place (st. 2; other songs of Zion are 46, 48, 76, 87, 122, 125, and 137). Pleading to be restored to the temple—if only to a humble place of service (st. 3)—the psalmist confidently declares that God is gracious to those who trust and serve the LORD (st. 4). Ada Roeper-Boulogne (PHH 18) versified this psalm in 1979 for the *Psalter Hymnal.* Another setting of Psalm 84 is at 243.

Scripture References
st. 1 = vv. 1-4
st. 2 = vv. 5-7
st. 3 = vv. 8-10
st. 4 = vv. 11-12

Tune
GENEVAN 84 first appeared in the 1562 edition of the Genevan Psalter; Howard Slenk (PHH 3) harmonized it in 1985. The rhythm of the first phrase is altered to match that of the second and final phrase. (The original first phrase began with two half notes followed by four quarter notes.) This loved Genevan psalm features much rhythmic vitality and should be sung with firm organ accompaniment that inspires confident singing.

Liturgical Use
Beginning of worship; expressions of longing for the new Jerusalem.

85

LORD, You Have Lavished on Your Land

*A communal prayer requesting God's forgiveness and the full experience
of his saving love and faithfulness.*

Text

In a time of distress after being restored from captivity, the people
of God pray for a renewal of God's mercies. If the restoration
referred to is Israel's return from Babylon, the troubles are
probably those alluded to in Nehemiah and Malachi—verse 12
suggests a severe drought. As you have pardoned and restored us
before, prays the psalmist, show us your grace once more (st. 1).

Scripture References
st. 1 = vv. 1-3
st. 2 = vv. 4-7
st. 3 = vv. 8-9
st. 4 = vv. 10-13

Forgive, revive, and bless us in your mercy, O God (st. 2). Surely the LORD's salvation is
near and unfailing (st. 3). God's love and faithfulness and righteousness and peace all
come together in God's grace (st. 4). The beautiful imagery of love and faithfulness
meeting together while "righteousness and peace kiss each other" (v. 10) has made
Psalm 85 a favorite for God's people everywhere. Marie J. Post (PHH 5) versified this
psalm in 1985 for the *Psalter Hymnal*.

Tune

William Hayes (b. Gloucester, England, 1708; d. Oxford, England, 1777) first published
NEW 113TH in his *Sixteen Metrical Psalms . . . for Use in Magdalen College Chapel* (1774) as a
setting for a versification of Psalm 134. (Any relationship with Psalm 113, as indicated by
the tune name, has never been discovered.) NEW 113TH requires solid harmony singing
and a sense of one broad beat per bar to support its somewhat meandering melody.
The suggested alternate tune, ST. PETERSBURG (50), may be better known and more
accessible to some congregations.

   As a boy Hayes was a chorister at Gloucester Cathedral. He served as organist of St.
Mary Church in Shrewsbury and at Worcester Cathedral but spent most of his career as
organist, choirmaster, and professor of music at Magdalen College, Oxford (1734-
1777). He received his doctorate at Oxford in 1749, a time when the opening of the
Radcliffe Library was being celebrated. That celebration included the first performance of George Frideric Handel's *Messiah* in Oxford—Hayes introduced Handel's
works to many areas of England. Hayes composed mostly choral music, some of which
is light-hearted, and his publications include various canons and psalm tunes.

Liturgical Use

A favorite in traditional Christian liturgies for the Advent season; many other occasions.

86

LORD, My Petition Heed

*A prayer for God's forgiving mercy and for deliverance from the threat of
ruthless enemies—to the praise of God's greatness and goodness.*

Text

This psalm is fitting for any of God's people threatened by
those who would rob them of their security as children of God.
The psalmist's hope and plea is that God will graciously forgive
his children and deliver them as well. "Poor and needy" in a
time of great peril, the psalmist pleads for God's help as a
servant who trusts confidently in the LORD (st. 1). With the
psalmist, we pray for God's mercy on us and for the comfort of
forgiveness in a time of need (st. 1-2). O LORD, you far out-
shine all other gods, says the psalmist (st. 3); you command the
praise of all people (st. 4). The psalmist asks for guidance in the way of truth and vows
to praise and glorify the LORD forever (st. 5; v. 12). Then he praises God for abundant
love and grace and returns to a plea for help (st. 6), mercy, renewed strength, deliverance, and comfort—so that enemies may be put to shame in the knowledge that the
LORD is our friend (st. 7). Bert Polman (PHH 37) versified this psalm in 1983 for the
Psalter Hymnal, retaining several lines from the 1912 *Psalter.*

Scripture References
st. 1 = vv. 1-3
st. 2 = vv. 4-5
st. 3 = vv. 6-8
st. 4 = vv. 9-10
st. 5 = vv. 11-12
st. 6 = vv. 13-16
st. 7 = vv. 16-17

Tune

MASON, by William F. Sherwin (PHH 8), was published as a setting for the first three
stanzas of Psalm 86 in the 1912 *Psalter* and in all previous editions of the *Psalter Hymnal.*
Since he studied with Lowell Mason (PHH 96), Sherwin could well have named the
tune after him. Dale Grotenhuis (PHH 4) harmonized MASON in 1985. The seven
phrases of this tune should be sung with the sense of two very long lines. Antiphony is
useful in singing the entire psalm.

Liturgical Use

When the church suffers threats to its security and well-being, and many other occasions. Stanzas 4 and 5 make a fine doxology for the conclusion of worship.

87

Our Gracious God

GENEVAN 87
♩ = 69

A celebration of the glory of Zion as the city of God, whose citizens, gathered from all nations, enjoy God's sure protection and unfailing blessings.

Text

This song about Zion has historically been understood as anticipating the gathering of the nations into the people of God (in harmony with many of the prophetic books from Isaiah to Zechariah). As the "city of God," Zion represented the earthly royal city of God's emerging kingdom (see also 46, 48, 76, 84, 122, 125, and 137)—citizenship in Zion signified all the benefits of God's blessing and protection. Most likely this psalm was composed for use in the liturgy of an annual religious festival drawing the pious in great throngs to Jerusalem. The psalmist notes God's special love for Zion (st. 1) and extols its glory as the city that draws the nations (st. 2-3). God will recognize as citizens of Zion all who come to confess their faith in the LORD (st. 4), and their response will be praise and adoration (st. 5). William Kuipers (b. Rochester, NY, 1883; d. Passaic, NJ, 1933) versified this psalm in 1931 for the 1934 *Psalter Hymnal;* it was reprinted in the 1987 *Psalter Hymnal* with only a few changes. Another setting of Psalm 87 is at 168.

Scripture References
st. 1 = vv. 1-2
st. 2 = vv. 3-4a
st. 3 = v. 4b
st. 4 = vv. 5-6
st. 5 = v. 7

A graduate of Calvin College and Seminary, Grand Rapids, Michigan, Kuipers was ordained in the Christian Reformed Church. From 1914 to 1919 he served the Second Christian Reformed Church of Fremont, Michigan, a congregation organized to be an English-speaking church. Later he served Christian Reformed churches in Oakland, Michigan (1919-1923); Dennis Avenue, Grand Rapids (1923-1927); and Summer Street, Passaic, New Jersey (1927-1933). Kuipers wrote a number of poems, hymns, and psalm versifications.

Tune

GENEVAN 87 was first published in the 1562 edition of the Genevan Psalter; Jacobus J. K. Kloppers (b. Krugersdorp, Transvaal, South Africa, 1937) wrote the harmonization in 1985. In the Hypo-Mixolydian mode, this tune consists of four lines, each of which have their own rhythmic and melodic identity. A stately pace is appropriate.

Now a Canadian citizen, Kloppers has published works in Afrikaans, German, and English, and given organ recitals on three continents. Educated at Potchefstroom University, South Africa, and the Johann Wolfgang Goethe University in Frankfurt, Germany, he also studied organ with Helmut Walcha. Kloppers was organist and choir director at several Reformed churches in South Africa and at the Evangelisch Reformierte Kirche in Frankfurt. He taught in South Africa until 1976, after which he moved to Canada. Since 1976 he has been organist at St. John's Anglican Church in Edmonton, Alberta, and since 1979, professor of music at The King's College, also in Edmonton. Kloppers has published several works on J. S. Bach, including *The Interpretation and Rendering of the Organ Works of J. S. Bach* (1966), and was coeditor of *Liturgical Organ Music* (1973, 1975). His compositions include psalm and hymn arrangements for choir and organ and an organ concerto. He has performed many organ recitals, including several performances for the Canadian Broadcast Corporation.

Liturgical Use
Pentecost, mission contexts; emphasis on the worldwide kingdom of the Lord and on the new Jerusalem.

88

VERGEEF, O HEER
♩ = 56

O LORD, I Call for Help by Day

A cry from the depths for deliverance from death.

Text

Having lived an entire life in the shadow of the grave (v. 15), the psalmist cries out to God (st. 1, 6) from the brink of death (st. 2). Like Job, who was shown the back of God's hand for reasons unknown to him, the psalmist has experienced only unrelenting and harsh troubles, so that even friends and companions have withdrawn (st. 3). Held helpless in death's grip, the psalmist lifts hands to God (st. 4) and laments that in the realm of the dead there is no escape from death and no interaction with God (st. 5). Only those who have known such suffering and abandonment can call darkness their "closest friend" (st. 7). Still—and this is the one gleam of light in the darkness—they (and all of us in intercession) can call on the LORD, "the God who saves" (v. 1). Again like Job, who cried to the LORD, who was shown only trouble, and who was put "in the darkest depths" (v. 8), the psalmist ends in faith, trusting in the LORD, the only Savior from death. Stanley Wiersma (PHH 25) versified this darkest of all the psalms in 1982 for the *Psalter Hymnal*.

Scripture References
st. 1 = vv. 1-2
st. 2 = vv. 3-6
st. 3 = vv. 7-8a
st. 4 = vv. 8b-9
st. 5 = vv. 10-12
st. 6 = vv. 14b-16
st. 7 = vv. 17-18
st. 8 = vv. 13-14a

Tune

VERGEEF, O HEER, composed by Gerben Baaij (b. Amsterdam, the Netherlands, 1929), was first published in the Dutch hymnal *Liedboek voor de Kerken* (1973) as a setting for a translation of John Greenleaf Whittier's "Forgive, O Lord, Our Severing Ways." Baaij studied organ, voice, and composition at the Protestant Church Music School in

Utrecht. He is director of the Recreatie-centra of the Hervormde Kerk in the Netherlands and cantor and organist for the ecumenical services in the Doorn-Driebergen region.

Dale Grotenhuis (PHH 4) harmonized the tune in 1983. VERGEEF, O HEER is one of the few tunes in the *Psalter Hymnal* with only three lines; each is rhythmically unique, with the middle line providing the apex of the entire melodic curve. The song may be sung in parts or by two alternating groups, but stanzas 1 and 8 should always be sung by everyone.

Liturgical Use
Good Friday; as a prayer for those who are sick, especially those who suffer from a life-threatening illness.

89

Forever I Will Sing of Your Great Love, O LORD

GENEVAN 89
♩ = 69

A joyful exposition of God's covenant with David as the basis for Israel's security under the Davidic dynasty, and a bitter lament over God's apparent repudiation of that covenant.

Text

This psalm may have been written for one of several instances in which a Davidic king suffered a devastating defeat; most often proposed is Nebuchadnezzar's defeat of Jehoiachin, which spelled the destruction of Judah. Verses 1-37 offer the most extensive exposition and joyful celebration of God's covenant with David found anywhere in the Old Testament (see also 132). However, here the exposition serves only to heighten the shock of God's apparent repudiation of that covenant. The sudden transition at verse 38 and the unrelieved lament that follows makes this one of the most poignant psalm prayers. Praising God's love expressed in the covenant with David (st. 1), the psalmist declares God's faithfulness and mighty power as sung in the heavens (st. 2) and proclaims the blessedness and security of God's people (st. 3). The LORD promised to raise up David as a mighty warrior and king whose reign would never be overthrown and whose line would never be severed from God's favor (st. 4-5). But alas, laments the psalmist, God has abandoned David's throne and handed Israel over to scornful enemies (st. 6). In anguished prayer he pleads with God: See how your anointed one has been mocked by enemies. How long will it be, O LORD, before you restore "your former great love" to your covenant people

Scripture References
st. 1 = vv. 1-4
st. 2 = vv. 5-13
st. 3 = vv. 14-18
st. 4 = vv. 19-25
st. 5 = vv. 26-37
st. 6 = vv. 38-45
st. 7 = vv. 46-51
st. 8 = v. 52

(v. 49; st. 7)? A doxology extolling God's faithfulness to all who praise him closes Book III of the Psalms (st. 8). This versification is the combined work of John Stek (PHH 68), Henrietta Ten Harmsel (PHH 61), and Clarence P. Walhout (PHH 6). Other settings of Psalm 89 are at 169 and 593.

Tune

One of the best-known tunes from the Genevan Psalter, GENEVAN 89 was first published in the 1562 edition. Jacobus J. K. Kloppers (PHH 87) harmonized the tune for the *Psalter Hymnal* in 1985. The first line is repeated in the second, and all the lines have a similar rhythmic pattern, including the last line, which was changed from the original (the third and fourth notes were originally half notes). Much of the psalm should be sung jubilantly, but sing stanzas 6 and 7 in a subdued manner. Antiphony can be useful in singing the complete psalm.

Liturgical Use

The complete psalm is useful for services focusing on Old Testament redemptive history, especially its messianic theme. Stanzas 1, 2, 3, and 8 make a wonderful doxology.

90

STELLA
♩ = 116

LORD, You Have Been Our Dwelling Place

An appeal for God's wisdom and favor upon the sad state of humankind as sinners and mortals.

Text

Psalm 90 opens Book IV of the Psalms. No other psalm expresses so poignantly our melancholy state as sinful mortals before the face of a holy and eternal God. Yet the psalmist expresses no defiance. Honesty acknowledges guilt, and faith knows God's unfailing love. To that love we can appeal for mercies that bring joy and for blessings that make our work fruitful. The psalm opens by addressing the everlasting God as humanity's security and rest through all generations (st. 1) and quickly moves to contrast God's eternity with the shortness of the human lifespan (st. 2). God knows all our sins, and we suffer God's displeasure because of them (st. 3). We live perhaps seventy or eighty years; yet even so long a life brings no relief from sorrow and no escape from death (st. 4). The psalmist asks God to grant wisdom to us sinners and to have pity and mercy on us so that we may yet know joy (st. 5). He continues with a request that God reveal his glory to us and our children by showing favor to us and blessing our efforts in the LORD's service (st. 6). The versification is a 1985 revision by

Helen Otte (PHH 17) of the texts found at 245 and 246 of the 1912 *Psalter.* Another setting of Psalm 90 is at 170.

Tune
First published in Henri Frederick Hemy's *Easy Hymn Tunes for Catholic Schools* (1851), STELLA was a folk tune from northern England that Hemy heard sung by children in Stella, a village near Newcastle-upon-Tyme. In modified bar form (AA'B), the tune has an interesting rhythmic structure. Antiphonal performance and part singing help in singing the entire psalm.

Gerald Hocken Knight (b. Par, Cornwall, England, 1908; d. London, England, 1979) composed the harmonization in 1950 for *Hymns Ancient and Modern Revised* (1950). Knight studied at Peterhouse, Cambridge, England, and at the Royal College of Music in London. He was organist at Truro Cathedral and Canterbury Cathedral (1937-1952) as well as director of the Royal College of Music (1952-1972). A music editor of the 1950 edition of *Hymns Ancient and Modern,* he also served on the committees that compiled its two supplements, *100 Hymns for Today* (1969) and *More Hymns for Today* (1980).

Liturgical Use
Traditionally for Old/New Year services; funerals; many other occasions in Christian worship.

Scripture References
st. 1 = vv. 1-2
st. 2 = vv. 3-6
st. 3 = vv. 7-9
st. 4 = vv. 10-11
st. 5 = vv. 12-15
st. 6 = vv. 16-17

91

Whoever Shelters with the LORD

DEUS TUORUM MILITUM
♩ = 132

Assurance that God will surely keep safe those who take refuge under the LORD's wings.

Text
Composed for godly worshipers at the temple, Psalm 91 assures those who dwell "in the shelter of the Most High" (v. 1) that they need never be afraid (st. 1); the LORD will be their sure refuge from all enemies and dangers (st. 2). Though thousands perish around them, God's people will be safe (st. 3). God charges the angels to keep his people from harm (st. 4): I will keep you safe because you trust in me (st. 5). Satan applied verses 11 and 12 specifically to Jesus when he was being tempted in the wilderness, but the psalm is appropriate for all who confess, "The LORD . . . 'is my refuge and my fortress'" (v. 2). Calvin Seerveld (PHH 22) versified this psalm in 1985 for the *Psalter Hymnal.*

Tune

DEUS TUORUM MILITUM (sometimes called GRENOBLE) was published in France in the 1753 *Grenoble Antiphoner* as a setting for the text "Deus tuorum militum" ("The God of Your Soldiers"). One of the finest French diocesan tunes from the eighteenth century, it represents a departure in Roman Catholic hymnody from the older chant style. Sing with vigor.

Scripture References
st. 1 = vv. 1-2
st. 2 = vv. 3-6
st. 3 = vv. 7-10
st. 4 = vv. 11-13
st. 5 = vv. 14-16

Liturgical Use

Traditional for New Year celebrations. As a psalm of trust in the Lord's care and keeping, it has many applications in Christian worship.

92

MADRID
♩ = 69

How Good It Is to Thank the LORD

Praise of God for unfailing protection of those who trust in him, and a word of wisdom about the folly of the wicked and the prosperity of the righteous.

Text

A joyful celebration of God's righteous rule, Psalm 92 appears to rise out of an experience of God's deliverance from enemies who took no account of God's readiness and power to protect his own (st. 4). That experience moved the psalmist to note the appropriateness of praising God's love and faithfulness (st. 1) and all that the LORD has done (st. 2). The psalmist also uses the occasion to expound on the folly of the wicked, who defy God by their actions (st. 3), and on the flourishing of the righteous, who trust in God (st. 5). In the post-exilic liturgy of the temple, Psalm 92 was sung at the time of the morning sacrifice on the Sabbath. The versification (altered) is from the 1912 *Psalter.* Another setting of Psalm 92 is at 171.

Scripture References
st. 1 = vv. 1-3
st. 2 = vv. 4-5
st. 3 = vv. 6-9
st. 4 = vv. 10-11
st. 5 = vv. 12-15

Tune

William Matthews (b. Ilkeston, Derbyshire, England, 1759; d. Nottingham, England, 1830) composed MADRID (not to be confused with another tune of that name associated with "Come, Christians, Join to Sing") early in the nineteenth century, but it is not clear how the tune acquired its name. Matthews was a stocking-maker at Nottingham and served as choirmaster and music teacher. He also owned a music shop in Houndsditch. Little else is known about his life.

This decorative tune consists of six lines, each of which has its own character. Sing MADRID in harmony, with joy, and with a sense for the half note as the main beat.

Liturgical Use

Jewish use prescribes this psalm for the Sabbath service. Stanzas 1 and 2 are very fitting for the beginning of worship. Stanzas 3 and 5 focus on wisdom teaching.

93

The LORD Is King, Enthroned

RIALTO
♩ = 84

A celebration of the mighty power by which the LORD keeps creation's order secure.

Text

Psalm 93 is the most succinct of the cluster 92-100, all of which share the theme of the kingship of the LORD. This psalm was to be sung by the Levites in the liturgy of a high religious festival (perhaps the Feast of Tabernacles) celebrating the LORD's kingship over the whole world (st. 1). Because God has founded all creation, no chaotic power (such as the raging seas) can threaten or undo it (st. 2-3). Even God's moral order stands firm (st. 4). In the post-exilic liturgy of the temple, this psalm was sung at the time of the morning sacrifice on the sixth day of the week; Christians sing it to honor the reign of Christ. The versification (altered) is from the 1912 *Psalter.* Another setting of Psalm 93 is at 172.

Scripture References
st. 1 = v. 1a
st. 2 = vv. 1b-2
st. 3 = vv. 3-4
st. 4 = v. 5

Tune

George Frederick Root (b. Sheffield, MA, 1820; d. Bailey's Island, ME, 1895), who is better known for his Civil War songs, composed RIALTO in 1859; the tune is named after an island and bridge in Venice and a theater district in New York City (where Root worked for some years). An energetic tune (with the half note as basic beat), RIALTO cries for full harmony singing and a full organ registration. Strive for two long lines.

A music educator and publisher, Root became acquainted with Lowell Mason (PHH 96) when he was Mason's aide at the Boston Academy of Music. Root moved to New York in 1844 to become a singing teacher at Abbott's School for Young Ladies and organist at Mercer Street Presbyterian Church. A well-known teacher, he taught at several schools, including Union Theological Seminary and the New York Institute for the Blind, where one of his students was Fanny Crosby (PHH 473). Root went to Paris in 1850 to study piano and singing. Following his return to New York, he and William Bradbury (PHH 114) established the Normal Musical Institute, which was founded to instruct music teachers. He composed music for the Christy Minstrels under his German pseudonym, G. Friedrich Wurzel. In 1859 Root moved to Chicago to work with his brother at Root and Cady, Chicago's leading music publisher until the great fire of 1871. Thereafter he affiliated with the John Church Company in Cincinnati. Deeply religious throughout his life, Root became a Swedenborgian in 1864. He composed over two hundred songs, including Civil War favorites such as "The Battle Cry of Freedom" and "Tramp, Tramp, Tramp, the Boys Are Marching." He also compiled some seventy song collections and educational works about music. Nineteen of his hymn tunes were included in *Gospel Hymns No. 1-6 Complete* (1894).

Liturgical Use

Ascension celebrations; many other occasions in Christian worship.

94

ASPINWALL
♩ = *120*

Almighty LORD God, Who Judges the Earth

Israel's appeal to the LORD as "Judge of the earth" to relieve their oppression and judge the wickedness of their oppressors.

Text

God's people are under the heels of a ruthless foreign power that oppresses them by its laws and the corruption of its courts, thinking that the LORD will do nothing to save Israel (st. 2). But Israel appeals to God, the righteous and faithful Judge (st. 1), knowing the LORD will not fail to be their rock and refuge (st. 9). How foolish those enemies are to assume that God doesn't know what they are doing (st. 3)! God will bring Israel relief and dig a pit for their powerful and arrogant oppressors (st. 4). God's people have confidence in his faithful care and just rule (st. 5); they know they need the LORD's help (st. 6), and they know they can count on it

Scripture References
st. 1 = vv. 1-5
st. 2 = vv. 6-7
st. 3 = vv. 8-11
st. 4 = vv. 12-13
st. 5 = vv. 14-15
st. 6 = vv. 16-17
st. 7 = vv. 18-19
st. 8 = vv. 20-21
st. 9 = vv. 22-23

in times of faltering and doubt (st. 7). God's just rule is never compromised (st. 8). God will mercifully protect his people and ultimately, in the Great Day to come, will deal justly with their oppressors (st. 9). In the post-exilic liturgy of the temple, this psalm was sung at the morning sacrifice on the fourth day of the week.

Patricia Ann (Siebersma) Haveman (b. Orange City, IA, 1946) versified Psalm 94 in 1983 for the *Psalter Hymnal*. Educated at South Dakota State University, Brookings, and Dordt College, Sioux Center, Iowa, Haveman is a member of the Hope Christian Reformed Church, Hull, Iowa. Some of her poetry has been published by the Midwest Writer's Association.

Tune

ASPINWALL is another of the many hymn tunes composed by Charles H. Gabriel (PHH 24). It was published with Psalm 104 in the 1912 *Psalter* and earlier editions of the *Psalter Hymnal.* The tune title refers to Aspinwall, a village just northeast of Pittsburgh. Spiced with some chromaticism as the harmony progresses, this music requires clear articulation of the repeated tones in the melody and a sense of one broad beat per measure. Alternate between two groups when singing the entire psalm, and sing stanza 9 in stately unison.

Liturgical Use

When the church appeals to the LORD, the righteous Judge, to rule against human pride and oppression.

95

Now with Joyful Exultation

BEECHER
♩ = 56

A call to worship God as the LORD of all creation and as Israel's Redeemer, and a warning that worship must be accompanied by a life of obedience.

Text

The Levites sang this psalm in the liturgy of a high festival that annually celebrated the cosmic rule of the LORD (perhaps the Feast of Tabernacles). Worship leaders call the congregation of God's people to praise the LORD (st. 1) as the one true God and the King of all creation (st. 2). As Israel's Maker and Shepherd, the LORD is to be worshiped reverently (st. 3) and served in humble

Scripture References
st. 1 = vv. 1-2
st. 2 = vv. 3-5
st. 3 = vv. 6-7
st. 4 = vv. 8-11

obedience. God warns the people not to harden their hearts as their ancestors had done in the wilderness (vv. 8-10). The people will enter into the LORD's promised "rest" only if they live according to God's will (st. 4). The versification (altered) is from the 1912 *Psalter.* Another setting of Psalm 95 is at 173.

Tune

John Zundel's BEECHER (named after Henry Ward Beecher, his pastor) was first published in his *Christian Heart Songs* (1870) as a setting for Charles Wesley's "Love Divine, All Loves Excelling" (568). The tune is also known as ZUNDEL. Approximating the shape of a rounded bar form (AA'BA'), BEECHER is a strong tune with clean rhythms that should be sung in harmony and with solid organ support (st. 4 needs more modesty).

After receiving an education in Germany, Zundel (b. Hochdorf, Germany, 1815; d. Cannstadt, Germany, 1882) went to St. Petersburg, Russia, where he served as organist of St. Anne Lutheran Church and was bandmaster of the imperial horse guards. He came to New York in 1847 and became the organist at Plymouth Congregational Church in Brooklyn (1850-1878). Henry Ward Beecher, the famous abolitionist preacher, was pastor of that congregation, and their joint ministry caused the Plymouth Church to become well known for its preaching, organ playing, and congregational singing. Dissatisfied with existing hymnals, Beecher asked Zundel to help compile several new hymnals. *Temple Melodies* (1851) and the *Plymouth Collection of Hymns* (1855) were the result. Zundel provided twenty-eight hymns tunes for the *Plymouth Collection*. He also published *The Choral Friend* (1855), *Psalmody* (1855), and *Christian Heart Songs*, and he edited the *Monthly Choir and Organ Journal* until his retirement in Germany in 1880.

Liturgical Use
During Lent; beginning of worship (st. 1-3); during the service of confession (st. 4).

96

WESLEY
♩ = 116

Sing to the LORD, Sing His Praise

A call to all the nations to join Israel in the worship of the LORD.

Text
The Levites were to sing Psalm 96 in the liturgy of a high festival such as the Feast of Tabernacles (Ps. 96 appears also in 1 Chron. 16:23-33). Standing among the Israelite congregation at the temple, the Levitical choir (or one of its leaders) would call all the nations to join Israel in worshiping the LORD (st. 1, 4). The psalm also calls for proclaiming the wondrous works of the LORD (st. 2), and it contrasts the glory of the God of Israel with the so-called gods of the nations (st. 3). The LORD God created heaven and earth and rules

Scripture References
st. 1 = vv. 1-2
st. 2 = vv. 3-4
st. 3 = vv. 5-6
st. 4 = vv. 7-9
st. 5 = v. 10
st. 6 = vv. 11-13

over all nations in righteousness (st. 5). In such calls and proclamations Israel began, in principle, the evangelization of the world (st. 2, 5-6). The cosmic scope of this psalm is very appropriate to the Christian task in the whole world. The versification (altered) is from the 1912 *Psalter*.

Tune
Lowell Mason (b. Medfield, MA, 1792; d. Orange, NJ, 1872) composed WESLEY for Thomas Hastings's (PHH 538) "Hail to the Brightness of Zion's Glad Morning," and the two were published together in *Spiritual Songs for Social Worship* (1833). The tune name honors the founders of Methodism, John and Charles Wesley. WESLEY consists of

four lines—the first and third beginning identically, and the fourth providing a suitable climax to the melody. Sing this jubilant tune with lots of energy.

As a child Mason learned to play every musical instrument available to him. He bought music books and attended a singing school when he was thirteen, and soon began teaching singing schools and directing a church choir. In 1812 he moved to Savannah, Georgia, where he helped to establish the firm Stebbins and Mason, which sold musical instruments in addition to dry goods. Mason also adapted, composed, and harmonized tunes for *The Boston Handel and Haydn Society Collection of Church Music* (1821). This collection was widely used and resulted in public demand for Mason to lead the music at singing schools, concerts, and Sunday school conventions. He moved to Boston in 1827 to become the music director in three churches; later he became the choir director of the Bowdoin Street Church. In 1833 Mason helped to found the Boston Academy of Music, which was instrumental in introducing music education to the Boston public schools in 1838. An advocate of Pestalozzi's educational principles (an inductive teaching method), Mason frequently lectured in England and the United States. A major force in musical education in the United States and in the promotion of European models of church music (as opposed to the southern folk-hymn tradition), Mason also encouraged the change from exclusive psalm singing to the singing of hymns in the churches. In association with Thomas Hastings (PHH 538), George Webb (PHH 559), and others, Mason compiled some eighty hymnals and collections, including *The Juvenile Psalmist* (1829), *Spiritual Songs for Social Worship* (1832), and, most importantly, *Carmina Sacra* (1841, revised 1852). Mason composed over eleven hundred original hymn tunes and arranged another five hundred, mainly from European sources. He derived most of his tune names from the Old Testament.

Liturgical Use
Traditional for Advent and Christmas; mission emphasis; beginning of worship.

97

God Reigns: Let Earth Rejoice!

GENEVA 97
♩ = 66

A joyful celebration of the LORD's righteous rule over all the world.

Text

Singing Psalm 97 in the liturgy of a high festival such as the Feast of Tabernacles, the Levites exhorted all peoples of the earth to turn from their powerless idols (v. 7) and to rejoice in the LORD, whose reign is universal, righteous, and eternal (st. 1). Mighty displays of God's power over creation show the righteousness of

Scripture References
st. 1 = vv. 1-2
st. 2 = vv. 3-6
st. 3 = vv. 7-9
st. 4 = vv. 10-12

God's rule and the majesty of God's glory (st. 2). With the people of Israel, we rejoice that God is "Most High over all the earth" (st. 3), and we remember that the LORD grants favor and protection only to those who hate evil and are upright in heart (st. 4). Marie J. Post (PHH 5) versified this psalm in 1981 for the *Psalter Hymnal.*

Tune

First published in the 1562 edition of the Genevan Psalter, GENEVAN 97 is set in the Ionian mode (major) and consists of four long lines (with some internal repetition) and a coda-like final phrase. The harmonization (1985) is by Dale Grotenhuis (PHH 4). This tune bears spirited singing with full accompaniment but should not be rushed.

Liturgical Use

Christmas; Ascension; mission and evangelism celebrations.

98

GENEVAN 98/118
♩ = 66
Sing, Sing a New Song to the LORD God

A universal call for praise of the LORD's mighty acts of redemption
and for the coming of God's righteous rule over all the world.

Text

In the liturgy of a high festival that annually celebrated the LORD's cosmic rule (perhaps the Feast of Tabernacles), the Levites used Psalm 98 to call first the congregation at the temple (st. 1); then all the people of the earth (st. 2); and finally all creation (st. 2-3) to joyful praise of the LORD. This praise celebrates God's acts of redemption (st. 1) and God's future coming "in righteousness" (v. 9; st. 3).

Scripture References
st. 1 = vv. 1-3
st. 2 = vv. 4-7
st. 3 = vv. 8-9

    Dewey D. Westra (b. Holland, MI, 1899; d. Wyoming, MI, 1979) versified this psalm in 1931 for the 1934 *Psalter Hymnal;* some revisions were made for the 1987 *Psalter Hymnal.* Other settings of Psalm 98 are at 174, 175, and 337.

    Westra was a dedicated educator, writer, and musician who faithfully served the Christian Reformed Church. He attended Calvin College, Grand Rapids, Michigan, and Wayne State University in Detroit. In the 1920s and 30s he was a Christian school principal in Byron Center and Detroit, Michigan. During the 1940s he was involved in various ventures, including becoming a diesel instructor for the Ford Motor Company. After 1947 he became a principal again, serving at Christian schools in Sioux Center, Iowa; Randolph, Wisconsin; and Walker, Michigan. Westra wrote poetry in English, Dutch, and Frisian, and translated poetry into English from Dutch and Frisian. He arranged many songs and composed songs for children's choirs. He also versified all one hundred and fifty psalms and the Lord's Prayer, as well as the songs of Mary, Zechariah, and Simeon, in meters that fit the corresponding Genevan psalm tunes. His manuscripts are housed in the library of Calvin College. Seventeen of his psalm versifications and his paraphrases of the Lucan canticles were included in the 1934 and in the 1959 editions of the *Psalter Hymnal*. Much of the credit for keeping the Genevan psalms alive in the Christian Reformed Church goes to Westra.

Tune

For information on GENEVAN 98/118, see 118. The harmonization here was prepared by Dale Grotenhuis (PHH 4) in 1985. See 118 and 314 for other harmonizations of this tune; 314 is placed in the key of F.

Liturgical Use

Advent, Christmas, Easter, and other jubilant times of the church year.

99

The LORD God Reigns in Majesty

NONE BUT CHRIST
$\downarrow = 100$

A call to praise the thrice-holy sovereign God of Israel for his grace.

Text

The Levites used Psalm 99 in the liturgy of a yearly high religious festival celebrating the LORD's worldwide rule (perhaps the Feast of Tabernacles). The psalm opens with a call to all nations to praise the God of Israel (st. 1), exhorts Israel to exalt their mighty King for performing righteous deeds in their behalf (st. 2), and recalls examples of God's gracious response to Israel's need for deliverance. It closes with a grateful remembrance of God's forgiveness (st. 3). Verses 3, 5, and 9 close with "God is holy," a poetic echo of the trisagion (see Isa. 6:3) and a reflection of the ancient liturgical penchant for triple repetition. The versification (altered) is from the 1912 *Psalter.*

Scripture References
st. 1 = vv. 1-3
st. 2 = vv. 4-5
st. 3 = vv. 6-9

Tune

James McGranahan (b. Adamsville, PA, 1840; d. Kinsman, OH, 1907) first published NONE BUT CHRIST in his *Sacred Songs and Solos* (1883) as the setting for the anonymous text "O Christ, in Thee My Soul Hath Found." NONE BUT CHRIST is a dynamic tune; because three of the lines open as a fanfare, brass accompaniment would be very fitting. Keep the accompaniment strong and brisk on the repeated soprano notes.

Of Scottish-Irish descent, McGranahan grew up on the family farm, and his father expected him to become a farmer. Because he wanted to study music, McGranahan hired another person to do the farm work while he earned his own money for music study. He attended William Bradbury's (PHH 114) Normal Music School at Geneseo, New York, conducted singing schools in Pennsylvania and New York, and taught at and managed George F. Root's (PHH 93) Normal Musical Institution for three summers. In 1877 he became a song leader for evangelist Major D. W. Whittle (PHH 495) and toured England and the United States; their association lasted some eleven years. A fine singer himself, McGranahan was one of the first to use male choruses in evangelistic crusades. He published *The Gospel Male Choir* (1878, 1883) and served as editor and compiler of numerous collections, including *Gospel Hymns and Sacred Songs, No. 3-6* (1878-1891) with Ira D. Sankey (PHH 73) and George Stebbins (PHH 63).

Liturgical Use
Ascension (see also 47, 93, and 110); like the others in the cluster 92-100, this psalm is appropriate for many different worship occasions.

100

GENEVAN 100
♩ = 76

All People That on Earth Do Dwell

A call to praise the LORD for showing grace and faithfulness toward "the sheep of his pasture" (v. 3).

Text

Psalm 100 brings to a close a collection of psalms that celebrate the LORD's righteous rule over all creation (93, 95-99). Like the others, it was composed to be sung by the Levites at a high religious festival that annually celebrated the LORD's kingship over the entire world (perhaps the Feast of Tabernacles). Psalm 100 is the Hebrew equivalent of a cheerleader's shout—a strong call to worship the LORD with joyful song (st. 1, 3): the LORD is the one true God who made us to be "the sheep of his pasture" (st. 2), and God's love and faithfulness never fail (st. 4).

Scripture References
st. 1 = vv. 1-2
st. 2 = v. 3
st. 3 = v. 4
st. 4 = v. 5

The *Psalter Hymnal* includes both an English and a French versification. The English text by William Kethe (b. Scotland [?], date unknown; d. Dorset, England, c. 1594) is the oldest metrical psalm text in the *Psalter Hymnal*. It first appeared in the Anglo-Genevan Psalter of 1561 and in John Day's *Psalmes of David in English Metre* (PHH 69), also of 1561. Since then it has been published in virtually all English-language psalters and hymnals. The French text (opposite 101 in the *Psalter Hymnal*) is taken from the French hymnal *Psaumes et Cantiques* (1891); it is included as a tribute to the original language of the Calvinist Psalter.

Both the time and place of Kethe's birth and death are unknown, although scholars think he was a Scotsman. A Protestant, he fled to the continent during Queen Mary's persecution in the late 1550s. He lived in Geneva for some time but traveled to Basel and Strasbourg to maintain contact with other English refugees. Kethe is thought to be one of the scholars who translated and published the English-language Geneva Bible (1560), a version favored over the King James Bible by the Pilgrim fathers. The twenty-five psalm versifications Kethe prepared for the Anglo-Genevan Psalter of 1561 were also adopted into the Scottish Psalter of 1565. His versification of Psalm 100 is the only one that found its way into modern psalmody.

Tune

GENEVAN 100, by Louis Bourgeois (PHH 3), was first a setting for Psalm 131 in the 1551 edition of the Genevan Psalter; in the 1562 edition it was set to Psalms 100 and 142 as well. This is the second Genevan tune in the Phrygian mode (see also GENEVAN 51 at 51). Many people will associate Kethe's text with GENEVAN 134, the tune chosen in the Anglo-Genevan Psalter for Psalm 100 (hence GENEVAN 134 is usually named OLD HUNDREDTH). GENEVAN 100 is of more rhythmic interest and is worth the additional effort that may be required to learn and sing it well, though OLD HUNDREDTH is a useful alternative tune. This tune needs a majestic performance and bright organ support. Two harmonizations are given: one from 1985 by Dale Grotenhuis (PHH 4) and, on the next page, a 1554 setting by Claude Goudimel (PHH 6) with the melody in the tenor. The latter is useful as a choral setting (perhaps on stanza 2) or as an alternative organ accompaniment. Another setting of Psalm 100 is at 176.

Liturgical Use

Many uses beyond its traditional role at the beginning of worship.

101

I Praise Your Justice, LORD

GENEVAN 101
♩ = 69

A pledge of the LORD's anointed to govern God's people in righteousness.

Text

Psalm 101 is a king's pledge to reign righteously. As the LORD's anointed, the king praises God's love and justice and pledges to live a pure life (st. 1). In some detail, he repudiates the ways of perverse people (st. 2, 4) and declares—at the heart and center of his commitments—that only those "whose walk is blameless" (v. 6) will have access to him and serve his administration (st. 3). This psalm portrays the commitment to righteousness expected of the LORD's anointed (see

Scripture References
st. 1 = vv. 1-3a
st. 2 = vv. 3b-5
st. 3 = v. 6
st. 4 = vv. 7-8

also Ps. 72), an expectation perfectly fulfilled by Jesus Christ. Bert Witvoet (PHH 4) versified Psalm 101 in 1985 for the *Psalter Hymnal.*

Tune

GENEVAN 101 was first published in the 1551 edition of the Genevan Psalter. Claude Goudimel (PHH 6) harmonized the tune in 1564. Like most of Goudimel's harmonizations, the melody was originally in the tenor. The *Psalter Hymnal* Revision Committee changed some of the bass notes to provide first inversion chords; Goudimel's original bass provided all root position chords. GENEVAN 101 appears twice in the *Psalter Hymnal*: once here in its authentic, original Genevan form, and at 248 in its altered Anglo-Genevan form under the name JE TE SALUE. To avoid confusion when introducing the tune, organists should play it through once before the congregation sings. Use strong organ accompaniment, a brisk articulation, and a stately tempo.

Liturgical Use

Best used with reference to Christ, the only Son of David, who truly fulfilled the Psalm 101 commitment to rule God's people righteously.

102

SOCIAL BAND
♩ = 54

LORD, Hear My Prayer and Let My Cry

A prayer asking God to have compassion on Zion and the LORD's anointed and to rebuild the devastated city to the praise of God's glory among the nations.

Text

The psalmist opens with an appeal to God to hear his prayer (st. 1) and describes his mournful state because of God's wrath (st. 1-2). Still, he is confident that God will rebuild Zion, to the dismay of all its enemies (st. 3). The psalmist asks that God's deliverance be recorded for future generations so that the praise of the LORD will resound in Jerusalem when peoples and nations gather there for worship (st. 4). Finally the psalmist expresses confidence that though heaven and earth will perish (st. 5), God

Scripture References
st. 1 = vv. 1-3
st. 2 = vv. 4-11
st. 3 = vv. 12-17
st. 4 = vv. 18-22
st. 5 = vv. 23-26
st. 6 = vv. 1-2, 27-28

will remain the same; future generations of God's people will continue to live before the LORD (st. 6). Marie J. Post (PHH 5) altered stanzas 1 through 3 from the 1912 *Psalter* and versified stanzas 4 through 6 in 1985. Psalm 102 is one of the traditional group of penitential psalms (along with 6, 32, 38, 51, 130, and 143).

Tune

New England singing master Jeremiah Ingalls (b. Andover, MA, 1764; d. Hancock, VT, 1828) composed SOCIAL BAND and published it in his 1805 collection of folk hymns, *Christian Harmony*. SOCIAL BAND is a classically shaped rounded bar form (AABA). Its third line provides a fine contrast and climax to the other (repeated) line. Sing the tune in harmony.

Ingalls was a farmer, cooper, tavern keeper, and singing teacher. After settling in Vermont in 1791, he led the choir and played bass viol in the Congregational Church in Newbury. He moved to a farm between Rochester and Hancock, Vermont, in 1810. Ingalls composed several popular fuguing tunes and compiled *The Christian Harmony* (1805), one of the earliest collections of American tunebooks to contain a significant number of folk melodies.

The harmonization (1965) is by J. Harold Moyer (b. Newton, KS, 1927), professor of music at his alma mater, Bethel College, North Newton, Kansas. He also studied at George Peabody College in Nashville, Tennessee, and received his Ph.D. in music composition from the University of Iowa in 1958. Moyer was chair of the tune committee and composed hymn tunes and harmonizations for the *Mennonite Hymnal* (1969). He also contributed to *Hymnal, A Worship Book* (1992) of the Brethren and Mennonite churches.

Liturgical Use

Penitence; expressions of confidence in God's unfailing commitment to his church, even though it may suffer in a hostile world; Christian worship focusing on illness (st. 5).

103

Come, Praise the LORD, My Soul

GENEVAN 103
♩ = 76

A call to all creation to praise the LORD for his boundless compassion to his people as sinners and mortals.

Text

A hymn to God's love and compassion, Psalm 103 is a carefully crafted song. Not only is it composed of twenty-two lines, the number of letters in the Hebrew alphabet, but its opening and closing calls to praise (vv. 1-5, 20-22; st. 1, 5) also frame a uniquely structured center (vv. 6-19). Six verses honor God's compassionate and forgiving grace toward the Israelites as sinners (vv. 7-12; st. 2-3), and six verses celebrate God's everlasting love for these chosen

Scripture References
st. 1 = vv. 1-5
st. 2 = vv. 6-10
st. 3 = vv. 11-14
st. 4 = vv. 15-18
st. 5 = vv. 19-22

people, whose "days are like grass" (vv. 13-18; st. 3-4). Further framing this exposition of God's love are two verses (6, 19) that proclaim God's righteousness and justice, upon which the LORD has established his throne in heaven so that his kingdom rules over all. Moreover, according to the principle of describing the outer limits of something in order to refer to its whole (as one refers to a whole tree by speaking of its fruit above and its roots below, cf. Amos 2:9), the psalmist's opening call to "my soul" to praise the LORD and the closing call on God's angels to do the same invites all creation to praise its Maker and King. Helen Otte (PHH 17) versified this psalm in 1986 for the *Psalter Hymnal*. Other settings of Psalm 103 are at 297, 475, 583, and 627.

Tune

GENEVAN 103 was first published in 1539 in Strasbourg, where Calvin published a small collection of nineteen psalms. Howard Slenk (PHH 3) harmonized the tune in 1985. Psalm 103 is a favorite song in the Dutch Reformed tradition, partially because of its textual content, of course, but also because its Hypo-Mixolydian tune has great merit. The six long lines have satisfying melodic curves and two main rhythmic patterns supplied by lines 1 and 3 (the other lines are repeats of these). Not all stanzas are equally jubilant, but strong organ accompaniment is helpful throughout.

Liturgical Use

Covenant renewal/profession of faith services; conclusion of the Lord's Supper; Christian worship focusing on illness or other distresses that emphasize the frailty of human life; worship focusing on God's love and compassion.

104

HOUGHTEN
♩ = 129

Your Spirit, O LORD, Makes Life to Abound

Praise of God's glory displayed in creation.

Text

A creation hymn, Psalm 104 contains echoes of Genesis 1 but is not a poetic account of creation. Rather, it sings the praise of the Creator by recounting how the visible creation displays God's glory—creation is the glorious robe that clothes the invisible God (v. 1; st. 2). The author sees God's glory not so much in creation's beauty but in its majesty (vv. 2-4; st. 2-3), in the security of land though seemingly threatened by the oceans (vv. 5-9; st. 3-4), and especially in the varied manner in which God nourishes life through the gift of water (st. 5-7). God reveals further glory in the life-supporting pattern of days and seasons (st. 8-9) and in the vastness and benevolence of the earth

Scripture References
st. 1 = vv. 30-31
       (theme stanza)
st. 2 = vv. 1-3
st. 3 = vv. 3b-6
st. 4 = vv. 7-9
st. 5 = vv. 10-12
st. 6 = vv. 13-15
st. 7 = vv. 16-18
st. 8 = v. 19
st. 9 = vv. 20-23
st. 10 = vv. 24-26
st. 11 = vv. 27-29
st. 12 = vv. 32-33
st. 13 = vv. 34-35

and seas (st. 10). God's creation is a kingdom of life, which he abundantly sustains (vv. 27-28; st. 11). Even when God cuts life off, he renews it by his creative Spirit (vv. 29-30; st. 11, 1). Awed by the Creator's almighty power, the psalmist commits to a life of worship and praise (st. 12). But God's glorious robe is marred by an ugly stain, so the psalmist prays that it be removed: "May sinners vanish from the earth and the wicked be no more" (v. 35). Echoing his opening lines, the psalmist closes with a call for praise to the LORD (st. 13). The versification derives mainly from that in the 1912 *Psalter*. The *Psalter Hymnal* Revision Committee chose one stanza (st. 1, based on vv. 30-31) as a theme stanza to be sung as a refrain to mark the main divisions in the biblical text. A hymn based on Psalm 104 is at 428.

Tune

Henry John Gauntlett (b. Wellington, Shropshire, England, 1805; d. Kensington, London, England, 1876) originally composed HOUGHTEN for the text "O Worship the King" (428). Sing the theme stanza (st. 1) in parts and the other stanzas in unison, or vice versa. When singing the entire psalm, sing stanzas 2 through 13 antiphonally. Singing of only part of the psalm should always include the theme stanza.

When he was nine years old, Gauntlett became organist at his father's church in Olney, Buckinghamshire. At his father's insistence he studied law, practicing it until 1844, after which he chose to devote the rest of his life to music. He was an organist in various churches in the London area and became an important figure in the history of British pipe organs. A designer of organs for William Hill's company, Gauntlett extended the organ pedal range and in 1851 took out a patent on electric action for organs. Felix Mendelssohn chose him to play the organ part at the first performance of *Elijah* in Birmingham, England, in 1846. Gauntlett is said to have composed some ten thousand hymn tunes, most of which have been forgotten. A number of them, including HOUGHTEN (1861), were first published in various editions of *The Congregational Psalmist* (1858-1886). A supporter of the use of plainchant in the church, Gauntlett published the *Gregorian Hymnal of Matins and Evensong* (1844).

Liturgical Use
Praise of God as Creator and Provider, especially when celebrating God's gifts to his people.

105

Trumpet the Name! Praise Be to Our LORD!

An exhortation to Israel to worship, trust, and obey the LORD for all he has done in covenant faithfulness to them; a call to tell all the nations about their God.

Text

Psalm 105 was composed for the liturgy of one of Israel's annual religious festivals celebrating God's great acts of salvation, perhaps the Feast of Tabernacles but more likely the Feast of Weeks—see Deuteronomy 16:9-12. The psalmist exhorts Israel: Remember the LORD's saving acts and proclaim them to the world (st. 1); remember the wonders the LORD has done; and trust the LORD always in every need (st. 2). God has always remembered his covenant with Israel (vv. 8-11, 42-45; st. 3, 9—notice this frame around the main body of the psalm). Examples of this covenant faithfulness are God's ways with Abraham (st. 4), God's ways with Jacob and Joseph (st. 5), God's blessing upon the Israelites under Joseph's rule in Egypt (st. 6), God's deliverance of Israel from slavery in Egypt (st. 7), and God's provision for Israel in the desert (st. 8). The LORD not only delivered Israel out of Egypt but also gave them the promised land so that they would serve him (st. 9). Consistent with a basic Old Testament theme, this psalm reminds us that God's claim on our lives is grounded primarily on what God has done for us. Other psalms recounting Israel's history are 78, 106, 135, and 136. (See 1 Chron. 16:8-36 for an example of a psalm composed of other psalms—16:8-22 = Ps. 105:1-15; 16:23-33 = Ps. 96:1-13; 16:34-36 = Ps. 106:1, 47-48.) Calvin Seerveld (PHH 22) versified Psalm 105 in 1983 for the *Psalter Hymnal.*

Scripture References
st. 1 = vv. 1-3
st. 2 = vv. 4-6
st. 3 = vv. 7-11
st. 4 = vv. 12-15
st. 5 = vv. 16-20
st. 6 = vv. 21-24
st. 7 = vv. 25-38
st. 8 = vv. 39-42
st. 9 = vv. 43-45

Tune

GENEVAN 105 was first published in the 1562 edition of the Genevan Psalter as a setting for Theodore de Bèze's versification of Psalm 105. Howard Slenk (PHH 3) composed the harmonization in 1985. Another sturdy tune from Calvin's psalter, GENEVAN 105 is in Ionian mode (major) and consists of six lines, each pair of which has the same rhythmic pattern. The optional repeat of musical line 4 in stanza 7 permits the narration of the plagues in Egypt. The repetition will help the congregation yearn for deliverance from that musical phrase—giving them a taste of how the Hebrew people must have felt! The complete psalm may be sung antiphonally. Sing the tune with much vigor and with a majestic tempo.

Liturgical Use

Christian worship focusing on God's establishment of Israel in the promised land; baptism, stanzas 1-3, with their focus on God's covenant faithfulness.

106

O Praise the LORD, for He Is Good

SEDGWICK
♩ = 58

A penitential prayer recalling Israel's long history of rebellion and God's covenant faithfulness.

Text

Psalm 106 is a kind of twin to Psalm 105; it recalls Israel's history but focuses more on the people's rebellious acts while noting God's faithfulness despite their disobedience. The psalmist opens with a call to praise the LORD for his goodness and mighty acts and asks for God's covenant mercy upon himself and the people of Israel (st. 1). He goes on to tell of Israel's disobedience against the LORD: already in Egypt they forgot God's miracles (v. 7; st. 2). In the desert they complained against God, and some of the people rose up against Moses (st. 3). At Mount Horeb (Sinai) they made an idol, and if not for Moses' intercession for them, God would have destroyed them (st. 4). Israel rejected God's promise of a "pleasant land," so God determined to scatter them; they worshiped the fertility god Baal, so God sent a plague to destroy them—but relented when Phinehas intervened for the sake of God's glory (st. 5). Israel again angered the LORD at Meribah, and they worshiped idols in the promised land. God gave them up to their enemies, but once again he relented when they cried out for mercy (st. 6). God's faithfulness gives the psalmist hope: in closing he cries, "Save us, O LORD our God, and gather us from the nations" (v. 47; see also vv. 4-5) so that the people may ever have cause to praise and thank the LORD (st. 7; notice the echo of v. 1). Other psalms recounting Israel's history are 78, 105, 135, and 136. Marie J. Post (PHH 5) versified Psalm 106 in 1985 for the *Psalter Hymnal*.

Scripture References
st. 1 = vv. 1-5
st. 2 = vv. 6-12
st. 3 = vv. 13-18
st. 4 = vv. 19-23
st. 5 = vv. 24-31
st. 6 = vv. 32-46
st. 7 = vv. 47-48

Tune

SEDGWICK, composed by Lee Hastings Bristol, Jr. (b. Brooklyn, NY, 1923; d. Syracuse, NY, 1979), in 1951, was first published in *Hymns for Children and Grown-ups* (1952) as a setting for the text "My Master Was a Worker" by William G. Tarrant. Bristol coedited that hymnal with Harold W. Friedell. Virtually a rounded bar form (AA'BA"), SEDG-WICK is a well-crafted tune that inspires dynamic congregational singing in parts, but it must not be rushed.

After earning a B.A. degree from Hamilton College, Clinton, New York, Bristol studied organ at Trinity College of Music, London, England, and completed graduate work at the Institute for International Studies, Geneva. From 1948 to 1962 he worked primarily in advertising and public relations for the family business, the Bristol-Myers Company in New York, and then served as president of Westminster Choir College, Princeton, New Jersey, from 1962 to 1969. A recipient of eleven honorary degrees, Bristol composed a number of anthems and edited two hymnal supplements, *Songs for Liturgy* and *More Hymns and Spiritual Songs* (1972), for the joint commission on church music of the Protestant Episcopal Church. He also published *The Lamb and Other Carols* (1951) and *Hymns for Children and Grown-ups*. In 1972 Bristol was honored as a Fellow of the Hymn Society in the United States and Canada.

Liturgical Use
Worship that focuses on Israel's history; stanzas 1 and 7 can form a doxology.

107

GENEVAN 107
♩ = 84

"Thanks Be to God Our Savior"

Praise for God's unfailing deliverance of those who cry to him in the crises of their lives—even when they suffer the just consequences of their sins—and a call to ponder the ways of God.

Text

Psalm 107 opens Book V of the Psalms in their final arrangement, but its affinities with 105 and 106 suggest that the three once formed a trilogy. Psalm 107 was likely composed by a priest or Levite for liturgical use at the temple. Its date is uncertain, but this interpretation seems probable: having experienced God's mercies anew in the return from Babylonian exile (vv. 2-3), Israel is called to thank the LORD (st. 1) and to meditate on God's compassion toward those who cried out to him during a crisis.

Scripture References
st. 1 = vv. 1-3
st. 2 = vv. 4-9
st. 3 = vv. 10-16
st. 4 = vv. 17-22
st. 5 = vv. 23-32
st. 6 = vv. 33-43

The psalm focuses on four such crises (vv. 4-32). In the first, people are lost in a desert without food or water (vv. 4-9; st. 2), and in the last, they are caught in a perilous storm at sea (vv. 23-32; st. 5). In the second and third, they suffer for their rebellious ways—as captives forced to bitter labor (vv. 10-16; st. 3) and as victims of serious illness (vv. 17-22; st. 4). A supplement (vv. 33-42) recalls how God often sends famine followed by times of plenty, and oppression followed by deliverance—to the joy of the upright and the dismay of the wicked. All these things, says the psalmist, should move the wise and godly to ponder God's mercies (st. 6). David Diephouse (PHH 62) versified Psalm 107 in 1985 for the *Psalter Hymnal*.

Tune

GENEVAN 107 first appeared in the 1551 edition of the Genevan Psalter. Dale Grotenhuis (PHH 4) harmonized the tune in 1986. Composed in the Dorian mode, this Genevan tune consists of four long lines, each of which has two phrases; lines 1 and 2 share melodic and rhythmic patterns, and lines 3 and 4 also have similar rhythms. Psalm 107 is a joyous song that needs strong organ accompaniment. Signal the internal refrain in the last half of stanzas 2 through 5 ("Bless him, his love proclaim . . .") by changing organ registration or texture.

Liturgical Use

Thanksgiving for God's aid in times of friendlessness, homelessness, imprisonment, illness, or other crisis in the Christian community.

108

My Heart Is Firmly Fixed

ST. THOMAS
$\text{♩} = 54$

Praise of God's faithful mercies toward his people, and prayer for God's help against threatening foreign powers.

Text

With slight modifications, Psalm 108 is made up of Psalm 57:7-11 (vv. 1-5) and Psalm 60:5-12 (vv. 6-13). Scholars are not sure what occasioned this new combination, but it may have risen out of the crisis of a new threat from foreign enemies. Through praise the psalmist expresses confidence in God (st. 1) and vows to praise the LORD among the nations for being faithful and merciful (st. 2). The psalmist proclaims God's glory above the heavens and over all the earth (st. 3), and then prays, "Save us and help us" (v. 6), O God, from the threat of our enemy (st. 4). Recalling

Scripture References
st. 1 = vv. 1-2
st. 2 = vv. 3-4
st. 3 = v. 5
st. 4 = v. 6
st. 5 = vv. 7-9
st. 6 = vv. 10-11
st. 7 = vv. 12-13

God's commitments to parcel out the land of Canaan to the tribes of Israel (st. 5), the psalmist asks, Who will lead us in triumph if God has rejected us (st. 6)? Then comes this confession: Our only hope is God, and he will not fail us (st. 7). The versification is significantly altered from that in the 1912 *Psalter.*

Tune

ST. THOMAS is actually lines 5 through 8 of the sixteen-line tune HOLBORN, composed by Aaron Williams (b. London, England, 1731; d. London, 1776) and published in his *Collection* (1763, 1765) as a setting for Charles Wesley's text "Soldiers of Christ, Arise" (570). The harmonization is by Lowell Mason (PHH 96). Well-suited to part singing, ST. THOMAS must remain stately, with two broad beats per bar.

Williams was a singing teacher, music engraver, and clerk at the Scottish Church, London Wall. He published various church music collections, some intended for rural church choirs. Representative of his compilations are *The Universal Psalmodist* (1763)—published in the United States as *The American Harmony* (1769)—*The Royal Harmony* (1766), *The New Universal Psalmodist* (1770), and *Psalmody in Miniature* (1778). His *Harmonia Coelestis* (1775) included anthems by noted composers.

Liturgical Use
Because this is a composite psalm, stanzas 1 through 3 can stand alone as praise for God's steadfast love. The remainder of the psalm is useful for times when the church is threatened by enemies.

109

NUN LOB, MEIN SEEL
♩ = 50

Do Not Be Silent, LORD God

A plea asking God, the heavenly Judge, to deliver the psalmist from false accusers and to deal judicially with them.

Text

Often singled out as the most harsh of the so-called "imprecatory" psalms, Psalm 109 does not so much curse the psalmist's enemies as plead for appropriate judgment on them (what they intended to do to the psalmist can be learned from what he asks God to do to them). The psalmist is deeply aggrieved because

Scripture References
st. 1 = vv. 1-5, 15
st. 2 = vv. 6-19
st. 3 = vv. 20-31

his attackers are people he has long befriended (st. 1). He appeals to God to deal out appropriate judicial penalties (st. 2) and pleads for deliverance from his vicious tormentors, concluding with a vow to publicly thank and praise the LORD, who protects the meek and needy (vv. 30-31; st. 3). Calvin Seerveld (PHH 22) versified this psalm in 1985 for the *Psalter Hymnal.*

Tune

Johann (Hans) Kugelmann (b. Augsburg, Germany, c. 1495; d. Konigsberg, Germany, 1542) adapted NUN LOB, MEIN SEEL from the song "Weiss mir ein Blümlein blaue" and first published the tune in his *Concentus Novi* (1540). A bar form, this German chorale consists of six long lines sharing some similar melodic and rhythmic patterns. NUN LOB was originally associated with a setting of Psalm 103 ("My soul, now praise the LORD . . .") in the Lutheran tradition, but it has a solemnity appropriate for Psalm 109.

Johann Kugelmann was trumpeter, music director, and composer at the court of Margrave Albrecht V of Brandenburg. His compositions include music for two Königsberg songbooks as well as melodies and harmonizations for a manuscript collection of devotional songs by Heinrich von Miltitz. Kugelmann's best known work, *Concentus novi* (1540), contains thirty of his original compositions.

Liturgical Use

Appropriate when the church is under attack, especially in the form of slander intended to arouse hostility; Calvin Seerveld suggests singing this psalm "whenever atrocities and institutionalized evil in the world or land preoccupy people in their prayerful concern."

110

The LORD unto My Lord Has Said

ALL SAINTS NEW
♩ = 56

*A proclamation of the sure triumph and unfailing reign
of the LORD's anointed, the priest-king son of David.*

Text

Traditionally ascribed to David (Matt. 22:43-45), this was most likely a coronation psalm for the Davidic kings. The two authoritative words, or oracles, from God (vv. 1, 4) may be echoes of the covenant made with David concerning his dynasty (2 Sam. 7; Ps.

Scripture References
st. 1 = vv. 1-2
st. 2 = vv. 3-4
st. 3 = vv. 5-7

89:1-37). The first of these oracles proclaims the sure triumph of the LORD's anointed (st. 1) and the refreshing dedication of the king's servants. The second oracle proclaims the king's enduring priesthood "in the order of Melchizedek" (st. 2; see Heb. 5:6, 10; 7:15-22)—perhaps because the king in Jerusalem was responsible for building and maintaining the temple, for overseeing the work of the priests and Levites there, and for interceding for the nations. This blessed king would rule all the nations, judge them, and know unfailing vigor in his exalted eternal reign (st. 3). The New Testament uses Psalm 110 more than any other in reference to Jesus Christ as the anointed King filling this role. The versification (altered) is from the 1912 *Psalter.*

Tune

Henry Stephen Cutler (b. Boston, MA, 1824; d. Boston, 1902) composed ALL SAINTS NEW in 1872 for Reginald Heber's (PHH 249) text "The Son of God Goes Forth to War," and the two were published together in *Hymnal with Tunes, Old and New* (1872). That text refers to "the glorious band" of God's people, helping to explain the chosen tune title. The NEW is to distinguish this tune from others that are also called ALL SAINTS. ALL SAINTS NEW has a processional or martial character, inherited no doubt from Cutler's love for the British cathedral tradition of choir processions. Sing the tune in parts at a moderate tempo.

Cutler studied music in Frankfurt, Germany, in 1844. He moved to England, where he listened with interest to the cathedral choirs and came under the influence of the Oxford Movement. Returning to Boston in 1846, Cutler became organist of the Episcopal Church of the Advent and formed a choir of men and boys, to whom he introduced the wearing of liturgical robes. When he took a position at Trinity Church in New York City, he removed women from the choir and used the occasion of a visit by the Prince of Wales to the church to introduce his newly vested men and boys' choir. He also moved the choir from the gallery to the chancel and initiated the chanting of the psalms and the singing of part of the worship service. Cutler compiled *The Psalter, with Chants* (1858) and published *The Trinity Psalter* (1864) and *Trinity Anthems* (1865).

Liturgical Use
Ascension (see also 47, 93, and 99).

111

GERMANY
♩ = 120

O Give the LORD Wholehearted Praise

Praise of the righteousness of the LORD.

Text

The first of eight "hallelujah" psalms (111-118), 111 was probably composed in the post-exilic period by a priest or Levite for temple worship. In structure and theme it is a poetic twin of Psalm 112. But while Psalm 112 is a eulogy to the righteous one who fears the LORD, 111 praises God for his unfailing righteousness. The opening and closing verses frame the main thematic development with a call to praise (st. 1) and a word of instruction concerning true wisdom: "The fear of the LORD is the beginning of wisdom" (v. 10; st. 7). God's righteousness is the faithfulness and grace by which he remains true to his covenant. The saints delight in God's "mighty works and wondrous ways" (st. 2), which display the faithfulness of the LORD's love and grace (st. 3). God has been faithful in granting the people "the wealth of nations" (the promised land; st. 4). The LORD's deeds and orders for living are true and just (st. 5), and God's redemption shows his true covenant faithfulness. Let all revere God's holy name (st. 6), gain wisdom and understanding in the LORD, and praise his name forever (st. 7)! The 1912 *Psalter* is the source for this (altered) versification.

Scripture References
st. 1 = v. 1
st. 2 = vv. 2-3
st. 3 = v. 4
st. 4 = vv. 5-6
st. 5 = vv. 7-8
st. 6 = v. 9
st. 7 = v. 10

Tune

William Gardiner (b. Leicester, England, 1770; d. Leicester, 1853) first published GERMANY as a setting for the text "As a Shepherd Gently Leads Us" in his *Sacred Melodies* (vol. 2, 1815), in which he attributed it to Ludwig van Beethoven. The last phrase of this tune resembles a part of the first theme of the Allegretto movement of Beethoven's Piano Trio, Op. 7, No. 2. The first phrase is from the opening of the aria "Possenti Numi" in Mozart's *The Magic Flute.* The tune is also known by the names BEETHOVEN, FULDA, WALTON, or GARDINER. Sing GERMANY briskly to get the sense of two long lines rather than four shorter, choppy ones. Antiphony is helpful for singing the entire psalm.

The son of an English hosiery manufacturer, Gardiner took up his father's trade in addition to writing about music, composing, and editing. Having met Joseph Haydn and Ludwig van Beethoven on his business travels, Gardiner then proceeded to help popularize their compositions, especially Beethoven's, in England. He recorded his memories of various musicians in *Music and Friends* (3 volumes, 1838-1853). In the first two volumes of *Sacred Melodies* (1812, 1815), Gardiner turned melodies from composers such as Haydn, Mozart, and Beethoven into hymn tunes in an attempt to rejuvenate the singing of psalms. His work became an important model for American editors like Lowell Mason (PHH 96; see Mason's *Boston Handel and Haydn Collection,* 1822), and later hymnbook editors often turned to Gardiner as a source of tunes derived from classical music.

Liturgical Use
Beginning of worship; wisdom emphasis (especially st. 7); many other occasions in Christian worship.

112

How Blest Are Those Who Fear the LORD

MELCOMBE
♩ = 104

A praise song eulogizing the righteous.

Text

The second of the eight "hallelujah" psalms (111-118), 112 was probably composed in the post-exilic period by a priest or Levite for temple worship. In structure and theme it is a poetic twin of Psalm 111, but while 111 sings the praise of the righteous God, 112 eulogizes the righteous one who fears the LORD. The opening and closing verses frame the development of the main theme by contrasting the blessedness of the righteous (v. 1; st. 1) and the unhappy end of the wicked (v. 10; st. 6)—a common theme in Old Testament wisdom literature (see also 1, 34, 37, 49, and 73). The psalmist notes that the children of the righteous share in "their great reward" (st. 1) and that prosperity comes

Scripture References
st. 1 = vv. 1-2
st. 2 = vv. 3-4
st. 3 = vv. 5-6
st. 4 = vv. 7-8
st. 5 = v. 9
st. 6 = v. 10

to the merciful and pure (st. 2). Those who befriend the weak find peace and a good name (st. 3), and those who trust in God have security from all their foes (st. 4). The righteous are generous to the poor and are "lifted high in honor" (v. 9; st. 5), but the wicked and their ways will come to nothing (st. 6). The (altered) versification of this wisdom psalm comes from *The Book of Psalms* (1871), a text-only psalter that was later published with music in the 1887 *Psalter.*

Tune

MELCOMBE was first used as an anonymous chant tune (with figured bass) in the Roman Catholic Mass and was published in 1782 in *An Essay on the Church Plain Chant.* It was first ascribed to Samuel Webbe (the elder; b. London, England, 1740; d. London, 1816) and named MELCOMBE in Ralph Harrison's *Sacred Harmony* (1791), the first of many Protestant hymnals to contain this popular Roman Catholic tune. The tune title refers to Melcombe Regis, the northern part of Weymouth in Dorsetshire, England, made famous through frequent visits by King George III (1738-1820).

Webbe's father died soon after Samuel was born without providing financial security for the family. Thus Webbe received little education and was apprenticed to a cabinet-maker at the age of eleven. However, he was determined to study and taught himself Latin, Greek, Hebrew, French, German, and Italian while working on his apprentice-ship. He also worked as a music copyist and received musical training from Carl Barbant, organist at the Bavarian Embassy. Restricted at this time in England, Roman Catholic worship was freely permitted in the foreign embassies. Because Webbe was Roman Catholic, he became organist at the Portuguese Chapel and later at the Sardinian and Spanish chapels in their respective embassies. He wrote much music for Roman Catholic services and composed hymn tunes, motets, and madrigals. Webbe is considered an outstanding composer of glees and catches, as is evident in his nine published collections of these smaller choral works. He also published *A Collection of Sacred Music* (c. 1790), *A Collection of Masses for Small Choirs* (1792), and, with his son Samuel (the younger), *Antiphons in Six Books of Anthems* (1818).

MELCOMBE has a steady rhythmic structure and a lot of stepwise intervals. The original setting had one dotted rhythm in the third phrase, which is deleted in many hymnals, including the *Psalter Hymnal.* The harmony borrows from Webbe's original bass line and from William H. Monk's (PHH 332) harmonization of MELCOMBE for *Hymns Ancient and Modern* (1861). Sing this tune in two long lines, with a small pause at the end of the first to allow a breath before singing the second.

Liturgical Use

Wedding or family services; wisdom emphasis; many other occasions in Christian worship.

113

Praise God, You Servants of the LORD

FESTUS
♩ = 100

Praise to the LORD for his exalted glory and mercies to the lowly.

Text

The third of the eight "hallelujah" psalms (111-118), 113 was probably composed by a priest or Levite for use in the temple. This psalm also begins the "Egyptian Hallel" used in Jewish liturgy at the annual religious festivals prescribed in the Torah. At Passover, Psalms 113 and 114 were sung before the meal; 115 through 118

Scripture References
st. 1 = vv. 1-2
st. 2 = vv. 3-4
st. 3 = vv. 5-6
st. 4 = vv. 7-9

were sung after the meal. After opening with a call to praise the LORD (vv. 1-3; st. 1-2), the psalm celebrates the exalted glory of heaven's great King, who bends down to get involved in earth's affairs (vv. 4-6; st. 2-3). The LORD is merciful to the needy—seating the poor among princes and blessing the barren with children (st. 4). The (altered) versification is from the 1912 *Psalter.* Another setting of Psalm 113 is at 177.

Tune

FESTUS is an abridgement of a tune published in Johann A. Freylinghausen's (PHH 34) *Geistreiches Gesangbuch* (1704) as a setting for "O du Hüter Israel." The shortened tune was first published in the Bristol *Tune Book* (1863). The tune title presumbably honors Festus, the Roman procurator of Judea (Acts 25-26). Sing FESTUS with a bright organ registration, which is helpful in negotiating the larger intervals in the second half of the tune.

Liturgical Use

Used in many Jewish festivals, including Passover, Psalm 113 is equally appropriate for special days of the Christian church year, especially Ascension (st. 3), and is generally fitting at the beginning of worship.

114

ANDRE
♩ = 108

When Israel Fled from Egypt Land

A celebration of God's mighty power displayed in the redemption of Israel.

Text

The fourth of the "hallelujah" psalms (111-118), 114 was probably composed by a priest or Levite for use in the temple liturgy. It stands second in the "Egyptian Hallel" used in Jewish liturgy at the annual religious festivals prescribed in the Torah. At Passover, Psalms 113 and 114 were sung before the meal; 115 through 118 were sung after the meal. With vivid metaphor (mountains skipping like rams) and masterful compression, this little hymn celebrates the mighty power of God displayed in the Exodus, at Sinai, in the Israelites' desert wanderings, and at the entrance to the promised land. God united with Israel at the time of the Exodus, taking up residence with them (st. 1). Earth's imposing and powerful features—

Scripture References
st. 1 = vv. 1-2
st. 2 = vv. 3-4
st. 3 = vv. 5-6
st. 4 = vv. 7-8

mountains and sea—yielded in awe to the redemptive purposes of God (st. 2), and the psalmist asks them to reflect on why they submitted (st. 3). The psalmist then calls upon all creation to tremble before its Maker, who can still bring water out of dry, hard rock and provide for his people's every need (st. 4). Henrietta Ten Harmsel (PHH 61) versified this psalm in 1985 for the *Psalter Hymnal.*

Tune

ANDRE by William B. Bradbury (b. York, ME, 1816; d. Montclair, NJ, 1868) is a solid tune in which a simple harmonization supports melodic and rhythmic motives well suited to the story-like character of Psalm 114. In the 1912 *Psalter* and in earlier editions of the *Psalter Hymnal,* ANDRE was set to Psalm 113; for the 1987 edition, the tune was chosen for Psalm 114 and abridged from five to four phrases. Ten Harmsel suggests that "the parallel images make it especially suitable for antiphonal singing." One possible arrangement is to have all sing on stanza 1, men on stanza 2, a children's choir or women and children on stanza 3, and all again on stanza 4. A solid accompaniment for stanzas 1, 2, and 4 should give way to lighter playing for the questions of stanza 3, which is reminiscent of the Passover tradition in which children ask their parents why that night is different from all other nights.

Bradbury came from a musical family who encouraged him from an early age to learn to play various musical instruments. In 1830 his family moved to Boston. There he studied singing with Lowell Mason (PHH 96) and sang in Mason's Bowdoin Street Church choir. In 1841 Bradbury moved to Brooklyn, New York, and became the organist at the Baptist Tabernacle in New York City. He organized children's singing classes, which developed into annual singing festivals and stimulated the teaching of music in the New York public schools. In 1854 William joined his brother Edward and a German piano maker to begin a piano firm, which became the Bradbury Piano Company. Bradbury wrote or edited sixty collections of popular music and edited and published numerous song books, including *The Psalmodist* (1844) and *Golden Shower of Sunday School Melodies* (1862). He is sometimes known as "the father of Sunday school hymnody."

Liturgical Use

Reflection on the Exodus theme, especially during Easter Vigil, when Christians associate the Exodus with their own exodus from sin and death through Christ's victory.

115

Not Unto Us, O LORD of Heaven

GAIRNEY BRIDGE
♩ = 72

A liturgy of praise including an exhortation to
trust in the LORD, followed by a priestly benediction.

Text

Number five of the eight "hallelujah" psalms (111-118), 115 was
probably composed by a priest or Levite as a liturgy of praise for
temple worship. Some scholars suggest that it was originally used
at the dedication of the second temple (Ezra 6:16) after the return
from Babylonian exile. This psalm stands third in the "Egyptian
Hallel" used in Jewish liturgy at the annual religious festivals
prescribed in the Torah. At Passover, Psalms 113 and 114 were
sung before the meal; 115 through 118 were sung after the meal. In this psalm many
voices speak. Here is a probable scenario: vv. 1-8, 12-13, and 16-18—the people;
vv. 9-11—the Levitical choir; vv. 14-15—a priest. The psalmist praises God for his love,
faithfulness, and sovereign power (st. 1, 5). He belittles the idols of the nations (st. 2),
exhorts Israel to trust in the LORD (st. 3), and pronounces a blessing upon God's
people (st. 4). The (altered) versification is from the 1912 *Psalter.*

Scripture References
st. 1 = vv. 1-3
st. 2 = vv. 4-8
st. 3 = vv. 9-12
st. 4 = vv. 13-15
st. 5 = vv. 16-18

Tune

Ernest Richard Kroeger (b. St. Louis, MO, 1862; d. St. Louis, 1934) wrote GAIRNEY
BRIDGE in gospel-hymn style. The tune was set to Psalm 115 also in the 1912 *Psalter.*
The tune should be sung in harmony, ably supported by organ articulation that points
clearly to three beats per bar. The liturgical dialogue built into this psalm may be
expressed through antiphonal performance: stanzas 1, 2, and 5 by everyone; stanza 3 by
one group; and stanza 4 by another.

Kroeger left his mercantile business in 1885 and began formal studies in music,
although he had been organist of Grace Episcopal Church in St. Louis at the age of
fifteen. From 1878 to 1885 he served as organist for Trinity Episcopal Church and from
1885 to 1921 for the (Unitarian) Church of the Messiah. A founder of the Kroeger
School of Music, he was also director of music at Forest Park College for Women, and
he led a number of choirs in St. Louis. Kroeger composed orchestral works, string
quartets, and various pieces for organ and voices.

Liturgical Use

Beginning of worship; profession of faith, ordination/commissioning, marriage, and
family services (st. 3-5).

116

I Love the LORD, for He Has Heard My Voice

A thank offering of praise for deliverance from death in answer to prayer.

Text

This sixth of eight "hallelujah" psalms (111-118) stands fourth in the "Egyptian Hallel" used in Jewish liturgy at the annual religious festivals prescribed in the Torah. At Passover, Psalms 113 and 114 were sung before the meal; 115 through 118 were sung after the meal. In this liturgical use, the singular personal pronoun was understood corporately, and the references to "death" alluded to Israel's slavery in Egypt. The "cup of salvation" (v. 13; st. 4)

Scripture References
st. 1 = vv. 1-4
st. 2 = vv. 5-7
st. 3 = vv. 8-11
st. 4 = vv. 12-14
st. 5 = vv. 15-19

probably referred originally to the festal cup of wine that climaxed a thank offering for a special deliverance or blessing. When this psalm was used in the Passover celebration, the "cup of salvation" was no doubt understood to be the cup of wine accompanying that festal meal. In singing this psalm, we join the psalmist in confessing our love for the LORD for deliverance from death in answer to prayer (st. 1). And we praise God's gracious ways that encourage us to keep trusting and to rest in the LORD (st. 2). The psalmist notes that faith had not failed in the time of crisis (st. 3); together we vow to praise the LORD among the saints and continue to call upon God's name (st. 4-5). Helen Otte (PHH 17) wrote the unrhymed versification in 1980 for the *Psalter Hymnal*. Another setting of Psalm 116 is at 178.

Tune

GENEVAN 116 was first published in the 1562 edition of the Genevan Psalter, in which it was also the setting for Psalm 74. Seymour Swets (b. South Holland, IL, 1900; d. Grand Rapids, MI, 1982) harmonized the tune in 1954. This Mixolydian tune is one of the simplest, finest, and most loved of the Genevan repertoire. It is suitable for unison or part singing; sing in a majestic manner.

A 1922 graduate of Calvin College, Grand Rapids, Michigan, with a major in history, Swets received his M.A. from the University of Michigan in 1923. Later that year he was appointed to the Calvin College faculty to teach speech and to establish a music program. He taught at Calvin College until 1967 and was largely responsible for the remarkable growth of its music department. A chronicle of that era appears in his book, *Fifty Years of Music at Calvin College* (1973). Swets served on the committees that prepared the 1934 and the 1959 editions of the *Psalter Hymnal* and contributed harmonizations to both books.

Liturgical Use

Occasions of thanksgiving for healing; Lent; Easter; Lord's Supper (especially st. 4).

117

Hallelujah, Hallelujah

IN BABILONE
♩ = 56

A call to all nations to praise the LORD.

Text

The seventh of eight "hallelujah" psalms (111-118), 117 is an expanded "Praise the LORD." It was probably composed for use at the beginning or end of temple liturgies. It stands fifth in the "Egyptian Hallel" used in Jewish liturgy at the annual religious festivals prescribed in the Torah. At Passover, Psalms 113 and 114 were sung before the meal; 115 through 118 were sung after the meal. Psalm 117 is only one stanza in length, but in calling all nations to praise the LORD for being faithful to Israel, it powerfully anticipates the Great Commission (Matt. 28:18-20). Paul quotes verse 1 in Romans 15:11 as proof that the salvation of Gentiles was not a divine afterthought. The versification derives from *The Book of Psalms* (1871), a text-only psalter that was later published with music in the 1887 *Psalter.*

Tune

IN BABILONE is a traditional Dutch melody that appeared in *Oude en Nieuwe Hollantse Boerenlities en Contradansen* (*Old and New Dutch Peasant Songs and Country Dances*), c. 1710. Ralph Vaughan Williams (PHH 316) discovered this tune as arranged by Julius Röntgen (b. Leipzig, Germany, 1855; d. Utrecht, the Netherlands, 1932) and included it in *The English Hymnal* (1906), from which it gained widespread use. A rounded bar-form tune (AABA), IN BABILONE provides a fine setting for Psalm 117's cosmic scope. Because this song has only one stanza, use the tune as an alternate to other texts in 87 87 D so that congregations may sing it more often. Stretch the cadence a bit to catch a breath at the end of line 3 (ending in the word *accord).*

An important Dutch pianist, composer, conductor, scholar, and editor, Röntgen studied music in Leipzig with well-known German teachers. In 1877 he moved to Amsterdam, where he first taught at the Amsterdam Conservatory. In 1886 he became conductor of the Society for the Advancement of Musical Art. He returned to the Conservatory as director in 1918, then retired in 1924 to devote himself to composition. He was a friend of leading composers of his day, including Liszt, Brahms, and Grieg, and wrote a biography of Grieg. Röntgen's compositions include symphonies, chamber works, operas, and film scores.

Liturgical Use

As an expanded "hallelujah," Psalm 117 has many uses in worship—by itself or possibly as a frame for another hymn.

118

GENEVAN 98/118
♩ = 66

Give Thanks to God for All His Goodness

Praising God for delivering the people when they were attacked by many nations and for making "the stone the builders rejected" the foremost cornerstone.

Text

The last of eight "hallelujah" psalms (111-118), 118 is a hymn of thanksgiving for deliverance from enemies. It presupposes a triumphal procession into the city and the temple of God. Psalm 118 praises God for unfailing love (st. 1) and for deliverance from many enemies (st. 2). In praise to God for bringing victory, the king leads a triumphal entry into God's presence (st. 3); the people celebrate "the day" in which God has set up his corner-

Scripture References
st. 1 = vv. 1-4
st. 2 = vv. 5-14
st. 3 = vv. 15-21
st. 4 = vv. 22-25
st. 5 = vv. 26-29

stone—the stone the builders had rejected (st. 4). The people praise and joyfully salute the anointed one, "who comes triumphant in God's name." A final call to praise and thank the LORD for unfailing love echoes the psalm's opening statement (st. 5).

Psalm 118 closes the "Egyptian Hallel" used in Jewish liturgies for the annual religious festivals prescribed in the Torah. At Passover, Psalms 113 and 114 were sung before the meal; 115 through 118 were sung after the meal. As the last song in that liturgy, 118 may have been the hymn sung by Jesus and his disciples at the end of the Last Supper (Matt. 26:30). Jesus applied verse 22 ("the stone the builders rejected") to himself in Matthew 21:42 and Mark 12:10 (see also Acts 4:11). Stanley Wiersma (PHH 25) versified this psalm in 1982 for the *Psalter Hymnal;* he took the refrain from verses 1 through 4 and made it the final line of each stanza. Other settings of Psalm 118 are at 179 and 241.

Tune

GENEVAN 98/118 is the one tune in the *Psalter Hymnal* used for two psalms. It was first published in the 1551 Genevan Psalter as a setting for Psalm 118; in the 1562 edition it was also set to Psalm 98 (hence both numbers in the tune name). The tune is also often named RENDEZ A DIEU, the French incipit for Psalm 118.

This beloved tune is one of the finest and most widely sung of the Genevan psalm tunes (next to GENEVAN 134). Its clear melodic structure and vibrant rhythm call for firm accompaniment with bright organ registration, though some congregations may want to try unaccompanied singing on a stanza or two in the tradition of the sixteenth-century Reformers.

Many modern hymnals set this tune to versifications of Psalm 98 or to hymn texts such as the one at 314. The 1564 harmonization here by Claude Goudimel (PHH 6) originally placed the melody in the tenor. See 98 and 314 for other harmonizations of this tune; 314 is placed in the key of F.

Liturgical Use
Times of thanksgiving; Palm Sunday and Easter processionals; many other occasions in Christian worship.

119

Blessed Are Those Who Heed the Law of God

GENEVAN 119
$\downarrow = 76$

Professions of one who lives by God's Word.

Text
The longest of the psalms, 119 is an extended devotional on the Word of God, probably included in the Psalms as a model of true piety. The psalmist expresses passionate devotion to God's Word as the light upon his path, acknowledging his own heart's errant ways. He confesses his experience of both the pain and fruits of God's corrective discipline, reflecting that he has suffered much at the hands of those who have no regard for God's Word and who have made him the target of their persecution. The psalmist addresses most of his lines to God, mingling prayer with professions of love for God's Word. He perceives that Word as made up primarily of promises to be believed and directives to be followed, which is consistent with the theme found elsewhere that true godliness ("the fear of the LORD") consists of trust and obedience.

Blessed are those who live by God's law, says the psalmist (st. 1); I live by the Word of God (st. 2). Please, LORD, help me understand your will (st. 3). Protect me from scorners and guide me (st. 4); increase my faith and help me be obedient (st. 5). Sustain me with your love in the face of those who taunt me for loving your Word (st. 6). Your Word renews my hope, O God, though the wicked mock me. Their unjust scorning of your laws angers me (st. 7). Please be merciful to me, according to your promise; I will obey your law even if the wicked bind me with ropes (st. 8). Give me wisdom to keep from straying again, and protect me from the slanderous attacks of the arrogant (st. 9). Please bless me for serving you so that the godly are encouraged (st. 10). O God, I trust your promises and love your precepts; please deliver me from those who wish to harm me (st. 11). Your creative word upholds the whole creation, and your commandments secure life (st. 12); I love your law for the wisdom and joy it provides (st. 13). Your law is a lamp to guide my feet and a heritage to be cherished (st. 14). I want no association with evildoers; I love your law, and I know I can rely on your promises to defend me (st. 15). LORD, defend me from those who oppress out of disdain for your law (st. 16). Your law is the source of light and life and understanding (st. 17); your laws are righteous; your promises never fail (st. 18). Save me from the lawless, O God. I want to live by your commands forever; I meditate on them throughout the night (st. 19). Deliver me from my persecutors, for I love your precepts (st. 20). I find comfort in your promises when I am persecuted without cause. Those who love your law have great peace (st. 21). Help me according to your promise, O God, so that my praise and delight in your law may continue (st. 22).

In 1980 Clarence P. Walhout (PHH 6) accepted the challenge of preparing a metrical setting of this long psalm, working with the suitably long tune from the 1551 Genevan Psalter. By working without rhyme, he was able to provide one stanza for each of the eight-verse units, completing the entire psalm in twenty-two stanzas. The original Hebrew poetry is in acrostic form, in which each of the sections is headed by one of the twenty-two letters of the Hebrew alphabet, and the letter heading a section is also the letter beginning each line of that section. Other settings of parts of Psalm 119 are at 276 and 584.

Scripture References

st. 1 = vv. 1-8
st. 2 = vv. 9-16
st. 3 = vv. 17-24
st. 4 = vv. 25-32
st. 5 = vv. 33-40
st. 6 = vv. 41-48
st. 7 = vv. 49-56
st. 8 = vv. 57-64
st. 9 = vv. 65-72
st. 10 = vv. 73-80
st. 11 = vv. 81-88
st. 12 = vv. 89-96
st. 13 = vv. 97-104
st. 14 = vv. 105-112
st. 15 = vv. 113-120
st. 16 = vv. 121-128
st. 17 = vv. 129-136
st. 18 = vv. 137-144
st. 19 = vv. 145-152
st. 20 = vv. 153-160
st. 21 = vv. 161-168
st. 22 = vv. 169-176

Tune

GENEVAN 119, by Louis Bourgeois (PHH 3), was first published in the 1551 edition of the Genevan Psalter; Howard Slenk (PHH 3) harmonized the tune in 1985. GENEVAN 119 is in Hypo-Ionian mode (major). The six long lines of the melody use two slightly different rhythmic patterns and mostly stepwise motion. A bright but not loud organ registration helps this tune to "sing itself." Antiphonal performance is helpful in the singing of a select group of stanzas.

Liturgical Use

Focus upon the Word of the Lord—the choice of stanzas may vary from one occasion to another: stanzas 3, 5, 7, 13, 14, and 17 are specifically useful in conjunction with the reading of the Ten Commandments or as sung prayers of illumination prior to the main Scripture reading. Any number of stanzas are useful when preaching on the Decalogue.

120

In My Distress I Cry to God

SALVATION
♩ = 56

A prayer for deliverance from slanderers and the harm they cause.

Text

Psalm 120 is the first in a series of "Songs of Ascents" (120-134) sung by the Israelites as they went up to worship at the LORD's temple on Mount Zion. A prayer for deliverance from false accusers, the last verse (v. 7) suggests that the author was a king. If

Scripture References
st. 1 = vv. 1-4
st. 2 = vv. 5-7

so, his enemies were trying to discredit him at home or spread lies about him in foreign lands to fuel a concerted effort to attack him. For pilgrims to Jerusalem, this song could serve as a prayer for deliverance from those who spread false reports about them along the way. The psalmist pleads for God's deliverance from the barbed tongues of malicious slanderers (st. 1), noting the vulnerability and isolation of one slandered by associates (st. 2).

Clarence P. Walhout (PHH 6) versified this psalm in 1982 for the *Psalter Hymnal*.

Tune

SALVATION is an anonymous tune that was published in Ananias Davisson's *Kentucky Harmony* (1816), the first Southern shape-note tune book. The melody was originally in the tenor. A rounded bar form (AABA'), SALVATION must be sung solemnly but not too slowly; the half-note rhythms define the energy of this music.

The harmonization was composed by Kenneth John Munson (b. Galesburg, IL, 1916; d. Burlington, VT, 1986) and first appeared in the Unitarian Universalist *Hymns for the Celebration of Life* (1964) set to three different texts. Munson studied at Knox College, Galesburg, Illinois, and received a Ph.D. in music from Eastman School of Music, Rochester, New York. He served as chair of the music department at St. Lawrence University in Canton, New York, from 1942-1981, and was organist and choir director in several churches throughout his career.

Liturgical Use

In the context of false accusation—especially when the Christian community is discredited in the public eye by malicious slander.

121

To the Hills I Lift My Eyes

A profession of the LORD's sure protection of his people.

Text

Psalm 121 is one of fifteen "Songs of Ascents" (120-134), psalms the Israelites sang as they went up to worship at the temple in Jerusalem. Its main theme—that the LORD is the unfailing Protector of those who look to him—surely made it appropriate for such use. However, it is equally appropriate for God's pilgrims on the journey of life. We confess that our security comes from the LORD, the Maker and Ruler of all creation, and receive assurance that the LORD never sleeps (st. 1), but watches over us day and night to protect us from harm no matter where we go (st. 2). The (altered) versification is from the 1912 *Psalter.* Other settings of Psalm 121 are at 180 and 448.

Scripture References
st. 1 = vv. 1-4
st. 2 = vv. 5-8

Tune

Converted to Christianity as a youth at a mission in Buffalo, New York, Marcus Morris Wells (b. Cooperstown, NY, 1815; d. Hartwick, NY, 1895) spent most of his life near Hartwick as a farmer and maker of farm implements. He is remembered in hymnody for writing both the text and tune of "Holy Spirit, Faithful Guide." "On a Saturday afternoon, October 1858, while at work in my cornfield, the sentiment of the hymn came to me," writes Wells. "The next day, Sunday, being a very stormy day, I finished the hymn and wrote the tune for it and sent it to Prof. I. B. Woodbury." Isaac Woodbury was the editor of the *New York Musical Pioneer,* and the original text and tune were first published in that periodical's November 1858 issue.

GUIDE has been associated with Psalm 121 since the 1887 *Psalter.* GUIDE is a rounded bar form (AABA); it has basically one rhythmic pattern and a very simple harmony. One antiphonal arrangement that works nicely is to have a soloist ask the opening question and everyone sing the rest in reply. The tune's simplicity invites unaccompanied singing in harmony.

Liturgical Use

Whenever the Christian church confesses its assurance in God's care and keeping; stanza 2 makes a fine choral benediction.

122

I Was Glad They Came to Call Me

JESU JOY
♩ = 104

A hymn of joy over Jerusalem, and a prayer for the peace of the city of God.

Text

This is one of fifteen "Songs of Ascents" (120-134) the Israelites sang as they went up to worship at the temple in Jerusalem. Psalm 122 must have been intended for the moment when the pilgrims reached the city: "Our feet are standing in your gates, O Jerusalem" (v. 2). The psalm hails Jerusalem as the city where the tribes may go up to worship at the LORD's temple and where the divinely chosen house of David rules in justice over God's people (st. 1). As such, Jerusalem (Zion) is the earthly center of the kingdom of God, the focal point of the worship, life, and security of God's covenant nation (other psalms of Zion are 46, 48, 76, 84, 87, 125, and 137). It is most fitting, then, that out of their love for Jerusalem the pilgrims conclude this song with a prayer for the city's peace (st. 2). Calvin Seerveld (PHH 22) versified Psalm 122 in 1982 for the *Psalter Hymnal*.

Scripture References
st. 1 = vv. 1-5
st. 2 = vv. 6-9

Tune

JESU JOY is a form of the tune WERDE MUNTER, MEIN GEMUETE by Johann Schop (b. Hamburg [?],Germany, c. 1595; d. Hamburg, 1667). In 1614 Schop was appointed court musician in the Hofkapelle at Wolfenbüttel. A virtuoso violinist, he also played the lute, cornetto, and trombone. He became a musician for King Christian IV of Denmark in Copenhagen in 1618. When the plague swept through Copenhagen, Schop fled to find employment elsewhere. In 1621 he settled in Hamburg, where he became the principal violinist for the city and organist at St. James Church. Exposed to various national music styles in Hamburg and in his travels, Schop became a cosmopolitan composer, well known for his dance suites, church concertos, and songs. He composed forty-nine new melodies for Johann Rist's *Himmlische Lieder* (1641-1643), including WERDE MUNTER (1642).

The melody gained popularity through Johann S. Bach's (PHH 7) famous harmonization of the tune in his Cantata No. 147 (1723). JESU JOY is a rounded bar form (AABA'). In communities where this tune is well known, it would be delightful to use the Bach organ arrangement as introduction, interlude (between the two stanzas), and postlude to the singing of the psalm; Bach's setting is in G major, and the hymn setting is in F, so one or the other needs to be transposed to combine them. A song leader can conduct the entrances for the congregation.

Liturgical Use

Beginning of worship; expressions of the church's commitment to the city or kingdom of God; prayer for the coming of the kingdom.

SARAH
♩ = 112

To You, O LORD, I Lift My Eyes

A prayer to the LORD to sustain his people in the face of the world's contempt.

Text

Another of fifteen "Songs of Ascents" (120-134) the Israelites sang as they went up to worship at the temple in Jerusalem, Psalm 123 is a brief, well-balanced prayer in which Israel looks up to the mighty God enthroned in heaven to ask for mercy. Like slaves who look to their masters for help (st. 1), the saints plead for rescue in the face of contempt and ridicule by the arrogant world powers around them (st. 2). The versification of Psalm 123 derives from both the 1871 *Book of Psalms* (st. 1) and the 1912 *Psalter* (st. 2). Verse 1 of the psalm serves as a thematic frame for the two stanzas.

Scripture References
st. 1 = vv. 1-2
st. 2 = vv. 3-4, 1

Tune

Hughes M. Huffman's SARAH first appeared in *Hymns II* (1976) as a setting for Henry Collins's text "Jesus, My Lord, My God, My All." He wrote the tune for that text in 1975 and named it in memory of his sister, who died in 1974, only three years after receiving her doctorate in organ from Yale University. The tune was first sung in 1976 at Christ Church, Oak Brook, Illinois, where Huffman served as minister of music from 1965-1977. SARAH sings well in harmony because it has repeated melodic and rhythmic motives.

Huffman (b. Morganton, NC, 1942) received his education at Wheaton College, Illinois; Northern Baptist Seminary, Oak Brook, Illinois; and Northern Illinois University, De Kalb. He was coeditor of the InterVarsity *Hymns II* (1976) and *Carols* (1978). Since 1988 he has been minister of music at the First Presbyterian Church of Covina, California. He has composed over twenty hymn tunes and arrangements.

Liturgical Use

Whenever the Christian church prays for mercy, especially in the face of the world's contempt and persecution.

124

If God the LORD Were Not Our Constant Help

GENEVAN 124
♩ = 76

Praise for God's deliverance from the fierce hostility of the nations.

Text

One of the fifteen "Songs of Ascents" (120-134) the Israelites sang as they went up to worship at the temple in Jerusalem, Psalm 124 praises God for deliverance from the raging hostility of other nations. Thus it stands appropriately next to Psalm 123, which is a prayer for such deliverance. In two well-balanced stanzas, Israel first acknowledges that only the LORD could have delivered them when the "flood" of hostility attempted to "engulf" them (v. 4; st. 1), and then praises the LORD for deliverance (st. 2). The imagery of hostility shifts from that of a threatening flood in the first stanza to that of a fowler's snare and a threatening wild beast in the second stanza. From the closing verse comes the traditional "votum" of Reformed liturgy: "Our help is in the name of the LORD, the Maker of heaven and earth." Calvin Seerveld (PHH 22) prepared the unrhymed versification of this psalm in 1981 for the *Psalter Hymnal.*

Scripture References
st. 1 = vv. 1-5
st. 2 = vv. 6-8

Tune

GENEVAN 124 (also known as OLD 124TH) was first published in the 1551 edition of the Genevan Psalter. Dale Grotenhuis (PHH 4) harmonized the tune in 1985. One of the best known from the Genevan Psalter, the tune is published in most North American hymnals. By 1564 it was adopted in English and Scottish psalters and became known either as OLD 124TH or as the abridged TOULON, which omits the third line (see 521). Originally, the rhythm of the second line was the same as the fifth, and the third line contained a spritely syncopation: ♩ ♫ ♩ ♩ ♫ ♩ ♫ . The rhythm in the *Psalter Hymnal* follows that of most recent North American hymnals.

Liturgical Use

Contexts of gratitude for God's deliverance.

125

All Who with Heart Confiding

An assurance of security for those who trust in the LORD and are purehearted.

Text

Psalm 125 is one of fifteen "Songs of Ascents" (120-134) the
Israelites sang as they went up to worship at the temple in
Jerusalem. As a testimony to the security of those who trust the
LORD, this psalm appropriately follows 123 (a prayer for deliverance from the contempt of surrounding nations) and 124 (praise
for such deliverance). Recalling the security of Mount Zion as the city surrounded by
God's sure protection (see also 122 and other related Zion songs: 46, 48, 76, 84, 87, and
137), the psalmist assures all who trust in the LORD that God will similarly keep them
safe (st. 1), especially from foreign oppression. But only the pure in heart can take
comfort from this assurance (st. 2); those who cherish evil will perish with the wicked.
The psalm closes with a plea for peace upon the LORD's people (st. 3). The (altered)
versification is from the 1912 *Psalter.*

Scripture References
st. 1 = vv. 1-2
st. 2 = vv. 3-4
st. 3 = v. 5

Tune

KNOWHEAD, by Charles H. Gabriel (PHH 24), was the setting for Psalm 125 in the 1912
Psalter. For the 1987 *Psalter Hymnal,* KNOWHEAD was adapted from the original 6/8 to
4/4 meter, and its rhythmic patterns were made consistent from one line to another.
Harmony singing goes well when feeling two beats per measure.

Liturgical Use

Both as a benediction (from God to the people) and as a prayer for peace (from the
people to the LORD).

126

When God Brought Zion's Remnant Band

*Praise for God's restoration from exile, and a prayer that God's grace may
continue until the people's joy is complete.*

Text

Psalm 126 is another of the fifteen "Songs of Ascents" (120-134) the Israelites sang as
they went up to worship at the temple in Jerusalem. Here Israel celebrates their

restoration from exile, most likely the exile in Babylon. With joy so great that they felt as if they were dreaming, the people returned to Jerusalem full of laughter and praise for the great things God had done for them, evoking wonder even among unbelieving nations

Scripture References
st. 1 = vv. 1-3
st. 2 = vv. 4-6

(st. 1). Having been so favored, the worshipers pray that God's acts of restoration may continue until those who "sow in tears" bring in a bountiful harvest with "songs of joy" (vv. 5-6)—in other words, until God makes their joy complete (st. 2). Calvin Seerveld (PHH 22) paraphrased this psalm in 1985 for the *Psalter Hymnal*.

Tune

Ludwig Senfl (b. Basil, Switzerland, c.1486; d. Munich, Germany, 1543) composed MAG ICH UNGLÜCK for his secular text "Mag mir Unglück nit widerstan." Senfl was a choir-boy in the chapel choir of Emperor Maximilian I and therefore traveled with the emperor; after his voice broke, he may also have received a scholarship to study music in Vienna, which was the custom for choirboys. He followed Heinrich Isaac as director of the choir in 1513, but three years later the new emperor, Charles V, dismissed the musicians in favor of more Spanish music. Senfl became sympathetic to the Reformation; Luther knew of his work and asked him to write for the church. Eventually settling in Munich, Senfl was an important transitional figure, marking the high point of the old German music at the end of the Middle Ages and of new musical styles at the beginning of the Reformation.

MAG ICH UNGLÜCK was adapted for this text. Rewritten as a hymn (possibly by Luther), it was published in Joseph Klug's *Geistliche Lieder* (1535). The rewritten text began with the words "Mag ich Unglück . . ." and became known as the "Queen Mary of Hungary Song." Dale Grotenhuis (PHH 4) harmonized the tune in 1985. A sturdy German chorale, MAG ICH UNGLÜCK is shaped in a bar form (AAB) that gains interest through its dynamic rhythms. The tune needs confident and bright organ accompaniment. Try to group the shorter phrases into three very long lines.

Joseph Klug (b. Nürnberg [?], Germany, c. 1500; d. Wittenberg, Germany, 1552) was an important printer in Wittenberg during the Reformation. He published scholarly works as well as Lutheran books and tracts, including Bugenhagen's *Brunswick Church Order* (1528). His most significant contribution to hymnody was his publication of *Geistliche Lieder*, a hymnbook compiled by Martin Luther that appeared in a number of subsequent editions (1529, 1533, 1535, and 1543). Its contents and organization became the model for the next generation of Lutheran hymnals. Some scholars think Klug may have assisted Luther in choosing the hymns for this volume.

Liturgical Use

Advent; Lent; expressions of eschatalogical hope and joy.

127

CREDO
♩ = 104

If God Does Not Build Up the House

Godly wisdom teaches that all of life's securities are
gifts of God and not human achievements.

Text

One of fifteen "Songs of Ascents" (120-134) the Israelites sang as
they went up to worship at the temple in Jerusalem, Psalm 127
reflects themes of Old Testament wisdom, reminding Israel that all
of life's basic securities and blessings are gifts from God alone (see

Scripture References
st. 1 = vv. 1-2a
st. 2 = vv. 2b-5

also 128). Two basic themes develop in two balanced stanzas. The first focuses on God's
provision and sure care of the believer's house and of the city that fears the LORD
(st. 1), and the second cites children as God's gift of heritage and security to believing
parents (st. 2). In Hebrew, the words *house* and *children* are linked by their similar
sounds; in calling sons a "heritage from the LORD," the psalmist may have intended a
subtle reference to the guarantee that sons secured the family heritage of land in the
promised land. Using unrhymed verse, Calvin Seerveld (PHH 22) paraphrased Psalm
127 in 1980 for the *Psalter Hymnal.* He gave the last two lines of each stanza "an epigrammatic character, because the cast of the text is indeed proverbial, meant to capture a
truth in a memorable couplet."

Tune

John Stainer (b. Southwark, London, England, 1840; d. Verona, Italy, 1901) composed
CREDO for the text "We Saw Thee Not When Thou Didst Come"; the tune was published in *Hymns Ancient and Modern* (1875). CREDO, like some other Victorian tunes,
depends as much on its harmonization as on its melody for effectiveness. But the bold
gestures of the tune's final line also give it distinction. Part singing is essential. Pause for
a breath at the end of the first musical phrase. If a more familiar tune is needed for this
psalm (for example, at a wedding), consider using MELITA (425).

An influential composer and music scholar in the Victorian era, Stainer grew up in a
musical environment. As a young boy he took organ lessons from his father on their
small home chamber organ, and he became a chorister at St. Paul Cathedral in 1849. In
1856 Frederick Ousely, professor of music at Oxford, visited St. Paul's and heard the
young Stainer improvising at the organ. Ousely promptly offered him employment as
the organist of the College of St. Michael at Tenbury. One of England's leading
musicians, Stainer also held organist positions at Magdalen College (1860-1872),
University College (1861-1872), St. Paul's Cathedral (1872-1888), and the National
Training School of Music, now the Royal College of Music (1875-1888). He founded
the Oxford Philharmonic Society and conducted its first concert in 1866. His most

famous cantata, *The Crucifixion* (1887), was followed in 1888 by knighthood and honorary degrees from Durham and Oxford. Much of Stainer's church music was composed for St. Paul Cathedral, including many anthems, carols, and cantatas. He was also a prominent musicologist—his publications include *A Theory of Harmony* (1871), *Music of the Bible* (1879), and a study of Dufay. He composed some one hundred and fifty hymn tunes, published collectively as *Hymn Tunes* (1901). He also served as editor of the *Church Hymnary* (1888) and coeditor of the well-known *Christmas Carols* (1871) and *The Cathedral Prayer Book with Music* (1891).

Liturgical Use
Weddings; family life services; services that mark "beginnings."

128

How Blest Are All the People

GENEVAN 128
♩ = 72

A declaration of the domestic blessedness of those who fear the LORD.

Text

A "Song of Ascents" (among the cluster 120-134) that the Israelites sang as they went up to worship at the temple in Jerusalem, Psalm 128 is a partner with 127 in extolling the LORD for the blessings of family life. The psalmist teaches that domestic blessings are especially reserved for those who fear the LORD. Their labors will prosper, and their wives will bear children, thus magnifying the daily banquet of joy around the family table (st. 1). A closing benediction pronounces blessing on those who fear the LORD and adds a blessing on all God's people (st. 2). Calvin Seerveld (PHH 22) versified this psalm for the *Psalter Hymnal* in 1981.

Scripture References
st. 1 = vv. 1-3
st. 2 = vv. 4-6

Tune

GENEVAN 128 was first published in the 1543 edition of the Genevan Psalter. Claude Goudimel (PHH 6) harmonized the tune in 1564; originally the melody was in the tenor. In the Dorian mode, this tune consists of four long lines in two pairs, consisting of slightly different rhythmic patterns. A striking melody with larger intervals at the beginnings of lines 1 and 2, GENEVAN 128 is worth the effort it may require to learn.

Liturgical Use

Weddings; family life services; choral benediction. Seerveld suggests singing this psalm for baptism, especially if the grandparents of the infant are present: "One of the richest blessings for an Old Testament believer was to live long enough to see the grandchildren flowering in the faith of the fathers and mothers."

129

CLIFF TOWN
♩ = 56

Those Hating Zion Have Afflicted Me

*Praise for God's preservation of his people, and a prayer that all who
threaten them may come to nothing.*

Text

Psalm 129 is another of the fifteen "Songs of Ascents" (120-134)
the Israelites sang as they went up to worship at the temple in
Jerusalem. This post-exilic psalm calls on Israel to praise the LORD
for preserving them, in spite of the oppression they have suffered
from hostile powers throughout their history (vv. 1-4; st. 1-2).

Scripture References
st. 1 = vv. 1-2
st. 2 = vv. 3-5
st. 3 = vv. 6-8

Then follows a prayer that the enemies of Zion may wither before they reach maturity,
like grass that springs up where there is no depth of soil and no water to sustain it
(vv. 5-8; st. 2-3). In focus is the great issue of human history: whether God's people will
endure or whether the forces arrayed against them will have their way in the world.
While Psalms 127 and 128 are psalms of blessing, 129 is a prayer asking God to withhold
his blessing on enemies (v. 8). Churches who experience persecution, who understand
the saying "Vengeance is mine, I will repay, says the Lord" (Rom. 12:19; Deut. 32:35,
RSV) will want to use this psalm. Marie J. Post (PHH 5) versified Psalm 129 in 1985 for
the *Psalter Hymnal*.

Tune

Erik Routley (PHH 31) wrote CLIFF TOWN in 1943 to the text "Not Only for the Goodly
Fruit-Trees Tall" by E. S. Armitage; the tune was first published in *Congregational Praise*
(1951). CLIFF TOWN is named after the Congregational Church at Southend-on-Sea,
England. It is fitted with a harmonization suited to four-part singing; the opening
phrase returns at the end with a small cadential change. Keep it stately, with two broad
beats per measure.

Liturgical Use

Whenever the Christian church experiences or reflects on God's preserving care in the
face of opposition or persecution. North American Christians may want to sing this
psalm in solidarity with other Christians who suffer severely.

130

Out of the Depths I Cry, LORD

GENEVAN 130
♩ = 66

A cry from the depths, and a profession of confidence in God's gracious forgiveness and help.

Text

One of the fifteen "Songs of Ascents" (120-134) the Israelites sang as they went up to worship at the temple in Jerusalem, Psalm 130 may have been composed for worshipers who came to the temple to pray when suffering affliction (the "depths" referred to in v. 1).

Scripture References
st. 1 = vv. 1-4
st. 2 = vv. 5-8

These suffering worshipers acknowledge that their deepest need is for God's forgiveness, but that is also their hope and assurance, for the LORD forgives the sins of the people (st. 1). In that confidence, they eagerly "wait for the LORD" to be gracious and to deliver them from their trouble. And to all God's people they say, "Hope in the LORD, for . . . with him is full redemption" (v. 7; st. 2). In early Christian liturgy Psalm 130 was designated as one of the seven penitential psalms (the others are 6, 32, 38, 51, 102, and 143). Robert Swets (b. Minneapolis, MN, 1950) wrote the unrhymed versification of Psalm 130 in 1980 for the *Psalter Hymnal*. Another setting of Psalm 130 is at 256.

Educated at Calvin College, Grand Rapids, Michigan, and the University of Michigan, Ann Arbor, Swets served as choir director in several Reformed and Christian Reformed congregations in the Grand Rapids area. Swets has published *Sixteen Sonnets* (1975) and a number of other poems.

Tune

GENEVAN 130 was first published in the 1539 edition of the Genevan Psalter. The 1564 harmonization by Claude Goudimel (PHH 6) originally placed the melody in the tenor. GENEVAN 130 is a Dorian tune consisting of four long lines in which the rhythm of line 3 is a fitting contrast to the repeated rhythmic pattern of the other lines. Sing the first stanza in a subdued manner and the second stanza boldly, with bright, full organ registration.

Liturgical Use

Like the other penitential psalms, 130 is most useful in the service of confession/forgiveness of sin. It is particularly appropriate for Lent. See further comment at PHH 131.

131

LORD, My Heart Is Humbled Now

A profession of childlike trust in the LORD.

Text

Psalm 131 is one of the fifteen "Songs of Ascents" (120-134) sung   *Scripture References*
by the Israelites as they went up to worship at the temple in   st. 1 = vv. 1-2a
Jerusalem. The placement of this profession of childlike trust in   st. 2 = vv. 2b-3
God immediately after Psalm 130 seems deliberate. Here faith
renounces all claims to heroic self-reliance: the psalmist rests in the LORD (st. 1) like a
babe in its mother's arms and exhorts all God's people to do the same (st. 2). Calvin
Seerveld (PHH 22) versified this psalm in 1982 for the *Psalter Hymnal.*

Tune

AUS DER TIEFE (also called HEINLEIN) was published in the *Nürnbergisches Gesang-Buch*
(1676-77) as a setting for Christoph Schwämlein's text based on Psalm 130 "Aus der
Tiefe rufe ich" ("Out of the Depths I Cry"). In that songbook the tune was attributed to
"M. H.," initials that are generally accepted to refer to Martin Herbst (b. Rothenbach,
Germany, 1654; d. Eisleben, Germany, 1681). Herbst was educated in theology and
philosophy at the universities of Altdorf and Jena. In 1680 he became rector of the
gymnasium (high school) and pastor of St. Andrew Church in Eisleben. The following
year he died of the plague.

    In the *Psalter Hymnal,* AUS DER TIEFE is in isorhythm, but its harmonization helps to
keep it a "humble handmaiden" for the psalm text. Sing the tune in parts, and add a
Picardy third on the final chord of stanza 2. The key and opening notes are the same as
in Psalm 130; they share the same key and opening notes.

Liturgical Use

Confessions of humble trust in the Lord (130 and 131 can frame a service of confession); many other occasions in Christian worship.

132

God of Jacob, Please Remember

BLAENWERN
♩ = 126

A prayer for God's blessing on David's royal son, and God's reassuring answer.

Text

One of fifteen "Songs of Ascents" (120-134) sung by the Israelites as they went up to worship at the temple in Jerusalem, Psalm 132 was distinctly messianic for Israel as they waited for God's promised restoration of the throne of David. Central to the psalm is the prayer for God's blessing on David's royal Son (vv. 1, 10; st. 1, 3). This prayer comes out of David's deep commitment to provide a permanent "resting place" for the LORD's throne (the

Scripture References
st. 1 = vv. 1-5
st. 2 = vv. 6-9
st. 3 = vv. 10-12
st. 4 = vv. 13-16
st. 5 = vv. 17-18

ark of the covenant) in the midst of the people in order to make the LORD central in Israel's life (vv. 2-9; st. 1-2). The LORD's answer—I will ever uphold and prosper my anointed (vv. 17-18; st. 5)—is rooted in God's covenant oath to David (vv. 11-12; st. 3) and in God's own choice of Zion as his desired "resting place" (st. 4). Calvin Seerveld (PHH 22) paraphrased this psalm in 1983 for the *Psalter Hymnal*.

Tune

Composed by William Penfro Rowlands (b. Maenclochog, Pembrokeshire, Wales, 1860; d. Swansea, Glamorganshire, Wales, 1937) during the Welsh revival of 1904-1905, BLAENWERN was published in Henry H. Jones's *Cân a Moliant* (1915). The tune's name refers to a farm in Pembrokeshire where Rowlands convalesced in his youth.

A church musician of many talents, Rowlands was a teacher in several schools. He composed hymn tunes and anthems and was conductor of the famous Morriston United Choral Society of southern Wales and precentor of the Tabernacle Congregational Church in Morriston. BLAENWERN gained its current popularity through Billy Graham crusades when it was sung to "What a Friend We Have in Jesus" (579).

Play this majestic music with two broad beats per measure. Especially when sung with its fine harmonization, BLAENWERN gradually builds to a powerful climax at the end of phrase 3 and the beginning of phrase 4. Assign some stanzas for antiphonal singing in harmony, but have the entire group sing stanza 5 in unison, perhaps with a slightly slower tempo.

Liturgical Use

Because of its messianic import, Psalm 132 is appropriate in conjunction with preaching on salvation history and during Advent.

133

GENEVAN 133
♩ = 72

Behold, How Good,
How Pleasant Is the Union

*Acclaim for the good and beautiful unity of people knit
together in their commitment to the LORD.*

Text

Psalm 133 is another of the fifteen "Songs of Ascents" (120-134)
the Israelites sang as they went up to worship at the temple in
Jerusalem. The people's oneness of heart in commitment to the
LORD sanctifies them for the worship of God, as did the oil of
consecration poured on Aaron's head (st. 1). There on Mount Zion, God's blessing
falls upon the people like the life-refreshing dew on Mount Hermon (part of the
Lebanon range, st. 2). Bert Polman (PHH 37) versified this psalm in 1986 for the *Psalter
Hymnal.* Another setting of Psalm 133 is at 514.

Scripture References
st. 1 = vv. 1-2
st. 2 = v. 3

Tune

GENEVAN 133 first appeared in the 1551 edition of the Genevan Psalter. Howard Slenk
(PHH 3) harmonized the tune in 1985. Composed in the Ionian mode (major),
GENEVAN 133 consists of six lines that group into two very long melodic curves with
identical cadences at the ends of lines 3 and 6. Sing the tune at a brisk pace in a festive
manner with crisp organ articulation.

Liturgical Use

Reflections on the goodness and beauty of unity among God's people (especially
appropriate at ecumenical gatherings).

134

GENEVAN 134 (OLD HUNDREDTH)
♩ = 63

You Servants of the
LORD Our God

A closing liturgy at the temple.

Text

Psalm 134 is the last of fifteen "Songs of Ascents" (120-134) the
Israelites sang as they went up to worship at the temple in
Jerusalem. A brief parting exchange between the worshipers and
the temple personnel, this psalm is a fitting conclusion to that

Scripture References
st. 1 = vv. 1-2
st. 2 = v. 3

collection. Originally this little liturgy may have functioned as the closure to the daily evening sacrifices. As they are ready to depart, the people exhort the Levites to carry on God's praise (even into the night, v. 1; st. 1), and they receive a priestly benediction (st. 2). Calvin Seerveld (PHH 22) versified this psalm in 1981 for the *Psalter Hymnal.* Because verse 3 echoes the beginning of the Aaronic benediction (Num. 6:24), Seerveld incorporated part of that benediction in stanza 2.

Tune

GENEVAN 134 is one of the noblest and most loved tunes in all of Christendom. It was composed by Louis Bourgeois (PHH 3) and first published in the 1551 edition of the Genevan Psalter, which he also edited. In the Anglo-Genevan Psalter of 1561 it was set to William Kethe's versification of Psalm 100, "All People That on Earth Do Dwell" (100), and since then the popular name for the tune has been OLD HUNDREDTH. GENEVAN 134 is also traditionally associated with Thomas Ken's doxology text "Praise God, from Whom All Blessings Flow" (638). The *Psalter Hymnal* retains the slightly altered version introduced by sixteenth-century English psalters: the last phrase of the melody originally began with three half notes. During the last few centuries GENEVAN 134 was usually sung in isorhythm (all notes of equal value). The rhythmic version found in the *Psalter Hymnal* is certainly preferred to provide a musical vitality that the hymn and the doxology at 638 deserve.

Though GENEVAN 134 should be sung with conviction, its use for this text does not require the jubilant character of the doxology; the psalm text is rather a call to praise (st. 1) and a benediction (st. 2). Stanza 1 can be appropriately sung by the congregation in the traditional harmony, and stanza 2 by a minister or choir using the famous John Dowland setting (1621) with the melody in the tenor (opposite 135 in the hymnal). For festive occasions (such as an ordination or a wedding), the congregation can conclude the psalm by singing the doxology (638).

John Dowland (b. London [?], England, 1563; d. London, 1626) was a well-known composer, singer, and lute player during the Elizabethan era. His greatest ambition was to be a lute player at the royal court in London. When this position was denied him, he served as lutenist in Paris for the British ambassador and in other continental courts, including the court of Christian IV of Denmark (1598-1606). He returned to London and in 1612 was finally appointed lute player for King James I. Dowland wrote numerous songs with lute accompaniment, solo works for lute, and a few arrangements of psalm tunes, including this setting of GENEVAN 134 published in Ravenscroft's *Psalms* (PHH 59).

Liturgical Use

Close of worship (with st. 2 as a sung benediction); for festive occasions such as ordination and wedding services.

JANET
♩ = 92

Sing Praise to the LORD God Almighty

Praise of the LORD as Creator and Redeemer.

Text

In Jewish tradition, Psalms 135 and 136 served as an appendage to the "Songs of Ascents." The two psalms are also noteworthy for their recounting of Israel's history (see also 78, 105, and 106). In this post-exilic hymn, the psalmist first exhorts the temple personnel: Praise God; "proclaim all his glory abroad" (st. 1), for God, in his goodness, has chosen Israel to be his people (st. 2). Praise God as the Creator and as the King of creation (st. 3-4); praise the LORD for redeeming Israel and for giving them the promised land (st. 5-6). Praise God, who continues to sustain Israel (st. 7). The idols made by human hands are powerless, and so "shall their worshipers be" (st. 8). Praise God, all Israel and all you who fear the LORD; "sing praise to his glorious name" (st. 9). Thus all believers are urged to praise the LORD as the one true God: the great Maker and Ruler of all creation who proves that all other gods are powerless, and the great Redeemer who overwhelmed Egypt and destroyed many kingdoms to give Israel the promised land. The combination of these two themes is common throughout the psalms; together they constitute the mighty acts by which the LORD became Israel's God. The (altered) versification is from the 1912 *Psalter.* Another setting of Psalm 135 is at 181.

Scripture References
st. 1 = vv. 1-2
st. 2 = vv. 3-4
st. 3 = vv. 5-6
st. 4 = v. 7
st. 5 = vv. 8-9
st. 6 = vv. 10-12
st. 7 = vv. 13-14
st. 8 = vv. 15-18
st. 9 = vv. 19-21

Tune

JANET, by George C. Stebbins (PHH 63), is thought to have been composed for this psalm and was first published in the 1912 *Psalter.* Written in Stebbins's characteristic gospel-hymn style, JANET is a simple tune with simple harmonization but with a strong rhythmic effect. Sing it in parts and in alternating groups for stanzas 3 through 8, and have everyone sing stanzas 1, 2, and 9. The bulk of this psalm is narration of salvation history—don't rush the narrative! Stanzas 1-2 and 9 frame the narrative with choral calls to praise.

Liturgical Use

The entire psalm is appropriate to services focusing on Israel's history. A selection of stanzas (for example, 1-4 and 9) have more general use at the beginning of worship.

136

Let Us with a Gladsome Mind

GENEVAN 136
♩ = 80

A recital of praise of the LORD as Creator and as the Redeemer of Israel.

Text

In Jewish tradition, Psalm 136 served with 135 as an appendage to the "Songs of Ascents." Like 135, it is a liturgy of praise to the LORD as Creator and as Israel's Redeemer, noteworthy for its recounting of Israel's history (see also 78, 105, and 106). This song's obvious antiphonal form presupposes recitation by a Levite soloist (or choir) and responses by the worshiping congregation. The psalmist calls on the saints to thank and praise the LORD, the kind and true God (st. 1), the one who rules over all (st. 2). God is the Creator of heaven and earth (st. 3) and of the sun, moon, and stars (st. 4). The LORD struck down Egypt's firstborn and parted the Red Sea to lead Israel out of slavery (st. 5), and then brought the waters down upon Pharaoh and his army (st. 6). God sustained the Israelites in their journey through the wilderness and destroyed the kingdoms in the land of Canaan (st. 7) to give Israel their promised land (st. 8). God has ever rescued and sustained us, says the psalmist (st. 9); so let us thank and praise the LORD (st. 10). The versification of Psalm 136 is a 1985 revision by Marie J. Post (PHH 5) of the twenty-four-stanza versification written by John Milton (b. Cheapside, London, England, 1608; d. London, 1674) in 1623 when he was fourteen years old. The litany's refrain appears in the second half of each even-numbered stanza. Another setting of Psalm 136 is at 182.

Scripture References

st. 1	=	vv. 1-2
st. 2	=	vv. 3-4
st. 3	=	vv. 5-7
st. 4	=	vv. 8-9
st. 5	=	vv. 10-14
st. 6	=	v. 15
st. 7	=	vv. 16-20
st. 8	=	vv. 21-22
st. 9	=	vv. 23-25
st. 10	=	v. 26

The greatest English poet of the seventeenth century, Milton was also, at various times, a teacher, pamphleteer, and statesman. Educated at St. Paul's School and Christ College, Cambridge, he mastered Latin, Greek, and Hebrew, as well as most modern European languages. A voracious reader of literature and theological works, Milton was also a staunch supporter of Oliver Cromwell and the Puritans; he wrote fiery pamphlets defending their causes. He also wrote famous—though not always well-received—essays on freedom of expression and divorce on the basis of incompatibility. Cromwell appointed him Secretary of Foreign Tongues in 1649, but Milton fell from grace when Charles II returned to the throne in 1660. Although he had been a skillful poet throughout his life, Milton's greatest achievement came in his last years. After his political demise and the loss of his sight, he wrote *Paradise Lost* (1667) and *Paradise Regained* (1671). His nineteen psalm paraphrases were published in his *Poems in English and Latin* (1673 edition).

Tune

GENEVAN 136 was first published in the 1562 edition of the Genevan Psalter. The 1564 harmonization by Claude Goudimel (PHH 6) originally placed the melody in the tenor. One of the shortest and brightest tunes from Geneva, this music may be sung responsorially (with a soloist for the narrative stanzas and everyone on the refrain parts, that is, the second half of each even-numbered stanza) or antiphonally (with two groups alternating on the narration, and everyone singing the refrain parts). The tune is in Mixolydian mode and properly ends on D. However, to modern ears D may need resolution to G, the opening chord. For that reason and because of the short tune and narrative style, do not hold the last chord. Instead, continue the rhythmic motion between verses without a pause, especially when singing antiphonally or responsorially. A song leader will help to keep the congregation moving along. MONKLAND (223), which is also associated with Psalm 136 and John Milton's versification in some other hymnals, is a useful alternate to GENEVAN 136.

Liturgical Use

Psalm 136 in many ways parallels Psalm 135 and thus will have similar uses. Psalm 136 is the only psalm structured entirely in litany form. It serves well for Easter and for baptisms as a processional or gathering song, at the close of worship as a doxology (using the frame formed by st. 1-2 and 9-10), and at Thanksgiving (st. 1-4, 9-10).

137

LLEF
♩ = 72

Babylon Streams Received Our Tears

A profession of intense devotion to the city of the LORD by a people exiled and mocked in the land of their captors, who destroyed God's city.

Text

Israel speaks of its deep love of Zion, the city of God (see also 46, 48, 76, 84, 87, 122, and 125). The psalmist had probably only recently returned from exile in Babylon (other psalms from the exile period are 74 and 79). Lingering in his soul are bitter memories of the troubled years when Israel mourned over ruined Zion and suffered Babylon's taunts, weeping for the city of their God in songless grief (st. 1). When asked by their captors to

Scripture References
st. 1 = vv. 1-2
st. 2 = vv. 3-4
st. 3 = vv. 5-6
st. 4 = v. 7
st. 5 = vv. 8-9

entertain with songs of Zion, they could not comply, for that would have violated Zion's beloved memory (st. 2). They call down curses upon their ability to sing and play music if they neglect Zion as their chief joy (st. 3). Such devotion to the LORD's city cannot but commit its destroyers, Edom and Babylon, to God's avenging judgment (st. 4-5).

The psalmist's words are harsh (v. 9) but do not go beyond judgments announced by the prophets against Edom and Babylon (Isa. 13:16; Jer. 49:7-22; Jer. 50-51). In 1982 Calvin Seerveld (PHH 22) versified this psalm for the *Psalter Hymnal* with an ABCA rhyme scheme, which is somewhat unusual in metrical psalmody.

Tune

Griffith Hugh Jones (b. Ty Du, Llanberis, Wales, 1849; d. Rhiwddolion, Wales, 1919) composed LLEF in memory of his brother, Rev. D. H. Jones, and the tune was first sung (prior to publication) at a *Cymanfa*, a Welsh song festival. LLEF was first published in David Jenkins's *Gemau Mawl* (1890). The haunting quality of the tune fits the plaintive psalm text well; the tune means "cry." All four melodic phrases descend as they lead into their respective cadences. Sing LLEF in a reflective manner, perhaps without the harmony on some stanzas and without accompaniment on others.

Jones's early musical influence was his father, who was a precentor at Methodist Capel Coch in Llanberis for sixty years. When Welsh preacher and musician John Roberts became pastor of the Llanberis chapel and discovered Jones's potential, he began to give him music lessons. In 1869 Jones became master of Rhiwddolion Elementary School, a position he retained for fifty years. Every Friday he traveled five miles on foot to teach music at Capel Curing, Moel Siabod. A poet as well as musician, Jones was often a judge at the famous Welsh Eisteddfodau musical contests.

Liturgical Use

Introductory comments to remind worshipers of the intense devotion Israel had for Zion and of the agony the people suffered in exile among taunting enemies can be helpful before singing this psalm. Also noteworthy is the image of Babylon's destruction in the eschatological vision of Revelation 18-19.

138

With All My Heart I Thank You, LORD

Praise for God's deliverance from threatening foes in answer to prayer.

Text

Similar to Psalm 18, 138 is a song of thanksgiving for God's saving acts—especially against enemies. After first praising the LORD for answering prayer (v. 3; st. 1), the psalmist expresses a desire that all the kings of earth be moved to add their praise to God; they too should see the greatness of God's glory. Even though the LORD is *Scripture References*
st. 1 = vv. 1-3
st. 2 = vv. 4-6
st. 3 = vv. 7-8
"on high," God does not identify with the proud but looks favorably on the lowly (st. 2). God's deliverance of the psalmist is an example of this care. The psalmist professes

confidence in God's continued care and commits the future to the LORD in a closing prayer (st. 3). Stanley Wiersma (PHH 25) versified this psalm in 1981 for the *Psalter Hymnal*. Another setting of Psalm 138 is at 183.

Tune

GENEVAN 138 was first published in the 1551 edition of the Genevan Psalter. Dale Grotenhuis (PHH 4) harmonized the tune in 1985. See also the 1564 alternative harmonization by Claude Goudimel (PHH 6) with the melody in the tenor (facing page). This second setting can be useful for a choral stanza (for example, st. 2) or for an alternate organ accompaniment. A sturdy Ionian (major) tune, GENEVAN 138 is a bar form (AABC) that repeats lines 1-2 and 3-4. This joyful music should be supported by bright and full organ registration and sung majestically.

Liturgical Use

Occasions of gratitude to God; the universal scope of stanza 2 makes Psalm 138 appropriate to themes of mission and kingdom.

139

LEICESTER
♩ = 96

LORD, You Have Searched My Life and Know

A prayer for God's thorough examination.

Text

Psalm 139 is a profound prayer asking God to examine the psalmist's heart. It recognizes God's intimate knowledge of our lives, even before birth. It expresses as nowhere else how awesome it is to lay oneself open to God's full scrutiny. I open myself to your searching eye, O God, says the psalmist; you know every one of my thoughts, words, and deeds (st. 1). There is no hiding from you (st. 2). You put me together in the womb; you know me far better than I know myself (st. 3). My zeal for you sets me against all who are against you; search me, teach me, and lead me (st. 4). Perhaps the author's loyalty to the LORD has been put under suspicion, which makes him long for God's vindication. Or, being zealous for the LORD (vv. 19-22), yet knowing the deviousness of every heart, does the psalmist want God to root out "any offensive way" in order to be led "in the way everlasting" (v. 24)? Calvin Seerveld (PHH 22) versified this psalm in 1985 for the *Psalter Hymnal*.

Scripture References
st. 1 = vv. 1-6
st. 2 = vv. 7-12
st. 3 = vv. 13-18
st. 4 = vv. 19-24

Tune

John Bishop (b. England, 1665; d. Winchester, England, 1737) was lay vicar at King's College, Cambridge, England, in 1687. From 1695 to 1737 he served as organist at Winchester College and in 1697 was appointed lay clerk. He was also an organist at Winchester Cathedral. In 1710 or 1711, Bishop published *A Set of New Psalm Tunes in Four Parts* (c. 1710), a work that was reprinted several times. LEICESTER was a setting for Psalm 112 in that collection (where it was named BEDFORD); the tune is named after the British city in Leicester County. LEICESTER is a minor tune consisting of three long lines, not six choppy phrases. The melodic units of line 1 also appear as parts of lines 2 and 3.

The harmonization, well suited to part singing, is by Harry Ellis Wooldridge (b. Winchester, 1845; d. London, England, 1917). Wooldridge was accomplished in both the visual arts and in music; he studied painting at the Royal Academy and music in London and Oxford. In 1895 he became Slade Professor of Fine Arts at Oxford University. His publications include *An English Metrical Psalter* (1890), two volumes of the *Oxford History of Music* (1901, 1905), three volumes of church music by Henry Purcell, and the *Yattendon Hymnal* (1899), which he coedited with Robert Bridges (PHH 386).

Liturgical Use

During periods of self-examination such as Advent, Lent, and preparation for the Lord's Supper; during services focusing on the work of the Spirit (st. 1-2).

140

Deliver Me from Evil

ACCEPTANCE
$\lessdot = 60$

A prayer for deliverance from the plots and slander of unscrupulous enemies.

Text

This prayer for deliverance recalls Psalms 58 and 64. As in those psalms, the enemies' chief weapon is the tongue, which cannot be countered with sword and shield. Only God can protect from the deadly mischief the tongue can cause. The psalmist prays for protection from those who plot against him (st. 1), asking God to foil their plans (st. 2). But the God to whom the psalmist prays is no mere bodyguard on call. He is the heavenly Ruler and Judge, who "secures justice for the poor and upholds the cause of the needy" (v. 12) and punishes wrongdoers. The psalmist asks God to sentence the plotters with the same measures they would have inflicted upon him; he declares that such justice will bring God praise among the righteous (st. 3).

Scripture References
st. 1 = vv. 1-5
st. 2 = vv. 6-8
st. 3 = vv. 9-13

The versification of Psalm 140 is a 1985 revision by Bert Witvoet (PHH 4) of the text in the 1912 *Psalter.*

Tune

ACCEPTANCE, by John Ness Beck (b. Warren, OH, 1930; d. Columbus, OH, 1987), was published as a four-part anthem to "Help Us Accept Each Other" (1977) by Fred Kaan (PHH 277). The tune features a consistently syncopated rhythmic pattern in each of its four lines. The unison melody should be sung with intensity. The accompaniment harmonies should not overpower—play the alto and tenor parts on a separate manual. MUNICH (279) is a more familiar alternate tune for this psalm text.

Beck attended Ohio State University, where he studied science as an undergraduate and music composition as a graduate student. He taught music theory and harmony at Ohio State and served as director of the University Music House. He was also music director of the University Baptist Church in Columbus. Cofounder and president of Beckenhorst Press, a retail sheet music publisher, Beck was also board chairperson of the John Ness Beck Foundation for choral composers and arrangers of traditional American music. He published some 120 works, most of which are anthems, hymns, and vocal solos for church use.

Liturgical Use

Useful in the Christian's battle against sin and evil in public life as well as in private.

141

QUEBEC
♩ = 126

O LORD, Come Quickly; Hear Me Pray

A prayer asking for God's help to keep the psalmist from joining the evil ways of the wicked.

Text

Beginning with a plea that God hear his prayer (st. 1), the psalmist asks the LORD to keep him from yielding to wicked people's enticements to join them in their evil deeds (st. 2; see Prov. 1:10-19). It is better to suffer chastisement that turns from sinful ways than to enjoy the momentary fruits of wickedness (st. 3). They are a trap that can lead only to destruction (st. 4). Keep me from these ensnaring enticements, O LORD, says the psalmist, to preserve me from certain death (st. 5). Marie J. Post (PHH 5) versified Psalm 141 in 1985 for the *Psalter Hymnal.*

Scripture References
st. 1 = vv. 1-2
st. 2 = vv. 3-4
st. 3 = v. 5a
st. 4 = vv. 5b-7
st. 5 = vv. 8-10

Tune

Henry Baker (b. Nuneham, Oxfordshire, England, 1835; d. Wimbledon, England, 1910; not to be confused with Henry W. Baker) was educated as a civil engineer at Winchester and Cooper's Hill and was active in railroad building in India. In 1867 he completed a music degree at Exeter College, Oxford, England. Baker composed QUEBEC in 1854 when he was a student at Exeter. In 1861 the London *Penny Post* advertised for a suitable tune for John Keble's text "Sun of My Soul." Baker's tune was among the many that were submitted, but without his knowledge—a friend who had seen QUEBEC shortly after Baker had written it submitted the tune anonymously. QUEBEC was selected and was published in Rev. John Grey's *Hymnal for the Use of the English Church* (1866). Many of Baker's hymn tunes were published in Garrett Horder's *Worship Songs* (1905).

A serviceable long-meter tune, QUEBEC proves that a limited soprano range is not a handicap in a well-crafted hymn tune. The tune title's reference to the Canadian city and province is unknown. Also known as HESPERUS, QUEBEC shares similarities with MARYTON (573), PENTECOST (212), and especially ST. CRISPIN (276)—to name just three of the "generic" late-nineteenth-century British hymn tunes. For best results, sing the harmony parts.

Liturgical Use

Psalm 141 serves especially well to conclude an evening service. In churches that have a history of daily prayer services, this psalm is traditionally sung during evening prayer.

142

Hear My Cry and Supplication

HERR, ICH HABE MISGEHANDELT
♩ = 69

A prayer for deliverance from powerful enemies.

Text

Traditionally this prayer for deliverance from enemies is ascribed to David "when he was in the cave" (see also 57). Alone, imprisoned in a desperate situation caused by powerful enemies, the psalmist appeals to God to hear his cry and to lead him when he grows faint (st. 1). No one comes to his rescue (st. 2); the LORD is his only refuge (st. 3). Then the psalmist declares that he will

Scripture References
st. 1 = vv. 1-3a
st. 2 = vv. 3b-4
st. 3 = vv. 5-6
st. 4 = v. 7

praise the LORD for deliverance from this tribulation and that the righteous will join in the rejoicing (st. 4). Clarence P. Walhout (PHH 6) versified Psalm 142 in 1982 for the *Psalter Hymnal.*

Tune

Johann Crüger (PHH 42) composed HERR, ICH HABE MISGEHANDELT for a hymn text of the same name by Johann Franck and then published the two together in his *Geistliche Kirchen-Melodien* (1649), a collection of psalms and hymns set for four voices, two instruments, and continuo. The tune has appeared in many altered versions; the *Psalter Hymnal* version is shaped by a repetitive rhythmic pattern. The tune's four phrases may be sung in harmony.

Liturgical Use

Whenever Christians find themselves or the church at the mercy of forces hostile to the kingdom of God.

143

GENEVAN 143
♩ = 69

LORD, Hear My Prayer, My Supplication

A prayer for deliverance from enemies by one who knows his own moral frailty.

Text

The psalmist prays for rescue from enemies whose fierce hostility has crushed him to the ground and turned his life into a living death (st. 2). But he is honest with himself and with God; he knows he cannot ground his appeal on his own moral perfection. "Do not bring your servant into judgment," the psalmist pleads, "for no one living is righteous before you" (v. 2; st. 1); "teach me to do your will . . . may your good Spirit lead me on level ground" (v. 10; st. 5). Remembering all the LORD has done for Israel, the psalmist pleads for God's help (st. 3) and adds, Help me soon, or I will perish (st. 4); deliver me from my enemies, O LORD (st. 5). "For your name's sake" (v. 11), show me your covenant grace (st. 6). The psalmist can appeal only to his firm confidence in God's covenant faithfulness, righteousness, and love, anticipating Paul's teaching of justification by faith (Rom. 3-5). In early Christian liturgy Psalm 143 was grouped with the penitential psalms (the others are 6, 32, 38, 51, 102, and 130); it functioned as a prayer anticipating the last judgment. James Vanden Bosch (b. Zeeland, MI, 1948) prepared the unrhymed versification for this psalm in 1981 for the *Psalter Hymnal.*

Scripture References
st. 1 = vv. 1-2
st. 2 = vv. 3-4
st. 3 = vv. 5-6
st. 4 = vv. 7-8a
st. 5 = vv. 8a-10a
st. 6 = vv. 10b-12

Educated at Calvin College, Grand Rapids, Michigan; Ohio State University in Columbus; and the University of Chicago Divinity School, Illinois, Vanden Bosch taught English at Dordt College in Sioux Center, Iowa, and is now professor of English at his alma mater, Calvin College. He has a special interest in the teaching of rhetoric. Vanden Bosch is a member of Calvin Christian Reformed Church in Grand Rapids.

Tune

GENEVAN 143 was a setting for Psalm 143 in the first partial edition of the Genevan Psalter (1539) and was altered in subsequent editions to its present form. Howard Slenk (PHH 3) harmonized the tune in 1985. In the Dorian mode, GENEVAN 143 consists of five lines in which lines 1 and 3 are similar and lines 2 and 4 are identical. Though it is solemn, do not sing the tune too slowly.

Liturgical Use

As a penitential psalm, 143 may be used in the service of confession of sin and forgiveness; stanzas 4 through 6 make a fine prayer asking God to lead and guide in the Christian life. Traditionally sung at the Easter Vigil.

144

All Praise to the LORD

ST. DENIO
♩ = 126

A prayer for God to deliver his people from all foreign oppression.

Text

Psalm 144 appears to be a composite. Because verses 1 through 10 clearly echo Psalm 18 (see also 2 Sam. 22), it seems that a prayer of David has been augmented for post-exilic Israel. (Note also the similarities between v. 3 and Ps. 8:4 and between v. 4 and Ps. 39:5, 11.) In the first part (vv. 1-10) the psalmist praises the LORD for sustaining him (st. 1), appeals to God to burst forth from heaven in earthshaking power to deliver him from the treachery of his enemies (st. 2), and vows to praise the LORD for giving the victory (st. 3). Adding to this prayer, post-exilic Israel includes a vision of the blessedness God's people will enjoy when the redemption of David's kingdom is complete (st. 4). Helen Otte (PHH 17) versified this psalm in 1985 for the *Psalter Hymnal.*

Scripture References
st. 1 = vv. 1-4
st. 2 = vv. 5-8
st. 3 = vv. 9-11
st. 4 = vv. 12-15

Tune

ST. DENIO is based on "Can mlynedd i nawr" ("A Hundred Years from Now"), a traditional Welsh ballad popular in the early nineteenth century. It was first published as a hymn tune in John Roberts's *Caniadau y Cyssegr* (*Hymns of the Sanctuary,* 1839). The tune title refers to St. Denis, the patron saint of France.

ST. DENIO is a sturdy tune in rounded bar form (AABA'); its bright character in a major key should put to rest the notion that all Welsh tunes are sad and in minor key. It bears vigorous performance with singing in harmony supported by solid organ tone. The final stanza is a jubilant profession of how God blesses—save the extra reeds and mixtures for it!

John Roberts (b. Tanrhiwfelen, Penllwyn, near Aberystwyth, Wales, 1822; d. Vron, Caernarvon, Wales, 1877) is also known by his Welsh name, Ieuan Gwyllt (Wild John) to distinguish him from many other John Roberts. He began conducting choirs at the age of fourteen and was a schoolteacher at sixteen. Ordained in the (Calvinist) Methodist ministry in 1859, he served congregations in Aberdare and Llanberis. In 1859 he also founded the Welsh singing festival "Gymanfa ganu" and compiled the important Calvinist Methodist hymnal *Llyfr Tonau Cynulleidfaol* (1859, enlarged 1890), which preserved the tunes of many Welsh composers. Roberts edited various periodicals and issued a Welsh edition of a Dwight L. Moody and Ira D. Sankey (PHH 73) hymnal, *Swn y Iiwvili* (1874).

Liturgical Use
Easter; Ascension; whenever the church reflects on the final triumph of Christ's kingdom; whenever the church needs encouragement to persevere in the Christian pilgrimage.

145

JERUSALEM
♩ = 63

I Will Exalt My God and King

Abundant praise of the glory of God's reign.

Text
Psalm 145 is one of the most beautiful hymns of the psalter. I will exalt you and praise your name for your greatness and goodness, O God, sings the psalmist. Your people "will tell of your mighty acts" and goodness forever (st. 1-2). You show your grace to sinners, and you care for all your creatures (st. 3). "All you have made will praise you" (v. 10); your saints will proclaim your glorious and eternal reign (st. 4). O LORD, you are faithful in restoring the afflicted and providing food for all living things (st. 5). In your righteousness you never fail to care for those who trust and obey you (st. 6); you redeem your saints, and you overthrow the wicked. Let every creature praise God's name (st. 7). The (altered) versification is from the 1912 *Psalter.* Other settings of Psalm 145 are at 185 and 186.

Scripture References
st. 1 = vv. 1-4
st. 2 = vv. 5-7
st. 3 = vv. 8-9
st. 4 = vv. 10-13a
st. 5 = vv. 13b-16
st. 6 = vv. 17-19
st. 7 = vv. 20-21

Tune
Charles Hubert Hastings Parry (b. Bournemouth, England, 1848; d. Rustington, Sussex, England, 1918) originally wrote JERUSALEM in 1916 for the William Blake text "And Did Those Feet in Ancient Time" (which refers to the [new] Jerusalem being built on English soil). It was published in sheet form in 1916, and its first publication in a hymnbook was in *A Students' Hymnal* (1923). The Federation of Music Competition

Festivals adopted JERUSALEM as their national hymn. The tune gained additional popularity through its use in the 1981 film *Chariots of Fire*. Majestic and dignified, with a fine climax in the last long line, JERUSALEM calls for strong unison congregational singing and forceful organ accompaniment. Singing the entire psalm calls for antiphony: have everyone sing stanzas 1, 4, and 7; alternate groups can sing stanzas 2-3 and 5-6 respectively.

Parry was a major force in the revival of music in England in the late nineteenth century. He received an excellent musical education at Eton College and Exeter College, Oxford. Because his father did not want him to assume a musical career, he worked for Lloyd's Register of Shipping for three years. But ultimately his interest in music prevailed: he taught music at the Royal College of Music from 1883 to 1918 and at Oxford University from 1900 to 1918. Parry composed chamber music, piano and choral pieces, and English songs and symphonies. A cofounder of the Oxford University Music Club, he contributed articles to *Grove's Dictionary of Music and Musicians* and published *The Art of Music* (1893), *Style in Musical Art* (1911), and a biography of J. S. Bach (1909). A number of his hymn tunes were published in *Hymns Ancient and Modern* (1904).

Liturgical Use
As a processional psalm in Reformation services; many other occasions in Christian worship.

146

Praise the LORD! Sing Hallelujah!

RIPLEY
$\jmath = 80$

Praise to God for his unfailing help, and an exhortation to rely on God alone.

Text
Psalm 146 begins and ends as a hymn of praise. But the main body of the psalm exhorts God's people to put their trust wholly in the LORD. Human beings, whatever standing they may have in the world, are but frail mortals (st. 1); God is the almighty Creator of heaven and earth. Blessed are those who rely upon this Creator God, who delivers the oppressed (st. 2), provides for the needy, and protects the weak. The LORD loves the righteous (st. 3) and reigns as Zion's God forever; let his name be praised (st. 4). The versification of Psalm 146 is altered from that in *The Book of Psalms* (1871), a text-only psalter that was later published with music in 1887.

Scripture References
st. 1 = vv. 1-4
st. 2 = vv. 5-7a
st. 3 = vv. 7b-9
st. 4 = vv. 1-2, 10

Tune

RIPLEY, composed in 1839, comes from the prolific pen of Lowell Mason (PHH 96), the great American promoter and publisher of school, choral, and congregational music. The tune title, assigned later, presumably honors George Ripley (1802-1889), the famous New York literary critic and transcendentalist. RIPLEY is a classically shaped rounded bar form (AABA) in which the third line provides the contrast and climax to the other lines. It is an energetic tune that calls for jubilant singing in parts and, on festive occasions, the use of brass (probably in E-flat major).

Liturgical Use

Beginning of worship; Advent; whenever the church focuses on God's saving grace as exemplified in Christ's miracles.

147

HARTFORD
♩ = 60

Sing Praise to Our Creator

Praise of God, the benevolent LORD of creation,
who faithfully sustains and provides for his people.

Text

This post-exilic hymn may have been composed for the Levitical choir when Nehemiah dedicated the rebuilt walls of Jerusalem (v. 2; see Neh. 12:27-43). The psalmist sings the greatness and goodness of God—the Creator, Provider, and benevolent Ruler of creation, the Redeemer and faithful Keeper of his chosen people. For each aspect of God's work the psalmist cites a number of specific illustrations. As Creator (st. 1), God numbers the stars (st. 2) and governs the orderly cycle of the seasons (st. 4). As Provider, God sends rain on the earth so that all creatures have food (st. 3). As benevolent Ruler, the LORD heals the brokenhearted and raises up the lowly but casts down the arrogant and the wicked (st. 2-3). As Israel's Redeemer and Keeper, God gathers the exiles; rebuilds Jerusalem (v. 2; st. 1) and strengthens its defenses (v. 13); gives peace along its borders and abundant crops in the fields (v. 14; st. 4); and reveals to the people the LORD's laws and decrees (st. 5). Marie J. Post (PHH 5) versified this psalm in 1985 for the *Psalter Hymnal.* Another setting of Psalm 147 is at 187.

Scripture References
st. 1 = vv. 1-3
st. 2 = vv. 4-7
st. 3 = vv. 8-11
st. 4 = vv. 12-18
st. 5 = vv. 19-20, 1

Tune

John Bacchus Dykes (b. Kingston-upon-Hull, England, 1823; d. Ticehurst, Sussex, England, 1876) wrote HARTFORD in 1872 for the text "The Voice that Breathed o'er Eden" on the occasion of a friend's wedding. The American tune title HARTFORD refers to the capital of Connecticut. The tune is known in England as BLAIRGOWRIE, which refers to a small island town northwest of Dundee, Scotland. The tune became the setting for Psalm 147 in the 1912 *Psalter.* Surely intended for part singing, HARTFORD is a double-meter tune with dependable rhythms and ascending melodic motives. Singers should combine the eight short phrases into four long lines; accompanists will want to use lots of bright organ color—and other instruments for festive services.

As a young child Dykes took violin and piano lessons. At the age of ten he became the organist of St. John's in Hull, where his grandfather was vicar. After receiving a classics degree from St. Catherine College, Cambridge, England, he was ordained in the Church of England in 1847. In 1849 he became the precentor and choir director at Durham Cathedral, where he introduced reforms in the choir by insisting on consistent attendance, increasing rehearsals, and initiating music festivals. He served the parish of St. Oswald in Durham from 1862 until the year of his death. To the chagrin of his bishop, Dykes favored the high church practices associated with the Oxford Movement (choir robes, incense, and the like). A number of his three hundred hymn tunes are still respected as durable examples of Victorian hymnody. Most of his tunes were first published in Chope's *Congregational Hymn and Tune Book* (1857) and in early editions of the famous British hymnal, *Hymns Ancient and Modern.*

Liturgical Use
Especially appropriate for services focusing on God's providence; many other uses in Christian worship.

148

CHRIST CHURCH: SYDNOR
$\rfloor = 76$

Praise the LORD! O Heavens, Adore Him

A summons to a universal choir to praise the LORD,
the Creator of heaven and earth, who has redeemed his people.

Text

A post-exilic hymn, Psalm 148 maintains that God's glory displayed in creation and redemption is so great that the praise on Israel's lips (as in 149) needs to be supplemented by a chorus from all creation. Let everything created in the heavens praise God for the majesty and ordered goodness of the celestial realm (st. 1). Let all created things on earth and in the seas praise their Maker (st. 2). Let all people join in praising God for salvation "from sin and shame" (st. 3). The versification of stanzas 1 and 3b is from an anonymous leaflet appended to a collection of psalms,

Scripture References
st. 1 = vv. 1-6
st. 2 = vv. 7-10
st. 3 = vv. 11-14

hymns, and anthems for the Foundling Hospital in London (1796). Stanzas 2 and 3a (altered) are from the 1912 *Psalter.* Other settings of Psalm 148 are at 188 and 466.

Tune

Richard Wayne Dirksen (b. Freeport, IL, 1921) composed CHRIST CHURCH: SYDNOR in 1973. Rev. William Sydnor, then rector of Christ Episcopal Church in Alexandria, Virginia, asked Dirksen to compose something for the church's 200th anniversary in the winter of 1974. Dirksen composed an anthem, some chant settings, and the hymn tune CHRIST CHURCH: SYDNOR for the anniversary service, and he arranged all of the music for orchestra and organ accompaniment. CHRIST CHURCH: SYDNOR is a strong tune featuring melodic repetitions in lines 1 and 2 and again in lines 3 and 4. Singing in unison or in parts, performers should feel the half-note beat and should distinguish clearly between the equal quarter-note patterns and the dotted ones. Use full-bodied organ registration, but save a special mixture or reed for the final stanza. Other instruments will add much to the jubilant singing of this psalm on festive days. HYFRY-DOL (568) is a suggested alternate tune.

Dirksen received his musical training at the Peabody Conservatory, Baltimore, Maryland. Holding the positions of precentor, organist, and choirmaster, he served at the Protestant Episcopal Cathedral (National Cathedral) in Washington, D.C., for more than four decades (1942-1991). Dirksen also directed the Cathedral Choral Society and the glee clubs of the St. Alban and the National Cathedral Schools. He has composed many anthems, an oratorio, and five operettas.

Liturgical Use

This cosmic call to praise is fitting at the beginning of worship and for many other occasions; especially appropriate for Thanksgiving and for similar services focusing on how the creation around us praises the Lord.

149

HANOVER
♩ = 120

Sing Praise to the LORD

Praise for the victories God grants his people.

Text

Another post-exilic hymn, Psalm 149 summons God's people to praise their Maker and King (st. 1) with dancing and music for delivering them (st. 2) from all who oppose and oppress them (st. 3). God arms them to execute his sentence of judgment on all world powers that have set themselves against the LORD's kingdom (st. 3-4). As a hymn on Israel's lips amid the travails of their history,

Scripture References
st. 1 = vv. 1-2
st. 2 = vv. 3-4
st. 3 = vv. 5-9
st. 4 = vv. 6-9

this psalm was a confession of faith concerning things promised by the prophets and even foreshadowed in the people's past experience, but not yet seen. The (altered) versification is from the 1912 *Psalter.*

Tune

William Croft (b. Nether Ettington, Warwickshire, England, 1678; d. Bath, Somerset, England, 1727) was a boy chorister in the Chapel Royal in London and then an organist at St. Anne's, Soho. Later he became organist, composer, and master of the children of the Chapel Royal, and eventually organist at Westminster Abbey. His duties at the Chapel Royal were expanded in 1715 to include teaching boys reading, writing, and arithmetic, as well as composition and organ playing. Croft published a two-volume collection of his church music, *Musica sacra* (1724), in one score rather than in separate part books, and in his preface encouraged others to do likewise. He contributed psalm tunes to *The Divine Companion* (1707) and to the *Supplement to the New Version of Psalms by Dr. Brady and Mr. Tate* (1708), which included HANOVER. These tunes mark a new development in English psalm tunes. HANOVER was printed anonymously, but William Croft is generally credited with its composition. The name derives from the House of Hanover, the family of King George III.

The descant is by Alan Gray (b. York, England, 1855; d. Cambridge, England, 1935). Gray studied law and music at Trinity College, Cambridge. A composer of church music and works for organ and chamber groups, he was music director at Wellington College (1883-1892) and Trinity College (1892-1930). He also conducted the Cambridge University Music Society. His *A Book of Descants* (1923) became very popular.

HANOVER is a well-crafted tune, distinguished in part by its triple meter, which was still rare in hymn tunes in the early eighteenth century. Like the music of its immediate neighbors, Psalms 148 and 150, which also begin and end with hallelujahs, HANOVER calls for the full resources of voices and organ and other instruments. It should be sung in harmony throughout—or try harmony on the first three stanzas and unison voices and the descant on the final stanza to provide a strong conclusion to this powerful psalm.

Liturgical Use

Especially suitable as a psalm of praise at the close of worship; many other uses in Christian worship.

150

GENEVAN 150
♩ = *80*

Hallelu the LORD Our God

Hallelujah, Amen.

Text

This final great hallelujah may have been composed specifically to *Scripture References*
close the Psalms. In any event, Psalm 150 is the grand concluding   st. 1 = vv. 1-2, 6
doxology to this collection of prayer and praise (Book V; briefer   st. 2 = vv. 3-6
doxologies close each of the previous four books: see Ps. 41:13;
72:18-19; 89:52; 106:48). As in Psalm 148, the psalmist summons a universal choir—all
who are in the temple, all that are in the heavens, and everything that has breath on
earth (st. 1). Praise God, says the psalmist, with every instrument of song and with
dancing (st. 2). Calvin Seerveld (PHH 22) wrote the partially rhymed versification in
1981 for the *Psalter Hymnal*. He notes the inclusion of the word *Lamb* in stanza 2 this
way: "In order to honor the literary units of the psalm and to fill out the Genevan
melody twice, a New Testament echo of the psalm is woven into the text (Rev. 5:12)."
Other settings of Psalm 150 are at 189, 466, and 628.

Tune

GENEVAN 150 was first published in the 1562 edition of the Genevan Psalter. Dale
Grotenhuis (PHH 4) harmonized the tune in 1985. Demonstrating how well they were
in tune with the musical changes of the mid-sixteenth century, the Genevan musicians
chose the Ionian mode (major) for this great doxology of the psalms. GENEVAN 150 is a
majestic tune featuring some melodic repetitions and brisk rhythms. Like Psalm 149,
this music requires joyful singing in parts and the participation of many instruments
beyond full organ, but it should not be rushed.

Liturgical Use

An exultant doxology that unites our praise to the LORD God.

BIBLE
SONGS

151

In the Beginning

IN HET BEGIN
♩ = 96

Text

Somewhat similar to Psalm 104, "In the Beginning" tells the creation story from Genesis 1 in verse form. The first six stanzas are devoted to the six days of creation. Stanza 7 focuses on the LORD's day of rest and turns this narrative song into a prayer for all of God's children. Stanzas 1-6 were originally written in Dutch by Hanna Lam and published in all four volumes of *Alles wordt nieuw* (1966-1978).

Scripture References
st. 1 = Gen. 1:1-5
st. 2 = Gen. 1:6-8
st. 3 = Gen. 1:9-13
st. 4 = Gen. 1:14-19
st. 5 = Gen. 1:20-25
st. 6 = Gen. 1:26-31
st. 7 = Gen. 2:1-3

Johanna (Hanna) Lam (b. Utrecht, the Netherlands, 1928; d. Bunnik, the Netherlands, 1988) collaborated with composer Wim ter Burg in the writing of these popular collections of songs based on biblical teachings and stories. Lam received a degree in social education from the University of Amsterdam and was committed to preparing worship songs for children, particularly in congregations where her husband served as pastor in the Hervormde Kerk; their last parish was in the community of Bunnik. The songs were initially intended for children, but they have been widely accepted and sung by adults as well.

Stanley Wiersma (PHH 25), using the pen name Sietze Buning, translated the first volume into English in 1982 with the title *All Will Be New*. That same year, he also provided a new stanza 7 for the *Psalter Hymnal*.

Tune

Like many of the tunes by Dutch composer Willem (Wim) ter Burg (b. Utrecht, the Netherlands, 1914; d. Maarn, 1995), IN HET BEGIN is childlike, easy to sing by adults and children alike. This is one of the tunes he composed for the original Dutch text by Hanna Lam that began with those words (hence, the tune name, which means "in the beginning").

Wim ter Burg was a music therapist in the Bartimeushage Instituut, a school for mentally and physically disabled students in Doorn, the Netherlands. He was cantor and organist in the Reformed Church in Baarn, and earlier served congregations in Enkhuizen, Amsterdam, and Nijmegen. Ter Burg composed most of the tunes for the four volumes of *Alles wordt nieuw* (1966-1978).

The keyboard accompaniment (1982) by Bert Polman (PHH 37) is for organ trio style or for piano. For variety, play the tune an octave higher on a light and gentle registration for stanzas 4 and/or 5. Flute, recorder, oboe, or violin are suitable descant instruments; the guitar chords also suggest ostinato patterns for Orff instruments. When singing the entire song, assign stanzas 1 through 6 to alternate groups within the congregation and have everyone sing stanza 7 in a stately manner.

Liturgical Use

Creation-story focus; prayer services for crops and industry; harvest thanksgiving. The prayer in stanza 7 is appropriate for Labor Day and many other occasions in Christian worship.

152

TZENA
♩ = 58

I Will Sing unto the LORD

Text

This triumphant text paraphrases the beginning of the Song of Moses and Miriam in Exodus 15, which was identified in the medieval church as one of the "lesser" Old Testament canticles.

Scripture References
st. 1 = Ex. 15:1-2

The song celebrates the LORD's victory over the Egyptians after the Israelites crossed the Red Sea (Sea of Reeds). Jewish tradition calls for using the Song of Moses each Sabbath evening to commemorate the Exodus. The anonymous versification (including the optional Easter stanza) dates from the mid-twentieth century.

Tune

TZENA is a lively Israeli folk melody consisting of three phrases, each one repeated before the next begins. The tune title is a Hebrew verb meaning "to go forth." After singing the melody through once, proceed in four-part canon on a half-note pulse (but slower in large congregations). The keyboard accompaniment suggests organ trio style, but the ideal accompaniment consists of guitar, piano, violin, tambourine, and hand clapping. For starters, try a hand clap at the points of the two eighth rests in the last section: "The LORD is God, and (clap) I will praise him." Emily R. Brink (PHH 158) harmonized the tune in 1986 for the *Psalter Hymnal.*

Liturgical Use

As a brief chorus or a canon by itself; possibly as a frame around another hymn. The Easter stanza may be sung with stanza 1 (especially during Easter Vigil), by itself, or as a frame around "Christ the Lord Is Risen Today" (388).

153

The Ten Commandments

LES COMMANDEMENS

♩ = 72

Text

The Decalogue is given in Exodus 20:1-17 (also Deut. 5:6-21). These Ten Commandments summarize the covenant stipulations to be obeyed by God's people; Deuteronomy makes very clear that God's commandments are the people's principal obligations in their covenant with the LORD God. In the New Testament, Jesus clearly regards them that way as well (Matt. 5:21, 27; 19:17-19; Mark 10:19; Luke 18:20).

Scripture References
st. 1 = Ex. 20:1; 19:18-19
st. 2 = Ex. 20:2-3
st. 3 = Ex. 20:4-6
st. 4 = Ex. 20:7
st. 5 = Ex. 20:8-11
st. 6 = Ex. 20:12
st. 7 = Ex. 20:13-16
st. 8 = Ex. 20:17

John Calvin prescribed the singing of the Decalogue in his Strasbourg liturgy (1545) as a rule of thanksgiving following the confession of sin. It had the same role in the Dutch Reformed tradition, in which the Decalogue was one of the very few non-psalm texts set to music. In translating the one hundred and fifty Psalms from Dutch to English, Dewey Westra (PHH 98) also provided translations for the Decalogue and for the New Testament canticles. This translation is from *Het boek der psalmen* (1773), which was reprinted as late as 1942 by Eerdmans Publishing Company, Grand Rapids, Michigan. There were also nine stanzas in the original Dutch. Westra's versification (revised) was first published in the *Psalter Hymnal Supplement* (1974).

Tune

LES COMMANDEMENS (French for "the commandments"), a rich and graceful tune in the Hypo-Ionian mode (major), was used in the Genevan Psalter (1547) for the Decalogue and for Psalm 140, and later in British psalters and in the Lutheran tradition. The first setting in the *Psalter Hymnal* derives from Claude Goudimel's (PHH 6) 1564 harmonization; his original harmonization with the melody in the tenor (on facing page in the hymnal) may be used for unison or choral stanzas.

Here are two performance suggestions: (a) the congregation or choir can sing stanzas 1 and 9 as a frame around the solo reading of stanzas 2 through 8 or of the corresponding verses from Scripture; (b) all can sing stanzas 1 and 9 (with the choir singing in harmony from the second setting), and the congregation can sing stanzas 2 through 8 antiphonally in unison. Organists can find preludes by Lutheran composers under the German title for this chorale tune: WENN WIR IN HÖCHSTEN NÖTEN SEIN.

Liturgical Use

May be sung as part of the confession of sin—often done with responsorial or antiphonal singing of the Decalogue and the Kyrie (see 258, transposed to F major) with brief organ interludes. Because use of the Decalogue as a rule of thanksgiving is one of the strengths of the Reformed tradition, however, it may well be sung after the confession of sin as a commitment to godly living—which is how stanza 9 directs our use of the commandments.

154

TORONTO
♩ = 54

Be Just in Judgment, Fair to All

Text

Leviticus 19:15-18, on which "Be Just in Judgment" is based, is part of a series of laws the LORD gave to Israel through Moses, saying, "Be holy because I, the LORD your God, am holy" (19:2). The LORD commands the people to live holy lives—that is, in a wholesome manner with their neighbors to bring honor to God, who is holy.

Scripture References
st. 1 = Lev. 19:15
st. 2 = Lev. 19:16-17
st. 3 = Lev. 19:18

Calvin Seerveld (PHH 22) wrote this song in 1985 for the *Psalter Hymnal* as a challenge for the Institute for Christian Studies (ICS), Toronto, Canada (where he was a professor), and, more broadly, to all creatures, institutions, and cultural movements—to hear the enduring Word of the LORD.

Tune

Seerveld named his tune TORONTO, after his city of residence. This common-meter tune features an added fifth phrase that acts as a refrain. Sing lines 1 through 4 in harmony, but join together in unison on the refrain. Dale Grotenhuis (PHH 4) harmonized TORONTO in 1986.

Liturgical Use

By congregation or choir during the service of confession and forgiveness; other occasions inviting acts of dedication and commitment; services focusing on the roles of civil, business, academic, military, and ecclesiastical leaders.

155

FARRANT
♩ = 92

Love God with All Your Soul and Strength

Text

Known best as the "summary of the law" (Mark 12:28-31; Rom. 13:9; Gal. 5:14; James 2:8), the text derives from two Old Testament passages: Deuteronomy 6:5 and Leviticus

19:18. The almost direct quotation of these biblical texts comes from the hand of Isaac Watts (b. Southampton, England, 1674; d. London, England, 1748), who published his paraphrase in a relatively unknown volume, *Divine Songs Attempted in Easy Language, for the Use of Children* (1715). Watts originally wrote the poem in four stanzas of varying meter for the children of the Thomas Abney household, where he lived much of his life. The *Psalter Hymnal* uses only stanza 1, which is the only Scripture stanza and the only one in common meter.

Scripture References
st. = Deut. 6:5
Lev. 19:18

Watts was a precocious student and voracious reader. As a youth he studied Latin, Greek, French, and Hebrew. He declined an offer to study at Oxford and chose instead to attend an independent academy in Stoke Newington (1690-1694). From 1696 to 1701 Watts was tutor for the family of Sir John Hartopp, and in 1702 he became the pastor of Mark Lane Independent Chapel in London. However, ill health, which he had suffered for some years, took a serious turn in 1712. After that time he served the Mark Lane Chapel only on a part-time basis and moved into the estate of Sir Thomas Abney to became the family chaplain, a position he held for the rest of his life. During the following thirty-six years Watts was a prolific author—writing books about theology, philosophy (including an influential textbook, *Logic*), and education, as well as conducting a voluminous correspondence.

Today, Watts is best remembered for his psalm paraphrases and hymns. Many of his contemporaries were exclusive psalm singers. After complaining about the poor quality of many of the psalm paraphrases, the teenager Watts was challenged by his father, "Give us something better!" So he began to write new psalm versifications in which he deliberately chose not to follow closely the King James text but instead to interpret the Old Testament psalms through contemporary British Christian and New Testament eyes.

The next step was to write hymns rather than Scripture paraphrases. What he called "hymns of human composure" established him as the creator of the modern English hymn; he is known as the "father of English hymnody." Altogether, Watts wrote more than six hundred psalm and hymn texts, which were published in his *Horae Lyricae* (1706), *Hymns and Spiritual Songs* (1707), *Divine Songs . . . for the Use of Children* (1715), *The Psalms of David Imitated in the Language of the New Testament* (1719), and *Sermons and Hymns* (1721-1727). Most of Watts's texts use the traditional British ballad meters (Short Meter, Common Meter, and Long Meter) and state their theme in often memorable first lines. His work became immensely popular in the English-speaking world, including the United States, where, following the American Revolution, Watts's texts were edited by Timothy Dwight in 1801 to remove their British connotations. Several of his versifications and hymns are still found in most hymnals; especially loved are the paraphrase of Psalm 90, "O God, Our Help in Ages Past" (170), and the hymn "When I Survey the Wondrous Cross" (384).

Tune

FARRANT is adapted from the anthem "Lord, for Thy Tender Mercies' Sake," which is sometimes attributed to Richard Farrant (thus the tune's name) but is more likely written by his contemporary John Hilton, a seventeenth-century English composer. Edward Hodges (b. Bristol, England, 1796; d. Clifton, England, 1867) adapted the tune to Common Meter around 1835, and since its publication in Frances R. Havergal's *Old Church Psalmody* (1847), FARRANT has been in common use. In its current simple form, the tune is well suited to either part or unison singing.

Hodges received a Doctor of Music degree from Cambridge in 1825. Throughout his life he combined his interest in organ building and organ playing. He was organist in St. James Church and in St. Nicholas Church in Bristol, and he helped to remodel the organs in both churches. In 1838 he immigrated to Canada and was organist in Toronto's St. James Cathedral for one year. After he moved to New York City, he served as organist at St. John's Church (1839-1846) and Trinity Church (1846-1859) and designed the organ in the new Trinity building. A skilled organist, Hodges was known especially for his extemporaneous playing and for his interpretation of J. S. Bach's music. He composed anthems, liturgical music, and hymn tunes (he also adapted ODE TO JOY from Ludwig van Beethoven's Ninth Symphony as a hymn tune), and wrote several essays on church music.

Liturgical Use

As a sung "summary of the law" in the service of confession and forgiveness or after the reading of the Ten Commandments; as a frame surrounding a suitable hymn of dedication or commitment, such as 284 or 288.

156

BENEDICTION
♩ = 69

The LORD Bless You and Keep You

Text

The words of "The LORD Bless You and Keep You" come entirely from Numbers 6:24-26 (RSV), well known as the priestly blessing and the Aaronic benediction. Martin Bucer and John Calvin introduced the Aaronic blessing to Reformed worship after the example set by Martin Luther's *Formula Missae* ("Formula of the Mass," 1523).

Scripture References
st. = Num. 6:24-26

Tune

BENEDICTION was composed in 1900 by Peter Christian Lutkin (b. Thompsonville, WI, 1858; d. Evanston, IL, 1931). This music is more an anthem than a hymn; it was called a "Farewell Anthem with Sevenfold Amen." Without the original series of "Amens," the current setting is accessible to congregations. Choirs may still love to sing the entire anthem—or if the choir wishes to sing just the blessing, the congregation can respond with a simple "Amen" cadence. Sing this music with a sense that its text is divinely ordained in the manner of an authoritative proclamation. The song's inner parts require good leadership from the choir for well-executed congregational singing. The popularity of this song can be attributed in part to its use for many years at the end of the weekly radio broadcasts of the Back to God Hour, an international ministry of the Christian Reformed Church.

Orphaned at an early age, Lutkin was raised in Chicago and had his early musical training in the choir school of the St. James Episcopal Cathedral. He studied under prominent organ teachers in Chicago, continued his education in Europe (1881-1884), and earned a doctorate in music from Syracuse University in 1900. In Chicago he served as organist and choirmaster at St. Clements Episcopal Church (1884-1891) and St. James Cathedral (1891-1896) and taught music theory at the American Conservatory (1885-1895). Lutkin was one of the founders of the American Guild of Organists. He also established the Chicago North Shore Festivals and founded the Northwestern University School of Music, of which he was the first dean (1896-1920). At several different times Lutkin was president of the Music Teacher's National Association. A composer of organ and choral music, he served on the editorial committees for both the Methodist *Hymnal* (1905) and the Episcopal *Hymnal* (1918).

Liturgical Use
Conclusion of worship, in which case it need not be repeated by the pastor; also appropriate during baptism, ordination, marriage, and other special occasions in Christian worship.

157

Give Ear, O Earth, Attend My Songs

NEW 113TH
♩ = 112

Text
Deuteronomy 32 and 33, which form the basis of this song, compile a series of blessings and judgments that Moses chanted to God's people prior to his death. Like the better-known text in Exodus 15, Deuteronomy 32:1-43 is a Song of Moses (PHH 152). It was known in medieval Christianity as one of the "lesser" Old Testament canticles. In 1985 Calvin Seerveld (PHH 22) para-phrased some key passages from the two chapters—32:1, 3-4, 34-38, and 33:26-29—highlighting the praise due to God (st. 1), the death that results from disobedience (st. 2), and God's saving power for his chosen people (st. 3). Seerveld wanted to give voice to the Song of Moses, a song that the apostle John heard sung in heaven (Rev. 15:3).

Scripture References
st. 1 = Deut. 32:1, 3-4
st. 2 = Deut. 32:34-38
st. 3 = Deut. 33:26-29

Tune

See PHH 85 for information on NEW 113TH and William Hayes.

Liturgical Use

In presenting central themes of the gospel such as praise, judgment, and salvation, "Give Ear, O Earth" is appropriate in the service of the Word before or after the sermon. Its third stanza also suggests Advent. Seerveld notes that it is suitable as a song of thanksgiving whenever God's people overcome a difficult trial.

158

VIOLA
♩ = 60

Song of Hannah

Text

The "Song of Hannah," based on 1 Samuel 2:1-10, is another of the "lesser" Old Testament canticles. Hannah sang this prayer of praise and thanksgiving when she brought her son, Samuel, to the tabernacle to serve the LORD. Several of the themes in Hannah's song reappear in the Song of Mary (Luke 1:46-55): both women exalt the LORD for his saving power, for

Scripture References
st. 1 = 1 Sam. 2:1-2
st. 2 = 1 Sam. 2:3-4
st. 3 = 1 Sam. 2:4-8a
st. 4 = 1 Sam. 2:8b-10

raising the poor from the dust and humbling the proud, and for answering the prayers of his people. (The similarity between Hannah's and Mary's songs is all the more striking when one considers that Hannah first couldn't conceive, whereas Mary, being unmarried, wasn't supposed to!) Initially the term "anointed one" (st. 4) referred to the king of Israel, but later it acquired messianic meaning. New Testament Christians therefore find profound relevance in the Song of Hannah.

Emily Ruth Brink (b. Grand Rapids, MI, 1940) versified this song in 1986 for the *Psalter Hymnal.* Brink studied at Calvin College, Grand Rapids, and the University of Michigan and received a Ph.D. in music theory from Northwestern University, Evanston, Illinois. She taught music at Trinity Christian College, Palos Heights, Illinois (1967-74), and the University of Illinois, Champaign-Urbana (1974-83). Since 1983 she has served as music and liturgy editor for CRC Publications and in that capacity was editor of the 1987 *Psalter Hymnal* and *Songs for LiFE* (1994). She is also editor of the journal *Reformed Worship* and adjunct professor of worship and church music at Calvin Seminary. Throughout her career she has been active as a church organist and choir director, at Ebenezer CRC in Berwyn, Illinois (1967-1971); at Orland Park (IL) CRC (1972-1974); Hessel Park CRC in Champaign-Urbana (1975-1983); and currently at Eastern Avenue CRC in Grand Rapids.

Tune

Hughes M. Huffman (PHH 123) composed VIOLA in 1976. InterVarsity Christian Fellowship first published the tune in *Hymns II* (1976) and used it widely at the 1976 IVCF Urbana Conference as a setting for E. Margaret Clarkson's text "Our God Is Mighty." A strong tune with a bold harmonization that suits the "Song of Hannah" well, VIOLA is published in the *Psalter Hymnal* without its original refrain. Sing in unison with much joy and with bright, full organ registration, but keep a sustained tempo.

Liturgical Use

Occasions of praise to God, whose saving strength guards the "anointed one."

159

LORD God of Israel, Come Among Us

LOBE DEN HERREN, O MEINE SEELE
♩ = 120

Text

1 Kings 8:22-53 (and 2 Chron. 6:12-40) record the prayer of King Solomon at the dedication of the temple he had built for God. Though the immediate focus is always the temple, the prayer has far-reaching themes about the covenant (st. 1); worship and its elements—prayer, praise, and repentance (st. 2); daily life, war, and sickness (st. 3); and "the stranger" or "foreigner" (1 Kings 8:41) and repentant exiles (st. 4). Each stanza ends with a refrain: "we praise you, God; you are the LORD."

Scripture References
st. 1 = 1 Kings 8:23-26
st. 2 = 1 Kings 8:27-32
st. 3 = 1 Kings 8:33-40
st. 4 = 1 Kings 8:41-53

Calvin Seerveld (PHH 22) wrote the poetic summary of this temple prayer in 1985 for the *Psalter Hymnal*. He notes that the dedication of Solomon's temple comes at the high point of Israel's history, about midway between the Exodus from Egypt (1 Kings 6:1) and the return from Babylonian captivity.

Tune

LOBE DEN HERREN, O MEINE SEELE (not to be confused with the more familiar LOBE DEN HERREN at 253) is a German chorale in AAB bar form. Well-known in Germany but less so in North America, this anonymous tune was published in 1665 in an appendix to the hymnal *Neu-vermehrte Christlich Seelen-Harfe* (1664) as a setting for a versification of Psalm 103 ("Praise the LORD, O my soul . . ."; hence the tune title). Sing in parts or in unison with vigor and rhythmic precision, using two broad beats per measure.

Liturgical Use

Dedication of a new church building; inauguration of a new congregation; beginning of a new season of church activities. Because of its far-reaching themes, this prayer is also appropriate at many other occasions of Christian worship.

160

In the Presence of Your People

Text

Brent Sinclair Chambers (b. Napier, Hawkes Bay, New Zealand, 1948) composed this song after experiencing an evening of ethnic music and dance in 1977. Chambers attended the Bible College of New Zealand and Auckland University and then became a self-employed painting contractor and song writer. He has written or co-written over five hundred songs, a number of which have been recorded or published. He based the text on Psalm 22:3, 22 and Psalm 145:7, though the words of the first line could also have been taken from Psalm 52:9b. He named his tune CELEBRATION, and both text and music were published in *Scripture in Song* (1977), one of the most important Scripture-chorus collections (initially from New Zealand) of the 1970s. The vocable "lai," suggested for the descant line on the repetition of the music, can be replaced with combinations of "ah" and "alleluia." Other stanzas can be added as well.

Scripture References
st. = Ps. 22:3, 22;
52:9b; 145:7

   In 1986 Bert Polman (PHH 37) wrote two additional stanzas based on Psalm 22:3, 23-28. These additional stanzas were rejected by the copyright owners for the *Psalter Hymnal*, but were accepted later for publication in *Songs for LiFE* (CRC Publications, 1994):

2
All who love you sing your praises
and proclaim your power,
for alone you are holy,
enthroned on the praises of Israel.
You have not ignored our suffering,
but have heard our cry;
may your power be exalted
here on earth and in heaven above.

3
All who seek your rule will praise you
and be satisfied;
for alone you are holy,
enthroned on the praises of Israel.
All the peoples of the nations
will bow down to you;
may your rule be exalted
here on earth and in heaven above.

Tune

CELEBRATION is music in the style of the Jewish *hora,* that is, "dance music." Sing the tune with enthusiasm, beginning more slowly, and increasing the tempo for each repetition or new stanza. The accompaniment is best played with piano and/or guitars. The exuberant character of this music also invites hand clapping and the use of other instruments such as strings and tambourines. The descant may be performed instrumentally (on violin or oboe, for example) at pitch or an octave higher. This descant is unusual because it lies below the main tune much of the time. Once the congregation knows the melody, direct the whole choir to sing the descant in octaves.

Liturgical Use

Beginning of worship, especially at festive services.

161

The LORD's My Shepherd

BROTHER JAMES' AIR
♩ = 66

Text

Of all metrical versions of the psalms, this versification of Psalm 23 from the 1650 Scottish Psalter is probably the best known. Though one of the best examples of a Scottish psalm in meter, the grammatical structure of the text is twisted for the sake of rhyme— the mismatch of textual and musical phrases is especially problematic in stanza 1. But the rugged strength of the verse and the powerful imagery of this psalm have endeared this Scottish versification to many believers through the centuries. For further commentary on this psalm see PHH 23.

Scripture References
st. 1 = Ps. 23:1-2
st. 2 = Ps. 23:3
st. 3 = Ps. 23:4
st. 4 = Ps. 23:5
st. 5 = Ps. 23:6

Tune

BROTHER JAMES' AIR was composed by James Leith Macbeth Bain (b. Scotland, c. 1840; d. Liverpool, England, 1925), the healer, mystic, and poet known simply as Brother James. The tune was first published in his volume *The great peace: being a New Year's greeting* (1915). Born in a devout Christian home, Bain came to doubt the faith but later regained a mystical belief with the aid of the Christo Theosophic Society. He founded the Brotherhood of Healers, and he and his fellow healers often sang to their patients during healing sessions. In the latter years of his life he worked among the poor in the slums of Liverpool. He published a book on healing entitled *The Brotherhood of Healers . . .* (1906).

This well-loved tune is in bar form (AAB) with an unusual final phrase that rises to a high tonic cadence. Ideally suited to part singing, the harmonization is adapted from the popular arrangement by Gordon Jacob (b. Norwood, near London, England, 1895; d. Saffron Walden, Essex, England, 1984) published in 1934, which was also titled "Brother James' Air."

Jacob studied at Dulwich College and the Royal College of Music and received his doctorate in music from London University in 1935. He taught composition at the Royal College of Music from 1926 to 1966 and was respected both as a fine teacher and as a composer of orchestral, chamber, and choral music and film scores. Included in his publications are *Orchestral Technique* (1931) and *The Composer and His Art* (1960).

Liturgical Use
See PHH 23.

162

PASTOR
♩ = 54

My Shepherd Is the LORD
El Señor Es Mi Pastor

Text

Ricardo Villarreal composed the text and tune of this setting of Psalm 23, including only the first five (not all six) verses of Psalm 23 as well as a final doxology stanza. The Spanish text and music were published with a harmonization by Delbert Asay in an undated songbook (c. 1975) entitled *Nuevas Canciones Cristianas*

Scripture References
st. 1 = Ps. 23:1-2
st. 2 = Ps. 23:3-4
st. 3 = Ps. 23:5

(*New Christian Songs*), published by Centro de Música de la Iglesia Evangélica Metodista in Uruguay. It was first published in the United States in *Celebremos II*, a collection of Hispanic songs with English translations provided by a task force of United Methodist Hispanic congregations. The English translation was revised for the *Psalter Hymnal* by the revision committee. For further commentary on this psalm see PHH 23.

Tune

No information is available about Villarreal, but he may have been known to Delbert A. Asay (20th c.), who served the United Methodist Church for many years as a music missionary in Uruguay and Mexico. Asay's songs and arrangements have appeared in several Hispanic songbooks, including *Nuevas Canciones Cristianas*, published in Uruguay (1975).

The name PASTOR (which means "shepherd") was assigned to this tune in the *Psalter Hymnal*. The tune consists of an antiphon (refrain) and stanzas of two identical lines that in themselves contain a phrase repeated at a lower pitch. The form of the tune exhibits similarities to the Bolivian mestizo *huayno* dance. Try singing the music antiphonally by dividing each stanza into either two or four segments and having everyone join in on the refrain.

Liturgical Use
See PHH 23.

163

Lift Up Your Heads, O Gates

VINEYARD HAVEN
$\quad$♩ = 100

Text

This text owes its origin to the tune VINEYARD HAVEN and the original text of its refrain: "Hosanna, hosanna, rejoice, give thanks and sing." Because of the association of those words with processionals, Bert Polman (PHH 37) versified the processional part of Psalm 24 (vv. 7-10) in 1986 for VINEYARD HAVEN so that this grand tune could be included in the *Psalter Hymnal.* The text was first sung to this tune in one of Polman's evening hymn sings at Immanuel Christian Reformed Church, Hamilton, Ontario. For further commentary on this psalm see PHH 24.

Scripture References
st. 1 = Ps. 24:7
st. 2 = Ps. 24:8
st. 3 = Ps. 24:9
st. 4 = Ps. 24:10

Tune

Richard Dirksen (PHH 148) composed VINEYARD HAVEN in 1974 for the text "Rejoice, Ye Pure in Heart" as a processional choral anthem for the installation of Presiding Bishop John Maury Allin at the Washington (D.C.) Cathedral, also known as the National Cathedral. The anthem includes various harmonizations for different stanzas and is scored for choir and organ with optional brass and timpani accompaniment. VINEYARD HAVEN was first published as a hymn tune in *Ecumenical Praise* (1977). Dirksen wrote that the quality of rejoicing was intended to foreshadow the raising of "such 'Hosannas' forever in [God's] presence and with the company of heaven in the life eternal." The tune is named after the town on the island of Martha's Vineyard, Massachusetts, where the Very Reverend Francis B. Sayre, Jr., who was then Dean of Washington Cathedral, had his permanent home.

$\quad$Erik Routley (PHH 31) once stated that it is "safe to call [VINEYARD HAVEN] one of the greatest twentieth-century hymn tunes." After related phrases rise sequentially in pitch, the tune reaches its peak in the "hosanna" refrain and at that point exhibits the melodic and harmonic surprises which, though initially difficult for a congregation, endear this tune to many Christians today. VINEYARD HAVEN requires full, bright organ registration. Sing this majestic tune in unison. To capture the question-and-answer character of the psalm text, the choir or part of the congregation may sing the question in the first line of stanzas 2 and 4, and everyone can sing the responses.

Liturgical Use

As a processional hymn. See also PHH 24.

164

ARTHUR'S SEAT
♩ = 58

O LORD, You Are My Light

Text

This setting of Psalm 27:1-6 expresses great confidence in God's protection of his people, a confidence that leads the psalmist to bring "joyful offerings" (st. 4) to the LORD. The first stanza (originally "Jehovah is my light") was first published in *The Book of Psalms* (1871), a text-only psalter that was later published with music in 1887. Stanzas 2-4 (altered) are from the 1912 *Psalter,* which in turn had altered the 1871 text. For further commentary on this psalm see PHH 27.

Scripture References
st. 1 = Ps. 27:1
st. 2 = Ps. 27:4
st. 3 = Ps. 27:5
st. 4 = Ps. 27:5b-6

Tune

ARTHUR'S SEAT was composed by John Goss (b. Fareham, Hampshire, England, 1800; d. London, England, 1880). As a boy Goss was a chorister at the Chapel Royal and later sang in the opera chorus of the Covent Garden Theater. He was a professor of music at the Royal Academy of Music (1827-1874) and organist of St. Paul Cathedral, London (1838-1872); in both positions he exerted significant influence on the reform of British cathedral music. Goss published *Parochial Psalmody* (1826) and *Chants, Ancient and Modern* (1841); he edited William Mercer's *Church Psalter and Hymn Book* (1854). With James Turle he published a two-volume collection of anthems and Anglican service music (1854).

ARTHUR'S SEAT was first published in *Hymns and Songs of Praise* (New York, 1874) as arranged by one of the editors, Uzziah C. Burnap (b. Brooklyn, NY, 1834; d. Brooklyn, 1900). Burnap's vocation was in the dry goods business, but his avocation was music. As a young man he studied music at the University of Paris and then served the Reformed Church of Brooklyn Heights for thirty-seven years as organist. Burnap composed and arranged many hymn tunes and was the music editor of two hymnals used in the Reformed Church of America: *Hymns of the Church with Tunes* (1869) and *Hymns of Prayer and Praise* (1871).

ARTHUR'S SEAT is named after a hill overlooking Edinburgh, Scotland; the British prince Arthur defeated a Saxon army in that area. The tune starts energetically, subsides, and then builds to a strong climax in its final phrase.

Liturgical Use

Beginning of worship; during the dedication of offerings. See also PHH 27.

165

Send Out Your Light and Your Truth

LUX FIAT
♩ = 56

Text

The text for this prayer for divine guidance is a composite of
Psalm 43:3 and Psalm 139:24b. The versification (altered) is from
the 1912 *Psalter.* For further commentary on these psalms see PHH
42, 43, and 139.

Scripture References
st. 1 = Ps. 43:3
st. 2 = Ps. 139:24b

Tune

LUX FIAT is an excerpt from a choral work by Charles F. Gounod (b. Paris, France, 1818;
d. St. Cloud, France, 1893), first published in his 1878 collection *Chants Sacres.* The tune
has the characteristics of a twentieth-century Scripture chorus: short, simple, and
effective if not overused. LUX FIAT was first combined with the text from Psalm 43 in the
1892 Episcopal *Church Hymnal;* in fact, the tune's title comes from the Latin phrasing of
Psalm 43:3. The setting in the 1987 edition is abridged from earlier editions of the
Psalter Hymnal. Do not rush in the singing of this fervant prayer; sing rather quietly, in
harmony, perhaps without accompaniment.

Gounod was taught initially by his pianist mother. Later he studied at the Paris
Conservatory, won the "Grand Prix de Rome" in 1839, and continued his musical
training in Vienna, Berlin, and Leipzig. Though probably most famous for his opera
Faust (1859) and other instrumental music (including his *Méditation sur le Prelude de
Bach,* to which someone added the Ave Maria text for soprano solo), Gounod also
composed church music—four Masses, three Requiems, and a Magnificat. His smaller
works for church use were published as *Chants Sacres.* When he lived in England (1870-
1875), Gounod became familiar with British cathedral music and served as conductor
of what later became the Royal Choral Society.

Liturgical Use

As a sung prayer for illumination before the reading and exposition of Scripture,
especially for Epiphany; many other occasions in Christian worship.

166

Clap Your Hands

CLAP YOUR HANDS
♩ = 76

Text

This jubilant setting of Psalm 47:1 is coupled with hosannas from
Psalm 118:25. "Clap Your Hands" comes from the tradition of

Scripture References
st. = Ps. 47:1

Scripture-verse singing, a practice revived in the second half of the twentieth century, especially among American and British evangelical Christians. Jimmy Owens paraphrased the psalm texts and set them to music in 1972. It was published that year by Lexicon Music, Inc., as part of "Come Together," a liturgical teaching musical. Probably the most familiar use of "Hosanna!" ("Save us, we pray") is in the context of Jesus' triumphal entry into Jerusalem, in which the Jewish people quote Psalm 118:25-26, saying, "Hosanna! Blessed is he who comes in the name of the Lord!" (John 12:13). For further commentary on this psalm see PHH 47.

Tune

James Lloyd Owens (b. Clarksdale, MS, 1930) was educated at Millsaps College, Jackson, Mississippi, and began his musical career as a jazz performer and arranger for Stan Kenton. He served for fourteen years as a minister of music at three different California churches. An arranger-producer of some eighty recordings, Owens has also produced a dozen Christian musicals, including *If My People, The Witness,* and *Come Together.* He and his wife, Carol, founded and are directors of a music institute, the School of Music Ministries International, which travels worldwide.

CLAP YOUR HANDS is a four-part canon; it may be sung in unison with the given accompaniment or in two- or four-part canon, sung without the keyboard accompaniment. The incipit invites its own accompaniment—hand clapping! Orff instruments may also be used. One example of a pattern: feel half notes on the pitches (CG/CG/CC/GC). Other stanzas can be added when singing this chorus by itself. Here is one suggestion:

Clap your hands, all you people;
Christ has ascended into heaven!
Clap your hands, all you people;
Christ has ascended with shouts of joy!
Hosanna, hosanna!
Christ has ascended into heaven!
Praise him, praise him!
Christ has ascended with shouts of joy!

—Based on Psalm 47:1, 5; 118:25; and the Ascension gospel; vers. Bert Polman, 1987

Liturgical Use

As a chorus; as a frame surrounding a festive hymn such as 408 or 413, especially on Ascension Day. See also PHH 47.

167

O God, Be Gracious to Me in Your Love

SONG 24
♩ = 92

Text

Ian Pitt-Watson (b. Glasgow, Scotland, 1923; d. London, England, 1995) prepared "O God, Be Gracious" for Oxford's *Church Hymnary* (3rd ed., 1973), basing it on the New English Bible text of Psalm 51:1-12. This portion of Psalm 51 is the part most concerned with repentance, forgiveness, and restoration of a sinner before a merciful God. For further commentary on this psalm see PHH 51.

Scripture References
st. 1 = Ps. 51:1-3
st. 2 = Ps. 51:4, 7
st. 3 = Ps. 51:8, 10
st. 4 = Ps. 51:11-12

Pitt-Watson was educated at the University of Edinburgh and graduated from the Royal Academy of Music in London. Ordained to the Presbyterian ministry in 1950, he served the Cathedral Church of St. Giles in Edinburgh, Scotland (the church where John Knox had been preacher). From 1952 to 1958 he was chaplain of the University of Aberdeen and later served congregations in Dundee and Glasgow. He returned to teach at Aberdeen in 1974 before moving in 1980 to become professor of preaching and practical theology at Fuller Theological Seminary in Pasadena, California, where he remained until retirement. Pitt-Watson was a highly regarded scholar, expositor, and preacher in both Europe and North America. Among his published works are *Preaching: a Kind of Folly* (1976) and *A Primer for Preachers* (1986). Some of his psalm paraphrases were published in *The Church Hymnary* of 1973.

Tune

Orlando Gibbons (b. Oxford, England, 1583; d. Canterbury, England, 1625) composed SONG 24 as a setting for a paraphrase of Lamentations 1. The tune was number 24 (hence, the tune name) in his collection of hymn tunes composed for and published in George Wither's *The Hymnes and Songs of the Church* (1623).

Gibbons began his musical career at age twelve as a chorister at King's College, Cambridge. He studied music at Cambridge and became the organist at the Chapel Royal in 1605, remaining in that position until his sudden death. He was recognized as one of the outstanding composers and organists of his day. In addition to composing hymn tunes, Gibbons published a collection of his music, *Madrigals and Motets* (1612), and is noted for his anthems and other liturgical music for the Anglican Church.

Mainly in the Dorian mode, SONG 24 is a beautiful tune most fitting for the penitential Psalm 51. As in most modern hymnals containing this tune, the original third and fourth phrases are omitted. The soprano and bass parts are by Gibbons; the inner voices are from *The English Hymnal* (1906). Sing this tune in unison or harmony; where resources permit, sing a stanza or two unaccompanied (perhaps using the E minor setting at 308).

Liturgical Use

See PHH 51.

168

WORCESTER
♩ = 54

Zion, Founded on the Mountain

Text

This setting of Psalm 87 is more a poetic summary than the versification in the psalter section (87). It derives from the 1912 *Psalter,* with stanzas 2 and 3 significantly revised for the *Psalter Hymnal.* For further commentary on this psalm see PHH 87.

Scripture References
st. 1 = Ps. 87:1-2
st. 2 = Ps. 87:3-5
st. 3 = Ps. 87:6-7

Tune

WORCESTER was composed in England by Walter G.Whinfield (b. South Elkington, Lincolnshire, England, 1865; d. Dodford, Bromsgrove, Worcestershire, England, 1919); it was published in the United States in the Episcopal *Church Hymnal* (1892). The tune is distinguished by its "rocket" motif—the rapid ascent of the first two lines—and by its stately cadence. Whinfield received both a B.A. and a B.Mus. from Magdalen College in Oxford. Ordained a priest in the Church of England in 1891, he served several parishes and published a collection of his hymn tunes in 1902. WORCESTER is named after the English county Hereford-Worcester, in which Whinfield served as a pastor in the parishes of Bromsgrove and Dodford for some twenty years.

The harmony by Paul Bunjes (PHH 79) was prepared for *Lutheran Worship* (Concordia, 1982). The tune is well suited to harmony singing and calls for solid organ accompaniment that emphasizes legato.

Liturgical Use

See PHH 87.

169

FILLMORE
♩ = 52

I Will Sing of the Mercies of the LORD

Text

Composed by James Fillmore around the turn of the century, this song became popular during the 1960s and, later, in the movement to sing the Scriptures in simple chorus settings. Stanza 1 is identical to the King James Version for Psalm 89:1. Marie J. Post (PHH 5) added a second stanza based partially on 89:5, 8 in 1983. The biblical text versified in this song expresses the praise due to God from all creatures—both earthly and angelic—for his covenant faithfulness and mercy. For further commentary on this psalm see PHH 89.

Scripture References
st. 1 = Ps. 89:1
st. 2 = Ps. 89:5, 8, 1

Tune

James Henry Fillmore (b. Cincinnati, OH, 1849; d. Cincinnati, 1936) began his musical career by teaching music classes in a singing school and by selling music books (mainly those published by his father). The success of these early sales enabled him to establish, with his brother Frank, the Fillmore Brothers Music House of Cincinnati (sold to Carl Fischer in 1951). The company became very successful, especially in the publishing of Sunday school music, gospel songs, temperance and prohibition songs, and general sheet music. Fillmore issued a monthly periodical, *The Musical Messenger,* in which he initially published his hymns before issuing them in hymnals such as *Songs of Glory* (1874), *New Christian Hymn and Tune-Book* (1882), and *The Praise Hymnal* (1912).

FILLMORE is one of the most popular Scripture songs of the later twentieth century. The diatonic tune and simple harmonization is effective—if not overused. Accompany with guitar and/or keyboard. Organ accompaniment should be rhythmically crisp over a legato pedal.

Liturgical Use

Beginning of worship and other points of praise in worship; baptisms (especially easy for children to learn); after confession of sin and reassurance of forgiveness, when worshipers will want to praise God for his mercy. See also PHH 89.

170

O God, Our Help in Ages Past

ST. ANNE
$\downarrow = 88$

Text

Considered one of the finest paraphrases written by Isaac Watts (PHH 155), "O God, Our Help in Ages Past" expresses a strong note of assurance, promise, and hope in the LORD as recorded in the first part of Psalm 90, even though the entire psalm has a recurring theme of lament. Watts wrote the paraphrase in nine stanzas around 1714 and first published the text in his *Psalms of David* (1719). The *Psalter Hymnal* includes the most well-known stanzas. The first line, originally "Our God, our help . . . ," was changed to "O God, our help . . . " by John Wesley in his *Collection of Psalms and Hymns* (1738). For further commentary on this psalm see PHH 90.

Scripture References
st. 1 = Ps. 90:1
st. 2 = Ps. 90:1
st. 3 = Ps. 90:2
st. 4 = Ps. 90:4
st. 5 = Ps. 90:5
st. 6 = Ps. 90:1

Tune

Though no firm documentation exists, ST. ANNE was probably composed by William Croft (PHH 149), possibly when he was organist from 1700-1711 at St. Anne's Church in Soho, London, England. (According to tradition, St. Anne was the mother of the virgin Mary.) The tune was first published in *A Supplement to the New Version* (6th ed., 1708) as a setting for Psalm 42. ST. ANNE became a setting for "O God, Our Help in Ages Past" in *Hymns Ancient and Modern* (1861), and the two have been inseparable ever since.

ST. ANNE shares its first melodic motif with a number of other tunes from the early eighteenth century; one example is Bach's great fugue in E-flat, nicknamed "St. Anne," though it uses only the first motif of ST. ANNE. The original "gathering notes" (where the first note of each phrase is doubled in length) have been changed to equal the tune's prevailing quarter-note rhythms. ST. ANNE is a strong tune that must not be sung too rapidly. On the final stanza, sing in a stately manner and try unison singing on the alternative accompaniment by David Johnson (PHH 433), which was first published in *Free Organ Accompaniments to Festival Hymns,* Vol. 1 (1963).

Liturgical Use

Because it has great stature in the British Commonwealth and virtually serves as a second national anthem, "O God, Our Help in Ages Past" is suitable for various civic occasions in addition to its more common liturgical use. See also PHH 90.

171

ELLESDIE
♩ = 54

It Is Good to Sing Your Praises

Text

This versification is a poetic summary of Psalm 92 that derives from the 1912 *Psalter* with minor alterations. See PHH 92 for textual commentary on Psalm 92.

Scripture References
st. 1 = Ps. 92:1-3
st. 2 = Ps. 92:4-11
st. 3 = Ps. 92:12-15

Tune

ELLESDIE was set to this text in the 1912 *Psalter* and in every edition of the *Psalter Hymnal.* The anonymous tune (with bass line) dates from a collection of evangelistic hymns compiled by Joshua Leavitt (b. Heath, MA, 1794; d. New York, NY, 1873). After receiving a degree in law from Yale University, Leavitt worked as a teacher and lawyer. He returned to Yale to study for the ministry and in 1825 was ordained in the Congregational Church in Stratford, Connecticut. In 1830 he began publishing *The Evangelist,* a weekly newspaper that printed many articles on antislavery, temperance, and religious revivals. That same year he edited and copublished *The Christian Lyre,* a popular shape-note tunebook.

ELLESDIE was published in the second volume of *Christian Lyre* (1833); there the tune was named DISCIPLE. The meaning of the tune name ELLESDIE is unclear—Robert McCutchan suggests that it stands for L.S.D., perhaps the initials of an unidentified person associated with this tune. ELLESDIE consists of four long lines in a modified rounded bar form (AA'BA'). Sing this tune in harmony with much enthusiasm.

Hubert P. Main (b. Ridgefield, CT, 1839; d. Newark, NJ, 1925) provided the harmony, first published in *Winnowed Hymns* (1873; that collection attributed the tune to Mozart, though no evidence supports that claim). Main came from a musical family: his father, Sylvester, was a singing schoolteacher and gospel song composer who had moved to the United States from England. Although he only completed elementary school, Main was a prolific composer. Beginning at the age of fifteen, he produced more than a thousand hymn and anthem settings, as well as secular music. Many of his harmonizations stem from his editorial work on a variety of hymnals and his association with music publishers, including William Bradbury (PHH 114). He spent many years in the service of the firm that eventually became Hope Publishing Company.

Liturgical Use
See PHH 92.

172

The LORD Is King

GENEVAN 93
♩ = 72

Text

Clarence P. Walhout (PHH 6) was a member of the Poets' Workshop that prepared many of the versifications for the *Psalter Hymnal.* His setting of this royal psalm was written to be sung to the tune GENEVAN 93, chosen because it had long been a favorite in the Dutch psalm-singing tradition. Earlier editions of the *Psalter Hymnal* had not included this tune. For commentary on this royal psalm see PHH 93.

Scripture References
st. 1 = Ps. 93:1-2
st. 2 = Ps. 93:3-4
st. 3 = Ps. 93:5

Tune

First published in the 1562 edition of the Genevan Psalter, GENEVAN 93 is in Hypo-Mixolydian mode and consists of four lines, each of which has a unique rhythmic pattern. This joyful music is well suited to part singing and festive occasions with brass accompaniment. The 1564 harmonization (altered) is by Claude Goudimel (PHH 6), who originally placed the melody in the tenor.

Liturgical Use
See PHH 93.

173

Come, Sing for Joy to the LORD God

Text

This unrhymed versification of Psalm 95 was written primarily by
Cor Wm. Barendrecht (PHH 326) and Calvin Seerveld (PHH 22),
both members of the group of writers who worked on the psalter
section. Like the previous song (172), this psalm text was prepared
to be sung to its Genevan psalm tune because of its long associa-
tion in the Dutch Reformed tradition. Earlier editions of the *Psalter Hymnal* had not
included this tune. For commentary on this psalm see PHH 95.

Scripture References
st. 1 = Ps. 95:1-2
st. 2 = Ps. 95:3-7
st. 3 = Ps. 95:7b-11

Tune

GENEVAN 95, composed in the Dorian mode, was first published in the 1542 Genevan
Psalter. It gained popularity in the Dutch Reformed tradition because of Psalm 95's
historic association with the beginning of morning worship. The tune is challenging;
almost every musical phrase has its own rhythm and unique melodic structure. But it is
worth some extra effort. In fact, it is the only tune in the Genevan Psalter used as a
setting for four psalms: 24, 62, 95, and 111 (see chart on p. 33).

Liturgical Use

Beginning of worship (especially st. 1-2); during confession of sin or as a sung prayer
for illumination (st. 3). See also PHH 95.

174

Sing a New Song to the LORD God

Text

The text is a versification of Psalm 98 altered from the 1912 *Psalter.*
For textual commentary on this psalm see PHH 98.

Scripture References
st. 1 = Ps. 98:1-2
st. 2 = Ps. 98:3-6
st. 3 = Ps. 98:7-9

Tune

The 1912 *Psalter* and earlier editions of the *Psalter Hymnal* set this text to the tune
AUSTRIAN HYMN by Franz J. Haydn. However, because of the tune's association with the
Nazi regime of World War II, several North American immigrants and Jewish Christians
suggested that it be removed from the hymnal. Synod 1986 of the Christian Reformed
Church agreed, and the tune HERMON was chosen. This strong tune features an
effective "rocket" (rapidly ascending) figure in three of its four lines. The tune title

presumably refers to Mount Hermon, often mentioned in the Bible as a geographical point of reference and noted in Psalm 133 for its natural beauty; the mountain is located to the north of the Golan Heights in Israel.

The scholar/musician and Anglican bishop Charles V. Pilcher (b. Oxford, England, 1879; d. Sydney, Australia, 1961) composed HERMON in Canada in 1935 for his own hymn text "King of Love, O Christ, We Crown Thee." Pilcher was educated at Hertford College, Oxford, ordained in the Church of England in 1903, and briefly served as curate in St. Thomas Church in Birmingham. After moving to Toronto, Canada, in 1906, he began a distinguished career, teaching Greek, Old Testament, and New Testament at Wycliffe College. In 1936 Pilcher was appointed bishop-coadjutor in Sydney in the Anglican Church of Australia, a position he held until 1956. A scholar of Icelandic literature, he published *Passion Hymns of Iceland* (1913) and *Icelandic Christian Classics* (1950). Pilcher was also an accomplished musician. He played bass clarinet in the Toronto Symphony Orchestra and served as precentor in several churches. He wrote a number of hymn texts and tunes and contributed them to the Canadian *Book of Common Praise* (1938) and the Australian *Supplement* (1947) to the *Book of Common Praise*. Pilcher also served as secretary to the committee for the Australian hymnbook.

Walter Lewis MacNutt (b. Charlottetown, P.E.I., Canada, 1910) harmonized HERMON in 1968; his arrangement was first published in the Canadian Anglican-United *Hymn Book* (1971). MacNutt was a student of Healey Willan at the Toronto Conservatory of Music from 1929 to 1932. He was organist and choirmaster at Trinity Church in Barrie, Ontario, Canada (1931-1935), and the Church of the Holy Trinity in Toronto (1935-1941). After serving in the Canadian Armed Forces during World War II, he was church musician in Winnipeg, Windsor, and at the Thomas Anglican Church in Toronto (1954-1977); he continued there as organist emeritus until 1987. MacNutt composed descants, choral anthems, and hymn tunes; *Five Hymn Tunes* was published in 1965.

Liturgical Use
Jubilant times of the church year. See also PHH 98.

175

Unto God Our Savior

MERRIAL
♩ = 72

Text

A versification of Psalm 98, "Unto God Our Savior" comes from the 1912 *Psalter* with minor alterations. See PHH 98 for textual commentary on Psalm 98.

Scripture References
st. 1 = Ps. 98:1-3
st. 2 = Ps. 98:4-6
st. 3 = Ps. 98:7-9

Tune

MERRIAL (sometimes known as LYNDHURST) is a fine tune by Frederic William Blunt (b. Mayfair, Westminster, Middlesex, England, 1839; d. Kensington, London, England, 1921). Not much is known about Blunt except that he was a London solicitor by profession and a musician by avocation. He originally composed the tune in 1871 for James Montgomery's "In the Hour of Trial." MERRIAL was published in the British collection *Church Praise, with Tunes* (1883) as a setting for Sabine Baring-Gould's "Now the Day Is Over." MERRIAL increases in dramatic intensity as it progresses. Sing it in parts on a firm half-note pulse.

MERRIAL should not be confused with the popular tune of the same name by Joseph Barnby (438) set to "Now the Day Is Over" in 1869, but with no tune name given. When introducing Barnby's tune to the United States in *Spiritual Songs* (1878), Charles S. Robinson named it EMMELAR, after the initials of his daughter, M.L.R. He later renamed it MERRIAL, for his daughter Mary L.

Liturgical Use

Jubilant times of the church year.

176

DEISS 100
♩ = 66

All the Earth, Proclaim the LORD

Text

This lively setting of Psalm 100 was composed by Lucien A. Deiss (b. Paris, France, 1921), a missionary, biblical scholar, liturgical expert, hymn writer, and composer who is recognized worldwide for his leadership in biblical studies and the renewal of worship. He was in the forefront of the movement in the Roman Catholic Church to sing congregationally in the vernacular. "All the Earth" is one of Deiss's most effective settings and has gained popularity far beyond its original Roman Catholic context. It was first published in French in *Sur la lyre a dix cordes* (1952); the English version was published in volume 1 of *Biblical Hymns and Psalms*. The refrain comes from Psalm 100:1, stanzas 1 through 5 cover the rest of the psalm, and stanza 6 is the customary trinitarian doxology (see PHH 246 for a brief explanation of trinitarian structure). See PHH 100 for textual commentary on Psalm 100.

Scripture References
ref. = Ps. 100:1
st. 1 = Ps. 100:2
st. 2 = Ps. 100:3
st. 3 = Ps. 100:3
st. 4 = Ps. 100:4
st. 5 = Ps. 100:5

Educated at the Gregorian University in Rome and a member of the Holy Spirit Fathers, Deiss taught theology at the Grand Scholasticat of Cheville, Paris, and was influential in the liturgical reform of the Second Vatican Council and of the Roman Catholic Church. A frequent lecturer and workshop leader, Deiss specialized in worship, church music, and liturgical dance. He regularly appeared on Vatican radio and on French television. His works are widely published (and translated), including *Early Sources of the Liturgy* (1967), *It's the Lord's Supper* (1976), and *Spring Time of the Liturgy* (1979). Under his supervision, his best-known worship songs were translated in *Biblical Hymns and Psalms* (2 vols., 1965, 1970; revised 1973), *A Child Is Born* (1974), and *Sing for the Lord* (1977); these and others hymns were also issued on at least twenty recordings. He and Gloria Weyman have collaborated on work in liturgical dance.

Tune

The name DEISS 100 was assigned by the editor of the *Psalter Hymnal*. Like virtually all of Deiss's music, this tune is intended for responsorial singing involving a cantor on the stanzas and everyone on the refrain. The whole song should be sung without pauses between the refrain and the stanzas. Because the rhythm never stops long enough for a good breath, it is best not to have the congregation sing it entirely. Choose choir or a soloist for the stanzas with everyone on the refrain. Groups within the congregation could sing the entire psalm antiphonally, but then sing the refrain in parts and the stanzas in unison. The refrain will need strong accompaniment, possibly with brass instruments; the stanzas can take a lighter accompaniment. Hand clapping and handbells also fit well with this ancient Hebrew "cheering" song. This is jubilant music—keep the energy and rhythms going!

Liturgical Use

Suitable as a processional psalm (see also 100); Thanksgiving, Epiphany and missions services. See also PHH 100.

177

Praise the LORD!

LAUDATE PUERI
♩ = 54

Text

Stanza 1 of "Praise the LORD!" is directly from Psalm 113:1-2 (RSV); Marjorie A. Jillson (b. Detroit, MI, 1931) wrote the remaining stanzas in 1970 at the request of Heinz W. Zimmermann as a poetic summary of 113:3-9 to be set to his melody for the psalm. It was first sung at the Grosse Point Memorial Church (Presbyterian), where she was a member. See PHH 113 for textual commentary on Psalm 113.

Scripture References
st. 1 = Ps. 113:1-2
st. 2 = Ps. 113:3-4
st. 3 = Ps. 113:5-8
st. 4 = Ps. 113:9

   Jillson was educated at the College of Wooster, Wooster, Ohio, and Wayne State University, Detroit, Michigan. She worked as a secretary for the joint chiefs of staff in Washington, D.C., and as a dental secretary in Detroit. Jillson's hymn texts are paired with previously composed tunes by Heinz W. Zimmerman in *Three Simple Melodies* (1972) and *Five Hymns* (1973).

Tune

LAUDATE PUERI was composed by Heinz Werner Zimmermann (b. Freiburg, Germany, 1930), a widely published composer of music written in a jazz-influenced style. LAUDATE PUERI is intended for unison singing, and, like the other church works by Zimmermann, it features some vocal syncopations contrasted by a strong bass line (originally for pizzicato string bass, a favorite device of this jazz-oriented composer). The original SATB version published in *Five Hymns* (1973) is useful for choirs and as a concertato. This is rhythmically exciting music! A bright organ registration will help, but keep the rhythms crisp and exact. The tune name LAUDATE PUERI is the Latin incipit of Psalm 113.

Zimmermann studied at the Heidelberg School of Sacred Music, the University of Heidelberg, and the State Music Academy in Freiburg. After teaching music composition at the Heidelberg School of Sacred Music (1954-1963) and directing the Spandau Church Music School in Berlin (1963-1975), he was appointed professor of music theory and composition at the State Music Academy in Frankfurt-am-Main (1975). He has also lectured in Great Britain and the United States for extended periods and received numerous prizes for his compositions.

Regarding his hymn settings, Zimmermann wrote, "In my own hymnodic attempts I always proceed from a Bible verse. The prose of this Bible verse becomes the prototype in number of syllables and sequence of accents for the subsequent stanzas" (*The Hymn*, April 1973, p. 50). Zimmermann then "derives" a melody according to the declamation of the text. He mentions Jillson in connection with this setting of Psalm 113, saying, "[She wrote] three additional stanzas to my melody." So Zimmermann's tune predates Jillson's text; both were written in 1970. Zimmermann also wrote in a note to his 1957 *Psalmkonzert* that the jazz idiom is the only modern style that can express true religious joy.

Liturgical Use

See PHH 113.

178

What Shall I Render to the LORD

ROCKINGHAM
♩ = 100

Text

This setting of the second half of Psalm 116 is one of the most loved from the 1912 *Psalter*. The text focuses on the "vow of praise" section of this festive psalm of thanksgiving. See PHH 116 for textual commentary on Psalm 116.

Scripture References
st. 1 = Ps. 116:12
st. 2 = Ps. 116:13-14
st. 3 = Ps. 116:15-16
st. 4 = Ps. 116:17-18
st. 5 = Ps. 116:19

Tune

Edward Miller (b. Norwich, England, 1735; d. Doncaster, Yorkshire, England, 1807) adapted ROCKINGHAM from an earlier tune, TUNEBRIDGE, which had been published in Aaron Williams's *A Second Supplement to Psalmody in Miniature* (c. 1780). ROCKINGHAM has long associations in Great Britain and North America with Isaac Watts's "When I Survey the Wondrous Cross" (384). The tune title refers to a friend and patron of Edward Miller, the Marquis of Rockingham, who served twice as Great Britain's prime minister.

Miller's father had made his living laying brick roads, and the young Edward became an apprentice in the same trade. Unhappy with that profession, however, he ran away to the town of Lynn and studied music with Charles Burney, the most prominent music historian of his day. A competent flute and organ player, he was organist at the parish church in Doncaster from 1756 to 1807. Miller was active in the musical life of the Doncaster region and composed keyboard sonatas and church music. His most influential publications were *The Psalms of David for the Use of Parish Churches* (1790), in which he sought to reform metrical psalmody (and which included ROCKINGHAM), and *David's Harp* (1805), an important Methodist tunebook issued by Miller with his son.

ROCKINGHAM (or ROCKINGHAM OLD) is one of the finest long-meter tunes in the history of church music and is much loved by those who sing in harmony. A slight hold (stretching rather than adding a beat) is appropriate at the end of the second phrase and helps to provide a sense of two long musical lines. Stanzas 4 and 5 need the full resources of organ and other instruments. Keep the music stately and awe-inspiring with respect to the marvelous salvation of which the text sings.

Liturgical Use

Particularly suitable during the Lord's Supper (*eucharista* means "thanksgiving," which is the theme of this psalm) or during the bringing of offerings (esp. st. 4). See also PHH 116.

179

ZERAH
♩ = 92

The Glorious Gates of Righteousness

Text

Based on the processional part of Psalm 118, this text is from the 1912 *Psalter*. See PHH 118 for textual commentary on Psalm 118.

Scripture References
st. 1 = Ps. 118:19
st. 2 = Ps. 118:20-21
st. 3 = Ps. 118:22-23
st. 4 = Ps. 118:25-26
st. 5 = Ps. 118:29

Tune

ZERAH was composed by Lowell Mason (PHH 96) and first published in his *Boston Academy's Collection of Church Music* (1837). This six-line common-meter tune was set to "The Glorious Gates of Righteousness" in the 1912 *Psalter* and all editions of the *Psalter Hymnal*. The tune title is a biblical name that presumably refers to one of the twins born to Judah (Gen. 38:30; Num. 26:20) or perhaps to the Cushite (Ethiopian) king who battled Asa, king of Judah (2 Chron. 14:9-13)—Mason often assigned biblical names (even obscure ones!) to his tunes (see Gen. 36:17; Num. 26:13; 1 Chron. 6:21, and 6:41 for references to other Zerahs in the Bible). ZERAH builds to an effective melodic and harmonic climax. Musicians will want to distinguish clearly between the even eighth notes and the dotted pattern. The dotted rhythms and simple harmony invite treatment by brass instruments.

Liturgical Use

See PHH 118.

180

GENEVAN 121
♩ = 66

I Lift My Eyes Up to the Hills

Text

A versification of Psalm 121, this text is a composite of the 1931 rhymed versification by Dewey Westra (PHH 98) found in earlier editions of the *Psalter Hymnal* and an unrhymed draft (1981) by Calvin Seerveld (PHH 22). See PHH 121 for textual commentary on Psalm 121.

Scripture References
st. 1 = Ps. 121:1-4
st. 2 = Ps. 121:5-6
st. 3 = Ps. 121:7-8

Tune

First published in the 1551 edition of the Genevan Psalter, GENEVAN 121 is in Hypo-Mixolydian mode. Howard Slenk (PHH 3) provided the harmonization.

GENEVAN 121 is presented in original rhythm rather than in all even notes, as it had been in earlier editions of the *Psalter Hymnal*. The melody consists of two groups of three phrases in which phrases 2 and 3 are linked without a break. Because each phrase has its own rhythmic pattern, this tune may be difficult for some people to sing. That difficulty is balanced by the ease of the melodic intervals, which are almost always stepwise. Sing the tune with confidence, especially after the question in stanza 1.

Liturgical Use

See PHH 121. Use stanzas 2 and 3 as a choral benediction.

181

Exalt the LORD, His Praise Proclaim

CREATION
♩ = 76

Text

This versification of parts of Psalm 135 comes from the *The Book of Psalms* (1871), a text-only psalter that was later published with music in 1887. Minor alterations were made in various later psalters, including that of 1912. These stanzas are basically the call-to-praise sections that frame Psalm 135. For further commentary on this psalm see PHH 135.

Scripture References
st. 1 = Ps. 135:1-4
st. 2 = Ps. 135:5-7
st. 3 = Ps. 135:1-2, 19-21

Tune

The tune CREATION is taken from the chorus "The Heavens Are Telling" from the well-known oratorio *The Creation* (1798) by Franz Joseph Haydn (b. Rohrau, Austria, 1732; d. Vienna, Austria, 1809). Haydn's life was relatively uneventful, but his artistic legacy was truly astounding. He began his musical career as a choirboy in St. Stephen's Cathedral, Vienna, spent some years in that city making a precarious living as a music teacher and composer, and then served as music director for the Esterhazy family from 1761 to 1790. Haydn became a most productive and widely respected composer of symphonies, chamber music, and piano sonatas. In his retirement years he took two extended tours to England, which resulted in his "London" symphonies and (because of G. F. Handel's influence) in oratorios. Haydn's church music includes six great Masses and a few original hymn tunes. Hymnal editors have also arranged hymn tunes from various themes in Haydn's music.

William Gardiner (PHH 111) altered CREATION to long-meter double in 1812; it was published in its present form in 1848 in Mason and Webb's *The National Psalmist*. CREATION is essentially a bar form (AABB') with a harmony well-suited to part singing; take it on a half-note pulse.

Liturgical Use

Beginning of worship or similar situations calling for festive praise; see also PHH 135.

182

CONSTANCE
♩ = 60

Give Thanks to God, for Good Is He

Text

This hymn of thankful praise is based on sections from Psalm 136, the great litany psalm. The litany refrain is captured in two alternating phrases about God's love and mercy that endure forever. The versification dates from the 1912 *Psalter*. See PHH 136 for more information on Psalm 136.

Scripture References
st. 1 = Ps. 136:1-4
st. 2 = Ps. 136:5-9
st. 3 = Ps. 136:23-26

Tune

Arthur S. Sullivan (PHH 46) composed CONSTANCE for James G. Small's hymn text "I've Found a Friend, O Such a Friend"; the sentiment of that text explains the tune title. That text and tune were published in the Swedenborgian *New Church Hymn Book* (1874). CONSTANCE is a solid Victorian tune with a fine climax in the melody of its final line. Though not specifically designed for the responsorial performance Psalm 136 requires, CONSTANCE can be performed in a dramatic manner that would please its operatically oriented composer. Organists could change registration or let the congregation sing unaccompanied on the refrain phrases. Or have one part of the congregation (or the choir or a good soloist) sing the first half of each line, and have everyone respond with the second half of each line, preferably by singing in parts. Emily R. Brink (PHH 158) composed the alternative harmonization in 1987 for the *Psalter Hymnal*.

Liturgical Use

See PHH 136.

183

With Grateful Heart My Thanks I Bring

SOLID ROCK
♩ = 80

Text

Based on Psalm 138, this versification (slightly altered) is from the 1912 *Psalter.* See PHH 138 for textual commentary on Psalm 138.

Scripture References
st. 1 = Ps. 138:1-2
st. 2 = Ps. 138:3-5
st. 3 = Ps. 138:6-7a
st. 4 = Ps. 138:7b-8

Tune

The Sunday school hymn writer William B. Bradbury (PHH 114) composed SOLID ROCK in 1863 for Edward Mote's "My Hope Is Built on Nothing Less." The tune name derives from that song's refrain: "On Christ, the solid rock, I stand. . . . " Bradbury published SOLID ROCK in his 1864 children's collection *The Golden Censor.* The tune exhibits a bar form (AAB) with a coda added to its final line, allowing a repeat of the final phrase in the versification. The final line was originally the refrain line in Mote's gospel hymn. SOLID ROCK is well-suited to singing in harmony; festival use of instruments other than organ heightens the thanksgiving mood of the psalm text.

Liturgical Use

See PHH 138.

184

LORD, You Have Searched Me

FEDERAL STREET
♩ = 80

Text

A versification of much of Psalm 139, "LORD, You Have Searched Me" comes from the 1912 *Psalter;* Marie J. Post (PHH 5) modified it in 1986 for the *Psalter Hymnal.* Stanzas 1 and 5, following verses 1 and 23-24 of the biblical text, frame the entire psalm. See PHH 139 for further commentary on Psalm 139.

Scripture References
st. 1 = Ps. 139:1-6
st. 2 = Ps. 139:7-10
st. 3 = Ps. 139:13-14
st. 4 = Ps. 139:15-16
st. 5 = Ps. 139:23-24

Text

Henry Kemble Oliver (b. Beverly, MA, 1800; d. Salem, MA, 1885) composed FEDERAL STREET in 1832, possibly as an imitation of earlier psalm tunes in long meter. He took it to a music class taught by Lowell Mason (who may have contributed to the harmony); Mason (PHH 96) published it in his *Boston Academy Collection of Church Music* (1836). The tune name refers to the street in Boston where Oliver's boyhood church stood, and to the street in Salem where Oliver's wife, Sally, was "reared, wooed, won, and married."

Kemble was educated at Harvard and Dartmouth. He taught in the public schools of Salem (1818-1842) and was superintendent of the Atlantic Cotton Mills in Lawrence, Massachusetts (1848-1858). His civic service included being mayor of Lawrence (1859-1861) and Salem (1877-1880), state treasurer (1861-1865), and organizer of the Massachusetts Bureau of Statistics and Labor (1867-1873). Oliver was organist at several churches, including Park Street Congregational Church in Boston, North Church in Salem, and the Unitarian Church in Lawrence. A founder of the Mozart Association and several choral societies in Salem, he published his hymn tunes in *Hymn and Psalm Tunes* (1860) and *Original Hymn Tunes* (1875).

While the text in this song often consists of two long lines, this tune unfortunately insists on four phrases. Trained choirs can easily couple the short phrases into the longer units the text calls for, but congregations may need persistent help from the organist or choir to complete the longer lines. Sing this tune in harmony. Try the alternate tune MELCOMBE (274) for a closer match of textual lines to musical phrases.

Liturgical Use
See PHH 139.

185

NOEL
♩ = 56

I Will Extol You, O My God

Text
Based on Psalm 145:1-8, "I Will Extol You" is reprinted, with a few alterations, from the 1912 *Psalter.* This part of the psalm centers on the well-known Hebrew confession "God is great, God is good!" See PHH 145 for further commentary on Psalm 145.

Scripture References
st. 1 = Ps. 145:1-3
st. 2 = Ps. 145:4-6
st. 3 = Ps. 145:6-8

Tune
For information about Arthur S. Sullivan and the tune NOEL, see PHH 46.

Liturgical Use
See PHH 145.

186

I Will Exalt My God, My King
Te Exaltaré, Mi Dios, Mi Rey

ECUADOR
♩ = 92

Text

Casiodoro Cardenas, an Ecuadoran, based this song on Psalm 145:1-3. The English translation of the text includes work in 1985 by Frank Sawyer (PHH 250) and in 1986 by Bert Polman (PHH 37). "Te Exaltaré" was published in Ecuador in 1975 in *Tiempo de Cantar* (vol. 2) and in the United States in *Celebremos I* (1979), a collection of Hispanic songs produced by the United Methodist Church. See PHH 145 for textual commentary on Psalm 145.

Scripture References
st. = Ps. 145:1-3

Tune

ECUADOR, composed by Cardenas, consists of four musical phrases repeated and combined in various ways. The tune was arranged by Raquel Mora Martinez (b. Allende, Coahuila, Mexico, 1940) for *Celebremos;* she served on the editorial committee that prepared that collection of Hispanic songs and also supervised the revision of *Himmnario Metodista* (1973), both United Methodist publications. Martinez, a church musician and editor for Word, Inc., received a B.A. in music education from the University of Texas in El Paso, Texas, and a Master of Sacred Music degree from the Perkins School of Theology, Dallas, Texas. She also studied at the Manhattan School of Music in New York City.

This music shares characteristics with the *sanjuanito* dance found in Ecuador (thus the tune title) and has the infectious rhythms common to other Latin dances such as the *rumba, samba,* and *conga.* ECUADOR is intended for unison singing, for keyboard (preferably piano or organ without pedals), and guitar. Hand clapping and ostinati on Orff instruments can be improvised in addition to the given percussion patterns.

Liturgical Use

At the beginning of worship as an entrance psalm of praise, at the offering as a psalm of dedication, or at the conclusion as a psalm of commitment to honor the Lord. See also PHH 145.

187

O Praise the LORD, for It Is Good

Text

The people of Jerusalem (v. 2) become the "church" (st. 1) in this hymn-like versification of Psalm 147. With minor alterations in each stanza, the versification comes from the 1912 *Psalter.* See PHH 147 for further commentary on Psalm 147.

Scripture References
st. 1 = Ps. 147:1-3
st. 2 = Ps. 147:4-9
st. 3 = Ps. 147:10-13

Tune

John H. Stockton (b. New Hope, PA, 1813; d. Philadelphia, PA, 1877) composed MINERVA for one of his own gospel-hymn texts, "Come, Every Soul by Sin Oppressed." The tune was published in his *Salvation Melodies No. 1* (1874); however, it had also been published earlier in *Joyful Songs Nos. 1-3 Combined* (1869) with the note "arr. by W. G. Fischer, by permission."

The significance of the tune title MINERVA is unknown, unless for some reason it refers to the mythical Roman goddess of wisdom. It is also sometimes known as STOCK-TON, after its composer.

Although born into a Presbyterian home, Stockton was converted at the age of twenty-one in a Methodist revival meeting. He became a lay preacher in the Methodist Church in 1844 and was ordained in 1857. After serving several pastorates in New Jersey, he retired in 1874 due to ill health. Throughout his ministry he was strongly interested in evangelism and music. When Dwight L. Moody and Ira D. Sankey held their revival meetings in Philadelphia, Stockton assisted them and wrote several gospel songs and tunes for their use. He published two collections of hymns: *Salvation Melodies* (1874) and *Precious Songs* (1875).

MINERVA is a simple tune in ABB'B form with one consistent rhythmic pattern and the simple harmonization common to many gospel hymns—and thus is easy for guitar. Sing this tune in harmony at a lively tempo using crisp rhythms over a legato organ pedal. The descant was composed by Dale Grotenhuis (PHH 4) in 1976 as part of a collection of descants for the 1959 edition of the *Psalter Hymnal.*

Liturgical Use

See PHH 147.

188

Praise the LORD, Sing Hallelujah

PRAISE JEHOVAH
♩ = 63 *(perhaps slightly slower on st. 4)*

Text

This versification of Psalm 148 is found in various later nineteenth-century Presbyterian psalters in the United States. All editions of the *Psalter Hymnal* have included this text to the tune PRAISE JEHOVAH as combined in the 1927 United Presbyterian *Bible Songs Hymnal.* See PHH 148 for textual commentary on Psalm 148.

Scripture References
st. 1 = Ps. 148:1-4
st. 2 = Ps. 148:5-8
st. 3 = Ps. 148:9-12
ref. = Ps. 148:13-14

Tune

PRAISE JEHOVAH was composed by William J. Kirkpatrick (b. Duncannon, PA, 1838; d. Philadelphia, PA, 1921) and joined in the 1890s to this versification of Psalm 148, with the original seventh stanza becoming the refrain. The tune was published with an 1899 copyright date in *Life Songs,* a 1916 publication of the Mennonite Publishing House.

Kirkpatrick received his musical training from his father and several other private teachers. A carpenter by trade, he engaged in the furniture business from 1862 to 1878. He left that profession to dedicate his life to music, serving as music director at Grace Methodist Church in Philadelphia. Kirkpatrick compiled some one hundred gospel song collections; his first, *Devotional Melodies* (1859), was published when he was only twenty-one years old. Many of these collections were first published by the John Hood Company and later by Kirkpatrick's own Praise Publishing Company, both in Philadelphia.

PRAISE JEHOVAH (also known as KIRKPATRICK and AINOS) is a splendid example of the best of gospel hymn writing: a strong melody, a variety of rhythms, and some independence in the harmony parts (especially in the refrain). Well-suited to part singing, PRAISE JEHOVAH can be sung in the common stanza-refrain pattern, but the order of the text would suggest singing the refrain (which can also be considered st. 4) only after stanzas 1 through 3. Try antiphonal singing on the three stanzas; have everyone sing the refrain. Sing the dotted rhythms crisply to distinguish them clearly from the regular eighth notes.

Liturgical Use

See PHH 148.

189

ORIENTIS PARTIBUS
♩ = 66

Hallelujah, Praise the LORD

Text

Marie J. Post (PHH 5) wrote this versification of Psalm 150 in 1972; *Scripture References*
it was first published in the 1974 *Psalter Hymnal Supplement.* The st. 1 = Ps. 150:2
"Hallelujah" coda was added for the 1987 *Psalter Hymnal.* Psalm st. 2 = Ps. 150:1, 6
150 was Post's favorite psalm; she said the lyrics came very easily to st. 3 = Ps. 150:3-5
her for this versification. See PHH 150 for textual commentary on st. 4 = Ps. 150:3-5
Psalm 150.

Tune

ORIENTIS PARTIBUS derives from a French medieval folk-dance song, *Orientis partibus Adventavit asinus,* originally associated with the Feast of the Ass, a church festival in some parts of France held each January 14 commemorating the flight of Joseph and Mary with Jesus into Egypt. The tune became well known in a duple-rhythm arrangement by Richard Redhead (PHH 255) published in his *Church Hymn Tunes* (1853). The triple rhythms—a good choice in keeping with the tune's folk-dance origins—in the *Psalter Hymnal* date from the arrangement by Ralph Vaughan Williams (PHH 316) for the 1906 *English Hymnal.* Sing the tune with a strong lilting rhythm, use other instruments (handbells, tambourines, recorders, flutes, Orff instruments), and let this music be a joyful expression of the text itself. This tune is popular and very useful with children!

Liturgical Use

A marvelous processional—alternate the singing of stanzas with instrumental-only versions of the tune. See also PHH 150.

190

MACHS MIT MIR
♩ = 126

God's Gift It Is to Eat and Drink

Text

"God's Gift It Is" voices one of the central themes of the book *Scripture References*
of Ecclesiastes—life centered on God is not "vanity" but st. 1 = Eccles. 3:13-14
brings joy and has meaning. In all circumstances, God is in st. 2 = Eccles. 7:14
control and guides our lives (see Answer 1 of the Heidelberg st. 3 = Eccles. 3:15
Catechism: "I . . . belong . . . in life and in death—to my

faithful Savior . . ."). The song's refrain picks up on this theme. In the biblical text this theme occurs in Ecclesiastes 2:24-26; 3:12-13; 5:18-20; 7:14; 8:15.

Calvin Seerveld (PHH 22) paraphrased Ecclesiastes 3:13-15 and 7:14 in 1985 for the *Psalter Hymnal*—and specifically for the tune MACHS MIT MIR. Except for the wisdom psalms, this is one of the few wisdom texts in the *Psalter Hymnal*.

Tune

MACHS MIT MIR was first published in the collection of music *Das ander Theil des andern newen Operis Geistlicher Deutscher Lieder* (1605) by Bartholomäus Gesius (b. München-berg, near Frankfurt, Germany, c. 1555; d. Franfurt, 1613). A prolific composer, Gesius wrote almost exclusively for the church. Gesius studied theology at the University of Frankfurt and pursued his musical studies privately. He was a cantor in Münchenberg, a private tutor for a poet's family in Muskau, and a cantor at the Marienkirche in Frankfurt from 1593 until his death. He composed numerous settings for pre-Reformation Latin songs and for Reformation hymns (with Luther's hymns well represented) and published them in ten volumes, including his *Psalmodia Choralis* and *Geistliche deutsche Lieder* (1601). He also wrote a *St. John Passion* (1588), a *St. Matthew Passion* (1613), important settings of the Magnificat (1607), and a theoretical work, *Synopsis musicae practicae* (1609).

Johann H. Schein later adapted Gesius's tune for his own hymn text "Machs mit mir, Gott" (1628)—from which the tune got its name—and published it in the second edition of his famous *Cantional* (1645). Johann S. Bach (PHH 7) used the tune in his *St. John Passion* (1724) and in his *Cantatas 139* and *156*. An isorhythmic version of the tune was published in the 1959 *Psalter Hymnal* under the name EISENACH. Dale Grotenhuis (PHH 4) prepared the harmonization in 1985 for the 1987 *Psalter Hymnal*.

Like so many chorales, MACHS MIT MIR is in bar form (AAB); its rhythms alternate between duple and triple—in this case the use of the two main forms of musical rhythm is a nice way of suggesting that God's providence covers all! Unison singing may be best on the stanzas, with harmonizing optional on the refrain. Sing this tune with much energy to an animating tempo.

Liturgical Use

Because this song focuses on God's providence, it will find frequent use in Christian worship—for example, springtime prayer for crops and industry, fall harvest thanksgiv-ing, Sunday near Labor Day, commemoration of events at the end of the year or season, times of prosperity and times of adversity.

WARRINGTON
$\downarrow = 116$

Hear Us, O People, Hear Our Plea

Text

"Hear Us, O People" focuses on two of the main themes of the Song of Songs: that love should not be awakened until it is ready, and that love cannot be bought. The first is a recurring refrain in the Song—2:7; 3:5; 8:4—and is captured in stanzas 1 and 4. The second theme is the vow of true love the lovers exchange in 8:6-7—captured in stanzas 2 and 3.

Scripture References
st. 1 = Song of Songs 2:7
Song of Songs 3:5
Song of Songs 8:4
st. 2 = Song of Songs 8:6
st. 3 = Song of Songs 8:7
st. 4 = Song of Songs 2:7
Song of Songs 3:5
Song of Songs 8:4

Calvin Seerveld (PHH 22) wrote this paraphrase in 1984 for use at a wedding of friends. In addition to scholarly work on this book, Seerveld earlier wrote the libretto for an oratorio on the Song of Songs entitled *The Greatest Song: In Critique of Solomon* (1967; rev. 1989).

Tune

WARRINGTON was composed by Ralph Harrison (b. Chinley, Derbyshire, England, 1748; d. Manchester, Lancashire, England, 1810) and published in his collection of psalm tunes, *Sacred Harmony* (1784). The tune's rising inflections help to accent words such as *erotic* (probably the only time this word has been used in a hymn!).

Harrison was educated at Warrington Academy (hence the tune title), a school associated with the Unitarian Church. He became an independent minister, spending most of his life serving the Cross Street Chapel in Manchester. He also taught classics at the Manchester Academy, a school he established, and published two volumes of church music entitled *Sacred Harmony* (1784, 1791), which include a number of his own psalm and hymn tunes.

Here are two suggestions for use of this hymn at a wedding: (a) bride and groom (or their representatives) sing a duet, alternating on stanzas 2 and 3; (b) bride and groom sing stanzas 2 and 3 in unison, and the congregation sings stanzas 1 and 4—possibly with this change in line 1 of stanza 4: "With all who hear *this* solemn vow. . . ." Better-known tunes for this text are WINCHESTER NEW (593) and OLD HUNDREDTH (134 and 638).

Liturgical Use

Whenever preaching focuses on the Song of Songs; more common use will be at weddings or in services that focus on marriage, anniversaries, or marriage renewal.

192

The People Who in Darkness Walked

LOBT GOTT, IHR CHRISTEN
♩ = 104

Text

The well-known messianic prophecy from Isaiah 9:2-7 was fulfilled
in the coming of Christ and in the rule of his kingdom. This
passage was versified by John Morison (b. Cairne, Aberdeenshire,
Scotland, 1750; d. Canisbay, Caithness, Scotland, 1798) for the
1781 version of the Scottish Paraphrases; it originally began "The
race that long in darkness pined." Morison's text has since been
altered by many hymnal editors; it is published in the *Psalter
Hymnal* without the stanza for Isaiah 9:4-5. This text is one of a handful of the sixty-
seven Scottish Paraphrases still in popular use today.

Scripture References
st. 1 = Isa. 9:2
st. 2 = Isa. 9:3
st. 3 = Isa. 9:6
st. 4 = Isa. 9:6
st. 5 = Isa. 9:7

Morison studied at King's College in Aberdeen and at the University of Edinburgh.
A schoolteacher before he became ordained in the Presbyterian Church, he served as
pastor in Canisbay from 1780 until his death. Morison served on the editorial committee of the 1781 Scottish Paraphrases and contributed seven of the sixty-seven paraphrases to that popular collection, which added significantly to the exclusively psalm-song
repertoire of the Scottish Presbyterian tradition.

Tune

LOBT GOTT, IHR CHRISTEN is a relatively short tune for a German chorale, but it is
distinguished by insistently repeated soprano tones and a charming rising-scale motif
that leads into the final phrase. The tune was composed by Nikolaus Herman
(b. Altdorf, near Nuremberg, Germany, c. 1485; d. Joachimsthal, Bohemia, 1561) and
first published in *Ein Christlicher Abentreien* (1554) as a setting for a children's hymn by
Herman about John the Baptist. The tune's name derives from its use since 1561 with
the chorale text "Lobt Gott, ihr Christen allzugleich." The harmonization by Johann S.
Bach (PHH 7) was taken from his Cantata 151 (1725). Bach also used the tune in his
Cantata 195; organists may also know one of Bach's preludes on this tune in his
Orgelbüchlein (Little Organ Book). Harmony singing is challenging but rewarding. Keep
the tempo moving.

Herman spent most of his life (1518-1560) in the mining town of Joachimsthal,
where he served as schoolmaster in the Latin School and organist and choirmaster in
the Lutheran Church. After a careful study of Martin Luther's writings, he adopted the
Protestant faith. Many of his 190 hymn texts were inspired by the sermons of Johannes
Mathesius, pastor of the Lutheran Church where Herman worked. A writer of hymn
tunes as well as texts, he often wrote his hymns for use in homes and schools, but they

gained acceptance as well in a number of Lutheran churches. His texts and tunes were included in *Die Sontags-Evangelia* (1560) and *Die Historien von der Sindfludt* (1562).

Liturgical Use
Advent; Epiphany.

193

Surely It Is God Who Saves Me

Text

Isaiah 12 consists of two stanzas of praise (12:1-3 and 4-6). *Scripture References*
Together they make up the "First Song of Isaiah," one of the st. 1 = Isa. 12:2-4a
"lesser" Old Testament canticles used by the medieval church. As st. 2 = Isa. 12:4b-6
songs of joy and praise for God's deliverance, these stanzas are the
climax to a group of prophecies spanning Isaiah 7-11. In stanza l, Isaiah 12:2 echoes
Exodus 15:2 of the Song of Moses (see also 152), and 12:3 uses the "wells of living
water" image, often a biblical symbol of salvation (John 4:10). Stanza 2 reflects the
praise language that abounds in the book of Psalms. Carl P. Daw, Jr. (b. Louisville, KY,
1944), versified these passages in 1981 for *The Hymnal 1982*, the Episcopal Church
hymnal published in 1985.

Daw was born into a Baptist preacher's family. He received degrees in English from
Rice University and the University of Virginia (Ph.D. in 1970), and taught English at the
College of William and Mary, Williamsburg, Virginia (1970-1978). In 1981 he received
a divinity degree from the University of the South, Sewanee, Tennessee. After ordina-
tion in the Protestant Episcopal Church, he served Episcopal congregations in Virginia,
Connecticut, and Pennsylvania. In 1996 he was appointed executive director of the
Hymn Society in the United States and Canada. Daw is a widely respected and often
published author of numerous hymns and hymn articles. His texts were collected in *A
Year of Grace* (1990), *To Sing God's Praise* (1992), and *New Psalms and Hymns and Spiritual
Songs* (1996).

Tune

LORD, REVIVE US is an anonymous American tune first used for the hymn text "Savior,
Visit Thy Plantation" by John Newton (PHH 462) in the 1868 Methodist collection *The
Revivalist*, compiled by Joseph Hillman. The tune title derives from Newton's text,
which uses the phrase "revive us" five times in its refrain. LORD, REVIVE US seems related
to earlier nineteenth-century tunes such as HOLY MANNA (322) and PLEADING SAVIOR
(603).

Dale Grotenhuis (PHH 4) harmonized the tune in 1985 for the *Psalter Hymnal*. In rounded bar form (AABA'), the music is well suited to part singing and also works well in canon (one measure); when singing in canon, do not use the harmony.

Liturgical Use
Daw suggests this song is suitable for baptism and as a general hymn of assurance; stanza 2 has a mission theme and may also reinforce Advent or Christmas themes, mentioning God's incarnation; Isaiah 12 is also one of the canticles appointed for daily morning prayer in various Christian prayer books.

194

Comfort, Comfort Now My People

GENEVAN 42
♩ = 80

Text

This song is a versification of Isaiah 40:1-5, the passage that opens the final large group of prophecies in Isaiah 40-66. Many of these prophecies express consolation and hope that Judah's exile in Babylon is almost over. That is certainly the tone of 40:1-5—words of comfort forecasting a new reign but also words that call for proper preparation—that is, repentance.

Scripture References
st. 1 = Isa. 40:1-2
st. 2 = Isa. 40:3-4
st. 3 = Isa. 40:3-5

Johannes Olearius (b. Halle, Germany, 1611; d. Weissenfels, Germany, 1684) originally versified the passage in German in honor of Saint John the Baptist Day and published it in his *Geistliche Singe-Kunst* (1671), a collection of more than twelve hundred hymns—three hundred of them by Olearius himself. Born into a family of Lutheran theologians, Olearius received his education at the University of Wittenberg and later taught theology there. He was ordained a Lutheran pastor and appointed court preacher to Duke August of Sachsen-Weissenfels in Halle and later to Duke Johann Adolph in Weissenfels. Olearius wrote a commentary on the entire Bible, published various devotional books, and produced a translation of the *Imitatio Christi* by Thomas á Kempis. In the history of church music Olearius is mainly remembered for his hymn collection, which was widely used in Lutheran churches.

Olearius's text was translated into English by Catherine Winkworth (b. Holborn, London, England, 1827; d. Monnetier, Savoy, France, 1878) and published in her *Chorale Book for England* (1863); the first line originally read "Comfort, Comfort Ye My People." Winkworth is well known for her English translations of German hymns; her translations were polished and yet remained close to the original. Educated initially by her mother, she lived with relatives in Dresden, Germany, in 1845, where she acquired her knowledge of German and interest in German hymnody. After residing near Manchester until 1862, she moved to Clifton, near Bristol. A pioneer in promoting women's rights, Winkworth put much of her energy into the encouragement of higher education for women. She translated a large number of German hymn texts from hymnals owned by a friend, Baron Bunsen. Though often altered, these translations continue to be used in many modern hymnals. Her work was published in two series of *Lyra Germanica* (1855, 1858) and in *The Chorale Book for England* (1863), which included the appropriate German tune with each text as provided by Sterndale Bennett and Otto Goldschmidt. Winkworth also translated biographies of German Christians who promoted ministries to the poor and sick and compiled a handbook of biographies of German hymn authors, *Christian Singers of Germany* (1869).

Tune

Louis Bourgeois (PHH 3) composed or adapted this tune for Psalm 42 for the Genevan Psalter. The 1564 harmonization by Claude Goudimel (PHH 6) originally placed the melody in the tenor. An alternate harmonization with descants by Johann Crüger (PHH 42) can be found opposite 41 in the *Psalter Hymnal*. (See also notes at PHH 42.)

Since the character of Isaiah 40 is very different from the lament of Psalm 42, for which the tune was written, the tempo should be faster here than at 42. Sing with a buoyant and lilting rhythm. Organists will find preludes to this tune under GENEVAN 42 in Dutch works or under FREU DICH SEHR in German works.

Liturgical Use

Traditional during Advent as applicable to Isaiah's and John the Baptist's calls to repentance.

195

OUR GOD REIGNS
♩ = 72

Our God Reigns

Text

Isaiah 52:7 speaks of "good news," originally referring to Israel's   *Scripture References*
delivery from captivity and return to Jerusalem. Today Christians   st. = Isa. 52:7
sing these words to celebrate our delivery from sin through Christ
(Rom. 10:15-16), who brings salvation and a restoration of God's rule, resulting in peace and happiness. The song text combines Isaiah's message with the theme that rings throughout the Psalms: God reigns!

Leonard E. Smith, Jr., (b. Philadelphia, PA, 1942) composed this song in 1973 in Riverton, New Jersey. Educated at Mount St. Mary's Seminary in Emmitsburg, Maryland, where he received a B.A. in philosophy, Smith first taught in public high schools, but his evangelical efforts in the schools created problems, resulting in his dismissal. He then began painting houses to support his family. One night as he was reading Isaiah 52 he was overwhelmed by the conviction that God was in control of his life and of all creation; he wrote this song that night in just five minutes. The song was first sung at New Covenant Community Church, where Smith served as worship leader. Though not published for some time, it became known internationally when evangelist Bob Mumford included it in his crusades. It was first published in a Servant Publications hymnal, *Songs of Praise* (vol. 2, 1977). In 1978 Smith added four additional verses. He has published over 130 Scripture songs with New Jerusalem Music Co.

Tune

OUR GOD REIGNS is an effective tune that gains its strength and popularity from its powerful chorus, in which hammer-stroke chords (in the style of George F. Handel's oratorios) proclaim "Our God reigns!"

Dale Grotenhuis (PHH 4) harmonized the tune in 1984 for the *Psalter Hymnal*. OUR GOD REIGNS lends itself to either unison or part singing. One of the most widely used Scripture choruses of praise, "Our God Reigns" gained popularity in the Christian Reformed Church when it was a theme song for Christian Reformed Home Missions.

Liturgical Use

Mission services; ordination services; Epiphany; Pentecost; Ascension. The chorus alone can be used as an acclamation, especially in informal services, or it can be used as a frame to surround another hymn such as "Sing Praise to the Lord" (466), or, if transposed to C major, added to Psalm 93 or 97.

196

See, Christ Was Wounded for Our Sake

KABODE
♩ = 63

Text

Brian Foley (b. Waterloo, near Liverpool, England, 1919) wrote this paraphrase of Isaiah 53:2-9, which is part of the "suffering servant" passage (Isaiah 52:13-53:12), the longest of the four "servant songs" in Isaiah (the others are in chapters 42, 49, and 50). The "suffering servant song" is the central text in Isaiah 40-66, and this part is quoted more frequently in the New Testament than any other non-psalm text from the Old Testament. Foley

Scripture References
st. 1 = Isa. 53:4-5
st. 2 = Isa. 53:2-3
st. 3 = Isa. 53:6-7
st. 4 = Isa. 53:8-9
st. 5 = Isa. 53:5-6

clearly followed New Testament use of this passage, referring directly to Christ as the "suffering servant." The song text is one of fourteen Foley versifications published in the 1971 British *New Catholic Hymnal,* a volume he helped to compile.

Foley received his theological education at the Upholland Roman Catholic College and Seminary and was ordained in 1945. After serving churches in the Liverpool diocese, he became the parish priest of Clayton Green, Chorley, Lancashire, in 1971, where he remained for many years. Although he regretted the loss of plainsong and the traditional Roman Catholic style of worship (a result of the changes approved by the Second Vatican Council), Foley began writing hymns in the 1950s.

Tune
Joyce Recker (b. Hammond, IN, 1951) composed KABODE in 1983 for Fred Pratt Green's "O Christ, the Healer" while she was a music student at The King's College, Edmonton, Alberta. She coined the title to represent the Edmonton co-op house she and her husband lived in at the time; the letter *k*, present in all the occupants' names, combined with the word *abode* to make *kabode*. Later they realized that in Hebrew *kabode* means "the glory of God." Recker received a bachelor's degree in fine arts from Aquinas College, Grand Rapids, Michigan. She is currently a piano teacher and free-lance artist living in Grand Rapids.

KABODE was first published in the 1987 *Psalter Hymnal*. A long-meter tune in minor tonality (an uncommon combination), it features consistent rhythms in its four lines. Sing in unison or harmony to a solemn tempo.

Liturgical Use
Lent, especially during Holy Week; also with sermons on Christ's redemption.

197

TREES OF THE FIELD
♩ = 92

The Trees of the Field

Text
Paraphrasing only verse 12 from Isaiah 55—a chapter rich with invitation, comfort, and wisdom—Steffi G. Rubin (b. The Bronx, NY, 1950) wrote "The Trees of the Field" in 1975. Verse 12 refers

Scripture References
st. = Isa. 55:12

to the "going out" from Babylon, the Israelites' return from exile. More generally, and certainly as seen through New Testament eyes, the passage sings of the joy resulting from God's salvation, a joy so far-reaching that even the "trees of the field will clap their hands," and fruitful trees and bushes will grow instead of thorns and briers.

Rubin has written many songs, a number of which have been published and record-ed by Jews for Jesus and its performance ensemble, the Liberated Wailing Wall. She received a B.A. degree in English from Simpson College in San Francisco, California. At one time an artist and creative director for Jews for Jesus, she has been self-employed in the graphic arts field since 1980. Rubin is also a music leader at Emmanuel Messianic Congregation and is active in Remnant, a group that sings Messianic music.

In 1985 Bert Polman (PHH 37) prepared an additional stanza based on Isaiah 55:13 to point out that the rejoicing is a testimony to the saving acts of God. This additional stanza was rejected by the copyright owners for the *Psalter Hymnal*, but was accepted later for publication in *Songs for LiFE* (1994):

> The fir and cypress trees will grow instead of thorns;
> the myrtle will replace the briers and nettles:
> this will be a sign, a sign of God's mighty name,
> that will not be destroyed. *Refrain*

Tune

The song's popularity is no doubt due to the Jewish-style music by Stuart Dauermann (b. Brooklyn, NY, 1944). Both text and tune were written for the Liberated Wailing Wall, the touring singing group of Jews for Jesus. It was first published in *Scriptures to Sing* (Lillenas, 1975). The infectious tune with its syncopations and hand clapping makes it a winner among contemporary Scripture choruses. Sing "The Trees of the Field" in unison at a good tempo on a half-note pulse. Use stringed instruments (guitars, violins), tambourines, hand clapping, and even some foot stomping! It may well be sung more than once, perhaps the second time (or with the additional stanza above) at a slightly faster tempo.

Dauermann was a senior staff missionary and music director of Jews for Jesus from 1973-1989; he also directed the Liberated Wailing Wall for five years. Educated in music theory (B.A.) and music education (M.M.) at the Manhattan School of Music, he also completed a master's degree in missiology at Fuller Theological Seminary in 1992. His songs appear on ten different record albums and have been published in various songbooks by Lillenas Publishing and Jews for Jesus. Dauermann currently serves on the staff of the A Havat Zion Messianic Synagogue, Beverly Hills, California.

Liturgical Use

Festive, highly celebrative, and joyful occasions.

198

Arise, Shine, for Your Light Is Come

ARISE, SHINE
♩ = 100

Text

Isaiah 60, the text for "Arise, Shine," concerns the glory of Zion, that is, Jerusalem and all of Israel. Many interpreters also understand the chapter to be a far-reaching prophecy, similar to passages in Revelation that describe the new Jerusalem. With New Testament eyes we can catch a glimpse of the new city of God and of the glory of a new heaven and a new earth. Parts of this song also have ongoing significance—for example, the ingathering of the church mentioned in stanzas 2 and 3. As is common with prophetic texts, parts are fulfilled already, but other parts (and sometimes even the same parts) will have their final fulfillment sometime in the future. The prophecy mentioned in stanza 1, for example, is fulfilled at the first coming of Christ but waits for its final completion at his second coming.

Scripture References
st. 1 = Isa. 60:2
st. 2 = Isa. 60:3, 14b
st. 3 = Isa. 60:4
st. 4 = Isa. 60:5
st. 5 = Isa. 60:19-20
ref. = Isa. 60:1

Composed by Eric Glass (a pseudonym for David Loden) in 1974, this song gained rightful popularity after being published in *Cry Hosanna* (1980) with instructions for hand gestures. The text, originally based on the King James Version, was revised for the *Psalter Hymnal*. The text is unrhymed and metrically irregular but not as difficult to sing as it first appears on the printed page. Little is known about the composer, who apparently lives in Israel.

Tune
The tune ARISE, SHINE is Israeli in character, moving with speech-like rhythms on the stanzas. The basic and regular half-note movement of the melody contains many repeated notes according to the varying numbers of syllables in the text. Dale Grotenhuis (PHH 4) prepared the harmonization. Have a cantor or choir (in unison) sing the stanzas with the congregation joining on the refrain in unison or harmony. Other instruments are helpful: guitar, strings, and tambourine (on the refrain only). Begin rather quietly, and build each stanza in volume and instrumental activity.

Liturgical Use
Advent; Epiphany; also for services focusing on missions, the church worldwide, and the new Jerusalem.

199

RUSSIA
♩ = 60

I Am the LORD Your God

Text
Helen Otte (PHH 17) prepared this versification of Jeremiah 31 in 1985 at the request of the *Psalter Hymnal* Revision Committee so that Jeremiah's famous "new covenant" passage could be included in the *Psalter Hymnal*. She chose to focus on God's salvation (st. 1), God's ingathering of his people from all parts of the earth (st. 2), and God's new covenant with the people (st. 3); all of these are main focal points in Jeremiah 31.

Scripture References
st. 1 = Jer. 31:1-2, 10
st. 2 = Jer. 31:7-9a, 13
st. 3 = Jer. 31:31-34

Tune

Alexey Feodorovitch Lvov (b. Reval [now Tallin], Estonia, 1799; d. Romanovo, near Kovno [now Kaunas], Lithuania, 1870) composed RUSSIA in 1833 one night "on the spur of the moment," according to his memoirs, after Czar Nicholas I asked him to compose a truly Russian national anthem (rather than continuing to sing a Russian text to the English melody for "God Save Our Gracious King"!). Lvov's tune was accepted and has been featured as the Russian anthem in various compositions (including Tchaikovsky's *1812 Overture*). Also used as a hymn tune ever since its 1842 publication in John Pyke Hullah's *Part Music*, RUSSIA is today often associated with the hymn text "God the Omnipotent!" Given its origin as a national anthem, the tune does have a majestic character and suggests brass instruments for accompaniment. Part singing is glorious! To highlight the change of voice from stanza 1 to stanza 2, have a soloist or choir sing stanza 1, and ask everyone to join in on stanzas 2 and 3—or perhaps have half the congregation sing 1; the other half, 2; and all together sing 3.

Lvov served in the Russian army from 1818 to 1837, advancing to personal adjutant to Czar Nicholas I as a major-general. In 1837 he succeeded his father as director of the imperial court chapel choir in St. Petersburg, a post he retained until 1861. A fine violinist, Lvov played Mendelssohn's violin concerto in Leipzig with the composer conducting in 1840. He toured with his own string quartet until deafness forced his retirement in 1867. Lvov composed much church music for the imperial choir as well as a violin concerto and several operas. He also compiled a collection of church music for the Orthodox church year, but is best known as the composer of the tune for the Russian national anthem.

Liturgical Use

Services focusing on renewal, profession of faith, restoration or healing, and the worldwide church and its evangelical task; also appropriate for baptism.

200

O My People, Turn to Me

HOSEA
$\quad$ = 84

Text

Based on Hosea 14, "O My People" is a call for repentance which, if sincerely made, will bring blessings—portrayed beautifully in images of fruitfulness. Marie J. Post (PHH 5) wrote this paraphrase in 1981 as a memorial to her mother; this passage was marked in her mother's Bible.

Scripture References
st. 1 = Hos. 14:1, 4-5a
st. 2 = Hos. 14:1, 5b-7

Tune

The *Psalter Hymnal* Revision Committee announced a tune search for this text; HOSEA, composed by Norm Jonkman (b. Paterson, NJ, 1944) in 1984, was selected from among several tunes submitted. HOSEA is a rounded bar form tune (AABA') in a minor tonality. It has characteristics similar to Appalachian tunes of the southeastern United States. HOSEA can be sung by a children's choir, a soloist, or in unison with rather light accompaniment over a sustained pedal line.

Jonkman studied music education at Calvin College, Grand Rapids, Michigan, and taught music at Whitinsville (MA) Christian School and Eastern Christian School in Paterson, New Jersey. Since 1975 he has been an electronic organ technician for the McIntyre Organ Service in Seattle, Washington. He has composed several pieces, including a Mass for choir and orchestra in 1995, which he dedicated to the choir he directs at Overlake Park Presbyterian Church in Bellevue, Washington.

Liturgical Use

Service of confession and forgiveness; evangelistic services.

201

CLAY
♩ = 63

Fear Not, Rejoice and Be Glad

Text

Priscilla Wright (b. Dallas, TX, 1928) based this song on Joel 2:18-32 and 3:17-21, passages that record the blessings God promises to his repentant people: the blessing of a bountiful harvest and the blessing of his Spirit. Because the apostle Peter used part of Joel's prophecy in Acts 2:16-21, the Spirit's outpouring becomes the controlling theme of this song and finds effective expression in the refrain. Wright wrote that she composed the song in 1971 as "an expression of joy for what the Holy Spirit was doing among the body of believers of which I was a member, [at] the Episcopal Church of the Redeemer in Houston, Texas." It became popular when The Fisherfolk recorded it (1972), and it was published in *Sound of Living Waters: Songs of the Spirit* (U.S. edition, 1974).

Scripture References
ref. = Joel 2:21, 28-29
st. 1 = Joel 2:22-24
Joel 3:13a
st. 2 = Joel 2:26
Joel 3:18
st. 3 = Joel 2:27-28

Wright studied at community colleges in Denver and Dallas and also studied theology at Christ for the Nations Institute of Biblical Studies in Dallas. She worked in inner-city social services for the Church of the Redeemer in Dallas and was the house director for the Dallas Ronald McDonald House, a residence for families of hospitalized children. Wright cites her association with the Church of the Redeemer (Episcopal) as the most prominent influence in her life: "There was always the awesome awareness that God was orchestrating a new thing [in charismatic Christian worship], and in retrospect it is evident that the renewal which took place there was a catalyst for renewal in many other parts of the world."

Tune

Like several Bible songs in the *Psalter Hymnal,* CLAY has a Jewish flavor. Wright designed the tune to flow without pause from the refrain into each stanza and on to the refrain again in continual motion. Dale Grotenhuis (PHH 4) harmonized the tune in 1986 for the *Psalter Hymnal.* Here are two performance suggestions: (a) everyone sing the refrain in unison, and one or more soloists or possibly a choir sing the stanzas; (b) everyone sing the refrain in parts, and antiphonal groups alternate on the stanzas. CLAY works well with tambourine, guitar, strings, or possibly hand clapping. The Fisherfolk often perform it with liturgical dance in the style of Hebrew folk dancing.

Liturgical Use

Pentecost; Thanksgiving; mission services.

202

Song of Jonah

EIFIONYDD
♩ = 96

Text

Paraphrasing Jonah 2, Calvin Seerveld (PHH 22) wrote "Song of Jonah" in 1982 for the *Psalter Hymnal.* Long-known in medieval liturgies as one of the "lesser" Old Testament canticles, Jonah's song is a psalm of thanksgiving similar in literary form and theme to Psalms 18, 30, 116, and 138, to give just a few examples. Jonah recalls his prayer for help to God, testifies that God answered his prayer and rescued him from drowning (st. 1-2), and honors his vow to praise and thank the LORD (st. 3). Seerveld also included a fourth stanza to capture

Scripture References
st. 1 = Jon. 2:1-4
st. 2 = Jon. 2:5-6
st. 3 = Jon. 2:7-9
st. 4 = Matt. 12:40
1 Cor. 15:20-28
Rom. 8:9-11
Rev. 1:17-18

New Testament references related to the Jonah story, especially in terms of the death and resurrection of Christ: Matthew 12:38-40; 1 Corinthians 15:20-28; Romans 8:9-11; and Revelation 1:17-18.

Tune

John Ambrose Lloyd (b. Mold, Flintshire, Wales, 1815; d. Liverpool, England, 1874) first published EIFIONYDD in his *Casgliad o Donau (A Collection of Tunes)* in 1843. The tune later appeared in Ieuan Gwyllt's (John Roberts's) important tune book *Llyfr Tonau Cynulleidfaol* (1859). Largely self-taught, Lloyd was a major presence in the Welsh music scene of his day. He was an adjudicator at the National Eisteddfodan (singing festival) in Wales and at other choral festivals and was founder of the Welsh Choral Union of

Liverpool. Lloyd composed three cantatas, including *The Prayer of Habakkuk*, and published two collections of hymn tunes: *Casgliad o Donau* (1843) and *Aberth Moliant* (1870).

Joseph Parry (PHH 18) judged EIFIONYDD the best hymn tune by a Welsh composer. The tune is named after a district in North Wales famous for its poets during the nineteenth century. In rounded bar form (AABA') and in minor tonality, the tune is eminently suited to part singing, though that may be reserved for stanza 3b and stanza 4. The final stanza could conclude with a Picardy third (a raised third on the final chord). Another option (unusual, but not unheard of with other Welsh tunes) is to shift to G major for the entire fourth stanza! That may require a bit of practice on the part of the organist and choir, however, and should follow only a suitable interlude that indicates clearly the change to major tonality.

Liturgical Use
Worship services focusing on Jonah; Easter Vigil; Easter Sunday.

203

DIR, DIR, JEHOVA
♩ = 92

The Day Is Coming—
God Has Promised

Text

This song is based on Micah 4:1-4, in which the prophet announces the rule of the LORD God in the last days, when the nations will flock to worship the LORD and peace shall reign. This prophecy will reach its fullest expression in the new heaven and earth, but Christians already see evidence of God's kingdom today wherever the Word of the LORD is proclaimed.

Scripture References
st. 1 = Mic. 4:1-2
st. 2 = Mic. 4:3
st. 3 = Mic. 4:3-4
ref. = Mic. 4:2

Calvin Seerveld (PHH 22) versified Micah's prophecy for the *Psalter Hymnal* in 1985 "to put this deeply comforting promise (found also in Isaiah 2:2-4) to song for God's people to sing."

Tune

DIR, DIR, JEHOVA was published anonymously in Georg Wittwe's *Musikalisches Handbuch der Geistlichen Melodien* (1690). The bar form (AAB) melody was expanded in Johann A. Freylinghausen's *Geistreiches Gesangbuch* (1704), where it was set to a hymn by Bärtholomaus Crasselius, "Dir, dir, Jehovah, vill ich singen" ("To thee, Jehovah, will I sing"); it maintains basically that shape in the *Psalter Hymnal*. Dale Grotenhuis (PHH 4) composed the harmonization. WINCHESTER NEW (593) is a long-meter adaptation of the same tune; that tune's familiarity may help in learning this more rhythmically varied one. Though the entire piece could be sung in harmony, try this alternative: sing the stanzas in unison and the refrain in harmony—then choral harmony should indicate the "end of strife"!

Liturgical Use
Advent; worship services focusing on justice and peace, God's kingdom, or the end of war; prayer for peace efforts by governments, leaders, or organizations.

204
Little Bethlehem of Judah

WESTRIDGE
♩ = 54

Text
Micah 5:2-4 singles out Bethlehem as the source of the Messiah, the One whose rule would bring reconciliation and initiate the kingdom of God. Calvin Seerveld (PHH 22) paraphrased this passage in 1986 for the *Psalter Hymnal.*

Scripture References
st. 1 = Mic. 5:2
st. 2 = Mic. 5:3
st. 3 = Mic. 5:4

Tune
WESTRIDGE is a charming two-line tune, effective precisely because "small is beautiful." Martin F. Shaw (PHH 49) composed it in 1929 for a children's hymn, "Jesus, Friend of Little Children," and the tune was published in *Songs of Praise for Boys and Girls* (1930). Sing it in unison and use light accompaniment, possibly even reducing the texture to three parts. Seerveld suggests a well-trained child's voice with piano accompaniment as a performance option.

Liturgical Use
Advent; service of Christmas lessons and carols.

205

THOMAS
♩ = 100

The LORD Is Saying

Text
Zechariah 8 records ten blessings, each one beginning with the words "This is what the LORD Almighty says: . . . " Calvin Seerveld (PHH 22) highlighted five of those blessings in this 1984 partially rhymed versification of Zechariah 8:2-8 for the *Psalter Hymnal.* The blessings pertain to Jerusalem, especially as an encourage-

Scripture References
st. 1 = Zech. 8:3-4
st. 2 = Zech. 8:5-7
st. 3 = Zech. 8:2, 8

ment to the Jewish remnant to rebuild the temple, but they are also messianic, so their true fulfillment occurs in the coming of Christ and his kingdom.

Tune

Dale Grotenhuis (PHH 4) composed THOMAS in 1986 for the *Psalter Hymnal.* In contrast to the composer's typical choral style of songwriting, THOMAS is intended for unison singing. Grotenhuis named the tune after his youngest son.

Liturgical Use

Advent; occasions when songs of encouragement and blessing are appropriate; services of renewal; services focusing on Christ's second coming. Seerveld suggests that the song is especially suitable for God's children in urban settings.

206

WIRKSWORTH
♩ = 80

Blest Are the Contrite Hearts

Text

With the tune WIRKSWORTH in mind, Calvin Seerveld (PHH 22) prepared this unrhymed versification of Matthew 5:3-16 in 1984 for the *Psalter Hymnal.* The passage includes the well-known Beatitudes (vv. 3-12; st. 1-5), which recount the blessings of the righteous and the "salt and light" metaphors (vv. 13-16; st. 6-7), which call the righteous to show their faith so that others may praise the Lord.

Scripture References
st. 1 = Matt. 5:3-4
st. 2 = Matt. 5:5-6
st. 3 = Matt. 5:7-8
st. 4 = Matt. 5:9-10
st. 5 = Matt. 5:11-12
st. 6 = Matt. 5:13-16
st. 7 = Matt. 5:16

Tune

WIRKSWORTH was first published in John Chetham's collection *A Book of Psalmody* (1718) and gained its present shape in James Green's *Book of Psalm Tunes* (1724). Set in minor tonality, WIRKSWORTH has a folklike charm. The tune's name derives from the town Wirksworth in Derbyshire, England. Antiphonal performance is desirable for singing the entire group of seven stanzas; each stanza could also be divided so that each group sings one of the Beatitudes. Another option is to alternate unison and harmony singing throughout. Everyone should sing the final stanza.

Samuel S. Wesley (b. London, England, 1810; d. Gloucester, England, 1876) harmonized the tune and published it in his *European Psalmist* (1872). A grandson of Charles Wesley (PHH 267), Samuel Sebastian was a chorister at the Chapel Royal and sang in St. Paul's Cathedral. He learned composition and organ from his father, Samuel (PHH 1), completed a doctorate in music at Oxford, and composed for piano, organ, and choir. He was organist at Exeter Cathedral (1835-1842), Leeds Parish Church (1842-1849), Winchester Cathedral (1849-1865), and Gloucester Cathedral (1865-1876).

Wesley strove to improve the standards of church music and the status of church musicians; his observations and plans for reform were published as *A Few Words on Cathedral Music and the Music System of the Church* (1849). He was the musical editor of Charles Kemble's *A Selection of Psalms and Hymns* (1864) and of the *Wellburn Appendix of Original Hymns and Tunes* (1875) but is best known as the compiler of *The European Psalmist* (1872), in which some 130 of the 733 hymn tunes were written by him.

Liturgical Use

Worship services focusing on the kingdom of God, the Sermon on the Mount—or, more specifically, the Beatitudes (st. 1-5) or the "salt and light" passage (st. 6-7).

207

The Lord's Prayer

LANGDON
See commentary

Text

This is the first of three settings based on the Lord's Prayer (see also 208 and 562). The Lord's Prayer, recorded in Matthew 6:9-13 and Luke 11:2-4, is the prayer taught by Christ himself as a model for our prayers. It lies at the heart of Christian piety and has a rich tradition in Christian liturgy. Later manuscripts added the doxological ending "for yours is the kingdom and the power and the glory forever. Amen," reflecting a Jewish practice. Except for the addition of one word to fit the rhythm of the chant setting (the word *and* before the phrase "forgive us our debts"), the text follows exactly from the New International Version.

Scripture References
st. = Matt. 6:9-13

Tune

LANGDON is the only example of Anglican chant in the *Psalter Hymnal.* Published in a group of twenty anonymous chants at the end of Richard Langdon's *Divine Harmony, a Collection in Score of Psalms and Anthems* (1774), it is considered to be Langdon's own composition because all the other chants can be traced to other composers. The melody is constructed with three statements of a basic formula; after the first statement, "Give us today . . . " and "And lead us not . . . " each begins the pattern again. In keeping with the Anglican style and tradition, sing in harmony; organ accompaniment should be light (until the final phrases), though unaccompanied singing is very appropriate. The rhythmical notation is approximate, for in this style of chant, speech rhythms determine musical ones.

Little is known about Richard Langdon (b. Exeter, England, c. 1729; d. Exeter, 1803) other than that he filled a series of organist positions. His family had a long involvement in the music program at Exeter Cathedral, and he was organist there from 1753-1777; he also served as Master of the Choristers during much of that time.

Liturgical Use

Traditional as a corporate conclusion to spoken prayer; as part of special liturgies or services.

208

♩ = 88

Our Father, Lord of Heaven and Earth

Text

The second of three settings based on the Lord's Prayer (see 207 and 562), "Our Father, Lord of Heaven and Earth" is a concise and yet rhymed metrical two-stanza versification of Matthew 6:9-13. Henry J. de Jong (b. Sarnia, ON, Canada, 1956) prepared the versification in 1982; it was first sung at First Christian Reformed Church, Toronto, Ontario. De Jong studied harpsichord and voice at the Royal Conservatory of Music, Toronto; church music at the Sweelinck Conservatory, Amsterdam; and aesthetics at the Institute for Christian Studies, Toronto. He worked in layout and design at the Knight Publishing Company in St. Catharines, Ontario. Since 1985 he has been a partner in a computer services company.

Scripture References
st. 1 = Matt. 6:9-11
st. 2 = Matt. 6:12-13

Tune

Martin Luther's versification of the Lord's Prayer was set to this tune in Valentin Schumann's hymnal, *Geistliche Lieder* (1539); the tune, whose composer remains unknown, had some earlier use. The tune name derives from Luther's German incipit: "Vater unser im Himmelreich. . . ." Because VATER UNSER found later use in British and Scottish psalters as a setting for Psalm 112, it acquired the alternate title OLD 112TH in some hymnals.

Johann S. Bach (PHH 7) used this tune in his *St. John Passion* (1724)—from which the *Psalter Hymnal* gets its harmonization—and in *Cantatas 90, 101,* and *102,* among others. Bach also wrote organ preludes on the melody. Felix Mendelssohn arranged a famous organ treatment on this tune in his *Sixth Organ Sonata.* One of the classic chorales, VATER UNSER features phrases grouped into three long lines. Use solid organ tone and sing in harmony if resources permit.

Liturgical Use

Traditional as a corporate conclusion to spoken prayers; as part of special liturgies or services. De Jong suggests also singing this setting in homes as a table grace.

209

Seek Ye First the Kingdom

LAFFERTY
♩ = 80

Text

Karen Lafferty (b. Alamogordo, NM, 1948) wrote this song one night after attending a Bible study on Matthew 6:33 in 1971 at Calvary Chapel, Costa Mesa, California. Struggling with financial difficulties after recently starting a full-time music ministry, she returned home that night with new encouragement. Others appreciated its beauty and simplicity, and the song soon gained popularity, eventually providing the support that permitted her to continue and develop her ministry. Other stanzas, also based on well-known quotations of Jesus, were written anonymously. Stanza 2 is based on Matthew 7:7, and stanza 3 on Matthew 4:4 (quoting Deut. 8:3). The first two quotations are from the Sermon on the Mount, and the third is Jesus' response to his first temptation in the desert. The addition of anonymous stanzas is a phenomenon related to the oral tradition in which many Scripture songs have developed. The three stanzas together persistently and fervently direct our attention to the things of God in the context of living praise ("alleluia"), indicating that such a manner of life is necessary before God. Maranatha! Music published the composite and recorded it on their initial *Praise* album (1972).

Scripture References
st. 1 = Matt. 6:33
st. 2 = Matt. 7:7
st. 3 = Matt. 4:4

    A musical missionary, Lafferty has been based in Amsterdam since 1981, when she became founder and director of Musicians for Missions, an international ministry of Youth with a Mission. She received a degree in music education at Eastern New Mexico University, Portales, New Mexico. From 1971 to 1981 she was a member of Calvary Chapel in Costa Mesa, California, where she served as a worship leader and became part of a fellowship of musicians, Maranatha! Music (which later became a Christian music company). Lafferty has recorded several solo albums and a music video. Her musical style is reminiscent of the folk music of such singers and groups as Joni Mitchell, the Kingston Trio, and Peter, Paul, and Mary. She and Musicians for Missions travel worldwide with their music ministry.

Tune

Named after its composer, LAFFERTY is a "simple is beautiful" tune consisting of one repeated musical line accompanied by a descant that encourages even the smallest congregation to sing in two-part harmony. A popular Scripture chorus published in many informal collections, it was one of the first to be included in recent denominational hymnals. LAFFERTY can be sung in different ways; one elaborate (though easy to learn) performance that extends the song is to treat the descant like a refrain in a two-part round; when the first group finishes the first stanza, it begins the alleluias as the second group begins stanza 1. Flute and guitar provide beautiful accompaniment; Karen herself plays guitar and oboe—try that for variety!

Liturgical Use
Before the reading of Scripture; appropriate in many kinds of services and at various points in the liturgy.

210

WHATSOEVER YOU DO
♩ = 46

Whatsoever You Do to the Least

Text

This Scripture song is based on Matthew 25:35-36, 40, part of Christ's story about the sheep and the goats at the final judgment (25:31-46). Jesus teaches here that the basis for judging is whether love has been shown to God's people—even to the least of them (see also 1 John 3:14-15). Rewards in the kingdom of God go to those who serve without claiming any merit themselves.

Scripture References
ref. = Matt. 25:40
st. 1 = Matt. 25:35-36
st. 2 = Matt. 25:36

Willard F. Jabusch (b. Chicago, IL, 1930) composed the text and tune in 1965 for a youth Mass at St. Celestine's Church, Elmwood Park, Illinois. Jabusch was one of many Roman Catholic priests who provided church music with English texts after Vatican II began the use of vernacular in worship. He is well-known for many Scripture paraphrases, and many of these are set to folk tunes—especially eastern European ones, because of Jabusch's familiarity with multiethnic parishes in the Chicago area (see also 370). This song was published with eleven stanzas in *Hymnal for Young Christians* (1966). The *Psalter Hymnal* includes the original stanzas 1, 2, 3, and 5 (the biblically based ones), combined in two longer stanzas.

Jabusch received degrees from St. Mary of the Lake Seminary, Mundelein, Illinois, and Loyola University, Chicago. He also earned a doctorate at Northwestern University, Evanston, Illinois (1986), and studied music at the Chicago Conservatory and the University of London. A parish priest at St. James Roman Catholic Church in Chicago from 1956 to 1961, he taught at Niles College of Loyola University from 1963 to 1966 and at the Mundelein Seminary from 1968 to 1990. Since 1990 Jabusch has been director of Calvert House, the Roman Catholic student center at the University of Chicago. His theological publications include *The Person in the Pulpit* (1980), *Walk Where Jesus Walked* (1986), and *The Spoken Christ* (1990). He has written some forty tunes and one hundred hymn texts, often pairing them with eastern European and Israeli folk tunes.

Tune

WHATSOEVER YOU DO begins with a refrain that surrounds each stanza. A simple melody, it is designed for unison singing, although the refrain could easily be adapted for part singing. Because the entire text is a quotation from Jesus, the song should be sung through by *one* body: soloist, choir, or congregation, possibly distinguishing only the refrain by singing harmony. This music is written to flow in continual motion, so be careful not to pause between stanzas and refrain. Keep it moving at one pulse per bar, and use light organ registration or folk instruments.

Liturgical Use

Lord's Supper; funeral services; worship services focusing on the final judgment or stressing the social implications of living the gospel.

211

The Lord Is Risen Indeed

OPGESTAAN
$\downarrow = 72$

Text

This song is based on the Easter story in Matthew 28:1-10 (also in Mark 16 and Luke 24). The original Dutch versification was a group effort by those who prepared many Bible songs for children (see also PHH 151); it was first published in volume 1 of *Alles wordt nieuw* (1966), part of a series of Dutch children's hymnals. Using the pen name Sietze Buning, Stanley Wiersma (PHH 25) translated that volume into English to produce *All Will Be New* (vol. 1, 1982). The refrain captures something of the traditional Easter greeting:

Scripture References
ref. = see commentary
st. 1 = see commentary
st. 2 = Matt. 28:1
st. 3 = Matt. 28:5-6
st. 4 = Matt. 28:6
st. 5 = Matt. 28:6-7
    (Luke 24:5)

> Christ the Lord is risen!
> He is risen indeed! Alleluia!

Stanza 1 sets the context of the song by offering a theological summary about the significance of Christ's resurrection, and stanzas 2 through 5 narrate the Easter story.

Tune

The Dutch musician Wim ter Burg (PHH 151) composed OPGESTAAN, a spritely melody designed for unison singing in continual motion, that is, without pauses between the stanzas and refrain. OPGESTAAN, the Dutch word for "resurrection," has a nice touch of imitation in the harmony of the refrain, where the bass part begins by imitating the melody. Use a variety of instruments on the refrain with its descant, including bells, recorder, flute, and trumpet. Orff instruments and recorders work nicely as accompaniment for small congregations or children's choir. For variety, a soloist or children's choir can sing the angel's words (in quotation marks). Keep the energy going!

Liturgical Use

Easter—sing stanzas 2 through 5 and the refrain to focus only on the narrative part of the song, or, alternatively, sing the entire song and repeat stanza 1 after stanza 5 to set the narrative in a theological frame.

212

PENTECOST
$\quad$ ♩ = 132

Song of Mary

Text

The Song of Mary recorded in Luke 1:46-55 is the first of the three "great" canticles recorded in Luke 1 and 2. It features similarities to the Song of Hannah (158) and echoes many other Old Testament passages. Commonly known as the Magnificat (after its Latin incipit), Mary's song is a bold text uttered by a young woman who wasn't supposed to become pregnant—and yet it compares in many ways with an Old Testament song

Scripture References
st. 1 = Luke 1:46-48
st. 2 = Luke 1:48-49
st. 3 = Luke 1:50-51
st. 4 = Luke 1:52-53
st. 5 = Luke 1:54-55

uttered by a woman (Hannah) who at first couldn't become pregnant. Mary's song has all the characteristics of a psalm of thanksgiving, praising God for his mighty acts of salvation, for being merciful toward the poor and hungry and humble, and for being faithful to his people. In 1931 Dewey Westra (PHH 98) versified Mary's song in Detroit for the 1934 *Psalter Hymnal*. The text was revised by the *Psalter Hymnal* Revision Committee for the 1987 edition. A hymnic paraphrase of Mary's song is at 478, and a canonic setting is at 622.

Tune

William Boyd (b. Montego Bay, Jamaica, 1847; d. Paddington, England, 1928) composed PENTECOST in 1864 for the hymn text "Come, Holy Ghost, Our Souls Inspire"; it was published in 1868 in *Thirty-Two Hymn Tunes Composed by Members of the University of Oxford*. The name PENTECOST derives from the subject matter of that hymn text. Boyd was educated at Hurstpierpoint, where the hymn writer Sabine Baring-Gould (PHH 522) was one of his teachers, and at Worcester College, Oxford. He was ordained in the Church of England and served the Church of All Saints, Norfolk Square, London, from 1893-1918.

$\quad$ The tune PENTECOST was retained from the 1959 *Psalter Hymnal*, though Dewey Westra originally versified Mary's song for the tune DUKE STREET (412). The humble, meditative character of PENTECOST stands in contrast to the spirit of rejoicing found in

DUKE STREET and the settings at 478 and 622. The text can also be sung to PUER NOBIS
(327). A simple chant-like tune with a range of only five tones in the melody, PENTE-
COST is one of the "generic" Victorian tunes of its time (see also QUEBEC, 141, 307;
ST. CRISPIN, 276; MORECAMBE 419; and MARYTON, 573). Sing it in harmony, perhaps
unaccompanied, but with a firm pulse and not too slowly.

Liturgical Use

Advent; Christmas; occasions of thanksgiving for God's grace. In churches that have
daily prayer services, this canticle is sung during evening prayer.

213

Song of Zechariah

AN WASSERFLÜSSEN BABYLON
$\d = 76$

Text

The Song of Zechariah is the second "great" canticle recorded
by Luke (1:68-79), well-known as the Benedictus, after its incipit
in the Latin Vulgate. Zechariah uttered his song as prophecy
and praise upon the naming of his son, John the Baptist. Stanza

Scripture References

st. 1 = Luke 1:68-75
st. 2 = Luke 1:76-79

1 praises God for bringing deliverance from evil and being true to his word spoken by
earlier prophets; stanza 2 addresses John, the forerunner of the Messiah, Jesus Christ,
who would "guide our feet in ways of peace." Zechariah's reference to "the rising sun"
(Luke 1:78) caused the early church to use this canticle in morning services, initially at
Lauds, the hour of early morning praise. The song is still used for morning prayer by
churches with a tradition of daily prayer services (see PHH 247 for more information
on this tradition). Bert Polman (PHH 37) versified Zechariah's song in 1986 specifically
for the tune AN WASSERFLÜSSEN BABYLON in an attempt to include a concise paraphrase of this long canticle in the 1987 *Psalter Hymnal*.

Tune

The tune AN WASSERFLÜSSEN BABYLON was composed by Wolfgang Dachstein
(b. Offenburg an der Kinzig, Germany, 1487; d. Strasbourg, Germany, 1553) and
published in the *Strassburger Kirchenampt* (1525), edited by Dachstein and his friend
Matthäus Greiter. In that collection it was the setting for Dachstein's German versification of Psalm 137, from which the tune name derives (in English, "By the rivers of
Babylon"). The tune is similar in character to Genevan psalm tunes that were published
slightly later, and it has always been associated with the Song of Zechariah in the
Genevan psalm-singing tradition, which did permit the singing of the Lukan canticles.
In bar form (AAB) with a long and complex B section, AN WASSERFLÜSSEN BABYLON is
a challenging tune for congregations, but well loved by those who were nurtured in the

Genevan tradition. The melisma in the final phrase effectively produces a strong ending.

Dachstein came from a long line of theologians and musicians originally from the town of Dachstein near Strasbourg. In 1503 he studied theology in Erfurt (Martin Luther was in that city in 1503 as well) and became a Dominican monk. He was an organist at both the Cathedral and the St. Thomas Church in Strasbourg and lived there at the same time as John Calvin, who was working on the Genevan Psalter. Converted to Protestantism in 1523, he became the assistant pastor at St. Thomas Church but later returned to Roman Catholicism to retain his position as organist at the Cathedral. Dachstein and Matthäus Greiter coedited the *Teutsch Kirchenamt mit Lobgesengen* (1525), one of the earliest Lutheran prayer and hymnbooks.

Liturgical Use
Advent; morning worship services.

214

ERE ZIJ GOD
$\downarrow = 60$

Glory to God
Ere zij God

Text

The third "great" canticle in Luke's gospel (2:14) records the song the angels sang at the birth of Jesus. However, it is sometimes not counted as a canticle because it was expanded in later liturgical use into the Gloria, a longer text that began with this verse and became a regular part of the daily Mass (see PHH 247 for the complete Gloria text). The Latin incipit of this text, "Gloria in excelsis Deo," is often used independently as a chorus of praise, as in the refrain of 347 and other Christmas carols.

Scripture References
st. = Luke 2:14

A certain F. A. Schultz prepared the text and music for "Ere zij God"; it was published in Bickers's *Het Nachtegaaltje* and in the numerous editions of the popular *Zangbundel* compiled by Johannes De Heer in the first half of the twentieth century. Those collections provided a means for those who sang only psalms in church to sing many popular hymns at home. "Ere zij God" is the best-known Dutch carol in the Netherlands, and many Christian Reformed congregations with and without Dutch immigrants have made this song part of their Christmas celebration.

Jan Luth, current director of the Liturgical Institute at the University of Groningen in the Netherlands, suggests that the composer may have been Franz Albert Schultz (b. Neustettin, Germany, 1692; d. 1763), a German Lutheran theologian educated in Halle. In 1732 he became a professor of theology at Konigsberg in East Prussia, where he spearheaded reforms in the Prussian church and educational system according to an ideal of "active Christianity." Further research is needed to determine whether or not this carol was perhaps translated from German into Dutch.

The composite English versification prepared for the 1987 *Psalter Hymnal* follows the New International Version, which restricts God's favor to his chosen people. "Glory to God" is a fine hymn of praise to God, who brings peace to his people on earth through the birth of the Messiah.

Tune

ERE ZIJ GOD is a tune "stretched" into rounded binary form and concluded with a double "amen" coda. Although it's ideally sung unaccompanied and in harmony, festive instruments, such as a brass quartet, can add a celebrative accent.

Liturgical Use

Christmas Day services and other occasions celebrating the significance of Christ's birth.

215

While Shepherds Watched Their Flocks

WINCHESTER OLD
♩ = 96

Text

The story of the shepherds and the angels is told in this famous paraphrase of Luke 2:8-14 by Nahum Tate (b. Dublin, Ireland, 1652; d. Southwark, London, England, 1715). It was first published in 1700 in a supplement to the *New Version of the Psalms* by Tate and Nicholas Brady. Tate's straightforward telling of the nativity story is an example of paraphrasing at its best: poetry that conveys the text well without undue liberties or additions and is easy to understand and sing. Adopted by virtually all hymnals since its writing, this narrative song simply tells the Christmas gospel as the shepherds heard it. A similarly narrative song based on the same gospel text is at 339.

Scripture References
st. 1 = Luke 2:8-9
st. 2 = Luke 2:9-10
st. 3 = Luke 2:11-12
st. 4 = Luke 2:12
st. 5 = Luke 2:13
st. 6 = Luke 2:14

Although born in Ireland, Tate spent all of his adult life in London, where he was known primarily as a playwright and poet. Most of his dramas were not original plays but adaptations of the works of others. Honored by being named poet laureate in 1692, Tate wrote poetry celebrating important national events. He was also appointed the official royal historian in 1702. Intemperate throughout his life, Tate died while living at the Suffolk House, a refuge for debtors in London. In the history of church music Tate and Brady are known for their *New Version* (1696), which replaced the "Old Version" of Sternhold and Hopkins published by John Day in 1562. Reprinted frequently and supplemented with some hymns, the new versification became the standard psalter of the Church of England and influenced psalmody well into the nineteenth century.

Tune

WINCHESTER OLD is a famous common-meter psalm tune, presumably arranged by George Kirbye (b. Suffolk, England, c. 1560; d. Bury St. Edmunds, Suffolk, England, 1634) from a melody in Christopher Tye's *Acts of the Apostles* and published in T. Este's *The Whole Book of Psalmes* (1592) set to Psalm 84. Kirbye was responsible for most of the harmonizations in that psalter. A musician at the estate of Sir Robert Jermyn near Bury St. Edmunds, Kirbye apparently also served as church warden of the local St. Mary's Church and composed several volumes of madrigals that were very popular in his time.

WINCHESTER OLD has been associated with Nahum Tate's Christmas text ever since it was published in *Hymns Ancient and Modern* (1861). The tune title refers to Winchester, an ancient town in Hampshire, England. The song could be sung as a miniature oratorio, with the choir doing the narration (st. 1, 2a, 5), a soloist singing the angel's words (st. 2-4), and on the final stanza (st. 6) the entire congregation becoming the "throng of angels" and the choir singing descant—with all the stops pulled out!

Liturgical Use

Christmas; stanza 5 makes an excellent doxology for the two Sundays following Christmas.

216

NUNC DIMITTIS
♩ = 72

Song of Simeon

Text

Recorded in Luke 2:29-32, Simeon's song is the final (fourth) "great" canticle in Luke 1-2 (see also 212, 213, and 214). This song of joy and peace is part of the gospel account of the presentation of Jesus in the temple, involving first Simeon and

Scripture References
st. 1 = Luke 2:29-30
st. 2 = Luke 2:31-32

then Anna (vv. 21-40), who express thanks that salvation in Christ is for Jew and Gentile alike. Simeon's song is often called the Nunc Dimittis, after its incipit in Latin. Dewey Westra (PHH 98) versified the text in Detroit in 1931 for the 1934 *Psalter Hymnal;* it was revised slightly for the 1987 edition.

The Nunc Dimittis has traditionally been paired with the Magnificat for Vespers or evening services and is still sung daily in churches with a tradition of daily prayer services (see 247 for more information on this tradition). John Calvin used it at the end of the Lord's Supper. In the Scottish *Kirk,* if communion was served at both services, Psalm 103 would be used at the end of the morning Lord's Supper and the Song of Simeon at the end of the afternoon or evening Lord's Supper.

Tune

Louis Bourgeois (PHH 3) composed NUNC DIMITTIS for the Song of Simeon; the tune was first published in the 1547 edition of the Genevan Psalter. Claude Goudimel (PHH 6) wrote the harmonization in 1564 with the melody originally in the tenor voice. Some Christian denominations associate this tune with the ancient Greek "Candlelight Hymn," which begins with the words "O gladsome Light, O grace" in the translation by Matthew Bridges (PHH 410).

Liturgical Use

Suitable as a hymn for dismissal, especially after the Lord's Supper, and during Epiphany, since it brings to focus the worldwide character and task of the church. Also appropriate for funerals.

217

Jesus, Remember Me

JESUS, REMEMBER ME
♩ = 76

Text

One of the robbers crucified with the Savior cried out, "Jesus, remember me when you come into your kingdom" (Luke 23:42). Jesus responded, "I tell you the truth, today you will be with me in paradise" (v. 43). This humble plea of a sinner for divine mercy is all the more poignant today as our Savior in heaven continues to pray for his people.

Scripture References
st. = Luke 23:42

"Jesus, Remember Me" comes from the Taizé community, an ecumenical community in France with Reformed roots. In the Taizé tradition, short songs are often sung repeatedly with various descants (as here and at 312); others are canons (see 622). The Taizé and many other Christian communities and churches use this song as a meditative chant in communal prayers. The text and tune are from *Music from Taizé* (vol. 1, 1981), published by G.I.A. Publications, Inc.

Tune

JESUS, REMEMBER ME (1978) is a simple tune from the hand of Jacques Berthier (b. Auxerre, France, 1923; d. Paris, France, 1994), one of the primary composers associated with the Taizé community. Consisting of just two phrases in melodic sequence, the tune is intended for singing in harmony, with repeats optional at the discretion of the performers. One can forgo the quarter rest at the middle of each line, singing basically two long lines for the entire song. In a meditative service, repeat the song a number of times (with some use of the two descants)—sometimes softly, sometimes forcefully, sometimes only humming. The song can also be sung as a "frame" surrounding spoken or silent prayers, or as a refrain to a series of spoken prayers.

A son of musical parents, Berthier studied music at the École César Franck in Paris. From 1961 until his death he served as organist at St. Ignace Church, Paris. Although his published works include numerous compositions for organ, voice, and instruments, Berthier is best known as the composer of service music for the Taizé community near Cluny, Burgundy. Influenced by the French liturgist and church musician Joseph Gelineau, Berthier began writing songs for equal voices in 1955 for the services of the then nascent community of twenty brothers at Taizé. As the Taizé community grew, Berthier continued to compose most of the mini-hymns, canons, and various associated instrumental arrangements, which are now universally known as the Taizé repertoire. In the past two decades this repertoire has become widely used in North American church music in both Roman Catholic and Protestant traditions.

Liturgical Use
Good Friday; as a prayer song in a meditative service.

218

LINDESFARNE
♩ = 80
In the Beginning Was the Word Eternal

Text

In the prologue to his gospel account, John declares explicitly that Christ has been with God and is God from time eternal, and that Christ has been at work in creation and re-creation making known the true God. This profound passage is filled with theologically rich terms such as "Word," "light," "became flesh," and "full of grace and truth." "In the Beginning" is a setting of John 1:1-5, 9-14, 17-18, covering most of John's prologue.

Scripture References
st. 1 = John 1:1-4
st. 2 = John 1:5, 9-11
st. 3 = John 1:12-13
st. 4 = John 1:14, 17-18

Bert Polman (PHH 37) versified these passages in 1985 for use by Fellowship Christian Reformed Church, Rexdale, Ontario, where he was organist at the time. The versification is unrhymed in order to include many direct quotations from John 1.

Tune

Polman wrote the text with the Israeli folk tune LINDESFARNE in mind. The tune was published in its current arrangement in the Oxford children's hymnal *Their Words My Thoughts* (1983). A charming tune in minor tonality, LINDESFARNE features a striking climax at the end of the second line that creates an effective melodic contour for the entire tune. It is intended for unison singing with accompaniment by keyboard or a variety of instruments; the tempo should be solid and majestic.

The tune was arranged by Francesca Leftley (b. Southend-on-Sea, Essex, England, 1955), who presumably named the tune for the English island famous for its religious history and its castle; Lindesfarne, also known as Holy Island, is located in the North Sea off England's Northumberland coast and south of Berwick-upon-Tweed. Leftley graduated from Digby Stuart College of Education, London, England, with a degree in music education. She has directed choirs and orchestras and has been active in church music at the local parish level. Her many songs have been published in a number of collections. Leftley was also involved in revising and composing new works for the *Veritas Religious Education Syllabus* used by Roman Catholic schools in Great Britain and Ireland.

Liturgical Use
Advent; Christmas; Epiphany; a sung confession of faith as an alternate to the Apostles' or Nicene Creed.

219

As Moses Raised the Serpent Up

O WALY WALY
$\downharpoonright$ = 76

Text

John 3:14-17, part of Jesus' nighttime discourse with Nicodemus, forms the basis of this song and includes that famous profession of faith "God so loved the world . . . ," one of the best-known and most frequently memorized verses in the entire Bible. In this setting that profession is used virtually as a refrain but is numbered as stanzas 2 and 4 for emphasis. Marie J. Post (PHH 5) prepared the versification in 1985 for use with the tune O WALY WALY in the *Psalter Hymnal.* She said this versification was one of her easiest assignments: "The lines simply fell into the music!"

Scripture References
st. 1 = John 3:14-15
st. 2 = John 3:16
st. 3 = John 3:17
st. 4 = John 3:16

Tune

O WALY WALY is a traditional English melody associated with the song "O Waly, Waly, gin love be bony," the words of which date back at least to Ramsay's *Tea Table Miscellany* (1724-1732), and as the setting for a folk ballad about Jamie Douglas. It is also well known in the Appalachian region of the United States.

Hal H. Hopson (b. White Mound, TX, 1933) adapted and arranged O WALY WALY as an anthem in 1971 for his setting of 1 Corinthians 13, "Gift of Love"; his version become known as GIFT OF LOVE. That copyrighted version of the tune can be sung in canon after one measure, especially on the "refrain" stanzas (2 and 4) and ideally by the choir or by a small part of the congregation, somewhat in the manner of a descant. Keep the phrases moving to help create four lines instead of eight choppy phrases. In fact, the tune has a difficult time when *not* sung in canon; more recent hymnals have begun publishing this tune in triple meter, contrary to the publisher's request, in order to avoid the long-held notes. (The *Companion to the United Methodist Hymnal* noted that their committee's request for permission to use triple meter was denied, but that "in an assertion of free will over predestination, *The Presbyterian Hymnal,* 1990, included the text with a triple-meter form of the tune," p. 636.)

Hopson was educated at Baylor University, Waco, Texas, and Southern Baptist Seminary, Louisville, Kentucky. He served various churches in the Nashville area as organist and choir director. He has also taught at Westminster Choir College, Princeton, New Jersey, and Scarritt Graduate School, Nashville, Tennessee. Over eight hundred of Hopson's hymn tunes and keyboard and choral compositions have been published. He takes an active role in many conferences and music clinics and was a major contributor to the Presbyterian *Psalter* (1994).

Liturgical Use
During the Lord's Supper; as a response to the preached Word; as a communal confession of faith, possibly in an evangelistic setting.

220

LOVE UNKNOWN
♩ = 63

I Am the Holy Vine

Text
Based on John 15:1-5, "I Am the Holy Vine" versifies Jesus' teaching about leading fruitful lives. Using the common Old Testament symbol of a vineyard (Ps. 80; Isa. 5; Jer. 2:21), Jesus points out that love can be produced only by being rooted in the source of true love, Christ, in the Father's vineyard. Whereas the Old Testament vineyard is sometimes pictured as unfruitful, Jesus casts himself as "the true vine" that produces good fruit.

Scripture References
st. 1 = John 15:1-2
st. 2 = John 15:4
st. 3 = John 15:5

James Quinn (b. Glasgow, Scotland, 1919) wrote this unrhymed versification and published it in his *New Hymns for All Seasons* (1969). Quinn is one of the most respected and increasingly published Scottish hymn authors; he frequently paraphrases or quotes Scripture in his hymns. Educated at St. Aloysius College, the University of Glasgow, and Heythrop College, Oxfordshire, Quinn became a member of the Jesuit Order in 1939 and was ordained in 1950. He served in various academic positions, two of which were classics master at Wimbledon College and spiritual advisor at Beda College, Rome (1976-1980). In the Roman Catholic Church, Quinn has been involved in ecumenical relationships—he was an observer at the 1964 assembly of the World Alliance of Reformed Churches in Frankfurt and a consultant to the World Council of Churches' Faith and Order conference at Louvain in 1972. A member of the Scottish Religious Advisory Committee of the BBC (1973-1976) and participant in various ecumenical dialogues for the British Council of Churches, he was also an advisor for the International Commission on English in the Liturgy (1972-1976). Quinn has written on a wide variety of theological issues. His writings include *The Theology of the Eucharist* (1973) and numerous articles for encyclopedias. He is also one of the leading writers of contemporary hymn texts, many of which are collected in his *New Hymns for All Seasons* (1969) and *Praise for All Seasons* (1994).

Tune

John Ireland (b. Bowdon, Cheshire, England, 1879; d. Rock Mill, Washington, Sussex, England, 1962) composed LOVE UNKNOWN in 1918 for the text "My song is love un- known"; the tune was first published in *The Public School Hymn Book* of 1919. A letter in the London *Daily Telegraph* of April 5, 1950, claims that Ireland wrote LOVE UNKNOWN within fifteen minutes on a scrap of paper upon receiving the request to compose it from Geoffrey Shaw, one of the editors of that 1919 hymnal. LOVE UNKNOWN has since appeared in many hymnals as a setting for a number of different texts.

Trained at the Royal College of Music, Ireland served as organist at St. Luke's, Chelsea (1904-1926), and taught at the Royal College of Music from 1923 to 1939. He became known as one of the best composers and teachers of his era, but his personal life was often troubled. Although his piano works, chamber music, and smaller orches- tral works remain popular, Ireland is mainly remembered for his song cycles of poetry by Shakespeare, Blake, Hardy, and other English poets. His songs often have carefully wrought accompaniments—as is certainly the case for LOVE UNKNOWN. Sing this fine tune in unison with firm legato organ support, or in harmony, possibly even unaccom- panied on a stanza, if resources permit.

Liturgical Use

Baptism; services emphasizing the communion of saints—for example, the reception of new members, observance of the Lord's Supper, celebrations of the church of all nations.

221

We Know That God Works Things for Good

LESTER
♩ = 60

Text

The often-quoted Scripture passage Romans 8:28-39 says that God chose some to be his people, that he justified them in Jesus Christ, and that nothing whatsoever can separate them—us— from the love of God in Christ. Calvin Seerveld (PHH 22) paraphrased this passage in 1985 and set it to a tune he com-

Scripture References
st. 1 = Rom. 8:28
st. 2 = Rom. 8:29-30
st. 3 = Rom. 8:31-34
st. 4 = Rom. 8:35
st. 5 = Rom. 8:37-39

posed and dedicated in tribute to the Christian faith of his father, Lester. The song was first published in the 1987 *Psalter Hymnal.*

Tune
Seerveld's LESTER is a common-meter tune in minor tonality and features an effective syncopation in its final phrase. Everyone should sing stanzas 1, 2, and 5; stanzas 3 and 4 could be sung a choir to highlight the questions in the text. The harmony was composed by Dale Grotenhuis (PHH 4) in 1986.

Liturgical Use
As a sung confession of faith, an alternative to reciting the Apostles' or Nicene Creed; also suitable for funerals (using the tune ST. ANNE; 170).

222

CAPETOWN
♩ = 52

If I Speak a Foreign Tongue

Text

"If I Speak" is a paraphrase of the Bible's famous chapter on love in 1 Corinthians 13. After discussing various spiritual gifts and their use in the Christian community (chap. 12), the apostle Paul turns to describe "the most excellent way"—the way of love. Love is the most profound fruit of the Holy Spirit, and it should characterize every facet of the Christian life. Using metaphor, hyperbole, and both positive and negative description, Paul describes this kind of *agape* love in a succinct and beautiful chapter.

Scripture References
st. 1 = 1 Cor. 13:1
st. 2 = 1 Cor. 13:2
st. 3 = 1 Cor. 13:3
st. 4 = 1 Cor. 13:4
st. 5 = 1 Cor. 13:8, 13

Bert Polman (PHH 37) paraphrased parts of the chapter for a Pentecost hymn festival at Fellowship Christian Reformed Church, Rexdale, Ontario, in 1986. Polman began by revising Christopher Wordsworth's hymn on the same text, "Gracious Spirit, Holy Ghost," published in Wordsworth's *The Holy Year* (1862), but ended up with this new paraphrase.

Tune

CAPETOWN was originally composed by Friedrich Filitz (b. Arnstadt, Thuringia, Germany, 1804; d. Munich, Germany, 1876) as a setting for the text "Morgenglanz der Ewigkeit"; that text and tune were included in *Vierstimmiges Choralbuch* (1847), a hymnal compiled by Baron Christian von Bunsen and published by Filitz. After earning a doctorate of philosophy, Filitz became active in music editing and publishing in Berlin, where he lived from 1843 to 1847, and in Munich, where he lived from 1848 to 1876. He also published a collection of sixteenth- and seventeenth-century hymns, *Vierstimmige Choralsätze* (1845).

CAPETOWN was soon published in England; Peter Maurice arranged it for publication in his *Choral Harmony* (1854) as a setting for Reginald Heber's litany "Lord of Mercy and of Might." CAPETOWN is presumably named after the legislative capital of South Africa. It is a simple but elegant tune in an unusual meter. Sing stanzas 1 through 4 in parts, reserving stanza 5 for a stately unison finale with an additional bright stop on the organ. This tune needs to move on a half-note pulse and slightly slower on stanza 5.

Liturgical Use
Any worship service focusing on God's command to love one another, the communion of saints, or spiritual gifts and their exercise; weddings or other family services.

223

For the Glories of God's Grace

MONKLAND
♩ = 58

Text
In 2 Corinthians 5:18-21 the apostle Paul concludes a description of the ministry of reconciliation: we who have received God's reconciliation through Christ now have the joyful task of being God's agents of reconciliation in the world. So we urge others to believe and join us in singing, "We are reconciled to God." Marie J. Post (PHH 5) composed a poetic summary of this Scripture passage in 1985.

Scripture References
all st. = 2 Cor. 5:18-21

Tune
The tune MONKLAND has a fascinating if complex history. Rooted in a tune for the text "Fahre fort" in Johann A. Freylinghausen's (PHH 34) famous hymnal, *Geistreiches Gesangbuch* (1704), it then was significantly altered by John Antes (b. Frederick, PA, 1740; d. Bristol, England, 1811) in a Moravian manuscript, *A Collection of Hymn Tunes* (c. 1800). Antes was a missionary, watchmaker, business manager, and composer. Born near the Moravian community of Bethlehem, Pennsylvania, he was trained at the Moravian boys' school and later received religious education and further training as a watchmaker in Herrnhut, Germany. From 1770 to 1781 he served as a missionary in Egypt and from 1783 until his death was the business manager of the Moravian community in Fullneck, England. Although music was his avocation, Antes was a fine composer and musician. Among his compositions are a number of anthems, several string trios, and over fifty hymn tunes.

MONKLAND received its present shape at the hands of John Lees in another Moravian hymnal, *Hymn Tunes of the United Brethren* (1824). From there John Wilkes (b. England, date unknown; d. England, 1882) simplified it and introduced it to Henry W. Baker (PHH 342), who published it in the the English *Hymns Ancient and Modern*

(1861) to his own harvest-theme text, "Praise, O Praise Our God and King." Wilkes named the tune after the village where he was organist and Baker was vicar—Monkland—located near Leominster in Herefordshire, England. Wilkes died around 1882; he should not be confused with the better-known John Bernard Wilkes (1785-1869).

MONKLAND's well-designed melodic contour is a good match for the text. Sing the tune in parts, except on the refrain line, which is appropriately sung in unison.

Liturgical Use
During the service of confession and forgiveness; worship services focusing on justification.

224

The Fruit of the Spirit

ROBERT
♩ = 84

Text
Based on the well-known listing of the fruit of the Spirit in Galatians 5:22-23, this song is almost entirely a direct quotation from Scripture. The first three lines come directly from the New International Version, and the fourth serves as a summary of the Scripture passage. The text of this short Scripture song was prepared by Dale Grotenhuis (PHH 4), the composer of the tune. (Other passages listing spiritual fruits are 2 Cor. 6:6; Eph. 4:2; 5:9; Col. 3:12-15.)

Scripture References
st. = Gal. 5:22-23

Tune
Dale Grotenhuis composed ROBERT in 1985 as a setting for this text in the *Psalter Hymnal*. The tune is named after Grotenhuis's second son. A simple but effective chorus, it should not be rushed.

Liturgical Use
Pentecost; weddings; any worship service that stresses Christian character and lifestyle. The song can function on its own as a chorus or response, or it can be used as a frame around another song (for example, 222).

225

Give Thanks to God, the Father

DU MEINE SEELE SINGE
♩ = 58

Text

The Scottish Jesuit priest James Quinn (PHH 220) wrote this paraphrase of Ephesians 1:3-14 "sometime before 1978." In the original Greek this Scripture passage is an extended doxology in one very long sentence. Quinn set the doxology in five stanzas of praise to God for blessings the Father has given us in Christ the Son through the Holy Spirit. The text is filled with profound theological confessions about each member of the Trinity. Like much of Quinn's work, the song text is unrhymed in order to preserve many well-known biblical phrases. The text was first published in *Resource Collection of Hymns and Service Music for the Liturgy* (1981).

Scripture References
st. 1 = Eph. 1:3-4
st. 2 = Eph. 1:5-7a
st. 3 = Eph. 1:7b-10
st. 4 = Eph. 1:11-13a
st. 5 = Eph. 1:13b-14

Tune

Johann G. Ebeling (b. Lüneburg, Germany, 1637; d. Stettin, Pomerania, Germany, 1676) originally composed DU MEINE SEELE SINGE for the text "Merkt auf, merkt Himmel, Erde" by Paul Gerhardt (PHH 331). A promising student of both music and theology, Ebeling succeeded the famous Johann Crüger (PHH 42) as cantor at St. Nicholas Church in Berlin at the age of twenty-five. In 1667 he moved to Stettin, where he taught music as well as Greek and poetry in the Caroline Gymnasium (high school). Providing most of the lively melodies and all the harmonizations, Ebeling published two collections of the hymn texts of Paul Gerhardt: *Pauli Gerhardi geistliche Andachten* (1667) and *Evangelischer Lustgarten Herrn Pauli Gerhardts* (1669).

This tune was published in the 1667 collection for another Gerhardt text, "Du meine Seele, singe," based on Psalm 146, and from that text the tune got its name. A majestic German chorale in bar form (AABC), DU MEINE SEELE SINGE has an attractive "rocket" motif in the first two lines and a solid climax in the final line. It is well suited to part singing, and antiphonal performance may help the singing of the entire text. Jacobus J. Kloppers (PHH 87) initially wrote the 1987 harmonization for use by The King's College Choir, Edmonton, Alberta, and subsequently included it in a hymn concertato.

Liturgical Use

As a doxology, also suitable as a hymn of praise at the beginning of worship, especially when focusing on the Trinity.

O Father, from Your Glorious Riches

Text

Ephesians 3:14-21 is a prayer uttered by the apostle Paul for the
Ephesian church; its two key words are *power* and *love*. Christ
possesses the power and love Paul talks about, but these can also
be ours if Christ's Spirit dwells in us. Paul concludes his prayer
with words of confidence and a doxology. Trudy Vander Veen
(nee Van Der Hyde; b. Long Island, NY, 1929) paraphrased this

Scripture References
st. 1 = Eph. 3:16-17
st. 2 = Eph. 3:18-19
st. 3 = Eph. 3:20
st. 4 = Eph. 3:21

text in 1984 (originally using first-person pronouns with the title "My Prayer") after
teaching a Bible class for one season on Paul's letter to the Ephesians.

Vander Veen is a member of the Third Christian Reformed Church, Denver,
Colorado, where she has been a leader in a neighborhood Bible studies and a church
school teacher in a local Cambodian church. For many years she was a secretary at the
Bethesda Pastoral Counseling Center in Denver. Vander Veen wrote the lyrics for a
musical based on the book of Ruth and has published a number of articles in periodicals such as *Discipleship*.

Tune

Roy Hopp (PHH 11) initially composed the tune for Daniel Meeter's versification of
the Ten Commandments, "The LORD Is God, There Is No Other," published in *Rejoice
in the Lord* (1985). He named the tune DENVER after he learned it was being considered
for publication in the *Psalter Hymnal* as a setting for Vander Veen's text. He had been
living in Denver, Colorado, when he composed the tune, and he knew Vander Veen,
who lived next door to his parents-in-law there. Hopp's distinctive cadences carry the
energy from one line of DENVER to the next. Keep the organ registration bright on this
unison tune but not necessarily loud, except at the doxological end of stanza 4.

Liturgical Use

This sung prayer is best used as part of communal prayers or as a dismissal prayer,
ending as it does with a doxology.

227

Christer, Who Is in the Form of God

BISHOP
♩ = 56

Text

Several songs have been composed on the poetic passage from Philippians 2:6-11; in addition to this setting of the biblical text, a hymn is at 467: "At the Name of Jesus," and a chorus setting is at 633: "He Is Lord." Some commentators suggest that Paul is quoting here from an early Christian hymn. A marvelous profession of faith, this creedal statement lays out the Christian beliefs about the Savior's humiliation and exaltation: though fully God, Christ "emptied himself" to become human and to take up our death, and therefore God exalted him so that everyone will "confess that Jesus Christ is Lord." The context makes clear that Christ's attitude is to be our model for Christian living.

Scripture References
st. 1 = Phil. 2:6-7
st. 2 = Phil. 2:8
st. 3 = Phil. 2:9
st. 4 = Phil. 2:10-11

David T. Koyzis (b. Oak Park, IL, 1955) paraphrased this Scripture passage in 1984 in South Bend, Indiana. The text is first published in the 1987 *Psalter Hymnal*. Koyzis's interest in poetry, hymnody, and psalmody was nurtured at an early age. His father wrote poems in both Greek and English, many of which were published in English- and Greek-language periodicals on the island of Cyprus, his place of birth. Koyzis has written a number of hymn texts and tunes as well as Scripture versifications, some of which are published in *Songs of Rejoicing* (1989). He studied at Bethel College, St. Paul, Minnesota, and the Institute for Christian Studies, Toronto, Canada; in 1986 he received a Ph.D. degree from Notre Dame University. Since 1987 he has taught political science at Redeemer College, Ancaster, Ontario, Canada.

Tune

Little is known about the composer of BISHOP, Joseph P. Holbrook (b. near Boston, MA, 1822; d. U.S.A., 1888); he did serve as editor of several hymn collections, including *Songs of the Church* (1862) and *Hymnal of the Methodist Episcopal Church with Tunes* (1878), to which he contributed a number of his own tunes.

Holbrook's tune BISHOP was first published in Duryea's *The Presbyterian Hymnal* (1874). No specific bishop has been identified in relation to the tune title. It is a serviceable tune with some dramatic flair in the second phrase that matches the text particularly well. Lines 1 and 3 are identical. BISHOP has the character of early Puritan psalm tunes; the humility of this melody helps one focus on the song text. It is ideally sung in harmony and in its entirety: all the stanzas belong together, and stanza 3 continues into stanza 4. Though the music consists of four lines, the textual units usually cover two; try to sing in two long lines, feeling two beats per bar, so that the textual lines prevail.

Liturgical Use

Christmas; Lent; Ascension; also as a sung confession of faith (an alternate to the Apostles' or Nicene Creed); "Worthy Is Christ" (629) provides a suitable frame for this song.

228

REJOICE
$\mathbf{J} = 84$

Rejoice in the Lord Always

Text

"Rejoice in the Lord Always" is almost a direct quotation of Philippians 4:4 (see also Phil. 3:1). The apostle Paul's encouragement to rejoice always, regardless of our circumstances, is an exhortation we sing cheerfully to each other in this song, often in the form of a round. The textual adaptation and the original tune are anonymous, products of the oral tradition associated with Scripture songs. The same oral tradition has produced minor variants on the tune, just one of which is included in the *Psalter Hymnal;* some congregations may know different versions of the tune. The text has been published in many of the early booklets and leaflets of the Scripture-chorus movement and appears now in a number of hymnals.

Scripture References
st. = Phil. 4:4

Tune

Sing REJOICE as written with the keyboard accompaniment composed by Dale Grotenhuis (PHH 4) in 1985. Or to increase the joy, divide the congregation into two or four sections, and sing as a four-part round with enthusiasm and vigor, with or without accompaniment, possibly using guitar and Orff xylophones.

Liturgical Use

As an acclamation; as an exhortation to be joyful; in medley with other hymns (for example, 569); many other occasions in Christian worship.

229

ARIRANG
$\mathbf{J} = 80$

Christ, You Are the Fullness

Text

"Christ, You Are the Fullness" is an unrhymed paraphrase of three essential passages in Paul's letter to the Colossians: 1:15-18, about the supremacy of Christ (st. 1); 3:1-4, about our position in Christ (st. 2); and 3:15-17, about thankful (doxological) living (st. 3). Bert Polman (PHH 37) versified these Scriptures in 1986 to be

Scripture References
st. 1 = Col. 1:15-18
st. 2 = Col. 3:1-4
st. 3 = Col. 3:15-17

sung with the Korean tune ARIRANG so that the hymnal would include at least one Korean tune. A Korean musician recommended this tune as one that all Koreans would know.

Tune

The tune ARIRANG is named after a Korean folk song that has long been a favorite in Korea and became known by many American soldiers during the Korean War (1950-1953). The song was probably composed around 1865, when laborers were conscripted from all over Korea to rebuild the Kyonbok Palace in Seoul. These workers brought their regional folk songs with them; this one presumably came from the legendary Arirang mountains, which in Korean culture symbolize the sometimes bitter separation of loved ones. Arirang is a lament with romantic connotations; the original text can be translated:

> As the stars, my tears are countless
> as they ceaselessly flow!
> You, so faithless, are leaving me alone and pale.
> May your feet pain you at the end of the trail!

ARIRANG is a fascinating tune featuring repeats of complete phrases and small motifs. Polman changed one of the original cadence patterns to make four clear phrases for this song, which is intended for unison singing. The 1986 keyboard harmonization by Dale Grotenhuis (PHH 4) features a drone (held note) in the bass, a device common in much Asian music. Because of the irregular number of syllables in each stanza, have a soloist or choir introduce it to the congregation.

Liturgical Use

Suitable in any parts or occasions of Christian worship focusing on Christ's kingship or kingdom, God's glory, the church, peace and purity, or doxological praise.

230

Since Our Great High Priest, Christ Jesus

ALL SAINTS
$\downarrow = 50$

Text

Based on several texts in the letter to the Hebrews—1:3-4, 4:14-16, and 12:2—this song incorporates parts of the book's lengthy discussion about Jesus Christ as our High Priest and about his absolute supremacy and sufficiency as the Mediator of God's grace. Because we have such a Priest/Mediator, who identifies with our weaknesses but is without sin, we can confidently approach God's throne of grace and find help for our

Scripture References
st. 1 = Heb. 4:14; 1:4
st. 2 = Heb. 4:15-16
st. 3 = Heb. 1:3-4; 12:2; 4:15
st. 4 = Heb. 12:2; 4:15

needs. Christopher M. Idle (PHH 20) wrote this song in London in 1971; it was first published in the British collection *Psalm Praise* (1973) as an Ascension canticle.

Tune

Unfortunately, the name ALL SAINTS was given to this tune in the *Psalter Hymnal*, a confusing name since it has been assigned historically to several tunes, including this one. The first three phrases of this bright German chorale tune can be traced to an anonymous melody in a Catholic hymnal (Bamberg, 1732). The Catholic hymnal *Tochter Sion* (Cologne, 1741) set the text "Lasst die weissen Flaggen wehen" to another variant of this tune. That is the variant found in the *Psalter Hymnal*. Other contemporary hymnals, for example *Rejoice in the Lord* (1985), name this version WEISSE FLAGGEN. William H. Monk (PHH 332) did yet another adaptation for *Hymns Ancient and Modern* (1861); that version, named ALL SAINTS, however, is not the one in the *Psalter Hymnal*. ALL SAINTS—or WEISSE FLAGGEN—is a stately tune with a demanding harmony that a congregation or choir may want to sing in parts. A setting of this tune in B-flat is at 277.

Liturgical Use

Ascension Day; whenever the church focuses on Christ's role as High Priest and ascended Lord.

231

ANNO DOMINI
♩ = 92

How Great Is the Love of the Father

Text

In his first letter to early Christian believers, the apostle John writes an exposition on righteousness and love as essential requirements for Christian living. In the midst of this exposition we find 1 John 3:1-3, a declaration of awe and praise for God's wondrous grace in making us his children. Based on this passage, "How Great Is the Love of the Father" describes how we become children of God (st. 1); how we should live as children of God (st. 2); and what we shall become in glory as children of God (st. 3).

Scripture References
st. 1 = 1 John 3:1
st. 2 = 1 John 3:1, 3
st. 3 = 1 John 3:2

Edna W. Sikkema (b. Grijpskerk, Groningen, the Netherlands, 1931; d. Grand Rapids, MI, 1994) prepared this versification specifically for the tune ANNO DOMINI in 1986 for the *Psalter Hymnal*. After working as a registered nurse, Sikkema graduated from Calvin College, Grand Rapids. She received her M.A. in 1965 from Ohio State University, and completed additional studies in Germany and the Netherlands. On the faculty of Hartwick College, Oneonta, New York, and later Trinity Christian College, Palos Heights, Illinois, Sikkema taught German, Dutch, and linguistics. After 1975 she returned to a career in health care and in real estate.

Tune

James C. Ward (PHH 56) originally composed ANNO DOMINI (1985) for the *Psalter Hymnal* versification of Psalm 11, but the *Psalter Hymnal* Revision Committee chose instead to use the tune as a setting for the versification of 1 John 3:1-3—the childlike simplicity of this tender tune is just right for this text. Ward, a professional composer and performer, named the tune after his booking agency in Grand Rapids, which takes its name from the Latin phrase meaning "in the year of the Lord." On Ward's recording *Blue Believer*, he sang the final three words of this song an octave higher than written, providing a joyful ending. Sing ANNO DOMINI in unison, and use other instruments for accompaniment: handbells, Orff xylophones, guitar, and piano.

Liturgical Use

For baptism, as a funeral hymn, and for many points in the order of worship.

232

You Are Worthy

WORTHY
♩ = 120

Text

Based on Revelation 4:11, "You Are Worthy" is a setting of one of several doxologies recorded in God's revelation to the apostle John on the island of Patmos. This doxology is sung by the twenty-four elders gathered around God's throne. Usually taken to be representatives of all of God's people, these elders lay their crowns before the throne as a sign of their submission to God's rule and then burst into song, praising God for his creative acts. A similar "You are worthy . . ." occurs in Revelation 5 (233, st. 2)—a doxology praising the Lamb's redemptive acts.

Scripture References
st. = Rev. 4:11

Pauline Michael Mills (b. Portland, IN, 1898) drew the versification almost verbatim from the King James Version in 1963. She reported that she composed the tune "on the spot" at a church meeting "somewhere in Oregon." The song was published in the chorus book *Asaph Praise* (1964), and the language was cast into more modern English in *Hymns for Today's Church* (1982), along with minor adjustments in the music. These revisions were adopted for publication in the *Psalter Hymnal*.

A graduate of the L.I.F.E. Bible School, Mills became an ordained minister in the Foursquare International Church. She served as a music director and exhorter in various churches and traveled widely, ministering to women's groups. Mills has written over three hundred Scripture songs and love songs, some of which were published in *Asaph Psalter* (1970).

Tune

WORTHY is a simple chorus that is best sung unaccompanied and in harmony. Performance tempos on this song vary immensely, but bear in mind that it must not be rushed. Keep one pulse per measure. The song must convey a sense of dignity, awe, and majesty. It is common in the tradition of Scripture singing to repeat such a chorus. It is also common to add more stanzas. Here is one example:

You are worthy, you are worthy,
you are worthy, O Lord!
You are worthy to receive glory,
glory and honor and power:
for you have redeemed us,
from all tribes and nations,
for you purchased us with your blood,
to be your servants, ruling creation;
you are worthy, O Lord!

—Revelation 4:11a; 5:9-10; vers. Bert Polman, 1987

Liturgical Use

As a doxology or acclamation; as a frame around another song (for example, the Te Deum, 504).

233

BETHANY
♩ = 56

Heavenly Hosts in Ceaseless Worship

Text

This versification of Revelation 4:8-11 and 5:9-13 incorporates phrases from the five doxologies recorded in Revelation 4-5: the four living creatures sing, "Holy, holy, holy . . ." (4:8); the twenty-four elders sing, "You are worthy . . ." (4:11; see also 232); the four

Scripture References
st. 1 = Rev. 4:8-11
st. 2 = Rev. 5:9-13

living creatures and the twenty-four elders together sing a new song: "You are worthy . . ." (5:9-10); a multitude of angels sing, "Worthy is the Lamb . . ." (5:12); and all creatures in heaven and on earth sing, "To him who sits on the throne . . ." (5:13). This is an awesome vision in which ever-greater numbers of creatures gather to sing praise to God and to the Lamb. Our singing could follow the same plan by gradually adding voices and instruments every two lines, until reaching a glorious conclusion to this powerful doxology. A three-stanza version could begin with a few singers on stanza 2, then more singers on stanza 1, this time in harmony.

Timothy Dudley-Smith (b. Manchester, England, 1926) versified this passage in 1972; it was first published in the British collection *Psalm Praise* (1973). Educated at Pembroke College and Ridley Hall, Cambridge, Dudley-Smith has served the Church of England since his ordination in 1950. He has occupied a number of church positions, including parish priest in the diocese of Southwark (1953-1962), archdeacon of Norwich (1973-1981), and bishop of Thetford, Norfolk, from 1981 until his retirement in 1992. He also edited a Christian magazine, *Crusade,* which was founded after Billy Graham's 1955 London crusade. Dudley-Smith began writing comic verse while a student at Cambridge; he did not begin to write hymns until the 1960s. Many of his several hundred hymn texts have been collected in *Lift Every Heart: Collected Hymns 1961-1983* (1984), *Songs of Deliverance: Thirty-six New Hymns* (1988), and *A Voice of Singing* (1993). The writer of *Christian Literature and the Church* (1963), *Someone Who Beckons* (1978), and *Praying with the English Hymn Writers* (1989), Dudley-Smith has also served on various editorial committees, including the committee that published *Psalm Praise* (1973).

Tune

BETHANY, named after the village near Jerusalem, is a suitably dramatic tune for the song text. It was composed by Henry Smart (b. Marylebone, London, England, 1813; d. Hampstead, London, 1879), a capable composer of church music who wrote some very fine hymn tunes (REGENT SQUARE, 354, is the best-known). He originally composed BETHANY for the text "Jesus, I My Cross Have Taken"; it was first published in *Psalms and Hymns for Divine Worship* (1867). Though Smart favored unison singing, which works well, especially with all the stops pulled out and the tempo increased on stanza 2, the harmonization is quite accessible to part singing. (*Note:* this BETHANY should not be confused with one composed by Lowell Mason in 1856 and first published as a setting for "Nearer, My God, to Thee.")

Smart gave up a career in the legal profession for one in music. Although largely self-taught, he became proficient in organ playing and composition, and he was a music teacher and critic. Organist in a number of London churches, including St. Luke's, Old Street (1844-1864), and St. Pancras (1864-1869), Smart was famous for his extemporizations and for his accompaniment of congregational singing. He became completely blind at the age of fifty-two, but his remarkable memory enabled him to continue playing the organ. Fascinated by organs as a youth, Smart designed organs for important places such as St. Andrew Hall in Glasgow and the Town Hall in Leeds. He composed an opera, oratorios, part-songs, some instrumental music, and many hymn tunes, as well as a large number of works for organ and choir. He edited the *Choralebook* (1858), the English Presbyterian *Psalms and Hymns for Divine Worship* (1867), and the Scottish *Presbyterian Hymnal* (1875). Some of his hymn tunes were first published in *Hymns Ancient and Modern* (1861).

Liturgical Use

As a song of praise and worship at the beginning of the service, or (more likely) as a doxology at the end—great for worship services focusing on Christ's second coming.

234

ALABARE

♩ = 108

Alleluia
Alabaré

Text

This joyful bilingual song versifies Revelation 5:11-14, focusing on the last two of the five doxologies in Revelation 4-5 praising God and the Lamb "who was slain" (see 233 for more information on this passage). This folk-like song possibly originated in Puerto Rico; it was first published in *Favoritos Juveniles*

Scripture References
st. 1 = Rev. 5:11
st. 2 = Rev. 5:11-12
st. 3 = Rev. 5:13-14

(Singspiration, 1968) and in *Canciones Carismáticas* (Ediciones Musical PAX, 1979). A revised version of this song was published in *Celebremos II* (1983). The Spanish text is by Manuel José Alonso, about whom no information is available. The English versification of the same biblical text was prepared by Bert Polman (PHH 37) in 1986 for the *Psalter Hymnal.*

Tune

José Pagán-López (b. Fortuna, Murcia, Spain, 1916) composed ALABARE in the style of a folk song; the short phrases, the singing in parallel thirds, and the rhythmic style are clearly Hispanic in flavor. Make use of the little echo phrases in the refrain. The accompaniment is for piano or guitar; hand clapping or other light percussion (tambourine) may be added on the refrain. Sing ALABARE at a joyful tempo, perhaps with solo or group on the fast-moving text of the stanzas, but with all on the refrain. English-speaking congregations can easily learn to sing (at least) the refrain in Spanish; "Alabaré" fits the melodic rhythm much better than "Alleluia." (*Note:* Be sure to warn unfamiliar singers that this song covers three pages in the *Psalter Hymnal.*)

Pagán-López was professor of harmony at the Higher Royal Conservatory of Music of Madrid for eighteen years and cofounder of the Association for the Promotion of Religious Music, for which he served as national secretary and later, treasurer. He has composed music for the cinema and documentaries for television, directed several recording projects, and published a variety of compositions.

Liturgical Use

As a narrative-based song in conjunction with preaching on Revelation 4-5 (or Rev. 21-22); also as a doxology on various praise occasions. Hispanic choruses such as this one are often combined in medley; "Alabaré" is often linked with 517 and 629.

235

Here from All Nations

O QUANTA QUALIA
♩ = 60

Text

In Revelation 7:9-17 the apostle John records his vision of a great multitude of God's children "from every nation, tribe, people, and language" standing before the Lamb and singing doxologies. The text is a most comforting description of the end of human troubles: no more thirst or hunger, no more griefs or trials. Now the people live by streams of living water under the care of their Shepherd—the complete fulfillment of Psalm 23!

Scripture References
st. 1 = Rev. 7:9-10
st. 2 = Rev. 7:14-15a
st. 3 = Rev. 7:15b-17a
st. 4 = Rev. 7:17
st. 5 = Rev. 7:12

Christopher M. Idle (PHH 20) effectively captures this awe-inspiring vision in his paraphrase "Here from All Nations," written in London in 1972 and first published with O QUANTA QUALIA in the British collection *Psalm Praise* (1973).

Tune

O QUANTA QUALIA is a chant tune from the Paris *Antiphoner* of 1681 and represents the "new" breed of French Roman Catholic diocesan tunes of the seventeenth and eighteenth centuries. The tune is often associated with Peter Abelard's twelfth-century hymn "O What Their Joy and Their Glory Must Be," which also has a new-heaven-and-earth focus. The tune name comes from the original Latin incipit of Abelard's text: "O quanta qualia. . . . " Antiphonal singing may be desirable, as is singing in harmony, but the final stanza should be sung in unison and at a majestic pace as a finale/doxology—preferably with other instruments to enhance the festivity.

Liturgical Use

In worship focusing on the worldwide nature of the church; as words of encouragement and comfort for those in the midst of troubles and/or martyrdom; as an exultant doxology; Advent; times when the church focuses on Christ's return and the new heaven and new earth; All Saints' Day; Reformation Day.

NEW HEAVEN
♩ = 104

Then I Saw a New Heaven and Earth

Text

In Revelation 21-22 we read about John's vision of the new heaven and new earth, of the new Jerusalem, and of the river of life where trees grow leaves "for the healing of the nations." This vision brings together features of Jerusalem and the Garden of Eden—both recreated! In pictorial language John describes the awe-inspiring cosmic renewal at the end of time.

Scripture References
st. 1 = Rev. 21:1-3
st. 2 = Rev. 21:4-6a
st. 3 = Rev. 21:6b-14, 18-21
st. 4 = Rev. 21:15-17, 22-23
st. 5 = Rev. 22:1-5

Christopher M. Idle (PHH 20) versified this passage in London in 1972; his paraphrase was first published in the British collection *Psalm Praise* (1973) with the tune NEW HEAVEN by Norman L. Warren (PHH 15). It quickly came across the Atlantic and was published in *Hymns for the Living Church* (1974). The editor of that hymnal, Donald Hustad, had come across the song in the pews of All Souls' Church, London, England, late in 1972 while practicing for his Royal College of Organists exams. Since that time it has appeared in various other hymnals.

Tune

NEW HEAVEN has a folk-like charm; in some ways the first part reminds one of Appalachian tunes. It is one of the few tunes in the *Psalter Hymnal* that begins in minor and changes to major (another is ST. ANDREW OF CRETE, 575). Idle's text generally warrants this change. Warren wrote that "these marvelous words from Revelation 21 set metrically by Christopher Idle came to me early one Saturday in 1969 as I was just setting off with my children for their weekly swimming lesson. I wrote the tune in about ten minutes in the gallery of the Baths. The first four phrases have a mystery about them and I set the tune in D minor [actually, in the Dorian mode]. The last four lines move into a great sense of joy, so the tune moves to a major key and to a joyful and secure melody. The last three notes invert the opening phrase to add completeness."

The structure of NEW HEAVEN invites unison responsorial singing. A solo or small group could do the minor sections, and a larger group the major sections, with everyone singing stanza 5. Or try the following arrangement: stanza 1—soloist (or small group); stanza 2a—everyone; stanza 2b—soloist (or small group); stanza 3—everyone; stanza 4a—soloist (or small group); stanza 4b—everyone; stanza 5a—soloist (or small group); stanza 5b—everyone. Complement this arrangement with the necessary changes in organ accompaniment, or in volume when using other instruments.

Liturgical Use

In worship focusing on the worldwide nature of the church; as words of encouragement and comfort for those in the midst of troubles and/or martyrdom; as an exultant doxology; Advent or other times when the church focuses on Christ's return and the new heaven and new earth; All Saints' Day; Reformation Day.

HYMNS

237

We Praise You, O God

KREMSER
♩ = 112

Text

This hymn of praise combines present and past to give hope for the future: we humbly and thankfully sing God's praise (st. 1), we praise God for his protection throughout our lives (st. 2), and we go forward under God's guiding hand (st. 3).

Scripture References
st. 2 = Deut. 31:6
(Heb. 13:5)
Ps. 48:14

The text was written at the request of J. Archer Gibson, organist at Brick Presbyterian Church in New York City. Gibson asked Julia Buckley Cady Cory (b. New York, NY, 1882; d. Englewood, NJ, 1963) to write a text to the tune KREMSER to replace the older text associated with that tune, "We Gather Together." The new hymn was first sung at Thanksgiving Day services in 1902 at the Brick Presbyterian Church and Church of the Covenant, both in New York City. It was first published in *Hymns of the Living Church* (1910) and has been the first hymn in every edition of the *Psalter Hymnal.*

Cory was the daughter of a prominent New York architect, J. Cleveland Cady. Her father was also a Sunday school superintendent and amateur hymnologist. Partly because of his influence Julia began to write hymns at an early age. She was a member of the Brick Presbyterian Church; after moving to Englewood, New Jersey, she joined the First Presbyterian Church. She married Robert Haskell Cory in 1911.

Tune

The tune KREMSER owes its origin to a sixteenth-century Dutch folk song "Ey, wilder den wilt." Later the tune was combined with the Dutch patriotic hymn "Wilt heden nu treden" in Adrianus Valerius's *Nederlandtsch Gedenckclanck,* published posthumously in 1626. "Wilt heden nu treden," which celebrated Dutch freedom from Spanish rule, was always popular in the Netherlands, but gained international popularity through an arrangement by Eduard Kremser in his *Sechs Altniederlandische Volkslieder* (1877) for men's voices. This collection of six songs in German translation from Valerius's anthology was the source of the older English text, "We Gather Together." Keep a firm but stately tempo with strong, solid organ registration.

Liturgical Use

Heritage festivals and harvest thanksgiving; beginning of worship; doxology during the offering of gifts.

EASTVIEW
♩ = 60

We Come, O Christ, to You

Text

Full of biblical phrases from the New Testament, "We Come, O Christ, to You" is a hymn of praise to Christ, who is the source of our life (st. 1), the Way (st. 2), the Truth (st. 3), the Life (st. 4), and the one we worship as Savior and King (st. 5).

Scripture References
st.1 = Acts 17:28
Col. 1:16
st. 2-4 = John 14:6
st. 4 = John 10:10

E. Margaret Clarkson (b. Melville, Saskatchewan, Canada, 1915) wrote the text during the summer and fall of 1946 at the request of Stacey Woods, general director of InterVarsity Christian Fellowship (IVCF) in Canada and the United States, who wanted a theme hymn for the scattered student groups of the still-young IVCF organization. The song was first sung at IVCF's first Missionary Convention (December 1946, Toronto; precursor of the IVCF Urbana conferences) and first published in IVCF's *Hymns* (2nd printing, 1947).

"We Come, O Christ" is undoubtedly the best known of Clarkson's hymns; it appears in many modern hymnals and has been translated into other languages. Clarkson herself revised the text to the modern second-person singular ("you") in 1984.

In 1919 Margaret Clarkson moved to Toronto, where she has lived for much of her life. Educated at Toronto Teachers' College, she taught elementary school in Barwick, Ontario (1935-37), and was supervisor of public school music in Kirkland Lake, Ontario (1937-42). From 1942 to 1973 she taught in various elementary schools in Toronto. Clarkson has published seventeen books, including *The Creative Classroom* (1958), *Rivers Among the Rocks* (1967), *Destined for Glory: the Meaning of Suffering* (1983), and *All Nature Sings* (1986). Her hymns were published in *A Singing Heart: The Collected Hymns of Margaret Clarkson* (1987). She has been a strong supporter of IVCF and wrote a number of the theme hymns for their Urbana Mission Conferences. In 1993 Clarkson was honored as a Fellow of the Hymn Society in the United States and Canada.

Tune

James Vernon Lee (b. Hove, Sussex, England, 1892; d. Southampton, England, 1959) originally composed EASTVIEW for the text "Rejoice, the Lord Is King" for his mother's eightieth birthday. Lee was an officer in the Brighton Battalion of the Boys' Brigade from 1910 to 1914. After service in the British armed forces during World War I he was the bursar at Caterham College (1919 1939). He also worked as a professional magician, earning the Gold Star of the Magic Circle in 1940. Lee served as organist in several churches and composed a number of hymn tunes as well as Masonic graces.

The British hymnal *Congregational Praise* first published EASTVIEW in 1951. Sing it in three long phrases, and use solid organ accompaniment.

Liturgical Use

Beginning of worship; after assurance of pardon; before proclamation of the Word; also as a wedding processional.

239

Amid the Thronging Worshipers

BOVINA
$\rfloor = 56$

Text

"Amid the Thronging Worshipers" is a versification from the concluding part of Psalm 22, that great psalm of lament most quoted in the New Testament. The conclusion of Psalm 22 features vows of strong praise made in the sure faith that God will deliver the believer and answer prayer. Like many psalms, this text is cosmic in scope, moving from the singular "I" (st. 1) to "his people" and "saints" (st. 1-2) to "all the earth" (st. 3). The versification is from the 1912 *Psalter.* See PHH 22 for further commentary on Psalm 22.

Scripture References
st. 1 = Ps. 22:22-23
st. 2 = Ps. 22:24-25
st. 3 = Ps. 22:26-28

Tune

Laura A. Tate composed the tune BOVINA, which was first published with this text in the 1912 *Psalter* published by the United Presbyterian Church (UPC). No information is known about her, but since her tune was copyrighted by the UPC in 1904 she may have been associated with that denomination. Sing in four broad phrases, perhaps in harmony.

Liturgical Use

Beginning of worship; praise occasions.

240

Come, All Who Fear the Lord God

TOURS
$\rfloor = 101$

Text

Like 239, this text is based on the concluding portion of Psalm 22. This versification stresses the communal aspect of praise and worship and highlights the righteousness that is part of the Lord's sovereign rule. The New Testament interpretation includes direct references to Christ and to the church, whose mission is to spread the praise of the Lord. The versification originally began "Come, ye

Scripture References
st. 1 = Ps. 22:23-26
st. 2 = Ps. 22:27-28
st. 3 = Ps. 22:29-31

that fear Jehovah" and was first published in the 1912 *Psalter.* See PHH 22 and 239 for other comments on Psalm 22.

Tune

The tune was named after its composer and published in the British volume *The Hymnary* (1872). TOURS has four broad phrases. Its repetitions of melodic and rhythmic units make it accessible and loved. The harmony suggests a stately tempo.

Berthold Tours (b. Rotterdam, the Netherlands, 1838; d. Fulham, London, England, 1897) received an early musical education from his father, a well-known Dutch organist of the St. Laurents Kerk, Rotterdam, and continued his training in conservatories in Leipzig and Brussels. He also spent two years studying in Russia. Given the opportunity to teach violin in London and to play in several orchestras, he moved to London in 1861 and settled there permanently. In 1862 Tours became organist of the Swiss Church (Holborne) in London. From 1878 on he served as an editor and arranger for Novello, the well-known music publisher. Tours wrote piano arrangements of operas and oratorios but is best remembered for his hymn tunes, anthems, and liturgical service music.

Liturgical Use

Beginning of worship; praise occasions.

241

This Is the Day

Text

With its first stanza based on Psalm 118:24, "This Is the Day" celebrates God's mighty acts of redemption (originally referring to the Passover before the Exodus), hailing "the day" as a special day of the Lord. Stanzas 2 and 3 refer to other special celebrations of God's acts—Easter and Pentecost—leading to the implication of Sunday as a special day for worship. Other popular versions of this hymn use "I will rejoice," even though the biblical text is clearly in the plural "we."

Scripture References
st. 1 = Ps. 118:24
st. 2 = Matt. 28:1-7
st. 3 = Acts 2:1-4
Rev. 1:10

Stanza 1, paraphrased by Leslie Norman Garrett (b. Matamata, North Island, New Zealand, 1943), was first published in his collection *Scripture in Song* (vol. 1, 1967). Les Garrett became a pastor after graduating from the Word of Faith Bible School. Currently he ministers at the Christian Family Center in Maddington (Perth), Australia. He is also a lecturer at Hebron Bible College and has traveled throughout the world speaking at conventions and churches. Garrett promotes the singing of Scripture choruses in books such as *Scripture in Song*.

The anonymous second and third stanzas grew out of the oral tradition surrounding Scripture-chorus singing. In the continuing spirit of oral tradition, many groups have written other stanzas, such as

> These are our friends,
> that the Lord has made;
> we will rejoice
> and be glad with them.

Tune

THIS IS THE DAY is presumably a folk tune from Fiji, arranged by Les Garrett for use with stanza 1. Antiphonal performance between two parts of the congregation works well. Rather than give verbal instructions, a song leader can direct simply by signaling to each group when they are to sing. For example, for stanza 1,

(group 1)
This is the day,
that the Lord has made,
we will rejoice,
and be glad in it,

(group 2)
this is the day
that the Lord has made;
we will rejoice
and be glad in it.

(both)
This is the day that the Lord has made,
we will rejoice and be glad in it;

(1)
this is the day,

(2)
this is the day

(both)
that the Lord has made.

When a song leader sings the first part as a solo, the congregation can follow from memory, without having to open songbooks. Use a light organ registration or preferably folk instruments such as guitar and/or tambourine. The syncopations give the tune rhythmic interest and unity. Take care not to rush the tempo.

Liturgical Use
Praise occasions.

242

ADOWA
♩ = 60

Come, All You People, Praise Our God

Text

Though this versification is based on Psalm 66:8-20, it doesn't
incorporate the strong literary images of the biblical text (66).
Still, "Come, All You People" does pick up significant themes
common to praise psalms: praise to God for deliverance (st. 1),
fulfillment of vows and dedication to God's service (st. 2), and
public testimony to God's salvation and care (st. 3). Stanzas 1 and 2 use the plural case,
calling all people to communal and consecrated worship of God, and stanza 3 uses the
singular, relating the psalmist's personal experience with God for the benefit of "all
who fear the Lord."

Scripture References
st. 1 = Ps. 66:8-12
st. 2 = Ps. 66:13-15
st. 3 = Ps. 66:16-20

The versification (altered) is from the 1912 *Psalter* and originally began with the words
"Come, all ye people, bless our God." See PHH 66 for other comments on Psalm 66.

Tune

ADOWA was composed by Charles H. Gabriel (PHH 24), the noted gospel songwriter,
during the Billy Sunday-Homer Rodeheaver evangelistic crusades of the 1910s, and was
published with this text in the 1912 *Psalter.* Sing the tune in two very long phrases.

Liturgical Use

Beginning of worship; offering of gifts; times of turmoil; thanksgiving for deliverance.

243

ST. EDITH
♩ = 54

How Lovely Is Your Dwelling

Text

Taken from Psalm 84:1-7, "How Lovely Is Your Dwelling" is a
prayer of longing for God's house and for the blessing of serving
God there. Stanza 1 describes the beauty of God's house and the
soul's longing for the joy and comfort of that holy place. Stanza 2
highlights God's care of his people, combining the images of
sparrow and swallow from Psalm 84:3 with the image of God's sheltering wings found in
other psalms (36:7; 57:1; 61:4; 91:4). Stanza 3 extols the blessedness of being God's
people in Zion or the New Jerusalem.

Scripture References
st. 1 = Ps. 84:1-2
st. 2 = Ps. 84:3
st. 3 = Ps. 84:4-7

The versification is from the 1912 *Psalter;* the original first line read "O Lord of hosts,
how lovely." See PHH 84 for other comments on Psalm 84.

Tune

The original form of ST. EDITH (also known as ST. HILDA) was composed in 1793 by Justin Heinrich Knecht for the text "Der niedern Menschhiet Hülle." It was published in *Vollstandige Sammlung . . . Choralmelodien* (1799), edited by Johann Friedrich Christmann and Knecht, who composed ninety-seven of the tunes in the collection.

Knecht (b. Biberach, Germany, 1752; d. Biberach, 1817) mastered the flute, oboe, trumpet, violin, and organ. He taught literature in Biberach and became the town's music director in 1792, pioneering the use of program notes in his public concerts. After serving as director of the theater orchestra in Stuttgart (1807-1809), he returned to Biberach for the rest of his life. Knecht was a prolific composer of songs for the stage, church music for organ and choir, and instrumental pieces. He also wrote several theoretical works on music and method books for organ playing.

Edward Husband (b. Hampshire, England, 1843; d. Folkestone, Kent, England, 1908) exchanged two lines of the original tune with two lines of his own in 1871 to produce the current setting. Educated at St. Aidan's College, Birkenhead, Husband was ordained in the Church of England in 1867. He was a pastor in Atherton from 1866 to 1872, after which he served at St. Michael and All Angels' Church in Folkestone. In 1885 he compiled an *Appendix* of hymn tunes for the Folkestone church. An organ teacher as well as pastor, Husband edited *The Mission Hymnal* (1874) and *Supplemental Tunes to Popular Hymns* (1882).

The tune title refers to the tenth-century British virgin Edith of Wilton (near Salisbury, Wiltshire), who refused various important positions and instead served the poor. Sing this tune in four broad phrases with rhythmic precision.

Liturgical Use

Beginning of worship; expressions of longing for the New Jerusalem.

244

God Himself Is with Us

ARNSBERG
♩ = 63

Text

Gerhardt Tersteegen (b. Mörs, Prussia, Germany, 1697; d. Mühlheim, Germany, 1769) wrote this hymn ("Gott ist gegenwärtig") in eight stanzas after his conversion experience in 1724, designing it to fit this tune by Neander. The hymn was first published in Tersteegen's *Geistliches Blumengärtlein* (1729) with the heading "Remembrance of the glorious and delightful presence of God."

Scripture References
st. 1 = Gen. 28:16-17
Ps. 95:6
Hab. 2:20
st. 2 = Isa. 6:3
Rev. 4:8-11

Stanzas 1 and 2 summon worshipers to praise and adore God, and stanza 2 (with an allusion to Isa. 6) begins a prayer for sanctification that continues through stanza 3. Though judged inadequate when compared with Tersteegen's mystical original, the translation (with the current selection of stanzas) is a favorite in many hymnals. While many of Tersteegen's hymns may be more suitable for private meditation, this one is a fine vehicle for public praise to God.

Tersteegen was a renowned representative of the Christian tradition of mysticism in German Reformed hymnody. He received a gymnasium (high school) education, but after his father's death, family poverty kept him from university training. He became a merchant and then a weaver, producing silk ribbons. Reared in the Reformed church, Tersteegen was influenced by a Pietist group but experienced a spiritual depression until 1724, when he dedicated his life to God in a confession written in his own blood. After this he began to conduct prayer meetings. Attracted to mysticism, Tersteegen became an important spiritual leader to many, and from 1727 until late in his life, he ran a retreat center in Otterbeck, near Mühlheim. He preached in Prussia and the Netherlands and kept up an extensive correspondence. When it was necessary, Tersteegen was supported by his followers, and in turn he shared his goods and simple medicines with the poor, becoming known as the "physician of the poor and the forsaken." Because his ministry was outside the established church, he often experienced the displeasure of church and civic authorities. His writings include translations into German from Latin and French mystics, sermons and meditations, and over one hundred hymns published in *Geistliche Blumen-Gärtlein* (1729 and later editions).

The composite translation in the *Psalter Hymnal* is mostly the work of Frederick W. Foster (1760-1835), John Miller (1756-1810), and William Mercer (1811-1873); see PHH 357 for information on Mercer.

Tune

ARNSBERG (also known as GOTT IST GEGENWÄRTIG and WUNDERBARER KÖNIG) was composed by Joachim Neander (b. Bremen, Germany, 1650; d. Bremen, 1680) and published in his *Glaub- und Liebesübung* (1680) for his hymn "Wunderbarer König." This bar-form (AAB) tune has undergone both rhythmic and melodic change in earlier hymnals. Keep it rhythmic, with a moving tempo. Observe the full length of the whole notes at the ends of the first two long phrases and extend the final chord into a whole note. For stanza 2 try a solo registration on the melody line with lighter accompaniment—or unaccompanied—and with the congregation singing in harmony.

Before writing this hymn, Neander had scoffed at his religious upbringing and led a careless, licentious life as a student in Bremen. One Sunday in 1670 he and his friends attended a service at St. Martin's Church—mainly to criticize and mock the preacher. However, he came under the spell of Theodore Under-Eyck's preaching and was converted from his wayward life. Enamored with Pietism, Neander associated with the Pietist leader Spener in Frankfurt. In 1674 Neander became headmaster of the Latin School in Düsseldorf and conducted pastoral duties in the Calvinistic congregation.

But his Pietist leanings prompted him to organize separate church services and to abstain from the Lord's Supper. These practices forced the authorities to suspend him in 1677. After recanting his views, Neander returned to his ordinary duties. But he was no longer happy in Düsseldorf, and he gladly accepted the opportunity to become Under-Eyck's assistant at St. Martin's Church in Bremen in 1679. He died soon afterward of tuberculosis. Neander loved nature and would often go for long walks. In fact, the valley of the Düssel near Mettmann was named Neanderthal after him; in 1856 a skeleton of the "Neanderthal man" was found there, and that coincidence has produced a number of apocryphal stories about Neander. He wrote about sixty hymn texts and some tunes, published in *Alpha und Omega* (1680, expanded posthumously, 1689).

Liturgical Use
Beginning of worship (useful as a choral introit); stanza 3 fits well after the service of confession and assurance.

245

Jesus, We Love to Meet

JESU A FE PADE
♩ = 96

Text

A marvelous gathering hymn, especially for gathering around the Word of God for Sunday worship, "Jesus, We Love to Meet" explains *why* we come together and *how* we are to worship and serve our God. Elizabeth Parson (b. Tavistock, England, 1812; d. Plymouth, England, 1873) wrote the text in the early 1840s for her Sunday-evening Bible class for youth (known as the "Willing Class"—whose members came voluntarily) at the Congregational church in Tavistock, England, where her father, W. Rooker, was pastor. She taught that class for some years before her marriage to T. Edgecombe Parson in 1844. Altogether Parson wrote eighteen hymns for this class, which were later published in various children's hymnals and hymn collections during the second half of the nineteenth century, such as the Baptist *Psalms and Hymns* (1858).

Scripture References
st. 3 = Eph. 2:8

Abraham Taiwo Olajide Olude (b. Ebute-Metta, Lagos, Nigeria, 1908; d. Lagos, 1986) learned the song at a missionary school in Nigeria during the 1940s. He translated the text into Yoruba and composed a tune for it. The new setting was first performed at Abeokuta, Nigeria, in 1949 at a service designed to popularize indigenous Yoruban music in Christian worship. Educated at Wesley College, Ibadan, and at the Mindola Training School in Nigeria, Olude became a pioneer in using African music in Christian worship. He believed that the "white" hymnody introduced by European and American missionaries was an intrusion into African culture, and he proposed that African music, including the extensive use of drums and other indigenous instruments, be a part of religious services. Olude served a number of churches as both pastor and choir director and from 1937 to 1950 made frequent tours all over Nigeria with his choirs. He was honored by the University of Nigeria with a Mus.D. degree.

The hymn came to North America in 1962 when the American hymnologist and composer Austin Lovelace received a number of indigenous African hymn tunes to consider for publication. Especially pleased with this tune of Olude, Lovelace contacted the United Nations to ask if someone there could help him translate the text into English. He was delighted to find that Biodun Adebesin, who was then serving at the U.N., could not only help but also knew Olude, having sung in his choir years earlier! Adebesin translated the text into English prose, which Lovelace then versified to the meter of the Nigerian tune. Neither of them knew the text had originally been written in English. The result of their work, "Jesus, We Want to Meet," was published in *The Methodist Hymnal* (1964) and later in *Hymns for the Living Church* (1974).

When the *Psalter Hymnal* Revision Committee inquired for permission to publish the English translation, it learned that someone had discovered an earlier English poem that was clearly related to Olude's text. That poem was none other than the one Elizabeth Parson had written in the 1840s. The revision committee found a printed copy of her poem in *A Private House of Prayer* (Weatherhead, 1958) and decided to use the original text. Parson's English text and Olude's Nigerian music, then, are first published together in the 1987 *Psalter Hymnal*. The only textual changes are from the pronouns "thee" and "thy" to "you" and "your."

Tune

The tune name JESU A FE PADE is the incipit of the Yoruba text; the phrase means "worship (or praise) to Jesus." African characteristics in the tune include the polyrhythmic combination of the quarter note and the dotted quarter note in 3/4 and 6/8 time, and the call/response structure in the first, second, and fourth phrases, suggesting responsorial or antiphonal performance.

A soloist or choir should sing the lines marked "unison," and the responding group (choir or congregation) should sing the "harmony" lines. Use small hand drums, bongo drums, tambourines, woodblocks, or "shakers" (gourds, rattles) for the optional but very effective rhythmic parts.

Liturgical Use

Opening of worship; as a sung prayer for illumination; as a refrain at three points in the worship service: stanza 1 at the beginning, stanza 2 before proclaiming the Word, and stanza 3 at the end.

246

Come, Thou Almighty King

ITALIAN HYMN
♩ = 120

Text

The anonymous text dates from before 1757, when it was published in a leaflet and bound into the 1757 edition of George
Whitefield's *Collection of Hymns for Social Worship*. The text appears
to be patterned after the British national anthem, "God Save the King." Filled with
names for members of the Godhead, this song exhibits a common trinitarian structure,
addressing God the Father (st. 1), God the Son (st. 2), and God the Holy Spirit (st. 3),
concluding with a doxology to the Trinity (st. 4).

Scripture References
st. 3 = John 15:26

The text has often been attributed to Charles Wesley, since the leaflet also included a
hymn text from his pen ("Jesus, Let Thy Pitying Eye"); however, "Come, Thou Almighty
King" was never printed in any of the Wesley hymnals, and no other Wesley text is
written in such an unusual meter.

Tune

Felice de Giardini (b. Turin, Italy, 1716; d. Moscow, Russia, 1796) composed ITALIAN
HYMN in three parts for this text at the request of Selina Shirley, the famous evangelical-
ly minded Countess of Huntingdon. Giardini was living in London at the time and
contributed this tune and three others to Martin Madan's *Collection of Psalm and Hymn
Tunes* (1769), published to benefit the Lock Hospital in London where Madan was
chaplain.

Giardini achieved great musical fame throughout Europe, especially in England. He
studied violin, harpsichord, voice, and composition in Milan and Turin; from 1748 to
1750 he conducted a very successful solo violin tour on the continent. He came to
England in 1750 and for the next forty years lived in London, where he was a prominent violinist in several orchestras. Giardini also taught and composed operas and
instrumental music. In 1784 he traveled to Italy, but when he returned to London in
1790, Giardini was no longer popular. His subsequent tour to Russia also failed, and he
died there in poverty.

ITALIAN HYMN appears in most hymnals, sometimes with small variants when
compared to the original melody, as in the *Psalter Hymnal*. Named for its composer's
homeland, ITALIAN HYMN is also known as MOSCOW (where Giardini died) and TRINITY
(after the theme of the hymn text).

This vigorous tune needs strong rhythmic accompaniment. Think one broad beat
per measure. The doxological stanza can be taken more majestically.

Liturgical Use

Beginning of worship; as a doxology (st. 4).

ALLEIN GOTT
♩ = 132

All Glory Be to God on High

Text

A translation of the fourth-century Latin text "Gloria in excelsis Deo," this song is a series of acclamations to God in a pattern that was common in doxologies used in the Greek liturgies of the early Christian church. Stanza 1 consists of an opening antiphon from Luke 2:14 and an acclamation to God the Father. Stanzas 2 and 3 are both acclamations to God the Son. Stanza 2 contains echoes from both the Agnus Dei and the Kyrie (257 and 258). A modern ecumenical translation reads as follows:

Scripture References
st. 1 = Luke 2:14
st. 2 = John 1:29
Rom. 8:34
Heb. 7:25
st. 3 = Col. 1:17

> Glory to God in the highest,
> and peace to God's people on earth.
> Lord God, heavenly King,
> almighty God and Father,
>   we worship you, we give you thanks,
>   we praise you for your glory.
>
> Lord Jesus Christ, only Son of the Father,
> Lord God, Lamb of God,
> you take away the sin of the world:
>   have mercy on us;
> you are seated at the right hand of the Father:
>   receive our prayer.
>
> For you alone are the Holy One,
> you alone are the Lord,
> you alone are the Most High,
>   Jesus Christ,
>   with the Holy Spirit,
>   in the glory of God the Father. Amen.

—*English Language Consultation, from* Praying Together, *1988*

In the Greek-speaking church the text of "Gloria in excelsis Deo" (or Gloria, as the song is commonly known) at first included only the words of Luke 2:14. The fifth-century "Liturgy of St. James," still used in some parts of the Orthodox Church today, preserves the Gloria in its short form, but the song is also used in various longer forms. One of the earliest long forms is recorded in the Greek *Codex Alexandrinus,* which dates from the late fifth century. The Gloria presumably entered the Roman church in the fourth century under the influence of Hilary, Bishop of Poitiers, France, and it was translated into Latin. It became a standard part of the Roman Mass from the sixth century onward and became known as the "Greater Doxology" (as compared with the "Lesser Doxology," or Gloria Patri, 635 and 636).

Very early in the Reformation, Nikolaus Decius (b. Hof, Franconia, Bavaria, c. 1485; d. Germany, after 1546) prepared a rhymed version of the Gloria, published in Low German in Joachim Slüter's Rostock *Gesangbuch* (1525) and in High German in Valentin Schumann's *Geistliche Lieder* (1539). Often used in the Lutheran tradition, Decius's text added an acclamation to the Holy Spirit in a fourth stanza, which, though not unwelcome, is not part of the original text as shown above. (The 1959 *Psalter Hymnal* also includes Decius's four stanzas at 319.)

Educated in a Latin school in Hof and at the University of Leipzig, Germany, Decius became a monk and served as head of the Benedictine Monastery at Steterburg. In 1523 he studied theology at the University of Wittenburg under Martin Luther. At Luther's recommendation he became a pastor in Stettin in 1524 and moved to Mühlhausen in 1534, where he was influenced by Dutch Calvinist refugees. He also served as church musician and preacher at the Königsberg court of Duke Albrecht of Prussia. Decius is credited with German hymnic versifications of "ordinary" parts of the Mass—the Kyrie (258), Gloria, Credo (520), Sanctus (626), and Agnus Dei (257), which he originally prepared to fit their corresponding chant tunes.

Ulrich Zwingli also made use of the Gloria, having worshipers recite it antiphonally between Scripture lessons. Thomas Cranmer introduced it into Anglican worship by including it in *The Book of Common Prayer* (1549).

The English translation in the *Psalter Hymnal* is primarily by Francis Bland Tucker (b. Norfolk, VA, 1895; d. Savannah, GA, 1984), prepared in 1977 for publication in the American Protestant Episcopal *Hymnal 1982* (1985). Bert Polman (PHH 37) altered the text slightly to bring it even closer to the Latin original.

An Episcopal priest, Tucker has been called "the dean of American hymn writers." He was educated at the University of Virginia and Virginia Theological Seminary. During World War I he served as an operating room assistant at Verdun. Ordained in 1920, Tucker had two long pastorates: St. John's Church in Georgetown, Washington, D.C. (1925-1945), and Christ Church in Savannah, Georgia (1945-1967), where, earlier, John Wesley had briefly served. Tucker was active in the Civil Rights Movement and in various civic organizations. He served on the committee for the Episcopal *Hymnal 1940*, which published six of his hymn texts and translations, and on the committee for the *Hymnal 1982*. In 1980 he was honored as a Fellow of the Hymn Society in the United States and Canada.

Tune

The tune name ALLEIN GOTT derives from the opening words of Decius's rhymed text in High German. The tune was first published in Schumann's *Geistliche Lieder.* Decius adapted the tune from a tenth-century Easter chant for the Gloria text, beginning at the part accompanying the words "et in terra pax . . . " ("and on earth, peace . . . ").

Because the Gloria became part of the *ordinary* (the unvarying parts) of the Roman Catholic Mass, there are many choral settings of the Latin text. Anglican composers have set the English text in their "great services," while Lutheran composers have written various chorale preludes on ALLEIN GOTT for organ. Bach used the hymn in cantatas 85, 104, 112, and 128 and composed about ten preludes on the tune. Typical of many Lutheran chorales, ALLEIN GOTT is in bar form (AAB).

Liturgical Use
Sung daily during Morning Prayer in the Eastern Church, at the beginning of worship in every Roman Catholic Mass, and in many historic Protestant liturgies; for the opening of worship; also suitable as a doxology.

248

JE TE SALUE
♩ = 72

I Greet My Sure Redeemer

Text

The strong text of "I Greet My Sure Redeemer" features many themes suitable to various times and places of Christian worship—indeed, to all Christian living: Jesus is my Redeemer, whom I love (st. 1); Jesus is King of kings and Lord of lords (st. 2); Jesus lives in us and enables us to live (st. 3); Jesus is our model for personal growth and community (st. 4); Jesus is revealed in the Scriptures (st. 5).

Scripture References
st. 1 = Isa. 12:2
    Isa. 40:1-2
st. 2 = Luke 1:78-79
    Isa. 60:20
st. 3 = Acts 17:28
st. 4 = Eph. 4:3

The original French text, "Je te salue, mon certain Redempteur," was published in the 1545 Strasbourg edition of Clément Marot's *Psalms* and appears to be a Protestant version of the Roman Catholic hymn "Salve Regina." The French text was later printed in *Opera,* volume 6 of an 1868 edition of John Calvin's works, and has been attributed to Calvin himself. However, modern scholars such as Pierre Pidoux have found no real proof for Calvin's authorship, and Calvin (unlike Luther) left no heritage of adapting Roman Catholic texts. The translation (1868) is mostly the work of Elizabeth L. Smith; it was published in Philip Schaff's *Christ in Song* (New York, 1869).

Elizabeth Lee Allen Smith (b. Hanover, NH, 1817; d. New York, 1898) was the daughter of the theologian, college president, and hymn writer William Allen (who published his *Psalms and Hymns* in 1835). In 1843 she married Henry Boynton Smith, who served on the faculty of Union Theological Seminary in New York City (1850-1877). Well-versed in various languages, she traveled with her husband in Europe in 1869, where he sought to recuperate from physical and mental collapse. Writer of her husband's memoirs, she also inherited an interest in hymnody from her father and translated hymns from German and French.

Smith's translation of this text came to eight stanzas in the same meter as the French original (10 10 666 666) and began with the words "I greet Thee, who my sure Redeemer art." It is not known who condensed the text to fit the 10 10 10 10 meter found in modern hymnals. The stanzas in the *Psalter Hymnal* are adapted from Smith's first five stanzas.

Tune

JE TE SALUE is named after the original French text and is an altered version of GENEVAN 101 (101). Louis Bourgeois (PHH 3) composed the original GENEVAN 101 for the 1551 Genevan Psalter. A comparison of 248 and 101 will show how the original tune has been extended to fit four textual lines of ten metrical feet. It is unknown who adapted the tune this way. To avoid confusion between this tune and GENEVAN 101, play it through entirely before signaling the congregation to sing. The suggested alternate tune, TOULON (521), is also an adaptation of a Genevan tune (for Ps. 124).

Liturgical Use
Many occasions in Christian worship.

249

Holy, Holy, Holy! Lord God Almighty

NICAEA
♩ = 54

Text

Using reverent and apocalyptic language, "Holy, Holy, Holy!" alludes to Revelation 4:6-11; 5:13; 15:2-4; and Isaiah 6:1-3 to sing the great majesty of the triune God. Note the cosmic scope of the text: human beings (st. 1), saints and angels in glory (st. 2), and all creation (st. 4) praise the name of the Lord! Though God's holiness, love, and purity are cloaked in mystery, we can still experience God's mercy and mighty power, and we can participate in praising God. The text is trinitarian in theme, but not in structure.

Scripture References
st. 1 = Isa. 6:3
    Rev. 4:8
st. 2 = Isa. 6:2-3
    Rev. 4:6-10
st. 3 = Isa. 6:3-4
    Rev. 4:11
    Rev. 15:4
st. 4 = Rev. 4:8
    Rev. 5:13

Reginald Heber (b. Malpas, Chesire, England, 1783; d. Trichinopoly, India, 1826) wrote the text for Trinity Sunday, the day for which lectionary in the Church of England's *Book of Common Prayer* prescribes the reading of Revelation 4. It was first published in the third edition (1826) of *A Selection of Psalms and Hymns for the Parish Church of Banbury* and was also published posthumously in Heber's *Hymns Written and Adapted to the Weekly Church Services of the*

Year (1827). The unusual single rhyme (all on the "ee" sound) and the uneven number of syllables in some lines have not detracted from the hymn's popularity.

Educated at Brasenose College, Oxford, Heber was ordained in the Church of England in 1807. He first served his family's parish in Hodnet, Shropshire (1807-1823), and in 1823 his dream of being a missionary was fulfilled when he was appointed bishop of Calcutta. He worked and traveled ceaselessly until his sudden death in 1826. Heber began writing hymns partly because of his dissatisfaction with the poor psalm singing in his congregation and partly because he was influenced by the vital hymn singing among Methodists and Baptists. He wrote hymns while in Hodnet and expressed a desire to compile a hymnbook with its contents appropriate to the church year. His fifty-seven hymn texts were published posthumously by his wife in *Hymns Written and Adapted to the Weekly Church Services of the Year* (1827), a hymnbook that began a tradition of arranging the contents of hymn collections according to the church year.

Tune
The tune NICAEA is named after the Council of Nicaea (A.D. 325) at which church leaders began to formulate the doctrine of the Trinity to oppose the heresies of Arius. NICAEA is one of the finest tunes composed by John B. Dykes (PHH 147) and the only one of his many tunes that resembles the style of the Lutheran chorale—its similarity to WACHET AUF (613) is noted by various scholars. Dykes wrote NICAEA as a setting for Reginald's text, and ever since their first publication together in *Hymns Ancient and Modern* (1861), the text and tune have been virtually inseparable.

Organists should articulate the repeated melody notes clearly but tie over a number of the repeated accompaniment notes. Sing at a stately tempo with solid organ tone. Use the descant once or twice a year on festive occasions.

Liturgical Use
Beginning of worship; worship services emphasizing the Trinity.

250

TE VENGO
♩ = 69

I've Come to Tell
Te Vengo a Decir

Text
"I've Come to Tell" is a testimonial hymn, a personal confession of love for the Lord Jesus describing feelings of joy and sorrow, happiness and peace. Juan M. Isáis (b. Zacatecas, Mexico, 1926) composed the song for a small church in Acapulco, Mexico; in 1967 the song was used during an evangelistic crusade in Lima, Peru. "Te Vengo a Decir" was first published in the Venezuelan hymnal *Cante Conmigo* (1971); it

was also published in *Celebremos I* (1979), a Hispanic hymnal of the United Methodist
Church in the United States.

A member of the National Presbyterian Church of Mexico, Isáis graduated from the
Central American Bible Institute, Guatemala City, Guatemala, in 1952. He serves as
director of the Latin America mission organization in Mexico and is involved in the
evangelism in-depth program and an urban mission project, Christ for the Cities. He
has published books and articles in English and Spanish and composed a number of
hymns and choruses. Isáis has written two other stanzas to this song, retaining the
second half of stanza 1 as a refrain:

2
Te quiero seguir, te quiero seguir, oh mi Salvador,
y darte mi ser, y darte mi ser, mi amigo, mi Dios.
Te quiero seguir, te quiero seguir, mi Rey, mi Señor.
Te vengo a poner todo lo que soy; recíbelo, oh Dios. *Refrain*

3
Doquiera Señor, doquiera Señor, yo te seguiré.
Y hasta el final, y hasta el final, tu siervo seré.
Envíame Señor, envíame Señor, doquiera yo iré.
Sé que nada soy, sé que nada soy, pero fiel te seré. *Refrain*

2
I'll follow you, I'll follow you, O Savior divine,
and give you my all, and give you my all, my friend and my God.
I'll follow you, I'll follow you, my King and my Lord.
Before you I place all that I am; receive me, O God. *Refrain*

3
Wherever you lead, wherever you lead, I'll follow you.
Until the end, until the end, your servant I'll be.
Send me, O Lord, send me, O Lord, and show me the way.
I'm nothing at all, I'm nothing at all, but faithful I'll be. *Refrain*

Tune
L. Frank Sawyer (b. Victoria, BC, Canada, 1946) translated the text into English in
1984. Then a Christian Reformed missionary in Latin America, Sawyer reminds us of
the Spanish oral tradition, in which "there are many choruses like this . . . sung to the
accompaniment of a guitar. Almost no one has any written music; local congregations
sing songs they pick up from neighboring Christians. It is common to hear three or
four variations to one tune." In 1986 Sawyer became a seminary professor, first for
Iglesia Cristiana Reformada in Tegucigalpa, Honduras, and more recently for
Reformatus Teologia Akademia in Sarospatak, Hungary. A pastor in Zoetermeer, the
Netherlands, from 1977 to 1980, he was also a missionary in Puerto Rico (1982-1985)

for Christian Reformed World Missions. Sawyer was educated at Calvin College, Grand Rapids, Michigan, and at the Reformed Seminary in Kampen, the Netherlands.

Though marked for unison singing, TE VENGO may be sung in two parts, a common practice in the Hispanic tradition, by following the alto or tenor part in parallel below the melody. The harmonization by Dale Grotenhuis (PHH 4) in 1984 retains the Spanish flavor of parallel thirds and sixths. Use piano or a light organ registration or preferably more folk-like instruments such as the guitar, flute, and tambourine.

Liturgical Use
Similar to Old Testament psalms written in the first-person singular ("I"), this testimony hymn is suitable for various occasions in corporate worship.

251

TOKYO
♩ = 88

Here, O Lord, Your Servants Gather

Text

This hymn expresses Christian unity in diversity, especially cultural or ethnic diversity. As servants of the Lord, believers sing of hope amid change and turmoil. They find rest in the Lord's peace and proclaim their purpose by living the way of Christ. Based on Jesus' words in John 14:6 and on Christ-centered teachings such as those in Romans 10:12-13 and Ephesians 1:7-14, "Here, O Lord" states that Jesus, our Savior, is the Way (st. 1); Jesus, our Teacher, is the Truth (st. 2); and Jesus, our Healer, is the Life (st. 3). The song closes with a prayer asking Jesus, our Master, for continued help and guidance (st. 4).

Scripture References
all st. = John 14:6
st. 2 = Rom. 10:12-13

While serving as a pastor of the United Church of Christ in Toyohashi, Japan, Tokuo Yamaguchi (b. Tomie-cho, Fukue Island, Nagasaki-Pref., Japan, 1900; d. Aichi-Pref., Japan, 1995) wrote the text for the fourteenth International Christian Education Conference held in Tokyo in 1958, just one year after the launching of Sputnik and the resulting new emphasis on education. The theme of that conference was "Christ, the Way, the Truth, and the Life." Everett M. Stowe (b. 1897) translated the Japanese text into English. The hymn was sung in both Japanese and English at the conference. No other information is available on Stowe.

Yamaguchi was a Methodist pastor in Sawara, Tanimura, Fujieda, and Asahikawa, following his graduation with a theology degree from Aoyama Gakuin University in 1924. His longest term of service was as pastor of the United Church of Christ in Toyohashi in the Aichi Prefecture (1937-1979). He translated *The Journal of John Wesley* into Japanese in 1961 and was honored by the Christian Literature Society of Japan in 1983 for his translation work.

Tune

The tune TOKYO is based on the ancient Japanese *Gagaku* mode of musical composition. *Gagaku* is the name for all traditional Japanese court music, much of it dating back to the eighth century, with previous roots in Chinese music. Composed by Isao Koizumi (b. 1907; d. Toyko, Japan, 1992) for Yamaguchi's text, TOKYO was first published in the English-language Japanese hymnal *Hymns of the Church* (1963).

Koizumi graduated from the Osaka University of Commerce in 1932. For the next ten years he taught at that school, was an organist in Tokyo, and then went on to work in the import-export business. He has served as the conductor of the Tokyo Choral Society and edited various hymnals, including *The Hymnal 1954* for the United Church of Christ in Japan, *The Sunday School Hymnal* (1954), and *Hymns of Praise* (1967 edition). A writer and translator of books and articles on church music, Koizumi has also composed and arranged hymn tunes. He is considered a leading figure in modern Japanese hymnody.

Like much Asian music, TOKYO consists of only five pitches and is meant for unison singing. I-to-Loh, editor of *Hymns from the Four Winds* (1983), a collection of Asian-American hymns, suggests that "ethnic instruments may be employed to double the melody or to accompany the piece." For this hymn he suggests an oboe, plucked lute, or zither, commenting that "an experienced accompanist may be able to simplify or improvise the accompaniment within the appropriate style after the congregation feels comfortable in singing the hymn." In any case, a keyboard accompaniment should be light, with no filling in of (Western) thirds in this open-fifth style.

Liturgical Use

Beginning of worship; Worldwide Communion Sunday; All Nations Heritage celebrations; mission emphasis; similar worship services that stress the "communion of the saints."

252

Father in Heaven

Text

Featuring a trinitarian structure, this hymn is a prayer for God's presence in both worship and life. It was written in 1961 by Elena G. Maquiso (b. Guindulman, Bohol, Philippines, 1914). She was educated both in the Philippines and the United States, received a doctorate from the Hartford Theological Foundation in 1960, and taught at Silliman University in Mumaguete, Philippines, where she directed its Ulahingan Research Project. Her publications, related to indigenous folklore and hymnody, include *Awitan Ta Ang Dyos* (1962), *Mga Sugilanon Sa Negros* (1980), and *Ulahingan: Epic of the Southern Philippines* (1992).

Daniel Thambyrajah Niles (b. Telipallai, Ceylon, 1908; d. Vellore Christian Medical College, India, 1970) translated this hymn text for the *EACC Hymnal* (1964), which he produced almost single-handedly. That hymnal includes forty-four of his own hymns and translations and adaptations of others. Niles began studies in law at Ceylon Christian University, but changed his course of study to the ministry, due in part to a devout Hindu warden at the University who greatly influenced him. Niles was ordained in the United Methodist Church in 1932. After serving in Ceylon, he became the president of the East Asia Christian Conference (EACC), and later the evangelism secretary for the World Council of Churches in Geneva.

A few word changes are included in the text published in the *Psalter Hymnal;* some other modern hymnals have changed the first line to "O God in heaven."

Tune
A simple, attractive tune, RESTORATION features the pentatonic (five-pitch) style typical of Appalachian music. It was first published in *Southern Harmony* (1835), published by William Walker (PHH 44). The tune name derives from "Mercy, O Thou Son of David," the text to which this tune was set in Walker's book.

Sing this music in four phrases at a good tempo. It is suitable for guitar or light organ registration. Try introducing it on folk instruments—for example, play the melody on recorder or flute (up an octave) and the harmony on guitar or Orff instruments. The most simple Orff accompaniment, which children can easily handle, is the playing of repeated rhythmic ostinati on the B and E pitches throughout.

Gary Warmink (b. Everson, WA, 1940) harmonized this tune in 1973 when serving as a member of the *Psalter Hymnal* Supplement Committee; his arrangement was first published in the 1974 *Psalter Hymnal Supplement.* A graduate of Calvin College, Grand Rapids, Michigan, and the University of Washington, Warmink also received a Ph.D. from Ohio State University. He taught music at Dordt College, Sioux Center, Iowa (1963-1980), Southwestern University, Georgetown, Texas (1980-1984), and was minister of music at First Presbyterian Church in Austin, Texas (1984-1996). He is currently pursuing a variety of service projects in Russia and Romania, including organ-building projects there and in Texas.

Liturgical Use
Beginning of worship; before the proclamation of the Word; with spoken prayers following the sermon; as a short sung prayer; Lord's Supper.

253

Praise to the Lord, the Almighty

Text

Loosely based on Psalm 103:1-6 and Psalm 150, with echoes from other psalms, this is a strong hymn of praise to our covenant God, who heals, provides for, and defends us. Let "all that has life and breath" sing praise to the Lord! According to the American hymnologist and composer Austin Lovelace, the exuberance of the text is matched by its "galloping dactylic rhythm."

Scripture References
st. 1 = Ps. 103:1
st. 2 = Ps. 17:8
st. 3 = Ps. 23:6
st. 4 = Ps. 106:48
Ps. 150:6

Joachim Neander (PHH 244) wrote this German chorale of five stanzas and published it in his *Glaub und Liebesübung* (1680). Stanzas 1 through 3 in the *Psalter Hymnal* are a translation by Catherine Winkworth (PHH 194) of the original stanzas 1, 2, and 4; these are taken from her *Chorale Book for England* (1863). Stanza 4 in the *Psalter Hymnal* is an anonymous translation. Various modern-language alterations from other hymnals and editors are included in the text published in the *Psalter Hymnal.*

Tune

LOBE DEN HERREN (not to be confused with LOBE DEN HERREN, O MEINE SEELE, 159) is originally from the Stralsund, Germany, *Ander Theil des Erneuerten Gesangbuch*, Part II (1665), where it was published with the text "Hast du denn, Liebster, dein Angesicht gänzlich verborgen." Neander altered the tune in 1680 to fit his own text, and his German incipit generated the name LOBE DEN HERREN. A magnificent tune in bar form (AAB), LOBE DEN HERREN is one of the finest and most popular tunes of the Lutheran repertoire. Bach used the tune in cantatas 57 and 137; a great variety of composers have created chorale preludes on it as well, testifying to the tune's enduring strength and usefulness.

The tune consists of two very long phrases at the beginning (probably the longest in all popular hymnody) matched by three shorter phrases at the end, with a well-positioned high note for climax. Sing it with rhythmic clarity, especially on the repeating melody notes. Use a strong full registration on the organ (with some bright mixtures and/or reeds); keep the rhythmic energy moving!

For festive occasions, use brass instruments and the descant composed by Craig S. Lang (b. Hastings, New Zealand, 1891; d. London, England, 1971). Lang was educated at Clifton College, Bristol, England, and earned his D.Mus. at the Royal College of Music in London. Throughout his life he was an organist and a music educator as well as a composer of organ, piano, and choral works. Lang was also music editor of *The Public School Hymn Book* (1949). He named many of his hymn tunes after Cornish villages.

Liturgical Use

Many occasions in Christian worship, for praise to God is our "duty and delight" in all circumstances of life.

254

GORTON
♩ = 132

Remember Not, O God

Text

A versification of part of Psalm 79, "Remember Not, O God"
comes from the 1912 *Psalter* with minor alterations. In lament
style, this prayer asks for deliverance from sin and then vows to
praise God forever. See PHH 79 for further commentary on Psalm
79.

Scripture References
st. 1 = 79:8
st. 2 = 79:9
st. 3 = 79:13

Tune

The tune GORTON derives from the second movement of Ludwig van Beethoven's
Piano Sonata No. 23, Opus 57 (1807); however, the arranger and any significance to the
tune title are unknown. GORTON was published with this versification of Psalm 79 in the
1912 *Psalter.* Sing this tune in parts, beginning very quietly and building to a fuller
sound on each successive stanza. Try the first stanza in parts but unaccompanied after a
chord or two on the organ to get the congregation started. Sing two long lines for each
stanza.

   A giant in the history of music, Beethoven (b. Bonn, Germany, 1770; d. Vienna,
Austria, 1827) progressed from early musical promise to worldwide, lasting fame. By the
age of fourteen he was an accomplished viola and organ player, but he became famous
primarily because of his compositions, including nine symphonies, eleven overtures,
thirty piano sonatas, sixteen string quartets, the *Mass in C,* and the *Missa Solemnis.* He
wrote no music for congregational use, but various arrangers, including Gardiner
(PHH 111), adapted some of his musical themes as hymn tunes; the most famous of
these is ODE TO JOY from the Ninth Symphony. Although it would appear that the great
calamity of Beethoven's life was his loss of hearing, which turned to total deafness
during the last decade of his life, he composed his greatest works during this period.

Liturgical Use

Service of confession and forgiveness. See also PHH 79.

255

REDHEAD 76
♩ = 96

God, Be Merciful to Me

Text

Based on Psalm 51, the best-known of the penitential psalms, "God, Be Merciful" is a
collation from the complete versification of the psalm in the 1912 *Psalter.* Making

various alterations, especially in stanza 3, Bert Polman (PHH 37) prepared the collation to provide a shortened version of this well-known psalm and tune for the *Psalter Hymnal*. Other settings of Psalm 51 are at 51 and 167.

Scripture References
st. 1 = vv. 1-3
st. 2 = vv. 4, 8
st. 3 = vv. 10-12
st. 4 = vv. 13-14, 17, 19

Tune

REDHEAD 76 is named for its composer, who published it as number 76 in his influential *Church Hymn Tunes, Ancient and Modern* (1853) as a setting for the hymn text "Rock of Ages." It has been associated with Psalm 51 since the 1912 *Psalter*, where the tune was named AJALON. The tune is also known as PETRA from its association with "Rock of Ages," and GETHSEMANE, which derives from the text "Go to Dark Gethsemane" (381).

Of the three long lines constituting REDHEAD 76, the last is almost identical to the first, and the middle line has an internal repeat. Well-suited to singing in parts, this music is also appropriate for unaccompanied singing.

Richard Redhead (b. Harrow, Middlesex, England, 1820; d. Hellingley, Sussex, England, 1901) was a chorister at Magdalen College, Oxford. At age nineteen he was invited to become organist at Margaret Chapel (later All Saints Church), London. Greatly influencing the musical tradition of the church, he remained in that position for twenty-five years as organist and an excellent trainer of the boys' choirs. Redhead and the church's rector, Frederick Oakeley (PHH 340), were strongly committed to the Oxford Movement, which favored the introduction of Roman elements into Anglican worship. Together they produced the first Anglican plainsong psalter, *Laudes Diurnae* (1843). Redhead spent the latter part of his career as organist at St. Mary Magdalene Church in Paddington (1864-1894).

Liturgical Use

Service of confession and forgiveness; a sung prayer for renewal (st. 3); offering of gifts (st. 4). See also PHH 51.

256

Out of the Depths I Cry

SANDON
♩ = 66

Text

Psalm 130, from which this hymn derives, is one of the traditional penitential psalms. The versification (altered) is from the 1912 *Psalter*. See PHH 130 for further commentary on Psalm 130.

Scripture References
st. 1 = vv. 1-4
st. 2 = vv. 5-6
st. 3 = vv. 7-8

Tune

Charles H. Purday (b. Folkestone, Kent, England, 1799; d. Kensington, London, England, 1885) composed SANDON for John Henry Newman's text "Lead, Kindly Light, amid the Encircling Gloom." Other hymnals use the tune for John D. S. Campbell's paraphrase of Psalm 121, "Unto the Hills Around Do I Lift Up," a setting much loved in Canada.

Respected and loved by many, SANDON is a bar-form tune (AABC) with a fine sense of climax in its fourth line. Try antiphonal singing on stanzas 1 and 2, and ask everyone to join in on stanza 3.

A publisher, composer, lecturer, and writer, Purday had a special interest in church music. He published *Crown Court Psalmody* (1854), *Church and Home Metrical Psalter and Hymnal* (1860), which included SANDON, and, with Frances Havergal (PHH 288), *Songs of Peace and Joy* (1879). A precentor in the Scottish Church in Crown Court, London, Purday sang at the coronation of Queen Victoria. In the publishing field he is known as a strong proponent of better copyright laws to protect the works of authors and publishers.

Liturgical Use
Advent; Lent; service of confession and forgiveness; other occasions of penitence. See also PHH 130.

257

CHRISTE, DU LAMM GOTTES
♩ = 100

O Christ, the Lamb of God

Text
The Agnus Dei is an ancient church text that developed from John the Baptist's salutation of Christ: "Look, the Lamb of God, who takes away the sin of the world!" (John 1:29; Isa. 53:7; Rev. 5:6-14). By the late seventh century this Latin text was introduced into the Roman Catholic Mass at a point just prior to the reception of communion. In the tenth century the Agnus Dei's third clause was changed to its present wording, *"dona nobis pacem"* ("grant us peace").

Scripture References
st. = John 1:29
Matt. 20:30
Ps. 123:3

The translation of the text into German included the uniquely Lutheran addition of "Christe" to the beginning of each clause. This translation was first published in Low German in 1528 in Johannes Bugenhagen's manual *Der Erbarn Stadt Brunswig Christlike Ordeninge*. The English version in the *Psalter Hymnal* is an adaptation of the Lutheran text mixed with a translation provided by the International Committee on English in the Liturgy, a Roman Catholic group that has been active ever since Vatican II (1962-65). In any language the text is a profound but short prayer for mercy and peace.

Tune

The chorale tune CHRISTE, DU LAMM GOTTES was published as the setting for the Agnus Dei in Bugenhagen's 1528 manual. The tune name comes from the opening words in the German text. Ulrich S. Leupold, editor of Martin Luther's hymns and liturgies (vol. 53 of *Luther's Works,* 1965), suggests that Luther may be the tune's arranger. It seems to derive from a Kyrie melody (Gregorian Tone 1) that Luther used in his German Mass of 1526 (see PHH 258 for information on the Kyrie).

The 1984 arrangement is by Dale Grotenhuis (PHH 4), who modeled it after a setting by Carl Hirsch (1858-1918) published in *Redeeming Love* (rev. ed., Concordia, 1963), a collection of Lenten and funeral music. Grotenhuis's arrangement is a fine antiphonal setting of the historic text: the first and second clauses are for two-part singing by women and men, respectively; the final clause is for everyone in four-part harmony. The hymn concludes with an "Amen" set to a delightfully challenging melisma.

Liturgical Use

Lord's Supper; Lent, though traditionally used in any season; service of confession and forgiveness.

258

Lord, Have Mercy upon Us

WILLAN KYRIE
♩ = 84

Text

The Kyrie translates into English as follows:

Kyrie eleison; *Lord, have mercy;*
Christe eleison; *Christ, have mercy;*
Kyrie eleison. *Lord, have mercy.*

Scripture References
st. = Matt. 20:30
Ps. 51:1
Ps. 57:1
Ps. 123:3

This ritual song dates from early Greek (Eastern) Christian liturgies and has retained its Greek text in the Latin (Western) rite. In the Eastern tradition the Kyrie is still used in its initial capacity, as a response in litanies. By the end of the eighth century in the Roman (Western) church, the Kyrie was used as a separate song, often in a nine-fold form—a three-time repetition of its three lines, in which the priest uttered the first line, the congregation or (more likely) a choir responded with the second, and the priest responded with the third. The Kyrie became part of the Ordinary (the unvarying parts) of the Roman Catholic Mass, chanted at the very beginning of the service.

Some liturgies of the Reformation continued to use the Kyrie in connection with confession of sin or with the reading of the Ten Commandments. Like other ancient biblical and liturgical expressions (such as "amen," "alleluia," "hosanna," "maranatha"), the Kyrie is a prayer that ties us to Christians from all times and places.

Tune

The music for this short prayer is just one segment from the *Missa de Sancta Maria Magdalena*, an Anglican service composed by Healey Willan (b. Balham, Surrey, England, 1880; d. Toronto, ON, Canada, 1968) in 1928 and named in honor of Saint Mary Magdalene Church in Toronto, where Willan served as organist and choirmaster for forty-seven years. The *Psalter Hymnal* Revision Committee assigned the title WILLAN KYRIE to this piece in honor of its composer. Willan composed his *Missa* in D major for unison voices with simple organ accompaniment. Sing in unison with a clear but light organ tone.

Willan spent his early years in England as a student from 1888 to 1895 at St. Saviour Choir School in Eastbourne and later as organist and choirmaster for several churches in and near London. In 1913 he became head of the music theory department for the conservatory of the University of Toronto. Thus began a long and distinguished career with that university, where he was influential as a teacher of composition and university organist and choral conductor. Willan retired in 1950. An outstanding composer, he wrote for orchestra, piano, organ, and voice. He was the musical director for the Hart House Theater and wrote incidental music for fifteen plays.

Willan's contribution to church music was equally impressive. He served as organist-choirmaster at St. Paul Anglican Church (1913-1921) and at the Church of St. Mary Magdalene (1921-1968), both in Toronto. He promoted the use of plainsong throughout his career. In addition to his organ preludes Willan wrote liturgical music, motets, anthems, and some thirty hymn tunes. A number of those tunes, as well as settings of biblical canticles and harmonizations of plainsong melodies, were first published in *The Hymnary of the United Church of Canada* (1930) and *The Book of Common Praise* (1938) of the Anglican Church in Canada. Willan was also music editor of *The Hymnbook for Children* (1962).

Liturgical Use

As a sung prayer for mercy in the service of confession and forgiveness; as part of a litany, sung after each petition (as in the oldest traditions); as a frame around spoken prayers.

259

GATHERING
♩ = 58

Out of Need and Out of Custom

Text and Tune

Intended as a hymn for the beginning of worship when the Christian community gathers around the Word, "Out of Need and Out of Custom" is a somewhat unusual text. It bears reading through several times and may also require some introductory comments prior to public singing. Stanza 2 points out that gathering for worship requires removing the

Scripture References
st. 2 = Eph. 4:15

masks behind which we often hide from God and from each other. We come to the Word with faith but also with doubts, and with joys but also with sorrows (st. 1)—and all of this we lay open to the Word, to Christ. The "searching" of stanzas 1 and 2 is our searching of the Word of God. Stanza 3 acknowledges our familiarity with God's message and directs us to pray for illumination.

Both the text and the music are by Ken Medema (born Kenneth Peter Medema, Grand Rapids, MI, 1943). He wrote stanza 1 in 1972 in Baltimore, Maryland, as part of a youth service in which some disillusioned young people wanted to tell their parents that "church is boring; church is a drag" and that being a church can be simply a custom or an artificial tradition. The words were sung to a familiar tune. Medema added two more stanzas later and composed a new tune for the text; the song was published in a larger score called *The Gathering* (1977). The tune name derives from that score title. GATHERING is a modified rounded bar-form tune (AA'BA'); it is well suited to part singing at a moderate tempo.

Blind from birth, Medema showed an early penchant for music. Educated in Christian schools in Grand Rapids, he also studied voice, piano, and music theory at Michigan State University. He worked as a music therapist in Fort Wayne, Indiana, and Cedar Grove, New Jersey, for five years before beginning his full-time concert career in 1973. A gifted improviser, Medema writes his own lyrics and tunes, many of which are published and available on recordings. He tours extensively throughout the United States and Canada.

Liturgical Use
Beginning of worship, but because the complete hymn takes us through the gathering and the confession and on to the prayer for illumination, it is best used in the service of confession and forgiveness just before the reading of Scripture.

260

Not What My Hands Have Done

LEOMINSTER
$\downarrow = 58$

Text

The famous Scottish preacher and hymn author Horatius Bonar (b. Edinburgh, Scotland, 1808; d. Edinburgh, 1889) wrote this text in twelve four-line stanzas, each beginning with the line "Not what these hands have done." He first published the text in his *Hymns of Faith and Hope* (2nd series, 1861). The *Psalter Hymnal* collates the most popular stanzas and includes minor textual changes.

Scripture References
st. 1 = Tit. 3:5
st. 2 = Eph. 1:7
Eph. 2:8-9
Heb. 9:11-12
st. 3 = John 14:19
1 John 4:10, 19

Bonar subtitled the text "Salvation through Christ alone," and that is surely its theme: my salvation is entirely due to the grace of God, my own works have no merit at all, and nothing but the blood of Christ will do (st. 1-2); my natural response, then, is praise, for "my Lord has saved my life" (st. 3)! Bonar was a staunch Calvinist; in writing this hymn he stood resolutely behind John Calvin in the Calvin-Arminius controversy (see the introduction to the Canons of Dort in the *Psalter Hymnal* for a brief explanation about Calvin's and Arminius's teachings).

Bonar was educated at the University of Edinburgh. At the age of thirty he became a preacher in the Presbyterian Church of Scotland, a church that underwent a schism — "The Disruption"— in 1843. A major question in the controversy was whether a minister could be forced on a congregation by an aristocratic sponsor. Many church leaders and the government agreed that he could, but one-third of the ministers, including Bonar, disagreed, and in 1843 this group formed the Free Church of Scotland. Bonar was a prolific, popular author of tracts, sermons, and hymns (even though his congregation sang exclusively psalms during much of his life). One of Bonar's great interests was biblical prophecy and the return of Christ, an interest reflected in some of his hymns. He published several hundred hymns in collections such as *The Bible Hymn Book* (1845), *Hymns of Faith and Hope* (1857, 1861), and *Hymns of the Nativity* (1879). Many were written casually, illustrating very little interest in poetic finesse, but a few have had staying power and are still found in many modern hymnals.

Tune
George William Martin (b. London, England, 1825; d. London, 1881) composed LEOMINSTER, named for a town in the county of Hereford and Worcester (formerly Herefordshire), England. The tune was first published in *The Journal of Part Music* (vol. 2, 1862), in which it was titled THE PILGRIM'S SONG. Martin was editor of that publication from 1861 to 1862. As a boy Martin was a chorister in St. Patrick's Cathedral. He taught music at the Normal College for Army Schoolmasters in Chelsea and at St. John's Training College in Battersea. In 1849 he became organist at Christ Church, Battersea. Well-known for his skill in training children's choirs, Martin also conducted mass choirs, such as the Metropolitan Schools Choral Society. He composed glees, madrigals, and part-songs, and edited oratorios of Handel and Haydn.

Arthur S. Sullivan (PHH 46) later arranged and harmonized the tune and labeled it as an "Old Melody" in his *Church Hymns with Tunes* (1874). LEOMINSTER's many repeated tones in lines 1 and 3 give way to the more dramatic shape of lines 2 and 4. The tune's simplicity allows for bringing in harmony, perhaps with stanza 2 unaccompanied. Accompany stanza 3 with a bright and strong organ registration.

Liturgical Use
Service of confession and forgiveness—either sing all three stanzas without interruption (since the hymn basically moves through confession/forgiveness/response) or intersperse spoken words between the stanzas.

261

Lord, We Cry to You for Help

HERR, NUN HEB
♩ = 120

Text

Although Ulrich Zwingli's famous Swiss battle hymn, "Herr, nun heb den Wagen selb!" originally written in three stanzas, is usually dated 1529, Markus Jenny, a Zwingli scholar, thinks Zwingli must have composed it in 1525 or 1526. The English text in the *Psalter Hymnal* is a loose translation by Helen A. Dickinson (b. Port Elmsley, ON, Canada, 1875; d. Tucson, AR, 1957). She deleted a "chariot" image, inserted a *kyrie* ("Lord, have mercy on us," st. 2), and changed the character of the hymn from a battle song into a more general lament

Scripture References
st. 1 = Ps. 6:2-4
    Ps. 102:1-2
st. 2 = Ps. 51:1, 4
    Ps. 123:3 (Kyrie)
st. 3 = Ps. 51:7, 10, 12
    Ps. 143:8, 11
st. 4 = Ps. 102:12-22
    Ps. 143:11-12

and prayer for peace. The resulting text is a prayer similar to the penitential psalms (especially Ps. 51), which usually include a cry for help, healing, or peace (st. 1); confession of sin (st. 2); a prayer for purity or cleansing (st. 3); and a prayer for God's glory or victory (st. 4). For further commentary on the penitential psalms, see PHH 6, 32, 38, 51, 102, 130, and 143.

Zwingli (b. Wildhaus, Switzerland, 1484; d. Kappel, Switzerland, 1531) was ordained a priest in the Roman Catholic Church after study in Vienna and Basel. He served briefly as a chaplain in the Swiss army and in 1518 became priest of the Great Church in Zurich, a position he retained for the rest of his life. Zwingli's rift with Rome was a gradual process. Influenced more by Erasmus than by Luther, he first began preaching against some of the abuses in the church and then developed his own theological views based on Scripture and the writings of the Church Fathers. By 1519 he was preaching against purgatory and praying to the saints. In 1522 he advocated freedom from the papacy and caused the Zurich church to abolish the Mass in 1525. Eventually the break with Rome was complete—the Zurich church and several of the other cantons became Protestant. However, some of the Swiss cantons remained loyal to Rome, and a military struggle ensued—the Forest Cantons attacked the Zurich forces. In the battle at Kappel the Zurich army was routed, and Zwingli, the banner-bearing chaplain, was killed.

In matters of worship Zwingli is of interest especially on two issues. He disagreed with both Calvin and Luther as far as the Lord's Supper was concerned, believing it to be strictly a memorial meal rather than a means of grace. However, in his later writings he acknowledges the "spiritual presence" of Christ in the Supper. His view on church music also set him apart from the other reformers. Zwingli was a fine singer, instrumentalist, and composer. He encouraged singing in his home, but he came to the conclusion that singing during public worship was not appropriate. He banned not only choral and instrumental music but congregational singing as well, believing that the emphasis in the liturgy ought to be on silent, spiritual worship. For Zwingli, music was largely a physical activity with great psychological power, which would distract from spiritual worship.

Tune

Zwingli arranged HERR, NUN HEB from a folk melody; thus it is a *contrafactum* (in other words, adapted from a folk/court setting for use in worship). The tune is named after the opening words of Zwingli's text. HERR, NUN HEB consists of four lines: lines 2 and 3 are identical, but the opening and closing lines provide a suitable contrast to that repetition. The *Psalter Hymnal* setting deleted an extended melisma from the final line. Sing this tune quietly in unison or in parts, but increase volume and strength on the final stanza.

Clarence Dickinson (b. Lafayette, IN, 1873; d. New York, NY, 1969) harmonized the tune, and it was published as a setting for his wife's English paraphrase in a choral anthem in 1940. They often colaborated on hymns and anthems, with Helen providing texts and Clarence composing the music. Their most significant collaboration and lasting contribution was the establishment of the School of Sacred Music at Union Theological Seminary. Clarence served as professor of music and served as its long-time director. Earlier he had studied at Miami University, Oxford, Ohio, and at Northwestern University, Evanston, Illinois, as well as in Berlin and Paris. As a church organist he served St. James Episcopal Church in Chicago, Illinois, and the Presbyterian Brick Church in New York. Editor of the Presbyterian *The Hymnal* (1933), Dickinson composed music for organ and choir; many anthems had texts written by his wife.

For her part, Helen Dickinson was educated at Queens University, Kingston, Ontario, and at the University of Heidelberg, where she was the first woman student to be admitted to the doctoral program in philosophy. She devoted much of her life to lecturing and publishing about church art and architecture and the history of church music, including *A Treasury of Worship*. In 1946 Clarence and Helen Dickinson were both honored as Fellows of the Hymn Society in the United States and Canada.

Liturgical Use

Service of confession and forgiveness, as with the penitential psalms; as a prayer for deliverance and for peace.

262

My Faith Looks Up to Thee

OLIVET
♩ = 60

Text

Ray Palmer (b. Little Compton, RI, 1808; d. Newark, NJ, 1887)
wrote these words while employed as a teacher at a private
girls' school in New York. He had experienced a difficult year
of illness and loneliness and was inspired to write this verse one
night after meditating on a German poem that depicted a
sinner kneeling before the cross of Christ. He later stated, "The
words for these stanzas were born out of my own soul with very little effort. I recall that I
wrote the verses with tender emotion. . . . When writing the last line, "O bear me safe
above, a ransomed soul!" the thought that the whole work of redemption and salvation
was involved in those words . . . brought me to a degree of emotion that brought
abundant tears."

Scripture References
st. 3 = Heb. 12:1-2
st. 4 = 2 Cor. 4:16
1 Thess. 4:17
Heb. 2:15; 12:1

Palmer jotted the text into a notebook, which he shared two years later while visiting
with the composer Lowell Mason (PHH 96) in Boston. Mason's prophecy that Palmer
"will be best known to posterity as the author of 'My Faith Looks Up to Thee'" has
certainly come true. A hymn of prayer, this song asks for forgiveness (st. 1), for purity of
love (st. 2), for divine guidance (st. 3), and for safe homecoming into glory (st. 4).
Stanzas 1 and 2 are popularly judged the best and the most useful. The gloom of stanza
3 is similar to some Old Testament laments. The *Psalter Hymnal* Revision Committee
altered stanza 4 to capture a more Reformed theology.

Palmer is often considered to be one of America's best nineteenth-century hymn
writers. After completing grammar school he worked in a Boston dry goods store, but a
religious awakening prodded him to study for the ministry. He attended Yale College
(supporting himself by teaching) and was ordained in 1835. A pastor in Congregational
churches in Bath, Maine (1835-1850), and Albany, New York (1850-1865), he also
served as secretary of the American Congregational Union (1865-1878). Palmer was a
popular preacher and author, writing original poetry as well as translating hymns. He
published several volumes of poetry and hymns, including *Sabbath Hymn Book* (1858),
Hymns and Sacred Pieces (1865), and *Hymns of My Holy Hours* (1868). His complete
poetical works were published in 1876.

Tune

Lowell Mason (PHH 96) composed OLIVET in three-part harmony for Palmer's text;
the two were published together in *Spiritual Songs for Social Worship* (1831). Mason, who
often assigned biblical names to his tunes, named this tune for the Mount of Olives.

OLIVET consists of a long line followed by two slightly shorter ones; the last line descends from an initial climax. The harmonization is straightforward: sing it in parts, perhaps without accompaniment on the inner stanzas.

Liturgical Use

Stanzas 1 and 2 are most useful in the service of confession and forgiveness—stanza 1 can initiate the confession; stanza 2 can be a response to words of forgiveness and assurance. Stanzas 3 and 4 are prayers for guidance as the Christian continues the pilgrimage toward glory.

263

WOODWORTH
♩ = 112

Just as I Am, without One Plea

Text

At the age of 32, Charlotte Elliott (b. Clapham, London, England, 1789; d. Brighton, East Sussex, England, 1871) suffered a serious illness that left her a semi-invalid for the rest of her life. Within a year she went through a spiritual crisis and confessed to the Swiss evangelist Henri A. César Malan (PHH 288) that she did not know how to come to Christ. He answered, "Come to him just as you are." Thinking back on that experience twelve years later, in 1834, she wrote "Just as I Am" as a statement of her faith.

Scripture References
all st. = John 6:37
Rev. 22:17

Hymn writing provided a way for Elliot to cope with her pain and depression— she wrote approximately 150 hymns, which were published in her *Invalid's Hymn Book* (several editions, 1834-1854), *Hymns for a Week* (1839), and *Thoughts in Verse on Sacred Subjects* (1869). Many of her hymns reflect her chronic pain and illness but also reveal that faith gave her perseverance and hope.

"Just as I Am" was first published in the 1836 edition of *Invalid's Hymn Book* with the subheading "Him that cometh unto me I will in no wise cast out" (John 6:37). She added a seventh stanza that same year, when the hymn was also published in her *Hours of Sorrow Cheered and Comforted* (1836). The *Psalter Hymnal* prints the four most common stanzas. Widely translated, this hymn has brought consolation to millions.

Tune

William B. Bradbury (PHH 114) originally composed WOODWORTH for Elizabeth Scott's text "The God of Love Will Sure Indulge," published in the *Mendelssohn Collection* (1849). Later Bradbury adapted Elliott's text (originally written as 88 86) by repeating the words "I come" in order to fit his long-meter tune; he published this adaptation in his *Eclectic Tune Book* (1860). The union of this text and tune became a standard in the hymnals used by Dwight L. Moody and Ira D. Sankey (PHH 73) and achieved great popularity through use in Billy Graham Crusades as a hymn of invitation.

This simple music is best sung in parts. Use light registration, and keep the tempo moving with two pulses per bar.

Liturgical Use

Service of confession and forgiveness; in response to preaching; for the Lord's Supper; in evangelistic services as a hymn of invitation.

264

Lord, I Want to Be a Christian

Text

In *Negro Slave Songs in the United States* (1953), Miles Mark Fisher suggests that this African American spiritual could well have originated in Virginia in the 1750s, based on this story from Hanover, Virginia, 1756: "A black slave asked Presbyterian preacher William Davies, 'I come to you, sir, that you may tell me some good things concerning Jesus Christ and my duty to God, for I am resolved not to live any more as I have done . . . Lord [Sir], I want to be a Christian.'" Apparently the story fits well with the ministry style of Davies in Virginia between 1748 and 1759.

Scripture References
st. 2 = 1 Thess. 3:12
st. 3 = 1 Thess. 3:13

Stanza 1 is a prayer expressing the initial desire to become a Christian; the others are prayers for growth in Christian character: to be more loving (st. 2), to be more holy (st. 3), and to be like Jesus (st. 4).

Tune

Both text and tune were first published in *Folk Songs of the American Negro* (1907), compiled by brothers Frederick J. Work and John W. Work, Jr. (PHH 476). This music is an example of the slow, sustained, long-phrased tune found in a number of African American spirituals. In the manner of many such spirituals, this is a call-and-response song, in which a soloist (or choir in unison) sings the stanzas (first two lines) and everyone responds by singing the chorus (last two lines) in four-part harmony. The soloist's lines could be sung rather freely, and the rest in more regular rhythm, but not fast. This music is intended to be reverent, with little, if any, accompaniment (perhaps piano).

Liturgical Use

As a hymn of response to hearing the Word of the Lord—the Word that calls for commitment to become a Christian and challenges all of us to mature in our walk with God; stanzas 2 through 4 can be used separately in the service of confession and forgiveness. Use the entire song as a hymn of encouragement or invitation in evangelistic services.

265

STANDING
♩ = 52

Standing in the Need of Prayer

Text
Like 264, "Standing in the Need" is an African American spiritual, and, like many folk songs, its origin is unknown. Both text and tune became well known after their publication in *The Book of American Negro Spirituals* (1925), compiled by James Weldon Johnson and his brother, J. Rosamond Johnson.

Using hyperbole, or exaggerating to make a point, the text brings a very specific message: "I need prayer!" Obviously all the other persons mentioned in the text need prayer as well—yet the text stresses the individual's need for prayer. Such an understanding of this text permits its use in corporate worship—in which we all realize that *each* of us needs prayer just as much as *all* of us need prayer. The text emphasizes personal responsibility within a larger context of community.

Tune
STANDING is a call-and-response tune; the *Psalter Hymnal* has marked clearly the solo lead parts and the congregational-response parts, which are to be sung in harmony. Since most African American spirituals were originally sung unaccompanied, have the choir or even the congregation hum the accompaniment to the solo lines.

Liturgical Use
As a call to prayer, this song should be part of a time of sung and spoken and silent prayers—for forgiveness, of course, but also for healing, for gratitude, for more fervent faith, and so on.

266

DUNFERMLINE
♩ = 56

"Forgive Our Sins As We Forgive"

Text
Rosamond E. Herklots (b. Masuri, India, 1905; d. Bromley, Kent, England, 1987) wrote these words in 1966 after digging out weeds in her garden and thinking how bitterness, hatred, and resentment are like poisonous weeds growing in the

Scripture References
all st. = Matt. 18:21-35
st. 1 = Matt. 6:12
Col. 3:13

407

Christian garden of life. "Forgive Our Sins" is a hymn about being ready to forgive others again and again—as Jesus said, seventy-times-seven times! We have many hymns about God's forgiveness of our sins, but this one adds a most helpful guide in forgiving others' sins.

Herklots revised her own text into the second-person singular ("you") in 1967. That text was first published in 1969 in the British supplementary hymnal *100 Hymns for Today* with the subhead "The Unforgiving Heart." It quickly became her best-known hymn, included in most recent hymnals.

Trained as a teacher at Leeds University, Herklots taught school briefly but from 1930 to 1980 worked as a medical secretary for a London neurologist. She had written poetry since childhood, and after encouragement by members of the Hymn Society of Great Britain and Ireland and by Oxford University Press she wrote about a hundred hymns. Some were published initially in various British hymnals and supplements, and some were contest-winners sung on BBC-TV.

Tune

DUNFERMLINE is one of the "common" tunes from Andro Hart's psalter *The CL Psalms of David*, Edinburgh (1615)—a "common" tune was one that was not matched with a specific text in a songbook. Millar Patrick, author of *Four Centuries of Scottish Psalmody* (London, 1949) and *The Story of the Church's Song* (1927, rev. 1962), attributes this tune to John Angus, one-time precentor at the Dunfermline Abbey (Scotland) during the Reformation. The tune takes its name from that abbey.

Sing DUNFERMLINE in unison or in harmony with the sense of two long lines for each stanza.

Liturgical Use

Early in the service of confession and forgiveness; as a call to forgiving each other— especially prior to the Lord's Supper or to the offering of gifts.

267

And Can It Be

SAGINA
♩ = 76

Text

In a compact poetic manner, this text exclaims the mystery of God's grace extended to sinners who turn to Christ in faith. These sinners receive the righteousness of Christ and can approach the Lord's throne in confidence. Such is the amazing love of God in Christ! Charles Wesley (b. Epworth, Lincolnshire, England, 1707; d. Marylebone, London, England, 1788) wrote

Scripture References
st. 2 = Phil. 2:7-8
st. 3 = Acts 12:6-8
    Acts 16:25-26
st. 4 = Rom. 8:1
    Heb. 4:16

his powerful and joyful hymn text in 1738 in the days immediately following his conversion to belief in Christ (May 21); he sang it with his brother John (b. Epworth, 1703; d. London, 1791) shortly after John's "Aldersgate experience."

"And Can It Be" was first published in John Wesley's *Psalms and Hymns* (1738). It is subtitled "Free Grace" in John and Charles Wesley's *Hymns and Sacred Poems* (1739). Traditionally one of the great hymns of Methodism, this text appears in a number of modern hymnals.

Like so many of Charles Wesley's hymn texts, "And Can It Be" is full of allusions to and quotations from Scripture; a few of the more obvious texts are Philippians 2:7, Acts 12:6-8, Romans 8:1, and Hebrews 4:16. Wesley's use of metaphors is also noteworthy— he deftly contrasts light and darkness, life and death, slavery and freedom, and especially Christ's righteousness and our unrighteousness.

Note. Further biographical information on Charles and John Wesley follows the musical information about this hymn.

Tune

SAGINA, by Thomas Campbell (b. Sheffield, England, 1777; d. England [?], 1844), is almost universally associated with "And Can It Be." Little is known of Campbell other than his publication *The Bouquet* (1825), in which each of twenty-three tunes has a horticultural name. SAGINA borrows its name from a genus of the pink family of herbs, which includes baby's breath and the carnation. Sing this tune vigorously and in parts, especially at the refrain; singers should be sure to keep the melismas legato, especially in lines 5 and 6.

Liturgical Use

Service of confession and forgiveness; adult baptism; in conjunction with doctrinal preaching; many other occasions.

* * * * * * *

Several members of the Wesley family are significant figures in the history of English hymnody, and none more so than Charles Wesley. Charles was the eighteenth child of Samuel and Susanna Wesley, who educated him when he was young. After attending Westminster School, he studied at Christ Church College, Oxford. It was there that he and George Whitefield formed the Oxford "Holy Club," which Wesley's brother John soon joined. Their purpose was to study the Bible in a disciplined manner, to improve Christian worship and the celebration of the Lord's Supper, and to help the needy. Because of their methods for observing the Christian life, they earned the name "Methodists."

Charles Wesley was ordained a minister in the Church of England in 1735 but found spiritual conditions in the church deplorable. Charles and John served briefly as missionaries to the British colony in Georgia. Enroute they came upon a group of

Moravian missionaries, whose spirituality impressed the Wesleys. They returned to England, and, strongly influenced by the ministry of the Moravians, both Charles and John had conversion experiences in 1738 (see more on this below). The brothers began preaching at revival meetings, often outdoors. These meetings were pivotal in the mid-eighteenth-century "Great Awakening" in England.

Though neither Charles nor John Wesley ever left the Church of England themselves, they are the founders of Methodism. Charles wrote some sixty-five hundred hymns, which were published in sixty-four volumes during his lifetime; these include *Collection of Psalms and Hymns* (1741), *Hymns on the Lord's Supper* (1745), *Hymns and Spiritual Songs* (1753), and *Collection of Hymns for the Use of the People called Methodists* (1780). Charles's hymns are famous for their frequent quotations and allusions from the Bible, for their creedal orthodoxy and their subjective expression of Christian living, and for their use of some forty-five different meters, which inspired new hymn tunes in England. Numerous hymn texts by Wesley are standard entries in most modern hymnals; fourteen are included in the *Psalter Hymnal*.

Charles's elder brother John also studied at Christ Church College, Oxford, and was ordained a priest in the Church of England in 1728. A tutor at Lincoln College in Oxford from 1729 to 1735, Wesley became the leader of the Oxford "Holy Club" mentioned above. After his contact with the Moravian missionaries, Wesley began translating Moravian hymns from German and published his first hymnal, *Collection of Psalms and Hymns*, in Charleston, South Carolina (1737); this hymnal was the first English hymnal ever published for use in worship. Upon his return to England in 1738 Wesley "felt his heart strangely warmed" at a meeting on Aldersgate Street, London, when Peter Bohler, a Moravian, read from Martin Luther's preface to his commentary on the epistle to the Romans. It was at that meeting that John received the assurance that Christ had truly taken away his sins. That conversion experience (followed a few days later by a similar experience by his brother Charles) led to his becoming the great itinerant evangelist and administrator of the Methodist "societies," which would eventually become the Methodist Church. An Anglican all his life, John Wesley wished to reform the Church of England and regretted the need to found a new denomination. Most of the hymnals he prepared with his brother Charles were intended for Christians in all denominations; their *Collection of Hymns for the Use of the People called Methodists* (1780) is one of the few specifically so designated. John was not only a great preacher and organizer, he was also a prolific author, editor, and translator. He translated many classic texts, wrote grammars and dictionaries, and edited the works of John Bunyan and Richard Baxter. In hymnody he is best known for his translation of selections from the German hymnals of Johann Crüger ("Jesus, thy boundless love to me"), Freylinghausen, and von Zinzendorf ("Jesus, thy blood and righteousness"), and for his famous "Directions for Singing," which are still printed in Methodist hymnals. Most significant, however, is his well-known strong hand in editing and often strengthening his brother Charles's hymn texts before they copublished them in their numerous hymnals.

KLOKJE KLINKT
♩ = 60

Lord, I Pray

Text

Originally a children's hymn for morning devotions, "Lord, I   *Scripture References*
Pray" is suitable for God's children of all ages. It is a prayer   st. 1 = Rom. 12:17
requesting a forgiving heart (st. 1), grateful living (st. 2), and   st. 2 = 1 Thess. 5:15-18
obedience and comfort through intimacy with God (st. 3).   st. 3 = Ps. 5:8

Jean C. Keegstra-De Boer (b. Grand Rapids, MI, 1922;
d. Worth, IL, 1982) wrote the text in four stanzas in 1949; it was published in *The
Children's Hymnbook* (NUCS/Eerdmans, 1962). The *Psalter Hymnal* includes the first
three of the original four stanzas, with minor alterations.

Keegstra-De Boer studied at Calvin College, Grand Rapids, and worked for a time as
an editor for Zondervan Publishing. She published several books of verse, including
Bible ABC's in Rhyme (1946). Some of her hymns appeared in *Let Youth Praise Him*
(1949).

Tune

The tune KLOKJE KLINKT is a traditional Dutch melody, often associated in the
Netherlands with the folk song "Klokje klinkt, vogel zingt" ("Clocks do ring, birds do
sing"). Use light organ accompaniment and sing in unison or harmony. The melody
may also be sung as a round after two measures, provided this accompaniment is not
used. Try stanza 3 as a round without accompaniment. Keep the sense of two long
musical lines.

AnnaMae Meyer Bush (b. Paterson, NJ, 1947) harmonized the tune in 1985 at the
request of the *Psalter Hymnal* Revision Committee. A graduate of Calvin College, Bush is
a member of Church of the Servant in Grand Rapids, a congregation that publishes its
own hymnal. Bush helped to compile and continues to update that hymnal. She has
written many hymn texts and tunes for initial use in her congregation, which celebrates
the Lord's Supper every week. Thus a number of her hymns are meant to be sung with
the celebration of the eucharist. Several of her hymns are published in *Songs of Rejoicing*
(1989) and *New Songs of Rejoicing* (1994).

Liturgical Use

Service of confession and forgiveness; as a prayer early in the morning service; as a sung
prayer that is part of the congregational prayer, especially in the morning.

269

Baptized in Water, Sealed by the Spirit

BUNESSAN
♩ = 60

Text

Michael Saward (PHH 16) wrote "Baptized in Water" in London on May 29, 1981, a few days after the twenty-fifth anniversary of his ordination to the ministry. The text was first published in *Hymns for Today's Church* (1982), a hymnal on which Saward worked as text editor.

Scripture References
st. 1 = Titus 3:5-7
Heb. 10:14
st. 2 = Rom. 6:3-4;
Col. 2:12
st. 3 = Rom. 8:15-16
Eph. 4:5-6

This song explains the New Testament theology on baptism in a rather compact way. The first line in each stanza alludes to John 3:5, Ephesians 1:13, and 1 Peter 3:21. The rest of each stanza explains the process symbolized by baptism: being cleansed by Christ's blood for salvation and godly living (st. 1); dying and being buried with Christ and rising again, free and forgiven (st. 2); and gaining the privilege of becoming God's children through Christ (st. 3). Each stanza also finishes with a note of praise to God. The text is powerful precisely because it is biblical.

Tune

BUNESSAN is a Gaelic tune that was first published (melody only) in Lachlan Macbean's *Songs and Hymns of the Gael* (1888) as a setting for Mary Macdonald's carol "Child in the Manger." The tune is named after Macdonald's birthplace on the Isle of Mull, Scotland. BUNESSAN is also well known as the setting for Eleanor Farjeon's "Morning Has Broken" (1931), published in many hymnals and widely popularized by Cat Stevens, who recorded an arrangement of the tune in 1971.

BUNESSAN is intended for unison singing; use a light accompaniment on the organ (or organ trio style) or folk instruments. Dale Grotenhuis (PHH 4) harmonized the tune for the *Psalter Hymnal* in 1985.

Liturgical Use

Infant or adult baptism. An excellent example of a "triumphant hymn" called for in the second form for Baptism of Children and the second form for Baptism of Adults in the *Psalter Hymnal*.

270

NAOMI
♩ = 84

Our Children, Lord, in Faith and Prayer

Text

A prayer asking for God's covenant faithfulness on the children   *Scripture References*
we baptize, this song is adapted from a baptism text written by   st. 1 = Col. 2:11-13
Thomas Haweis (b. Redruth, Cornwall, England, 1734; d. Bath,   st. 2 = Mark 10:13-16
England, 1820) and published in the enlarged edition of his
Carmina Christo (1808). The *Psalter Hymnal* Revision Committee made some significant
changes in the text to express more modern Reformed theological ideas about
baptism.

    Initially apprenticed to a surgeon and pharmacist, Haweis decided to study for the
ministry at Oxford and was ordained in the Church of England in 1757. He served as
curate of St. Mary Magdalen Church, Oxford, but was removed by the bishop from that
position because of his Methodist leanings. He also was an assistant to Martin Madan at
Locke Hospital, London. In 1764 he became rector of All Saints Church in Aldwinkle,
Northamptonshire, and later served as administrator at Trevecca College, Wales, a
school founded by the Countess of Huntingdon, whom Haweis served as chaplain.
After completing advanced studies at Cambridge, he published a Bible commentary
and a volume on church history. Haweis was strongly interested in missions and helped
to found the London Mission Society. His hymn texts and tunes were published in
Carmino Christo, or *Hymns to the Savior* (1792, expanded 1808).

Tune

NAOMI was a melody that Lowell Mason (PHH 96) brought to the United States from
Europe and arranged as a hymn tune; the arrangement was first published in the
periodical *Occasional Psalm and Hymn Tunes* (1836). Some scholars have attributed the
original melody to Johann G. Nägeli (PHH 315), but there is little evidence to substan-
tiate this claim. The name NAOMI has no specific significance, though Mason did often
assign biblical names to his hymn tunes. Sing this typically serviceable Mason tune in
parts, possibly unaccompanied, and keep the tempo moving.

Liturgical Use

Infant baptism.

271

We Know That Christ Is Raised

WALLACE
♩ = 66

Text

The author, John B. Geyer, writes,

Scripture References
st. 2 = Rom 6:3-5
Col. 2:12

"We Know That Christ Is Raised" was written in 1967, when I was tutor at Cheshunt College, Cambridge, U.K. At that time a good deal of work was going on 'round the corner (involving a number of American research students) producing living cells ("the baby in the test tube"). The hymn attempted to illustrate the Christian doctrine of baptism in relation to those experiments.

John B. Geyer (b. Wakefield, Yorkshire, England, 1932) is an Old Testament scholar who has written widely in his field. He wrote a commentary on *The Wisdom of Solomon* (1973) as well as a number of hymns that were first published in various British supplementary hymnals. Educated at Queen's College, Cambridge, and Mansfield College, Oxford, he also studied Old Testament under Gerhard von Rad in Heidelberg. In 1959 Geyer was ordained in the Congregational Union of Scotland. He served as a chaplain at the University of St. Andrews, pastor of Drumchapel Congregational Church in Glasgow, Scotland, and a college tutor. In 1969 Geyer became minister in the (now) United Reformed Church in Little Baddow. Since 1980 he has served as pastor at Weoley Hill, Birmingham, and as chaplain at the University of Birmingham, England.

The text was first published in the British Methodist supplementary hymnal *Hymns and Songs* (1969) but has since been altered in various other hymnals, including the *Psalter Hymnal.* The controlling thought comes from Romans 6:3-5, in which Paul teaches that in baptism we are united with Christ in his resurrection—that is the basis for our new life. Like 269, this song ends each stanza with a note of praise—in this case with an "alleluia" refrain line.

Tune

Composed by C. Keith Landis (b. Chicago, IL, 1922), WALLACE first appeared in *Sixty Hymns from Songs of Zion* (Praise Publications, Inc., 1977). It was first sung at the American Guild of Organists Southern California Conference in 1978. The tune was named for a family friend. Landis was a pastor in the Los Angeles area with a Bachelor of Music degree from Northwestern University, Evanston, Illinois (1946), and a Bachelor of Divinity degree from the Church Divinity School of the Pacific, Berkeley, California (1958).

WALLACE was harmonized by Jeffrey H. Rickard (b. Pasadena, CA, 1942), who received both his B.M. and M.M. from the University of Redlands in California and is currently director of choral activities there. Composer of many choral works, he is also minister of music at Trinity Episcopal Church, Redlands, California, and associate director of publications and musical editor for Praise Publications, Whittier, California.

WALLACE calls for solid organ support. Sing the stanzas in unison, perhaps with the "alleluia" refrain in harmony. Those alleluias should tax the resources of your organ and, if possible, a brass ensemble! Work up an animated pace. Many hymnals set Geyer's text to Charles V. Stanford's ENGELBERG (512), the tune Geyer intended for his text. ENGELBERG may be a bit more difficult —and although it's an older tune, it sounds more modern than WALLACE—but is another fine match for the text.

Liturgical Use
Infant or adult baptism; Easter.

272

JANNA
♩ = 54

You Are Our God; We Are Your People

Text

David A. Hoekema (b. Paterson, NJ, 1950) composed both the text and the tune for this hymn in June 1978 in Grand Rapids, Michigan, for the baptism of his daughter Janna, for whom he named the tune. Hoekema states,

Scripture References
st. 1 = Gen. 7
     Gen. 9:13-15
     1 Pet. 3:18-22
st. 2 = Gen. 15:5
     Gen. 17:1-8
     Gen. 21:1-7
st. 3 = Heb. 8
st. 4 = Acts 2:38-39

> One morning in June, while I walked the half-mile up the hill from my home to my office, a spirited little tune hummed its way into my mind, and at the same time some words and ideas that I had toyed with took clearer shape in relation to the tune. During the next week or so I added the harmony—a dissonant but rolling harmony that seemed to fit the tune especially well—and refined the text. I believe that this hymn was a gift given to me to celebrate my daughter's baptism.

Originally titled "Covenant Song," Hoekema's storylike text recounts various points in salvation history when God made covenant promises with his people: to Noah (st. 1; in Gen. 9 and also 1 Pet. 3, where Peter relates the flood story to baptism), to Abraham and Sarah (st. 2), and to us in the new covenant in Christ (st. 3), with baptism the sign of our union with Christ and his body, the people of God (st. 4). This hymn was first published in the 1987 *Psalter Hymnal.*

Tune

JANNA is a strong tune built with some repeated phrases and sequences; a unique rhythmic pattern carries this song along resolutely from beginning to end. Sing JANNA in unison with lots of energy on a half-note pulse. This tune also makes a fine solo anthem. Sing stanzas 1 and 2 in antiphonal groups and stanzas 3 and 4 all together.

Hoekema is currently an academic dean at his alma mater, Calvin College, Grand Rapids, Michigan. He received a Ph.D. from Princeton University, taught philosophy at St. Olaf College, Northfield, Minnesota (1977-1984), and was executive director of the American Philosophical Association while teaching philosophy at the University of Delaware (1984-1993). In addition to many journal articles on philosophical issues, he has published *Rights and Wrongs: Coercion, Punishment and the State* (1986).

Liturgical Use
Infant or adult baptism; in conjunction with preaching on covenant history. Hoekema says it is also fitting after a week of rain!

273

Almighty Father, Covenant God

WYATT
♩ = 54

Text
Marie J. Post (PHH 5) wrote "Almighty Father, Covenant God" in 1975 for the baptism of her grandson Wyatt L. Worst. Both text and tune were first published in the 1987 *Psalter Hymnal.*

The text includes both Old Testament covenant language, such as "the seed of Abraham" (st. 4), and New Testament images for baptism, such as being grafted into Christ and being adopted as children of God (st. 2). Stanza 5 is a trinitarian doxology (see PHH 246 for a brief explanation of trinitarian structure).

Tune
WYATT is a tune that Dale Grotenhuis (PHH 4) originally composed for an Easter cantata. When Marie J. Post asked him to provide music for her baptism hymn, Grotenhuis used this tune. At Post's request, he named it WYATT in honor of her grandson.

WYATT has an effective melodic contour that rises to its highest point in the tune's final phrase. Sing this tune in unison or in harmony at a good pace. Try singing stanza 5 in a slightly more stately manner and with extra reeds and mixtures in the organ accompaniment.

Liturgical Use
Infant baptism.

274

MELCOMBE
♩ = 100

O God, Great Father, Lord and King

Text

"O God, Great Father" alludes to the gospel story of bringing little children to Jesus, especially in stanzas 1 and 3 (Mark 10:13-16). The Reformed view of God's covenant shows up in stanza 2, and the work of the Holy Spirit appears in stanza 4. Stanza 5 is similar to the consecration prayer that follows the act of baptism in the *Psalter Hymnal's* baptism forms.

Scripture References
st. 1 = Mark 10:13-16
st. 2 = Gen. 17:7
st. 3 = Mark 10:13-16
st. 4 = Titus 3:5
st. 5 = Ps. 119:133, 135

Methodist Bishop Elijah Embree Hoss (b. Washington County, TN, 1849; d. Muskogee, OK, 1919) composed these words for a baptismal service he conducted in Walnut Ridge, Arkansas, in November 1903. The text was printed in the Nashville *Christian Advocate* in early 1904 and subsequently published in *The Methodist Hymnal* of 1905; Hoss served on the Joint Commission that produced this hymnal. An ordained minister in the Methodist Episcopal Church South, Hoss served parishes in Knoxville, Tennessee; San Francisco, California; and Asheville, North Carolina. He was also professor of church history at Vanderbilt University, Nashville, Tennessee, and president of Emory and Henry College, Emory, Virginia.

Tune

MELCOMBE was composed by Samuel Webbe (1740-1816). See PHH 112 for information on MELCOMBE and on Webbe.

Liturgical Use

Infant baptism.

275

ARDEN
♩ = 116

The Lord Our God in Mercy Spoke

Text

Isaac Watts (PHH 155) first published this baptism hymn in his *Hymns and Spiritual Songs* (1707). The *Psalter Hymnal* has omitted Watts's original third stanza and has altered the text considerably to update the language. Originally the first line read "Thus saith the mercy of the Lord."

Scripture References
st. 1 = Gen. 17:7
st. 2 = Gen. 22
st. 3 = Acts 2:38-39

The song's four stanzas in the *Psalter Hymnal* are a "sung theology" of God's covenant with Abraham and his descendants (Gen. 17:7) expressed in the context of baptism. Stanza 4 offers an unusual apocalyptic view of the meaning of baptism.

Tune

ARDEN is a noble, singable, somewhat dramatic tune set to a fine accompaniment suited to harmony singing. Try having a soloist sing the words attributed to God in stanza 1.

George T. Thalben-Ball (b. Sidney, Australia, 1896; d. London, England, 1987) composed ARDEN for the *BBC Hymn Book* of 1951, on which he worked as an editor. In that volume ARDEN was a setting for Charles Wesley's "Oh, for a Thousand Tongues to Sing" (501). The tune is named for the district in Warwickshire, England, where the committee who compiled the *BBC Hymn Book* often met.

Thalben-Ball moved with his family from Australia to England when he was a child. His promise as an organist was evident early on: after studying at the Royal College of Music in London in 1910, he became organist at several London churches. At the age of sixteen he became a Fellow of the Royal College of Organists. In 1923 he became the permanent organist of the Temple Church in London, a position he retained for many years. This church was largely destroyed during World War II, but it was restored in 1954 with an organ built under Thalben-Ball's supervision. An internationally known recitalist and an organist for the BBC, he helped shape the daily religious broadcasts of the BBC and contributed to the *The BBC Hymn Book*. He also became city and university organist in Birmingham, served as an examiner for the Royal School of Church Music, taught organ at the Royal College of Music, and was famous for his choral recordings at the Temple Church. Thalben-Ball was knighted in 1982.

Liturgical Use

Most often for infant baptism.

276

Teach Me, O Lord, Your Way of Truth

ST. CRISPIN
♩ = 138

Text

The five stanzas of "Teach Me, O Lord" come from three long-meter settings for Psalm 119 in the 1912 *Psalter*. That psalter included a separate musical setting for each of Psalm 119's twenty-two biblical stanzas. The *Psalter Hymnal* Revision Committee chose these five stanzas because they are especially useful as prayers for illumination. With the psalmist, we sing: Teach us your way, O Lord (st. 1); the path of your command-

Scripture References
st. 1 = Ps. 119:33-34
st. 2 = Ps. 119:35-36
st. 3 = Ps. 119:105-106
st. 4 = Ps. 119:129-130
st. 5 = Ps. 119:131-132

ments is our delight (st. 2); your Word is a lamp to our feet (st. 3); we obey and honor your truthful and clear Word (st. 4); as we thirst for it, Lord, we ask for the mercy you have promised us (st. 5). See PHH 119 for further commentary on Psalm 119.

Tune
Composed by George J. Elvey (PHH 48) in 1862 for "Just as I Am, without One Plea" (263), ST. CRISPIN was first published in the 1863 edition of Edward Thorne's *Selection of Psalm and Hymn Tunes.* The tune title honors a third-century Roman martyr, Crispin, who, along with Crispinian, preached in Gaul (modern-day France); these two missionaries are the patron saints of shoemakers and leather workers.

ST. CRISPIN has an attractive melodic contour. Its repeated notes are typical of other "generic" British hymn tunes from the later nineteenth century (for example, QUEBEC, 141, 307; PENTECOST, 212; MORECAMBE, 419; and MARYTON, 573). Sing it in harmony, perhaps unaccompanied on one of the inner stanzas. The parallel structure of the text also invites singing stanzas in alternation between either men and women or two sides of the congregation.

Liturgical Use
As a sung prayer for illumination; whenever God's people meditate on the centrality of the Word.

277

ALL SAINTS
♩ = 50

God Who Spoke in the Beginning

Text
Fred (Frederick Herman) Kaan (b. Haarlem, the Netherlands, 1929) skillfully conveys through his hymn text that when God speaks, things happen. God spoke the creation into being (st. 1); God has spoken throughout history and supremely through Christ, the Son (st. 2); and God still speaks today through the Word Incarnate (Christ) and through the words and deeds of Christians who are stirred to action through his Holy Spirit (st. 3).

Scripture References
st. 1 = Gen. 1-2
st. 2 = Heb. 1:1-2

Under the title "The First and Final Word" the text was first published in *Pilgrim Praise* (1968), a compilation of Kaan's hymns.

Baptized in the historic St. Bavo Church in Haarlem, Kaan began his theological education at the University of Utrecht but moved to England in 1952 and completed his studies at Bristol University. Ordained by the (now) United Reformed Church in 1955, he served the Windsor Road Congregational Church in Barry, Wales (1955-1963), and the Pilgrim Church, Plymouth, England (1963-1968). From 1968 to 1978 he was initially minister-secretary of the International Congregational Council in Geneva, Switzerland, and then executive secretary of the World Alliance of Reformed Churches. He returned to England in 1978 to become the moderator of the Western Midlands Province of the United Reformed Church, after which he served the Central Church in Swindon and the Penhill United Reformed Church (1985-1989). As an ecumenist Kaan has associations with Christian communities and social action groups throughout the world. He began to write hymns because he wanted to "fill the gaps" not covered by traditional hymnals especially in the area of the social responsibility demanded by the gospel. Considered one of the important contributors to the recent "explosion" in English hymn writing, Kaan has written some two hundred hymns and translations. His hymns were collected in *Pilgrim Praise* (1968,1972), *Break Not the Circle* (1975), *The Hymn Texts of Fred Kaan* (1985), and *Planting Trees and Sowing Seeds* (1989), as well as in most recent hymnals. Kaan's 1984 doctoral dissertation (Geneva Theological College) is called "Emerging Language in Hymnody."

Tune

ALL SAINTS is a stately tune with a demanding harmony that a good singing congregation or choir will want to sing in parts. See PHH 230 for background information on ALL SAINTS; the setting there is also in a lower key.

Liturgical Use

Probably most useful before or after the sermon, but also suitable in many other contexts.

278

Holy Spirit, Mighty God

LAUDS
♩ = 52

Text

Written by Calvin Seerveld (PHH 22) in 1983, "Holy Spirit, Mighty God" was first published in the 1987 *Psalter Hymnal*. The unrhymed text is a prayer asking the Holy Spirit to help us hear the Word (st. 1), to move us to live the Christian life in deeds of love (st. 2), and to grant us the shalom of communion with God (st. 3). Each stanza ends with a request for wisdom.

Scripture References
all st. = 1 Cor. 2:13

Tune

Spritely and bright, LAUDS fits well with Seerveld's text. The melody features an effective tonal and rhythmic climax in the last phrase. Use light organ accompaniment to sing the tune in unison. Harmony singing works well too. Keep a dotted half note pulse throughout. A descant by Wilson for this tune was also published in Hymns for Celebration and in the Agape (Hope Publishing Co.) Hymnal Supplement.

John W. Wilson (b. Bournville, Birmingham, England, 1905; d. Guildford, Surrey, England, 1992) composed LAUDS in 1967 to be published with James Montgomery's (PHH 72) text "Songs of Praise the Angels Sang" in the British Methodist supplementary hymnal *Hymns and Songs* (1969). The tune's name derives from the praise theme of that text. Ever since a 1972 hymn sing organized by the Royal School of Church Music, London, however, LAUDS has been associated with Brian A. Wren's (PHH 311) text "There's a Spirit in the Air." LAUDS was published with that text in the British collection *Hymns for Celebration* (1974). It was this latter combination that inspired Calvin Seerveld in 1983 to write another text about the Holy Spirit for this tune.

Wilson was a major force in the modern British "hymn explosion." After receiving an education in mathematics and physics at Cambridge University, he turned his attention to music and studied at the Royal College of Music in London. He was director of music at Charterhouse, a famous British school (1947-1965), and taught music at the Royal College of Music (1965-1980). Treasurer of the Hymn Society of Great Britain and Ireland from 1965 to 1990, he organized and directed the popular "Come and Sing" hymn festivals at Westminster Abbey. Wilson edited many British hymnals, including the *Clarendon Hymn Book* (1936), *Hymns for Church and School* (1964), and, most extensively, the Methodist *Hymns and Psalms* (1983). In addition he contributed his editorial expertise to a number of hymnal supplements and his encouragement to various modern hymn authors and composers. His own tunes have been published in a variety of British and American hymnals. Wilson was honored as a Fellow of the Hymn Society in the United States and Canada in 1985.

Liturgical Use

As a prayer for illumination; during Pentecost; whenever Christian worship focuses on obedience, comfort, wisdom, or other evidence of the Spirit's presence.

279

MUNICH
♩ = 54

O Word of God Incarnate

Text

The prevalent image in this hymn is light: God is the Light; his Word is a light for our path; and we, the church, must be a light for the nations. The author, William W. How (b. Shrewsbury, Shropshire, England, 1823; d. Leenane, County Mayo, Ireland, 1897), first published it with a subhead quotation from Proverbs 6:23: "For the commandment is a

Scripture References
st. 1 = Ps. 119:105, 130
John 1:1-14
st. 2 = 2 Tim. 3:15-17
st. 3 = Matt. 5:14-16
1 Cor. 13:12

lamp: and the law is light; and reproofs of instruction are the way of life" (KJV). Some hymnodists have stated that the song is based on Psalm 119:105, which contains nearly the same imagery: "Your word is a lamp to my feet and a light for my path." Using intriguing word play, the hymn praises Christ as the "Word of God incarnate" and as the "Light" who has given us Scripture (often referred to as God's Word) as a "light" ("lantern") to guide the church (st. 1-2) and to inspire it to be a "lamp" for shining God's "light" to all the world (st. 2-3). The text also includes travel imagery: "footsteps" (st. 1), "chart and compass," "voyage" (st. 2), and "pilgrims" (st. 3). Singing this text, we pray that the church, the people of God, will always be led by the Scriptures to seek Christ, to whom the Scriptures point, and to bring the good news of his Word to the nations. This text was first published in the 1867 addition to *Psalms and Hymns* (1854), a supplementary collection How edited with Thomas B. Morrell.

How studied at Wadham College, Oxford, and Durham University and was ordained in the Church of England in 1847. He served various congregations and became Suffragan Bishop in east London in 1879 and Bishop of Wakefield in 1888. Called both the "poor man's bishop" and "the children's bishop," How was known for his work among the destitute in the London slums and among the factory workers in west Yorkshire. He wrote a number of theological works about controversies surrounding the Oxford Movement and attempted to reconcile biblical creation with the theory of evolution. He was joint editor of *Psalms and Hymns* (1854) and *Church Hymns* (1871). While rector in Whittington, How wrote some sixty hymns, including many for children. His collected *Poems and Hymns* were published in 1886.

Tune

MUNICH has a colorful history. Traces of it run as far back as 1593 in the Dresden, Germany, *Gesangbuch* in conjunction with the text "Wir Christenleut." A version from a Meiningen *Gesangbuch* (1693) is still used in Lutheranism for "O Gott, du frommer Gott." Felix Mendelssohn's adaptation of that tune for the quartet "Cast Thy Burden upon the Lord" in the oratorio *Elijah* (1846) is the most recent step in shaping MUNICH as we find it in the *Psalter Hymnal* and other modern English hymnals.

Felix Mendelssohn-Bartholdy (b. Hamburg, Germany, 1809; d. Leipzig, Germany, 1847) was the son of banker Abraham Mendelssohn and the grandson of philosopher Moses Mendelssohn. His Jewish family became Christian and took the Bartholdy name (name of the estate of Mendelssohn's uncle) when baptized into the Lutheran church. The children all received an excellent musical education. Mendelssohn had his first public performance at the age of nine and by the age of sixteen had written several symphonies. Profoundly influenced by J. S. Bach's music, he conducted a performance of the *St. Matthew Passion* in 1829 (at age 20!)—the first performance since Bach's death, thus reintroducing Bach to the world. Mendelssohn organized the Domchor in Berlin and founded the Leipzig Conservatory of Music in 1843. Traveling widely, he not only became familiar with various styles of music but also became well known himself in countries other than Germany, especially in England. He left a rich treasury of music:

organ and piano works, overtures and incidental music, oratorios (including *St. Paul* and *Elijah* and choral works, and symphonies. He harmonized a number of hymn tunes himself, but hymnbook editors also arranged some of his other tunes into hymn tunes.

Given its geographical roots, we may be fairly confident that the tune is named after the German city Munich, although the city's name in German is München.

Like many other chorales, MUNICH is in bar form (AABA'). Try singing it in harmony and possibly unaccompanied on stanza 2.

Liturgical Use

As a sung prayer for illumination and for the preservation and mission of the church.

280

LIEBSTER JESU
♩ = 52

Blessed Jesus, at Your Word

Text

Essentially a prayer asking for illumination by the Holy Spirit as the Christian community gathers around the Lord's Word, "Blessed Jesus" is a pre-sermon hymn by Tobias Clausnitzer (b. Thum, Saxony, Germany, 1619; d. Weiden, Upper Palatine, Germany, 1684). It was first published in the *Altdorffisches Gesang-Büchlein* (1663) and first attributed to Clausnitzer in the Nüremberg, Germany, *Gesangbuch* (1676). Catherine Winkworth (PHH 194) translated the text and published it in English in her *Lyra Germanica* (2nd series, 1858).

Clausnitzer graduated from the University of Leipzig and became a chaplain in the Swedish army. He preached two sermons at memorable occasions: when Queen Christina ascended the Swedish throne in 1645 and when the Peace of Westphalia, which ended the Thirty Years War, was celebrated in 1648. Clausnitzer became a pastor in Weiden in 1648, where he remained until his death. In addition to "Blessed Jesus, at Your Word," his creedal hymn, "We Believe in One True God," is found in many modern hymnals.

Tune

LIEBSTER JESU is a rather serene German chorale that is ideally sung in three long lines and in parts with light organ accompaniment. In rounded bar form (AABA') LIEBSTER JESU (also called DESSAU and NÜRENBERG) was originally one of Johann R. Ahle's "sacred arias," first published with Franz J. Burmeister's Advent hymn text "Ja, er ist's, das Heil der Welt" in the Mühlhausen, Germany, *Neue geistliche auf die Sonntage . . . Andachten* (1664). The tune was later modified and published in the Darmstadt, Germany, *Das grosse Cantional* (1687) as a setting for a baptism hymn by Benjamin Schmolck that had the same first line as Clausnitzer's text: "Liebster Jesu, wir sind hier."

Because several sources say that LIEBSTER JESU was first associated with Clausnitzer's hymn in the 1671 *Altdorfer Gesangbuch,* it seems probable that the tune name derives from that hymn text.

While studying at the university in Erfurt, Ahle (b. Mühlhausen, Thuringia, Germany, 1625; d. Mühlhausen, 1673) was a cantor at St. Andrew Church and director of the music school. In 1654 he became organist at St. Blasius Church in Mühlhausen, a position he held until his death. During those years Ahle also served as a councilman and mayor of the city. Ahle's compositions, often ornate and strongly dramatic, reflected some of the features of Italian opera; he called his religious vocal pieces "sacred arias." Although sometimes scorned by more traditional musicians, Ahle's music helped to revitalize the church music of his day.

Liturgical Use
As a sung prayer for illumination prior to the reading or preaching of the Word.

281

Thanks to God Whose Word Was Spoken

ERIN
$\quad \downarrow = 100$

Text
Reginald T. Brooks (b. Wandsworth, London, England, 1918; d. London, 1985) wrote this hymn in 1954 for the 150th anniversary of the British and Foreign Bible Society; it was first published in the 1964 *Methodist Hymnal.* The text has been altered for publication in the *Psalter Hymnal.* More comprehensive than the similar text at 277, Brooks's hymn

Scripture References
all st. = Hebrews 1:1-2
st. 1 = Zech. 13:9
st. 2 = John 1:14
st. 3 = Rom. 16:25-26

helps us offer thanks to God for the various ways in which the Word comes to us: through creation (st. 1); through Christ, the incarnate Word (st. 2); through the Bible, God's written Word, published in many languages (st. 3-4); and through the Holy Spirit, who speaks to us within (st. 5).

Brooks was an ordained minister in the United Reformed Church in England and served as a radio and television producer for the Religious Broadcasting Department of the BBC. Always known as R. T. Brooks, he was educated at the London School of Economics and studied theology at Mansfield College, Oxford, England.

Tune
Paul T. Langston (b. Marianna, FL, 1928) composed ERIN on request in 1974 for the 1975 *Baptist Hymnal,* in which it was published as a setting for W. Nantlais Williams's urban hymn "Jesus, Friend of Thronging Pilgrims." Langston named the tune after his daughter. Brooks originally wrote his text in 87 87 47, without the textual repeat in the

final line, but the addition of that repeat to accommodate ERIN fits very well with the tune's closing sequence. Composed in bar form (AAB), ERIN is a tune in minor that shifts to melodic minor (almost major) in its final line for a brilliant ending. Stanzas 2 and 3 may be sung by alternating groups (men and women, or two sides of the congregation) with everyone joining in each time on "God has spoken. . . ." For festive use, add trumpets or a full brass choir. Bright, full organ music is also helpful.

Langston is a music educator and a composer of both organ and choral works. He studied composition with Nadia Boulanger and received his education from the University of Florida, Gainesville, and Southern Baptist Theological Seminary, Louisville, Kentucky. In 1963 he earned a doctorate at Union Theological Seminary, New York City. An organist and choirmaster at several churches, Langston has also been a professor at Davidson College in North Carolina and Stetson University in Florida.

Liturgical Use
The entire song is suitable for festive use at high points in the church year and for special events such as ordination, profession of faith, missions, Reformation, and more. Stanzas 1 through 3 (and perhaps 4) are suitable before the sermon, and stanza 5 is a fitting post-sermon response.

282

BREAD OF LIFE
♩ = 60

Break Now the Bread of Life

Text
Mary A. Lathbury (b. Manchester, NY, 1841; d. East Orange, NJ, 1913) is known primarily for two hymns: this one (originally "Break Thou the Bread of Life") and "Day Is Dying in the West." She wrote both at the request of Bishop John H. Vincent for use in the services of the Chautauqua Assembly, well-known in the late nineteenth and early twentieth centuries as a conference center that offered a rich fare of Bible study, Sunday school teaching methods, concerts, and plays. Vincent, the secretary of the Methodist Sunday School Union, founded the Chautauqua Institution on Chautauqua Lake in upper New York State in an effort to educate Sunday school teachers. An assistant to Vincent at the camp, Lathbury was also a well-known writer, editor, and illustrator of children's books. Her literary skills earned her the nickname "Poet Laureate of Chautauqua."

Lathbury wrote stanzas 1 and 2 in 1877; they were first published in *Chautauqua Carols* (1878). Alexander Groves (b. Newport, Isle of Wight, England, 1842; d. Henley-on-Thames, Oxfordshire, England, 1909) added stanzas 3 and 4 later, and they were first published in the *Wesleyan Methodist Magazine* (London, Sept. 1913). Groves's career

Scripture References
st. 1-2 = Matt. 14:13-21
st. 3   = John 6:33-35
st. 4   = Matt. 9:27-30
          Matt. 20:30-34

included being a grocer and accountant as well as a trustee, auditor, and actuary for the Henley Savings Bank. He served as organist of the Henley Wesleyan Chapel but later in life became a member of the Anglican Church in Henley.

Some expressions in "Break Now the Bread of Life" may not satisfy everyone in the Reformed community, but these verses were not written to define doctrine in sharp detail. They were intended to be used as a simple prayer for illumination for Bible study groups and in the meetings of the Chautauqua Literary and Scientific Circle. Tradition also calls for the hymn's use during Sunday-evening vespers at the Lake Chautauqua assembly grounds.

The hymn text draws on biblical images to depict Scripture's role in our lives. Stanzas 1 and 2 recall the breaking and the blessing of the bread at Jesus' feeding of the five thousand. Stanza 3 confesses Christ as the bread of life. Stanza 4 calls for the Spirit's presence and alludes to Christ's healings of various blind people.

Tune

William F. Sherwin (PHH 8) composed BREAD OF LIFE in 1877 for the stanzas by Lathbury when he was the music director for the Chautauqua Institution.

A good fit for the hymn text, BREAD OF LIFE is a quiet tune, meditative in tone but with a fine climax in its final phrase. Sing this tune in harmony at a firm tempo.

Liturgical Use

A simple prayer for illumination; vespers. (Though it uses the "bread of life" image, this is not ordinarily a hymn for the Lord's Supper.)

283

The Lord Almighty Spoke the Word

ROK NOVY
$\downarrow = 60$

Text

One of the best short hymns in the hymnal's Word of God section, "The Lord Almighty Spoke" is a crisp text, striking in its simplicity and its thought pattern. Stanza 1 extols God's creative word; stanza 2 celebrates the victory of Christ, the Word made flesh; and stanza 3 appeals to the Trinity to proclaim the coming kingdom.

Scripture References
st. 1 = Gen. 1
Job 38:7
st. 2 = John 1:14
1 Cor. 15

Charles E. Watson (b. Cleethorpes, Lincolnshire, England, 1869; d. Stroud, Gloucestershire, England, 1942) left the Church of England to study for the ministry in the Congregational Church. Beginning in 1898 he served Congregational churches at Lymm in Cheshire, Oakhill; in Somerset; and for the last thirty-three years of his life, the Rodborough Tabernacle United Reformed Church in Gloucestershire. He wrote two hymns and a prayer book for his congregation at

Rodborough Tabernacle. This hymn was published in the *Rodborough Hymnal* in 1964. Stanza 3 was altered for publication in the *Psalter Hymnal*.

Tune

ROK NOVY is an anonymous Slovak tune that was first published in Tobias Zavorka's *Kancional* of 1602, though it may date back into the fifteenth century. The tune title means "new year" and is the incipit of the Slovak Old/New Year text "Rok novy zase k nam prisel," traditionally associated with this music (PHH 444). Zavorka served as a pastor and dean in the Bohemian city of Dubrava. *Kancional* was an important Bohemian Brethren hymnal containing 770 tunes (usually dated 1602, the year in which work on the hymnal began, although it was published around 1606).

The tune is a fine match for the striking text: a short initial phrase launches the remainder of the melody, which flows on in one long line. The harmony, prepared in 1984 by choral composer Dale Grotenhuis (PHH 4), is well suited to part singing. Raise the final tenor note at the end of stanza 3 to conclude with a bright major chord.

Liturgical Use

Because stanzas 1 and 2 are designed for teaching (only st. 3 addresses God), this hymn is most useful in conjunction with reading Scripture and preaching the Word. But it can be used at many points in the worship service, including the beginning and end.

284

MARANATHA
♩ = 58

Father, I Adore You

Text

"Father, I Adore You" is one of the more enduring praise choruses of the latter part of the twentieth century, partly because it's a humble and simple text and partly because it's enjoyable to sing as a round. The text expresses praise, subjection, and love to the triune God. Out of the oral tradition in which choruses like this one prevail, the song's trinitarian text has prompted an additional, concluding stanza: "Three-in-One, I adore you." Some hymnals use the plural form, "Father, *we* adore you."

Terrye Coelho (b. Camp Roberts, CA, 1952) states that she composed both text and tune for this hymn in 1972 "while driving a car and worshiping God." The song was first performed, published, and recorded at Calvary Chapel, Costa Mesa, California, in 1972. In 1971 Coelho was converted to Christianity, joined Calvary Chapel, and became a singer for Maranatha! Music. Educated at Arizona State University and at a medical assistant's program in Anaheim, California, Coelho is a songwriter and homemaker. She has written many lyrics, most of which are unpublished.

Tune

The tune title MARANATHA is an Aramaic expression meaning "Come, O Lord!" or "Our Lord has come." "Maranatha!" became an acclamation in the early church (see 1 Cor. 16:22; Rev. 22:20) and is also part of the name of the Christian music publisher Maranatha! Music, which began as a ministry of Calvary Chapel.

Sing this hymn in three stanzas, or preferably as a three-part round. Use very light registration, just strong enough to provide a steady tempo, and maintain the pulse between stanzas. Guitars are appropriate, with perhaps flute or other melody instruments improvising a descant by playing the alto or tenor part an octave higher.

Because the song is so simple, people can divide into groups to sing it as a round; to avoid the distraction of spoken directions, the song leader can simply gesture to signal when each group should begin. Try singing stanza 1 together; then continue with stanzas 2 and 3 in a round.

Liturgical Use

Offering of gifts; adult baptism; profession of faith; ordination; commissioning; Lord's Supper; many other occasions in Christian worship.

285

O Jesus, I Have Promised

NYLAND
$\downarrow = 58$

Text

John E. Bode (b. St. Pancras, England, 1816; d. Castle Camps, Cambridgeshire, England, 1874) wrote this hymn of consecration in 1866 on the occasion of the confirmation (profession of faith and first communion) of his daughter and two sons. The text was printed in 1868 by the Society for the Promotion of Christian Knowledge in a leaflet entitled "A Hymn for the Newly Confirmed" and was later published in an appendix to that society's *Psalms and Hymns* (1869).

Scripture References
st. 1 = Luke 9:57
Rom. 6:13
st. 4 = John 12:26

A fine student at Christ Church, Oxford, England, and a prominent scholar who gave the famous Bampton Lectures ("for the exposition and defense of the Christian faith") at Oxford in 1855, Bode was a rector in Westwell, Oxfordshire, and in Castle Camps. This gifted poet and hymn writer published *Hymns for the Gospel of the Day, for Each Sunday and Festivals of Our Lord* in 1860.

Nearly all hymnals, including the *Psalter Hymnal*, delete two of Bode's original six stanzas. The hymn originally began with the words "O Jesus, *we* have promised" and included a reference to Luke 9:57: "I will follow you wherever you go." The text, especially stanza 4, has been altered for publication in the *Psalter Hymnal*.

The word "promised" in stanza 1 refers to the vows taken at confirmation/profession of faith. This hymn is a prayer for Christ's presence on the Christian pilgrimage—in the face of temptation and external sin (st. 2) and internal guilt (st. 3)—and it assures us that our promises (st. 1) come in response to the promises of Christ (st. 4).

Tune

NYLAND, named for a province in Finland, is a folk melody from Kuortane, South Ostrobothnia, Finland. In fact, the tune is also known as KUORTANE. NYLAND was first published with a hymn text in an appendix to the 1909 edition of the Finnish *Suomen Evankelis Luterilaisen Kirken Koraalikirja*. It gained popularity in the English-speaking world after David Evans's use of it in the British *Church Hymnary* of 1927 as a setting for Anna L. Waring's text "In Heavenly Love Abiding." Evans (b. Resolven, Glamorganshire, Wales, 1874; d. Rosllannerchrugog, Denbighshire, Wales, 1948) edited that hymnal, which was the source of a number of his harmonizations, including this one.

David Evans was an important leader in Welsh church music. Educated at Arnold College, Swansea, and at University College, Cardiff, he received a doctorate in music from Oxford University. His longest professional post was as professor of music at University College in Cardiff (1903-1939), where he organized a large music department. He was also a well-known and respected judge at Welsh hymn-singing festivals and a composer of many orchestral and choral works, anthems, service music, and hymn tunes.

NYLAND is a modified rounded bar-form tune (AA'BA') with a wide-ranging melodic contour and a fine harmonization for part singing. It needs good singers for the harmony and requires organ phrasing that produces four long lines.

Liturgical Use

Profession of faith; adult baptism; ordination; as a hymn of dedication following the sermon.

286

MINIVER
♩ = 112
Lord of Creation, to You Be All Praise

Text

"Lord of Creation" begins by voicing praise to God for his mighty deeds (st. 1), and in keeping with the "summary of the law" (Mark 12:28-31; see also 155), it directs each one of us to sing, "I give you my will" (st. 2), "my mind" (st. 3), "my heart" (st. 4), and "my all" (st. 5). Note also the use of paradox in stanza 2.

Scripture References
st. 3 = 1 Cor. 2:9-10

John (Jack) Copley Winslow (b. Hanworth, Middlesex, England, 1882; d. Godalming, Surrey, England, 1974) wrote this hymn of dedication and first published it in his *Garland of Verse* (1961). Alterations to the text have been made in various hymnals, including the *Psalter Hymnal*. Winslow was educated at Balliol College in Oxford and Wells Theological College, and was ordained a priest in the Church of England in 1908. After serving at Wimbledon and lecturing at St. Augustine's College in Canterbury, he worked as a missionary in India (1914-1934). He returned to England and served as parish priest and chaplain at a number of churches, including Lee Abbey in Lynton (1948-1962). His publications include *The Church in Action* (1936), *The Christian Approach to the Hindus* (1958), and *Modern Miracles* (1968). His hymns were published in *Hymns Ancient and Modern* (1950) as well as in various other hymnals.

Tune

MINIVER is a strong tune that makes good use of several repeated melodic motives. Sing stanzas 1 and 5 in unison and stanzas 2 through 4 in parts. Support the melody line with a bright solo stop on the organ. Composed by Cyril V. Taylor (b. Wigan, Lancashire, England, 1907; d. Petersfield, England, 1992), MINIVER was published with Jan Struther's "Lord of All Hopefulness" (558) in the *BBC Hymn Book* (1951). The tune is named after Struther's novel *Mrs. Miniver* (1939).

Taylor was a chorister at Magdalen College School, Oxford, and studied at Christ Church, Oxford, and Westcott House, Cambridge. Ordained a priest in the Church of England in 1932, he served the church as both pastor and musician. His positions included being a producer in the religious broadcasting department of the BBC (1939-1953), chaplain of the Royal School of Church Music (1953-1958), vicar of Cerne Abbas in Dorsetshire (1958-1969), and precentor of Salisbury Cathedral (1969-1975). He contributed twenty hymn tunes to the *BBC Hymn Book* (1951), which he edited, and other tunes to the Methodist *Hymns and Psalms* (1983). He also edited *100 Hymns for Today* (1969) and *More Hymns for Today* (1980). Writer of the booklet *Hymns for Today Discussed* (1984), Taylor was chairman of the Hymn Society of Great Britain and Ireland from 1975 to 1980.

Liturgical Use

As an offertory hymn; as a hymn of commitment following the reading of the Ten Commandments; as a response to the sermon.

ADELAIDE
♩ = 58

Have Thine Own Way, Lord

Text

Periodically distressed after being unable to raise money to go to Africa as a missionary in the late 1890s, Adelaide A. Pollard (b. Bloomfield, IA, 1862; d. New York, NY, 1934) attended a prayer meeting in 1902 and was inspired after hearing an older woman pray, "It really doesn't matter what you do with us, Lord—just have your way with our lives." Pollard went home and meditated on the potter's story in Jeremiah 18 (the same image is also in Isa. 64:8) and wrote the consecration hymn "Have Thine Own Way, Lord." Repeating the words "Have thine own way," each stanza emphasizes the believer's harmony with God's will. This is a deeply personal prayer that culminates in a strong plea that others may see Christ in the believer through the power of the Holy Spirit (st. 4).

Scripture References
st. 1 = Jer. 18:6
Isa. 64:8
st. 2 = Ps. 139:23-24

Originally called Sarah, Pollard chose the name Adelaide for herself. She studied speech at the Boston School of Oratory and taught in several girls' schools in Chicago, Illinois. Influenced by the evangelist R. A. Torrey, she enrolled as a student at the Moody Bible Institute in Chicago and later taught at the Missionary Training School of the Christian Missionary Alliance in Nyack-on-the Hudson, New York. A missionary in Africa prior to World War I, she devoted the last years of her life to Christian mysticism.

Tune

George C. Stebbins (PHH 63) composed ADELAIDE for these words of Pollard and named the tune in her honor. Loved by many Christians, both text and tune were first published in 1907 in Stebbins's collection *Northfield Hymnal with Alexander's Supplement;* they were also published in several of Ira D. Sankey's hymnals that same year.

Though the melody is certainly serviceable, ADELAIDE is perhaps best sung in parts. Give this music a shot of energy: do not sing it too slowly.

Liturgical Use

For believers to dedicate themselves individually and collectively to follow the will of the Lord; stanza 2 suggests use in the service of confession and forgiveness, but as a whole the song fits best as a post-sermon hymn.

288

Take My Life and Let It Be

HENDON
♩ = 56

Text

Frances R. Havergal (b. Astley, Worcestershire, England, 1836; d. Oystermouth, Glamorganshire, Wales, 1879) originally composed her text in eleven couplets as a hymn of "self-consecration to Christ" on February 4, 1874. She told the following story about writing this hymn:

Scripture References
all st. = Isa. 6:8
  Phil. 1:20-21
  Rom. 12:1
st. 4 = Luke 21:2-3 (KJV)

> I went for a little visit of five days [to Areley House, Worcestershire, in December 1873]. There were ten persons in the house, some unconverted and long prayed for, some converted but not rejoicing Christians. [God] gave me the prayer, "Lord, give me *all* this house." And He just did! Before I left the house, everyone had got a blessing. The last night of my visit . . . I was too happy to sleep and passed most of the night in praise and renewal of my own consecration, and these little couplets formed themselves and chimed in my heart, one after another, till they finished with "Ever, only, all, for Thee."

The text is a "catalog" hymn that lists aspects of our lives and offers them in Christ's service.

"Take My Life and Let It Be" was first published in the 1874 appendix to Charles B. Snepp's *Songs of Grace and Glory* (1872). A twelfth couplet was added at some later point, producing the six stanzas published in the *Psalter Hymnal*.

Although her formal education was sporadic because of poor health, Havergal learned six foreign languages, including Greek and Hebrew, and was well read in many subjects. She began writing poetry at an early age and was also an accomplished singer and pianist. The daughter of a clergyman, she had a conversion experience at the age of fourteen and was confirmed in the Church of England in 1853. Taking seriously her own words "take my silver and my gold," she sent all her jewelry to the Church Mission Society to be sold. She also supported other charitable organizations. Her more than one hundred hymns were originally published in leaflets and later gathered into seven collections: *Ministry of Song* (1869), *Twelve Sacred Songs for Little Singers* (1870), *Under the Surface* (1874), *Loyal Responses* (1878), *Life Mosaic* (1879), *Life Chords* (1880), and *Life Echoes* (1883), as well as in one large volume, *Poetical Works* (1884).

Tune

HENDON was composed by Henri A. César Malan (b. Geneva, Switzerland, 1787; d. Vandoeuvres, Switzerland, 1864) and included in a series of his own hymn texts and tunes that he began to publish in France in 1823, and which ultimately became his great hymnal *Chants de Sion* (1841). HENDON is thought to date from 1827. Lowell Mason (PHH 96) brought the tune to North America and published it in his *Carmina Sacra* (1841); that version is the one published in the *Psalter Hymnal*. Hendon is a village in Middlesex, England.

Because HENDON has five phrases, the text has to repeat its fourth line in each stanza to fit the music. Try singing in two units, grouping the first two phrases together and then the last three. Articulate the repeated tones clearly on the organ. Malan's harmonization is a good one for part singing by the entire congregation. Antiphonal performance may be best when singing the entire six stanzas; stanza 3 is a perfect candidate for unaccompanied singing.

Educated at the College of Geneva, Malan intended to become a businessman but instead was led to a ministerial career. In 1810 he was ordained in the National Reformed Church of Switzerland. A popular preacher at the Chapelle du Temoignage in Geneva, he attacked the formalism and liberalism of the national church and urged both a return to strict Calvinism and the need for conversion. When the church forbade him access to its pulpits, Malan had a church built in his garden and continued to preach to a large congregation. In his later years he devoted much of his energy to revival preaching. He traveled in Switzerland, France, the Netherlands, Belgium, England, and Scotland, where he conducted six revival tours and preached to a large following. A writer of several books and countless tracts, many of them translated into English, Malan also wrote the texts and tunes of over a thousand hymns, many of which became popular in the French Protestant churches.

Liturgical Use

Christian worship that emphasizes dedication, offering, or commitment—for example, after the sermon, as an offertory hymn, for ordination or commissioning, for profession of faith, for the dedication or anniversary of a church or congregation; fits well with many stewardship themes.

289

TEBBEN
♩ = 80

Take My Life That It May Be

Text

This text is an updated version of Frances R. Havergal's "Take My Life and Let It Be" (288) and is partly modeled after a revision of Havergal's text published in *Hymns for Today's Church* (1982).

Scripture References
all st. = Isa. 6:8
Phil. 1:20-21
Rom. 12:1
st. 4 = Luke 21:2-3

Tune

Timothy L. Hoekman (b. Racine, WI, 1954) composed TEBBEN in 1979 for the text "Take My Life and Let It Be" (288), and it was first sung by the Ann

Arbor (MI) Christian Reformed Church on May 13, 1979. Hoekman dedicated the tune to his grandfather on his mother's side, Kasjen Tebben, who was a Christian Reformed minister for fifty-nine years. Hoekman received his education at Calvin College, Grand Rapids, Michigan; Peabody Conservatory, Baltimore, Maryland; and the University of Michigan (D.M.A.). From 1982 to 1984 he taught at East Carolina University and since 1984 has been a professor of vocal coaching and accompanying at Florida State University, Tallahassee. He is also artistic director for the South Georgia Opera Company and assistant conductor and vocal coach for the Glimmerglass Opera Company, Cooperstown, New York. His published work includes *Seven Housman Songs* (1988).

TEBBEN consists of four phrases with connecting harmonic links from one phrase to the next. This haunting tune may be sung in unison, but is particularly beautiful sung in harmony, especially when sung in two long flowing lines with a sustained tempo. See 5 for a setting of this tune in a lower key.

Liturgical Use
See PHH 288.

290

Give Us This Day Our Daily Bread

BARBARA
♩ = 60

Text

Beginning with the fourth petition of the Lord's Prayer (Matt. 6:11; Luke 11:3), "Give Us This Day Our Daily Bread" asks God to meet our daily needs and moves quickly to ask that God help us share from our abundance with "a world in need" (st. 1). The text makes clear that our sharing must involve not only daily needs but also the message and example of Christ's love, as we are loved. The text swings full circle by returning to the image of bread (from John 6)—Christ is the "living bread" (st. 2) who feeds the hungry multitudes.

Scripture References
st. 1 = Matt. 6:11
Luke 11:3
st. 2 = John 6:35

At the request of the *Psalter Hymnal* Revision Committee, Helen Otte (PHH 17) wrote this text in 1986 for the tune BARBARA, a well-known setting for a text on the same theme: Grace N. Crowell's "Because I Have Been Given Much."

Tune

In modified bar-form (AA'B), BARBARA consists of two long lines and a third, longer line that comes to a strong cadence by means of a melisma. Sing this music in unison with firm organ tone. The tune also makes a fine choral prayer during the offertory, perhaps sung without accompaniment.

BARBARA was composed by Harold W. Friedell (b. Jamaica, NY, 1905; d. Hastings-on-Hudson, NY, 1958) and published in *Hymns for Children and Grownups* (Farrar, Straus, and Young, 1953) as a setting for "Because I Have Been Given Much." The tune was published with the same text in *New Songs for the Junior Choir* (Concordia, 1961).

Friedell taught music theory and composition at the Guilmant Organ School, the School of Sacred Music at Union Theological Seminary, and the Juilliard School of Music. He also served as organist at the Calvary Episcopal Church and St. Bartholomew Church, both in New York City, and at St. John Episcopal Church in Jersey City, New Jersey. Friedell composed a number of hymn tunes, carols, anthems, and service music.

Liturgical Use
A splendid offertory hymn (st. 1 and 2 also make a fine choral response at the offertory, but do not overuse); also useful in conjunction with stewardship themes.

291

ST. LEONARDS
♩ = 54

May the Mind of Christ, My Savior

Text
In the first four stanzas of this "catalog" hymn the believer asks, "May the mind of Christ," the "word of God," the "peace of God," and the "love of Jesus" live in my heart throughout each day, in "all I do and say." Stanza 5 invokes the race-running imagery of Hebrews 12:1-2.

Scripture References
st. 1 = Phil. 2:5
st. 3 = Col. 3:15
st. 5 = Heb. 12:1-2

The *Psalter Hymnal* Revision Committee omitted the final stanza for publication in the *Psalter Hymnal* and changed stanza 5 to the first-person plural ("we/us") to provide a corporate finale. The song was first published in the London children's hymnbook *Golden Bells* (1925) and has gained popularity in recent hymnals.

This text is attributed to Kate Barclay Wilkinson (b. England, 1859; d. Kensington, England, 1928). She wrote this text in 1912 in six stanzas, inspired by Philippians 2:5: "Let this mind be in you, which was also in Christ Jesus" (KJV). Little is known about Wilkinson's life: a member of the Church of England, she was involved in a ministry to girls in London and a participant in the Keswick Convention Movement. She was married to Frederick Barclay Wilkinson.

Tune
A. Cyril Barham-Gould (b. England, 1891; d. Turnbridge Wells, Kent, England, 1953) composed ST. LEONARDS for Wilkinson's text while living at St. Leonards-on-Sea, England; it was published as the setting for that text in *Golden Bells*. The St. Leonard for whom St. Leonards-on-Sea is named and to whom the tune title indirectly refers is the

fifth-century French bishop Leonard of Limosin, the patron saint for pregnant women and prisoners of war. Barham-Gould was educated at Ridley Hall, Cambridge, and ordained a priest in the Church of England in 1928. He worked in several churches in and near London and served as vicar of St. Paul's, Onslow Square, from 1936 until his death in 1953.

Sing ST. LEONARDS in two long lines. The first four stanzas can be sung antiphonally by groups within the congregation, but stanza 5 is for everyone together. Reserve the descant, by Emily R. Brink (PHH 158), 1986, and unison singing for stanza 5.

Liturgical Use
Dismissal at close of worship; immediately following the sermon. Change the "me/my" of stanzas 1 through 4 to "you/your" for use as a sung blessing on a wedding couple, on new members of the church, for sending out missionaries, for ordination of church officers, and so on.

292

Living for Jesus

LIVING FOR JESUS
♩ = 80

Text
Composer C. Harold Lowden stated the following about this hymn:

> In 1915 I wrote a "light and summery" type of gospel song entitled "The Sunshine Song" for children's services. It became quite popular, and many pastors wrote to me that the music should be saved, and more general words wedded to it. I came across a copy of it in my files in 1917 and played it over. The rhythm and tempo suggested the words "Living for Jesus." . . . I decided to ask T. O. Chisholm to write the words. I mailed him a copy of the music and suggested the title and the type of refrain which I thought it deserved. In a day or so, Mr. Chisholm returned it to me, saying he didn't have the slightest idea as to the method used in writing words to music. I sent the material back to him immediately, telling him I believed God had led me to select him, and suggesting that he permit God to write the poem. Within a couple of weeks he had completed the writing of the words.

Thus the author, Thomas O. Chisholm (b. Franklin, KY, 1866; d. Ocean Grove, NJ, 1960), wrote "Living for Jesus" in 1917. Although he had little formal education, Chisholm served at various times as a teacher, editor, and pastor. He also wrote more than twelve hundred poems and hymn texts. Chisholm's accomplishments included being associate editor of his hometown newspaper, *The Franklin Advocate*, and editor of the *Pentecostal Herald*. He was ordained in the Methodist Church but served only briefly as a pastor in Scottsville, Kentucky, because of poor health. After that he sold life insurance in Winona Lake, Indiana, and Vineland, New Jersey. His devotional poetry and hymn texts were published primarily in religious periodicals.

His wrote his text to fit Lowden's tune in four stanzas and a refrain. Stanza 3 in the *Psalter Hymnal* collates phrases from stanzas 3 and 4 of Chisholm's original text. The text and tune were first published together in *Uplifting Songs* (1917), a hymnal compiled by Lowden and Rufus W. Miller.

This is a hymn of total consecration and dedication in which we commit to "living for Jesus" in all that we do (st. 1) and wherever we are (st. 3) in response to Christ's sacrifice (st. 2; refrain). "Living for Jesus" is well known in the Christian Reformed Church as the theme song of the Calvinist Cadet Corps, a church-related organization for young boys.

Tune

LIVING FOR JESUS is a gospel hymn tune distinguishable by its dactylic rhythm for the stanzas and its straightforward iambic refrain. The guitar chords avoid some of the chromaticism of the original harmony; when using guitar, do not use keyboard. Singing the refrain only once—at the end of stanza 3—will constitute a fine climax. Singers may want to observe a *ritardando* or a *fermata* in the final phrase of the refrain.

C. Harold Lowden (b. Burlington, NJ, 1883; d. Collingwood, NJ, 1963) wrote his first songs when he was only twelve years old. He continued to write hymns for the rest of his life and edited a number of hymnals. A musical editor for the Evangelical and Reformed Church board, Lowden taught music at the Bible Institute of Pennsylvania (now Philadelphia College of Bible). He capped his career by serving for twenty-eight years, until his retirement in 1961, as minister of music of the Linden Baptist Church in Camden, New Jersey.

Liturgical Use

Most often as a post-sermon hymn; also as a hymn of dedication or commitment at a suitable place in the worship service.

293

SHARPTHORNE
♩ = 54

What Does the Lord Require

Text

Early in 1949 Albert F. Bayly (b. Bexhill-on-Sea, Sussex, England, 1901; d. Chichester, England, 1984) wrote a hymn text based on Micah 6:6-8 as one of a series of seventeen hymns he was writing   *Scripture References*
      all st. = Micah 6:6-8

on the Old Testament prophets. His objective was to present the prophets "in the light of the climax and fulfillment of the Old Testament revelation in the coming of Christ."

"What Does the Lord Require" asks questions and states commands as if Micah were a modern-day prophet. The refrain line "Do justly . . ." subtly shifts from the imperative voice in stanzas 1 through 4 to a corporate confession in stanza 5. The text was first published in Bayly's *Rejoice, O People* (1951) and is included in the *Psalter Hymnal* with minor alterations.

Bayly studied briefly at the Royal Dockyard School at Portsmouth to prepare himself for the shipbuilding industry. However, in 1925 he began studying for the ministry at Mansfield College, Oxford. He became a Congregationalist minister and served seven churches. Bayly wrote missionary pageants and numerous hymns, many of which used more contemporary language and concepts than had been customary in previous hymn writing. Because of the publication of his collection *Again I Say Rejoice* (1967), Bayly is often acknowledged as the pioneer of the revival of British hymn writing in the 1960s and 70s. His hymns were published in four collections: *Rejoice, O People* (1951), *Again I Say Rejoice* (1967), *Rejoice Always* (1971), and *Rejoice in God* (1978).

Tune

Erik Routley (PHH 31) composed SHARPTHORNE in 1968 to be published as a setting for Bayly's text in the British supplementary hymnal *100 Hymns for Today* (1969). SHARPTHORNE is actually a revision of another Routley tune, TYES CROSS, which was the setting for Bayly's text in the 1951 *Rejoice, O People*. Routley said SHARPTHORNE is "a sort of paraphrase in the minor key" of TYES CROSS. Sharpthorne and Tyes Cross are both villages in Routley's native county of Sussex, England.

SHARPTHORNE is a rugged tune (one of Routley's best!) with several repeated motives and sequences; it fits well with the stern prophetic message as interpreted by Bayly. The tune is best sung in unison. One way to sing it is to have a choir or soloist sing the first two lines of each stanza and have everyone sing the refrain line, at which time the organ should thunder its support! An even more dramatic performance can be arranged as follows: a soloist can walk among the aisles of the church singing the prophet's lines in stanzas 1 through 3, a choir can sing stanza 4, and everyone can join in on stanza 5.

Liturgical Use

As part of the service of confession in conjunction with sermons from Micah, Amos, Isaiah 1, or similar passages; as a hymn for social justice, especially for civic festivals or national-holiday celebrations; times of penitence and renewal such as Advent and Lent.

REGWAL
♩ = 80
As Saints of Old Their Firstfruits Brought

Text

Frank von Christierson (b. Lovisa, near Helsinki, Finland, 1900) stated the following about this hymn:

Scripture References
st. 1 = Deut. 26:1-15
st. 2 = 1 John 3:18
James 1:22

> As pastor of two new churches, with small memberships and great financial needs, I have been deeply concerned with stewardship, also because I am deeply concerned about missions and the outreach of the church to "all the world," [and] also because stewardship is a very important phase of the Christian life. No one is deeply Christian until he is a "good steward."

This hymn text (more explicitly than 296) puts our human stewardship of money and other prized resources (st. 1) into the larger context of the worldwide mission of the church, in view of the coming of Christ's kingdom (st. 2). We must always integrate our giving of gifts with our giving of ourselves for Christian service (st. 3).

Christierson wrote the text in 1960 and submitted it to a hymn search conducted jointly by the Department of Stewardship & Benevolence of the National Council of Churches of Christ in the USA and the Hymn Society of America (HSA). It was accepted and was first published in the HSA booklet *Ten New Stewardship Hymns* (1961). Altered (especially in st. 2) for publication in the *Psalter Hymnal,* the song originally began with the words "As men of old . . ."

Christierson's family immigrated to the United States in 1905. He received his education at Stanford University and San Francisco Theological Seminary and was ordained in the Presbyterian Church in 1929. A moderator of regional presbyteries, he served several Presbyterian churches in California and was founding pastor of the Trinity Community Presbyterian Church in North Hollywood (1944-1961). He wrote some 140 hymns, a number of which have been published by the Hymn Society of America as well as in his *Make a Joyful Noise* (1987). In 1982 Christierson was honored as a Fellow of the Hymn Society in the United States and Canada.

Tune

REGWAL was published with von Christierson's text in 1963 in an anthem setting composed by Leland B. Sateren (b. Everett, WA, 1913). The tune consists of four lines, the first of which reminds us of GENEVAN 124's opening phrase (see also TOULON, 521). The final line rises to an impressive climax. Sing stanzas 1 and 2 antiphonally in unison, and bring everyone together in harmony for stanza 3, with some extra color from the organ.

A noted Lutheran musician, Sateren has long been associated with Augsburg College in Minneapolis, Minnesota. He received his B.A. there in 1935 and, after further study at the University of Minnesota, became a member of Augsburg's music faculty in 1946—a position he retained until his retirement. Chairman of the music department from 1950 to 1973, Sateren also directed the Augsburg Choir. He has conducted choral schools throughout Scandinavia, has often served as judge at music festivals, and was active in the American Choral Directors' Association. Publisher of over three hundred choral works and many professional articles on music and music education, he also served on the committees that produced the *Service Book and Hymnal* (1958) and the *Lutheran Book of Worship* (1978).

Liturgical Use
As an offertory hymn; stewardship themes; emphasis on missions.

295

Lord of All Good

MORESTEAD
𝅗𝅥 = 63

Text
Albert F. Bayly (PHH 293) included this text in his collection *Again I Say Rejoice* (1967); he originally wrote it for a Christmas fair at Eccleston Congregational Church, St. Helens, Lancashire, England, where Bayly served as minister from 1956 to 1962. The *Psalter Hymnal* Revision Committee modernized second-person singular pronouns throughout the hymn text.

Scripture References
st. 2 = Rom. 12:1
st. 3 = 2 Cor. 9:7

"Lord of All Good" expresses that not our gifts alone but our entire selves are to be an offering for God's service (st. 1) and for his glory (st. 2) out of gratitude and praise to the triune God who creates, saves, and sustains us (st. 3). This excellent hymn of dedication proceeds with certainty toward the doxology of its final stanza.

Tune
Sydney Watson (b. Manchester, England, 1903; d. Banbury, Oxfordshire, England, 1991) composed MORESTEAD, which is considered one of his best tunes. Its initial "rocket" motif, its melodic contour, and its "walking" bass are a fine match for Bayly's text. Intended for unison singing at two beats (not four) per measure, this tune has an active pedal part for organists with two feet! Save your bright mixtures or colorful reeds for stanza 3, and sing that stanza at a slightly slower pace than the first two.

MORESTEAD was published in the British *Hymns for Church and School* (1964) as a setting for Henry M. Butler's "Lift Up Your Hearts." The tune is named after a village in

Hampshire, England, just southeast of Winchester, where Watson often rode his bicycle.

Educated at the Royal College of Music in London, Keble College, and Oxford University, Watson had a distinguished career in music education and church music. Organist at New College, Oxford, from 1933 to 1938, he also taught music at Winchester College (1938-1946) and at Eaton (1946-1955). Later Watson was conductor of the Oxford Bach Choir and Orchestra and organist at Christ Church Cathedral in Oxford (1955-1970).

Liturgical Use

A great offertory hymn! Also useful at the close of the worship service, bringing together our whole-life dedication and a strong doxology; special occasions of consecration and dedication such as adult baptism, profession of faith, ordination, renewal of vows, and so on.

296

SCHUMANN
♩ = 63

We Give You But Your Own

Text

When he wrote this hymn, Bishop William W. How (PHH 279) appended a reference to Proverbs 19:17: "Whoever has pity on the poor lends to the Lord"—a Scripture that characterizes not only this hymn text but also much of How's ministry to the poor in the east side of London, England.

Scripture References
st. 1 = 1 Chron. 29:14
        1 Peter 4:10
st. 2 = Deut. 26:1-5
st. 3-4 = Matt. 25:35-40

"We Give You But Your Own" is a hymn about stewardship, about bringing our gifts to be used for the church's ministry of word and deed to needy people—in other words, *our* ministry for Christ. Like Psalm 50 and Isaiah 1, this text declares that everything in creation already belongs to God and that what we give and what we keep are all to be used gratefully in God's service (st. 5). See also 294.

How wrote the text in six stanzas in 1858; it was first published in *Psalms and Hymns* (2nd ed., 1864), edited by How and Thomas B. Morrell. The *Psalter Hymnal* omits How's original stanza 3 and includes many alterations to the text.

Tune

SCHUMANN is one of many hymn tunes arranged by Lowell Mason (PHH 96). He first published the arrangement in *Cantica Laudis* (1850), a collection he edited with George J. Webb (PHH 559). First called WHITE, the tune was marked "Arr. from Schumann" and was thus ascribed to the German composer Robert A. Schumann.

Although Clara Schumann doubted that it came from her husband's music, the tune's name derives from that early association with Schumann's name.

SCHUMANN builds to an effective climax in its final line—the first line is unfortunately broken into two short phrases, but sensitive organists and singers will try to tie these into one long line. Try antiphonal singing or a combination of unison and harmony stanzas when singing the entire hymn.

Liturgical Use
As an offertory hymn (st. 1 and 2 also make a fine choral response at the offertory, but do not overuse); as a post-sermon hymn in conjunction with stewardship themes.

297

O Come, My Soul, Sing Praise to God

TIDINGS
♩ = 76

Text
"O Come, My Soul" is a paraphrase of Psalm 103. The lengthy meter (11 10 11 10) makes possible a clear flow of thoughts and images, and the refrain continually reminds us of the praise running through this much-loved psalm. The versification comes from the 1912 *Psalter* with minor alterations. See PHH 103 for further commentary on Psalm 103.

Scripture References
st. 1 = Ps. 103:1-4
st. 2 = Ps. 103:8-12
st. 3 = Ps. 103:13-14
st. 4 = Ps. 103:15-18
st. 5 = Ps. 103:19, 22
ref. = Psalm 103:20-21

Tune
James Walch (b. Edgerton, Lancashire, England, 1837; d. Llandudno, Caernarvon, Wales, 1901) composed TIDINGS in 1875 for Frederick W. Faber's hymn text "Hark, Hark, My Soul! Angelic Songs Are Swelling"; the tune was first published in *The Hymnal Companion to the Book of Common Prayer* (1877). TIDINGS is often associated with Mary A. Thomson's "O Zion, Haste, Thy Mission High Fulfilling"; in fact, the tune name derives from the word "tidings" in Thomson's refrain (see 525). TIDINGS is a fairly dramatic tune, a good match for Psalm 103. Sing in parts if you like, and add extra musical forces for the refrain. Stanza 3 sings well without accompaniment.

Walch received a musical education from his father and from the famous organist and organ builder Henry Smart (PHH 233). He served as organist at Duke's Alley Congregational Church (1851-1857), Bridge Street Wesleyan Chapel (1858-1863), and St. George's Parish Church (1863-1877)—all in Bolton. He conducted for the Bolton Philharmonic Society from 1870 to 1877 and near the end of his life was a music dealer in Barrow-in-Furness. Walch composed a number of hymn tunes and other church music.

Liturgical Use

Psalm 103 is read at the end of some communion liturgies (see *Psalter Hymnal* pp. 975, 981, 986); that reading could be replaced by a joyful singing of the psalm, using 297 or other settings of Psalm 103 (103, 475, 583, 627). See PHH 103 for other liturgical uses.

298

BANGOR
♩ = 80

According to Thy Gracious Word

Text

One of the best-loved hymns of James Montgomery (PHH 72), "According to Thy Gracious Word" was published in six stanzas in *The Christian Psalmist* (1825) under the subtitle "This do in remembrance of me," Jesus' words from Luke 22:19. The *Psalter Hymnal* omits the original stanza 5.

Scripture References
st. 1 = Luke 22:19
st. 2 = 1 Cor. 11:24-25
st. 3 = Matt. 26:36-39
Luke 22:44
st. 4 = Isa. 53:6-7
John 1:29
st. 5 = Luke 23:42

Reflective and meditative, the text focuses on the memorial aspect of the Lord's Supper—each stanza concludes with the word *remember.* Our memory of Jesus can be taken two ways, of course: in the active sense, as in ancient liturgies and in the Reformation teachings of John Calvin; or in the passive sense, as in liturgies espoused by Ulrich Zwingli. Montgomery underlined "I will remember thee" in his manuscript, possibly indicating that he intended to promote the classic, active sense of *anamnesis.* (This untranslatable Greek word refers to the active way in which Christ is present with us in the Lord's Supper.) The text is strong and effective because of its biblical quotations and allusions (see Scripture references).

Tune

Traditionally used for Montgomery's text and for Peter Abelard's "Alone Thou Goest Forth, O Lord," BANGOR comes from William Tans'ur's *A Compleat Melody: or the Harmony of Syon* (the preface of which is dated 1734). In that collection the tune was a three-part setting for Psalm 12 (and for Psalm 11 in a 1738 reprint). Possibly alluding to an earlier origin, the tune title recalls the Welsh borough and city Bangor. The tune was popular in Scotland: Robert Burns refers to it in his poem "The Ordination": "an' skirl up the Bangor."

BANGOR is a solemn but expressive tune, though not mournful. It is sturdy and supportive of the classic *anamnesis* interpretation of Montgomery's text. Sing in harmony on stanzas 1 through 4, and sing in unison on stanza 5—or try singing the first three phrases in harmony and the fourth in unison to highlight the important concluding phrase in each stanza.

Tans'ur (originally Tanzer; b. Dunchurch, Warwickshire, England, 1706; d. St. Neots, Huntingdonshire, England, 1783) was an itinerant music teacher and song leader who served as occasional organist in churches in Barnes, Ewell, Cambridge, Stamford, and Boston (England). Later he lived in St. Neots, where he was a bookseller and music teacher. He published numerous pedagogical works on music as well as psalm books, including *A Compleat Melody: or Harmony of Syon* (1734), *The Psalm Singer's Jewel* (1760), and *Melodia Sacra* (1771); many of his books were reprinted numerous times. It is not always clear which tunes in these collections Tans'ur composed himself or which he adapted from other sources. A selection from his tunebooks was published in the United States as *The American Harmony* (1771), a book that influenced William Billings in his composing of psalm tunes.

Liturgical Use
During the Lord's Supper as a meditative hymn; Lent; Holy Week; also makes a fine Passion hymn (without st. 2).

299

As We Walk Along Beside You

BURNING HEART
♩ = 88

Text
Michael A. Perry's text draws from the Emmaus story in Luke 24:13-35. As we sing it, we experience the journey to Emmaus and discover Christ in the Word (st. 1), in the breaking of bread (st. 2), and in our service to him (st. 3). The Easter "alleluias" framing this hymn were not part of the original text, which Perry (b. Beckenham, Kent, England, 1942; d. England, 1996) wrote in 1981 in Southampton, England.

Initially studying mathematics and physics at Dulwich College, Perry was headed for a career in the sciences. However, after one year of study in physics at the University of London, he transferred to Oak Hill College to study theology. He also studied at Ridley Hall, Cambridge, and received a M.Phil. from the University of Southhampton in 1973. Ordained a priest in the Church of England in 1966, Perry served the parish of St. Helen's in Liverpool as a youth worker and evangelist. From 1972 to 1981 he was the vicar of Bitterne in Southhampton and from 1981 to 1989, rector of Eversley in Hampshire and chaplain at the Police Staff College. He then became vicar of Tonbridge in Kent, where he remained until his death from a brain tumor in 1996. Perry published widely in the areas of Bible study and worship. He edited Jubilate publications such as *Hymns for Today's Church* (1982), *Carols for Today* (1986), *Come Rejoice!* (1989), and *Psalms for Today* (1990). Composer of the musical drama *Coming Home* (1987), he also wrote more than two hundred hymns and Bible versifications.

Tune

Norman L. Warren (PHH 15) wrote BURNING HEART for Perry's text in 1981 and added the "alleluia" frame. Both text and tune were first published in the British *Hymns for Today's Church* (1982). The tune title derives from Luke 24:32: "Were not our hearts burning within us while he talked with us on the road and opened the Scriptures to us?"

BURNING HEART is a unison tune with three melodic sequences; it is ably supported by a harmony featuring effective accented nonharmonic tones. Sing the initial "alleluias" gently, and gradually increase intensity and crescendo throughout the stanzas so that the final "alleluia" may be jubilant. The format of this hymn is similar to that of "O Sons and Daughters" (393).

Liturgical Use

Lord's Supper, especially at Easter or at any time in conjunction with the Emmaus reading.

300

BICENTENNIAL
♩ = 76

Gift of Finest Wheat

Text

This beautiful song has become widely recognized as one of the finest recent Lord's Supper hymns, primarily because of its use of biblical images (see Scripture references). The stanzas introduce each of these images in turn, and the refrain repeatedly brings us back to the hymn's controlling thought: God's "gift of finest wheat" is Christ, "the bread of life" (Ps. 81:16; John 6:35). The solid theological text aptly presents many of the central meanings of the sacrament of the Lord's Supper.

Scripture References
ref. = Ps. 81:16
  John 6:35
st. 1 = John 10:14-16
st. 2 = Ps. 34:1
st. 3 = 1 Cor. 10:16
st. 4 = Col. 1:27
st. 5 = John 13:14-15

Cincinnati poet and publisher Omer Westendorf (b. Cincinnati, OH, 1916) submitted "Gift of Finest Wheat" to a eucharistic-hymn competition that judged it the best out of more than two hundred entries. Westendorf's text and the tune BICENTENNIAL were then printed on a song sheet for use at the 41st Eucharistic Congress, a Roman Catholic convention on the eucharist held in Philadelphia, Pennsylvania, in 1976 (the year of the U.S.A.'s bicentennial). Both text and tune have recently been published in various hymnals.

Westendorf has had a rich and varied career in music. Educated at the College-Conservatory of the University of Cincinnati, he served as organist and choirmaster of St. Bonaventure Church in Cincinnati (1936-1976). His freelance Bonaventure Choir appeared in many concerts and made numerous recordings. He also taught music in several Cincinnati schools and founded the World Library of Sacred Music in 1950 and World Library Publications in 1957. Since 1976 he has operated his own consulting agency on church music. Westendorf has written some thirty-five hymn texts and compiled four hymnals, including the *People's Mass Book* (1964), which was the first vernacular hymnal in the United States to implement the changes in Roman Catholic worship that Second Vatican Council (1962-1965) had approved.

Tune
Robert E. Kreutz (b. La Crosse, WI, 1922; d. Golden, Colorado, 1996) carefully crafted BICENTENNIAL for this text in Denver, Colorado, in 1976. Though the meter changes frequently, the sung text flows very naturally, with the changing meters unified by melodic and rhythmic motifs. Singing the refrain and the stanzas in two long lines instead of four short ones brings out the beauty of the text. The entire hymn may be sung in unison, but a choral harmonization of the refrain adds a beautiful effect. The stanzas can be sung antiphonally in a variety of ways: by two or more groups in the congregation, or perhaps by a cantor or soloist(s) singing the stanzas and everyone singing the refrain. For further variety, improvise a descant for the refrain and use instruments other than organ.

Kreutz received a bachelor's degree from the American Conservatory of Music, Chicago, and a master's degree from the University of Colorado, Denver. He also studied composition with Arnold Schoenberg, Leo Sowerby, and Norman Lockwood. A resident of Golden, Kreutz worked for many years for the Gates Rubber Company as a development engineer and also directed the choir at St. Bernadette Church in Lakewood, Colorado, for more than twenty-five years. He published some three hundred choral and instrumental compositions, including many psalm settings and other liturgical music.

Liturgical Use
Lord's Supper, especially during distribution of the bread and wine.

301

Taste and See

ANTHEA
$\downarrow = 100$

Text
Written in 1981, "Taste and See" was one of the first songs written by Carol Vriend Petter (b. Amsterdam, the Netherlands, 1954) for worship at Church of the Servant, a Christian Reformed church in Grand Rapids, Michigan, that celebrates the Lord's Supper weekly. The text makes good use of both Old Testament

Scripture References
st. 1 = 1 Cor. 10:16
ref. = Ps. 33:22
    Ps. 34:3b, 8a

and New Testament images. In covenant with God, we taste and see his love as we share in the Lord's Supper (st. 1; ref.), experiencing the blessings of pardon, grace, and kingdom inheritance (st. 2), at the same time reminding ourselves of our mission to share God's love with the spiritually and physically needy (st. 3).

A graduate of Calvin College, Grand Rapids, Petter is currently a retirement plan administrator for First Michigan Bank in Grand Rapids. She is a member of Church of the Servant, and some of her hymns are published in that congregation's hymnal supplement, *Joyful Noises*.

Tune

Wim Mennes (b. Amsterdam, the Netherlands, 1917; d. Noordwolde, 1996) composed ANTHEA for Petter's text in 1984 in Noordwolde, the Netherlands; his tune was selected by the *Psalter Hymnal* Revision Committee from among several tunes submitted as part of a hymn search for this text. He named the tune after a granddaughter.

Sing the stanzas of this bar-form tune (AABB') in unison, with organ trio style accompaniment, using manuals only, but sing the refrain in full harmony accompanied by a larger organ registration, including pedal. The refrain should be legato, with repeated notes tied; it also functions well at the beginning of the music. If you like, use the refrain separately as a chorus (possibly sung repeatedly) or as a frame around another psalm or hymn such as 34, 178, or 220.

Born into a family of musicians, Mennes graduated from the Conservatory of Amsterdam in 1941. He was organist in the Gereformeerde Church of Amsterdam South and in the Andreas Church of Zwolle and was a professor of music in a teachers' college in Zwolle. A writer of some fifty hymns, Mennes was a leader in promoting contemporary hymnody in the Netherlands.

Liturgical Use

Lord's Supper, during distribution of the bread and wine.

302

KINGDOM
♩ = 69

In the Quiet Consecration

Text

This fine Lord's Supper hymn combines a number of important images: intimate union with Christ (st. 1), participation in the sacrament "by faith and with thanksgiving" (st. 2), the support and strength of Christ's resurrection life (st. 3), and the sacrament's foretaste of the heavenly feast with the Lamb (st. 4). Gently but firmly supported by the

Scripture References
st. 2 = John 6:51
st. 3 = John 6:56

447

tune KINGDOM, the reflective text is for "quiet consecration" and meditation. The song also stands out as a Lord's Supper hymn with an apocalyptic focus.

Constance H. Coote (b. England, 1844; d. Turnbridge Wells, Kent, England, 1936) wrote "In the Quiet Consecration" in 1910 and first published it in her *At His Table* (1913); later the hymn found wider circulation when published in *The Church Hymnal for the Christian Year* (1917).

Although Coote spent much of her life as a single woman and a widow, she is known mainly because of her marriage to Algernon Coote, a pastor who later became Sir Algernon, a baronet. Throughout her life she wrote hymns and other devotional poetry.

Tune

KINGDOM features a gentle melodic contour and subtle changes in rhythmic structure that soften the trochaic meter of the text. Sing this tune in harmony and in two long lines. This communion hymn can be framed by the equally meditative "Alleluia" (see 640). Good singers may improvise additional parts (especially a higher descant) on the "Alleluia" setting. Sing it once at the beginning of the hymn and again after the fourth stanza, or perhaps have everyone sing the "Alleluia" setting and have the choir sing the hymn stanzas.

V. Earle Copes (b. Norfolk, VA, 1921) composed KINGDOM in 1959 for the hymn text "For the Bread Which Thou Hast Broken," written by Louis F. Benson; the tune name derives from the word "kingdom" in the final line of that text. KINGDOM was first used publicly at the 1960 National Convocation of Methodist Youth, and it was later published as an anthem. The first hymnal to publish it was *The Methodist Hymnal* (1964).

An ordained Methodist minister, Copes has served mainly in the musical ministry of the church. He was educated at Davidson College and Union Theological Seminary, obtaining degrees in both church music and theology. From 1946 to 1949 he was minister of music at the Highland Park Methodist Church, Dallas, Texas, and at Christ United Methodist Church, Dayton, Ohio. In subsequent years he taught organ and church music at Hendrix College, Conway, Arizona, and at Cornell College, Mt. Vernon, Iowa. Copes also edited the Methodist periodical *Music Ministry* (1958-1967), taught at Birmingham Southern College in Alabama (1967-1973), and served as minister of music at Christ United Methodist Church, Kettering, Ohio (1973-1986). Now retired, Copes has published numerous works for organ and choir.

Liturgical Use
During the Lord's Supper.

303

A VA DE
♩ = 88

Come, Let Us Eat

Text

Billema Kwillia (b. Liberia, c. 1925) composed both the text and the tune of this hymn during the 1960s when he was a literacy teacher and evangelist. The text's rather cryptic phrases highlight central themes of the Lord's Supper. Stanzas 1 and 2 issue the invitation "Come . . . ," stanza 3 draws us into an appropriate meditative mood in the Lord's presence, and stanza 4 dismisses us with the reminder to "spread abroad God's mighty Word."

A speaker of the Loma language, Kwillia learned to read the language as an adult through a church literacy program. In the early 1960s he became a literacy teacher himself. After being baptized as a Christian, he served as a preacher and evangelist.

The text and tune of this hymn were originally transcribed from a recorded church service. Margaret D. Miller (b. Clifton Springs, NY, 1927) translated stanzas 1 through 3 from the Loma language into English in 1969, and that translation was first published in 1970 in the Lutheran World Federation hymnal *Laudamus* (4th ed.). Miller was educated at the Lankenau School for Girls in Philadelphia while her widowed mother served as a missionary in Liberia. After graduation from college, Miller followed her mother's example and became a missionary in Liberia, serving there as a literacy worker and translator of the Wozi language as well as an editor of the bilingual Loma newspaper, *Weekly.* She has done graduate work in linguistics and anthropology at the Hartford Seminary Foundation, Hartford, Connecticut.

Gilbert E. Doan (b. Bethlehem, PA, 1930) added stanza 4 prior to the hymn's publication in the Lutheran hymnal *Contemporary Worship-4* (1972). A prominent Lutheran clergyman, Doan served as campus pastor in Philadelphia from 1955 to 1961. He was northeastern director for the National Lutheran Campus Ministry from 1961 to 1984 and more recently was pastor of the Lutheran Church of the Holy Communion, Philadelphia. A graduate of Harvard College (B.A. in geology) and Lutheran Theological Seminary, Philadelphia (D.B.), he also received an master's degree in American civilization from the University of Pennsylvania. He has written *Renewal in the Pulpit* (1966), edited *The Preaching of Frederick W. Robertson* (1964), and was chair of the hymn texts committee of the Inter-Lutheran Commission on Worship (1967-1978).

Tune

The tune title A VA DE is the incipit of Kwillia's original text in the Loma language. "Come, Let Us Eat" is an excellent choice for congregations that celebrate communion with various groups of people coming forward to stand or sit around the Lord's table (in the old Dutch Reformed manner). The hymn can be sung in a call-and-response manner, with a soloist singing the first line and the congregation responding with the repetition. The congregation can sing easily without books while coming forward. Sing without pauses between stanzas.

Leland B. Sateren (PHH 294) arranged the music for optional singing as a two-part round and harmonized it for *Contemporary Worship-4*. The round is at two measures, and its second part should be sung by a smaller group in the manner of an echo. The tune itself has two phrases, each of which repeats once. Sing this lively music in unison or as a two-part round, and accompany it with guitars, flutes, and especially percussion instruments such as hand drums, woodblocks, or tambourines.

Liturgical Use

Lord's Supper—sing stanzas 1 through 3 during distribution of the bread and wine, and sing stanza 4 as a dismissal after the sacrament.

304

Let Us Break Bread Together

BREAK BREAD TOGETHER
♩ = 96

Text

Some of the stanzas of this African American spiritual may date back to the eighteenth century. Other stanzas have been added by oral tradition. A look through modern hymnals will reveal an array of variations on the text. The most notable alteration in the *Psalter Hymnal* is the phrase "to the Lord of life" in place of the original "to the rising sun," in which "sun" was an ambiguous metaphor referring to God. The song's use at communion services probably dates from after the American Civil War. Miles Mark Fisher notes in *Negro Slave Songs in the United States* (1953),

> [Originally the hymn] relates hardly at all to holy communion, which does not necessarily require early morning administration or a devotee who faces east. [This] it seems was a signal song of Virginia slaves during the eighteenth century who used it and similar ones to convene their secret meetings.

The text discerns participation in the Lord's Supper as a humble act in which we not only eat the bread (st. 1) and drink the wine (st. 2) but also praise our God (st. 3) "on our knees." The refrain ends with a prayer for mercy, an African American *kyrie* (see PHH 258) that reminds us of the tax collector's prayer in Luke 18:13.

Tune

The tune BREAK BREAD TOGETHER, like the text, has been subject to variation. It became widely known after publication in *The Second Book of Negro Spirituals* (1926), compiled by the brothers James Weldon Johnson and J. Rosamond Johnson. The tune gained further popularity through a variety of choral arrangements; it can be found in many hymnals dating after 1955, when it was published in the American Presbyterian/

Reformed *Hymnbook*. Dale Grotenhuis (PHH 4) harmonized the tune in 1984 for the *Psalter Hymnal*.

Arranged without the call-and-response pattern that often characterizes African American spirituals, BREAK BREAD TOGETHER in the *Psalter Hymnal* takes the shape of a regular hymn, with part singing on the stanzas and refrain. If you like, however, sing stanzas 1 and 2 in unison and the refrain and stanza 3 in parts—a higher melody line for stanza 3 is published in *The Hymnal 1982* (1985), a revision of the American Protestant Episcopal *Hymnal 1940*. In addition, try singing the entire song without accompaniment.

Liturgical Use
Lord's Supper—during preparation for the sacrament or during distribution of the bread and wine.

305

SCHMÜCKE DICH
♩ = 72 # Clothe Yourself, My Soul, with Gladness

Text

The first stanza of "Schmücke dich, O liebe Seele" by Johann Franck was published in Johann Crüger's *Geistliche Kirchen-Melodien* (1649). Crüger and C. Runge published the complete hymn in nine stanzas in their 1653 *Gesangbuch*. The hymn has since appeared in virtually all German hymnals and in many English-language ones. The English text in the *Psalter Hymnal* is a revision of select stanzas from two translations by Catherine Winkworth (PHH 194), one published in her *Lyra Germanica* (2nd series, 1858) and the other in her *Chorale Book for England* (1863). Winkworth's first line read "Deck thyself, my soul, with gladness."

Scripture References
st. 1 = Isa. 61:10
Rev. 21:3
st. 2 = Rev. 3:20
st. 4 = Rev. 19:9

The dominant tone of this text is one of deep joy enhanced by a sense of awe. We express joy and praise for "this wondrous banquet" (st. 1), and we show reverence in receiving Christ (st. 2). Thankful for "heavenly food" and drink (st. 3), we rejoice in Christ's love for us and in its power to unite us (st. 4). Often considered the best and most popular of the Lutheran chorales for the Lord's Supper, this text, according to John Julian,

> is an exhortation to the soul to arise and draw near to partake of the Heavenly Food and to meditate on the wonders of Heavenly Love; ending with a prayer for final reception at the Eternal Feast.
>
> —A Dictionary of Hymnology *(2nd ed., 1907), p. 1014*

Johann Franck (b. Guben, Brandenburg, Germany, 1618; d. Guben, 1677) was a law student at the University of Köningsberg and practiced law during the Thirty Years'

War. He held several positions in civil service, including councillor and mayor of Guben. A significant poet, second only to Paul Gerhardt (PHH 331) in his day, Franck wrote some 110 hymns, many of which were published by his friend Johann Crüger in various editions of the *Praxis pietatis melica*. All were included in the first part of Franck's *Teutsche Gedichte bestehend im geistliche Sion* (1672).

Tune

Johann Crüger (PHH 42) composed SCHMÜCKE DICH for Franck's text and first published the tune as a setting for Franck's first stanza in *Geistliche Kirchen-Melodien*. The tune name is the incipit of the original German text. Johann S. Bach (PHH 7) used this tune in his *Cantata 180;* he and many other composers have written organ preludes on the melody.

Like many chorale tunes, SCHMÜCKE DICH is in bar form (AABC); it has a melodic repeat and a delightful, though challenging, change of rhythm in its third line. This music serves well for unison or part singing; a good pace and light accompaniment help to create the joyful intimacy and wonder expressed by the text. "Leave the gloomy haunts of sadness"; in other words, avoid the funereal tone that sometimes characterizes Reformed observances of the Lord's Supper—this is dance music for a feast!

Liturgical Use

Lord's Supper—probably most effective during distribution of the bread and wine.

306

Now the Solemn Feast Is Done

SONNE DER GERECHTIGKEIT
$\downarrow = 72$

Text

Calvin Seerveld (PHH 22) wrote these words in Toronto in 1985; they were first published in the 1987 *Psalter Hymnal*. He offered the text as an alternate to "At the Lamb's High Feast We Sing," which is often associated with the tune SONNE DER GERECHTIGKEIT. Seerveld created an effective, festive dismissal hymn in the conviction that the Lord's Supper is best concluded with a jubilee song instead of spoken words.

All three stanzas end with the theme "Christ sets us free." The joyful character of the text comes from remembering the death of Christ in the light of his resurrection, as Paul instructs in 1 Corinthians 15. Christ gave himself freely as the sacrifice (st. 1) required to set us free from sin (st. 2), and because of new life in him, we are free to laugh (st. 3)!

Tune

SONNE DER GERECHTIGKEIT was originally the tune to a fifteenth-century folk song, "Der reich Mann war geritten aus," and it was adopted by the Bohemian Brethren for their 1566 hymnal, *Kirchengeseng*. The tune is thus a *contrafactum*, changed from folk/court use to church use. The title is the German incipit for the chorale most commonly associated with the tune.

SONNE DER GERECHTIGKEIT is a bright tune characterized by a rising initial motif and forceful rhythms. Sing it in unison to a full organ registration and at a good tempo. Use brass and timpani for very festive singing.

Liturgical Use

As a dismissal hymn after the Lord's Supper; also very useful at an Easter Lord's Supper service or at the end of the Easter Vigil, after communion. Since every Sunday is a "little Easter," sing it anytime as a post-communion hymn, but not during Lent or Holy Week.

307

QUEBEC
♩ = 126

O Jesus, Joy of Loving Hearts

Text

This pious, evangelical hymn expresses a yearning for the feeding-by-faith symbolized in the Lord's Supper. Christ is the focal point as "the fount of life" (st. 1) and the Light of the World (st. 1, 4).

Scripture References
st. 2 = Joel 2:32
Acts 2:21
Rom. 10:13

The original source of this devotional hymn is the Latin poem "Jesu, dulcis memoria" from the late twelfth century. The evangelical fervor of the Latin text has caused some hymnodists to attribute the poem to Bernard of Clairveaux, but without sufficient proof. Ray Palmer (PHH 262) freely translated selected stanzas (4, 3, 20, 28, 10) from the poem. These were published in the *Sabbath Hymn Book* (1858), beginning with the words "Jesus, thou joy of loving hearts" (see PHH 480). The translated text has been altered for publication in the *Psalter Hymnal*.

Tune

Information on QUEBEC and on the composer can be found at PHH 141. QUEBEC is better suited to the lament character of Psalm 141 than to this Lord's Supper text. GERMANY (111), ROCKINGHAM (178), and WAREHAM (463) are more melodic settings that can be used as alternates. When using QUEBEC, sing in harmony with clean rhythmic articulation on repeated tones; add volume and strength for stanza 5.

Liturgical Use

As a partial substitute for one of the Lord's Supper prayers; during distribution of the bread and wine; many other occasions on non-communion Sundays (without st. 3).

308

Come, Risen Lord, as Guest among Your Own

SONG 24
♩ = 96

Text

This fine text celebrates the presence of Christ in the Lord's Supper. Stanzas 1 and 4 allude to the part of the Emmaus story (Luke 24:28-35) in which the two disciples invite Jesus to be their guest, but then Jesus becomes their host. Stanza 2 focuses on our partaking of the sacrament and stanzas 3 and 4 on the oneness we share with all believers in this world and in heaven.

Scripture References
st. 1 = Luke 24:28-31
st. 2 = Luke 22:12ff.
    1 Cor. 11:23-26
st. 3 = 1 Cor. 10:16-17
st. 4 = Luke 24:35
    1 Cor. 12:27

Originally written as "Come, risen Lord, and deign to be our guest," the text by George W. Briggs (b. Kirkby, Nottingham County, England, 1875; d. Hindhead, Surrey, England, 1959) was first published in the original edition of the British hymnbook *Songs of Praise* (1925). Briggs, however, regretted a change suggested by Percy Dearmer (PHH 595), editor of that hymnal—from "thine own sacrament" to "this our sacrament" in stanza 1—so he later published the text in its original form in his own *Songs of Faith* (1945). The *Psalter Hymnal* text is slightly altered from the revision published in *Hymns for Today's Church* (1982).

Educated at Emmanuel College, Cambridge, Briggs was a well-known twentieth-century hymn writer. A clergyman in the Church of England, he served a number of parishes and was a chaplain in the Royal Navy. He was especially interested in promoting meaningful worship in the British schools and consequently wrote *Prayers and Hymns for Use in Schools* (1927) and *Prayers and Hymns for Junior Schools* (1933). Briggs was a founding member of the Hymn Society of Great Britain and Ireland.

Tune

For information on SONG 24 and Orlando Gibbons see PHH 167; the setting there is in D minor. The tempo indicated there is deliberately faster than at 167.

Liturgical Use

Lord's Supper services—fits well as a congregational song either before the sacrament or during distribution of the bread and wine; also makes a fine choir anthem, preferably unaccompanied, during the sacrament.

SING ALLELUIA
♩ = 92

Lift Up Your Hearts unto the Lord

Text

Immensely popular, this praise chorus has been included in hundreds of songbooks, both in North America and in other continents. Linda L. Stassen-Benjamin (b. La Porte, IN, 1951) originally composed what is now stanza 5 rather instantaneously (while she was in the shower!) in June 1974. The song was published and recorded by Maranatha! Music, a ministry of Calvary Chapel, Costa Mesa, California, of which Stassen-Benjamin is a member. Stassen-Benjamin was educated at Ball State University, Muncie, Indiana, and El Camino College, Torrence, California. During the 1970s she sang and recorded for various ensembles, including David and New Song. Since 1981 she has been secretary, songwriter, and vocalist with New Song Ministries in Costa Mesa.

Following both oral tradition and the format in various published hymnals (including *Hymns for Today's Church*, 1982), the *Psalter Hymnal* precedes Stassen-Benjamin's stanza with four other stanzas derived from early Christian liturgies and the "Easter Canticle," which quotes from 1 Corinthians 5:7-8 and 15:20-22. So the text contains biblical and liturgical phrasing familiar to all English-speaking Christians. Together these textual ingredients make a powerful praise chorus. Following the tradition of many praise choruses, other stanzas can be added, for example:

> Jesus is risen from the dead!
> Christ is the Lord of heav'n and earth.
> Praise be to God forevermore!

Tune

Stassen-Benjamin's music appears in various collections with slight variations in the second part. The version here permits continuous singing of the two parts at the distance of one measure. The second part imitates the first part initially and again at the close, but the middle line of the second part is independent. Dale Grotenhuis (PHH 4) provided the harmonization in 1986.

The song can be sung in various ways: (a) have the congregation sing the main melody, and have a choir or any small group sing the second part in the manner of an echo or descant; (b) divide the singing of the two parts between similar-size groups within the congregation, such as left side and right side, or men and women; (c) use other instruments such as guitars, trumpet, recorder, and handbells, and improvise some percussion rhythms. Sing this music at a moving tempo without breaks between stanzas.

Liturgical Use

Before or during the Lord's Supper; especially useful during Easter season; the "feast" in stanza 4 is clearly the Lord's Supper, but it could also refer to other festivals of the church year.

310

Bread of the World, in Mercy Broken

EUCHARISTIC HYMN
♩ = 108

Text

Written by Reginald Heber (PHH 249), "Bread of the World" was first published posthumously in his *Hymns written and adapted to the Weekly Church Service of the Year* (1827); it was subtitled "Before the Sacrament."

Scripture References
all st. = John 6:33-35
Rom. 6:11

The text is a prayer asking Christ to look on us with mercy and to feed us with his grace. Though written in two stanzas, it is one continuous thought. A devotional text with strong poetic images—"bread of the world" and "wine of the soul"—this hymn invites confession of sin and the acceptance of divine grace.

Tune

John Sebastian Bach Hodges (b. Bristol, Gloucestershire, England, 1830; d. Baltimore, MD, 1915) composed EUCHARISTIC HYMN for Heber's text in 1868, while he was rector at Grace Episcopal Church, Newark, New Jersey. He first published the tune in his *Book of Common Praise* (1869) and named it after the sacramental service for which Heber wrote the text. Sing EUCHARISTIC HYMN in harmony, preferably without accompaniment and always in its entirety. It also makes a fine communion motet for a choir.

The son of Edward Hodges (PHH 155), John came to the United States at the age of fifteen. Educated at Columbia University, New York City, and General Theological Seminary, New York City, he was ordained in 1855. After having served Episcopal churches in Pittsburgh, Chicago, and Newark, he devoted the remainder of his career to St. Paul Church in Baltimore (1870-1906). There Hodges replaced the mixed choir with a choir of men and boys. He composed over a hundred hymns and anthems and compiled *The Book of Common Praise* (1869) and the revised edition of *Hymn Tunes* (1903). He was also active on the committees that produced the Episcopal *Hymnal* (1874) and *Hymnal* (1892).

Since the publication of William Mercer's *Church Psalter and Hymn Book* (1854), many hymnals have set Heber's text to GENEVAN 98/118 (see 98, 118, or 314) in one long stanza. That tune—much loved in the Reformed tradition—is a useful alternate because it helps to bind together the two short stanzas into one longer prayer. To create a longer Lord's Supper hymn, combine 310 and 314 into one song or choral anthem using GENEVAN 98/118.

Liturgical Use

As Heber said, "Before the sacrament"—use this hymn as part of the service of confession and forgiveness or during the communion liturgy as a substitute for the traditional singing of the Agnus Dei.

311

LAND OF REST
♩ = 56

I Come with Joy to Meet My Lord

Text

Brian A. Wren (b. Romford, Essex, England, 1936) wrote this communion hymn in Hockley, Essex, England, in July 1968 and revised it in 1970. The text was first published in the Canadian Anglican-United *Hymn Book* (1971); he revised it again in 1982 and 1995. Wren wrote this text to summarize a series of sermons on the meaning of the Lord's Supper, specifically as a post-sermon hymn to help illustrate the presence of Christ in the sacrament. He states that he wanted to express this

Scripture References
st. 1 = Gal. 1:4

> as simply as possible, in a way that would take the worshipper (probably without
> . . . recognizing it) from the usual individualistic approach to communion
> ("I come") to an understanding of its essential corporateness ("we'll go").

Wren has carefully worked out the progression from "I" to "we." This text contains themes of remembrance (st. 1), of sharing the bread and wine in communion with the saints (st. 2-3) and with Christ in his presence (st. 4), and of Christian service (st. 5), but the prevailing tone is one of joy and praise.

Wren is a major British figure in the revival of contemporary hymn writing. He studied French literature at New College and theology at Mansfield College in Oxford, England. Ordained in 1965, he was pastor of the Congregational Church (now United Reformed) in Hockley and Hawkwell, Essex, from 1965 to 1970. He worked for the British Council of Churches and several other organizations involved in fighting poverty and promoting peace and justice. This work resulted in his writing of *Education for Justice* (1977) and *Patriotism and Peace* (1983). With a ministry throughout the English-speaking world, Wren now resides in the United States where he is active as a freelance lecturer, preacher, and full-time hymn writer. His hymn texts are published in his *Faith Looking Forward* (1983), *Praising a Mystery* (1986), *Bring Many Names* (1989), *New Beginnings* (1993), and *Faith Renewed: 33 Hymns Reissued and Revised* (1995), as well as in many modern hymnals. He has also produced *What Language Shall I Borrow?* (1989), a discussion guide to inclusive language in Christian worship.

Tune

LAND OF REST is an American folk tune with roots in the ballads of northern England and Scotland. It was known throughout the Appalachians; a shape-note version of the tune was published in *The Sacred Harp* (1844) and titled NEW PROSPECT as the setting for "O land of rest! for thee I sigh." The tune was published again with that same text in J. R. Graves's *Little Seraph* (Memphis, 1873). The name LAND OF REST derives from the tune's association with that text.

The tune was known to Annabel M. Buchanan (b. Groesbeck, TX, 1888; d. Paducah, KY, 1983), whose grandmother sang it to her as a child. She harmonized the tune and published it in her *Folk Hymns of America* (1938), noting similarities between this tune and the tune for "Swing Low, Sweet Chariot" (616).

Known especially as a musicologist of American folk music, Buchanan was educated at the Landon Conservatory, Dallas, Texas, and the Guilmant Organ School, New York City. She taught at several colleges, including Stonewall Jackson College, Abingdon, Virginia. Buchanan published numerous articles on folk traditions of the Appalachian area of the United States. She also lectured widely on this topic and gave recitals of folk music. Her own compositions also show the influence of folk music.

Like many other folk tunes, LAND OF REST should be sung rather lightly and energetically with two pulses per measure, and faster in a small group. Sing stanzas 1 and 2 in unison (or using a soloist) and stanzas 3 through 5 in harmony.

Liturgical Use

Lord's Supper—sing entire hymn before or during the Lord's Supper; perhaps save stanza 5 for a doxology afterwards.

312

Eat This Bread, Drink This Cup

EAT THIS BREAD
$\quad$ = 72

Text

The first volume of *Music from Taizé* included mostly Latin texts; when preparing the second volume, G.I.A. president Robert J. Batastini was interested in providing more English texts as well.

Scripture References
st. = John 6:35

Working with Brother Robert and Jacques Berthier of the Taizé Community in France, Batastini adapted "Eat This Bread" from John 6:35 on the morning of October 7, 1983, and Berthier composed the music that same afternoon. The volume they were working on was published in 1984. (See PHH 217 for more information about the Taizé Community and their music.)

Batastini intended the hymn for communion processionals that call for a chorus that is easily memorized and sung while people come forward for the communion bread and wine. The *Psalter Hymnal* prints only the refrain; five stanzas taken from John 6, to be sung by a soloist, are published in *Music from Taizé* (vol. 2, 1984). The original text of the refrain portrays Christ as the speaker: "Come to me" and "Trust in me."

Tune

Like JESUS, REMEMBER ME (217), EAT THIS BREAD is a meditative chorus intended to be sung repeatedly and accompanied with various descants; repetitions are more natural when sung as refrains to the solo stanzas. Sing this chorus in harmony without accompaniment, with a song leader indicating dynamics, sometimes *forte*, sometimes *piano*. After several repetitions, intersperse humming to enhance the meditative effect of the singing. Add oboe, flute, recorder, or violin for the instrumental descants. The number of repetitions (with or without stanzas and instrumental descants) may be determined by the worship leaders. It should not be rushed. Use a combination of choir and congregational singing, if you like, perhaps interspersed with instrumentals and humming. One manner of performance is recorded on *We Come, O Christ, to You* (1985), a CRC Publications cassette recording of hymns for worship. Additional descant melodies are published in *Music from Taizé* (vol. 2; *Instrumental Edition*, G-2778A).

Liturgical Use

Lord's Supper, during distribution of the bread and wine.

313

ALLES IST AN GOTTES SEGEN
♩ = 58

Praise the Lord, Rise Up Rejoicing

Text

This post-communion text was first published in the British supplementary hymnal *100 Hymns for Today* (1969). As a hymn of thanksgiving, fitting for the eucharistic (thanksgiving) character of the Lord's Supper, the text rejoices in the victory of Christ on the cross (st. 1), the ingathering of Christ's people, his body (st. 2), and the Christian's task in the world (st. 3).

Howard C. A. Gaunt (b. Birmingham, England, 1902; d. Winchester, England, 1983) wrote this hymn during his tenure as precentor at Winchester Cathedral in southern England. "Tom" Gaunt was ordained in the Church of England and spent much of his career in education. He was headmaster of Malvern College (1937-1953) and head of the English department at Winchester College (1953-1963). He was also chaplain, then precentor at Winchester Cathedral until retirement in 1973. A number of his hymn texts were first published in *100 Hymns for Today*.

Tune

ALLES IST AN GOTTES SEGEN is a splendid tune that matches Gaunt's text well, giving it a lot of lift. Sing it in unison on stanzas 1 and 3 and in harmony on stanza 2. Use a cheerful trumpet stop, and keep the articulation crisp on repeating tones.

Johann Löhner (b. Nuremberg, Germany, 1645; d. Nuremberg, 1705) composed the first-known version of ALLES IST AN GOTTES SEGEN, published in *Der Geistlichen Erquick-Stunden . . . Poetischer Andacht-Klang* (1691). Löhner's parents died before he was fifteen, and he was adopted by his sister and brother-in-law, who also became his organ teacher. From 1670-1672 he traveled to Vienna, Salzburg, and Leipzig, both to study and to perform, but then returned to Nuremberg, where he remained the rest of his life. Löhner served as a singer (tenor) and organist in several churches, including the Frauenkirche (1672-1682), the Spitalkirche (1682-1694), and the Lorenzkirche (1694-1705). Known especially for his devotional songs for home singing, he also composed small operas, canons, and hymn tunes.

ALLES IST AN GOTTES SEGEN was altered in Johann B. König's (PHH 45) *Harmonischer Lieder-Schatz* (1738) and set to the text "Alles ist an Gottes Segen," from which the tune's name derives. Some other modern hymnals use the tune as revised in Johann A. Hiller's *Allgemeines Choral-Melodienbuch* (1793). The harmonization is by Johann S. Bach (PHH 7).

Liturgical Use

After the Lord's Supper, to thank God for the salvation and unity that the sacrament represents in our lives; also appropriate for dismissal after the sacrament.

314

Father, We Give You Thanks, Who Planted

GENEVAN 98/118
♩ = 72

Text

This hymn text is rooted in the early Christian church, all the way back to the Greek-language *Didache* (the *Teaching of the Twelve Apostles*), a Christian manual from the Church of Antioch, Syria, which some scholars date as early as A.D. 110. To produce this hymn text, F. Bland Tucker (PHH 247) translated selected prayers from chapters 9 and 10 of the *Didache*.

Scripture References
all st. = John 6:58
2 Cor. 4:6
Eph. 5:25-27; 6:6-7
2 Tim. 1:10
1 John 5:20

Stanzas 1 and 2a are from a post-communion prayer, and stanza 2b is from a prayer intended during distribution of the bread. The whole is essentially a hymn of thanksgiving and praise (st. 1) concluded with a petition for the unity of the church (st. 2), which reminds us of Christ's prayer that all believers "may be one" (John 17:21). That unity should be obvious when Christians gather around the Lord's table, but it should also extend within and between Christian denominations.

Tucker's 1939 translation was first published in the American Protestant Episcopal *Hymnal 1940*. The original first line read, "Father, we thank thee who hast planted." The modernized text in the *Psalter Hymnal* is the same as that published in the Australian hymnal *With One Voice* (1977).

Tune

For information on GENEVAN 98/118, see PHH 118. The harmonization here is from the *Pilgrim Hymnal* (1931); other harmonizations are found at 98 and 118.

Liturgical Use

Lord's Supper—as a post-communion hymn of thanksgiving; perhaps combined with the text of 310 (as the first stanza) whenever a longer hymn is needed, especially as a choral motet during communion.

315

DENNIS
♩ = 120

Blest Be the Tie That Binds

Text

An orphan at the age of twelve, John Fawcett (b. Lidget Green, Yorkshire, England, 1740; d. Hebden Bridge, Yorkshire, 1817) became apprenticed to a tailor and was largely self-educated. He was converted by the preaching of George Whitefield at the age of sixteen and began preaching soon thereafter. In 1765 Fawcett was called to a small, poor, Baptist country church in Wainsgate, Yorkshire. Seven years later he received a call from the large and influential Carter's Lane Church in London, England. Fawcett accepted the call and preached his farewell sermon. The day of departure came, and his family's belongings were loaded on carts, but the distraught congregation begged him to stay. In *Singers and Songs of the Church* (1869), Josiah Miller tells the story associated with this text:

Scripture References
st. 1-3 = Gal. 3:28
st. 3 = Gal. 6:2

> This favorite hymn is said to have been written in 1772, to commemorate the determination of its author to remain with his attached people at Wainsgate. The farewell sermon was preached, the wagons were loaded, when love and tears prevailed, and Dr. Fawcett sacrificed the attraction of a London pulpit to the affection of his poor but devoted flock.

Fawcett continued to serve in Wainsgate and in the nearby village of Hebden Bridge for the remainder of his active ministry.

Fawcett titled this hymn "Brotherly Love." It is essentially about the communion of saints, bound together in love (st. 1), united in worship (st. 2), sharing each other's burdens (st. 3), and encouraging each other with the hope of eternal life in glory, where we will be reunited with departed friends and freed "from sorrow, toil, and pain, and sin" (st. 4-6).

He wrote most of his hymns to be sung by his congregation at the conclusion of the sermon. They were published in *Hymns adapted to the Circumstances of Public Worship and Private Devotion* (1782). In the preface to his collection Fawcett apologized to "persons of an elevated genius" for his "plain verses" but expressed the hope that they would edify "humble Christians."

Tune

Lowell Mason (PHH 96) arranged DENNIS and first published it in *The Psaltery* (1845), a hymnal he compiled with George J. Webb (PHH 559). Mason attributed the tune to Johann G. Nägeli (b. Wetzikon, near Zurich, Switzerland, 1773; d. Wetzikon, 1836) but included no source reference. Nägeli presumably published the original melody as the setting for "O selig, selig, wer vor dir" in his *Christliches Gesangbuch* (1828). Nägeli was an influential music educator who lectured throughout Germany and France. Influenced by Johann Pestalozzi, he published his theories of music education in *Gangbildungslehre* (1810), a book that made a strong impact on Lowell Mason. Nägeli composed mainly choral works, including settings of Goethe's poetry. He received his early instruction from his father, then in Zurich, where he concentrated on the music of J. S. Bach. In Zurich he also established a lending library and a publishing house, which published first editions of Beethoven's piano sonatas and music by Bach, Handel, and Frescobaldi.

The tune name DENNIS is thought to refer to a town in Massachusetts. It is a simple tune, initially built with several sequences. Sing stanzas 1 and 6 in unison and the others in parts, perhaps using no accompaniment on stanza 4 for occasions of sorrowful parting. Two groups can also sing the entire hymn antiphonally, by half-stanzas, especially if one group is parting from the other. Sing the tune in two long lines, with one pulse per measure.

Liturgical Use

Worship services that stress unity or the communion of saints; occasions of departure; encouragement for mutual prayer, fellowship, and burden bearing; close of the worship service or other church meetings; funerals.

316

God Be with You Till We Meet Again

Text

Jeremiah E. Rankin (b. Thornton, NH, 1828; d. Cleveland, OH, 1904) says of his hymn text,

Scripture References
st. 1 = Acts 20:32
st. 3 = Deut. 33:27
st. 4 = Song of Songs 2:4

It was written as a Christian good-bye; it was called forth by no person or occasion, but was deliberately composed as a Christian hymn on the basis of the etymology of "good-bye," which means "God be with you." The first stanza was sent to two different composers, one of musical note, the other [William G. Tomer] wholly unknown and not thoroughly educated in music. I selected the composition of the latter, and with some slight changes it was published.

The first stanza was published in 1880 with the tune GOD BE WITH YOU by William G. Tomer in *Gospel Bells;* the 1883 edition of that hymnal included eight stanzas. A popular hymn, "God Be with You" gained currency through the evangelistic crusades of Dwight L. Moody and Ira D. Sankey (PHH 73). Modern hymnals usually print only four stanzas.

The text is essentially a parting blessing, a prayer that God will guide you (st. 1), feed you (st. 2), and protect you in life and in death (st. 3-4). Each stanza is framed by the phrase "God be with you till we meet again."

A graduate of Middlebury College, Vermont, and of Andover Theological Seminary, Newton Center, Massachusetts, Rankin served Congregational churches in New York, Vermont, Massachusetts, Washington, D.C., and New Jersey (1855-1889). In 1889 he became president of Howard University, Washington, D.C., a school famous for its many prominent African American graduates. Rankin issued three volumes of poetry and hymn texts (of which "God Be with You" is his most well-known), collaborated in the compilation of hymnals such as *The Gospel Temperance Hymnal* (1878) and *Gospel Bells* (1880), and published *German-English Lyrics, Sacred and Secular* (1897).

Tune

Though the gospel tune by Tomer has enjoyed popularity, its overly sentimental character prompted a search for alternatives. Ralph Vaughan Williams (b. Down Ampney, Gloucestershire, England, 1872; d. St. Marylebone, London, England, 1958) composed the distinguished tune RANDOLPH for Rankin's text. The tune was first published in *The English Hymnal* (1906). In it Vaughan Williams matched the repetition of the first and last textual phrases with a repeated musical phrase.

Though written for unison singing and best accompanied with clear organ sounds, several stanzas sing well in parts, possibly even without accompaniment. Or sing the first and final phrases in unison and the inner phrases in harmony. Because the first and last phrases are identical for each stanza, this hymn is very effective when two groups alternate between stanzas, perhaps even facing each other.

Through his composing, conducting, collecting, editing, and teaching, Vaughan Williams became the chief figure in the realm of English music and church music in the first half of the twentieth century. His education included instruction at the Royal College of Music in London and Trinity College, Cambridge, as well as additional studies in Berlin and Paris. During World War I he served in the army medical corps in France. Vaughan Williams taught music at the Royal College of Music (1920-1940), conducted the Bach Choir in London (1920-1927), and directed the Leith Hill Music Festival in Dorking (1905-1953). A major influence in his life was the English folk song. A knowledgeable collector of folk songs, he was also a member of the Folksong Society and a supporter of the English Folk Dance Society. Vaughan Williams wrote various articles and books, including *National Music* (1935), and composed numerous arrangements of folk songs; many of his compositions show the impact of folk rhythms and melodic modes. His original compositions cover nearly all musical genres, from orchestral symphonies and concertos to choral works, from songs to operas, and from chamber music to music for films. Vaughan Williams's church music includes anthems; choral-orchestral works, such as *Magnificat* (1932), *Dona Nobis Pacem* (1936), and *Hodie* (1953); and hymn tune settings for organ. But most important to the history of hymnody, he was music editor of the most influential British hymnal at the beginning of the twentieth century, *The English Hymnal* (1906), and coeditor (with Martin Shaw) of *Songs of Praise* (1925, 1931) and the *Oxford Book of Carols* (1928).

Liturgical Use
Though traditionally used when ministers, missionaries, or others take their leave from a congregation, this hymn is generally useful as a dismissal hymn, as a prayer for blessing, and as a sung benediction.

317

Go Now in Peace

GO NOW IN PEACE
♩ = 50

Text
Natalie Sleeth (b. Evanston, IL, 1930; d. Denver, CO, 1992) wrote this charming round in 1975 when she was employed in the church school of Highland Park United Methodist Church, Dallas, Texas, dedicating it to one of her Orff instrumentalist friends. Sleeth published the text and music of this hymn in 1976 in her *Sunday Songbook,* compiled for use by church school groups and young choirs. Sleeth's work consists of many anthems that involve two-, three-, or four-part rounds.

The text is a simple blessing or benediction: go in peace under God's loving care.

Tune

The beauty of GO NOW IN PEACE lies in its simplicity of melody and in the many possibilities of enhancing a performance with a variety of instruments. The hymn is a wonderful "little anthem" for a children's choir accompanied by elementary school instrumentalists. Use Orff instruments or try handbells for the repeated patterns. Sing altogether once, and on the repeat, sing this hymn as a three-part round; four parts are also possible if the round begins every two bars.

A respected author and composer of hymns, anthems, and rounds, Sleeth composed almost two hundred works for a variety of publishers from 1969 until her death. Educated at Wellesley College in Massachusetts, in 1952 she married Ronald E. Sleeth, a Methodist minister and homiletics professor; they resided in seminary communities in Nashville, Dallas, Evanston, and Denver. Sleeth published a devotional book, *Adventures for the Soul* (1987), which describes some of her compositions. She was the subject of the video *Words and Music* (1990). Some of her anthems were published as hymns in *Songs for LiFE* (1994).

Liturgical Use

A parting blessing; a sung benediction at the close of a worship service; generally useful at any Sunday worship service, but probably most fitting at a festive service because of the extra effort required for instrumentation; could also be a recessional in which each group begins to leave after completing its part of the round.

318

ST. CLEMENT
♩ = 104

The Day You Gave Us, Lord, Is Ended

Text

John Ellerton (b. London, England, 1826; d. Torquay, Devonshire, England, 1893) wrote this evening hymn (and 319) in 1870 for *A Liturgy for Missionary Meetings*. The text's dominant theme is the

Scripture References
st. 3 = Ps. 113:3

growing worldwide fellowship of the Christian church and its unbroken, unceasing offering of praise and prayer to God. Even though Victoria may have chosen the hymn to symbolize the British Empire, stanza 4 wisely reminds us that earthly kingdoms pass away—only the kingdom of God stands and grows forever.

Ellerton borrowed the hymn's first line from an anonymous text in *Church Poetry* (1843). He then revised his text for the hymn's publication in the Society for the Promotion of Christian Knowledge's *Church Hymns* (1871), of which he was coeditor. Possibly prompted by the suitability of the worldwide church image as a symbol for the British Empire "on which the sun never sets," Queen Victoria chose this hymn to celebrate her Diamond Jubilee in 1897. Victoria's use of the hymn assured its popularity in the English-speaking world.

Educated at King William's College on the Isle of Man and at Trinity College, Cambridge, England, Ellerton was ordained in the Church of England in 1851. He served six parishes, spending the longest time in Crewe Green (1860-1872), a church of steelworkers and farmers. Ellerton wrote and translated about eighty hymns, many of which are still sung today. He helped to compile *Church Hymns* and wrote its handbook, *Notes and Illustrations to Church Hymns* (1882). Some of his other hymn texts were published in *The London Mission Hymn Book* (1884).

Tune

ST. CLEMENT was composed for this text by Rev. Clement C. Scholefield (b. Edgbaston, near Birmingham, Warwickshire, England, 1839; d. Goldalming, Surrey, England, 1904). ST. CLEMENT was published in Arthur S. Sullivan's 1874 hymnal, *Church Hymns with Tunes;* of his own accord Sullivan (PHH 46) "canonized" his curate, Scholefield, by naming this tune ST. CLEMENT. Educated at St. John's College, Cambridge, Scholefield was ordained in the Church of England in 1867. He served at Hove, Brighton, St. Peter's in Kensington (1869-1879), and briefly at St. Luke's in Chelsea. From 1880 to 1890 he was chaplain at Eton College and from 1890 to 1895 vicar of Holy Trinity in Knightsbridge. Mainly self-taught as a musician, Scholefield became an accomplished pianist and composed some songs and hymn tunes, of which ST. CLEMENT is the only one in common use today; it is always joined to Ellerton's text.

Although some people object to the waltz-like rhythms of ST. CLEMENT, most love the melody with its slurred tones. Sing with solid organ support or accompaniment. For the fourth stanza, the organist could slow down slightly and add the most brilliant mixture and reeds available.

Liturgical Use

An evening hymn at the close of worship (st. 1 is only for evening use); a missionary hymn; at festivals of the church: Pentecost, worldwide communion, All Saints/Reformation Day.

319

Savior, Again to Your Dear Name We Raise

ELLERS
$\srJ = 60$

Text

John Ellerton (PHH 318) wrote this hymn in 1866 as a concluding hymn for the festival of the Malpas, Middlewich, and Nantwich Choral Association. Ellerton revised the text and reduced it from six to four stanzas for the Appendix to the original edition of *Hymns Ancient and Modern* (1868).

The text is a prayer for peace: peace at the conclusion of worship (st. 1), when homeward bound (st. 2), during the night (st. 3), and throughout our lives (st. 4).

This hymn differs from Ellerton's other evening hymn, "The Day You Gave Us, Lord, Is Ended" (318) in that its focus is peace rather than missions.

Tune

Composed by Edward J. Hopkins (b. Westminster, London, England, 1818; d. St. Pancras, London, 1901) as a unison melody with varied organ accompaniments, ELLERS has been traditionally associated with this text. The tune was published in 1869 in Brown-Borthwick's *The Supplemental Hymn and Tune Book.* The harmony, slightly revised, is from Hopkin's four-part arrangement for singers, taken from his first stanza organ part. It was published in the Appendix to the *Bradford Tune Book* (1872).

The tune has a wave motion, rising to its climax at midpoint and then descending to end on a D. Since the hymn is a prayer, use clear but light organ registration.

Hopkins began his musical career as a chorister at the Chapel Royal and at St. Paul's Cathedral while also developing his skill at the organ. At the age of sixteen he received his first organist position—at the Mitcham Church in Surrey. In 1843 he was appointed organist and choirmaster at the Temple Church, London, where he remained for fifty-five years. During that time the men and boys choir achieved great fame for its outstanding services. Also active in other musical areas, Hopkins founded (with others) the Royal College of Organists, founded and edited the periodical *The Organist and Choirmaster,* and with E. F. Rimbault coauthored a standard text, *The Organ: Its History and Construction* (1855). He composed a large number of anthems, liturgical music, and hymn tunes. Some of his tunes were published in the *Cathedral Psalter* (1855) and *The Temple Choral Service Book* (1867). Hopkins also served as music editor for various hymnals produced in England, Scotland, and Canada.

Liturgical Use

Dismissal hymn sung prior to the spoken benediction, especially in evening worship; stanzas 1 and 4 could be sung at a similar place in morning worship; stanza 4 alone is appropriate at a funeral service (it was sung at Ellerton's funeral on June 20, 1893).

320

SICILIAN MARINERS
♩ = 88
Lord, Dismiss Us with Your Blessing

Text

First published anonymously in *A Supplement to the Shawbury Hymn Book* (1773), this hymn text was attributed to John Fawcett (PHH 315) in the 1791 Harris hymnal *A Collection of Psalms and Hymns.* That hymnbook included three stanzas, but most modern hymnals print only stanzas 1 and 2. (Stanza 3 concerns parting at death.)

Scripture References
st. 1 = Num. 6:24
Luke 2:29
Acts 20:32

"Lord, Dismiss Us with Your Blessing" is a prayer hymn to be used at the close of worship. It asks the Lord for a parting blessing (st. 1), praises the Lord for salvation, and asks for fruitfulness and obedience in our lives (st. 2).

Tune

SICILIAN MARINERS is traditionally used for the Roman Catholic Marian hymn "O Sanctissima." According to tradition, Sicilian seamen ended each day on their ships by singing this hymn in unison. The tune probably traveled from Italy to Germany to England, where *The European Magazine* and *London Review* first published it in 1792. The tune was associated with the German Christmas carol "O du Fröhliche, O du Selige." The tune also appears to have had an influence on the African American song "We Shall Overcome."

SICILIAN MARINERS is a bar-form tune (AAB) with a florid soprano line and an active harmonization. Sing it either vigorously or reflectively; singing rather deliberately will increase the hymn's dignity. A traditional version of the tune includes dotted rhythms, which encourage a more meditative approach to singing.

Liturgical Use

At the close of worship just prior to the benediction; or sing stanza 1 before and stanza 2 after the benediction.

321

Lord, Dismiss Us with Your Blessing

JULION
♩ = 72

Text

For text commentary see PHH 320.

Tune

David Hurd (b. Brooklyn, NY, 1950) composed JULION in 1974. The harmony is rich (up to six parts with the descant) and well suited to a rich, smooth organ sonority, including strings. The descant is difficult and will need rehearsing, but it can be effectively sung by a choir or played by instruments above the congregational unison on stanza 2.

Hurd was a boy soprano at St. Gabriel's Church in Hollis, Long Island, New York. Educated at Oberlin College and the University of North Carolina, he has been professor of church music and organist at General Theological Seminary in New York since 1976. In 1985 he also became director of music for All Saints Episcopal Church, New York. Hurd is an outstanding recitalist and improvisor and a composer of organ, choral, and instrumental music. He has served on several committees of the Standing Commission on Church Music of the Episcopal Church, and a number of his tunes were included in *The Hymnal 1982.* To date two collections of his hymn tunes have been published: *The David Hurd Hymnary* (1983) and *The David Hurd Hymnary Supplement* (1985).

Liturgical Use
See PHH 320.

322

God, the Father of Your People

Text

This hymn is unusual because two different and very short hymn texts, written two centuries apart, were combined to form a composite text. Both contain the themes of parting, peace, and unity. Stanza 1 is a prayer that God's people may be one body as they serve and witness. Stanza 2 is borrowed in part from 2 Corinthians 13:14; it invokes a blessing on all God's people.

Scripture References
st. 2 = 2 Cor. 13:14

Alfred E. Mulder (b. Ireton, IA, 1936) wrote stanza 1 in 1978, during his days as a minister among the Navajo and Zuni people, as a versification of the ministry statement of Bethany Christian Reformed Church, Gallup, New Mexico. Mulder received his education at Calvin College and Seminary, Grand Rapids, Michigan, and studied counseling at the University of New Mexico in Albuquerque. Ordained a pastor in the Christian Reformed Church, he served congregations in Luctor, Kansas (1960-1964), and Brigham City, Utah (1964-1968), and was a missionary pastor in Gallup, New Mexico (1968-1984). Since 1984 he has held the position of director of new church development for Christian Reformed Home Missions.

John Newton (PHH 462) wrote the text of stanza 2. It was one of his "short hymns," first published in *Olney Hymns* (1779) in a section entitled "After Sermon."

Tune

HOLY MANNA is an Appalachian tune, published in William Moore's four-shape tune book *The Columbian Harmony* in 1825. Moore (from Wilson County in west Tennessee) claimed authorship of eighteen of the tunes in that collection, including HOLY MANNA, which was set to "Brethren,We Have Met to Worship." HOLY MANNA was a very popular tune, given various names and set to various texts in many collections.

Shaped in rounded bar form (AABA), HOLY MANNA was originally meant to be sung in unison. The pentatonic (five-note) melody is well suited for canonic singing. The choir can effectively sing stanza 2, beginning one measure after the congregation, with the organ playing the last measure two times to complete the canon. Use light accompaniment or play the melody on a solo manual.

The harmonization by Norman E. Johnson (b. Smolan, KS, 1928; d. Grand Rapids, MI, 1983) was first published in the 1973 *Covenant Hymnal.* Johnson attended Bethany College, Lindsborg, Kansas; North Park Theological Seminary, Chicago, Illinois; and received a Master of Church Music degree from the University of California. A senior music editor for Singspiration Music, Johnson also served the Evangelical Covenant Church of Grand Rapids as minister of music. He edited several hymnals, including *The Covenant Hymnal* (1973), to which he also contributed some texts and tunes.

Liturgical Use

Just prior to a spoken benediction; at the close of worship (the spoken benediction should be some blessing other than the familiar apostolic form; instead use the Aaronic blessing from Numbers 6:24-26); an appropriate blessing on a marriage, with the following changes: "us" to "them," "we" to "they," and in the last line of stanza 1—"as one body we will serve you" to "as one body let them serve you" (or the bridal couple could sing stanza 1, and the congregation, stanza 2).

323

Forth in the Peace of Christ We Go

ANGELUS
♩ = 116

Text

Irish Jesuit James Quinn (PHH 220) wrote the text to this hymn in Edinburgh, Scotland, as poetic commentary on sections of Vatican II's "Constitution on the Church" (chap. IV, sec. 34-36; and chap. I, sec. 1). The text was first published in Quinn's *New Hymns for All Seasons* (1969).

Scripture References
st. 3-4 = 1 Pet. 2:9

"Forth in the Peace of Christ We Go" emphasizes our responsibility as Christians to spread the gospel: we go to the world preaching Christ with joy (st. 1); we go as kings to show our servanthood to the King and to all people (st. 2); we go as priests to minister with the message of God's healing grace (st. 3); we go as prophets to speak his word (st. 4); we go as the church to bring Christ's peace and love (st. 5).

Tune

ANGELUS is attributed to Georg Joseph (Germany, 17th century), a musician at the court of the prince-bishop of Breslau. It was published in the 1657 hymnal *Heilige Seelen-Lust,* edited by Joseph. In that hymnal the tune was associated with the Johann Scheffler text "Du meiner Seelen güldne Ziehr." In fact, the tune's name comes from the name Scheffler took after his conversion to Roman Catholicism: Angelus Silesius. Joseph provided most of the musical settings for Scheffler's texts; their joint work was published in the four books of *Heilige Seelenlust* (1657, expanded to five books, 1668). In the nineteenth century the tune was adapted to its present form and was published in the Munich hymnal *Cantica Spiritualia* (1847).

Sing stanzas 1 and 5 in unison and stanzas 2-4 in harmony. Or, for stanzas 2-4, divide the congregation into three groups representing prophets, priests, and kings, and have them sing their corresponding stanzas. Reginald Thatcher's more modern WILDERNESS (608) is a suggested alternate tune for this text.

Liturgical Use

As a dismissal or recessional hymn; in conjunction with sermons on "prophet, priest, and king"; at high festivals of the church.

324

GONFALON ROYAL
♩ = 100

Forth in Your Name, O Lord, I Go

Text

Charles Wesley (PHH 267) wrote the text of this hymn and published it in *Hymns and Sacred Poems* (1749) as a hymn "for believers." It was entitled "Before Work."

Scripture References
st. 2 = Ps. 139:2
Rom. 12:1-2
st. 3 = Ps. 16:8
st. 4 = Matt. 11:30
Matt. 26:41

The hymn originally had six stanzas. Following John Wesley's example in his *Collection* (1780), most modern hymnals, including the *Psalter Hymnal*, omit the original stanza 3.

Recognizing the significance of daily work for the Christian, Charles Wesley wrote and sang hymns not only for Sunday but also for daily use. The text of this hymn reflects Wesley's views about work: we are to do our work in the name of the Lord (st. 1); God calls us to our work in obedience to his will (st. 2); we may offer all our work to God (st. 3); as we journey from this life to glory, we may always view our work as part of the coming of God's kingdom (st. 4); we may gratefully use all God's gifts for his glory (st. 5).

Tune

Percy C. Buck (b. West Ham, Essex, England, 1871; d. Hindhead, Haslemere, Surrey, England, 1947), director of music at the well-known British boys' academy Harrow School, wrote GONFALON ROYAL for "The royal banners forward go" (*gonfalon* is an ancient Anglo-Norman word meaning *banner*). Buck published the tune in 1913 in his *Fourteen Hymn Tunes*.

Each stanza moves toward a rhythmically intense but inconclusive ending, propelling the singer on to the next stanza. The final ending is reserved for the "Amen," which appropriately concludes this sung prayer. Sing boldly in unison (the usual practice for the boys at Harrow School) with strong organ or piano accompaniment.

Buck studied at the Guildhall School of Music, the Royal College of Music, and Worcester College, Oxford, England, where he received his doctorate. An organist at Worcester College and at Wells and Bristol Cathedrals, he served as director of music at Harrow School from 1901-1927, taught at Dublin University, and then taught at the University of London until his retirement in 1937. He was also knighted that year. Buck wrote pedagogical books on the history and theory of music, on acoustics, and on the psychology of music. A composer of chamber music, anthems, and hymn tunes, he also edited *The English Psalter* (1925), *The Oxford Song Book* (1929), and *The Oxford Nursery Song Book* (1934).

Liturgical Use

Close of worship; worship services in which labor is stressed (Labor Day Sunday); springtime prayer services for crops and industry; New Year's Day; ordination; profession of faith; commissioning services; when used during the Easter season, substitute an "Alleluia" for the final "Amen."

325

Go Forth for God

ANIMA CHRISTI
$\quad = 60$

Text

"Go Forth for God" is a wonderful parting hymn of encouragement. It exhorts believers to "go forth for God" to the world in peace (st. 1), "in love" (st. 2), "in strength" (stanza 3), and "in joy" (st. 4), using phrases from Romans 12:9-21 and 1 Thessalonians 5:13b-22—biblical texts containing Paul's instructions about how Christians should act in the world.

John R. Peacey (b. Hove, Brighton, Sussex, England, 1896; d. Brighton, Sussex, 1971) wrote the original text to this hymn in 1968. The 1987 *Psalter Hymnal* version of the text, however, is a result of revisions made by Peacey in 1970 and by the editors of the *English Hymnal* supplement, *English Praise* (1975). Educated in theology at Selwyn College, Cambridge, Peacey was ordained in the Church of England in 1923. In addition to serving several churches in England, he was also headmaster and principal of the Bishop Cotton School in Simla, India (1927-1945), and principal of Bishop's College in Calcutta, India (1935-1945). Peacey concluded his career at Bristol Cathedral (1945-1966). Written mainly during his retirement years, his hymn texts were published posthumously in *Go Forth for God* (1981).

Tune

ANIMA CHRISTI became popular in the latter half of the nineteenth century in British Roman Catholic churches, where it was used for evening benediction services. It is believed that Jesuit priest William J. Maher (b. Bristol, Gloucestershire, England, 1823; d. Paris, France, 1877) composed the tune around 1863 for a fourteenth-century Latin hymn, "Anima Christi sanctifica me." The obscure British collection *Mission Hymns* (1864) first published ANIMA CHRISTI for use with an anonymous English translation of this Latin text. Maher both studied and taught at Stonyhurst College. He entered the Jesuit Order in 1841, was ordained in 1856, and became an evangelist in London. The editor of Francis Trappes's *Hymns for the Liturgical Year* (1865), Maher died in Paris while en route to Lourdes to seek a cure for his cancer.

ANIMA CHRISTI builds slowly to its high point in line 3. Try singing the first line of each stanza in unison and all other lines in harmony. Each succeeding stanza should build in intensity. Accompany the hymn with some sense of marcato so that the music supports the text. Try the organ trumpet stop or, better yet, a trio of real trumpets playing from different balconies or church corners.

For more rousing tunes, use WOODLANDS (478), MORESTEAD (295), or the more familiar TOULON (521) with this text.

Liturgical Use

Dismissal; especially effective for a profession of faith or commissioning service.

326

HESSEL PARK
$\quad$ = 56

We Lift Our Hearts to God

Text

This text is a fitting confession for Christians who must leave the comfortable pew and venture into God's world. The text of stanza 1 says that we go out to serve, "to work in church and kingdom," under God's protection and with God's blessing of peace. In stanza 2 author Cornelius (Cor) Wm. Barendrecht (b. The Hague, the Netherlands, 1934) quotes from the Heidelberg Catechism (Q&A 32) to say that serving God is a whole-life act of worship, "a living sacrifice."

Scripture References
st. 1 = Phil. 4:7
st. 2 = Rom. 12:1

Also quoting New Testament phrases, poet Barendrecht wrote this unrhymed verse text, his first hymn, in Grand Rapids, Michigan, in 1975. Educated at Grand Valley State University and Calvin College, both in Grand Rapids, Barendrecht is a writer and has served as editor for several Christian publications. He was cofounder and editor of the Christian literary magazine *For the Time Being* (1970-1978) and is currently director of business and communication of the Grand Rapids Area Ministries and editor of *Grace Notes*.

Tune

Psalter Hymnal editor Emily R. Brink (PHH 158) wrote HESSEL PARK for the Barendrecht text in 1976; the text and tune were first published in *For the Time Being*. The tune is named for the Hessel Park Christian Reformed Church, Champaign, Illinois, where Brink was music director while teaching at the University of Illinois, Champaign-Urbana.

HESSEL PARK consists of two long melodic units, each with its own pattern of dramatic rising phrases and descents to the tonic. Sing this tune in unison at a moderate pace with a large organ plenum as supporting cast.

Liturgical Use

As a parting hymn at the close of worship.

327

On Jordan's Bank the Baptist's Cry

PUER NOBIS
♩ = 132

Text

John the Baptist's announcement "Prepare the way for the Lord" (Matt. 3:3, a quote from Isa. 40:3) is the primary basis for this Advent hymn. Stanzas 1 and 2 apply that message to people today; stanza 3 is a confession by God's people of their need for salvation; stanza 4 is a prayer for healing and love; stanza 5 is a doxology. This much-loved Advent text is laced with various scriptural phrases.

Scripture References
st. 1-2 = Isa. 40:3, 9
Matt. 3:3
Mark 1:3
Luke 3:3-4
st. 3 = Ps. 46:1
Isa. 40:7

Charles Coffin (b. Buzancy, Ardennes, France, 1676; d. Paris, France, 1749) wrote this text in Latin ("Jordanis oras praevia") for the Paris *Breviary* (1736), a famous Roman Catholic liturgical collection of psalms, hymns, and prayers. Coffin was partially responsible for the compilation of that hymnbook. Latin remained the language of scholarship and of the Roman Catholic liturgy in the eighteenth century. Working in that tradition, Coffin was an accomplished Latin scholar and writer of Latin poems and hymns. Educated at Deplessis College of the University of Paris, he served on the faculty and was university rector at the College of Doirmans-Beauvais, the University of Paris. He collected a hundred of his hymns and published them in *Hymni Sacri* (1736); a number of these have found their way into English language hymnals, including this Advent hymn.

The English translation is a composite work based on a translation by John Chandler (PHH 485), who published it in his *Hymns of the Primitive Church* (1837). (Chandler thought it was a medieval text!) Since 1837, various hymnal editors have revised the text in attempts to bring the translation closer to Coffin's original.

Tune

PUER NOBIS is a melody from a fifteenth-century manuscript from Trier. However, the tune probably dates from an earlier time and may even have folk roots. PUER NOBIS was altered in Spangenberg's *Christliches Gesangbüchlein* (1568), in Petri's famous *Piae Cantiones* (1582), and again in Praetorius's (PHH 351) *Musae Sioniae* (Part VI, 1609), which is the basis for the triple-meter version used in the 1987 *Psalter Hymnal*. Another form of the tune in duple meter is usually called PUER NOBIS NASCITUR. The tune name is taken from the incipit of the original Latin Christmas text, which was translated into German by the mid-sixteenth century as "Uns ist geborn ein Kindelein," and later in English as "Unto Us a Boy Is Born." The harmonization is from the 1902 edition of George R. Woodward's (PHH 403) *Cowley Carol Book*.

PUER NOBIS is a splendid tune in arch form that lifts and then propels itself along to its final note.

Try having the choir sing stanzas 1 and 2 in unison. Then all could sing stanzas 3 and 4 in unison with the choir providing the harmony. Stanza 4 could also be sung in canon at one measure, with either a strictly unison accompaniment or one composed to accommodate the canon. All worshipers could sing stanza 5 in unison again. Use a rather light organ registration, but change to a full one for stanza 5.

Liturgical Use

During Advent, especially in worship services on John the Baptist; sermons on repentance and renewal. The final stanza makes a fitting doxology for the four Sundays in Advent as well as for Christmas.

328

VENI IMMANUEL
♩ = 60

O Come, O Come, Immanuel

Text

This ancient Advent hymn may date back to a community of fifth-century Jewish Christians and perhaps was part of their Hanukkah festival. The text does include many elements of the Hanukkah celebration—remembrance of wilderness wandering, darkness and death, but also celebration of light (the use of candles) and, above all, wonderment about the hope for Christ's return ("O").

In the ninth century the text entered the Roman liturgy for use during Advent. In the week before Christmas the medieval church regularly sang seven "Great 'O' Antiphons" in conjunction with the Magnificat during Vespers. Each of these antiphons included an Old Testament name for the coming Messiah. During the twelfth or thirteenth century these words were put in hymn form, in Latin, and the "Rejoice" refrain was added. The stanzas included in the *Psalter Hymnal* were historically scheduled for December 23 (st. 1, Immanuel); Dec. 17 (st. 2, Wisdom); December 18 (st. 3, Lord of might); December 19 (st. 4, Branch of Jesse); December 20 (st. 5, Key of David); December 21 (st. 6, Bright Morning Star); December 22 (st. 7, Desire of Nations).

John Mason Neale (PHH 342) translated this Latin verse into English and published it in his *Medieval Hymns and Sequences* (1851). In subsequent years other hymnal editors made various changes, including changing the order of the stanzas. Neale also gave copious scriptural references for the text in his *Words of the Hymnal Noted* (1855).

Although the Latin phrase in the refrain "nascetur pro te, Israel" has been translated "shall come to you," it really means "shall be born to you." Thus the original Latin hymn celebrated the first coming of the Christ. The translation, however, permits use of the hymn to celebrate both first and second comings.

Scripture References
st. 1 = Isa. 7:14
    Matt. 1:23
st. 2 = Isa. 11:2
    1 Cor. 1:30
st. 3 = Deut. 10:17
    1 Tim. 6:15
    Ex. 19:16-20
st. 4 = Isa. 11:1, 10
    Rom. 15:12
st. 5 = Isa. 22:22
    Rev. 3:7
st. 6 = Num. 24:17
    Rev. 22:16
st. 7 = Jer. 10:7
    Rev. 15:4
ref. = Isa. 59:20

Tune

VENI IMMANUEL was originally music for a Requiem Mass in a fifteenth-century French Franciscan *Processional*. Thomas Helmore (b. Kidderminster, Worcestershire, England, 1811; d. Westminster, London, England, 1890) adapted this chant tune and published it in Part II of his *The Hymnal Noted* (1854). A graduate of Magdalen College, Oxford, England, Helmore was ordained a priest in the Church of England, but his main contribution to the church was in music. He was precentor at St. Mark's College, Chelsea (1842-1877), and master of the choristers in the Chapel Royal for many years. He promoted unaccompanied choral services and played an important part in the revival of plainchant in the Anglican Church. Helmore was involved in various publications of hymns, chants, and carols, ncluding *A Manual of Plainsong* (1850) and *The Hymnal Noted* (with John Mason Neale).

VENI IMMANUEL is in the Dorian mode and could be sung in harmony throughout, but the preferred practice is to sing the stanzas in unison and the refrain in parts. For example, sing the hymn antiphonally, perhaps including organ-alone stanzas. On stanza 4 the organ could play an arrangement of the tune while the congregation meditates on the text.

Chant tunes are intended to be sung in speech-rhythm, so sing this hymn freely and do not hesitate to let the "Rejoice" phrases ring through the church! Use light accompaniment on the stanzas and full, bright accompaniment on the refrain. Play and sing the line "Immanuel shall come to you" as one phrase. Organists may want to use an accompaniment in more of a chant style; for example, *Hymnal 1982* (56) contains an accompaniment suited to unison singing of the stanzas. Accompanists could still use the *Psalter Hymnal* harmonization for part singing on the refrain.

Liturgical Use

During Advent, singing the hymn in full or choosing certain stanzas for different Sundays; an Advent hymn festival using various arrangements from other hymnals such as *Carols for Choirs*.

329

STUTTGART
♩ = 52

Come, Thou Long-Expected Jesus

Text

Charles Wesley (PHH 267) wrote this Advent hymn and printed it in his *Hymns for the Nativity of our Lord* (1744). Like so many of Wesley's texts, "Come, Thou Long-Expected Jesus" alludes to one or more Scripture passages in virtually every phrase. The double nature of Advent is reflected in this text, in which we remember Christ's first coming even while praying for his return. Stanzas 1 and 2 recall Advent prophecies in the Old Testament; stanza 3 speaks of Christ's birth and kingdom, and stanza 4 is a prayer for Christ's rule in our hearts.

Scripture References
st. 1   = 2 Cor. 4:14
        Rev. 3:21
st. 3-4 = Isa. 61:1-2
        Luke 4:18-19
        Rom. 6:22

Tune

STUTTGART was included in *Psalmodia Sacra* (1715), one of the most significant hymnals of the early sixteenth century. Christian F. Witt (b. Altenburg, Germany, c. 1660; d. Altenburg, 1716) was an editor and compiler of that collection; about 100 (of the 774) tunes in that collection are considered to be composed by him, including STUTTGART, which was set to the text "Sollt' es gleich." Witt was chamber organist and later Kapellmeister at the Gotha court. He composed vocal and instrumental music, including some sixty-five cantatas.

The tune title STUTTGART relates to a story about Rev. C. A. Dann's banishment from his pulpit at St. Leonard's Church in Stuttgart in the early nineteenth century. When Dann was eventually invited back to his church, his congregation greeted him with the singing of "Sollt' es gleich." Henry J. Gauntlett (PHH 104) put the tune into its present isorhythmic (all equal rhythms) form for *Hymns Ancient and Modern* (1861).

A simple tune of two long lines and a number of repeated tones, STUTTGART has true congregational appeal. This tune has been traditionally used for "Come, Thou Long-Expected Jesus." Sing the hymn in harmony in a broad tempo. Or try singing stanza 3 unaccompanied and in parts, and stanza 4 in unison with alternate harmonization or with the descant (1983) by John Wilson (278). Use clear articulation on the organ with cheerful stops.

Liturgical Use

Advent; Christmas and Christmas carol/lesson worship services; worship that stresses the second coming.

330

O Christ! Come Back to Save Your Folk

O HEILAND, REISS DIE HIMMEL AUF
♩ = 126

Text

Calvin Seerveld (PHH 22) wrote this text in 1983 for a Christian Reformed congregation in his home city of Toronto, Ontario. Seerveld's impetus for writing the text was his belief that during Advent Christians should focus on Christ's second coming as well as on his first. All five stanzas are a prayer for Christ's return. Seerveld uses fresh language based on traditional biblical images of the Lord's making a new heaven and a new earth.

Scripture References
st. 3 = Rev. 7:17
Rev. 21:4
st. 4 = Luke 18:42
Ps. 35:5

Written to match O HEILAND, REISS DIE HIMMEL AUF, this text was first published in the 1987 *Psalter Hymnal.*

Tune

O HEILAND, REISS DIE HIMMEL AUF is a German chorale melody published anonymously in *Rheinfelsisches Deutsches Catholisches Gesangbuch* (1666 ed.). *Psalter Hymnal* Revision Committee member Dale Grotenhuis (PHH 4) prepared the harmonization in 1985.

The tune is in Dorian mode and exhibits two main rhythmic patterns within its four lines. Try singing stanzas 1, 3, and 5 in unison. Have stanzas 2 and 4 sung in harmony by antiphonal groups or by the choir. Use strong rhythmic organ or piano accompaniment. Sing with one pulse per bar.

Liturgical Use

During Advent when the focus is on Christ's return.

331

O Lord, How Shall I Meet You

Text

Paul Gerhardt (b. Gräfenhainichen, Saxony, Germany, 1607; d. Lübben, Germany, 1676), famous author of Lutheran evangelical hymns, wrote this German text in ten stanzas, published in Crüger and Runge's *Luthers . . . geistliche Lieder und Psalmen* (1653). The *Psalter Hymnal* contains three of those ten stanzas.

The original text was inspired by Matthew 21:1-9, the Gospel reading for the first Sunday of Advent in the old Lutheran lectionary. Like so many of the psalms that use the first-person pronoun ("I"), this text moves from the personal welcome of the Savior (st. 1), to a confession of the reason for Christ's incarnation (st. 2), to the church's expectation of Christ's return (st. 3).

The English translation of stanzas 1 and 2 is based on that of Catherine Winkworth (PHH 194) in her *Chorale Book for England* (1863). Bert Polman (PHH 37) translated stanza 3 for the 1987 *Psalter Hymnal.*

Gerhardt studied theology and hymnody at the University of Wittenberg and then was a tutor in Berlin, where he became friends with Johann Crüger (PHH 42). He served the Lutheran parish of Mittenwalde near Berlin (1651-1657) and the great St. Nicholas' Church in Berlin (1657-1666). Friederich William, the Calvinist elector, had issued an edict that forbade the various Protestant groups to fight each other. Although Gerhardt did not want strife between the churches, he refused to comply with the edict because he thought it opposed the Lutheran "Formula of Concord," which condemned some Calvinist doctrines. Consequently, he was released from his position in Berlin in 1666. With the support of friends he became archdeacon at Lübben in 1669 and remained there until his death. Gerhardt experienced much suffering in his life—he and his parishioners lived in the era of the Thirty Years' War, and his family experienced incredible tragedy: four of his five children died young, and his wife died after a prolonged illness. In the history of hymnody Gerhardt is considered a transitional figure—he wrote at a time when hymns were changing from a more objective, confessional, and corporate focus to a pietistic, devotional, and personal one. Like other German hymns, Gerhardt's were lengthy and intended for use throughout a service, a group of stanzas at a time. More than 130 of his hymns were published in various editions of Crüger's *Praxis Pietatis Melica,* the Crüger-Runge *Gesangbuch* (1653), and Ebeling's *Das andere Dutzend geistliche Andachtslieder Herrn Paul Gerhardts* (1666-1667). John Wesley (PHH 267) and Catherine Winkworth (PHH 194) both made famous English translations of Gerhardt's texts.

Tune

Johann Crüger composed WIE SOLL ICH DICH EMPFANGEN for Gerhardt's text and published the tune in 1653; the tune name is the German incipit of Gerhardt's text. Enhancing a sense of personal and communal meditation, the tune gives reflective support to this text. The tune is in isorhythmic form (all equal rhythms) as well as rounded bar form (AABA). It is well suited for part singing.

Liturgical Use

Worship services of renewal and penitence during Advent; worship that focuses on Christ's return; Palm Sunday, especially with the alternate tune ST. THEODOLPH (375 and 376).

332

Hark! A Thrilling Voice Is Sounding

MERTON
♩ = 104

Text

Although earliest manuscript copy dates from the tenth century, this text is possibly as old as the fifth century. It is based on the Latin hymn "Vox clara ecce intonat" and its 1632 revision "En clara vox redarguit." The text in the *Psalter Hymnal* is a revision of both Edward Caswall's (PHH 438) translation in his *Lyra Catholica* (1849) and the translation in *Hymns Ancient and Modern* (1861).

Scripture References
st. 1 = Rom. 13:11-12
st. 2 = 2 Pet. 1:19
st. 3 = John 1:29
st. 4 = Luke 21:25-28
st. 5 = Rev. 5:13

The hymn is most useful for Advent because it permits various interpretations of Christ's coming. Stanzas 1-3 contain references to Christ's first coming, but they can be used to celebrate his second coming as well. Stanza 4 surely refers to the second coming, and stanza 5, the only stanza addressed to God, is a doxology.

Tune

William H. Monk (b. Brompton, London, England, 1823; d. London, 1889) composed MERTON and published it in *The Parish Choir* (1850). The tune has been associated with this text since the 1861 edition of *Hymns Ancient and Modern*. The tune's title is thought to refer to Walter de Merton, founder of Merton College, Oxford, England.

Monk is best known for his music editing of *Hymns Ancient and Modern* (1861, 1868, 1875, and 1889 editions). He also adapted music from plainsong and added accompaniments for *Introits for Use Throughout the Year*, a book issued with that famous hymnal. Beginning in his teenage years, Monk held a number of musical positions. He became choirmaster at King's College in London in 1847 and was organist and choirmaster at St. Matthias, Stoke Newington, from 1852 to 1889, where he was influenced by the

Oxford Movement. At St. Matthias, Monk also began daily choral services with the choir leading the congregation in music chosen according to the church year, including psalms chanted to plainsong. He composed over fifty hymn tunes and edited *The Scottish Hymnal* (1872 edition) and Wordsworth's *Hymns for the Holy Year* (1862) as well as the periodical *Parish Choir* (1840-1851).

MERTON consists of two long lines. It has an attractive rising figure at the opening, and it features consistent quarter-note rhythms. Sing the inner stanzas in a subdued manner, rising on stanza 4 to prepare for the climactic doxology in stanza 5. The hymn is suitable for part singing, but sing stanza 5 in unison with a choir singing the descant; add trumpets if possible.

Liturgical Use
During Advent for worship services that stress Christ's second coming; use stanza 5 as an Advent doxology.

333

GREENLAND
♩ = 60

Rejoice, Rejoice, Believers

Text
Considered to be one of the finest hymn writers of the Pietistic period, Laurentius Laurenti wrote this text based on the *Scripture References* st. 1-2 = Matt. 25:1-13 parable of the wise and foolish maidens (Matt. 25:1-13; see also 613). Stanzas 1 and 2 focus on the expected coming of the bridegroom; stanza 3 is a prayer for Christ's return to complete the work of redemption and to set his people free.

Born Lorenz Lorenzen (b. Husum, Schleswig, Germany, 1660; d. Bremen, Germany, 1722) in Schleswig (which at various times has been ruled by Denmark), Laurenti studied at the University of Rostock and in Kiel. In 1684 he moved to Bremen, where he was appointed music director and cantor in the Lutheran Cathedral Church. A well known writer of German hymns in the Pietist tradition, Laurenti based most of his hymn texts on the gospel lessons for the church year. They were published in *Evangelia Melodica* (1700).

Sarah Borthwick Findlater (b. Edinburgh, Scotland, 1823; d. Torquay, England, 1907) translated the text into English and published it in *Hymns from the Land of Luther* (1854), a collection of 122 hymns translated by her (53 hymns) and her sister Jane Borthwick. Findlater was a fine linguist; as a translator of German chorales, she is considered second only to Catherine Winkworth (PHH 194). Findlater's husband, Eric John, was a pastor in the Free Church of Scotland in Lochearnhead, Perthshire. The Findlater parsonage was known as being literate and hospitable.

Tune

GREENLAND, an example of the popular nineteenth-century practice of creating hymn tunes from the works of classical composers, is thought to be originally from one of J. Michael Haydn's (PHH 67) "Deutschen Kirchen Messen." The tune acquired its title from its occasional association with the text "From Greenland's Icy Mountains" by Reginald Heber (PHH 249).

The harmonization is from Benjamin Jacob's *National Psalmody* (1819). Jacob (b. London, England, 1778; d. London, 1829) became the organist of Salem Chapel in Soho, London, at age ten. Known as one of the best organists of his day, he was also active as a pianist and conductor. He included his own tunes and harmonizations as well as those of others in the 1819 hymnbook he compiled.

GREENLAND has a large range, strong high points, and a rising "rocket" figure at the beginning of the fourth line. It is well suited to choral harmony with brass accompaniment. Because the first two stanzas are sung by believers to believers, the congregation could divide as follows: women on stanza 1; men on stanza 2; all on stanza 3. Sing the hymn with a great sense of rejoicing, but note the change (st. 2-3) to a sense of hopeful expectation that Christ will soon return.

Liturgical Use

During Advent, focusing on Christ's second coming.

334

The Prophets Came to Israel

FIVE CANDLES
$\bemol = 60$

Text

Bert Witvoet (PHH 4) wrote this text and tune in 1980 for use at Fellowship Christian Reformed Church, Toronto, Ontario. Bert Polman (PHH 37), Fellowship's organist, prepared the harmonization in 1981. The hymn was first published in Christian Schools International's *Hymn of the Month* (set 5, 1981). Witvoet intended that the hymn be used during Advent as part of the lighting of candles on an Advent wreath. Although there are various traditions of readings and names for the Advent candles, the pattern associated with this hymn is as follows:

Scripture References
st. 1 = Isa. 9:6-7
st. 2 = Mic. 5:2-4
st. 3 = Luke 2:8-12
st. 4 = Luke 2:13-14
st. 5 = Luke 2:4-7

First Sunday of Advent: the prophets' candle, st. 1
Second Sunday of Advent: the Bethlehem candle, st. 2
Third Sunday of Advent: the shepherds' candle, st. 3
Fourth Sunday of Advent: the angels' candle, st. 4
Christmas Day: the Christ candle, st. 5

The procedure for the lighting of Advent candles is as follows: on the first Sunday of Advent, light one candle, read the Bible passage for stanza 1, and then sing the stanza. On the second Sunday review the meaning of the first candle and light the second candle. Read the Bible passage and sing stanzas 1 and 2. Follow the same pattern on the third and fourth Sundays of Advent. On Christmas Day review the meaning of all the candles and light the Christ candle. Sing all five stanzas of the hymn.

As the first candle is lit, think of the prophets who foretold the coming of Christ. When the Bethlehem candle is lit, think of Micah foretelling that Christ would be born in Bethlehem. On the third Sunday remember that in Bethlehem lived shepherds who expected the Messiah. On the fourth Sunday of Advent think of the angels bringing the message of Christ's birth to those shepherds. And on Christmas Day think of Christ's birth and what it means to you.

Properly observed, the Advent wreath carries with it a cumulative effect. Each week more light shines, symbolic of that "light" that John 1: 9 says "was coming into the world."

Tune

FIVE CANDLES is a simple tune; the three-part harmonization is preferably played on two manuals and pedal with light registration. Use light accompaniment or accompany the hymn with recorders and/or Orff instruments.

Liturgical Use

For worship services on the four Advent Sundays and on Christmas Day.

335

RICHMOND
♩ = 112
Hark, the Glad Sound! The Savior Comes

Text

"Hark, the Glad Sound!" is a fine Christological hymn; it uses the Old Testament text as Christ himself did. Stanza 1 speaks about the Savior's coming. Stanzas 2 and 3 quote the Isaiah and Luke passages about Christ's mission to release those in prison, to heal the wounded, and to enrich the poor. Stanza 4 concludes with a glad response of welcome and praise to our Savior.

Scripture References
st. 1 = Luke 4:18-19
st. 2-3 = Isa. 61:1-3

Philip Doddridge (b. London, England, 1702; d. Lisbon, Portugal, 1751) wrote this text in 1735 with the heading "Christ's message from Luke 4:18-19" (where Christ quotes from Isaiah 61:1-2). The text was revised and published in the 1745 and the 1781 editions of the Scottish *Translations and Paraphrases*. It was also published in Job Orton's

Hymns, Founded on Various Texts in the Holy Scriptures (1755). As is customary in modern hymnals, the *Psalter Hymnal* prints four (1, 3, 5, and 7) of the original seven stanzas.

Doddridge belonged to the Non-conformist Church (not associated with the Church of England). Its members were frequently the focus of discrimination. Offered an education by a rich patron to prepare him for ordination in the Church of England, Doddridge chose instead to remain in the Non-conformist Church. For twenty years he pastored a poor parish in Northampton, where he opened an academy for training Non-conformist ministers and taught most of the subjects himself. Doddridge suffered from tuberculosis, and when Lady Huntington, one of his patrons, offered to finance a trip to Lisbon for his health, he is reputed to have said, "I can as well go to heaven from Lisbon as from Northampton." He died in Lisbon soon after his arrival. Doddridge wrote some four hundred hymn texts, generally to accompany his sermons. These hymns were published posthumously in *Hymns, Founded on Various Texts in the Holy Scriptures* (1755); relatively few are still sung today.

Tune

RICHMOND (also known as CHESTERFIELD) is a florid tune originally written by Thomas Haweis (PHH 270) and published in his collection *Carmina Christo* (1792). Samuel Webbe, Jr., adapted and shortened the tune and published it in his *Collection of Psalm Tunes* (1808). It was reprinted in 1853 in *Webbe's Psalmody*. Webbe named the tune after Rev. Leigh Richmond, a friend of Haweis's. The CHESTERFIELD name comes from Lord Chesterfield, a statesman who frequently visited Selina Hastings, Countess of Huntingdon, for whom Haweis worked as a chaplain.

At its opening the tune has a "rocket" motif radiating a sense of confidence. With its various revisions the melody has lost its original florid character, but the harmonization (from *Hymns Ancient and Modern Revised,* 1950) provides strength and vigor, and the descant by Craig S. Lang (PHH 253) introduces another florid line for festive singing of stanza 4.

Sing stanza 1 in unison and stanzas 2 and 3 with jubilant accompaniment. Because stanza 4 is the only one directed to Christ, it should receive a different musical treatment than the other stanzas. Strong unison singing, a full accompaniment, and the use of the vocal or instrumental descant will help the "glad hosannas . . . ring."

Like his father Samuel, Sr. (PHH 112), Samuel Webbe, Jr. (b. London, 1770; d. London, 1843), was very active in both sacred and secular music. Together they published *A Collection of Motetts and Antiphons* (1792). He was active as organist in Liverpool and London at both Unitarian and Roman Catholic churches.

Liturgical Use

During Advent; as a processional for Palm Sunday.

336

Savior of the Nations, Come

Text

As attested by Augustine in 372, as well as by other early writers, Ambrose wrote this hymn in Latin ("Veni, Redemptor gentium") in the fourth century. The text appears in a number of eighth- and ninth-century manuscripts. Martin

Scripture References
st. 1-3 = Luke 1:26-45
st. 4   = Phil. 2:6-11

Luther (b. Eisleben, Saxony, Germany, 1483; d. Eisleben, 1546) translated this text into German ("Nun komm, der Heiden Heiland") in 1523 and included it in the Erfurt *Enchiridia* (1524). Consequently "Savior of the Nations" has become possibly the best known of the Lutheran Advent hymns. Various English translations are found in modern hymnals, many of which use, at least in part, William M. Reynolds's translation from his *Hymns, Original and Selected* (1851). Using the Latin and German texts as well as several English translations, Calvin Seerveld (PHH 22) prepared the translation that appears in the *Psalter Hymnal* in Toronto, Ontario, in 1984.

Stanzas 1-3 explain in hymn form what the Apostles' Creed confesses: he was "conceived by the power of the Holy Spirit and born of the virgin Mary" (see also Luke 1:26-45). Stanza 4 alludes to Philippians 2:6-11, which speaks of Christ's humiliation and exaltation. Stanza 5 is a prayer for faithfulness, and stanza 6 is a plea that Christ continue to intercede for his people. Stanza 7, a doxology, points to Christ's second coming and the coming of his eternal "lasting kingdom."

Ambrose (b. Treves, Germany, 340; d. Milan, Italy, 397), one of the great Latin church fathers, is remembered best for his preaching, his struggle against the Arian heresy, and his introduction of metrical and antiphonal singing into the Western church. Ambrose was trained in legal studies and distinguished himself in a civic career, becoming a consul in Northern Italy. When the bishop of Milan, an Arian, died in 374, the people demanded that Ambrose, who was not ordained or even baptized, become the bishop. He was promptly baptized and ordained, and he remained bishop of Milan until his death. Ambrose successfully resisted the Arian heresy and the attempts of the Roman emperors to dominate the church. His most famous convert and disciple was Augustine. Of the many hymns sometimes attributed to Ambrose, only a handful are thought to be authentic.

The influence of Martin Luther was monumental in biblical studies, theology, and the course of church history, but his influence was equally important in the worship and music of the church. He was educated at Magdeburg, Eisenach, and Erfurt and intended to enter the legal profession. But at the age of twenty-two he decided to become a monk and entered the Augustinian monastery in Erfurt. There he underwent the required rigors of spiritual training and was ordained in 1507. In 1510 he was commissioned to go to Rome to discuss a controversy within the Augustinian order.

While in Rome, Luther was shocked by the worldliness and commercialism of the Italian clergy and the ostentation of the papacy.

After his return to Germany, Luther was appointed professor of sacred Scriptures at the University of Wittenberg, a position he retained until his death. In his lectures and preaching Luther began to teach the biblical and Augustinian doctrines of salvation by grace through faith in Christ, and he began to urge reforms of the abuses in the church. This call for reform came to a head when the Dominican friar Johann Tetzel appeared selling indulgences. Luther protested the whole system of salvation as taught by the church and published his "Ninety-five Theses" in 1517. This challenge resulted in a condemnation from Rome, and Luther found himself on a collision course with the church. He devoted the rest of his life to working out the implications of his stance and to assuming the leadership of the Protestant Reformation. Luther embodied his teachings in sermons, lectures, debates, table conversations, devotions, letters, and songs. His collected works number over fifty volumes (in English translation), not including one of his greatest contributions—the translation of the Bible into German.

Luther also became involved in the reformation of the worship of the church. It is generally recognized that in his liturgy Luther remained much closer to the Roman Catholic Church than did Calvin. However, both his Latin Mass ("Formula missae," 1523) and German Mass ("Deutscher messe," 1526) incorporated the basic teachings of the Reformation and became the model of worship for later Lutheran (and other) churches. Luther also promoted congregational singing and wrote thirty-five hymns, many based on the psalms and others on early hymns. Scholars are not completely certain how many hymn tunes he composed himself or arranged from other sources, but more are attributed to Luther now than in the past. Luther was a fine singer and lute player, and his love of music influenced the Lutheran tradition. In cooperation with a number of associates, Luther supervised the compilation of various hymnals, ranging from the *Achtliederbuch* (1524) to Babst's *Geystliche Lieder* (1545).

Tune

NUN KOMM DER HEIDEN HEILAND is a chorale derived from a chant. Among the simplest of the Lutheran repertoire, it is framed by identical lines—1 and 4. Sing the entire hymn with antiphonal groups (the practice its original Latin author, Ambrose, strongly promoted). Sing some stanzas in unison and others in harmony. Always reserve stanza 7, the doxology, for a strong unison with full accompaniment. Play this music in two long lines to match the couplet structure of the textual lines.

The tune dates from a twelfth- or thirteenth-century Einsiedeln manuscript. Presumably by Johann Walther (PHH 398), the adaptation of the tune was published in the 1524 Erfurt *Enchiridia*. Johann S. Bach (PHH 7) used the tune for preludes in the *Clavierübung* and *Orgelbüchlein* and in his cantatas 36 and 62.

The harmonization in the *Psalter Hymnal* comes from Seth Calvisius's *Hymni Sacri* (1594). Originally named Seth Kalwitz, Calvisius (b. Gorsleben, Thuringia, Germany, 1556; d. Leipzig, Germany, 1615) became known as the leading music theoretician of his time. He was educated at the universities of Helmstedt and Leipzig and spent much of his life teaching and writing about music history and theory. He taught at the Fürstenschule in Schulpforta from 1582 to 1594 and at the University of Leipzig from 1594 until his death. He also served as cantor at several churches. In addition to his theoretical work, Calvisius wrote psalm and hymn tunes and anthems, and he edited the first hymnbook published in Leipzig, *Harmonia cantionum ecclesiasticarum* (1597).

Liturgical Use

During Advent or for Christmas Day (on Christmas Day st. 1-6 could be sung during the worship service, with st. 7 reserved for the doxology); stanzas 4-7 could also be used during Lent and for Easter Sunday.

337

ANTIOCH
♩ = 96

Joy to the World! The Lord Is Come

Text

Isaac Watts (PHH 155) wrote this text as a paraphrase of Psalm 98. He published it in his *Psalms of David Imitated* (1719) under the heading "The Messiah's Coming and Kingdom."

Scripture References
st. 1-3 = Ps. 98
st. 2 = Ps. 96:11-12
st. 3 = Gen. 3:17-18

The paraphrase is Watts's Christological interpretation. Consequently, he does not emphasize with equal weight the various themes of Psalm 98. In stanzas 1 and 2 Watts writes of heaven and earth rejoicing at the coming of the king. An interlude that depends more on Watts's interpretation than the psalm text, stanza 3 speaks of Christ's blessings extending victoriously over the realm of sin. The cheerful repetition of the non-psalm phrase "far as the curse is found" has caused this stanza to be omitted from some hymnals. But the line makes joyful sense when understood from the New Testament eyes through which Watts interprets the psalm. Stanza 4 celebrates Christ's rule over the nations.

Tune

ANTIOCH borrows ideas from two choruses and a tenor recitative from Handel's *Messiah*—"Lift Up Your Heads," "Glory to God in the Highest," and "Comfort Ye My People." The hymn tune is essentially an adaptation and arrangement by Lowell Mason (PHH 96), published in his *Occasional Psalms and Hymn Tunes* (1836). Mason named the tune ANTIOCH after the New Testament city in which the "followers of the Way" were first called Christians.

With its exuberant air and melodic repeats and sequences, requiring the repetition of textual lines, ANTIOCH has become an enduring favorite for the Watts text. Sing stanzas 1 and 3 in harmony and give tenors and basses solid accompaniment on their entries in the third line. Sing stanza 4 in unison, possibly with an alternate harmonization on full organ.

Liturgical Use
Christmas Day, but also at any other time of year in relation to Psalm 98. Raised eyebrows at singing "Joy to the World!" in July will lower as soon as the relationship to Psalm 98 becomes clear.

338
Come and Stand Amazed, You People
KOMT, VERWONDERT
♩ = 88

Text
Although many Christmas hymns are narratives of the Christmas story and theologically light, this translation of an old Dutch text is theologically profound. Because it makes excellent use of paradox, the text should be read before it is sung. Stanzas 1 and 2 are an amplification of Philippians 2:6-8; stanza 3 is a prayer.

Scripture References
st. 1 = Phil. 2:6-8
st. 2 = Luke 2:7, 14
st. 3 = John 1:5, 14

The original Dutch text, "Komt, verwondert U hier, mensen," may have medieval roots. The text was first published in *Blijden-wegh tot Bethlehem* (Antwerp, 1645) in four stanzas. The original third stanza is omitted in the *Psalter Hymnal*.

The English translation, dating from the late 1960s, is mainly the work of Klaas Hart (b. Zedaandam, the Netherlands, 1906; d. Toronto, Canada, 1977). Hart began his ministry in 1935 by serving churches successively in Oostwold, Velp, and Utrecht, the Netherlands. He was actively involved in the resistance movement during World War II, and his name was high on the "honor roll" of those wanted by the German police. In 1953 he immigrated to Canada and served Christian Reformed congregations in Wallaceburg, Petersborough, and Ingersoll, all in Ontario. His manuscript collection includes both original hymns and English translations of Dutch hymns.

Tune
Although the tune has Baroque characteristics of the early eighteenth century, KOMT, VERWONDERT could possibly be as old as the text. The tune was first published in 1856 in the Edmond de Coussemaker collection *Chants Populaires des Flamands de France*.

KOMT, VERWONDERT is a florid tune with a number of rising figures, giving the tune lots of lift. The Dale Grotenhuis (PHH 4) harmonization is well suited to part singing. Use light organ support or piano accompaniment.

Liturgical Use
Christmas season, either for congregational singing or as a choral anthem (worship leader could point out some paradoxes in the text).

339

VOM HIMMEL HOCH
♩ = 96 From Heaven Above to Earth I Come

Text
Written by Martin Luther (PHH 336) for his family's Christmas *Scripture References*
Eve devotions, this text (originally "Vom Himmel hoch da   all st. = Luke 2:10-14
komm ich her") was first published in Joseph Klug's (PHH
126) *Geistliche Lieder* (1535) in fifteen stanzas. Luther intended that stanzas 1-7 be sung by a man dressed as an angel and stanzas 8-15 by children.

As the basis for his first stanza, Luther revised the old folk song "Aus Fremden Landenkomm ich hier." Also called a "garland" song, "Aus Fremden" was used traditionally as a chorus in a game of riddles that involved the taking of garlands if a riddle was not solved.

The English translation is primarily the work of Catherine Winkworth (PHH 194), from her *Lyra Germanica* (1855). However, numerous hymnal editors have revised her translation. From the original fifteen stanzas the *Psalter Hymnal* Revision Committee chose to include five—the familiar narrative stanzas based on Luke 2:10-14.

Stanzas 1-4 contain the angels' words to the shepherds. Stanza 5 is the angel chorus (Luke 2:14), which we all sing as we share in the shepherds' and angels' joy. (For a similar narrative Christmas hymn on the same biblical text, see 215.)

Tune
Initially Luther used the folk melody associated with his first stanza as the tune for this hymn. Later he composed this new tune for his text. VOM HIMMEL HOCH was first published in Valentin Schumann's *Geistliche Lieder* in 1539. Johann S. Bach (PHH 7) used Luther's melody in three places in his well-known and loved Christmas Oratorio. VOM HIMMEL HOCH is a simple but spritely melody. Try having either a soloist (with an angelic voice) or a small choir, in harmony and unaccompanied, sing stanzas 1-4. The entire group or congregation could then sing stanza 5 in unison. Add strong accompaniment, possibly using one of the elaborate Bach harmonizations.

Liturgical Use
Christmas Day worship service; Christmas festival of lessons and carols, especially with the dramatic performance style Luther intended (suggested above); church school programs.

340

O Come, All Ye Faithful

ADESTE FIDELES
♩ = 60

Text

In this well-known and loved Christmas hymn, we are invited as God's faithful people to go to Bethlehem and adore Christ the Lord (st. 1). We sing words borrowed from the Nicene Creed to express the Christian faith about the incarnation (st. 2). Then after exhorting the angels to sing their praise (st. 3), we greet Christ on his birthday (st. 4). The text has two unusual features for such a popular hymn: it is unrhymed and has an irregular meter.

Scripture References
st. 1 = Luke 2:4-7
st. 3 = Luke 2:13-14
st. 4 = John 1:14

John Francis Wade (b. England, c. 1711; d. Douay, France, 1786) is now generally recognized as both author and composer of this hymn, originally written in Latin in four stanzas. The earliest manuscript signed by Wade is dated about 1743. By the early nineteenth century, however, four additional stanzas had been added by other writers. A Roman Catholic, Wade apparently moved to France because of discrimination against Roman Catholics in eighteenth-century England—especially so after the Jacobite Rebellion of 1745. He taught music at an English college in Douay and hand copied and sold chant music for use in the chapels of wealthy families. Wade's copied manuscripts were published as *Cantus Diversi pro Dominicis et Festis per annum* (1751).

The translation in the *Psalter Hymnal* is based primarily on the work of Frederick Oakeley (b. Shrewsbury, Worcester, England, 1802; d. Islington, London, England, 1880), who translated the text for use at the Margaret Street Chapel (now All Saints', Margaret Street) in London (1841). It is also based on translations found in both F. H. Murray's *A Hymnal for Use in the English Church* (1852) and William Mercer's (PHH 357) *Church Psalter and Hymn Book* (1854).

Educated at Christ Church, Oxford, England, Oakeley was ordained in the Church of England in 1826. He served at Balliol College, Lichfield Cathedral, Whitehall, and Margaret Street Chapel in London. Influenced by the Oxford Movement, Oakeley and Richard Redhead (PHH 255), organist of Margaret Chapel, instituted "high" liturgies there, eliciting the charge of "Romanism." Oakeley also asserted in a pamphlet that even though he would not "teach," he certainly should be allowed to "hold" all Roman Catholic doctrines. These views caused him to be suspended from his office. Rather than retract his statement, he joined the Roman Catholic Church in 1845 and associated himself with John Henry Newman. Following his reordination in the Roman Catholic Church, Oakeley worked among the poor in the Westminster area of London. In his writings he defended the Roman theology and practices of worship. He also wrote four volumes of verse as well as *Historical Notes on the Tractarian Movement* (1865).

Tune

Some scholars have suggested that Wade fashioned ADESTE FIDELES from melodic fragments of stage music. In the original Wade manuscripts the tune was in triple meter. It was changed to its present form by 1782 and published in the elder Samuel Webbe's (PHH 112) *Essay on the Church Plain Chant*.

Some Protestant hymnals have published ADESTE FIDELES as a setting for other texts; for example, Ira D. Sankey (PHH 73) used this tune for "How Firm a Foundation." But the tune and text are now commonly used together, and "O Come, All Ye Faithful" remains one of the most-loved Christmas hymns.

The tune is a fuguing tune; it begins chordally and uses some imitation in the refrain. The harmonization in the *Psalter Hymnal* is from *The English Hymnal* (1906); the descant is from *Hymns Ancient and Modern* (revised ed., 1947). Sing the stanzas in unison and the refrain in parts.

Liturgical Use

Christmas Day; a "must" hymn for a Christmas festival of lessons and carols (especially in more elaborate performances involving choir and instruments).

341

PICARDY
♩ = 60

Let All Mortal Flesh Keep Silence

Text

Evidence suggests that the Greek text of "Let All Mortal Flesh" may date back to the fifth century. The present text is from the Liturgy of St. James, a Syrian rite thought to have been written by St. James the Less, first Bishop of Jerusalem. It is based on a prayer chanted by the priest when the bread and wine are brought to the table of the Lord.

Scripture References
st. 1 = Hab. 2:20
Zech. 2:13
st. 2 = Rev. 19:16
Luke 22:19-20
st. 3 = Matt. 16:27
st. 4 = Isa. 6:2-3

The text expresses awe at Christ's coming (st. 1) and the mystery of our perception of Christ in the body and blood (st. 2). With images from Isaiah 6 and Revelation 5, it portrays the glory of Christ (sung to by angels) and his victory over sin (st. 3-4). Although it has eucharistic emphasis, the text pictures the nativity of Christ in a majestic manner and in a much larger context than just his birth in Bethlehem. We are drawn into the awe and mystery with our own "alleluias."

Gerard Moultrie (b. Rugby, Warnickshire, England, 1829; d. Southleigh, England, 1885) translated the text from the Greek; his English paraphrase was first published in Orby Shipley's *Lyra Eucharistica* (1864) and entitled "Prayer of the Cherubic Hymn." The *Psalter Hymnal* alters that paraphrase in part to solve Reformed sensitivities about eucharistic theology. Moultrie's great-grandfather had settled in South Carolina, but after siding with England during the American Revolution, he had moved back to Britain. Educated at Exeter College, Oxford, England, Moultrie served as a pastor and chaplain in the Church of England. In addition to writing his own hymns he prepared translations of Greek, Latin, and German hymns. He also edited several hymnals, including *Hymns and Lyrics for the Seasons and Saints' Days* (1867) and *Cantica Sanctorum, or Hymns for the Black Letter Saints' Days in the English and Scottish Calendars* (1880).

Tune

PICARDY is a French "noel," a carol tune thought to date back to the seventeenth century. The tune was first published in *Chansons Populaires des Provences de France* (vol. IV, Paris, 1860); the melody was written down as sung by a Madame Pierre Dupont in Champfleury-Wekerlin to "Jesus Christ s'habille en pauvre," a folk song she remembered from her childhood in Picardy, an old province in northern France. PICARDY was first published with "Let All Mortal Flesh" in *The English Hymnal* (1906).

The tune is more solemn than other French carols (see 347). With its minor tonality PICARDY is a fine vehicle for supporting the majesty expressed in this text. Sing in unison with some sense of contemplation, mystery, and awe. Use restraint on the organ (or any accompaniment) throughout the first two stanzas, but let it become more brilliant on stanza 3. Pull out all the stops on the "alleluias" of stanza 4.

Liturgical Use

Ideal to use during Lord's Supper services at Christmastime, but may be used at any time during the Christmas season; Lord's Supper at other times of the church year (especially as a sung part of the Great Prayer of Thanksgiving at the beginning of the eucharistic liturgy).

342

Of the Father's Love Begotten

DIVINUM MYSTERIUM

Text

This hymn, with very ancient roots, is a confession of faith about the Christ, the eternal Son of God, whose birth and saving ministry were the fulfillment of ancient prophecies (st. 1-3). The final stanzas are a doxology inspired by John's visions recorded in Revelation 4-7 (st. 4-5). The text is based on "Corde natus ex parentis," a Latin poem by Marcus Aurelius C. Prudentius (b. Saragossa [?], Northern Spain, 348; d. c. 413).

Prudentius was the greatest Christian poet of his time. We know little of his life—only what he tells us in his own writings. He received a fine education, served as a judge, and "twice ruled noble cities." He also tells of an appointment at the imperial court in

Rome. But at the age of fifty-seven Prudentius bade farewell to this successful, prosperous life and vowed to spend the rest of his days in poverty. He served the church by meditating and writing, presumably at an unnamed monastery. All of his writings are in poetic form, including learned discussions in theology and apologetics. Most of the English hymns derived from his works, including "Of the Father's Love Begotten," were taken from his *Liber Cathemerinon* (c. 405), which consists of twelve extended poems meant for personal devotions, six for use throughout the hours of the day and six for special feasts.

Scripture References
st. 1 = Rev. 22:13
Rev. 1:8
Rev. 21:6
Ps. 2:7
Heb. 1:5
st. 2 = Luke 1:35
Luke 2:11
Matt. 1:18, 21
st. 3 = Luke 1:70
st. 4 = Ps. 148:1-2
Ps. 150:6

Working from the Latin text, John Mason Neale (b. London, England, 1818; d. East Grinstead, Sussex, England, 1866) prepared a translation and published it as a six-stanza hymn in his *The Hymnal Noted* (1854). He retained the refrain "Evermore and evermore," an eleventh-century addition to the orginal Latin text.

Neale's life is a study in contrasts: born into an evangelical home, he had sympathies toward Rome; in perpetual ill health, he was incredibly productive; of scholarly temperament, he devoted much time to improving social conditions in his area; often ignored or despised by his contemporaries, he is lauded today for his contributions to the church and hymnody. Neale's gifts came to expression early—he won the Seatonian prize for religious poetry eleven times while a student at Trinity College, Cambridge, England. He was ordained in the Church of England in 1842, but ill health and his strong support of the Oxford Movement kept him from ordinary parish ministry. So Neale spent the years between 1846 and 1866 as a warden of Sackville College in East Grinstead, a retirement home for poor men. There he served the men faithfully and expanded Sackville's ministry to indigent women and orphans. He also founded the Sisterhood of St. Margaret, which became one of the finest English training orders for nurses.

Laboring in relative obscurity, Neale turned out a prodigious number of books and articles on liturgy and church history, including *A History of the So-Called Jansenist Church of Holland* (1858); an account of the Roman Catholic Church of Utrecht and its break from Rome in the 1700s; and his scholarly *Essays on Liturgiology and Church History* (1863). Neale contributed to church music by writing original hymns, including two volumes of *Hymns for Children* (1842, 1846), but especially by translating Greek and Latin hymns into English. These translations appeared in *Medieval Hymns and Sequences* (1851, 1863, 1867), *The Hymnal Noted* (1852, 1854), *Hymns of the Eastern Church* (1862), and *Hymns Chiefly Medieval* (1865). Because a number of Neale's translations were judged unsingable, editors usually amended his work, as evident already in the 1861 edition of *Hymns Ancient and Modern;* Neale claimed no rights to his texts and was pleased that his translations could contribute to hymnody as the "common property of Christendom."

The story of "Of the Father's Love Begotten" continues with the 1859 nine-stanza revision by Henry W. Baker (b. Vauxhall, Lambeth, Surrey, England, 1821; d. Monkland, England, 1877), published in *Hymns Ancient and Modern* (1861). Educated at Trinity College, Cambridge, Baker was ordained in the Church of England in 1844. He became the vicar of the Monkland parish in 1851, where he remained until his death. Because of his high-church beliefs in the celibacy of the clergy, Baker was unmarried. In the history of hymnody Baker is well known as the editor and chairman of the committee that compiled *Hymns Ancient and Modern*, the most significant British hymnal of the nineteenth century. Baker devoted at least twenty years of his life to this endeavor. Considered an autocratic editor in his time, Baker freely changed hymn texts, but many of his decisions have proven themselves over time. The 1875 edition of *Hymns Ancient and Modern* contained thirty-three of Baker's original hymns and translations.

Tune

DIVINUM MYSTERIUM is a plainsong, or chant, associated with the "Divinum mysterium" text in manuscripts dating from the twelfth to fifteenth centuries. The tune was published in triple meter in Theodoricis Petri's *Piae Cantiones* (1582). Some hymnals retain the dance-like triple meter, while others keep the original unmeasured form of the chant. (It is one of the few chants in the *Psalter Hymnal*.)

Strong wave shapes characterize DIVINUM MYSTERIUM. Sing in unison with the accompaniment preferably played on manuals only. Sing also in speech rhythms, with some freedom in phrasing and tempo—not in the block-chord style of regular metered singing (thus no metronome marking).

The accompaniment was composed by Charles Winfred Douglas (b. Oswego, NY, 1867; d. Santa Rosa, CA, 1944), an influential leader in Episcopalian liturgical and musical life. Educated at Syracuse University and St. Andrews Divinity School, Syracuse, New York, he moved to Colorado for his health. There he studied at St. Matthew's Hall, Denver, and founded the Mission of the Transfiguration in Evergreen (1897). Ordained a priest in the Episcopal Church in 1899, he also studied in France, Germany, and England, where he spent time with the Benedictines of Solesmes on the Island of Wight (1903-1906). For much of his life Douglas served as director of music at the Community of St. Mary in Peekskill, New York, and had associations with cathedrals in Denver, Colorado, and Fond du Lac, Wisconsin. He promoted chanting and plainsong in the Episcopal Church through workshops and publications such as *The American Psalter* (1929), the *Plainsong Psalter* (1932), and the *Monastic Diurnal* (1932). His writings include program notes for the Denver Symphony Orchestra, various hymn preludes for organ, as well as the book, *Church Music in History and Practice* (1937). He was editor of both the *Hymnal 1916* and its significant successor, *Hymnal 1940*, of the Episcopal Church. Douglas's other achievements include a thorough knowledge of the life and culture of Hopi and Navajo natives, among whom he lived for a number of years.

Liturgical Use

Christmas season; without stanza 2 on many other occasions; because the original Latin poem concerns Christ's miracles, could be sung during Epiphany or at worship services when the New Testament gospel is preached; stanzas 4 and 5 make a fine doxology for the close of any service.

343

Break Forth, O Beauteous Heavenly Light

ERMUNTRE DICH
♩ = 80

Text

Inspired by Isaiah 9:2-7 and Luke 2, Johann Rist (b. Ottensen, near Hamburg, Germany, 1607; d. Wedel, Germany, 1667) wrote a twelve-stanza hymn on the incarnation of Christ. Rist's text began with the words "Ermuntre dich, mein schwacher Geist." The text was first published in Rist's *Himlischer Lieder* (1641).

Scripture References
st. 1 = Luke 2:8-11
st. 2 = John 1:14
Matt. 1:23

Stanza 1 is a paraphrase of Rist's original ninth stanza; the rather free paraphrase is a composite effort of John Troutbeck and others. Borrowing more from John 1, Norman E. Johnson (PHH 322) prepared a second stanza, which was first published in the 1973 *Covenant Hymnal*. The composite text then views the Christmas story both through the perspective of Luke 2 (st. 1) and John 1 (st. 2).

Rist was a man of many gifts and accomplishments. He studied at the universities of Rinteln and Rostock, published widely on contemporary events, and became poet laureate for Emperor Ferdinand III in 1644. He served as both pastor and physician in Wedel (1635-1667) but lost his musical and scientific instruments during the Thirty Years' War. Although a successful pastor who was often honored for his work, Rist refused positions of greater prestige and income. In collections published from 1641 to 1656 he produced some 680 hymn texts for use in private devotions. Eventually German churches used a number of his hymns in public worship.

John Troutbeck (b. Blencowe, Cumberland, England, 1832; d. Westminster, London, England, 1899) was educated at University College, Oxford, England, and ordained a priest in the Church of England in 1856. He was precentor at Manchester Cathedral from 1865 to 1869 and then held a similar position at Westminster Abbey. Troutbeck served as chaplain to Queen Victoria and was secretary for the New Testament Revision Committee (1870-1881). His greatest claim to fame arises from his translation into English of German, French, and Italian operas, songs, and oratorios (including cantatas and chorales set by J. S. Bach) for the British music publisher Novello. An editor of *The Manchester Psalter* (1867), *Westminster Abbey Hymn Book* (1883), and several chant books, he was also the author of *Church Choir Training* (1879).

Tune

Johann Schop (PHH 122) composed ERMUNTRE DICH in triple meter for the Rist text with which it was published in *Himmlische Lieder* (1641). Johann Crüger (PHH 42) adapted the tune for his *Praxis Pietatis Melica* (1648). The isorhythmic (all equal rhythms) setting in the *Psalter Hymnal* is the Johann S. Bach (PHH 7) arrangement from his Christmas Oratorio (1734).

ERMUNTRE DICH is a bar form (AAB) tune consisting of four long, majestic, and stately lines. Often congregations will sing this hymn in unison, but Bach's rich harmonization could be an interesting challenge for choir. When the hymn is sung in harmony, the tempo should be slower. Use lots of bright mixtures on the organ. The harmonization is one of the more difficult ones in the *Psalter Hymnal* but is well worth the effort.

Liturgical Use

Christmas season; Christmas festival of lessons and carols; a fine choir anthem.

344

Silent Night! Holy Night!

STILLE NACHT
♪ = 112

Text

With a mixture of reflection and awe, the writer evokes the night of Christ's birth, recalling not only the birth but also its meaning: the Christ who is born in Bethlehem is our Savior and our King!

Scripture References
all st. = Luke 2:1-20

Parish priest Joseph Mohr (b. Salzburg, Austria, 1792; d. Wagrein, Austria, 1848) wrote the original German text in six stanzas in Oberndorf, Austria, on December 24, 1818, for St. Nicholas's Church. Because the church organ had broken down that day, Mohr and his parish organist, Franz Gruber (b. Unterweizberg, near Hochburg, Austria, 1787; d. Hallein, near Salzburg, Austria, 1863), composed this beloved hymn to be accompanied on guitar for the Christmas Eve service.

After organ repairman Karl Mauracher heard the hymn, he took the manuscript to the Tyrol region. Because it was sung by various Tyrol folk groups (including the touring Strasser "sisters" and the Rainer family), "Silent Night" became known as a "Tyrolean carol." The hymn's widespread use enhanced its popularity throughout Europe and North America during the middle nineteenth century. Without attributing the hymn's composition to Mohr and Gruber, the Leipzig *Katholisches Gesang-und Gebetbuch* first published the hymn in 1838; because of the efforts of Gruber's grandson, the author and composer were soon recognized.

Author Joseph Mohr was born into a humble family—his mother was a seamstress and his father, an army musketeer. A choirboy in Salzburg Cathedral as a youth, Mohr studied at Salzburg University and was ordained in the Roman Catholic Church in

1815. Mohr was a priest in various churches near Salzburg, including St. Nicholas Church. He spent his later years in Hintersee and Wagrein.

Various English translations abound, some of which are rather free paraphrases. The familiar stanzas 1, 3, and 4 in the *Psalter Hymnal* come from the popular English translation by John F. Young, first published in John C. Hollister's *Sunday School Service and Tune Book* (1863). Henrietta Ten Harmsel (PHH 61) wrote stanza 2 and made other alterations in the text in 1984 to "stress the paradoxes and deeper meanings of Christmas."

Tune
Although he composed nearly one hundred works, Franz Gruber is remembered for only one—the tune of "Silent Night," composed on Christmas Eve, 1818. He scored the tune for tenor and bass soli (sung by Mohr and Gruber on that night) with the final phrase to be repeated in harmony (sung by the village choir girls); the singing was accompanied by guitar. In 1854 he wrote an account of the history of "Stille Nacht, heilige Nacht," accompanied by a score (dated 1833) for two solo voices, chorus, organ, pizzicato strings, and two horns.

Gruber was born into a linen weaver's family and studied violin and organ even though his father wanted him to work in the family business. In addition to serving as parish organist for St. Nicholas Church in Obendorf, he taught school in nearby Arnsdorf (1807-1829) and Berndorf (1829-1833). He spent the balance of his career as organist and choir director in Hallein, where he founded the famous Hallein Choral Society.

STILLE NACHT is a pastoral tune in the style of a landler or Austrian siciliano (slow waltz). The tune is intended for gentle singing with light accompaniment (recall its historic performance on guitar). The *Psalter Hymnal* harmonization is mainly the work of Carl Reinecke (1910).

Sing in four parts, perhaps unaccompanied. Or you may want to try only two-part singing (soprano and alto) for some stanzas. Try using a flute or recorder descant; there are many published settings for these instruments. In smaller worship settings try guitar and flute or recorder. Or have children sing some stanzas in alternation with the congregation. Sing in two pulses per bar.

Liturgical Use
Candlelight worship services on Christmas Eve; church school programs; "carols from many lands" choral services.

345

Hark! The Herald Angels Sing

MENDELSSOHN
♩ = 54

Text

Charles Wesley (PHH 267) wrote this text in ten four-line stanzas and published it in *Hymns and Sacred Poems* (1739). Originally entitled "Hymn for Christmas Day," this most popular of Wesley's Christmas hymns began with the following words:

Scripture References
st. 1 = Luke 2:14
    2 Cor. 5:19
st. 2 = Gal. 4:4
    John 1:14
st. 3 = Isa. 9:6
    Mal. 4:2
    Phil. 2:7-8
    1 Pet. 1:3

> Hark, how all the welkin [heavens] rings
> Glory to the King of Kings.

George Whitefield changed the first line to "Hark! The herald angels sing" and published the text with additional alterations in his *Collection* (1753). In 1782 the revised opening couplet became repeated as the refrain. The text was extensively changed and shortened by various other eighteenth-century editors as well. With a few word changes the *Psalter Hymnal* version is essentially the same as the one published in John Kempthorne's *Select Portions of Psalms . . . and Hymns* (1810).

Containing biblical phrases from Luke, John, and Paul, the text is a curious mixture of exclamation, exhortation, and theological reflection. The focus shifts rapidly from angels, to us, to nations. The text's strength may not lie so much in any orderly sequence of thought but in its use of Scripture to teach its theology. That teaching surely produces in us a childlike response of faith; we too can sing "Glory to the newborn King!"

Tune

The tune is from the second chorus of Felix Mendelssohn's (PHH 279) *Festgesang* (Op. 68) for male voices and brass; it was first performed in 1840 at the Gutenberg Festival in Leipzig, a festival celebrating the anniversary of Gutenberg's invention of the printing press. Mendelssohn's tune is similar to another that appeared one hundred years earlier in "The Song of Mars" from the John Pepusch opera *Venus and Adonis*.

Mendelssohn once wrote of this music, "It will *never* do to sacred words." William H. Cummings (b. Sidbury, Devonshire, England, 1831; d. Dulwich, London, England, 1915) may not have been aware of Mendelssohn's opinion; he adapted the tune to Wesley's text in 1856. When they were placed together in *Hymns Ancient and Modern* (1861), "Hark! The Herald Angels Sing" became a very popular hymn.

Cummings had a lifelong love of Felix Mendelssohn, sparked when he sang at age sixteen in the first London performance of *Elijah*, which was directed by Mendelssohn himself. As a young boy, Cummings had been a chorister at St. Paul's Cathedral and later sang in the choirs of the Temple Church, Westminster Abbey, and the Chapel Royal. Cummings became a famous tenor—he sang in oratorios and was especially known for his evangelist role in the Bach passions. He taught voice at the Royal Academy of Music and the Royal Normal College and School for the Blind in London and was also an accomplished organist. Cummings wrote books and articles on music history, wrote a biography of Henry Purcell and edited his music, and composed many choral pieces.

MENDELSSOHN is an excellent match for Wesley's text. It is a rousing tune, even martial in some of its phrases. Sing with lots of enthusiasm; do not drown out the stanzas with too much organ—save that extra stop for the refrain and the final stanza.

Let the final stanza soar with the descant and the alternate harmonization by David Willcocks (b. Newquay, England, 1919), published in *Carols for Choir I* (1961). Willcocks has had a highly distinguished musical career. A chorister at Westminster Abbey, he continued his education at Clifton College, the Royal College of Music, and King's College, Cambridge, England. He was organist of Worcester Cathedral (1950-1957) and conductor of the Bradford Festival Choral Society (1955-1974). Under his leadership as director of music and organist of King's College, Cambridge, from 1957 to 1974, the King's College Choir began a series of recordings which, among other repertoires, made famous the annual Festival of Lessons and Carols. Beginning in 1960 Willcocks conducted the Bach Choir of London, and in 1973 he became director of the Royal College of Music. Mainly a composer of church music, Willcocks has also made arrangements of carols, many of which were published in the various Oxford's *Carols for Choirs* publications. He makes frequent trips to North America for choral festivals.

Liturgical Use
Christmas Day; another of the "must" hymns for an annual lesson/carol festival.

346

IRBY
♩ = 80

Once in Royal David's City

Text

To help children understand the Apostles' Creed words "who was conceived by the Holy Spirit, born of the virgin Mary," Cecil F. Alexander (b. Redcross, County Wicklow, Ireland, 1818; d. Londonderry, Ireland, 1895) wrote this text and published it in her *Hymns for Little Children* (1848). Five of her six stanzas are included; the third stanza is omitted.

Scripture References
st. 1-2 = Luke 2:4-7
st. 4 = Mark 10:14
st. 5 = Rom. 8:34

A good mingling of the biblical story and Christian theology, the text sets the nativity of Christ into a much larger framework—the history of salvation. Alexander's words enable us to look back and to look forward from this historic event. Stanzas 1 and 2 recall Christ's humble birth. Stanza 3 focuses on Christ's childhood and identity with humanity. Stanzas 4 and 5 look forward to the sharing of Christ's glory with his children.

As a small girl, Cecil Frances Humphries wrote poetry in her school's journal. In 1850 she married Rev. William Alexander, who later became the Anglican primate (chief bishop) of Ireland. She showed her concern for disadvantaged people by traveling many miles each day to visit the sick and the poor, providing food, warm clothes, and medical supplies. She and her sister also founded a school for the deaf. Alexander was strongly influenced by the Oxford Movement and by John Keble's *Christian Year*. Her first book of poetry, *Verses for Seasons*, was a "Christian Year" for children. She wrote hymns based on the Apostles' Creed, baptism, the Lord's Supper, the Ten Commandments, and prayer, writing in simple language for children. Her more than four hundred hymn texts were published in *Verses from the Holy Scripture* (1846), *Hymns for Little Children* (1848), and *Hymns Descriptive and Devotional* (1858).

Tune

Henry J. Gauntlett (PHH 104) composed IRBY for the text and published it in the pamphlet *Christmas Carols, Four Numbers* (1849) in a unison setting with piano accompaniment. Because of the hymn's traditional use (since 1918) as a processional hymn for the annual lessons and carols festival at King's College, Cambridge, various composers have provided glorious harmonizations for the tune, including the descant setting by David Willcocks (PHH 325) in the *Psalter Hymnal* and the Arthur Mann setting found in many modern hymnals. In the King's College festival a boy soprano sings the first stanza unaccompanied—a stunningly beautiful effect!

Named after a village in Lincolnshire, England, IRBY is a graceful tune that returns to the tonic in five out of six phrases. It is in rounded bar form (AABA). This hymn is a good candidate for antiphonal singing. Try having the children sing stanzas 1 and 3, the choir or full congregation sing stanzas 2 and 4, and the entire group sing stanza 5 in unison, with the choir singing the descant.

Liturgical Use

Christmas Eve or Christmas Day worship services, especially as a glorious processional; anytime during the church year in conjunction with worship services in which this part of the creed or eschatological themes (st. 5) are preached; church school programs.

347

Angels We Have Heard on High
Les Anges Dans Nos Campagnes

GLORIA
♩ = 58

Text

"Les anges" is a French noel (from the Languedoc region) believed to date from the eighteenth century. Its text and tune were first published in the *Nouveau Recueil de Cantiques* in 1855.

Scripture References
all st. = Luke 2:8-15

The English translation originated as a free imitation from the French by James Chadwick, which was adapted by Henri Hemy in his Roman Catholic collection, *Crown of Jesus Music* (1862). Of the original eight-stanza French text, stanzas 1, 2, and 4 are included.

The Christmas gospel in Luke 2:8-15 is the basis for the text. The hymn's refrain, "Gloria in excelsis Deo" is the first part of the angels' chorus in Luke 2:14; it is one of the few Latin phrases in common use in Protestant churches.

Tune
GLORIA is the French noel tune traditionally associated with this text. The popularity of this carol stems from its refrain—all those cascading phrases in which human beings imitate the angels' chorus. Try using the refrain by itself as a short choral introit during the Christmas season, perhaps with the Baroque performance practice of dotted rhythms to add a subtle touch of beauty! The repeat of the melody in the refrain permits variation in performance; for example, a small choir in the balcony could sing the first refrain line, and the entire group could join in on the second refrain line (the effect of a few angels beginning the hymn and then being joined by more and more angels). Play with light organ registration until the refrain.

The tune is also known as IRIS because of its association with James Montgomery's "Angels from the Realms of Glory" (354), which was first printed in the *Sheffield Iris* (Montgomery, ed.).

The harmonization is by Edward S. Barnes (b. Seabright, NJ, 1887; d. Idyllwild, CA, 1958) and was first published in *The New Church Hymnal* (1937). Barnes studied at the Lawrenceville School, Yale University, and the Schola Cantorum in Paris. He was organist and choirmaster at two New York City churches—Church of the Incarnation and Rutgers Presbyterian—and in Philadelphia at St. Stephen's Episcopal Church. From 1938 to 1954 he served as organist at the First Presbyterian Church in Santa Monica, California. Barnes contributed to the Presbyterian *Handbook to the Hymnal* (1935) and wrote piano and vocal works as well as anthems and liturgical music.

Liturgical Use
Christmas season; in "carols from many lands" choral services.

348

AWAY IN A MANGER
♩ = 112

Away in a Manger

Text
Stanzas 1 and 2 of this anonymous children's hymn were first published in the Lutheran compilation *Little Children's Book for Schools and Families* (Philadelphia, 1885). Charles H. Gabriel

Scripture References
st. 1 = Luke 2:4-7

(PHH 24) published the text with an additional third stanza, also anonymously written, in his *Vineyard Songs* (1892).

Though obviously a children's hymn, "Away in a Manger" is a charming favorite of many people, regardless of age. When people object to the "no crying" phrase in stanza 2, seeing it as a denial of Christ's humanity, they've really missed the childlike nature of this hymn. "Away in a Manger" has a lullaby character in stanzas 1 and 2; stanza 3 is an evening bedtime prayer.

Tune

With the original two-stanza text, AWAY IN A MANGER was first published in James R. Murray's *Dainty Songs for Little Lads and Lasses* (1887) and initialed "J. R. M." Murray (b. Andover, MA, 1841; d. Cincinatti, OH, 1905) compiled the songbook and is now thought to be the tune's composer. However, Murray's hymnbook erroneously described this song as: "Luther's Cradle Hymn. Composed by Martin Luther for his children, and still sung by German mothers to their little ones." As a result, the hymn was wrongly attributed to Luther for many years.

As a young man taught by such famous music teachers as Lowell Mason (PHH 96), George Root (PHH 93), and William Bradbury (PHH 114), Murray also studied at the Musical Institute in North Reading, Massachusetts. From 1868 until the Chicago fire of 1871 destroyed the company, he edited the *Song Messenger* for the publishing firm of Root and Cady. He then returned to his birth place, Andover, and taught music in the public schools. From 1881 to 1905 he was an editor for the John Church Company of Cincinatti, an important publisher of church school materials and gospel music, including the monthly *Musical Visitor*. Murray composed many gospel songs and tunes and compiled a number of church school songbooks that contained his music.

AWAY IN A MANGER is a simple tune in ABAC form, probably best performed with light organ accompaniment and/or with flute, recorder, guitar, or Orff instruments. "Away in a Manger" is a fine young children's choir anthem; it could be sung by children alone, with adults humming the harmony.

The hymn is suitable for two-part, four-part, or unison singing. Try also to sing unaccompanied. Maintain one pulse per bar.

Liturgical Use

Christmas season, perhaps best on Christmas Eve or on a similar evening worship service.

349

CRADLE SONG
♩ = 96

Away in a Manger

Text

For text commentary see PHH 348.

Scripture References
st. 1 = Luke 2:4-7

Tune

William J. Kirkpatrick (PHH 188) composed CRADLE SONG, which was first published in *Around the World with Christmas* (1895). Like AWAY IN A MANGER, CRADLE SONG is a simple tune in ABAB form, but with a slightly more adventurous harmony. Try singing this childlike song in harmony; without accompaniment or with only light organ registration; or with flutes and guitar.

Liturgical Use

See PHH 348.

350

YORKSHIRE
♩ = 80

Christians, Awake

Text

John Byrom (b. Broughton, Manchester, England, 1692; d. Manchester, 1763) wrote this text in 1749 as a Christmas present for his daughter Dorothy. Originally in eight stanzas, "Christians, Awake" was printed in broadsheet around 1750 and then in Byrom's posthumous *Miscellaneous Poems* (1773).

Scripture References
all st. = Luke 2:1-20

The original stanzas 1-6 were all narrative. Many hymnals delete at least some stanzas, primarily as a gesture of goodwill to congregations who would find it difficult to sing all eight stanzas in this very long meter! The *Psalter Hymnal* version of the text includes Byrom's first and second stanzas, based on the familiar Christmas story in Luke 2:1-20. Stanza 3, a combination of Byrom's original stanzas 7 and 8, is a theological commentary on this narrative.

Byrom studied at Trinity College, Cambridge, England, and then received a medical degree in Montpellier, France, although he never practiced medicine. Instead, he made his living teaching a form of shorthand he had devised, for which he received a parliamentary monopoly for twenty-one years. John and Charles Wesley (PHH 267) were among his pupils—John used this shorthand for his voluminous journal entries and Charles for jotting down hymns at unusual times and places. Byrom was attracted initially to Methodism and later to the Quakers. He wrote many poems, some of which became hymn texts. His collected *Miscellaneous Poems* were published posthumously in 1773.

Tune

John Wainwright (b. Stockport, England, 1723; d. Stockport, 1768) wrote YORKSHIRE for this text in 1750. The tune was first sung on Christmas Day, 1750, in the parish church of Stockport; it was first published in Caleb Ashworth's *Collection of Tunes* (1760) and then in Wainwright's *Collection of Psalm-Tunes, Anthems, Hymns and Chants* (1766). Because it was first named after the town in Lancashire where Wainwright was organist, in England, YORKSHIRE is better known as STOCKPORT.

Little is known of Wainwright's early life. He moved to Manchester in 1746 to become assistant organist and eventually organist and "singing man" at the Collegiate Church. He returned to Stockport in 1750 and served the parish church there as organist. Also a violinist, Wainwright published a *Collection of Psalm Tunes, Anthems, Hymns and Chants for 1, 2, 3, and 4 Voices* in 1766. His sons also became well-known musicians.

YORKSHIRE has some marvelous ascending phrases. The second line repeats in the final line with a happy rhythmic change. Try having a small group (a choir or two antiphonal groups) sing stanzas 1 and 2, or begin with a small group and then add singers every two lines. The entire congregation could then sing stanza 3. The hymn also works well as a processional. See 80 for a setting of this tune in the key of B-flat.

Liturgical Use

Christmas Day worship service, especially as the opening hymn on Christmas morning.

351

Lo, How a Rose E'er Blooming

ES IST EIN ROS
$\downarrow = 54$

Text

This "Twelfth Night" German carol from the Rhineland region combines the story of Luke 1-2 and Matthew 2 with Isaiah's prophecies about the "rose" from the "stem of Jesse" (Isa. 11:1; 35:1-2). Stanzas 1 and 2 are a combination of folklore ("amid the cold of winter") and Christological interpretation of Isaiah 11:1 and 35:1-2. Stanza 3 introduces imagery from John 1.

Scripture References
st. 1-2 = Isa. 11:1
Isa. 35:1-2
Luke 1-2
Matt. 2
st. 3 = John 1

Originally "Es ist ein Ros entsprungen," the carol may date back to the fifteenth century. However, the earliest manuscript containing the text, found in St. Alban's Carthusian monastery in Trier and preserved in the Trier municipal library, is dated around 1580. It was first published with twenty-three stanzas in *Alte catholische geistliche Kirchengesänge* (Cologne, 1599). Originally stanza 2 interpreted the "rose" as being Mary, mother of Jesus. But in *Musae Sionae* (1609) Michael Praetorius changed the interpretation to point to Christ as the rose in accord with actual biblical imagery. In that hymnbook Praetorius published only stanzas 1 and 2.

The English translation of stanzas 1 and 2 in the *Psalter Hymnal* are by Theodore Baker (b. New York, NY, 1851; d. Dresden, Germany, 1934) and are possibly from an anthem setting published by G. Schirmer, Inc., in 1894 when Baker was music editor there. Baker is well known as the compiler of *Baker's Biographical Dictionary of Musicians* (first ed. 1900), the first major music reference work that included American composers. Baker studied music in Leipzig, Germany, and wrote a dissertation on the music of the Seneca people of New York State—one of the first studies of the music of American Indians. From 1892 until his retirement in 1926, Baker was a literary editor and translator for G. Schirmer, Inc., in New York City. In 1926, he returned to Germany.

Stanza 3 is a translation by Gracia Grindal (b. Powers Lake, ND, 1943), originally published in the *Lutheran Book of Worship* (1978). Grindal was educated at Augsburg College, Minneapolis, Minnesota; the University of Arkansas; and Luther-Northwestern Seminary, St. Paul, Minnesota, where she has served since 1984 as a professor of pastoral theology and communications. From 1968 to 1984 she was a professor of English and poet-in-residence at Luther College, Decorah, Iowa. Included in her publications are *Sketches Against the Dark* (1981), *Scandinavian Folksongs* (1983), *Lessons in Hymnwriting* (1986, 1991), and *We Are One in Christ: Hymns, Paraphrases, and Translations* (1996). She was instrumental in producing the *Lutheran Book of Worship* (1978) and the *The United Methodist Hymnal* (1989).

Tune

First published with the text in the Cologne *Gesangbuch* of 1599 (see above), ES IST EIN ROS is a rounded bar form tune (AABA). The tune has characteristics of a Renaissance madrigal; it invites performance by an unaccompanied choir so that all the fine part writing and subtle rhythms can be clearly heard. ES IST EIN ROS is also a fine congregational tune or a children's choir anthem. Sing in unison with delicate accompaniment. Be sure to articulate carefully on the organ or piano those repeated melody tones.

The revised text and new harmonization by Michael Praetorius (b. Kreutzburg, Thuringia, Germany, 1571; d. Wolfenbüttel, near Brunswick, Germany, 1621) turned "Lo, How a Rose" into a beautiful and popular hymn. Born into a staunchly Lutheran family, Praetorius was educated at the University of Frankfort-an-der-Oder. In 1595 he began a long association with Duke Heinrich Julius of Brunswick, when he was appointed court organist and later music director and secretary. The duke resided in Wolfenbüttel, and Praetorius spent much of his time at the court there, eventually establishing his own residence in Wolfenbüttel as well. When the duke died, Praetorius officially retained his position, but he spent long periods of time engaged in various musical appointments in Dresden, Magdeburg, and Halle. Praetorius produced a prodigious amount of music and music theory. His church music consists of over one thousand titles, including the sixteen-volume *Musae Sionae* (1605-1612), which contains Lutheran hymns in settings ranging from two voices to multiple choirs. His *Syntagma Musicum* (1614-1619) is a veritable encyclopedia of music and includes valuable information about the musical instruments of his time.

Liturgical Use

Advent and the Christmas season; useful as a response to the Isaiah 11 passage, especially in services of lessons and carols or "carols from many lands."

352

That Boy-Child of Mary

BLANTYRE
♩ = 63

Text

Scripture References
st. 2 = Matt. 1:21, 23

African missionary Thomas S. Colvin (b. Glasgow, Scotland, 1925) wrote this text in 1967 for use at St. Michael's Cathedral in Blantyre, Malawi. In his missionary work Colvin learned that the name given to a child often expresses hopes for the child as well as events associated with his or her birth. The significance of Christ's birth and name, expressed in this text, is patterned after that African practice.

Stanza 1 asks about the identity of Jesus; stanzas 2-4 explain who Jesus is; and stanza 5 offers our praise and service to "that boy-child of Mary." The simple and direct text is for God's children of all ages.

Colvin was trained as an engineer and worked in that profession in Burma and Singapore from 1945 to 1948. After studying theology at Trinity College, Glasgow University, he was ordained in the Church of Scotland in 1954. He served as missionary in Nyasaland (now Malawi) from 1954 to 1958, in Ghana from 1958 to 1964, and again in Nyasaland from 1964 to 1974. His work there included preaching, education, and community development. After completing his missionary work, Colvin became a minister in the United Reformed Church of England and served an inner-city church in London. He returned to Africa in 1984 as a development consultant to the Zimbabwe Christian Council. He is now retired in Edinburgh. Colvin's writings include *Christ's Work in Free Africa* (1964) and three collections of hymns, many written in collaboration with African Christians—*Free to Serve* (1966), *Leap My Soul* (1976), and *Fill Us with Your Love* (1983).

Tune

Colvin adapted a traditional Malawian melody for this text and named the tune for the Blantyre Synod in Malawi. BLANTRYE is in a call-and-response form; therefore, it is best to alternate between soloists or small choir and the entire group or congregation. Try having a soloist sing stanza 1, the choir sing in parts on stanzas 2-4 (adjusting the hymnal harmonization, or using a published arrangment), and the entire group sing stanza 5 as well as the refrain. Another possibility would be to have young children gather to sing the refrain and the whole congregation sing the stanzas. Use very light accompaniment (if any at all), but support the tune with improvised percussion patterns: drums, tambourines, shakers, or clapping; Orff xylophones would also work well. This hymn is another one of those perpetual energy songs with no breaks between the refrain and the stanzas.

Liturgical Use
Christmas season; church school programs and carol worship services of various kinds.

353

W ZLOBIE LEZY
♩ = 76

Infant Holy, Infant Lowly

Text

Evoking the atmosphere at the manger (st. 1) and among the shepherds (st. 2), this traditional Polish carol tells the Christmas story in short phrases with tight rhymes. A final refrain sums up the significance of the event: Christ the child, Lord of all, was born for our salvation!

Scripture References
all st. = Luke 2:1-20

"W Zlobie Lezy" ("In a manger lies") may date back to the thirteenth or fourteenth century. However, it was not published until the early twentieth century, when it was included with its traditional tune in *Spiewniczek Piesni Koscielne* (1908). Edith M. Gellibrand Reed (b. Islington, Middlesex, England, 1885; d. Barnet, Hertfordshire, England, 1935) translated the text into English and published it in *Music and Youth* (vol. 1, Dec. 1921), a journal that she edited.

Reed was educated at the Guildhall School of Music in London, England, and devoted her life to the musical education of children. In association with Percy Scholes she edited various magazines such as *Music and Youth, The Music Student,* and *Pan's Pipes.* Her publications include *Story Lives of Great Composers* (1925) and several Christmas dramas. She also contributed to the *Kingsway Carol Book* and various church school songbooks.

Tune

The Polish tune is a rounded bar form (AABA). Its lines consist of short figures and phrases bound together by the consistent rhythmic pattern of the Polish mazurka (made famous by Frederic Chopin). Note especially the third line with its fine sequences and harmonic suspensions. Sing in parts with adults or in unison with young children. Use light organ accompaniment, preferably played on two manuals and pedal. Add handbells (or even sleigh bells) on the first beat of each bar. Sing in four long lines and avoid the choppiness suggested by the short melodic phrases.

Liturgical Use

Christmas season, in regular worship services, or in carol and candlelight services, especially those that feature carols from many lands.

354

Angels from the Realms of Glory

REGENT SQUARE
♩ = 58

Text

A writer of many Christian hymns, James Montgomery (PHH 72) composed this Christmas and Epiphany text and published it on Christmas Eve, 1816, in the *Sheffield Iris,* a newspaper he edited. Montgomery based the text in part on the French carol "Angels We Have Heard on High" (347); it was sung to that tune for over fifty years. Entitling it "Good Tidings of Great Joy to All People," Montgomery republished the text with small alterations in his *Christian Psalmist* (1825).

Scripture References
st. 1-3 = Luke 2
Matt. 2
st. 4 = Joel 3:2
Phil. 2:10

Perhaps because he knew the psalms so well, Montgomery expresses a cosmic sense in this text: he reaches from Christ's incarnation to the final great day. The text successively incorporates all creatures—the angels (st. 1), the shepherds (st. 2), the wise men (st. 3), all nations (st. 4), and all people (st. 5)—in the call to "come and worship Christ, the newborn King!"

The text was originally in five stanzas, although many hymnals now delete the fifth stanza. Stanzas 1-3 are from Montgomery's text, which was inspired by the Christmas stories in Luke 2 and Matthew 2. Stanza 4 comes from another Montgomery carol inspired by Philippians 2. Stanza 5 is a doxology (not written by Montgomery) from the *Salisbury Hymn Book* (1857).

Tune

Henry T. Smart (PHH 233) composed REGENT SQUARE for the Horatius Bonar (PHH 260) doxology "Glory be to God the Father." The tune was first published in the English Presbyterian Church's *Psalms and Hymns for Divine Worship* (1867), of which Smart was music editor. Because the text editor of that hymnal, James Hamilton, was minister of the Regent Square Church, the "Presbyterian cathedral" of London, the tune was given this title. At times Montgomery's text is sung to GLORIA (347), but it is usually associated with this tune.

REGENT SQUARE is a splendid tune with lots of lift and some repeated phrases. For variety, try having small groups sing stanzas 1-3, with all on the refrains; stanza 4 sung by all in harmony; and stanza 5 in unison, perhaps with an alternative accompaniment.

Liturgical Use

Christmas Day worship service; during the Christmas season and Epiphany (not only for the Christmas story, but also for the hymn's obvious mission focus in stanza 4).

IN DULCI JUBILO
♩ = 60

Good Christian Friends, Rejoice

Text

Expressing the good news of Christ's birth who is born to save, this medieval carol calls all Christians to "rejoice with heart and soul and voice!" The earliest manuscript of the text dates from around 1400 (Leipzig), though the carol wasn't published until 1533 in Joseph Klug's *Geistliche Lieder* (PHH 126). Mention of the carol, however, was made by a fourteenth-century writer who claimed that angels sang this hymn while dancing with the mystic Heinrich Suso (d. 1366). The carol is part of the late medieval tradition of teaching Bible stories to peasants by means of folk music. The original bilingual text combined Latin and German.

Scripture References
st. 1 = Luke 2:11

John M. Neale (PHH 342) provided a rather free English paraphrase that was published in his *Carols for Christmastide* (1853). The English text originally began "Good Christian men, rejoice" and also included additional words because Neale's associate, Thomas Helmore (PHH 328), made an error in transcribing the rhythm of the tune.

Tune

IN DULCI JUBILO was originally a folk dance; it is filled with rhythmic energy. There are many organ and choral arrangements of this tune. Sing this lilting lively carol in unison or in parts with bright flute accompaniment (either real flutes or flute stops on the organ). Observe a ritardando only in the final phrase of stanza 3. Sing with two pulses per bar.

Liturgical Use

Christmas Day or Christmas Eve worship services, especially early in the service; festivals of lessons and carols; "carols from many lands" services; church school programs.

356

GO TELL IT
♩ = 69

Go, Tell It on the Mountain

Text

The text of this beloved spiritual was first published in *Folk Song of the American Negro* (1907), a study of African American folk music by John Wesley Work, Jr. (PHH 476). The song may date back to earlier sources, but evidently the original text was lost. According to Edith McFall Work, widow of John Wesley Work, III,

Scripture References
all st. = Luke 2:8-20
ref.   = Matt. 28:19

the verses of these songs were published by John Work, II, in place of the original ones which could not be found. In 1940 John Work, III, had the songs copyrighted and published [at 215] in his book *American Negro Songs*.

—*Companion to the* United Methodist Hymnal, *p. 360*

In *American Negro Songs and Spirituals* (1940), John Wesley Work, III, attributes the newer text to his uncle Frederick J. Work. "He may have composed it" [the tune], wrote J. W. Work, III. "I know he composed the verses." John, III, recalled that when he was a child, the students at Fisk University began singing this before daybreak on Christmas morning, going from building to building. Later, his arrangement for use in choral concerts by the Fisk Jubilee Singers helped to popularize the spiritual.

The refrain theme comes from Old Testament passages in which praise to God for his acts of deliverance was often shouted, both literally and metaphorically, from the mountaintops (Isa. 42:11). While the three stanzas tell the essence of the Christmas story, the refrain underscores the missionary impetus of the Christian church: "go and make disciples of all nations" (Matt. 28:19). The "go, tell," which initially applied to the singers caroling on the university campus, is a signal for us to leave the comfortable confines of Christian worship and "go, tell" the message of Christ's redemption to the whole world.

Because of the spiritual's oral tradition, variants in text and melody exist. A textual variant for "Go, Tell It" is an Easter version with the following refrain text:

Go, tell it on the mountain,
Over the hills and everywhere;
Go, tell it on the mountain
That Jesus lives again.

Tune

Some scholars have discovered similarities between GO TELL IT and white folk songs from the Civil War era. The setting by Hale Smith (b. Cleveland, OH, 1925) was published in *Hymns III* (1978), an American Episcopal supplementary hymnal. Smith attended the Cleveland Institute of Music, where he received a M.Mus. degree in composition. He moved to New York City in 1958 and worked as an editor for several music publishing companies. During that time he also arranged music for several famous jazz performers and composed music for radio, films, and television. In 1968 he began teaching at the C. W. Post College of Long Island University, New York, and in 1970 began teaching music at the University of Connecticut at Storrs.

Smith's setting features a gospel style in the refrain and a common melodic version of the tune (your congregation may involuntarily sing another variant). Try having a soloist, a small group, or a choir (with a different harmonization) sing the stanzas and the congregation sing the refrain. Piano is the most appropriate accompaniment for this African American gospel style.

Liturgical Use

Christmas morning; a Christmas candlelight service; "carols from many lands" service; the refrain could be used by itself as a chorus on Christmas Day, or it could be combined with the Easter refrain version (see above) and used during worship services that focus on missions.

357

How Bright Appears the Morning Star

Text

This text is based on the famous Lutheran chorale "Wie schön leuchtet der Morgenstern" by Philipp Nicolai, published in his *Frewden-Spiegel dess ewigen Lebens* (1599).

Scripture References
st. 1 = Rev. 22:16
st. 2 = John 1:14

Philipp Nicolai (b. Mengeringhausen, Waldeck, Germany, 1556; d. Hamburg, Germany, 1608) described his text as "a Spiritual bridal song of the believing soul concerning her Heavenly Bridegroom, founded in the 45th Psalm of the Prophet David." He wrote the text in 1597, the year after the Black Plague had ravaged Germany. Even though this chorale arose out of sadness, it became popular for weddings in Germany. The chorale is often called the "Queen of the Chorales"; his "Wake, Awake" (613) is named "King of the Chorales."

Nicolai lived an eventful life—he fled from the Spanish army, sparred with Roman Catholic and Calvinist opponents, and ministered to plague-stricken congregations. Educated at Wittenberg University, he was ordained a Lutheran pastor in 1583 in the city of Herdecke. However, he was soon at odds with the Roman Catholic town council, and when Spanish troops arrived to reestablish Roman dominance, Nicolai fled. In 1588 he became chief pastor at Altwildungen and court preacher to Countess Margaretha of Waldeck. During that time Nicolai battled with Calvinists, who disagreed with him about the theology of the real presence of Christ in the Lord's Supper. These doctrinal controversies were renewed when he served the church in Unna, Westphalia. During his time as a pastor there, the plague struck twice, and Nicolai wrote both "How Bright Appears the Morning Star" and "Wake, Awake." Nicolai's last years were spent as pastor of St. Katherine's Church in Hamburg.

The English text, only loosely translated from the original German, is mainly the work of William Mercer (b. Barnard Castle, Durham, England, 1811; d. Leavy Green, Sheffield, England, 1873). First published in *Church Psalter and Hymn Book* (1856) and revised substantially in 1859, Mercer's text incorporates some lines from a translation of Nicolai's chorale by John C. Jacobi published in Jacobi's *Psalmodia Germanica* (1722).

Mercer's text includes certain Nicolai phrases, omits Nicolai's love-song imagery, and emphasizes objective praise and prayer.

Educated at Trinity College, Cambridge, England, Mercer was ordained in the Church of England and served the parish of St. George's, Sheffield (1840-1873). He translated and paraphrased several hymns from Latin and German, but his main contribution to church music was as compiler, with John Goss (PHH 164), of the most popular psalter and hymnal in the Church of England in the mid-nineteenth century. This collection had the imposing title *The Church Psalter and Hymn Book, comprising the Psalter, or Psalms of David, together with the Canticles, Pointed for Chanting; Four Hundred Metrical Hymns and Six Responses to the Commandments; the whole united to appropriate Chants and Tunes, for the Use of Congregations and Families* (1854, enlarged 1856, and published with an Appendix 1872).

Stanza 1 begins with the words "Morning Star" from Revelation 22:16 and proceeds to give Old Testament names for the Messiah—"O Righteous Branch," "O Jesse's Rod." Stanza 2 relates how Christ left his glory to become human for our salvation. Both stanzas 1 and 2 end with a prayer of petition. Stanza 3, with a prayer of praise, rejoices in Christ's incarnation and exhorts the Incarnate God to "ride on, great Conqueror, till all know your salvation."

Tune
Adapting a tune written for Psalm 100 found in Wolff Köphel's *Psalter* (1538), Nicolai composed WIE SCHÖN LEUCHTET, which was published with the text in 1599. Although the tune was originally more varied rhythmically, the hymnal version here is isorhythmic (all equal rhythms) and set to the rich harmonization of Johann S. Bach (PHH 7). That setting will delight all choristers and challenge the organist's feet! Bach also used this tune in his cantatas 1, 36, 37, 61, and 172 and wrote a chorale prelude based on it (as have many other—especially Lutheran—composers).

A rounded bar form (AABA) tune, WIE SCHÖN LEUCHTET is a noble melody that has lost some of its strength due to isorhythm but has regained new color and vigor through the Bach harmonization. Try having the congregation sing this hymn in unison with harmony sung by the choir or played by brass instruments.

Liturgical Use
Epiphany; Christmas season; any worship service that focuses on Christ as Lord.

358

As with Gladness Men of Old

Text

Inspired by the Epiphany gospel, Matthew 1:1-11, William C.
Dix (b. Bristol, England, 1837; d. Cheddar, Somerset, England,
1898) wrote this text in 1858 while recuperating from illness.
The text was first published in A. H. Ward's *Hymns for Public
Worship and Private Devotion* (1860). The following year it was
published in both Dix's *Hymns of Love and Joy* and *Hymns Ancient and Modern*.

Scripture References
st. 1-3 = Matt. 1:1-12
st. 4-5 = Rev. 21:23
Rev. 22:5

Taking Matthew 1:1-11 as his theme for stanzas 1-3, Dix likens the journey of the wise
men who came to worship the Christ to our own Christian pilgrimage. The pattern of
these stanzas is "as they . . . so may we." Stanzas 4 and 5 are a prayer that our journey on
the "narrow way" may bring us finally to glory where Christ is the light (Rev. 21:23) and
where we may perfectly sing his praise.

Most British hymn writers in the nineteenth century were clergymen, but Dix was a
notable exception. Trained in the business world, he became the manager of a marine
insurance company in Glasgow, Scotland. Dix published various volumes of his hymns,
such as *Hymns of Love and Joy* (1861) and *Altar Songs: Verses on the Holy Eucharist* (1867). A
number of his texts were first published in *Hymns Ancient and Modern* (1861). In
addition to the two printed in the *Psalter Hymnal* (also 406), another popular hymn by
Dix is "What Child Is This."

Tune

An early form of the tune DIX was composed by Conrad Kocher (b. Ditzingen,
Wurttemberg, Germany, 1786; d. Stuttgart, Germany, 1872). Trained as a teacher,
Kocher moved to St. Petersburg, Russia, to work as a tutor at the age of seventeen. But
his love for the music of Haydn and Mozart impelled him to a career in music. He
moved back to Germany in 1811, settled in Stuttgart, and remained there for most of
his life. The prestigious Cotta music firm published some of his early compositions and
sent him to study music in Italy, where he came under the influence of Palestrina's
music. In 1821 Kocher founded the School for Sacred Song in Stuttgart, which popularized four-part singing in the churches of that region. He was organist and choir
director at the Striftsckirche in Stuttgart from 1827 to 1865. Kocher wrote a treatise on
church music, *Die Tonkunst in der Kirche* (1823), collected a large number of chorales in
Zions Harfe (1855), and composed an oratorio, two operas, and some sonatas.

William H. Monk (PHH 332) created the current form of DIX by revising and
shortening Conrad Kocher's chorale melody for "Treuer Heiland, wir sind hir," found
in Kocher's *Stimmen aus den Reiche Gottes* (1838). Monk's tune was published with Dix's
text in the 1861 edition of *Hymns Ancient and Modern*, of which Monk was music editor.

Dix regretted the use of this tune for his text, but the combination has proven a good match—"As with Gladness" is the most popular Epiphany hymn today.

DIX is a simple bar form tune (AAB) with a wavelike contour in each of its three lines. Sing in three long lines rather than six short ones in order to reflect the longer phrases of the text. Sing stanzas 1-4 in unison or in harmony. In stanza 5 add the descant from Sydney H. Nicholson's Royal School of Church Music collection *Music for Boys' Voices* (1944).

Sydney H. Nicholson (b. St. Marylebone, London, England, 1875; d. Ashford, Kent, England, 1947) was an organist and church music educator who greatly influenced English hymnody. Educated at Oxford's New College, the Royal College of Music in London, and in Frankfurt, Germany, he became organist at several famous cathedrals, including Westminster Abbey (1919-1928). Nicholson founded and administered the School of English Church Music at Chislehurst in 1927; this important institution, with branches throughout the English-speaking world, was renamed the Royal School of Church Music in 1945. Located in Canterbury after World War II, its headquarters were moved to Addington Palace, Croydon, in 1954. Nicholson was music advisor for the 1916 *Supplement* of *Hymns Ancient and Modern* and prepared the way for its 1950 edition. He wrote *Church Music: a Practical Handbook* (1920) and *Quires and Places Where They Sing* (1932) and composed operettas, anthems, and hymn tunes. In 1938 he was knighted for his contributions to church music.

Liturgical Use
Epiphany; Christmas season.

359

Christ Is the King and He Shall Reign

NATIVITY
♩ = 58

Text

A paraphrase of Psalm 72:8-15, this Epiphany text comes from the 1912 *Psalter.* (For general comments on this psalm, see PHH 72.)

Scripture References
st. 1 = Ps. 72:8
st. 2 = Ps. 72:9
st. 3 = Ps. 72:10-11
st. 4 = Ps. 72:12-14
st. 5 = Ps. 72:15

The text begins with a Christological interpretation of what was originally a Hebrew royal psalm (st. 1). It goes on to say that distant tribes and foreign kings (all nations) will bring tribute to Christ, and he will subdue his enemies (st. 2-3), that Christ's rule will bring redress for the poor and needy (st. 4), and that like those foreign kings, we too may bring our "gold" and our offerings of praise to Christ (st. 5). Psalm 72:8-15 fits well with the Epiphany gospel of the wise men bringing their gifts to the infant Jesus. It is also fitting testimony to Christ's cosmic rule, which should spur us to ongoing missionary work.

Tune

Henry Lahee (b. Chelsea, London, England, 1826; d. Croydon, London, 1912) composed NATIVITY, which was first published in 1855 and set to a nativity hymn (thus the tune's title), "High let us swell our tuneful notes," by Philip Doddridge (PHH 335). Because NATIVITY was published with Isaac Watts's (PHH 155) "Come let us join our cheerful songs" in the 1875 edition of *Hymns Ancient and Modern*, it has often been set to that text. NATIVITY is the only Lahee tune still in common use.

After studying music privately, Lahee became organist at several churches. His most prominent position was at Holy Trinity Church, Brompton, England, where he was organist from 1847-1874. While in that position he joined his vicar, W. J. Irons, in producing *The Metrical Psalter* (1855); NATIVITY was included in an appendix to that collection. A composer of cantatas and many madrigals and glees, Lahee also compiled *One Hundred Hymn Tunes* (1857) for use with a collection of hymn texts edited by Irons.

A cheerful tune, NATIVITY is distinguished both by its brevity and by its opening dramatic "rocket" figure. Sing in two long lines with stanzas 1 and 5 in unison and stanzas 2-4 in harmony. The fanfare-like opening and royal character of this psalm invite brass accompaniment.

For the final stanza, add the fine descant by Florence Mary Spencer Palmer ("Peggy"; b. Thornbury, Gloucestershire, England, 1900; d. Bristol, England, 1987) from the *Anglican Hymn Book*, 1965. Palmer studied piano and composition in her youth and later taught those disciplines, both privately and at various schools in the Bristol area. In addition to her many hymn tunes she composed music for piano, cello, and voice.

Liturgical Use

For any worship service (see PHH 72 for other comments on use); Epiphany Sunday, especially stanzas 3 and 5.

360

DEJLIG ER DEN HIMMEL BLAA
♩ = 66

Bright and Glorious Is the Sky

Text

The great Danish hymn writer Nikolai F. S. Grundtvig (b. Udby, Denmark, 1783; d. Vartov, Denmark, 1872) wrote this hymn for Christmas, 1810. One of his earliest texts, it was first published in Knud L. Rahbek's *Sandsigeren* on April 10, 1811. Based on the Epiphany gospel (Matt. 1:1-11), the text speaks about the wise men coming from the East and being led by the star to worship the Christ child (st. 1-4a). It compares the light of the star to the Bible—the light that leads us to the Christ (st. 4b-5).

Scripture References
st. 1-4 = Matt. 2:1-12
st. 4-5 = Ps. 119:105

Grundtvig was a famous Danish preacher, educator, and hymn writer. Although he had studied theology at the University of Copenhagen, because of the influence of rationalist theology he lost his faith. After a period of intense spiritual reflection he regained both his faith and renewed appreciation for his orthodox Lutheran heritage. His ordination in 1811 was delayed for a year because he preached a sermon in which he criticized the rationalist theology of the Danish clergy. Later he experienced other confrontations with the established church leaders and for some ten years did not have a regular parish. But in 1839 he was appointed pastor to Vartov. An effective preacher and a much-loved author of hymns, Grundtvig finally was accepted by the church and upon his golden jubilee was given the title of bishop.

The most influential and prolific writer of devotional poems and orthodox hymns in nineteenth-century Scandinavia, he published two significant hymnals, *Sang-Vark til den Danske Kirke* (1837) and *Festsalmer* (1850). All of his hymns and poems were published posthumously in five volumes. As an educator Grundtvig was instrumental in initiating public high schools in some Danish cities and raising educational standards; these schools became very popular and were copied in neighboring countries. Consequently Grundtvig is often called the "father of public schools" in Scandinavia.

The translation combines Jens C. Aaberg's translation from the *Hymnal for Church and Home* (1927) and Fred C. M. Hansen's and Thorvald O. Burntvedt's from the *Service Book and Hymnal* (1958). Aaberg (b. Moberg, Denmark, 1877; d. Minneapolis, MN, 1970) immigrated to the United States in 1901. Educated at Grand View College and Seminary in Des Moines, Iowa, he entered the ministry of the Danish Evangelical Lutheran Church in America and served congregations in Marinette, Wisconsin; Dwight, Illinois; and Minneapolis, Minnesota. Aaberg wrote *Hymns and Hymnwriters of Denmark* (1945), translated at least eighty hymns from Danish into English, and served on four hymnal committees. In 1947 King Frederick of Denmark awarded him the Knight Cross of Denmark.

Tune

DEJLIG ER DEN HIMMEL BLAA is an anonymous Danish tune said to be the work of an old man unversed in music composition (around 1840). The tune was first published in Andreas Berggren's *Melodier til den af Roeskildes Praesteconvent udgivne Psalmebog* (1853).

A charming tune, DEJLIG ER DEN HIMMEL BLAA is built with several repetitions and sequences. It has a fine "rising star" figure in the first phrase and provides its own ritardando in the rhythm of the final phrase. Sing in harmony or in unison. To lighten the texture of this dance-like tune (especially on st. 3), play in three voices (omitting the tenor) on a light, bright organ registration.

Liturgical Use

Epiphany Sunday; stanza 5 could be sung just prior to the reading of Scripture.

361

SALZBURG
♩ = 58

Songs of Thankfulness and Praise

Text

Christopher Wordsworth (b. Lambeth, London, England, 1807; d. Harewood, Yorkshire, England, 1885), nephew of the great Romantic poet William Wordsworth, wrote this hymn in five stanzas. It was published in his *Holy Year* (1862) with the heading "Sixth Sunday after Epiphany." Wordsworth described the text as follows:

Scripture References
st. 1 = Matt. 2:1-12
st. 2 = John 2:1-11
John 3:13-17
st. 3 = Matt. 4:1-11, 23-24
ref. = Mark 8:29
John 1:14

[It is a] recapitulation of the successive manifestations of Christ, which have already been presented in the services of the former weeks throughout the season of Epiphany; and anticipation of that future great and glorious Epiphany, at which Christ will be manifest to all, when he will appear again to judge the world.

The didactic text teaches the meaning of Epiphany—the manifestation of Christ in his birth (st. 1), baptism, miracle at Cana (st. 2), healing of the sick, power over evil, and coming as judge (st. 3). Originally the refrain line was "Anthems be to thee addressed, God in man made manifest." The revised refrain borrows Peter's confession, "You are the Christ!" (Mark 8:29), and makes that our corporate confession as we acknowledge the "Word become flesh" who lived among us.

Wordsworth was a prolific author and the most renowned Greek scholar of his day. Included in his works are *Memoirs of William Wordsworth* (1851), *Commentary on the Whole Bible* (1856-1870), *Church History* (1881-1883), innumerable sermons and pamphlets, and *The Holy Year* (1862), which contained 117 of his original hymns as well as 82 others written for all the Sundays and Christian holy days according to the *Book of Common Prayer.* Wordsworth was educated at Trinity College, Cambridge, England, where he distinguished himself as a brilliant student. He later taught at Trinity College and was headmaster of Harrow School (1836-1844). Ordained a priest in the Church of England in 1835, he was canon of Westminster in 1844, a country priest in Stanford-in-the-Vale, Berkshire (1850-1869), and then Bishop of Lincoln (1869-1885).

Tune

The tune SALZBURG, named after the Austrian city made famous by Wolfgang Amadeus Mozart, was first published anonymously in the nineteenth edition of *Praxis Pietatis Melica* (1678); in that hymnbook's twenty-fourth edition (1690) the tune was attributed to Jakob Hintze (b. Bernau, Germany, 1622; d. Berlin, Germany, 1702). Partly as a result of the Thirty Years' War and partly to further his musical education, Hintze traveled widely as a youth, including trips to Sweden and Lithuania. In 1659 he settled in Berlin, where he served as court musician to the Elector of Brandenburg from 1666 to 1695.

Hintze is known mainly for his editing of the later editions of Johann Crüger's (PHH 42) *Praxis Pietatis Melica*, to which he contributed some sixty-five of his original tunes.

The harmonization by Johann S. Bach (PHH 7) is simplified from his setting in his *Choralgesänge* (*Rejoice in the Lord* [231] and *The Hymnal 1982* [135] both contain Bach's full harmonization). The tune is a rounded bar form (AABA) easily sung in harmony. But sing the refrain line in unison with full organ registration.

Liturgical Use
Throughout the Epiphany season.

362

Lord of the Universe

STONEHENGE
♩ = 120

Text

Margaret Clarkson (PHH 238) wrote this text of partially rhymed verse in Toronto, Canada. This is how she explained how she came to write the text:

Scripture References
st. 1 = John 1:14
          1 Tim. 2:6
st. 2 = Heb. 4:14-16
st. 3 = Ps. 43:3
st. 4 = Rom. 8:18-25

> The theme for the IVCF [Inter-Varsity Christian Fellowship] missions conference Urbana '73 had been announced as "Jesus Christ—Lord of the Universe, Hope of the World," and a contest had been launched among Inter-Varsity's student groups for a song to be written on that theme. Not being a student, I couldn't enter, but every time I saw the theme words in print during the last part of 1972 and the early part of 1973, I had to hold myself back from starting to write—the beauty and scope of those majestic words was almost too much to withstand. They were a song in themselves, so thrilling and rhythmic that they burned themselves more and more deeply into my very heart and soul. However, I managed to refrain from bursting forth in a hymn. In March of 1973 (after receiving correspondence emblazoned with the theme words) . . . I could no longer restrain myself. Forgetting about lunch, I grabbed clipboard and pencil and began to write. Faster than I could put the words down on paper they came pouring out, accompanied in the back of my mind by a melody; they almost came out singing. By mid-afternoon I had before me a finished hymn. . . . I had been "acted upon" by the Holy Spirit of God in a way I have never experienced before or since (*A Singing Heart*, Hope, 1987).

Although the contest winners' hymns were sung at Urbana '73, Clarkson's text became the convention hymn. "Lord of the Universe" was published in the Urbana songbook *Sounds* (1973) as well as in IVCF's *Hymnal II* (1976).

The four stanzas start with the theme phrase, "Lord of the universe, hope of the world." Stanza 1 recalls Christ's incarnation and stanza 2, his earthly ministry; stanza 3 enjoins us to be serious about our missionary task; stanza 4 looks forward to Christ's coming again. The refrain turns this hymn of confession into an anthem of praise.

Tune
At the *Psalter Hymnal* Revision Committee's request William P. Rowan (b. San Diego, CA, 1950) wrote STONEHENGE for Clarkson's text in 1985 (the tune's name was chosen because of the "monolithic" proportions of the text). The hymn was first published in the 1987 *Psalter Hymnal.*

Rowan built this rounded bar form (AABA) tune by combining several melodic and rhythmic figures and dividing them asymmetrically over a five-line stanza and a three-line refrain. The musical setting is best suited to unison singing. Use strong organ accompaniment with a full registration for the refrain, and add a Picardy (major) third on the final cadence for the last time through the refrain. Sing the hymn in a more stately manner that final time, but always try to sing at a moderate pace with two pulses per bar.

Rowan received his musical education at Southern Illinois University, Carbondale, and the University of Michigan, Ann Arbor. He has served various churches in Michigan and is currently the director of music ministries at St. Mary Cathedral in Lansing, Michigan, and music consultant for the Roman Catholic diocese there. A composer of numerous anthems and organ works, he has also published hymn tunes in *Together Met, Together Bound, Hymn Settings by William Rowan* (1993).

Liturgical Use
Throughout Epiphany (with its ministry/mission theme); on many other occasions when the "Lord of the universe, hope of the world" theme fits.

363

ST. MICHAEL'S
♩ = 60
Your Hands, O Lord, in Days of Old

Text
Edward H. Plumptre (b. Bloomsbury, London, England, 1821; d. Wells, Somersetshire, England, 1891) wrote this text in 1864 during his tenure as chaplain at King's College, London. Considered to be one of the finest on the theme of health and healing, the text was first printed as the leaflet *A Hymn Used in the Chapel of King's College Hospital*. Published the following year in the second edition of Plumptre's *Lazarus and Other Poems*, "Your Hands, O Lord" also appeared in the 1868 Appendix to *Hymns*

Scripture References
st. 1 = Matt. 14:35-36
st. 2 = Mark 6:55-56

Ancient and Modern. Originally the text's first line read, "Thine arm, O Lord, in days of old."

Stanzas 1 and 2a recount the healing miracles of Christ. Stanzas 2b and 3 are a prayer for that same healing power of Christ to be present today.

Plumptre was an eminent classical and biblical scholar who gained prominence in both church and university. Educated at King's College, London, and University College, Oxford, he was ordained in the Church of England in 1846. Plumptre served as a preacher at Oxford and a professor of pastoral theology at King's College, and held a number of other prestigious positions. His writings include *A Life of Bishop Ken* (1888), translations from Greek and Latin classics, and poetry and hymns. Plumptre was also a member of the committee that produced the Revised Version of the Bible.

Tune

ST. MICHAEL'S is an anonymous tune first published by William Gawler (b. Lambeth, London, England, 1750; d. London, 1809) in 1789 in his London collection *Hymns and Psalms Used at the Asylum for Female Orphans* (1785-1789). Gawler was organist at the Asylum of Refuge for French Orphans in Lambeth, the first such residence in England for homeless girls. He published a variety of voluntaries for organ.

In some hymnals the tune has been attributed to Mozart or Haydn. ST. MICHAEL'S (which refers to the archangel Michael in the Bible) is also known as ST. MICHEL'S, MOZART, or GOSHEN. Some hymnals set this text to ST. MATTHEW, a useful alternate tune (see 21).

The tune is a rounded bar form (AABA), which displays the symmetry of phrases and the cadences often associated with the classical style. Sing in harmony. Perhaps a choir could sing stanzas 1 and 2a, which tell the story, with the congregation joining in with the prayer in stanzas 2b and 3.

Liturgical Use

Latter part of the Epiphany season; Lent; worship services that focus on Christ's miracles of healing; at healing services or prayer services for the sick.

364

O Love, How Deep, How Broad, How High

DEO GRACIAS
♩ = 132

Text

The original anonymous text in Latin ("O amor quam ecstaticus") comes from a fifteenth-century manuscript from Karlsruhe. The twenty-three-stanza text has been attributed to Thomas à Kempis because of its similarities to writings of the Moderna

Devotio Movement associated with à Kempis (that movement was an important precursor of the Reformation in the Netherlands). However, there is insufficient proof that he actually wrote this text.

Scripture References
st. 1 = Eph. 3:18-19
Phil. 2:7
st. 2 = Matt. 3:13
Matt. 4:1-11
st. 3 = John 17:9
st. 4 = Rom. 4:25
1 Pet. 2:24
st. 5 = Rom. 8:34
John 16:7, 13

Benjamin Webb (b. London, England, 1819; d. Marylebone, London, 1885) translated the text in eight stanzas. It was published in *The Hymnal Noted* (1852), produced by his friend John Mason Neale (PHH 342). Webb received his education at Trinity College, Cambridge, England, and became a priest in the Church of England in 1843. Among the parishes he served was St. Andrews, Wells Street, London, where he worked from 1862 to 1881. Webb's years there coincided with the service of the talented choir director and organist Joseph Barnby (PHH 438), and the church became known for its excellent music program. Webb edited *The Ecclesiologist,* a periodical of the Cambridge Ecclesiological Society (1842-1868). A composer of anthems, Webb also wrote hymns and hymn translations and served as one of the editors of *The Hymnary* (1872).

The text has a wide scope, taking in all of Jesus's incarnate life: his birth (st. 1); identification with human affairs (st. 2); daily ministry (st. 3); crucifixion (st. 4); resurrection, ascension, and gift of the Spirit (st. 5); the final stanza is a doxology (st. 6). Thus the text summarizes Christ's life in the same manner as the Apostles' Creed. A striking feature is the text's emphasis on the fact that Jesus accomplished all of this "for us"; "for us" occurs at least a dozen times! The redemptive work of Christ is very personally, very corporately applied.

Tune
DEO GRACIAS is a fifteenth-century English ballad tune sung to commemorate the Battle at Agincourt in 1415. The Agincourt ballad began with the refrain (popularized by E. Power Biggs in an organ fanfare arrangement) "Deo gracias Anglia Redde pro victoria" ("Render thanks to God, England, for victory"). Stanza 1 originally began "Owre kynge went forth to Normandy." Also known as AGINCOURT, the tune was adapted for congregational singing in the 1906 *English Hymnal* by dropping a closing melisma.

DEO GRACIAS is a vigorous tune, even martial with this harmonization by Carl Schalk (PHH 10) written for the Lutheran *Worship Supplement* (1969). Support the unison singing line with solid organ tone and crisp rhythmic accompaniment. Try having antiphonal groups sing stanzas 1-5 and the entire congregation sing stanza 6. Use brass instruments for fanfares and/or accompaniment. Maintain one pulse per bar.

Liturgical Use

Epiphany, especially later in the season; Lent, Holy Week, Easter, Ascension, and at many other times; the final stanza makes a good doxology for Epiphany, Lent, or the Easter season.

365

Amen

AMEN
♩ = 66

Text

A traditional African American spiritual, "Amen" arose from oral tradition; thus different hymnals contain variations in the text. Donald Hustad believes "Amen" probably comes from the twentieth century. With a choral arrangement by long-time promoter of spirituals Jester Hairston, this hymn was the theme song for the film *Lilies of the Field* (1963) starring Sidney Poitier.

The text gives glimpses into Jesus' life: his birth (st. 1); his wisdom as a twelve-year-old, which astounded the temple rulers (st. 2); his preaching and healing ministry (st. 3); his suffering in Gethsemane (st. 4); and his crucifixion and victorious resurrection (st. 5). All text is framed by the repeated "Amen" responses; as we sing we reaffirm that "truly, truly, this is the gospel!"

Scripture References
st. 1 = Luke 2:6-7
st. 2 = Luke 2:46-47
st. 3 = Mark 3:7-12
    Mark 6:53-56
st. 4 = Matt. 26:36-46
    Mark 14:32-42
    Luke 22:39-46
st. 5 = Matt. 27:32-35
    Matt. 28:1
    Mark 15:21-26
    Mark 16:1-7
    Luke 23:26-34
    Luke 24:1-8
    John 19:16-18
    John 20:1-2

Tune

The traditional call-and-response structure calls for a soloist on the text, with everyone singing the ostinato pattern of "Amens," either in unison or harmony. The soloist may apply rhythmic and melodic freedom to the lines. If possible, sing unaccompanied, or use piano, guitars, and/or string bass for accompaniment rather than organ. Everyone but the soloist should sing without a book in front of them!

The arrangement is by Richard Smallwood (b. Washington, D.C., 1948), a composer, arranger, pianist, and innovator in the African American gospel style. Many of his arrangements of gospel hymns appear in *Lift Every Voice and Sing* (1981). Organized by Smallwood in 1967, the Richard Smallwood Singers have sung and recorded many of his arrangements. He remains their current director. Smallwood has a B.M. degree from Howard University, Washington, D.C.

Liturgical Use

Christmas Day; Epiphany; Lent; Easter; anytime with children; whenever you need a
simple attractive synopsis of Christ's life set to essentially two-part music.

366

LITTLE FLOCK
♩ = 76

Have No Fear, Little Flock

Text

Heinz W. Zimmermann (PHH 177) chose the words of Jesus
from Luke 12:32 as his basis for writing stanza 1 in 1971.
Marjorie A. Jillson (PHH 177) wrote stanzas 2-4 in 1972. The
complete hymn, published by Concordia in *Five Hymns* (1973),
features unison and SATB stanzas, which choir directors and
organists will want to consult as alternate settings.

Scripture References
st. 1 = Luke 12:32
st. 1-4 = Matt. 17:1-8
Mark 9:2-8

   The text has the character of a benediction: the Father has chosen to give you the
kingdom (st. 1); the Father will keep you in his love forever (st. 2); the Lord stoops
down to heal, uplift, and restore you (st. 3); God stays close beside you to work with you
(st. 4). Stanza 3 has special significance for Jillson who says, "What I learned from my
own illness is that God will restore you, even if your body has to die first."

Tune

Composed by Zimmermann in 1971, LITTLE FLOCK features the syncopations typical of
his jazz-flavored church music. Sing in unison accompanied by bright organ tones with
crisp articulation to help carry the syncopations. Play on manuals only and add pedal
for the final short phrase. Or use two manuals and pedal throughout, possibly alternating with the published SATB setting in *Five Hymns*. Do not rush!

Liturgical Use

Use as a sung benediction; in conjunction with "Sermon on the Mount" preaching; for
services with a theme of encouragement.

367

Oh, I Know the Lord Laid His Hands on Me

I KNOW THE LORD
♩ = 108

Text

A traditional African American spiritual, this hymn was published in *The Second Book of Negro Spirituals* compiled by James Weldon Johnson and J. Rosamund Johnson (1926).

The stanzas selected (of the various ones in oral and written tradition) focus on Christ's ministry: his preaching (st. 1), his saving (st. 2), and his healing (st. 3). The refrain finds comfort in the biblical image of "the hands of the Lord," which guide, protect, and uphold. The text makes Christ's ministries very personal to the believer: it is the same Lord who preaches, saves, and heals, who has his hands on me!

Scripture References
st. 1 = Luke 4:18
Luke 7:22
Matt. 11:5
st. 2 = Luke 7:48
st. 3 = Luke 4:18
Luke 7:22
Matt. 11:5

Tune

Like many spirituals, "Oh, I Know the Lord" was written for responsorial singing. The refrains are sung by the entire group, and a soloist sings the stanzas with melodic and rhythmic freedom. (The soloist's melody descends, like the Lord reaching down his hands!) Sing either unaccompanied (perhaps with E-flat drone humming during the soloist's lines) or with minimal keyboard accompaniment.

Edward Boatner's arrangement was published in *Lift Every Voice and Sing* (1981). Boatner (b. New Orleans, LA, 1894; d. unknown, 1981) was a composer, educator, choral director, and concert singer. He studied music at Western University, Boston Conservatory, and New England Conservatory, and received a Bachelor of Music degree from the Chicago Musical College, Illinois, in 1932. Best known for his compositions and arrangements of spirituals, Boatner served as the director of music for the National Baptist Convention from 1925 to 1931 and taught at two Texas institutions, Samuel Houston College and Wiley College, in the 1930s.

Liturgical Use

Epiphany; in worship services during other seasons that focus on Christ's ministry; profession of faith; adult baptism.

368

THORNBURY
♩ = 54

O Son of God the Father

Text

Written by William W. How (PHH 279), this text was originally
called "O One with God the Father." It was published in the
Society for the Promotion of Christian Knowledge's *Church
Hymns* (1871), of which How was editor. Because the "One" in
the original title seemed very impersonal, the first line was altered to strengthen the
reference to Christ.

Scripture References
st. 1-3 = 1 John 1:5-7
st. 3   = Mal. 4:2

   The controlling metaphor in this text comes from Jesus' own words, "I am the light
of the world" (John 8:12; light is an important metaphor for Christ throughout John's
gospel). The three stanzas of this text constitute a prayer in which we confess that Jesus
is the light (st. 1), that we see "but dimly" (st. 2), and that we need the light of Christ to
illumine our way (st. 3).

Tune

See PHH 509 for information on Basil Harwood and THORNBURY. The harmonization
there retains the original richer texture for the final line.

Liturgical Use

Epiphany; any service that focuses on the "light of the world" theme.

369

TRANSFIGURATION
♩ = 120

Christ, upon the Mountain Peak

Text

Brian Wren (PHH 311) wrote this text at Mansfield College,
Oxford, England, in 1962. Published in the British supplement
100 Hymns for Today (1959), "Christ, upon the Mountain Peak" was
the second hymn text that Wren wrote.

Scripture References
st. = Luke 9:28-36

   The text is based on the gospel story of Christ's transfiguration from Matthew 17:1-8,
Mark 9:2-8, and Luke 9:28-36. Powerfully poetic, the text not only captures something
of the awe in the event—we share in the awe as we sing "Alleluia"—but also presents a
cosmic picture: the saints, angels, prophets, all nations, and the whole creation bring
praise to the true Son of God! In the style of the transfiguration celebration in the
Eastern Orthodox Church, the entire focus is on Christ, the Alpha and Omega (st. 4).

Tune

The *Psalter Hymnal* Revision Committee announced a tune search for this text, and TRANSFIGURATION, composed by Norm Jonkman (PHH 200) in 1984, was chosen from among several submitted. TRANSFIGURATION, moving between triple and duple meter, has a rather rugged (mountainous) melodic contour and concludes with two rhythmically exciting "Alleluia" figures. Sing in unison, possibly with harmony on the "Alleluias," at which point the brighter organ stops should help to proclaim those "Alleluias." Reserve the most powerful reed or mixture for stanza 4 and build in a solid ritardando for the final "Alleluias." Congregations may need some encouragement with the tune at first, but they will find the extra effort worthwhile.

Liturgical Use

In worship services that focus on the transfiguration (at the end of the Epiphany season or early in Lent); useful at other occasions that emphasize the cosmic awe proper before God's beloved Son.

370

The King of Glory Comes

PROMISED ONE
♩ = 96

Text

Roman Catholic priest Willard F. Jabusch (PHH 210) wrote this text in five stanzas in 1965 in Niles, Illinois, for use by the parish folk-music ensemble of St. Celestine's Roman Catholic Church in Elmwood Park, Illinois. The text was published in *Hymnal for Young Christians* (1966), one of the first English Roman Catholic hymnals published in the United States after Vatican II.

Stanza 1 and the refrain are based on Psalm 24:7-8; stanzas 2 and 3 recall Jesus' ministry and his death to atone for sin; stanza 4 confesses Christ's victory over death and the coming of his kingdom. The original third stanza was not included.

Scripture References
st. 1 = Ps. 24:8
Isa. 7:14
st. 2 = Matt. 4:23
st. 3 = Isa. 53:12
st. 4 = 1 Cor. 15:57
John 14:2
ref. = Ps. 24:7
Ps. 67:4

Tune

Jabusch wrote his text to correspond to PROMISED ONE, an Israeli folk tune. Probably of Hasidic origin, PROMISED ONE was associated with the folk song "Gilu Hagalilim," brought by Zionist settlers to Israel after World War I. *The Fireside Book of Folk Songs* (1947) contains the tune with a different text but with the "Lift up your voices" phrase in its refrain.

This joyful minor tune has the syncopated rhythm associated with the Jewish hora dance and derives its melodic phrases from variations of the first line. PROMISED ONE is an exciting tune intended to be sung with perpetual energy and without pauses between refrain and stanza and refrain. Sing in unison and try using a faster tempo for each succeeding stanza. Accompany with guitar, various percussion instruments, hand clapping, and/or Orff instruments on the ostinati patterns or improvise similar patterns. Try adding a simple descant for the final two measures of the refrain by going up the scale as follows: B, C-sharp, D-sharp, E, E.

John Ferguson (b. Cleveland, OH, 1941) prepared the setting for Advent services at the United Church of Christ, Kent, Ohio, in 1973. That setting was published the following year in the UCC's *Hymnal,* of which Ferguson was music editor. Known for his skill as a music clinician and for his organ concerts and improvisations, Ferguson has devoted much of his professional life to church music. He was educated at Oberlin College, Kent State University, and the Eastman School of Music, where he received a Doctor of Musical Arts in 1976. From 1965 to 1978 he was professor of music at Kent State University and organist and choirmaster at the United Church of Christ. He served as music director and organist at Central Lutheran Church in Minneapolis, Minnesota, from 1978 to 1983. Since 1983 Ferguson has been professor of church music and organ at St. Olaf College, Northfield, Minnesota. He has published numerous choral anthems and hymn arrangements for organ and issued various recordings of hymn festivals. His published works include *A Musician's Guide to Church Music* (1981) and *Worship Blueprints: Guide to Planning Worship Music* (1983).

Liturgical Use
Epiphany; Advent; Palm Sunday, or anytime; a great processional hymn at the beginning of a worship service.

371

JESU, MEINES LEBENS LEBEN
♩ = 52
Christ, the Life of All the Living

Text
Ernst C. Homburg (b. Mihla, near Eisenach, Germany, 1605; d. Naumberg, Germany, 1681) wrote this German chorale text ("Jesu, meines Lebens Leben"), which was published in Part One of his *Geistliche Lieder* (1658). Homburg, who wrote most of his hymns for his own devotions, described his eight-stanza text as a "hymn of thanksgiving to his Redeemer and Savior for his bitter sufferings." In early life Homburg was a writer of love and drinking songs. After a difficult time of family illness he experienced a religious conversion, and his poetry took a more serious turn. A lawyer by profession, he wrote hymns to express and strengthen his own faith rather than for public use. Some 150 of his hymn texts were published in his *Geistliche Lieder.*

The translation of selected stanzas is by Catherine Winkworth (PHH 194), who published them in her *Chorale Book for England* (1863).

The text is a meditation on the suffering and death of Christ, which brought eternal life to believers (st. 1), provided full atonement for our sin (st. 2), and mortified our "old nature" (st. 3). The tone of unending gratitude to God reflected in the refrain line—"thousand, thousand thanks are due"—runs throughout the entire text.

Tune

The composer of the tune is unknown; it was first published in *Das grosse Cantional: oder Kirchen-Gesangbuch* (Darmstadt, 1687) to the text "Alle Menschen mussen sterben" by J. G. Albinus; some Baroque organ works are associated with that text. The tune became associated with Homburg's text since they were published together in *Anhang, An das Gothaische Cantional* (1776). The meditative tune is a good match for this text. It is in bar form (AAB) with a dotted pattern in each of the four lines, which provides rhythmic interest. Sing either in parts or in unison. Use a larger organ registration for the refrain. The tune is easily adapted for organ trio-style accompaniment (played on two manuals and pedal).

Liturgical Use

Lent, especially Holy Week; any worship service with a thanksgiving focus.

372

O Christ, Our Lord, Dear Son of God

ORMEAU
♩ = 50

Text

Calvin Seerveld (PHH 22) wrote this fresh and vivid text in Toronto, Ontario, 1977, to fit the tune ORMEAU. With the assurance that both Good Friday's crucifixion and Easter's resurrection are historical fact, the text helps us focus on the discipline of Lent. Stanza 1 confesses that Christ has died and rose again in victory over sin and hell; stanza 2 is a prayer to the Father for guidance and wisdom in living the Christian life; stanza 3 asks the Holy Spirit to help us live in true repentance during Lent.

Tune

William Davies (b. Bolton, Lancashire, England, 1921) composed ORMEAU, one of several tunes he contributed to the British supplement *Praise for Today* (1975) on whose editorial committee he served. He also served as the conductor of the North Ireland BBC Orchestra in Belfast.

ORMEAU contains variations on the bold opening figure. Like the text, the tune is in two distinct halves: the first half in G major and the second half in G minor, with a minor ending for the first two stanzas. The third stanza has a new, bright ending—the only cadence on G major—appropriately set to the final "shouts of praise!" Sing in unison with strong organ accompaniment to help the congregational singing. Although the tune has a few surprises, it is well worth the effort to learn.

Liturgical Use

Lent.

373

Lift High the Cross

Text

George W. Kitchin (b. Naughton, Suffolk, England, 1827;
d. Durham, England, 1912) wrote the original version of this text
in 1887 for the Society for the Propagation of the Gospel. The
hymn was intended to be used for a festival service at Winchester
Cathedral, England. Michael R. Newbolt (b. Dymock,
Gloucestershire, England, 1874; d. Bierton, Buckinghamshire,
England, 1956) revised the text in twelve couplets for the 1916
Supplement to *Hymns Ancient and Modern* where it was set to
CRUCIFER. Eight of his couplets are included in the seven stanzas
and refrain.

Scripture References
st. 1 = Matt. 16:24
1 Pet. 2:21
st. 2 = Rev. 7:3
st. 3 = Ps. 107:1-3
st. 4 = John 12:32
st. 5 = Matt. 1:21
st. 6 = Ps. 103:19
Matt. 25:31
st. 7 = 2 Cor. 2:14
Col. 2:15
ref. = John 3:14

Perhaps similar to Constantine's vision of Christ's cross, this
text makes clear that the cross is a symbol of Christ's love. As
Stanley L. Osborne (PHH 395) states, "[The text's] images are
biblical, its moods expectant, its promises courageous, and its demands costly" (*If Such
Holy Song*, 321). "Lift High the Cross" reveals many implications of Christ's cross: Christ
rallies his people behind him (st. 1-2); Christ gathers his people from throughout the
world
(st. 3-5); Christ gives healing to the despair of the world (st. 6); Christ's victory enjoins
our praise to him (st. 7).

A scholar and Anglican clergyman, Kitchin spent most of his life in academic institutions. Educated at Christ Church, Oxford, England, he was ordained in the Church of
England in 1852. He served initially as a headmaster in Twyford, Hampshire, and then as
a tutor at Oxford (1863-1883). Dean of Winchester Cathedral from 1883 to 1894 and of
Durham Cathedral from 1894 to 1912, Kitchin was also chancellor of Durham University
the last few years of his life. His publications include *A Life of Pope Pius II* (1881), a three-
volume work entitled *A History of France* (1877), and archeological writings.

Michael R. Newbolt was educated at St. John's College, Oxford, and ordained as
priest in the Church of England in 1900. He ministered at several churches during the
early part of his career and then became principal of the Missionary College in
Dorchester (1910-1916). From 1916 to 1927 he served St. Michael and All Angels
Church in Brighton and from 1927 to 1946 was canon of Chester Cathedral. Newbolt
wrote several theological works, including a commentary on the Book of Revelation.

Tune

Sydney H. Nicholson (PHH 358) composed CRUCIFER for the text as revised by Newbolt. The tune name means "cross-bearer" and refers to one who carries the cross in a liturgical procession. The hymn was published in the 1916 Supplement to *Hymns Ancient and Modern*.

Often considered Nicholson's finest tune, CRUCIFER has broad melodic gestures and an effective cadence to the stanzas, which leads right back into the refrain without interruption, pause, or slowing down. Try having the congregation or choir sing harmony on the stanzas and unison on the refrain with select use of the descant. Use of the entire hymn as a processional or on other festive occasions will merit antiphonal groupings for the stanzas or, perhaps, use of a published concertato. Sing and accompany with stateliness and majesty.

The descant was composed by Richard Proulx (b. St. Paul, MN, 1937). A composer, conductor, and teacher, Proulx was director of music at the Holy Name Cathedral in Chicago, Illinois (1980-1997); before that he was organist and choirmaster at St. Thomas' Episcopal Church in Seattle, Washington. He contributed his expertise to the Roman Catholic *Worship III* (1986), the Episcopal *Hymnal 1982*, *The United Methodist Hymnal* (1989), and the ecumenical *A New Hymnal for Colleges and Schools* (1992). He was educated at the University of Minnesota, MacPhail College of Music in Minneapolis, Minnesota, St. John's Abbey in Collegeville, Minnesota, and the Royal School of Church Music in England. He has composed more than 250 works and recently retired to devote more time to composition.

Liturgical Use

Lent; Holy Week; profession of faith; baptism and similar consecration/renewal worship services; missions (thus for Epiphany or Pentecost); many other occasions, especially as an opening or closing hymn.

374

No Weight of Gold or Silver

PASTORALE
♪ = 144

Text

Timothy Dudley-Smith (PHH 233) wrote this text during August 1972 at his seaside summer home in Ruan Minor, Cornwall, England. The text was first published in the British collection *Psalm Praise* (1973) as a psalm for Passion week.

Scripture References
st. 1 = 1 Pet. 1:18-19
st. 2 = Isa. 53:3-6
John 1:29
st. 3 = 2 Cor. 5:14, 17

This strong text of testimony and encouragement points all sinners to Christ, the Lamb of God. It also encourages believers to continue the journey that will ultimately bring them to the throne of the Lamb in glory. The repeated phrase "Lamb of God" is John the Baptist's description of Christ as the fulfillment of the Old Testament Passover (John 1:29).

Tune

PASTORALE is a rounded bar form (AABA) tune with a melodic contour colored by gentle ornateness. Sing in unison or in harmony. Use a confident but not exuberant accompaniment with a legato pedal line tying many of the repeated notes in the bass part. Keep two pulses per measure, and slow down slightly in the last phrase of stanza 3.

Adrian Hartog (b. Orange City, IA, 1899; d. Edgerton, MN, 1964) composed PASTORALE in 1954. The tune was first published in the 1959 *Psalter Hymnal* with a version of Psalm 23 (thus its title). A member of the committee that produced the 1959 edition, Hartog also contributed the tune for the Christian Reformed Church centennial hymn (see 486 in that edition).

Hartog learned to play a reed (pump) organ from his father, organist at the First Christian Reformed Church, Orange City, Iowa. After the family moved to Edgerton, Minnesota, when he was fifteen, Hartog assisted and later succeeded his father as organist at the First Christian Reformed Church.

He became owner of a grocery store that sold pianos and organs out of a back room; this business eventually grew into the Hartog Piano and Organ Company. Conductor of a community choir known as the Temple Choir, Hartog also published a handbook for organ students, *A Comprehensive Manual on Organ Playing*.

Liturgical Use

Lent; Holy Week; Easter; worship services of confession/forgiveness as well as other times in which we reflect on Christ's redemptive work.

375, 376

ST. THEODULPH
♩ = 58

All Glory, Laud, and Honor

Text

Theodulph, bishop of Orleans, wrote this text around 820 while he was imprisoned at Angers, France, for conspiring against King Louis the Pious. A probably apocryphal story from the early sixteenth century states that in a Palm Sunday procession King Louis passed the prison in which Theodulph was housed and heard the imprisoned bishop singing this hymn. According to the legend the king was so moved that he freed Theodulph and decreed the singing of "All Glory, Laud, and Honor" on all subsequent Palm Sundays.

Scripture References
st. 1-3 = Matt. 21:1-17
Mark 11:1-10
Luke 19:28-38
John 12:12-13
st. 2 = Rev. 5:11-12

The text was originally in thirty-nine Latin couplets, although only the first twelve lines were sung in ancient liturgical use (since a late-ninth-century manuscript from St. Gall). John M. Neale (PHH 342) translated the text into English in his *Medieval Hymns and Sequences* (1851). Neale revised that translation for *The Hymnal Noted* (1854); a further altered text was included in the original edition of *Hymns Ancient and Modern* (1861).

Based on Matthew 21:1-11 (and similar passages in Mark 11, Luke 19, and John 12), the text was originally written for a Palm Sunday procession. Thus it reflects on the original Palm Sunday's hymns of praise by the Jews as well as on our praise today.

Tune

Now often named ST. THEODULPH because of its association with this text, the tune is also known, especially in organ literature, as VALET WILL ICH DIR GEBEN. It was composed by Melchior Teschner (b. Fraustadt [now Wschowa, Poland], Silesia, 1584; d. Oberpritschen, near Fraustadt, 1635) for "Valet will ich dir geben," Valerius Herberger's hymn for the dying. Teschner composed the tune in two five-voice settings, published in the leaflet *Ein andächtiges Gebet* in 1615.

Teschner studied philosophy, theology, and music at the University of Frankfurt an-der-Oder and later studied at the universities of Helmstedt and Wittenberg, Germany. From 1609 until 1614 he served as cantor in the Lutheran church in Fraustadt, and from 1614 until his death he was pastor of the church in Oberpritschen.

ST. THEODULPH is a vigorous, bar form (AAB) tune with a strong ascending figure in the opening line. The tune has an exuberance marred only by the low-pitched ending; some congregations may prefer C major.

Two harmonizations are provided. The one at 375 by William H. Monk (PHH 332) was first published in *Hymns Ancient and Modern* (1861). The harmonization at 376 is by Johann S. Bach (PHH 7), taken from his *St. John Passion*. For either one use a large organ registration, perhaps with brass fanfares/interludes. Try using the fine double descant by Randall De Bruyn (b. Portland, OR, 1947) for stanza 3 with a ritardando at the very end of the stanza (376).

De Bruyn attended Lewis and Clark College, Portland, Oregon, and the University of Illinois (M.M. and D.M.A.). Many of his compositions and arrangements have been published by Oregon Catholic Press, where he has been music editor and currently serves as staff composer and arranger. His *Traditional Choral Praise* (1992) contains at least 160 hymn arrangements for SATB and SAB choirs with vocal and instrumental descants.

Many composers have composed organ music on this tune. Hal Hopson's *The Singing Bishop,* a children's musical based on this hymn, could provide an effective prelude for a Palm Sunday service.

Liturgical Use

Palm Sunday morning processional; possibly during Advent.

377

WERE YOU THERE
♩ = 50

Were You There

Text

An African American spiritual that probably predates the
Civil War, "Were You There" was first published in William
Barton's *Old Plantation Hymns* (1899). The spiritual's
earlier roots include a white spiritual known in Tennessee
as "Have you heard how they crucified my Lord?"
Additional stanzas are available from oral and written tradition:

Scripture References
st. 1-2 = Matt. 27:55-56
st. 3 = Luke 23:55
st. 4 = Matt. 28:1-7

> Were you there when they pierced him in the side?
> Were you there when the sun refused to shine?

Just as modern Jews identify with the Hebrew slaves in Egypt at their Passover Seder
("When I was in Egypt"), we are encouraged in this text to identify with the witnesses to
Christ's death and resurrection. With distances of geography and time removed, we
become part of that great body of people who come trembling to the cross of Christ for
salvation. ("Tree" in stanza 2 refers, of course, to the cross, but it was undoubtedly
significant to black slaves who witnessed lynchings.)

Tune

The congregation could sing the entire spiritual, but the tune has a call-and-response
structure; try singing unaccompanied with a soloist asking the initial questions in each
stanza and the congregation joining in at "Oh, sometimes." The soloist could take
significant liberty with the melody and rhythm, and congregations could also treat the
"tremble" figure with freedom. Try having the choir hum the parts as background for
the solo voice. Although the preferred practice is to sing unaccompanied, "Were You
There" could be accompanied by flute or guitar. The harmony was composed by
C. Winfred Douglas (PHH 342).

Liturgical Use

Stanzas 1-3 on Good Friday; stanzas 1-4 during the Paschal Vigil or at Easter sunrise
services.

378

Hosanna, Loud Hosanna

ELLACOMBE
♩ = 63

Text

Like "All Glory, Laud, and Honor" (375/376), this text is based on Christ's triumphal entry on Palm Sunday. However, "Hosanna, Loud Hosanna" focuses more on the children's role in that event. The text was written by Jeannette Threlfall (b. Blackburn, Lancashire, England, 1821; d. Westminster, London, 1880) in an "idle moment" (as she says she wrote all of her hymns, all others of which have been forgotten). Undoubtedly, Threlfall had Mark 11 in mind when she wrote this text, but she also alludes to Jesus' welcoming of the children in Mark 10:13-16. Stanzas 1 and 2 tell how the children shared in the songs during Christ's procession into Jerusalem. Stanza 3 is our cue to participate in praising our Redeemer.

Scripture References
st. 1-3 = Matt. 21:1-17
Mark 11:1-10
Luke 19:28-38
John 12:12-13

Threlfall's life was extremely difficult: she was orphaned at an early age, and two serious accidents caused her to be an invalid for life. But she bore her misfortune with grace and fortitude and maintained a ministry to many people who came in contact with her. Threlfall wrote devotional verse, which was published anonymously in various periodicals and later collected in *Woodsorrel, or Leaves from a Retired Home* (1856) and *Sunshine and Shadow* (1873), which included "Hosanna, Loud Hosanna."

Tune

Published in a chapel hymnal for the Duke of Würtemberg (*Gesangbuch der Herzogl,* 1784), ELLACOMBE (the name of a village in Devonshire, England) was first set to the words "Ave Maria, klarer und lichter Morgenstern." During the first half of the nineteenth century various German hymnals altered the tune. Since ELLACOMBE's inclusion in the 1868 Appendix to *Hymns Ancient and Modern,* where it was set to John Daniell's children's hymn "Come, Sing with Holy Gladness," its use throughout the English-speaking world has spread.

ELLACOMBE is a rounded bar form (AABA), rather cheerful in character, and easily sung in harmony. Try having a soloist sing the story in stanzas 1 and 2, with the children (or entire congregation) joining in on stanza 3.

Liturgical Use

Palm Sunday, in conjunction with the Palm Sunday gospel reading or the children's message.

♩ = 60

What Wondrous Love

Text

Although various sources have attributed this text to a number of different writers, it remains anonymous. "What Wondrous Love" was first published in both Stith Mead's hymnal for Methodists, *A General Selection of the Newest and Most Admired Hymns and Spiritual Songs* (1811), and in Starke Dupuy's hymnal for Baptists, *Hymns and Spiritual Songs* (1811).

Scripture References
all st. = Rev. 5

Like 103 and 305, the text is addressed to the soul. It meditates on Christ's wonderful love (st. 1), which brought about our salvation (st. 2), a love to which we and the "millions" respond with eternal praise (st. 3-4).

Tune

WONDROUS LOVE was first set to this text in William Walker's (PHH 44) second edition of *Southern Harmony* (1840). Publication of the hymn in B. F. White's *The Sacred Harp* (1844) further promoted the combination of text and tune. The meter of "What Wondrous Love" derives from an old English ballad about the infamous pirate Captain Kidd:

My name was Robert Kidd, when I sailed, when I sailed;
My name was Robert Kidd, when I sailed;
My name was Robert Kidd, God's laws I did forbid,
So wickedly I did when I sailed, when I sailed
So wickedly I did when I sailed.

Described by Erik Routley (PHH 31) as "incomparably beautiful," the tune is in ABA form and in Dorian or Aeolian mode (depending on which version is used or which "authentic" performance is heard). The setting is by Emily R. Brink (PHH 158). *The Hymnal 1982* (439) includes the original three-part setting with the melody in the tenor; that setting could be useful for choirs alternating with the congregation on the hymnal setting. Sing unaccompanied, or use light accompaniment for stanzas 1 and 2, gradually becoming more forceful through stanza 3, and use full organ (or piano) for stanza 4.

Liturgical Use

Lent; stanzas 1-3 for services of confession/forgiveness; funeral services (entire hymn); stanza 2 with preaching about Jonah; stanza 3 as a doxology.

380

O Perfect Life of Love

SOUTHWELL
♩ = 52

Text

Because of how well biblical phrases and theological statements are packed into such short meter, John Julian calls this a text "of much merit." Written by Henry W. Baker (PHH 342) in seven stanzas, "O Perfect Life of Love" was first published in the 1875 edition of *Hymns Ancient and Modern* as a hymn for Passiontide.

Scripture References
st. 1-5 = John 19:30

The text meditates on the suffering and death of Christ, "that he might make us whole" (st. 1-5), confesses our total dependence on the merits of Christ (st. 6), and prays that our response to Christ's love may be a life of love and service (st. 7).

Tune

SOUTHWELL first appeared as a setting for Psalm 45 in John Bull's unauthorized publication of William Daman's *The Psalmes of David* (1579).

Lord Buckhorst, an English music patron who supported an international group of musicians, brought William Daman (b. Liège, Belgium, c. 1540; d. London, England, 1591) to England in 1565 to serve as a musician in his court. In 1579 Daman became one of the court musicians to Queen Elizabeth. His greatest contribution to hymnody was his harmonizations of the tunes found in the *Sternhold and Hopkins Psalter,* published as *The Psalmes of David in English Meter, with Notes of Foure Partes set unto them* (1579, 1591). In this work's second volume Daman often placed the main tune in the soprano rather than in the more traditional tenor part.

SOUTHWELL, with the melody in the tenor, was included in Daman's 1591 collection as a setting for Psalm 45. In his 1612 *Psalter* Thomas Ravenscroft named the tune after the cathedral city in Nottinghamshire, England. The simple Dorian tune is one of the earliest in short meter (66 86). It consists of two opening phrases followed by a long closing line. The original version contained more rhythmic interest, particularly in the third phrase, than the isorhythmic (all equal rhythms) version in most modern hymnals. Sing in parts and assign various stanzas to antiphonal groups in the congregation. Reserve stanzas 6 and 7 for the entire congregation to sing in unison.

Liturgical Use

Holy Week; stanzas 6 and 7 in worship services of confession/forgiveness or in other prayer services (including times other than Holy Week).

381

Go to Dark Gethsemane

Text

James Montgomery (PHH 72) wrote two versions of "Go to Dark Gethsemane," the first of which appeared in Thomas Cotterill's *Selection of Psalms and Hymns* in 1820. The second version, originally published in his *Christian Psalmist* (1825), is the more common one found in hymnals today. Small alterations have been made in the text, most notably the change from a command ("learn of Jesus Christ to pray") to a prayer of petition in the final phrase in each stanza. Many hymnals delete his original fourth stanza, which focused on Christ's resurrection.

Scripture References
st. 1 = Mark 14:32-42
st. 2 = John 18:28
John 19:16
1 Pet. 2:21
st. 3 = John 19:17-30

The text exhorts us to follow Christ as we meditate on his sorrow in the Garden of Gethsemane (st. 1), on his suffering on the cross (st. 2), and on his sacrificial death (st. 3); each stanza ends with a corresponding petition.

Tune

For commentary on Richard Redhead and REDHEAD 76, see PHH 255 (there the tune is in E-flat rather than in D). Sing the stanzas in parts, but sing in unison on the petition phrases that conclude each stanza.

Liturgical Use

Holy Week, especially on Good Friday.

382

Ride On, Ride On in Majesty

Text

Henry H. Milman (b. St. James, London, England, 1791; d. Sunninghill, Berkshire, England, 1868) wrote this text around 1822. It was first published in Reginald Heber's (PHH 249) *Hymns Written and Adapted to the Weekly Church Services of the Year* (1827). Of the text of this fine Palm Sunday hymn, Stanley L. Osborne (PHH 395) has written,

Scripture References
all st. = Matt. 21:1-17

> Objective, robust, confident, and stirring, it possesses that peculiar combination of tragedy and victory which draws the singer into the very centre of the drama. It is this which gives the hymn its power and its challenge (*If Such Holy Song*, 449).

The text unites meekness and majesty, sacrifice and conquest, suffering and glory—all central to the gospel for Palm Sunday. Each stanza begins with "Ride on, ride on in majesty." Majesty is the text's theme as the writer helps us to experience the combination of victory and tragedy that characterizes the Triumphal Entry. Christ is hailed with "Hosanna" as he rides forth to be crucified (st. 1). That death spells victory: it is his triumph "o'er captive death and conquered sin" (st. 2). God the Father awaits Christ's victory with expectation (st. 3). Finally, Christ rides forth to take his "power . . . and reign!" (Note how "reign" is subtly offered as both noun and verb.) The original third stanza was not included.

Milman was a playwright, professor of poetry, historian, theologian, churchman, and hymn writer—and he was successful in all these areas. He graduated from Brasenose College, Oxford, England, in 1816, and by 1823 had written three popular plays with religious themes. He was appointed professor of poetry at Oxford in 1821 but turned to the study of church history after 1827. His *History of the Jews* (1829), which raised vehement protest from reviewers, was influenced by the new critical German methods. Ordained in 1817, Milman served St. Mary's Church in Reading and St. Margaret's Church in London; his most illustrious church appointment was as dean of St. Paul's Cathedral, London, a position he held from 1849 until his death. His finest scholarly work is his *History of Latin Christianity* (1854). Milman wrote thirteen hymns, all published in Bishop Heber's *Hymns* (1827).

Tune

Henry B. Hays (b. Clarksville, TN, 1920) composed CHICKAHOMINY, which was published in his collection of hymn tunes, *Swayed Pines Song Book* (1981). Hays was raised in the Protestant tradition but since the 1950s has been a Benedictine monk at St. John's Abbey in Collegeville, Minnesota. A Civil War devotee, he has derived his hymn tune titles from names of battles or places associated with that war.

CHICKAHOMINY is a stirring tune that fits well with this text. The tune is marked by well-placed descending and ascending melodic figures; the final phrase was rhythmically simplified. Although part singing is possible on the middle stanzas, try having the group or congregation sing in unison throughout (but especially on st. 1 and 4). The hymn needs forceful accompaniment and surely requires a raised third on the final chord of stanza 4!

Liturgical Use

Obligatory for every Palm Sunday morning worship service (with 375/376).

383

O Sacred Head, Now Wounded

Text

Originally from a Latin poem beginning "Salve mundi salutare" and attributed to either Bernard of Clairvaux (twelfth century) or Arnulf von Loewen (thirteenth century), "O Sacred Head" is one of seven sections to be used for meditation during Holy Week. Each section focuses on one aspect of Christ's dying body.

Scripture References
st. 1 = Matt. 27:29
Mark 15:17-18
John 19: 2-3
Isa. 53:3-5

Paul Gerhardt (PHH 331) translated the seventh section ("Salve caput cruenta-tum"), which addresses Christ's head, into German ("O Haupt voll Blut und Wunden"). His ten-stanza translation was published in Johann Crüger's (PHH 42) *Praxis Pietatis Melica* (1656).

The English translation is mainly the work of James W. Alexander (b. Hopewell, Louisa County, VA, 1804; d. Sweetsprings, VA, 1859). It was published in Joshua Leavitt's *The Christian Lyre* (1830) and revised by Henry W. Baker (PHH 342) for *Hymns Ancient and Modern* (1861). Alexander was often overshadowed by his father, the renowned Archibald Alexander, first professor at Princeton Theological Seminary. But James Alexander was also a fine preacher, teacher, and writer. He studied at New Jersey College (now Princeton University) and Princeton Seminary. Ordained in the Presbyterian Church, he alternated his career between teaching and pastoring; for two years (1849-1851) he was professor of ecclesiastical history and church government at Princeton Seminary. Alexander translated a number of hymns from Greek, Latin, and German but is mainly known today for his translation of "O Sacred Head."

"O Sacred Head" has enjoyed great popularity since 1656; the hymn appears in all modern hymnals, in many languages and translations, and with various numbers of stanzas. Deeply devotional, the text makes a very personal application of Christ's atoning death (st. 1-2) and confesses our gratitude and commitment to Christ (st. 3).

Tune

The tune HERZLICH TUT MICH VERLANGEN has been associated with Gerhardt's text since they were first published together in 1656. The tune's first association with a sacred text was its attachment in 1913 to Christoph Knoll's funeral text "Herzlich tut mich verlangen" (hence the tune name). It was originally a court song by the great Renaissance composer Hans Leo Hassler (b. Nüremberg, Germany, 1564; d. Frankfurt, Germany, 1612), published in his *Lustgarten neuer teutscher Gesäng* (1601).

Hassler came from a family of famous musicians. He received his early education from his father in Nüremberg, then studied in Venice with Andrea Gabrieli and became friends with Giovanni Gabrieli. In Venice he learned the polychoral style, for

which the Gabrielis were justly famous, and brought this practice back with him to
Germany. Hassler served as organist and composer for Octavian Fugger, the princely
art patron of Augsburg (1585-1601), as director of town music and organist in the
Frauenkirche in Nürëmberg (1601-1608), and finally as court musician for the Elector
of Saxony in Dresden (1608-1612). A Lutheran, Hassler composed for both the Roman
Catholic liturgy and for Lutheran churches. Among his many works are two volumes of
motets (1591, 1601), a famous collection of court songs, *Lustgarten neuer Deutscher
Gesang* (1601), chorale motets, *Psalmen und christliche Gesänge* (1607), and a volume of
simpler hymn settings, *Kirchengesänge, Psalmen und geistliche Lieder* (1608).

The isorhythmic (all equal rhythms) setting was adapted from one of the harmonizations composed by Johann S. Bach (PHH 7) for his *St. Matthew Passion* (1729). Many
composers have written organ music based on this tune; various melodic and rhythmic
versions exist.

HERZLICH TUT MICH VERLANGEN (also known as ACH HERR, MICH ARMEN SUNDER,
and PASSION CHORALE) is a bar form tune (AAB) with a glorious melody whose beauty
has done much to fit the private devotional text onto the lips of congregations. Sing
stanzas 1 and 3 in unison and stanza 2 in harmony (possibly unaccompanied with a
confident congregation or choir). Keep a subdued registration on the organ and always
accompany at a sustained pace.

Liturgical Use
Good Friday.

384

When I Survey the Wondrous Cross

Text
Many consider "When I Survey" to be the finest hymn text written
by Isaac Watts (PHH 155). In fact, Charles Wesley (PHH 267) is
said to have thought it was better than any of his own hymn texts.
Watts published it in *Hymns and Spiritual Songs* (1707) as part of a
group of hymns for the Lord's Supper. The text arose out of
Watts's meditation on Galatians 6:14: "May I never boast except in
the cross of our Lord Jesus Christ. . . ." Originally in five stanzas (the fourth is commonly omitted), the text was subtitled "Crucifixion to the World, by the Cross of Christ."

Scripture References
st. 1 = Phil. 3:7-8
st. 2 = Gal. 6:14
st. 3 = Matt. 27:29
st. 4 = Rom. 12:1

The text is a meditation on Christ's atoning death: at the cross God's love is revealed
to each believer, requiring total commitment to Christ—"my soul, my life, my all!" Watts's
profound and awe-inspiring words provide an excellent example of how a hymn text by a
fine writer can pack a great amount of systematic theology into a few memorable lines.

Tune

Lowell Mason (PHH 96) composed HAMBURG (named after the German city) in 1824. The tune was published in the 1825 edition of Mason's *Handel and Haydn Society Collection of Church Music.* Mason indicated that the tune was based on a chant in the first Gregorian tone.

HAMBURG is a very simple tune with only five tones; its simplicity allows us to focus entirely on the text. Sing stanzas 1-3 in harmony and stanza 4 in unison. Try singing one of the middle stanzas unaccompanied. Although some prefer larger organ accompaniment on stanza 4, Watts's profound text can also suggest a more quiet and humble treatment.

The suggested alternate tune ROCKINGHAM (178) is also closely associated with this text, especially in British and Canadian hymnals.

Liturgical Use

Lent; Holy Week; Lord's Supper; many other occasions—perhaps profession of faith, adult baptism, and similar times of consecration and renewal—especially with the unqualified commitment of stanza 4.

385

MARTYRDOM
♩ = 44

Alas! And Did My Savior Bleed

Text

Written by Isaac Watts (PHH 155) in six stanzas, this text was published in Watts's *Hymns and Spiritual Songs* in 1707. The final line in stanza 1 originally read, "for such a worm as I."

Scripture References
st. 2 = Mark 15:34
st. 3 = Mark 15:33

Watts's original heading for the text, "Godly sorrow arising from the suffering of Christ," fits stanzas 1-3 well. Stanza 3 contains the profound paradox of God the creator dying for the sin of human creatures: "Christ, the mighty Maker, died for his own creatures' sin." Stanza 4 moves from penitent sorrow to gratitude and tears of joy.

Tune

MARTYRDOM was originally an eighteenth-century Scottish folk melody used for the ballad "Helen of Kirkconnel." Hugh Wilson (b. Fenwick, Ayrshire, Scotland, c. 1766; d. Duntocher, Scotland, 1824) adapted MARTYRDOM into a hymn tune in duple meter around 1800. A triple-meter version of the tune was first published by Robert A. Smith (b. Reading, Berkshire, England, 1780; d. Edinburgh, Scotland, 1829) in his *Sacred Music* in 1825, a year after Wilson's death. A legal dispute concerning who was the actual composer of MARTYRDOM arose and was settled in favor of Wilson. However, Smith's triple-meter arrangement is the one chosen most often. The tune's title presumably refers to the martyred Scottish Covenantor James Fenwick, whose last name is also the name of the town where Wilson lived. Consequently, in Scotland this tune has always had melancholy associations.

Hugh Wilson learned the shoemaker trade from his father. He also studied music and mathematics and became proficient enough in various subjects to become a part-time teacher to the villagers. Around 1800 he moved to Pollokshaws to work in the cotton mills and later moved to Duntocher, where he became a draftsman in the local mill. He also made sundials and composed hymn tunes as a hobby. Wilson was a member of the Secession Church, which had separated from the Church of Scotland. He served as a manager and precentor in the church in Duntocher and helped found its first Sunday school. It is thought that he composed and adapted a number of psalm tunes, but only two have survived because he gave instructions shortly before his death that all his music manuscripts were to be destroyed.

Although largely self-taught, Robert Smith was an excellent musician. By the age of ten he played the violin, cello, and flute, and was a church chorister. From 1802 to 1817 he taught music in Paisley and was precentor at the Abbey; from 1823 until his death he was precentor and choirmaster in St. George's Church, Edinburgh. He enlarged the repertoire of tunes for psalm singing in Scotland, raised the precentor skills to a fine art, and greatly improved the singing of the church choirs he directed. Smith published his church music in *Sacred Harmony* (1820, 1825) and compiled a six-volume collection of Scottish songs, *The Scottish Minstrel* (1820-1824).

MARTYRDOM has an effective melodic contour. Sing in harmony with subdued accompaniment. One pulse per bar permits singing in two long lines rather than four phrases.

Liturgical Use
Holy Week; with sermons on atonement and redemption.

386

Ah, Holy Jesus, How Have You Offended

HERZLIEBSTER JESU
$\downarrow = 52$

Text
Using imagery from Isaiah 53 as well as from other Bible passages, the text sets forth the Christian doctrine of Christ's atonement: Christ died for the sin of the world in a substitutionary death on the cross. The most striking aspect of the text is its personalization: it was for my sin that Christ died! Thus a generic doctrine has become a deeply personal confession and profound meditation.

Scripture References
st. 1 = Isa. 53:3
 John 1:11
st. 2 = Matt. 26:21-22
st. 3 = John 3:16-17
 John 10:14-15
 Gal. 2:20

Johann Heermann (b. Raudten, Silesia, Austria, 1585; d. Lissa, Posen [now Poland], 1647) wrote this text during the misery of the Thirty Years' War (1618-48). The fifteen-stanza German text ("Herzliebster Jesu, was hast du verbrochen") was published in Heermann's *Devoti Musica Cordis* in 1630 with the heading "The cause of the bitter sufferings of Jesus Christ, and consolation from his love and grace. From Augustine." Heermann based his text on the seventh meditation from Jean de Fécamp's *Meditationes,* a Latin work wrongly attributed by many scholars, including Heermann, to St. Augustine.

Heermann's own suffering and family tragedy led him to meditate on Christ's undeserved suffering. The only surviving child of a poor furrier and his wife, Heermann fulfilled his mother's vow at his birth that, if he lived, he would become a pastor. Initially a teacher, Heermann became a minister in the Lutheran Church in Köben in 1611 but had to stop preaching in 1634 due to a severe throat infection. He retired in 1638. Much of his ministry took place during the Thirty Years' War. At times he had to flee for his life and on several occasions lost all his possessions. Although Heermann wrote many of his hymns and poems during these devastating times, his personal faith and trust in God continued to be reflected in his lyrics. He is judged to be the finest hymn writer in the era between Martin Luther and Paul Gerhardt, one whose work marks a transition from the objective hymns of the Reformation to the more subjective hymns of the seventeenth century. His hymn texts were published in collections such as *Devoti Musica Cordis, Hauss- und Hertz-Musica* (1630, expanded in 1636, 1644), and *Sontags- und Fest-evangelia* (1636).

Based on both Latin and German sources, the rather free translation is by Robert S. Bridges (b. Walmer, Kent, England, 1844; d. Boar's Hill, Abingdon, Berkshire, England, 1930). That translation was first published in five stanzas in 1897 in *Hymns in Four Parts,* a hymnbook reissued in 1899 as the famous *Yattendon Hymnal.* In a modern listing of important poets Bridges's name is often omitted, but in his generation he was considered a great poet and fine scholar. He studied medicine and practiced as a physician until 1881, when he moved to the village of Yattendon. He had already written some poetry, but after 1881 his literary career became a full-time occupation, and in 1913 he was awarded the position of poet laureate in England. Bridges published *The Yattendon Hymnal* (1899), a collection of one hundred hymns (forty-four written or translated by him) with settings mainly from the Genevan psalter, arranged for unaccompanied singing. In addition to volumes of poetry, Bridges also published *A Practical Discourse on Some Principles of Hymn-Singing* (1899) and *About Hymns* (1911).

Tune

Partially based on earlier melodies (including the Genevan tune for Psalm 23), HERZLIEBSTER JESU was composed by Johann Crüger (PHH 42) and published in his *Neues vollkömliches Gesangbuch* (1640). Johann S. Bach (PHH 7) used the tune in both his *St. Matthew Passion* and *St. John Passion,* and various other composers have written preludes on the chorale.

HERZLIEBSTER JESU is a sober tune in minor tonality; it provides a strong match for Heermann's text. Sing with solemnity. Accompany in a subdued manner except at the final phrase of stanza 3, "for my salvation," a phrase that merits full organ accompaniment.

Liturgical Use
Lent; Holy Week; Lord's Supper.

387

Alleluia! Alleluia!

EBENEZER
♩ = 84

Text

Christopher Wordsworth (PHH 361) believed it was "the first duty of a hymn to teach sound doctrine, and thus to save souls." Consequently, many of Wordsworth's texts, including this one, are virtually short sermons in verse form. "Alleluia! Alleluia!" is one of two Easter hymns by Wordsworth in his *Holy Year* (1862). The text was originally in five stanzas; the original second stanza was not included.

Scripture References
st. 2 = 1 Cor. 15:3-4
st. 3 = 1 Cor. 15:20-23

The text proclaims the meaning of Christ's resurrection. The "alleluias" that begin stanzas 1, 2, and 4 and run throughout stanza 4 lift this teaching hymn to a high level of praise. The entire text is influenced by Paul's resurrection discourse in 1 Corinthians 15:1-28.

Tune

EBENEZER originally came from the second movement of an anthem ("Goleu yn y Glyn" or "Light in the Valley") by Welsh composer Thomas John Williams (b. Ynysmeudwy, Glamorganshire, Wales, 1869; d. Llanelly, Carmarthenshire, Wales, 1944). EBENEZER (meaning "stone of help" in the Bible) is named for the chapel in Rhos, Pontardawe, which Williams attended at the time he composed the tune. Although his primary vocation was in the insurance business, Williams studied with David Evans (PHH 285) at Cardiff and later was organist and choirmaster at Zion Church (1903-1913) and Calfaria Church (1913-1931), both in Llanelly. He composed a number of hymn tunes and a few anthems.

First published as a hymn tune in the *Baptist Book of Praise* (1901), EBENEZER is often associated in Wales with "Guide Me, O Thou Great Jehovah" (543). Because an English folksinger claimed that the tune had been washed up on the Welsh coast in a bottle, the tune is known in some hymnals as TON-Y-BOTL (tune in a bottle). In the United States, the tune gained popularity as a setting for the text "Once to Every Man and Nation."

Developed out of the opening motif, EBENEZER is a glorious tune built with just six notes and an energetic rhythmic pattern involving triplets. The tune is a rounded bar form (AABA) in which the "B" lines move momentarily into major. Sing stanzas 1 and 4 in unison and stanzas 2 and 3 in harmony. Sing with vigor and majesty, but do not rush! In Welsh practice the triplet is sung heavily; do not worry about making the dotted rhythms distinct from the triplets. Use rhythmically energetic accompaniment with fairly full organ, adding a crowning mixture and/or reed for stanza 4. Try finishing the final stanza with a major chord.

Liturgical Use
Easter; anytime, because every Sunday is a "little Easter." Stanza 4 is a fine doxology, thus the hymn is most useful at the close of services throughout the Easter season.

388

EASTER HYMN
♩ = 60
Christ the Lord Is Risen Today

Text

Charles Wesley (PHH 267) composed this "Hymn for Easter Day" in eleven stanzas. First sung at the famous Foundry Meeting House, the text was published in *Hymns and Sacred Poems* (1739). The "alleluia" responses, reflecting ancient Jewish and Christian practice, were added by later editors to fit the tune. Wesley's stanzas 1-2a and 3b-6 are included.

Scripture References
st. 1 = Matt. 28:1-10
st. 2 = Acts 2:24
st. 3 = Hosea 13:14
1 Cor. 15:55
st. 4 = Phil. 3:10-11
st. 5 = Phil. 2:10

The text contains some of the most familiar Easter themes: all creatures rejoice in Christ's resurrection (st. 1); the work of redemption is complete (st. 2); death is vanquished (st. 3); we have new life in Christ now (st. 4); we praise the victorious Christ (st. 5). The "alleluias," which remind us of the ancient Easter greeting, do more than interrupt the textual flow: they provide the framework for praising God with each line of text.

Tune

EASTER HYMN originally appeared in the John Walsh collection *Lyra Davidica* (1708) as a rather florid tune. Tempered to its present version by John Arnold in his *Compleat Psalmodist* (1749), EASTER HYMN is now one of the best and most joyous Easter tunes.

Composed by Paul Sjolund (b. Minneapolis, MN, 1935), the descant comes from *Hymns for the Family of God* (1976), which also provides additional parts for two trumpets. A composer, conductor, and festival director, Sjolund has had several hundred of his compositions published. He was minister of music at two Los Angeles churches: Bel Air Presbyterian Church (1959-1968) and La Canada Presbyterian Church (1968-1980). He has also been a consultant and contributor to several modern hymnals.

Wonderfully decorating the "alleluias," the melismas add a depth to our praise that a spoken "alleluia" cannot approximate (and that can be exceeded only by dancing such "alleluias"). The structure of text and music invites antiphonal performance. Try having small groups sing Wesley's words and the entire group sing the "alleluias." If the congregation wants to sing the entire hymn—and it often does—organists could point out the antiphonal character by playing the regular lines with a lighter accompaniment, or unison melody on some stanzas, and by changing to full organ and/or harmony for the "alleluias." Be sure to add the descant, especially on stanza 5, perhaps taking that stanza a bit slower.

Liturgical Use
Easter Sunday morning; a great processional hymn.

389

Come, You Faithful, Raise the Strain

ST. KEVIN
♩ = 66

Text

Eighth-century Greek poet John of Damascus (b. Damascus, c. 675; d. St. Sabas, near Jerusalem, c. 754) is especially known for his writing of six canons for the major festivals of the church year. (A canon is a form of Greek hymnody based on biblical canticles consisting of nine odes, each with six to nine stanzas.) His "Golden Canon" is the source of Easter hymns (see also 390). Written around 750 and inspired by the Song of Moses in Exodus 15, this text is John's first ode from the canon for the Sunday after Easter.

Scripture References
st. 1 = 1 Cor. 15: 20-28
st. 2 = Matt. 28:1-9

John's father, a Christian, was an important official at the court of the Muslim caliph in Damascus. After his father's death, John assumed that position and lived in wealth and honor. At about the age of forty, however, he became dissatisfied with his life, gave away his possessions, freed his slaves, and entered the monastery of St. Sabas in the desert near Jerusalem. One of the last of the Greek fathers, John became a great theologian in the Eastern church. He defended the church's use of icons, codified the practices of Byzantine chant, and wrote about science, philosophy, and theology.

All canons in the Greek church demonstrated how Old Testament prophecies were fulfilled in Christ's resurrection. The first ode of each canon was based on the Passover event and on Exodus 15 as the metaphor for Christ's delivery of his people from the slavery of sin and death (seen more clearly at 390). That metaphor lies behind stanza 1. Stanza 2 uses images of spring and sunshine as metaphors for the new life and light of Christ. Stanza 3 concludes the text with an Easter doxology.

John M. Neale (PHH 342) translated the text in his article on Greek hymnology in the *Christian Remembrancer* (April, 1859) and reprinted it in his *Hymns of the Eastern Church* in 1862.

The three stanzas are taken from Neale's stanzas 1a and 3b (st. 1), his stanza 2 (st. 2), and a doxology from the 1868 edition of *Hymns Ancient and Modern* (st. 3).

Tune

Better known as an operatic composer than a hymn-tune composer, Arthur S. Sullivan (PHH 46) composed ST. KEVIN for this text. Named by Sullivan after a seventh-century Irish monk, the tune was published in Joseph Barnaby's *Hymnary* (1872) as well as in Sullivan's *Church Hymns with Tunes* (1874).

For the sake of the text, sing and play in four long lines rather than eight choppy ones. Sing stanzas 1 and 2 in harmony and stanza 3 in unison.

Liturgical Use

Easter season.

390

FARMER
♩ = 72

The Day of Resurrection

Text

See PHH 389 for information about the origins of this text and John of Damascus.

This text also comes from John's first ode of the "Golden Canon," recognized as his finest work and written around 750. It was traditionally sung at midnight on Easter with the lighting of candles.

John M. Neale's (PHH 342) rather free English translation was published in his *Hymns of the Eastern Church* (1862). The first stanza uses the Old Testament Passover story as a metaphor for Christ's resurrection (as is customary in all the first odes of a Greek canon). In stanza 2 we, like the New Testament disciples, become witnesses to the risen Lord. Stanza 3 invites the entire cosmos to join in praise to the risen Christ.

Scripture References
st. 2 = Rev. 1:16
Matt. 28:9
st. 3 = Ps. 19:1
Ps. 150:6
John 16:22

Tune

The tune FARMER is marked by dramatically ascending melodic phrases and energetic rhythms in its opening lines. Sing in harmony throughout, possibly reserving unison for the third stanza. Use solid organ accompaniment; accompany with brass if possible.

Presumably, the source of FARMER is John Farmer's *Hymns and Chorales* (1892). A self-taught pianist, violinist, and harpist, Farmer (b. Nottingham, England, 1836; d. Oxford, England, 1901) studied music in Leipzig, Germany, and Coburg, Germany.

He taught in Zurich from 1857 to 1861 but then returned to England, where he taught at Harrow School—not in a traditional, academic manner but through lighthearted choral singing. In 1885 he became organist at Balliol College, Oxford, a position he retained until his death. At Balliol he introduced Sunday evening performances of classical music despite the objections of many church folk. He also wrote many songs for the Harrow School as well as oratorios and operas. Farmer was a major force in introducing Bach and Brahms to the English public. He edited works of Bach as well as *Hymns and Chorales for Schools and Colleges* (1892).

Liturgical Use

Easter, but this marvelous text may be sung any Sunday.

391

The Strife Is O'er, the Battle Done

VICTORY
♩ = 132

Text

This Easter hymn pictures Christ's death as the final battle with the powers of evil, but Christ is the victor; his resurrection marks the decisive outcome of that battle. Each stanza begins with some aspect of Christ's resurrection and moves to our response of praise. A poetic commentary on and summary of Paul's resurrection discourse in 1 Corinthians 15, the entire text is framed with "alleluias" (like some of the psalms).

Scripture References
st. 1 = 1 Cor. 15:20
st. 2 = 2 Tim. 1:10
Col. 2:15
st. 3 = Luke 24:26
st. 4 = Rev. 1:18
st. 5 = 1 Cor. 15:55

Although John M. Neale (PHH 342) believed this text came from the twelfth century, no medieval manuscript containing the text has been found. Based on a Latin hymn ("Finita iam sunt proelia"), "The Strife Is O'er" first appeared in the Jesuit collection *Symphonia Sirenum Selectarum* in 1695.

Francis Pott (b. Southwark, Surrey, England, 1832; d. Speldhurst, Kent, England, 1909) translated the text around 1859. The text was published in five stanzas in two 1861 hymnals: Pott's *Hymns Fitted to the Order of Common Prayer* and *Hymns Ancient and Modern* (with a few changes). Educated at Brasenose College, Oxford, England, Pott was ordained in the Church of England in 1856. However, his severe hearing loss caused his retirement from a pastorate at Norhill in Ely (1866-1891). A member of the committee that produced *Hymns Ancient and Modern* (1861), Pott also published original hymns, translations from Latin, and Syriac hymns in *Hymns Fitted to the Order of Common Prayer* (1861). During his retirement he devoted himself to improvements in worship and singing, and he edited *The Free Rhythm Psalter* (1898).

Tune

The origin of this tune lies in a choral mass by the great Italian Renaissance composer Giovanni Pierluigi da Palestrina (b. Palestrina, Italy, c. 1525; d. Rome, Italy, 1594). One of the most gifted composers of his age, Palestrina influenced church music for many centuries. He began his musical training at the age of nine when he went to Rome to become a chorister in the Church of Santa Maria Maggiori. By 1544 he was a singing teacher and organist at the cathedral in his hometown of Palestrina and had begun composing. In 1551 the bishop of Palestrina became Pope Julius III, and he took the musician with him to Rome.

Palestrina lived in Rome until his death. As his fame as choirmaster and composer grew, he held a series of increasingly prestigious positions—teacher at the Jesuit seminary from 1565 to 1571 and choirmaster at the Capella Giulia at St. Peter's from 1571 to 1594. His first decade in Rome was difficult: during that time he lost two sons and two brothers to epidemics, and in 1580 his wife died. Although Palestrina had begun preparation to enter the priesthood in 1581, he instead married the rich widow of a fur and leather merchant and then helped to conduct her business. A prolific composer, mainly of church music, he wrote one hundred masses and four hundred motets. For many years after the Council of Trent, Palestrina was considered the model composer for Roman Catholic liturgical music.

William H. Monk (PHH 332) adapted the first phrases of the Gloria Patri in Palestrina's *Magnificat Tertii Toni* (1591) to create VICTORY. Monk added his own "alleluia" at the close of the text. His arrangement was published in *Hymns Ancient and Modern* (1861).

Also known as PALESTRINA, the tune is rather sober but surrounded by festive "alleluias." The first three "alleluias" should be sung once at the beginning and once at the conclusion of the hymn; each stanza ends with its own "alleluia." Have everyone sing the "alleluias" in unison, but assign stanzas to antiphonal groups. Organists need to observe the rest in the final line of the stanza (just before the single closing "alleluia") with much care. This hymn is a good candidate for a brass ensemble, especially on the "alleluias."

GELOBT SEI GOTT (397) is a good alternate tune—it does not include the initial "alleluias" but does place three "alleluias" at the end of each stanza.

Liturgical Use

Easter; funerals.

392

A Shout Rings Out, a Joyful Voice
Daar juicht een toon

DAAR JUICHT EEN TOON
♩ = 60

Text

Eduard Gerdes (b. Kleef, the Netherlands, 1821; d. Doetichem, the Netherlands, 1898) wrote the Dutch text of this Easter carol ("Daar juicht een toon"). Text and tune were published in numerous editions of the Dutch *Zangbundel,* a hymnal compiled by Johannes De Heer and used in homes but never adopted by any Dutch Reformed denomination. Dutch immigrants who came to North America after World War II brought this song with them (see also 214). The text is a testimonial, a witness to the meaning of Easter: Christ Jesus has risen victoriously from the grave in triumph over death and hell (st. 1-3a); believers may claim Christ's victory now and forever (st. 3b-4).

Scripture References
st. 1 = Zeph. 3:14
st. 3 = 1 Cor. 15:55
st. 4 = Eph. 5:8

Evangelist, journalist, educational author, and hymn writer, Gerdes was an untiring worker for the church. His main vocation was as a preacher in evangelistic services, both among the laboring classes in Amsterdam and among the peat farmers in northern Holland. Born into a Lutheran home, Gerdes worked in Baptist as well as in Dutch Reformed Secessionist congregations. His writings include books on the study of foreign languages, stories for children, evangelistic tracts, and a number of hymns. His most popular hymn was "Er ruist langs de wolken" (1857), a Christmas hymn included by Canadian Leendert Kooi in *50 Favorite Dutch Hymns* (1986); the composite English translation there begins "There Rings Through the Clouds."

Tune

DAAR JUICHT EEN TOON is attributed to Henri A. C. Malan (PHH 288), renowned nineteenth-century Swiss reformer and evangelist. The tune consists of two long lines with ascending melodic phrases and strong cadential rhythms. Sing in harmony with strong organ accompaniment.

Liturgical Use

Easter season, but especially on Easter Sunday.

393

O Sons and Daughters

Text

This hymn was written in Latin by Franciscan (Minorite) friar Jean Tisserand (b. France, 15th century; d. 1494); it was found in an untitled booklet printed in Paris between 1518 and 1536. Tisserand's text, which began "O filii et filiae, Rex coelestis," was preceded by three "alleluias" and concluded by one. Several additional Latin stanzas were added at a later date. A popular preacher, Tisserand also composed other hymns in French and Latin. In 1492 he founded the Refuge of St. Madeleine, an institution for the rehabilitation of prostitutes.

Scripture References
st. 1 = 1 Cor. 15:55
st. 2 = Matt. 28:1
st. 3 = Matt. 28:2-7
st. 4 = John 20:24-25
st. 5 = John 20:26
st. 6 = John 20:27
st. 7 = John 20:28
st. 8 = John 20:29

John M. Neale (PHH 342) translated the text into twelve stanzas, which were published in his *Medieval Hymns and Sequences* (1851). That translation appeared in an altered form in *Hymns Ancient and Modern* (1861) and in various other hymnals. Neale's stanzas 1, 3, 5-7, and 8-10 form the present text.

Like 211, this hymn is a narrative Easter carol; it begins with the Easter gospel from Matthew 28:1-10 (st. 1-3) and concludes with the doubting Thomas story from John 20:19-29 (st. 4-8). This hymn and 394 are the two Easter hymns dealing with Thomas.

Tune

Although it was not published until 1623 in the Parisian collection *Airs sur les hymnes sacrez, odes et noëls* in four parts, O FILII ET FILIAE is thought to be contemporaneous with the text. The tune appears with small variations in a number of later songbooks and hymnals.

A joyful tune, O FILII ET FILIAE is appropriate for unison singing, but some of the stanzas and the final set of "alleluias" could easily be sung in parts. Sing the opening "alleluias," which frame the entire carol, once at the beginning and once again at the conclusion. Use strong accompaniment for the "alleluias" and lighter accompaniment for the stanzas. This folk-dance tune needs to proceed with one pulse per bar. Harmony singing and accompaniment must not slow down the tune's dance-like character.

Liturgical Use

Because the narrative covers two Easter season Sundays, the stanzas can be divided as follows: for Easter Sunday morning, stanzas 1-3, 5, and 8; for Easter evening, stanzas 1-4 and 8; for the Sunday after Easter (which usually includes the doubting Thomas story), stanzas 1 and 4-8. Stanza 8 is appropriate at any time as a sung beatitude.

394

These Things Did Thomas Count as Real
MERLE MARIE
♩ = 96

Text

Thomas H. Troeger (b. Suffern, NY, 1945) says, "I wrote [this] hymn to help people sing their way past doubt and skepticism to belief in the risen Christ." Inspired by the doubting Thomas story (usually read on the Sunday after Easter), Troeger wrote the text during a Lenten week he spent in the White Mountains of New Hampshire in 1983. Both text and tune were published in the Troeger/Carol Doran collection *New Hymns for the Lectionary—To Glorify the Maker's Name* (1986). "These Things Did Thomas Count" is one of the finest of Troeger's texts and indeed of the latter twentieth century.

Scripture References
all st. = John 20:24-29

Stanzas 1 and 2 describe Thomas's view of reality—so close to our own materialistic conception—in fresh language that recalls Christ's crucifixion. Stanza 3 depicts the movement from doubt to faith with that wonderful line, "until his fingers read like braille the markings of the spear and nail." Stanza 4 is a prayer for true faith to receive the Christ, who holds out his hands to us as he did to Thomas.

Following his education at Yale University, New Haven, Connecticut, and Colgate Rochester Divinity School, New York, Troeger was associate pastor of the Presbyterian Church in New Hartford, New York, from 1970 to 1977. In 1977 he became professor of preaching and parish ministry at his alma mater, now called Colgate Rochester Divinity/Bexley Hall/Crozer Theological Seminary. Since 1991 he has taught homiletics and communication at Iliff School of Theology in Denver, Colorado. Troeger is an active leader of workshops and seminars on worship and often does so in association with Carol Doran. Troeger and Doran have published several hymn collections: *Open to Glory* (1983), *New Hymns for the Lectionary* (1986), and *New Hymns for the Life of the Church* (1992), with texts by Troeger and tunes by Doran. Troeger has also written several other books, including *Are You Saved: Answers for the Awkward Question* (1980) and *Creating Fresh Images for Preaching* (1982).

Tune

Carol Ann Doran (b. Philadelphia, PA, 1936) composed the unison tune MERLE MARIE for this text in Rochester, New York, in 1983. The tune is named in honor of Troeger's wife. The symmetrical melody shifts between C major and B-flat major. Doran intended that this shift depict the two realities with which Thomas was struggling. Because this tune may not be easy for many congregations to sing, it would be helpful if organists could provide clear enunciation of the tune on a solo registration. A number of more familiar tunes might make this text more accessible, including BISHOP (227) or TRURO (413). MERLE MARIE works well with this text as a choir anthem.

Doran received a degree in music education from West Chester State University, Pennsylvania, and a Doctor of Musical Arts in organ and church music from the Eastman School of Music, Rochester. She was organist and choir director at the Twelve Corners Presbyterian Church, Rochester (1964-1969), and at the Episcopal Church of the Incarnation in Penfield, New York (1969-1982). Since 1975 she has taught church music at the Colgate Rochester/Bexley Hall/Crozer Theological Seminary. Doran has published three collections of her hymn tunes in cooperation with Thomas Troeger (listed above). She has written many articles and has established programs of study for both professional and amateur church musicians. Doran and Troeger frequently conduct workshops together on church music and renewal in worship.

Liturgical Use

Sunday after Easter (like 393); other services that focus on issues of doubt and faith; the text is also useful for individual study or for sermon material.

395

ARFON
$\rfrac{1}{2} = 54$

Hail, O Once-Despised Jesus

Text

The original two-stanza version of this text, now attributed to John Bakewell (b. Brailsford, Derbyshire, England, 1721; d. Lewisham, England, 1819), was published anonymously in the 1757 London pamphlet *A Collection of Hymns Addressed to the Holy, Holy, Triune God*. Bakewell was a lay evangelist and itinerant preacher in the Methodist tradition. He was personally acquainted with John and Charles Wesley (PHH 267) as well as with Augustus Toplady (PHH 497). Although he wrote several hymns and other devotional poetry, only "Hail, Thou Once-Despised Jesus" remains in common use.

Scripture References
st. 1 = Isa. 53:3-5
st. 2 = Rom. 5:11
st. 3 = Acts 5:31
Rom. 8:34
Heb. 7:25
st. 4 = Rev. 4:11
Rev. 5:12

Martin Madan altered and extended the text for his *Collection of Psalms and Hymns* (1760); later hymnal editors further altered the text. The present version is derived from the modernized text in *Hymns for Today's Church* (1982).

Described by Austin Lovelace as "rhymed theology," the text moves from Christ's suffering and death (st. 1-2) to his exaltation at the Father's right hand (st. 3-4); from our redemption and forgiveness (st. 1-2) to Christ's intercession for us (st. 3). Finally, we join in a cosmic praise of the Savior (st. 4).

Tune

ARFON is originally a six-phrase Welsh folk tune in minor tonality entitled "Tros y Garreg." Named for a district on the mainland of northern Wales opposite Mon and Anglesey, the tune was published in Edward Jones's *Relicks of the Welsh Bards* (1784). In the later nineteenth century ARFON was associated in France with the Christmas texts "Un nouveaux présent des cieux" and "Joseph est bien marié."

The tune is a rounded bar form (AABA), set here in major tonality. The harmonization, prepared by Stanley L. Osborne (b. Clarke Township, ON, Canada, 1907) in 1970, was published in the *Hymn Book* (1971), which was published by two Canadian denominations, the Anglican Church and the United Church. Osborne intended his harmonization first of all for a recorder ensemble and only secondarily for organ or voices. Use a clean, light accompaniment for stanzas 1 and 2 and a broader treatment for stanzas 3 and 4. Sing the middle stanzas in parts. Use trumpet accompaniment for stanza 4.

Osborne's interest in both pastoral work and church music is reflected in his education and career. Educated in music at Victoria University, Toronto, and in theology at Emmanuel College, Toronto, he received a Mus.D. from the University of Toronto in 1945 and a Th.D. from Victoria University in 1954. He was ordained in the United Church of Canada in 1932 and served five pastorates. In 1948 he became principal of the Ontario Ladies College (now Trafalgar Castle School), Whitby, Ontario, and in 1968, the full-time secretary of the committee that prepared the *Hymn Book* (1971). Osborne also published a handbook to that hymnal, *If Such Holy Song* (1976), which is characterized not only by solid scholarship but also by the expression of strong personal opinions. In 1986 he was appointed a Fellow of the Hymn Society in the United States and Canada.

Liturgical Use

Lent; Holy Week; Easter; Ascension; as a processional hymn for the beginning of worship services.

396

Low in the Grave Christ Lay

CHRIST AROSE
$\quad = 58$

Text

Robert S. Lowry (b. Philadelphia, PA, 1826; d. Plainfield, NJ, 1899) composed both text and tune of this Easter gospel hymn in 1874 while he was pastor of the First Baptist Church, Lewisburg, Pennsylvania. The hymn was published in *Brightest*

Scripture References
st. 1 = Matt. 27:59-60
st. 2 = Matt. 27:66
st. 3 = Acts 2:24
ref. = Matt. 28:2-10

and Best (1875), a church school songbook edited by Lowry and William Doane (PHH 473).

The meditative stanzas of this testimony hymn contrast with its dramatic refrain—"He arose!" That refrain recalls for us the angel's announcement: "He is not here; he has risen!" (Luke 24:6a). Originally the first line read, "Low in the grave He lay."

Although Lowry valued his preaching ministry much more than his writing of hymns, he attained a lasting name in the gospel music tradition. Educated at Bucknell University, he returned there to become a professor of rhetoric from 1869-1875. He was also a pastor at Baptist churches in Pennsylvania, New York, and New Jersey. Known nationally as the editor of numerous Sunday school song collections for publishers Biglow and Maine in New York, Lowry also collaborated with William H. Doane to produce gospel hymnals and Sunday school songbooks such as *Bright Jewels* (1869), *Hymn Service* (1871-1873), *Welcome Tidings* (1877), *Gospel Hymn and Tune Book* (1879), and *Glad Refrain* (1886).

Tune
The gospel tune CHRIST AROSE captures well the drama of Christ's resurrection with the ascending ("rocket") figures in the refrain. Undoubtedly, the refrain line has greatly enhanced this hymn's popularity. Sing in harmony with crisp rhythms and marcato accompaniment on the refrain. After the final stanza hold back the tempo on the last line of the refrain. Finish with "Christ arose" in three crashing chords with full organ. Sing the stanzas at a subdued pace, the refrain a bit faster.

Liturgical Use
Easter morning; for sunrise services play in the B-flat setting; for Easter morning worship at the usual hour look for a setting in C major (see 1959 *Psalter Hymnal*)—Easter mornings can bear that extra lift!

397

CHRIST AROSE
♩ = 58
Good Christians All, Rejoice and Sing

Text
While Headmaster of Eton College, Cyril A. Alington (b. Ipswich, England, 1872; d. St. Leonards, Hertfordshire, England, 1955) wrote this text for Melchior Vulpius's tune GELOBT SEI GOTT. The hymn was published in *Songs of Praise* (1931). Stanley L. Osborne (PHH 395) has written of Alington's stanzas, "They vibrate with excitement, they utter the encouragement of victory, and they stir the heart to praise and thanksgiving" (*If Such Holy Song*, 469). This text should not be mistaken for its Christmas counter-

part "Good Christian Friends, Rejoice" (355); both texts originally began, "Good Christian men, rejoice."

A strong text for Easter, "Good Christians All" rings in the victory of Christ's resurrections so that "all the world" will know the news. Each stanza encourages us to tell the good news and praise the "Lord of life," and ends with an exciting three-fold "alleluia."

Educated at Trinity College, Oxford, England, Alington was ordained a priest in the Church of England in 1901. He had a teaching career that included being headmaster at Shrewsbury School and Eton College. He was dean of Durham from 1933-1951 as well as chaplain to the king of England. His writings include literary works and *Christianity in England, Good News* (1945). Many of his hymns appeared in various twentieth-century editions of the famous British hymnal, *Hymns Ancient and Modern*.

Tune

Melchior Vulpius (b. Wasungen, Henneberg, Germany, c. 1570; d. Weimar, Germany, 1615) composed this tune as a setting for Michael Weisse's hymn "Gelobt sei Gott in höchsten Thron." Weisse's text was published with the tune in Vulpius's *Ein Schön Geistlich Gesangbuch* (1609). Because the text dates from the early sixteenth century, some scholars think the tune may have older roots.

Born into a poor family named Fuchs, Vulpius had only limited educational opportunities and did not attend the university. He taught Latin in the school in Schleusingen, where he Latinized his surname, and from 1596 until his death served as a Lutheran cantor and teacher in Weimar. A distinguished composer, Vulpius wrote a St. Matthew Passion (1613), nearly two hundred motets in German and Latin, and over four hundred hymn tunes, many of which became popular in Lutheran churches, and some of which introduced the lively Italian balletto rhythms into the German hymn tunes. His music was published in *Cantiones Sacrae* (1602, 1604), *Kirchengesang und Geistliche Lieder* (1604, enlarged as *Ein schön geistlich Gesangbuch*, 1609), and posthumously in *Cantionale Sacrum* (1646).

An exuberant tune, GELOBT SEI GOTT (also known as VULPIUS) is in triple meter. It reveals a Baroque playfulness in the syncopations in lines 2 and 3. Although the refrain is barred in triple meter, Germans would have sung it in duple meter with an accent on the second syllable of "alleluia."

Sing in unison or in parts. Try an antiphonal performance in which the choir or antiphonal groups sing the stanzas and the congregation sings the refrain. Choir sopranos could sing the descant by Emily R. Brink (PHH 158) on the refrain. Try also to sing one of the middle stanzas unaccompanied. Use strong, rhythmically precise organ accompaniment, especially on the cadences in phrases 2 and 3. On an average Sunday C major is a suitable key, but try D major on Easter Sunday or other festive days because that key is brighter. "Good Christians All" is also a wonderful piece for a brass choir.

Liturgical Use

Easter season; many other worship services.

398

Christ Jesus Lay in
Death's Strong Bands

Text

In preparing songs for congregational singing during the early
years of the Reformation, Martin Luther (PHH 336) often
turned to earlier sources. His intention with this chorale,
published in the Erfurt *Enchiridia* (1524), was to "improve" an
older German hymn—"Christ ist erstanden"—that was in turn
based on a medieval sequence, "Victimae Paschali laudes,"
attributed to Wipo, chaplain to Emperor Henry III (1017-
1056). Luther drew more on the original Latin text than on the German.

Scripture References
st. 1 = Acts 2:24
st. 2 = 1 Cor. 15:54-55
Isa. 25:8
Hos. 13:14
st. 4 = 1 Cor. 5:7-8

The English translation by Richard Massie (b. Chester, Cheshire, England, 1800;
d. Pulford Hall, Coddington, England, 1887) was published in Massie's *Martin Luther's
Spiritual Songs* (1854). Massie was the oldest of twenty-two children. Raised in the
rectory of St. Bride's in Chester, he remained in the Chester area his entire life, inherited two estates, and had the luxury of being able to devote much of his time to literary
pursuits. He taught himself German and translated many German hymns into English.
His publications include *Luther's Geistliche Lieder* (1854), two volumes of Carl Spitta's
hymns, *Lyra Domestica* (1860, 1864), and translations of chorales by Paul Gerhardt
(PHH 331). Many of his translations were first published in William Mercer's (PHH
357) *Church Psalter and Hymn Book* (1854).

The text emphasizes Christ's conquest of death, breaking of Satan's power, and
victory over the rule of evil (st. 1-3); it calls us to celebrate Christ's victory and his life-
giving sacrifice of himself at the feast of the Lord's Supper (st. 4-5). The reference in
stanza 4 and 5 to 1 Corinthians 5:7b-8, however, could be interpreted in a more general,
non-sacramental way.

Tune

CHRIST LAG IN TODESBANDEN is an adaptation of a medieval chant used for "Victimae
Paschali laudes" (the same chant is the source for CHRIST IST ERSTANDEN, 407). The
tune's arrangement is credited to Johann Walther (b. Kahla, Thuringia, Germany,
1496; d. Torgau, Germany, 1570), in whose 1524 *Geystliche Gesangk Buchleyn* it was first
published. But it is possible that Luther also had a hand in its arrangement.

Walther was one of the great early influences in Lutheran church music. At first he
seemed destined to be primarily a court musician. A singer in the choir of the Elector
of Saxony in the Torgau court in 1521, he became the court's music director in 1525.

After the court orchestra was disbanded in 1530 and reconstituted by the town, Walther became cantor at the local school in 1534 and directed the music in several churches. He served the Elector of Saxony at the Dresden court from 1548 to 1554 and then retired in Torgau.

Walther met Martin Luther in 1525 and lived with him for three weeks to help in the preparation of Luther's German Mass. In 1524 Walther published the first edition of a collection of German hymns, *Geystliche gesangk Buchleyn*. This collection and several later hymnals compiled by Walther went through many later editions and made a permanent impact on Lutheran hymnody.

One of the earliest and best-known Lutheran chorales, CHRIST LAG IN TODESBAN-DEN is a magnificent tune in rounded bar form (AABA) with a vigor and lightness characteristic of Easter carols. Many organ compositions are based on this tune; Johann S. Bach (PHH 7) incorporated it extensively in his cantatas 4 and 158.

Liturgical Use
Easter season; Lord's Supper.

399

Jesus Lives, and So Do We

JESUS, MEINE ZUVERSICHT
$\downharpoonleft = 69$

Text

Christian F. Gellert (b. Hainichen, Saxony, Germany, 1715; d. Leipzig, Germany, 1769) wrote the original German text ("Jesus lebt, mit ihm auch ich") in six stanzas. Published in Gellert's *Geistliche Oden und Lieder* (1757), the text is similar to "Jesus, meine Zuversicht," a chorale text often attributed to Dutch writer Luise Henriette of Brandenburg.

Scripture References
st. 1 = John 14:19
1 Cor. 15:55
st. 4 = Rom. 8:38-39
st. 5 = 1 Cor. 15:54
John 16:33

Gellert studied theology at the University of Leipzig and planned to become a pastor. Due to "congenital timidity" and poor memory, which made preaching impossible for him (the Lutheran Church in that era did not encourage pastors to read their sermons but to preach them from memory), he became a tutor. He went on to study philosophy at the University of Leipzig, where he was later appointed to the philosophy faculty. He became a popular lecturer and included among his students Goethe and Lessing. Gellert published various literary works, including the classic *Tales and Fables* (1746, 1748).

Calvin Seerveld (PHH 22) translated the text in 1985 in Toronto, Ontario; he borrowed the last line of each stanza from the translation by Australian John D. Lang, published in Lang's *Aurora Australis* (1826). It was first published in the 1987 *Psalter Hymnal*.

A strong text of comfort in Christ's resurrection, "Jesus Lives and So Do We" was inspired by John 14:19b, "Because I live, you also will live." Each stanza begins with the Easter faith: Jesus lives! We sing of Christ conquering death (st. 1), of his rule as king over all (st. 2), of his forgiveness of sin (st. 3), and of our security in his love (st. 4-5).

Tune

First published in Johann Crüger's *Praxis Pietatis Melica* (1653) without attribution, JESUS, MEINE ZUVERSICHT was credited to Crüger (PHH 42) in the 1668 edition of that hymnal. (The later isorhythmic RATISBON is related to this tune; see 34.) JESUS, MEINE ZUVERSICHT is named for its association with the text attributed to Luise Henriette (see above).

This splendid bar form (AAB) tune is set in its original rhythm. Sing stanzas 1-4 in harmony and stanza 5 in unison. Use solid organ tone to support the music.

Liturgical Use

Easter season; to comfort the sick and dying; funerals.

400

UPP, MIN TUNGA
♩ = 50

Praise the Savior Now and Ever

Text

Traditionally dated the year 569, the original Latin text "Pange, lingua, gloriosi proelium," was written by Venantius H. Fortunatus for the Holy Week offices of the medieval church.

Scripture References
st. 2 = Rom. 5:1-11
st. 3 = Gen. 3:15

Venantius Honorius Clematianus Fortunatus (b. Cenada, near Treviso, Italy, c. 530; d. Poitiers, France, 609) was educated at Ravenna and Milan and was converted to the Christian faith at an early age. Legend has it that while a student at Ravenna he contracted a disease of the eye and became nearly blind. But he was miraculously healed after anointing his eyes with oil from a lamp burning before the altar of St. Martin of Tours. In gratitude Fortunatus made a pilgrimage to that saint's shrine in Tours and spent the rest of his life in Gaul (France), at first traveling and composing love songs. He developed a platonic affection for Queen Rhadegonda, joined her Abbey of St. Croix in Poitiers, and became its bishop in 599. His *Hymns for all the Festivals of the Christian Year* is lost, but some of his best hymns on his favorite topic, the cross of Jesus, are still respected today, in part because of their erotic mysticism.

One English translation by John M. Neale (PHH 342) appears in many modern hymnals as "Sing, My Tongue, the Glorious Battle." But the version here comes through a Swedish translation ("Upp, min tunga, att lovsjunga") published in *Andeliga Psalmer och Wijsor* (1614). Johan O. Wallin revised the Swedish text, changing the Passiontide focus to an Easter focus.

Wallin's version, published in the *Svenska Psalmboken* (1816), was translated into English by Augustus Nelson (b. Asarum, Bleking, Sweden, 1863; d. Mankato, MN, 1949); it is one of seven Swedish hymns he prepared for the *Hymnal* (1925) of the Augustana Lutheran Synod. A revised version appeared in the 1958 *Service Book and Hymnal.*

Nelson graduated from Gustavus Adolphus College in St. Peter, Minnesota, and did graduate work in philosophy and history at Yale University and at Augustana Theological Seminary, Rock Island, Illinois. During his ministry he served parishes in Michigan, Illinois, Connecticut, Wisconsin, and Minnesota.

The text sets forth the gospel of Easter: Christ who died has risen in victory (st. 1), has set us free from sin (st. 2), and has conquered death and hell itself (st. 3); to that confession we respond with our praise—a doxology to the Trinity (st. 4).

Tune

UPP, MIN TUNGA was published anonymously in the 1697 edition of the *Swenska Psalmboken* in dotted rhythms rather than the present isorhythmic form (all equal rhythms).

A bar form (AAB) tune, UPP, MIN TUNGA consists of three long lines. Avoid turning the initial phrases of these lines into choppy phrases—strive for the longer lines! Sing this majestic chorale in harmony on stanzas 1-3 and in unison on stanza 4.

Liturgical Use

Easter; many other times.

401

Oh, How Good Is Christ the Lord
Oh, Qué Bueno Es Jesús

OH QUE BUENO
♩ = 66

Text

This hymn is one of a number of Spanish folk hymns sung by evangelical Christians throughout Central and South America. No other published source is known. Transcribed from a tape recording of a small Bible study group in Puerto Rico, the song was presented by a Hispanic task force charged with recommending Spanish-language hymns for the *Psalter Hymnal.*

The text presents the heart of the Christian confession of faith: Christ who died for our sin has risen again! We respond to this confession, "Glory be to Jesus." This acclamation is similar to the traditional liturgical response to the reading of the gospel text. To continue the confession, Bert Polman (PHH 37) wrote an additional stanza in 1987:

Oh, how good is Christ the Lord! He has sent his Spirit here
to lead us along the way. Glory be to Jesus!
Glory be to Jesus! Glory be to Jesus!
For his kingdom has no end. Glory be to Jesus!

Tune

OH QUE BUENO is a simple tune with musical phrases bound by one syncopated rhythm, a typical trait of many popular tunes from Latin America. The tune is a fine example of the Puerto Rican corito ("a little song"). It is intended for unison singing, but choirs may wish to try singing in harmony. Dale Grotenhuis (PHH 4) prepared the harmonization in 1985. Use light accompaniment with guitars or piano; improvise some additional percussion rhythms.

Liturgical Use

Easter season; as a short, sung confession of faith.

402

CHURCH STREET
♩ = 108

Alleluia, Alleluia! Give Thanks

Text

Surrounded by "alleluias," the text presents the good news of Easter: Christ is risen! In this hymn we sing Pauline phrases that proclaim the new life we have in the risen Christ.

Scripture References
st. 3 = Rom. 6:6
Gal. 2:20

Donald E. Fishel (b. Hart, MI, 1950) composed both text and tune "rather spontaneously" during the summer of 1971 in a house on Church Street in Ann Arbor, Michigan. The hymn was first sung in services of the Word of God Community in Ann Arbor, a charismatic Roman Catholic congregation that Fishel had then recently joined; he later served that community as publications editor of *Servant Music* (1973-1981). Fishel received a bachelor's degree in instrumental music education from the University of Michigan in 1972 and a degree in computer science from Eastern Michigan University in 1983. Since then he has worked in the computer industry.

Tune

CHURCH STREET has an ABA form with the A line being the antiphon or refrain. Also well known as ALLELUIA NO. 1, CHURCH STREET is a simple but effective folk-like tune.

Sing without pauses between the refrain and its stanzas. The setting is for harmony singing on the refrain and unison singing on the stanzas. See *Hymnal 1982* for a setting in the key of E with descant and piano accompaniment. Try using this hymn as an acclamation with the gospel reading during the Easter season: each Sunday during that season sing the refrain, a different stanza, and the refrain again. Make sure organ accompaniment is light; other instruments such as guitar, piano, and flute also work well.

Liturgical Use

Easter; suitable for many other occasions, including baptism and profession of faith.

403

This Joyful Eastertide

VRUCHTEN
♩ = 69 *(possibly faster with a small group of singers)*

Text

George R. Woodward (b. Birkenhead, Cheshire, England, 1848; d. Highgate, London, England, 1934) wrote the text of this Easter carol to fit the VRUCHTEN tune. The text expresses the joy Christ's resurrection brings to believers (st. 1); that joy provides a sense of security throughout our lives (st. 2) and gives confidence even in the face of death (st. 3). The hymn was first published in Woodward's *Carols for Easter and Ascension* (1894), which later became a part of the 1902 edition of his famous *Cowley Carol Book.*

Scripture References
st. 2 = 1 Cor. 15:51-52
ref. = 1 Cor. 15:14, 20

Educated at Caius College in Cambridge, England, Woodward was ordained in the Church of England in 1874. He served in six parishes in London, Norfolk, and Suffolk. He was a gifted linguist and translator of a large number of hymns from Greek, Latin, and German. But Woodward's theory of translation was a rigid one—he held that the translation ought to reproduce the meter and rhyme scheme of the original as well as its contents. This practice did not always produce singable hymns; his translations are therefore used more often today as valuable resources than as congregational hymns. With Charles Wood he published three series of *The Cowley Carol Book* (1901, 1902, 1919), two editions of *Songs of Syon* (1904, 1910), *An Italian Carol Book* (1920), and the *Cambridge Carol Book* (1924). Much of the unfamiliar music introduced in *The English Hymnal* (1906) resulted from Woodward's research. He also produced an edition of the *Piae Cantiones* of 1582 (1910) and published a number of his translations in *Hymns of the Greek Church* (1922).

Tune

VRUCHTEN is originally a seventeenth-century Dutch folk tune for the love song "De liefde Voortgebracht." It became a hymn tune in Joachim Oudaen's *David's Psalmen* (1685) as a setting for "Hoe groot de vruchten zijn."

The tune is distinguished by the melismas that mark the end of stanza lines and by the rising sequences in the refrain, which provide a fitting word painting for "arisen." Although the melody has a wide range, it has become a popular Easter carol in modern hymnals. The harmonization by Dale Grotenhuis (PHH 4) makes for glorious part singing (many hymnals use a harmonization by Charles Wood). Use medium organ accompaniment, possibly with a trumpet stop or real trumpets.

Liturgical Use

Easter season; funerals.

404

LYNGHAM
♩ = 76

Sing, Choirs of New Jerusalem

Text

Written in Latin by Bishop Fulbert of Chartres (b. Italy, c. 960; d. Chartres, France, 1028) early in the eleventh century, this Easter text originally began "Chorus novae Jerusalem." The text was used in British cathedrals and monasteries during the Easter season.

Scripture References
st. 2 = Rev. 5:5
Gen. 3:15
st. 3 = Col. 1:15-18

After studying at Rheims, Fulbert became head of the Cathedral School in Chartres. He lectured on various subjects, including medicine, and was able to attract many well-known scholars to the school; thus the Chartres institution was one of the best schools of its time. Appointed bishop of Chartres in 1007, Fulbert entered into the political and theological controversies of his day. He left a substantial body of writings, including hymns, some of which were used in the British medieval *Sarum Breviary*.

Robert Campbell's English translation in six stanzas, which originally began "Ye choirs of new Jerusalem," was published in Campbell's *Hymns and Anthems* (1850). The original stanzas 3 and 5 are omitted.

Referring to the songs of Revelation 4, 5, and 7, stanza 1 expresses the triumph of Christ's "paschal victory"; stanza 2 speaks of Christ as "Judah's Lion," who has "crushed the serpent's head"; stanza 3 is inspired by Colossians 1:15 18, and stanza 4 is a familiar Trinitarian doxology.

Tune

LYNGHAM is a fuguing tune by Thomas Jarman (b. Clipston, Northamptonshire, England, 1776; d. Clipston, 1862), published in his *Sacred Music* (around 1803). Jarman was a tailor by vocation, but he much preferred his musical avocation. He composed many hymn tunes, which were published in seventeen collections, including *The Northamptonshire Harmony* (1826), as well as in *The Wesleyan Methodist* periodical. Jarman was a popular choral director at the Clipston Baptist Chapel and at music festivals in neighboring villages.

Typical of fuguing tunes, LYNGHAM begins chordally and then moves to imitative lines that require part singing as well as repetition of some of the textual phrases. The tune has also been effectively set to "Oh, for a Thousand Tongues to Sing" (501).

The tune works well for choral singing and for congregational singing in parts. The rhythmic vitality of the music needs brisk organ accompaniment, but keep the accompaniment light as well as vigorous!

Liturgical Use

Easter; Ascension; other occasions when a more elaborate musical setting would be helpful to ascribe glory to Jesus; the final stanza makes a fine doxology for any service.

405

I Serve a Risen Savior

ACKLEY
♩ = 76

Text

Written by Presbyterian minister Alfred H. Ackley (b. Spring Hill, PA, 1887; d. Whittier, CA, 1960), both text and tune were published in the Rodeheaver hymnal *Triumphant Service Songs* (1933). (Rodeheaver was a gospel song publisher.) As told by hymnal editor George Sanville, the following incident provided the spark for Ackley's inspiration: a young Jewish man asked evangelist/musician Ackley, "Why should I worship a dead Jew?" To which Ackley replied,

Scripture References
ref. = Luke 24:6

But Jesus lives! He lives! I tell you. He is not dead, but lives here and now. Jesus Christ is more alive today than ever before. I can prove it by my own experience, as well as by the testimony of countless thousands.

Sanville goes on to explain,

Mr. Ackley's forthright, emphatic answer, together with his subsequent triumphant effort to win the man for Christ, flowered forth into song and crystallized into a convincing sermon on "He lives!" . . . The scriptural evidence, his own heart, and the testimony of history matched the glorious experience of an innumerable cloud of witnesses that "He lives," so he sat down at the piano and voiced that conclusion in song.

—Forty Gospel Hymn Stories, *1943*

Ackley wrote the words and/or tunes to at least a thousand gospel songs and hymns in collaboration with his brother Bentley. Trained at the Royal Academy of Music in London, he was an accomplished cellist. Ackley graduated from Westminster Theological Seminary in Maryland and served Presbyterian churches in California and Pennsylvania. In addition to writing his own hymns, he edited hymnals and gospel song-books for the Rodeheaver Publishing Company.

Tune

Composed in gospel-song style, ACKLEY is supported by a simple harmonization intended for part singing. Some rubato may be observed in the refrain's final line. Observe two pulses per bar.

Liturgical Use

Easter; equally useful on many other occasions of worship.

406

LOWELL
♩ = 63

Alleluia! Sing to Jesus

Text

In 1866 William C. Dix (PHH 358) wrote this text for the celebration of the Lord's Supper at Ascension services. Originally entitled "Redemption by the Precious Blood," the five-stanza text, in which stanza 5 was a repeat of stanza 1, was published in Dix's *Altar Songs, Verses on the Eucharist* (1867). The original stanza 4 as well as the repeated stanza are omitted here. As in earlier editions of the *Psalter Hymnal,* stanza 3 changes the original text, which was "Alleluia! Bread of heaven, Thou on earth our food, our stay."

Scripture References
st. 1 = Rev. 5:9
st. 2 = John 14:18
Acts. 1:9
Matt. 28:20

The "alleluias" that begin each stanza create a joyful tone of praise for the entire hymn. As we sing, we acclaim the glory of Christ now that the work of redemption is finished (st. 1); we are reminded that Christ has ascended but is always present with his people by his Spirit (st. 2); and we petition Christ to hear the cry of sinners and be our "Intercessor" (st. 3).

Tune

Composed in 1905 by H. Ernest Nichol (b. Hull, Yorkshire, England, 1862; d. Skirlaugh, Yorkshire, England, 1926), LOWELL was first introduced in the Christian Reformed Church when it was included in the *New Christian Hymnal* in 1929.

Nichol had begun a study program in civil engineering when he decided to study music instead. In 1888 he received a bachelor's degree in music from Oxford University. Nichol wrote some 130 hymn tunes and texts, many under the pseudonym

"Colin Sterne" (derived from his middle and last name); many were first sung at church school programs.

A strong tune, LOWELL consists of several dramatic melodic phrases that are repeated and varied. Sing stanza 1 in unison with full, bright accompaniment; sing stanzas 2 and 3 in harmony, preferably unaccompanied; then sing stanza 1 again in unison with full accompaniment, thus concluding the hymn in a more jubilant fashion (in tune with what Dix intended). Many other hymnals use HYFRYDOL (568) as a setting for this text.

Liturgical Use
Ascension Day, many other occasions.

407

Christ the Lord Ascends to Reign

CHRIST IST ERSTANDEN
♩ = 63

Text
As a basis for his text "Christus ist erstanden," Michael Weisse (b. Neisse, Silesia, Poland, c. 1480; d. Landskron, Bohemia, Czechoslovakia, 1534) turned to the same earlier sources that Martin Luther had turned to just a few years earlier (PHH 398). Weisse also reworked the older chorale "Christ ist erstanden," at

Scripture References
st. 2 = Rom. 8:34
Heb. 7:25
st. 4 = John 3:5

that time a popular "leise"—a song that included a "Kyrie eleison" refrain shortened to "kirleis" or "leis." The original "Christ is erstanden" was developed from the Latin sequence "Victimae Paschali laudes" (c. 1100). Weisse's chorale was published in the first German-language Bohemian hymnal *Ein Neugesängbuchlein* (1531), which he edited. The hymnal contained 155 hymns, with some original texts written by Weisse and others translated by him from Bohemian. Many of Weisse's hymn texts also found their way into later German hymnals.

Weisse was a monk in Breslau when he came in contact with the writings of Martin Luther. After leaving the Roman Catholic Church, he joined the Bohemian Brethren, spiritual descendants of John Hus, who were later called Moravians. A leader among the Bohemian Brethren, Weisse established a number of their German-speaking communities and was sent to consult with Luther on issues of theology.

Catherine Winkworth (PHH 194) translated Weisse's text, which was published in her *Lyra Germanica* (1858). Originally entitled "Song of Triumph," the translation began with the words, "Christ the Lord is risen again." The *Psalter Hymnal* includes Winkworth's stanzas 1, 3, 7, and 6 (in that order).

Stanzas 1 and 2 focus on the Christ, who suffered death on the cross but who is now exalted in glory as our mediator. Stanza 3 is a prayer especially suited for celebration of the Lord's Supper. Stanza 4 encourages us to preach the good news to extend Christ's kingdom. Each stanza concludes with an "alleluia." The final refrain rings in even more "alleluias" and includes the cosmic testimony "the Lamb is King of kings!"

Tune
CHRIST IST ERSTANDEN is derived from the twelfth-century chant melody for "Victimae Paschali laudes" (which also produced CHRIST LAG IN TODESBANDEN, 398). The tune was first published in Joseph Klug's (PHH 126) *Geistliche Lieder* (1533).

This ancient tune, originally in Dorian mode, consists of several melodic units that are repeated and varied. Dale Grotenhuis (PHH 4) wrote the harmonization in 1984. Sing stanzas 1-4 in unison with light accompaniment, but sing the "alleluia" at the end of each stanza in harmony. Use full accompaniment on the final refrain. Try also to sing some of the "alleluias" unaccompanied and/or incorporate the use of antiphonal groups.

Liturgical Use
Easter; Ascension; Lord's Supper.

408

DARWALL'S 148TH
♩ = 66

Rejoice, the Lord Is King

Text

Charles Wesley (PHH 267) wrote this text for Easter and Ascension in six stanzas. First published in John Wesley's *Moral and Sacred Poems* (1744), the text was also published in Charles Wesley's *Hymns for our Lord's Resurrection* (1746). The original stanzas 2 and 5 are not included.

Scripture References
st. 2 = Rev. 1:18
st. 3 = Acts 5:31
   Heb. 1:3
st. 4 = 1 Cor. 15:52
   1 Thess. 4:16
   Rev. 20:11-15
ref. = Phil. 4:4

The text rejoices in the kingship of Christ (st. 1) whose rule extends "o'er earth and heaven" (st. 2). All will bow the knee to Christ (st. 3) when he returns in glory to judge "the living and the dead" (st. 4). The refrain line based on Philippians 4:4, "Rejoice in the Lord always. I will say it again: Rejoice," is the keynote of the entire text.

Tune

Composed by John Darwall (b. Haughton, Staffordshire, England, 1731; d. Walsall, Staffordshire, England, 1789), DARWALL'S 148TH was first published as a setting for Psalm 148 in Aaron William's *New Universal Psalmodist* (1770) with only soprano and bass parts. The harmonization dates from the nineteenth century.

The son of a pastor, Darwall attended Manchester Grammar School and Brasenose College, Oxford, England (1752-1756). He became the curate and later the vicar of St.

Matthew's Parish Church in Walsall, where he remained until his death. Darwall was a poet and amateur musician. He composed a soprano tune and bass line for each of the 150 psalm versifications in the Tate and Brady *New Version of the Psalms of David* (1696). In an organ dedication speech in 1773 Darwall advocated singing the "Psalm tunes in quicker time than common [in order that] six verses might be sung in the same space of time that four generally are."

The only Darwall tune still in common use, DARWALL'S 148TH is marked by both its dramatic opening figure (outlining the tonic chord) and by the convincing ascent of the final line. Sing in unison or in parts at a lively tempo. Try adding trumpets both to the melody as well as to the descant by Sydney H. Nicholson (PHH 358) on stanza 4.

Liturgical Use
Ascension; Easter; a great hymn of praise suitable for any worship service (fits well with the royal psalms in the Old Testament); funeral or memorial service.

409

Hail the Day That Sees Him Rise

LLANFAIR
♩ = 66

Text
Considered to be the most popular of all Ascension texts in English-language worship, "Hail the Day" was written by Charles Wesley (PHH 267) in ten stanzas and published in his *Hymns and Sacred Poems* (1739). Thomas Cotterill (b. Cannock, Staffordshire, England, 1779; d. Sheffield, Yorkshire, England, 1823) altered the text and published his version in *Selection of Psalms and Hymns* (1820); the "alleluias" were added in George White's *Hymns and Introits* (1852). Included here with further alterations are original stanzas 1, 2, 4, 6, and 10.

Scripture References
st. 1 = Acts 1:9-11
st. 2 = Ps. 24:7-10
st. 4 = Rom. 8:34
　Heb. 7:25
　John 14:2
　1 Cor. 15:20-23
st. 5 = 2 Tim. 2:12

"Hail the Day" sings out its "alleluias" for Christ's triumphal entry into glory after he accomplished his saving work on earth (st. 1-2) and for Christ's work of interceding and preparing a place for his people (st. 3-4). The text concludes by hailing the great day when we shall rule with Christ (st. 5).

Thomas Cotterill studied at St. John's College, Cambridge, England, and became an Anglican clergyman. A central figure in the dispute about the propriety of singing hymns, Cotterill published a popular collection of hymns (including many of his own as well as alterations of other hymns), *Selection of Psalms and Hymns* in 1810. But when he tried to introduce a later edition of this book in Sheffield in 1819, his congregation protested. Many believed strongly that the Church of England should maintain its tradition of exclusive psalm singing. In a church court the Archbishop of York and

Cotterill reached a compromise: the later edition of *Selection* was withdrawn, and Cotterill was invited to submit a new edition for the archbishop's approval. The new edition was published in 1820 and approved as the first hymnal for the Anglican Church of that region. Cotterill's suppressed book, however, set the pattern for Anglican hymnals for the next generation, and many of its hymns are still found in modern hymnals.

Tune

LLANFAIR is usually attributed to Welsh singer Robert Williams (b. Mynydd Ithel, Anglesey, Wales, 1781; d. Mynydd Ithel, 1821), whose manuscript, dated July 14, 1817, included the tune. Williams lived on the island of Anglesey. A basket weaver with great innate musical ability, Williams, who was blind, could write out a tune after hearing it just once. He sang hymns at public occasions and was a composer of hymn tunes.

LLANFAIR was first published with a harmonization by John Roberts in John Parry's *Peroriaeth Hyfryd (Sweet Music)* (1837). The tune has been associated with the Wesley/Cotterill text since its publication with the text in *The English Hymnal* (1906). LLANFAIR is actually a common Welsh name, but some scholars believe that in this case the tune's name refers to the Montgomery County village in Wales where Williams was born.

A rounded bar form (AABA) tune, LLANFAIR features the common Welsh device of building a melody on the tones of the tonic triad. The tune is in a major key (not all Welsh tunes are in minor keys!). The melismas give fitting shape to the "alleluias." Use brisk accompaniment for this cheerful tune. LLANFAIR has a similar pattern to that of EASTER HYMN (388); see suggestions there for antiphonal style performance.

Liturgical Use

Ascension; other services that emphasize Christ's reign.

410

DIADEMATA
♩ = 60

Crown Him with Many Crowns

Text

This text is a composite of texts by two different authors, both of whom were inspired by the words from Revelation 19:12, "On his head are many crowns." Matthew Bridges's six-stanza text was published in his *Hymns of the Heart* in 1851. Asked to improve on Bridges's text, Godfrey Thring wrote a new text instead, which was published in his *Hymns and Sacred Lyrics* in 1874. Drawing from both authors' texts, the *Church of England Hymn Book* published a composite version of "Crown Him" in 1880.

Scripture References
st. 1 = Rev. 19:12
st. 3 = Isa. 2:4
Ps. 46:9

Most hymnals follow that example and include stanzas written by both Bridges and Thring; stanzas 1 and 3 are by Bridges, and stanza 2 is by Thring.

The text is a magnificent celebration of Christ's victory over sin and death and of his rule in the world. The "crown," which in Revelation refers to both the crown of royalty/kingship and the wreath of victory given to an athlete, symbolizes both the victory and the rule.

Matthew Bridges (b. Malden, Essex, England, 1800; d. Sidmouth, Devonshire, England, 1894) was raised in the Church of England. Though he wrote the anti-Roman Catholic book *The Roman Empire under Constantine the Great* in 1829, he came under the influence of the Oxford Movement and left the Church of England to become Roman Catholic. Bridges wrote a number of historical works, as well as poetry and hymns, and published them in collections such as *Hymns of the Heart* (1847) and *The Passion of Jesus* (1852). He lived in Quebec, Canada, for some time but returned to England before his death.

Geoffrey Thring (b. Alford, Somersetshire, England, 1823; d. Shamley Green, Guilford, Surrey, England, 1903) was born in the parsonage of Alford, where his father was rector. Educated at Balliol College, Oxford, England, he was ordained a priest in the Church of England in 1847. After serving in several other parishes, Thring returned to Alford and Hornblotten in 1858 to succeed his father as rector, a position he retained until his own retirement in 1893. He was also associated with Wells Cathedral (1867-1893). After 1861 Thring wrote many hymns and published several hymnals, including *Hymns Congregational* (1866), *Hymns and Sacred Lyrics* (1874), and the respected *A Church of England Hymn Book Adapted to the Daily Services of the Church Throughout the Year* (1880), which was enlarged as *The Church of England Hymn Book* (1882).

Tune
Composed for Bridges's text by George J. Elvey (PHH 48), DIADEMATA was first published in the 1868 *Appendix* to *Hymns Ancient and Modern*. Since that publication, the tune has retained its association with this text. The name DIADEMATA is derived from the Greek word for "crowns."

The tune is lively and buoyant (though the harmony lacks life, especially the inner voices). Sing a strong unison on stanza 3 if using the Hal H. Hopson (PHH 219) descant. A number of good choral and brass arrangements, useful for festive occasions, are available.

Liturgical Use
A fine doxology for festive worship services (especially Easter and Ascension); many other times of jubilant praise and adoration.

411

The Head That Once Was Crowned with Thorns

Text

Thomas Kelly (b. Kellyville, County Queens, Ireland, 1769; d. Dublin, Ireland, 1855) wrote some 760 hymn texts and composed a number of hymn tunes. Of all his texts, this is his finest; it is usually included without any alteration in hymnals today. It was published in the 1820 edition of Kelly's *Hymns on Various Passages of Scripture*.

Scripture References
st. 1 = Mark 15:17
Heb. 2:9
Rev. 19:12
st. 2 = Phil. 2:9
Rev. 19:16
st. 4 = Luke 10:20
st. 5 = 2 Tim. 2:12

A poetic commentary on Hebrews 2:9-10, the text was initially entitled "Christ Perfect Through Sufferings." The opening couplet is probably borrowed from a John Bunyan poem (from "One Thing is Needful," c. 1664) which begins:

The head that once was crowned with thorns
Shall now with glory shine;
The heart that broken was with scorns
Shall flow with life divine.

Kelly's text is an ideal teaching hymn, of which Erik Routley (PHH 31) says: "All the joy and hope of the Ascension, as seen by us through Pentecost, needs to be expressed in the singing of this hymn." We move from Christ's mock crowning by Roman soldiers to his celestial crowning: from his suffering to his glory. We learn that the way of Christ is the way of discipleship: those who bear the cross of suffering for Christ will also share in his glory and reign. Here we find all the joy and hope of the Ascension! The Timothy passage referred to in stanza 5 was probably an early Christian hymn.

A brilliant student, Kelly studied law at Trinity College, Dublin, but then experienced a religious conversion, which initially turned him into an ascetic. After further study he was ordained in the Church of Ireland (1792) and began preaching in Dublin. Judged by the archbishop of Dublin to be too evangelistic, Kelly was barred from preaching. He became an independent preacher and was instrumental in building three chapels, financed largely from his own and his wife's inheritances. He also shared his means generously with the poor of Ireland, especially during the famine of the late 1840s. He published *A Collection of Psalms and Hymns* (1802), *Hymns on Various Passages of Scripture* (1804), and *Hymns by Thomas Kelly, Not Before Published* (1815); his hymns became popular in Ireland, England, and America.

Tune

ST. MAGNUS first appeared in Henry Playford's *Divine Companion* (1707 ed.) as an anonymous tune with soprano and bass parts. The tune was later credited to Jeremiah Clark (b. London, England, c. 1670; d. London, 1707), who was a chorister in the Chapel Royal and sang at the coronation of James II in 1685. Later he served as organist in Winchester College, St. Paul's Cathedral, and the Chapel Royal. He shot himself to death in a fit of depression, apparently because of an unhappy romance. Supported by Queen Anne, Clark was a prominent composer in his day, writing songs for the stage as well as anthems, psalm tunes, and harpsichord works. One well-known piece, the *Trumpet Voluntary*, was long attributed to his contemporary Henry Purcell (PHH 612) but is now recognized as Clark's composition. Robert Bridges (PHH 386) and Ralph Vaughan Williams (PHH 316) reintroduced Clark's hymn tunes for congregational use in the twentieth century in the *Yattendon Hymnal* (1899) and *The English Hymnal* (1906).

Although ST. MAGNUS was originally used as a setting for Psalm 117, it has been associated with this text since they were combined in the 1868 *Appendix* to *Hymns Ancient and Modern*. The tune is named for the Church of St. Magnus the Martyr, built by Christopher Wren in 1676 on Lower Thames Street near the old London Bridge, England.

ST. MAGNUS consists of two long lines, each of which has its own sense of climax. The octave leap in the final phrase has a stunning effect, like a vault in a Gothic cathedral. Assign stanzas for antiphonal singing in unison and/or in harmony. Organ accompaniment should be lively, with full, bright registration.

Liturgical Use

Easter; Ascension; other festive worship services.

412

Jesus Shall Reign

DUKE STREET
♩ = 72

Text

Isaac Watts (PHH 155) based this hymn text on Psalm 72:12-19 and referred to verses 5 and 8 of the psalm as well. (For general comments on this psalm see PHH 72.) Originally in eight stanzas entitled "Christ's Kingdom among the Gentiles," the text was published in Watts's *Psalms of David, Imitated* (1719). The original stanzas 2, 3, and 7 are omitted, as is customary in modern hymnals.

Scripture References
st. 1 = Ps. 72:5, 8, 17
st. 2 = Ps. 72:15
st. 3 = Ps. 72:10-11
st. 4 = Ps. 72:12-14
st. 5 = Ps. 72:19
Rev. 5:11-14

Watts's text is a strong Christological interpretation of Psalm 72. We sing of the worldwide reign of Christ (st. 1), who is praised by all creatures (st. 2 and 5), and whose rule results in blessings on people "of every tongue" (st. 3) and redemption for the outcasts (st. 4). The text has a strong missionary focus.

Tune
First published anonymously in Henry Boyd's *Select Collection of Psalm and Hymn Tunes* (1793), DUKE STREET was credited to John Hatton (b. Warrington, England, c. 1710; d. St. Helen's, Lancaster, England, 1793) in William Dixon's *Euphonia* (1805). Virtually nothing is known about Hatton, its composer, other than that he lived on Duke Street in St. Helen's and that his funeral was conducted at the Presbyterian chapel there.

A sturdy and much loved tune, DUKE STREET has a generic resemblance to TRURO (413, 539) and to the African American gospel-style doxology (637). Sing stanzas 1 and 5 in unison; stanzas 2, 3, and 4 in harmony. The final stanza is a doxology that would be enhanced by a descant; it would also benefit from a stately tempo. Use strong and vigorous accompaniment with trumpets if possible.

Liturgical Use
Advent; Epiphany; Ascension; with mission themes; stanza 5 as a doxology; (see also suggestions at PHH 72).

413

TRURO
♩ = 88

Christ Is Alive! Let Christians Sing

Text
Brian A. Wren (PHH 311) wrote the text in Hockley, Essex, England, during April of 1968. Wren writes:

Scripture References
st. 1 = Zech. 8:18-23

It was written for Easter Sunday, two weeks after the assassination of Dr. Martin Luther King, Jr. I could not let Easter go by without speaking of this tragic event which was on all our minds. . . . The hymn tries to see God's love winning over tragedy and suffering in the world. . . . There is tension and tragedy in these words, not just Easter rejoicing.

First published in the British supplement *New Church Praise* (1975), the text was revised by Wren in 1978.

"Christ Is Alive" is a joyful celebration of Christ's resurrection (st. 1) and of his personal rule in a human world in which pain, war, and injustice abound (st. 2-4). Christ's transcendent and immanent reign is empowered by the Holy Spirit and will ultimately bring about a new creation (st. 5).

Tune

TRURO is an anonymous tune, first published in Thomas Williams's *Psalmodia Evangelica* (second vol., 1789) as a setting for Isaac Watts's "Now to the Lord a noble song." Virtually nothing is known about this eighteenth-century British editor of the two-volume *Psalmodia Evangelica,* a collection of three-part psalm and hymn tunes for "Churches, Chapels, and Dissenting Meetings in England, Scotland, and Ireland." The tune is named for an ancient city in Cornwall, England, famous for its cathedral and for its pottery.

TRURO's opening phrase ascends the octave. The entire tune is influenced by George F. Handel's style and bears relationship to similar tunes (see comments at PHH 412). Sing stanzas 1 and 5 in unison, stanzas 2-4 in harmony with stanza 4 unaccompanied. Use clear articulation on the organ and a moderate tempo. Try also to frame the singing of this hymn with "Clap Your Hands" (166); that rendition would be very fitting for Ascension services. Wren believes that more meditative tunes than TRURO are also appropriate for this text; try the familiar ROCKINGHAM (178).

Liturgical Use

Easter; Ascension; other worship services that focus on contemporary human conditions.

414

REX GLORIAE

$\mathord{\downarrow} = 60$

See, the Conqueror Mounts in Triumph

Text

Replete with biblical imagery and allusion, this text by Christopher Wordsworth (PHH 361) was published in his *Holy Year* (1862) in ten stanzas. John Julian considers "See, the Conqueror" to be one of Wordsworth's finest hymn texts.

The text views the ascending Lord being sung to by angels at heaven's gates (st. 1), recalls Christ's suffering, death, resurrection, and ascension (st. 2), and looks forward to our reign with Christ in glory (st. 3). The text emphasizes not only the event of the Ascension but also its meaning for us: in Christ's ascension, "we by faith can see our own."

Scripture References
st. 1 = Ps. 24:7
st. 2 = Luke 24:50-51
Acts 1:9
st. 3 = Eph. 2:6
Heb. 1:8
Ps. 68:18

Tune

Henry T. Smart (PHH 233) composed REX GLORIAE for this text; the hymn was published in the 1868 *Appendix* to *Hymns Ancient and Modern.* Stanley L. Osborne (PHH 395) suggests that Smart initially intended REX GLORIAE as a tune for children. Derived from the topic of Wordsworth's text, the tune's name means "King of Glory."

A festive tune, REX GLORIAE is in rounded bar form (AABA). Sing in unison and use vigorous accompaniment bordering on marcato.

Liturgical Use

Easter; Ascension; many other worship services.

415

SUNRISE
♩ = 56

Spirit, Working in Creation

Text

With John Stainer's ALL FOR JESUS tune in mind, John Richards (b. Bournemouth, Hampshire, England, 1939) wrote this text in 1978. It was published in *Cry Hosanna* (1980) in ten four-line stanzas. The original stanzas 1 and 2, 4 and 5, and 8 and 10 are included in three eight-line stanzas.

Scripture References
st. 1 = Gen. 1:2
    2 Pet. 1:21
st. 2 = Matt. 3:16
    Matt. 4:1
    Mark 1:10, 12
    Luke 3:22; 4:1
    John 1:32-33
st. 3 = John 20:22

Like 416, this text is a biblical study of the ministry of the Holy Spirit: in creation and inspiration (st. 1), in the life of Christ and his people (st. 2), and in the church (st. 3). Although the emphasis is on the work of the Spirit, the text clearly recognizes that the Spirit always points to Christ.

Richards received his education at St. John's College in Durham, Emmanuel College in Cambridge, England, and Queen's College in Birmingham, England. Having served as the curate at several parishes in southern England and as a school chaplain, he is currently the director of Renewal Services, a parachurch organization. Richards has published several books, including *Exorcism, Deliverance and Healing* (1976) and *The Church's Healing Ministry* (1986).

Tune

Sometimes known as OMNI DIE, SUNRISE was first published in the 1768 *Supplementum* to the Luxembourg *Kyriale*. After its inclusion in *Gesang und Gebetbuch* (Trier, 1847), the tune gained popularity. sunrise attained its name because of its publication with William Bright's morning hymn "At thy feet, O Christ we lay" in *Hymns Ancient and Modern Revised* (1950).

A bar form (AAB) tune, SUNRISE is marked by a number of repeated tones. The active harmonization will delight choirs and challenge part-singing congregations. Sing stanzas 1 and 3 in unison with brisk accompaniment; sing stanza 2 in harmony unaccompanied.

Liturgical Use

Pentecost (entire hymn); other times of the church year—stanzas 1 and 3 as a sung prayer for illumination or as response to the sermon, stanza 3b as a doxology.

416

For Your Gift of God the Spirit

BLAENWERN
♩ = 126

Text

Margaret Clarkson (PHH 238) wrote this text about the work
of the Holy Spirit during the summer of 1959 at the Severn
River, Ontario, Canada. Requested by Stacey Woods, General
Secretary of Inter-Varsity Christian Fellowship in Canada and
the United States, the text was first published in *Anywhere
Songs* (IVCF songbook, 1960). Clarkson revised the text for
use in IVCF's *Hymns II* in 1976 and made final revisions in 1984.

Scripture References
st. 2 = Gen. 1:2
st. 3 = Rom. 8:26-27
st. 5 = Eph. 4:30
1 Thess. 5:19

If "Veni, Creator Spiritus" (425 and 426) is the classic prayer text to the Holy Spirit,
"For Your Gift" is the best teaching text on the Holy Spirit. Inspired by biblical passages
about the work of the Spirit in creation, the church, and our personal lives, this text
reads like a study of the doctrine of the Holy Spirit. It is a splendid example of sung
theology, which brings our heart's confession onto our lips.

Tune

For information on the tune and composer, see PHH 132.

Liturgical Use

Pentecost; appropriate for many other services.

417

Filled with the Spirit's Power

FARLEY CASTLE
𝅗𝅥 = 56

Text

Believing that there were too many hymns about the Holy Spirit
that focused on the individual believer and too few about the
work of the Spirit in the community of saints, John R. Peacey
(PHH 325) wrote this text in 1967. Peacey's text includes two
common biblical expressions about the Spirit's work: "the
fellowship of the Holy Spirit" (2 Cor. 13:14) and "the unity of
the Spirit" (Eph. 4:3). Written after Peacey's retirement from
missionary service in India, "Filled with the Spirit's Power" was first published in *100
Hymns for Today* (1969), a supplement to *Hymns Ancient and Modern.*

Scripture References
st. 1 = Acts 2:2-3
2 Cor. 13:14
st. 2 = John 17:21
Acts 4:32
Eph. 4:3

The text is a prayer for true unity, for a spirit of servanthood, and for a genuine love
that is able to "embrace the people of all lands and every race." But only the Holy Spirit

can accomplish this work. Just as the New Testament church described in Acts 2:42-47 experienced "the fellowship of the Holy Spirit," we, too, can see the Spirit's work in the Christian community.

Tune

FARLEY CASTLE, composed by Henry Lawes (b. Dinton, Wiltshire, England, 1596; d. London, England, 1662), was first published in treble and bass parts as a setting for Psalm 72 in George Sandys's *Paraphrase upon the Divine Poems* (1638). In the British tradition the tune is used as a setting for Horatius Bonar's communion hymn "Here, O My Lord, I See Thee," but now the tune is also often set to Peacey's text.

Lawes was a well-known composer, singer, and teacher in seventeenth-century England. His teaching career began with his appointment as music tutor to the daughters of the Earl of Bridgewater. Later he was a voice teacher to professional singers. In 1631 he was appointed musician in the court of King Charles I; he lost this position during Cromwell's reign but was reappointed at the Restoration. Lawes was known as a composer of some four hundred songs, many of which were used in stage productions. He and John Milton (PHH 136) collaborated on the famous masque *Comus* (1634). The writer of about twenty anthems, including one for the coronation of Charles II in 1660, Lawes also contributed tunes to George Sandys's *Psalms* (1638) and to *Choice Psalms put into Musick for three Voices* (1648), which he published with his brother. Lawes's tunes were reintroduced to modern hymnody when Ralph Vaughan Williams (PHH 316) included five of them in *The English Hymnal* (1906).

FARLEY CASTLE has a rather angular contour; its active harmony is suited to part singing. Use light accompaniment and a measured pace for this prayer hymn.

Liturgical Use

Pentecost; worship that focuses on the church, its unity, and worldwide ministries.

418

BEFIEHL DU DEINE WEGE
♩ = 56

The Spirit Came, As Promised

Text

James E. Seddon (PHH 15) based this Pentecost hymn entirely on references to the Holy Spirit in Ephesians. Essentially a teaching hymn about the Holy Spirit (see also 415 and 416), the text was first published in the British *Psalm Praise* (1973).

Scripture References
st. 1 = Eph. 1:13, 17-19
Eph. 2:18
st. 2 = Eph. 2:21-22
Eph. 3:16-19
1 Cor. 6:19
st. 3 = Eph. 4:3-4, 11-13, 29-31
st. 4 = Eph. 5:8-20
Eph. 6:17-18

Tune

Dutch organist Johannes G. Bastiaans (b. Wilp, the Netherlands, 1812; d. Haarlem, the Netherlands, 1875) composed BEFIEHL DU DEINE WEGE as a setting for the Dutch translation (by Bernard ter Haar) of Paul Gerhardt's (PHH 42) German text "Befiehl du deine Wege." Each of the tune's four lines are melodically unique but are bound together by one consistent rhythmic pattern. The tune was published with that translation in the Dutch *Vervolgbundel op de Evangelische Gezangen* (1868); some thirty of his tunes were included in that hymnal.

Born near the city of Deventer, Bastiaans had his early musical training there. From 1836 to 1838 he studied organ and composition in Germany. After returning to the Netherlands, Bastiaans served as organist in Deventer and Amsterdam and, from 1858 until his death, was the municipal organist and carillonist in Haarlem. He also taught music at the Institute for the Blind in Amsterdam and gave private lessons in composition and organ. In addition to being an accomplished organist, Bastiaans was well known for his organ compositions. Moreover, he was primarily responsible for introducing J. S. Bach to the Netherlands, both through his Bach recitals and his founding of the Bach Society in Amsterdam.

Liturgical Use

In any service as a teaching hymn about the work of the Holy Spirit, especially with sermons from Ephesians; as a sermon summary, response, or confessional hymn (sung confession of faith); select stanzas in many different places in the order of worship.

419

Spirit of God, Who Dwells within My Heart

MORECAMBE
$\quad = 63$

Text

This hymn is an intense, personal prayer for the working of the Holy Spirit (st. 1), for illumination (st. 2), for more fervent love for Christ (st. 3), for greater holiness in our walk with the Lord (st. 4), and for the fullness of the Spirit (st. 5). The first line was changed from "Spirit of God, descend upon my heart" to "Spirit of God, who dwells within my heart."

This text was ascribed posthumously to George Croly (b. Dublin, Ireland, 1780; d. Holborn, London, England, 1860) when it was published in Charles Rogers's *Lyra Britannica* (1867). Croly was educated at Trinity College, Dublin. After serving in Irish Anglican churches from 1804-1810, he moved to London and began a successful literary career as poet,

Scripture References
st. 1 = Ps. 51:10-12
Rom. 8:26
Eph. 3:16
st. 2 = Luke 11:13
st. 3 = Matt. 22:37
st. 4 = Ezek. 36:27
st. 5 = Rom. 5:5

novelist, conservative journalist, and editor of *The Universal Review*. In 1835 he returned to pastoral work and served a poor parish in London, where he became a very popular preacher. Croly published a number of his hymns in a collection he edited, *Psalms and Hymns for Public Worship* (1854).

Tune

MORECAMBE was composed in 1870 by Frederick C. Atkinson (b. Norwich, England, 1841; d. East Dereham, England, 1896) as a setting for Henry Lyte's "Abide with Me" (442). It was first published in G. S. Barrett and E. J. Hopkins's *Congregational Church Hymnal* (1887). The tune is named for a coastal town on Morecambe Bay near Lancaster, England, a town not far from Bradford, where Atkinson served as organist.

As a boy Atkinson was a chorister and assistant organist at Norwich Cathedral. In 1867 he graduated with a Bachelor of Music degree from Cambridge and then served as organist and choirmaster in St. Luke's Church, Manningham, Bradford. He also held that position at Norwich Cathedral and at St. Mary's Parish Church in Lewisham. Atkinson wrote hymn tunes, anthems, and complete Anglican services, as well as songs and piano pieces.

MORECAMBE has a good melodic contour and a strong rise to its climax but then concludes rather weakly. (See comments on the generic group of tunes that includes MORECAMBE at PHH 276.) Try singing this fervent prayer to MORESTEAD (295), a tune with a very different character that will shed new light on the text.

Liturgical Use

Pentecost; worship services at other times of the year because anytime is renewal time!

420

TRENTHAM
♩ = 126

Breathe on Me, Breath of God

Text

The text is a prayer for renewal by God's Spirit (like Ps. 51:10-12), a renewal that is to be expressed in a life of love (st. 1), in purity of heart and will (st. 2), and in an intimacy with God that heralds the perfection of eternal life (st. 3). In both Hebrew and Greek the word for "spirit" is the same as "wind/air/breath"; thus in this text the Spirit of God is referred to as "Breath of God."

Scripture References
st. 1   = Ezek. 36:27
st. 1-3 = Joel 2:28
              John 20:22

Intended as a hymn for ordination, this text by Edwin Hatch (b. Derby, England, 1835; d. Oxford, England, 1889) was privately printed in 1878 and then published in Henry Allon's *The Congregational Psalmist Hymnal* in 1886. Hatch evidently had a simple and childlike faith; that description fits this text as well.

Hatch grew up in a Non-conformist home, was educated at Pembroke College, Oxford, England, and ordained in the Church of England in 1859. A teacher of classics and church history, he taught at Trinity College, Toronto, Canada (1859-1862), and at a high school in Quebec City (1862-1867). In 1867 he returned to Oxford, where he served the academic world with great distinction, particularly as a specialist on early Christian history. His few hymn texts were published posthumously in *Towards Fields of Light* (1890).

Tune
Robert Jackson (b. Oldham, Lancashire, England, 1842; d. Oldham, 1914) originally composed TRENTHAM as a setting for Henry W. Baker's "O Perfect Life of Love" (380). Named for a village in Staffordshire, England, close to the town in which Jackson was born, the tune was published with the Baker text in *Fifty Sacred Leaflets* (1888).

After receiving his musical training at the Royal Academy of Music, Jackson worked briefly as organist at St. Mark's Church, Grosvenor Square, in London. But he spent most of his life as organist at St. Peter's Church in Oldham (1868-1914), where his father had previously been organist for forty-eight years. A composer of hymn tunes, Jackson was also the conductor of the Oldham Music Society and Werneth Vocal Society.

By the turn of the twentieth century, TRENTHAM became associated with the Hatch text. TRENTHAM is a serviceable tune in the mannerist tradition of Victorian hymnody (see PHH 276), but it is barely adequate for the fervor of this text. Nonetheless, the tune is loved by many. Sing in harmony and maintain one pulse per bar.

Liturgical Use
Pentecost; as a prayer for renewal; ordination and other commissioning services; profession of faith.

421

Spirit Divine, Inspire Our Prayer

GRÄFENBERG
$\downarrow$ = 66

Text
Although the text was written by Andrew Reed (b. St. Clement Danes, London, England, 1787; d. Hackney, London, 1862), it was published anonymously in the *Evangelical Magazine,* June 1829, with the heading "Hymn to the Spirit, Sung on the late Day appointed for solemn Prayer and Humiliation." The "late Day" referred to Good Friday of that year, which had been set aside by the Congregational clergy of London for prayer for "the renewal of religion in the British churches." The original text began

Scripture References
st. 1 = Rom. 8:26
Eph. 3:16
st. 2 = John 16:13
st. 3 = Ps. 51:10-12
Ezek. 36:26
Acts 2:2-3

"Spirit divine, attend our prayers" and had seven stanzas (st. 7 was a virtual repeat of st. 1). His stanzas 1-3 and 6 are included in modernized form.

The text begins with a prayer for the working of the Holy Spirit in our hearts (st. 1). It then uses the metaphors of light, fire, and the dove to enable us to see the Spirit's work more clearly: "Come as the light" is a prayer for illumination (st. 2); "Come as the fire" is a prayer for cleansing (st. 3); and "Come as the dove" is a prayer for peace and unity (st. 4).

The son of a watchmaker, Reed entered that profession until he felt a call to the ministry. Educated at Hackney College, London, he became a Congregational minister in 1811. He served a flourishing congregation in St. George's-in-the-East, London (later named Wycliffe Chapel), until his retirement in 1861. Known for his administrative skills, Reed founded various charitable institutions such as the London Orphan Asylum, the Asylum for Fatherless Children, the Royal Hospital for Incurables, the Infant Orphan Asylum, and the Asylum for Idiots. He published a *Supplement* (1817) to Isaac Watts's (PHH 155) hymns, which was enlarged in 1825 and called *The Hymn Book;* it included twenty-one hymn texts by Reed and twenty anonymous texts by Reed's wife (not properly credited until the *Wycliffe Chapel Supplement* of 1872). In 1842 Reed issued *The Hymn Book,* a compilation of his hymns as well as those by Watts and others.

Tune

Composed by Johann Crüger (PHH 42) as a setting for Paul Gerhardt's "Nun danket all' und bringet Ehr," GRÄFENBERG was first published in the 1647 edition of Crüger's *Praxis Pietatis Melica.* The tune is arbitrarily named after a water-cure spa in Silesia, Austria, which became famous in the 1820s.

The rhythmic structure of Crüger's tune has been altered in most hymnals by the adoption of "gathering" notes (longer beginning notes to every phrase) in the style of British psalm tunes. Originally the second and fourth phrases began with a quarter rest and quarter note. Sing in harmony or in unison with light accompaniment suited to this prayer hymn.

Liturgical Use

Pentecost; other services of prayer for the work of the Holy Spirit.

422

FOREST GREEN
♩ = 96

Eternal Spirit, God of Truth

Text

Originally entitled "For a well-grounded hope of salvation," this text by Thomas Cotterill (PHH 409) was published in Cotterill's *Selection of Psalms and Hymns* (1810). The text's original first line began "Eternal Spirit, source of truth."

Scripture References
st. 1 = Ps. 51:10-12, 17
st. 2 = Rom. 8:9-17

Stanza 1 is a prayer for renewal by the Holy Spirit (see PHH 420); stanza 2 continues this prayer with allusions to Romans 8:9-17.

Tune
FOREST GREEN is an English folk tune associated with the ballad "The Ploughboy's Dream." Ralph Vaughan Williams (PHH 316) turned FOREST GREEN into a hymn tune for *The English Hymnal* (1906), using it as a setting for "O Little Town of Bethlehem."

Shaped in rounded bar form (AABA), FOREST GREEN has the cheerful characteristics of folk tunes. Those characteristics help to support the humanness of this text: we are to be the children (folk) of God! Sing in unison or in harmony, but given the tune's many eighth notes, do not rush. Congregations used to certain rhythmic patterns in hymn tunes will be challenged by the new rhythms at the transition from line 3 to line 4; accompanists should give leadership there.

Liturgical Use
Pentecost; as a prayer for comfort at many other services.

423

Holy Spirit, Truth Divine

SONG 13
♩ = 56

Text
Samuel Longfellow (b. Portland, ME, 1819; d. Portland, 1892) wrote this text with the heading "Prayer for Inspiration." It was published in the Unitarian hymnal *Hymns of the Spirit* in 1864.

Scripture References
all st. = Luke 11:13
John 15:26
John 16:13
st. 6 = Num. 21:17
John 4:10

Like "O Come, O Come, Immanuel" (328), this text is a catalog: it lists attributes of the Holy Spirit in successive stanzas. The text is a prayer that the application of the Spirit's attributes may result in more vibrant Christian living, which will then be manifest in discernment of God's will (st. 1), holiness and purity (st. 2), courageous servanthood (st. 3), obedience to God's rule (st. 4), peace and restfulness (st. 5), and the experience of joy (st. 6). The final stanza alludes to Numbers 21:17 ("song of the well") and to John 4:10 ("living water"). Note that this hymn addresses the Holy Spirit without any reference to the Trinity, a Unitarian position that should not, however, hamper its use.

Samuel Longfellow is not as famous as his brother, poet Henry Wadsworth Longfellow, about whom he wrote a biography that was published in 1886. In his time, however, Samuel was well known as a Unitarian preacher and hymn writer. Educated at Harvard College and Harvard Divinity School, he became a minister in 1848 and served Unitarian congregations in Fall River, Massachusetts (1848-1851), Brooklyn,

New York (1853-1860), and Germantown, Pennsylvania (1860-1883). With Samuel Johnson he compiled two hymnals: *A Book of Hymns for Public and Private Devotion* (1846) and *Hymns of the Spirit* (1864). He also published a number of his hymn texts in *A Book of Hymns and Tunes* (1860).

Tune
Orlando Gibbons (PHH 167) composed SONG 13 in soprano and bass parts. Used as a setting for a text from the Song of Songs, the tune was published in George Withers's *Hymnes and Songs of the Church* (1623) as hymn number 13 (hence the tune name).

As in other hymnals, the melody is presented in a simplified isorhythmic (all equal rhythms) form; the more rhythmically varied original also had more notes and was better suited to solo singing. Sing all the stanzas in antiphonal groups with select use of part singing. Use light accompaniment.

Liturgical Use
Pentecost; many other worship services: entire hymn or select stanzas at the opening of worship, as a response to the Decalogue, as a prayer for illumination, as a hymn of dedication following the sermon.

424

IVERSON
♩ = 56
Spirit of the Living God

Text
The composite hymn text is a prayer for the Holy Spirit to work renewal in the individual heart (st. 1) and to make these renewed people one in love and service (st. 2).

Scripture References
all st. = Acts 10:44

Daniel Iverson (b. Brunswick, GA, 1890; d. Asheville, NC, 1977) wrote the first stanza and tune of this hymn after hearing a sermon on the Holy Spirit during an evangelism crusade by the George Stephans Evangelistic Team in Orlando, Florida, 1926. The hymn was sung at the crusade and then printed in leaflets for use at other services. Published anonymously in Robert H. Coleman's *Revival Songs* (1929) with alterations in the tune, this short hymn gained much popularity by the middle of the century. Since the 1960s it has again been properly credited to Iverson.

Iverson studied at the University of Georgia, Moody Bible Institute, Columbia Theological Seminary, and the University of South Carolina. Ordained in the Presbyterian Church in 1914, he served congregations in Georgia and in North and South Carolina. In 1927 he founded the Shenandoah Presbyterian Church in Miami, Florida, and served there until his retirement in 1951. An evangelist as well as a preacher, Iverson planted seven new congregations during his ministry in Miami.

Michael Baughen (b. Borehamwood, Hertfordshire, England, 1930) added a second stanza to the text in 1980. That stanza's emphasis on the Spirit moving "among us all" provides a necessary complement to the first stanza's focus on the Spirit's work in the individual ("fall afresh on me"). The stanzas were first published together in the British *Hymns for Today's Church* (1982).

Baughen was a priest in the Church of England since 1964 and Bishop of Chester from 1982 until he retired in 1996. He now lives in London. Educated at London University and Oak Hill Theological College, he served as rector of Holy Trinity Church in Rushholme, Manchester (1964-1970), and All Saints, Langham Place, London (1970-1982). Baughen has written four books including *Chained to the Gospel* (1986) and *The Prayer Principle* (1981). He also founded the Jubilate Group and served as editor of four hymnals: *Youth Praise* (1966), *Youth Praise II* (1969), *Psalm Praise* (1973), and *Hymns for Today's Church* (1982).

Tune

IVERSON is a simple chorus; its original melody line was altered in 1929 (see above). Southern Baptist leader Baylus B. McKinney wrote the harmony, which was published in his *Songs of Victory* (1937).

Sing in harmony unaccompanied or accompany with organ or guitars. When used as a frame around prayers (see Liturgical Use), accompany the first line of each stanza, and then allow the singing to proceed unaccompanied.

Liturgical Use

Pentecost; renewal services; profession of faith; ordination; special dedication/consecration of persons and organizations to Christian ministry; in worship services of confession/forgiveness or as a sung prayer for illumination; as a frame around the congregational prayers—sing stanza 1 at the beginning and stanza 2 at the conclusion of spoken prayers.

425

Creator Spirit, by Whose Aid

MELITA
♩ = 50

Text

The ninth-century Latin hymn "Veni, Creator Spiritus" is the basis for this text as well as 426. Almost as well known as the earlier "Te Deum Laudamus" (504), "Veni, Creator Spiritus" is an anonymous hymn; it has been attributed to Rhabanus Maurus (776-856), but with no solid proof to date. *The Hymnal 1982 Companion* provides the following information:

Scripture References
st. 1 = Gen. 1:2
1 Cor. 6:19
st. 2 = John 14:16

Of all Latin Hymns, this has probably been the most familiar to Anglicans throughout the centuries. Most likely written in the ninth century, it has been in continuous use in English coronation rites since the accession of Edward II in 1307. . . . Its original use is unknown, but it has been sung at various Pentecost offices at least since the tenth century and at ordination services at least since the eleventh (Vol. Three B, pp. 502-503).

Several translations are in use, all rather free paraphrases from the Latin. The translation provided here is by John Dryden (b. Aldwinkle, Northamptonshire, England, 1631; d. London, England, 1700), published in his *Miscellany Poems* (1693). One of the prime literary figures of his time, Dryden received his education at Trinity College, Cambridge, England. His first major poem was "Heroic Stanzas on the Death of Oliver Cromwell." After James I was restored to the throne, Dryden became both a royalist and Roman Catholic. At the height of his career he was appointed poet laureate and royal historian. Because he remained a Roman Catholic when the Protestants William and Mary came to the throne in 1688, he lost his official positions. A writer of plays, poems, odes, and satires, Dryden also translated the works of classical poets such as Virgil and Bocaccio. His English translations of Latin hymns were published posthumously in *The Primer of Office* (1706).

The text is a prayer for the creative, dynamic work of the Holy Spirit in God's people. The prayer is cast in older English expressions: "Paraclete" is Greek for comforter, advocate, or counselor (st. 2); "sevenfold energy" is based on the medieval reading of Isaiah 11:2, in which the Hebrew list of six characteristics of the Spirit was mistakenly translated into the Latin *Vulgate* as seven traits, thereby spawning a medieval tradition of "sevenfold . . . of the Spirit" (st. 3).

Tune

The original chant melody associated with this text is found in most hymnals of denominations where chant has played a role, including the Lutheran tradition, which has produced much organ music on this well-known chant.

The setting here is by John B. Dykes (PHH 147), originally composed as a setting for William Whiting's "Eternal Father, Strong to Save." Published in *Hymns Ancient and Modern* (1861) with that text, MELITA is often referred to as the "navy hymn." The tune is named after the island of Malta where Paul was shipwrecked.

A fine tune, MELITA is marked by good use of melodic sequences and a harmony that features several dominant sevenths (both are Dykes's trademarks). Sing in harmony; because the lines flow into each other in almost breathless fashion, use a stately tempo.

Liturgical Use

Pentecost; ordination or commissioning services; baptism; profession of faith. ·

426

O Holy Spirit, by Whose Breath

DAS NEUGEBORNE KINDELEIN
♩ = 116

Text

Like 425, this text is based on the Latin hymn "Veni, Creator Spiritus" (see PHH 425). More a translation than the paraphrase at 425, this text by John W. Grant was written in 1968 and published in the Canadian Anglican and United *Hymn Book* (1971). Stanley L. Osborne (PHH 395) writes, "The vividness and freshness of its expression combined with its faithfulness to the spirit of the original text marks it as one of the finest translations ever to come out of this century" (*If Such Holy Song* 246).

Scripture References
all st. = John 15:26

Although the ancient text acquires a modern face with the freshness of Grant's translation, the ancient and biblical images are still very much present: we sing of the Spirit as "breath" and "fire" (st. 1); as "giver and Lord of life" (st. 2); as "energy" and giver of gifts (st. 3); as source of light and love (st. 4); and as bringer of peace, fullness, and unity (st. 5). The text concludes with a fine Trinitarian doxology (st. 6).

John Webster Grant (b. Truro, Nova Scotia, Canada, 1919) received his education at Dalhousie University and Pine Hill Divinity Hall in Halifax, Nova Scotia. Ordained in the United Church of Canada in 1943, he became a Rhodes scholar after World War II and earned a doctoral degree at Oxford. He taught church history at Union College, British Columbia, Vancouver, (1949-1959); served as editor in chief of Ryerson Press (1959-1963); and from 1963-1984 taught church history at Emmanuel College, Victoria University, Toronto. Grant served as a member of the committee that produced *The Hymn Book* (1971), published by the United Church and the Anglican Church. His writings include *Free Churchmanship in England, 1870-1940* (1955), *The Canadian Experience of Church Union* (1967), *The Church in the Canadian Era* (1972), and *Moon of Wintertime* (1984).

Tune

Also known as JENA, DAS NEUGEBORNE KINDELEIN was originally a chorale melody for Cyriacus Schneegass's text "Das neugeborne Kindelein." Composed by Melchior Vulpius (PHH 397) and published in his *Ein Schön Geistlich Gesangbuch* (Jena, 1609), the tune was introduced to English congregations primarily because of its inclusion in George R. Woodward's (PHH 403) *Cowley Carol Book* (1901 ed.). The harmony is simplified from a setting by Johann S. Bach (PHH 7) in his Cantata 122.

DAS NEUGEBORNE KINDELEIN is a beautiful carol tune that allows contemplation of this vibrant text on the Spirit's work. Sing stanza 1 in unison and stanzas 2-5 in parts, possibly with some antiphonal singing. Return to unison singing for stanza 6 with strong accompaniment. Use lighter accompaniment on stanzas 1-5; maintain one pulse per bar. Note how stanza 5 propels into stanza 6!

Liturgical Use

See PHH 425; because 426 is a more precise and detailed translation of the original Latin, it is preferred for ordination, baptism, and profession of faith services. Try using an alternate tune such as WINCHESTER NEW (593) for ecumenical services.

427

Dwell in Me, O Blessed Spirit

Text

The writer of this text is listed as Martha J. Lankton, one of the many pseudonyms used by Fanny J. Crosby (PHH 473). The hymn was first published in the *Sunday School Hymnal* (1899) of the Reformed Church in the U.S.A. In 1941 it was published in the *Hymnal* of the Evangelical and Reformed Church.

Though it appears now in virtually no other hymnal, this hymn is beloved in the Christian Reformed Church and has appeared in every edition of the *Psalter Hymnal*. For the 1987 edition the original stanza 2 was deleted, and the final line of the refrain was changed from "For the home of bliss that waits me" to "For the kingdom work that calls me."

Patterned after Psalm 51:10-12, "Dwell in Me" is a prayer that the Spirit keep us "in the way of life eternal" (st. 1), comfort us, and prod us on to service (st. 2). The refrain sends us out of the church into the kingdom.

Tune

Composed by Georgia Guiney Berky (nineteenth century), DWELL IN ME is a gospel tune in verse/refrain pattern with a simple harmonization. Virtually no information is available about her other than that she was married to A. G. Berky and is thought to have been a member of the Reformed Church in the U.S.A. Sing in harmony with a gentle legato accompaniment suitable for this prayer. Maintain a moderate tempo.

Liturgical Use

As a sung prayer following the sermon at Pentecost or other Sunday worship; the refrain can be used as an independent chorus or as a frame around hymns such as 574 or 597.

428

O Worship the King

LYONS
♩ = 126

Text

Robert Grant (b. Bengal, India, 1779; d. Dalpoorie, India, 1838) was influenced in writing this text by William Kethe's (PHH 100) paraphrase of Psalm 104 in the Anglo-Genevan Psalter (1561). Grant's text was first published in Edward Bickersteth's *Christian Psalmody* (1833) with several unauthorized alterations. In 1835 his original six-stanza text was published in Henry Elliott's *Psalms and Hymns*. Stanza 3 was omitted in the *Psalter Hymnal.*

Scripture References
st. 1 = Ps. 18:2
    Dan. 7:9, 13, 22
st. 2 = Ps. 18:9-12
    Ps. 104:1-3
st. 3 = Ps. 104:7-10
st. 5 = Ps. 145:10

Rather than being a paraphrase or versification, the text is a meditation on the creation theme of Psalm 104. Stanzas 1-3, which allude to Psalm 104:1-6, focus on God's creation as a testimony to his "measureless Might." More personal in tone, stanzas 4 and 5 confess the compassion of God toward his creatures and affirm with apocalyptic vision that the "ransomed creation, with glory ablaze" will join with angels to hymn its praise to God.

Of Scottish ancestry, Grant was born in India, where his father was a director of the East India Company. He attended Magdalen College, Cambridge, and was called to the bar in 1807. He had a distinguished public career as Governor of Bombay and as a member of the British Parliament, where he sponsored a bill to remove civil restrictions on Jews. Grant was knighted in 1834. His hymn texts were published in the *Christian Observer* (1806-1815), in Elliott's *Psalms and Hymns* (1835), and posthumously by his brother as *Sacred Poems* (1839).

Tune

LYONS, named for the French city Lyons, appeared with a reference to "Haydn" in volume 2 of William Gardiner's (PHH 111) *Sacred Melodies.* However, the tune was never found in the works of Franz Joseph Haydn or those of his younger brother Johann Michael Haydn. Recent research revealed that the tune was composed by Joseph Martin Kraus, a German composer who settled in Sweden and who traveled widely throughout Europe. *Die Werke von Joseph Martin Kraus systematisch-thematisches Werkvereichnis,* by Bertil H. Van Boer, Jr. (Stockholm, 1988), includes information on Kraus's *"Tema con variazioni (Scherzo),"* a work composed around 1785 in London with an incipit that clearly matches the opening measures of LYONS. The work was published as a set of twelve variations for piano and violin in London in 1791. The violin part may have been an addition by another composer, perhaps a "G. Haydn," since a subsequent London edition (c. 1808) was entitled "Sonatina with Twelve Variations for the Piano Forte with Violin Accompaniments, composed by G. Haydn."

Joseph Martin Kraus (b. Miltenberg am Main, Germany, 1756; d. Stockholm, Sweden, 1792) spent his youth in Germany, but in 1778 moved to Stockholm. He was elected to the Swedish Academy of Music and became the conductor of the court orchestra and eventually the best-known composer associated with the court of Gustavus III. On his travels, Kraus did meet Franz Joseph Haydn, who considered Kraus "one of the greatest geniuses I have met." Kraus wrote operas as well as many vocal and instrumental works.

A bright melody, LYONS is much loved by many congregations. Lines 1, 2, and 4 are similar in shape; lines 2 and 4 are identical. The climbing melody and dominant pedal-point of line 3 provides contrast. Sing stanzas 1, 3, and 5 in solid unison and stanzas 2 and 4 in harmony. Use clear, bright accompaniment. Maintain one pulse per bar. LYONS's opening figure is similar to that of HANOVER (149 and 477), a good alternate tune.

Liturgical Use
An opening hymn of praise; because of the hymn's relationship to Psalm 104, see suggestions for use at PHH 104.

429

FAITHFUL
♩ = 63

The Heavens Declare Your Glory

Text
This paraphrase of the opening verses of Psalm 19 was written by British scholar Thomas R. Birks (b. Staveley, Derbyshire, England, 1810; d. Cambridge, England, 1883), who published it in his *Companion Psalter* (1874). Birks was educated at Trinity College, Cambridge. After ordination in the Church of England, he served two churches and was a professor of moral philosophy at Cambridge. He wrote about a number of biblical subjects, especially prophecy, and prepared at least a hundred versifications of psalms.

Scripture References
st. 1 = Ps. 19:1-2
st. 2 = Ps. 19:4-6
st. 3 = Ps. 19:14

Following the example of Psalm 19:1-6, this text takes as its theme the praise that all creation gives to its Creator. In typical nineteenth-century fashion Birks provides a moral: just as the physical universe around me praises the Lord God, so I must praise the Creator with all my thoughts, words, and deeds (st. 3). The modernized version in the *Psalter Hymnal* reflects current pronoun usage. (For additional comments on this psalm see PHH 19.)

Tune

FAITHFUL is an adaptation of a tune from Johann S. Bach's (PHH 7) well-known aria "Mein gläubiges Herze" ("My heart ever faithful"), found in his Cantata 68. The tune's title is derived from the English translation of the aria's opening words.

A charming tune, FAITHFUL consists of repetitions and variations of just a few motives. Sing in unison with light accompaniment.

Liturgical Use

An opening hymn of praise; for more suggestions see PHH 19.

430

We Sing the Mighty Power of God

KINGSFOLD
$\sf{\downarrow}$ = 60

Text

Written by Isaac Watts (PHH 155), this eight-stanza text originally began "I sing the almighty power of God." The text was published in *Divine and Moral Songs for the Use of Children* (1715; the first hymnal intended primarily for children) with the heading "Praise for Creation and Providence." The *Psalter Hymnal* omits the original stanzas 7 and 8 and combines the other six original stanzas into three long ones.

Scripture References
all st. = Gen. 1
Job 26
Ps. 104

Although it was written for children, this is also a great hymn for adults. The text presents a wonderful view of God's creation sketched in vivid pictorial language. The creation around us is a beautiful panorama that testifies to its Creator, whose power and wisdom (st. 1), goodness and wonders (st. 2), and providence and omnipresence (st. 3) we confess with awe and praise.

Tune

Thought by some scholars to date back to the Middle Ages, KINGSFOLD is a folk tune set to a variety of texts in England and Ireland. The tune was published in *English Country Songs* (1893), an anthology compiled by Lucy E. Broadwood and J. A. Fuller Maitland. After having heard the tune in Kingsfold, Sussex, England (thus its name), Ralph Vaughan Williams (PHH 316) introduced it as a hymn tune in *The English Hymnal* (1906) as a setting for Horatius Bonar's "I Heard the Voice of Jesus Say" (488).

Shaped in classic rounded bar form (AABA), KINGSFOLD has modal character and is both dignified and strong. It is well suited to either unison or harmony singing. Use bright organ tone. Try playing on two manuals and pedal on the middle stanzas.

Liturgical Use

On many occasions at the beginning of worship; services that focus on creation and providence (including harvest thanksgiving).

431

LASST UNS ERFREUEN
♩ = 80

All Creatures of Our God and King

Text

Virtually blind and unable to endure daylight, St. Francis (b. Assisi, Italy, c. 1182; d. Assisi, 1226) wrote this nature hymn during the summer of 1225 in the seclusion of a hut near San Damiano, Italy. The text is a meditation on Psalm 145 (although it also reflects Psalm 148 as well as the Canticle of the Three Young Men in the Furnace—an apocryphal addition to Dan. 3). Originally in Italian ("Laudato sia Dio mio Signore"), the text is known as the "Song of All Creatures" and as the "Canticle of the Sun."

Scripture References
st. 1 = Job 12:7-10
Ps. 148:3
st. 2 = Ps. 148:8
st. 4 = Ps. 148:9
st. 5 = Ps. 148:11-13

St. Francis of Assisi is universally known for preaching to the birds and urging them to praise God. But his whole life was one of service to God and humanity. The son of a wealthy cloth merchant, Francis led a carefree, adventurous life as a youth, but after an illness and a pilgrimage to Rome in 1205, he voluntarily began a traveling life of poverty. He restored run-down chapels and shrines, preached, sang devotional "laudi spirituali" (adapted from Italian folk songs), and helped the poor and the lepers. Other young men joined him, and Francis founded the order named after him; the Franciscans were approved by the Pope in 1210. Legends about Francis abound, and various stories, prayers, and visions are attributed to him.

William H. Draper (b. Kenilworth, Warwickshire, England, 1855; d. Clifton, Bristol, England, 1933) translated—or rather paraphrased—the text (which appears in virtually all English hymnals) for a children's Whitsuntide (Pentecost) Festival in Leeds, England, around 1910. Originally in seven stanzas, Draper's translation was published with the tune LASST UNS ERFREUEN in the *Public School Hymn Book* (1919). The modernized version in the *Psalter Hymnal* omits the original stanza 6 (about death) and combines the original stanzas 5 and 7 into one (now st. 5).

Educated at Cheltenham College and Keble College, Oxford, England, Draper was ordained in the Church of England in 1880. He served at least six churches during his lifetime, including the Temple Church in London (1919-1930). He is known for his sixty translations of Latin, Greek, and German hymns, many published in *The Victoria Book of Hymns* (1897) and *Hymns for Holy Week* (1899).

"All Creatures" is a catalog text that enumerates various features of the creation and summons all to praise the Lord with their "alleluias." Although not found in the original text, the "alleluias" make splendid sense and are necessary for the tune. Repeating the words "O praise him" each stanza emphasizes the cosmic praise of all creation: the sun and moon (st. 1); wind, clouds, and light (st. 2); water and fire (st. 3); the earth and its produce (st. 4); all creatures (st. 5).

Tune

LASST UNS ERFREUEN derives its opening line and several other melodic ideas from GENEVAN 68 (68). The tune was first published with the Easter text "Lasst uns erfreuen herzlich sehr" in the Jesuit hymnal *Ausserlesene Catholische Geistliche Kirchengesänge* (Cologne, 1623). LASST UNS ERFREUEN appeared in later hymnals with variations in the "alleluia" phrases.

The setting is by Ralph Vaughan Williams (PHH 316); first published in *The English Hymnal* (1906), it has become the most popular version of LASST UNS ERFREUEN. In that hymnal the tune was set to Athelstan Riley's "Ye watchers and ye holy ones" (thus it is sometimes known as VIGILES ET SANCTI).

In this hymn a great text is matched by an equally strong and effective tune. Try these two possibilities of antiphonal singing: divide stanzas between women and men, or assign the verses to one group and the "alleluias" to another. Accompanists can signal such antiphonal effects in their use of varied registration. Registration changes also will help interpret the text; for example, the third stanza can begin with a lighter registration and move to a "blazing" sound on the second half.

Try having the congregation sing some stanzas unaccompanied but add organ (with full stops) at the "alleluias." Or, for a fine effect, have the congregation sing some stanzas in unison with accompaniment and the choir sing the "alleluias" in harmony unaccompanied, as indicated in the *Psalter Hymnal*. It is musically correct and pastorally wise to observe a fermata at the end of the second "alleluia" on the second system by turning that half note into a whole note. No ritard is necessary at the end of the hymn; it is built right into the final "alleluia" phrase. Try adding instruments to enhance this magnificent tune; there are several fine concertato versions in print that involve trumpets and/or full brass scoring.

Liturgical Use

Many occasions as a strong opening hymn of praise; a congregational call to worship; springtime prayer services for crops/industry and for harvest thanksgiving (especially st. 4); festive processionals (use a concertato arrangement with brass and choral parts).

432

DIX
♩ *= 54*

For the Beauty of the Earth

Text

In the spring of 1863 Folliott S. Pierpont (b. Bath, Somerset, England, 1835; d. Newport, Monmouthshire, England, 1917) sat on a hilltop outside his native city of Bath, England, admiring the country view and the winding Avon River. Inspired by the view to think about God's gifts in creation and in the church, Pierpont wrote this text. Pierpont was educated at Queen's College, Cambridge, England, and periodically taught classics at Somersetshire College. But because he had received an inheritance, he did not need a regular teaching position and could afford the leisure of personal study and writing. His three volumes of poetry were collected in 1878; he contributed hymns to *The Hymnal Noted* (1852) and *Lyra Eucharistica* (1864).

Scripture References
all st. = Ps. 33:4-9
Ps. 145
Col. 1:15:18
James 1:17

"For the Beauty of the Earth" is the only Pierpont hymn still sung today. The eight-stanza text, which had as its original refrain "Christ, our God, to thee we raise this, our sacrifice of praise," was intended to be a hymn for the Lord's Supper. Entitled "The Sacrifice of Praise" (Heb. 13:15), the text was published in Orby Shipley's *Lyra Eucharistica* (1864).

The *Psalter Hymnal* includes his original stanzas 1-2 and 4-5 with several changes; most notable is the altered refrain (also found in other modern hymnals), which turns what once was a eucharistic text into a general thanksgiving.

"For the Beauty" helps us to thank the Lord for the beauty of creation around us (st. 1-2); for the joyful love of family and friends (st. 3); and for God's greatest gift, Christ Jesus (st. 4), to whom "we raise this, our hymn of grateful praise."

Tune

For comments on DIX see PHH 358; for information on the composer see PHH 332.

DIX is a fine setting for part singing. Be sure to sing the refrain as one long line. Use a fairly strong organ registration for the stanzas and add a mixture and/or reed stop for the refrain.

Liturgical Use

Many occasions of praise and thanksgiving (including harvest thanksgiving); stanza 4 for Lord's Supper services; stanza 3 for worship that focuses on the family.

433

Earth and All Stars

EARTH AND ALL STARS
♩ = 132

Text

Herbert Brokering (b. Beatrice, NE, 1926) wrote this text for the ninetieth anniversary of St. Olaf College, Northfield, Minnesota, in 1964. It was published in David Johnson's *Twelve Folksongs and Spirituals* in 1968 and in the Lutheran hymnal *Contemporary Worship I* in 1969. About his writing of the text Brokering says:

Scripture References
all st. = Ps. 96:1
Ps. 98
Ps. 150

> I tried to gather into a hymn of praise the many facets of life which emerge in the life of community. So there are the references to building, nature, learning, family, war, festivity. Seasons, emotions, death and resurrection, bread, wine, water, wind, sun, spirit . . . have made great impressions on my imagination.

Like 431 and 435, "Earth and All Stars" is a catalog text, inviting us to join with a whole host of natural and cultural phenomena to "sing to the Lord a new song!" The text alludes to Psalm 96:1 in each stanza and to Psalm 98:1 in the refrain. But Brokering presents a modern list of natural, manufactured, and inanimate things that join in praising the Lord: planets in cosmic order (st. 1); weather and vegetation (st. 2); musical instruments (st. 3); technology and building (st. 4); learning and athletics (st. 5); wisdom, and all of God's people (st. 6).

A prolific author, Brokering is currently a freelance consultant on worship and ministry. Specializing in religious education, he studied at Wartburg College, Waverly, Iowa; the Lutheran Theological Seminary, Columbus, Ohio; the University of Iowa; and the University of Erlangen, Germany. Brokering is a prominent figure in the Lutheran World Federation and the World Council of Churches and has served as a parish pastor in several Lutheran congregations. His writings include *Lord, Be with Me* (1969), *Lord, If* (1977), and texts for hymns, anthems, cantatas, and musicals.

Tune

David Johnson (b. San Antonio, TX, 1922; d. Phoenix, AZ, 1987), former music department chairman at St. Olaf College, composed EARTH AND ALL STARS and published it in his *Twelve Folksongs and Spirituals* (1968). Johnson studied at Trinity University, San Antonio, Texas, and received his master's and doctoral degrees in music from Syracuse University, New York. In addition to St. Olaf, he taught at Syracuse University; Alfred University, Alfred, New York; and Arizona State University. Johnson was organist at Syracuse University and organist and choir director at Trinity Episcopal Cathedral in Phoenix. His publications include *Instruction Book for Beginning Organists* and *Organ Teacher's Guide;* his compositions number over three hundred and include hymn tunes, varied harmonizations, and hymn preludes.

The tune, distinguished by its use of melismas, is intended for unison singing. Dale Grotenhuis (PHH 4) prepared the harmonization in 1984. Try assigning various stanzas to different groups, but have the entire group sing the refrain. Each stanza could also be divided in half and assigned to smaller groups. Then each group would conclude with "Sing to the Lord a new song," but the entire congregation would still sing the refrain. Some may want to sing the refrain only after the final stanza. Use strong, briskly energetic accompaniment.

Liturgical Use

Many uses as a modern hymn of praise. Sing the entire hymn or use a selection of stanzas as follows: stanzas 1-2 for worship that focuses on nature; other stanzas for worship that focuses on work, education, festivity/worship.

434

DUNDEE
♩ = 52

God Moves in a Mysterious Way

Text

William Cowper (pronounced "Cooper"; b. Berkampstead, Hertfordshire, England, 1731; d. East Dereham, Norfolk, England, 1800) is regarded as one of the best early Romantic poets. To biographers he is also known as "mad Cowper." His literary talents produced some of the finest English hymn texts,

Scripture References
st. 1   = Rom. 11:33
            Ps. 77:19
st. 3-4 = Ps. 62:1-8

but his chronic depression accounts for the somber tone of many of those texts. Educated to become an attorney, Cowper was called to the bar in 1754 but never practiced law. In 1763 he had the opportunity to become a clerk for the House of Lords, but the dread of the required public examination triggered his tendency to depression, and he attempted suicide. His subsequent hospitalization and friendship with Morley and Mary Unwin provided emotional stability, but the periods of severe depression returned. His depression was deepened by a religious bent, which often stressed the wrath of God, and at times Cowper felt that God had predestined him to damnation.

For the last two decades of his life Cowper lived in Olney, where John Newton (PHH 462) became his pastor. There he assisted Newton in his pastoral duties, and the two collaborated on the important hymn collection *Olney Hymns* (1779), to which Cowper contributed sixty-eight hymn texts. In addition to his two hymns (also 551) in the *Psalter Hymnal,* "There Is a Fountain Filled with Blood" is also often included in modern hymnals.

Erik Routley (PHH 31) compared this text to a Rembrandt painting, saying it had a dark background with a strong streak of light falling across it. That is an apt analogy.

Cowper wrote "God Moves in a Mysterious Way" in 1773 prior to the onset of one of his severely depressive states, which later that year led him to an unsuccessful suicide attempt. The text was published in Newton's *Twenty-six Letters on Religious Subjects; to which are added Hymns* (1774). It was also included in *Olney Hymns* with the heading "light shining out of darkness" and accompanied by a reference to John 13:7 in which Jesus says, "You do not realize now what I am doing, but later you will understand." The original stanza 4, omitted in the *Psalter Hymnal,* contained the couplet "behind a frowning providence/He hides a smiling face."

The first line indicates the focus of the entire text: God's ways may well be mysterious to us, but God does act! He "works his sovereign will" (st. 2), and someday "he will make it plain" (st. 5). In the meantime, even in periods of profound doubt and despair, we may trust God's wisdom.

Tune

DUNDEE first appeared in the 1615 edition of the Scottish Psalter published in Edinburgh by Andro Hart. Called a "French" tune (thus it also goes by the name of FRENCH), DUNDEE was one of that hymnal's twelve "common tunes"; that is, it was not associated with a specific psalm. In the *Psalter Hymnal* the tune is in isorhythmic form (all equal rhythms) and has a harmonization that was published in Thomas Ravenscroft's (PHH 59) *Whole Booke of Psalmes* (1621). The tune's name comes from the city of Dundee, known as the "Scottish Geneva" during the era of the Scottish Reformation.

DUNDEE fits the meditative character of the text; its smooth lines invite part singing.

Liturgical Use

This fine hymn on divine providence is useful on many occasions of worship.

435

All Things Bright and Beautiful

ROYAL OAK
$\downarrow = 66$

Text

Cecil F. Alexander (PHH 346) wrote a number of hymn texts on articles of the Apostles' Creed. This text, whose biblical source is Genesis 1:31 ("and God saw all that he had made, and it was very good"), is Alexander's explanation of the Creed's phrase "Maker of heaven and earth." The text was first published in her *Hymns for Little Children* (1848) in seven stanzas, one of which was

Scripture References
st. 1 = Matt. 6:28-29
all st. = Gen. 1:31
Eccles. 3:11
Neh. 9:6
Ps. 148

The rich man in his castle,
The poor man at his gate,
God made them high and lowly
And ordered their estate.

In the currently familiar form of this hymn Alexander's original first stanza has been turned into the refrain, and her stanzas 3 and 6 have been omitted.

The vivid images depicting the creedal statement are easily understood by God's children of all ages. It is a catalog text (see also 431 and 433) because it enumerates various creatures God has made: flowers and birds (st. 1); mountains, rivers, daylight, and evening (st. 2); summer, winter, and harvest (st. 4). The final stanza and the refrain teach us that the creation points to and praises the Creator, for "the Lord God made them all." Note that "all" is used four times in the refrain!

Tune

ROYAL OAK is presumably named for a tree at Boscobel, Shropshire, England, in which King Charles II hid during the Battle of Worcester, 1651. A folk song that may well be older than the seventeenth century, ROYAL OAK was associated in the 1600s with the loyalist song "The Twenty-Ninth of May," a song that celebrated the restoration of the monarchy under Charles II on May 29, 1660. Originally found in *The Dancing Master* (1686), the tune was arranged as a hymn setting by Martin F. Shaw and published in his *Song Time* (1915). ROYAL OAK is usually associated with the Alexander text in modern hymnals.

John Worst (b. Grand Rapids, MI, 1940) prepared the harmonization, first published in the *Psalter Hymnal Supplement* in 1974. Worst is a composer as well as professor of music at Calvin College, Grand Rapids, a position he has held since 1966. Previously he taught at Dordt College, Sioux Center, Iowa, and the University of Michigan. Educated at Calvin College, Ohio State University, and the University of Michigan (Ph.D.), Worst was an editor of *Songs of Rejoicing: Hymns for Worship, Meditation and Praise* (1989). He was also one of the contributors to *Youth, Electronic Media, and Popular Art* and the arranger of the *Hymn of the Month*, sets 1-4, for Christian Schools International.

This light, bright, and energetic tune is well suited to the colorful text. It requires unison singing throughout, although with a few simple changes the refrain could be sung in parts. Use light accompaniment. Try accompanying with guitars, flutes, or recorders, or use just three-part texture on the organ for the stanzas and four-part texture on the refrain. This is a great children's hymn— be sure to have them sing a stanza or two by themselves and then have the congregation join in on the refrain.

Liturgical Use

As a creation hymn, especially for children but also suitable for adults; with Heidelberg Catechism, Lord's Day 9, as a hymn of confession of faith.

436

This Is My Father's World

TERRA BEATA
♩ = 63

Text

When he went walking along the shores of Lake Ontario, Maltbie
D. Babcock (b. Syracuse, NY, 1858; d. Naples, Italy, 1901) would
say, "I'm going out to see my Father's world." He wrote this poem,
originally in sixteen stanzas of four lines each; it was published
posthumously in Babcock's *Thoughts for Everyday Living* (1901).
Parts of his long poem were joined to form stanzas 1 and 3 in the
Psalter Hymnal. Mary Babcock Crawford (b. Salem, OR, 1909), Babcock's granddaughter, wrote stanza 2 in 1972 at a time of increased ecological awareness and concern.
That stanza was originally published in the Episcopal *Hymnal* (1982).

Scripture References
all st. = Gen. 1
Ps. 24
Ps. 104
Acts 4:24

The text is a confession of faith and trust, a testimony that all creation around us is
the handiwork of our Father, who made the creation (st. 1), charged us to take good
care of it (st. 2), and continues to exercise his kingship over it (st. 3; also see 19 for this
theme). The phrase "music of the spheres" in stanza 1 refers to the ancient belief that
the planets made music or harmony as they revolved in the universe.

Babcock graduated from Syracuse University, New York, and Auburn Theological
Seminary (now associated with Union Theological Seminary in New York) and became
a Presbyterian minister. He served the Brown Memorial Presbyterian Church in
Baltimore, Maryland, and the Brick Presbyterian Church in New York City. In
Baltimore he was especially popular with students from Johns Hopkins University, but
he ministered to people from all walks of life. Babcock wrote hymn texts and devotional
poems, some of which were published in *The School Hymnal* (1899).

Mary Babacock Crawford attended Occidental College, Los Angeles, California, and
received master's degrees from both San Francisco Theological Seminary and Columbia
University, New York City. She has held administrative posts at Occidental College and at
Furman University, Greenville, South Carolina. A United Methodist, she retired in
Pebble Beach, California, where she was active in choral music well into her seventies.

Tune

TERRA BEATA was originally a traditional English folk tune, a variant of which, entitled
RUSPER, appeared in *The English Hymnal* in 1906. Franklin L. Sheppard (b. Philadelphia, PA, 1852; d. Germantown, PA, 1930) arranged the tune for Babcock's text and
published it in the Presbyterian church school hymnal *Alleluia* (1915), edited by
Sheppard (Babcock and Sheppard were friends).

After graduating from the University of Pennsylvania, Philadelphia, Sheppard
entered the family foundry business in Baltimore, Maryland, in 1875. He was organist
at Zion Episcopal Church and later was an elder and music director of the Second

Presbyterian Church in Baltimore. President of the Presbyterian Board of Publications, Sheppard also served on the committee that prepared the Presbyterian *Hymnal* of 1911. In the history of hymnody he is remembered primarily for arranging the tune TERRA BEATA for "This Is My Father's World."

TERRA BEATA (also called TERRA PATRIS) is Latin for "beautiful world." A lively melody with an extended range, the tune requires a light manner of performance as well as light accompaniment. Try using guitars and recorders. Harmony singing is fine as long as voices stay light and energetic. Organists, choose light and bright foundation stops, not heavy diapasons. Easily learned by children, this is a vivacious hymn that would be hampered by plodding or weightiness. Observe a ritard only on the last line of stanza 3.

Liturgical Use

Many worship settings but especially those that focus on creation, providence, and stewardship of nature; fits well with springtime prayer services for crops/industry and for fall harvest thanksgiving; as a hymn of praise and a teaching hymn about God and creation.

437

PENET
♩ = 80

Thank You, God, for Water, Soil, and Air

Text

Since its inclusion in the British supplementary hymnal *New Church Praise* in 1975, this hymn has been widely regarded as one of the best "ecology hymns." Brian Wren (PHH 311) wrote the text in September 1973 in Colchester, England.

Scripture References
all st. = Ps. 104:30

The stanzas have basically the same pattern. Each one begins with gratitude to God for some aspect of the physical creation: water, soil, and air (st. 1); minerals and ores (st. 2); petroleum and atomic energy (st. 3); the delicate ecological networks that bind all creation together. The first four stanzas conclude with a prayer for forgiveness for our sinful abuse of these resources and a petition that God will "help us renew the face of the earth." The final stanza (st. 5), with apocalyptic faith, concludes the text with the prayer that God himself will come to "renew the face of the earth" (a reference to Ps. 104:30). This text combines thankfulness with overt admission of our responsibility for ecological stewardship—so necessary in modern times (see 455 for this theme as well).

Tune

William P. Rowan (PHH 362) composed PENET in 1985 for this text; they are published together for the first time in the 1987 *Psalter Hymnal.* PENET, named for friends of Rowan, is distinguished by rhythmic contrasts between the steady, fairly slow beginning and the faster conclusion of each phrase. It would be best for the congregation to sing this hymn in unison. Try having men alternate with women on different stanzas, or the congregation in unison alternate with the choir in harmony. Because our gratitude for God's good earth is tempered here by our confession of sin, this tune needs modest treatment from the organ. Maintain a moderate tempo.

Liturgical Use

Harvest thanksgiving; springtime prayer services for crops/industry; other occasions of worship that focus on our stewardship of earth's resources (such as occasions of nuclear accidents or oil spills).

438

When Morning Gilds the Sky

LAUDES DOMINI
$\frac{1}{2} = 66$

Text

This litany of praise to Christ was translated from an anonymous German text, "Beim frühen Morgenlicht," thought to date from around 1800 (perhaps even the mid-1700s). The German text was first published in Sebastian Portner's *Katholisches Gesangbuch* (1828) in fourteen stanzas of couplets with a refrain line.

Scripture References
st. 1 = Ps. 34:1
st. 2 = Rev. 5:6-14
st. 3 = Ps. 19:1
ref. = Heb. 13:15

Edward Caswall's English translation, prepared from one of several variants of the text, was published in six stanzas in Henry Formby's *Catholic Hymns* (1854). Caswall (b. Yately, Hampshire, England, 1814; d. Edgebaston, Birmingham, England, 1878) published another eight stanzas in his *Masque of Mary* (1858). Like most other hymnals, the *Psalter Hymnal* provides a text taken from various parts of the Caswall translation.

A morning hymn (st. 1) as well as an evening hymn (st. 4), the text presents praise to Christ from angels and human creatures (st. 2) and from the elements of earth to the farthest reach of the cosmos (st. 3). In fact, this text is for all times and places: "Be this the eternal song"!

Caswell, the son of an Anglican clergyman, studied for the priesthood at Brasenose College, Oxford, England. He was ordained in 1839 and served the church in Stratford-sub-Castle but resigned his position in 1847. By this time he had become deeply involved in the Oxford Movement, an Anglican movement with strong Roman Catholic leanings. In 1847 Caswell and his wife traveled to Rome, where they were received into the Roman Catholic Church. After his wife's death Caswell became a Roman Catholic priest and joined the Oratory of St. Philip Neri in Birmingham, a group supervised by John Henry Newman, an earlier Roman Catholic convert from the Church of England. Caswell then devoted himself to two main tasks—serving the poor of Birmingham and writing and translating hymns, mainly from the Latin office-books and from German sources. Many of his translations were published in his *Lyra Catholica* (1849) and, with revisions, in *Hymns and Poems* (1873).

Tune

Joseph Barnby (b. York, England, 1838; d. London, England, 1896) composed LAUDES DOMINI for this text. Tune and text were published together in the 1868 *Appendix* to *Hymns Ancient and Modern* and they have been inseperable ever since.

An accomplished and popular choral director in England, Barnby showed his musical genius early: he was an organist and choirmaster at the age of twelve. He became organist at St. Andrews, Wells Street, London, where he developed an outstanding choral program (at times nicknamed "the Sunday Opera"). Barnby introduced annual performances of J. S. Bach's *St. John Passion* in St. Anne's, Soho, and directed the first performance in an English church of the *St. Matthew Passion*. He was also active in regional music festivals, conducted the Royal Choral Society, and composed and edited music (mainly for Novello and Company). In 1892 he was knighted by Queen Victoria. His compositions include many anthems and service music for the Anglican liturgy, as well as 246 hymn tunes (published posthumously in 1897). He edited four hymnals, including *The Hymnary* (1872) and *The Congregational Sunday School Hymnal* (1891), and coedited *The Cathedral Psalter* (1873).

LAUDES DOMINI is one of Barnby's better tunes; many others have been forgotten or charitably retired by hymnal committees. The tune's Latin title, which means "the praises of the Lord," is derived from the litany refrain.

LAUDES DOMINI's most notable element is its built-in retard in the final phrase. Sing the stanzas in antiphonal fashion but have the entire congregation sing the refrain. Use strong organ accompaniment with a bit more stately tempo on the fifth stanza. Do not add any further ritardando to the final phrase; the composer has already provided it.

Liturgical Use

Many occasions as a hymn of praise to Christ; a hymn for all seasons and all times of worship—morning, midday, or evening; could also frame the day of worship with stanzas 1-3 used at the beginning of morning worship and stanzas 4-5 used as a doxology for evening worship.

439

We Come to Thank You, God, by Singing

Text

Herman A. Bruining (b. Rotterdam, the Netherlands, 1738; d. Veere, the Netherlands, 1811) wrote a five-stanza Dutch evening hymn that began "'k Wil U, O God, mijn dank betalen." It was published in the Dutch hymnal *Evangelische Gezangeng* (1806). Luther's instructions in his Little Catechism about evening devotions were undoubtedly the inspiration for this text.

Scripture References
st. 1 = Ps. 103:13
st. 2 = Phil. 4:6
st. 3 = Ps. 46:1

Bruining studied at the University of Utrecht, the Netherlands, and became a pastor in the Reformed Church, serving congregations in Kolham, Workum, and Veere. He was widely respected for his theological and biblical studies.

Arie Verduijn (b. Oudshoorn, the Netherlands, 1911; d. Burlington, ON, Canada, 1992) translated Bruining's stanzas 1 and 5 (now st. 1 and 3) into English in 1969 as an expression of "my thanks for all my blessings after God took home my wife, Eeke." It was first sung at an Old Years' service in First Christian Reformed Church, Hamilton, Ontario, on December 31, 1969. He translated stanza 2 in 1986. Following the original Dutch, Verduijn's translation began "I want to thank you, God," but the *Psalter Hymnal* Revision Committee changed all singular pronouns to plural ones.

An engineer by profession, Verduijn always had a lively interest in church music and served as organist in several churches in the Netherlands. After immigrating to Canada in 1952, he was organist in several Christian Reformed and Presbyterian churches in Ontario. Trained at the Technical College in Leeuwarden, the Netherlands, Verduijn worked at the Philips Company in Eindhoven as well as at other Dutch firms. In Canada he worked as an industrial engineer for the Steel Company of Canada, Hamilton, Ontario (1955-1976). He has published many articles in technical publications as well as a family chronicle and autobiography, *Sojourners* (1981).

Like many vesper hymns, the text contrasts the fading daylight and approaching darkness with the eternal light of Christ. Stanzas 1 and 2 express gratitude to God for his blessings that come our way during the days of our lives. Stanza 3 turns "evening" into a metaphor for the closing years of earthly life when we may "rest our hope for the brighter morning" on the Lord of eternal life and light.

Tune

DIE TUGEND WIRD is derived from the more ornamented version found in Johann Freylinghausen's (PHH 34) *Geistreiches Gesangbuch* (1704), where it was used as a setting for "Die Tugend wird am Kreus geubet." The tune is a rounded bar form (AABA) with harmony suited to part singing. Congregational singing will benefit from firm organ support.

Johanna Wagenaar (b. Utrecht, the Netherlands, 1900) prepared the isorhythmic (all equal rhythms) setting for the choral edition of *Psalmen en Gezangen* of the Dutch Hervormde Kerk (1938).

Wagenaar first studied music (mainly theory and church music) with her father, who was organist at the Domkerk in Utrecht, the Netherlands. After completing formal studies in Utrecht, she continued music studies in Berlin. Wagenaar returned to the Netherlands, where she taught harmony, counterpoint, and piano at the Koninklijk Conservatorium of Music in The Hague. Composing new tunes and supplying harmonizations for existing tunes, she was active on hymnal commissions for the Hervormde Kerk and the Nederlandse Protestanten Bond.

Liturgical Use
An evening hymn of thankfulness for God's providence; New Year's Eve services; funerals; as a hymn of gratitude and consolation.

440

TRYGGARE KAN INGEN VARA
♩ = 69
Children of the Heavenly Father

Text
The author of this text, Caroline W. Sandell Berg (b. Fröderyd, Sweden, 1832; d. Stockholm, Sweden, 1903), is better known as Lina Sandell, the "Fanny Crosby of Sweden." Originally in Swedish ("Tryggare kan ingen vara"), the text was first published in Sandell-Berg's *Andeliga daggdroppar*

Scripture References
st. 1-2 = Psalm 84
st. 3 = Rom. 8:38-39
st. 4 = Job 1:21

(1855). Ernst W. Olson (b. Skane, Sweden, 1870; d. Chicago, IL, 1958) prepared the English translation for the 1925 *Hymnal* of the Lutheran Augustana Synod.

The four-stanza text is a confession of humble but confident trust in God's providence in the lives of his people. It reflects Lord's Day 1 of the Heidelberg Catechism—"in life and in death I belong to my faithful Savior."

"Lina" Wilhelmina Sandell Berg was the daughter of a Lutheran pastor to whom she was very close; she wrote hymns partly to cope with the fact that she witnessed his tragic death by drowning. Many of her 650 hymns were used in the revival services of Carl O. Rosenius, and a number of them gained popularity particularly because of the musical settings written by gospel singer Oskar Ahnfelt. Jenny Lind, the famous Swedish soprano, underwrote the cost of publishing a collection of Ahnfelt's music, *Andeliga Sänger* (1850), which consisted mainly of Berg's hymn texts.

As editor, writer, poet, and translator, Olson made a valuable contribution to Swedish-American culture and to church music. His family immigrated to Nebraska when he was five years old, but he spent much of his life in the Chicago area. Educated at Augustana College, Rock Island, Illinois, he was editor of several Swedish-American newspapers and spent most of his professional career as an editor for the Augustana Book Concern (1911-1949). Olson wrote *A History of the Swedes in Illinois* (1908). He also contributed four original hymns and twenty-eight translations to *The Hymnal* (1925) of the Evangelical Lutheran Augustana Synod and served on the committee that produced the Lutheran *Service Book and Hymnal* (1958).

Tune

First associated with this text in Fredrik Engelke's *Lofsånger och andeliga wisor* (1873), TRYGGARE KAN INGEN VARA is probably a Swedish folk song, but versions of the tune were also sung in Germany in the early 1800s.

This charmingly simple tune needs light accompaniment, perhaps just recorders and guitars. It is well suited to part singing and could be sung unaccompanied.

Liturgical Use

As a confession of faith in God's providence; for many other occasions, including baptisms or funerals.

441

All Praise to You, My God, This Night

TALLIS CANON
♩ = 96

Text

Anglican bishop Thomas Ken (b. Berkampstead, Hertfordshire, England, 1637; d. Longleat, Wiltshire, England, 1711) wrote a group of three hymns for morning, evening, and midnight devotions for the students at Winchester College; this is the evening hymn. Ken suggested that the students sing these hymns

Scripture References
st. 1 = Ps. 91:4
st. 2 = Prov. 3:24
st. 3 = Ps. 4:8

"in your chamber devoutly." Although an unauthorized pamphlet version of the evening hymn appeared in 1692, the text was first published in Henry Playford's *Harmonia Sacra* (1693). Ken published the text in his *Manual of Prayers* (1695 ed.) and revised it for his 1709 edition. That edition is the source of the *Psalter Hymnal* version, which presents a modernized text of four of the original twelve stanzas (st. 1, 2, 4, and 12). Some hymnals begin the text with these words: "Glory to Thee, my God, this night," a line from Ken's 1695 publication. Typical of the piety of Ken's day, the original stanza 3 read:

Teach me to live, that I may dread
The grave as little as my bed;
Teach me to die, that so I may
Rise glorious at the awful day.

The oldest and most popular of the traditional English evening hymns, "All Praise to You" has standard features of an evening hymn: thanksgiving for the day that is past (st. 1), penitence for sin committed (st. 2), prayer for peaceful sleep (st. 3), and confidence in God's care and keeping (st. 1-3). The final stanza (st. 4) has become the most famous doxology in the English language (also found at 637 and 638).

Thomas Ken studied at Winchester College, Hart Hall, and New College, Oxford, England. Ordained in the Church of England in 1662, he served variously as pastor, chaplain at Winchester College (1669-1679), chaplain to Princess (later Queen) Mary in The Hague, and bishop of Bath and Wells (1685-1691). He was a man of conscience and independent mind who did not shirk from confrontations with royalty. When King Charles II came to visit Winchester, he took along his mistress, the famous actress Nell Gwynne. Ken was asked to provide lodging for her. The story is told that Ken quickly declared his house under repair and had a builder take off the roof! He later was dismissed from the court at The Hague when he protested a case of immorality. Then, later in 1688, Bishop Ken refused to read King James II's Declaration of Indulgence in the churches, which granted greater religious freedom in England, and he was briefly imprisoned in the Tower of London. A few years later he refused to swear allegiance to King William, and he lost his bishopric.

Ken wrote many hymns, which were published posthumously in 1721 and republished in 1868 as *Bishop Ken's Christian Year, or Hymns and Poems for the Holy Days and Festivals of the Church*. But he is best known for his morning, evening, and midnight hymns, each of which have as their final stanza the famous doxology "Praise God, from Whom All Blessings Flow."

Tune
TALLIS CANON is one of nine tunes Thomas Tallis (PHH 62) contributed to Matthew Parker's *Psalter* (around 1561). There it was used as a setting for Psalm 67. In the original tune the melody began in the tenor, followed by the soprano, and featured repeated phrases. Thomas Ravenscroft (PHH 59) published the tune, with the repeated phrases omitted, in his *Whole Book of Psalmes* (1621). The Ravenscroft version is the setting that virtually all modern hymnals use for this text.

TALLIS CANON is a round most congregations can easily sing in two parts, especially when women sing the first part and men sing the second. The congregation could also sing the hymn as a four-part round (each entry at four beats). Try also to sing unaccompanied (organists could sound the first phrase of each entry and then sing along).

Liturgical Use

A fine evening hymn well suited to the close of evening worship; midweek prayer meetings; Old Year's Eve services ("night" would then be used in the figurative sense).

442

Abide with Me

EVENTIDE
♩ = 56

Text

Henry Francis Lyte (b. Ednam, near Kelso, Rosburghshire, Scotland, 1793; d. Nice, France, 1847) wrote this text in the late summer of 1847; he died in November of that year (various other stories about Lyte's writing of this text do not appear to be reliable). First printed in a leaflet in 1847, the text was published posthumously in Lyte's *Remains* (1850). Most hymnals, including the *Psalter Hymnal,* customarily omit three of the original eight stanzas. The *Psalter Hymnal* also contains other alterations; for example, stanza 4 originally read, "Ills have no weight, and tears no bitterness."

Scripture References
st. 1 = Luke 24:29
Ps. 27:9
st. 2 = James 1:17
Ps. 102:26-27
st. 3 = Rom. 16:20
st. 4 = Ps. 27:1
1 Cor. 15:55
st. 5 = 2 Pet. 1:19

The text was inspired by Luke 24:29, in which the two travelers to Emmaus ask Jesus to "stay with us, for it is nearly evening." But "Abide with Me" is not a hymn for the evening of a day; instead evening is a metaphor for the close of life, a transition from life's "little day" (st. 2) to "Heaven's morning" (st. 5), which Lyte himself was quickly approaching. The text is a prayer for God's abiding care when friends fail (st. 1), when everything seems to change and decay (st. 2), when the devil attacks (st. 3), when death approaches (st. 4), and when we pass from this life to heaven's glory (st. 5).

Lyte was orphaned at an early age. He decided to pursue a medical career, although he also had an early interest in poetry. At Trinity College, Dublin, Scotland, he was awarded a prize for his poems on three different occasions. While at Trinity, he decided to become a minister and in 1815 was ordained in the Church of England. He served a number of parishes, including Lower Brixham, a small fishing village in Devonshire (1823-1847). Lyte wrote a considerable body of poetry, hymns, and psalm paraphrases, which were published in *Tales on the Lord's Prayer in Verse* (1826), *Poems, Chiefly Religious* (1833, 1845, slightly enlarged posthumously as *Miscellaneous Poems,* 1868), and *The Spirit of the Psalms* (1834, 1836). Because of ill health Lyte made winter visits to the French Riviera from 1844 until his death there in 1847.

Tune

According to some sources, William H. Monk (PHH 332) wrote EVENTIDE for Lyte's text in ten minutes. As the story goes, Monk was attending a hymnal committee meeting for the 1861 edition of *Hymns Ancient and Modern* of which he was music editor. Realizing that this text had no tune, Monk sat down at the piano and composed EVENTIDE. The hymn was then published in that edition of *Hymns Ancient and Modern.* The tune has always been associated with this text.

EVENTIDE is a modest tune, much loved in the Christian church. Though often used for solemn occasions, the tune must not be sung too slowly. Try singing one of the middle stanzas without accompaniment. Organists should keep a firm and steady tempo.

Liturgical Use
Funerals and memorial services; healing services; Easter evening (given st. 4); New Year's Eve services; many other occasions.

443

O DU LIEBE MEINER LIEBE
♩ = 58
Hours and Days and Years and Ages

Text

Dutch poet Rhijnvis Feith (b. Zwolle, the Netherlands, 1753; d. Zwolle, 1824) wrote this text in six stanzas; it was published in the Dutch *Evangelische Gezangen* (1806). An English translation by Leonard P. Brink (b. East Saugatuck, MI, 1876; d. Pomeroy,

Scripture References
all st. = Ps. 90
Ps. 103:13-18

WA, 1936) was published in *The New Christian Hymnal* compiled by Henry J. Kuiper in 1929. Going back to the Dutch original, Henrietta Ten Harmsel (PHH 61) thoroughly revised the Brink translation in 1984 for the *Psalter Hymnal.*

The text contrasts the changing character and frailty of human life with the everlasting love of our changeless God. Though "life's dangers overwhelm us," we have confidence in God's guidance and protection. The text helps us to give voice to our own trust in divine providence, to bring comfort to those in distress, and to express our hope for "everlasting peace."

Rhijnvis Feith received a law degree from the University of Leiden in 1770 and was mayor of Zwolle. An ardent Dutch patriot and a man of letters who lamented the Napoleonic occupation of the Netherlands, Feith wrote nineteen volumes of prose and poetry, much of it highly romantic, as well as theological and philosophic essays. He also wrote a number of hymns, thirty-five of which were included in the Dutch hymnal *Evangelische Gezangen* (1806), which he helped to compile.

Leonard P. Brink, a graduate of Calvin Seminary, Grand Rapids, Michigan (1900), spent much of his life as a missionary among the Navajo people. He translated Bible books and hymns into the Navajo language and wrote a catechism for the Navajo people. He also translated Dutch poetry and hymns into English.

Tune

Originally a folk song ("Sollen nun die grünen Jahre") dating from around 1700, O DU LIEBE MEINER LIEBE was used as a hymn tune in the Catholic hymnal *Bambergisches Gesangbuch* (1732). The tune name is the incipit of the text to which it was set in Johann Thommen's *Erbaulicher Musicalischer Christen-Schatz oder 500 Geistliche Lieder* (1745). The *Psalter Hymnal* version is from a manuscript chorale book of the Moravian Brethren compiled in Herrnhut in 1735.

The tune is a rounded bar form (AABA) with simple stepwise melodic motion. Sing in harmony. Another harmonization in G major (see 513) could provide an alternative setting, perhaps for a higher and fuller sound on stanza 4.

Liturgical Use

Old Year's Eve services; worship that focuses on God's providence; funerals; church anniversaries.

444

Greet Now the Swiftly Changing Year

ROK NOVY
♩ = 60

Text

The original text of this anonymous Slovak hymn ("Rok novy zase k nam prisel") was found in Tobias Závorka's Czech hymnal *Kancionál* (1602). A revision of that text was published in 1636 in Juraj Tranovsky's *Pisne Duchovni Stare I Move,* a Slovak Lutheran hymnal usually known as the *Cithara Sanctorum.* Jaroslav J. Vajda (b. Lorain, OH, 1919) prepared the English translation in 1968 for the *Worship Supplement* to *The Lutheran Hymnal.* This hymn remains very popular for New Year's Day celebrations in every Slovak home and church.

Scripture References
all st. = Ps. 90
st. 6 = Luke 2:14

Stanza 1 immediately alerts us that this is a hymn for New Year's Day as we "Rejoice!" and "with thanks embrace another year of grace." Stanzas 2-5 remind us of our blessing in Christ. In stanza 6 we join once more with the Christmas angels in their chorus of glory and peace. Stanza 7 is a prayer for continued blessings in "this new year of grace."

Born of Czechoslovakian parents, Vajda was educated at Concordia College in Fort Wayne, Indiana, and Concordia Theological Seminary in St. Louis, Missouri. Ordained a Lutheran pastor in 1944, he served congregations in Pennsylvania and Indiana until 1963. He was editor of the periodicals *The Lutheran Beacon* (1959-1963) and *This Day* (1963-1971) and book editor and developer for Concordia Publishing House in St. Louis from 1971 until his retirement in 1986. Working mainly with hymn texts, Vajda served on several Lutheran commissions of worship. A writer of original poetry since his teens, he is the author of *They Followed the King* (1965) and *Follow the King* (1977).

His translations from Slovak include *Bloody Sonnets* (1950), *Slovak Christmas* (1960), *An Anthology of Slovak Literature* (1977), and contributions to the Lutheran *Worship Supplement* (1969) and the *Lutheran Book of Worship* (1978). A collection of his hymn texts, carols, and hymn translations was issued as *Now the Joyful Celebration* (1987); its sequel is *So Much to Sing About* (1991). Vajda's hymns are included in many modern hymnals, and he was honored as a Fellow of the Hymn Society in the United States and Canada in 1988.

Tune

ROK NOVY, which means "New Year" in Czech, was named by translator Vajda after the first two words of the original text. For historical data about this tune see PHH 283; the setting at 233 is in F minor.

The harmonization here is by Theodore Beck (b. River Forest, IL, 1929). Beck is a graduate of Concordia Teachers College in River Forest, Illinois, and earned master's and Ph.D. degrees at Northwestern University, Evanston, Illinois. He has taught at Concordia Teachers College in Seward, Nebraska, since 1953. A published composer of organ and choral works, Beck served on the music committee for the Lutheran *Worship Supplement* (1969).

Sing antiphonally, assigning stanzas to groups within the congregation; for example, assign the first halves of stanzas 1-4 and 6 to antiphonal groups but have the entire congregation sing the second halves and all of stanzas 5 and 7. Accompanists, try taking a quick "breath" at the end of the first couplet in each stanza (just before "Rejoice") and be sure to help congregations phrase the final couplet of each stanza into one long line. Stanza 7 is a prayer; a fuller accompaniment will help highlight the change of address.

Liturgical Use

New Year's Day; New Year's Eve watch-night service.

445

GREGOR'S 112TH METRE
♩ = 58

Our Faithful God

Text

Dutch pastor Hendrik Pierson (b. Amsterdam, the Netherlands, 1834; d. Groningen, the Netherlands, 1923) wrote the original text, "God is getrouw, zijn plannen falen niet," and published it in *Vluchtheuvel Gezangen* (1904), which he compiled for the Vluchtheuvel Church in Zetten. It was also published in the *Psalmen en Gezangen* (1938) of the Dutch Hervormde Kerk and then brought to North America by Dutch-Canadian

Scripture References
st. 1 = Rom. 8:30
st. 3 = Col. 1:9

immigrants after World War II. Stanley M. Wiersma's (PHH 25) translation was first published in the *Psalter Hymnal Supplement* in 1974.

The three stanzas display a Trinitarian pattern: stanza 1 is about God's providence; stanza 2, Christ's victorious rule; stanza 3, the Spirit's leading of the church. Together the stanzas portray a powerful vision of God's providence as a doctrine that brings comfort to Christians.

Pierson not only served as a pastor in Heinenoord and Hertogenbosch, he was also a director of the Heldring Institute in Zetten, which operated halfway houses and schools for girls and young women. He was a leader in various social movements in the Netherlands, especially militating against legalized prostitution. In his life and work he maintained a fine balance between theology, worship, and the diaconal work of the church. Pierson wrote a number of hymns.

Tune

Christian Gregor, Moravian minister and musician (b. Dirsdorf, Silesia 1723; d. Berthelsdorf, near Herrnhut, Saxony, 1801), wrote GREGOR'S 112TH METRE as a setting for "Er wird es tun, der fromme treue Gott" and published it in his *Choralbuch* in 1784 (hymn no. 112). That hymnal was a supplement to the 1778 *Gesangbuch der evangelische Brueder-Gemeinen*. Dutch musician Leonard J. Mens (1879-1960) prepared the harmonization for the *Psalmen en Gezangen* (1938), where this tune was set to Pierson's text.

The tune has bar form shape (AAB) common in many chorales. The melody also has a sensitive balance between stepwise motion and larger, dramatic intervals. Sing in harmony and use a firm, bright organ registration.

Gregor became uncomfortable as a Protestant in predominantly Roman Catholic Silesia, and he joined the Moravian settlement in Herrnhut in 1742. There his many gifts came to expression: he became a noted spiritual leader, church musician, and hymnal editor. He traveled to Moravian communities and mission outposts in Europe and the United States, served as organist for the Moravians in Zeist, the Netherlands (1749-1753), and became a Moravian bishop in Herrnhut in 1789. The principal editor of the Moravian *Gesangbuch* (1778), Gregor supplied some three hundred of his own texts as well as adaptations to its contents of 1,750 hymns. He also compiled a tunebook for that hymnal, entitled *Choralbuch* (1784), in which a number of tunes are also attributed to him.

Liturgical Use

Worship that focuses on God's providence or the Trinity; ordination/commissioning services; church dedications and anniversaries; new ventures in church ministries.

446

If You But Trust in God to Guide You

Text

Georg Neumark (b. Langensalza, Thuringia, Germany, 1621; d. Weimar, Germany, 1681) lived during the time of the Thirty Years' War, when social and economic conditions were deplorable. He had personal trials as well. On his way to Königsberg to study at the university, traveling in the comparative safety of a group of merchants, he was robbed of nearly all his possessions. During the next two years he spent much of his time looking for employment. He finally secured a tutoring position in Kiel. When he had saved enough money, he returned to the University of Königsberg and studied there for five years. In Königsberg he again lost all his belongings, this time in a fire. Despite his personal suffering Neumark wrote many hymns in which he expressed his absolute trust in God. In 1651 he settled in Weimar, Thuringia, where he became court poet and archivist to Duke Johann Ernst and librarian and registrar of the city. Neumark wrote thirty-four hymns, of which "If You But Trust in God to Guide You" has become a classic.

Scripture References
all st. = Ps. 55:22
Ps. 56:11
Prov. 3:5-6

Neumark wrote this text at age twenty, just after he had finally been able to find employment as a tutor for a judge in Kiel. Neumark was so relieved and grateful to God by his change in circumstance that he wrote this text, saying, "This good fortune, which came so suddenly and, as it were, from heaven, so rejoiced my heart that I wrote my hymn 'Wer nur . . .' to the glory of my God on that first day."

Written in Kiel, Germany, in 1641, the seven-stanza text ("Wer nur den lieben Gott lasst walten") had the following heading: "a hymn of consolation, that God will care for and preserve his own in his own time; after the saying 'cast thy burden upon the Lord and He shall sustain thee.' Psalm 55:22." The text was published with the tune, also composed by Neumark, in *Fortgepflanzter Musikalisch-Poetischer Lustwald* (1657).

Catherine Winkworth (PHH 194) prepared two translations of the original German text: one published in her *Lyra Germanica* (1855) and one published with substantial revision in her *Chorale Book for England* (1863), in which the first stanza began "If thou but suffer God to guide thee." Winkworth's revised translation of Neumark's original stanzas 1, 3, and 7 is the basis for the three stanzas found in the *Psalter Hymnal.*

A classic German chorale, this fine text focuses on trust in God's care in all of life's circumstances, both prosperous times and "evil days." As Christians we are counseled to be confident (st. 1), to have patience (st. 2), and to be faithful in service (st. 3).

Tune

Published in 1657 (see above) WER NUR DEN LIEBEN GOTT is also known as NEUMARK. Johann S. Bach (PHH 7) used the tune in its isorhythmic shape (all equal rhythms) in his cantatas 21, 27, 84, 88, 93, 166, 179, and 197. Many Lutheran composers have also written organ preludes on this tune.

WER NUR DEN LIEBEN GOTT is a bar form (AAB) with rhythmic interest and mainly stepwise melodic lines. Sing in a steady unison on stanzas 1 and 3 and in harmony on stanza 2 with a quieter organ registration.

Liturgical Use

Many occasions in Christian worship when profound trust and hope in God's providence and faithfulness needs to be affirmed as only song can express it.

447

Eternal God beyond All Time

JORDAN
$\downarrow = 54$

Text

Written by Marie J. Post (PHH 5) in 1979 for the profession of faith of her daughter Meredith, this text was first published in the 1987 *Psalter Hymnal*.

Scripture References
st. 1 = Ps. 90:1

The text expresses thanks to God for his leading in past years (st. 1), for his presence in our lives today by his Word (st. 2), and for hope of blessing in future years (st. 3). As we sing, we address the God of yesterday, today, and tomorrow, and we dedicate ourselves to his service.

Tune

One of the 246 hymn tunes by Joseph Barnby (PHH 438), JORDAN was published in *The Hymnary* (1872) as a setting for "Sing to the Lord a Joyful Song." JORDAN contains several repeated phrases. Barnby originally composed the tune to be sung in harmony, with phrases 5 and 7 sung in unison, although the full accompaniment was included for organ. But have the congregation sing in unison throughout, perhaps with one stanza in harmony.

Liturgical Use

Profession of faith; sermon response; hymn of dedication; for worship that focuses on the family; Reformation services; church anniversaries; graduation ceremonies (from schools or church classes).

448

LUZON
♩ = 144

I Lift Up My Eyes to the Mountains

Text

Written by Henry Zylstra (PHH 82) in 1953, this text is a versification of Psalm 121. It was first published in the 1959 *Psalter Hymnal*
and is one of the few texts in that hymnal in amphibrachic meter.
(For other settings of Psalm 121 see 121 and 180; for further
analysis of the text see PHH 121.)

Scripture References
st. 1 = Ps. 121:1-2
st. 2 = Ps. 121:3-4
st. 3 = Ps. 121:5-6
st. 4 = Ps. 121:7-8

Tune

Dick L. Van Halsema (PHH 2) composed LUZON in 1954. The tune was published with
the Zylstra text in the 1959 *Psalter Hymnal* on whose committee both writer and composer served. Zylstra and Van Halsema also served together as United States servicemen
stationed on the Philippine island of Luzon at the end of World War II (hence the
name of this tune). At that time both men experienced the truth of Psalm 121 in their
lives.

The tune and harmonization make use of repeated tones and pedal points to
portray the stability and dependability of God's care; the final phrase of the melody
originally repeated one note throughout. The E-flat chord in the third line provides a
delightful touch of color. LUZON is suitable for either unison or harmony singing.
Maintain one pulse per measure.

Liturgical Use

See comments at PHH 121.

449

FRANCES
♩ = 66

O Righteous, in the Lord Rejoice

Text

A paraphrase of a number of verses in Psalm 33 (1-3, 13-15, and
18-20), this text was originally published in the 1912 *Psalter.*
Marie J. Post (PHH 5) revised parts of that text for the 1959
Psalter Hymnal, a revision that was further altered for the 1987
edition. (See PHH 33 for a setting of the complete psalm and for
additional general comments.)

Scripture References
st. 1 = Ps. 33:1-3
st. 2 = Ps. 33:13-15
st. 3 = Ps. 33:18-20

The text testifies with joy that God's people are safe and secure in his hands and under his rule. Stanza 1 calls us to praise, stanza 2 confesses God's omniscience, and stanza 3 confesses God's providence.

Tune

Better known for his gospel songs than his hymn tunes, James McGranahan (PHH 99) wrote FRANCES in the latter part of the nineteenth century. Copyrighted in 1901 by McGranahan, the tune was set to this text in the 1912 *Psalter* and in every edition of the *Psalter Hymnal*.

FRANCIS is a rousing tune with strong ascending figures and a rhythmic drive that produces two very long musical lines. Sing in harmony; use bright organ registration and crisp articulation to support this energetic melody.

Liturgical Use

See PHH 33 for many uses; however, these stanzas do focus more specifically on God's intimate knowledge of our lives and on his guidance and protection.

450

O God, Our Father, We Come

CENTENNIAL PRAYER
♩ = 96

Text

John H. Kromminga (b. Grundy Center, IA, 1918; d. Grand Rapids, MI, 1994) wrote this text in 1956, the same year he became president of Calvin Seminary, Grand Rapids. He and his wife, Claire, who composed the tune, submitted this text in the centennial hymn contest held as a part of the 100th anniversary celebration of the Christian Reformed Church in 1957. Marie J.

Scripture References
st. 1 = Ps. 100:4
st. 2 = Ps. 115:1
st. 3 = Ps. 46:1
st. 4 = Matt. 6:13

Post's "O Lord, Beneath Thy Guiding Hand" set to an Adrian Hartog tune (1959 *Psalter Hymnal* 486) was the winning entry. But the *Psalter Hymnal* Revision Committee chose to publish the Kromminga hymn, not the Post/Hartog hymn, in the 1987 *Psalter Hymnal*.

The first three stanzas reveal a Trinitarian pattern of praise: to God the Father, whom we have come to worship (st. 1); to Jesus Christ, who died for our sin (st. 2); and to the Holy Spirit, who guides us by the Word (st. 3). The final stanza affirms that our praise to God—our doxology—is orthodox (right praise) only when it is accompanied by our daily obedience in witness and service.

Kromminga studied at Calvin College and Calvin Seminary and received his Th.D. from Princeton Seminary, Princeton, New Jersey, in 1946. He was a pastor in three Christian Reformed Church congregations before he joined his alma mater, Calvin Seminary, as professor of church history (1952-1983) and then as president (1956-

1983). After his retirement in 1983 he served as president of International Theological Seminary in Pasadena, California. He wrote many articles and four books, including *The Christian Reformed Church: A Study in Orthodoxy* (1949).

Tune

Claire Ottenhoff Kromminga (b. Chicago, IL, 1919; d. Grand Rapids, MI, 1995) first composed CENTENNIAL PRAYER in a music theory class at Calvin College in 1939 and then revised it for submission in the 1957 contest (see above). Kromminga studied at Chicago Music College and received a B.A. from Calvin College, Grand Rapids. She was an elementary school teacher from 1941 to 1944 in Muskegon, Michigan, and Newton, New Jersey, and then returned to Michigan.

Dale Grotenhuis (PHH 4) prepared the harmonization for the 1987 *Psalter Hymnal*. Sing stanzas 1-3 in harmony and stanza 4 in unison.

Liturgical Use

General hymn of praise for many occasions (like the anniversary service for which it was written); profession of faith; marriage; ordination; stanzas 1-3 at the beginning of worship, stanza 4 at the end of worship.

451

WAS GOTT TUT
♩ = 54

What God Ordains Is Always Right

Text

Samuel Rodigast (b. Gröben, Thuringia, Germany, 1649; d. Berlin, Germany, 1708) wrote the text ("Was Gott tut, das ist wohlgetan!") in six stanzas for his seriously ill friend, Severus Gastorius. The text was published in the Appendix to *Das Hannoverische Gesangbuch* (1676). Gracia Grindal (PHH 351) translated four of the original stanzas for the 1978 *Lutheran Book of Worship*.

Scripture References
all st. = Rom. 8:38-39
st. 1 = Deut. 32:4
st. 2 = Deut. 31:6
Heb. 13:5
John 8:12; 14:18
st. 3 = Eph. 2:20
st. 4 = Luke 1:79

A sermon on Deuteronomy 32:4 in hymn form, the text is a confession of unshakable trust in God's providence in our lives (see 440 and 446 as well as confessions found in Rom. 8:38-39 and Lord's Day 1 for a similar theme). The text expresses the kind of devout faith that produced Lutheran Pietism (which began around 1670) and provides a worthy vehicle for congregations to affirm trust in God's care.

Rodigast studied at the University of Jena and briefly served as an instructor in philosophy there. But for most of his professional life he was associated with the Greyfriars Gymnasium (high school) in Berlin, as joint rector from 1680 to 1698 and as rector from 1698 until his death. A fine scholar and administrator, Rodigast was offered a position at the University of Jena, but he preferred to stay at the gymnasium. He is known to have written only two hymn texts, of which "What God Ordains" has become a classic.

Tune
WAS GOTT TUT is usually attributed to Severus Gastorius (b. Ottern, near Weimar, Germany, 1646; d. Jena, Germany, 1682), who presumably composed the tune during a convalescence in 1675 (see above). The tune was published in *Ausserlesenes Weimarisches Gesangbuch* (1681). Educated at the University of Jena, Gastorius became cantor of Jena in 1677, a post he held until his death. He wrote a variety of church music, including five funeral motets, but he is known primarily for composing WAS GOTT TUT.

The tune is a classic example of a seventeenth-century German chorale setting in bar form (AAB). Sing in sturdy unison, changing to harmony for some of the stanzas. Do not rush, but sing with stately fervor. Observing fermatas at the ends of the first two long lines will help to bring a sense of patience to this melody by giving more breathing time.

Liturgical Use
As a sung confession of faith in God's care and keeping and in his wisdom as he directs our lives; a healing service; many other occasions of worship.

452

He Leadeth Me

AUCHTON
♩ = 56

Text
Like the psalm on which it is based, this text confesses absolute trust in the Lord's guidance and care, a trust that is sufficient even for "the valley of the shadow of death" (st. 4). Joseph H. Gilmore (b. Boston, MA, 1834; d. Rochester, NY, 1918) noted the following about his writing of this text:

Scripture References
all st. = Ps. 23

> I was supplying for a couple of Sundays the pulpit of the First Baptist Church in Philadelphia. At the midweek service of March 26, 1862, I set out to give the people an exposition of the 23rd Psalm, but I got no further than the words "He leadeth me." Those words took hold of me as they had never done before. I saw in them a significance and beauty of which I had never dreamed. . . . At the close of the meeting a few of us kept on talking about the thoughts which I had empha-sized; and then and there, on a back page of my sermon notes, I penciled the hymn just as it stands today, handed it to my wife, and thought no more of it. . . .

She sent it without my knowledge to the *Watchman and Reflector* magazine, and there it first appeared in print December 4, 1862.

While visiting a church in Rochester, New York, in 1865, Gilmore saw his hymn in print for the first time set to William B. Bradbury's tune (see below). The text was also published in Gilmore's *He Leadeth Me, and Other Religious Poems* (1877).

Educated at Brown University, Providence, Rhode Island, and Newton Theological Seminary, Newton, Massachusetts, Gilmore was ordained to the Baptist ministry in 1862. He served churches in Fisherville, New Hampshire, and Rochester, New York. In 1868 he was appointed to the English faculty at the University of Rochester, where he served until retirement in 1911. He published various literary works, including *Outlines of English and American Literature* (1905).

Tune

After seeing Gilmore's text in the Boston *Watchman and Reflector*, William B. Bradbury (PHH 114) composed AUCHTON for those words. Bradbury arranged the text into a stanza/refrain structure, added the final line of the refrain, and published the hymn in his *The Golden Censor* in 1864. AUCHTON (also known as HE LEADETH ME) means "unknown."

The tune is a gospel melody in typical verse/refrain pattern; it has a simple harmonization. AUCHTON consists of two main lines formed into an AABB pattern. Sing in harmony. Fermatas, if any are observed, should come at the ends of the lines and not in the middle of line 2, as some soloists prefer.

Liturgical Use

Various occasions of worship; funerals.

453

ASH GROVE
♩ = 116

Let All Things Now Living

Text

Katherine K. Davis (PHH 57) wrote this text for the tune ASH GROVE in the 1920s. The text was first published as an anthem and descant setting in 1939 (by E. C. Schirmer) under the name John Cowley, one of her pseudonyms. (Davis wrote "The Little Drummer Boy," 1941, as well as many other songs under this and other pseudonyms.)

Scripture References
all st. = Gen. 1
Job 26:7-14; 38

Employing Old Testament images, the text calls forth praise from all creatures and directs that praise to God the Creator. We praise God because he made us and provides for us (st. 1); we join our praise to that of the entire universe in a song of "hosanna and praise" (st. 2).

Tune

ASH GROVE first appeared in print in the collection *Bardic Museum* compiled by Edward Jones and published in London in 1802. It has been suggested that the tune is similar to a melody found in the *Beggar's Opera* (1728), an opera that includes many arrangements of well-known folk tunes. ASH GROVE is, however, a harp tune rather than a folk song, and its associations in Wales are entirely secular.

Katherine K. Davis related that she found this tune in the *Book of National Songs,* a pamphlet published by Novello. She wrote the harmonization and a descant for the tune and published them with her text in 1939 (see above). Since that time the hymn has been a favorite of many church choirs and congregations.

ASH GROVE is in classic rounded bar form (AABA). Sing in harmony and add the descant at stanza 2, perhaps also with instruments like flutes or recorders.

Liturgical Use

For many worship services of praise and thanksgiving including, but by no means limited to, harvest thanksgiving; a doxology at the close of worship.

454

Now Thank We All Our God

NUN DANKET
♩ = 56

Text

Martin Rinkart (b. Eilenburg, Saxony, Germany, 1586; d. Eilenburg, 1649) was a pastor during the horrors of the Thirty Years' War, and that difficult ministry inspired him to both sacrificial service and to the writing of hymns of praise and confidence in God.

Scripture References
st. 1 = 1 Chron. 29:13
Ps. 107:1, 8
st. 2 = Phil. 4:7

As a youth he was a choirboy at the St. Thomas Church in Leipzig, Germany, and then studied at the university there. He became a schoolmaster and cantor, held several pastorates, and became the archdeacon in Eilenburg in 1617, a position he held until his death. Because of the war the walled city of Eilenburg was overflowing with refugees, causing widespread disease and famine. During the epidemic of 1637 Rinkart officiated at over four thousand funerals, including his wife's; at times he presided at fifty burials a day. But in spite of these incredible demands on his ministry, he wrote many theological works and sixty hymns, of which "Now Thank We All Our God" is best known.

The text was published in the 1663 edition of his *Jesu Heartz-Büchlein;* it was presumably published in the earlier 1636 edition, but no copy of that edition is extant. The translation by Catherine Winkworth (PHH 194) was published in her *Lyra Germanica* in 1858 and again in her *Chorale Book for England* in 1863.

The text alludes to the apocryphal book of Ecclesiasticus 50:22-24 (part of the Lutheran Bible), which reads: "Now bless the God of all, who in every way does great things." Stanza 1 thanks God for what he has done in the past; stanza 2 prays for God's guidance in the future; stanza 3 is a Trinitarian doxology styled after the "Gloria Patri." Stanzas 1 and 2 were originally meant to be sung as a table grace; stanza 3 was added later as a Trinitarian doxology. (Stories that Rinkart wrote his text for the Peace of Westphalia of 1648 are incorrect, although this hymn was used in the celebrations of that year.)

Tune
NUN DANKET, named for the incipit of Rinkart's text, has been associated with this text ever since they were published together by Johann Crüger (PHH 42) in his *Praxis Pietatis Melica* (1647). Like most modern hymnals, the *Psalter Hymnal* prints the isorhythmic (all equal rhythms) version. The tune was used by Johann S. Bach (PHH 7) in his cantatas 79 and 192 and by Felix Mendelssohn (PHH 279) in the Lobgesang movement of his *Symphony No. 2* (1840); the harmonization is based on the one in six voices by Mendelssohn in that work. There are also many organ compositions based on NUN DANKET.

A bar form (AAB), NUN DANKET is a splendid tune for majestic occasions of thanksgiving. Sing stanzas 1 and 2 in either unison or harmony, but sing the doxology in stanza 3 in unison, preferably with a descant. Observe a fermata at the ends of the first two systems. This tune needs a broad tempo.

Liturgical Use
Most commonly at the conclusion of worship; useful for many occasions of thanksgiving: regular worship services, weddings, harvest thanksgiving.

455

EAST ACKLAM
♩ = 56

For the Fruits of His Creation

Text
Fred Pratt Green (b. Roby, Liverpool, Lancashire, England, 1903) wrote the text specifically for the tune EAST ACKLAM with its somewhat unusual meter. Pratt Green carefully matched the "Thanks be to God" phrases to fit the short but powerful cadential motifs in Francis Jackson's tune. The text was first published in the British *Methodist Recorder* in August 1970. "For the Fruits" has become a popular harvest thanksgiving hymn.

Scripture References
st. 2 = Matt. 20:1-16
　　 Matt. 25:37-45
st. 3 = Gal. 5:22

The text's theme is thanksgiving: in stanza 1 for the natural harvest and in stanza 3 for the spiritual harvest. That thanksgiving tone, however, functions as a frame around stanza 2, which reminds us that thanksgiving must also be shown in our deeds of sharing God's bounty with those in need. Although the text is a modern one, it expresses the same message as did the Old Testament prophets: offerings of thanksgiving are acceptable to God only if "the orphans and the widows" have received loving care (see Isa. 1:10-17; Amos 5:21-24; Micah 6:6-8). That message is so necessary at North American harvest feasts!

Already in the 1970s Erik Routley (PHH 31) considered Fred Pratt Green to be the most important British hymn writer since Charles Wesley, and most commentators regard Green as the leader of the British "hymn explosion." Green was educated at Didsbury Theological College, Manchester, England, and in 1928 began forty years of ministry in the Methodist Church, serving churches mainly in the Yorkshire and London areas. A playwright and poet, he published his works in numerous periodicals. His poetry was also published collectively in three volumes, including *The Skating Parson* (1963) and *The Old Couple* (1976). Though he had written a few hymns earlier, Green started writing prolifically after 1966, when he joined a committee to prepare the Methodist hymnal supplement *Hymns and Songs* (1969) and was asked to submit hymn texts for subjects that were not well represented. His hymn texts, numbering over three hundred, have appeared in most recent hymnals and supplements and have been collected in *26 Hymns* (1971), *The Hymns and Ballads of Fred Pratt Green* (1982), and *Later Hymns and Ballads* (1989). In 1982 Green was honored as a Fellow of the Hymn Society in the United States and Canada.

Tune

Francis Jackson (b. Malton, Yorkshire, England, 1917) wrote EAST ACKLAM in 1957 at York Minster Abbey, where he had a long and distinguished career as organist and music master (1946-1982). The tune's name refers to the hamlet northeast of York, England, where Jackson has lived since 1982. Jackson received his early musical training at the York Minster School, later studied with Edward Bairstow, and received his doctorate from Durham University (1940). From 1947 to 1980 he conducted both the York Musical Society and the York Symphony Orchestra. He has published a wide array of organ and church music and was very popular as an organ recitalist.

Jackson originally wrote the tune as a setting for Reginald Heber's (PHH 249) "God, that madest earth and heaven," which was usually sung to the popular Welsh tune AR HYD Y NOS. Now matched to Pratt Green's text in several modern hymnals, EAST ACKLAM was first published in the British supplement *Hymns and Songs* (1969).

The tune has several striking features: the hammer-blow chords at the end of lines 1, 2, and 4; the melodic sequences; and the stunning melodic rise to the climax in lines 3 and 4. Although good choirs may enjoy the challenge of the harmony, the tune is best sung in unison by congregations. Use solid accompaniment and observe a ritardando at the very end of stanza 3.

Liturgical Use

For harvest thanksgiving but also for Labor Day services and other occasions that focus on social justice.

456

WIR PFLÜGEN
♩ = 60

We Plow the Fields and Scatter

Text

Matthias Claudius (b. Reinfeld, Holstein, Germany, 1740; d. Hamburg, Germany, 1815) grew up in the home of a Lutheran pastor and studied briefly for the ministry at the University of Jena. During his twenties and thirties he seems to have forsaken the faith, influenced by the rationalistic thought of the time. He became seriously ill in 1777, and this crisis was instrumental in returning him to his childhood faith. He

Scripture References
st. 1 = Ps. 145:16
Ezek. 34:26-27
st. 2 = Ps. 104
Acts 14:17
st. 3 = Gen. 8:22

worked briefly as commissioner of agriculture and manufacture of Hesse-Darmstadt (1776-1777) and in 1778 was appointed an auditor of the Schleswig-Holstein Bank in Altona. Most of his life was spent as a journalist, editor, and writer on general culture, much of it as editor of *Der Wansbecker Bote (The Wansbeck Messenger)*.

Claudius also wrote many devotional poems, of which this is the only one in common use as hymn text. Originally a poem in seventeen stanzas with a refrain that began "Im Anfang war's auf Erden," the poem was the peasants' song in Claudius's sketch "Paul Erdmann's Feast," published in *Asinus omnia sua secum portans* (1782). It was popularized in various nineteenth-century German hymnals where it appeared with fewer stanzas, often beginning with Claudius's third stanza "Wir pflugen und wir streuen."

The English text is based on Jane Montgomery-Campbell's free translation of his original stanzas 3, 5, 7, 9, 10, and 13, first published in Charles S. Bere's *A Garland of Songs* (1861). Campbell (b. Paddington, London, England, 1817; d. Bovey Tracey, South Devon, England, 1878) was proficient in both music and German. She translated a number of German hymns into English, which were first published in Charles Bere's *Garland of Songs, or an English Liederkranz* (1862) and his *Children's Chorale Book* (1869). The writer of *A Handbook for Singers* (undated), Campbell also taught singing to the children in her parish school, St. James in Paddington, where her father was rector.

The text affirms that, while we need to plow the land and sow the seed, it is God who provides the increase; he sends the rain and the sunshine to produce a harvest. God also sustains his creation, for "all good gifts around us are sent from heaven above." Thus praise bursts from our "humble, thankful hearts."

Tune

WIR PFLÜGEN (named after the incipit of Schulz's original third stanza) was published anonymously in the Hanover collection *Lieder für Volksschulen* (1800). But it was credited to Johann A. P. Schulz in Lindner's Berlin songbook *Jungenfreund* (1812). The harmonization by John B. Dykes (PHH 147) was first published in the 1861 edition of *Hymns Ancient and Modern*.

The tune is noted for its opening phrase, which encompasses a very wide range, but that doesn't appear to discourage most congregations from singing it. Sing the stanzas in unison (note that lines 1 and 4 are unison) and the refrain in harmony. Change the organ registration before stanza 3 to highlight the change of focus in the text: as we sing stanzas 1 and 2, we address each other, but in stanza 3 we address God.

Johann Abraham Peter Schulz (b. Luneburg, Germany, 1747; d. Schwedt an der Oder, Germany, 1800) had a distinguished career in music, though his father wanted him to become a pastor. At the age of fifteen Schulz traveled to Berlin by himself to seek out a good music teacher. He persevered in his musical training under the composer and theorist Johann Philipp Kirnberger. Appointed accompanist and music teacher to the Polish princess Sophia Woiwodin in 1768, Schulz traveled all through Europe and was exposed to many different kinds of music. After 1775 he had a number of prestigious positions, including director of the Royal French Theater in Berlin (1776-1780), director of music for Prince Henry of Prussia (1780-1787), and director of the Royal Danish Theater (1787-1795). Schulz composed operas, instrumental works, church music, and song settings in a folk-music style, often setting the poems of great literary figures to music.

Liturgical Use

Harvest thanksgiving; as a hymn of creation; the final stanza as an offertory hymn.

457

He's Got the Whole World in His Hands

WHOLE WORLD
♩ = 100

Text

This anonymous spiritual rose out of the oral tradition of African Americans and has become one of the most widely known and loved spirituals, sung by young and old everywhere. Like other songs arising out of an oral tradition, it has many variations in both text and tune. Creating new stanzas would also be consistent with the tradition.

Scripture References
all st. = Ps. 47; 93-99

The text confesses the same theme of the Lord's cosmic rule that is proclaimed in kingship psalms such as Psalms 47 and 93-99: "The Lord reigns!" The stanzas give examples of aspects of the "whole world"—nature, human creatures, and in fact, everything and everybody.

Tune

WHOLE WORLD is characterized by one recurring melodic and rhythmic motif. The tune is intended for unison singing and possibly some solo singing (for example, on st. 4-5), with light accompaniment on guitar or piano. Try singing some stanzas unaccompanied, clapping on beats two and four.

Liturgical Use

Various occasions of worship: services that focus on creation, God's rule and providence, family life (st. 3-5), and communion of saints (st. 6); as a hymn of assurance.

458

WIE LIEBLICH IST DER MAIEN
♩ = 60

Sing to the Lord of Harvest

Text

In simple, vivid language derived from biblical images in the second half of Psalm 65, this text thanks the Lord for the harvest (st. 1-2) and offers to God the harvest of our lives (st. 3). Written

Scripture References
all st. = Ps. 65:9-13

by John S. B. Monsell in four stanzas, this text was published in Monsell's *Hymns of Love and Praise* in 1866.

John Samuel Bewley Monsell (b. St. Colomb's, Londonderry, Ireland, 1811; d. Guilford, Surrey, England, 1875) was educated at Trinity College in Dublin and served as a chaplain and rector of several churches in Ireland after his ordination in 1835. Transferred to England in 1853, he became rector of Egham in Surrey and was rector of St. Nicholas Church in Guilford from 1870 until his death (caused by a construction accident at his church). A prolific poet, Monsell published his verse in eleven volumes. His three hundred hymns, many celebrating the seasons of the church year, were issued in collections such as *Hymns and Miscellaneous Poems* (1837), *Spiritual Songs* (1857), *Hymns of Love and Praise* (1863), and *The Parish Hymnal* (1873).

Tune

This tune was originally a love song composed in 1575 by Johann Steurlein (b. Schmalkalden, Thuringia, Germany, 1546; d. Meiningen, Germany, 1613) as a setting for "Mit Lieb bin ich umfangen." Steurlein studied law at the University of Wittenberg. From 1569 to 1589 he lived in Wasungen near Meiningen, where he served as town clerk as well as cantor and organist in the Lutheran church. From 1589 until his death he lived in Meiningen, where at various times he served as notary public, mayor, and secretary to the Elector of Saxony. A gifted poet and musician, Steurlein rhymed both the Old and

New Testaments in German. A number of his hymn tunes and harmonizations were published in *Geistliche Lieder* (1575) and *Sieben und Zwantzig Neue Geistliche Gesenge* (1588).

His tune WIE LIEBLICH IST DER MAIEN gets its name from its original use as a setting for Martin Behm's hymn text that began with those words in 1581; text and tune were published together in Gregor Gunderreitter's *David's Himlische Harpffen*. The Steurlein tune was later set to Monsell's text in W. Garrett Horder's *Worship Song* in 1905 and popularized through the 1954 anthem by Healey Willan (PHH 258). The harmonization is by Willan, simplified from his anthem.

The tune is a rounded bar form (AABA) whose melodic variation in the fourth line sometimes confuses congregations. Use bright organ tone on that line to support the tune, but use a lighter touch on other lines. The tune can be sung in harmony by agile voices, but congregations may prefer to sing in unison.

Liturgical Use

Harvest thanksgiving and similar services; offertory hymn; hymn of dedication; stanza 3 is fitting for dedication of our gifts and our whole lives for kingdom service/missions.

459

Our World Belongs to God

RHOSYMEDRE
♩ = 63

Text

At the request of the *Psalter Hymnal* Revision Committee, Marie J. Post (PHH 5) wrote this text in March 1986 based on sections of *Our World Belongs to God*, a Contemporary Testimony (see p. 857; for the complete text, see pp. 1019-1038 of the worship edition of the *Psalter Hymnal* 1987).

Scripture References
st. 1 = Gen. 1
Ps. 33:1-11
st. 2 = John 3:16
st. 3 = Rev. 21:4

The text focuses on main themes in the contemporary testimony: God's creation of the world and his providence (par. 8 and 13, st. 1); human sin and God's plan of salvation in Christ (par. 36, 19, 24, 27, st. 2); our hope for a God-glorifying, renewed creation (par. 56 and 58, st. 3).

Tune

John David Edwards (b. Penderlwyngoch, Cardiganshire, Wales, 1805; d. Llanddoget, Denbighshire, North Wales, 1885) was educated at Jesus College, Oxford, England, and ordained an Anglican priest in 1833. He served parishes in Rhosymedre and Llanddoget and published a collection of hymn tunes, *Original Sacred Music* (2 vols., 1836, 1843), for use in Anglican churches in Wales.

RHOSYMEDRE was published in the 1836 collection. The tune's title is derived from the Welsh parish where Edwards was pastor for some years after 1843. In Wales this tune is associated with Easter and is thought of as a jubilant hymn tune. Outside of Wales, however, it often receives a more devotional treatment.

RHOSYMEDRE is characterized by mainly stepwise motion and by repeated tones. It is a bar form tune (AAB). Sing this fine harmonization in parts. Use firm accompaniment, and play at a moderate pace.

Liturgical Use
Congregations can sing this brief choral confession of faith as a profession of faith (in lieu of saying the Apostles' Creed or Nicene Creed); could be sung before or after confessing a section of the Contemporary Testimony.

460

ST. DENIO
♩ = 126

Immortal, Invisible, God Only Wise

Text
Walter C. Smith based this text on 1 Timothy 1:17: "Now to the King eternal, immortal, invisible, the only God, be honor and glory for ever and ever." The six-stanza text was published in Smith's *Hymns of Christ and the Christian Life* (1867) and, after having been revised by Smith, in W. Garrett Horder's *Congregational Hymns* (1884). Further revisions were made by the *Psalter Hymnal* Revision Committee.

"Immortal, Invisible" is a strong text of praise to God, who created and sustains the lives of all his creatures. The text focuses on the Creator of the universe, the invisible God whose visible works in nature testify to his glory and majesty. "Light" is the prevailing image in stanzas 1, 2, and 4 (see also Ps. 104:2); our inability to see God is not because of insufficient light but because the "splendor of light hides [God] from view."

Walter Chalmbers Smith (b. Aberdeen, Scotland, 1824; d. Kinbuck, Perthshire, Scotland, 1908) was educated at the University of Aberdeen and New College, Edinburgh, and became a Presbyterian pastor in the Free Church of Scotland in 1850. He served four congregations, including the Free High Church in Edinburgh (1876-1894). Moderator of his denomination in 1893, Smith was a man of wide interests. His poetry was published in some six volumes entitled *Poetical Works* (1902), and his hymn texts were published in *Hymns of Christ and the Christian Life* (1886).

Tune
ST. DENIO is a much-loved Welsh tune commonly associated with this text. Sing stanzas 1 and 4 in unison and stanzas 2 and 3 in harmony. Pull out all the stops for stanza 4. Use one strong pulse per measure.

For historical information on ST. DENIO see PHH 144.

Liturgical Use

As a festive hymn of praise to God; for various other worship services, especially at the beginning of the service; with stanza 3 for services that focus on the brevity of life.

461

Beautiful Savior

ST. ELIZABETH
♩ = 60

Text

This hymn expresses love and praise for Christ, the King of creation. The beauty of God's creation is readily affirmed, but the greater praise goes to the King of that creation, the same Christ who is the Lord of the nations! The framing stanzas (1 and 4) constitute a fine doxology.

Scripture References
st. 1 = 1 Tim. 1:17
1 Tim. 6:16
Dan. 7:9, 13, 22
st. 3 = Isa. 40:28
Isa. 64:6
st. 4 = Isa. 6:2

The original German text ("Schönster Herr Jesu") appeared anonymously in a manuscript dated 1662 in Münster, Germany. It was published in the Roman Catholic *Munsterisch Gesangbuch* (1677) and, with a number of alterations, in the *Schlesische Volkslieder* (1842), a hymnbook compiled by Hoffman and Richter.

The translation, primarily the work of Joseph A. Seiss (b. Graceham, MD, 1823; d. Philadelphia, PA, 1904), was based on the 1842 edition and first published in the *Sunday School Book for the use of Evangelical Lutheran Congregations* (1873). Another well-known translation based on the 1842 version is the anonymous "Fairest Lord Jesus," published in Richard S. Willis's *Church Chorals and Choir Studies* (1850).

Seiss was born and raised in a Moravian home with the original family name of Seuss. After studying at Pennsylvania College in Gettysburg and completing his theological education with tutors and through private study, Seiss became a Lutheran pastor in 1842. He served several Lutheran congregations in Virginia and Maryland and then became pastor of St. John's Lutheran Church (1858-1874) and the Church of the Holy Communion (1874-1904), both in Philadelphia. Known as an eloquent and popular preacher, Seiss was also a prolific author and editor of some eighty volumes, which include *The Last Times* (1856), *The Evangelical Psalmist* (1859), *Ecclesia Lutherana* (1868), *Lectures on the Gospels* (1868-1872), and *Lectures on the Epistles* (1885). He contributed to and compiled several hymnals.

Tune

ST. ELIZABETH appears to be an eighteenth-century tune from the Glaz area of Silesia. It has always been associated with this text. No factual data exists for the legend that this text and tune date back to the twelfth-century crusades, although those apocryphal stories explain one of the names by which this tune is known, namely,

CRUSADER'S HYMN. After Franz Liszt used the tune for a crusaders' march in his oratorio *The Legend of St. Elizabeth* (1862), the tune also became known as ST. ELIZABETH.

The tune consists primarily of a few melodic sequences and their variations. It could either be sung gently, perhaps with guitar and flute accompaniment, or it could be sung with great power with almost full organ for stanzas 1 and 4. Try singing in harmony with no accompaniment at all for stanzas 2 and 3. Sing in four long lines rather than eight short phrases.

Liturgical Use
The entire text as a hymn of praise at the beginning of worship or as a sermon response; stanzas 1 and 4 (both doxologies) at the end of worship.

462

NEW BRITAIN
♩ = 112
Amazing Grace—How Sweet the Sound

Text

One of the best loved and most often sung hymns in North America, this hymn expresses John Newton's personal experience of conversion from sin as an act of God's grace. At the end of his life, Newton (b. London, England, 1725; d. London, 1807) said, "There are two things I'll never forget: that I was a great sinner, and that Jesus Christ is a greater Savior!" This hymn is Newton's spiritual autobiography, but the truth it affirms—that we are saved by grace alone—is one that all Christians may confess with joy and gratitude.

Scripture References
all st. = Eph. 1:3-14
st. 1 = Eph. 2:8
          John 9:25
st. 3 = Ps. 142:5

Newton was born into a Christian home, but his godly mother died when he was seven, and he joined his father at sea when he was eleven. His licentious and tumultuous sailing life included a flogging for attempted desertion from the Royal Navy and captivity by a slave trader in West Africa. After his escape he himself became the captain of a slave ship. Several factors contributed to Newton's conversion: a near-drowning in 1748, the piety of his friend Mary Catlett, (whom he married in 1750), and his reading of Thomas á Kempis's *Imitation of Christ*. In 1754 he gave up the slave trade and, in association with William Wilberforce, eventually became an ardent abolitionist. After becoming a tide-surveyor in Liverpool, England, Newton came under the influence of George Whitefield and John and Charles Wesley (PHH 267) and began to study for the ministry. He was ordained in the Church of England and served in Olney (1764-1780) and St. Mary Woolnoth, London (1780-1807). His legacy to the Christian church includes his hymns as well as his collaboration with William Cowper (PHH 434) in publishing *Olney Hymns* (1779), to which Newton contributed 280 hymns, including "Amazing Grace."

"Amazing Grace" was published in six stanzas with the heading "1 Chronicles 17:16-17, Faith's review and expectation."

Four of his original stanzas are included in the *Psalter Hymnal* along with a fifth anonymous and apocalyptic stanza first found in *A Collection of Sacred Ballads* (1790). The fifth stanza was first published separately in the 1859 edition of *The Sacred Harp* and joined to Newton's text in Edwin O. Excell's *Coronation Hymns* (1910); it has been associated with Newton's text ever since. *The Hymnal 1982 Companion* calls it "an example of a 'wandering' stanza in [common meter] that appears at the end of a variety of hymns in nineteeth-century hymnals" (Vol. Three B, 671).

Tune

NEW BRITAIN (also known as AMAZING GRACE) was originally a folk tune, probably sung slowly with grace notes and melodic embellishments. Typical of the Appalachian tunes from the southern United States, NEW BRITAIN is pentatonic with melodic figures that outline triads. It was first published as a hymn tune in shape notes in *Columbian Harmony* (1829) to the text "Arise, my soul, my joyful pow'rs." It was first set to "Amazing Grace" in William Walker's (PHH 44) *Southern Harmony* (1835) (see facsimile at p. 85).

The setting is from Edwin O. Excell's *Make His Praise Glorious* (1900). Excell (b. Stark County, OH, 1851; d. Louisville, KY, 1921) grew up in a German Reformed parsonage and worked as a bricklayer as a young man. In 1871 he became a singing school teacher. Soon after, while leading the music and singing solos in a Methodist revival, he experienced a conversion. Excell joined evangelist Sam P. Jones as a song leader, and the two traveled the United States as an evangelistic team. An important figure in the Sunday school movement, Excell wrote over two thousand gospel songs and edited ninety songbooks. He became a very successful publisher of hymnbooks in Chicago; his company, the Biglow-Main-Excell Company, eventually merged with Hope Publishing Company.

Since NEW BRITAIN is pentatonic, it can be sung unaccompanied in a two- or even four-part canon, with groups entering after one or two measures. Sing stanzas 1 and 5 in unison and stanzas 2 and 3 in harmony, and to illustrate the text, try stanza 4 in canon. Use light accompaniment, but consider singing stanza 3 unaccompanied.

Some recordings of "Amazing Grace" by recent pop singers have cast a sentimental shadow over this hymn, presumably because those performers do not understand the experience of salvation that so amazed Newton. Christians should sing this hymn with some vigor and a moderate tempo that supports their convictions.

Liturgical Use

Many occasions of worship when we need to confess with joy that we're saved by God's grace alone; as a hymn of response to forgiveness of sin or as an assurance of pardon; as a confession of faith or after the sermon.

463

WAREHAM
♩ = 126

O Love of God, How Strong and True

Text

One of Horatius Bonar's (PHH 260) best hymn texts, "O Love of God" was published in his *Hymns of Faith and Hope* (1861) in ten stanzas. The *Psalter Hymnal* includes the original stanzas 1, 3-6, 9, and 10.

Scripture References
st. 1 = Jer. 31:3
Lam. 3:22-23
st. 3 = Eph. 3:17-18
st. 5 = Col. 1:19-20
st. 7 = Ps. 33:20

The text's theme is God's love, which we cannot comprehend but do experience (st. 1-2). We may observe God's love in the creation around us (st. 3-4), but we find his love most clearly expressed in the sacrifice of Christ (st. 5-6); it is in this redemptive love that we find our eternal rest (st. 7).

Tune

William Knapp (b. Wareham, Dorsetshire, England, 1698; d. Poole, Dorsetshire, 1768) composed WAREHAM, so named for his birthplace. A glover by trade, Knapp served as the parish clerk at St. James's Church in Poole (1729-1768) and was organist in both Wareham and Poole. Known in his time as the "country psalm-singer," Knapp published *A Set of New Psalm Tunes and Anthems* (1738) and *New Church Melody* (1753). WAREHAM was published in his 1738 collection with the melody in the tenor as a setting for Psalm 36. Its slightly simplified form appears in nearly all modern hymnals. The tune is easy to sing because of its almost continuous stepwise motion and smooth melodic contour. Try assigning the stanzas as follows for antiphonal singing: stanzas 1 and 2 to one group, stanzas 3 and 4 to another, and the remaining three stanzas to the entire congregation. Sing in harmony for the even-numbered stanzas, but the strength of unison singing is necessary for stanza 7.

Liturgical Use

The theme of God's redemptive love is fitting for many worship services, particularly as a hymn between confession and assurance and the service of the word; worship that focuses on creation (st. 1, 3-5); healing services (st. 1-2, 5, 7); funerals (st. 1-2, 5-7); Easter Sunday (st. 5-7).

464

Father, Long before Creation

CORONAE
♩ = 60

Text

This anonymous Chinese text was initially used as a theme song by
Chinese Christians who kept the faith while the Cultural
Revolution was in full swing. The hymn was sung in a Bible-study
center in Peking during the winter of 1952-53. In 1953, Bliss

Scripture References
st. 1 = Eph. 1:4
st. 3 = John 3:16

Wyant, scholar of Chinese music and culture, gave the text to Francis P. Jones (b.
Wisconsin [?] 1890; d. Claremont, CA, 1965 [?]), a missionary to China from 1915 to
1950. Jones translated the text into English and published it in the *China Bulletin* of the
National Council of Churches (1953). After it appeared in *The Hymnbook* in 1955, the
text was published in a number of other hymnals.

With various references to Ephesians 1:3-14, the text confesses the Christian faith.
That confession is all the more bold when it is seen against the background of the
Chinese Cultural Revolution. Stanza 2 states that "Though the world may change its
fashion, you will still remain the same." Stanza 3 concludes with a line from John 3:16,
"God so loved us that he gave his only Son." The entire text affirms God's electing love
and redemptive grace and leads to a final stanza in which we sing "glory to the Lamb
upon the throne."

Francis P. Jones studied at Wisconsin State College, Northwestern University, the
University of Chicago, Garrett Bible Institute, and Union Theological Seminary. After
returning from China, he lectured at Drew Theological Seminary in Madison, New
Jersey, edited the *China Bulletin,* translated Christian classics into Chinese, and made
lecture tours to Taiwan and Hong Kong, retiring in 1965. His publications include
some twenty-six volumes in addition to articles for periodicals and some hymn
translations.

Tune

William H. Monk (PHH 332) composed CORONAE in 1871. The following year it was
published in J. Ireland Tucker's *Hymnal with Tunes Old and New* as a setting for Thomas
Kelly's text "Look, ye saints, the sight is glorious." That text had "Crown him!" in each
stanza, thus the title for this tune.

A bar form tune (AAB), CORONAE is noteworthy for the rhythmic structure of its
final line. Sing stanzas 1 and 4 in unison and stanzas 2 and 3 in harmony. Apply crisp
articulation on the repeated melody tones and use bold accompaniment.

Liturgical Use

As a sung confession of faith in God's electing love.

465

Sing Praise to God Who Reigns Above

Text

Johann J. Schütz (b. Frankfurt-am-Main, Germany, 1640;   *Scripture References*
d. Frankfurt-am-Main, 1690) wrote the original German text in   st. 1 = Ps. 146:6-10
nine stanzas, which began, "Sei Lob und Ehr' dem höchsten Gut."   st. 2 = Ps. 121
The text was published in his *Christliches Gedenckbüchlein* (1675)   Ps. 91
with the heading "Hymn of Thanksgiving" and with a reference to
Deuteronomy 32:3: "I will proclaim the name of the Lord; O praise the greatness of
our God!"

Trained at Tübingen, Schütz practiced law in Frankfurt his entire professional life.
He was a close friend of Philipp Jakob Spener, the major force in the Pietist movement
in Germany. The Pietists criticized the formalism of the Lutheran Church, stressed
conversion and personal piety, and became famous for their prayer meetings and
orphanages. Schütz was among the Pietists who left the Lutheran Church in 1686 to
join the Moravians. His hymn texts were published in *Christliche Gedenckbüchlein* (1675)
and *Christliche Levensregeln* (1677), but only his "Sing Praise to God" is found today in
English-language hymnals.

The translation by Francis Elizabeth Cox (b. Oxford, England, 1812; d. Headington,
England, 1897) was published in Orby Shipley's *Lyra Eucharistica* and in Cox's *Hymns
from the German* (both 1864). Cox wrote a number of original hymns, but few of these
have survived; instead she is known for her translations of German hymns into English.
She translated about eighty texts, many of which were published in her 1864 collection.
Her choice of hymns was often determined by her friend, Baron Bunsen, the Prussian
ambassador to England. Cox and Catherine Winkworth (PHH 194) are regarded as the
best translators of German chorales into English.

Stanzas 1-4 in the *Psalter Hymnal* are derived from Cox's translation of the original
stanzas 1, 3, 4, and 8. The text is an expansion in hymn form of the Old Testament
theme found in the psalms: "God is great, and God is good!" As we sing, we affirm
God's power in creation, his love in redemption, his mercy toward his people, and the
comfort he gives to those in grief. He is truly God, steadfast in mercy and abounding in
love. For all these blessings we offer "to God all praise and glory!"

Tune

MIT FREUDEN ZART has some similarities to the French chanson "Une pastourelle
gentille" (published by Pierre Attaingnant in 1529) and to GENEVAN 138 (138). The
tune was published in the Bohemian Brethren hymnal *Kirchengesänge* (1566) with
Vetter's text "Mit Freuden zart su dieser Fahrt."

Splendid music for a great text, this rounded bar form tune (AABA) is one of the great hymn tunes of the Reformation. Sing the outer stanzas in unison and the middle ones in harmony, although the final phrase, "to God all praise and glory," could be sung consistently in unison.

Liturgical Use

As a hymn of thanksgiving and praise for God's providential care, especially for deliverance, comfort, and peace of mind (the "distress" in st. 3 could be seen as personal or corporate, local or national); funerals.

466

Sing Praise to the Lord

LAUDATE DOMINUM
♩ = 108

Text

Originally "O Praise Ye the Lord," this text is considered to be one of finest written by Henry W. Baker (PHH 342). It was published in the 1875 edition of *Hymns Ancient and Modern* (Baker was editor of both the 1861 and 1875 editions).

Scripture References
st. 1 = Ps. 148:1-6
st. 2 = Ps. 148:11-14
st. 3 = Ps. 150:3-6

The entire text is an amplification in hymn form of the "alleluia" phrases that frame Psalm 148 and 150. While stanzas 1-3 are based on various verses in those psalms, stanza 4 is a summary: "For love in creation, for heaven restored, for grace of salvation, sing praise to the Lord!"

Tune

LAUDATE DOMINUM (Latin words for the opening phrase of Psalm 150) comes from the end of the anthem "Hear My Words, O Ye People" by C. Hubert H. Parry (PHH 145), an anthem he composed in 1894 for a festival of the Salisbury Diocesan Choral Association. Parry's tune was set to Baker's text in the 1916 *Supplement* of *Hymns Ancient and Modern,* replacing an earlier LAUDATE DOMINUM by Henry J. Gauntlett for Baker's text. Parry's tune is an inspired melody from a great tune writer who rarely came to church but who produced some of the best hymn tunes in the later Victorian era.

Sing this noble tune with vigor and excitement; accompany it on the organ with a full registration and a touch of marcato. Sing stanza 1 in unison, stanzas 2 and 3 in parts (possibly one of them unaccompanied), and stanza 4 in unison again. For a real treat use Parry's majestic alternate harmonization with a "walking bass" on the final stanza; that harmonization is found in *The Hymnal 1982* (432) and requires a slower tempo (half note = 88).

Liturgical Use

Any occasion of praise when Psalm 148 or 150 could also be used; a glorious (although long) doxology for harvest thanksgiving; a choral festival or similar praise service.

467

At the Name of Jesus

Text

Caroline Marie Noel (b. Teston, Kent, England, 1817; d. St. Marylebone, London, England, 1877) wrote this spiritually powerful text. The daughter of an Anglican clergyman and hymn writer, she began to write poetry in her late teens but then abandoned it until she was in her forties. During those years she suffered frequent bouts of illness and eventually became an invalid. To encourage both herself and others who were ill or incapacitated, Noel began to write devotional verse again. Her poems were collected in *The Name of Jesus and Other Verses for the Sick and Lonely* (1861, enlarged in 1870).

Scripture References
st. 1 = Phil. 2:6-11
John 1:1
st. 2 = Ps. 33:6-9
st. 3 = Col. 2:15
st. 6 = Acts 1:11

One of the hymns in the 1870 collection was this text (originally beginning "In the Name of Jesus"), designed for use as a processional hymn on Ascension Day. The *Psalter Hymnal* includes stanzas 1, 3-5, and 7-8 of Noel's original eight stanzas.

The text is based on the confession of faith that Paul quotes in Philippians 2:6-11, which may well have been an early Christian hymn. Stanza 1 announces the triumph of the ascended Christ to whom "every knee should bow" (Phil. 2:10). In stanza 2 Christ is the "mighty Word" (see John 1:1-4) through whom "creation sprang at once to sight." Stanzas 3 and 4 look back to Christ's humiliation, death, resurrection, and ascension (Phil. 2:6-9). Stanza 5 is an encouragement for submission to Christ, for us to have the "mind of Christ," and stanza 6 looks forward to Christ's return as "King of glory." The text is not only concerned with the name "Jesus," whose saving work it confesses, but also with the glory and majesty that attends "the name of Jesus."

Tune

Ralph Vaughan Williams (PHH 316) composed KING'S WESTON for this text. It was published in *Songs of Praise* (1925). The combination of text and tune in a festive hymn-anthem by Vaughan Williams has become a favorite of many church choirs. The tune's title refers to a manor house on the Avon River near Bristol, England.

KING'S WESTON is a great tune marked by distinctive rhythmic structures and a soaring climax in the final two lines. Like many of Vaughan Williams's tunes, it is best sung in unison with moderate accompaniment to support this vigorous melody. For festive services use the descant in Vaughan Williams's anthem for stanza 4, or combine select choral stanzas from this anthem with congregational stanzas in the manner of a hymn concertato, using E minor throughout.

Liturgical Use
Advent; Easter; Ascension; Epiphany; as a sung confession of faith; many other occasions of worship.

468

God Is Our Fortress and Our Rock

EIN FESTE BURG
♩ = *88*

Text

Martin Luther (PHH 336) wrote both the tune and the original   *Scripture References*
German text ("Ein' feste Burg ist unser Gott"), which was inspired   all st. = Ps. 46
by Psalm 46. The chorale is known to have been published in the
1529 edition of Joseph Klug's (PHH 126) *Geistliche Lieder* although no copy is extant. It also appeared in both High and Low German versions in various Lutheran hymnals. Just as Genevan Psalm 68 has had great significance for many Calvinists, this hymn, which became "the battle hymn" of the Reformation, has been immensely important to Lutherans and other Protestants.

With the help of Annamarie von Rad, Michael A. Perry (PHH 299) translated the four-stanza German text into three stanzas at Eversley, Hampshire, England, in 1981. His translation was published in the British *Hymns for Today's Church* (1982). Perry captures well the strong battle images that Luther's text magnified from Psalm 46: as we fight against the powers of evil, our hope is fixed on Christ whose "kingdom is immortal!" (A different translation is at 469.)

Tune

Some scholars surmise that Luther adapted preexisting melodies when composing EIN FESTE BURG. They also suspect that the popularity of this hymn not only contributed to the spread of the Reformation but also to the increasing importance of the Ionian mode (major) as opposed to the older church modes.

The melody is in a rounded bar form (AABA); the setting at 468 is in the original rhythm; the setting at 469 is adapted. If the rhythmic setting of 468 is unfamiliar, use it as a choir anthem at first. Perhaps the organist could play one of the many organ preludes that employ this authentic rhythm. Accompany with a moderate organ registration for the first two stanzas, but enlarge the registration for stanza 3. Be sure to play at a moderately fast pace and keep rhythms crisp; this tune must sparkle with energy. Use brass for festive services.

Liturgical Use

Many occasions of worship throughout the church year, but especially Reformation Sunday, Old/New Year services, and times when the church faces persecution or spiritual battles.

469

EIN FESTE BURG
♩ = *100*

A Mighty Fortress Is Our God

Text

See PHH 468 for a brief history of the original text and tune. This English translation of Luther's German text is by Frederick H. Hedge (b. Cambridge, MA, 1805; d. Cambridge, 1890); it was published in Furness's *Gems of German Verse* (1852) and in *Hymns for the Church of Christ* (1853), a hymnal edited by Hedge and Frederick Huntington. Hedge's translation, which closely follows Luther's words, is the one usually found in North American hymnals.

Scripture References
all st. = Ps. 46
st. 3 = 1 Pet. 5:8

Hedge was a precocious child who read Latin and Greek classics at an early age. Between the ages of twelve and sixteen he was in Germany, where he studied German literature. Educated at Harvard University and Divinity School, he became a Unitarian minister in 1829. Hedge served congregations in Maine, Rhode Island, and Massachusetts, and taught church history at Harvard Divinity School (1857-1876) and German literature at Harvard University (1872-1884). A respected transcendentalist and a famous German scholar, he published the monumental *Prose Writers of Germany* (1848). His original hymns and translations were published in *Hymns for the Church of Christ* (1853), which he compiled with F. Dan Huntington. He is remembered primarily for his translation of Luther's famous hymn.

Stanzas 1-3 of the original text were inspired by Psalm 46; stanza 4 arose directly from Luther's persecution experience. The text expresses trust in God's protection amidst the battle that Christians wage against the devil. "Earthly powers" in stanza four undoubtedly referred to the Roman Catholic authorities of Luther's day, but modern Christians may identify other "powers" that oppose the rule of Christ. The closing line of the text provides much comfort: "God's truth abideth still; his kingdom is forever!"

Tune

The original rhythms of EIN FESTE BURG (see 469) had already reached their familiar isorhythmic (all equal rhythms) shape by the time of Johann S. Bach (PHH 7) in the eighteenth century. The harmonization is taken from his Cantata 80. Many organ and choral works are based on this chorale, including Felix Mendelssohn (PHH 279) in his *Fifth Symphony* and Giacomo Meyerbeer in his opera *Les Huguenots*.

This rhythmic setting needs a more majestic approach than the one found at 468. Sing in harmony on stanzas 2 and 3 and in unison on stanzas 1 and 4. Support the singing with strong accompaniment on the organ and/or with use of a brass ensemble.

Liturgical Use
See PHH 468.

470

All Hail the Power of Jesus' Name

MILES LANE
♩ = 54

Text

Edward Perronet began writing this text in 1779. Its first stanza was published with the MILES LANE tune later that year in the November issue of the *Gospel Magazine* without attribution. The completed eight-stanza text was published with Perronet's name as author in the April 1780 edition of that magazine. John Rippon revised parts of the original text and replaced some stanzas with new ones that he wrote; his version was published in his *Selection of Hymns* (1787). Perronet's stanzas 1, 5, and 8, and Rippon's stanza 7 are included with minor alterations.

Scripture References
st. 1 = Rev. 7:11
st. 2 = 1 Tim. 2:5-6
st. 3 = Isa. 66:18
st. 4 = Rev. 7:11-12

Originally headed "On the Resurrection, the Lord Is King," this fine coronation hymn affirms the kingship of Christ and calls on all creatures to "crown him Lord of all." The "power of Jesus' Name" is hailed by angels (st. 1), by converted Jews (st. 2), by all humankind (st. 3), and by ourselves (st. 4). (Rippon actually entitled each stanza "Angels," "Converted Jews," "Sinners of Every Nation," "Ourselves," etc.) The middle stanzas highlight redemption and conversion from sin as the grounds for the exuberant refrain.

Edward Perronet (b. Sundridge, Kent, England, 1726; d. Canterbury, England, 1792) came from a family of Huguenots who had fled from France to England around 1680. His father was sympathetic to the cause of the Wesleys, and in 1746 Perronet and his brother became Methodist itinerant preachers. Too independent and irascible to function under anyone's supervision, Perronet differed with the Wesleys about the Methodists' relationship to the Church of England: the Wesleys wished to remain in the church and did not permit their unordained itinerant preachers to administer the sacraments. Perronet, however, did administer communion and urged the people to shun the Anglican Church. Matters became worse when he published a scathing attack on the Church of England in the satiric poem *The Mitre* (1757). The Wesleys were able to suppress the book and avoid wide circulation, but the damage had been done. Soon after, Perronet left the Methodists and later became the pastor of a Congregational chapel in Canterbury. During his ministry he wrote a number of hymns and Scripture versifications, which were published anonymously in three small volumes: *Select Passages of the Old and New Testament, Versified* (1756), *A Small Collection of Hymns* (1782), and *Occasional Verses* (1785). His "All Hail the Power of Jesus' Name" is the only hymn that remains in common use.

John Rippon (b. Tiverton, Devonshire, England, 1751; d. London, England, 1836) was pastor of the Baptist Church in Carter Lane, London; he began in 1772 as an interim pastor and then stayed for sixty-three years as head pastor. He also edited the *Baptist Annual Register* (1790-1802). His main contribution to hymnody was his compiling of *A Selection of Hymns from the Best Authors, Intended As an Appendix to Dr. Watts's Psalms and Hymns* (1787) and *A Selection of Psalm and Hymn Tunes* (1791). These publications became popular in both England and America. However, later hymnologists have often been frustrated by Rippon's work because he frequently did not indicate the authors of the hymns and often altered the texts without acknowledging his changes.

Tune

MILES LANE is one of three tunes that are closely associated with this well-known and beloved text; CORONATION is found at 471. Other hymnals also include the more florid DIADEM, composed by James Ellor in 1838 and noted for its elaborate choral harmonization.

MILES LANE was published anonymously with Perronet's first stanza in the November 1779 issue of the *Gospel Magazine*. The tune appeared in three parts with the melody in the middle part. Each "Crown him" was meant to be sung by a different part, first by the bass, then by the treble, and finally by the tenor. Thus MILES LANE was a fuguing tune. Stephen Addington identified William Perronet as the composer in his *Collection of Psalm Tunes* (1780). The tune's title comes from the traditional English corruption of St. Michael's Lane, the London street where the Miles' Lane Meeting House was located, of which Addington was minister.

William Shrubsole (b. Canterbury, Kent, England, 1760; d. London, England, 1806) composed MILES LANE when he was only nineteen. A chorister in Canterbury Cathedral from 1770 to 1777, Shrubsole was appointed organist at Bangor Cathedral in 1782. However, he was dismissed in 1783 for associating too closely with religious dissenters. In 1784 he became a music teacher in London and organist at Lady Huntingdon's Spa Fields Chapel, Clerkenwell, a position he retained until his death.

Shrubsole is the subject of a famous essay (1943) by Ralph Vaughan Williams (PHH 316), who called MILES LANE a "superb" tune and composed a concertato arrangement of it in 1938. Edward Elgar called it "the finest tune in English hymnody." MILES LANE has a wide melodic range and a most effective climax in the refrain, which could benefit from some rubato, especially at the end of stanza 4. Accompany and sing in a majestic manner.

Liturgical Use
Useful for many different services as a great hymn of praise for redemption in Christ; a doxology; a processional or recessional hymn for Ascension Day or similar worship services that emphasize the kingship of Christ.

471

All Hail the Power of Jesus' Name

Text
See PHH 470 for discussion of the text.

Tune
Like MILES LANE (470), CORONATION was written for this text. Oliver Holden (b. Shirley, MA, 1765; d. Charlestown, MA, 1844) composed the tune in four parts with a duet in the third phrase. The tune, whose title comes from the theme of Perronet's text, was published in Holden's *Union Harmony* (1793). It is the one eighteenth-century American tune that has enjoyed uninterrupted popularity—from the singing schools of that era to today's congregational worship.

CORONATION is a vigorous marching tune with many repeated tones that delighted Holden's contemporaries. The tune requires the jubilant repetition of the last couplet of text for each stanza. Sing in parts and accompany with a firm sense of rhythm.

Holden was reared in a small rural community and had only a minimal formal education—a few months in a "common school" in Groton, Massachusetts. He worked as a carpenter and was involved in community service in Charlestown, holding posts in the Anti-Slavery Society and serving in the Massachusetts House of Representatives. In addition he worked very profitably as a merchant and real estate dealer, and served as a Puritan lay preacher. Very interested in music, Holden became a composer and singing-school teacher in the tradition of William Billings. He was involved in publishing various tunebooks, including *The American Harmony* (1792), *The Massachusetts Compiler* (1795), *Plain Psalmody* (1800), and *The Charlestown Collection of Sacred Songs* (1803).

Liturgical Use
See PHH 470.

O Jesus, We Adore You

Text

Written by Arthur T. Russell (b. Northampton, England, 1806; *Scripture References*
d. Southwick, Brighton, England, 1874), this text focuses on the st. 1 = Acts 4:12
redemptive work of Christ on the cross, which means, as one st. 2 = Isa. 53:3-6
Lord's Supper formulary describes it, "that he was condemned st. 3 = Matt. 27:41-43
to die that we might be pardoned, that he endured the suffer-
ing and death of the cross that we might live through him, and that he was once
forsaken by God that we might forever be accepted by him" (979).

As we sing this hymn, we praise Christ for his saving work (st. 1), confess our sinfulness which "nailed [Christ] to the tree" (st. 2), and pray for the completion of our
redemption in life everlasting (st. 3). The phrase "pass by" in stanzas 2 and 3 comes
from Lamentations 1:12, a passage that is often used liturgically in conjunction with the
gospel narratives of Christ's passion.

Although Russell's family name was originally Clout, his father changed it to Russell.
Educated at Manchester College, York, and St. John's College, Cambridge, Russell was
ordained in the Church of England in 1829 and served parishes in Hunts, Caxton,
Whaddon, and Wrockwardine Wood. His theology was influenced by Augustine, and he
changed from a very high-church to a moderate-Calvinist perspective. His new views
came to expression when he wrote several articles against proponents of the Oxford
Movement, who wanted the Church of England to move closer to Roman Catholicism.
A prolific writer on theological and biographical topics, Russell also wrote 140 hymns
and 150 hymn translations and composed some hymn tunes. He compiled a number of
hymnals, such as *Hymn Tunes, Original and Selected* (c. 1840), *Hymns for Public Worship*
(1848), and *Psalms and Hymns* (1851), a book that included many of his translations of
German hymns and also "O Jesus, We Adore Thee."

Tune

For information on the tune and composer, see PHH 82, where the setting is in the key
of D.

Liturgical Use

Holy Week; Lent; worship that focuses on the doctrine of redemption (Lord's Day 23 of
the Heidelberg Catechism).

473

To God Be the Glory

TO GOD BE THE GLORY
♩ = 126

Text

Prodigious writer of hymn texts, Fanny J. Crosby (b. Putnam County, NY, 1820; d. Bridgeport, CT, 1915) wrote this hymn, which was first published with Doane's tune in *Songs of Devotion* (1870). This text and "Blessed Assurance" (490) are among the best-known and most-loved hymn texts of the thousands Crosby produced. Initially ignored in the United States, the hymn was sung in British churches after its inclusion in Ira D. Sankey's *Sacred Songs and Solos* (1903). Because of its use in the Billy Graham Crusades beginning in 1954, the hymn gained great popularity in Britain and Australia as well as in the United States.

Scripture References
st. 1 = Ps. 126:2-3
John 3:16
1 John 2:2
Matt. 7:13-14
ref. = John 14:6

In contrast to many gospel hymns (including the majority of Crosby's texts), "To God Be the Glory" directs our attention away from personal experience to the glory of God. God so loved the world that he gave us his Son to make atonement for sin (st. 1); all who believe in Christ will receive pardon (st. 2) and will rejoice now and through all eternity because of the "great things he has done" (st. 3). The refrain borrows its praise in part from the Old Testament psalms. The phrase "when Jesus we see" (st. 3) must have meant something special to Crosby, who was blinded when she was seven weeks old.

Fanny (Francis) Jane Crosby attended the New York City School for the Blind, where she later became a teacher. She began writing poetry when she was eight and published several volumes, such as *A Blind Girl, and Other Poems* (1844). Married to musician Alexander Van Alstyne, who was also blind, Crosby began writing hymn texts when she was in her forties. She published at least eight thousand hymns (some under various pseudonyms; see PHH 427); at times she was under contract to her publisher to write three hymns a week and often wrote six or seven a day. Crosby's texts were set to music by prominent gospel song composers such as William B. Bradbury (PHH 114), William H. Doane, Robert S. Lowry (PHH 396), Ira D. Sankey (PHH 73), and William J. Kirkpatrick (PHH 188). Her hymns were distributed widely and popularized at evangelistic services in both America and Great Britain. Crosby was one of the most respected women of her era and the friend of many prominent persons, including presidents of the United States.

Tune

The strength of Crosby's text is enhanced by the cheerful gospel music of TO GOD BE THE GLORY, composed for this text by William H. Doane (b. Preston, CT, 1832; d. South Orange, NJ, 1915), writer of many tunes for Crosby's texts.

An industrialist and philanthropist, Doane was also a staunch supporter of evangelistic campaigns and a prolific writer of hymn tunes. He was head of a large woodworking machinery plant in Cincinnati and a civic leader in that city. He showed his devotion to the church by supporting the work of the evangelistic team of Dwight L. Moody and Ira D. Sankey and by endowing Moody Bible Institute in Chicago and Denison University in Granville, Ohio. An amateur composer, Doane wrote over twenty-two hundred hymn and gospel song tunes, and he edited over forty songbooks.

The rounded bar form tune (AABA) has a verse/refrain structure. Sing the harmony parts with joy and vigor. Be sure to distinguish clearly between the regular eighth rhythms and the dotted ones. Because the harmonic rhythm is slow, the singing tempo can be quite animated. Maintain one pulse per measure.

Liturgical Use

Suitable for many worship services as a superb hymn of praise for God's mighty acts of redemption in Christ; baptism; profession of faith; assurance of pardon.

474

RATHBUN
♩ = 126

In the Cross of Christ I Glory

Text

John Bowring's text was inspired by Galatians 6:14: "May I never boast except in the cross of our Lord Jesus Christ." Originally in five stanzas (st. 5 was a repeat of st. 1), it was initially entitled "The Cross of Christ" but later came to be known as "Glorying in the Cross." (The often-told story that Bowring wrote this hymn text after seeing a cross on top of a ruined cathedral on the island of Macao near Hong Kong is not true; Bowring went to Hong Kong twenty-four years after writing the text.)

Scripture References
st. 1 = Gal. 6:14
1 Cor. 2:2
st. 2 = 1 Cor. 1:18

The first stanza affirms that the cross of Christ stands at the center of history; it is the key to the meaning of the history of events or civilizations that are the "wrecks of time." Stanzas 2 and 3 confess the comfort, peace, and joy that Christ's cross brings to our troubled personal lives. Stanza 4 concludes that "bane and blessing, pain and pleasure" become a profound experience of unending peace and joy when "sanctified by the cross."

John Bowring (b. Exeter, England, 1792; d. Exeter, 1872) was a businessman who spent much of his life in public service. From 1828 to 1835 he worked for the British government as a political economist in the Netherlands, France, and Belgium. A member of Parliament, he worked for the British government in China in 1849 and completed his government career as governor of Hong Kong. Bowring's literary output was phenomenal: he published thirty-six volumes on topics ranging from economics to biography, science, religion, and poetry. In practice a devout Christian, he belonged to the Unitarian Church. Bowring studied two hundred languages and claimed to speak one hundred. Included in his writings are two collections of hymns, *Matins and Vespers with Occasional Devotional Pieces* (1823) and *Hymns as a Sequel to Matins* (1825), which included "In the Cross of Christ I Glory."

Tune
This story is associated with the writing of RATHBUN: One Sunday in 1849 Ithamar Conkey (b. Shutesbury, MA, 1815; d. Elizabeth, NJ, 1867) walked out of the morning service at Central Baptist Church, Norwich, Connecticut, where he was choir director and organist, frustrated because only one soprano from his choir had come that morning. The next Sunday the minister preached a Lenten message on the words of Christ on the cross. One of the hymns to be sung was Bowring's "In the Cross of Christ I Glory." Later that day Conkey's discouragement changed to inspiration, and he composed a new tune for that text. He named the tune after that one faithful soprano, Mrs. Beriah S. Rathbun. The tune was published in Henry W. Greatorex's *Collection of Psalm and Hymn Tunes* (1851). In 1850 Conkey moved to New York City and became bass soloist at Calvary Episcopal Church. Later he was bass soloist and conductor of the quartet choir at the Madison Avenue Baptist Church. He also sang frequently in oratorio performances.

RATHBUN is easily sung in parts. To sense the joy that breathes through the text, do not sing too slowly. Some hymnals set this text to STUTTGART (329), a helpful alternate choice.

Liturgical Use
Lent and Holy Week; other services that focus on the meaning of Christ's cross for us.

475

Praise, My Soul, the King of Heaven

LAUDA ANIMA
♩ = 104

Text
One of two hymn texts that Henry F. Lyte (PHH 442) based on Psalm 103, this text was published in Lyte's *Spirit of the Psalms* (1834) in five stanzas. Following the pattern of many modern hymnals, the *Psalter Hymnal* omits the original fourth stanza.

Scripture References
all st. = Ps. 103

This text captures the spirit of Psalm 103: sing praise to the King who redeems us (st. 1 = vv. 1-4); praise him for his steadfast love (st. 2 = vv. 6-10); praise him for his compassion (st. 3 = vv. 13-14); let angels and all creatures praise God (st. 4 = vv. 20-22). The text contains a number of memorable lines: "Ransomed, healed, restored, forgiven" (st. 1); "slow to chide and swift to bless" (st. 2); "Father-like he tends and spares us" (st. 3). (See additional notes about the psalm at 103.)

Tune

John Goss (PHH 164) composed LAUDA ANIMA (Latin for the opening words of Psalm 103) for this text in 1868. Along with his original harmonizations, intended to interpret the different stanzas, the tune was also included in the appendix to Robert Brown-Borthwick's *Supplemental Hymn and Tune Book* (1869). LAUDA ANIMA is one of the finest tunes that arose out of the Victorian era. A reviewer in *The Musical Times,* June 1869, said, "It is at once the most beautiful and dignified hymn tune which has lately come under our notice."

Try singing in concertato fashion: the unison stanzas sung by the congregation and stanza 2 as well as the original stanza 4 (see below) sung by the choir in harmony, preferably unaccompanied.

Frail as summer's flower we flourish,
blows the wind and it is gone;
but while mortals rise and perish,
God endures unchanging on.
Alleluia, alleluia,
praise the High Eternal One.

—based on Psalm 103:15-17

Singers and accompanists will want to emphasize the melodic contours and not the marching rhythms emphasized by the bar lines. Organists, take advantage of Goss's interpretation of the various stanzas by playing the first stanza with solid and firm foundation stops, the second (if accompanied) with quieter sound, and the third with a very legato gentle sound on strings. Then open all the stops for a majestic conclusion on the fourth stanza.

Liturgical Use

See suggestions for use at PHH 103; other settings of Psalm 103 are at 297, 583, and 627.

476

GO DOWN, MOSES
♩ = 80

When Israel Was in Egypt's Land

Text

This African American spiritual dates from before the Civil War. It was published in the *Jubilee Songs* (1872), made popular by the Jubilee Singers of Fisk University in their concert tours (see also PHH 356). Often known by its refrain line, "Go down, Moses," the spiritual was also published in J. B. T. Marsh's *The Story of the Jubilee Singers with their Songs* (1876). "When Israel Was in Egypt's Land" originally had twenty-four stanzas of which the *Psalter*

Scripture References
all st. = Ex. 7

Hymnal (as well as other modern hymnals) includes four narrative stanzas and one stanza of application. Commenting on the spiritual's message, John Lovell, Jr., writes:

> "Go Down, Moses" does not employ the undercurrent symbolism of "Steal Away to Jesus" and other such poems. Only a very obtuse listener can miss its point. It says flatly that Moses freed these Egyptian slaves boldly and justly because slavery is wrong. It clearly projects the principles of this experience to all the world: wherever men are held in bondage, they must and shall be freed. The "Let my people go!" refrain is thunderous. It does not argue economic, sociological, historical, and racial points. . . . It wastes no words and moves relentlessly toward its goal of filling every listener with a pervasive contempt for oppression and a resounding enthusiasm for freedom.
>
> —*from* Black Song, *1972, pp. 326-327*

A stanza not printed in the *Psalter Hymnal* reiterates Lovell's point:

We need not always weep and moan
Let my people go!
And wear these slavery chains forlorn
Let my people go!

The final stanza in the *Psalter Hymnal* is a prayer to God for freedom for all who are oppressed, a petition for liberation in Christ.

Tune

The spiritual is in the call-and-response pattern: a leader sings the verses with some rhythmic freedom, either unaccompanied or with only light accompaniment; the entire congregation sings the phrases "Let my people go!" and the refrain, probably in harmony. That practice fits well for stanzas 1-4, but the entire group should sing all of stanza 5.

The harmonization by John W. Work, Jr. (b. Nashville, TN, 1872; d. Nashville, 1925), was originally published in *The Story of the Jubilee Singers* (1896). Work is well known for his pioneering studies of African American folk music and for his leadership in the performance of spirituals. He studied music at Fisk University in Nashville and classics at Harvard and then taught Latin, Greek, and history at Fisk from 1898 to 1923. Director of the Jubilee Singers at Fisk, Work also sang tenor in the Fisk Jubilee Quartet, which toured the country after 1909 and made commercial recordings. He was president of Roger Williams University in Nashville during the last two years of his life. Work and his brother Frederick Jerome Work (1879-1942) were devoted to collecting, arranging, and publishing African American slave songs and spirituals. They published two collections: *New Jubilee Songs as Sung by the Fisk Jubilee Singers* (1901) and *Folk Songs of the American Negro* (1907).

Liturgical Use

Worship that focuses on the Old Testament Exodus event or on redemption for the oppressed and freedom in Christ; Easter Vigil service.

477

You Servants of God, Your Master Proclaim

HANOVER
♩ = 120

Text

The year this text was written, 1744, was a year of political and religious turmoil in Britain. The newly formed Methodist societies were suspected of being merely disguised Roman Catholic societies and were accused of attempting to overthrow the Crown. To strengthen and reassure his Methodist followers, Charles Wesley (PHH 267) anonymously published *Hymns for Times of Trouble and Persecution* (1744). This text, in seventeen stanzas, was the first of the "Hymns to be Sung in a Tumult." Of those stanzas, 1 and 4-6 of Wesley's Part I are included; the battle-song stanzas, which the small but heroic Methodist groups sang in the face of violent opposition, are omitted.

Scripture References
st. 1 = Deut. 32:3
Ps. 148:13
Ps. 145:11-13
st. 3 = Rev. 5:12-14
Rev. 7:10

The text is a hymn of thankful praise to Christ for his victorious reign and for providing salvation for his people. It reveals the cosmic scope of Christ's kingdom (st. 1) and helps us to join our voices with the great doxology to Christ, the Lamb, as foretold in Revelation 5:9-14 (st. 2-4). In the first stanza "servants" refers to all Christians, not just clergy, to those made "to be a kingdom and priests to serve our God" (Rev. 5:10).

Tune

For information on the tune and composer, see PHH 149; a descant is also given there that would be very appropriate for stanza 4 of Wesley's text.

Liturgical Use

A great doxology for festive services such as Easter; with eschatological preaching during Advent; other services that focus on Christ's work of redemption and his glory.

478

Tell Out, My Soul

WOODLANDS
♩ = 116

Text

One of the first hymn texts written by Timothy Dudley-Smith
(PHH 233), this free paraphrase of the Song of Mary from Luke
1:46-55 is his best known. It was first published in the *Anglican
Hymn Book* (1965). Dudley-Smith writes of this text:

Scripture References
all st. = Luke 1:46-55

> I did not think of myself . . . as having in any way the gifts of a hymn-writer when
> in May 1961 I jotted down a set of verses, beginning "Tell out, my soul, the
> greatness of the Lord." I was reading a review copy of the New English Bible New
> Testament, in which that line appears exactly as I have put it above; I saw in it the
> first line of a poem, and speedily wrote the rest (Dudley-Smith 1984).

The text calls us to proclaim the greatness "of the Lord" (st. 1), "of his name" (st. 2),
"of his might" (st. 3), and "of his word" (st. 4). The text's strong language captures the
spirit of Mary's exuberant song of praise to God. The powerful text contrasts with the
humble meditative setting of the Song of Mary at 212. A third, partial setting of Mary's
Song is found at 622—sung to a Taizé round.

Tune

WOODLANDS is a perfect match for the bold text. Walter Greatorex (b. Mansfield,
Nottinghamshire, England, 1877; d. Bournemouth, Hampshire, England, 1949)
composed this tune in 1916, and it was published in the *Public School Hymn Book* in 1919.
The tune's title refers to one of the schoolhouses at Gresham's School, Holt, Norfolk,
where Greatorex was director of music from 1911-1936. Before that he served as
assistant music master at Uppingham School in Rutland (1900-1910). Greatorex's
musical education began as a chorister at King's College, Cambridge, England, and he
received his university music training at St. John's College, Cambridge.

A dramatic tune, WOODLANDS is marked by irresistible melodic gestures and by the
"breathless" cadence of line 2, which propels us forward into line 3. The alternate
harmonization provided is his original; use that for stanza 4. Sing in strong unison
throughout with a full organ and brass for festive services. Try having the full choir sing
up an octave for the final two measures of stanzas 3 and 4.

Liturgical Use

Advent; Christmas; other services in which a jubilant setting of the Song of Mary is
appropriate; Mary's Song is traditionally appointed for vespers; see additional comments at PHH 212.

479

I Will Sing of My Redeemer

Text

Near the end of 1876, Philip P. Bliss (PHH 482) and his wife
were traveling to Chicago to sing for the evangelistic services
led by Daniel W. Whittle at Dwight L. Moody's Tabernacle. But
a train wreck and fire en route claimed their lives. Their trunk,
which was spared, contained this hymn text by Bliss.

Scripture References
all st. = Ps. 89:1
Eph. 5:19-20
Titus 2:13-14

In four stanzas with refrain, the text was set to a gospel tune by James McGranaham
(PHH 99), who subsequently succeeded Bliss as song leader for Whittle. The text and
McGranaham's tune were published in *Welcome Tidings, a New Collection for Sunday
School,* compiled by Robert S. Lowry (PHH 396), William H. Doane (PHH 473), and Ira
D. Sankey (PHH 73) in 1877.

The text is a fine statement in hymn form of Christian teachings on the saving work
of Christ, whose atoning death "sealed my pardon, paid the debt, and made me free."
The *Psalter Hymnal* Revision Committee reordered original text into three stanzas to fit
the tune HYFRYDOL; the original refrain appears in stanzas 1 and 3.

Tune

One of the most loved Welsh tunes, HYFRYDOL was composed by Rowland Hugh
Prichard (b. Graienyn, near Bala, Merionetshire, Wales, 1811; d. Holywell, Flintshire,
Wales, 1887) in 1830 when he was only nineteen. It was published with about forty of
his other tunes in his children's hymnal *Cyfaill y Cantorion (The Singers' Friend)* in 1844.

Prichard (sometimes spelled Pritchard) was a textile worker and an amateur
musician. He had a good singing voice and was appointed precentor in Graienyn. Many
of his tunes were published in Welsh periodicals. In 1880 Prichard became a loom
tender's assistant at the Welsh Flannel Manufacturing Company in Holywell.

HYFRYDOL (Welsh for "tuneful" or "pleasant") is often set to Charles Wesley's "Love
Divine, All Loves Excelling" (568) and William C. Dix's "Alleluia! Sing to Jesus" (406).
More recently the tune has appeared in several hymnals with Bliss's text.

A simple bar form (AAB) tune with the narrow range of a sixth, HYFRYDOL builds to
a stunning climax by sequential use of melodic motives. Sing in unison or harmony,
and observe one pulse per measure.

Liturgical Use

A glorious testimony hymn about salvation in Christ useful for many worship services;
Lent.

480

Jesus, the Very Thought of You

ST. AGNES
♩ = 108

Text

The extended (forty-two stanzas) Latin poem "Jesu, dulcis memo- *Scripture References*
ria" is the source of this text (see discussion at PHH 307, which   all st. = Eph. 3:19
includes its traditional attribution to Bernard of Clairveaux).
Although some scholars believe the poem was written by Bernard, others suggest that it
originated in Britain at the end of the twelfth century. Most agree, however, that the
poem's fervor was influenced by the famous Bernard. The English text is taken from a
fifty-stanza translation by Edward Caswall (PHH 438) published in his *Lyra Catholica*
(1849), where the opening line read "Jesu, the very thought of Thee."

Displaying a passionate devotion to Christ, the text provides a clear hint of its
original use as a text for personal devotion. Its focus is entirely on Christ and his saving
love, a love that gives hope, joy, and rest to believers (st. 1, 3), a love that excels any
human love (st. 2, 4).

Tune

John B. Dykes (PHH 147) composed ST. AGNES for this text. Dykes named the tune
after a young Roman Christian woman who was martyred in A.D. 304 during the reign
of Diocletian. St. Agnes was sentenced to death for refusing to marry a nobleman to
whom she said, "I am already engaged *to Christ,* to Him alone I keep my troth." The
tune was published in John Grey's *Hymnal for Use in the English Church* (1866).

ST. AGNES is a simple tune, best sung in two long lines and in harmony. To encourage meditation on the text (as was the practice with its Latin original), consider having
the congregation follow the text of stanza 2 ("No voice can sing") without singing, but
simply listening to it as played by the organ.

Liturgical Use

Worship that focuses on Christ's redemptive work; Lord's Supper; Lent.

481

Christ, Whose Glory Fills the Skies

LUX PRIMA
♩ = 60

Text

Written by the great hymn writer Charles Wesley (PHH 267), this text was published in
three stanzas in *Hymns and Sacred Poems,* compiled in 1740 by Charles Wesley and his
brother John. James Montgomery called it "one of Charles Wesley's loveliest progeny."

Titled "Morning Hymn" by Wesley, it is unusual in that it does not contain the customary reference to the previous night's rest or to the work and dangers of the day ahead. The text begins by placing the focus entirely on Christ, the "light of the world," the "Sun of Righteousness who rises with healing in his wings"; he is the "Dayspring" and "Daystar." Thus the "light of Christ" is to fill our lives and lead us forward "to the perfect day."

Scripture References
st. 1 = John 8:12
2 Pet. 1:19
Luke 1:78
Mal. 4:2
Ps. 27:1

Tune

French romanticist composer Charles F. Gounod (PHH 165) wrote LUX PRIMA, which means "first light" in Latin. When the Franco-Prussian War broke out in 1870, Gounod left his native Paris and settled in England for five years. This sturdy tune was published in the Scottish *Hymnary* in 1872.

It uses several melodic sequences and builds to a climax in its last line. Sing in parts throughout with moderate to strong accompaniment. RATISBON, the suggested alternate tune, is found with this text in many other hymnals, but its isorhythmic (all equal rhythms) shape doesn't fit this text as well as Gounod's more lively LUX PRIMA.

Liturgical Use

As a morning hymn during the Easter vigil service and during Advent; other services that have as their theme Christ as "light."

482

HALLELUJAH! WHAT A SAVIOR
♩ = 104

Man of Sorrows—What a Name

Text

Philip P. Bliss (b. Clearfield County, PA, 1838; d. Ashtabula, OH, 1876) wrote both text and tune of this hymn that was published in *The International Lessons Monthly* of 1875 with the title "Redemption."

Scripture References
st. 1 = Isa. 53:3-6
st. 4 = John 19:30

"Man of Sorrows" is a reference to the prophet Isaiah's depiction of the "suffering servant" (Isa. 52:13-53:12). The full text draws on that prophetic vision and on the gospel narratives of Christ's crucifixion and atoning death. While much of the text affirms objectively the redemptive work of Christ, stanza 2 makes a very personal confession (like 386): "in my place condemned he stood, sealed my pardon with his blood." Stanzas 4 and 5 move from Christ's death to his exaltation at the right hand of God and to his return as "glorious King." Each stanza concludes with an "alleluia" to so great a Savior.

Bliss left home as a young boy to make a living by working on farms and in lumber camps, all while trying to continue his schooling. He was converted at a revival meeting at age twelve. Bliss became an itinerant music teacher, making house calls on horseback during the winter, and during the summer attending the Normal Academy of Music in Genesco, New York. His first song was published in 1864, and in 1868 Dwight L. Moody advised him to become a singing evangelist. For the last two years of his life Bliss traveled with Major D. W. Whittle and led the music at revival meetings in the midwest and southern United States. Bliss and Ira D. Sankey (PHH 73) published a popular series of hymn collections entitled *Gospel Hymns*. The first book of the series, *Gospel Songs*, was published in 1874. The story of Bliss's tragic death at the age of thirty-eight is told at PHH 479.

Tune

HALLELUJAH! WHAT A SAVIOR, composed by Bliss, is sometimes called GETHSEMANE. This strong tune is characterized by repeated tones and by rhythmic interest in the final phrase. Sing stanzas 1-4 in harmony in fairly strict rhythm. Sing stanza 5 in unison with some rhythmic freedom on the final phrase.

Liturgical Use

A hymn of redemption useful on many occasions of worship; Lord's Supper; Lent; because of the "Hallelujah" refrain avoid using during Holy Week (so as not to "steal the thunder" of the Easter "alleluias").

483

How Great Thou Art

O STORE GUD
♩ = 66

Text

This text has an international history. Its first source is a Swedish text by Carl G. Boberg ("O store Gud"—"O great God"), who wrote its nine stanzas one summer evening in 1885 after he had admired the beauty of nature and the sound of church bells. Boberg published the text in

Scripture References
all st. = Ps. 121
st. 3 = Heb. 12:1-2
st. 4 = 1 Thess. 4:16-17

Mönsterås Tidningen (1886). Several years later, after hearing his text sung to a Swedish folk tune, Boberg published text and tune in *Sanningsvittnet* (April 16, 1891), the weekly journal he edited.

Manfred von Glehn, an Estonian, prepared a German translation of the text in 1907, which became the basis for a Russian translation by Ivan S. Prokhanoff in 1912. The Russian translation first appeared in the booklet *Kimvali* ("Cymbals") and then in the larger volume *The Songs of a Christian*, published in 1922 with support from

Prokhanoff's friends in the American Bible Society (reprinted in 1927). Several English translations also appeared in the early twentieth century, but these had limited exposure.

The Russian text came to the attention of Stuart Wesley Keene Hine (b. London, England, 1899; d. Somerset, England, 1989) when he and his wife were missionaries in the Ukraine; they often sang it together as a duet. Earlier, Hine had served in the British Army in France during World War I and then entered the Methodist ministry. Starting in 1923 he was a missionary in Poland, Czechoslovakia, Romania, and Russia. In 1939 he returned to England and ministered to displaced persons who had come from eastern European countries. From 1950-1959 he conducted weekly meetings with various Slav immigrants in Earls Court. Hine wrote evangelistic tracts as well as a number of popular hymns, of which "How Great Thou Art" is best known, and the book *Not You, But God: A Testimony to God's Faithfulness* (1982).

Hine prepared the English translation from the Russian: stanzas 1 and 2, while he and his wife worked amidst the impressive scenery of the Carpathian Mountains; stanza 3, while they were involved with village evangelism; and stanza 4 in 1948, while they ministered to displaced persons in England. The complete English text and its Swedish tune were published in 1949 in the Russian missions magazine *Grace and Peace*. Because much of Boberg's original text was lost in the multiple translations, the English text in modern hymnals is usually credited to Hine. The hymn gained great popularity after George Beverly Shea began singing it in the Billy Graham Crusades, beginning with the Toronto Crusade of 1955.

Hine's text vividly combines a sense of awe of nature and of its Creator (see also Ps. 8) with the New Testament gospel of Christ's atoning death and glorious return.

Tune
Originally in triple meter, the Swedish tune O STORE GUD is in bar form (AAB). The first section has a very limited range of four notes; the more meditative stanzas give way to a dramatic refrain with an expanded range. Sing in parts and observe some rhythmic freedom in the last line of the refrain, preferably only after stanza 4 (unless George Beverly Shea is the soloist!).

Liturgical Use
Many appropriate times in Christian worship.

484

Humble Praises, Holy Jesus

VESPER HYMN
♩ = 52

Text

Sometimes labeled as a "composite," this anonymous text was published in the Augustana Lutheran *Hymnal* (1925) and in Henry J. Kuiper's *New Christian Hymnal* (1929). It was introduced to many Christian school children in *Let Youth Praise Him* (1949) and was included in the 1959 *Psalter Hymnal*. In 1985, *Psalter Hymnal* editor Emily R. Brink (PHH 158) revised the text for the 1987 edition.

All stanzas use the biblical imagery of the shepherd (Jesus) and his lambs (children) in a petition for guidance and protection. The refrain adds its "alleluia to our King" as evidence of the "humble praises." The entire text is an effective prayer of petition and praise.

Tune

VESPER HYMN appeared in John A. Stevenson's *Selection of Popular National Airs* (1818) as a setting for Thomas Moore's "Hark! The Vesper Hymn Is Stealing." A footnote in that hymnal explained that Stevenson had added what is now the first line of the refrain to a "Russian Air." Some later hymnals attributed the tune to Dimitri Bortniansky, but no tune resembling this one has been found in that Russian composer's published works. Stevenson is generally recognized as being the arranger if not also the composer.

As a youth, Stevenson (b. Dublin, Ireland, 1761; d. Kells, Ireland, 1833) was a chorister at Christ Church Cathedral and St. Patrick's Cathedral, Dublin. He later worked as a church musician in both cathedrals: at St. Patrick's from 1783 to 1800 and at Christ Church from 1800 to 1814. In 1814 he became organist and musical director at the Castle Chapel. Stevenson published *Morning and Evening Services and Anthems* (1825) and an oratorio, *Thanksgiving* (1831). But he is better known for his operas and songs for the stage and his collection of *Irish Melodies* (1807-1809) to lyrics by Thomas Moore.

This bar form (AAB) tune reaches an early climax in its refrain. Preferably sing with children, but begin and end with the refrain as a frame sung by the entire congregation. For choral singing at a special service, try having the sopranos sing the final line of the refrain up an octave.

Liturgical Use

Many occasions of worship; though it works well with younger children, suitable for all God's children, regardless of age.

485

O Christ, Our Hope, Our Heart's Desire

Text

Although manuscript copies do not appear until the eleventh century, the Latin source for this Ascension text ("Jesu, nostra redemptio, amor et desiderium") is thought to date from the seventh or eighth century. A five-stanza English translation by John Chandler was published in his *Hymns of the Primitive Church* (1837), and a doxology stanza was added later. Of those stanzas, 1-3 and 5 are included with a few word changes.

Scripture References
st. 2 = 1 Pet. 2:24
st. 3 = 1 Tim. 2:6
st. 4 = 1 Pet. 1:8

This short but comprehensive text honors Christ as creator of the world (st. 1); meditates on his love, which led to his atoning death (st. 2); voices our worship to the ascended Christ for his victory over death (st. 3); and offers our prayer to keep Christ central in our lives (st. 4).

John Chandler (b. Witley, Godalming, Surrey, England, 1806; d. Putney, Surrey, 1876) spent most of his life in Witley, where his father was the vicar. After theological studies at Corpus Christi College, Oxford, England, he assumed his father's position in Witley in 1837. Noting that many of the prayers of the Anglican Church were English translations of early Latin prayers, Chandler decided that the church should sing hymns from that era as well. Because he did not find many suitable English translations, he made his own and published them in *The Hymns of the Primitive Church* (1837) and, with revisions, in *The Hymns of the Church, mostly Primitive* (1841). Some of the Latin hymns he translated, however, were not as ancient as the words "Primitive Church" might suggest; he also included translations of hymns from the *Paris Breviary* (1736).

Tune

MANOAH was first published in Henry W. Greatorex's *Collection of Psalm and Hymn Tunes* (1851). This anthology (later editions had alternate titles) contained one of the best tune collections of its era and included thirty-seven original compositions and arrangements by compiler Greatorex as well as melodies by his father, Thomas, and grandfather Anthony. Because no other source has been traced, it is believed that Greatorex composed MANOAH.

Greatorex (b. Burton-on-Trent, Staffordshire, England, 1813; d. Charleston, SC, 1858) received his early music training from his father, who was organist at Westminster Abbey. After moving to the United States in 1839, he served as organist at the Center Congregational Church and at St. John's Church, both in Hartford, Connecticut. He accepted the position of organist at St. Paul's Episcopal Church around 1846 and later became organist and choirmaster of the Calvary Episcopal Church, both in New York City. His final musical position was at the Episcopal Church in Charleston.

The composer gave arbitrary names to his tunes: Manoah was the father of Samson in the Old Testament. This well-crafted common-meter tune features some repetition of melodic motives and a harmonization that invites part singing. Sing in harmony in two long lines rather than four short phrases. Use moderate organ accompaniment at first, but make sure it swells for stanza 4.

Liturgical Use

A hymn of response after the sermon; Easter; Ascension; many other worship services.

486

Come, Thou Fount of Every Blessing

NETTLETON
♩ = 88

Text

Robert Robinson (b. Swaffham, Norfolk, England, 1735; d. Birmingham, England, 1790) wrote this text in four stanzas for Pentecost Sunday in 1758 when he was a pastor in Norwich. The text was published in *A Collection of Hymns used by the Church of Christ in Angel-Alley, Bishopsgate* (1759). Three of his four stanzas are included with some alterations, especially in stanza 2, which originally began "Here I raise my Ebenezer" (see 1 Sam. 7:12).

Scripture References
st. 1 = Rev. 21:6
Rev. 7:17
st. 2 = 1 Pet. 2:9-10
Col. 1:21-22
st. 3 = Eph. 2:7-8
1 Cor. 1:22

In his youth, Robinson was apprenticed to a London barber. Although raised in the Church of England, he did not become a Christian until 1755 after hearing a sermon on "the wrath to come" by George Whitefield. He then became a pastor and briefly served a Calvinist Methodist chapel in Mildenhall, Suffolk, England, and an Independent congregation in Norwich. In 1759 he was rebaptized and began a long association with the Stone Yard Baptist Church in Cambridge, England. Following his retirement in Birmingham in 1790, he was influenced by Unitarianism. Robinson published a new edition of William Barton's *Psalms* (1768) and *A History of Baptism* (1790) and wrote thirteen hymns.

This fine text about divine grace and providence contains various biblical images: Christ is the "fountain of life" (Ps. 36:9; Zech. 13:1) from which "streams of mercy" come. But Christ is also our "rock" (often used in the psalms along with "mount" or "Ebenezer," which means "stone of help"); he "rescues me from danger." Christ also "sought me when a stranger" (Col. 1:21) and "binds" or "seals" his own even when they are "prone to wander" (see Matt. 18:11-14). That phrase may have had special meaning for Robinson, who became successively a Calvinist Methodist, Congregationalist, Baptist, and finally a Unitarian.

Tune

NETTLETON is a rounded bar form (AABA) with a harmonization easily sung in parts by congregations. Named for nineteenth-century evangelist Ahasel Nettleton, the tune was published anonymously with this text in John Wyeth's collection of folk hymnody, *Repository of Sacred Music, Part Second* (1813). The tune may possibly be related to a group of folk melodies used for "Go Tell Aunt Rhody Her Old Grey Goose Is Dead."

A printer by trade, Wyeth (b. Cambridge, MA, 1770; d. Philadelphia, PA, 1858) is important in the history of hymnody as a compiler and publisher of early shape-note tunebooks. He worked briefly in Santo Domingo but had to flee when a revolt occurred. In 1792 he settled in Harrisburg, Pennsylvania, where he lived for much of the rest of his life. A Unitarian, he was coeditor for some thirty-five years of the Federalist newspaper *Oracle of Dauphin*, a prominent source of news and opinion. Not a musician himself, Wyeth published *Repository of Sacred Music* (1810) and, with the help of Methodist preacher and musician Elkanah Kelsay Dare, *Repository of Music, Part Second* (1813). Intended for Methodist and Baptist camp meetings, these tunebooks contained a number of anonymous folk tunes as well as music by a number of composers, including William Billings. The two volumes influenced the next generation of tunebooks, such as *Southern Harmony*, and a number of the folk tunes have survived as hymn tunes in various modern hymnals.

Liturgical Use

A testimony hymn about Christ's love for us, which could be used throughout the church year at the beginning of worship, after confession/assurance, or after the sermon.

487

ST. PETER
♩ = 56

How Sweet the Name of Jesus Sounds

Text

With the heading "The Name of Jesus," this text by John Newton (PHH 462) was published in the *Olney Hymns* (1779), where it was part of a group of hymns inspired by scriptural passages. The text is a fine example of Newton's evangelical piety and his skill at incorporating biblical phrases or allusions into his hymn texts. Of his original seven stanzas, 1, 2, and 5-7 are included.

Newton said that Song of Songs 1:3 ("your name is like perfume poured out") was the inspiration for this text: stanzas 1 and 2 compare perfume, with its sweet fragrance and healing properties, to the name of Jesus, which "soothes" and "heals." With its many biblical names for the Savior, stanza 3 evokes a variety of images about the person and ministry of Christ. The final stanzas confess that though our worship of Christ may be weak and imperfect, we will use our resources to praise him and testify to his love.

Tune

Composed by Alexander R. Reinagle (b. Brighton, Sussex, England, 1799; d. Kidlington, Oxfordshire, England, 1877), ST. PETER was published as a setting for Psalm 118 in Reinagle's *Psalm Tunes for the Voice and Pianoforte* (c. 1836). The tune first appeared with Newton's text in *Hymns Ancient and Modern* (1861); it is now usually associated with this text, for which it is a better match than for Psalm 118. The tune was named after St. Peter-in-the-East, the church in Oxford, England, where Reinagle was organist from 1822-1853.

Little is known of Reinagle's early life. Of Austrian descent, he came from a family of musicians and became a well-known organ teacher. A writer of teaching manuals for string instruments, Reinagle also compiled two books of hymn tunes, the 1836 collection and *A Collection of Psalm and Hymn Tunes* (1840). He also composed a piano sonata and some church music.

ST. PETER features descending motion after an initial rise. Sing stanzas 1-2 and 4-5 in parts, but sing the crucial middle stanza in unison. This music needs to express the fervor of the text without any festive fanfares.

Liturgical Use

Many occasions of worship, probably after the sermon as a hymn of testimony and encouragement.

Scripture References
st. 1 = Acts 4:12
Jer. 30:17
Rom. 10:13
Joel 2:32
1 John 4:18
Ps. 147:3
st. 2 = John 16:20
John 6:31-33
Matt. 11:28
st. 3 = John 10:11
John 15:13-14
John 4:19
John 14:6
Heb. 4:14
Rev. 17:14

488

I Heard the Voice of Jesus Say

RESTING PLACE
♩ = 54

Text

While pastor of a Presbyterian church in Kelso, Scotland, Horatius Bonar (PHH 260) wrote this text, which he intended to be a children's hymn. Entitled "The Voice from Galilee," the text was published in Bonar's *Hymns Original and Selected* (1846) with a reference to John 1:16 ("From the fullness of his grace we have all received one blessing after another"). The truth of the biblical imagery and the spiritual depth of the personal responses to Christ cap-

Scripture References
st. 1 = Matt. 11:28-29
st. 2 = John 4:14
st. 3 = John 8:12
John 9:5

tured in this text have made this a hymn much loved by children and adults. It is often considered to be among the finest of Bonar's many hymn texts.

Each of the three stanzas has two parts: the first half quotes Jesus' words, and the second half testifies to the personal experience of responding to Christ. The entire text invites us to accept what Jesus offers: rest from our burdens (st. 1), living water to quench our thirst (st. 2), and light for life's journey (st. 3).

Tune

Christian Reformed Church minister Henry Vander Werp (b. Bedum, Groningen, the Netherlands, 1846; d. Grand Rapids, MI, 1918) composed RESTING PLACE, which first appeared in his privately published *The Psalms, New Metrical Version, with Tunes New and Old* (Hudsonville, MI, 1911). The tune was first set to Bonar's text in the *New Christian Hymnal* (1929).

Orphaned at age three when his parents died of cholera, Vander Werp was raised by relatives. He trained to be a schoolteacher, did further studies in modern languages, and became a tutor to a wealthy family in Rotterdam. A member of the Dutch Seceder Church, he continued his studies at the theological seminary in Kampen and then took a pastorate in Beverwijk (1879-1881). After immigrating to the United States, Vander Werp served a Christian Reformed congregation in Noordeloos, Michigan (1882). Later he was pastor at Christian Reformed churches in Chicago, Cincinnati, South Dakota, and Michigan until his retirement in 1913. Vander Werp left a considerable body of writings in both Dutch and English, including poetry, editorials, many articles in the Christian Reformed periodicals *De Wachter* and *The Banner*, two catechism books, and children's stories. His privately published psalm book (see above) contained a number of his psalm tunes with texts from the 1909 draft of the United Presbyterian *Psalter*. He had hoped that the Christian Reformed Church would accept his book as its official English-language psalter because of its use of Genevan tunes, but the synod of 1914 decided instead to accept the United Presbyterian 1912 *Psalter* (with over four hundred tunes but virtually no Genevan tunes).

For regular congregational use of this isorhythmic tune (all equal rhythms) sing in harmony. Organists could highlight Jesus' quotations by a change in registration. For a more dramatic performance, try having the choir begin each stanza and then hum the parts while a soloist sings the words of Christ; the congregation could join in singing the second half of each stanza.

Liturgical Use
Regular Sunday worship services; evangelistic meetings.

489

When Peace like a River

VILLE DU HAVRE
♩ = 58

Text

Late in 1873 Horatio G. Spafford (b. North Troy, NY, 1828; d. Jerusalem, 1888) and his family were scheduled to travel from the United States to Europe. Delayed by pressing business, Spafford sent his wife and daughters ahead on the French liner *Ville du Havre*. The ship collided with the English ship *Lochearn* on November 22 and sank in just twelve minutes. Spafford's wife was saved, but his daughters perished. After arriving in Wales, Mrs. Spafford cabled her husband, "Saved alone." Spafford then left by boat to meet her. Near the tragic scene on the high seas he wrote this text. Upon hearing the news, evangelist Dwight L. Moody, a friend of the Spaffords, traveled to England to comfort them. He reported that Spafford said about the tragic event, "It is well; the will of God be done." Philip P. Bliss, another family friend, wrote the tune for Spafford's text. Both text and tune were published in *Gospel Hymns No. 2* (1876), a hymnal compiled by Ira D. Sankey (PHH 73) and Bliss.

Scripture References
st. 1 = Phil. 4:7
st. 3 = Col. 2:14
st. 4 = Isa. 34:4
1 Cor. 15:52

   The text conveys a sense of trust and ultimate peace with God's plan for our lives. Even in the face of "sorrows" and Satan's temptations, the Christian believes "it is well with my soul" (st. 1-2). That experience of trust and peace derives from knowing with certainty that Christ has paid the penalty for "my sin, not in part, but the whole" (st. 3). The final stanza affirms that it will also be "well with my soul" on the great day of Christ's return. This hymn has brought comfort to many Christians.

   In 1856, several years before writing this text, Spafford had moved to Chicago, Illinois, where he established a law practice and became a professor of medical jurisprudence at Lind University (now the Chicago Medical College). Active in the YMCA and as a Sunday school teacher, he served as director and trustee for the Presbyterian Theological Seminary of the Northwest in Chicago. Spafford became acquainted with Dr. Piazza Smith, a Scottish astronomer, and through him became interested in biblical archeology. Heavy losses in the Chicago fire of 1871, the death of his four daughters in 1873, and the death of his son in 1880 caused Spafford to be accused of some secret sin by uncharitable church members. In 1881 he, his wife, and some friends moved to Jerusalem and founded an American colony there; the family's story was told by another daughter, Bertha Spafford Vester, in *Our Jerusalem*.

Tune

The gospel tune by Philip Bliss (PHH 482) was named after the ship on which his friends died; VILLE DU HAVRE (also called IT IS WELL) is best sung in harmony throughout. The refrain may be sung only once—after stanza 4 as a final testimony. Use a moderate organ accompaniment to support confident singing of this testimonial hymn.

Liturgical Use

As a testimonial hymn, often after tragic events, when we want to confess our faith in God's providence even when we don't understand the "whys" of life.

490

ASSURANCE
♩ = 72

Blessed Assurance: Jesus Is Mine

Text

This text and "To God Be the Glory" (473) are probably the best-known texts by Fanny J. Crosby (PHH 473). She said the following about her writing of the text:

Scripture References
all st. = 1 Pet. 1:8
1 John 3:1-3

> Sometimes a tune is furnished me for which to write the words. The hymn titled "Blessed Assurance" was made in this manner. My dear friend Phoebe Palmer Knapp (Mrs. Joseph), so well-known as a writer and singer of most excellent music and as an aid and inspiration to all who knew her, had composed the tune; and it seemed to me one of the sweetest I had heard for a long time. She asked me what it said. I replied, "Blessed assurance." I felt while bringing the words and tones together that the air and the hymn were intended for each other
>
> —*from* Fanny Crosby's Memories

Crosby's text and Knapp's tune were published in John R. Sweney's *Gems of Praise* in 1873. The hymn was also published in both the American and British editions of the Ira D. Sankey (PHH 73) hymnals and was more recently featured in Billy Graham Crusades. It is an immensely popular hymn in English-speaking Christendom. The *Psalter Hymnal* includes the original stanzas 1 and 3, but stanza 2 by Marie J. Post (PHH 5) is substituted for Crosby's "rapture" stanza.

"Blessed Assurance" is a typical gospel hymn of the late nineteenth century. It is simple, truly evangelical in spirit, and has an emotional appeal that comes from its rousing tune and from the personal experience described in the text. It is a fine testimonial hymn of praise to Christ for his work of redemption (st. 1), for the Spirit's work of sanctification (st. 2), and for the joy of serving Jesus (st. 3).

Tune

The eight phrases of ASSURANCE use, with just one slight variation in the second phrase, the same rhythmic pattern throughout, sung over a static bass line. Sing in parts. Observe a moderate pace for the slow-moving harmony.

ASSURANCE is one of several tunes composed for Crosby's texts by Phoebe Palmer Knapp (b. New York, NY, 1839; d. Poland Springs, ME, 1908). As a young girl Knapp displayed great musical talent; she composed and sang children's songs at an early age. The daughter of the Methodist evangelist Walter C. Palmer, she was married to John Fairfield Knapp at the age of sixteen. She was a founder of the Metropolitan Life Insurance Company, and after her husband's death shared her considerable inherited wealth with various charitable organizations. She composed over five hundred gospel songs, of which the tunes for "Blessed Assurance" and "Open the Gates of the Temple" are still popular today.

Liturgical Use
Many occasions in worship and in daily life.

491

Our Lives Are Filled with Sorrows

ES KOMMT EIN SCHIFF GELADEN
♩ = 60

Text
Calvin Seerveld (PHH 22) wrote this text in Toronto, Ontario, in 1983, specifically for use with this tune, which he had found in a German chorale book. In a note on the original manuscript Seerveld indicated that he had written this text "for singing at the funerals of believing people (over fifty years of age)."

Scripture References
st. 1 = Ps. 90:1
st. 2 = 1 Cor. 15:54
st. 3 = Rev. 7:9-10
st. 4 = Job. 19:26

There are a number of biblical allusions in the text, the most obvious in the final phrase—a fitting reference to Job 19:25-26. The text clearly recognizes the finality of death (st. 2), the joy of the redeemed in glory (st. 3), and the reality of consolation for the believers who remain on earth (st. 1, 4). To personalize the text, stanzas 2 and 3 offer alternative readings, referring to either "brother's" and "brother," or "sister's" and "sister."

Tune
The tune ES KOMMT EIN SCHIFF GELADEN was originally part of a German Maria-lied, or love song to Mary. The tune became a carol when it was set to a text attributed to the mystic Johannes Tauler (around 1300-1361). It was published with Tauler's text in the Roman Catholic *Andernacher Gesangbuch* of 1608. *Psalter Hymnal* editor Emily R. Brink (PHH 158) composed the harmonization in 1985 on the birthday of one of her sisters, whose husband was missing at that time and later found murdered.

This Renaissance melody begins in triple meter but then changes to duple at the midpoint—the only time this happens in the entire *Psalter Hymnal!* The tune's meter requires keeping a constant two pulses per bar, both in the triple- and duple-meter sections. Sing in unison with sturdy organ support, or try having a choir sing unaccompanied. If this tune is unfamiliar, consider the alternate tune at 565 or sing the text in two long stanzas to a longer tune (7676D).

Seerveld wants to have this hymn sung at his own funeral. But he has requested that a New Orleans jazz-style interlude be improvised between stanzas 3 and 4 in the tradition of African American funerals in the southern United States. In those funerals sad music is traditionally played en route to the cemetery, but upbeat, joyful jazz is played as the mourners return home to emphasize their sure belief in a Christian resurrection.

Liturgical Use
Funerals.

492

WELLINGTON SQUARE
♩ = 54

Our Voice Would Be a Useless Cry

Text

Marie J. Post (PHH 5) wrote this text in 1970 and entered it in a hymn-writing contest sponsored by the *Missionary Monthly* magazine (it received honorable mention). It was first published in the *Psalter Hymnal Supplement* (1974).

Scripture References
st. 2 = Mark 4:35-41
Matt. 8:23-27
Luke 8:22-25
st. 3 = Rev. 5:11-12

The text incites our devotion to God, whose Holy Spirit is active in all Christian work. The Spirit equips us for ministry in the world and produces fruit from our human efforts (st. 2). God in Christ works in us and empowers us to labor in his name (st. 2). The same Spirit who inspires our preaching of God's Word has already revealed to us the great victory song of Revelation 5 and 7 (st. 3).

Tune

An energetic tune in minor tonality, WELLINGTON SQUARE is a rounded bar form (AABA) built around variations on the first four notes. Though it could be sung in parts by a choir, have the congregation sing in unison with confident tones from the organ.

Guy Warrack (b. Edinburgh, Scotland, 1900; d. Englefield Green, Surrey, England, 1986) composed WELLINGTON SQUARE for the 1931 edition of the British *Songs of Praise*. In that hymnal it was set to a text by Jan Struther (pseudonym for Joyce Torrens-Graham), "When Stephen, Full of Power and Grace."

Warrack studied at Magdalen College, Oxford, England, and at the Royal College of Music, where he was a student of Ralph Vaughan Williams. A teacher at the Royal

College of Music from 1925 to 1935, Warrack also held a number of important conducting posts. He was conductor of the BBC Scottish Orchestra and musical director of the Sadler's Wells Theater Ballet. Warrack composed many orchestral pieces, including his *Symphony in C minor* and film scores for documentaries.

Liturgical Use
Pentecost; Epiphany; services that focus on missions or similar kingdom themes (for mission festivals or ecumenical services use the better-known alternate tune ALL SAINTS NEW found at 110).

493

Precious Lord, Take My Hand

PRECIOUS LORD
♩ = 66

Text
In 1932, a week after the death of his wife in childbirth and the subsequent death of his newborn son, Thomas Andrew Dorsey (b. Villa Rica, GA, 1899; d. Chicago, IL, 1993) wrote this text. He also arranged the George N. Allen tune PRECIOUS LORD to match his text. Dorsey is considered the "father" of the African American gospel tradition (in distinction from the spiritual tradition) and was an active writer in this style from the 1920s through the 1950s. "Precious Lord" is the most popular of the early group of gospel songs that arose in the United States. Martin Luther King, Jr., chose the hymn as one of the "freedom anthems" of the Civil Rights Movement; since that time it has been included in many hymnals.

Scripture References
st. 1 = Ps. 139:10

Given the circumstances surrounding Dorsey's writing of this text, it is not surprising that it has the character of the Old Testament lament psalms: we confess our own helplessness (st. 1), and we utter a cry for divine help (st. 2), but even in the face of death we are confident of God's saving power (st. 3).

Born into a Baptist preacher's family, Dorsey moved to Atlanta when he was five. There he studied music and came under the influence of local blues pianists. He moved to Chicago in 1915, where he studied at the Chicago College of Composition and Arranging and played in nightclubs as "Georgia Tom" or "Barrelhouse Tom," accompanying blues singers such as Tampa Red, Ma Rainey, and Bessie Smith. Because of his skill as composer, arranger, and pianist, he was in great demand. He also formed his own band, Wildcat's Jazz Band. After suffering from a severe illness in 1926, Dorsey became more involved with the Pilgrim Baptist Church and in 1932 began a forty-year tenure as the church's choral director. He wrote at least two hundred gospel songs (his total works number more than a thousand), organized and was president of the National Convention of Gospel Choirs and Choruses, and frequently directed other ensembles, including the Gospel Choral Union. His gospel songs were popularized by singers such as Mahalia Jackson, Roberta Martin, and Clara Ward.

Tune
The intense spirituality of African American gospel music like PRECIOUS LORD thrives on musical improvisation and flexibility in performance; this is especially true when it is performed by a soloist or a trained choir. When led by improvisation at the keyboard, sing this hymn in unison. Otherwise the congregation may well sing in harmony, even unaccompanied, in the tradition of African American spirituals. Traditional gospel accompaniment consists of piano, or piano and organ together, often with drums and guitars; all these instruments would assist in coloring the harmonization with additional chords, rhythmic figures, and melodic ornaments.

Dorsey slightly adapted the tune MAITLAND, composed by George Nelson Allan (b. Mansfield, OH, 1812; d. Cincinnati, OH, 1877), which was first published in his 1844 collection of hymn texts and tunes, *The Oberlin Social and Sabbath School Hymn Book*. Nearly all of Allen's adult life was associated with Oberlin College. After his graduation from Oberlin in 1837, he became a faculty member, teaching music and geology. His most lasting contribution was the introduction of choral and instrumental programs, which later developed into the Oberlin Conservatory of Music.

Liturgical Use
Similar to uses for Old Testament lament psalms: times of personal tragedy, communal disasters, international conflicts; services in which Christians want to express solidarity with the oppressed and those who experience "the valley of the shadow of death."

494

BALM IN GILEAD
♩ = 88

There Is a Balm in Gilead

Text
This anonymous African American spiritual probably took shape during outdoor revival meetings in the early nineteenth century. The text draws on the image of Gilead, which in biblical times was a source of spices and medicinal ointments. The refrain states in positive terms what the prophet Jeremiah asks negatively, "Is there no balm in Gilead?" "Balm" becomes a metaphor for redemption in Christ.

Scripture References
all st. = Gen. 37:25
Jer. 46:11
ref. = Jer. 8:22

One of its most memorable phrases, "the sin-sick soul," was taken from hymns by Charles Wesley (267) and John Newton (462). The refrain alone was published in the *Revivalist* (upstate New York, 1868) and the complete spiritual in *Folk Songs of the American Negro* (1907), compiled by brothers Frederick J. Work and John W. Work, Jr.

(PHH 476). Of those stanzas, the two are included that concern the Spirit's encouragement of discouraged Christians and the task of every Christian to be a witness to Christ's love.

Tune

BALM IN GILEAD consists of two melodic lines, each of which is repeated in varied form. Have the congregation sing either in parts or in unison. It is also possible to adapt the call-and-response technique, so common in spirituals, to this hymn: a soloist sings the stanzas, and the entire congregation sings the refrain.

Liturgical Use

A hymn of comfort in times of discouragement or of encouragement for professing Christians; healing services; the refrain could be used as a chorus of invitation during evangelistic services.

495

I Know Not Why God's Wondrous Grace

EL NATHAN
$\downarrow = 56$

Text

American evangelist Daniel Webster Whittle (b. Chicopee Falls, MA, 1840; d. Northfield, MA, 1901) wrote this text based on 2 Timothy 1:12, which is quoted in the refrain (King James Version). It was published with EL NATHAN in *Gospel Hymns No. 4* (1883).

Scripture References
ref. = 2 Tim. 1:12

The text contrasts the "I know not" stanzas with the certainty of the "I know" refrain. We cannot understand God's saving grace to us (st. 1); we cannot explain our spiritual birth (st. 2); we are unable to comprehend the work of God's Spirit (st. 3); and we do not perceive clearly the future of our earthly lives (st. 4). But we do know by faith that God is true to his word!

Whittle was a bank cashier, Civil War soldier, and company treasurer before he became an evangelist. Earning the title of major during his military career, he was called Major Whittle throughout his life. Because of the influence of Dwight L. Moody, whom he met during the war, Whittle became an itinerant evangelist in 1873. He conducted evangelistic campaigns in North America and Great Britain, often accompanied by popular gospel singers such as Philip P. Bliss (PHH 482), James McGranahan, and George Stebbins (PHH 63). These men not only sang at Whittle's evangelistic meetings but also set to music many of his two hundred hymn texts (which he usually wrote under the pseudonym "El Nathan").

Tune

James McGranahan (PHH 99), Whittle's song leader, composed EL NATHAN. The tune's title is a pseudonym used by Whittle. A typical gospel hymn tune, EL NATHAN is constructed with a few melodic lines and a very simple harmony, but it is marked by some rhythmic interest. The tune is easily sung in parts. Try singing the stanzas in two long lines. The text of the refrain calls for one long extended phrase; accompanists and choirs using staggered breathing can demonstrate the effectiveness of a musical "communion of the saints" by performing the entire refrain without a break.

Liturgical Use

As a hymn of response to preaching; for times of renewal; profession of faith; other testimonial services.

496

CALCUTTA
♩ = 58

My Lord, I Did Not Choose You

Text

Originally beginning "'Tis not that I did choose thee," this hymn by Josiah Conder (b. Aldersgate, London, England, 1789; d. St. John's Wood, London, 1855) was published in Leifchild's *Original Hymns* (1843). Although not as well known as other hymn texts by Conder (e.g., "Bread of Heaven, On Thee We Feed" or "The Lord Is King, Lift Up Thy Voice"), this

Scripture References
st. 1 = John 15:16
Eph. 1:4
2 Thess. 2:13
st. 2 = 1 John 4:10, 19

text has been treasured in the songbooks of the Christian Reformed Church because of its focus on the doctrine of election. The text simply confesses that God chose us as his people long before any of us responded to his love.

A prolific poet and author of books on a variety of topics, Conder was a Congregational layman who took over his father's bookshop and for some twenty years edited the *Eclectic Review.* His hymns were published posthumously in *Hymns of Praise, Prayer, and Devout Meditation* (1856). Isaac Watts's (PHH 155) hymns had dominated the Congregational Church for many years, but in 1836 the Congregationalist Union published *The Congregational Hymn Book, a supplement to Dr. Watts' Psalms and Hymns,* edited by Conder. That hymnbook contained fifty-six of Conder's hymns.

Tune

Said to be a "Greek Air," CALCUTTA was one of the popular national tunes used by Dublin's Thomas Moore (1779-1852) in his *Sacred Songs* (1816). Arthur S. Sullivan (PHH 46) adapted it for congregational singing and published it in his *Church Hymns with Tunes* (1874). The tune is named CALCUTTA because of its association with "From

Greenland's Icy Mountains," a text by Reginald Heber (PHH 249), who was the Anglican bishop of Calcutta at the time of his death.

CALCUTTA is a bar form (AAB) with a harmonization that invites part singing.

Liturgical Use
During the service of confession/assurance; with confessional preaching on the doctrine of election.

497

How Vast the Benefits Divine

BETHLEHEM
♩ = 60

Text
Written by ardent Calvinist Augustus M. Toplady (b. Farnham, Surrey, England, 1740; d. Kensington, London, England, 1778), this text was published in the *Gospel Magazine* (Dec. 1774). Dewey Westra (PHH 98) revised Toplady's text in 1931 for the first edition of the *Psalter Hymnal* (1934).

Scripture References
st. 2 = Eph. 1:4

This teaching text presents in song the essential points of the doctrine of redemption (like 496 but more comprehensively): only in Christ are we saved, for we have no merit of our own. Our redemption was ordained "before the world began" (see election texts referred to in 496), and our salvation ultimately leads to ruling with Christ in his kingdom.

Toplady is primarily known for writing "Rock of Ages" and for being an outspoken Calvinist opponent of John Wesley (PHH 267). After his father's death, Toplady moved with his mother to Ireland, where he studied at Trinity College, Dublin. He experienced a conversion while listening to the Wesleyan Methodist lay preacher James Morris. Ordained in the Church of England in 1762, Toplady served several congregations, including Broadhembury in Devonshire (1770-1775) and the Chapel of the French Calvinists in Leicester Fields, London, from 1775 on. Although converted under the preaching of a Methodist, Toplady became a bitter opponent in sermons and print of John Wesley and his Arminian teaching. Often using scurrilous language, such as "Wesley is guilty of Satanic shamelessness," he pressed his Calvinistic interpretation of the Bible, to which Wesley responded with equal disdain. Toplady wrote 130 hymn texts and produced *Poems on Sacred Subjects* (1769) and *Psalms and Hymns for Public and Private Worship* (1776).

Tune
Gottfried W. Fink (b. Sulza, Thuringia, Germany, 1783; d. Leipzig, Germany, 1846) composed BETHLEHEM in 1842 as a setting for Matthias Claudius's text "War einst ein

Riese Goliath." The tune was published with that text in Fink's *Musikalischer Hausschatz der Deutschen* (1843).

After studying theology at the University of Leipzig, Fink was ordained in 1809 and became an assistant pastor in that city. His main career, however, was in music. A composer for the piano, violin, and voice, Fink served as director of music and taught at the University of Leipzig. But he was especially prominent as a music scholar and critic. Editor of the influential periodical *Allgemeine musikalische Zeitung*, Fink also wrote and edited a number of works on music theory and history. Arthur S. Sullivan (PHH 46) arranged the tune and published it as a setting for "While Shepherds Watched Their Flocks By Night" (thus the tune's title) in his *Church Hymns with Tunes* (1874).

BETHLEHEM is a rounded bar form (AABA) with a distinctive third line. Sing the teaching stanzas (1 and 3) in unison and the middle stanza, addressed to Christ, in harmony. This tune requires a certain majesty of tempo.

Liturgical Use
With preaching on redemption, probably after the sermon; Lent.

498

FINLANDIA
♩ = 60

I Sought the Lord, and Afterward I Knew

Text

Said by some scholars to have been written in 1878, this anonymous text was published in *Holy Songs, Carols, and Sacred Ballads,* compiled by the Roberts brothers in Boston (1880). Austin Lovelace says of this text: "'He first loved us.' This simple yet profound thought is the basis for the hymn. God loved us long before we knew it. We seek God, but already God is holding out a hand waiting for us to take hold of it and be rescued from the seas of life" (Lovelace, *Hymn Notes*).

Scripture References
st. 2 = Matt. 14:22-33
st. 3 = 1 John 4:10, 19
Jer. 31:3

Stanza 2 alludes to the scene in which Christ saves Peter from drowning (see Matt. 14:22-33).

Tune

In 1899 Finnish composer Jean Sibelius (b. Hameenlina, Tavastehus, Finland, 1865; d. Järvenpää, near Helsingfors, Finland, 1957) wrote a musical score for six historical tableaux in a pageant that celebrated and supported the Finnish press against Russian oppression. In 1900 Sibelius revised the music from the final tableau into FINLANDIA, a tone poem for orchestra. The chorale-like theme that emerges out of the turbulent beginning of this tone poem became the hymn tune.

FINLANDIA was first used as a hymn tune in the Scottish *Church Hymnary* (1927) and in the Presbyterian *Hymnal* (1933). The melody features several repeated and varied melody lines. It is clearly an instrumental tune, but with diligent leadership by organists, congregations can sing the various cadential tones to their proper length. Because of the long lines, accompanists must work to keep the tempo moving. The tune is a glorious setting for harmony singing by choirs. This tune is also often set to the hymn text of Katharina Von Schlegel, "Stille, mein Wille, dein Jesus hilft siegen" ("Be Still, My Soul, The Lord Is On Thy Side").

Sibelius began music studies on the piano, then violin, and at one time thought of becoming a concert violinist. But he began composing at the age of ten, and his later career in music was primarily in composition. Finland's most famous composer, Sibelius used native mythology and geography in his composition, which became a rallying point for Finland's nationalism and patriotism. In 1897 the government awarded him a pension for life for his contribution to his country. From 1900 until the outbreak of World War I he traveled extensively in Europe, often as conductor of his own works. In 1914 he visited the United States, where he was a popular conductor, and where he received an honorary degree from Yale University and taught briefly at the New England Conservatory in Boston. He did not compose during the last twenty-six years of his life. Sibelius is known especially for his symphonic music, but he also composed many songs and theater music, as well as music for piano and chamber ensembles. His only compositions for devotional use are *Five Christmas Songs* (1895-1913) and "You Are Mighty, O Lord" (1927) for mixed choir.

Liturgical Use
See PHH 496 and PHH 497.

499

My God, How Wonderful You Are

ST. ETHELDREDA
♩ = 50

Text

Frederick W. Faber (b. Calverly, Yorkshire, England, 1814; d. Kensington, London, England, 1863) wrote "My God, how wonderful thou art," a hymn published in his *Jesus and Mary; or Catholic Hymns* (1849). Of the original nine stanzas, 1, 3-5, 7, and 9 are included in modernized form.

Scripture References
st. 1 = Ps. 113:5
st. 5 = Ps. 103:13

Presenting a magnificent view of God, this text is particularly appropriate for the late twentieth century, a time in which humankind has lost its sense of wonder. As we sing, we contemplate the glory and majesty of God (st. 1-2), which in turn inspires our holy fear, penitence, and love (st. 3-4). The text alludes to Psalm 103:13 (st. 5) and gives us an apocalyptic vision of worshiping God face to face (st. 6).

Raised in the Church of England, Faber came from a Huguenot and strict Calvinistic family background. He was educated at Balliol College, Oxford, and ordained in the

Church of England in 1839. Influenced by the teaching of John Henry Newman, Faber followed Newman into the Roman Catholic Church in 1845 and served under Newman's supervision in the Oratory of St. Philip Neri. Because he believed that Roman Catholics should sing hymns like those written by John Newton (PHH 462), Charles Wesley (PHH 267), and William Cowper (PHH 434), Faber wrote 150 hymns himself. One of his best known, "Faith of Our Fathers," originally had these words in its third stanza: "Faith of Our Fathers! Mary's prayers/Shall win our country back to thee." He published his hymns in various volumes and finally collected all of them in *Hymns* (1862).

Tune

Thomas Turton (b. Hatfield, Yorkshire, England, 1780; d. Westminster, Middlesex, England, 1864) composed ST. ETHELDREDA in 1860; it was published in James Turle's *Psalms and Hymns for Public Worship* (1863). Educated at Catharine Hall, Cambridge, England, Turton became a professor of mathematics at Cambridge in 1822 and five years later a professor of divinity at the same school. In 1830 he left Cambridge to become Dean of Peterborough. He also served as Dean of Westminster (1842-1845) and as Bishop of Ely from 1845 until his death. Turton wrote many polemical tracts and composed some church music.

This simple but charming tune is in the style of the older English psalm tunes. Sing much of the hymn in harmony, possibly with some antiphonal stanzas, but sing stanza 7 in unison. The singing and its accompaniment should contribute to the sense of awe inherent in the text.

Liturgical Use

As a hymn of adoration at the beginning of worship, or as a response after preaching.

500

FOUNDATION
♩ = 72

How Firm a Foundation

Text

Based on Isaiah 43:1-5, this text was given the heading "Exceeding great and precious Promises. II Peter 3:4" in John Rippon's *A Selection of Hymns* (1787). The author was listed simply as "K." Although some scholars are not convinced of this attribution, "K" presumably refers to Richard Keen, song leader in the London church where Rippon was minister. With minor alterations, stanzas 1, 3-5, and 7 are included from the original seven stanzas.

Scripture References
st. 1 = 1 Cor. 3:11
st. 2 = Isa. 41:10
st. 3-4 = Isa. 43:2
st. 5 = Rom. 8:35-39
Heb. 13:5
Deut. 31:6

"How Firm a Foundation" is a noble text, full of comfort for God's people whose "foundation" of faith is rooted in the Word (st. 1) and whose lives experience divine protection when they face "deep waters" and "fiery trials" (st. 2-4). The final stanza clearly moves beyond the text's Old Testament source and proclaims the certainty of redemption in Christ.

A Baptist minister, Rippon (b. Tiverton, Devonshire, England, 1751; d. London, England, 1836) was called to the Baptist Church in Carter Lane, London, in 1772 as an interim pastor. After becoming head pastor, he stayed in that position for sixty-three years. He also edited the *Baptist Annual Register* (1790-1802). His main contribution to hymnody was his compiling of *A Selection of Hymns from the Best Authors, Intended As an Appendix to Dr. Watts's Psalms and Hymns* (1787) and *A Selection of Psalm and Hymn Tunes* (1791). These publications became popular in both England and America. However, later hymnologists have often been frustrated by Rippon's work because he frequently did not indicate the authors of the hymns and often altered the texts without acknowledging his changes.

Tune

The anonymous tune FOUNDATION first appeared in Joseph Funk's *A Compilation of Genuine Church Music* (1832) as a setting for this text (there it was called PROTECTION). The tune was also published with the text in *Southern Harmony* and *Sacred Harp*.

The ancestors of Joseph Funk (b. Lancaster County, PA, 1778; d. Mountain Valley, a.k.a. Singers Glen, VA, 1862) were German Mennonites who had settled in eastern Pennsylvania. Around 1780 the Funk family moved to the Shenandoah Valley close to Harrisonburg, Virginia. Funk became a farmer and a teacher in a schoolhouse on his property. An itinerant singing-school teacher and music publisher, he also issued the monthly music journal *Southern Musical Advocate and Singer's Friend* before the Civil War (the journal was continued later by his sons). Funk published *Choral-Music* (1816) and *A Compilation of Genuine Church Music* (1832). The revised twenty-fourth edition (1980) is still in use by Mennonites in the Shenandoah Valley today. Funk's life was the focus of Alice Parker's opera *Singers Glen* (1978).

The harmonization is by Dale Grotenhuis (PHH 4). There are several options for singing: congregation throughout, soloists on the middle stanzas, or in canon. Like many folk tunes, FOUNDATION is pentatonic and should be sung with vigor. It can be sung either in two-part canon (two measures apart) or in four parts (one measure apart). Try having the choir's men and women sing in canon on the inner stanzas, perhaps following a soloist. For the final stanza, try dividing the entire congregation into four groups for a stirring conclusion. When singing in canon, sing unaccompanied or use the Busarow settings for canon in *All Praise to You, Eternal God* (Augsburg, 1980); do not use the hymnal accompaniment.

Liturgical Use

Many occasions of worship that focus on redemption and providence; as a hymn of comfort for those in difficult or tragic circumstances; baptism; profession of faith; prior to reading of Scripture.

501

Oh, for a Thousand Tongues to Sing

Text

In 1739, for the first anniversary of his conversion, Charles Wesley (PHH 267) wrote an eighteen-stanza text beginning "Glory to God, and praise and love." It was published in *Hymns and Sacred Poems* (1740), a hymnal compiled by Wesley and his brother John. The familiar hymn "Oh, for a Thousand Tongues" comes from stanzas 1 and 7-12 of this longer text (this pattern already occurs in Richard Conyers's *Collection of Psalms and Hymns*, 1772). Stanza 7 is the doxology stanza that began the original hymn. Wesley acquired the title phrase of this text from Peter Böhler, a Moravian, who said to Wesley, "If I had a thousand tongues, I would praise Christ with them all" (Böhler was actually quoting from Johann Mentzner's German hymn "O dass ich tausend Zungen hätte").

Scripture References

st. 1-2	=	Ps. 145:10-12
st. 2	=	Luke 4:18-19
		Isa. 61:1-2
st. 3	=	Acts 3:16
		Rom. 5:1
st. 4	=	Col. 2:14
st. 5	=	Heb. 2:4
st. 6	=	Matt. 11:5
		Isa. 35:6
		Acts 3:8
st. 7	=	Rev. 5:13

Through this jubilant, partly autobiographical text Wesley exalts his Redeemer and Lord. With its many biblical allusions it has become a great favorite of many Christians.

Tune

Lowell Mason (PHH 96) adapted AZMON from a melody composed by Carl G. Gläser in 1828. Mason published a duple-meter version in his *Modern Psalmist* (1839) but changed it to triple meter in his later publications. Mason used (often obscure) biblical names for his tune titles; Azmon, a city south of Canaan, appears in Numbers 34:4-5.

AZMON is the preferred tune for this text in the United States. The British often use RICHMOND (335), which offers a descant, or LYNGHAM (404), a fuguing tune. Either of these would make fine alternate tunes.

This great hymn of praise and rejoicing calls for exuberant singing and strong, full accompaniment. Assign some stanzas to antiphonal groups singing in harmony; reserve the final stanza for unison with descant.

Liturgical Use

Many types of services; profession of faith; baptism; other times of renewal; Pentecost.

502

The Church's One Foundation

AURELIA
♩ *= 116*

Text

This well-known hymn arose out of a theological controversy in the mid-nineteenth century. John W. Colenso, Anglican bishop of Natal, South Africa, wrote a book that expressed critical views of the historicity of parts of Scripture and questioned some articles of the Christian faith. Samuel J. Stone (b. Whitmore, Staffordshire, England, 1839; d. London, England, 1900), a clergyman in Windsor, England, was one of the people who defended the orthodox Christian faith. He did so in part by publishing his *Lyra Fidelium; Twelve Hymns on the Twelve Articles of the Apostles' Creed* (1866). "The Church's One Foundation" was his hymn on the article "the holy catholic church, the communion of saints." Stone's text originally had seven stanzas, but he added three more in 1885 for processional use at Salisbury Cathedral. Of those ten stanzas, 1, 2, 4, and 5 are the usual stanzas included in modern hymnals.

Scripture References
st. 1 = Eph. 1:22-23
    Col. 1:18
    1 Cor. 3:11
    Eph. 2:20
    Eph. 5:26-27
st. 2 = Eph. 4:4-6
st. 3 = Rev. 6:10

The text portrays the Christian church as rooted in the Savior, Jesus Christ, through the water of baptism and the Word of God (st. 1). In accord with the ninth article of the Apostles' Creed, we confess through this text that the church is catholic (universal) and united by "one Lord, one faith, one baptism" (Eph. 4:5). As we sing, we lament the "heresies" that "distress" the church (st. 3); although this is a direct reference to the Colenso controversy, the stanza fits many other situations in church history as well. The final stanza ends on a hopeful tone: the church will finally be at peace and at rest.

Stone attended schools at Charterhouse and Pembroke College in Oxford, England. Ordained in the Church of England in 1862, he became curate of Windsor, a position he held until he joined his father in ministry at St. Paul's in Haggerston, London, in 1870. He succeeded his father as vicar at Haggerston in 1874, staying until 1890. From 1890 until his death he served All-Hallows-on-the Wall in London, which he turned into a haven for working girls and women. In addition to his collection of hymns, Stone's publications include *Sonnets of the Christian Year* (1875), *Hymns* (1886), and *Iona* (1898). He served as a member of the committee that prepared *Hymns Ancient and Modern* (1909). His *Collected Hymns and Poems* were published posthumously.

Tune

Composed by Samuel S. Wesley (PHH 206), AURELIA (meaning "golden") was published as a setting for "Jerusalem the Golden" in *Selection of Psalms and Hymns,* which was compiled by Charles Kemble and Wesley in 1864. Though opinions vary concerning the tune's merits (Henry J. Gauntlett once condemned it as "secular twaddle"), it has been firmly associated with Stone's text since tune and text first appeared together in the 1868 edition of *Hymns Ancient and Modern*. However, Erik Routley (PHH 31) suggests rejuvenating this text by singing it to ST. THEODULPH (375/376).

Sing stanzas 1-3 in parts and stanza 4 in unison. Support with crisp organ articulation on the repeated soprano tones.

Liturgical Use

With Lord's Day 21; Reformation celebrations; church festivals; ecumenical services; in times of theological controversy.

503

KIRKEN
$\ =46$

Built on the Rock

Text

This hymn is a great favorite among Scandinavian Christians, second only to Martin Luther's "A Mighty Fortress." Written by Nicolai F. S. Grundtvig (PHH 360) in seven stanzas ("Kirken den er et gammelt Hus"), the text was published in *Sang-Värk til den Danske Kirke* (1837) and later revised by Grundtvig for publication in the 1854 edition of his *Festsalmer.*

Scripture References
st. 1 = Matt. 16:18
st. 2 = Isa. 57:15
1 Cor. 6:19
st. 3 = 1 Pet. 2:5

Carl Döving (b. Norddalen, Norway, 1867; d. Chicago, IL, 1937) translated Grundtvig's hymn in 1909. Döving immigrated to the United States in 1890 and studied at Luther College, Decorah, Iowa, and Luther Seminary, St. Paul, Minnesota. He served Lutheran parishes in Minnesota and New York and concluded his career as a city missionary in Chicago. A competent linguist and fine hymnologist, he contributed more than thirty-two English translations of German and Scandinavian hymns to *The Lutheran Hymnary* (1913), including "Built on the Rock."

The current version is a revision of Döving's translation prepared by Fred C. M. Hansen for the *Hymnal for Church and Home* (1927). This text may well have been the model for the modern hymn "I Am the Church, You Are the Church" by Richard Avery and Donald Marsh (1972).

Drawing on biblical texts, "Built on the Rock" emphasizes certain characteristics of the Christian church: Christ is the foundation and builder of his church (st. 1); the church is not primarily a building but people loved and inhabited by God (st. 2); these people are blessed through their whole-life worship of God (st. 3).

Tune

Composed for this text by Ludwig M. Lindeman (b. Trondheim, Norway, 1812; d. Oslo, Norway, 1887), KIRKEN was published in Wilhelm A. Wexel's *Christelige Psalmer* (1840). A bar form (AAB) tune in the Dorian mode, it is a suitably rugged, folk-like tune for this text, with a satisfying climax in line 6. Sing in harmony throughout and support with energetic accompaniment.

KIRKEN (also called LINDEMAN) was the first hymn tune Lindeman wrote. Born into a family of musicians, Lindeman received his early organ training from his father, for whom he became a substitute organist at the age of twelve. Although he studied theology in Oslo (then called Christiana), after 1839 he turned to a career in music. He was the organist of the Church of the Savior in Oslo (1839-1887) and became a virtuoso performer. In 1871 he was invited to come to London to give inaugural recitals on the new organ in Albert Hall. Lindeman published hymn collections and organ works as well as the influential *Koralbog* (1877), which contained tunes (restored to rhythmic shape) for Landstad's hymnal of 1869. He was also an excellent teacher and founded an organ school (later the Oslo Conservatory) with his son in 1883. A scholarly collector of Norwegian folk music, Lindeman traveled the country collecting folk songs, which he published in a series of volumes (1853-1867) and which influenced the works of composer Edvard Grieg.

Liturgical Use
With Lord's Day 21; Reformation celebrations; church festivals, anniversaries, and ecumenical services.

504

Holy God, We Praise Your Name

GROSSER GOTT
♩ = 120

Text
This text is based on the anonymous fourth-century Latin hymn "Te Deum Laudamus," which in one modern English prose translation reads:

Scripture References
st. 2 = Isa. 6:3
Rev. 4:8

We praise you, O God,
we acclaim you as Lord;
all creation worships you,
the Father everlasting.
To you all angels, all the powers of heaven,
the cherubim and seraphim, sing in endless praise:
    Holy, holy, holy Lord, God of power and might,
    heaven and earth are full of your glory.
The glorious company of apostles praise you.
The noble fellowship of prophets praise you.
The white-robed army of martyrs praise you.

Throughout the world the holy Church acclaims you:
    Father, of majesty unbounded,
    your true and only Son, worthy of all praise,
    the Holy Spirit, advocate and guide.

You, Christ, are the king of glory,
the eternal Son of the Father.
When you took our flesh to set us free
you humbly chose the virgin's womb.
You overcame the sting of death,
and opened the kingdom of heaven to all believers.
You are seated at God's right hand in glory.
We believe that you will come to be our judge.
    Come then, Lord, and help your people,
    bought with the price of your own blood,
    and bring us with your saints
    to glory everlasting.

—English Language Liturgical Commission, from Praying Together, *1988*

A classic text of the church, "Te Deum Laudamus" has been a staple item in many liturgies and is sometimes extended with versicles and responses. It is loved by all traditions of Christendom: Eastern, Roman Catholic, and Protestant. Much of the text consists of liturgical phrases and acclamations, including some from the "Gloria in excelsis Deo" (see 247). Over the centuries many composers have set this text in large choral works; it has been translated and versified into many languages and expressed in numerous hymns.

A German versification of the "Te Deum" ("Grosser Gott, wir loben dich") appeared anonymously in the *Katholisches Gesangbuch* (Vienna, around 1774) at the request of Empress Maria Theresa of Austria. Four years later that versification was also published by Ignaz Franz (b. Protzau, Silesia, 1719; d. Breslau [Poland], 1790) with small alterations; thus it is attributed to Franz in some modern sources. Franz was a Roman Catholic priest who studied at Glas and Breslau. He held a number of church positions, the longest (1766 until his death) as an assistant in the ecclesiastical court in Breslau. Franz published ten books, the most important a Roman Catholic hymnal, *Katholisches Gesangbuch* (c. 1774), which contained forty-seven of his hymns.

A rather free English translation of the German and Latin by Clarence A. Walworth (b. Plattsburg, NY, 1820; d. Albany, NY, 1900) was published in a Redemptorist Father's hymnal in 1853 and was reprinted in Dublin's *Catholic Psalmist* in 1858.

Walworth was born into a Presbyterian home. After studying at Union College in Schenectady, New York, he was admitted to the bar in 1841. His interest in theology led to studies for the Episcopalian ministry at General Theological Seminary in New York City, but under the influence of the Oxford Movement he became a Roman Catholic in 1845 and joined the Redemptorist Order. In 1848 he was ordained as "Clarence Alphonsus" at the Redemptorist college in Wittem, the Netherlands. Walworth served as a priest in Troy, New York and in Albany, New York. One of the founders of the Paulist Order, he fought industrial abuses, took up the cause of Native Americans on the St. Regis reservation, and wrote poetry and hymns. He was stricken with blindness during the last ten years of his life. His best-known publication is *The Oxford Movement in America* (1895).

The *Psalter Hymnal* includes Walworth's stanzas 1-4, which cover only the first half of the "Te Deum." We and all creation praise our God and Lord (st. 1); all the angels sing their praise to God (st. 2); saints in heaven and the church on earth praise God (st. 3); we praise the triune God (st. 4). The two halves of this part of the "Te Deum" are carefully balanced: stanza 2 ends with the angels' threefold Sanctus; stanza 4 concludes with a Gloria Patri.

Tune

GROSSER GOTT was set to the German versification in the *Katholisches Gesangbuch* (see above). Variants of the tune abound; the version found in the *Psalter Hymnal* came from Johann Schicht's *Allgemeines Choralbuch* (1819), and the harmonization came from Conrad Kocher's (PHH 358) setting in his *Zions Harfe* (1855). William H. Monk's (PHH 332) shortened version of this tune (HURSLEY) is often associated with John Keble's evening hymn "Sun of My Soul."

A sturdy melody, GROSSER GOTT is in simple bar form (AAB). Sing in parts on stanzas 1-3 and add the descant by Emily R. Brink (PHH 158) to unison singing on stanza 4. Use full organ tone with some festive mixtures.

Liturgical Use

An opening hymn at Sunday morning worship services (as is traditional for the "Te Deum"); an extended doxology for festive occasions.

505

For All the Saints

SINE NOMINE
♩ = 60

Text

"For All the Saints" is considered to be William W. How's (PHH 279) finest hymn text. Originally in eleven stanzas, it was published in Earl Nelson's *Hymns for Saints' Days* (1864) with the heading, "Saints' Day Hymn. A Cloud of Witnesses. Heb. 12:1." The *Psalter Hymnal* includes the original stanzas 1-2, 6-8, and 10-11, with modernized pronouns. (Among the stanzas omitted in most hymnals are those that begin "for all the apostles," "for all the evangelists," and "for all the martyrs.")

Scripture References
st. 1 = Rev. 14:13
     Heb. 12:1-2
st. 3 = Rev. 2:10
st. 4 = John 17:22
st. 6 = Prov. 4:18
st. 7 = Rev. 7:9-17

The text begins with a proclamation of thanksgiving for the saints ("the cloud of witnesses") who confessed Christ and found in him protection and inspiration (st. 1-2). That proclamation is followed by a prayer for Christ's soldiers on earth to be "faithful, true, and bold" (st. 3). At the crux of the text is the confession of a "blest communion" of saints in heaven and on earth (st. 4). Though the holy warfare may be "fierce and long" (st. 5), "all the saints" may take courage from the vision of a victorious church that worships the triune God on that "more glorious day" (st. 6-7).

Tune

Ralph Vaughan Williams (PHH 316) composed SINE NOMINE for this text and published it in the *English Hymnal* in 1906. Vaughan Williams wrote two harmonizations— one for unison stanzas and one for choral stanzas. The tune's title means "without name" and follows the Renaissance tradition of naming certain compositions "Sine Nomine" if they were not settings for preexisting tunes.

Equipped with a "walking" bass, SINE NOMINE is a glorious marching tune for this great text. Many consider this tune to be among the finest of twentieth-century hymn tunes (it is, perhaps, the cathedral's equivalent to "When the Saints Go Marching In"). Allowing the "alleluia" phrase to enter before our expectation of it is a typical and very effective Vaughan Williams touch.

Sing the unison and harmony stanzas as given in the *Psalter Hymnal*. Try assigning the various stanzas to antiphonal groups: a "heavenly" ensemble for stanzas 1-2, an "earthly" ensemble for stanzas 3 and 5, and the entire congregation on stanzas 4, 6, and 7.

Liturgical Use

Traditionally for All Saints Day (the first Sunday in November) and similar church festivals; worship that emphasizes the church as militant and triumphant; funerals.

506

RUSTINGTON
♩ = 108

Glorious Things of You Are Spoken

Text

Written in five stanzas by John Newton (PHH 462), this text was published in the *Olney Hymns* (1779). There it was part of a group of hymns inspired by Scripture passages (Newton referred to Isa. 33:20-22). The original stanzas 1-3 and 5 are printed in the *Psalter Hymnal* (with "you" in place of the original "thee"). The hymn has been described as the "one truly joyful hymn" in the Olney collection and the evangelical equivalent to the more catholic "The Church's One Foundation." John Julian ranks "Glorious Things" with the finest hymns in the English language.

The text uses the metaphor of Zion, the (new) city of God (see Heb. 12:22) for the church or people of God. Founded securely on Christ's salvation, God's people experience his presence, protection, and guidance, and share in his glory.

Tune

C. Hubert H. Parry's (PHH 145) RUSTINGTON was first published in the *Westminster Abbey Hymn Book* (1897) as a setting for Benjamin Webb's "Praise the Rock of Our Salvation." The tune is named for the village in Sussex, England, where Parry lived for some years and where he died.

This is such a distinguished melody that it is probably best to sing all the stanzas in unison, although confident choirs will want to sing the harmony of the middle stanzas. Organists, use bright mixtures. The tune AUSTRIA is most commonly associated with this text, as it was in earlier editions of the *Psalter Hymnal*. In 1985, however, the synod of the Christian Reformed Church rejected the use of AUSTRIA in its hymnal because Dutch immigrants and Jewish Christians associate that tune with its use by Nazis during World War II.

Liturgical Use

With preaching on ecclesiology (Lord's Day 21, etc.); profession of faith; ordination/commissioning services; church festivals, anniversaries, and ecumenical services.

Scripture References
st. 1 = Ps. 87:1-3
Ps. 132:13-14
Matt. 16:18
Isa. 26:1
st. 2 = Ps. 46:4
Rev. 7:17
Rev. 22:1
st. 3 = Ex. 13:21-22
Ex. 16:14-16
Isa. 4:5-6
Ps. 105:39-41
st. 4 = Gal. 6:14
Matt. 6:19-21
Ps. 87:6

507

The Son of God, through His Spirit

HEIDELBERG 54
$\quad \downarrow = 112$

Text

Psalter Hymnal editor Emily R. Brink (PHH 158) composed several musical settings for important segments of the Heidelberg Catechism, one of the primary confessional statements of the Christian Reformed Church. Two of these settings are included in the *Psalter Hymnal:* this text about the church and the comforting text from Lord's Day 1 (549). (The entire Heidelberg Catechism is found in the worship edition of the *Psalter Hymnal* on pp. 861-925, with a helpful historical introduction on p. 860.)

Based on Lord's Day 21, Q&A 54 (p. 883) of the Heidelberg Catechism (thus the tune's title), this text provides an explanation of the apostolic confession about the "holy catholic church." Although it makes a strongly objective statement about Christ's

Scripture References
st. = John 10:28-30
Rom. 8:28-30

church, the text also presents a deeply personal confession in its final line ("Of this community I am and always will be a living member").

Tune
Emily R. Brink composed HEIDELBERG 54 in 1977. The tune has chantlike features at its beginning but develops larger melodic gestures toward the end. Because of its use of several melodic motives, the tune is accessible to many congregations. Either for initial learning or for regular use, try having the choir sing much of this setting in harmony, but have the congregation join in singing the personal final line (at the double bar). The long lines of this text demand careful choral leadership. Try also to sing this hymn unaccompanied or have those making profession of faith sing with just guitar as accompaniment.

Liturgical Use
Baptism; profession of faith; as a sung creed; church festivals and anniversaries; Reformation services; ecumenical gatherings.

508

GOWER'S LITANY
♩ = 104

Jesus, with Your Church Abide

Text
John Julian explains that the author of this text, Thomas B. Pollock (b. Strathallan, Isle of Man, England, 1836; d. Birmingham, England, 1896), was a most successful writer of metrical litanies. Many of them were published in Pollock's *Metrical Litanies for Special Services and General Use* (1870) and appeared in a variety of mainly Anglican hymnals. Originally written for a prayer day organized by the Society for the Propagation of the Gospel, this text was published in eighteen stanzas in Pollock's 1871 *Appendix* to his *Metrical Litanies* and was revised for the 1875 edition of *Hymns Ancient and Modern*. Like other modern hymnals, the *Psalter Hymnal* provides various parts of these different versions in a five-stanza text.

A litany is a form of prayer that has a number of petitions but usually only one response or refrain (see Ps. 136 for this structure). This text, Pollock's "Litany of the Church," has that pattern: the stanzas offer various prayers for the church, its members, and its ministries. Each prayer concludes with the response "Lord, our Savior, hear us" (originally, "We beseech thee, hear us").

Educated at Trinity College, Dublin, Ireland, Pollock first studied medicine, but he changed his studies to theology and was ordained in the Church of England in 1861. In 1865, after serving several parishes, Pollock took the position of curate at St. Alban Mission Church in Birmingham, where his brother had the higher position of vicar.

Remaining curate for thirty years, Pollock became vicar after his brother's death but died a year later. Although he had many opportunities to serve in more prestigious positions, he chose to work among the poor of Birmingham. He was a member of the committee that compiled the 1861 edition of *Hymns Ancient and Modern.*

Tune
GOWER'S LITANY comes from John H. Gower's *Original Tunes* (1890). This serviceable tune works with the text but unfortunately lacks a suitable harmonization (the worst of Gower's chromatic harmony has been removed from the *Psalter Hymnal*). Try singing the hymn in true litany style: have a soloist or a choir in unison sing the petitions and the congregation sing the response (at which point the choir could sing in harmony). Use a light accompaniment and observe a ritardando on the response line.

John H. Gower (b. Rugby, Warwickshire, England, 1855; d. Denver, CO, 1922) became assistant organist at Windsor Castle at the age of twelve. After studying at Oxford, he became organist and music director in 1876 at Trent College, Nottingham, England. He moved to the United States in 1887 and became involved in the mining industry in Colorado but also continued his musical career at the Cathedral of St. John in the Wilderness, the Central Presbyterian Church, and the Unity Church, all in Denver.

Liturgical Use
As a part of the main prayers of a worship service; church meetings and mission services, especially when sung in true litany fashion.

509

Your Hand, O God, Has Guided

THORNBURY
♩ = *104*

Text
Edward H. Plumptre (PHH 363) wrote this text entitled "Church Defence" and published it in Plumptre's *Lazarus and Other Poems* (1865). Republished in the 1889 *Supplement* to *Hymns Ancient and Modern,* the text has gained much popularity in England. Of the original six stanzas, the *Psalter Hymnal* provides stanzas 1, 2, and 6 in modern language.

Scripture References
ref. = Eph. 4:4-6

The text affirms God's faithful hand of guidance and blessing on the church (st. 1), a church that has continually proclaimed the gospel of the kingdom (st. 2), and that, by God's power, will ultimately be victorious in its mission (st. 3). Each stanza leads directly into the powerful refrain line taken from Ephesians 4:4-5: "There is one body [the church of Christ] . . . one Lord, one faith. . . ."

Tune

Basil Harwood (b. Woodhouse, Olveston, Gloucestershire, England, 1859; d. Kensington, London, England, 1949) composed THORNBURY for this text. The manuscript states that the tune was "begun in New College Garden, finished at Christ Church Oxford, June 28, 1898 . . . for the twenty-fifth Annual Festival of the London Church Choir Association, held in St. Paul's Cathedral, November 17th 1898."

THORNBURY was printed in the Association's Festival Book (1898) and was later published in Harwood's *Hymn Tunes Original and Selected* (1905).

Named after a town in Gloucestershire, England, this strong and stately tune in bar form shape (AAB) has elongated rhythms in its refrain line that are a perfect match for the text. The three stanzas may be sung in harmony, but the refrain line should always be sung in unison until the final choral cadence.

The festival origin of THORNBURY is evident: it is a "big tune" with stately accompaniment (Harwood's tunes are often more contemplative). Whether sung in unison or in harmony, this tune needs firm organ support and a majestic tempo.

Harwood was educated at Trinity College, Oxford, England, and at the Leipzig Conservatory. He served as organist at several churches before becoming organist at Ely Cathedral (1887-1892) and Christ Church, Oxford (1892-1909). The first conductor of the Oxford Bach Choir and precentor at Keble College, Harwood composed some ninety hymn tunes as well as anthems and other liturgical music. He was the editor of the *Oxford Hymn Book* (1908).

Liturgical Use

Festivals of the church; church anniversaries; mission services; Reformation celebrations; ordination/commissioning services.

510

ST. THOMAS
♩ = 104

I Love Your Church, O Lord

Text

Timothy Dwight (b. Northampton, MA, 1752; d. Philadelphia, PA, 1817) was a grandson of Jonathan Edwards who became a Congregationalist pastor, a Revolutionary War army chaplain, a tutor and professor at Yale College, and president of Yale from 1795 to 1817. As president he continued to teach and serve as chaplain and was instrumental in improving both the academic and the spiritual life of the college.

Scripture References
st. 1 = Ps. 17:8
Deut. 32:10
Isa. 49:16
st. 2 = Ps. 137:5-6

Because the British emphasis of Isaac Watts's psalms and hymns became politically incorrect in the United States following the American Revolution, the Congregational and Presbyterian churches of Connecticut asked Dwight to revise Watts's collection. The title of Dwight's volume explains its contents: *The Psalms of David . . . by I. Watts. A New Edition in which the Psalms omitted by Dr. Watts are versified, local passages are altered, and a number of Psalms are versified anew in proper metres. By Timothy Dwight. . . . To the Psalms is added a Selection of Hymns* (1801). This edition, known as "Dwight's Watts," became a popular collection in the United States, although Dwight's own versifications of psalms were often very free even by late eighteenth-century standards.

Inspired by Psalm 137:5-6, Dwight's text was published in eight stanzas; the first line was originally "I love your kingdom, Lord" (Dwight equated the kingdom of God with the church of God). The *Psalter Hymnal* includes his stanzas 1-2 and 6.

Dwight's text is the oldest hymn text by an American author in common use today. In three compact stanzas "I Love Your Church" proclaims a profound love for the church of God, for its members (st. 1) who are saved by Christ (st. 3), and who express their communion in whole-life worship (st. 2).

Tune

For information on ST. THOMAS and Aaron Williams, see PHH 108.

ST. THOMAS is a joyful tune with a confident contour that fits well with this text. Sing in harmony throughout with firm accompaniment. Like many other short-meter tunes, ST. THOMAS must not be rushed.

Liturgical Use

Regular worship services; special occasions in the life and worship of the church.

511

These Are the Facts As We Have Received Them

YVONNE
$\quad = 84$

Text

Michael Saward (PHH 16) wrote this creedal text about the mighty acts of God in 1971. It was published in the British *Psalm Praise* (1973) as an alternate text to the liturgical Easter canticle "Christ Our Passover Is Sacrificed for Us."

Drawing mainly on Paul's resurrection discourse in 1 Corinthians 15, the text confesses the basic doctrines of Christianity and helps us focus on the objective truth of what God has done for his people in Christ. "These Are the Facts" simply states the biblical facts of Christ's death and resurrection and of his work of redemption, which is the heart of the Christian gospel.

Scripture References
st. 1 = 1 Cor. 15:1-4
st. 2 = 1 Cor. 15:3, 22
st. 3 = Gal. 2:20
Rom. 8:10-11
st. 4 = 1 Cor. 15:51-57
st. 5 = 1 Cor. 15:1-4

Tune

Norman L. Warren (PHH 15), a clergyman in Leamington Spa, England, composed YVONNE in 1972 for this text. Text and tune were published together in *Psalm Praise* (1973). The tune is named in honor of Warren's wife.

With its stepwise motion and strong rhythmic patterns, YVONNE is easily singable. Sing the framing stanzas in unison and the three middle stanzas in parts.

Liturgical Use

A creedal hymn or canticle for Easter and other festive worship services; substitute this hymn for saying or singing one of the other creeds.

512

ENGELBERG
♩ = 54

When in Our Music God Is Glorified

Text

At the request of John W. Wilson (PHH 278), Fred Pratt Green (PHH 455) wrote this text in Norwich, England, in 1971. It was intended for use with Charles V. Stanford's ENGELBERG at a London conference of the Methodist Church Music Society. Originally entitled "When in Man's Music God Is Glorified," the text was first published in Pratt Green's *26 Hymns* (1971). This hymn has been widely accepted in many recent hymnals and is sung in numerous choral festivals.

Scripture References
st. 3 = 1 Chron. 16:42
st. 4 = Matt. 26:30
Mark 14:26
st. 5 = Ps. 150
Eph. 5:19-20
Col. 3:16

"When in Our Music" is the only hymn text in Christendom that explains the reasons for church music while simultaneously offering "alleluias" to God. The various stanzas deal with our humility in performance (st. 1), the aesthetics of musical worship (st. 2), and the history of church music (st. 3). The final two stanzas present a biblical model (st. 4) and quote Psalm 150 (st. 5). (A fruitful study could be made of this text and the Christian Reformed Church "Statement of Principle on Church Music" and its implications and practice, *Psalter Hymnal*, pp. 11-15.)

Tune

Charles V. Stanford (b. Dublin, Ireland, 1852; d. Marylebone, London, England, 1924) composed ENGELBERG as a setting for William W. How's "For All the Saints" (505). The tune was published in the 1904 edition of *Hymns Ancient and Modern* with no less than six different musical settings. It is clearly a fine congregational hymn but also a stunning choral anthem when used with some of the additional settings that Stanford supplied.

ENGELBERG is an attractive, energetic melody with many ascending motives, designed for unison singing with no pauses between stanzas. Try using other instruments in addition to organ (as stanza 5 suggests). Accompanists could play the third and fourth stanzas in a more subdued manner and then play the climactic final stanza with great strength and vigor.

A distinguished composer and teacher of composition, Stanford began his musical career at an early age. Before the age of ten he had composed several pieces and given piano recitals of works by Handel and Bach. He studied at Queen's College, Cambridge, England, as well as in Leipzig and Berlin. At the age of twenty-one he was asked to become organist at the famous Trinity College, Cambridge. At that time he also began a prestigious career in conducting, which included appearances with the London Bach Choir from 1885 to 1902, and he traveled widely in England, Europe, and the United States. His teaching career was equally impressive. Stanford taught composition at both the Royal College of Music and Cambridge University; among his students were Ralph Vaughan Williams (PHH 316) and Gustav Holst. He was knighted in 1902. Stanford wrote over two hundred compositions in nearly all musical genres, including symphonies, operas, chamber music, and songs. Most notable in his church music are several complete services, anthems, and unison hymn tunes.

Liturgical Use
Regular worship services, but most often at special praise services, choral liturgies, worship conferences, and other "musical feasts"; appropriate for recognizing the work of church musicians.

513

Christian Hearts in Love United

O DU LIEBE MEINER LIEBE
♩ = 54

Text
In 1723 Count Nicolaus L. von Zinzendorf (b. Dresden, Germany, 1700; d. Herrnhut, Germany, 1760) wrote an extended poem, "Die letzten Reden unsers Herrn," of 320 stanzas on the teachings of Jesus found in John 14-17. A hymn text beginning "Herz und Herz vereint zusammen" was taken from this work and published in various early Moravian hymnals.

Scripture References
st. 1 = Eph. 4:15-16
st. 2 = John 13:34
John 15:5

Zinzendorf's career, achievements, and influence were of great import, both in his own community and worldwide. Although his family insisted that he be trained in law, his inclination was always toward religious matters. A devout youth who was influenced by Philipp Spener and the Pietists, he wrote his first hymn at the age of twelve. After his graduation from Wittenberg University in 1719, he became the official poet for the Saxon court.

His life took focus in 1722 when a small group of persecuted Bohemian Brethren, or Moravians (spiritual descendants of John Hus), sought a place of refuge. Zinzendorf granted them protection on his estate in Bertelsdorf; they called their new home "Herrnhut," or "the Lord's shelter." The settlement grew to over two hundred homes and became an outstanding Christian community of piety, worship, and mission. Some of these missionaries influenced John and Charles Wesley (PHH 267). Zinzendorf became their bishop in 1737 but then was banished for a decade from Saxony by Saxon officials because of his evangelical convictions; he returned to Herrnhut in 1748. During his banishment he traveled throughout Europe, to St. Petersburg in Russia, and to the United States and the West Indies in order to establish and encourage Moravian mission centers.

He promoted the tradition of congregational singing at Herrnhut and elsewhere and frequently led long hymn sings in an improvised medley format, which included hymn fragments or choruses. Some two thousand hymn texts are attributed to him, but many are judged to be too subjective for congregational use today. *Das Gesang-Buch der Gemeine Herrnhut* (1735), with its almost one thousand texts, was compiled under his supervision and contained some two hundred of his own hymns. He also produced a two-volume hymnal in London, *Alt- und Neuer Bruder-Gesang* (1753-1754), which contained over three thousand German hymn texts grouped in chronological order.

The three stanzas in the *Psalter Hymnal* come from a composite translation that depends on English versions by Frederick W. Foster and John Miller (Johannes Müller) in the *Moravian Hymn Book* (1789, with revisions in the 1886 ed.) and by Walter Klaassen in *The Mennonite Hymnal* (1969). This text gained great significance at the Herrnhut settlement, where it was often used after the healing of internal conflict.

This distinguished text about the church's "communion of saints" proclaims that Christians live in union with Christ (st. 1), love each other (st. 2), and serve and witness in the world (st. 3).

Tune

For information about O DU LIEBE MEINER LIEBE see PHH 443.

This rounded bar form tune (AABA) with mostly stepwise motion has a harmonization that invites part singing. Organ accompaniment should use a moderate registration. Because the middle stanza is a sung prayer to God, try singing it unaccompanied.

Liturgical Use

Regular Sunday worship services; times of renewal and reconciliation; profession of faith; ecumenical services and church conventions; church festivals.

514

How Good and Pleasant Is the Sight

PRESSLY
♩ = 96

Text

A paraphrase of Psalm 133, this text is a revised version of the one found in the 1912 *Psalter.* (See further discussion of this psalm's text at PHH 133.) Using metaphors such as oil and dew, "How Good and Pleasant" extols the blessings of unity and love among God's people.

Scripture References
st. 1 = Ps. 133:1-2
st. 2 = Ps. 133:3

Tune

PRESSLY is one of the many (now often forgotten) hymn tunes and gospel songs composed by Charles H. Gabriel (PHH 24). With a copyright date of 1901, the tune first appeared with this text in the 1912 *Psalter.*

Sing in harmony as a testimony of our harmonious love! Well-trained choirs should lead the congregation in singing this hymn in two long lines rather than six short phrases.

Liturgical Use

Regular Sunday worship; ecumenical gatherings; other occasions of "communion of the saints."

515

Lift Your Heart to the Lord

SALVE FESTA DIES
𝅗𝅥 = 54

Text

Written by John E. Bowers (b. London, England, 1923), this text was first published in *More Hymns for Today,* a 1980 supplement to *Hymns Ancient and Modern.* Originally entitled "The House of God," the first stanza began "Christians, lift up your hearts." The seven-stanza text dealt with various aspects of Christian worship such as gathering, praising God, confessing and forgiving, preaching, taking the sacraments, and departing to serve. The *Psalter Hymnal* includes Bower's stanzas 1 (now the refrain), 3, 4, and 6.

Scripture References
st. 2 = Rom. 6:4
st. 3 = Luke 24:35
ref. – Ps. 118:14, 24

The refrain's text borrows from the Sursum Corda ("Lift up your hearts") of the Lord's Supper liturgy and from Psalm 118:14, 24. Like Q&A 65 of Lord's Day 25 in the Heidelberg Catechism, the three stanzas focus on preaching and the sacraments (st. 1), baptism, and the Lord's Supper (st. 2 and 3).

Bowers served in the British and Indian army during World War II and then studied at King's College, London University, England, from 1947 to 1951. Ordained a priest in the Church of England in 1952, he served both as a chaplain in the territorial army and as a priest in various parishes in the diocese of Leicester. He retired in 1988.

Tune

Ralph Vaughan Williams (PHH 316) composed SALVE FESTA DIES as a setting for Venantius H. Fortunatus's (PHH 400) famous text "Hail Thee, Festival Day." The tune, whose title comes from the opening words of that text, was published in *The English Hymnal* of 1906.

Like SINE NOMINE (505), this tune is vigorous and jubilant with a rhythmic energy characteristic of Vaughan Williams's hymn tunes. Its broad dimensions and use of triplets may appear formidable, but it is a glorious tune that can be sung in unison by congregations who have good choral and organ leadership. Try singing antiphonally with a choir of children or adults singing the stanzas and the entire congregation singing the refrain. Note how Vaughan Williams has neatly steered the stanzas right back into the refrain without a pause. Accompany with a sense of majesty and strength.

Liturgical Use

The opening of regular Sunday worship; baptism; Lord's Supper; a choral processional at festive church services and worship conferences (in this case choirs may want to learn additional stanzas and add a descant; see other hymnal settings of "Hail Thee, Festival Day").

516

ST. JOHN'S QUADRA
♩ = 100

God Is Here

Text

Fred Pratt Green (PHH 455) wrote this text early in 1978 in Norwich, England. Russell Schulz-Widmar had requested that Pratt Green write a hymn text to be sung at the closing service of an eight-month festival on worship, music, and the arts, held at the University United Methodist Church in Austin, Texas.

Scripture References
st. 1 = 1 Cor. 12:27-31
st. 2 = 2 Cor. 4:5
st. 3 = 2 Thess. 2:15
st. 4 = Titus 2:14

In that service on April 30, 1978, the church dedicated its new chancel furniture (thus st. 2), and the people rededicated themselves to God. The text was first published in the British/Methodist supplementary volume *Partners in Praise* (1979).

"God Is Here" helps us celebrate what it means to be a church: to offer praise and prayer to God with "all our varied skills and arts" (st. 1), to preach the Word and participate in the sacraments (st. 2), to foster faith and service (st. 3), and to live lives in "church and kingdom" that bring glory to our Lord (st. 4). This text presents a catalog of the central tasks of the church (see also 515) and emphasizes the relationship between Sunday worship and daily living.

Tune

Peter Janson (b. Aalst-Waalre, Noord Brabant, the Netherlands, 1957) composed ST. JOHN'S QUADRA in Victoria, British Columbia, Canada, in 1982 as a setting for "Praise the Lord! Ye Heavens Adore Him" (148). The tune was the winner in a hymn-writing contest held by the Royal Canadian College of Organists in 1983. First published in the 1987 *Psalter Hymnal*, the tune is named for St. John's Anglican Church on Quadra Street, Victoria, British Columbia, where it was first performed.

A well-crafted, modern tune, ST. JOHN'S QUADRA is built with variations of one melodic and rhythmic motive, which gives a majestic and joyful sense to the text. Sing in unison throughout. If there are confident harmony singers in your group, sing the outer stanzas in unison and the inner ones in harmony.

Jansen came to Canada as a child and received his musical education at the University of Victoria. He has served as organist and choirmaster at the Church of St. Aidan in Victoria, British Columbia, since 1985. Mainly a composer of church music, he has also written some articles on music history.

Liturgical Use

Regular Sunday worship; festivals, dedications, anniversaries of the church; worship conferences and missions.

517

There's No God as Great
No Hay Dios tan Grande

NO HAY DIOS

$\quad = 108$

Text

One of the marks of any folk song is that its origins cannot be traced. That is certainly the case for this infectiously joyful song. "There's No God as Great" is known all over Central and South America by evangelical Christians who love to sing one song after the other, often stringing them together in medley fashion. This hymn is built in four sections, almost like a little medley in itself. Each section is repeated and is based on a different Scripture passage.

Scripture References
st. = Ps. 77:13-14
Hosea 1:7
Zech. 4:6
Rom. 8:9, 11, 21

The text confesses the greatness of our Lord; he does "mighty wonders" by his Spirit in leading his people, the church.

Tune

Like much Hispanic folk music, NO HAY DIOS has simple harmonies. The melody is matched by a parallel line found alternately in the alto and tenor line. That parallel line, either the interval of a third or a sixth below the melody, makes for good duet possibilities (sec. 1 and 3—soprano and tenor duet, sec. 2 and 4—soprano and alto duet). Because the range of both tenor and alto is just an octave (from A to A), that harmony part would be accessible to either altos or tenors, who could switch back and forth from treble to bass clefs. Accompaniment is designed for piano, guitars, and some rhythm instruments, including maracas, castanets, and woodblocks. Try making up rhythmic patterns that reflect the joyful confidence of this song. Use a light registration if organ is the only available instrument. In the medley fashion typical of Hispanic performance, try pairing "There's No God as Great" with some of the eight other Hispanic songs in the *Psalter Hymnal* (234, 186, and 629 would work well).

Liturgical Use

A chorus to be sung prior to Scripture reading or the sermon; a sung confession of faith or response to preaching; Pentecost season; church festivals and ecumenical services.

518

CREEDAL SONG
♩ = 58

In God the Father I Believe

Text

There are two musical settings of the Apostles' Creed in the *Psalter Hymnal:* this versification in meter and a prose setting (519). The full text of this ancient creed appears in the *Psalter Hymnal* on page 813 with a footnote about its "sublime simplicity, unsurpassable brevity, beautiful order, and liturgical solemnity." The Apostles' Creed is also explained in Lord's Days 8-22 of the Heidelberg Catechism.

Scripture References
st. 1 = Gen. 1:1
  Matt. 1:20-21
st. 2 = Mark 15-16
  Luke 24:51
  Eph. 1:20
  John 14:16-17
st. 4 = 1 Cor. 12:4-7, 12-13
  Phil. 3:21

Frank De Vries (b. Langsa, Sumatra, Indonesia, 1929) wrote this versification of the creed in Houston, British Columbia, Canada, in 1969 after Christian Reformed Church minister Mel Pool suggested that the creed should be sung as well as spoken. De Vries also composed a tune for his text; both were published in Vancouver, British Columbia, in a Shalom

Productions booklet, *Believe It, Or . . .* (1972) and in the second printing of the *Psalter Hymnal Supplement* (1976).

The four stanzas of "In God the Father" adhere closely to the text of the Apostles' Creed. That fact and the buoyant musical setting undoubtedly account for the hymn's popularity in the Christian Reformed Church and its acceptance in other denominations.

A Christian school educator, DeVries served for many years as a principal in several Canadian schools, including fourteen years (1970-1984) as principal of Vancouver Christian School. He has written a number of songs, some of which were published in *Tiny Little Spider* (1976).

Tune

Bert Polman (PHH 37) wrote the three-part harmonization for De Vries's CREEDAL SONG in Toronto, Canada, in 1975 (also published in the 1976 *Psalter Hymnal Supplement).* The tune gets its well-proportioned outline mainly from variations on the opening motive. Sing in unison throughout. Organists may want to play on two manuals with a sixteen-foot stop for the left hand.

Liturgical Use

Singing or speaking one of the ancient confessions of faith has been a regular ingredient of public worship since the days of the early church. The Apostles' Creed was historically associated with baptism, the Nicene Creed with the Lord's Supper. The traditional place in historic Christian worship for reciting both creeds was after hearing God's Word—the creed then becomes our response of faith.

519

Apostles' Creed

SCHOUTEN
♩ = 80

Text

This second setting of the Apostles' Creed (see also 518) includes the entire text in prose form.

Tune

The music consists of a chant formula that is repeated and varied to suit the textual phrases. Sing in unison with rhythmically crisp accompaniment on the keyboard or with guitars and flutes/recorders. The notation in eighth and quarter notes does not imply a strict meter or tempo; let the speech rhythms overrule any yearning for a marching beat.

Scripture References
st. = Gen. 1:1
Matt. 1:20-21
Mark 15-16
Luke 24:51
Eph. 1:20
John 14:16-17
1 Cor. 12:4-7, 12-13
Phil. 3:21

The melody was originally a chant used for the Credo of the Roman Catholic Mass during the seventeenth century (*Credo* is Latin for "I believe," the first words of the creed). Dutch organist Paul C. Van Westering published a sheet music adaptation of the chant for a Dutch version of the Apostles' Creed. The tune SCHOUTEN was named for Maria Henneveld Schouten (b. The Hague, the Netherlands, 1929), who arranged that Dutch setting of the tune to fit the English text of the creed. Schouten was raised in a musical family and in her early years studied organ and piano, first in the Netherlands and later at the Royal Conservatory of Toronto in Canada. She currently lives in Clearbrook, British Columbia, Canada.

John Hamersma (b. Hawthorne, NJ, 1929) harmonized Schouten's arrangement for publication in the *Psalter Hymnal Supplement* (1974). Hamersma attended Calvin College, Grand Rapids, Michigan, and received his master's degree and doctorate in sacred music from Union Theological Seminary, New York City. Since 1954 he has been professor of music and college organist at Calvin College. He has given many organ recitals in the United States and Germany and served as a music consultant for *The Children's Hymnbook* (1962) and music editor for *Hymns for Youth* (1966). Hamersma was a member of the 1987 *Psalter Hymnal* Revision Committee and currently serves as organist and choirmaster at Grace Episcopal Church in Grand Rapids.

Liturgical Use
See PHH 518.

520

DRAESEL
♩ = 108; 88

Nicene Creed

Text

While the familiar Apostles' Creed is associated with baptism (see 518 and 519), the Nicene Creed is associated particularly with the Lord's Supper and is professed weekly throughout the world by many churches, including Roman Catholic, Episcopal, and Lutheran congregations. See also page 842 for a discussion of this ecumenical creed; the text is found in the *Psalter Hymnal* (p. 814) with a brief historical footnote (note that the hymn text differs from the modern translation of the creed in a few phrases).

Scripture References
st. = Gen. 1:1
John 1:14
Matt. 1:20-21
Mark 15-16
Luke 24:51
Eph. 1:20
John 14:16-17
1 Cor. 12:4-7, 12-13
Rom. 6:4
1 Cor. 15:21

Tune

Because the Latin text is the Credo (Latin for "I believe"),
one part of the Ordinary of the Roman Catholic Mass, the Nicene Creed has been set to music with Latin texts by numerous composers over the centuries. But one of the

changes introduced by Vatican II, a major Roman Catholic council during the 1960s, was to encourage worship in vernacular languages, creating a need for new settings.

Many Roman Catholic churches began to replace the historic Latin Mass settings with hymnody and choral music influenced by the commercial "folk style." Geoffrey Beaumont, a founder of the "20th Century Church Light Music Group," initiated this trend in England when he composed his *20th Century Folk Mass* in 1956. Musicians throughout the world in both Roman Catholic and Protestant communities soon followed his example, including Herbert G. Draesel, Jr. (b. Jersey City, NJ, 1940), who composed this setting.

Draesel's setting is from his folk mass *Rejoice* (1964), which enjoyed popularity for some time in youth services. Draesel studied at Trinity College, Hartford, Connecticut, and in 1964 received a divinity degree from General Theological Seminary in New York City. He was a curate and rector of the House of Prayer in Newark, New Jersey, and since 1975 has been rector of Grace Church, White Plains, New York.

The melody uses several chantlike melodic patterns, which are repeated and varied to carry the text. The tune also includes syncopations, a trademark of this musical style. If led by a choir, congregations should be able to learn this setting. Note that two metronome markings are given; the middle section should be sung more slowly. Some may prefer to use this creedal song primarily as a profession of faith sung by a youth choir accompanied with guitars (its original style).

Verlyn Schultz (b. Edgerton, MN, 1932) prepared the keyboard setting in 1985. A church organist, Schultz was a member and secretary of the *Psalter Hymnal* Revision Committee. He taught music at the Christian school in Fremont, Michigan, from 1959 to 1980, and since 1982 has been employed at the Christian Music Center in Grand Rapids, Michigan.

Liturgical Use
See PHH 518.

521

God of the Prophets

TOULON
♩ = 116

Text

Denis Wortman (b. Hopewell, NY, 1835; d. East Orange, NJ, 1922) wrote the poem "God of the Prophets! Bless the Prophets' Sons" in 1884 for the one-hundredth anniversary of New Brunswick Theological Seminary, from which he had graduated in 1860. Wortman entitled his poem "Prayer for Young Ministers" and sent it with the following note to the seminary:

Scripture References
st. 1 = 2 Kings 2:8-14
st. 3 = 1 Pet. 2:5, 9
st. 5 = Rom. 1:1-6

May I take the liberty of sending you the enclosed verses; a very humble attempt to express the prayer that our Class of 1860, and indeed all loyal sons of New Brunswick Seminary, lift to God at this unusual anniversary, for his blessing upon her and all who go forth from her instructions.

Also educated at Amherst College, Wortman served a number of Reformed Church in America congregations, mainly in New York State. He was the denomination's secretary of ministerial relief from 1901 to 1922 and served as president of General Synod in 1901. His publications include *Reliques of Christ* (1888), *The Divine Processional* (1903), and this one hymn text.

His hymn text was first published in the Episcopal *Church Hymnal* (1892) in six stanzas. Of those, stanzas 1-2 and 4-5 are retained with many revisions. Carl P. Daw, Jr. (PHH 193), wrote the third stanza in 1981 for *The Hymnal 1982*.

All the stanzas were originally cast in third person ("Anoint them") since the hymn was written for clergymen; the revised text in first person ("Anoint us") now includes all God's people as ministers or servants. The text refers to various biblical offices to depict Christian ministries: prophets, priests, kings (all Old Testament offices), and apostles (the only New Testament office mentioned in this text).

Tune

TOULON was originally an adaptation of the Genevan Psalter melody for Psalm 124 (124). In one melodic variant or another and with squared-off rhythms, the tune was used in English and Scottish psalters for various psalm texts. It was published in the United States in its four-line abridged form (called MONTAGUE) by Lowell Mason (PHH 96) and George J. Webb (PHH 559) in *The National Psalmist* (1848). That version, now called TOULON, is named quite arbitrarily after the French city.
Sing the outer stanzas in unison and the middle stanzas in harmony. On the fifth stanza add the descant by Emily R. Brink (PHH 158). TOULON is a fine tune for accompaniment by brass quartet. It should be sung and played with power and dignity.

Liturgical Use

Renewal services; for commissioning the entire congregation at the beginning of a church season; for an ordination service one or several of the middle stanzas could be sung in the older form—"Anoint them prophets. . . ."

522

Onward, Christian Soldiers

ST. GERTRUDE
♩ = 60

Text

Sabine Baring-Gould (b. Exeter, England, 1834; d. Lew-
Trenchard, England, 1924), curate of a mission church at
Horbury Bridge, Yorkshire, England, wrote this text in 1864 for a
children's Pentecost Sunday procession. Baring-Gould said the
following about his writing of the text:

Scripture References
st. 1 = Deut. 31: 6
1 Tim. 6:12
st. 2 = Eph. 4:4
st. 3 = Matt. 16:18

> For a Whitsuntide [Pentecost] procession it was arranged that our school should
> join forces with that of a neighboring village. I wanted the children to sing when
> marching from one village to another, but couldn't think of anything quite
> suitable, so I sat up at night and resolved to write something myself. "Onward,
> Christian Soldiers" was the result. It was written in great haste. . . . I am certain
> that nothing surprised me more than its popularity.

Entitled "Hymn for Procession with Cross and Banners," the text was published in
The Church Times (Oct. 15, 1864) in six stanzas and refrain. His stanzas 1, 3, 5-6 are
included with small alterations.

As indicated in the refrain, "Onward, Christian Soldiers" is a processional hymn with
a cross as the head of the procession (see also 373). It is also a children's hymn; the line
in stanza 2 "We are not divided; all one body we" initially referred simply to the children
from the several villages (the hymn obviously does not provide a realistic analysis of
church unity on a larger scale). And "Onward, Christian Soldiers" is clearly a nineteenth-century text that reveals some of the British triumphalism of that era. Its martial
imagery, though drawn from biblical texts such as Ephesians 6:10-18, has often been
misinterpreted as militaristic. Thus various opinions exist about the modern usefulness
of this text. All agree, however, that stanza 3, which quotes Jesus' promise in Matthew
16:18, is the hymn's finest verse.

Baring-Gould is remembered today especially for this hymn, though he was also the
author of some eighty volumes, including books about travel, popular theology, and
English folk songs. Educated at Clare College, Cambridge, England, he was a curate
and rector in the Church of England. He inherited a large estate but married a mill-
hand girl after paying for her education. Many of his hymns were written for the
children of his congregations, often for their marches around the village in procession
with crosses and banners. Baring-Gould compiled several collections of folk songs,
which were an important part of the English folk-music movement, including *Songs and
Ballads of the West* (1889-1891) and *A Garland of Country Song* (1894).

Tune

The popularity of this hymn is partly due to ST. GERTRUDE, the marching tune that Arthur S. Sullivan (PHH 46) composed for this text. The tune was published in the *Musical Times* of December 1871 in an advertisement for Joseph Barnby's (PHH 438) forthcoming *Hymnary,* which published both text and tune in 1872. ST. GERTRUDE is named for Gertrude Clay-Ker-Seymer, at whose home in Hanford, Dorsetshire, England, Sullivan composed the tune.

Though some will want to sing the instrumental-style harmony, try singing in unison. Be sure to sing lightly in the manner of children's voices (not like Sherman tanks!).

Liturgical Use

Services dealing with spiritual warfare, with greatest emphasis on stanzas 3 and 4.

523

ABBOT'S LEIGH
♩ = 112

Lord, You Give the Great Commission

Text

Jeffery W. Rowthorn (b. Newport, Gwent, Wales, 1934) wrote this text in 1978 while he was Chapel Minister at Yale Divinity School, New Haven, Connecticut. The text was first published in *Laudamus* (1980), a hymnal supplement edited by Rowthorn and used at the Yale Divinity School.

Scripture References
st. 1 = Matt. 10:7-8
st. 2 = Matt. 28:19-20
st. 3 = Matt. 26:26-28
st. 4 = Luke 23:34
st. 5 = Matt. 28:20
ref. = 1 Cor. 12:4-11
Eph. 4:12

This powerful text about the various ministries of the Christian church has two striking features: each stanza includes a quotation of Christ's words (usually from Matthew), and a concluding refrain line turns each stanza into a prayer. Christ's words are applied to the tasks of God's people in the world with a fervent prayer that the Spirit equip the saints to carry out these ministries faithfully.

Rowthorn graduated from Cambridge and Oxford Universities, Union Theological Seminary in New York, and Cuddeson Theological College in Oxford. Ordained in 1963 in the Church of England, he served several congregations in England before immigrating to the United States, where he was chaplain at Union Theological Seminary and a faculty member in liturgics at the Yale Institute of Sacred Music, which he helped to establish. He was then elected Suffragan Bishop of the Episcopal Diocese of Connecticut. The writer of several hymns, Rowthorn was also coeditor with Russell Schulz-Widmar of *A New Hymnal for Colleges and Schools* (1991). Rowthorn has since moved to Paris, where he is Bishop in Charge of the American Churches in Europe.

Tune

Cyril V. Taylor (PHH 286) composed ABBOT'S LEIGH in May of 1941 when he was working for the Religious Broadcasting Department of the British Broadcasting Corporation (BBC). The BBC had received complaints about the use of AUSTRIA (tune for the Austrian national hymn) during this time of war, a tune then set to "Glorious Things of You Are Spoken" (506). Thus Taylor originally composed his tune for that text. First printed in a leaflet, ABBOT'S LEIGH was published in *Hymns Ancient and Modern Revised* (1950), *Congregational Praise* (1951), and the *BBC Hymn Book* (1951), of which Taylor was editor. No modern hymnal would want to omit this great twentieth-century tune! ABBOT'S LEIGH is named for a village near Bristol, England, where Taylor composed the tune (Bristol was wartime headquarters for the BBC).

This dramatic tune with bold melodic gestures and a bar form shape (AAB) is suitable for unison or harmony singing. Use strong accompaniment with a stately tempo.

Liturgical Use

Pentecost; profession of faith; Reformation Sunday; ordination and commissioning services (for specific offices or for all of God's people); festivals of the church (dedications, anniversaries); church conferences and mission meetings.

524

Hope of the World

VICAR
♩ = 60

Text

Of the hundreds of hymns submitted in a search for new hymns for the Second Assembly of the World Council of Churches (held in Evanston, IL, in August 1954), "Hope of the World" was chosen as the winner by the Hymn Society of America. Theologian Georgia E. Harkness (b. Harkness, NY, 1891;

Scripture References
all st. = Rom. 15:13
st. 2 = John 6:35
st. 3 = John 8:12

d. Claremont, CA, 1974) wrote the text to coincide with the Assembly's theme, "Jesus Christ, Hope of the World." First published in a Hymn Society of America pamphlet, *Eleven Ecumenical Hymns* (1954) and in *The Hymn* (July 1954), the text has since appeared in many North American hymnals. Translated into several languages, it has also been published in hymnals in various other countries.

This prayer text entreats Christ, "the hope of the world," to reconcile those now involved in conflict and strife (st. 1-2) and to direct the ministry of the church to be faithful to his gospel (st. 3-5). Recognizing the brokenness of the church and the temptations of the world, this sung prayer also presents the hope and challenge of ministering in Christ's name.

Harkness studied at Cornell University, Ithaca, New York, received a doctoral degree from Boston University (1923), and did further studies at Harvard, Yale, and Union Theological Seminary. She taught at Elmira (NY) College (1922-1937); Mount Holyoke College, South Hadley, Massachusetts (1937-1939); Garret School of Theology, Evanston, Illinois (1939-50); and the Pacific School of Religion, Berkeley, California (1950-61). The first woman in the United States to be appointed a full professor in a theological seminary, Harkness was ordained in the Methodist Church in 1926. Partly because of her work in the World Council of Churches, her influence was wide-ranging. The recipient of many honors and awards, she wrote thirty-seven books, including *John Calvin: The Man and His Ethics* (1931), *Prayer and the Common Life* (1947), *The Providence of God* (1960), and *Women in Church and Society* (1972). Her hymn texts and other poetry were published in *Holy Flame* (1935), *The Glory of God* (1943), and *Be Still and Know* (1953).

Tune

GENEVAN 12 (or DONNE SECOURS, see 12) was the tune originally selected for the text for singing at the Evanston Assembly. That tune is set to the Harkness text in many hymnals.

V. Earle Copes (PHH 302) composed VICAR in 1963 as a setting for Harkness's text for inclusion in the American *Methodist Hymnal* of 1966. The tune is named for the composer's father, Archie Vicar Copes (usually called by his middle name).

VICAR is a vigorous unison tune with distinctive rhythms and a colorful harmonization, and is representative of what Erik Routley (PHH 31) called the "clean-limbed" style. Organists should favor the soprano line to support this fervent prayer. Try having the choir's sopranos sing the tenor line an octave higher as a descant on stanza 5.

Liturgical Use

A sung prayer appropriate for many occasions of worship; Reformation services; church festivals; mission conferences.

525

TIDINGS
♩ = 76

O Christians, Haste

Text

About her writing of this text, Mary A. Thomson (b. London, England, 1834; d. Philadelphia, PA, 1923) stated:

Scripture References
st. 1 = 2 Pet. 3:9

I wrote the greater part of the hymn "O Sion, haste" in the year 1868. I had written many hymns before, and one night, while I was sitting up with one of my children, who was ill with typhoid fever, I thought I should like to write a missionary hymn to the tune of "Hark, hark my soul! angelic songs are swelling," as I was fond of that tune; but as I could not then get a refrain I liked, I left the hymn unfinished and about three years later finished it by writing the refrain which now forms a part of it. I do not think my hymn, "O Sion, haste," is ever sung to the tune for which I wrote it. Mr. Anketell told me, and I am sure he was right, that it is better for a hymn to have a tune of its own and I feel much indebted to the author of the tune TIDINGS for writing so inspiring a tune to my words.

—William B. Bodine, Some Hymns and Hymn Writers, p. 224

Thomson's text was published with the tune TIDINGS in Charles Hutchins's Episcopal *Church Hymnal* (1892). Of the original six stanzas, 1, 4, and 5 are included.

The text boldly urges the church to its missionary task to "every people, tongue, and nation." The third stanza clearly indicates what the missions commitment involves: we must send missionaries from among us and support them with our wealth and prayers. The heart of the Christian gospel is announced in the refrain.

Born in England, Thomson moved to the United States as a girl and married John Thomson, the first librarian of the famous Free Library in Philadelphia. The Thomsons were members of the Episcopal Church of the Annunciation in Philadelphia, where John served as treasurer. Mary wrote poetry and some forty hymns, which appeared in religious magazines such as New York's *The Churchman* and Chicago's *The Living Church*.

Tune
For information about this tune see PHH 297.

Liturgical Use
Regular Sunday worship; Epiphany and Pentecost seasons; All Nations Sunday; missions festivals; ordination/commissioning of missionaries to home or foreign fields.

526

Come, Labor On

ORA LABORA
♩ = 66

Text
Jane L. Borthwick (b. Edinburgh, Scotland, 1813; d. Edinburgh, 1897) wrote this text and published it in her *Thoughts for Thoughtful Hours* (1859) in seven, six-line stanzas. Borthwick revised the text into its present five-line form and published that version in her *Thoughts for Thoughtful Hours* of 1863. The *Psalter Hymnal* includes stanzas 1, 2, 4, and 6 from her revised version.

Inspired by the gospel parables that liken the coming of God's kingdom to the sowing of seed and harvesting of grain

Scripture References
st. 1 = Matt. 20:6-7
st. 2 = Matt. 13:24-26
　　Ps. 121:3-4
st. 3 = John 4:34
st. 4 = Eph. 5:16
st. 5 = Matt. 25:21

(see Matt. 9:37-38; Matt. 13; John 4:35-38), the text calls us to work for God's cause even in the face of Satan's opposition. Because our earthly time is limited, we must use our resources wisely and be diligent in our kingdom tasks until we hear the final "Well done, good and faithful servant" (Matt. 25:21).

Borthwick was a member of the Presbyterian Free Church of Scotland and had a strong interest in the church's mission work. She also supported Moravian missions in Labrador, Canada, and was involved in social service work in Edinburgh. Both Jane and her younger sister Sarah Findlater Borthwick (PHH 333) are well-known translators of German chorales.

Tune

T. (Thomas) Tertius Noble (b. Bath, England, 1867; d. Rockport, MA, 1953) composed ORA LABORA for Borthwick's text when it was accepted in 1916 for inclusion in the Episcopal hymnal, on whose commission Noble served. ORA LABORA, which means "pray and work," was also published in *The New Hymnal* of 1918.

Sing this distinguished cathedral-style tune in unison. Use strong, majestic organ accompaniment and a moderate tempo. (The phrase "No time for rest" in st. 5 merits a thoughtful pause in our workaholic society!)

As a youth Noble attended a boarding school but found the curriculum so ill-suited to his abilities (the school offered no music) that he was allowed to come home. A pastor took the thirteen-year-old boy under his wing, supervised his education, and secured him a position at All Saints Church of Colchester. After attending the Royal College of Music in London, England, Noble became organist and choirmaster at Ely Cathedral (1892-1898) and York Minster (1898-1912). In 1913 he was invited to become the organist and to establish a cathedral music program at St. Thomas Episcopal Church in New York City. The church had been recently renovated, and a new organ was built under Noble's direction. He also established a famous choir school for boys there in 1919. Noble served that church until his retirement in 1942. He composed orchestral pieces, choral works, anthems, service music for the Anglican liturgy, and hymn tunes. A member of the Episcopal Church's Joint Commission on Church Music (1916-1943), he published two collections (1946, 1949) of free harmonizations of hymn tunes used in the *Hymnal 1940*.

Liturgical Use

Ordination for church offices and for missionaries (although this text applies to all of God's people, not only to church workers); many occasions of worship that focus on our task in the world and in missions; profession of faith; at the beginning of a church season.

527

Come, You Thankful People, Come

ST. GEORGE'S WINDSOR
♩ = 58

Text

Henry Alford (b. London, England, 1810; d. Canterbury, England, 1871) wrote this text and published it in seven stanzas in his *Psalms and Hymns* (1844). He revised and shortened it for publication in his *Poetical Works* (1865) and made final changes for his *Year of Praise* (1867). The latter version is the source of the further revised *Psalter Hymnal* text.

Scripture References
st. 2 = Mark 4:28
st. 3 = Matt. 13:41-43
st. 4 = Rev. 22:20

Written for village harvest festivals in England, the text uses imagery found in two gospel parables: the growing seed (Mark 4:26-29) and the wheat and the weeds (Matt. 13:24-30, 36-43). However, the initial agricultural harvest theme becomes an eschatological metaphor for the final judgment when the angels will gather God's chosen people into the "glorious harvest home" and cast the evil "weeds" into the "fire." Thus the text provocatively combines language and imagery that represent annual harvests as well as the ultimate consummation of history.

Alford was born into a family of clergy. He received his education at Trinity College, Cambridge, England, and was ordained in the Church of England in 1833. He became dean of Canterbury Cathedral in 1857, a position he held until his death. A renowned scholar, Alford wrote a four-volume commentary on the Greek New Testament, which became a standard work in its field. He was also a voluminous poet and hymn writer and published *Poetical Works* (2 vols, 1845) and *Hymns for the Sundays and Festivals Throughout the Year* (1836).

Tune

George J. Elvey (PHH 48) composed ST. GEORGE'S WINDSOR as a setting for James Montgomery's text "Hark! The Song of Jubilee," with which it was published in Edward H. Thorne's *Selection of Psalm and Hymn Tunes* (1858). The tune has been associated with Alford's text since publication of the hymn in the 1861 edition of *Hymns Ancient and Modern*. ST. GEORGE'S WINDSOR is named after the chapel in Windsor, England, where Elvey was organist for forty-seven years.

This serviceable Victorian tune is held together by the rhythmic motive of the opening phrase. Sing the opening stanzas in parts, but sing the prayer of stanza 4 in unison. Use of the descant by C. S. Lang (PHH 253) with stanza 4 may suggest a foretaste of heaven's glory.

Liturgical Use

Best suited for services that focus on the task or mission of the church in the world; associated in popular thought with harvest thanksgiving services, its use on such occasions merits some comment about the meaning of the harvest metaphor. Also use for Pentecost season; worship that focuses on Christ's second coming.

528

CANONBURY
♩ = 54

Lord, Speak to Me That I May Speak

Text

Francis R. Havergal (PHH 288) wrote this text at Winterdyne, England, on April 28, 1872. With the heading "A Worker's Prayer" and with a reference to Romans 14:7 ("none of us lives to himself alone"), the seven-stanza text was first published as one of William Parlane's musical leaflets. It was then republished in Havergal's *Under the Surface* in 1874. The *Psalter Hymnal* includes the original stanzas 1, 2, 4, and 7 in modern English.

Scripture References
st. 1 = Jer. 1:9
st. 3 = Isa. 50:4
st. 4 = 1 Cor. 12:4-11

"Lord, Speak to Me" is a prayer that God will speak to, lead, and teach each of us so that we may do the same to others who need Jesus Christ (st. 1-3). The text also expresses our commitment to full-time kingdom service ("use me, Lord . . . just as you will, and when, and where"), an ongoing task that ultimately leads us to eternal "rest," "joy," and "glory" (st. 4).

Tune

Derived from the fourth piano piece in Robert A. Schumann's *Nachtstücke,* Opus 23 (1839), CANONBURY first appeared as a hymn tune in J. Ireland Tucker's *Hymnal with Tunes, Old and New* (1872). The tune, whose title refers to a street and square in Islington, London, England, is often matched to Havergal's text.

CANONBURY has a simple binary form, which consists of two versions of the same long melody. Sing in parts, ideally with a sense of two long lines rather than four choppy phrases, possibly with a fermata at the end of the first long line.

Robert Schumann (b. Zwickau, Saxony, Germany, 1810; d. Endenich, near Bonn, Germany, 1856) wrote no hymn tunes himself, though a few of his lyrical melodies were adapted into hymn tunes by hymnal editors. One of the greatest musicians of the Romantic period, Schumann did not at first seem destined for a musical career. Although he was a precocious piano player, his mother and his guardian insisted that he study for a legal career. From 1828 to 1830 he studied law at Leipzig and Heidelberg Universities, but much of his time was consumed with music and poetry. From 1830 until his death Schumann devoted his life to music. After a finger injury terminated his concert career as a pianist in 1832, he turned completely to composition. Schumann composed successfully in many genres but became especially famous for his piano works and song cycles. In 1840 he married Clara Wieck, whom he had known since

1828; she was a famous pianist and composer in her own right who inspired many of Schumann's songs. He suffered from depression for much of his adult life and in 1854, after an unsuccessful suicide attempt, was admitted to a mental institution, where he later died. Schumann founded the magazine *Neue Zeitschrift für Musik* and edited it for ten years.

Liturgical Use
Worship that focuses on missions and evangelism (during Pentecost season) and on the "equipping of the saints for ministry."

529

Speak Forth Your Word, O Father

DURROW
$\downarrow = 54$

Text
Charles J. Jeffries (b. London, England, 1896; d. Bromley, Kent, England, 1972) wrote this hymn text in 1967, revealing a zeal for the mission of the church that he also expressed in his life and work. After studies at Malvern College and Magdalen College, Oxford, England, he served on the continent in World War I and was seriously injured; his voice was also damaged. He spent his career as a public servant in the Colonial Office, rising to joint deputy under secretary of state. Knighted in 1956, he served on the boards of the Society for the Promotion of Christian Knowledge and the British and Foreign Bible Society.

Scripture References
st. 1 = Deut. 8:3
Matt. 4:4
st. 4 = Rom. 10:14-17
2 Tim. 4:2

Versions of his text were published in the Lutheran *Worship Supplement* (1969) and in the Canadian Anglican and United *Hymn Book* (1971), where it was set to the tune DURROW. Of the five original stanzas, 1-3 are included and a fourth stanza combines parts of Jeffries's stanzas 4 and 5.

Inspired by Deuteronomy 8:3, which is quoted by Christ in Matthew 4:4—"One does not live by bread alone, but by every word that comes from the mouth of God" (NRSV)—this text is a prayer that all modern means of communication be used to spread the gospel. As we sing the final stanza, we dedicate ourselves to be effective witnesses for the cause of Christ.

Tune
DURROW was originally a traditional Irish folk melody associated with "Captain Thomson," a sea song from Ireland's Limerick region (Durrow is the name of a town in Ireland between Port Laoise and Kilkenny). The tune first appeared as a hymn tune in *Church Hymnary* of 1927.

The harmonization by William France (b. New Liskeard, Ontario, Canada, 1912; d. Ottawa, Ontario, 1985) was taken from the Anglican and United *Hymn Book* (1971), for which he served on the hymnal committee. Educated at the University of Toronto, France was skilled in organ and piano as well as choral conducting and composition. He was organist and choirmaster at several United Church of Canada congregations and had a long and distinguished tenure at the Dominion-Chalmers United Church in Ottawa. France composed for piano and organ and wrote anthems and part songs.

Like many Irish tunes, DURROW is hexatonic (six tones, no A-flat in the melody). The tune has a wide range and a rounded bar form shape (AABA) with repeated melodic phrases that make it readily accessible. Sing the outer stanzas in unison and the middle ones in harmony.

Liturgical Use

Services that focus on modern missions and evangelism, encouraging the use of contemporary media to spread the gospel; ordination/commissioning of mission personnel.

530

HANKEY
♩ = 63

I Love to Tell the Story

Text

"I Love to Tell the Story" is one of two hymn texts derived from a long poem on the life of Christ written by A. (Annabelle) Catherine Hankey (b. Clapham, England, 1834; d. Westminster, London, England, 1911) in 1866. Hankey wrote the poem during a long period of convalescence following a serious illness. The first part of the poem, "The Story Wanted," is the source of the children's gospel song "Tell Me the Old, Old Story," while the second part, "The Story Told," contains this text. Beginning in 1866 different versions of the full poem were printed in various publications. This hymn text, with the tune HANKEY and a refrain written by William G. Fischer, were published in *Joyful Songs* (1869).

Scripture References
all st. = Ps. 66:16
John 15:27

Apart from the context of the larger poem, some of the couplets of this text appear rather shallow or repetitious; thus the *Psalter Hymnal* includes only the original stanzas 1, 3, and 4. But the entire original poem provides a fine autobiographical testimony to Hankey's evangelical fervor, which she expressed in her writings and in her support of foreign and home missions (she taught church school classes to the rich and poor of London). The text simply affirms the Christian's zeal to "tell the old, old story of Jesus and his love" to the unsaved as well as to the saved, here on earth and in glory.

Hankey was the daughter of a wealthy banker and was associated with the Clapham sect of William Wilberforce, a group of prominent evangelical Anglicans from the Clapham area. This group helped to establish the British and Foreign Bible Society, promoted the abolition of slavery, and was involved in improving the lot of England's working classes. Hankey taught Bible classes for shop girls in London, visited the sick in local hospitals, and used the proceeds of her writings to support various mission causes. Her publications include *Heart to Heart* (1870) and *The Old, Old Story and Other Verses* (1879).

Tune

HANKEY has many characteristics of a gospel song: stepwise melodic motion, verse-refrain form, and simple harmony. After hearing both hymn texts from Hankey's poems quoted by one of the speakers at an 1867 YMCA convention in Montreal, Quebec, gospel hymn writer William H. Doane (PHH 473) was inspired to set both texts to music. However, Doane's tune for "I Love to Tell the Story" was soon replaced by the tune HANKEY by William G. Fischer, who also added a refrain to the original text. The tune set to Hankey's text was published in *Joyful Songs* (1869) and in many gospel hymnals. The hymn was popularized through its use in the Ira D. Sankey (PHH 73) and Dwight L. Moody crusades.

In his youth, Fischer (b. Baltimore, MD, 1835; d. Philadelphia, PA, 1912) developed an interest in music while attending singing schools. His career included working in the book bindery of J. B. Lippencott Publishing Company, teaching music at Girard College, and co-owning a piano business and music store—all in Philadelphia. Fischer eventually became a popular director of music at revival meetings and choral festivals. In 1876 he conducted a thousand-voice choir at the Dwight L. Moody/Ira D. Sankey revival meeting in Philadelphia. Fischer composed some two hundred tunes for Sunday school hymns and gospel songs.

Liturgical Use

Worship that expresses missionary fervor; children's church school classes.

531

How Shall They Hear the Word of God

O JESU
♩ = 54

Text

In 1980 Michael A. Perry (PHH 299) wrote this text in Southhampton, England, for use at a tenth anniversary service for "Radio Solent," a celebration held in Winchester Cathedral in 1981. The text was first published in *Hymns for Today's Church* (1982).

Scripture References
st. 1-2 = Rom. 10:14
st. 3 = Rom. 10:15

Inspired by Romans 10:14-17, "How Shall They Hear" is a missions text. The first line of each stanza poses a question in the manner of the Pauline passage, and the final line is a prayer that constitutes a personal commitment to be witnesses for Christ "with life and voice." That personal commitment is our answer to the questions posed earlier.

Tune

O JESU first appeared in an organ collection, *Sammlung alter und neuer Melodien evangelischen Lieder* (1747), compiled by Johann B. Reimann for use with texts found in the *Hirschberger evangelischen Gesangbuch* (1741). Often attributed to Reimann, the tune was set to "O Jesu, warum legst du mir so viele Lasten auf." O JESU originally had half notes at the beginning and end of each line.

This simple bar form (AAB) tune invites part singing. For a more dramatic performance, try having one or several soloists sing the questions in each stanza with the entire congregation singing the prayer responses.

Liturgical Use

Services that promote missions and evangelism (during Epiphany and Pentecost seasons); ordination/commissioning of missionaries; prayer meetings prior to evangelistic campaigns.

532

RUSTINGTON
♩ = 108

We Have Told the Blessed Tidings

Text

Marie J. Post (PHH 5) originally wrote this text for a Pentecost hymn contest sponsored by the *Missionary Monthly* magazine in 1969. Although it was not the contest winner (of the two winners one was "Sweet Gift of God" by Post), this text was first published in the May 1970 issue of that magazine and later in the *Psalter Hymnal Supplement* (1974). It gained popularity because of its use as a theme hymn for missions conferences.

Scripture References
st. 1 = Acts 1:8
st. 2 = 2 Cor. 5:18-21

The text affirms the work of the Holy Spirit in the missionary enterprise of the church. Our missions task reaches from our immediate surroundings (st. 2) to the remotest regions of the world (st. 1); it requires a selfless use of our varied skills and resources (st. 3).

Tune

See PHH 506 for discussion of RUSTINGTON.

Liturgical Use

Pentecost season; services that focus on the missionary task of the church; ordination of missionaries and evangelists; as a teaching hymn about commitment to missions.

533

Church of God, Elect and Glorious

MEAD HOUSE
♩ = 56

Text

Written by James E. Seddon (PHH 15), this text is based on the *Scripture References* well-known passage in 1 Peter 2:9-12 where Peter calls the church "a chosen people, a royal priesthood, a holy nation, a people belonging to God" (v. 9). Each stanza of the text begins with one or more of these memorable phrases and then, following Peter's pattern, explains why the church should be such a holy people. Because it is the recipient of God's mercy, the church must be consecrated to holy living as a testimony of praise to God and as a convincing witness to the unsaved.

Scripture References
all st. = 1 Pet. 2:9-12

The text was first published in *Hymns for Today's Church* (1982).

Tune

Cyril V. Taylor (PHH 286) composed MEAD HOUSE as a setting for Christopher Wordsworth's "Alleluia, Alleluia!" (387). Named for a house in Redhill, Surrey, England, where Taylor often stayed as a boy, the tune was one of twenty tunes by Taylor published in the *BBC Hymn Book* (1951).

MEAD HOUSE is a rounded bar form (AABA) with an opening melodic motive that permeates the entire tune and leads to an impressive climax. This is a glorious tune for unison singing, though some may want to sing the harmony on certain stanzas. Try using brass instruments as accompaniment.

Liturgical Use

Regular Sunday worship; special occasions in the life of the church: anniversaries, dedications, ordinations; with confessional preaching on the doctrine of election; baptism; profession of faith; missions services.

534

Come, You Sinners, Poor and Needy

ARISE
♩ = 96

Text

In this invitation hymn, "poor and needy" sinners are welcomed to *Scripture References* "arise and go to Jesus." The final stanza alludes to Christ's parable of the prodigal son who returns to his loving father's arms.

Scripture References
st. 1 = Matt. 9:13
st. 3 = Matt. 11:28
st. 4 = Luke 15:11-32

The hymn has autobiographical overtones. Raised in a Christian home, Joseph Hart (b. London, England, 1712;

d. London, 1768) left the faith and for a time lived a life he described as "carnal and spiritual wickedness, irreligious and profane." He was converted in 1757 at a Moravian chapel in London. From 1759 until his death he served as pastor of the independent chapel on Jewin Street, London, where he preached staunchly Calvinistic sermons to large crowds. Hart's approximately two hundred hymns were published as *Hymns Composed on Various Subjects* (1759, with supplements, 1762, 1765); for a time his hymns were as popular as those of Isaac Watts (PHH 155).

Originally in seven, six-line stanzas, this hymn from his 1759 collection was entitled "Come, and Welcome, to Jesus Christ," beginning with the words, "Come, ye sinners, poor and wretched." Stanzas 1-3 are made up of various lines from the original stanzas 1, 3, and 4. The fourth stanza is taken from the refrain of an anonymous ballad about the prodigal son that appeared in several nineteenth-century American songbooks. Beginning with the words, "Far, far away from my loving Father," the ballad had as its refrain, "I will arise and go to Jesus." Philip P. Bliss (PHH 482) added that refrain line to Hart's text and set the entire text to the tune ARISE in his *Gospel Songs* (1874).

Tune

ARISE is an anonymous American folk melody. Set to "Mercy, O Thou Son of David," the tune was published in William Walker's (PHH 44) *Southern Harmony* (1835) with the title RESTORATION. Its name was changed to ARISE (after the refrain in the ballad about the prodigal son) when it was set to Hart's text.

Like many folk tunes, ARISE is pentatonic and could be sung in two-part canon (at one measure), but then the accompaniment should not be used. Sing in unison on stanza 1, with the choir in canon on stanza 2. Try having the entire group sing in harmony on stanzas 3 and 4. When singing and accompanying, be sure to retain the sturdiness of this folk melody.

Liturgical Use

As an invitation hymn in evangelistic services, possibly with altar calls or with the Lord's Supper; useful in the service of confession/forgiveness.

535

INVITATION
♩ = 60

Come to the Savior Now

Text

John M. Wigner (b. King's Lynn, Norfolk, England, 1844; d. London, England, 1911) wrote this text in 1871 for use with the young people of the church where his father was a Baptist minister. The hymn was published in his father's *Supplement* to the Baptist *Psalms and Hymns* in 1880 (Wigner's father had also compiled the original edition of this hymnal in 1858). Educated

Scripture References
st. 2 = Isa. 53:6
st. 4 = Matt. 11:28-30
Ps. 55:22
1 Pet. 5:7

at London University, Wigner served in various capacities at his church, especially working with young people. After 1876 Wigner was employed in the Indian Home Office in London.

Like 534, this invitation hymn makes use of biblical phrases and imagery. We are called to come to the Savior in repentance and for renewal. The text makes an urgent, direct appeal (st. 3) to come to Christ for salvation, relief from our burdens, and eternal rest.

Tune

Frederick C. Maker (b. Bristol, Gloucestershire, England, 1844; d. Bristol, 1927) composed INVITATION for this text. Also known as COME TO THE SAVIOR, the tune was published in the *Bristol Tune Book* (1881), edited by Alfred Stone and others. Well matched to the text, INVITATION begins gently but involves more dramatic melodic gestures in its final half. Sing in parts, perhaps unaccompanied.

Maker received his early musical training as a chorister at Bristol Cathedral. He pursued a career as organist and choirmaster—most of it spent in Methodist and Congregational churches in Bristol. His longest tenure was at Redland Park Congregational Church, where he was organist from 1882-1910. Maker also conducted the Bristol Free Church Choir Association and was a long-time visiting professor of music at Clifton College. He wrote hymn tunes, anthems, and a cantata, *Moses in the Bulrushes*.

Liturgical Use

As an invitation hymn in evangelistic services, possibly with altar calls or with the Lord's Supper; useful in the service of confession/forgiveness.

536

Lord Jesus Is Calling to All Who Will Hear

RADWELL
♩ = 120

Text

Vernon Luchies (b. Fremont, MI, 1927) wrote this text during his years as an inner-city pastor in Kalamazoo, Michigan (1969-1978). Written to complement a sermon on the Holy Spirit, the hymn was intended to be sung at the conclusion of worship. "Lord Jesus Is Calling" was first published in the *Psalter Hymnal Supplement* of 1974.

Scripture References
st. 1 = Rev. 22:17
st. 2 = John 4:14; 7:37
st. 3 = John 16:33

This invitation hymn (see also 534 and 535) uses the "living water" image from Christ's words in John 4:10-13 and 7:37-39. The text makes clear that this "water" is a metaphor for the Holy Spirit, who instills joy in the hearts of believers and enables them to witness to others about salvation in Christ.

Educated at Calvin College and Calvin Seminary, Grand Rapids, Michigan, Luchies also served other congregations in Iowa, South Dakota, British Columbia, New York, and Kentucky before retiring in 1989. Luchies has had several hymns published and has written many articles for periodicals and newspapers.

Tune

After serving in the armed forces during World War I, Hilary P. Chadwyck-Healey (b. London, England, 1888; d. Harrow, London, 1976) entered the electrical business, a position he retained until his retirement in 1956. He also retained his strong interest in composition and published choral, piano, and organ works. He served as a director of the Royal Academy of Music and as a vice-president of the Royal School of Church Music.

Chadwyck-Healey composed RADWELL around 1940 in London as a setting for Reginald Heber's (PHH 249) "Brightest and Best of the Sons of the Morning." RADWELL was set to a variety of texts in *Hymns Ancient and Modern Revised* (1950) and in several later hymnals, including the Canadian Anglican and United *Hymn Book* (1971).

RADWELL is distinguished by an effective climax at the end of its third line. Sing in unison.

Liturgical Use

As an invitation hymn during evangelistic services or for regular Sunday worship; Pentecost season.

537

ONTWAAK
♩ = 132

Awake, All Who Sleep

Text

Petro Parson (b. Amsterdam, the Netherlands, 1803; d. Steenwijk, the Netherlands, 1878) wrote this text ("Ontwaak, gij die slaapt") during his long tenure as a pastor in Steenwijk (1831-1875). After studies at theological schools in Amsterdam, Utrecht, and Leiden, he briefly served one other congregation in Kuinre (1829-1831) before moving to Steenwijk, where he lived until retirement.

Scripture References
st. 1 = Eph. 5:14
st. 3 = Acts 17:30-31

The best of Parson's devotional poetry, this text was first published in the *Christelijke Gezangen der Herstelde Evangelisch Lutherse Gemeente in Nederland* (1857) and then in the *Vervolgbundel op de Evangelische Gezangen* (1868). Stanley M. Wiersma (PHH 25) translated the text into English in 1982.

The primary image of "Awake, All Who Sleep" comes from Ephesians 5:14, in which Paul is thought to quote an early Christian hymn, "Wake Up, O Sleeper, Rise from the Dead, and Christ Will Shine on You." The text presents an urgent, insistent reveille, a call to arise and turn to Christ now for eternal life, or face him later as the judge who condemns unbelievers to eternal death.

Tune

Johannes G. Bastiaans (PHH 418) composed ONTWAAK (awake) in 1866 for the original Dutch text. The tune was one of thirty that Bastiaans provided for the *Vervolgbundel op de Evangelische Gezangen* (1868) after being commissioned to do so by the Nederlandse Hervormde Kerk. ONTWAAK is also one of several of Bastiaans's tunes that remain popular to this day in the Dutch Reformed churches.

The tune is a bar form (AAB), a rarity in Bastiaans's tunes. Its melodic contour consists of a delicate balance of larger intervals and stepwise motion. Sing either in unison or in harmony. A more dramatic rendition might involve soloists singing stanzas 1-3 and the entire group singing stanza 4.

Liturgical Use

As an invitation hymn in evangelistic services, or possibly during regular Sunday worship after the sermon (when the cry "Awake" could do double duty!); useful during the Easter Vigil or Easter season.

538

Come, You Disconsolate

CONSOLATION
𝅗𝅥 = 56

Text

Like the previous four hymns, "Come, You Disconsolate" is an invitation, a call for sinners to come to Christ with their sorrows and find healing (st. 1), experience hope and comfort (st. 2), and participate in the feast of the Lamb (st. 3). The text emphasizes the consolation that Christ offers to those who turn to him in faith.

Scripture References
st. 1 = Heb. 4:14-16
st. 2 = Isa. 54:7
John 14:18

Entitled "Relief in Prayer," this text by Thomas Moore (b. Dublin, Ireland, 1779; d. Devizes, Wiltshire, England, 1852) was first published in three stanzas in Moore's *Sacred Songs, Duets and Trios* (1816), one of his thirty-two hymn texts in that collection. Minor changes were made for the 1824 edition.

Although born and educated in Ireland, Moore spent much of his adult life in England. In 1804 he began a civil service appointment in Bermuda but delegated it to a deputy, who embezzled money that Moore had to pay back! He traveled throughout the eastern United States and Canada in 1840 but then returned to London. Moore became known for two achievements—playing and singing Irish folk songs in aristocratic homes and writing poetry. His publications include a biography of Lord Byron and *A Selection of Irish Melodies* (1807-1834).

The American composer Thomas Hastings (b. Washington, Litchfield County, CT, 1784; d. New York, NY, 1872) revised Moore's stanzas 1 and 2 and substituted his own third stanza when he published the hymn in *Spiritual Songs for Social Worship* (1831), compiled by Hastings and Lowell Mason (PHH 96). Like Lowell Mason, Hastings was a tireless writer, composer, and promoter of church music in the European style (he thought the shape-note tradition "unscientific"). He wrote some six hundred hymn texts and composed about a thousand tunes, most of which have been forgotten. From 1823 to 1832 he lived in Utica, New York, where he directed the Oneida County Choir and was editor of a religious magazine, *The Western Recorder.* In 1832 Hastings was invited by twelve churches to come to New York City to improve their psalm singing. He stayed there the rest of his life, composing, writing, teaching, and directing. He published some fifty volumes, including his *Utica Collection* (1816, later expanded as *Musica Sacra*), *Spiritual Songs for Social Worship* (with Mason, 1833), and *Church Melodies* (1858).

Tune

CONSOLATION was originally set for solo voice to "Alma redemptoris mater" by Samuel Webbe, Sr. (PHH 112), in his *Collection of Motetts and Antiphons* (1792). Thomas Hastings adapted the tune for use with Moore's text in *Spiritual Songs for Social Worship* (1831). CONSOLATION is also known as ALMA and CONSOLATOR.

With lyric sweetness and urgent rhythms, this tune has the character to support the solace offered in this text. Sing in parts or in unison (reminiscent of its vocal solo origins). Accompany with enough rhythmic firmness to offset any inherent sentimentality.

Liturgical Use

As an invitation hymn in evangelistic services, possibly with altar calls or with the Lord's Supper (note st. 3); useful in the service of confession/forgiveness and comfort/encouragement.

539

Shout, for the Blessed Jesus Reigns

TRURO
♩ = 92

Text

The text "shouts" the cosmic reign of Christ over all nations, a reign that is joyfully confessed by his chosen people on earth and celebrated by saints and angels in heaven. In the midst of these powerful exclamations of praise to Christ the Lamb comes a prayer for the increase of the church (st. 4). This is presumably one of the earliest "church growth" hymns!

Scripture References
st. 2-3 = Isa. 66:20
Zech. 8:18-23
st. 5 = Rev. 19:1-8

Benjamin Beddome (b. Henley-in Arden, Warwickshire, England, 1717; d. Bourton, Gloucestershire, England, 1795), a British Baptist preacher, wrote this text. It was published in the Bristol *Collection of Hymns adapted to Public Worship* (1769), compiled by John Ash and Caleb Evans.

Beddome originally pursued a medical degree and was apprenticed to a surgeon. However, after his conversion at age twenty, he became pastor of the Baptist congregation at Bourton-on-the-Water in Gloucestershire, where he remained until his death. (The following story is told about Beddome: When he received a caller from London asking him to accept a call from a much more prestigious church, one of his parishioners went to the parsonage, confronted the London caller with the line "robbers of churches are the worst sort of robbers," and turned loose the man's horse!) Beddome wrote more than eight hundred hymn texts, many of which were composed to be sung by his congregation after the morning sermon.

Tune

For a discussion of TRURO see PHH 413.

Sing the outer stanzas in unison, the middle ones in harmony. This tune needs brisk accompaniment and would be enhanced by brass instruments.

Liturgical Use

A fine hymn of praise or doxology for general use; fitting for church festivals like Worldwide Communion and All Nations Sunday; during Epiphany.

MC KEE
♩ = 100

In Christ There Is No East or West

Text

Many hymnals contain William A. Dunkerley's "In Christ There Is No East or West," a hymn text written in 1908 by Dunkerley under the pseudonym of John Oxenham. However, it is ironic that this text about the worldwide church has been considered by many in the twentieth century to have an exclusively male emphasis. Consequently, various recent hymnal editors have altered the text. Michael A. Perry (PHH 299) concluded that the revision needed to be so radical that an entirely new text would be a better choice. Thus Perry kept only Dunkerley's opening line and wrote a new text on the same theme. Perry's text was published in *Hymns for Today's Church* in 1982.

Scripture References
st. 1 = Isa. 49:12
Luke 13:29
Acts 17:26
Col. 3:11
Gal. 3:28
st. 2 = 2 Cor. 5:18-19

Based on New Testament passages such as Galatians 3:28 and 1 John 4:7-12, this text describes certain ideal characteristics of the church: its comprehensiveness (st. 1), unity (st. 2, 5), love (st. 3), and holiness (st. 4), ideals for which we must continually work and pray. Perry says of his text, "The spirit of reconciliation was invoked from the Pauline Epistles, and the spirit of fellowship from the Johanine."

Tune

MC KEE has an interesting history. According to a letter from Charles V. Stanford (PHH 512) to Samuel Coleridge-Taylor (who arranged the tune for piano in his *Twenty-Four Negro Melodies*, 1905), MC KEE was originally an Irish tune taken to the United States and adapted by African American slaves. It became associated with the spiritual "I Know the Angels Done Changed My Name," which appeared in J. B. T. Marsh's *The Story of the Jubilee Singers with their Songs* (1876).

Harry T. Burleigh (b. Erie, PA, 1866; d. Stamford, CT, 1949) arranged the tune to fit Dunkerley's text in 1939. As a setting for that text, the tune was published in *The Hymnal 1940*. Burleigh named the tune after Elmer M. Mc Kee, rector of St. George's Episcopal Church, New York, where Burleigh was the baritone soloist from 1894-1946.

Burleigh began his musical career as a choirboy in St. Paul's Cathedral, Erie, Pennsylvania. He also studied at the National Conservatory of Music, New York City, where he was befriended by Anton Dvorak and, according to tradition, provided Dvorak with some African American musical themes that became part of Dvorak's *New World Symphony*. Burleigh composed at least two hundred works but is most remembered for his vocal solo arrangements of African American spirituals. In 1944 Burleigh was honored as a Fellow of the Hymn Society in the United States and Canada.

Sing stanzas 1, 2, and 5 in unison, the others in harmony. The instruction in *The Hymnal 1940* for this tune is still helpful: sing this hymn "with dignity."

Liturgical Use
For Worldwide Communion, All Nations Sunday, All Saints Day, and other church festivals such as Pentecost; splendid for ecumenical services.

541

Christ Shall Have Dominion

KING OF GLORY
$\downarrow = 56$

Text
Found in the 1912 *Psalter* and in every edition of the *Psalter Hymnal,* this mission hymn is based on Psalm 72:8-19 (for comments on Psalm 72 see PHH 72).

Scripture References
st. 1 = Ps. 72:8-11
st. 2 = Ps. 72:12-14
st. 3 = Ps. 72:15-17
st. 4 = Ps. 72:18-19

The paraphrase in New Testament language proclaims the worldwide rule of Christ over all peoples and kingdoms (st. 1, vv. 8-11); his saving mercy to the needy and oppressed (st. 2, vv. 12-14); and the blessings of his endless reign (st. 3, vv. 15-17). The final stanza is a doxology (originally the doxology that ended Book II of the psalms; see Psalm 72:19). This beloved royal psalm has several settings in the *Psalter Hymnal* (72, 359, 412, and 630).

Tune
Albert Piersma (b. Friesland, the Netherlands, 1901; d. Grand Rapids, MI, 1960) composed KING OF GLORY in 1933 as a setting for Caroline M. Noel's "At the Name of Jesus" (467), which has "King of Glory" in its final stanza—thus the tune's title. The tune was published with Noel's text in the 1934 and 1959 editions of the *Psalter Hymnal.* Piersma lived in Grandville, Michigan, where he worked for the Kindle Bed Furniture Company. He was the senior organist of Grandville Avenue Christian Reformed Church for over thirty years. In addition to hymn tunes, Piersma wrote several poems, which were published in *The Banner.*

KING OF GLORY is a stately tune that builds to a solid climax in its final line. Sing the first three stanzas in parts but sing in unison on stanza 4. That stanza also needs a descant; if the accompanist cannot compose one, try having the sopranos sing the tenor line an octave higher. Use your best mixture or reed stop on the organ. For festive occasions add brass instruments.

Liturgical Use

This great messianic psalm is appropriate for Advent, Epiphany, and Ascension; useful in missions services, ecumenical gatherings, and church festivals such as Worldwide Communion, All Nations Sunday, and All Saints Day or Reformation.

542

VISION
♩ = 96

The Ends of All the Earth Shall Hear

Text

The text is based on Psalm 22:27-31, the "vow of praise" part of this lament psalm (see PHH 22 for further comments on Psalm 22). It was first published with Doane's tune in the 1912 *Psalter* and in every edition of the *Psalter Hymnal.*

Like 541, this text confesses with great certainty the worldwide rule of Christ, the Lord of lords and King of kings. All peoples and nations will submit to his reign (st. 1-2), for both rich and poor and future generations will confess the mighty deeds of the Lord (st. 3-4).

Scripture References
st. 1 = Ps. 22:27
st. 2 = Ps. 22:28
st. 3 = Ps. 22:29
st. 4 = Ps. 22:30-31

Tune

VISION, composed by William H. Doane (PHH 473), was first published in the 1883 *Baptist Hymnal,* of which Doane was musical editor. There the tune, named GOD OF OUR STRENGTH, was set to the 1882 Francis J. Van Alstyne (pseudonym for Fanny J. Crosby, PHH 473) text "God of Our Strength, Enthroned Above." In the 1912 *Psalter* and all subsequent editions of the *Psalter Hymnal,* VISION was set to "The Ends of All the Earth Shall Hear." Presumably its name comes from the visionary nature of this text.

Sing in harmony with forceful accompaniment. Use brass instruments for festive services.

Liturgical Use

At the beginning or end of regular Sunday worship; mission services; ecumenical events; during Epiphany and Pentecost seasons; fitting for Worldwide Communion, All Nations Sunday, and similar church festivals.

543

Guide Me, O My Great Redeemer

CWM RHONDDA
♩ = 100

Text

The great circuit-riding preacher/poet William Williams (b. Cefn-y-Coed, Carmarthenshire, Wales, 1717; d. Pantycelyn, Carmarthenshire, 1791) wrote the original Welsh text "Arglwydd, arwain trwy'r anialwch"—"Lord, Lead Me Through the Wilderness." It was published in his *Alleluia* (1745) and in his *Caniadau* (1762) with the title, "A prayer for strength to go through the wilderness of the world." Translated into some seventy-five languages, Williams's text has become universally popular in Christendom (and with the tune CWM RHONDDA, a favorite at Welsh rugby matches).

Scripture References
st. 1 = Ps. 48:14
Ps. 73:23-24
John 6:31-35
Ex. 16:4
st. 2 = Ex. 13:21-22
Ps. 28:7

The English translation by Peter Williams (b. Llansadurnin, Carmarthanshire, Wales, 1722; d. Llandyfeilog, Wales, 1796), which began "Guide me, O thou great Jehovah," was published in his *Hymns on Various Subjects* (1771). That first stanza is still in use, but the remaining stanzas come from William Williams's own translation, which he prepared for *The Collection of Hymns Sung in the Countess of Huntingdon's Chapels* (1771).

Pilgrimage is a much-used metaphor in Williams's texts. "Guide Me, O My Great Redeemer" draws on images from the Exodus story in the Old Testament: "bread of heaven" (Ex. 16), "crystal fountain" (Ex. 17), "fire and cloudy pillar" (Ex. 13:21-22). But the New Testament, Christocentric focus of the text is equally clear in the repeated final line of each stanza: Jesus is the "bread of heaven" (or "bread of life," John 6), the "rock" who is our "strength and shield" (1 Cor. 10:4), and the victor over "death . . . and hell's destruction" (Rev. 1:18). Thus the change from the original "Jehovah" of the first line to "Redeemer" makes eminent sense.

William Williams and Peter Williams were contemporaries with a similar background. William Williams is usually considered to be the greatest Welsh hymn writer of the eighteenth century. He had begun to prepare himself for a medical profession, but the course of his life was altered when he was influenced by the ministry of Howell Harris, an evangelist associated with George Whitefield. Williams began to study for the ministry and in 1740 was ordained a deacon in the Church of England. After being refused ordination as a priest because of his evangelical beliefs, he joined the Calvinist Methodists in 1744. He became an itinerant evangelist and for the next forty-five years served as a leading figure in the revival movement in Wales. Williams's evangelistic preaching was greatly aided by his hymns, which were sung with great enthusiasm at revival and "society" meetings. Known as the "sweet singer of Wales," he wrote about eight hundred hymn texts in Welsh and over one hundred in English. They were published in *Alleluia* (1744), *Hosanna i Fab Dafydd* (1754), *Hosanna to the Son of David* (1759), *Y Mor o Wydr* (1762), and *Gloria in Excelsis* (1771).

Peter Williams was converted to Christianity by the preaching of George Whitefield and was ordained in the Church of England in 1744. His evangelical convictions soon made him suspect, however, and he left the state church to join the Calvinist Methodists in 1746. He served as an itinerant preacher for many years and was a primary figure in the Welsh revival of the eighteenth century. After being expelled by the Methodists in 1791 on a charge of heresy, he ministered in his own chapel during the last years of his life. He published the first Welsh Bible commentary (1767-1770) and a Bible concordance (1773); he was also one of the annotators for John Canne's Welsh Bible (1790). In addition Williams published a Welsh hymnal, *Rhai Hymnau ac Odlau Ysbrydol* (1759), as well as *Hymns on Various Subjects* (1771).

Tune
The popularity of Williams's text is undoubtedly aided by its association with CWM RHONDDA, composed in 1905 by John Hughes (b. Dowlais, Glamorganshire, Wales, 1873; d. Llantwit Fardre, Wales, 1932) during a church service for a Baptist *Cymanfa Ganu* (song festival) in Capel Rhondda, Pontypridd, Wales. Hughes received little formal education; at age twelve he was already working as a doorboy at a local mining company in Llantwit Fardre. He eventually became an official in the traffic department of the Great Western Railway. Much of his energy was devoted to the Salem Baptist Church in Pontypridd, where he served as both deacon and precentor. Hughes composed two anthems, a number of Sunday school marches, and a few hymn tunes, of which CWM RHONDDA is universally known.

At first widely disseminated in leaflet form, CWM RHONDDA gradually was adopted into various hymnals. The tune is named after the valley of the Rhondda River, a coal mining area in Wales. Though composed with simple melodic means, CWM RHONDDA is a vigorous melody in major tonality (contrary to the popular belief that most Welsh tunes are minor). Sing in harmony. The altos and basses may wish to sing the little notes on the last line as they repeat the words "evermore," "strength and shield," and "sing to you." Accompany in a forceful, confident manner.

Liturgical Use
As a hymn of pilgrimage and prayer for divine providence; for various services and occasions on the Christian journey, including Old/New Year and the Easter season (given its Exodus theme).

544

Lead Me, Guide Me

LEAD ME
♩ = 92

Text

Doris M. Akers (b. Brookfield, MO, 1922) wrote both text and tune of this African American gospel hymn in 1953 in Oakland, California. The text is an earnest plea for an intimate walk with God, who is asked to lead, guide, and protect the believer. The deeply personal stanzas emphasize that divine guidance is essential because of our lack of strength, our blindness, and Satan's temptations. Only God can lead us on the narrow path and through all the complexities and challenges of earthly life.

Scripture References
ref. = Ps. 5:8
    Luke 1:79
st. 2 = Ps. 23:3

Like many of the psalms, this text pours out in prayer the yearning of the individual Christian, a prayer that reminds us of these words of the psalmist:

Lead me, Lord, lead me in thy righteousness;
make thy way plain before my face.
For it is thou, Lord, thou, Lord only
that makest me dwell in safety.

—*Psalm 4:8; 5:8 (KJV) as set to music by Samuel S. Wesley (PHH 206)*

Akers had an active career as singer, choir director, and songwriter. She wrote her first song at age ten and since that time has composed more than three hundred gospel songs and hymns, most of which were published by Manna Music (including "There's a Sweet, Sweet Spirit in this Place"). She resides in Columbus, Ohio.

Tune

LEAD ME is representative of the first generation of African American gospel music, a generation that began with Thomas Dorsey (PHH 493) and includes gospel artists such as Roberta Martin, Lucie Campbell, Kenneth Morris, Theodore Frye, and Doris M. Akers. The core of this style is improvisation. Thus the printed notes are intended only as guides to the creativity of singers and accompanists. The piano arrangement by Richard Smallwood (PHH 365) from *Lift Every Voice and Sing* (1981) suggests some additional chords and triplet rhythms, but further improvisation would certainly be appropriate.

The unison vocal setting could easily be sung by a congregation or, using a responsorial pattern, by a congregation on the refrain and one or several soloists on the stanzas.

Liturgical Use

Many occasions of worship, especially those in which personal testimony and prayer for divine guidance are appropriate.

TEMPLE
♩ = 84

Make Me a Channel of Your Peace

Text

This text is based on a well-known prayer attributed to Francis
of Assisi (PHH 431), founder of the Franciscan Order.
Originally in Latin, the prayer appeared in various nineteenth-
century documents (the English translation begins "Lord,
make me an instrument of thy peace").

Scripture References
all st. = Phil. 2:12-13
ref.   = Acts. 20:35

Like 544, "Make Me a Channel" is a fervent, personal prayer but one that is overtly
social in its application. In it the believer asks to be a vehicle of divine peace and biblical
shalom, one through whom God works "to will and to act according to his good
purpose" (Phil. 2:12b-13). The fruit of the Spirit, including love, faith, hope, and joy,
will be the channel of reconciliation and peace to a world troubled by hatred, doubt,
despair, and sadness. The refrain's theme is characteristic of Francis's Christian ministry and reflects the meaning of Jesus' words quoted by Luke in Acts 20:35, "It is more
blessed to give than to receive."

The versification and melody of this setting are the work of Johann Sebastian
Temple (b. Pretoria, Transvaal, South Africa, 1928), a member of the Franciscan Order.
By the time he was fifteen, Temple had published a novel and two books of poems in
Afrikaans. He studied anthropology at the University of South Africa and pre-
Renaissance art in Italy. After living in England for six years, he became a monk in a
yoga monastery in India. When he moved to the United States, he entered the
Franciscan Order. Temple is a singer and a songwriter who has recorded his songs on
twelve albums.

Tune

TEMPLE was composed in the ballad and guitar style typical of 1960s folk music. After
Vatican II permitted the use of languages other than Latin in worship, a number of
Roman Catholic composers adopted this style, sometimes fusing it with a chant style
(note the repeated melody tones), when they set vernacular texts to music (see 520).

This setting is for unison singing, though the refrain lines could easily be sung in
harmony if more variety in texture is desired. The accompaniment suggests the use of
guitars, but light accompaniment on piano or organ is also possible. Sing with two
pulses per measure.

Liturgical Use

Many occasions of worship that focus on the Christian virtues that Francis enumerates;
as a sung part of other spoken prayers at the beginning or end of the congregational
prayer.

546

Make Me a Captive, Lord

ST. BRIDE
♩ = 108

Text

This text is the finest example of sustained use of paradox in
the *Psalter Hymnal.* It is built on a series of paradoxes that
amplify the New Testament concept of freedom, which can be
achieved only by being a servant, or prisoner, of Christ (see 2
Cor. 12:9-10). By their cumulative effect the contrasts between
"captive" and "free"; "sink" and "stand"; "my own" and "thine"; "unbent" and "leaned"
grip our imagination and powerfully affirm our servanthood to Christ.

Scripture References
st. 1 = 2 Cor. 12:9-10
Rom. 6:18, 22
st. 2 = Phil. 4:13

George Matheson (b. Glasgow, Scotland, 1842; d. North Berwick, Scotland, 1906)
wrote the text during his stay at Row, Dunbartonshire, Scotland, in 1890. It was published that same year in his collection of poems and hymns, *Sacred Songs,* with the
heading, "Christian freedom: Paul the prisoner of Jesus Christ (Eph. 3:1)." The four
short-meter stanzas are taken from the first and fourth stanzas of Matheson's original
short-meter-double text.

A brilliant student of philosophy at the University of Glasgow and its divinity school,
Matheson wrote several important theological and devotional works, including *Aids to
the Study of German Theology* (1874). This achievement is especially noteworthy because
of his failing eyesight during his teen years and virtual blindness by the age of eighteen.
He had to rely on others, especially his sisters, for all his reading, research, and writing.
Matheson was a very able preacher, serving Presbyterian churches in Glasgow;
Clydeside Church in Innellan, Argyllshire (1868-1886); and finally St. Bernard's
Church in Edinburgh (1886-1899).

Tune

Samuel Howard (b. London, England, 1710; d. London, 1782) composed ST. BRIDE as a
setting for Psalm 130 in William Riley's London psalter, *Parochial Harmony* (1762). The
melody originally began with "gathering" notes at the beginning of each phrase. The
tune's title is a contraction of St. Bridget, the London church on Fleet Street where
Howard was organist (the church was destroyed in an air raid in 1940).

Howard was a chorister in the Chapel Royal and later sang tenor in a chorus for
Georg Friederich Handel. But his main career was as an organist: he held concurrent
organist positions at St. Bride, Fleet Street (1736-1782), and St. Clement Dane, The
Strand (1769-1782). A composer of many songs, cantatas, and theater music, Howard
assisted William Boyce (PHH 553) in the compiling of *Cathedral Music* (1760-1773). His
church music includes a number of anthems and hymn tunes.

Erik Routley (PHH 31) described ST. BRIDE as "one of the best short-meter tunes
available" because of the "girder-like effect of the long downward scale contrasting with

the arch-like shape of the other three phrases" (*The Music of Christian Hymns,* p. 71).
The tune is constructed with a sensitive balance of melodic steps and leaps. Sing in
harmony at a deliberate pace that permits consideration of the literary device in the
text.

Liturgical Use
Many occasions of worship, especially after the sermon; adult baptism; profession of
faith; ordination; times of testimony to the joy of being "captives" of Christ.

547

ELLACOMBE
♩ = 58
Fill Thou My Life, O Lord, My God

Text
Horatius Bonar (PHH 260), famous Scottish evangelical preacher   *Scripture References*
and poet, wrote this text in twelve, four-line stanzas. Entitled   st. 1 = Ps. 34:1
"Life's Praise," the text was published in the third series of Bonar's   Ps. 71:8
Hymns of Faith and Hope (1866). Like most other hymnals the
Psalter Hymnal includes only half of the original text with minor alterations (the most
obvious being the change from "intercourse" to "fellowship" in st. 2, which is more in
accord today with Bonar's meaning).

The text's theme is the consecration of all life as a doxology to God—the equivalent
in hymn form of the neo-Calvinist concept that all of life is religion. Echoing an
emphasis of the Old Testament prophets (see Ps. 50 or Isa. 1), this text affirms that "lip
service" or an orthodox heart is not enough; we must live our Christianity in every
aspect of our lives each day. That sanctity of life includes the intimate setting of family
life and, by extension, the entire family of God, the church (st. 2). Such a holy lifestyle
is possible only in communion with God, in "fellowship with thee."

Tune
For a discussion of ELLACOMBE see PHH 378. Bright organ stops and brass instruments
will immensely enhance the conviction expressed in this text. Some hymnals still
provide four-line stanzas for this text and offer RICHMOND (335) as the tune.

Liturgical Use
Because the whole of Christian life should be a true doxology to the Lord, many
occasions of worship.

548

When We Walk with the Lord

TRUST AND OBEY
♩ = 42

Text

Daniel B. Towner, composer of the tune, writes about the origins of this well-known gospel hymn:

Scripture References
st. 1 = 1 John 5:2-3
Prov. 16:20
st. 2 = Ex. 19:5

> Mr. Moody [Dwight L.] was conducting a series of meetings in Brockton, Massachusetts [presumably in 1886] and I had the pleasure of singing for him there. One night a young man rose in a testimony meeting and said, "I am not quite sure—but I am going to trust, and I am going to obey." I just jotted that sentence down, and sent it with the little story to the Rev. John H. Sammis, a Presbyterian minister. He wrote the hymn, and the tune was born.

—*Ira D. Sankey*, The Story of the Gospel Hymns, *1906*

John Henry Sammis (b. Brooklyn, NY, 1846; d. Los Angeles, CA, 1919) wrote the chorus lines first and then the five stanzas, after which Towner composed the tune. The hymn was published in *Hymns Old and New* (1887). Because of its use in the Dwight L. Moody and Ira D. Sankey crusades and its printing in Sankey hymnals, "When We Walk with the Lord" became widely known.

The refrain provides the text's theme: trust and obey the Lord (Prov. 16:20). The three stanzas develop this theme: we show our trust by walking with God in accord with his Word and with total commitment to his will for our lives.

Sammis was a successful businessman in Logansport, Indiana, and active as a Christian layman. His volunteer work for the YMCA eventually led to a change of career. He studied at McCormick Theological Seminary in Chicago, Illinois, graduated from Lane Theological Seminary, and was ordained in the Presbyterian Church in 1880. He served congregations in Glidden, Iowa; Indianapolis, Indiana; Grand Haven, Michigan; Red Wing, Minnesota; and Sullivan, Indiana. From 1909 until his death he was a teacher at the Bible Institute of Los Angeles.

Tune

One of the sturdiest of the some two thousand tunes Daniel Brink Towner (b. Rome, PA, 1850; d. Longwood, MO, 1919) composed, TRUST AND OBEY is also among the most popular. It is cast in the verse-refrain form typical of gospel hymns.

Sing in harmony throughout. Though the use of a fermata in the refrain (on "Jesus") prevails in some congregations, hymnals, and recordings, the text is one unit and should be performed as one long musical phrase without undue breaths or pauses. Observe one broad beat per measure.

Towner was educated musically by his father and later trained by gospel musicians such as George Root (PHH 93) and George Webb (PHH 559). He served as music director for the Centenary Methodist Church in Binghamton, New York (1870-1882), the York Street Methodist Church in Cincinnati, Ohio (1882-1884), and briefly at the Union Methodist Church in Covington, Kentucky. In 1885 he joined Dwight L. Moody's evangelistic campaigns as a baritone soloist and choral conductor. From 1893 until his death he was head of the music department of Moody Bible Institute in Chicago, where he strongly influenced several generations of students. Towner compiled fourteen hymn collections.

Liturgical Use

With Scripture reading before or after the sermon; on various occasions of worship as a hymn of encouragement, commitment and dedication, and testimony.

549

HEIDELBERG 1
♩ = 88

My Only Comfort

Text

The Heidelberg Catechism (1563) is the "most ecumenical of the Reformed catechisms and confessions . . . and is the most widely used and most warmly praised catechism of the Reformation period" (*Psalter Hymnal,* p. 860).

Scripture References
st. 1 = 1 Cor. 6:19-20
Rom. 14:7-9
st. 2 = 1 Pet. 1:18-19
Heb. 2:14-15
st. 3 = Matt. 10:29-31
st. 4 = Rom. 8:28
st. 5 = 2 Cor. 1:21-22

The text of this prose hymn is Q&A 1 from Lord's Day 1 of the Heidelberg Catechism (thus the tune's title). Though the entire catechism is sometimes treated simply as a pedagogical document, the opening paragraphs in this Lord's Day clearly indicate that this confession was intended to be much more—it is a creed of comfort, hope, and encouragement. In a few sentences this text summarizes the essential components of the Christian faith and walk with the Lord. Many Christians have memorized this part of the catechism; perhaps this musical setting will aid in further memorization.

Tune

Emily R. Brink (PHH 158) composed the HEIDELBERG 1 for this text in Champaign, Illinois, in 1975 (the year that the new translation of the catechism was adopted by the Christian Reformed Church). Brink composed the tune, along with a setting for the final "Amen" answer in the Heidelberg Catechism, for a hymn contest celebrating the hundredth anniversary of Calvin College in 1976. Although no submitted hymns were selected as the centennial hymn, eight of Brink's settings for various Q&As of the catechism (see also 507) were published in *Bible Landmarks: A Study of the Heidelberg Catechism,* part of the Bible Way curriculum published by CRC Publications in 1977.

HEIDELBERG 1 consists of one flexible chantlike formula, which is applied to stanzas 1-4, and another set of derived motives, which shape stanza 5. Either sing in unison throughout or sing stanzas 1-4 in unison and stanza 5 in harmony. Organ accompaniment initially calls for two manuals and pedal with a clear stop for the soprano part; the increased texture in four parts in stanza 5 suggests a fuller registration.

Liturgical Use
As a sung confession of faith (could be a substitute for one of the other sung creeds, see 518-520); with sermons on the Heidelberg Catechism in which this sung Lord's Day could be paired with any of the other spoken Lord's Days; for festive events—Old/New Year services, special seasons of prayer, Reformation celebrations; funerals.

550

My Shepherd Will Supply My Need

RESIGNATION
♩ = 104

Text
Psalm 23 has inspired numerous paraphrases and hymn texts, including this text by Isaac Watts (PHH 155). Watts included it in his large 1719 collection of psalm paraphrases, *The Psalms of David Imitated.*

Scripture References
st. 1 = Ps. 23:1-3
st. 2 = Ps. 23:4-5
st. 3 = Ps. 23:6

For general comments on this beloved psalm, see PHH 23; other settings are also at 161 and 452.

Tune
RESIGNATION is another of the anonymous tunes from the shape-note hymnal tradition in the Southern United States; William Walker (PHH 44) included it in his *Southern Harmony* (1835) set to Watts's text. That association of text and tune has been maintained in many hymnals and anthems, including a famous choral setting by Virgil Thompson.

Like so many American folk tunes, RESIGNATION is pentatonic. This rounded bar form tune (AABA) has a sturdy harmonization. Sing in unison or harmony.

Liturgical Use
See suggestions at PHH 23, 161, and 162.

551

Oh, for a Closer Walk with God

Text

William Cowper (PHH 434) wrote this text on December 9, 1769, during the illness of his long-time friend and housekeeper, Mrs. Unwin. In a letter written the next day Cowper voiced his anxieties about her condition and about what might happen to him if she died. Saying that he composed the text "to surrender up to the Lord" all his "dearest comforts," Cowper added,

Scripture References
st. 3-4 = Ps. 51:12
Job 29:2-3
st. 5 = Heb. 12:14

> Her illness has been a sharp trial to me. Oh, that it may have a sanctifying effect!
> . . . I began to compose the verses yesterday morning before daybreak, but fell
> asleep at the end of the first two lines; when I awoke again, the third and fourth
> were whispered to my heart in a way which I have often experienced.

The text was published in Richard Conyers's *Collection of Psalms and Hymns* (1772) and, with some revision, in the *Olney Hymns* (1779). There it had the heading "Walk with God" and included a reference to Enoch in Genesis 5:24. The original fourth stanza is omitted.

Although Cowper frequently battled depression, doubt, and melancholy, this text speaks of a very intimate walk with the Lord. That walk is rooted in Scripture (st. 1), rejoices in conversion (st. 2-3), and denounces all idols that would usurp God's sovereignty (st. 4). The text concludes with a return to the prayer of the first stanza, but now that prayer is sung with increased confidence and serenity.

Tune

Composed by John B. Dykes (PHH 147), BEATITUDO was published in the revised edition of *Hymns Ancient and Modern* (1875), where it was set to Isaac Watts's "How Bright Those Glorious Spirits Shine." Originally a word coined by Cicero, BEATITUDO means "the condition of blessedness."

Like many of Dykes's tunes, BEATITUDO has a convincing melodic contour and a somewhat chromatic harmonization. Sing the outer, framing stanzas in unison and the middle ones in parts. Use just enough organ to keep this hymn moving. Maintain one pulse per measure.

Liturgical Use

For occasions of aspiration, hope, and encouragement for a more intimate walk with God; a fine testimonial hymn.

552

The Blood Will Never Lose Its Power

THE BLOOD
♩ = 92

Text

African American gospel musician Andraé Crouch (b. Los Angeles, CA, 1945) wrote both text and tune in 1962. An arrangement of the text by Thursten G. Frazier entitled "It Will Never Lose Its Power" was published as a choral piece that same year by the Frazier-Cleveland Company.

Scripture References
all st. = Eph. 1:7

Like other familiar hymns about the blood of Jesus (383, "O Sacred Head" and 384, "When I Survey the Wondrous Cross") this text presents the blood of Jesus as a metaphor for Christ's atonement for our sin. That atonement gives "me strength from day to day" and "will never lose its power." Certainty about the efficacy of Christ's sacrifice (st. 1) "soothes [our] doubts and calms [our] fears" (st. 2) and helps us negotiate "the highest mountain" and "the lowest valley" in our experiences of life in Christ.

Tune

Crouch's musical setting of THE BLOOD provides a skeleton script for a piano accompaniment that welcomes additional or substitute chords, arpeggios, runs, and ornaments. This hymn is appropriate for regular congregational singing, choral part singing, and/or the use of a soloist on the stanzas. Keep the dotted rhythms crisp and sing majestically.

The African American gospel style began in the 1920s with Thomas Dorsey (PHH 493). Along with Edwin Hawkins, Jessye Dixon, James Cleveland, Dannibelle, and Curtis Burrell (to name a few), Crouch represents a more recent generation of such gospel musicians.

Andraé Crouch is a leader in contemporary gospel music. He began performing as a teen in his church, directed a choir at a Teen Challenge drug rehabilitation center, and then formed a singing group for the Church of God in Christ denomination. As a singer he has toured with his "Disciples" ensemble throughout the world for twenty-five years; his recordings have won Grammy and Dove awards. He has written more than three hundred gospel songs, many of which have become standards in gospel music. He has also written an autobiography, *Through It All: A Biography* (1974).

Liturgical Use

Worship that focuses on Christ's sacrifice, atonement, and power; Lord's Supper.

553

Jesus Calls Us; O'er the Tumult

Text

Irish hymn writer Cecil F. Alexander (PHH 346) wrote this text for St. Andrew's Day. The appointed gospel reading for that day in the church year concerned Jesus' calling of Simon Peter and Andrew (Matt. 4:18-20). Her text was published in the Society for the Promotion of Christian Knowledge's (SPCK) *Hymns for Public Worship* (1852). Though written for a relatively minor saint's day, this hymn quickly gained popularity. It was frequently altered (sometimes mutilated) in later hymnals; Alexander herself prepared an inferior revision about twenty years after the text's first publication. The original third stanza is omitted.

Scripture References
st. 1-2 = Matt. 4:18-20
　　　　 Mark 1:16-18
st. 3　 = John 21:15
st. 4　 = Rom. 12:1

The thread that binds the stanzas together is the call of Christ. Just as Jesus called the fishermen to be his disciples, he still calls us today to be his followers and obedient servants. His call is for total commitment, a "follow me" that overrides all our earthly "cares and pleasures."

Tune

HALTON HOLGATE (also called SHARON) is a version of a psalm tune originally composed by William Boyce (b. London, England, 1710; d. Kensington, London, 1779) and published around 1765 in his *Collection of Melodies,* including tunes by various composers for Christopher Smart's paraphrases of the psalms.

William Boyce was an organist, a composer for both church and theater, and a music editor. He began his musical career as a chorister in St. Paul Cathedral, London, and later served as organist in a number of churches, including the Chapel Royal. However, increasing deafness affected his organ playing, and the last church he served (St. Michael's, Cornhill) asked him to resign. Boyce wrote songs for the stage, odes for important occasions for the royal house, church services, anthems, and hymn tunes. In the history of church music he is also remembered for his *Cathedral Music* (1760, 1773), a three-volume collection of church music by English composers from the sixteenth to eighteenth centuries.

Adding melodic tones to the orginal, the current version of this sturdy tune dates from 1789, where it was included in Thomas Williams's *Psalmodia Evangelica* (PHH 413). The harmonization is by Samuel S. Wesley (PHH 206). Though the entire hymn may be sung by the whole congregation, the drama of the stanzas suggests that the initial stanzas be sung by a choir or soloists and the final stanza by everyone in unison.

Alexander's text is set to Edward J. Hopkins's WRAYBURY in the British tradition and to William H. Jude's GALILEE in many American hymnals (including the 1959 *Psalter Hymnal*).

Liturgical Use

Worship that focuses on God's call, his summons to obedience; profession of faith; ordination and commissioning; evangelistic meetings.

554

In Sweet Communion, Lord, with You

PRAYER
♩ = 120

Text

This text is a paraphrase of the final segment of a wisdom psalm, Psalm 73:23-28 (for general comments on this psalm see PHH 73). The versification of the text (usually one biblical verse per stanza) is a revision of that found in the 1912 *Psalter.*

Scripture References
st. 1 = Ps. 73:23
st. 2 = Ps. 73:24
st. 3 = Ps. 73:25
st. 4 = Ps. 73:26
st. 5 = Ps. 73:27-28

"In Sweet Communion" sets forth the joy of walking closely with God (st. 1 and 5), following his directives (st. 2), shunning earthly distractions (st. 3), and experiencing his comfort and power. The final stanza proclaims the wisdom theme of the psalm: "To live apart from God is death; 'tis good his face to seek."

Tune

William U. Butcher (U.S.A., nineteenth century) composed PRAYER in 1860. Except for the fact that he had some association with the Oliver Ditson Music Company, no information is available about Butcher.

This simple but serviceable tune has an elementary harmonization that invites singing in harmony. To emphasize the theme, sing the final stanza in unison both at the beginning and the end as a frame with an alternate organ setting. Sing all other stanzas in parts. Maintain one broad pulse per bar.

Liturgical Use

Worship that focuses on the teaching "the fear of the Lord is the beginning of wisdom."

Lead On, O King Eternal

Text

With the encouragement of his fellow graduating classmates,
Ernest W. Shurtleff (Boston, MA, 1862; d. Paris, France, 1917)
wrote this text in 1887 for Andover Theological Seminary's
commencement ceremonies. Winning immediate acclaim, the
text was published in Shurtleff's *Hymns of the Faith* that same year.
Since that publication it has appeared in many American hymnals.

Scripture References
st. 1 = Eph. 6:10
st. 2 = Luke 4:18-19
Isa. 61:1-2
st. 3 = 2 Tim. 4:7-8

Graduation is one milestone on our life's journey, a road sign that points to the
future as much as it marks the end of formal education. Consequently, "Lead On, O
King Eternal" is a battle call to go forward in Christian service. Initially laced with war
imagery, the text moves on to biblical imagery—"deeds of love and mercy"—and
concludes with a note of eschatological hope. This message is as urgent today as it was a
hundred years ago.

Before studying at Andover, Shurtleff attended Harvard University. He served
Congregational churches in Ventura, California; Old Plymouth, Massachusetts; and
Minneapolis, Minnesota, before moving to Europe. In 1905 he established the
American Church in Frankfurt, and in 1906 he moved to Paris, where he was involved
in student ministry at the Academy Vitti. During World War I he and his wife were
active in refugee relief work in Paris. Shurtleff wrote a number of books, including
Poems (1883), *Easter Gleams* (1885), *Song of Hope* (1886), and *Song on the Waters* (1913).

Tune

LANCASHIRE is a suitably rousing march tune to accompany this text. Henry T. Smart
(PHH 233) composed the tune in 1835 for use at a missions festival at Blackburn,
Lancashire, England. For that festival, which celebrated the three-hundredth anniver-
sary of the Reformation in England, the tune was set to Reginald Heber's (PHH 249)
"From Greenland's Icy Mountains." First printed in leaflets, LANCASHIRE was published
in Smart's *Psalms and Hymns for Divine Worship* (1867). It was set to Shurtleff's text in the
1905 *Methodist Hymnal*. In some hymnals this tune is associated with "The Day of
Resurrection" (390).

Initially cast over a static bass, LANCASHIRE becomes quite animated in its third
phrase. Sing and accompany with much energy and rhythmic vitality.

Liturgical Use

A fine recessional hymn; appropriate many other times of worship, including ordina-
tion/commissioning, church education graduations, and occasions that mark the
beginning of a church program.

556

Great Is Thy Faithfulness

Text

"There is no circumstantial background for 'Great Is Thy Faithfulness,'" writes its author, Thomas O. Chisholm (PHH 292). He goes on to say that it was simply the result of his "morning by morning realization of God's personal faithfulness." Chisholm wrote the text in Vineland, New Jersey, in 1923, and sent it to his friend William M. Runyan, who composed the tune. Set to FAITHFULNESS, the text was published in Runyan's *Songs of Salvation and Service* (1923). "Great Is Thy Faithfulness" is a vibrant testimony to the faithfulness of God, a testimony Chisholm reaffirmed in 1941:

Scripture References
st. 1 = Lam. 3:22
James 1:17
st. 2 = Ps. 36:5
Ps. 104:19
ref. = Lam. 3:23
James 1:17

> I must not fail to record here the unfailing faithfulness of a covenant-keeping God and that he has given me many wonderful displays of his providing care, for which I am filled with astonishing gratefulness.

The text emphasizes the immutability of God (st. 1), a constancy to which nature attests (st. 2). But the greatest evidence of God's unfailing love is his forgiveness and "presence to cheer and to guide" us each day of our walk with him (st. 3). The refrain was inspired by the comforting words of Lamentations 3:22-23.

Tune

William Marion Runyan (b. Marion, NY, 1870; d. Pittsburg, KS, 1957) composed FAITHFULNESS for Chisholm's text in Baldwin, Kansas, in 1923. Twenty years later Runyan wrote:

> Mr. Chisholm and I were devoted co-workers, and I wrote harmonies to some 20 or 25 of his poems. This particular poem held such an appeal that I prayed most earnestly that my tune might carry over its message in a worthy way, and the subsequent history of its use indicates that God answers prayer.

Showing early musical promise, Runyan was a substitute church organist by the age of twelve. He became a Methodist minister in 1891 and served several churches in Kansas but turned to evangelism in 1903; he worked for the Central Methodist Conference for the next twenty years. Following that service, Runyan became pastor at the Federated Church at John Brown University, Sulphur Springs, Arkansas. Editor of *Christian Workers Magazine*, he also served the Moody Bible Institute and was an editor for Hope Publishing Company until his retirement in 1948. Runyan wrote a number of hymn texts, gospel songs, and hymn tunes.

"Great Is Thy Faithfulness" became an unofficial school hymn at Moody Bible Institute, and it was featured in the Billy Graham crusades in England in 1954. Thus it attained popularity on both sides of the Atlantic Ocean.

Sing this distinguished gospel music in harmony at a moderate pace.

Liturgical Use
As a hymn of testimony to God's covenant faithfulness; weddings; funerals.

557

GORDON
♩ = 54

My Jesus, I Love Thee

Text

William R. Featherstone (b. Montreal, Quebec, Canada, 1846; d. Montreal, 1873) wrote this beloved devotional text in 1862 in Montreal at the age of sixteen (possibly at the time of his conversion and baptism). He incorporated these phrases from an old revival hymn into his text:

Scripture References
st. 1 = 1 Pet. 1:8
st. 2 = 1 John 4:10, 19

> O Jesus, my Savior! I know thou art mine.
> For thee all the pleasures of earth I resign.

Featherstone sent "My Jesus, I Love Thee" to an aunt in Los Angeles, California, who presumably encouraged its distribution. But the text was first published anonymously in the *London Hymn Book* (1864), set to a now-forgotten tune. It was also published in Dwight L. Moody's *Northwestern Hymn Book* (1868). Very little is known about Featherstone. It appears that he lived in Montreal his whole life, where he was a member of the Wesleyan Methodist Church (now St. James United Church).

The refrain presents the theme of the text: "If ever I loved thee, my Jesus, 'tis now"— a testimony of fervent love for the Savior, a personal love that chooses for Christ and against sin (st. 1), a thankful love for Christ's salvation, a love born in response "because he first loved us" (1 John 4:19; st. 2), and a love that leads through death (st. 3) to a vision of glory in heaven (st. 4).

Tune

In 1870 Featherstone's text came to the attention of Adoniram J. Gordon (b. New Hampton, NH, 1836; d. Boston, MA, 1895), an evangelical preacher who was compiling a new Baptist hymnal. Because he was unhappy with the existing melody for this text, Gordon composed this tune; as he wrote, "in a moment of inspiration, a beautiful new air sang itself to me." Named for the composer, GORDON was first published in the 1876 edition of Caldwell and Gordon's *The Service of Song for Baptist Churches*.

Gordon, who was named after Adoniram Judson (1788-1850), the pioneering Baptist missionary to India and Burma, was educated at Brown University, Providence, Rhode Island, and Newton Theological Seminary, Newton, Massachusetts. After being ordained in 1863, he served the Baptist Church in Jamaica Plain, Massachusetts, and the Clarendon Street Baptist Church, Boston. A close friend of Dwight L. Moody, he promoted evangelism and edited *The Service of Song for Baptist Churches* (1871) as well as *The Vestry Hymn and Tune Book* (1872). Both Gordon College and Gordon-Conwell Theological Seminary are named after Gordon.

Sing this rounded bar form (AABA) tune in harmony throughout. It is a beautiful candidate for singing with little or no accompaniment. Do not rush the long phrases.

Liturgical Use

As a hymn of commitment and devotion to Christ for baptism, Lord's Supper, and many other occasions of worship.

558

Lord of All Hopefulness

SLANE
♩ = 100

Text

Joyce Torrens-Graham (b. Westminster, London, England, 1901; d. New York, NY, 1953) wrote many poems and essays under the pen name of Jan Struther (derived from her mother's maiden name, Eva Anstruther). She wrote this text at the request of Percy

Scripture References
st. 2 = Ps. 25:5
st. 4 = Ps. 4:8

Dearmer, with whom she prepared the enlarged edition of *Songs of Praise* (1931). It was first published in that hymnal to the tune SLANE. According to Frank Colquhoun, the text "is a work with a warm human touch, a healthy spiritual tone, and well merits its popularity." It is one of the best examples of the "all-day" hymn texts (dealing with the whole day, from morning to evening).

The four stanzas begin by addressing God in terms of his attributes and then ask for specific blessings for morning, noon, evening, and night. Displaying a consistent literary structure, the text, according to Dearmer, "is indeed a lovely example of the fitting together of thought, words and music."

In addition to her pen name, Struther also had the married names of Mrs. Anthony Maxtone Graham and, from a second marriage, Mrs. Adolf Kurt Placzek. During World War II she moved with her children to New York City and remained there until her death. In England she is best known for her novel *Mrs. Miniver* (1940), which consists of sketches of British family life before World War II. Immensely popular, the book was later made into a movie. Struther also wrote comic and serious poetry, essays, and short stories, published in *Betsinda Dances and Other Poems* (1931), *Try Anything Twice* (1938),

The Glass Blower (1941), and, posthumously, *The Children's Bells* (1957). *Songs of Praise* (1931) included twelve of her hymn texts.

Tune

SLANE is an old Irish folk tune associated with the ballad "With My Love Come on the Road" in Patrick W. Joyce's *Old Irish Folk Music and Songs* (1909). It became a hymn tune when it was arranged by David Evans (PHH 285) and set to the Irish hymn "Be Thou My Vision" published in the *Church Hymnary* (1927). SLANE is named for a hill in County Meath, Ireland, where St. Patrick's lighting of an Easter fire—an act of defiance against the pagan king Loegaire (fifth century)—led to his unlimited freedom to preach the gospel in Ireland.

SLANE is an attractive tune with phrases that demonstrate a wide range and creative melodic patterns. The harmonization, one of two settings in *The Hymnal 1982,* is accessible to good singers (especially to low basses!), but most congregations may prefer unison throughout. Support the singing with rather light but energetic accompaniment.

Liturgical Use

Occasions of worship that focus on trusting the Lord's guidance; the hymn's "all day" theme also permits a choice of stanzas for specific times.

559

WEBB
♩ = 56

Stand Up, Stand Up for Jesus

Text

George Duffield, Jr. (b. Carlisle, PA, 1818; d. Bloomfield, NJ, 1888), was inspired to write this text after hearing the dying words of a Presbyterian colleague, Dudley A. Tyng. Ousted from his own congregation for his strong anti-slavery stance, Tyng preached to large crowds in weekday meetings sponsored by the YMCA. His work spearheaded an evangelical revival in Philadelphia early in 1858. At Tyng's deathbed, caused by a farm accident in which he lost an arm, Duffield and others asked if he had any final message. Tyng replied, "Tell them to stand up for Jesus!" At Tyng's memorial service on April 25, 1858, Duffield preached on Ephesians 6:14 and concluded his sermon by reading his new hymn text, "Stand Up, Stand Up for Jesus." Several lines in that original text referred to Tyng's words and ministry. The six-stanza text was first distributed in leaflet form and then was published in *The Church Psalmist* (1859). The *Psalter Hymnal* follows

Scripture References
st. 1 = 2 Tim. 2:3
st. 2 = 1 Cor. 16:13
st. 3 = Eph. 6:10-17
st. 4 = Rev. 2:10
2 Tim. 4:7-8

the custom of most hymnals of including the original stanzas 1, 3, 4, and 6 with updated language.

The challenge of "Stand Up for Jesus" is proclaimed through the military metaphors Paul uses in Ephesians 6:10-18. Although some decry the warlike imagery, the spiritual battle that Christians must fight is very real. Christ's victory is assured even if we do not always move "from victory unto victory" in our earthly lives.

A graduate of Yale College and Union Theological Seminary, Duffield served eight Presbyterian churches in New York, New Jersey, Pennsylvania, Illinois, and Michigan. He was a regent for the University of Michigan for seven years, served as editor of the Presbyterian paper *Christian Observer,* and promoted evangelistic work with his personal wealth. Duffield's interest in hymnody influenced his son, Samuel W. Duffield, to publish *English Hymns, Their Authors and History* (1886).

Tune
George J. Webb (b. Rushmore Lodge, near Salisbury, Wiltshire, England, 1803; d. Orange, NJ, 1887) composed WEBB (also known as MORNING LIGHT) on a voyage from England to the United States. The tune was published in *The Odeon,* a collection of secular music compiled by Webb and Lowell Mason (PHH 96) in 1837. There it was set to "'Tis Dawn, the Lark Is Singing." WEBB was used as a hymn tune in *The Wesleyan Psalmist* (1842), where it was the setting for "The Morning Light Is Breaking" (thus its other title).

William B. Bradbury (PHH 114) paired WEBB to Duffield's text, an association that appeared in many of Ira D. Sankey's (PHH 73) hymnals. Hymnologist Stanley L. Osborne says that this tune "goes with a roar." A rounded bar form (AABA), WEBB has a very simple harmony. Sing the entire hymn in parts—standing, of course!

Although his parents had intended that he become a minister, Webb's early skills in music soon pointed toward a career in music. He studied organ at Salisbury Cathedral and became organist in a church in Falmouth. In 1830 he immigrated to the United States, settled in Boston, and became organist in the Old South Church, a position he held for the next forty years. In his later years Webb taught singing in Orange, New Jersey, and New York City and published two books on voice pedagogy. Working with Lowell Mason on a number of projects, including the publishing of *The National Psalmist* (1848), Webb also taught music at Mason's Boston Academy of Music and was president of the Handel and Haydn Society. In 1835 Webb joined the Swedenborgian Church and was influential in shaping its musical service book of 1836 as well as the book's revisions in 1854 and 1876. He also edited other songbooks such as *The Massachusetts Collection of Psalmody* (1840), *The Psaltery* (1845), *The Melodist* (1850), and *Cantica Ecclesiastica* (1859).

Liturgical Use
Profession of faith; adult baptism; ordination and commissioning services; various other times of worship.

560

Like a River Glorious

Text

Frances R. Havergal (PHH 288) wrote this text in 1874 in
Leamington, England. First appearing in leaflet form, the text
was published in a collection of her poems, *Loyal Responses* (1878),
without music. The *Psalter Hymnal* version is notably altered from
the original three stanzas.

Scripture References
st. 1 = Isa. 66:12
st. 2 = Ps. 37:24

Like "Trust and Obey" (548) and various psalms of trust, this text extols the blessing
of trusting in God's care and keeping. Such trust produces serenity (st. 1), strength to
face each day (st. 2), and "perfect peace and rest" (ref.).

Tune

James Mountain (b. Leeds, York, England, 1844; d. Tunbridge Wells, Kent, England,
1933) composed WYE VALLEY for Havergal's text on one of his first preaching tours
through Britain. Throughout his life Mountain was influenced by the Countess of
Huntington and her following of evangelical Pietists in the Anglican Church. He was
trained at the Pietist Rotterham College and later served the Countess's church in
Tunbridge Wells (1889-1897).

Strongly influenced by Dwight L. Moody and Ira D. Sankey's (PHH 73) evangelistic
tour of England, Mountain followed their example and did evangelistic work from 1874
to 1889, both in England and abroad. Later he became a Baptist and founded St. John's
Free Church in Tunbridge Wells. Mountain wrote a number of devotional works as well
as hymns and hymn tunes. Mountain also imitated Sankey's musical style. Assisted by
Frances Havergal, he compiled *Hymns of Consecration and Faith* (1876), which included
her text with the heading "Perfect Peace." WYE VALLEY is named for the district around
the village of Wye, near Ashford in Kent.

This relatively simple tune is marked by repeated melody tones. In fact, the refrain
melody is a repeat of the latter half of the tune for the stanzas. Sing in harmony
throughout in six long phrases rather than twelve short ones. Try singing unaccompanied on stanza 2.

Liturgical Use

As a hymn of trust for many occasions of worship; a sung benediction.

561

Rejoice, O Pure in Heart

MARION
♩ = 60

Text

Anglican clergyman Edward H. Plumptre (PHH 363) wrote this text for use as a processional hymn for the annual choral festival at Peterborough Cathedral, England (May 1865). "Rejoice, O Pure in Heart" was originally in eleven stanzas—long enough for all the choirs to process into the cathedral. It was published in the third edition of Plumptre's *Lazarus and Other Poems* (1868) and in the *Appendix* to *Hymns Ancient and Modern* (1868). Of the original eleven stanzas, 1, 2, 8, 9, and 11 are included.

Scripture References
st. 2 = Ps. 40:3
ref. = Phil. 4:4

In this text the imagery of a liturgical procession becomes a marching metaphor for the journey of life. The call to "rejoice, give thanks and sing" (st. 1) is extended to all people, "bright youth and snow-crowned age, both men and women" (st. 2), and on all occasions, "by night and day, in gladness and in woe" (st. 3). Life's pilgrimage has a specific goal, to be at rest in the new Jerusalem (st. 4) where all God's creatures will join in a great doxology (st. 5). The "rejoice" theme in the refrain is borrowed from Philippians 4:4.

Tune

Arthur H. Messiter (b. Frome, Somersetshire, England, 1834; d. New York, NY, 1916) composed MARION for this text in 1883 and named it after his wife. The tune was published in the *Hymnal with Music as Used in Trinity Church* (1893), a hymnal compiled by Messiter during his long term of service as organist/choirmaster at Trinity Church (Episcopal) in New York City (1866-1897).

Educated by private tutors in England, Messiter immigrated to the United States in 1863 and had an active musical career in Philadelphia, which included an organist position at St. James the Less. At Trinity Church in New York City, he modeled with distinction the British cathedral tradition of music. Messiter was an editor of the Episcopal *Hymnal* (1893), compiled the *Psalter* (1889) and *Choir Office Book* (1891), and wrote a musical history of Trinity Episcopal Church, New York (1906).

A short-meter tune, MARION is distinguished by an appealing melodic contour and an effective refrain line. Sing stanzas 1-4 in harmony and the final, doxological stanza in unison. The refrain would benefit from the use of a descant. Do not rush! Though MARION is the preferred tune for congregational singing of this text, choir directors may want to consider using Richard Dirksen's anthem on his VINEYARD HAVEN tune (163) for choral festivals.

Liturgical Use

As a processional or recessional hymn for festive occasions; the "pilgrimage" theme may be suitable for Old/New Year services and for funerals.

562

VATER UNSER
♩ = 95

Our Father, Clothed with Majesty

Text

This third setting of the Lord's Prayer is an extended prayer *Scripture References*
based on the Heidelberg Catechism's teaching on the meaning   all st. = Matt. 6:9-13
of the prayer (see pp. 918-925 in the worship edition of the *Psalter
Hymnal*). The other settings are a prose chant version (207) and a two-stanza metrical
version also set to VATER UNSER (208). For general comments about the Lord's Prayer
see PHH 207 and 208.

Psalter Hymnal Revision Committee member Marie J. Post (PHH 5) prepared this
eight-stanza metrical version in 1984, following an earlier paraphrase written in 1931 by
Dewey Westra (PHH 98) for the 1934 *Psalter Hymnal*. Post found "rich and profound
meaning" in the catechism's teaching. The relationship of this text to the Heidelberg
Catechism is as follows:

stanza 1: Lord's Day 46, Q&A 120-121
stanza 2: Lord's Day 47, Q&A 122
stanza 3: Lord's Day 48, Q&A 123
stanza 4: Lord's Day 49, Q&A 124
stanza 5: Lord's Day 50, Q&A 125
stanza 6: Lord's Day 51, Q&A 126
stanza 7: Lord's Day 52, Q&A 127
stanza 8: Lord's Day 52, Q&A 128-129

Tune

For a discussion of VATER UNSER see PHH 208.

Liturgical Use

Ordinarily used with selected stanzas in services that focus on the Lord's Prayer
segment of the Heidelberg Catechism.

563

SONG 67
♩ = 50

God Works His Purposes in Us

Text

In 1981, after participating in a Bible study of Paul's letter to the Philippians, *Psalter
Hymnal* Revision Committee member Dale Topp (b. Holland, MI, 1937) was inspired

to write this text, a paraphrase of portions of Paul's letter. The text was first published in the 1987 *Psalter Hymnal*.

Although the letter includes Paul's expression of gratitude to the Philippians for their gift to him, it is primarily a pastoral letter of Christian advice and encouragement. Paul's exhortations, using an early Christian creed or hymn , emphasize joy (see Phil. 2:6-11 and *Psalter Hymnal* 227, 467). The beginning phrase of each stanza, "God works his purposes in us," is derived from Philippians 2:13. Those with a literary bent will note with suitably Philippian joy the tight internal rhymes in the third phrase of each stanza.

Topp was educated at Calvin College, Grand Rapids, Michigan, and the University of Michigan, Ann Arbor, and began teaching music in the Zeeland (Michigan) Christian Schools. Since 1967 he has been a professor of music education at Calvin College. He has published several music guides for Christian Schools International, edited various "Hymn of the Month" collections, and he wrote *Music in the Christian Schools* (1975). Topp was chair of the tune committee that prepared the 1987 *Psalter Hymnal.*

Scripture References
st. 1 = Phil. 1:3-11
st. 2 = Phil. 1:19-26
st. 3 = Phil. 2 :15-16
st. 4 = Phil. 3:1-14
st. 5 = Phil. 4:4-13

Tune

SONG 67 was published as a setting for Psalm 1 in Edmund Prys's Welsh *Llyfr y Psalmau* (1621). Erik Routley (PHH 31) suggests that the tune should be ascribed to Prys.

Orlando Gibbons (PHH 167) supplied a new bass line for the melody when it was published with a number of his own tunes in George Withers's *Hymnes and Songs of the Church* (1623). There it was a setting for the sixty-seventh song (thus the title), a paraphrase of Acts 1:12-26. The tune originally had "gathering" (long) notes at the beginning of each of the four phrases.

A rather sturdy tune, SONG 67 is built on a few melodic motives. Sing in harmony in two broad musical lines rather than four short phrases.

Liturgical Use

With preaching on Philippians; as a response to the sermon.

564

Fount of Love, Our Savior God

MAN-CHIANG-HUNG
♩ = 80

Text

The author of this text, Ernest Y. L. Yang (b. Wuxi, Jiangsu, China, 1899; d. China, 1984), served on the committee that prepared the interdenominational Chinese hymnbook *Hymns of Universal Praise* (1936). He wrote over two hundred hymns,

Scripture References
st. 1 = 1 John 1:5-7
st. 5 = Matt. 7:13-14

including melodies, arrangements, translations, and original texts. Regarded as an outstanding musicologist in China, he is known especially for his important two-volume history of ancient music in China, *Zhongkuo Gudai Yinyue Shigao* (1944). A graduate of St. John's University in Shanghai and Guanghua University, Yang taught at Yanjing University, the National Conservatory of Music, and Jinling Women's University.

Yang's hymn was translated into English by Frank W. Price (b. Sinchang, Che, China, 1895; d. Lexington, VA, 1974). A missionary to China for thirty years (1919-1949), Price was imprisoned by the Communist Chinese government for three years. After returning to the United States in 1952, he became director of the Missionary Research Library at Union Theological Seminary, New York City. This text is one of a number of Chinese hymns from *Hymns of Universal Praise* that Price translated and published in *Chinese Hymns by Chinese Writers* (1953). The text was also included in the East Asian Christian Conference songbook, *EEAC Hymnal* (1963), and the Asian-American United Methodist anthology, *Hymns from the Four Winds* (1983).

This pilgrimage text presents the petition "Savior God, be our guide" in the refrain. Sprinkled with delightful metaphors, expressive words, and biblical phrases, the text asks for divine illumination and guidance amid the pitfalls of life, for wholehearted devotion to the "narrow gate . . . that leads to life" (Matt. 7:13-14). The first time it was sung from the *Psalter Hymnal* was at the Ann Arbor Campus Chapel the Sunday after the confrontation in Tienamin Square on June 4, 1989.

Tune

Based on an ancient Chinese Tsu melody, MAN-CHIANG-HUNG (meaning "all red the river") was associated with a patriotic poem written by General Yueh-Fei. In 1980 the Chinese scholar and musician I-to Loh (b. Tamsui, Taipei, Taiwan, 1936) arranged this popular melody into a hymn tune for publication in *Hymns from the Four Winds* (1983).

Pentatonic and built on several melodic patterns, MAN-CHIANG-HUNG should be sung in unison with rather light accompaniment, perhaps with plucked strings. Other instruments such as flutes could play some delicate variations and grace notes on the unison melody. The subtle interplay of motives, dissonances, and open chords in the Oriental harmonization are characteristic and should not be westernized with triadic chords.

A world-renowned scholar and hymn composer, I-to Loh has contributed greatly to the development of non-Western hymnody. Not content to let Asian and African churches continue to imitate European and North American hymns, he has encouraged the development of indigenous church music in his travels to many different countries. Loh received his theological training at Tainan Theological College in Taiwan, studied composition at Union Theological Seminary in New York, and in 1982 received a Ph.D. in music from the University of California, Los Angeles. He is professor of church music and ethnomusicology at the Asian Institute for Liturgy and Music in Manila and at Tainan Theological College. In addition to the the well-known *Hymns from the Four Winds* (1983), he has edited hymn collections such as *New Songs of Asian*

Cities (1972), *African Songs of Worship* (1987), *Asian Songs of Worship* (1988), and *Sound the Bamboo* (1990). A composer of tunes for over sixty hymns and anthems, Loh is also the author of *Teach Us to Praise: In Search of Contextualized Church Music* (1988).

Liturgical Use

The initial stanzas, as a sung prayer for illumination before preaching; the entire hymn, after the sermon as a prayer for God's guidance on our journey through life; a fine anthem for a children's choir with accompaniment of plucked strings and flutes.

565

Abide with Us, Our Savior

CHRISTUS, DER IST MEIN LEBEN
♩ = 96

Text

Originally in six stanzas, Josua Stegmann's German text ("Ach bleib mit deiner Gnade") was published in the third edition of his *Suspiria Temporum* (1628). Our version includes the original stanzas 1-3 and an anonymous doxological stanza.

Scripture References
st. 1-3 = Luke 24:29

    The English translation of the first two stanzas is an anonymous translation found in the Lutheran *Church Book* (Philadelphia, 1868). The third stanza is derived from a translation by August Crull, whose hymn texts were published in various nineteenth-century Lutheran hymnals in the United States.

    The opening phrases in stanzas 1-3 ("Abide with us") recall the Emmaus travelers (Luke 24:29). The text is a prayer for guidance on our life's journey and for obedience to God's Word, particularly in the face of Satan's temptations.

    Josua Stegmann (b. Sülzfeld, near Meiningen, Germany, 1588; d. Rinteln, Germany, 1632) was a brilliant scholar and church administrator whose life was greatly troubled by the political and religious disturbances of his time. Educated at the University of Leipzig, he became a pastor in the Lutheran church in Stadthagen and a teacher at the gymnasium (high school) there in 1617. When the gymnasium became a university and moved to Rinteln, Stegmann was appointed professor of theology, but he fled the town in 1623 because of local battles in the Thirty Years' War. He returned to Rinteln in 1625, but his career was interrupted by the Edict of Restitution (1629), which ordered that all church estates (secularized in 1552) be returned to the Roman Catholic Church. The local Benedictine monks claimed possession of the university and the lands, which had been used to pay the professors' salaries. Stegmann was also harassed by soldiers coming to his home to claim a refund on his salary. Soon after these incidents he succumbed to illness and died in 1632. His devotional writings include verse written in Latin and a few hymn texts written in German.

Tune

Melchior Vulpius (PHH 397) composed this short chorale tune, published as a setting for the anonymous funeral hymn "Christus, der ist mein Leben" ("For Me to Live Is Jesus") in Vulpius's *Ein Schön Geistlich Gesangbuch* (1609). Johann S. Bach (PHH 7) based his Cantata 95 on this tune and provided two harmonizations, one in duple and the other in triple meter, in his *Choralgesänge*.

Sing stanzas 1-3 in harmony with suitably prayerful accompaniment. Sing the final stanza in unison with a more full registration on the organ.

Liturgical Use

As a sung prayer for illumination before the Service of the Word; for evening services; the close of worship; Old/New Year services and other times when embarking on new ventures in the church's ministries.

566

IN DIR IST FREUDE
♩ = 54

In You Is Gladness

Text

Cantor Johann Lindemann (b. Gotha, Thuringia, Germany, 1549; d. Gotha, 1631) wrote this text to fit the tune IN DIR IST FREUDE. It was published in Lindemann's *Amorum Filii Dei Decades Duae* (1598). Lindemann attended the gymnasium (high school) in Gotha and then studied at the University of Jena. He returned to Gotha, where he served on the council and became a cantor in several churches (1580-1631). One of the signers of the Lutheran Formula of Concord (1577), Lindemann published *Amorum Filii Dei Decades Duae* (1598), which included his "In You Is Gladness." Catherine Winkworth (PHH 194) prepared the English translation for the second series of her *Lyra Germanica* (1858).

Scripture References
st. 2 = Rom. 8:35-39
Heb. 4:14-16

The text confesses with joy the Christian's security of walking intimately with God through the ups and downs of daily life. The two long stanzas consist of various short biblical phrases and allusions woven into an integrated pattern of praise and petition, confession and rejoicing. All are punctuated by periodic "alleluias." The words of the text suggest Q&A 1 of the Heidelberg Catechism.

Tune

IN DIR IST FREUDE is one of many balletti (dance-like songs) written by Giovanni G. Gastoldi, a priest and composer from Mantua, Italy. It was originally published in his *Balletti a cinqve voce* (1591), where it was set to "Alieta vita, Amor ciinuita," which like so many balletti had a "fa-la-la" refrain.

Gastoldi served as a deacon and singer in the chapel of the Gonzaga family in Mantua. Succeeding Giaches de Wert, he directed music in the Church of Santa Barbaras in Mantua from 1592 to 1608. Little is known about the rest of his life. Gastoldi composed a considerable body of court music, such as madrigals, and some church music, but he is best known for his *Balletti,* which influenced composers such as Monteverdi, Hassler, and Morley.

The melody consists of short phrases formed into two sections, each repeated. The well-known organ prelude on this tune by Johann S. Bach (PHH 7) is cast into complex counterpoint (found in his *Orgelbuchlein*). But congregational singing and accompaniment should reflect the original character of lighthearted dance music. Sing in a swinging lively manner and strive for long musical phrases. Part singing is appropriate throughout, or try changing from unison to part singing (or vice versa) at the repeats of the A and B musical phrases. Maintain one pulse per measure.

Liturgical Use
Many occasions of worship in which encouragement and joy in Christ's saving work are appropriate in the face of "sin or death or night"; after Lord's Supper; funerals.

567

We've Come This Far by Faith

WE'VE COME THIS FAR
♩ = 92

Text

In a manner similar to many of the Old Testament lament psalms, this text affirms God's saving power in the past; God's compassion and providential care for his people throughout history give us hope for the future. Thus the text becomes a marker or milestone on life's journey: "we've come this far by faith, leaning on the Lord" (1 Sam. 7:12, "Thus far has the Lord helped us"). With confidence in the Lord's help we can go forward and face "burdens . . . misery and strife."

Scripture References
st. = 1 Sam. 7:12

Albert A. Goodson (b. Los Angeles, CA, 1933) wrote both text and tune in 1956 for the Radio Choir of the Fellowship Baptist Church in Chicago, Illinois, where he served as minister of music. The hymn was published as a gospel anthem by Manna Music in 1963. Goodson received his education at the University of California in Los Angeles and served Baptist churches in the Los Angeles area as well as the Fellowship Baptist Church in Chicago. As organist and pianist, he toured with Mahalia Jackson and has been a prominent figure in the development of African American gospel music.

Tune

Goodson's gospel song was included in the African American hymnal *Lift Every Voice and Sing* (1981). The setting by Richard Smallwood (PHH 365) displays some of the chord structures, melodic decorations, and rhythmic figures that are common in the African American gospel style. The printed score of gospel songs only conveys a guideline to actual performance; improvisation is the operative word! The congregation should sing the refrain (framed by "We've come this far by faith") aided by a choir who could improvise a harmony part. A soloist could sing the stanza ("Don't be discouraged . . .") with additional improvisation in the melody line and accompaniment. Try accompanying with piano, guitars, and percussion instruments. Don't rush!

Liturgical Use

After corporate confession of faith or personal profession of faith; Old/New Year services; at the beginning of a new season of worship and ministry.

568

HYFRYDOL
♩ = 126

Love Divine, All Loves Excelling

Text

Considered by many to be among Charles Wesley's (PHH 267) finest texts, "Love Divine" was published in four stanzas in his *Hymns for those that seek, and those that have Redemption in the Blood of Christ* (1747). Many hymnals, including the *Psalter Hymnal,* omit the original second stanza, which contained the questionable line "take away our power of sinning." A verse from John Dryden's poem beginning with the words "Fairest isle, all isles excelling" used by Henry Purcell in his opera *King Arthur* were undoubtedly Wesley's inspiration for writing this text. In fact, "Love Divine" was set to a Purcell tune in John and Charles Wesley's *Sacred Melody* (1761).

Scripture References
st. 1 = Rev. 21:3
John 3:16
John 15:9
st. 2 = Mal. 3:1
st. 3 = 2 Cor. 3:18
2 Cor. 5:17
2 Pet. 3:14

Addressed to Christ, this text begins as a prayer for the indwelling of his love in our lives: "fix in us thy humble dwelling" and "let us all thy life receive" (st. 1-2). A tone of praise and adoration runs throughout the text. But the final stanza is clearly a prayer for sanctification, for consistently holy lives. Though this stanza was an outcome of the specifically Wesleyan doctrine of perfection, it is our fervent Christian prayer that our sanctification will ultimately lead to glorification. As is customary in a Charles Wesley text, biblical allusions abound.

Tune

See PHH 479 for a discussion of HYFRYDOL.

Sing in harmony on stanzas 1 and 2. You may also want to sing the middle stanza unaccompanied. On the third stanza sing in unison, perhaps with an alternate accompaniment.

Liturgical Use
As a sung prayer, probably towards the end of the service or, given its tone of praise, as a closing hymn; Advent.

569

Praise the Lord with the Sound of Trumpet

PRAISE THE LORD
♩ = 76

Text

Somewhat similar to Francis of Assisi's "All Creatures of Our God and King" (431) and Herbert Brokering's "Earth and All Stars" (433), this text is a wonderful catalog of things, times, and places. All instruments and all occasions can be used to sing our praise to the Lord. Note that God's praise is warranted not only in the good times but also in "the time of sorrow" or in "the peace and quiet" (st. 2).

Scripture References
st. 1-2 = Ps. 148
Ps. 150

Natalie Sleeth (PHH 317) wrote both text and tune of this fine praise hymn in 1975 when she worked with church school children and a junior choir at Highland Park United Methodist Church in Dallas, Texas. "Praise the Lord" was one of twelve hymns published in Sleeth's *Sunday Songbook* (1976). It is also available separately as a choral anthem.

Tune

PRAISE THE LORD is a stirring tune in rounded bar form (AABA). It may be sung in unison throughout or, as is true with so many of Sleeth's compositions, as a two-part round. The keyboard extension should be played each time the hymn is sung in canon. The accompaniment, preferably on piano, should preserve the light texture of this tune. Try to emphasize the outer parts, perhaps by using several soprano instruments and string bass or bass guitar in addition to keyboard. Keep the energy of this music quite lively.

Liturgical Use

As the text suggests, "praise the Lord anytime and anywhere" and "everywhere in every way"!

FROM STRENGTH TO STRENGTH
♩ = 120

Soldiers of Christ, Arise

Text

Charles Wesley (PHH 267) wrote this text about the church militant in sixteen long stanzas. With the heading "The Whole Armour of God. Ephesians 6," it was published in the section entitled "Hymns for Believers" in Charles and John Wesley's *Hymns and Sacred Poems* (1749). Many later hymnals have included various segments of Wesley's original stanzas. Our present version is derived primarily from the original stanzas 1, 2, and 16.

Scripture References
st. 1 = Eph. 6:10-11
st. 2 = Eph. 6:14-17
st. 3 = Eph. 6:12-13, 18

Paul's exhortations in Ephesians 6:10-18 for Christians to "put on the full armor of God" and to fight against "the powers of this dark world and . . . the spiritual forces of evil" are clearly the inspiration for the text. Though the ancient imagery of armor may not be current, the battle against evil is real and urgent; the encouragement to "wrestle, fight, and pray" (st. 3) is also as timely in our day as it was in Roman times and in the eighteenth century when Wesley and his fellow Methodists faced strife and trial. A note of hope and triumph appears in the final stanza: the spiritual battle has already been won by Christ. The church militant will ultimately be the church victorious!

Tune

Edward W. Naylor (b. Scarborough, Yorkshire, England, 1867; d. Cambridge, England, 1934) composed FROM STRENGTH TO STRENGTH for this text in 1902 for use at Emmanuel College, Cambridge, England. Once a student at Emmanual, Naylor returned to become organist and lecturer in music history, a position he held until his death more than thirty years later. Named for the opening phrase of the final stanza, the tune was published in *The Public School Hymn Book* (1919).

Naylor also studied at the Royal College of Music in London, England, then served as organist at St. Michael, Chester Square (1889-1896), and briefly at St. Mary, Kilburn. He returned to Cambridge in 1897, becoming assistant master at the Leys School before accepting the position at Emmanuel College. A composer of much service music and many anthems, Naylor also received acclaim for his cantatas and operas and was known for his writings about music, including *Shakespeare and Music* (1896) and *The Poets and Music* (1928).

One of the most thrilling unison tunes in the *Psalter Hymnal*, FROM STRENGTH TO STRENGTH opens with a hunting-horn figure (perfect fourth), which permeates the entire melody. Supported by a marching rhythm, the tune moves to a convincing climax in the fourth line. The tune's "strength, life, radiance, and thrust" (Stanley L. Osborne) force congregations to take the spiritual battle seriously. Crisp rhythms in the accompaniment and the use of trumpets will aid this battle call.

Liturgical Use

With preaching from Ephesians 6; other occasions of worship when Christians must exhort each other to obey God's call to fight the powers of evil.

571

Jesus Loves Me, This I Know

JESUS LOVES ME
♩ = 60

Text

Anna B. Warner (b. Long Island, NY, 1827; d. Constitution Island, near West Point, NY, 1915) wrote this beloved children's hymn text in 1859. It was published in *Say and Seal* (1860), a novel Warner wrote in collaboration with her sister Susan, author of another popular children's hymn, "Jesus Bids Us Shine." In this now-forgotten novel a dying boy, Johnny Fax, is comforted by his church school teacher, who sings to him the four original stanzas of this hymn. Warner and her sister Susan wrote popular novels under the pen names Amy Lothrop and Elizabeth Wetherell. They also taught Bible classes for the cadets at West Point, who were ferried to the Warner home on Constitution Island. After she died, Warner was buried with military honors at West Point in honor of this service. She wrote devotional poetry and compiled two collections: *Hymns of the Church Militant* (1858) and *Wayfaring Hymns, Original and Translated* (1869).

Scripture References
st. 1 = Eph. 5:2
Jer. 31:3
st. 2 = Gal. 2:20
st. 3 = Matt. 18:2-4
Matt. 19:13-15
Mark 10:13-16
Luke 18:15-17

Both Anna and Susan Warner's writings are marked by what some judge to be "undistinguished religious sentimentality." But those who are critical of the text's simplicity may do well to remember what the great theologian Karl Barth once said when asked about his most profound theological discovery:

> Jesus loves me, this I know,
> for the Bible tells me so.

The text has been translated into many other languages. Our version includes the original stanzas 1 and 2 and adds a stanza derived from David R. McGuire's rewriting of the text, which he prepared for the Canadian Anglican and United *Hymn Book* (1971).

McGuire (b. St. Catherines, ON, Canada, 1929; d. Richmond Hill, ON, Canada, 1971) was educated at University College and Wycliffe College, both at the University of Toronto. Ordained in the Anglican Church, he served four congregations in Ontario, including Church of Christ the King in Etobicoke, Toronto (1959-1969). McGuire was strongly interested in hymnody and was on the committee that produced *The Hymn Book* (1971), published by two Canadian denominations—the Anglican Church and the United Church. He also edited a collection of contemporary folk hymns, *Sing I* (1972).

"Jesus Loves Me" weaves together some of the most basic truths of the childlike Christian's experience with the Lord: Jesus loves me, Jesus saves me, and Jesus invites me to come to him. The refrain simply emphasizes that we know Jesus' love from the Bible.

Tune
William B. Bradbury (PHH 114) added a refrain line to Warner's stanzas and wrote the tune JESUS LOVES ME in 1861. The hymn was published in Bradbury's church school collection *The Golden Shower* (1862). The tune is also known as CHINA in some hymnals, presumably because of its popularity among missionaries to that land.

Liturgical Use
A fine children's hymn of testimony to Jesus' love but also appropriate for children of God of all ages.

572

JESU, MEINE FREUDE
♩ = 96

Jesus, Priceless Treasure

Text

The original German text "Jesu, meine Freude" by Johann Franck (PHH 305) first appeared in Johann Crüger's *Praxis Pietatis Melica* (1653) in six long stanzas. The text was modeled in part after a love song found in Heinrich Albert's *Arein* (1641), "Flora, meine Freude, meiner Seele Weide."

Scripture References
st. 1 = Matt. 13:44-46
John 15:1-4
st. 3 = Ps. 73:25
Phil. 3:8

Catherine Winkworth (PHH 194) translated the text into English and published it in her *Chorale Book for England* (1863). Our version includes the original stanzas 1, 2, 4, and 6. Much loved by Christians from various traditions, "Jesus, Priceless Treasure" is one of the finest examples of German piety in a devotional hymn. The intensity of emotional expression found here provides a suitable counterbalance to the cerebral character of much Reformed worship.

Inspired by Jesus' parables of the great treasure and fine pearl (Matt. 13:44-46) and other New Testament references to the metaphor "treasure," this text is strongly Christocentric. Stanza 1 confesses with mystical ecstasy that Christ is the source of purest pleasure (a bold affirmation that counters the hedonism of this world). Stanza 2 expands the metaphor: Christ our treasure is also our fortress, our defense and protector from the "sin and hell" that would "assail" us. Stanza 3 contrasts the eternal pleasures of knowing Jesus with the "empty" delights of this world. And stanza 4 affirms that, despite the fears and sorrow we must bear, Jesus remains our greatest treasure and source of profound joy.

Tune

Johann Crüger (PHH 42) composed JESU, MEINE FREUDE, a bar form tune (AAB) written for this text. Johann S. Bach (PHH 7) incorporated the tune into his cantatas 12, 64, 81, and 87 and composed a beautiful motet and several organ preludes on the melody.

Sing this great chorale in harmony throughout. For more elaborate and meditative use intersperse the sung stanzas with organ preludes on the tune.

Liturgical Use

As a hymn of devotion and trust and a testimony of our joyous commitment to Christ amid the temptations of contemporary life; after Lord's Supper; profession of faith.

573

O Master, Let Me Walk with Thee

MARYTON
♩ = 112

Text

Washington Gladden (b. Pottsgrove, PA, 1836; d. Columbus, OH, 1918) wrote the original poem from which this text was taken. It was published in three long stanzas in the magazine he edited, *The Sunday Afternoon* (March 1879), with the title

Scripture References
st. 1 = 1 John 2:5-6
st. 3 = Gal. 5:16

"Walking with God." Gladden explained that his poem "had no liturgical purpose" but was intended as "an honest cry of human need, of the need for divine companionship."

Interestingly enough, this meditative text on Christian service (with a gentle quality confirmed by the use of the MARYTON tune) is the work of a man who, by the end of the nineteenth century, was considered to be a powerful spokesman and activist for the liberal "social gospel." Ordained in 1860, Gladden was a Congregational minister who served churches in New York, Massachusetts, and Ohio. He gained national prominence during his pastorate at the First Congregational Church in Columbus, Ohio (1882-1914), because of his advocacy of the church's strong role in issues of social justice for the laboring people and because of his use of modern methods of biblical criticism. Educated at Williams College, Williamstown, Massachusetts, Gladden edited the New York *Independent* and was one of the editors of the *Pilgrim Hymnal* (1904). Included in his many writings are *The Christian Way* (1877), *Applied Christianity* (1887), *Christianity and Socialism* (1905), and a fascinating essay, "Tainted Money" (1905), in which he criticized his denomination for accepting a $100,000 gift from Standard Oil's Rockefeller.

Charles H. Richards revised stanzas 1 and 3 of Gladden's poem and published them as a hymn text in four shorter stanzas in his *Songs of Christian Praise* (1880). Richards's revision appears in most modern hymnals. The text emphasizes that an intimate walk with God is expressed in Christian service to our neighbors: in bearing burdens (st. 1), in actions of love and patient leadership (st. 2-3), and in striving for hope and peace (st. 4).

Tune
After various tunes had been set to this text, Gladden insisted on the use of MARYTON. Composed by H. Percy Smith (b. Malta, 1825; d. Bournemouth, Hampshire, England, 1898), the tune was originally published as a setting for John Keble's "Sun of My Soul" in Arthur S. Sullivan's *Church Hymns with Tunes* (1874).

Henry Percy Smith was educated at Balliol College, Oxford, England, and ordained a priest in the Church of England in 1850. He served five churches, including St. Michael's York Town in Farnborough (1851-1868), Great Barton in Suffolk (1868-1882), Christ Church in Cannes, France (1882-1892), and the Cathedral in Gibraltar (1892-1898). MARYTON is his only tune found in contemporary hymnals and is thought to be the only tune he published.

MARYTON is a serviceable but generic nineteenth-century hymn tune; its wide-ranged melody reaches a high point in the middle phrases. Sing the first and final stanzas in unison and the middle stanzas in parts. Because textual and musical phrases are often at odds with each other in this hymn, a competent choir may aid the singing by following the punctuation and not breathing in the middle of textual phrases. Keep the tempo moving!

Liturgical Use
As a post-sermon hymn or prayer hymn; fitting for worship that focuses on Christian ministries in the world.

574

DARMSTADT
♩ = 92

O God, My Faithful God

Text
During the difficulties of the Thirty Years' War in the late 1620s, Johann Heermann (PHH 386) wrote the original German text ("O Gott, du frommer Gott") in his Silesian home of Koben. Entitled "A Daily Prayer," the text was published in Heermann's

Scripture References
st. 3 = Ps. 141:3
Isa. 50:4

Devoti Musica Cordis (1630). Nineteenth-century German hymnologist A. F. W. Fischer has said of this text, "It is one of the poet's most widely used and signally blessed hymns and has been not unjustly called his 'master song.' If it is somewhat 'home baked,' yet it is excellent, nourishing bread. It gives training in practical Christianity . . . in godly living."

Catherine Winkworth (PHH 194) translated the text into English and published it in her *Lyra Germanica* (second series, 1858). Our version includes the original stanzas 1-4. The text is a prayer for a Christlike mind (st. 1), obedience to our Lord's commands (st. 2), proper speech (st. 3), and a life of patience and peace (st. 4).

Tune

Composed by Ahasuerus Fritsch (b. Mücheln on the Geissel, near Merseburg, Germany, 1629; d. Rudolstadt, Germany, 1701), DARMSTADT first appeared in his *Himmels-Lust und Welt-Unlust* (1679). The melody was altered when it was published in the 1698 Darmstadt *Geistreiches Gesangbuch* and in several other eighteenth-century German hymnals. The tune is also known as O GOTT, DU FROMMER GOTT (named after the Heermann text) and as WAS FRAG ICH NACH DER WELT (named after an association with a text in the Darmstadt hymnal).

Fritsch grew up during the turbulent time of the Thirty Years' War, and his family was often forced to flee for their lives. He was educated at the University of Jena and later became chancellor of that university. He also served as president of the church's consistory in Rudolstadt and edited two collections of hymns.

The harmonization comes from Cantata 45 by Johann S. Bach (PHH 7); he also used the tune in cantatas 64, 94, and 133. This noble tune has short phrases that should be sung in four long lines; observe small fermatas at the end of each of the first two lines. Use solid organ tone to support congregational singing in unison or in parts. Keep the energy lively.

Liturgical Use

As a hymn of petition for Christian virtues either after the sermon or as part of a cycle of sung and spoken prayers; profession of faith; ordination/commissioning services.

575

Christian, Do You Struggle

ST. ANDREW OF CRETE
♩ = 54

Text

The original version of this text, "Christian, Dost Thou See Them," was published by John M. Neale (PHH 342) in his *Hymns of the Eastern Church* (1862). There it was said to be a translation of a Greek hymn by Andrew of Crete (660-732). Because no such Greek text has ever been found, most scholars now assume that Neale wrote the text. But it does reflect the spirit of St. Andrew, who battled vigorously for the gospel in early Christian history. Various hymnal editors have made small

Scripture References
st. 1 = Eph. 6:10-17
st. 2 = Mark 14:38
Col. 4:2

alterations in the text. Bert Polman prepared a modernized version in 1985 for the 1987 *Psalter Hymnal.*

"Christian, Do You Struggle" is one of a number of Christian battle hymns that uses the spiritual warfare imagery Paul sets forth in Ephesians 6:10-18. The Christian battle is "not against flesh and blood" but against the "powers of this dark world and against the spiritual forces of evil." It is a deadly serious battle that requires Christians to "put on the full armor of God," which his Word and Spirit provide. This spiritual warfare is against sinful cultures and their authorities in the external world (st. 1) but also against the tempting powers of sin within (st. 2), which may lead to doubt and unbelief (st. 3). Each stanza concludes by taking seriously Paul's advice to "put on the full armor of God," "stand firm," and "pray in the Spirit."

Tune

John B. Dykes (PHH 147) composed ST. ANDREW OF CRETE for this text. The hymn was published in the 1868 *Appendix* to *Hymns Ancient and Modern.*

ST. ANDREW OF CRETE is one of a few tunes in the *Psalter Hymnal* that shifts from minor to major tonality (see also CREDO, 127 and NEW HEAVEN, 236). The initial soprano monotone is mercifully balanced by more interesting harmony. Erik Routley (PHH 31) claims that the "prowling" harmony is an example of Dykes's attempt at word painting. Sing in parts throughout. A fine alternate tune for congregational singing in unison is the more inspired KING'S WESTON by Ralph Vaughan Williams (467).

Liturgical Use

The tone of encouragement and hope in this hymn will be useful in various personal contexts of Christian warfare against evil; may also serve as a battle cry and prayer for the entire Christian community.

576

GENEVAN 51
♩ = 72

A Congregational Lament

Text

In 1983 Calvin Seerveld (PHH 22) wrote this prayer hymn in Toronto, Canada, for use with GENEVAN 51; he revised it in 1986 for publication in the 1987 *Psalter Hymnal.*

Scripture References
st. 1 = Ps. 44:9-26

The text is a modern lament, a contemporary prayer in the style of the biblical laments in the psalms. Most Old Testament laments cry to God for help in some situation of need and offer words of encouragement and trust in God's saving deeds. Much Christian hymnody is devoid of such biblical lamenting in specific times of need and pain—the psalms clearly fill this void.

As the *Psalter Hymnal* indicates, gender-specific terms may be used interchangeably as appropriate to the person(s) on whose behalf this lament is raised. The intention is that two stanzas will ordinarily be sung: always the first, which recognizes sin in our lives, and then a later stanza, which suits a specific situation—imprisonment (st. 2), illness (st. 3), divorce (st. 4), untimely death (st. 5), and other occasions of pain and sorrow (st. 6). Although the stanzas would not ordinarily be sung in sequence, Seerveld does provide a common refrain in the latter half of each of the "situation" stanzas.

Tune
See discussion of the hauntingly beautiful GENEVAN 51 at 51; Psalm 51 is one of the psalms of lament. Unison may be most appropriate for congregational singing of this lament. Though suitably solemn, this melody should not be sung too slowly.

Liturgical Use
Always sing the first stanza and one other stanza; fitting for confession of sin early in worship or as part of the congregational prayers (a spoken introduction that refers to the specific situation may be helpful); funerals.

577

Beams of Heaven

SOME DAY
♩ = 80

Text
African American preacher Charles A. Tindley (b. Berlin, MD, 1851; d. Philadelphia, PA, 1933) was also a composer who wrote most of his church music for the East Calvary Methodist Episcopal Church, which he founded in Philadelphia. His church choir performed many gospel concerts.

Scripture References
st. 1 = 1 John 1:5-7
st. 3 = 2 Cor. 4:8-10
Rev. 22:1-6

Although probably written earlier in the century, Tindley's "Beams of Heaven" was published in 1916 in his *New Songs of Paradise* (copy available in the Library of Congress). Strongly apocalyptic, the text expresses the Christian's confidence that when "Jesus leads me, I shall get home someday." That ultimate certainty gives hope and encouragement for our daily walk with God. Stanzas 1 and 2 use the rich Old Testament Exodus imagery of light and darkness to refer to times of joy and sorrow. The third stanza points from current troubles (see 2 Cor. 4:8-10) to the vision of a new creation, to "that land of peace and glory" (see Rev. 22:1-6).

The son of slave parents, Tindley taught himself to read and write and moved to Philadelphia, where he worked initially as a janitor for the John Wesley Methodist Church (later Calvary Methodist) and took correspondence courses from Boston University School of Theology. Ordained a Methodist pastor in 1885, he served several congregations in Delaware, Maryland, and New Jersey before returning in 1902 to

Calvary Methodist in Philadelphia. Under his ministry the church thrived as a multi-ethnic congregation. Tindley wrote the texts and tunes to forty-five gospel hymns, including "I'll Overcome Some Day" (1901), which became the inspiration for the well-known Civil Rights Movement theme song "We Shall Overcome."

Tune

Tindley's early twentieth-century gospel music is often considered to be the immediate forerunner of the rise of the African American gospel style associated with Thomas Dorsey (PHH 493).

SOME DAY consists of a few melodic motives, which are varied in triple meter. The refrain melody is a repeat of the latter half of the tune. The hymnal arrangement was prepared by Dale Grotenhuis (PHH 4). Sing in parts.

Liturgical Use

As a testimonial and visionary hymn about God's guidance of our lives from this world to eternity; also for funerals and other homecoming/going occasions.

578

ABERYSTWYTH
♩ = 92

Jesus, Lover of My Soul

Text

Charles Wesley (PHH 267) wrote this text sometime after his conversion in 1738. The five-stanza text was published in John and Charles Wesley's *Hymns and Sacred Poems* (1740). Because the words of the original opening couplets were considered to be too intimate for public worship, many hymnal editors made textual changes before publishing "Jesus, Lover of My Soul" in various nineteenth-century hymnals.

Originally entitled "In Temptation," this text develops the imagery of the troubled person adrift in a storm of temptation. That person can find a sure refuge only in Jesus Christ.

Scripture References
st. 1 = Ps. 57:1
Ps. 32:6-7
Matt. 11:28
st. 2 = Ps. 91:4
Ps. 141:8
st. 3 = Ps. 32:1-2
Rev. 21:6b
John 4:14

Tune

For a discussion of ABERYSTWYTH see PHH 18.

The tune's musical contour is a fine match for this text. It climbs from its initial minor phrases through a touch of major to a convincing high point in the final line before settling to a solemn close. Sing in parts throughout at a restrained pace to permit all the eighth notes to sound clearly. ABERYSTWYTH is set in the key of D at 18, which also provides a canonic harmonization that could be used effectively on stanza 2.

Liturgical Use

For times of temptation (as Wesley suggests); as a hymn of prayer following the sermon; with sermons on crossing the Red Sea, Jonah drowning, Peter walking on water, and other situations in which the cosmological imagery of refuge from the waters of chaos is appropriate.

579

What a Friend We Have in Jesus

BEACH SPRING
♩ = 80

Text

Joseph M. Scriven (b. Seapatrick, County Down, Ireland, 1819; d. Bewdley, Rice Lake, ON, Canada, 1886), an Irish immigrant to Canada, wrote this text near Port Hope, Ontario, in 1855. Because his life was filled with grief and trials, Scriven often needed the solace of the Lord as described in his famous hymn. Educated at Trinity College, Dublin, Ireland, he enrolled in a military college to prepare for an army career. However, poor health forced him to give up that ambition. Soon after came a second blow—his fiancee died in a drowning accident on the eve of their wedding in 1844. Later that year he moved to Ontario, where he taught school in Woodstock and Brantford. His plans for marriage were dashed again when his new bride-to-be died after a short illness in 1855. Following this calamity Scriven seldom had a regular income, and he was forced to live in the homes of others. He also experienced mistrust from neighbors who did not appreciate his eccentricities or his work with the underprivileged. A member of the Plymouth Brethren, he tried to live according to the Sermon on the Mount as literally as possible, giving and sharing all he had and often doing menial tasks for the poor and physically disabled. Because Scriven suffered from depression, no one knew if his death by drowning in Rice Lake was suicide or an accident.

Scripture References
st. 1 = John 15:15
Eph. 6:18
1 Thess. 5:17
st. 3 = Matt. 11:28-30

Scriven wrote "What a Friend" to comfort his sick mother in Dublin, possibly right after the death of his second fiancee. When asked by a neighbor about his writing of the text, Scriven modestly commented, "The Lord and I did it between us." The text was published anonymously in Horace Hastings's *Social Hymns, Original and Selected* (1865), but Scriven was given proper credit in Hastings's *Songs of Pilgrimage* (1886). Ira D. Sankey (PHH 73) included the text, set to the familiar tune by Charles C. Converse, in his various hymnals (from 1875 on).

Scriven's text clearly arises from his own experiences in life. Although not great poetry, the text has spiritual appeal and an effective repeated phrase, "take it to the Lord in prayer." Because of its simple encouragement to "pray without ceasing," the text is much loved in many circles of Christendom. A collection of his poetry was published in *Hymns and Other Verses* (1869).

Tune

British hymnals have set Scriven's text to various tunes, including BLAENWERN (416), a fine alternate choice. The choice of BEACH SPRING represents a change from the text's traditional association in North America with CONVERSE, a tune written in 1868 for "What a Friend" by Charles C. Converse. Although that combination is also found in previous editions of the *Psalter Hymnal,* the revision committee decided to use BEACH SPRING for this text.

BEACH SPRING was first published in *The Sacred Harp* (1844) as a setting for Joseph Hart's "Come, Ye Sinners, Poor and Wretched" (534). The tune appears in *The Sacred Harp* (1844) with note values almost identical to those in the *Psalter Hymnal* but barred in duple rather than triple meter.

Benjamin F. White (b. Spartanburg, SC, 1800; d. Atlanta, GA, 1879), coeditor of *The Sacred Harp* (1844), was listed as the composer. The tune is named after the Beach Spring Baptist Church in Harris County, Georgia, where White lived. He came from a family of fourteen children and was largely self-taught. Eventually White became a popular singing-school teacher and editor of the weekly Harris County newspaper.

BEACH SPRING is a strong, pentatonic tune cast into a rounded bar form (AABA). A. Royce Eckhardt (b. Scottsbluff, Nebraska, 1937) wrote the harmonization, which was first published in *The Covenant Hymnal.* A graduate of North Park College, Chicago, Illinois, and the University of Hartford in Connecticut, Eckhardt has served as minister of music in Covenant Church congregations in Washington, Connecticut, and Illinois. He has also taught at North Park Theological Seminary in Chicago and was music editor of the *Covenant Hymnal* (1973).

Liturgical Use

As a hymn of encouragement to pray amid the "sins and griefs" we encounter on our journey of life.

580

O Perfect Love

O PERFECT LOVE
♩ = 58

Text

One Sunday evening in 1884 at Pull Wyke, Cumberland, England, Dorothy Francis Blomfield (later Gurney; b. London, England, 1858; d. Kensington, London, 1932) wrote this text for her sister's wedding. The hymn tune STRENGTH AND STAY

Scripture References
st. 1 = Matt. 19:4-6
Eph. 3:19
1 Cor. 13:7, 13

by John B. Dykes (PHH 147) was her sister's favorite, but that hymn's text (by Ellerton and Hort) included the line "the brightness of a holy death-bed," which made it inappropriate for a wedding. So her sister challenged her to write a new text to fit that tune.

At a later time Gurney said:

> After about 15 minutes I came back with the hymn, "O Perfect Love," and there and then we all sang it to the tune of "O Strength and Stay." . . . The writing of it was no effort whatever after the initial idea came to me of the two-fold aspect of a perfect union, love and life, and I have always felt that God helped me to write it.

The text was published in the 1889 *Supplement* to *Hymns Ancient and Modern* with a reference to Ruth 1:17. Because of its use at the wedding of Princess Louise and the Duke of Fife that same year, it gained much popularity. Thereafter its place in many hymnals and at many weddings was assured.

"O Perfect Love" is a prayer that Christ's love and life may infuse a wedding couple's new life together. The text, however, would be stronger if it contained a direct address to God or Christ in more customary biblical terms.

In 1897, several years after her sister's wedding, Dorothy Blomfield also married. She and her husband, Gerald Gurney, were both children of Anglican clergymen. Initially an actor, Gerald was later ordained in the Church of England. But in 1919 Gerald and Dorothy joined the Roman Catholic community at Farnborough Abbey. Dorothy Gurney wrote several volumes of verse, including *A Little Book of Quiet,* which contained the once well-known poem "God's Garden."

Tune

Joseph Barnby (PHH 438) composed O PERFECT LOVE and said it was a "hymn tune in the natural style and idiom . . . of our own time." Originally an anthem, O PERFECT LOVE was shortened into a hymn tune for publication in *The Hymnal Companion* (1890) and in the *Church Hymnary* (1898). The tune is also known as FIFE and SANDRINGHAM.

Erik Routley (PHH 31) calls Barnby's hymn tunes "shamelessly sentimental." O PERFECT LOVE is surely an example of what he means (Barnby's tunes at 438 and 447 are not). Sometimes thought to be the most notorious product of the Victorian composers, this tune is often performed with too much rubato and in a sentimental manner too often associated with weddings. Sing it in unison at a cheerful pace.

Liturgical Use

Weddings (sparingly); renewal of wedding vows in family services with a marriage renewal emphasis.

581

CROSS OF JESUS
♩ = 96

Lord, Today Bless This New Marriage

Text
Marie J. Post (PHH 5) wrote this text in 1966 in Grand Rapids, Michigan, for her son Jack's wedding. It was first published in the *Psalter Hymnal Supplement* (1974) and revised for publication in the 1987 *Psalter Hymnal.*

The text's phrases were inspired by words from the prayer that concludes the traditional wedding formulary of the Christian Reformed Church (*Psalter Hymnal,* pp. 1008-1009).

Tune
Composed by John Stainer (PHH 127), CROSS OF JESUS comes from his oratorio *The Crucifixion* (1887), where it was a setting for J. Sparrow-Simpson's text "Cross of Jesus, cross of sorrow" (thus the tune's title).

CROSS OF JESUS is an excellent congregational tune with a strong harmonization. Sing in unison with confident organ support. A better known and more accessible alternate tune for wedding services is STUTTGART.

Liturgical Use
Towards the close of a wedding service as a sung prayer.

582

JUDAS MACCABEUS
♩ = 63

Praised Be the Father

Text
Calvin Seerveld (PHH 22) wrote this celebratory text for his own wedding ceremony (he married Ines C. N. ten Cate on Sep. 8, 1956, in Den Haag, the Netherlands). Because George F. Handel's JUDAS MACCABEUS was his fiancee's favorite tune, Seerveld wrote this text to fit that tune. A church choir from Hoorn, the Netherlands, helped the Dutch congregation sing the hymn during the ceremony. Set to Handel's tune, the text was first published in the *Psalter Hymnal Supplement* (1974).

"Praised Be the Father" is a wedding prayer that fittingly combines praise and petition. The stanzas are in a trinitarian pattern. Each one is structured in the design of a liturgical collect: the divinity is praised for some attribute or quality, petitions are made, and a doxology is sung.

Tune

JUDAS MACCABEUS is an arrangement of a tune from the chorus "See, the Conquering Hero Comes" in Handel's oratorio *Judas Maccabeus* (first performed without this chorus in 1746). Handel initially used the tune in his oratorio *Joshua* (1747) but transferred it to *Judas Maccabeus* in 1751; such changes were common in Handel's operas and oratorios. Handel is reported to have said to a friend, "you will live to see it [the tune] a greater favorite with the people than my other finer things."

The tune's first appearance in a hymnal was probably in Thomas Butts's *Harmonia Sacra* (around 1760) where it was set to Charles Wesley's "Christ the Lord Is Risen Today" (388). This melody, also known as MACCABEUS, is the setting for Edmond Budry's Easter text "A toi la gloire" ("Thine Be the Glory") in a number of modern hymnals.

Including the refrain, JUDAS MACCABEUS is cast in a rounded bar form (AABA). Sing in unison or in parts. This tune merits the use of trumpets or a brass ensemble in addition to festive, crisp articulation of organ tones.

Georg Friederich Handel (b. Halle, Germany, 1685; d. London, England, 1759) became a musician and composer despite objections from his father, who wanted him to become a lawyer. Handel studied music with Zachau, organist at the Halle Cathedral, and became an accomplished violinist and keyboard performer. He traveled and studied in Italy for some time and then settled permanently in England in 1713. Although he wrote a large number of instrumental works, he is known mainly for his Italian operas, oratorios (including *Messiah*, 1741), various anthems for church and royal festivities, and organ concertos, which he interpolated into his oratorio performances. He composed only three hymn tunes, one of which (GOPSAL) still appears in some modern hymnals. A number of hymnal editors, including Lowell Mason (PHH 96), took themes from some of Handel's oratorios and turned them into hymn tunes (see ANTIOCH, 337).

Liturgical Use

As a processional or initial hymn at wedding services; for renewal of wedding vows in family services with a marriage renewal emphasis.

583

The Tender Love a Father Has

TALLIS' ORDINAL
♩ = 54

Text

Psalm 103 is one of the most beloved in the entire psalter. This paraphrase from the 1912 *Psalter* includes verses 13-18, which emphasize God's love for his frail human creatures. Such love is an example for our relationships in family life and, by extension, in all of God's family, his church. Other settings of this psalm are found at 103, 297, and 475.

Scripture References
st. 1 = Ps. 103:13
st. 2 = Ps. 103:14-15a
st. 3 = Ps. 103:15b-16
st. 4 = Ps. 103:17a
st. 5 = Ps. 103:17b-18

Tune

TALLIS' ORDINAL is one of nine psalm tunes Thomas Tallis (PHH 62) composed for Matthew Parker's *The Whole Psalter translated into English Metre* (undated, but around 1567). This collection also included TALLIS CANON (441). TALLIS' ORDINAL received its name from its association with a revised translation of the Latin hymn "Veni, Creator Spiritus" (425, 426) in the Ordinal (Ordination Liturgy) of the 1549 Prayer Book.

The earliest-known hymn tune in common meter, it was published with the melody in the upper voice, although at that time the primary melody was usually assigned to the tenor. The tune's structure is very simple: first and third phrases are identical, and the fourth phrase repeats the second one at the interval of a fifth below. Tallis provided the harmonization except for some added thirds in opening and cadence chords (try omitting those thirds for a more "authentic" sound). Sing in parts, perhaps reserving unison for the final stanza. A gentle accompaniment fits this text.

Liturgical Use

Worship that emphasizes God's compassion for his people; family life services; see PHH 103 for other suggestions.

584

BROOKSIDE
♩ = 116

How Shall the Young Direct Their Way?

Text

This text from the 1912 *Psalter* is a paraphrase of the "Beth" (second letter of the Hebrew alphabet) stanza of Psalm 119. In these verses of the psalm (9-16), directed specifically at the young, the psalmist professes delight in God's word (or law) as a guide for living. But that word also calls for obedience from all God's creatures, young and old alike. (See 119 and 276 for other settings of Psalm 119.)

Scripture References
st. 1 = Ps. 119:9
st. 2 = Ps. 119:10-11
st. 3 = Ps. 119:12-14
st. 4 = Ps. 119:15-16

Tune

Roy Hopp (PHH 11) composed BROOKSIDE in May 1981 for use with "O Jesus, Joy of Loving Hearts" (307) at a communion service. The tune is named for Brookside Christian Reformed Church, Grand Rapids, Michigan, where Hopp was choir director when he wrote the tune.

BROOKSIDE has a somewhat angular melodic contour; it has strong ascending intervals and a comforting stepwise descent in the final phrase. The harmonization invites part singing.

Liturgical Use

Before or after the reading of the Decalogue or another law text (consider using just st. 3-4 at this time); the entire hymn is appropriate for services that emphasize youth or Christian education.

585

WEYMOUTH
♩ = *116*

Let Children Hear the Mighty Deeds

Text

This versification of Psalm 78:1-8 is a modernized form of Isaac Watts's (PHH 155) version, published in his *Psalms of David Imitated* (1719). Psalm 78 is a didactic psalm of history. It teaches all of God's people to remember God's merciful dealings with them, to refrain from repeating the sins Israel committed in olden days, and to obey the word of the Lord (see PHH 78 for further comments on the psalm).

Scripture References
st. 1 = Ps. 78:1-4
st. 2 = Ps. 78:5-7

The text emphasizes the joyful covenant responsibility of parents to teach diligently the ways of the Lord to their children. Its theme comes from verses 4-5; there the biblical text combines a stress on God's savings deeds, which lead to faith, and God's commandments, which demand obedience. The command to "tell your children" runs throughout the Pentateuch (Ex. 10:2; Deut. 4:9).

Tune

See PHH 75 for discussion of WEYMOUTH.

Liturgical Use

Baptism; other occasions of worship that stress the covenant responsibility of one generation to teach the next generation not to forget God's deeds but to keep his commands (see Ps. 78:6-7); family life emphases; beginning of church school season.

586

In Our Households, Heavenly Father

CAPTIVITY
♩ = *80*

Text

Psalter Hymnal Revision Committee member Marie J. Post (PHH 5) wrote this text for publication in the 1974 *Psalter Hymnal Supplement*. It was written to fill a gap in the 1959 *Psalter Hymnal*,

Scripture References
st. 3 = 1 Pet. 4:9

which contained very few hymns with an emphasis on home and family. The 1987 *Psalter Hymnal* includes stanzas 1-3 of the original text.

"In Our Households" is a prayer for love, peace, joy, and charity in the home; for obedience to divine discipline; and a life of hospitality and service. Because this prayer seemed to focus mainly on married people, Rolf Bouma added a new third stanza in 1991 when he was pastor of Eastern Avenue Christian Reformed Church, Grand Rapids, Michigan, to acknowledge the increasing number of single adults and parents who also form households:

> And in single life or married,
> make us open to your call
> to encourage, comfort others,
> and show love to one and all.

Tune
CAPTIVITY is a traditional Latvian folk tune; it is also known as KAS DZIEDAJA from the Latvian poem associated with the tune. The title CAPTIVITY is derived from its more recent use (especially in post-Vatican II Roman Catholicism) with Ewald Bash's para-phrase of Psalm 137, which begins "By the Babylonian rivers."

CAPTIVITY is a rather reflective tune, almost haunting in its minor mode. It has a stunning octave rise at the beginning of the second long line. The tune is suitable for either unison or part singing. Accompany with modest organ tones or strings (guitars).

Liturgical Use
The family theme of this hymn can and should be extended to mean all of God's family throughout the world; family life services; weddings; cell groups or household worship times.

587

LEICESTER
♩ = 52

O God in Heaven

Text
The British editor of *The Baptist Hymn Book Companion,* Hugh Martin (b. Glasgow, Scotland, 1890; d. East Grinstead, Sussex, England, 1964), wrote this text. It was chosen as one of thirteen finalists from among some 450 new texts submitted to the Hymn Society of America on the topic of "Home and Family." The text was first published in a Hymn Society pamphlet, *Thirteen New Marriage and Family Life Hymns* (1961). This publication was the result of a joint project by the Department of Family Life of the National Council of Churches (U.S.), the Canadian Council of Churches, and the Hymn Society of America. Their mandate was to find new hymns that "recognize the

fundamental nature of marriage and family life; express the Christian ideals which should guide such relationships; and stress the responsibility of the church for developing and maintaining such ideals."

"O God in Heaven" is united by the refrain's prayer for divine blessing on family life. The four stanzas confirm God's care in our lives when he gave us Christian parents and homes and fellowship in times of "joy and sorrow, work and play" (st. 1-2). The text presents a prayer for forgiveness and wisdom as young and old relate together (st. 3) and a prayer for joy in doing daily tasks—"housework," which every member should share with "delight" (st. 4). The humble gratitude for the ordinary aspects of family living and the sensitivity to the good and bad times exhibited in this text are attitudes that seem increasingly scarce in our hurried and often broken family lives.

Educated at Glasgow University, Martin studied for the Baptist ministry. From 1914 to 1950 he was active in the Student Christian Movement and served as the editor of its press. He later served as the moderator of the Free Church Federal Council and chairman of the executive committee of the British Council of Churches. One of his many publications, *They Wrote Our Hymns* (1961), is a notable book about the work of the great hymn writers.

Tune
See discussion of LEICESTER at PHH 139.

Liturgical Use
As a homemaker's prayer in family life services of various kinds (also fitting for doing the laundry and other chores during weekdays).

588

Tell Your Children

TELL YOUR CHILDREN
♩ = 58

Text
J. Grace Hawthorne (b. Salem, NJ, 1946) wrote this text based on the main theme of the Hebrew acrostic hymn, Psalm 145: all peoples should praise God for his mighty acts, which testify to his compassion and his great power. This hymn thus becomes our cheerleading song as we "Glorify the living Lord above [and] magnify his holy name."

Hawthorne is a freelance writer living in Atlanta, Georgia. Educated as a journalist at Louisiana State University, she has also worked as a newspaper writer and as an editor in the book division of Time, Inc. Her publications include hymn texts and lyrics for opera and children's musicals, including *It's Cool in the Furnace* (1973).

Tune

Thomas E. Fettke (b. Bronx, New York City, 1941), a senior editor for Word Inc., composed TELL YOUR CHILDREN for this text. The hymn was published in *Lord, We Believe* (1980).

Educated at Oakland City College and California State University, Hayward, Fettke has taught in several public and Christian high schools and served as minister of music in various churches, all in California. He has published over eight hundred compositions and arrangements (some under the pseudonyms Robert F. Douglas and David J. Allen) and produced a number of recordings. Fettke was the senior editor of *The Hymnal for Worship and Celebration* (1986).

The tune TELL YOUR CHILDREN is framed by a repeated opening line and a repeated closing phrase. The refrain builds to a solid climax with its highest tone on the word "Lord," to whom this song directs our praise. TELL YOUR CHILDREN is suitable for either unison or part singing, but the refrain needs a convincing sense of power and majesty from singers and accompanists. This is a great piece for a brass ensemble.

Liturgical Use

After infant baptism; profession of faith by young people; family life services; beginning of church school seasons and Vacation Bible School.

589

ST. BOTOLPH
♩ = 120

Our Father, Whose Creative Love

Text

Albert F. Bayly (PHH 293) wrote this text in February 1966 and published it in his *Again I Say Rejoice* (1967). The *Psalter Hymnal* includes his original stanzas 1-3 and 5.

The text is a prayer hymn by and for parents for divine blessing on the raising of children and youth. As we sing stanza 1, we recognize God's gift of life in the act of procreation and his image in the life of each child. In stanzas 2 and 3 we pray that parents will be faithful in their covenant obligations in raising children to be wholesome persons, whose bodies and souls are nourished by biblical wisdom. Stanza 4 concludes this prayer with a petition for the consecrating work of the Holy Spirit in the dealings of all parents with their children.

Tune

ST. BOTOLPH was composed by Gordon A. Slater (b. Harrogate, Yorkshire, England, 1896; d. Lincoln, England, 1979) and first published in *Songs of Praise for Boys and Girls* (1930).

The tune was named for St. Botolph's Parish Church in Boston, Lincolnshire, England, where Slater was organist from 1919 to 1927, following his service in the British army in France during World War I. That church honors St. Botolph, the seventh-century abbot of an influential monastery thought to have been near Iken, northeast of Ipswich in Suffolk, a monastery destroyed during the Danish invasions. Also from 1919 to 1927, Slater was conductor of the Boston Choral Society. He then served at Leicester Cathedral from 1927 to 1930. Organist and choirmaster at Lincoln Cathedral from 1930 to 1966, Slater supervised the rebuilding of the cathedral's organ in 1960. During those years he was also the conductor of the Lincoln Symphony Orchestra. He taught at various British colleges and universities and was a well-known organ recitalist for the BBC. In addition to piano and organ music, Slater composed anthems and hymn tunes.

As originally intended by Slater, ST. BOTOLPH is best sung in unison. Music theory students may delight in finding some parallel fifths in the harmonization. Sing and accompany in two long lines rather than in four short phrases. "Jesus, the Very Thought of You" (480) is often sung to ST. BOTOLPH in British churches..

Liturgical Use
Infant baptism; family life services (note that the emphasis is on parents).

590

Jesus, Our Mighty Lord

ROSE-MARIE
♩ = 112

Text
Titus Flavius Clemens, known as Clement of Alexandria (b. Athens, Greece, c. 170; d. Palestine [?], c. 220), was a student of Greek philosophy who was converted to the Christian faith. One of his poems, translated as "Hymn of the Savior Christ," featured a series of metaphors, some biblical, addressed to Christ, and became one of the earliest known Christian hymn texts. It was appended to the third section of a treatise called *The Tutor* (around 200); both the treatise and the hymn were evidently used in the catechizing of new converts to Christianity. An important philosopher and theologian in the Eastern church, Clement became head of the famous catechetical school in Alexandria, where he stressed Christ, the Word, as the true teacher. In 202 Clement fled from Alexandria to Palestine because the Christians were being persecuted. Little is known of his later life.

Scripture References
st. 2 = Ezek. 34:11-16
st. 3 = Eph. 5:19-20

The traditional translation of his Greek text begins "Shepherd of Tender Youth." An English version was prepared by Henry Dexter in 1846 (see the 1959 *Psalter Hymnal*, 414). Like other recent hymnals, the 1987 *Psalter Hymnal* provides a paraphrase of the text by F. Bland Tucker (PHH 247). That version, prepared for *The Hymnal 1982*, borrows from Tucker's older paraphrase of Clement's text, which appeared as "Master of Eager Youth" in *The Hymnal 1940*.

Tucker's more recent paraphrase includes some of the most important New Testament expressions for the Savior: Jesus, our Lord, is the Word (st. 1); the Good Shepherd and the Way (st. 2); and the God of peace (st. 3).

Tune

ROSE-MARIE was one of several tunes submitted for this text during a hymn search announced by the *Psalter Hymnal* Revision Committee. Dutch musician Wim Mennes composed ROSE-MARIE for this text in 1984 in Noordwolde, the Netherlands. The tune is named in honor of Mennes's daughter.

ROSE-MARIE thrives on melodic repetitions and sequences. Sing in unison. Accompany modestly at first but use greater force for the final stanza.

Liturgical Use

With preaching on New Testament texts that concern Christ as the Word, Shepherd, Way, King, and Savior; profession of faith by young people; family life and youth services.

591

RHUDDLAN
♩ = 56

Savior, Like a Shepherd Lead Us

Text

Although sometimes ascribed to either Henry F. Lyte (PHH 442) or Dorothy A. Thrupp, in whose *Hymns for the Young* (fourth ed., 1836) it appeared, this text is the work of an unknown author. The original four stanzas appear in the *Psalter Hymnal* with the modern pronouns ("you" rather than "thou").

Scripture References
st. 1-2 = Ps. 23
John 10:18

The text is a prayer for divine guidance and obedience to God's will. Psalm 23 and the parable of the good shepherd (John 10:18) were the inspiration for stanzas 1 and 2; the remaining stanzas contain other biblical phrases.

Tune

RHUDDLAN is a traditional Welsh tune used by harp-playing folk musicians. Named after the historic village in northern Wales, the tune was published in the musical edition of Edward Jones's *Musical and Poetical Relicks of the Welsh Bards* (1800). The harmonization is from the 1906 *English Hymnal*.

Sing this bar form (AAB) tune in unison or in parts with sensitivity to the energy of the melodic and rhythmic patterns.

Liturgical Use

With and for children (perhaps using PICARDY, 341, or the more traditional BRADBURY tune found in earlier editions of the *Psalter Hymnal);* family life services; baptism; beginning of church school seasons or Vacation Bible School; other times when the theme is God's guidance or providence.

592

O God, Your Constant Care and Love

MORNING HYMN
♩ = 54

Text

This text by H. Glen Lanier (b. Welcome, NC, 1925; d. Statesville, NC, 1978), was the result of a search conducted by the Hymn Society of America for new hymns that "celebrate the later years of life and the meaning of aging." The search was conducted in cooperation with the Church Relations Department of the National Retired Teachers Association and the American Association of Retired Persons. "O God, Your Constant Care" was one of ten entries from among some twelve hundred submissions that were published in the Hymn Society of America's pamphlet *Ten New Hymns on Aging and the Later Years* (1976).

The text rejoices in God's care in our lives "from infancy to later age" (st. 1); thanks God for the various experiences of life (st. 2); and prays for continued faithfulness, freshness, and contentment in our walk with God when we are older (st. 3-4). The meaning and application found in this strong text are suitable for God's people of all times and ages.

A minister in the United Methodist Church, Lanier served churches throughout North Carolina. Educated at High Point College, North Carolina, and Duke Divinity School, Durham, North Carolina, Lanier wrote over one thousand poems and two books of published poetry: *The Seasons of Life* (1960) and *Three Dozen Poems for Christmas* (1967).

Tune

During the early 1780s Francois H. Barthélémon (b. Bordeaux, France, 1741; d. Southwark, Surrey, England, 1808) wrote MORNING HYMN at the request of Jacob Duché, chaplain at the Female Orphan Asylum in London, England. Duché had requested that Barthélémon compose a tune for the well-known morning hymn by Thomas Ken (PHH 441), "Awake, My Soul." The tune was published in *A Supplement to the Hymns and Psalms Used at the Asylum or House of Refuge for Female Orphans* (undated, but printed between 1785-1789).

Born of a French father and Irish mother, Barthélémon had a brief military career in the Irish Brigade after which he studied music on the continent. He moved to

London in 1765. There he began a musical career as a composer, especially for opera and ballet, and as an outstanding violinist. A close friend of Joseph Haydn, Barthélémon composed theater music, some concertos, choral and chamber works, and a small amount of church music (some of it for use in the chapel of the Asylum for Female Orphans). Later in life he became interested in the philosopher Emanuel Swedenborg and joined the Swedenborgian Church.

Erik Routley (PHH 31) refers to MORNING HYMN as a children's tune, but its mainly stepwise motion and marching rhythms make it accessible to people of all age groups. Sing in parts at a moderate pace. Consider using the better-known WINCHESTER NEW (593) as an alternate tune.

Liturgical Use

The "graying" of our entire population makes this hymn eminently useful for various occasions of worship and fellowship; family life services; profession of faith; end-of-year services; church anniversaries; commencement or graduation ceremonies.

593

WINCHESTER NEW
♩ = 95

My Song Forever Shall Record

Text

Originally published in the 1912 *Psalter*, this text is a paraphrase of select verses from Psalm 89. That psalm unites a great hymn of praise for God's faithfulness, particularly to David and his dynasty, and a prayerful lament for the downfall of Israel (see also PHH 89).

Scripture References
st. 1 = Ps. 89:1
st. 2 = Ps. 89:2
st. 3 = Ps. 89:14
st. 4 = Ps. 89:15
st. 5 = Ps. 89:17-18

This paraphrase is taken from the psalm's first section, its hymn of praise. Stanzas 1 and 2 extol God's mercy and faithfulness, which he displays to his people at all times and in all places. Stanza 3 and 4 witness to the biblical cosmology in which God's justice and love are to be the model for the lifestyle of his people. The final stanza is a doxology.

Tune

The original version of WINCHESTER NEW appeared in *Musikalisches Handbuch der geistlichen Melodien,* published in Hamburg, Germany, in 1690 by Georg Wittwe. It was set to the text "Wer nur den lieben Gott" (see 446). An expanded version of the tune was a setting for "Dir, dir, Jehova" (see 203) in Johann Freylinghausen's *Geistreiches Gesangbuch* (1704). The melody was also used by John and Charles Wesley (PHH 267) for their texts and was reworked by William J. Havergal as a long-meter tune in his *Old Church Psalmody* (1864). Havergal's version closely resembled its original 1690 form.

Named for the ancient English city in Hampshire noted for its cathedral, the tune gained much popularity because of its extended use. It is called WINCHESTER NEW (also called CRASSELIUS) to distinguish it from WINCHESTER OLD (see 215 and 628).

Sing this dignified psalm tune in unison on the outer stanzas and in parts on the middle ones. Use solid organ tone and phrase in two long lines.

Liturgical Use
As a general hymn of praise at any time in the worship service; especially for occasions of worship that emphasize God's mercy, justice, and faithfulness as examples of how we as Christians should live and act in this world.

594

God Is Working His Purpose Out

PURPOSE
♩ = 54

Text
In 1894 Arthur C. Ainger (b. Blackheath, England, 1841; d. Eton, England, 1919) wrote the text in five irregular stanzas for use by the boys at Eton College, where Ainger was a popular schoolmaster from 1864-1901. Educated at Trinity College, Cambridge, England, Ainger wrote numerous songs and hymns for use at Eton.

Scripture References
st. 2 = Isa. 42:4
st. 4 = Ps. 127:1-2
ref. = Isa. 11:6-9
Hab. 2:14

Dedicated to Edward W. Benson, Archbishop of Canterbury, the text was first issued as a leaflet and then published in the *Hymn Book of the Church Missionary Society* (1899). The *Psalter Hymnal* includes the original stanzas 1, 2, 4, and 5.

Broadly defined as a missions hymn, this text is united by the closing biblical line of each stanza (similar to a refrain): "when the earth shall be filled with the glory of God as the waters cover the sea." "God Is Working" provides a clear testimony that God is the Lord of history, that he "is working his purposes out" (st. 1) even when we cannot fathom his ways. But it also presents a challenge: to press the cause of Christ throughout the whole world (st. 2), to let the gospel of Christ set free those who are captive to sin and sorrow (st. 3), and to make sure our deeds are worthy of God's blessing (st. 4). The entire text affirms the passage from Philippians 2 (12-13), where we are commanded to "work out your salvation with fear and trembling, for it is God who works in you to will and to act according to his good purpose."

Tune
Written by English composer Martin F. Shaw (PHH 49) for this text, PURPOSE was published in the 1931 edition of *Songs of Praise*. This is the tune usually sung to Ainger's

text in North America. In Britain, however, Millicent Kingham's BENSON is the preferred setting.

PURPOSE is a vigorous tune that suggests the folk idiom that Shaw loved so dearly. As indicated in the small print, the setting is canonic. Erik Routley (PHH 31) stated that this tune was "the best canon in hymnody since that of Tallis" (see 441). However, PURPOSE is not a strict canon; the full measure at the end of page 2 is condensed to two beats in the following measure, which is why the canon part had to be notated. Because of the tune's irregular meter, sing the first two stanzas in unison, but then sing stanzas 3 and 4 in canon between women and men's voices. Or, because of the tricky rhythmic change between the two parts, try having the congregation sing the first part and the choir the second part. Use trumpet and trombone accompaniment for added support. The entire hymn requires singing in long lines (lots of breath!) and a marcato articulation on the organ.

Liturgical Use

As a hymn of divine sovereignty and providence; worship that emphasizes the public task or kingdom work of Christians in the world.

595

SLAVA BOGU
♩ = 116

Praise to God in the Highest!

Text

Originally a Russian folk carol ("Slava Bogu na nebye"), this text was published by Yakushkin in 1815; it exists with many variants in Russian music collections. The English version of the selected
Scripture References
st. 2 = Ps. 126:2-3

stanzas included in the *Psalter Hymnal* was taken from a translation by A. F. D. in the *Oxford Book of Carols* (1928). According to editors at Oxford University Press, A. F. D. stood for Percy Dearmer (b. Kilburn, Middlesex, England, 1867; d. London, England, 1936), one of three editors of that hymnbook. Bert Polman added the final "alleluias" to complete this setting for the *Psalter Hymnal*.

Though Nicholas Rimsky-Korsakov called this a Christmas hymn (note st. 4 with its reference to Luke 2:14), the stanzas function as a general hymn of prayer suitable for all seasons of the year. Framed by a tone of praise to God and a recurring refrain, "Praise to you," the stanzas petition God for the blessings of guidance (st. 1), truthfulness and daily food (st. 2), goodness and rejoicing (st. 3), and peace (st. 4).

Educated at Christ Church, Oxford, England, Dearmer was ordained in the Church of England in 1892. He served a number of churches and was a Red Cross chaplain in Serbia, where his first wife died. Dearmer also lectured in England and abroad (including the United States) and from 1919-1936 was professor of ecclesiastical art at King's

College, London. Dearmer had many interests, and he published books on a wide range of topics—church history, faith healing, fasting, and art. But he is especially noted for his contribution to liturgy and church music. Along with others he edited *The English Hymnal* (1906), *Songs of Praise* (1925, enlarged 1931), and the *Oxford Book of Carols* (1928). He also wrote a hymnal handbook, *Songs of Praise Discussed* (1933), produced original hymns, and translated hymns from Latin and other languages into English.

Tune

A favorite Russian folk tune, SLAVA BOGU was used by several famous composers in their works. Ludwig van Beethoven incorporated the melody into the trio of his second Rasumovsky String Quartet (Op. 59), Rimsky-Korsakov used it in his cantata *Slava,* and Modest Mussorgsky employed the tune in the coronation scene of his opera *Boris Godunov.* Like Martin F. Shaw's setting in the *Oxford Book of Carols,* Dale Grotenhuis's (PHH 4) harmonization places the original Russian melody in the soprano in the first half and repeats it in the tenor line in the second half.

There are several ways to sing this Russian folk hymn. The congregation could sing as written, considering the soprano line as the melody throughout. An even simpler way would be to sing only the original melody, which is found in the first half, and consider this half to be musically complete, to be repeated for each of the eight sections of text. Then the melody would remain in the upper voice and be sung twice for each complete stanza. A third way, the most interesting musically, would be to sing antiphonally: the congregation could sing the first phrases followed by the choir, or the treble voices of the congregation could sing the first half of each stanza followed by the men singing the tenor melody. During the second half of each stanza the organist should support the tenor melody with a solo stop.

Liturgical Use

Because of its similarities in theme to the Lord's Prayer, as part of the spoken and sung prayers in many worship services, including Christmas Day.

596

From Ocean unto Ocean

FAR OFF LANDS
$\downarrow = 101$

Text

Robert Murray (b. Earltown, Colchester County, Nova Scotia, Canada, 1832; d. Halifax, Nova Scotia, 1910), editor of *The Presbyterian Witness* and an outstanding preacher, wrote this text. It was published with three other hymn texts, all identified with just the initial "M," in the first Canadian Presbyterian *Hymnal* of 1880.

Murray's text originally made reference to Canada's geography, but its opening lines, "From ocean unto ocean," recall the words of Psalm 72:8: "He will rule from sea to sea." Although many patriotic hymns express national pride, this text clearly affirms the sovereignty and healing power of God in human and national affairs and humbly admits human sin and folly. Stanza 1 confesses that the earth's natural resources will yield their bounty in praise to God (see Ps. 72:16), and stanzas 3 and 4 profess submission to the claims of Christ. This hymn helps us to say and sing that our service to God has an impact on our daily lives, on our stewardship of resources, on our living together in community, and on our hope for and experience of reconciliation in the marketplace and in political life.

Murray began writing poetry at the age of ten. Educated at the Free Church College of Halifax, he was licensed to preach in the Presbyterian Church of Canada. His life's vocation, however, was not in pastoral ministry. Instead he served as editor of *The Presbyterian Witness* for more than fifty years. A member of numerous denominational committees, Murray favored Canadian confederation and the temperance movement in his editorials. A number of his hymns were first published in *The Hymnal* (1880) of the Presbyterian Church in Canada and its successor, *The Book of Praise* (1918).

Tune

FAR OFF LANDS is a bar form tune (AAB) from the Bohemian Brethren or Moravian heritage. The Moravians were the people who established Herrnhut in the early eighteenth century and were famous for their missionary enterprises and musical fervor (see 513). Set to "Hur Ljuvt det är att komma," FAR OFF LANDS was published in the Swedish *Hemmets Koral Bok* (1921). The musical setting was originally prepared for the American *Hymnal 1940* by C. Winfred Douglas (PHH 342) for use with Percy Dearmer's (PHH 595) text "Remember All the People Who Live In Far Off Lands" (thus the tune's title).

Sing in unison or in parts with suitable energy; for a majestic ending add some ritardando on the final stanza.

Liturgical Use

Worship that focuses on stewardship of natural resources (including harvest thanksgiving) and on justice and charity in public life; patriotic occasions and other times of prayer for national life.

597

STOKESAY CASTLE
♩ = 56

The City Is Alive, O God

Text

Ideas about the mission of the church have gone through many changes in the twentieth century. Thus the Hymn Society of America conducted a search in 1968 for new hymns about the

Scripture References
st. 1 = Matt. 9:36
st. 3 = Matt. 11:28-30

task of the church in the world. The Society chose this hymn by William W. Reid, Jr. (b. New York, NY, 1923), as one of the best texts from the more than eight hundred submissions. It was published in the Hymn Society pamphlet, *Nine New Hymns on "The Mission of the Church"* (1969).

In Isaiah 61:1-3 the prophet foretells the coming of the Messiah, who will "preach good news to the poor . . . bind up the brokenhearted, proclaim freedom for the captives . . . and comfort those who mourn." This text takes that view of Christ's ministry and applies it to Christian service in the urban context. The major cities of the world are fascinating places, but they also contain "loneliness and greed and hate," and "crime and slums and lust abound." Just as Christ ministered "through healing touch, through word and cross," so must the church minister the gospel in word and deed throughout the whole world, but especially in the cities. "The City Is Alive" encourages us to be servants in those urban centers, to give Christian hope to the world, and to offer a new song of shalom to its citizens.

Reid was a Methodist minister serving congregations in Camptown, Pennsylvania (1950-1957); Carverton (near Wyoming), Pennsylvania (1957-1967); and the Central United Methodist Church in Wilkes-Barre, Pennsylvania (1967-1978), where he wrote this text. In 1978 he was appointed superintendent of the Wilkes-Barre district of the Methodist Church. Reid received his education at Oberlin College in Ohio, where he concentrated in botany. He served in the United States Army Medical Corps during World War II and survived imprisonment in a German prison camp. The recipient of a divinity degree from the Yale Divinity School, Reid was inspired to write hymns by his father, the founder and first executive secretary of the Hymn Society. A number of Reid's hymns were published in pamphlets issued by the Hymn Society in 1955, 1958, and 1959.

Tune
Eric H. Thiman (b. Ashford, Kent, England, 1900; d. Camden, London, England, 1975) composed STOKESAY CASTLE in 1923 as a setting for "Stand Up, Stand Up for Jesus." The tune was published with a variety of other texts in the British *Congregational Praise* (1951) and in the Canadian Anglican and United Church's *Hymn Book* (1971). The tune is named after an old fortified manor house near Church-Stretton, close to the Onny River on the border between England and Wales. Thiman was much impressed with that house when he visited there.

STOKESAY CASTLE is marked by strong motives and a march-like accompaniment. Sing with strong unison voices and use sturdy organ accompaniment to make this "city hymn" come alive.

Thiman's education included study at Trinity College of Music and the Guildhall School of Music; he also received a Doctor of Music degree from the University of London in 1927. In 1932 he became a teacher of harmony at the Royal Academy of Music and in 1956 was named dean of the faculty of music at the University of London. An accomplished organist, Thiman made frequent recital tours both in England and throughout the British Commonwealth. One of his many interests was choral singing by congregations; he served London's Park Chapel from 1927 to 1957 and City Temple Church from 1957 to 1975. A prolific composer, Thiman wrote piano and orchestral pieces and some fine part songs, but most of his work was church music: he composed services, cantatas (including *The Last Supper* and *The Temptation of Christ),* many anthems, organ pieces, and hymn tunes. Chair of the music committee for *Congregational Praise* (1951), he contributed tunes, descants, and harmonizations to that hymnbook. Thiman also wrote music textbooks, including a manual on varied organ harmonizations, *Varied Harmonies to Hymntunes* (1924); his many hymn tune harmonizations were published as *Varied Harmonies to 34 Well-Known Hymns* (1937), *Varied Harmonizations of Favorite Hymn Tunes* (1955), and *44 Hymn Tunes Freely Harmonized* (1969).

Liturgical Use

Worship that focuses on the variety of Christian ministries carried out in the world, especially in its cities.

598

ERHALT UNS, HERR
♩ = 54 ## Lord, Keep Us Steadfast in Your Word

Text

In 1541 the Turkish army was threatening to take Vienna. The German rulers called for special prayers for safety from these Islamic forces. Martin Luther (PHH 336) responded to this request by writing the original German text ("Erhalt uns, Herr, bei deinem Wort") for a prayer service in Wittenberg. Convinced that the church was threatened not only by the Turkish army of Sultan Suleiman but also by the Roman Catholic Pope, Luther began his text as follows (English translation):

Scripture References
st. 2 = John 17:11

> Lord, keep us in thy Word and work,
> Restrain the murderous Pope and Turk,
> Who fain would tear from off thy throne
> Christ Jesus, thy beloved Son.

After these threats to the church subsided, the text was altered: it eliminated the reference to the Pope and Turk and referred generally to all enemies of the Word. The text was published in Low German in the *Magdeburg Gesangbuch* (1542) and in High German in Joseph Klug's *Geistliche Lieder* (1543). The English translation by Catherine Winkworth (PHH 194) was published in her *Chorale Book for England* (1863).

The text is a fervent prayer in song cast into a Trinitarian mold. As we sing, we pray that God the Father will keep his kingdom from the powers of evil (st. 1), that God the

Son will rule the church (st. 2), and that God the Spirit will bring peace and unity on earth and will support us in our "final [earthly] strife," the doorway to eternal life (st. 3).

Tune
ERHALT UNS, HERR was adapted from an older chant tune associated with the text "Veni Redemptor gentium" (PHH 336). Some scholars assume that Luther did the arranging himself. The tune was published with Luther's text in Klug's *Geistliche Lieder* (1543). Johann S. Bach (PHH 7) composed Cantata 126 on this tune.

ERHALT UNS, HERR is an effective chorale and one of the shorter ones in the Lutheran chorale tradition. Sing in parts throughout.

Liturgical Use
In times of war and persecution that affect us or, perhaps more commonly, in solidarity with other people who experience such turmoil; as a prayer hymn before the proclamation of God's Word; peace services.

599
God of All Ages, Whose Almighty Hand
NATIONAL HYMN
♩ = 63

Text
Daniel C. Roberts (b. Bridgehampton, Long Island, NY, 1841; d. Concord, NH, 1907) wrote this patriotic hymn in 1876 for July 4 centennial celebrations in Brandon, Vermont, where he was rector at St. Thomas Episcopal Church. Originally entitled "God of Our Fathers," this text was later chosen as the theme hymn for the centennial celebration of the adoption of the United States Constitution. It was published in the Protestant Episcopal *Hymnal* of 1892.

Scripture References
st. 3 = Ps. 46:1

Educated at Kenyon College, Gambier, Ohio, Roberts served in the union army during the Civil War. He was ordained in the Episcopal Church as a priest in 1866 and ministered to several congregations in Vermont and Massachusetts. In 1878 he began a ministry at St. Paul Church in Concord, New Hampshire, that lasted for twenty-three years. For many years president of the New Hampshire State Historical Society, Roberts once wrote, "I remain a country parson, known only within my small world," but his hymn "God of Our Fathers" brought him widespread recognition.

Unlike many other nationalist hymns, this text keeps our focus on God. This is a God who created the universe, who leads and governs his people, who serves as our protector, and who refreshes his people with divine love. Presumably the text referred originally to white Anglo-Saxons, but in its present form it is fitting for all citizens and residents of any country. Christians too may sing this anthem, using it to recognize the national association we have on earth but remembering that the practice of "true religion" (st. 3) transcends earthly loyalties and promotes citizenship in the kingdom of heaven.

Tune

Roberts's text was initially sung to Alexy Lvov's RUSSIAN HYMN (199), but in 1892, right after the text was accepted for the Episcopal hymnal, George W. Warren (b. Albany, NY, 1828; d. New York, 1902) composed NATIONAL HYMN for Roberts's text. The new tune was published with Roberts's text in the *Hymnal Revised and Enlarged* (1894), compiled by J. Ireland Tucker and W. W. Rousseau.

Warren received his general education at Racine College in Wisconsin, but as a musician he was largely self-trained. An organist in a number of Episcopal churches, he played the organ for thirty years (1870-1900) at St. Thomas Church in New York City. Warren composed anthems and liturgical service music; his hymn tunes were collected in *Warren's Hymns and Tunes as Sung in St. Thomas Church* (1888).

Though the great hymnologist Erik Routley (PHH 31) dismissed NATIONAL HYMN as "a pretentious piece of bombast," many people enjoy singing it with the gusto appropriate to civic events. The tune includes martial trumpet fanfares, which may give too much of a triumphalistic effect in church. Use more humble musical forces, especially on the inner stanzas.

Liturgical Use

Worship that focuses on God's reign over the nations; civic celebrations.

600

ST. JOAN
♩. = 50

Christ Is the World's True Light

Text

George W. Briggs (PHH 308) wrote this text as a "missionary hymn" to emphasize one of the concepts of modern missions: "In Christ all races meet." The text was published in the Advent section of Oxford's *Songs of Praise* (1931) and in Briggs's *Songs of Faith* (1945), in which it was entitled "The Light of the World."

The text begins by affirming Christ's own saying, "I am the light of the world" (John 8:12). Christ is the light and daystar who brings his people salvation from the darkness of sin. Borrowing one of Paul's memorable teachings in Galatians 3:28 and Jesus' prayer for unity in John 17, the text confesses the essential unity of all humanity and especially the oneness of the

Scripture References
st. 1 = John 8:12
John 12:46
2 Pet. 1:19
st. 2 = Isa. 2:4
Mic. 4:1-5
Gal. 3:28
st. 3 = Isa. 9:5-7
1 John 2:2
Rom. 8:19-23

family of God. Only when the nations and all peoples submit to Christ's reign will our "groaning" world experience true peace and redemption.

Tune

Percy E. B. Coller (b. Liverpool, England, 1895; d. unknown) composed ST. JOAN and submitted it anonymously for publication in *The Hymnal 1940,* where it was set to Briggs's text. Coller must have enjoyed the companionship of a saintly wife because he named this tune in her honor. As a boy chorister Coller sang in the Liverpool and Oxford Cathedral choirs, and at the age of fifteen he became suborganist of Liverpool Cathedral. He was educated at Liverpool University and after World War I served as organist and choirmaster of St. Peter Church, Montreal, Canada.

Marked by ascending "rocket" motives and several sequences, ST. JOAN is intended for part singing. The tune requires confident organ accompaniment and a brisk tempo that thrives on one pulse per bar.

Liturgical Use

Worldwide communion; ecumenical and missions services; Advent; Epiphany; many other occasions of worship.

601

Jesu, Jesu, Fill Us with Your Love

CHEREPONI
♩ = 66

Text

Tom Colvin (PHH 352), long-term missionary to Africa, wrote this text in 1963 in Chereponi, northern Ghana, while he was attending a lay-training course in agriculture, development, and evangelism. New converts had brought a folk melody to this meeting, which they thought might be appropriate for a text about Christian love. Colvin explained his writing of the text as follows:

Scripture References
st. 1 = John 13:2-5

> Sitting there in the moonlight, I felt it simply had to be about black and white, rich and poor. I was ashamed of the wasteful affluence of my people but proud of the Gospel that transforms us into servants of one another. It is only when we who are rich learn to have the humility of the slave towards the poor of the world that we shall be able to learn from them; they have so much to teach us and share with us.

Colvin shared text and tune with the Iona Community in Scotland. After the hymn was published in their collection *Free to Serve: Hymns from Africa* (1968), its popularity spread to other Christian communities. It was also published in many other hymnbooks.

This fine text is based on Jesus' personalized object lesson on servanthood when he washed his disciples' feet (John 13:1-17) and on Jesus' parable of the good Samaritan. That parable was his response to the question "Who is my Neighbor?" (Luke 10:25-37).

Tune

CHEREPONI was originally a traditional Ghanaian love song. Colvin named the tune after the village in which he first heard it and in which he wrote his text. The traditional African performance for melodies like CHEREPONI involves a leader and a group as well as various percussion instruments and clapping. Such a practice can easily be implemented in congregations that have one or several soloists or a choir. If you have drummers in your church, have them improvise some ostinato rhythms on drums and/or tambourines. Because this is a perpetual energy kind of song, make sure that there are no rhythmic pauses between the refrain and the stanzas.

The hymnal harmony was prepared by Jane Marshall (b. Dallas, TX, 1924) for Colvin's collection *Fill Us with Your Love* (1983). A graduate of Southern Methodist University, Dallas, Marshall taught music theory at Southern Methodist's School of Music (1968-1975) and church music at the Perkins School of Theology at Southern Methodist (1975-1986). She was a church musician at several Presbyterian and United Methodist congregations in the Dallas area. Active in the American Guild of Organists, the Choristers Guild, and the American Choral Directors Association, Marshall has been honored for her leadership roles in the musical life of the United Methodist and the Southern Baptist denominations. She has composed many anthems, contributed to numerous choral collections, and published a number of hymn tunes.

Liturgical Use

Many occasions of worship in which Christian servanthood is the theme, thus missions services and services that focus on diaconal work.

602

GERMANY
♩ = 116

Where Cross the Crowded Ways of Life

Text

Caleb T. Winchester, an editor of the 1905 *Methodist Hymnal,* challenged Frank M. North (b. Lower Manhattan, New York, NY, 1850; d. Madison, NJ, 1935) to write a hymn text on city missions. North had intimate knowledge of urban life because of his work for the Methodist Church in New York City. Inspired by Jesus' words "Go to the street corners and invite to the banquet anyone you find" (Matt. 22:9), North wrote "Where

Scripture References
st. 1 = Matt. 9:36
st. 2 = Luke 19:41-42
st. 3 = Matt. 10:42
Mark 9:41
st. 5 = Rev. 21:2-4

Cross the Crowded Ways." After making various revisions and adding a title ("A Prayer for the Multitudes"), he published the text in *The Christian City* (June 1903), a missions journal he edited. The text was also published in the 1905 *Methodist Hymnal* and in many other twentieth-century hymnbooks. Modern hymnals have changed the original "thous" and "thees" to "yous."

One of the earliest and finest modern "city hymns," this text focuses on the ills of our great urban centers (and ignores their benefits) with the insight and compassion of a Christian worker in the city slums. North's descriptive phrases may have been startling at the turn of the century, but they are even more accurate descriptions of the massive cities in our world today. His prescription to follow in the footsteps of Christ and bring the gospel in word and deed is relevant as long as the Lord delays in bringing the new Jerusalem.

Primarily a churchman, North devoted himself to loyal service in the Methodist denomination and to various ecumenical ventures. He was educated at Wesleyan University, Middleton, Connecticut, and ordained in the Methodist Church in 1872. A minister in several churches in Florida, New York, and Connecticut, he also held administrative positions—secretary of the New York Church Extension and Missionary Society (1892-1912) and secretary of the Board of Foreign Missions of the Methodist Church (1912-1924). He was involved with the Federal Council of Churches of Christ in America (forerunner of the National Council of Churches) and was the council's president from 1916-1920. Editor of the periodical *Christian City*, North was active in many organizations that promoted and carried out Christian ministries in urban life. North contributed hymns to *Sursum Corda* (1898) and the *Methodist Hymnal* (1905) and was a charter member of the Hymn Society, which republished his eight hymns in a booklet in 1970.

Tune
See PHH 111 for a discussion of GERMANY. Sing the first three stanzas in parts but take stanzas 4 and 5 as one textual unit and sing it in unison. Observe two long phrases; sing and accompany in a brisk tempo.

Liturgical Use
For urban ministries and other occasions that emphasize missions and diaconal work.

603

Lord, Whose Love in Humble Service

PLEADING SAVIOR
$\quad$ ♩ = 56

Text
Albert F. Bayly (PHH 293) wrote this text in response to a Hymn *Scripture References*
Society of America search for new hymns on social welfare. It $\quad$ st. 4 = Matt. 25:34-40

was chosen as the theme hymn for the Second National Conference on the Churches and Social Welfare held in Cleveland, Ohio, October 23-27, 1961. The Hymn Society published the text in *Seven New Social Welfare Hymns* (1961).

The text begins with a recognition of Christ's ultimate sacrifice on the cross and then points to the continuing needs of the homeless, the hungry, the prisoners, and the mourners. Bayly's words remind us of modern refugees, AIDS patients, and famine victims who are as close as our doorstep or who are brought to our attention via the news media. The final two stanzas encourage us to move from Sunday worship to weekday service; such integrity in the Christian life is truly a liturgy of sacrifice, pleasing to God.

Tune
PLEADING SAVIOR is a pentatonic folk melody that was included in *The Christian Lyre*, compiled by Joshua Leavitt (PHH 171) in New York in 1830. The tune's title comes from the John Leland text "Now the Savior Stands A-pleading," to which it was set in that collection. The harmonization by Ralph Vaughan Williams (PHH 316) was first prepared for use in *The English Hymnal* (1906).

There are various options for singing this fine tune: sing in parts or in unison, or try one of the stanzas in canon, at two measures, unaccompanied. Observe one pulse per bar.

Liturgical Use
Services that emphasize missions, diaconal themes, and servanthood.

604

COMPASSION
♩ = 126

God of All Living

Text
Kenneth I. Morse (b. Altoona, PA, 1913) wrote this text in 1974 while he was a member of the denominational staff of the Church of the Brethren. Originally beginning "Brothers

Scripture References
st. 2-4 = Matt. 25:34-40

and sisters of mine are the hungry," the four-stanza text was published in a Church of the Brethren songbook, *Sisters and Brothers Sing* (1977). The *Psalter Hymnal* Revision Committee chose to use the final stanza as an opening stanza as well, thus creating a frame around the text.

"God of All Living" applies Jesus' words in Matthew 25:34-40 to our modern world, in which wastefulness abounds and the hungry and homeless populate our streets and the media. In this world Christians must minister to various needs in the name of Christ and for his sake. As is true of other hymns in this section, the images depicted here remind us that the starving child, the despairing drug addict, and the destitute home-less are our brothers and sisters; we must "open our hearts" and "reach out our hands" to them.

Morse graduated from Juniata College, Huntingdon, Pennsylvania, and earned a master's degree in English literature from Pennsylvania State University. He taught in public schools until 1943 and then worked on the denominational staff of the Church of the Brethren until his retirement in 1978. The editor of several books and maga-zines, he also wrote many poems and hymns, as well as a book on worship entitled *Move in Our Midst* (1977). Morse served on the committee that produced the *Hymnal, A Worship Book* (1992) of the Brethren and Mennonite churches.

Tune

Psalter Hymnal editor Emily R. Brink (PHH 158) composed COMPASSION for Morse's text in 1987. The *Psalter Hymnal* Revision Committee on which Brink served had tried various tunes for this text, but due to its unusual accents no successful match was found among preexisting melodies. In composing the tune Brink tried to create music that reflected a spirit of compassion and repentance as well as of hope. She named the tune COMPASSION after the theme of Morse's words.

COMPASSION consists of several melodic motives that are united by a regular alterna-tion of measures with three and five beats. Sing the outer, framing stanzas in unison and the middle ones in parts. Accompany with modest resources.

Liturgical Use

Worship that focuses on our mission task in the world and on those who assist in housing, feeding, counseling, and healing.

605

Creating God, Your Fingers Trace

KILLIBEGS
♩ = 66

Text

Jeffery W. Rowthorn (PHH 523) wrote this text based on Psalm 148 in 1974, the year he first started writing hymn texts. One of two winners in the Hymn Society of America's contest for "New Psalms for Today," the text was published in *The Hymn* of April 1979.

Scripture References
st. 1 = Ps. 147:4-5
Col. 1:16
st. 2 = Ps. 147:8

In Psalm 148 both heavenly and earthly creatures bring praise to God (see addition-al comments at PHH 148). Rowthorn uses the psalm as the backdrop for a text that is not so much a paraphrase in the traditional sense of that term but a new text that affirms four great tenets of the Christian faith: the God we worship created the entire cosmos (st. 1), sustains the ecology of life (st. 2), redeems his people from oppression and death (st. 3), and dwells by his Spirit in his people, the church (st. 4).

Tune
William Davies (PHH 372) composed KILLIBEGS for use in the British supplement *Praise for Today* (1975). Davies served on the compilation committee of that hymnbook. The tune is named after a fishing village in Donegal, Northern Ireland, where Davies vacationed while he was conductor of the BBC orchestra in Northern Ireland.

This fine modern tune is intended for unison singing. Its singable phrases are supported by a chordal accompaniment that emphasizes the duple meter. Let your voices soar on this melody. Use brilliant reeds on the organ.

Liturgical Use
The beginning of each stanza contains the themes of this text: creation, providence, redemption, and incarnation; in the light of these, the hymn has many possible uses in Christian worship.

606

LLANGLOFFAN
♩ = 58

O God of Every Nation

Text
In 1958 William W. Reid, Jr. (PHH 597), submitted this hymn text to a contest sponsored by the Hymn Society of America in conjunction with the Department of International Affairs of the National Council of Churches. The text won first place and was sung at the opening session of the Fifth World Order Study Conference held in Cleveland, Ohio, on November 13-21, 1958. It was published in the Hymn Society's *Twelve New World Order Hymns* (1958).

Scripture References
st. 2 = Isa. 2:4
st. 4 = Isa. 9:5-7

"O God of Every Nation" is a beautiful prayer for God's shalom to reign over the whole world; for truth, love, and justice to preside over human affairs; and for an end to warfare with its "trust in bombs that shower destruction" (st. 2). As war and rumors of war continue to plague our world; the final stanza holds before us the vision of a new heaven and earth in which "Christ shall rule victorious."

Tune
LLANGLOFFAN is a Welsh carol or ballad tune, which appeared as a hymn tune in *Llwybrau Moliant* (*The Paths of Praise*). That collection of tunes for use by Baptists was edited by Lewis Jones and published in Wrexham in 1872. LLANGLOFFAN is named for a town in Glamorgan, Wales, at one time presumably the location of a church that honored St. Cloffan.

This is a sturdy tune in a minor key. You may wish to modulate after stanza 3 into the major form of this tune (LLANFYLLIN) and sing the final stanza in that bright major key.

Liturgical Use

In times of war or when you want to express your solidarity with others who are in war-torn areas; peace services and similar occasions that stress Christian servanthood and social responsibilities; Advent.

607

Father, Help Your People

WHITWORTH
♩ = 96

Text

In the mid-1960s 1960s Fred Kaan (PHH 277) began writing hymn texts "to fill gaps" in traditional hymnody. He wrote this text in 1966 while he was pastor of the Pilgrim Church in Plymouth, England. It was published in his collection *Pilgrim Praise* (1968).

This "kingdom hymn" illustrates that Kaan was well versed in the Reformed understanding of the kingdom of God. "Father, Help Your People" is a prayer for the coming of God's kingdom wherever we are—in church, home, or marketplace—and with whatever gifts we have—in worship, work, or play. We are urged here to be Christ's servants in the world and thus to experience living as a feast, a foretaste of the great celebrations in the new heaven and earth.

Tune

Walter MacNutt (PHH 174) composed WHITWORTH in the mid-1960s when he was organist and choirmaster at St. Thomas Anglican Church in Toronto, Canada. Intended for an Epiphany processional, the tune was written for "Lo, the Pilgrim Magi." WHITWORTH was first published in the pamphlet *Five Hymn Tunes* (1970) and then included in *The Hymn Book* (1971) of the Canadian Anglican and United Church. The tune is named for Jack Whitworth, a long-time secretary at St. Thomas Church and a friend of MacNutt.

Stanley L. Osborne (PHH 395) says that this is "possibly the finest tune that MacNutt has written." This excellent melody invites unison singing, which should soar from inside a church building to far beyond the church walls. Use a strong organ registration to send this prayer on its way up to God.

Liturgical Use

A "kingdom hymn" for many occasions of worship; fitting for special times of prayer for the nation, industry, science, and the arts; observances of schooling, graduations, business, and domestic life, and Labor Day.

608

O God of Love, O King of Peace

Text

Written by Henry W. Baker (PHH 342) and entitled "The Lord
Shall Give His People the Blessing of Peace," this text was published in the 1861 edition of *Hymns Ancient and Modern*. Baker was
chairman of the committee that prepared this landmark hymnal.
The *Psalter Hymnal* omits the original fourth stanza.

Scripture References
st. 1 = Ps. 46:9
Isa. 2:4
Mic. 4:3
st. 2 = Ps. 78:3-4
ref. = Ps. 29:11

Because the sin of war is always present in our world, this
profound prayer for peace or shalom is continuously relevant. As
we sing, we pray for a cease-fire among hostile peoples, for reconciliation among
warring factions (st. 1). But it is only because of God's faithfulness and mercy, his
"works of old," and not from human efforts that true peace will come (st. 2). Like the
Old Testament psalms that affirm God's saving deeds, this text testifies that only God
can be trusted to provide a lasting peace (st. 3). "O God of Love" has an unforgettable
litany refrain, "Give peace, O God, give peace again!"

Tune

Reginald S. Thatcher (b. Salisbury, England, 1888; d. Cranleigh, Surrey, England,
1957) composed WILDERNESS when he was a musician at the famed Harrow Public
School in England. The tune was published in the *Clarendon Hymn Book* (1936), a
hymnal initially prepared for Charterhouse, another well-known British public school.

Sing in unison, although part singing on the refrain might effectively set off the
litany phrase. For an effective ending, consider turning the final chords (on "give peace
again") from minor to all major chords. Use full, firm, though not bright accompaniment.

Thatcher received his education at the Royal College of Music and at Worcester
College, Oxford, England. His career consisted of a series of music school appointments, including director of music at the Royal Naval College and principal of the
Royal Academy of Music. From 1954 to 1960 Thatcher was president of the Royal
College of Organists. He also served on the editorial committee of *The BBC Hymn Book*
(1951). In 1952 Thatcher was knighted for his contribution to British music and
culture.

Liturgical Use

Because war, revolution, strife, and the spirit of contention are rampant in our world
and because the Christian church should be engaged in peace efforts and prayers for
peace, this hymn is appropriate for many occasions of worship.

609

How Would the Lord Be Worshiped

HELDER
♩ = 56

Text

Inspired by a sermon on Isaiah 58:6-11, Marie J. Post (PHH 5) wrote this unrhymed hymn text to illustrate the prophet's concept of true worship. Written in Grand Rapids, Michigan, in 1982, the text was first published in the 1987 *Psalter Hymnal.*

Scripture References
st. 1 = Isa. 58:6
st. 2 = Isa. 58:7
st. 3 = Isa. 58:9b
st. 4 = Isa. 58:8-9a
st. 5 = Isa. 58:10b-11

The passage from Isaiah is a part of the prophet's sermon on the meaning of fasting. Through Isaiah's words God teaches his people that true worship consists not only in the proper rituals but also, and even more so, in the practice of righteousness in daily life. True worship requires fighting injustice, feeding the hungry, and clothing the destitute. The Old Testament prophets were insistent on this theme (Isa. 1:10-17; Jer. 7:21-26; Amos 5:21-24; Mic. 6:6-8). God will accept our Sunday worship and bless us only when such righteous deeds characterize our lives.

Tune

The *Psalter Hymnal* Revision Committee sent Post's text to various musicians and requested a tune. The tune selected was HELDER, composed by Brent Assink (b. Bellingham, WA, 1955) in St. Paul, Minnesota, in December 1984. The following year the Dordt College Alumni Choir, of which Assink was a member, sang the hymn in Sioux Center, Iowa (the choir's conductor, Dale Grotenhuis, was a *Psalter Hymnal* Revision Committee member). The tune was named in honor of Assink's childhood piano teacher, Martha Helder.

HELDER features some striking melodic and rhythmic motives. For the first three stanzas, consider having a soloist or choir sing the question with the congregation on the response. Then sing all together in unison on stanzas 4 and 5.

Educated in music and business administration at Dordt College, Sioux Center, Assink received a master's degree in musicology from the University of Minnesota. He served the St. Paul Chamber Orchestra first as assistant manager and then as artistic operations manager (1981-1990). From 1984 to 1990 he was also minister of music at Calvary Christian Reformed Church in Bloomington, Minnesota. Assink became general manager of the San Francisco Symphony in 1990 but returned to the twin cities in 1994 to take the position of president and managing director of the St. Paul Chamber Orchestra.

Liturgical Use
Worship that focuses on living the gospel in word and deed and on the meaning of worship; observances of world hunger, international relief operations, and urban ministries.

610

FUERZA
♩ = 92

God Is My Rock/El Señor Es Mi Fuerza

Text
Juan S. Espinosa (b. Villafranca de los Barros, Spain, 1940) wrote the original Spanish text and composed the tune in 1969. It was first published in Madrid in 1970 in *El Senor Es Mi Fuerza,* his most significant song collection, which included forty-two liturgical songs written both in Spain and in northern Peru, where Espinosa worked with peasants. Espinosa has said that he "composed to offer the Christian communities in their liturgical expression a few songs in consonance with the new spirit of Vatican II." Espinosa, who earned a degree in theology and philosophy and also studied music, published a number of song collections. The English translation was published in *Celebremos II* (1983), a Hispanic hymnal of the United Methodist Church in the United States.

Scripture References
ref. = Ps. 46:1
st. 1 = Ps. 23:3
st. 2 = Ps. 23:4

This hymn is based on Psalm 46:

God is our refuge and strength,
an ever-present help in trouble.
Therefore we will not fear, though
the earth give way. . . .
The Lord Almighty is with us;
the God of Jacob is our fortress.

As in the biblical psalm, the four stanzas of this text express an unshaken trust in God's guidance and protection of his people, especially when they face turmoil, injustice, and life's other trials. Thus the text is a testimony of confident faith, sure hope, and mutual encouragement. In the biblically proper sense of the term, this is a hymn text of "liberation theology."

Tune
FUERZA is the Spanish word for "fortress" or "refuge" (see both Psalm 46 and the text). The repeated refrain or antiphon is intended for unison singing, but the melody of the stanzas suggests two-part singing in typically Spanish parallel thirds. Try using a duet or two-part choir on the stanzas and have everyone sing the refrain. Since the stanzas are

rather high and the refrain rather low, have the congregation sing the refrain and a duet or two-part choir sing the stanzas. Also, since the refrain is repeated each time, try to sing the refrain in English the first time through and repeat it in Spanish.

Liturgical Use

As is true of Psalm 46, this hymn fits many occasions of worship; useful for Old/New Year services, but especially at prayer services for justice and peace and urban ministries.

611

As Stewards of a Vineyard

WORKERS' SONG
♩ = 63

Text

Canadian Christian day school teacher and principal Frank De Vries (PHH 518) composed both text and tune in 1970 in Burnaby, British Columbia. Entitled "Workers' Song," the hymn was chosen as a theme song by the Christian Labor Association of Canada. That organization also published the hymn in 1970 in their Toronto Convention booklet. About his writing of "As Stewards" De Vries says, "I wrote this hymn in reaction to 'Solidarity Forever,' that strident union song which is sung at every convention and demonstration by the secular labor unions."

Scripture References
st. 1 = Mic. 6:8
ref. = Ps. 127:1
1 Cor. 15:58

The *Psalter Hymnal* has omitted the original third stanza, which made specific reference to employer-employee relationships.

Tune

WORKERS' SONG was named in honor of "workers," specifically the many members of the Christian Labor Association of Canada.

Known for years in a melody-only score (sometimes with added guitar chords), this tune was harmonized for the *Psalter Hymnal* by Dale Grotenhuis. Sing in harmony with voices full of confidence and joy for the blessing of daily work done for Christ's sake.

Liturgical Use

Worship that emphasizes kingdom service in daily work, the pursuit of justice, reconciliation, and peace.

WESTMINSTER ABBEY
♩ = 46

Lo! He Comes,
with Clouds Descending

Text

In 1750 John Cennick, a friend of John and Charles Wesley (PHH 267), wrote an Advent hymn that began, "Lo! he cometh, countless trumpets blow before his bloody sign!" Cennick's hymn was published in his *Collection* (1752). Charles Wesley completely rewrote the text and published his version in *Hymns of Intercession for all Mankind* (1758) with the title "Thy Kingdom Come" (changed to "The Second Advent" in other editions). Though later hymnals occasionally mixed Cennick's lines with Wesley's, the *Psalter Hymnal* includes most of Wesley's original text.

Scripture References
st. 1 = Matt. 24:30
Rev. 5:11-13
st. 2 = Rev. 1:7
Zech. 12:10
John 19:37

Like so many of Wesley's texts, "Lo! He Comes" abounds with biblical imagery. Stanzas 1, 2, and 4 are based on the rich language of John's apocalyptic visions recorded in Revelation 1:7 and 5:11-13. The third stanza reminds us that Christ's wounds and atoning death should lead us to greater faith and ultimately to our worship of Christ in glory (as Christ himself reminded the doubting Thomas). Stanza 4 is a majestic doxology to Christ, our Savior and Lord.

Tune

WESTMINSTER ABBEY was composed by Henry Purcell (b. Westminster, London, England, 1659; d. Westminster, 1695), perhaps the greatest English composer who ever lived, though he only lived to the age of thirty-six. Purcell's first piece was published at age eight when he was also a chorister in the Chapel Royal. When his voice changed in 1673, he was appointed assistant to John Hingston, who built chamber organs and maintained the king's instruments. In 1674 Purcell began tuning the Westminster Abbey organ and was paid to copy organ music. Given the position of composer for the violins in 1677, he also became organist at Westminster Abbey in 1679 (at age twenty) and succeeded Hingston as maintainer of the king's instruments (1683). Purcell composed music for the theater (*Dido and Aeneas*, c. 1689) and for keyboards, provided music for royal coronations and other ceremonies, and wrote a substantial body of church music, including eighteen full anthems and fifty-six verse anthems.

WESTMINSTER ABBEY comes from the concluding "alleluias" in Purcell's verse anthem "O God, thou art my God" (c. 1692). That anthem was published in William Boyce's *Cathedral Music*, vol. 2, 1760. Ernest Hawkins arranged the "alleluias" as a hymn tune for use in Vincent Novello's *The Psalmist* (1843). The tune achieved great popularity after its publication in the 1939 *Shortened Music Edition of Hymns Ancient and Modern* and after its use at several British royal weddings. Often associated with "Christ Is Made the Sure Foundation," WESTMINSTER ABBEY is named after the famous cathedral in London. Originally in B-flat, Purcell's tune was transposed down in Hawkins's arrangment; consequently some adjustments were made in the part writing. This magnificent tune requires spirited singing and a fairly lively tempo. Yet the tempo should be majestic, swinging in two large beats per measure. Have the choir sing one stanza unaccompanied for variety.

Liturgical Use
Advent; other worship services that focus on Christ's coming again in glory.

613

"Wake, Awake, for Night Is Flying"

WACHET AUF
♩ = 76

Text
In 1597 the Westphalian (German) village where pastor Philipp Nicolai (PHH 357) lived experienced a terrible pestilence, which claimed some thirteen hundred lives in his parish alone. Nicolai turned from the constant tragedies and frequent funerals (at times he buried thirty people in one day) to meditate on "the noble, sublime doctrine of eternal life obtained through the blood of Christ." As he said, "This I allowed to dwell in my heart day and night and searched the Scriptures as to what they revealed on this matter." Nicolai also read Augustine's *City of God* before he wrote this great Advent text and arranged its tune.

Scripture References
st. 1 = Matt. 25:1-13
Isa. 52:1, 8
st. 2 = Rev. 22:16-20
st. 3 = Rev. 5:11-13
Rev. 21:21
Isa. 64:4
1 Cor. 2:9

The original German text ("Wachet auf! ruft uns die Stimme") and tune were published in Nicolai's collection of devotional poetry, *Frewden-Spiegel dess ewigen Lebens* (1599), with a title that read (translated into English), "Of the Voice at Midnight and the Wise Virgins who meet their Heavenly Bridegroom." Catherine Winkworth's (PHH 194) English translation was published in her *Lyra Germanica* (1858). The *Psalter Hymnal* includes that translation as altered in the *Lutheran Book of Worship* (1978).

The parable of the ten virgins (Matt. 25:1-13) was the inspiration for stanzas 1 and 2, and John's visions of the glory of Christ and the new Jerusalem (Rev. 19, 21, and 22) provide the basis for stanza 3. Erik Routley (PHH 31) says this hymn is filled with "pageantry, energy, light, color, and expectancy"; it is surely a great hymn about the joyful anticipation of Christ's coming again, and one that brings comfort and hope to Christians in all situations.

Tune

WACHET AUF is sometimes known as the "king of chorales," while Nicolai's other famous tune, WIE SCHON LEUCHTET (357) is known as the "queen of chorales." Nicolai's WACHET AUF is based on the "Silberweisse" tune (around 1513) by Hans Sachs, the famous Meistersinger from Nuremburg, Germany. The original form of the melody was more rhythmically varied, but by the eighteenth century, the isorhythmic (all equal rhythms) version is what Johann S. Bach (PHH 7) used in his Cantata 140 (1731); the harmonization is from the closing chorale of that cantata. There are also many organ preludes on the tune.

WACHET AUF calls for festive accompaniment, including brass instruments, so that the shouts of "alleluia" and "hosanna" may truly crescendo (as st. 3 suggests). Congregations will probably enjoy singing this hymn in unison, but choirs should try the harmony.

Liturgical Use

Advent; other times when our eyes of faith long for the return of Christ; with preaching on Matthew 25.

614

MEINE HOFFNUNG
♩ = 52

Day of Judgment! Day of Wonders!

Text

John Newton (PHH 462) wrote this text during "the most of two days" in 1774, and it was published in the *Olney Hymns* (1779). The *Psalter Hymnal* includes the original stanzas 1-3 and 6. Newton's text borrows phrases and concepts from the thirteenth-century Latin sequence "Dies irae, dies illa," which

Scripture References
st. 3 = Matt. 25:41-46
Rev. 20:11-14
st. 4 = Matt. 25:34-40

has sometimes been attributed to Thomas of Celano (without specific evidence), a friend of Francis of Assisi. The "Dies irae" became part of the Roman Catholic Requiem Mass and was often included in dramatic musical settings that emphasized the judgment of sinners. Many of the various popular English translations of that ancient Latin text begin with the words, "Day of wrath, O day of mourning."

Although the "Dies irae" holds out judgment for the unrepentant sinner, it also contains prayers for mercy for the believer. Newton clearly announces the judgment of God on sin and sinners in his hymn text (st. 1, 3), but he also transforms the original prayers for mercy into comforting words of assurance for believers in Christ (st. 2, 4). The text concludes with a paraphrase of Jesus' words in Matthew 25:34, "Come, you who are blessed by my Father; take your inheritance, the kingdom prepared for you since the creation of the world."

Tune

MEINE HOFFNUNG received its name from its association with Joachim Neander's (PHH 244) text "Meine Hoffnung stehet feste" ("All My Hope on God Is Founded"). The tune was published with Newton's text in Neander's *Alpha and Omega* (1680). (The chorale found in Johann S. Bach's Cantata 40 is very loosely based on MEINE HOFF-NUNG.)

To reflect the emphases in the text, sing stanzas 1 and 3 in unison and stanzas 2 and 4 in harmony. Singers and accompanists should note the built-in ritardando in the final long line; no further expressive device needs to be added in the final stanza.

Liturgical Use

Advent; other worship that focuses on Christ's return in glory "to judge the living and the dead."

615

The King Shall Come When Morning Dawns

MORNING SONG
$\lrcorner = 56$

Text

Infused with the imagery of morning light typical of early Greek hymnody, this Advent text stirs hope in the hearts of all who look forward to the return of Christ. "The King Shall Come" is a confession of faith in the sure return of our Lord; his coming again will occur in a blaze of glory, which will far surpass his earthly death and resurrection. The text concludes with a paraphrase of the ancient prayer of the church—"Maranatha," or "Lord, come quickly" (Rev. 22:20).

Scripture References
st. 1 = Luke 21:25-28
2 Pet. 1:19
st. 5 = Rev. 22:20

The text was included in *Hymns from the East* (1907), a collection by John Brownlie (b. Glasgow, Scotland, 1859; d. Crieff, Perthshire, Scotland, 1925) of translations and what he called "suggestions" of devotional material from the Eastern Orthodox tradition. Because no Greek original has ever been found, scholars now assume that the text is not a translation but a "suggestion": an original text by Brownlie that reflects his wide knowledge of Greek hymnody. The *Psalter Hymnal* includes the original stanzas 1-4 and 7.

A Presbyterian pastor in the Free Church of Scotland, Brownlie was educated at Glasgow University and at the Free Church College. He served for many years as pastor of the Free Church of Portpatrick, Wigtownshire. Brownlie's contribution to church music was significant: he published three volumes of original hymn texts, including *Pilgrim Songs* (1892); he wrote a handbook (1899) to the 1898 edition of the Scottish Presbyterian hymnal, *The Church Hymnary;* and he published several volumes of English translations of Greek and Latin hymns, including *Hymns from East and West* (1898) and *Hymns from the East* (1907).

Tune

MORNING SONG is a folk tune that has some resemblance to the traditional English tune for "Old King Cole." The tune appeared anonymously in Part II of John Wyeth's (PHH 486) *Repository of Sacred Music* (1813). In 1816 it was credited to "Mr. Dean," which some scholars believe was a misprinted reference to Elkanah K. Dare, a composer who contributed more than a dozen tunes to Wyeth's *Repository*. In the original harmonization the melody was in the tenor. The tune is also known as CONSOLATION (and KENTUCKY HARMONY), its title in Ananias Davisson's *Kentucky Harmony* (1816), where it was set to Isaac Watts's morning song, "Once More, My Soul, the Rising Day."

Jack Grotenhuis (PHH 17) composed the harmonization in Tempe, Arizona, in late November 1983 (a few weeks before his death). The Episcopal *Hymnal 1982* provides two additional settings. The music is suitable for either unison singing (especially on st. 1, 5) or part singing (especially on st. 2-4). The tune requires a sense of two long phrases rather than four short ones.

Liturgical Use

An eschatological text suitable as a morning hymn anytime in the church year, but especially for services (during Advent) that focus on Christ's return.

616

SAMANTHRA
$\quad\downarrow = 92$

Isaiah the Prophet Has Written of Old

Text

Written by Joy F. Patterson (b. Lansing, MI, 1931) in 1981, this text was one of seven winners in a hymn-writing contest for children's hymns sponsored jointly by the Choristers Guild and the Hymn Society of America. It was published in the Hymn Society leaflet "New Hymns for Children" (1982) and was first sung at the Society's convocation in Atlanta that same year. Patterson says of the text, "I have always loved the tune SAMANTHRA, and the images and words from Isaiah 11 seemed made for the tune. Thus scriptural language, a prayer for peace, and a good but little-used tune came together for me in this hymn."

Scripture References
st. 1 = Isa. 11:6-9
st. 2 = Isa. 55:12-13

Based on biblical imagery found in Isaiah, the text skillfully contrasts the evil and injustice in this world (st. 2a) with the vision of peace, harmony, and joy in the kingdom of God (st. 1). It concludes with a "Maranatha" prayer ("Lord, come quickly!") for peace, wisdom, justice, and joy (st. 2b).

Patterson grew up in LaGrange, Illinois, studied French language and literature at the University of Wisconsin, and spent a year at the University of Strasbourg, France, on a Fulbright scholarship. She taught French at the University of Wisconsin and worked as a homemaker and as a claims representative for the Social Security Administration. An elder in the Presbyterian Church, she was a member of the committee that prepared *The Presbyterian Hymnal* (1990). A writer of some thirty hymn texts and composer of hymn tunes, Patterson has also written choral music, including "On a Winter Night" (1974). A collection of her hymns, *Come, You People of the Promise,* was published in 1994.

Tune

SAMANTHRA is a beautiful melody from the southeastern Appalachian region of the United States. The tune appeared in Ananias Davisson's 1820 *Supplement to Kentucky Harmony* (see PHH 83), where it was set to the folk hymn "His Voice As the Sound of a Dulcimer Sweet" (thus the title, which means "listener" in Hebrew). The harmonization was composed by AnnaMae Meyer Bush (PHH 268). Sing this rounded bar form tune (AABA) in unison throughout. Keep the accompaniment light.

Liturgical Use

Advent; other worship that emphasizes the qualities of the kingdom of God, both here and to come.

617

Swing Low, Sweet Chariot

SWING LOW
♪ = 76

Text

This is one of the best-known African American spirituals in Christian history. Its source is the oral tradition of African Americans, but the concerts of the Fisk Jubilee Singers (PHH 476) and the Hampton Singers brought "Swing Low" to the attention of white audiences. J. B. T. Marsh includes an early version of text and tune in his *The Story of the Jubilee Singers, with their Songs* (1876 ed.).

Considered by Erik Routley (PHH 31) to be one of the "archetypal" African American spirituals, "Swing Low" welcomes death as the occasion "to carry me home" to glory. The text incorporates the imagery of "Jordan" and "chariot" from the Old Testament narratives of Elijah's ascent into heaven (2 Kings 2). In spite of the "ups" and "downs" of earthly life (st. 3), it is comforting for Christians to know with certainty that their final destination is the glory of a new heaven and earth.

Tune

A pentatonic melody, SWING LOW has the musical structure of "call and response" (solo and chorus), which is common in the rote practices associated with African American spirituals. Use a vocal soloist or a small group of voices for the marked unison segments and have the entire congregation sing the harmony parts. Although ideally this spiritual is sung unaccompanied, the continual changes from unison to harmony can also be emphasized with instruments. Some melodic and rhythmic liberties should be taken in singing the solo lines. Do not rush!

Liturgical Use
Advent; times of hardship; with preaching on 2 Kings 2 or on eschatological topics.

618

EWING
♩ = 54

Jerusalem the Golden

Text

This hymn was translated from part of a satiric poem of almost three thousand lines, "De Contemptu Mundi" ("the contemptable world"), written around 1145 by the twelfth-century monk Bernard of Cluny. Not to be confused with Bernard of Clairvaux, Bernard of Cluny is thought to have been born in Murles, France, supposedly of English parents. He spent the greater part of his adult

Scripture References
st. 1 = Rev. 21:1-2, 21
st. 2 = Rev. 21:12-14, 22-25
Rev. 22:1-2
st. 3 = Rev. 22:3-5
st. 4 = Heb. 11:13-16

life in the famous monastery of Cluny during the time that Peter the Venerable was its abbot (1122-1156). Founded in 910 with high standards of monastic observance, the monastery was wealthy—its abbey, with splendid worship services, was the largest of its time. In the twelfth century there were more than three hundred monasteries that had adopted the Cluny order. During his life Bernard was known for his published sermons and his piety, but his lasting fame rests on "De Contemptu Mundi."

In that poem Bernard applied dactylic hexameter (six groups of triplets) and intricate internal rhyme schemes to satirize the evils of his culture, as well as those of the church and his own monastery. Amazed at his own skill and discipline, Bernard said, "Unless the Spirit of wisdom and understanding had flowed in upon me, I could not have put together so long a work in so difficult a meter." To put sin in sharp relief, Bernard began his poem by focusing on the glories of heaven.

Seven hundred years later Richard C. Trench published the initial stanzas of the poem, beginning "Urbs Sion aurea, patria lactea," in his *Sacred Latin Poetry* (1849). John M. Neale (PHH 342) translated this portion of the poem into English and published it in his *Medieval Hymns and Sequences* (1851). Neale made revisions and additions to his earlier free translation when he published it in his *The Rhythm of Bernard* (1858). The text found in the *Psalter Hymnal* is the most popular of the four hymns derived from Neale's translation.

This text "of such rare beauty" (Neale's words) is based on the imagery of the new Jerusalem found in Revelation 21:22. Like the saints described in Hebrews 11:13-16, Christians today long "for a better country—a heavenly one. Therefore God . . . has prepared a city for them." As we sing "Jerusalem the Golden," we yearn for a fulfillment of this vision, for the Lord to come quickly so that we may be a part of "the city of God's presence."

Tune

Alexander Ewing (b. Old Aachar, Aberdeen, Scotland, 1830; d. Taunton, Somerset, England, 1895) originally composed EWING for "For Thee, O Dear, Dear Country," another hymn taken from Neale's translation of Bernard's poem. At first in triple meter, the tune was sung to that text by the Aberdeen Harmonic Choir (of which Ewing was a member) and published in leaflet form in 1853 and in Grey's *Manual of Psalms and Hymn-Tunes* (1857).

After having studied law, German, and music, Ewing served in the British army during the Crimean War and in the foreign service in Australia and China. An accomplished amateur musician (an excellent pianist), he was active in the Haydn Society of Aberdeen and in the Aberdeen Harmonic Choir. Ewing is known today only because of the one popular tune named after him.

EWING was recast into duple meter by William H. Monk (PHH 332) and set to "Jerusalem the Golden" in *Hymns Ancient and Modern* (1861). A strong tune for this text, EWING has a wide compass and a glorious ascent in its third line. Sing in harmony with robust dignity.

Liturgical Use

Any service in which the new creation (as symbolized in the celestial city) is the theme; as a song of comfort and hope; for meditation.

619

Ten Thousand Times Ten Thousand

ALFORD
♩ = 112

Text

Henry Alford (PHH 527) was Dean of Canterbury Cathedral when he wrote this text. Designating it for the twenty-first Sunday after Trinity, he published the three-stanza text in the magazine *Good Words* in March 1867 and later that same year in his *Year of Praise*. A fourth stanza was added when the hymn was reprinted in *The Lord's Prayer Illustrated*, prepared by Pickersgill and Alford in 1870. The *Psalter Hymnal* includes the revised, three-stanza version found in *Hymns for Today's Church* (1982).

Scripture References
st. 1 = Rev. 5:6-14
Dan. 7:9-10

A noted New Testament scholar, Alford drew his imagery for this text about the church triumphant from John's Revelation. Stanza 1 portrays the "ten thousand times ten thousand" angels who praise the victorious Lamb upon the throne and who are then joined by the "countless voices" of all creatures praising God (see Rev. 5:11-13). The second stanza is an exclamation of joy and comforting anticipation of the final victory of God's saints. Stanza 3 is a "Maranatha" prayer, which urges Christ to come quickly and usher in the consummation of his glorious kingdom ("Desire of Nations" is an Old Testament name for the Messiah; see Hag. 2:7).

Tune

John B. Dykes (PHH 147) composed ALFORD for this text. Tune and text were published in the revised edition of *Hymns Ancient and Modern* (1875). Typical in many ways of Victorian hymn tunes, ALFORD has a passable melody that is subjected to a harmony that periodically goes beyond shameless sentimentality. Sing in parts and use a bright solo stop on the organ.

Liturgical Use

Advent; with eschatological preaching; other occasions of worship when a "Maranatha" hymn is appropriate.

620

CRYSTAL
♩ = 58

By the Sea of Crystal

Text

Once, after hearing Edward Elgar's "Pomp and Circumstance" march, William Kuipers (PHH 87) decided to write a new hymn text that could be sung to it. At the time the march was associated with the patriotic hymn "Land of Hope and Glory." Kuipers wrote this text late in 1932 while he was pastor of the Summer Street Christian Reformed Church (CRC), Passaic, New Jersey. He submitted it to Henry J. Kuiper, editor of the Christian Reformed Church weekly, *The Banner*, and a member of the committee preparing the 1934 *Psalter Hymnal*, which was the first denominational collection including hymns (the CRC had previously sung only psalms in worship).

Scripture References
st. 1 = Rev. 4:6
st. 2 = Rev. 7:9
st. 3 = Rev. 7:10-17

Because Elgar's music was under copyright, *The Banner* held a contest to find a new tune for Kuipers's text. The magazine received 150 tune entries and recognized first, second, and third places, as well as six honorable mentions. First prize of $10 was awarded to Siebolt H. Frieswyk of Whitinsville, Massachusetts, and his tune was published with Kuipers's text in *The Banner*, May 5, 1933. However, an honorable-mention winner by John Vanderhoven was chosen as the setting for this text when the new *Psalter Hymnal* was printed in 1934. That association of text and tune has been continued in each of the following editions of the *Psalter Hymnal.* Because it was used as a theme song for the *Back to God Hour* broadcasts, this hymn became well known to a whole generation of radio listeners in the 1950s and 60s.

The text's theme is drawn from John's vision of the saints in glory singing one of their great doxologies (Rev. 7:9-17). The initial reference to the "sea of crystal" is from Revelation 4:6—"Also before the throne there was what looked like a sea of glass, clear as crystal." And the final (rhetorical) reference to the "King of kings" (st. 3) comes from Revelation 17:14.

Tune

John (born Johann Ludwig) Vanderhoven (b. Rotterdam, the Netherlands, 1887; d. Grand Rapids, MI, 1974) immigrated to the United States in 1912 and worked at various vocations. He concluded his career as owner of the Sterling Sponge and Chamois Company in Grand Rapids, Michigan (1951-1962). VanderHoven served as organist in several Christian Reformed congregations, including Burton Heights Christian Reformed Church in Grand Rapids from 1931 to 1942. A frequent improviser of preludes and offertory music for church, he also composed a number of hymn tunes and anthems.

CRYSTAL is a sturdy melody distinguished by occasional dotted rhythms and a fine climax in the last line (where the harmonization has a moment of Victorian chromaticism). Sing in parts on stanzas 1 and 2 and in unison with the support of bright organ tones on stanza 3. Organists might want to play in the original key of A major as found in earlier editions of the *Psalter Hymnal.*

Liturgical Use

Worship that focuses on the praise of God in glory; funerals; stanza 3 as a doxology.

621

The God of Abraham Praise

LEONI
♩ = 58

Text

This text is based on a Jewish doxology of thirteen articles formulated by Moses ben Maimon (Maimonides) in the latter part of the twelfth century. A fourteenth-century metrical version of that doxology, *Yigdal Elohim* ("magnify the Lord"), is traditionally used in daily morning synagogue services and during the Sabbath eve in Jewish family worship. That version is variously attributed to Daniel ben Judah or to Immanuel ben Solomon, both of whom lived in Rome. After hearing the Jewish cantor Meyer Lyon sing this *Yigdal* in the Duke's Place Synagogue, London, England, Thomas Olivers (b. Tregynon, Montgomeryshire, England, 1725; d. London, England, 1799) prepared an English paraphrase in twelve stanzas (around 1770). About his paraphrase, Olivers reportedly said, "I have rendered it from the Hebrew, giving it, as far as I could, a Christian character, and I have called on Leoni [the cantor Lyon] who has given me a synagogue melody to suit it."

Orphaned at the age of four, Olivers was negligently cared for by various relatives and received very little formal education. He worked as a cobbler but lived such a scandalous life that he was forced to leave his hometown. However, his life changed drastically after he was converted by a George Whitefield sermon on the text "Is not this a branch plucked out of the fire?" (Zech. 3:2). At first a follower of Whitefield, Olivers joined John and Charles Wesley (PHH 267) in 1753. He served as an itinerant Methodist preacher, traveling one hundred thousand miles on horseback through much of England, Scotland, and Ireland until 1777. He became editor of the *Arminian Magazine* in 1775, but John Wesley dismissed him in 1789 because of flagrant printing errors and the insertion of articles that Wesley did not approve. Olivers wrote only a few hymns, of which "The God of Abraham Praise" is most well-known.

His text with Leoni's tune was published as a leaflet, "A Hymn to the God of Abraham," in 1772. The hymn was also published by John Wesley in his *Sacred Harmony* (1780) and in 1830 in Joshua Leavitt's popular American frontier hymnal *The Christian Lyre* (PHH 171). It appears in most modern hymnals (but should not be confused with another hymnic translation of the *Yigdal* that begins, "Praise to the living God," by Max Landsberg, Newton Mann, and William Gannett). The *Psalter Hymnal* includes Olivers's stanzas 1, 4, 6, 7, and 12 in a modernized text borrowed in part from *Hymns for Today's Church* (1982).

Like the *Yigdal*, this text begins by praising God for his sovereignty and faithfulness to his people (st. 1-2). God gives his people a land "of milk and honey," an image that becomes a rich eschatological metaphor for the new creation (st. 3-4) in which angels sing "Holy, holy, holy," and all creatures join in praise to God (st. 5). Olivers appended many biblical references to the margin of his text. The primary ones for these stanzas are Exodus 3 and the great doxologies in Revelation 4, 5, and 7.

Scripture References
st. 1 = Ex. 3:6, 15
Dan. 7:9, 13, 22
st. 2 = Gen. 22:16-17
Mal. 3:6
st. 3 = Rev. 22:1-2
st. 4 = Jer. 23:6
Jer. 33:16
st. 5 = Isa. 6:3
Rev. 4:8-11

Tune

Named after the Jewish cantor whose performance of the *Yigdal* inspired Olivers to write this text, LEONI is the second of the seven historic Jewish melodies associated with the great Hebrew doxology, which were handed down orally from one cantor to another. Olivers adapted Lyon's version for congregational use. Known also by his liturgical name, Meyer Leoni (b. London, England, 1751; d. Kingston, Jamaica, 1797),

Lyon was a tenor at the Covent Garden and Drury Lane theaters in London and a cantor in several synagogues, including the Great Synagogue in Aldgate.

LEONI is a magnificent tune with lots of life and vibrant rhythms. Sing the outer stanzas in a full-voiced unison and the middle ones in harmony at a more moderate volume. The harmonization is taken from *Hymns Ancient and Modern* (1875). Because the *Yigdal* was traditionally sung in responsorial fashion, antiphonal singing might be appropriate.

Liturgical Use
As a monumental hymn of praise, especially at the close of a service; with eschatological preaching; during Advent.

622

Magnify the Lord

MAGNIFICAT
♩ = 58

Text
This delightful canon comes from the Taizé Community, an ecumenical, monastic retreat center in France (see also 217, 312, and 639). Like many of the first Taizé songs, "Magnify the Lord" was originally in Latin ("Magnificat Anima Mea"). It was published in France by the Taizé Community in 1978 and two years later in North America in the first volume of *Music from Taizé*. The original Latin text consisted entirely of repetitions of the opening phrase of the Song of Mary. In 1985 Bert Polman (PHH 37) prepared an English version of the text to which he added several other phrases from the opening verses of Mary's Song (Luke 1:46-47, 49). This English version was first published in the 1987 *Psalter Hymnal.*

Scripture References
st. = Luke 1:46-49

The text is one of three in the *Psalter Hymnal* taken from Mary's Song as recorded in Luke's gospel (see PHH 212 and 478 for further commentary on this profound biblical passage). The segment of the Song of Mary in this canon becomes for us a hymn of praise to Christ, an ascription of glory to the "Lord who is my Savior and my God!"

Tune
This canonic setting of the MAGNIFICAT appeared in *Music from Taizé* as a double canon: a principal canon in four parts (given in larger print in the *Psalter Hymnal*) and a secondary canon in four parts (given as a descant). The same score also provides two different four-part choral settings, which choir directors could consult and use for more elaborate performances of this festive canon. The options for singing range from simple unison to four-part canon (with or without descant) to double canon with full harmonizations (using separate choral harmonizations, which add fuller textures to the

harmony of the melodic canons). Bert Polman introduced the dotted rhythm to carry the English text. That rhythm needs to be sung crisply and distinguished from the regular eighth-note rhythms. Do not rush!

Liturgical Use
As a song (canon) of jubilant praise to God on various occasions of worship; during the Christmas season; traditionally as the New Testament canticle for vesper services.

623
Unto Christ, Who Loved Us

UNTO HIM THAT LOVED US
♩ = 76

Text
This text originally appeared in *The Daily Service* (1936), the full music edition of the British *Prayers and Hymns for Schools,* of which Ralph Vaughan Williams (PHH 316) was an editor. "Unto Christ" was included in the Order of Morning Prayer for Fridays.

Scripture References
st. = Rev. 1:5-6

The text is taken from Revelation 1:5-6, which contains a doxology attached to the opening greeting addressed to the "seven churches in the province of Asia." The first clause helps us focus our praise on Christ our Savior, who commissioned us to be his kings and priests (see Ex. 19:6). The final words, "glory and dominion for ever and ever," are part of the familiar formula for doxologies—our ascription of praise to our Lord Jesus Christ.

Tune
The fine composer, folk music scholar, and noted hymnal editor Ralph Vaughan Williams (PHH 316) composed this setting for the biblical text for Oxford University Press's *The Daily Service* (1936). This simple unison melody became familiar to Christian day-school students and Christian Reformed Churches because of its inclusion in *Hymns for Youth* (1966).

Sing with an energetic ascent toward the climax on "unto him be glory and dominion"; let the textual punctuation suggest the musical phrases.

Liturgical Use
Baptism; as a conclusion to spoken prayers; as a doxologic coda to another hymn (291, 573) or a doxology at the conclusion of worship.

624

Hear Our Prayer, O Lord

WHELPTON
♩ = 50

Text

The text of this prayer response is derived from Psalm 143:1, "O
Lord, hear my prayer, listen to my cry for mercy." Its final phrase,
"grant us your peace," is taken from the conclusion of the ancient
liturgical text *Agnus Dei* (see also 257) and is followed by an
"Amen." Taken together, these two phrases constitute an urgent petition for the Lord
God to hear our prayers and a confession of certainty that he will do so. Though there
is no proof, it can be assumed that the composer of the tune, George Whelpton, chose
these textual phrases when he composed this prayer chorus in 1897. The hymn was first
published in leaflet form and later appeared in *Hymns for American Youth* (1924),
compiled by H. Augustine Smith.

Scripture References
st. = Ps. 143:1
John 14:27

Tune

George Whelpton (b. Redbourne, England, 1847; d. Oxford, OH, 1930) immigrated to
the United States with his family in 1851. He enlisted in the Union army at the age of
sixteen, serving as an assistant pharmacist during the Civil War. Educated at the Lake
Chautauqua School of Music, he was a popular choir director in Buffalo, New York, for
some twenty years. Whelpton moved to New York City in 1903 to become an editor for
the Century Publishing Company. Among his editorial projects were *Hymns of Worship
and Service* and *The Church Hymnal*. He joined the editorial staff of the A. Barnes
Publishing Company in 1916 and served there until his retirement in 1925.

   WHELPTON is a simple prayer response, ideally sung unaccompanied, in harmony,
with a light registration on the organ.

Liturgical Use

As a conclusion to silent or congregational prayer; entirely or perhaps with only the first
phrase repeated as a refrain/response in a litany.

625

Lord, Listen to Your Children Praying

CHILDREN PRAYING
♩ = 66

Text

Author-composer-performer Ken Medema (PHH 259) says the
following about his writing of this prayer hymn:

Scripture References
st. = Ps. 55:1

"Lord, Listen to Your Children Praying" came out of my New Jersey years. One night [in 1970], I was with a youth group. We started talking about a young man who was in the hospital and who really needed our prayers. In the middle of our prayer time, the idea for this little chorus came to me. I started humming, then singing. Soon the kids were mumbling along with me. We sang that chorus, "Lord, listen to your children praying," several times over. Then I started adding verses, and the kids quickly joined me in singing the new words. So it was a song born out of our concern and prayer for a friend.

—Reformed Worship 9, Fall 1988, p. 4

The complete song was recorded on Medema's album *Son Shiny Day* (Word, 1973) and published in an accompanying songbook. As do other recent hymnals, the *Psalter Hymnal* includes only the chorus, not the various stanzas.

This chorus has become a popular sung prayer for the presence of the Holy Spirit, for the Father's love, and for the grace of Jesus Christ to direct our lives. The words "love," "power," and "grace" in the final line allude to the well-known New Testament benediction (see 2 Cor. 13:14).

Tune

CHILDREN PRAYING is easy to sing from memory, and that should be encouraged. Be sure to keep fairly strict rhythms on the whole and half notes—some congregations may be tempted to cut short the cadences; accompanists could help by improvising with additional rhythmic accompaniment on the longer notes.

Liturgical Use

As a song that concludes a prayer (for example, a silent prayer) or that frames a time of prayer; prayer meetings; ordination and commissioning services; baptism; a choral invocation at the beginning of worship.

626

MERENGUE
♩ = 84
"Holy, Holy, Holy"/"Santo, Santo, Santo"

Text

"Holy, Holy, Holy" is derived from the song of the angels in Isaiah's *Scripture References* vision (Isa. 6:3). The early Christian church added other liturgical   st. = Isa. 6:3 phrases such as "Hosanna" and "Blessed is he who comes in the name of the Lord" (Ps. 118:26) to the passage from Isaiah. That expanded text eventually became the Sanctus of the Roman Mass and is still sung in every Mass (now in the vernacular). The Sanctus was retained by the Lutheran tradition, appearing in chorale form (Martin Luther's "Jesaia, dem Propheten, das geschach") and in various plainsong and metrical settings. It is also the basis for other hymns such as "Holy, Holy, Holy, Lord God Almighty" (249).

This Spanish setting of the Sanctus was submitted by the Hispanic task force who selected music from Hispanic sources for the 1987 *Psalter Hymnal.* The song, typical of the many folk choruses known by evangelical Christians throughout Latin America, is often paired with "No Hay Dios" (517) in the Hispanic community, where the tradition is to sing several choruses together in medley fashion. Bert Polman (PHH 37) translated the Spanish text into English, and AnnaMae Meyer Bush (PHH 268) supplied the harmonization, both in 1985 for the 1987 *Psalter Hymnal.*

This hymn text is an ascription of holiness and glory to God by his angels and by us, God's people. It affirms that the whole cosmos testifies to God's glory (as in Ps. 19:1) and concludes with a prayer for salvation ("Hosanna" means "save us, O Lord").

Tune
The tune's title, MERENGUE, refers to a Hispanic dance form common in Cuba and Haiti; some of the dance's rhythmic characteristics are stylized in this music. Intended for rather majestic, unison singing, this chorus needs to be supported with strong accompaniment on keyboard and/or guitars. Hand clapping or the use of other percussion instruments would also be appropriate.

Liturgical Use
Traditionally the Sanctus is sung at the end of the Great Thanksgiving Prayer, which begins the liturgy for the Lord's Supper (see *Psalter Hymnal,* pp. 973-974), but this acclamation may also be used for praising God on many other occasions in Christian worship (including Palm Sunday).

627

Bless His Holy Name

BLESS THE LORD
♩ = 104

Text
Gospel musician Andraé Crouch (PHH 552) composed a song for the familiar opening phrases of Psalm 103, one of the much-loved Old Testament hymns about God's love and compassion for his people. Only the refrain, which frames his longer text, is included in the *Psalter Hymnal;* the same words provide a frame around the entire psalm. Crouch retains the conventional Hebrew custom of addressing oneself as "my soul." Crouch's phrase "He has done great things" is a summary reference to all the mighty and compassionate deeds of the Lord described in Psalm 103—God forgives, heals, provides, and redeems; and

Scripture References
st. = Ps. 103:1

he is gracious, patient, loving, and just (see PHH 103 for additional comments on the psalm).

Crouch and his ensemble, The Disciples, popularized this chorus by their numerous performances in the early 1970s. The hymn was recorded and published by Lexicon Music in 1973, both as a four-part choral octavo and as a solo piece.

Tune

Sing BLESS THE LORD with jubilant unison voices accompanied by a complement of African American gospel-style instruments: piano, electric organ, and drums. Several solo voices in the congregation could improvise alternate soprano melodies and/or substitute other lyrics for "He has done great things," especially if the song is repeated; alternate phrases derived from Psalm 103 include: he forgives my sins; he redeems my life; he renews my youth; he made known his ways; he is slow to anger; he abounds in love (other phrases from Ps. 103).

Liturgical Use

As a chorus of praise to God on many occasions of worship, especially on the great feast days of the church calendar, like Christmas and Easter, when we think of the "great things" God has done.

628

WINCHESTER OLD
♩ = 104
Praise God, You Angel Hosts Above

Text

This summary of Psalm 150 was adapted from a text first found in the 1912 *Psalter.* Like the psalm, "Praise God" invites the angels above, saints below, and all creation to glorify the Lord.

Scripture References
st. 1 = Ps. 150:1
st. 2 = Ps. 150:6

Tune

See PHH 215 for a discussion of WINCHESTER OLD.

This hymn becomes a festive doxology when sung in parts with suitably strong organ accompaniment. Consider using the descant at 215 for the second stanza. Because the original psalm calls upon various instruments to praise the Lord, on a festive occasion add instruments like trumpets, drums, and cymbals.

Liturgical Use

As a doxology—Psalm 150 is the great doxology of the entire book of Psalms.

629

Worthy Is Christ/Digno Es Jesús

DIGNO ES JESUS
♩ = 96

Text

Like many other Hispanic choruses, this is a true folk song in that
it has an anonymous author, composer, and source. "Worthy Is
Christ" was submitted by members of the Hispanic task force that
provided recommendations to the *Psalter Hymnal* Revision
Committee. The task force knew the song from memory and presented it to the
committee by singing it. *Psalter Hymnal* editor Emily R. Brink (PHH 158) notated the
hymn during the meeting.

Scripture References
st. 1 = Rev. 5:9
st. 2 = Rev. 5:12

   The text is a personal testimonial of praise derived from two of the great doxologies
in the last book of the New Testament, which are sung in praise of the Lamb, Jesus
Christ:

> You are worthy . . .
> because you were slain,
> and with your blood you purchased men for God
> from every tribe and language and people and nation. . . .
>
> Worthy is the Lamb, who was slain,
> to receive power and wealth and wisdom and strength
> and honor and glory and praise!

—Revelation 5:9, 12

Tune

Presumably a tune from oral tradition, DIGNO ES JESUS has a dignified choral harmonization that suggests part singing. Try using guitar accompaniment (it could be
accompanied with only three chords: F, B-flat, and C). The stanza-refrain character of
the text could be emphasized by singing the stanza line in unison and the refrain line in
harmony. Sing at a tempo that encourages meditative singing and do not rush.

Liturgical Use

As a sung response to Scripture reading; as a doxology anytime but, given the second
stanza, especially during Lent and at Easter services.

630

CORONATION
♩ = 56

Now Blessed Be the Lord Our God

Text

Each of the internal "books" or original anthologies within the book of Psalms concludes with its own doxology. Psalm 72, at the end of Book II, features a doxology at verses 18 and 19. That biblical text is paraphrased in this hymn, a paraphrase originally published in the 1650 edition of the Scottish Psalter. However, what was originally a standard four-line common-meter text has been stretched into common meter of six lines to suit the tune.

Scripture References
st. 1 = Ps. 72:18
st. 2 = Ps. 72:19

"Now Blessed Be" is cast in the *berakah* form common in Jewish worship. God is to be blessed, or praised, because of his wondrous works and mighty deeds (st. 1) and because his saving acts reveal his glory throughout the earth and throughout eternity (st. 2). Amen and Amen! So shall it be! (For further discussion of Psalm 72 see PHH 72.)

Tune

See PHH 471 for a discussion of CORONATION.

This doxology invites full voices with a vigorous accompaniment that grows in strength until the final "Amen."

Liturgical Use

As a doxology anytime, but because its basis is Psalm 72 (one of the finest messianic psalms), especially during Advent, Epiphany, and Ascension; missionary festivals.

631

LOBET UND PREISET
♩ = 54

Praise and Thanksgiving

Text

Stanza 1 of this text was originally a traditional German round from the Alsace region ("Lobet und preiset"). Edith Lovell Thomas (b. Eastford, CT, 1878; d. Claremont, CA, 1970) translated the text and published it in her *The Whole World Singing* (1950).

A graduate of Boston University and the School of Sacred Music at Union Theological Seminary in New York City, Thomas served as both educator and church musician. She taught music and worship at Boston University (1918-1932), directed church school music at Christ Church Methodist in New York City, and cofounded the Miss Thomas Preparatory School in Collingswood, New Jersey. Through much teaching and guest lecturing, she played an active role in promoting music and singing in church education. Her publications include several children's hymnals: *Singing Worship* (1935), *Sing, Children, Sing* (1939), and *The Whole World Singing* (1950), and the text-book *Music in Christian Education* (1953).

Marie J. Post (PHH 5) added two stanzas, and all three were then published in the *Psalter Hymnal Supplement* (1974). The first two stanzas call everyone to join in joyful song to praise God for his many blessings, "for every good thing." The final stanza is a prayer for all of us to live a Christian life of love in the world.

Tune
Congregations may want to try singing LOBET UND PREISET as a three-part round; that works well with a text that enjoins everyone to sing. In 1985 Dale Grotenhuis (PHH 4) provided the keyboard accompaniment, which is suitable for unison or canonic singing.

Liturgical Use
The entire hymn as a doxology at the close of worship; stanzas 1 and 2 as a call to worship, perhaps in unison, then concluding the service with stanza 3 in canon; as a hymn of praise for many joyful occasions.

632

To God Be the Glory

MY TRIBUTE
♩ = 88

Text
In 1971 African American gospel composer and performer Andraé Crouch (PHH 552) composed a choral work entitled *My Tribute* in which this song is the refrain. The text's opening lines are derived from Fanny J. Crosby's famous hymn text "To God Be the Glory, Great Things He Has Done" (473). The closing lines refer to two of the most important "things he has done"—providing salvation through Christ's atoning blood and granting new life to all believers in Christ's resurrection. Thus two essential doctrines of the Christian faith are forcefully and beautifully confessed in this simple song.

Tune
MY TRIBUTE requires strong accompaniment with crisp rhythms and exuberant voices from people who know how great God's saving deeds are! Try singing the hymn twice in succession. Add other instruments as desired or available, including percussion, which is customary in the African American gospel style. Do not rush!

Liturgical Use

Though especially appropriate during the Easter season, this joyful "cheerleading" chorus is appropriate for many different services and at various times in the service—with Scripture readings, spoken testimonies, the Lord's Supper, and at other times of thanksgiving for God's mighty acts in Christ.

633

He Is Lord

Text

One of numerous anonymous Scripture songs arising out of the charismatic movement during the 1960s and following, this popular song is drawn from the well-known confession of faith recorded in Philippians 2:10-11. There Paul appears to be quoting from an early Christian hymn that was used as a profession of faith. The following are additional stanzas, also anonymous, printed in the British Methodist *Hymns and Psalms* and in *The Worshiping Church* (1990); these may be freely reprinted in church bulletins:

Scripture References
st. = Phil. 2:10-11

He is King, he is King!
He will draw all nations to him, he is King;
and the time shall be when the world shall sing
that Jesus Christ is King!

He is Love, he is Love!
He has shown us by his life that he is Love.
All his people sing with one voice of joy
that Jesus Christ is Love!

He is Life, he is Life!
He has died to set us free and he is Life;
and he calls us all to live evermore,
for Jesus Christ is Life!

These additional stanzas use phrases from John's gospels to extol Christ as the king who draws all nations to him (John 12:32), as the source and model of love (1 John 3:16), and as the surety for eternal life (1 John 5:11).

Tune

HE IS LORD should be sung with great conviction as a bold testimony to all the world that "Jesus is Lord!" Use strong accompaniment, but do not rush the tempo. When the hymn is sung with some or all of the additional stanzas, conclude the singing with a repeat of the first stanza.

Liturgical Use

As a sung profession of faith in many different times and places of worship; during the Easter season; Lord's Supper.

634

Father, We Love You

GLORIFY YOUR NAME
♩ = 56

Text

Donna Adkins composed this fine song in 1976 and entitled it "Glorify Thy Name." The hymn was first published in a small booklet used at a pastor's conference and was later published by Maranatha! Music in 1981 in the collection *Praise 5*. It also appeared on the corresponding recording of the same name. Adkins writes the following about her composition of this hymn:

Scripture References
st. = John 12:28; 17:1-5
Ps. 108:5
Isa. 6:3

> One morning while reading the seventeenth chapter of John, I began to meditate on the prayer of Jesus. I saw in a new way that Jesus was not only praying for His disciples, but for *all* who would follow Him in years to come. He was actually praying for me! I was impressed that Jesus was placing great emphasis on the unity in the Godhead. I also saw that it was very important to Jesus that the Father's name be glorified, and that there seemed to be a correlation between glorifying the Father's name and achieving unity. In that same moment I was inspired to sit at the piano and write "Glorify Thy Name."

With a Trinitarian structure in its three stanzas, this popular hymn is one of the finest praise choruses as well as prayer hymns from the mid-1970s. "Father, We Love You" first expresses our humble love and devotion to God and then offers Jesus' own prayer, "glorify your name" (see John 12:28; 17:1-5). God's name is glorified in the completion of Christ's ministry on earth, in the faithful testimony of God's family, the church, and in the praises of angels and saints in heaven. As we sing, we also pray for God's glory to arise from "all the earth" (see Ps. 108:5 and Isa. 6:3). Thus the text has a biblically cosmic ring: "all the earth" refers to our whole lives, all the nations, and, in fact, the entire creation!

Donna Whobrey Adkins (b. Louisville, KY, 1940) began singing in public at the age of two and by the age of twelve was playing piano for the family quartet. Her parents were church musicians and traveling gospel singers. Educated at Asbury College in Wilmore, Kentucky, and the University of Louisville, Kentucky, she has served on the music staff of several churches and currently serves as the secretary to the senior pastor of the Covenant Church of Pittsburgh, Pennsylvania.

Tune

GLORIFY YOUR NAME is best sung in harmony, possibly without instrumental accompaniment, although instruments could be helpful in negotiating the longer cadences in lines 2 and 4. The hymn is really a glorious unaccompanied chorus! Try beginning the stanzas rather quietly and humbly and then increase the volume with each new repetition of the words "glorify your name." Sing prayerfully with an inner intensity that gives the hymn fervor and energy. Keep a majestic tempo and do not rush. Encourage your congregation to sing this song from memory.

Liturgical Use

As a fitting choral invocation at the beginning of worship and a beautiful prayer following sermons that set forth the glory of God; a doxology for many occasions of worship.

635

MEINEKE
♩ = 60

Glory Be to the Father

Text

This Gloria Patri text is usually known as the "Lesser Doxology" (what is known as the "Greater Doxology" begins "Gloria in excelsis Deo"; see 247). It is a liturgical text common to most Christian traditions and is often appended to the singing of Old Testament psalms or New Testament canticles. The traditional version of this text is found here, while a more modern translation occurs at 636.

The initial part of the Gloria Patri may be traced back to the Trinitarian baptismal formula recorded in Matthew 28:19; it was probably used by early Christians as an acclamation. The second part, which begins "as it was in the beginning," was added in the fourth century as a response to the Arian heresy. Thus the text reflects the orthodox insistence on the consubstantiality of the Son with the Father and the eternal unity and equality of the three persons in the Trinity.

Tune

Charles (Christoph) Meineke (b. Oldenburg, Germany, 1782; d. Baltimore, MD, 1850) immigrated from Germany to England in 1810, then came to the United States in 1820. He composed the MEINEKE chant for an "Evening Prayer" to be used at St. Paul Episcopal Church, Baltimore, where Meineke was organist. The tune was published in his collection of psalm and hymn tunes and service music for St. Paul's congregation, *Music for the Church* (1844).

Otherwise quite serviceable, MEINEKE is marred by one mismatched textual and musical phrase—the rhythms and melodic contour for "and to the Son" do not work well for those words. In spite of this obvious fault "Glory Be to the Father" is hallowed by tradition. Sing in harmony with conviction and with appropriate rhythmic vigor.

Liturgical Use
Traditionally used at the end of Old Testament psalms and New Testament canticles and at the conclusion of certain prayers or creedal statements; a general doxology.

636

Glory to the Father

BETHEL PARK
$\downarrow = 72$

Text
"Glory to the Father" is a modern translation of the traditional Latin Gloria Patri or "Lesser Doxology" (see PHH 635 for discussion of that text). This translation is similar to one recommended by the International Consultation on English Texts (ICET), which reads as follows:

Glory to the Father, and to the Son,
and to the Holy Spirit;
as it was in the beginning, is now,
and will be forever. Amen.

—ICET version, 1975

Tune
John Erickson (b. Ottawa, IL, 1938) composed BETHEL PARK in 1984 for use at Christ United Methodist Church in Bethel Park, Pennsylvania, where he was organist and director of worship. Although the setting of the Gloria Patri at 635 is intended for part singing, BETHEL PARK is meant for unison voices. Sing the half-note rhythms crisply and use bright organ sounds for accompaniment.

Erickson was educated at the American Conservatory of Music in Chicago, Illinois, and at Northwestern University in Evanston, Illinois. His choral music illustrates that he has been strongly influenced by the English tradition of cathedral music. He has served as music director in several churches and since 1982 has been organist and director of worship at Christ United Methodist Church.

Liturgical Use
See PHH 635.

637

Praise God, from Whom All Blessings Flow

Text

As indicated at 635 and 636, the practice of adding a Gloria Patri doxology to Old Testament psalms and New Testament canticles is an ancient tradition in the Christian church. After the Reformation, many Protestant groups kept up that practice; for example, Puritan psalters included various metrical versions of the Gloria Patri for use with the singing of the psalms in meter. This text (and 638) is the most famous of such metrical doxologies. It was written by Thomas Ken (PHH 441), possibly as early as 1674, for the conclusion of each of his "Three Hymns for Morning, Evening, and Midnight." The three hymns were published in the 1695 edition of Ken's *A Manual of Prayers* (for use at Winchester College) and revised in the 1709 edition. Eventually, this doxology began to be used independently of Ken's hymn texts.

Scripture References
st. = Ps. 150:1

The text calls forth praise to God from the whole universe, from creatures on earth and from saints and angels in heaven. Concluding with praise for the Trinity, this doxology is likely the most well-known expression of the doctrine of the Trinity in hymn form.

Tune

NEW DOXOLOGY is a musical setting from the oral traditions of the African American community. The first phrase of this tune is identical to DUKE STREET (412), and that may cause confusion in some congregations. The harmonization is unmistakably African American gospel style, however, and should be accompanied by piano and other instruments including drums (if played on the organ, this tune could be simplified by omitting some of the triplets, especially on the "Amen" line). Sing in unison; keep a majestic pace in the style of African American slow-meter hymns.

Liturgical Use

As a hymn of praise at the beginning of worship or doxology at the conclusion of worship; for many other occasions of special thanksgiving.

638

Praise God, from Whom All Blessings Flow

GENEVAN 134 (Old Hundredth)
♩ = 88

Text and Tune

See PHH 637 for discussion of the text and PHH 134 for a discussion of OLD HUN-
DREDTH (GENEVAN 134). The harmonization here differs slightly from that at 134.
In the past 150 years "Praise God, from Whom All Blessings Flow" sung to OLD HUN-
DREDTH has become the best known of all Christian doxologies.

Liturgical Use

See PHH 637.

639

Alleluia

TAIZÉ ALLELUIA
♩ = 80

Text

"Alleluia" is the Greek spelling of a Hebrew expression, "Hallelu Yah[weh]," which
simply means "praise the Lord." That phrase is found in the Old Testament as a frame
around a number of the psalms (Ps. 103-106; 146-150) and in the New Testament in
Revelation 19:1-6. In Christian liturgical use "alleluia" is usually sung in conjunction
with one of the Scripture readings as an acclamation (except during Lent). It is also
used during Easter and appears as a phrase in many hymns. Some musical settings of
"alleluia" are overtly jubilant; for example, George F. Handel's famous "Hallelujah"
chorus in *The Messiah*. But there are many ways to sing "alleluia"—note all the "alleluia"
hymns in the *Psalter Hymnal* (see the index of first lines).

Tune

Jacques Berthier composed TAIZÉ ALLELUIA for use at the Taizé Community (see PHH
217, 312, and 622 for further discussion of this community and its music). Known as
ALLELUIA VII in Taizé publications, the tune functions as the communal refrain for
stanzas that are sung by a cantor. It became better known in the English-speaking world
after its publication in *Music from Taizé* (vol. 2, 1984).

Sing in harmony with great inner intensity. This tune works well unaccompanied,
but in Taizé style various instruments would be used in repetitions of this short refrain.

Liturgical Use

As an independent acclamation traditionally with the reading of the gospel, but appropriate at many other times in worship; as a frame around another psalm or hymn, for example Psalm 70 (sing either "alleluia" or "maranatha").

640

Alleluia

Text

See PHH 639 for a discussion of the "alleluia" text. In the style of praise choruses the following anonymous stanzas were added after the original setting was composed (note that each phrase is sung four times):

2 He's my Savior, alleluia!
3 He is worthy, alleluia!
4 I will praise him, alleluia!
5 Maranatha, alleluia!

With these additional stanzas the theme of "alleluia" becomes the praise of Christ. Stanzas 2 and 3 explain the reasons for this praise: Jesus is our Savior (Matt. 1:21b), and he is worthy of all praise (Rev. 4:11; 5:12). Stanza 4 makes the "alleluia" directly personal, and the final stanza, "Maranatha," urges the Lord to come quickly to receive perfect praise from all his creatures.

Tune

Jerry Sinclair's (b. Calais, ME, 1943) tune SINCLAIR was initially published in several Scripture chorus booklets in 1972. Like the Taizé "Alleluia" (639) this simple chorus throbs with a solemn inner praise; that praise would be heightened by unaccompanied five-part singing (with some sopranos doubling the alto part an octave higher to create the fifth part) and should be disciplined by a restrained tempo. "Alleluia" thrives on such sobriety—the strength of its internalized praise may be lost with a fast tempo and/or external flamboyance.

Jerry Sinclair began writing songs when he was a teenager in northeastern Maine. During the early days of the Jesus Movement, he ministered with a singing group, The Chosen Ones, in various churches in the western United States, often in association with evangelists such as Arthur Blessitt. Later he became an executive of a cellular phone company and owned his own publishing business, Southern California Music.

Liturgical Use

Various occasions of praise to God, including the Lord's Supper; with the final stanza, "Maranatha," during Advent; see PHH 639 for additional suggestions.

641

Amen (three settings)

Text

"Amen" is a Hebrew expression that means "so be it" or "let it be true." The word connotes a sense of certainty and a conviction of truthfulness. The Old Testament Hebrew people used "amen" to affirm the rightness of God's judgments (see Deut. 27:15-26). But "amen" is also the New Testament believers' affirmation of God's promises, and the concluding acclamation to orthodox Christian praise and prayer (see 1 Cor. 14:16 and Rev. 5:14; 7:12).

"Amen" is familiar as the final word of prayers, a word of faith that portrays the strong conviction that God answers prayer. It is similarly used in some hymns, especially in select hymns of petition and certain hymns of profession of faith. Some hymnals still provide an "amen" for each hymn—a practice that arose in the nineteenth century when church choirs sang much of the service music and congregations added only their spoken or sung "amen." This practice is not followed in most modern hymnals.

Tune

"Twofold Amen"

This "Dresden Amen" is often attributed to Johann G. Naumann (1741-1801), a composer of operas and church music at the royal court in Dresden, Germany. The tune was used by Felix Mendelssohn (PHH 279) in his *Reformation Symphony* and by Richard Wagner in *Parsifal*.

"Threefold Amen"

This setting is of unknown origin, but its wide use, especially in Lutheran churches in Denmark, gave rise to the name "Danish Amen." In the *Companion to the United Methodist Hymnal* (1993), author Carlton R. Young gave a particularly apt description of the Danish Amen: "a Scandinavian breakfast pastry in G major for sleepy choirs" (p. 582).

"Fourfold Amen"

Attributed to John Stainer (PHH 127), this setting's first publication has not been traced. The 1873 date in the *Psalter Hymnal* would appear to be a reference to Stainer's more familiar "Sevenfold Amen," which was published in his *A Choir Book* in 1873.

Liturgical Use

As sung acclamations to spoken prayers and benedictions; congregations may want to sing the various settings at different times of the church year.

ECUMENICAL CREEDS AND DOCTRINAL STANDARDS

Apostles' Creed

Psalter Hymnal page 813   *by Harry Boonstra*

Text

Despite its name, there is no biblical or historical evidence to suggest that the apostles of Christ had any involvement in shaping the Apostles' Creed. Church historians trace its origins to the second century. It went through a long and slow development, crystallizing more or less into its present form as late as the seventh century. There are many minor variants of it even today. Some of these are due to differing doctrinal traditions. Others have developed through ongoing attempts by churches to update its language. The version found in the second and subsequent printings of the *Psalter Hymnal* is a fresh translation made from the Latin by a committee that reported to Synod 1988 of the Christian Reformed Church.

Although it does not come to us directly from the apostles, this creed certainly does carry biblical and apostolic content and authority. We can readily trace each one of its statements back to the New Testament. For example, the basic trinitarian structure of the creed echoes Christ's commission to baptize in the name of the Father, the Son, and the Holy Spirit (Matt. 28:19). The article confessing the return of our Lord repeats what Paul writes in 2 Timothy 4:1: that "Christ Jesus . . . will judge the living and the dead."

After the close of the apostolic period the church often felt the need to express its teaching in brief, basic statements. This greatly aided the teaching ministry of the church, as new converts, most of them illiterate, were taught the essentials of the faith. The early church required converts to summarize their faith at the time of their baptism. From this practice creeds (from *credo,* meaning "I believe") developed in the teaching and liturgical ministry of the church. A number of these early confessions contain statements very similar to those that we find in the Apostles' Creed. "Jesus is Lord" (1 Cor. 12:3) is one of the earliest and simplest of such creedal statements.

The church also had to formulate its faith in response to false teachings. Although the Apostles' Creed did not originate in the context of heresy proceedings, as did the Nicene and Athanasian Creeds, it is a deeply theological confession. It emphasizes that Jesus is both fully divine and fully human. That testimony strongly communicated that the church adamantly refused to allow any attack on this biblical teaching. Yet there are some differences in the formulation of the creed. For example, the phrase "he descended into hell" is omitted by Korean Christians.

The Apostles' Creed does not offer us a complete theology or summary of Scripture. Notable gaps include a lack of reference to the teachings of Christ. It also makes no reference to the atonement. Instead the Apostles' Creed offers us a succinct outline of the pivotal, crucial building blocks of our faith—a faith rooted in Jesus Christ, who gives us access to the Father, and who, through the Holy Spirit, builds his church.

The Apostles' Creed is both personal and universal. When we say or sing the creed, we profess our personal faith in God and recommit ourselves to him every time we confess it. But this creed is also universal. The church of all times and all places confesses it as well. The Apostles' Creed allows us to link hands with God's people around the globe and across the centuries.

Liturgical Use

As communal response to proclamation of God's Word; an important component of baptismal, public profession of faith, and Lord's Supper services. The creed may be recited in unison; sung, using *Psalter Hymnal* 518 or 519; or spoken responsively, using the following question-and-answer format:

> With all God's people throughout time and history,
> and gathered in this place today,
> we ask you to profess your faith in the triune God.
>
> Do you believe in God the Father?
> **I believe in God the Father, Almighty . . .**
>
> Do you believe in Jesus Christ, his only Son?
> **I believe in Jesus Christ, his only Son, our Lord . . .**
>
> Do you believe in God the Holy Spirit?
> **I believe in the Holy Spirit . . .**
>
> *—from* Agenda for Synod 1994, *(Christian Reformed Church in North America), p. 175*

On all occasions those who recite the Apostles' Creed stand, if they are able.

Nicene Creed

by Harry Boonstra   *Psalter Hymnal* page 814

Text

The Nicene Creed in many ways parallels the Apostles' Creed. It incorporates the same three-part division reflecting our belief in the triune God and devotes its largest section to its confession of Jesus Christ.

But there are some significant differences as well. These are rooted in the controversies that raged in the Christian church during the first centuries after the close of the apostolic age. At that time the church struggled to formulate correctly the biblical teaching of the nature and the relationship of the Father, the Son, and the Holy Spirit.

One prominent teacher, Arius from Alexandria (d. A.D. 336), taught that "the Son has a beginning but God is without beginning," and that the Son is not God. Rather, said Arius, Christ is an inferior "Word," a created being, called into existence by God before all time.

Arius and his followers were strongly opposed by others. When the controversy threatened to divide both the church and the Roman Empire, Emperor Constantine decided to intervene. In A.D. 325 he convened the Council of Nicea in Asia Minor. After heated controversy the council drew up a creedal statement that included explicit pronouncements against the Arian teaching. Phrases such as "very God from very God," "begotten, not made," and "being of one substance with the Father" emphasized the biblical teaching that Christ is *not* a creature, but *is* eternal God. The council added that the church curses those who refuse to confess what this creed confesses, judging the rejection of Christ's divinity to be a dangerous and deadly heresy.

The creedal statement that this council produced can be called the Creed of Nicea. But it is not identical with our Nicene Creed. The Nicene Creed as we have it today was formulated later in the century, perhaps at the Council of Constantinople in A.D. 381, and was officially adopted at the Council of Chalcedon in A.D. 451. The Nicene Creed we have today confesses the essence of the earlier creed, especially the unity of the Father and the Son. But it has dropped the curses that were attached to the Creed of Nicea.

One little phrase found in the Nicene Creed needs additional comment: "[The Holy Spirit] proceeds from the Father *and the Son* . . ." The Eastern Church refuses to accept the addition of the phrase "and the Son." It does not believe that the Spirit proceeds from the Son, but that both the Son and the Spirit proceed equally from the Father. In Latin "and the Son" reads "filioque," and this "filioque" difference was considered so important that it became the major doctrinal cause for the breach between the Eastern and Western branches of the church in A.D. 1054.

Whereas the Apostles' Creed is historically associated with baptism, the Nicene Creed has historically been associated with regular Sunday worship as a response to the Word and before the Lord's Supper. The place of the Nicene Creed in the worship of Reformed churches is very similar to that of the Apostles' Creed. Congregations in the Reformed tradition may want to recite it more often than they tend to, since, in one way, it is more ecumenical than the Apostles' Creed, having found its way into the liturgy of more churches. Its stately prose, confessing so pointedly the heart of our faith, ably commends it to that role.

Liturgical Use

As a communal response to proclamation of God's Word, especially when the Lord's Supper in celebrated; particularly suitable for use in services in which the identity and person of Christ are proclaimed and celebrated. The creed may be spoken or sun, using *Psalter Hymnal* 520. On all such occasions those who recite the Nicene Creed stand, if they are able.

Athanasian Creed

by Harry Boonstra

Text

Just as the titles to the Apostles' Creed and the Nicene Creed are not really accurate, neither is the title of the Athanasian Creed. Athanasius lived from A.D. 293-373. And the Athanasian Creed was not drawn up until the sixth century, probably by an unknown priest in Gaul. The creed was written at a time when the church was in disarray after the barbarian invasion of the Roman Empire. As a result the clergy received virtually no education. To meet this lack, the creed was intended to provide a summary of the doctrines of the Trinity and of the two natures of Christ. It used the formulations adopted by the great councils in the fourth and fifth centuries. Since Athanasius had been a chief defender of orthodox trinitarian views against Arius, it seemed plausible to believe that Athanasius had been the author of this creed.

The Athanasian Creed consists of forty-four statements, divided into two main sections. The first section (statements 3-28) teaches the mystery of the Trinity. It tries to warn against two dangerous misunderstandings of the doctrine of the Trinity. The first error describes the persons of God as so distinct that they are really seen as three separate gods. The second error describes the persons of God as so unified that Father, Son, and Holy Spirit can be seen only as one person who reveals himself in these three separate ways or roles. To counter these opposing views, statements fifteen and sixteen of the Athanasian Creed emphasize, "Thus the Father is God, the Son is God, the Holy Spirit is God. Yet there are not three Gods; there is but one God." Statement 27 adds, "So in everything, as was said earlier, we must worship their trinity in their unity and their unity in their trinity."

The second section of the creed, statements 29-43, deals with the mystery of the incarnation and of Jesus' divinity and humanity. It confesses that Jesus "is God from the essence of the Father, begotten before time; and he is human from the essence of his mother, born in time" (statement 31). Said differently: "Although he is God and human, yet Christ is not two, but one" (statement 34). The close of this section, statements 38-43, sounds very much like the Apostles' Creed. The language in which it confesses Christ's suffering, ascension, and return indicates that it was probably borrowed from that creed.

The Athanasian Creed is longer, more didactic, and more technical than the Apostles' and the Nicene creeds. This more elaborate structure probably accounts for the fact that it has not been nearly as influential. For example, the Eastern Church has never recognized it. Nor does it function as actively in churches that do recognize it. Churches do not recite or sing large portions of the Athanasian Creed as part of their liturgy. Its technical language makes it inappropriate in that context.

However, the Athanasian Creed does fit well in a collection of the creeds of the church. It ably sums up crucial doctrines that the church confesses. It lets us celebrate the joy of biblical light that shone so brightly even at a time of deep darkness. The three ecumenical creeds are all treasures of the church, but they function differently. The Apostles' and Nicene creeds are like familiar hymns that we use every Lord's Day to express our oneness with the church universal and to confess our faith. The Athanasian Creed is more like an old family Bible with old-fashioned printing. The language is not quite ours, but we do hold it dear because of the ageless truths we find there. Through it we experience the common bond we have with those who came before us, who through two millennia have shared our Christian faith.

Liturgical Use

Brief portions can be used in litanies or responsive readings as formulas that encapsulate biblical teaching on the Trinity and on the natures of Christ.

The Belgic Confession

Psalter Hymnal pages 817-59   *by Henry Zwaanstra*

Text

Guido de Brès wrote the Belgic Confession when the dreadful Spanish Inquisition was still operating in the Low Countries. An itinerant Flemish Reformed minister, de Brès had come to reside in the city of Doornik in 1559, in what today is the country of Belgium. Although independent from it, de Brès's confession is similar to the Gallic Confession adopted by the Reformed churches in France around that same time. In preparing his confession, de Brès must have consulted with other Reformed pastors and possibly also with the consistory of the Reformed church in Antwerpen.

The earliest printed version of the Belgic Confession dates from 1561. At that time the Low Countries were under Spanish Roman Catholic control, ruled locally by Margaret, Duchess of Parma, Regent for King Philip II of Spain. To assure the civil magistrates and Roman Catholic citizens of the nonrevolutionary character of the Reformed Protestant movement, de Brès attached copies of the confession to the city gates in Doornik. Margaret soon sent commissioners to investigate these "disturbances." Early in the morning of November 2, 1561, as the gates of the castle at Doornik were opened, Margaret's commissioners found a small, sealed package inside the exterior wall. The package contained a copy of the confession along with an introductory letter to King Philip. It also included an explanatory address to the civil magistrates.

These supporting documents clearly indicate the apologetic purpose for which the confession was written. In requesting religious toleration, de Brès wished to convince Philip and the local magistrates of the Reformers' loyalty to the gospel of Jesus Christ.

He also wanted to give assurance of their willingness to submit to the existing civil government by dissociating themselves from the Anabaptist movement. In 1567 de Brès died a martyr to the faith. During the struggle for the Reformation in the Netherlands, thousands of his fellow Reformed believers were executed as well.

The earliest recorded use of the Belgic Confession as a standard of Reformed orthodoxy requiring subscription on the part of church officers was a secret gathering of Walloon (French-speaking) Reformed "kruiskerken"—churches living and struggling under a cross of persecution. They met in Armentiers in 1563. At subsequent synods the confession was read in order to testify to the doctrinal unity of the assembled churches and to determine whether or not there was anything in the confession that needed to be amended. The National Synod of Dort reviewed and fixed the authoritative text for the Reformed churches in the Netherlands in 1619. The English translation presented in the *Psalter Hymnal* is based on the French text approved by that synod.

In thirty-seven articles the Belgic Confession summarizes the salient teachings of the Reformed churches. The articles express doctrinal continuity with the ancient church, creeds, and ecumenical councils in their representation of the doctrines of God, creation, the fall, and Christ. The ancient trinitarian and Christological errors as well as Pelagianism are explicitly rejected.

The confession also distinguishes Reformed Protestant teaching from Roman Catholic and Anabaptist doctrine: confessing the sovereignty of divine grace in salvation, the total depravity of humankind, and justification by faith alone. It also deals with the Reformed understanding of the church, the sacraments, and civil government.

Historically the Belgic Confession has occupied a more modest position in the public worship of the Reformed churches than the ecumenical creeds and the Heidelberg Catechism have. Recently Reformed ministers have preached the Word of God with assistance from the confession. Some of its articles lend themselves easily to sermonic treatment; others simply do not. Likewise, some articles or parts of articles may be effectively put to liturgical use. The Belgic Confession has many beautiful sections that are still contemporary and relevant for the faith-life of believers today.

Liturgical Use
As a guide for preaching the Word, substituting the Belgic Confession for the Heidelberg Catechism. Selected portions can be read in unison or responsively as a summary of biblical teaching or as a confession of faith, especially where a narrower focus and a more extensive treatment of a specific teaching or teachings is desirable.

The Heidelberg Catechism

Psalter Hymnal pages 816-925   *by Fred H. Klooster*

Text

The churches of the Reformation produced many booklets and manuals containing systematic summaries of religious doctrine in question-and-answer form. These were intended to instruct all church members, but especially children and new converts. They were called "catechisms" and were composed by all the major Reformers. The two catechisms of Martin Luther are still used in Lutheran churches throughout the world. The two Reformed catechisms still in use are the Westminster Shorter Catechism and the Heidelberg Catechism.

The city of Heidelberg, from which this catechism receives its name, was the capital of the important German province named *the Palatinate*. It had the distinction of having an elector as its civil ruler. An elector was one of six persons charged with the awesome responsibility of choosing the next emperor of the Holy Roman Empire. Because this territory was a stronghold of the Roman Catholic Church, the Palatinate was one of the most difficult areas of Germany for the Reformation to gain recognition in. Luther's 1518 visit to Heidelberg was the seed bed of the Reformation in Heidelberg, but more than twenty-five years passed before the struggling plant could flower.

In December 1545, as the congregation of the Church of the Holy Spirit in Heidelberg celebrated Roman Catholic mass, some members spontaneously began to sing the Reformation hymn "Salvation Has Come to Us, O Lord." This hymn celebrates justification by grace alone, through faith alone. However, political and ecclesiastical opposition suppressed popular desire. Another decade passed before the Reformation made progress in the Palatinate.

When Otto Henry became the elector in 1556, Lutheranism advanced. Upon his death he was succeeded by Frederick III. The Reformation flourished during his reign (1559-1576). Coming from a staunch Roman Catholic family, Frederick became a Protestant through the encouragement of his Lutheran wife and through his faithful Bible reading. He reflected the irenic spirit of Philipp Melanchthon, himself a son of the Palatinate.

During the early years of Frederick's reign tensions increased between strict Lutherans and followers of Melanchthon. Controversy focused on the Lord's Supper and related doctrines concerning Jesus Christ, especially the doctrine of "ubiquity" (the omnipresence of Christ in his human nature) embraced by the Lutherans. This development led Frederick to consider the need for a new catechism to replace those of Luther and Brenz. Early in 1562 Frederick III ordered its composition.

As noted in the introduction to the Heidelberg Catechism in the *Psalter Hymnal* (p. 860), tradition credits Zacharias Ursinus (1534-1583) and Caspar Olevianus (1536-1587) with primary authorship, but no one knows for sure who drafted the document.

Both political and ecclesiastical pressures from outside the Palatinate made it important that its publication reflect official policy. So its authorship was kept secret to reflect the fact that its composition was a team effort.

Although the need for a new catechism arose from doctrinal controversy and church squabbles, Frederick III wanted a catechism that was positive and, above all, biblical. Frederick ensured that it was designed to meet three important needs: as catechetical instruction, as a guide for preaching, and as a confessional form of unity. He urged preachers and teachers to "teach, and act, and live in accordance with it, in the assured hope that if our youth in early life are earnestly instructed and educated in the Word of God, it will please Almighty God also to grant reformation of public and private morals, and temporal and eternal welfare" (preface to the 1563 edition of the Heidelberg Catechism, as quoted in *Studies on the Heidelberg Catechism*, by G. Richards, p. 197, 199). Little did the elector know that it would one day become one of the most widely used and profoundly loved Reformed catechisms throughout the world. The introduction in the *Psalter Hymnal* briefly traces the spread of the Heidelberg Catechism and how it assumed its present form and usage within the Christian Reformed Church.

The Heidelberg Catechism is unique in its intentional structure and its warm, personal qualities. Catechisms generally included four main units—the Apostles' Creed, the Ten Commandments, the Lord's Prayer, and a section on the sacraments. The authors of the Heidelberg Catechism structured those four units into a marvelous pattern with the theme of *comfort*, using three divisions: *misery, deliverance*, and *gratitude*.

The comfort of the gospel, rediscovered in Scripture by the Reformers, permeates the entire catechism. The first section, on *misery*, uses the summary of the law as the teacher of sin and the pointer to Christ. The second section, on *deliverance*, follows the sequence of the Apostles' Creed and concludes with a section on the sacraments as God's gracious guarantees of our only comfort. The third part explains the thanks, the *gratitude*, that a believer shows to God for Christ's complete deliverance. That section includes an explanation of the Ten Commandments as the norm to follow in thankful living. Since prayer is "the most important part of the thankfulness God requires of us" (Q&A 116), the catechism concludes with a discussion of the Lord's Prayer.

The Heidelberg Catechism expresses much that was common to all branches of the Reformation. Members of the team project had firsthand acquaintance with Luther, Melanchthon, Heinrich Bullinger, John Calvin, and Théodore de Bèze, as well as with numerous earlier catechisms. Its authors have been likened to bees flitting from flower to flower to gather honey. The Heidelberg Catechism reflects the rich, ripe fruit of the entire Reformation. Yet it is clearly a Reformed catechism distancing itself from the ubiquity doctrine of Lutheranism and from other Protestant and Roman Catholic views of the sacraments.

Most important of all, the Heidelberg Catechism claims to be simply *biblical*. The Scripture passages listed in the margins of the early editions point out the biblical sources of the various answers. When opponents charged that the catechism was Calvinistic and had no right to exist under the terms of the 1555 peace of Augsburg,

Elector Frederick insisted that he had never read any of Calvin's writings. He challenged anyone to show where the catechism was inconsistent with Scripture. No suggestions were offered. His courageous defense of the Heidelberg Catechism before the emperor in 1566 earned him the nickname "Frederick the Pious." The catechism has stood the test of time. Its biblical faithfulness has made it one of the most loved catechisms of history.

Liturgical Use

As a regular means of proclaiming God's Word; portions can be recited in unison or responsively as a congregational response to the sermon or as a confession of faith (in this latter context, Lord's Day 1 is especially appropriate). Selections from the section dealing with the sacraments can be used in preparation for baptism and the Lord's Supper, the section on the Ten Commandments can be meaningfully incorporated into the service of reconciliation, and the answers to the questions on the Lord's Prayer can be incorporated into litanies and prayers.

The Canons of Dort

Psalter Hymnal pages 927-49   *by Donald Sinnema*

Text

The formal title of the Canons of Dort is even more daunting that its common one. Formally this document is named "The Decision of the Synod of Dort on the Five Main Points of Doctrine in Dispute in the Netherlands." It consists of statements of doctrine adopted by the Synod of Dort, which met in the Dutch city of Dordrecht in 1618-1619. This synod was held in the late sixteenth century to settle a serious controversy in the Dutch churches initiated by the rise of Arminianism.

The story begins with John Calvin a half-century earlier. Calvin (1509-1564) taught double predestination, a belief that God decides from eternity to save some people and to condemn others. Although this doctrine did not take center place in his theology, some of Calvin's followers, especially Théodore de Bèze, William Perkins, and Franciscus Gomarus, gave predestination a more prominent role in their theology. They developed an extreme form of this teaching called *supralapsarianism.* In this view God predestines people from eternity, without taking into consideration the fall of humanity.

Jacobus Arminius (1559-1609), who had studied in Geneva under de Bèze, questioned the teaching of Calvin and his followers on a number of points. He advocated a position that placed less emphasis on God's sovereignty in predestination and more emphasis on human responsibility. Controversy ignited while Arminius was serving as a minister of the Reformed church in Amsterdam. It heated up when he became a theological professor at Leiden University, where his views clashed with those of his supralapsarian colleague, Gomarus.

After Arminius's death his own followers presented their views in the Remonstrance of 1610. This document criticized Calvinistic views and spelled out the Arminian position in five articles, which declared that

- God has in Jesus Christ eternally decided to save sinners who believe and persevere in faith, and to condemn those who do not believe.
- Christ died and earned forgiveness for all people, but only those who believe will be saved.
- no one has saving faith by one's own free will; it is necessary to be regenerated and renewed by God in order to do what is truly good.
- all good works must be ascribed to God's grace, but this grace is not irresistible.
- by the aid of grace believers have the strength to persevere, but whether they are able to fall from grace completely must yet be determined from Scripture.

In later writings the Arminians more explicitly based election and reprobation on foreseen faith and unbelief, and they affirmed the possibility of a complete fall from a state of grace.

For a number of years the controversy around these five points continued to blaze in the church, school, and marketplace. Finally in 1618 the Dutch government called together the Synod of Dort in order to resolve them. The proceedings lasted for six-and-a-half months. Although this was a national synod of the Reformed church of the Netherlands, it had an international character. It was attended by fifty-eight Dutch delegates and by twenty-six Reformed theologians from eight other lands. In addition, the Dutch government sent eighteen civil delegates to supervise and to give advice on matters relating to politics. Over a dozen leading Arminians, headed by Simon Episcopius, were called before the synod to have their views examined and judged. The Arminians refused to acknowledge the synod as a legitimate judge of their case and sought a conference between the opposing parties instead. After about six weeks of heated debate, during which the Arminians refused to cooperate fully, they were expelled from the synod.

After months of deliberations, the synod debated a set of canons drafted by nine of its members. In the course of three weeks they were drafted in Latin, revised several times, adopted, and signed by all members of the synod. In light of the diverse viewpoints of the time, these Canons of Dort take a moderate Reformed stance on the disputed issues.

The synod also drew up forms of subscription by which officebearers of the Reformed churches were required to signify that these articles and points of doctrine fully agree with the Word of God. So the canons acquired a secondary purpose. They became a doctrinal standard for the Reformed churches of the Netherlands, alongside the Belgic Confession and the Heidelberg Catechism.

The First Main Point of the Canons of Dort offers a moderate treatment of God's election and reprobation. Against the Arminian view of election and reprobation based on foreseen faith and unbelief, the canons teach that God elects people solely as an act of grace, not as a response to human belief. God also reprobates others by his sovereign will, but they perish by their own fault. The canons deal with predestination in a sensitive manner so that this delicate teaching will be a comfort to believers rather than a threat. This way of presenting predestination is infralapsarian. It contends that in predestining God takes into consideration the fallen state of humanity. This First Main Point avoids—though it does not condemn—the harshness of the supralapsarian position.

The Second Main Point focuses on the nature and extent of Christ's atonement for sins. In the Arminian view, Christ died and obtained forgiveness for all people, even though only those who believe will be saved. The canons teach that Christ's atonement, while sufficient for all people, was made only for those whom God has chosen.

The Third and Fourth Main Points deal with human corruption and conversion to God. They stress that by the fall humanity became totally incapable on its own to return to God. While humans remain human, with intellect and will, their conversion does not occur by their own free choice. Conversion is the work of God by the power of the Holy Spirit through the gospel. According to the canons, God's grace works not only outwardly in the proclamation of the gospel. It also penetrates inwardly by the effective operation of the Holy Spirit, softening the heart, freeing the will, producing faith. It is this faith that enables the person to repent. The Arminians taught that this grace is resistible. The Third and Fourth Main Points assert that God's regenerating grace works irresistibly. It does not coerce a reluctant will by force, but it spiritually *reforms* the will, thus overcoming its resistance.

The Fifth Main Point teaches that believers will persevere in faith until the end of their lives. True, they are not entirely free from sin in this life, even though they are no longer enslaved to it. Their negligence can even lead them to stray into very serious sins. But God does not let them fall so far that they totally forfeit grace and thus perish—a plight that the Arminians considered entirely possible. Believers may rest assured that God will powerfully preserve them and renew them to repentance by his Word and Spirit. This assurance does not lead to false security or carelessness but provides a powerful incentive to greater godliness.

The Canons of Dort are often summarized in the so-called "five points of Calvinism," sometimes remembered by the acronym TULIP: Total depravity, Unconditional election, Limited atonement, Irresistible grace, and Perseverance (or preservation) of the saints. Though they help us remember the teachings of the canons, these labels oversimplify their nuanced teaching.

From its beginning in 1857 the Christian Reformed Church has accepted the Canons of Dort as one of its three doctrinal standards. In a world in which the Arminian perspective still flourishes, the canons continue to affirm boldly, yet sensitively, their central message. They teach us that salvation, from beginning to end, occurs wholly by God's gracious initiative. Yet this teaching in no way erodes our human responsibility for sin and its tragic consequences.

Liturgical Use

As a guide for preaching the Word, substituting the Canons of Dort for the Heidelberg Catechism. Selected portions can be read in unison or responsively as a summary of biblical teaching or as a confession of faith, especially where a narrower focus and a more extensive treatment of God's initiative in the work of salvation is desirable. The frequent inclusion of Scripture references in the canons also provides opportunity for a confessional response by the congregation to specific passages.

The Form of Subscription

by Robert De Moor   *Psalter Hymnal* page 950

Text

All officebearers in the Christian Reformed Church are required to signify their agreement with the doctrine of the church by signing the Form of Subscription. They are to do this when they are ordained or installed into office and when attending major assemblies.

The requirement of signing such a form dates back to the Synod of Dort in 1618-1619. The form drawn up by that synod was intended only for ministers of the Word—separate forms were devised for schoolteachers and professors of theology. Gradually elders and deacons were also required to sign the form intended for ministers. Evangelists and seminary professors who receive ordination are now also required to sign the present form, which has descended from that original one designed specifically for ministers. So while the original form used the term "servants of the divine Word" to refer only to ministers, its meaning has now been stretched to include all other officebearers as well.

The version adopted by the Synod of Dort was updated in Dutch in 1899 by H. H. Kuyper. That version, together with the English translation found in the 1976 edition of the *Psalter Hymnal,* formed the frame of reference for the updated Form of Subscription that has been in use since it was adopted by Synod 1988 of the Christian Reformed Church.

Need for the present translation arose for several reasons. Synodical interpretations of what the 1976 version meant had to be expressed more clearly (see "Guidelines as to the meaning of subscription . . . ," *Church Order 1996,* p. 25). Second, the inclusion of more cultural groups into the Christian Reformed Church required a more straightforward, contemporary version that would be understandable to those who do not use English as their primary language. Synod 1981 had already modified the 1976 version of the form to make it useful for Classis Red Mesa. As other cultural groups followed into the Christian Reformed Church, it became clear that a more readily understandable form should be adopted to serve all the churches. Synod 1987 appointed a committee to report back on this matter to Synod 1988. That committee's revised translation of the Form of Subscription was adopted and remains in use for all office-bearers in the CRC.

Liturgical Use
Optional use within the ordination service: officebearers come forward to sign a copy of the subscription form.

LITURGICAL FORMS AND RESOURCES

Commentary written by David J. Diephouse,
Carl G. Kromminga, and Bert Polman

Service for Baptism

Psalter Hymnal pages 953-56

Text

This model for a service including baptism was approved by Synod 1981. It is one of several that were prepared by the Christian Reformed Church Liturgical Committee and published as Part Three of the Service Book published in that year. This Service for Baptism incorporates the material of the Form for Baptism found on pages 960-962 of the *Psalter Hymnal* into a complete order of worship. It makes the celebration of baptism an integral part of the entire liturgy, instead of a mere appendage to it.

The service as a whole has a four-part structure: beginning, confession and assurance, proclamation of the Word, and response. It reflects the basic pattern of worship advocated in the Liturgical Committee Report adopted by Synod 1968. The model offered here integrates the baptismal liturgy into the service of confession and assurance. Similarly the formulary sections "The Institution" and "The Promises" serve to frame the congregation's confession and then lead into the celebration of baptism.

Placing the sacrament within the reconciliation part of the liturgy calls attention to the role of baptism as a sign and seal of cleansing from sin and the beginning of new life in Christ. This service indicates that it is through baptism that Christians ritualize their entry into the church, the family of God. That is why in many old churches baptism fonts were located at the entrance of the building.

The prayer of confession, beginning with "We confess to you, our God . . . ," contains allusions to several older sources. These include early Reformed service orders and forms of general confession found in the *Book of Common Prayer.* All of them, to some extent, are adaptations from medieval models of the confession spoken privately by priests at the beginning of the Roman Mass. The prayer of confession concludes with a quotation from the eucharistic *Agnus Dei* (see 257). In this way it provides an effective link between the two sacraments.

The service as a whole allows for considerable flexibility and adaptation to local circumstances. It would be possible, for example, to place the vows and celebration of baptism after the proclamation of the Word and to incorporate the instructional portion of the form into the sermon itself. This pattern of Word and sacrament, analogous to that used for the Lord's Supper (see PsH, pp. 972-975), seems to have been typical of early Christian liturgies (as evidenced by the third-century Apostolic Tradition of Hippolytus). The pattern can also be found in some historic Reformed service orders and in many recent baptismal liturgies. In this format the act of baptism functions as a response to God's grace proclaimed in the Word.

The Service for Baptism includes an optional recitation of the Apostles' Creed as part of the service of response (PsH, p. 956). This creed derived originally from baptismal formularies and remains a part of baptism in many Christian traditions (see

"The Apostles' Creed," PsH, p. 813). The Apostles' Creed should be a normal part of baptism in this service as well, either spoken or sung (see 518, 519). It can also be used after the congregation says "The Vows" and immediately before the actual baptism.

Liturgical Use
As a model for a service that integrates the administration of baptism within the liturgy; as a means of structuring the confession and assurance section of the liturgy on those occasions when it is followed by baptism. Although designed for children's baptism, this service can easily be adapted for use in adult baptism.

Baptism of Children

Psalter Hymnal pages 957-59

Text
This form was prepared in 1973 by the Christian Reformed Church Liturgical Committee. It is a translation of the traditional Dutch form for baptism that dates from 1566. In that year Peter Datheen published a Dutch version of the Genevan Psalter. Datheen's *Psalmboek* included a form for baptism, as well as a Dutch version of the recently developed Heidelberg Catechism. Datheen's Psalter was printed in Heidelberg for the refugees who had found shelter at nearby Frankenthal under the protection of Frederick III, elector of the Palatinate.

Datheen drew on several sources for his baptism form. He borrowed from the liturgy Calvin used in Geneva. He also drew on the liturgical writings of Johannes à Lasco, which had been used by the London congregation of Flemish refugees. A third source was the form for baptism found in the Church Order of the Palatinate (1563). These sources were themselves based in part on early Reformation formularies that can be traced back to Zwingli and ultimately to Martin Luther's baptismal liturgy. Luther's, in turn, was a revision of existing medieval forms. Many of the Reformation sources also drew inspiration from early Christian writings. These include sermons and treatises by church leaders such as Augustine, Tertullian, and Chrysostom.

Early Dutch synods made some alterations in Datheen's form. The Synod of Dort (1618-1619) established the version that remained in use in the Reformed churches of the Netherlands until recent times. In 1912 the synod of the Christian Reformed Church adopted an English translation of this form and made several additions to it. That translation had originally been prepared in the Netherlands for English and Scottish refugees and had long been used by the Reformed Church in America. This form was published in the 1914 *Psalter* used by the Christian Reformed Church and republished, with minor changes, in the 1934 *Psalter Hymnal.*

Synod 1976 adopted a new translation. In preparing it, the Liturgical Committee deliberately chose to work with the original Dutch text of 1566. This version, retained in the present *Psalter Hymnal,* attempts to render the "parent" version of the traditional form into contemporary English.

Like most traditional Calvinist formularies, the "Baptism of Children" has a strongly didactic flavor. It reflects the Reformers' concern to provide a proper doctrinal understanding of the sacrament and to eliminate unscriptural ceremonies associated with the Roman rite. That's why the form begins with an application of three central elements of Reformed doctrine—sin, salvation, and service—to baptism. This expository section concludes with an appeal to Scripture to defend and require the practice of infant baptism.

The next section focuses on the actual baptism. It begins with the historic *flood prayer,* originally composed by Martin Luther for the baptismal rite he introduced in 1523. Then follow the questions to the parents. Together with the parents' affirmation these questions constitute their baptismal vows. There is no specific renunciation of sin as occurs in classic baptismal rites. Nor does it include a complementary vow by the congregation—an element that really ought to be included (see the congregational vow, PsH, p. 961).

Immediately following the vows is the orthodox, trinitarian formula for baptism, as commanded by Christ in Matthew 28:19.

The prayer of thanksgiving that closes the formulary is one of the finest sections in the historic liturgy of the Reformed churches. It opens with gratitude for God's loving gift of salvation through Jesus Christ, for our adoption through the Holy Spirit, and for the confirmation of this adoption in the sacrament of baptism. The petitions that follow are carefully woven together into a fervent plea for the Spirit's governance and guidance of the baptized children. In the classic Christian baptism forms, this prayer affirms the sealing of the Holy Spirit, often accompanied by the laying-on of hands. The prayer then concludes in praise and glorification of the triune God.

Liturgical Use

As a segment of the worship service that prepares for and celebrates the administration of baptism, possibly doubling as the service of reconciliation. Suitable substitutions for the instructional section can be found in Lord's Days 26-27 of the Heidelberg Catechism, Article 34 of the Belgic Confession, and stanza 40 of *Our World Belongs to God.* The didactic character of this form can be balanced with suitable means of participation by family members of the child being baptized.

Baptism of Children

Psalter Hymnal pages 960-62

Text

Synod 1964 of the Christian Reformed Church asked the Liturgical Committee to develop a less didactic version of the 1934 formulary. First proposed in 1969, the new form was extensively revised during the next several years. Synod adopted it in 1976. It was published, with small editorial changes, in the 1987 *Psalter Hymnal.*

The traditional form failed to include any specific biblical warrant for the practice of baptism. Therefore this revision opens with Christ's words of institution from Matthew 28:18-20, making it parallel, in that respect, to the Lord's Supper forms. The revised form then offers a selection of biblical texts, which trace the promises of the covenant of grace. It reaches through redemptive history back to Abraham and forward to the day when the promises will be fulfilled in the reign of God's people with Christ in glory.

The form pays more attention than do earlier forms to the "water of baptism" and its intended symbolism. The references to the physical element of the sacrament occur primarily in the context of doctrinal instruction. In many other liturgies, both ancient and modern, these references are contained in a prayer of thanksgiving and consecration over the baptismal water. Alluding frequently to supporting scriptural passages, the instruction section further develops the themes of covenant and forgiveness. This section concludes by emphasizing that children are included in God's covenant along with believing adults.

The "Prayer of Preparation" that follows is clearly trinitarian. Its opening section contains echoes of the great "flood prayer" from Martin Luther's baptism form. It uses further imagery of water in Scripture to suggest our participation by baptism in the death and resurrection of Christ. It makes a touching plea that Christ "will always keep us and our little ones in the grip of his hand." The prayer concludes with a petition for the Spirit's aid in living the new life of faith in Christ.

The "Vows" to be affirmed by the parents reflect the three vows in the traditional Reformed formulary, with the order of the first two questions reversed. The first question now calls for reaffirmation of the parents' faith, and the second question calls for their conviction that their children ought to be baptized. In the third question the parents affirm their intent to nurture their children in the Christian life by diligent instruction and example. Following the parental vows, a vow is also required of the congregation. This practice parallels the support given by godparents in other Christian traditions.

The rite of baptism may be preceded by the quotation of Mark 10:14. Use of this verse is optional because "the relationship of this text to baptism is not equally and obviously clear to all" (*Acts of Synod 1976*, p. 345). The context is this verse is that of children being brought to Christ not for baptism but for a blessing. Yet the text commends its use in the baptismal service because Jesus teaches so clearly in Mark 10:15 that the invitation to enter the kingdom is extended only to those who do so "like a little child." As the child is baptized, the trinitarian formula is used, as commanded by Christ in Matthew 28:19.

Since the time of the early church, the act of baptism has often been followed by an act of blessing, in which the minister lays hands on each of the newly baptized and offers a prayer that they may receive the gifts of the Holy Spirit. But this form reflects the historic Reformed practice. It turns that classic blessing into a final prayer: "Fill them with your Spirit and make their lives fruitful."

Liturgical Use

As a segment of the worship service that prepares for and celebrates the administration of baptism, possibly doubling as the service of reconciliation. Other biblical passages of promise could be substituted for "The Promises" section, or the promises could be sung by the congregation using PsH 272. Suitable substitutions for the instructional section can be found in Lord's Days 26-27 of the Heidelberg Catechism, Article 34 of the Belgic Confession, and stanza 40 of *Our World Belongs to God*. Suitable means of participation by family members of the child being baptized can help to make the baptism more personal and festive.

Public Profession of Faith

Psalter Hymnal page 963

Text

The intent of any confession of Christian faith is for a person or a community to testify to belief in God. The practice of making verbal testimonies of faith as a part of living out our faith may be derived from a number of biblical texts such as Matthew 10:32 and Romans 10:9.

Initiation into the fellowship of believers in the early church included both baptism with water and an act of blessing or anointing. Over time these actions became separated into two distinct ceremonies the baptismal ceremony and a "confirmation" of baptism, observed a number of years later. Any priest was authorized to administer the sacrament of baptism. Confirmation, on the other hand, came to be seen as the prerogative of a bishop. In the medieval church this act gradually took on a separate sacramental significance of its own.

Protestant Reformers rejected the confirmation rite as unsupported by biblical evidence. They saw it as a denial of the once-for-all character of baptism. Luther required that children should give an account of their young faith as taught in the catechism, but he devised no ritual for such an event. Calvin had a similar view: he also wanted catechism instruction and a profession of faith, ideally by the age of ten. There was no formulary for this occasion.

The Reformers recognized the need for Christian instruction and the need of Christians—children as well as adults—to be able to give a clear testimony of their faith throughout their lives. Public profession of faith by young people was observed because theirs was a good age to begin to make such confessions of faith—and to continue doing so throughout their lives. But profession of faith was more a pastoral or consistorial matter than a liturgical act. Though important for admission to the Lord's Supper, profession of faith did not constitute a liturgical, sacramental step.

The churches that followed the thought and practice of Calvin held the same views. Converts to the Reformed faith and covenant children were carefully catechized. They were then examined with respect to their knowledge of the faith, and they were asked whether they agreed with the doctrines of the church, intended to live a godly life, and were willing to submit to the discipline of the church. A brief admonition to continue in their profession often followed, and then these persons were presented to the congregation and admitted to the Lord's table.

Although the questions asked on the occasion of profession of faith took on a traditional pattern, the Dutch churches did not adopt a specific form for this event. The Church Order of Dort, Article 61, prescribed simply that those desiring admittance to the table make "a profession of their faith in the Reformed religion, agreeable to the practice of the churches to which they are joined."

Prior to the 1930s, the Christian Reformed Church (CRC) had been using a simple set of three questions unaccompanied by any introduction or conclusion. The person making profession responded to them with a simple "yes."

The liturgical formulary that the CRC has used since 1932 was derived from a Dutch Reformed form of 1923. It was influenced in part by sixteenth-century sources such as the Church Order of the Palatinate and a Genevan form dating from 1553. It was revised by Synod 1986 of the CRC so that what was previously the third question has now become the first one.

The form begins with a brief expression of thanksgiving. Four questions follow immediately. A charge and welcome follow the "I do." An optional prayer concludes the event. This prayer expresses gratitude to the Lord for covenant promises fulfilled. It contains a moving plea that God will grant the confessors growth in grace and protection from the powers of temptation and evil. The prayer ends on a fine note of hope, asking that on the great day when the Lord makes up his jewels, those who have confessed him will also be set in his crown, "that they may shine as stars, to [God's] praise, forever and ever."

Liturgical Use
In the service as preparation for first communion; those making profession may add more self-expression to their testimony. It is also appropriate for the minister or another representative of the church to make a specific statement or presentation to

each person making profession. A song such as "O Jesus, I Have Promised" (285) or "Eternal God Beyond All Time" (447) can be sung by the congregation to join its voice with those making public profession. For people with mental impairments who are making public profession of faith, the content of this form and the questions should be simplified as appropriate—CRC Publications offers *Expressing Faith in Jesus,* a practical guide for how this can be done.

Public Profession of Faith

Psalter Hymnal pages 964-65

Text

Over the years public profession of faith in the Christian Reformed Church has come to include various meanings and functions:

- It is the means by which the congregation welcomes baptized church members, young and old, to participation in the Lord's Supper.
- For young adults it marks the transition to taking personal responsibility for their faith and life in Christ and to accepting adult responsibilities.
- It is the means by which new believers express the faith that forms the basis for their baptism and inclusion in the church.
- It is the ritual in which commitment is pledged to the doctrine and government of the church.

Recent decisions by synod to encourage younger children to make public profession of their faith has meant a separation of these elements in their case. These elements can still be combined for young adults and adults. But a younger child's profession of faith does not include a commitment to the confessions or to adult responsibilities. Such a commitment will be asked of younger confessing members when they reach the age of eighteen. Since the forms in the *Psalter Hymnal* are geared to older age levels, Synod 1995 adopted a new liturgical form suitable for the profession of faith of younger children. It can be found in the *Acts of Synod 1995* (pp. 715-716).

The second form in the *Psalter Hymnal* was prepared by the Liturgical Committee of the Christian Reformed Church and presented to Synod 1972. Synod granted provisional use for three years. It was adopted in slightly revised form by Synod 1976 and approved with minor additional changes by Synod 1986 for incorporation in the 1987 *Psalter Hymnal.*

The spirit of this form's introduction is joyful and celebrative. It expresses gratitude for God's covenant faithfulness in the confirmation of baptism of those making public profession, and for their desire to love and serve the Lord in the full life of the church's fellowship. The first three questions are similar to those in the earlier form. The fourth question seeks not only submission to the authority of the church but also faithful participation in "the work of the Lord everywhere." The form allows, but does not require, those who make profession to turn the questions ("The Vows") into declarations. It also welcomes additional self-expression.

After the minister has welcomed those who are making profession of faith to the "responsibilities, joys, and sufferings" of the church and has pronounced a benediction on them, the congregation pledges its "love, encouragement, and prayers" to the new communicant members. Then everyone joins in reciting the Apostles' Creed. The concluding prayer makes overt reference to the work of the Holy Spirit. The optional use of personal statements rather than questions, the pledge of support by the congregation, and the mutual confession of the Apostles' Creed all contribute to greater personal involvement on the part of all church members in sharing in this brief ceremony.

Liturgical Use
In the service as preparation for first communion; those who are professing their faith may add more self-expression to their testimony. It is also appropriate for the minister or another representative of the church to make a specific statement or presentation to each person making profession. A song such as "O Jesus, I Have Promised" (285) or "Eternal God Beyond All Time" (447) can be sung by the congregation with those making public profession. For people with mental impairments who are making public profession of faith, the content of this form and the questions should be simplified as appropriate—CRC Publications offers *Expressing Faith in Jesus,* a practical guide for how this can be done.

Baptism of Adults

Psalter Hymnal pages 966-68

Text
In 1978 synod adopted a new translation of the traditional form for celebrating the baptism of adults. The Dutch forms on which it is based originated around 1600, when several provincial synods in the Netherlands adapted the existing infant baptism form for use with the baptism of adults.

During the early history of the church, baptismal rites focused on adult converts who were admitted to full fellowship after completing a period of instruction. At the time of baptism candidates were required to renounce "Satan and all his works" and to give an account of their faith by responding to specific baptismal questions. These questions and responses eventually formed the basis of the Apostles' Creed. After Christianity was accepted as a state religion in the Netherlands, the focus shifted to infant baptism, with parents and godparents making the baptismal vows on a child's behalf.

In keeping with their covenant theology and in contrast to the Anabaptist insistence on "believers' baptism," Calvinist Reformers strongly affirmed the practice of infant baptism. The authors of the Reformed liturgies did not wish to create an entirely separate form for adult baptism. The fundamental doctrine of baptism was valid for baptism of adults as well as children. But by 1600 it had become clear in the Dutch churches that some adaptation had to be made to achieve uniformity of usage. To accomplish this, the Synod of Dort (1618-1619) addressed the issue and provided this form, which it adapted from the versions produced by several provincial synods.

For the most part, this formulary follows closely the traditional form for infant baptism (see PsH, pp. 957-959). Several sections are adapted for adults, such as the last part of the instructional section, the preparatory prayer, and the baptismal vows. The first four questions are essentially expanded versions of the three questions from the infant baptism vows, while the fifth question requires a clear rejection of "the world and its evil attractions." This is reminiscent of the act of renunciation of sin found in the classic sources and in many recent liturgies. Like the infant baptism form from which it was adapted, this form, unfortunately, has no congregational vow of support for the new Christian. The corresponding vow in the second form for the Baptism of Adults makes a very appropriate addition (see PsH, p. 971).

Liturgical Use
For the public profession of faith and baptism of an adult who has not yet received baptism. The instructional portion of the form can be substituted by portions read from Scripture or from the creeds or by the congregational singing of an appropriate hymn; a vow by the congregation may also be added (see PsH, p. 971). Opportunity should be given for the person being baptized to give an expression of his or her faith; family members and friends may also be involved in the baptism liturgy by reading part of the formulary, leading in prayer, making other statements of support, or contributing music, dance, or visual art appropriate to the occasion.

Baptism of Adults

Psalter Hymnal pages 969-71

Text
Synod 1976 of the Christian Reformed Church adopted an alternate form for the baptism of adults parallel to the form for infant baptism approved that same year (see PsH, p. 960-962). In recognition of the basic unity of the doctrine of baptism with respect to both children and adults, the basic content of the two forms is very similar.

This alternate form for adult baptism begins with "The Vows" section that makes explicit use of the expressions of commitment associated with public profession of faith. The adult baptism vows on page 969 of the *Psalter Hymnal* are identical to questions 1, 2, and 4 of the second form for Public Profession of Faith (PsH, p. 964). The subsequent sections of this second adult baptism form parallel those of the second form for infant baptism.

Just before their actual baptism candidates are asked whether they wish to be baptized. By adding this question, the church conforms to the ancient tradition grounded in Acts 8:36 about seeking consent from those who are being baptized.

This form includes an optional paragraph of instruction and two additional vows related to family baptism. This makes the form well suited to those who present not only themselves but also their children for baptism.

A congregational vow forms an important part of this formulary. After the act of baptism the minister welcomes the new members to "full participation in the life of the church," using a formula drawn from the form for Public Profession of Faith. The concluding prayer expands this theme of fellowship to encompass all believers throughout the ages who are united in "one faith, one hope, and one baptism."

To make their baptism meaningful, adults seeking baptism should be properly prepared. Their catechetical instruction should lead at some point directly into a planning session for their profession of faith and baptism. This will allow for an explanation of the significance of the vows they make, the responsibilities and privileges they assume, as well as the meaning of the rites themselves. It also allows adult baptism candidates to contribute to making the service personal, meaningful, and edifying for themselves, their family, and the congregation as a whole.

Liturgical Use
For the public profession of faith and baptism of an adult (including his or her children) who has not yet received baptism. The instructional portion of the form can be substituted by portions read from Scripture or from the creeds or by the congregational singing of an appropriate hymn. Opportunity should be given for the person being baptized to give an expression of his or her faith; family members and friends may also be involved in the baptism liturgy by reading part of the formulary, leading in prayer, making other statements of support, or contributing music, dance, or visual art appropriate to the occasion.

Service of Word and Sacrament

Psalter Hymnal pages 972-75

Text

This model service was drawn up by the Liturgical Committee of the Christian Reformed Church and approved for provisional use in 1978. It received final approval by Synod 1981. It follows the basic Word-and-sacrament structure advocated in the 1968 Liturgical Committee Report. This service makes use of a somewhat revised version of a new order for communion proposed in that report.

Both the general structure and many of the details of this service hark back to patristic forms and practices. Sometime before the middle of the second century the early church combined the service of Scripture and prayer with the celebration of the Lord's Supper, which was originally part of a separate fellowship meal—the *agape* meal. This basic pattern of Word and table was preserved from the time of the church fathers through the time of the Reformation and into the present. It squared fully with John Calvin's understanding that assemblies of believers invariably included "the Word, prayers, partaking of the Supper, and almsgiving" (*Institutes of the Christian Religion*, IV. 7.44). The Christian Reformed "Service of Word and Sacrament" therefore draws deeply from the wells of Christian tradition. It also bears a striking resemblance to recent liturgies from other churches, both Protestant and Roman Catholic.

Although ecumenical in form and spirit, the entire service bears distinct witness to the Reformed conception of biblical worship as a dialogue between God and the people. It also reflects the classic Reformation emphasis on the priesthood of all believers. Throughout the service the congregation takes an active part. Although there are solemn moments, the basic tone of this service is *eucharistic*, a thanksgiving for the benefits of God's great redemptive work in Christ so vividly communicated through both Word and table fellowship.

The service begins with a dialogue of invocation and blessing. In the Mass of the late Middle Ages such sentences were spoken privately by the priest before the actual service. The Reformers restored them to public use, in keeping with their understanding that in worship all believers share the priestly office. A recommended but optional response is the "passing of the peace." This act of fellowship, rooted in the "holy kiss" of the New Testament, seems to have been a normal part of early Christian worship.

The prayer of confession of sin is essentially an adaptation of a traditional Reformed type found in the Palatinate liturgy and attributed to Calvin, who derived it from an earlier form by Martin Bucer. The response to the declaration of pardon is the familiar *Gloria Patri*, which can be spoken or sung (635, 636). This service of confession concludes with a reading of the law, either the Ten Commandments or another appropriate scriptural passage. The law functions here in the characteristic Reformed role as a guide to grateful living, and it can be spoken or sung (153).

The "Proclamation of the Word" begins with another characteristically Reformed feature: a prayer for illumination. This prayer anticipates and parallels a second petition for the presence and work of God's Spirit in the service, namely the prayer of consecration in the communion, underscoring the relationship of Word and table. The response to the proclaimed Word consists of a song, recitation of the Apostles' or Nicene Creed, intercessory prayers, and the offertory.

The offertory serves as a natural transition to the second half of this liturgy: the service of the table. A rubric notes that the communion elements may be brought to the table during the offertory. This simple ceremony restores a practice common in the early church. It was customary for offerings to be given "in kind." The presider would frequently take the bread and wine for the supper from among the gifts brought by the people as their offering.

The communion liturgy itself is faithful to many aspects of early Christian eucharistic forms. A tone of joy prevails throughout this liturgy, emphasizing that the supper celebrates Christ's incarnation and resurrection as much as his death. The formulary has no didactic section (a striking departure from traditional Christian Reformed practice). In its 1968 report the Liturgical Committee argued that instruction in sacramental doctrine was properly the task of preaching rather than the task of the sacramental liturgy. The committee further argued that lengthy instruction constituted an obstacle to greater frequency of the supper and to its desired celebrative character.

The thanksgiving itself is prefaced by the *sursum corda* in its historic dialogue form. This call to "lift up your hearts" is reminiscent of the heavenly worship and the communion of saints throughout the ages, a major theme in most Reformed liturgies. The main body of this prayer follows a trinitarian structure: blessing the Father for the work of creation and providence; the Son for his redemptive life, death, and resurrection; and the Spirit for working in believers to build up the church.

The words of "Institution" that follow are woven into a renewed expression of thanksgiving, to which all respond with a memorial based on the "covenant exchange" portion of the traditional Dutch Reformed formulary. The consecration prayer restores the beautiful imagery of "grain . . . from many fields" and "grapes from many hills" found in ancient liturgies (such as the *Didache,* c. 100) and in the traditional Dutch form.

Following a dialogue between minister and people as the elements are prepared, the minister speaks the invitation, specifying who is eligible to come to the table. The nature of this invitation bears witness to the typically Reformed determination to both welcome believers to the table and "fence the table" against unworthy participants.

All join in a dedicatory offering of thanks, based on a traditional acclamation: "Christ has died, Christ has risen, Christ will come again!" Then the minister focuses the worshipers' attention on the elements and proclaims, "The gifts of God for the people of God."

The actual administration of communion and the concluding thanksgiving follow the traditional Dutch Reformed pattern. The entire service concludes with singing and a spoken benediction that commends the congregation to "go in peace."

Liturgical Use

As a model for a service that integrates the service of the Word and the sacrament of the Lord's Supper; as a means of celebrating the Lord's Supper in a more festive rather than didactic way. The form can be readily abbreviated and adapted for use with homebound persons and others who cannot participate in a wider church setting.

Preparatory Exhortation for the Lord's Supper

Psalter Hymnal pages 976-77

Text

The tradition of administering the Lord's Supper in the Christian Reformed Church includes a preparatory sermon and an applicatory sermon (old Art. 60c, Church Order). Because many churches no longer observe this practice, Synod 1988 agreed to drop it as a requirement. To help churches who wish to preserve that tradition, however, Synod 1981 approved a brief dialogue form that can be read responsively. This allows for the use of a preparatory exhortation even when churches increase the frequency of their Lord's Supper celebration from the traditional four times per year.

The "Preparatory Exhortion for the Lord's Supper" begins with a prayer inspired by the "Collect for Purity" found in the sixteenth-century *Book of Common Prayer.* It continues with an exhortation to self-examination based on the three Christian virtues of faith, hope, and love. These are followed in each case by appropriate petitions prayed by the congregation to God. A warning against presumptuous participation and an assurance of welcome to the penitent precede a final corporate petition for God's help, through the Holy Spirit, to prepare us for worthy partaking of the sacrament.

The preparatory exhortation as a call to self-examination is traditionally part of the "preparatory service" on the Sunday before the Lord's Supper, but it may also be used on communion Sunday itself. This particular preparatory exhortation (PsH, pp. 976-977) and the similar ones in the older formularies (PsH, pp. 978-979, 983-984) have the same function. They help believers prepare for coming to the table of the Lord, and they "fence the table" against unrepentant sinners. Today many worship leaders in the Reformed tradition question whether such an exhortation is essential. Our weekly act of confession and assurance and hearing the Word proclaimed should accomplish what these special preparations were intended to do.

However, we do have these preparatory exhortations as part of our liturgical heritage. There may be pastoral wisdom in continuing to use them in some settings. If used, they should be made an integral part of the confession and assurance segment of the service. Alternatively a preparatory exhortation could be used as a response to the proclaimed Word, especially during the more meditative or penitential seasons such as Advent and Lent.

This dialogic preparatory exhortation is the most liturgical and the least didactic of the versions in the *Psalter Hymnal*. This commends it more readily for use in the worship service.

Liturgical Use
On the Sunday before or on the Sunday of the celebration of the Lord's Supper, as an integral part of the service of confession and assurance or as a response to the sermon. Its use is optional, and when used, care should be taken to avoid duplication or lack of integration with other parts of the liturgy.

Celebration of the Lord's Supper

Psalter Hymnal pages 978-82

Text
This communion form is a substantially revised version of the formulary traditionally used in the Christian Reformed Church. Like the traditional form for infant baptism, its parent text was the English translation of a form originally included in the *Psalmboek* of Peter Datheen, which itself was little more than a translation into Dutch of the service order for the Palatinate churches. The Palatinate form is generally held to be the work of Caspar Olevianus, assisted by Zacharias Ursinus and perhaps others. Olevianus drew upon the church order of à Lasco, written earlier, as well as material from John Calvin and Micronius. He also made some use of a form from the churches of neighboring Württemburg, which combined Lutheran and Zwinglian influences. In many respects the Palatinate liturgy represented a synthesis of many of the major Reformation traditions—German, French, and Swiss; Calvinist, Zwinglian, and Lutheran.

The Palatinate form underwent minor editorial changes in the course of its translation into Dutch and, later, into English. An English translation used by the Reformed Church in America shaped the Christian Reformed version that was eventually incorporated into the 1934 *Psalter Hymnal*. During the 1950s several synods mandated committees to revise the form and to shorten it. Synod 1957 appointed a committee that was to maintain contact with the Reformed churches in the Netherlands in response to their request for cooperation in revising the communion form. For various reasons that cooperation did not materialize, and the committee produced two alternative forms of its own, both of which were adopted by Synod 1964.

Of the two 1964 versions, this one represents a more thoroughgoing revision of the traditional form. While it retains the basic structure of the original, the material is shortened considerably, and the language is made simple and direct. One obvious change is the division of the form into two sections, designed to make it possible for the section on self-examination to be used separately from communion—that is, on a preceding Sunday. The communion formulary itself follows much of the traditional Dutch form (discussed in more detail below), although the language has been substantially altered at many points.

The prayer of thanksgiving in this form has features that anticipate the new eucharistic prayer developed by the Liturgical Committee in 1968. The Lord's Prayer is used to conclude this prayer, presumably spoken in unison (it could also be sung—207, 208). Next the Apostles' Creed is recited as a common confession of faith before communing at the Lord's table (it, too, could be sung—518, 519). This formulary omits a traditional rubric recommending the reading of Scripture or the singing of psalms or hymns during the distribution of the elements. While retaining a strong didactic element, this form conveys a stronger sense of comfort and assurance than its parent version does.

Liturgical Use:

The Preparatory Exhortation in this form can be used either on the Sunday before or on the Sunday of the celebration of the Lord's Supper, as an integral part of the service of confession and assurance or as a response to the sermon. The Formulary portion is intended to structure the actual celebration of the Lord's Supper; when used, care should be taken to avoid duplication or lack of integration with other parts of the liturgy.

Celebration of the Lord's Supper

Psalter Hymnal pages 983-87

Text

This form contains numerous additions to, omissions from, and condensations and revisions of material from the traditional Dutch Reformed formulary. While it is not simply a new translation of the Dutch form, it does adhere to its main thoughts, retaining most of the emphases typical of the Reformed forms of the sixteenth century. It reflects the Reformers' fervent emphasis on the need for intelligible worship and informed participation on the part of the people. It also reflects their polemic against theological distortions associated with the Roman Mass. This historical context explains much of the form's didactic character.

The preparatory exhortation in this form constitutes a Reformed tradition dating at least to the service order of Johannes à Lasco in the 1550s. Originally this formed part of a separate service held on the Saturday before the celebration of the sacrament—the root of the Reformed preparatory service. The present version begins with the apostle Paul's account of Christ's institution of the supper. The first half of this institution account (1 Cor. 11:23-26) formed part of the canon (main prayer) of the Mass. Here it serves instead as a warrant for the celebration of the sacrament, and Paul's subsequent injunction to self-examination before coming to the table (1 Cor. 11:27-29) provides the basis for the exhortation that follows. Assurance that God welcomes all repentant believers to his table is balanced by an explicit warning against partaking by those who have not repented or who are defiled with certain "gross" sins. This heavy stress on worthy partaking and "fencing the table" is a theme inherited from early liturgies and the writings of church fathers such as Chrysostom and Tertullian.

The actual communion formulary begins with another reference to Christ's institution of the sacrament, which is omitted when the two parts of the form are used in a single service. This is followed by an extensive teaching section regarding the purpose for which Christ instituted the supper. Celebration of the supper is not intended to be a somber recollection or memorialization of a departed Jesus. Neither does it involve any repetition of the "perfect sacrifice, once offered on the cross." Rather, the events and meaning of Jesus' coming into the world, his life, suffering, and death, constitute the only ground of our salvation and the source of our nourishment to everlasting life.

A prayer of preparation follows. It represents a considerable reworking of patristic and medieval sources and includes an invocation of the Holy Spirit. Consonant with Reformed theology, the Spirit is here invoked to transform the hearts and lives of the communicants rather than the physical elements of communion. This strong emphasis on the role of the Spirit can be found in sources dating back at least to Hippolytus in the third century A.D.

The prayer is followed by the Apostles' Creed. Use of the creed at this point in the form represents one of the contributions of Calvin, who regarded the creed as a form of covenant pledge. Following the prayer comes a typically Calvinistic version of the *sursum corda* ("Lift up your hearts"), derived from a service book of Guillaume Farel. Instead of its ancient role as a call to prayer, here it becomes an exhortation to lift up our heart to Christ and be nourished by the "true bread from heaven . . . through the working of the Holy Spirit."

The words spoken during the breaking of the bread and the sharing of the cup come from the London liturgy of à Lasco. He, in turn, had borrowed them from Pollanus's version of the French Strasbourg liturgy published for French-speaking refugees in London in 1551. The language serves to emphasize the actions of the sacrament—breaking, eating, drinking—in contrast to the medieval tendency to focus on the elements themselves. Communion of both kinds is required, with both bread and wine to be shared by all believers. The Reformers considered the actual communion by the people to be the central component of the Lord's Supper. This is in contrast to the Roman Catholic focus on the consecration. As a result, while the Reformers failed to restore the custom of regular weekly communion as practiced in the early church, the typical Reformed frequency of four to six celebrations per year still constituted a sharp contrast to prevailing medieval practice, in which actual communion by the people was infrequent—as little as once a year. Even then the cup, in medieval practice, was reserved for the clergy and not shared with the people.

The Lord's Supper form concludes the celebration with the recitation of a beautiful chain of thanksgiving and praise drawn from parts of Psalm 103 and Revelation 5. These can also be sung (103, 297, 475). The concluding prayer acknowledges with gratitude the blessed actions of the three persons of the Trinity in connection with the supper. Rooted in the biblical accounts of the Last Supper, this post-communion thanksgiving also owes something, in both form and content, to the influence of the sermons of Chrysostom.

Liturgical Use

The Preparatory Exhortation in this form can be used either on the Sunday before or on the Sunday of the celebration of the Lord's Supper, as an integral part of the service of confession and assurance or as a response to the sermon. The Formulary portion is intended to structure the actual celebration of the Lord's Supper; when used, care should be taken to avoid duplication or lack of integration with other parts of the liturgy.

Excommunication

Psalter Hymnal pages 988-89

Text

The Reformation occurred in the context of a society in which virtually everyone was nominally a member of the church. This meant that the restoration and exercise of church discipline, inspired by the model of the early church, took on particular significance for the Reformers. The early synods of the Dutch Reformed churches dealt with many problems of a disciplinary nature. However, the Dutch liturgy did not include a form for excommunication. Such a form was not commended for use in the churches until the general Synod of Middelburg in 1581. The Synod of the Hague in 1586 also drew up a form for excommunication as well as one for readmission. These forms were entirely of local origin and were not based on other Reformed or Protestant models.

English versions of these forms first entered the liturgy of the Christian Reformed Church after 1912 by way of the translations used in the Reformed Church in America. Synod 1934 incorporated slightly revised versions of these forms into the 1934 *Psalter Hymnal*. New forms for excommunication and readmission prepared by the Liturgical Committee of the Christian Reformed Church were adopted by Synod 1982. Final versions were approved by Synod 1986. Only these newer forms appear in the present *Psalter Hymnal*.

After the publication of the 1987 edition of the *Psalter Hymnal*, Synod 1991 adopted a revision of both the form for excommunication—renaming it the "Form for Exclusion from Membership"—as well as the form for readmission. Previous synods had ruled that use of such forms were optional, as well as the entire practice of announcing excommunication or readmission in a worship service. However, where such forms are used, Synod 1991 insisted that the nature of the sin be kept confidential. It is important to note that the present church order expressly disallows the practice of naming the sin. It specifies that "special care should be observed in the wording of public announcements. The sin of the person should not be mentioned, but only that he/she is unrepentant" (Church Order, 1996). For this and other reasons, the form for excommunication was revised. **The forms, as found in the first seven printings of *Psalter Hymnal*, should not be used.** Instead, the forms as found in the *Acts of Synod 1991* (pp. 720-723) should be used. These forms are also available on electronic disk from CRC Publications and beginning with the eighth printing of the *Psalter Hymnal*.

In the Christian Reformed Church exclusion from membership has traditionally taken place in the worship service, although the present church order no longer requires that practice. It only requires that "the consistory shall inform the congregation and encourage its involvement in both the exclusion from and the readmission to membership" (Church Order, 1996). This leaves open the question of whether worship is the appropriate place for such a sad and wrenching action. Some church councils only announce exclusion from membership at a congregational meeting.

However, it is in the worshiping community that the Word is proclaimed, the sacraments are celebrated, and public profession of faith is made, including the vow to submit to the government of the church. Sad as any actual exclusion from membership is, it is appropriate that the council announce such an act in the public gathering for worship. In this way the sorrow and grief resulting from this action can be brought to the Lord in the setting of communal prayer and proclamation of the gospel. In this way the most explicit exercise of both the opening and shutting functions of the keys of the kingdom is carried out in the worshiping assembly (see the Heidelberg Catechism, Lord's Day 31).

Liturgical Use
As a means of solemnly declaring the exclusion of an impenitent person from membership in the church and of offering communal prayers for his or her repentance; appropriate placement in the liturgy would be in the context of the congregational prayer or of the confession of sin.

Readmission

Psalter Hymnal pages 990-91

Text

When it revised and renamed the form for excommunication (see previous page), Synod 1991 also revised the form for readmission that was printed in the 1987 *Psalter Hymnal.* **Both of these forms as they appear in the first seven printings of** *Psalter Hymnal* **should no longer be used.** Instead, the revised versions should be used as found in the *Acts of Synod 1991* (pp. 720-723). These revised forms are also available on computer disk from CRC Publications and beginning with the eighth printing of the *Psalter Hymnal.*

Because the revision of the form for readmission is not extensive, the following commentary applies equally to both the obsolete and the new versions.

The process for readmission takes place in two stages. First comes an announcement of the repentance of someone who has been previously excluded from membership and who expresses a desire to be readmitted to the full fellowship of the church. Actual readmission takes place a week or two later so that the congregation has opportunity to bring forward any lawful objections before that time.

The ceremony of readmission opens with a brief recollection of the biblical teaching on repentance, forgiveness, reconciliation, and the right and duty of the church to declare sins forgiven on the authority of Christ (see John 20:23). Appropriate questions are addressed to the person seeking readmission. The last question is the same as the final question asked of confessors in one of the formularies for Public Profession of Faith (PsH, p. 964). Following the "I do, God helping me," a solemn and joyful declaration of readmission is addressed to the person being readmitted. It includes words of assurance and a brief exhortation to the congregation to receive the person with joy and thanksgiving. The congregation rises as it expresses its thanks to God and vows its support to the person being restored. The form concludes with the recitation of the Apostles' Creed, which can also be sung (518, 519), and with an appropriate, unscripted prayer.

Liturgical Use

To declare and celebrate the readmission of a person who was previously excluded from membership; the act of readmission may be incorporated into the service of confession and assurance, where the creed is usually recited, or it could precede the congregational prayer. It may be appropriate and desirable in the act of readmission for the restored person to make an additional personal statement.

Ordination/Installation of Ministers of the Word

Psalter Hymnal pages 992-94

Text

Christian Reformed Church investiture terminology varies. For example, the words *ordination* and *installation* are often used interchangeably. But there is some consensus. *Ordination* here describes the ceremony in which a minister of the Word is inducted into office. In other forms this term describes the ceremonies for inducting evangelists, elders, and deacons (PsH, pp. 1002-1006). Because ministers continue in office, when they begin to serve in another congregation or ministerial position, the induction ceremony is referred to as *installation*. The same form is used in both cases.

Commissioning describes the ceremony in which church members are charged with ministries other than those of a minister, elder, deacon, or evangelist, such as specific positions relating to church teaching, outreach projects, youth work, or worship. The CRC has no approved or recommended forms for such commissioning.

In its generic sense, ordination is the ritual that celebrates and affirms the call of God and of the church for persons to engage in a variety of ministries. While all members of the church are called to the general office of believer, through ordination certain persons are set apart, consecrated, and appointed to carry out specific functions in the ministry of the church of Christ. Any distinctions among the general and special offices in the church are differences of function, not matters of essence. This larger context of a mutual ministry must be emphasized because some forms for ordination tend to give a much more narrow focus.

Ordination should be a celebration of the whole church in action, a vivid symbol of the unity of the church as all of God's saints engage in worship and service, intercessory prayer and proclamation, and teaching and caring. Ordination is

- an invocation of the Holy Spirit to equip those called
- an enactment of faith that God will use human means to accomplish his ends
- an act of commitment by the church to those who are ordained

From the earliest days in the history of the Dutch Reformed churches, the ordination of ministers of the Word was attended by a solemn interrogation of the prospective minister. These churches did not adopt a particular formulary for ordination until 1586, when the Synod of the Hague, using elements from the works of Johannes à Lasco and Micronius, approved a form that continued to serve the Dutch churches into the early twentieth century.

This ordination form in the *Psalter Hymnal* was prepared by the CRC Liturgical Committee and was referred to the churches by Synod 1983 for trial use and comment; it was adopted by Synod 1986. The development of this form came in response to instructions by Synod 1978 that a new ordination form be devised to reflect the

"Guidelines for Understanding the Nature of Ecclesiastical Office" (*Acts of Synod 1973*, pp. 62-64) and Articles 11-13 of the Church Order.

The form begins with an introduction stressing that while the entire church has been given the mandate "to proclaim the good news of salvation in Jesus Christ to the whole world," the complexity of that task led the early church to institute special offices, or "distinct ministries," one of which is the office of the minister of the Word. An expository section outlines the tasks that this ministry entails.

The questions addressed to the person to be ordained are virtually the same as those in the earlier formulary (1971). The address to the minister and to the congregation stresses the joy of the occasion and encourages both minister and congregation to be faithful to the Lord's calling and to the commitments they have made. The ceremony closes with a simple prayer of thanksgiving and petition.

Liturgical Use

At the ordination or installation of a minister of the Word and sacraments; most appropriate use is after the reading and proclamation of the Word. This form is specifically geared to ministers who serve in a congregational setting—it would require extensive modification if used for the ordination/installation of ministers called to other areas of ministerial service.

Ordination/Installation of Ministers of the Word

Psalter Hymnal pages 995-1001

Text

The traditional Dutch formulary for ministers of the Word was another of the many that the Christian Reformed Church borrowed in English translation from the Reformed Church in America after 1912. A revised version of that form was eventually adopted by synod and included in the 1934 and 1959 editions of the *Psalter Hymnal*. The form included variants for the ordination of missionaries and of professors of theology.

Synod 1961 appointed a committee to revise these ordination forms and to provide a new form for persons engaged in special kinds of service as ministers of the Word. In 1969 synod committed the materials submitted by that committee to the Liturgical Committee for editing. Synod 1971 adopted an amended version of their submission. In turn, the present form is an edited version of that form.

This form preserves the basic teaching about the task of the minister found in the traditional Dutch formulary. The opening section deals with basic scriptural teaching about the divine institution of the ministerial office and includes a summary statement of the duties of the minister in general. This form differs from the Dutch formulary in that it next presents four different sections that describe distinct positions of ministerial service: pastor of a congregation, foreign missionary, home missionary, and professor of theology.

The sections dealing with each of these variants contain the same "declaration of dependence," questions put to the prospective minister, directions for the ceremony of laying-on of hands, and solemn words spoken during that ritual.

The laying-on of hands is one of the oldest rites preserved in the church's liturgical forms. It was retained in most of the Reformed sources in the sixteenth century. It testifies to the genuinely catholic orientation of the Calvinist Reformers, who understood that while the people have a voice in the choice of the one to be ordained, the actual commission to office ultimately comes from God. It is expressed in the laying-on of hands by those who are already called and ordained to office.

The pledge of the congregation is found only in the section designated for a pastor in an established congregation. In all variants, both the material prefacing the ceremony and the charge to the minister are appropriately worded to reflect the special character of the pastor's, missionary's, or professor's task. The charge to the congregation and the prayer that follows are identical for both "home" and "foreign" missionaries, but for the others these two elements have been adjusted to fit their specific type of ministry.

The segment for a professor of theology is to be used only when the person assuming this position is to be ordained to the office of minister of the Word. For the appointment of professors of theology who are already ordained ministers, the form for the Teacher of Theology under "Forms for the Commissioning of Minister to Extraordinary Tasks" is to be used. That form is not in the *Psalter Hymnal* but may be found in the *Service Book* (Part II, p. 27) published by CRC Publications in 1981.

Liturgical Use

At the ordination or installation of a minister of the Word and sacraments; most appropriate use is after the reading and proclamation of the Word. This form is designed for use at the ordination or installation of those called to parish ministry as well as those called to serve in other areas of ministerial service.

Ordination of Evangelists

Psalter Hymnal pages 1002-3

Text

The formulary for the ordination of an evangelist was composed to meet a need created by the decision of Synod 1978 to "establish the office of evangelist with authority to administer the Word and sacraments in the work of evangelism of his calling church." The Liturgical Committee submitted a draft of this form in 1979. In a somewhat amended version it was commended by synod for use in the churches for a trial period of three years. The final version was adopted by Synod 1982.

This formulary is marked by directness and brevity. It describes the biblical origin of the task of the evangelist and how it functions in the church today. Synod's decision that an evangelist should serve also as an elder is reflected in the statement "In our congregation [name] will be acknowledged as an elder."

The form indicates that the laying-on of hands is optional when the declaration of ordination is spoken. The charge to the evangelist consists of a quotation of a substantial portion of 2 Timothy 4:1-2, 5. The charge to the congregation summons God's people to honor the evangelist in this task, to give support with gifts and assistance, and to provide prayer support. It also charges the congregation to accept the evangelist as the bearer of good news and to provide encouragement in difficult circumstances. After the congregation has responded with the vow "We do, God helping us," the ceremony is concluded with appropriate prayer for both the evangelist and the congregation.

Liturgical Use

At the ordination of an evangelist to a specific location or area of ministry; most appropriate use is after the reading and proclamation of the Word. The four questions can be recast as vows and voiced by the evangelist.

Ordination of Elders and Deacons

Psalter Hymnal pages 1004-6

Text

Churches in the Reformed tradition have always held to a presbyterian form of church government, in which authority is vested in those who are called and elected to serve in the special offices of minister, elder (presbyter), and deacon. Already by 1568, the Reformed churches in the Low Countries were insisting that persons elected to serve as elders should make public promises and be publicly charged with the duties and conduct of their office in much the same way as ministers of the Word. This was to be done before the consistory and, if possible, before the assembled congregation. Deacons were to be ordained in the same way.

In 1586 an ordination form for elders and deacons was adopted that remained in use virtually unchanged until recent times. The English translation that the Christian Reformed Church borrowed from the Reformed Church in America in 1912 underwent significant revisions before synod adopted it for inclusion in the 1934 *Psalter Hymnal;* substantial deletions were made, and a section that could be offensive to the poor was revised.

The CRC Liturgical Committee presented a new form for the ordination of elders and deacons to Synod 1979, which commended it for a three-year trial period; it was approved by Synod 1982. In offering this new form to the churches in 1979, the committee provided a rather extensive history of the older form and indicated some of its weaknesses. In addition, the committee gave a substantial rationale for the new form and proposed ways in which it could be "stretched" over an entire service. This form, slightly edited for style, was eventually included in the 1987 *Psalter Hymnal* as the sole form for the ordination of elders and deacons.

The form divides the teaching about the offices of elder and deacon between the expository section and the charge section. The questions seek an affirmation of the call to office, a profession of the Christian faith as taught in the Christian Reformed Church, and a commitment to the work and authority of the church with respect to the special offices. The ceremony of ordination is direct and simple; laying-on of hands is made optional. After the charges to the new elders and deacons, the congregation also receives a charge and pledges to receive these officebearers as "Christ's gift to the church." A brief prayer concludes the ceremony, requesting God's help so that the officebearers and the congregation can fulfill their respective duties.

Liturgical Use

At the ordination of elders and deacons; in the case of ordaining only elders or only deacons, only the appropriate segments of the form should be used.

Marriage

Psalter Hymnal pages 1007-9

Text

A Christian wedding is a public event during which a man and a woman declare their marriage covenant before God and other witnesses such as family, friends, the church, and the state. These join in acknowledging and affirming the vows of the couple. The wedding is more than a private ritual. Most Christian churches, including the Christian Reformed Church, observe certain traditions and follow certain rules for its solemnization (see Church Order, Art. 69).

No consistent pattern can be found in the history of the church's marriage observances. Unlike other aspects of church life, marriage was primarily seen as a covenant between the two marriage partners. Any liturgical ceremony accompanying the joining of husband and wife represented a secondary action, a blessing upon commitments already made between them and God. In some communities marriage was celebrated as part of the congregational service of worship on Sundays. In other traditions separate ceremonies were developed for weekday use by the families and friends of the couple. Both the Roman Catholic and Orthodox churches came to regard marriage as a sacrament and celebrated it in a nuptial mass.

The Reformers rejected the idea that marriage was a sacrament. However, they held the institution in high regard and believed that the commitment between spouses should find public expression and confirmation within the fellowship of God's people. Most service orders of the sixteenth century, including those in the Reformed tradition, included a formulary for the solemnization of marriage. These make clear that the church does not "marry" a couple, for the marriage is formed by the couple itself. The church's role is as an affirming witness.

The earliest Reformed service was one drawn up by Guillaume Farel in 1533. Much of it was later adopted by John Calvin. Calvin's form, along with those of Micronius and others, eventually made its way into the Palatinate liturgy. From there it was translated into Dutch for inclusion in Datheen's *Psalmboek*. The form in the *Psalter Hymnal* is an extensively revised version of this traditional Dutch form.

The original English translation of this form, in use since 1912, was considerably altered before its inclusion in the 1934 *Psalter Hymnal*. The form originally had the heading "Form for the Confirmation of Marriage Before the Church," clearly presupposing a ceremony as part of an official service of worship. The 1934 version of the form was headed "Form for the Solemnization of Marriage" and was worded in such a way that it could be used either in an official service of worship, as a private ceremony, or in an unofficial gathering of the congregation.

The present *Psalter Hymnal* version of this form has clear parallels in medieval sources, notably the Sarum rite, which provided the basis for the historic form in the *Book of Common Prayer*. The address recalls the divine institution of marriage—honored and confirmed by the Lord Jesus as a "lasting bond." It also recalls the apostle Paul's description of marriage as a symbol of the union of Christ and the church, the purposes of marriage, and the God-ordained relationship of husband and wife.

The ceremonial section begins with a declaration of intent and the optional "giving away" of the bride by her father or guardian—a remnant of old patriarchal tradition. Many couples dispense with this custom altogether, or alter it after the model of the "Parting from Parents" section in the more recent marriage form (PsH, p. 1010). These sections are followed by the actual marriage vows and an optional ring ceremony. An official pronouncement confirms the marriage in the name of the Trinity. The form concludes with an extensive prayer of petition for the couple and closes with the Lord's Prayer, which can be spoken in unison or sung (207, 208).

Liturgical Use

To solemnize a marriage either in an official worship service or in an informal setting; because the use of a form is not obligatory, pastors and couples should feel free to use this form as a model that can be revised as desired.

Marriage

Psalter Hymnal pages 1010-12

Text

This form was submitted to synod by the Liturgical Committee of the Christian Reformed Church in 1977 and was adopted by Synod 1979 (except for the final prayer). It is a form that honors tradition and yet takes account of contemporary developments in wedding styles and practices. The first element in this form is a declaration about the purpose of the gathering. Following a brief prayer is an optional section titled "Parting from Parents." This is an excellent substitute for the patriarchal custom of "giving away" the bride, permitting both sets of parents to give their blessing and support to the couple.

The instructional section affirms the covenant nature of marriage as instituted by God. It summarizes the apostle Paul's teaching about the mutual duties of husbands and wives and mentions the threats to marriage posed by sin. It concludes with reassurances of God's provision for them if they follow the biblical pattern for love.

The declaration of intent, the vows, the optional ring ceremony, and the pronouncement of marriage in the name of the Trinity are direct and simple. The form includes an optional promise of support by those in attendance. Using this promise is appropriate if the assembly consists primarily of Christians.

The form then calls for a message by the pastor. The ceremony concludes with a prayer of thanksgiving and petition.

While the form does not specify them, other elements can be added, such as singing, a candle-lighting ceremony, and the signing of legal documents.

Liturgical Use

To solemnize a marriage either in an official worship service or in an informal setting; because use of a form is not obligatory, pastors and couples should feel free to use this form as a model that can be revised as desired.

Responsive Readings of the Law

Psalter Hymnal pages 1013-18

Text

This section provides readings that were privately drafted and that have been in use in Christian Reformed congregations since the 1970s. They provide alternative, dialogical ways of proclaiming the Ten Commandments, which constitute a traditional part of the service of confession and assurance in Reformed worship.

These responsive readings, edited by the Liturgical Committee, were presented to Synod 1981. With some alterations they were approved by synod and commended to the churches for their use. The choice and sequence of some of the biblical texts has been questioned, usually on the grounds that contextual matters are not sufficiently respected in their compilation. Ministers and other worship leaders are free to use these readings as they are, to adapt them as desirable, and/or to combine them with appropriate song selections.

"(1) Words of Jesus from the Gospels" uses sayings of Jesus as responses to the commandments by the congregation. The Lord's injunctions are intended to parallel the Old Testament commandments. *Scripture References:* Matthew 4:10; John 4:24; Matthew 5:34-37; Mark 2:27-28; Matthew 15:4; 5:44-45; 5:28; 15:19-20; 12:34-37; Luke 12:15.

"(2) From the Epistles" bases the people's responses on the New Testament letters to churches. The structure of this reading is similar to that of the first; the injunctions and affirmations parallel Old Testament commandments. *Scripture References:* Romans 11:36; Colossians 1:14-15; Hebrews 13:15; Colossians 3:16; 3:20; Ephesians 4:32; 1 Corinthians 6:19-20; Ephesians 4:28; 4:15; Philippians 4:11.

"(3) From the Psalms" provides a reading that is responsive in the strict sense of that term. The minister or other worship leader speaks the commandments, and the people respond by affirming from the Psalms their desire to obey the Lord's Word. *Scripture References:* Psalm 51:4; 95:6-7; 51:15; 84:1, 10; 25:7; 139:23-24; 90:8; 51:1; 119:29; 119:36; 39:8; 145:18-19; 145:21.

"(4) As a Teacher of Sin" is most appropriate for use in penitential seasons such as Advent or Lent. Though the Calvinist Reformers held up the Ten Commandments as a rule of thankful and holy living, most of them also saw it as a teacher of sin. This reading begins with a brief dialogue drawn from the wisdom tradition of the Old Testament. Then follows the reading of the Ten Commandments by the leader, divided into the two traditional tables of the law. The people respond after each part. The prayer of confession after the first part is taken from Psalm 51:2-3; this prayer could be substituted with a song (255). The concluding petition for cleansing is taken from Psalm 130:3-4; this petition could also be substituted with a song (130, 256). *Scripture References:* Psalm 128:1; 119:105; 112:1; 119:35; 51:2-3; 130:3-4.

"(5) As a Rule of Gratitude" emphasizes the Reformation view of the Ten Commandments as a rule of gratitude to guide us into holy living. The leader proclaims each of the commandments, and the people respond with statements of commitment and obedience that are drawn or adapted from various biblical texts. The final text, from Micah 6:8, could be sung (293). *Scripture References:* Deuteronomy 5:1; Matthew 4:10; John 4:24; Psalm 29:2; 118:24; Luke 10:27; Ephesians 6:1-4; Romans 13:1; Ephesians 4:32; 5:3; 4:28; Zechariah 8:16-17; Philippians 4:11; Matthew 22:39; Micah 6:8.

"(6) As Summarized in Matthew 22:37-40" offers a reading that does not quote the Ten Commandments but uses the summary of the law drawn from Deuteronomy 6:5 and Leviticus 19:18, as quoted by Jesus in the gospels. This reading is structured into a simple dialogue between leader and people. Given its brevity, this reading may well be combined with a concluding psalm or hymn.

In addition to these readings, the Ten Commandments can also be sung. John Calvin prescribed its singing in his Strasbourg liturgy (1545) as a rule of thanksgiving following the confession of sin. The *Psalter Hymnal* provides a congregational setting (153). The ancient *Kyrie eleison* was used in some Reformation liturgies in connection with the confession of sin or with the reading of the Ten Commandments—sometimes in litany style. The singing of the *Kyrie* (258) could be used as a frame around the reading of the law: sung once at the beginning and again at the end. In addition, it could also be sung after the first part, or table, of the law.

Liturgical Use

In the service of confession and assurance as a variant for the reading of the Ten Commandments.

Our World Belongs to God: a Contemporary Testimony

by Morris N. Greidanus   *Psalter Hymnal* pages 1019-38

Text

This contemporary testimony provides the Christian Reformed Church with a modern statement of faith. It grew out of the church's responses to various requests for a new confession. The first request for a new confession came from Classis Chatham in 1971. It asked synod to replace the present doctrinal standards with a new expression of the faith of the church. Primary reasons for this request were (1) the fresh insights given by the Holy Spirit since the Synod of Dort and (2) modern heresies that are not specifically addressed in the confessions.

The idea of replacing the present doctrinal standards by a new confession frightened more church members than it persuaded. But the need to augment the traditional confessions with a more current statement became increasingly obvious to a succession of synods and study committees.

One committee developed the idea of calling the new work a *testimony*. This would signal a more tentative step than calling it a new confession. Another committee listed the issues that should be addressed and the approach that should be adopted. Based on their work the contemporary testimony committee drafted the actual text and a commentary on it. Synod 1983 adopted a draft of the testimony for provisional use in the worship, education, and outreach of the church. The final draft was approved in 1986 for inclusion in the 1987 edition of the *Psalter Hymnal*.

The major reason for drafting this contemporary testimony was the secular challenge posed by our time. Many people believe and act as if the world belongs to them. This testimony confesses the biblical perspective of the present and coming kingdom of God. *Our World Belongs to God* embraces and states this kingdom vision in many of its sections.

The contemporary testimony begins with a preamble that introduces the theme of God's kingdom. This is followed by sections on creation, the fall, redemption, and the new creation. The Psalter Hymnal Revision Committee followed this sequence in structuring the third group of hymns in the 1987 *Psalter Hymnal*—those numbered 428-641.

To promote the use of the contemporary testimony in church education, the committee that drafted it cooperated with the denominational Education Department. Together they produced a study version that is available from CRC Publications. That edition contains *Our World Belongs to God* together with a commentary on various contemporary issues and discussion questions that can be used by study groups. A newer survey for individual or group use, titled *Speaking of God . . . : A User's Guide to Our Contemporary Testimony* is also available from CRC Publications.

Liturgical Use
As a guide for preaching the Word, substituting *Our World Belongs to God* for the Heidelberg Catechism; selections can be read in unison or antiphonally as a confession of faith by the congregation or by those making public profession of faith. Appropriate passages can be used in the celebration of the sacraments or on special occasions; as a source for prayers or complete liturgies, such as British-style "Lessons and Carols" services; as a source for visual images, banners, or other church art.

INDEXES

Heidelberg Catechism: Song Suggestions

Items marked with an asterisk (*) are psalms for which the Psalter Hymnal *provides additional settings. References to these additional settings are provided below the psalm number in the* Psalter Hymnal.

Lord's Day	Q&A	*Psalter Hymnal* Suggestions	Lord's Day	Q&A	*Psalter Hymnal* Suggestions
1	1	*46, 62, 73, 194, 221, 549	12	31	21, 110, 229, 230, 395, 410, 541
	2	*130, 267		32	45, *72, 288, 289, 326, 521, 575, 594
2	3	19, *119, 584	13	33	2, 110, 231, 252, 340, 342
	4	40, 153, 154, 155, 293		34	*72, 195, 374, 395, 472, 633
	5	38, *51, 261, 263	14	35	*72, 218, 227, 342, 352, 362, 467
3	6	8, 33, 135, 148, 151		36	118, 193, 238, 267, 338, 462, 473, 479
	7	38, *51, 267, 386			
	8	25, 53, 86, *130, 614	15	37	22, 69, 196, 380, 383, 386
4	9	5, 38, 261, 544		38	22, 69, 196, 385, 395
	10	11, 50, 94, 537, 614		39	22, 69, 196, 384, 474
	11	58, 82, 200, 257, 258	16	40	88, 227, 380, 384, 385, 395
5	12	10, 52, 479, 482		41	202, 384, 387, 398
	13	*51, *130, 196		42	49, 285, 391, 392, 491, 493
	14	49, 260, 474		43	*103, 221, 287, 292, 371, 380, 479, 497
	15	85, 223, 230, 329, 485		44	22, 69, 196, 267, 372
6	16	25, *130, 260, 267, 395	17	45	30, *118, 271, 388, 392, 399, 511
	17	196, 223, 227, 467, 568			
	18	*72, 230, 379, 473, 479	18	46	47, 68, 406, 409, 414, 467
	19	40, 218, 277, 279, 571		47	230, 300, 405, 406, 492, 566
7	20	*87, 219, 488, 490, 533		48	230, 238, 413, 414
	21	16, 62, 262, 490, 495, 567		49	*72, 229, 408, 409
	22	90, 500, 540	19	50	2, 110, 247, 408
	23	511, 518, 519, 520, 549		51	*46, 229, 408, 411, 416, 418
8	24	252, 372, 605, 634		52	3, 10, *96, 203, 330, 614
	25	225, 246, 249, 283, 635, 636	20	53	*51, 104, 143, 201, 416, 418, 423
9	26	8, 104, 136, 148, 428, 430, 435, 436, 459	21	54	48, *87, 122, 504, 505, 507, 510, 516
10	27	*23, *46, 91, 190, 221, 457, 509, 556		55	*133, 225, 322, 528, 533, 586
	28	*33, 104, *147, 434, 446, 558, 567		56	32, *51, *103, *130, 223, 267, 473
11	29	18, 473, 482, 557, 572	22	57	16, 30, 235, 399, 408, 618
	30	2, 53, *95, 467, 537		58	16, *84, 236, 392, 472, 504

Lord's Day	Q&A	*Psalter Hymnal* Suggestions
45	116	65, *116, *147, 160, 265, 421, 579
	117	40, 86, 257, 422, 579, 624, 625
	118	*23, 27, 66, *138, 451
	119	207, 208, 562
46	120	*103, 231, 252, 284, 440, 450, 562:1, 634
	121	96, 445, 446, 450, 457, 460, 483, 499, 533
47	122	*89, 160, 186, 247, 249, 562:2, 621, 626, 634
48	123	2, *46, *72, 286, 542, 562:3, 598, 616
49	124	*119, *139, 261, 287, 324, 451, 546, 548, 562:4
50	125	*65, 81, 104, 127, 145, 190, 290, 446, 455, 456, 562:5
51	126	32, *51, *130, 257, 266, 562:6, 587
52	127	73, *103, 140, 141, 505, 522, 544, 559, 562:7, 575
	128	8, 247, 253, 286, 408, 428, 478, 542, 562:8, 632
	129	89:8, 365, 562:8, 630, 641

Heidelberg Catechism: Cross References to the Belgic Confession and Canons of Dort

This "Harmony of the Confessions," based on the order of the Heidelberg Catechism, is intended to serve as an aid in locating related statements of doctrine found in the other confessions.

Heidelberg Catechism (Lord's Day) (Question & Answer)		Belgic Confession (Article)	Canons of Dort (Head & Article) (RE = Rejection of Errors)
I	1	—	I, 12 - 14; RE I, 6, 7; III/IV, 11; V, 8-12; RE V, 5
	2	—	I, 1-4. (Note: Each chapter follows order of sin, deliverance, gratitude.)
II	3	—	III/IV, 5, 6
	4	—	—
	5	14, 15	III/IV, 3-6; V, 2, 3
III	6	14	III/IV, 1
	7	14, 15	I, 1; III/IV, 1-4
	8	14, 15, 24	III/IV, 3, 4
IV	9	14, 15, 16	I, 1; III/IV, 1
	10	15, 37	I, 4; II, 1; III/IV, 1
	11	16, 17, 20	I, 1-4; II, 1, 2
V	12	20	II, 1
	13	14	II, 2; III/IV, 1-4
	14	—	—
	15	19	II, 1-4
VI	16	18, 19, 20, 21	II, 1-4
	17	19	II, 1-4
	18	10, 18, 19, 20, 21	II, 1-4
	19	2, 3, 4, 5, 6, 7	I, 3; II, 5; III/IV, 6-8
VII	20	22	I, 1-5; II, 5-7; III/IV, 6
	21	23, 24	III/IV, 9-14; RE III/IV, 6
	22	7	I, 3; II, 5; III/IV, 6-8
	23	9	—
VIII	24	8, 9	—
	25	8, 9	—
IX	26	12, 13	—
X	27	13	—
	28	12, 13	—

Heidelberg Catechism		Belgic Confession	Canons of Dort
(Lord's Day)	(Question & Answer)	(Article)	(Head & Article)
			(RE = Rejection of Errors)
XI	29	21, 22	II, 3
	30	21, 22, 24	II, 5; RE II, 3-6
XII	31	21, 26	—
	32	—	V, 1, 2
XIII	33	10, 18, 19	—
	34	—	—
XIV	35	18, 19, 26	—
	36	18, 19	—
XV	37	20, 21	II, 2-4
	38	21	—
	39	20, 21	II, 2-4
XVI	40	20, 21	II, 3, 4; RE II, 7
	41	—	—
	42	—	—
	43	—	II, 8
	44	21	II, 4
XVII	45	20	RE, V, 1
XVIII	46	26	—
	47	19, 26	—
	48	19, 26	—
	49	26	—
XIX	50	26	—
	51	—	V, 1-15
	52	37	—
XX	53	11, 24	III/IV, 11, 12; RE III/IV, 5-8; V, 6, 7
XXI	54	16, 27, 28, 29	I, 1-18; II, 1-9; V, 9
	55	28, 30, 31	—
	56	22, 23	II, 7, 8; V, 5
XXII	57	37	—
	58	37	—
XXIII	59	21, 22, 23	II, 7, 8
	60	21, 22, 23	II, 7, 8
	61	21, 22, 23	II, 7, 8; RE II, 4
XXIV	62	23	II, 1; III/IV, 3-6; RE III/IV, 4, 5
	63	24	—
	64	24	III/IV, 11; V, 12, 13; RE V, 6

Heidelberg Catechism		Belgic Confession	Canons of Dort
(Lord's Day)	(Question & Answer)	(Article)	(Head & Article)
			(RE = Rejection of Errors)
XXV	65	24, 33	III/IV, 17; RE III/IV, 7-9; V, 14
	66	33	—
	67	33	—
	68	33	—
XXVI	69	15, 34	—
	70	15, 34	—
	71	15, 34	—
XXVII	72	34	—
	73	34	—
	74	15, 34	I, 17
XXVIII	75	35	—
	76	35	—
	77	—	—
XXIX	78	35	—
	79	35	—
XXX	80	35	—
	81	35	—
	82	35	—
XXXI	83	29, 30, 32	—
	84	29, 32	—
	85	29, 32	—
XXXII	86	24	III/IV, 11, 12; V, 10, 12
	87	24	—
XXXIII	88	24	III/IV, 11, 12; V, 5, 7
	89	24	III/IV, 11, 12; V, 5, 7
	90	24	III/IV, 11, 12; V, 5, 7
	91	24, 25	—
XXXIV	92	—	—
	93	—	—
	94	1	—
	95	1	—
XXXV	96	32	—
	97	—	—
	98	7	III/IV, 17; V, 14
XXXVI	99	—	—
	100	—	—
XXXVII	101	36	—
	102	—	—

INDEXES

Heidelberg Catechism		Belgic Confession	Canons of Dort
(Lord's Day)	(Question & Answer)	(Article)	(Head & Article) (RE = Rejection of Errors)
XXXVIII	103	—	V, 14
XXXIX	104	36	—
XL	105	36	—
	106	—	—
	107	—	—
XLI	108	—	—
	109	—	—
XLII	110	—	—
	111	—	—
XLIII	112	—	—
XLIV	113	—	—
	114	24, 29	V, 4
	115	25	III/IV, 17
XLV	116	—	—
	117	—	—
	118	—	—
	119	—	—
XLVI	120	12, 13, 36	—
	121	13	—
XLVII	122	2, 7	—
XLVIII	123	36, 37	—
XLIX	124	12, 24	III/IV, 11, 16
L	125	13	—
LI	126	15, 21, 22, 23	II, 7
LII	127	26	V, 6-8
	128	26	—
	129	—	—

The *Revised Common Lectionary* with Related Songs

A lectionary is a schedule of Scripture readings. The *Revised Common Lectionary* (RCL) is a three-year schedule prepared by the Consultation on Common Texts, an ecumenical forum for liturgical dialogue and renewal among many denominations in North America. This index includes *Psalter Hymnal* songs based on the assigned Scriptures. For additional resources on the RCL, including an index of all scripture references, consult the *Handbook for the Revised Common Lectionary*, Peter C. Bower, editor (Louisville: Westminster/John Knox Press, 1996).

The three years (designated A, B, and C) include several Scripture readings for each day: an Old Testament lesson; a psalm, preferably sung, which serves as a reflection on the Old Testament reading; a reading from one of the New Testament epistles; and, finally, a reading from one of the four gospels—Matthew in Year A, Mark in Year B, and Luke in Year C. Readings from the gospel of John are included in all three years. Over the three years, at least one reading from each book of the Bible is included. When used regularly, the lectionary functions in a similar way to the historic Reformed use of the Heidelberg Catechism: a disciplined approach to covering the whole range of Scripture. (A table for Years A, B, and C, highlighting important dates in the liturgical calendar through the year 2040, is found on p. 880.)

CHRISTMAS CYCLE

Advent

Advent is a time of preparation, beginning with the Sunday nearest November 30. On the four Sundays of Advent, the church both looks forward to celebrating the birth of Christ and prepares for the return of Christ. The liturgical color is purple or dark blue.

1st Sunday of Advent
Year A
- Isa. 2:1-5 .... 410, 600,606, 608
- Ps. 122 122
- Rom. 13:11-14 .... 332, 481
- Matt. 24:36-44 .... ——

Year B
- Isa. 64:1-9 287
- Ps. 80:1-7, 17-19 80
- 1 Cor. 1:3-9 .... ——
- Mark 13:24-37 .... 333, 612

Year C
- Jer. 33:14-16 .... ——
- Ps. 25:1-10 25
- 1 Thess. 3:9-13 264
- Luke 21:25-36 .... 612, 615

2nd Sunday of Advent
Year A
- Isa. 11:1-10 .... 328, 351, 616
- Ps. 72:1-7, 18-19 .... 72, 412, 541
- Rom. 15:4-13 600
- Matt. 3:1-12 327

Year B
- Isa. 40:1-11 194
- Ps. 85:1-2, 8-13 85
- 2 Pet. 3:8-15a 525
- Mark 1:1-8 327

Year C
- Mal. 3:1-4 .... ——
- Luke 1:68-79 213
- Phil. 1:3-11 .... ——
- Luke 3:1-6 .... 194, 327, 332

3rd Sunday of Advent
Year A
- Isa. 35:1-10 .... ——
- Ps. 146:5-10 or Luke 1:47-55 ...... 146 or 212, 478, 622
- James 5:7-10 329
- Matt. 11:2-11 335

869

Christmas

Christmas is the festival of the birth of Christ, of
the incarnation. The twelve days of Christmas
begin on Christmas Eve and end on the celebration of the Epiphany (January 6). The liturgical
colors are white and gold.

EPIPHANY SEASON/ORDINARY TIME

The Sundays between the Epiphany of the Lord
and Ash Wednesday are sometimes called the
Epiphany Season; they are also called Ordinary
Time, since those Sundays are not associated with a
major festival day. The liturgical color for Ordinary
Time is green, except on the first and last Sundays—
the Baptism of the Lord and the Transfiguration of
the Lord—for which the color is white.

Note: Depending on the date for Easter, this period
of Ordinary Time may include six or more
Sundays. The Transfiguration of the Lord is
scheduled for the Sunday preceding Lent.

Baptism of the Lord
(1st Sunday in Ordinary Time, Jan. 7-13)
Year A
- Isa. 42:1-9............................594
- Ps. 29 29
- Acts 10:34-43.........................—
- Matt. 3:13-17.........................—

Year B
- Gen. 1:1-15...................151, 430, 453
- Ps. 29 29
- Acts 19:1-7.......................269, 417
- Mark 1:4-11..........................327

Year C
- Isa. 43:1-7............................500
- Ps. 29 29
- Acts 8:14-17..........................417
- Luke 3:15-17, 21-22 415

2nd Sunday after the Epiphany
(2nd Sunday in Ordinary Time, Jan. 14-20)
Year A
- Isa. 49:1-7............................—
- Ps. 40:1-11 40
- 1 Cor. 1:1-9 ....—
- John 1:29-42..................247, 257, 415

Year B
- 1 Sam. 3:1-10 (11-20).................—
- Ps. 139:1-6, 13-18...................139, 184
- 1 Cor. 6:12-20.....................425, 503
- John 1:43-51.......................528, 553

Year C
- Isa. 62:1-5............................—
- Ps. 36:5-10 36
- 1 Cor. 12:1-11 528
- John 2:1-11 361

3rd Sunday after the Epiphany
(3rd Sunday in Ordinary Time, Jan. 21-27)
Year A
- Isa. 9:1-4............................192
- Ps. 27:1, 4-9........................27, 164
- 1 Cor. 1:10-18 ....—
- Matt. 4:12-23......................285, 553

Year B
- Jon. 3:1-5, 10........................—
- Ps. 62:5-12 62
- 1 Cor. 7:29-31 ....—
- Mark 1:14-20..........................553

Year C
- Neh. 8:1-3, 5-6, 8-10................276, 584
- Ps. 19 ....19, 429
- 1 Cor. 12:12-31a...............288, 289, 308
- Luke 4:14-21......................335, 501

4th Sunday after the Epiphany
(4th Sunday in Ordinary Time, Jan. 28-Feb. 3)
Year A
- Mic. 6:1-8............................293
- Ps. 15 15
- 1 Cor. 1:18-31.................384, 474, 600
- Matt. 5:1-12..........................206

Year B
- Deut. 18:15-20 ....—
- Ps. 111 111
- 1 Cor. 8:1-13 ....—
- Mark 1:21-28..........................361

Year C
- Jer. 1:4-10............................528
- Ps. 71:1-6 71
- 1 Cor. 13:1-13 222
- Luke 4:21-30..........................364

5th Sunday after the Epiphany
(5th Sunday in Ordinary Time, Feb. 4-10)
Year A
- Isa. 58:1-9a (9b-12) 609
- Ps. 112:1-9 (10)......................112
- 1 Cor. 2:1-12 (13-16) ....—
- Matt. 5:13-20.........................206

Year B
- Isa. 40:21-31 460
- Ps. 147:1-11, 20c..................147, 187
- 1 Cor. 9:16-23 ....—
- Mark 1:29-39 ....361, 363, 501

Year C
- Isa. 6:1-8 (9-13) 244, 288, 289, 504
- Ps. 138 ....138, 183
- 1 Cor. 15:1-11 ....400, 462, 498, 511
- Luke 5:1-11.......................477, 525

6th Sunday after the Epiphany
(6th Sunday in Ordinary Time, Feb. 11-17)
Year A
- Deut. 30:15-20 446
- Ps. 119:1-8 119
- 1 Cor. 3:1-9 325
- Matt. 5:21-37......................545, 574

Year B
- 2 Kings 5:1-14 ....—
- Ps. 30 30
- 1 Cor. 9:24-27.....................291, 563
- Mark 1:40-45 ....361, 363, 501

EASTER CYCLE

Lent

Like Advent, Lent is a time of preparation. For forty days and six Sundays beginning on Ash Wednesday, the church proclaims and remembers the atoning work of Christ and what it means to follow Jesus. Historically this period was one in which those new to the faith were prepared for baptism on Easter Sunday.

The week from Palm/Passion Sunday to Easter Sunday is traditionally called Holy Week. And the final three days from Maundy Thursday through the Easter Vigil form a unit of remembering the death and resurrection of Christ; they are sometimes called the Three Days.

The liturgical color for Lent is purple but may also be red on Palm/Passion Sunday. Traditionally the church is stripped of all decoration on Maundy Thursday, so no color is designated for Good Friday.

Easter

The Easter season is a period of fifty days—forty days from Easter Sunday to the ascension of Christ, and ten more from Ascension Day to Pentecost. The Easter season celebrates the triumph of Christ over death and his ruling power over all creation. The liturgical colors, like those of Christmas, are white and gold. The liturgical color for the day of Pentecost is red.

ORDINARY TIME

After the Easter cycle, a longer period of Ordinary Time—almost half the year—follows Pentecost Sunday until Advent. The first Sunday in this period is Trinity Sunday; the last Sunday is Christ the King Sunday. The liturgical color for Ordinary Time is green, except on those first and last Sundays, for which the color is white.

Trinity Sunday (*1st Sunday after Pentecost*)

If the Sunday falling in the period of May 24-28 follows Trinity Sunday, the readings for the 8th Sunday in Ordinary Time (8th Sunday after Epiphany) are used.

9th Sunday in Ordinary Time

(May 29-June 4, if after Trinity Sunday)

10th Sunday in Ordinary Time

(June 5-11, if after Trinity Sunday)

11th Sunday in Ordinary Time

(June 12-18, if after Trinity Sunday)

Year C
  1 Kings 21:1-10 (11-14) 15-21a. . . . . ——
  Ps. 5:1-8 5
  Gal. 2:15-21 . . . . 373, 402, 571, 578
  Luke 7:36-8:3 499

12th Sunday in Ordinary Time
(June 19-25, if after Trinity Sunday)
Year A
  Gen. 21:8-21 . . . . ——
  Ps. 86:1-10, 16-17 86
  Rom. 6:1b-11 . . . . 269, 271, 402, 515
  Matt. 10:24-39 477
Year B
  1 Sam. 17:(1a, 4-11, 19-23), 32-49 559
  Ps. 9:9-20 9
  2 Cor. 6:1-13 544
  Mark 4:35-41 572
Year C
  1 Kings 19:1-4 (5-7) 8-15a . . . . ——
  Ps. 42-43. . . . . 42, 43
  Gal. 3:23-29. . . . . 271, 315
  Luke 8:26-39 363

13th Sunday in Ordinary Time (June 26-July 2)
Year A
  Gen. 22:1-14 621
  Ps. 13 13
  Rom. 6:12-23 . . . . 285, 546
  Matt. 10:40-42 602
Year B
  2 Sam. 1:1, 17-27 . . . . ——
  Ps. 130. . . . . 130, 256
  2 Cor. 8:7-15 . . . . 290, 294
  Mark 5:21-43. . . . . 363, 501
Year C
  2 Kings 2:1-2, 6-14 521
  Ps. 77:1-2, 11-20 77
  Gal. 5:1, 13-25. 224, 374
  Luke 9:51-62. . . . . 285, 553

14th Sunday in Ordinary Time (July 3-9)
Year A
  Gen. 24:34-38, 42-49, 58-67 . . . . ——
  Ps. 45:10-17 or Song of Songs 2:8-13. 45
  Rom. 7:15-25a. . . . . ——
  Matt. 11:16-19, 25-30 . . . . 324, 488, 578, 579
Year B
  2 Sam. 5:1-5, 9-10 . . . . ——
  Ps. 48 48
  2 Cor. 12:2-10. 500, 546
  Mark 6:1-13 . . . . 508, 523, 524

Year C
  2 Kings 5:1-14 . . . . ——
  Ps. 30 30
  Gal. 6:(1-6) 7-16. . . . . 315, 602
  Luke 10:1-11, 16-20. . . . . 523, 526

15th Sunday in Ordinary Time (July 10-16)
Year A
  Gen. 25:19-34 . . . . ——
  Ps. 119:105-112. 119
  Rom. 8:1-11 267
  Matt. 13:1-9, 18-23 . . . . ——
Year B
  2 Sam. 6:1-5, 12b-19 . . . . ——
  Ps. 24 . . . . 24, 163
  Eph. 1:3-14. . . . . 225, 464, 497
  Mark 6:14-29 . . . . ——
Year C
  Amos 7:7-17. . . . . ——
  Ps. 82 82
  Col. 1:1-14 445
  Luke 10:25-37 . . . . 154, 155, 311, 601

16th Sunday in Ordinary Time (July 17-23)
Year A
  Gen. 28:10-19a . . . . ——
  Ps. 139:1-12, 23-24 . . . . 139, 184
  Rom. 8:12-25. 416
  Matt. 13:24-30, 36-43 . . . . 526, 527
Year B
  2 Sam. 7:1-14a. . . . . ——
  Ps. 89:20-37. . . . . 89, 593
  Eph. 2:11-22 . . . . 418, 502
  Mark 6:30-34, 53-56. . . . . 363, 524
Year C
  Amos 8:1-12. . . . . ——
  Ps. 52 52
  Col. 1:15-28. . . . . 229, 238
  Luke 10:38-42. 293

17th Sunday in Ordinary Time (July 24-30)
Year A
  Gen. 29:15-28 . . . . ——
  Ps. 105:1-11, 45b or Ps. 128 . . . . 105 or 128
  Rom. 8:26-39 . . . . 221, 399, 440
  Matt. 13:31-33, 44-52 572
Year B
  2 Sam. 11:1-15. . . . . ——
  Ps. 14 14
  Eph. 3:14-21 . . . . 226, 364
  John 6:1-21 282

Year B

    2 Sam. 23:1-7 . . . . ——

    Ps. 132:1-12 (13-18) 132

    Rev. 1:4b-8 . . . . 612, 623

    John 18:33-37 . . . . 408, 410

Year C

    Jer. 23:1-6 . . . . 619, 621

    Luke 1:68-79 213

    Col. 1:11-20 229

    Luke 23:33-43 . . . . 298, 381

Thanksgiving Day *(last Thursday in November—U.S.;*
second Monday in October—Can.)

Year A

    Deut. 8:7-18 . . . . 294, 455

    Ps. 65 . . . . 65, 458

    2 Cor. 9:6-15 . . . . ——

    Luke 17:11-19 . . . . ——

Year B

    Joel 2:21-27 201

    Ps. 126 126

    1 Tim. 2:1-7 609

    Matt. 6:25-33 . . . . 209, 435

Year C

    Deut. 26:1-11 294

    Ps. 100 . . . . 100, 176

    Phil. 4:4-9 . . . . 228, 326, 561

    John 6:25-35 . . . . 282, 524

Dates in the Liturgical Calendar Until the Year 2040

Year	1st Sunday of Advent	Ash Wednesday	Easter	Ascension	Pentecost
A	Nov. 29, 1998	Feb. 17, 1999	Apr. 4, 1999	May 13, 1999	May 23, 1999
B	Nov. 28, 1999	Mar. 9, 2000	Apr. 23, 2000	June 1, 2000	June 11, 2000
C	Dec. 3, 2000	Feb. 28, 2001	Apr. 15, 2001	May 24, 2001	June 3, 2001
A	Dec. 2, 2001	Feb. 13, 2002	Mar. 31, 2002	May 9, 2002	May 19, 2002
B	Dec. 1, 2002	Mar. 5, 2003	Apr. 20, 2003	May 29, 2003	June 8, 2003
C	Nov. 30, 2003	Feb. 25, 2004	Apr. 11, 2004	May 20, 2004	May 30, 2004
A	Nov. 28, 2004	Feb. 9, 2005	Mar. 27, 2005	May 5, 2005	May 15, 2005
B	Nov. 27, 2005	Mar. 1, 2006	Apr. 16, 2006	May 25, 2006	June 4, 2006
C	Dec. 3, 2006	Feb. 21, 2007	Apr. 8, 2007	May 17, 2007	May 27, 2007
A	Dec. 2, 2007	Feb. 6, 2008	Mar. 23, 2008	May 1, 2008	May 11, 2008
B	Nov. 30, 2008	Feb. 25, 2009	Apr. 12, 2009	May 21, 2009	May 31, 2009
C	Nov. 29, 2009	Feb. 17, 2010	Apr. 4, 2010	May 13, 2010	May 23, 2010
A	Nov. 28, 2010	Mar. 9, 2011	Apr. 24, 2011	June 2, 2011	June 12, 2011
B	Nov. 27, 2011	Feb. 22, 2012	Apr. 8, 2012	May 17, 2012	May 27, 2012
C	Dec. 2, 2012	Feb. 13, 2013	Mar. 31, 2013	May 9, 2013	May 19, 2013
A	Dec. 1, 2013	Mar. 5, 2014	Apr. 20, 2014	May 29, 2014	June 8, 2014
B	Nov. 30, 2014	Feb. 18, 2015	Apr. 5, 2015	May 14, 2015	May 24, 2015
C	Nov. 29, 2015	Feb. 10, 2016	Mar. 27, 2016	May 5, 2016	May 15, 2016
A	Nov. 27, 2016	Mar. 1, 2017	Apr. 16, 2017	May 25, 2017	June 4, 2017
B	Dec. 3, 2017	Feb. 14, 2018	Apr. 1, 2018	May 10, 2018	May 20, 2018
C	Dec. 2, 2018	Mar. 6, 2019	Apr. 21, 2019	May 30, 2019	June 9, 2019
A	Dec. 1, 2019	Feb. 26, 2020	Apr. 12, 2020	May 21, 2020	May 31, 2020
B	Nov. 29, 2020	Feb. 17, 2021	Apr. 4, 2021	May 13, 2021	May 23, 2021
C	Nov. 28, 2021	Mar. 2, 2022	Apr. 17, 2022	May 26, 2022	June 5, 2022
A	Nov. 27, 2022	Feb. 22, 2023	Apr. 9, 2023	May 18, 2023	May 28, 2023
B	Dec. 3, 2023	Feb. 14, 2024	Mar. 31, 2024	May 9, 2024	May 19, 2024
C	Dec. 1, 2024	Mar. 5, 2025	Apr. 20, 2025	May 29, 2025	June 8, 2025
A	Nov. 30, 2025	Feb. 18, 2026	Apr. 5, 2026	May 14, 2026	May 24, 2026
B	Nov. 29, 2026	Feb. 10, 2027	Mar. 28, 2027	May 6, 2027	May 16, 2027
C	Nov. 28, 2027	Mar. 2, 2028	Apr. 16, 2028	May 25, 2028	June 4, 2028
A	Dec. 3, 2028	Feb. 14, 2029	Apr. 1, 2029	May 10, 2029	May 20, 2029
B	Dec. 2, 2029	Mar. 6, 2030	Apr. 21, 2030	May 30, 2030	June 9, 2030
C	Dec. 1, 2030	Feb. 26, 2031	Apr. 13, 2031	May 22, 2031	June 1, 2031
A	Nov. 30, 2031	Feb. 11, 2032	Mar. 28, 2032	May 6, 2032	May 16, 2032
B	Nov. 28, 2032	Mar. 2, 2033	Apr. 17, 2033	May 26, 2033	June 5, 2033
C	Nov. 27, 2033	Feb. 22, 2034	Apr. 9, 2034	May 18, 2034	May 28, 2034
A	Dec. 3, 2034	Feb. 7, 2035	Mar. 25, 2035	May 3, 2035	May 13, 2035
B	Dec. 2, 2035	Feb. 27, 2036	Apr. 13, 2036	May 22, 2036	June 1, 2036
C	Nov. 30, 2036	Feb. 18, 2037	Apr. 5, 2037	May 14, 2037	May 24, 2037
A	Nov. 29, 2037	Mar. 10, 2038	Apr. 25, 2038	June 3, 2038	June 13, 2038
B	Nov. 28, 2038	Feb. 23, 2039	Apr. 10, 2039	May 19, 2039	May 29, 2039
C	Nov. 27, 2039	Feb. 15, 2040	Apr. 1, 2040	May 10, 2040	May 20, 2040

Songs with Guitar Chords

(By Key)

(By First Line and Title)

General Index to Essays

Numbers refer to pages in the Historical Essays section of the handbook.

Authors, Composers, and Sources

*Biographical information is usually found in the first reference. A **bold print** number indicates that biographical information is found at that number rather than in the first reference.*

Dykes, John B. (1823-1876) 147, 235, 249, 425,
456, 480, 551, 575, 619
Easy Hymns (1851) 90
Ebeling, Johann (1637-1676)................ 225
Eckhardt, A. Royce (b. 1937)................ 579
Edwards, John D. (1806-1885)............... 459
Ellerton, John (1826-1893) 318, 319
Elliott, Charlotte (1789-1871) 263
Elvey, George J. (1816-1893)..... 48, 276, 410, 527
English 46, 155, 185, 219, 364, 422, 430, 436
English Praise (1975)......................... 325
Erfurt, *Enchiridia* (1524) 336
Erickson, John F. (b. 1938).................. 636
Ernewerten Gesangbuch, Stralsund (1665) 253
Espinosa, Juan A. (20th cent.) 610
Essenberg, Benjamin (1890-1976) 68
Este, *Whole Book of Psalmes* (1592) 215
Evangelisches Gesangbuch, Hirschberg (1741)... 531
Evans, David (1874-1948)................ 22, **285**
Ewing, Alexander C. (1830-1895)............ 618
Excell, Edwin O. (1851-1921) 462
Faber, Frederick W. (1814-1863)............. 499
Farmer, John (1836-1901) 390
Fawcett, John (1740-1817) 315, 320, 321
Featherstone, William R. (1846-1873) 557
Feith, Rhijnvis (1753-1824) 443
Ferguson, John (b. 1941) 370
Ferris, Theodore P. (b. 1908) 75, 585
Fettke, Thomas E. (b. 1941)................ 588
Filitz, Friedrich (1804-1876) 222
Fillmore, James H. (1849-1936) 169
Findlater, Sarah B. (1823-1907)............. 333
Fink, Gottfried W. (1783-1846) 497
Finnish 285
Fischer, William G. (1835-1912) 530
Fishel, Donald E. (b. 1950) 402
Foley, Brian (b. 1919) 196
Fortunatus, Venantius Honorius (c. 530-609) .. 400
Foundling Hospital Collection (1796) 148
France, William (1912-1985) 529
Francis of Assisi (1182-1226) 431, 545
Franck, Johann (1618-1677) 305, 572
Franz, Ignaz (1719-1790) 504
French 189, 248, 311, 347
Freylinghausen, *Gesangbuch* (1704) ... 34, 223, 439
Friedell, Harold W. (1905-1958) 290
Fritsch, Ahasuerus (1629-1701)............... 574
Frizzoni, *Canzuns Spirituaelas* (1765) 54
Fulbert of Chartres (c. 960-1028) 404
Funk, *A Compilation of Genuine Church Music*
(1832) 500

Gabriel, Charles H. (1856-1932) 24, 29, 94,
125, 242, 514
Gaelic.................................... 269
Gardiner, *Sacred Melodies* (1815)..... 111, 428, 602
Garrett, Les (b. 1943) 241
Gastoldi, Giovanni (1556-1622) 566
Gastorius, Severus (1646-1682)............. 451
Gaunt, Howard C. A. (1902-1983) 313
Gauntlett, Henry J. (1805-1876) 104, 329, 346
Gawler, *Hymns and Psalms* (1789) 363
Gay, Annabeth McClelland (b. 1925).......... 58
Geist und Lehr-reiches Kirchen . . . Buch,
Dresden (1694) 7
Geistliche Volkslieder, Paderborn (1850) 79
Geistreiches Gesangbuch, Halle (1704).......... 113
Gellert, Christian F. (1715-1769)............. 399
Genevan Psalter (1539-1562)... 3, 6, 12, 19, 25, 27,
33, 42, 43, 47, 65, 68, 77, 81, 84,
87, 89, 97, 98, 103, 105, 107,
116, 118, 119, 124, 128, 130,
133, 134, 136, 143, 150, 153,
172, 173, 180, 314, 521, 576, 638
Gerdes, Eduard (1821-1898) 392
Gerhardt, Paul (1607-1676)............. 331, 383
German 35, 72, 351, 355, 438
Gesangbuch, Augsburg (1666) 330
Gesangbuch, Darmstadt (1698) 230, 277
Gesangbuch, Meiningen (1693) 279
Gesangbuch, Munster (1677)................ 461
Gesangbuch, Trier (1695)................... 415
Gesangbuch, Wittenberg (1784).......... 378, 547
Gesius, Bartholomaus (1555-1613)........... 190
Geyer, John B. (b. 1933) 271
Ghanaian................................. 601
Giardini, Felice de (1716-1796).............. 246
Gibbons, Orlando (1583-1625) 167, 308, 423
Gilmore, Joseph H. (1834-1918)............. 452
Gladden, Washington (1836-1908)........... 573
Gläser, Carl G. (1784-1829) 501
Glass, Eric (20th cent.) 198
Gloria in excelsis Deo......................... 247
Gloria Patri (2nd cent.) 635, 636
Goodson, Albert A. 567
Cordon, Adoniram J. (1836-1895) 557
Goss, John (1800-1880) 164, 475
Goudimel, Claude (c. 1505-1572).... 6, 33, 43, 47,
51, 68, 77, 100, 101, 118,
128, 130, 136, 153, 172,
194, 216, 248, 576
Gounod, Charles F. (1818-1893)......... 165, 481
Gower, John H. (1855-1922) 508

Tune Names

First Lines and Titles of Songs

*indicates first lines or titles by which some hymns in this book may also be known

911

Glossary

Aeolian mode. *See* **modal system.**

Agnus Dei. Latin for "Lamb of God." Incipit for the fifth item of the Ordinary (q.v.) of the Mass. Based on John 1:29 (257).

alternatum praxis. Performance by two or more alternating groups. Often used in early Lutheran services for the performance of chorales with many stanzas. Similar to antiphony (q.v.).

Anglican chant. An Anglican practice of chanting the psalms according to psalm tones (q.v.) arranged in four-part harmony (207).

antiphon. Literally, "sung before"; use in *Psalter Hymnal* similar to a refrain, but also preceding the first stanza (176).

antiphony, antiphonal. Performance by two or more alternating groups. To be distinguished from responsorial (q.v.) performance.

bar form. A musical structure in which the first section is repeated before a second different section (AAB). Common in early German songs and many hymns.

Benedictus. The Latin incipit for the Song of Zechariah, Luke 1:68-79.

cadence. The closing formula of a musical phrase or an entire piece.

canon. A composition in which the parts enter successively in exact imitation of the leading part. A round is a type of canon in that each part may return immediately to the beginning and repeat the process as many times as desired.

canticle. Biblical songs other than the psalms.

cantional. Congregational singing with the melody in the soprano rather than in the tenor, which was the traditional placement until the late sixteenth century.

cantor. "Chief singer"; still used in Jewish worship; in Christian worship also called "precentor" during Reformation times; fell into disuse as first organists, then music/worship leaders took over role of "lead singer." The advantage of the term "cantor" is that it highlights the central role of the lead musician to encourage congregational song.

"catalog" hymn. A hymn that lists several aspects of a given subject (e.g., 433)

church modes. *See* **modal system.**

coda. Literally, "tail"—a concluding section of a piece of music that gives a strong sense of closure.

common meter. (CM) Four-line stanza structure with lines of 8, 6, 8, and 6 syllables. Very common in English hymnody.

common meter double. (CMD) Two CM stanzas combined to form one eight-line stanza.

concertato. A hymn arranged for varied stanza treatments with congregation, choir, and instruments.

continuo. A type of accompaniment typical of Baroque music consisting of a bass instrument (cello, bassoon, etc.) and a chordal instrument (harpsichord, organ, lute, guitar, etc.).

Credo. Latin for "I believe." Incipit for the Nicene Creed, the third item of the Ordinary (q.v.) of the Mass; also the incipit of the Apostles' Creed.

dactylic. Metrical foot of three syllables, the first stressed.

descant. A counter melody, usually placed above the main melody.

Dorian mode. *See* **modal system.**

double meter. e.g., a four-line meter doubled to create eight lines (CM becomes CMD).

doxology. Song of praise to God.

duple. Rhythmic unit of two pulses.

enjambment. Disagreement between poetic and musical stresses and cadence points (e.g., 161).

faux-bourdon. Four-part harmony with the melody in the tenor rather than soprano.

fermata. Symbol [⌢] to show the end of a phrase and/or to extend the note value beyond its normal length.

fuguing tune. A type of hymn or psalm tune particularly popular in 18th century America. Typically in ABB form in which the A part is homophonic (q.v.) and the B parts begin with each voice-part entering in turn like the beginning of a round (404).

gathering notes. A lengthened first note to give people time to "gather" on it before proceding to sing together in tempo.

Gloria. Latin for "glory." Incipit for the second item of the Ordinary (q.v.) of the Mass; it begins with the song of the angels to the shepherds (Luke 2:14). See PHH 247.

Gregorian chant. *See* plainsong.

heterophany. A musical texture in which all participants are performing the same melody in varying versions at the same time. This is typical in improvised music and in the performance of monophonic music in cultures without musical notation.

homophony, homophonic. Musical texture of one main melody supported by other parts; e.g., SATB; more chordal than polyphony (q.v.), which is more linear.

Hypo- Prefix for modes (e.g., Hypodorian) with a range that begins a fourth below the final. See **modal system**.

iambic pentameter. In metered poetry, a structure of five poetic feet per line, each with two syllables, the second stressed.

incipit. The opening words to a song; Latin for "beginning." Pronounced "in-chip-it."

Ionian mode. *See* modal system.

isorhythm. All the notes of equal rhythmic value.

Kyrie. Greek for "Lord, have mercy." Incipit for the first item of the Ordinary (q.v.) of the Mass (258).

Lauds. *See* Office Hours.

Lectionary. A schedule of scripture readings over a given period; the *Revised Common Lectionary* (RCL) is a three-year schedule of readings; the complete RCL is included in the index on page 867.

Lining out. A method of leading unaccompanied singing when a precentor (q.v.) sings phrase by phrase, or line by line, followed in turn by the congregation.

Long meter. (LM) Four-line stanza with each line including eight syllables (88 88).

Long meter double. (LMD) Two LM stanzas combined.

Lydian mode. *See* modal system.

Magnificat. The Latin incipit for the Song of Mary, Luke 1:46-55.

Matins. *See* Office Hours.

melisma. A string of two or more notes for one syllable of text, in distinction from syllabic structure typical of hymns.

metrical psalmody. An arrangement for singing the psalms. The psalm text is poetically paraphrased into stanzas having the same metrical structure so that each stanzas can be sung to the same melody; i.e., the same structure as traditional hymns.

Mixolydian mode. *See* modal system.

modal system. Pitch structures in Greek, Asian, medieval, and many folk musics, more varied than the major and minor constructs of the later major-minor tonal system. Eight medieval church modes used pitches in relationships related to the white notes on a keyboard as follows: Dorian (mode I), final on d and range d-d; Hypodorian (mode II), final on a and range d-d; Phrygian (mode III), final on e and range e-e; Hypophrygian (mode IV), final on e and range b-b; Lydian (mode V), final on f and range f-f; Hypolydian (mode VI), final on f and range c-c; Mixolydian (mode VII), final on g and range g-g; and Hypomixolydian (mode VIII), final on g and range d-d.

Renaissance theorists began recognizing four additional modes: Aeolian (mode IX), final on a and range a-a (what is now called "natural minor"); Hypoaeolian (mode X), final on a and range e-e; Ionian (mode XI), final on c and range c-c (what is now called "major"); Hypoionian (mode XII), final on c and range g-g.

monophony, monophonic. Unison texture; everyone singing the same melody.

Nunc Dimittis. Latin incipit for the Song of Simeon, Luke 2:29-32.

Office Hours. Periods of worship throughout the day and night consisting mainly of prayer, scripture reading, and chanting of the psalms and canticles. The full-fledged system of Office Hours as observed in monastic communities consisted of eight services: Matins (i.e., Morning Prayer) during the night; Lauds, at daybreak; Prime, c. 6:00 a.m.; Terce, c. 9:00 a.m.; Sext, noon; None ("the ninth hour" [of daylight]), c. 3:00 a.m.; Vespers (i.e., Evening Prayer), in the evening; and Compline, before retiring.

Ordinary. In contrast to the Proper (q.v.) of the Mass, the Ordinary of the Mass consists of those texts that are always (ordinarily) found in the Mass, regardless of the day. There are five principle texts that belong to the Ordinary: the Kyrie, Gloria, Credo, Sanctus and Benedictus, and Agnus Dei. Since the fifteenth century, so many composers have set these five texts to music that a Mass in music means a musical setting of these five texts.

Ordinary Time. That part of the Christian year that is not associated with the Christmas and Easter cycles; i.e., from Epiphany until the beginning of Lent, and from Pentecost until the beginning of Advent.

organ trio style. The melody is played on one manual, the inner voice(s) on another, and the bass in the pedal.

ostinato, ostinati. A persistently repeated short pattern, especially rhythmic.

pentatonic. Five-tone melody commonly found in folk tunes, rather than the seven pitches typical of Western music. Often the melodies can be played entirely on the black keys of a piano.

plainsong. Monophonic singing of liturgical texts according to the modal system (q.v.) and with free unmetered rhythms. Also called plain-chant. Gregorian chant is the name given to the repertory of plainchant that has had the official sanction of the Roman Catholic Church since the time of Charlemagne (8th century).

polyphony, polyphonic. In contrast to monophony (q.v.), a texture of several voices singing melodic lines simultaneously, as in soprano, alto, tenor, and bass.

Phrygian. *See* **modal system.**

precentor. Literally, one who sings before; in Protestant worship of Reformation times unaccompanied psalm singing was sometimes led by one person who sang the psalms "lined out" (q.v.) the melody phrase by phrase; *see also* **cantor.**

Proper. In contrast to the Ordinary (q.v.) of the Mass, the Proper consists of those parts of the service that vary according to a day or season (e.g., Scripture readings and prayers).

psalm tones. Melodic formulas for chanting the psalms; usually in two halves (or four, called "double tones") that match the parallel structure of Hebrew poetry. The *Lutheran Book of Worship* (1978) includes ten psalm tones.

responsorial psalmody. A method of singing the psalms where one group (usually the congregation) sings a refrain at the beginning and after sections of the psalm, which is read or sung by another group or soloist or cantor.

rounded bar form. AABA; *see also* **bar form.**

Sanctus. Latin for "holy"; the incipit of part of the fourth part of the Ordinary (q.v.) of the Mass. Based on Isaiah 6:3.

sequence. A type of chant for the Mass that proliferated during the high Middle Ages. It is typically a syllabic setting of a long poetic text in double-line stanzas, but unlike a hymn, the melody was not repeated for each stanza of text. During the Counter-Reformation, the Council of Trent abolished all but four of the sequences.

shape notes. A system of notation for learning to sight-sing by distinguishing shapes; *for an example, see p. 85.*

st. Stanza(s), the unit of division for hymn texts, in distinction from verse(s), used for biblical text divisions.

trisagion. A Greek version of the same text as the Sanctus (q.v.).

v., vv. Verse(s), the unit of division in biblical texts, in distinction from stanzas, used for hymn texts.

voorzanger. Dutch word for precentor (q.v.).